CLASSICS OF YOUNG ADULT LITERATURE

EDITED BY

CHARLES H. FREY
PROFESSOR
University of Washington

LUCY ROLLIN
PROFESSOR EMERITUS
Clemson University

PEARSON
Prentice
Hall

Upper Saddle River, New Jersey 07458

Library of Congress Cataloging-in-Publication Data

Frey, Charles H.

   Classics of young adult literature / Charles H. Frey, Lucy Rollin.
      p. cm.
Includes index
    ISBN 0–13–094218–9
   1. Young adult literature, American—History and criticism.   2. Canon
(Literature)   I. Rollin, Lucy.   II. Title.
   PS490 .F74 2003
     810.9'9283—dc21

                            2003003648

Editor-in-Chief: Leah Jewell
Assistant Editor: Karen A. Schultz
Editorial Assistant: Jennifer Migueis
Production Liaison: Fran Russello
Editorial/Production Supervision: Bruce Hobart (Pine Tree Composition, Inc.)
Manufacturing Manager: Mary Ann Gloriande
Prepress and Manufacturing Buyer: Brian Mackey
Marketing Director: Beth Gillett Mejia
Marketing Manager: Rachel Falk
Cover Designer: Robert Farrar-Wagner

This book was set in 10/12 Janson by Pine Tree Composition, Inc. and was printed and bound by Courier Companies, Inc. The cover was printed by Phoenix Graphics.

Credits appear on page 1177, which constitutes a continuation of the copyright page.

   ©2004 by Pearson Education, Inc.
             Upper Saddle River, NJ 07458

Printed in the United States of America
10 9 8 7 6 5 4 3 2 1

ISBN: 0-13-094218-9

Pearson Education Ltd., London
Pearson Education Australia PTY. Limited, Sydney
Pearson Education Singapore, Pte. Ltd
Pearson Education North Asia Ltd, Hong Kong
Pearson Education Canada, Ltd., Toronto
Pearson Educación de Mexico, S.A. de C.V.
Pearson Education—Japan, Tokyo
Pearson Education Malaysia, Pte. Ltd
Pearson Education, Upper Saddle River, New Jersey

For

Professor Mark I. West,

Friend and Colleague

CONTENTS

L. M. MONTGOMERY 189
(1874–1942)

Anne of Green Gables 192

MAUREEN DALY   361
(1921–)

Seventeenth Summer   365

S. E. HINTON   497
(1948–)

The Outsiders   501

ALICE CHILDRESS   579
(1920–1994)

A Hero Ain't Nothin' but a Sandwich   582

viii

PREFACE

In North American colleges and universities, courses in English, Education, and Information Science often include the subject of Young Adult, or Adolescent, Literature. Most of the works commonly taught in such courses are realistic novels written during the last three or four decades, particularly those taught in any high school or junior high school today. As a consequence of this curriculum-materials approach, classic works revealing the long and rich history of young adult literature and classic works that challenge censorship often are not read in their entirety, if at all. Students tend not to realize that there is indeed a core group of young adult novels and authors respected for creating a tradition of historical depth and integrity. No anthology has heretofore existed to collect such novels and authors and to provide a history and analysis of relations among them. Instead, courses in Young Adult Literature have presented disparate scatterings of recent paperbacks, often with no overlaps at all among reading lists. What could and should be a true literature and a true subject of inquiry becomes a number of discrete reading experiences.

This anthology is designed to encourage the teaching of Young Adult Literature as a long-standing and valuable cultural phenomenon offering profound social and psychological exploration as well as artistic worth. It is a coming-of-age literature spanning at least a century and a half, a literature that presents significant situations, themes, and emotions shared by youths from diverse families and subcultures. We, the editors, believe it is time for Young Adult Literature to assert its rightful, valuable place in the teaching of classic, or enduring, literature, and we believe that this anthology can aid many teachers and their students in sharing their informed respect for such classics studied in relation to each other.

The chief problem we faced as we embarked on this project was, of course, deciding what to include. As with any anthology, practical problems of length, availability, and cost became intertwined with issues of quality and taste. We struggled with many lists of possible works, developing our criteria a little at a time. Finally we settled on these: we would include about eleven complete works (partial works were never considered); each work should have been intended, in the mind of the author or the publisher, for a teen audience; the work should have a young adult protagonist, a reasonably complex plot and complex characters, and themes that touch not only on teen concerns but on basic human issues; the author's style should be characterized by such maturity bad one. The suffix *–escence* or *–escent* usually means "becoming," or growing; it well conveys the essential quality of this literature, and certainly one must take the psychology of the adolescent into account if one is to think seriously about fiction describing it. (On the other hand, the age delineation of adolescence varies. Twelve used to be the entry, and eighteen the exit point; in recent years sociologists and psychologists, acknowledging significant changes in Western physique and lifestyle, suggest that adolescence may begin at ten or eleven and continue until age 22 at least.)

In the turbulent 1960s, to high school students and college freshmen becoming more politically and sexually outspoken, terms such as "juvenile" and "adolescent" sounded like insults. Young people demanded to be heard and respected; they also demanded a literature that accurately reflected their lives. Publishers responded by creating the term "Young Adult" and actively seeking writers who would address modern teen concerns. Thus the term worked its way into the reviewing journals and into the libraries, and "YA Literature" was officially born. The age delineation for Young Adults varies depending on who uses it, but for our purposes, in this anthology, we have thought in terms of ages thirteen to twenty. The winners of the Newbery Medal for excellence in Children's Literature are a gray area. While they appeal to readers up to and including age fourteen, and while many students, teachers, and critics count works such as *Holes* and *The Giver* among the very best of YA novels (for good reason; these are extraordinary works that speak to children, adults, and everyone in between), we have elected not to include them here but to concentrate on works for older readers. We have also elected to include novels *written or published* with an audience of young readers in mind, though we recognize that the definition of YA can certainly include what young readers *choose* to read.

As the brief history below will show, Young Adult literature has from its inception been intertwined with *popular* literature—that is, literature deliberately written to sell to a particular audience or literature that has achieved phenomenal success in the marketplace, as distinguished from the artistic creation of an individual not primarily interested in profit. This connection constantly raises questions of value among critics whether they are talking about Horatio Alger or Judy Blume: can a book written "to order" really achieve literary excellence? For many, the answer is a flat "No." Books that non-academic readers buy in huge quantities, too, whether or not they were written with the market in mind (Stephen King and Danielle Steel, for example), are suspect. In this anthology, we acknowledge this Gordian knot of value, prejudice, taste, and history not by offering clear answers (there aren't any) but by providing a range of Young Adult books demonstrating the complexity of this issue. We hope they will stimulate discussion about the distinction between popular and elite culture and all the problems it raises.

A Brief History of Young Adult Literature

Although the term "Young Adult Literature" emerged in the late 1960s, literature designed for readers no longer children but not quite adults emerged most clearly in America about two centuries ago, resulting from the new concept of adolescence. Speaking very generally, before then children were children until they became adults. Since we have no formal rite of passage as some cultures do, leaving school was probably the most significant marker of maturity, and of those few who went to school at all, many left shortly after their first decade of life, went to work, and took on the full responsibilities of adults soon thereafter. But as our society became less agrarian and more affluent and literate, school time lengthened; the child's financial dependence on the family correspondingly lengthened, and that sheltered yet increasingly liberated period we call adolescence took shape.

As the population became larger and more varied, religion loosened its hold on education and reading, opening the way for pleasure reading (though to a large portion of adults this activity remained suspect for years to come). William Taylor Adams, who wrote under the pseudonym Oliver Optic, began providing such pleasure in the 1850s with his novels, stories, and magazines for young readers. In a scenario that characterizes Young Adult literature still, his popularity caused parents and librarians to ban his work from their shelves. But in 1867, Horatio Alger, Jr., entered the game with his story of street life in New York City, *Ragged Dick*. Its success (and his own financial troubles) encouraged him to write other books like it, and the series novel—a genre that has played a major role in Young Adult Literature and attracted its share of nervous critics— was born.

The cataclysm of the American Civil War forced very young men into military service, leaving girls at home to work out a different sort of life, a daily routine not primarily concerned with either school or marriage. Louisa May Alcott, already an accomplished writer for adults, was invited to try her hand at a "girls' book," and this she did in 1868, conveying with vibrant prose and unforgettable characters an all-female Civil War household. *Little Women* resembled the sentimental domestic novel that dominated girls' and women's reading, but transcended it with its complexity, thoughtfulness, and fully-realized characters. It was immediately popular with girls, and has remained so to this day.

One particularly American form of literature emerged in the popular market during the second half of the nineteenth century: the dime novel. Though "trashy" novels had been around for years, the 1860 publication of *Malaeska* by the New York firm run by Erastus and Irwin Beadle, heralded a new kind of popular literature. Short, encased in cheap paper covers, and selling for a dime, the books offered action and excitement; like *Malaeska* they were often set in the Old West where lawlessness ruled and rough brave men shot it out in saloons, though by the end of the century their most popular stories concerned hard-boiled private detectives. Most of the books were written by hacks who could crank them out at the rate of four a year (ironically, Alcott wrote some dime novels for cash), but the Beadles insisted on high standards for writing, and for morality. *Malaeska* represents the best such work. Predictably, however, the popularity of these action-packed tales among young readers, especially boys, alerted parents, librarians, clergy, and even newspaper editors to their "dangers," and many public campaigns were waged against them. They died out around 1900, replaced in the hearts of the young by the series books of the Stratemeyer Syndicate.

From 1899 until about 1940, popular series books from Edward Stratemeyer's stable of writers formed the bulk of Young Adult reading. As a young man in the late nineteenth century, Stratemeyer determined to follow in Horatio Alger's footsteps and write for a market of teen boys. Because he was both fast and good at it, publishing opportunities presented themselves so often that

3

he realized he could publish more by hiring people to do the actual writing while he supplied the outlines of plot and character as well as a fictional name for the otherwise anonymous author (who had to sign a contract agreeing never to divulge his or her identity). The syndicate system he launched enabled him to produce hundreds of books each year, selling them for fifty cents each and raking in a huge profit. They supplied what teens wanted to read: short novels about teenage protagonists enjoying independence, action, and adventure, in an easy-to-read style and a predictable format. One of his earliest and longest-running successes was The Rover Boys series, which followed the adventures of three teenaged boys through thirty volumes by "Arthur Winfield." The Tom Swift series, by "Victor Appleton," focused on teenaged Tom who always moved quickly thanks to various interesting vehicles. The Motion Picture Boys, The Moving Picture Girls, The Motor Girls, The Bobbsey Twins, Ruth Field-ing, and many other series were created by Stratemeyer and written by hundreds of nameless authors across the country. In 1929 he created The Hardy Boys, by "Franklin W. Dixon," and in 1930, his greatest success, Nancy Drew, by "Carolyn Keene." Stratemeyer died shortly after Nancy appeared and his daughters took over the syndicate. One of them, Harriet Stratemeyer Adams, for many years claimed that she had written the Nancy Drew books, but in the 1980s Mildred Wirt Benson, a Midwestern newspaperwoman, revealed that she was the true and original "Carolyn Keene." Benson died in 2002. Meanwhile the syndicate system still produces many favorite series books for teen and pre-teen readers, and still, as it did in the early 1900s, attracts the distrust and even the ire of many adults who believe the books are, essentially, junk.

By the late 1930s several fine writers were producing novels for Young Adults, anticipating the full flowering of the genre in the 1960s. Florence Crannell Means wrote sensitive, thoughtful works with minority teens—black, Navajo, Japanese-American—as protagonists. Among her best is *Shuttered Windows*, about a black girl from the North who attends school on a South Carolina island and struggles against identifying with the other girls at the school. Maureen Daly's 1942 novel *Seventeenth Summer*, begun before the author herself was twenty, showed that a romance for teen girls could be serious and subtle, poetic and psychologically realistic. John R. Tunis set his tales in gymnasiums and playing fields, but he wrote no ordinary sports books, choosing instead to tackle issues such as anti-Semitism as well as the sometimes unreasonable pressures on high school athletes. Such writers approached their chosen audience with dignity; they had faith that young people could enjoy a serious novel as much as a series mystery.

Beginning in 1945 and accelerating through the 1950s, the concept of the *teenager* dominated the popular media. As opposed to the *adolescent* struggling seriously with assimilation into the adult world, the *teenager* lived in the present as a joyful consumer—of music, cars, and fashion. The high school increasingly became a place apart, not so much where teenagers tested their skills as potential adults but where they bonded with each other and maintained their own language, social hierarchy, and goals. Many book publishers responded to this image by producing pleasant, unchallenging reading for teens, such as *Double Date* by Rosamond du Jardin, *Going on Sixteen* by Betty Cavanna, *Junior Miss* by Sally Benson, and *Hot Rod* by Henry Gregor Felsen. For serious fare, reading teens turned to adult novels such as *Cry, the Beloved Country* (1948) and *Lord of the Flies* (1955).

Probably the most famous literary adolescent of them all, Holden Caulfield, stumbled into existence in 1951. One of the loneliest teenage characters in fiction (and one of the funniest, though he himself has no sense of humor), Holden tells his own story—of a three-day weekend in New York after being thrown out of prep school again—in the language that teens really used. J. D. Salinger intended *Catcher in the Rye* for adult readers, but it soon made its way into college classrooms, then into the reading lives of teenagers all over the country who embraced its authenticity. When it arrived in some high school senior English classes, however, it became the most censored book in America. It still remains at the top of any list of challenged books in the country, usually alongside Mark Twain's *The Adventures of Huckleberry Finn*, which it resembles in its indictment of adult values. *Catcher* is the premier example of a work not designed for Young Adult readers, but discovered by them and absorbed into the canon of favorite and most representative works. Countless succeeding YA novels have imitated its slangy first-person style, its profanity, and its suffering protagonist, though none has yet achieved its brilliance. It remains one of the most honest representations of adolescent language and emotion in American literature.

It is clear thus far that Young Adult Literature existed before 1967, but that year seemed to gather together all that had gone before, clarify its focus, and propel it into the 1970s, where YA established itself as a genuine presence in American literature. That year, S. E. Hinton published the novel that many believe is the first official work of Young Adult Literature: *The Outsiders*. Editors had by this time recognized that teen voices had to be heard, and here was the real thing: Susie Hinton, a teenager from Tulsa, Oklahoma, writing about drive-ins, switchblades, greasers, and rumbles, and turning it all into a romance of ideals and sacrifice. That same year, Ann Head published *Mr. and Mrs. Bo Jo Jones*, a novel that faced the reality of unplanned teen pregnancy, and Robert Lipsyte published *The Contender*, the spare story of a ghetto boy trying to become a boxer. Publishers' doors had opened and editors were inviting good writers to submit timely, honest novels with believable teen protagonists. Librarians and reviewers were equally welcoming and interested in such books.

Thus, by 1972, we had *The Pigman* by Paul Zindel; *His Own Where* by June Jordan; *Dinky Hocker Shoots Smack* by M. E. Kerr; *A Wizard of Earthsea* by Ursula LeGuin; and *The Man Without a Face* by Isabelle Holland. 1973 brought *Summer of My German Soldier* by Bette Greene; *The Friends* by Rosa Guy; and *A Hero Ain't Nothin' But a Sandwich* by Alice Childress. 1974 brought *The Chocolate War* by Robert Cormier and *House of Stairs* by William Sleator. In 1975 we had S. E. Hinton's *Rumble Fish*, Judy Blume's *Forever*, M. E. Kerr's *Is That You, Miss Blue?*, and Lawrence Yep's *Dragonwings*. Sue Ellen Bridgers gave us *Home Before Dark* and Richard Peck gave us *Are You in the House Alone?* in 1976. The decade also produced *Words By Heart* by Ouida Sebestyen, *Beauty* by Robin McKinley, and more books by Richard Peck, Robert Cormier, Sue Ellen Bridgers, Rosa Guy, Robert Lipsyte, and S. E. Hinton.

Such an outpouring of fine novels clearly intended and published for Young Adults was unprecedented. The 1970s is sometimes called "The Golden Age" of YA Literature, as the period from 1865 to 1910 in England is called "The Golden Age" of Children's Literature for the same reason: something in the Zeitgeist produced a series of books for this audience that raised the standard of the art for those who came after. Richard Peck, one of the first and best spokespersons for YA, believes that "some of the best fiction of the last quarter century is in our pages," because as YA writers, "we don't allow ourselves five-hundred pages, and we can't resort to pornography to mask weak writing or to keep the pacing peppy" (Preface, *St. James Guide to Young Adult Writers* 1999).

Of course, not all YA novels published in the 1970s were superior works of fiction. Some reviewers and critics recognized a certain sameness in what we might call the "second tier" of YA books: they centered around some kind of problem—divorce, alcohol, sex, peer pressure, etc.; they were told in a casual first-person voice; they included a few curse words. The parents in them were flawed people; the protagonist discovered an older adult outside the family who dispensed the wisdom needed to solve the problem. The mood of the books was generally unrelieved by humor. Their literary style was undistinguished. They *felt* as if they had been written with a formula. These books acquired the label "problem novels," a term that for a time was applied to almost any YA novel despite the complexity of, for example, Robert Cormier's work. Some novels for young readers during this period seemed so overburdened with "problems" as to suggest their authors were less interested in producing literature than in making sociological statements.

In the 1980s and 1990s, many of the writers mentioned above continued to write excellent fiction for YA audiences, while new ones were attracted to the genre. Chris Crutcher, Bruce Brooks, Gary Paulsen, Cynthia Voigt, Walter Dean Myers, and Brock Cole—along with Cormier, Lipsyte, and others mentioned above—freed the genre from the "problem novel" label with their complex characters and plots, their touches of humor, their honesty and their artistry. Several writers took new risks with their work. Annette Curtis Klaus combined the romance with the vampire tale in *The Silver Kiss* (1990); Francesca Lia Block created a funny, moving punk fairy tale in her brilliant *Weetzie Bat* (1989). In *The Arizona Kid* (1988), Ron Koertge combined a boy's first heterosexual experience and a sympathetic depiction of his uncle's homosexuality without being heavy-handed about either. Jacqueline Woodson's *I Hadn't Meant to Tell You This* (1995) treated the subject of incest. Books offering insights into other cultures also appeared more frequently. Suzanne Fisher Staples took us into modern-day Pakistan with her touching coming-of-age tale *Shabanu* (1989) and into a modern harem with its exciting sequel, *Haveli* (1993). Linda Crew depicted the difficulties of a Cambodian girl's entry into American culture in *Children of the River* (1989). In one of the best such books, Victor Martinez offered a touching glimpse into the life of a Mexican-American boy in *Parrot in the Oven* (1996). The sexual frankness of today's television programs and films, our increasingly multicultural society, and the lure and power of the Internet cause Richard Peck to confess, "We write for the people we never were . . . I write in awe of what being young is today, of the choices I never had to make" (Preface, *St. James Guide to Young Adult Writers*, 1999).

Still, he writes, as do many others who continually test the boundaries of what Young Adult Literature means, and who consequently face repeated challenges from readers fearing such fiction. Which of their books will have the shelf life of *The Chocolate War* or *The Outsiders* remains to be seen. What is clear is that the latest Chris Crutcher novel could not be on the shelves without all the YA writers that have preceded him and helped to create his editor, publisher, reading audience, and reviewer. As with all human endeavors, some things about YA Literature have undergone great change; other things have

hardly changed at all. The chief function of this brief history, and of this anthology as a whole, is to bring that contrast into focus.

Censorship

Literature for the young has always been a convenient target for censors. Parents are naturally frightened as their children approach puberty, encounter peer
pressure, and seek the loosening of family ties. Compared to movies, television,
cars, drugs, and now the Internet, a book seems an easy thing control. The difficulties come when those adults wish to control not only what their children
read but what other children read as well. Such control is an infringement on
the First Amendment rights of all Americans. When the target is a trashy dime
novel, or the horror comics of the 1950s that prompted congressional hearings,
the fears of such adults may be, to some degree, understandable. But sophisticated literary works—*Huckleberry Finn* and *Catcher in the Rye* for instance—are
just as often suspect.

By the 1960s, as Young Adult Literature became a separate genre, those who
would ban or restrict the reading of all young people recognized the warning
signals: increasing sexual frankness in teen novels; more curse words; more
parental characters who were unattractive or even dangerous; the suggestion,
subtle or overt, that teens could get along without much adult supervision, and
in some cases might be better off without it. Three books from this decade remain at the top of most lists of challenged books. In 1971 came Beatrice Sparks'
Go Ask Alice, which was published as though it were the authentic diary of a girl
on drugs. In 1973 Alice Childress published *A Hero Ain't Nothin' But a Sandwich*, the story of a thirteen-year-old boy hooked on heroin, told in Harlem
street language. Then in 1974 came Cormier's *The Chocolate War*, which many
believe is the premier YA novel, the one that set the highest literary standard
for such fiction, but which depicts corruption in a Catholic school. In 1975 Judy
Blume's *Forever* was published, the first novel for teens to suggest that they
could have responsible sex lives.

It can be no accident that the incident which prompted the most important
Supreme Court decision regarding the right to read, took place in 1976, when a
group of school board members from the Island Trees, New York, school district removed several books from the school library shelves because they were
"anti-American, anti-Christian, anti-Semitic, and just plain filthy" (quoted in
Donelson and Nilsen, *Literature for Today's Young Adults* 1993, 526). A student,
Stephen Pico, along with others who protested this action, brought suit; the
U.S. Supreme Court heard the case in 1979. In a very mixed verdict, the Court
upheld the students' and librarians' rights, but asserted the right of school
boards to have a say in classroom reading material. There have been other
courtroom conflicts over this issue (see Donelson and Nilsen 519–531 for a
thorough discussion), but none has produced any lasting solution. Librarians
everywhere, and teachers like Gloria Pipkin and Claudia Johnson in Florida,
Cecilia Lacks in Missouri, and Alfred Wilder in Colorado, along with guidance
counselor Mike Dishnow in Wisconsin (who was fired for defending Blume's
Forever) still must fight individual battles.

When a political climate encourages, condones, or just ignores attacks on
free reading, the price is high for writers themselves. In a book of stories

collected by Judy Blume and dedicated to the National Coalition Against Censorship, Norma Fox Mazer says, "Where once I went to my writing without a backward glance, now I sometimes have to clear my mind of those shadowy censorious presences. That's bad for me as a writer, bad for you as a reader" (*Places I Never Meant to Be* 1999, 33). Katherine Paterson comments, "These days . . . I look more closely at certain words or paragraphs that I realize may cause trouble for teachers or librarians who use or recommend my books. It is very painful for me when someone else has to put her or his reputation or livelihood on the line because of something I have written" (*Places* 70). Walter Dean Myers observes that much censorship is "by omission," preventing certain ideas from ever being written, a kind of censorship that "corrupts the development of the writer" (*Places* 113). He finds this especially true among African American writers, whose work may be suppressed before it is ever published.

Young Adult Literature will not be free of challenges like these. It *cannot*, if it remains true to its purpose of reflecting honestly the lives of those making the transition from childhood to adulthood. Young adults *must* question the world they are about to enter. Their task is to make it better, and so they must explore new values and ideas, revisit the old ones, and make careful choices. They must also question themselves. Many of the choices they face are the same today as they were a century ago; many are entirely new. YA Literature at its best offers an honest approach to those choices and a safe place to ponder both the future and the past.

Fantasy and Romance

Although Young Adult Literature is most represented by the genre of the short realistic novel, young adult readers of course enjoy other genres. In the case of fantasy and romance, they often "cross over"—that is, read adult or children's novels as well as YA. Readers who like fantasy might turn to Stephen King, Anne Rice, or Robert Jordan as well as to Madeleine L'Engle, Susan Cooper, Lloyd Alexander, or C. S. Lewis. Romance has long been a popular genre for adult women, and teen girls who grew up with the Sweet Valley High series, as young adults may enjoy Daphne du Maurier's works or those of Danielle Steel and V. C. Andrews. Thus, despite the number of fantasies and romances written and published for YA readers, issues of taste and quality connected with popular culture tend to arise most frequently in these genres.

What is frequently labeled "high fantasy" is distinguished by its Arthurian origins. Set in the misty past, often echoing Welsh mythology in its language and proper names, it tends to depict a young male on a quest and to culminate in a great struggle between good and evil. J. R. R. Tolkien's *Lord of the Rings* trilogy is the touchstone for such fantasies and the inspiration for one of the finest works of high fantasy written for young adults: Ursula LeGuin's *A Wizard of Earthsea* (1968). Set in a primitive land of islands, where wizards are trained and sent out to perform various necessary magical services for the populace, LeGuin's tale has the dignity and scope of a true classic, and her theme—a young person's search for himself—reverberates in some form through all YA literature. Jane Yolen and Robin McKinley more often focus on a female protagonist as they reshape familiar fairy patterns into tales for young adults, thereby unveiling the true nature of these tales: although they have come to be associated with children, they are almost invariably about young adults experiencing the wider world for the first time.

Many young adult readers also enjoy science fiction, a genre which explores what our future might become. One can argue that no genre is more important to young readers today, as their lives move rapidly into an age dominated by computers. No longer characterized only by the "space cowboy" tales from the pulp magazines of the 1940s, this genre has gained dignity especially through the work of Ray Bradbury in the thoughtful fables of his *Martian Chronicles* (1950) and the social critique of *Fahrenheit 451* (1953). Among writers of science fiction for young adults, Sylvia Engdahl advanced the genre with *Enchantress from the Stars* (1970), as did British writer Peter Dickinson with *Eva* (1989). A favorite with American readers, *Eva* depicts the life of a girl whose brain is placed in the body of a chimpanzee. Like all good science fiction, this novel relies on sound research and sends a warning about the future, in this case by depicting the decline of human sympathy for other species in an overpopulated world.

Probably no genre is as popular among girls and women of all ages, ethnic groups, and educational levels as the romance, and no genre attracts as much negative criticism—no coincidence, surely. The term *romance* began to acquire its negative connotations as early as the eighteenth century when it was distinguished from the novel, the genre that depicted "real life." Holman and Harmon's *Handbook to Literature* (1992) still sounds negative when it defines the popular term thus: "In common usage, it refers to works with extravagant characters, remote and exotic places, highly exciting and heroic events, passionate love, or mysterious and supernatural experiences" (413). Today the term is most used as a synonym for "love story." Such tales have appealed to female readers since the English novel was first "invented," by Samuel Richardson when he wrote *Pamela* in 1740, the story of a virtuous girl fending off the advances of her lascivious employer. American readers finally received their own version of this kind of romance in 1867 when Augusta Jane Evans Wilson, known as the "American Bronte," published *St. Elmo*, a similar tale of a virtuous girl searching for true love. It sold in the thousands and opened a market that remains robust.

The romance written specifically for young adult readers is a more recent phenomenon. Maureen Daly's *Seventeenth Summer* was published in 1942 on adult lists. But other briefer, less sophisticated romances for teens were beginning to appear, as publishers acknowledged the post-war growth of teen consumerism in all areas. Romances by Mary Stolz, Betty Cavanna, and Rosamund du Jardin attracted teen girls all during the 1940s and 1950s. With the 1960s and 1970s came romances less centered on the malt shop, the prom, and the right dress, and more attuned to the psychological and physical difficulties of romantic relationships, especially the pressures of sex. Paul Zindel's *My Darling, My Hamburger* (1971) faced the reality of abortion. Judy Blume wrote *Forever* (1975) to demonstrate that teens could have sex responsibly but still might suffer the loss of love. Rosa Guy's *Ruby* (1976) detailed with sympathy a doomed lesbian romance.

In the 1980s, however, came a phenomenal resurgence of the kind of romances popular in the 1940s and 1950s: books in which summer fun and innocent boy–girl romance occupied center stage. Publishers rushed to capitalize on the trend; the book world was startled when in 1985 a Sweet Valley High book, an entry in the popular series by Francine Pascal, reached the *New York Times*

9

MALAESKA

THE INDIAN WIFE OF THE WHITE HUNTER

PUBLISHERS' NOTICE FROM THE FIRST EDITION

WE TAKE pleasure in introducing the reader to the following romance by Mrs. Ann S. Stephens. It is one of the most interesting and fascinating works of this eminent author. It is chosen as the initial volume of the Dime Novel series, from the chaste character of its delineations, from the interest which attaches to its fine pictures of border life and Indian adventure, and from the real romance of its incidents. It is American in all its features, pure in its tone, elevating in its sentiments; and may be referred to as a work representative of the series that is to follow—every volume of which will be of the highest order of merit, from the pens of authors whose intellectual and moral excellencies have already given the writers an enviable name, in this country and in Europe. By the publication of the series contemplated, it is hoped to reach all classes, old and young, male and female, in a manner at once to captivate and to enliven—to answer to the popular demand for works of romance, but also to instil a pure and elevating sentiment in the hearts and minds of the people.

BEADLE & CO.

New York,
June, 1860.

CHAPTER 1

The brake hung low on the rifted rock
  With sweet and holy dread;
The wild-flowers trembled to the shock
  Of the red man's stealthy tread;
And all around fell a fitful gleam
  Through the light and quivering spray,
While the noise of a restless mountain-stream
  Rush'd out on the stilly day.

THE TRAVELER who has stopped at Catskill, on his way up the Hudson, will remember that a creek of no insignificant breadth washes one side of the village, and that a heavy stone dwelling stands a little up from the water on a point of verdant meadow-land, which forms a lip of the stream, where it empties into the more majestic river. This farm-house is the only object that breaks the green and luxuriant beauty of the point, on that side, and its quiet and entire loneliness contrasts pleasantly with the bustling and crowded little village on the opposite body of land. There is much to attract attention to that dwelling. Besides occupying one of the most lovely sites on the river, it is remarkable for an appearance of old-fashioned comfort at variance with the pillared houses and rustic cottages which meet the eye everywhere on the banks of the Hudson. There are no flowers to fling fragrance about it, and but little of embellishment is manifest in its grounds; but it is surrounded by an abundance of thrifty fruit-trees; an extensive orchard sheds its rich foliage to the sunshine on the bank, and the sward is thick and heavy which slopes greenly from the front door down to the river's brink.

The interior of the house retains an air of substantial comfort which answers well to the promise conveyed without. The heavy furniture has grown old with its occupants; rich it has been in its time, and now it possesses the rare quality of fitness, and of being in harmony with surrounding things. Every thing about that house is in perfect keeping with the character and appearance of its owner. The occupant himself, is a fine stately farmer of the old class—shrewd, penetrating, and intelligent—one of those men who contrive to keep the heart green when the frost of age is chilling the blood and whitening upon the brow. He has already numbered more than the threescore years and ten allotted to man. His habits and the fashion of his attire are those of fifty years ago. He still clings to huge wood-fires, apples, and cider in the winter-season, and allows a bevy of fine cows to pasture on the rich grass in front of his dwelling in the summer. All the hospitable feeling of former years remains warm at his heart. He is indeed a fine specimen of the staunch old republican farmer of the last century, occupying the house which his father erected, and enjoying a fresh old age beneath the roof tree which shadowed his infancy.

During a sojourn in this vicinity last season, it was one of our greatest pleasures to spend an evening with the old gentleman, listening to legends of the Indians, reminiscences of the Revolution, and pithy remarks on the present age, with which he loved to entertain us, while we occasionally interrupted him by comparing knitting-work with the kind old lady, his wife, or by the praises of a sweet little grandchild, who would cling about his knees and play with the silver buckles on his shoes as he talked. That tall, stately old man, and the sweet child made a beautiful picture of "age at play with infancy," when the fire-light flickered over them, to the ancient family pictures, painted in Holland, hanging on the wall behind us, in the old-fashioned oval frames, which, with the heavy Dutch Bible, which lay on the stand, secured with hasps and brass hinges, ponderous as the fastenings of a prison-door, were family relics precious to the old gentleman from antiquity and association. Yes, the picture was pleasant to look upon; but there was pleasure in listening to his legends and stories. If the one here related is not exactly as he told it, he will not fail to recognize the beautiful young Indian girl, whom he described to us, in the character of Malaeska.

At the time of our story, the beautiful expanse of country which stretches from the foot of the Catskill mountains to the Hudson was one dense wilderness. The noble stream glided on in the solemn stillness of nature, shadowed with trees that had battled with storms for centuries, its surface as yet unbroken, save by the light prow of the Indian's canoe. The lofty rampart of mountains frowned against the sky as they do now, but rendered more gloomy by the thick growth of timber which clothed them at the base; they loomed up from the dense sea of foliage like the outposts of a darker world. Of all the cultivated acres which at the present day sustain thousands with their products, one little clearing alone smiled up from the heart of the wilderness. A few hundred acres had been cleared by a hardy band of settlers, and a cluster of log-houses was erected in the heart of the little valley which now contains Catskill village. Although in the neighborhood of a savage Indian tribe, the little band of pioneers remained unmolested in their humble occupations, gradually clearing the land around their settlement, and sustaining their families on the game which was found in abundance in the mountains. They held little intercourse with the Indians, but hitherto no act of hostility on either side had aroused discontent between the settler and the savages.

It was early in May, about a year after the first settlement of the whites, when some six or eight of the stoutest men started for the woods in search of game. A bear had been seen on the brink of the clearing at break of day, and while the greater number struck off in search of more humble game, three of the most resolute followed his trail, which led to the mountains.

The foremost of the three hunters was an Englishman of about forty, habited in a threadbare suit of blue broadcloth, with drab gaiters buttoned up to his knees, and a hat sadly shorn of its original nap. His hunting apparatus bespoke the peculiar care which all of his country so abundantly bestow on their implements of sport. The other two were much younger, and dressed in home-made cloth, over which were loose frocks manufactured from the refuse flax or swingled tow.[1] Both were handsome, but different in the cast of their features. The character of the first might be read in his gay air and springy step, as he followed close to the Englishman, dashing away the brushwood with the muzzle of his gun, and detecting with a quick eye the broken twigs or disturbed leaves which betrayed the course of the hunted bear. There was also something characteristic in the wearing of his dress, in the fox-skin cap thrown carelessly on one side of his superb head, exposing a mass of short brown curls around the left ear and temple, and in the bosom of his coarse frock, thrown open so as to give free motion to a neck Apollo might have coveted. He was a hunter, who had occasionally visited the settlement of late, but spent whole weeks in the

---

1 *swingeled tow*   flax fibers scraped clean with a wooden knife or swingle.

woods, professedly in collecting furs by his own efforts, or by purchase from the tribe of Indians encamped at the foot of the mountains.

The last was more sedate in his looks, and less buoyant in his air. There was an intellectual expression in his high, thoughtful brow, embrowned though it was by exposure. A depth of thought in his serious eye, and a graceful dignity in his carriage, bespoke him as one of those who hide deep feeling under an appearance of coldness and apathy. He had been a schoolmaster in the Bay State,[2] from whence he had been drawn by the bright eyes and merry laugh of one Martha Fellows, a maiden of seventeen, whose father had moved to the settlement at Catskill the preceding summer, and to whom, report said, he was to be married whenever a minister, authorized to perform the ceremony, should find his way to the settlement.

The three hunters bent their way in a southwestern direction from the settlement, till the forest suddenly opened into a beautiful and secluded piece of meadow-land, known to this day by its Dutch title of "the Straka," which means, our aged friend informed us, a strip of land. The Straka lay before them of an oblong form, some eight or ten acres in expanse, with all its luxuriance of trees, grass, and flowers, bathed in the dew and sunshine of a warm summer's morning. It presented a lovely contrast to the dense wilderness from which the hunters emerged, and they halted for a moment beneath the boughs of a tall hickory to enjoy its delicious freshness. The surface of the inclosure was not exactly level, but down the whole length it curved gently up from the middle, on either side, to the magnificent trees that hedged it in with a beautiful and leafy rampart. The margin was irregular; here and there a clump of trees shot down into the inclosure, and the clearing occasionally ran up into the forest in tiny glades and little grassy nooks, in which the sunlight slumbered like smiles on the face of a dreaming infant. On every side the trunks of huge trees shot up along the margin beneath their magnificent canopy of leaves, like the ivied columns of a ruin, or fell back in the misty perspective of the forest, scarcely discernible in its gloom of shadow. The heavy piles of foliage, which fell amid the boughs like a wealth of drapery flung in masses to the summer wind, was thrifty and ripe with the warm breath of August. No spirit of decay had as yet shed a gorgeous breath over its deep, rich green, but all was wet with dew, and kindled up by the sunlight to a thousand varying tints of the same color. A bright spring gushed from a swell of ground in the upper part of the inclosure, and the whole surface of the beautiful spot was covered with a vigorous growth of tall meadow-grass, which rose thicker and brighter and of a more delicate green down the middle, where the spring curved onward in a graceful rivulet, musical as the laugh of a child. As if called to life by the chime of a little brook, a host of white wild-flowers unfolded their starry blossoms along the margin, and clumps of swamp-lilies shed an azure hue along the grass.

Until that day, our hunters had ever found "the Straka" silent and untenanted, save by singing-birds, and wild deer which came down from the mountains to feed on its rich verdure; but now a dozen wreaths of smoke curled up from the trees at the northern extremity, and a camp of newly-erected wigwams might be seen through a vista in the wood. One or two were built even on the edge of the clearing; the grass was much trampled around them, and three or four half-naked Indian children lay rolling upon it, laughing, shouting, and

---

2 *Bay State*   Massachusetts colony.

flinging up their limbs in the pleasant morning air. One young Indian woman was also frolicking among them, tossing an infant in her arms, caroling and playing with it. Her laugh was musical as a bird song, and as she darted to and fro, now into the forest and then out into the sunshine, her long hair glowed like the wing of a raven, and her motion was graceful as an untamed gazelle. They could see that the child, too, was very beautiful, even from the distance at which they stood, and occasionally, as the wind swept toward them, his shout came ringing upon it like the gush of waters leaping from their fount.

"This is a little *too* bad," muttered the Englishman, fingering his gun-lock. "Can they find no spot to burrow in but 'the Straka?' St. George! but I have a mind to shoot the squaw and wring the neck of every red imp among them."

"Do it!" exclaimed Danforth, turning furiously upon him; "touch but a hair of her head, and by the Lord that made me, I will bespatter that tree with your brains!"

The Englishman dropped the stock of his musket hard to the ground, and a spot of fiery red flashed into his cheek at this savage burst of anger so uncalled for and so insolent. He gazed a moment on the frowning face of the young hunter, and then lifting his gun, turned carelessly away.

"Tut, man, have done with this," he said; "I did but jest. Come, we have lost the trail, and shall miss the game, too, if we tarry longer; come."

The Englishman shouldered his musket, as he spoke, and turned into the woods. Jones followed, but Danforth lingered behind.

"I must see what this means," he muttered, glancing after his companions, and then at the group of young Indians; "what can have brought them so near the settlement?"

He gave another quick glance toward the hunters, and then hurried across "the Straka" toward the wigwams. Jones and the Englishman had reached the little lake or pond, which lies about a mile south of "the Straka," when they were again joined by Danforth. His brow was unclouded, and he seemed anxious to do away the effect of his late violence by more than ordinary cheerfulness. Harmony was restored, and they again struck into the trail of the bear, and pursued toward the mountains.

Noon found our hunters deep in the ravines which cut into the ridge of the Catskill on which the Mountain House now stands. Occupied by the wild scenery which surrounded him, Jones became separated from his companions, and long before he was aware of it, they had proceeded far beyond the reach of his voice. When he became sensible of his situation, he found himself in a deep ravine sunk into the very heart of the mountains. A small stream crept along the rocky bottom, untouched by a single sun's ray, though it was now high noon. Every thing about him was wild and fearfully sublime, but the shadows were refreshing and cool, and the stream, rippling along its rocky bed, sent up a pleasant murmur as he passed. Gradually a soft, flowing sound, like the rush of a current of air through a labyrinth of leaves and blossoms, came gently to his ear. As he proceeded, it became more musical and liquid, swelled upon the ear gradually and with a richer burden of sound, till he knew that it was the rush and leap of waters at no great distance. The ravine had sunk deeper and deeper, and fragments of rock lay thickly in the bed of the stream. Arthur Jones paused, and looked about him bewildered, and yet with a lofty, poetical feeling at his heart, aroused by a sense of the glorious handiwork of the Almighty encompassing him. He stood within the heart of the mountain, and it seemed to heave and tremble beneath his feet with some unknown influence as he gazed. Precipices, and rocks piled on rocks were heaped to the sky on either side. Large forest-trees stood rooted in the wide clefts, and waved their heavy boughs abroad like torn banners streaming upon the air. A strip of the blue heavens arched gently over the whole, and that was beautiful. It smiled softly, and like a promise of love over that sunless ravine. Another step, and the waterfall was before him. It was sublime, but beautiful—oh, very beautiful—that little body of water, curling and foaming downward like a wreath of snow sifted from the clouds, breaking in a shower of spray over the shelf of rocks which stayed its progress, then leaping a second foaming mass, down, down, like a deluge of flowing light, another hundred feet to the shadowy depths of the ravine. A shower of sunlight played amid the foliage far overhead, and upon the top of the curving precipice where the waters made their first leap. As the hunter became more calm, he remarked how harmoniously the beautiful and sublime were blended in the scene. The precipices were rugged and frowning, but soft, rich mosses and patches of delicate white wild-flowers clung about them. So profusely were those gentle flowers lavished upon the rocks, that it seemed as if the very spray drops were breaking into blossoms as they fell. The hunter's heart swelled with pleasure as he drank in the extreme beauty of the scene. He rested his gun against a fragment of rock, and sat down with his eyes fixed on the waterfall. As he gazed, it seemed as if the precipices were moving upward—upward to the very sky. He was pondering on this strange optical illusion, which has puzzled many a dizzy brain since, when the click of a gunlock struck sharply on his ear. He sprang to his feet. A bullet whistled by his head, cutting through the dark locks which curled in heavy masses above his temples, and as a sense of giddiness cleared from his brain, he saw a half-naked savage crouching upon the ledge of rocks which ran along the foot of the fall. The spray fell upon his bronzed shoulders and sprinkled the stock of his musket as he lifted it to discharge the other barrel. With the quickness of thought, Jones drew his musket to his eye and fired. The savage sent forth a fierce, wild yell of agony, and springing up with the bound of a wild animal, fell headlong from the shelf. Trembling with excitement, yet firm and courageous, the hunter reloaded his gun, and stood ready to sell his life as dearly as possible, for he believed that the ravine was full of concealed savages, who would fall upon him like a pack of wolves. But every thing remained quiet, and when he found that he was alone, a terrible consciousness of bloodshed came upon him. His knees trembled, his cheek burned, and, with an impulse of fierce excitement, he leaped over the intervening rocks and stood by the slain savage. He was lying with his face to the earth, quite dead; Jones drew forth his knife, and lifting the long, black hair, cut it away from the crown. With the trophy in his hand, he sprang across the ravine. The fearless spirit of a madness seemed upon him, for he rushed up the steep ascent, and plunged into the forest, apparently careless what direction he took. The sound of a musket stopped his aimless career. He listened, and bent his steps more calmly toward the eminence on which the Mountain House now stands. Here he found the Englishman with the carcass of a huge bear stretched at his feet, gazing on the glorious expanse of country, spread out like a map, hundreds of fathoms beneath him. His face was flushed, and the perspiration rolled freely from his forehead. Danforth stood beside him, also bearing traces of recent conflict.

"So you have come to claim a share of the meat," said the old hunter, as Jones approached. "It is brave to leave your skulking-place in the bushes, when the danger is over. Bless me, lad! what have you there?" he exclaimed, starting up and pointing to the scalp.

Jones related his encounter with the savage. The Englishman shook his head forebodingly.

"We shall have hot work for this job before the week is over," he said. "It was a foolish shot; but keep a good heart, my lad, for, hang me, if I should not have done the same thing if the red devil had sent a bullet so near my head. Come, we will go and bury the fellow the best way we can."

Jones led the way to the fall, but they found only a few scattered locks of black hair, and a pool of blood half washed from the rock by the spray. The body of the savage and his rifle had disappeared—how, it was in vain to conjecture.

One of the largest log-houses in the settlement had been appropriated as a kind of tavern, or place of meeting for the settlers when they returned from their hunting excursions. Here a store of spirits was kept, under the care of John Fellows and pretty Martha Fellows, his daughter, the maiden before mentioned. As the sun went down, the men who had gone to the woods in the morning, began to collect with their game. Two stags, raccoons and meaner game in abundance, were lying before the door, when the three hunters came in with the slain bear. They were greeted with a boisterous shout, and the hunters crowded eagerly forward to examine the prize; but when Jones cast the Indian's scalp on the pile, they looked in each other's faces with ominous silence, while the young hunter stood pale and collected before them. It was the first time that Indian life had been taken by any of their number, and they felt that in the shedding of red blood, the barriers of their protection were broken down.

"It is a bad business," said one of the elder settlers, waving his head and breaking the general silence. "There'll be no clear hunting in the woods after this; but how did it all come about, Jones? Let us know how you came by that scalp—did the varmint fire at you, or how was it?"

The hunters gathered around Jones, who was about to account for his possession of the scalp, when the door of the house was opened, and he happened to look into the little room thus exposed. It was scantily furnished with a few benches and stools; a bed was in one corner, and Martha Fellows, his promised wife, stood by a rough deal table,[3] on which were two or three drinking-cups, a couple of half-empty bottles, with a pitcher of water, backed by a broken mug, filled to the fractured top with maple molasses. Nothing of the kind could have been more beautiful than pretty Martha as she bent forward, listening with rapt attention to the animated whisper of William Danforth, who stood by her, divested of his coarse frock,[4] his cap lying on the table before him, and his athletic figure displayed to the best advantage by the roundabout[5] buttoned closely over his bosom. A red silk handkerchief, tied like a scarf round his waist, gave a picturesque gracefulness to his costume, altogether in harmony with his fine proportions, and with the bold cast of his head, which certainly was a model of muscular beauty.

A flash of anger shot athwart Arthur Jones' forehead, and a strange jealous feeling came to his heart. He began a confused account of his adventure, but the Englishman interrupted him, and took it upon himself to gratify the clamorous curiosity of the hunters, leaving Jones at liberty to scrutinize each look

---

3 *deal table*   made of fir or pine planks.
4 *frock*   robe.
5 *roundabout*   short jacket.

and motion of his lady-love. He watched with a jealous feeling the blush as it deepened and glowed on her embrowned cheek; he saw the sparkling pleasure of her hazel eyes, and the pretty dimples gathering about her red lips, like spots of sunlight flickering through the leaves of a red rose, and his heart sickened with distrust. But when the handsome hunter laid his hand on hers and bent his head, till the short curls on his temples almost mingled with her glossy ringlets, the lover could bear the sight no more. Breaking from the little band of hunters, he stalked majestically into the house, and approaching the object of his uneasiness, exclaimed, "Martha Fellows," in a voice which caused the pretty culprit to snatch her hand from under the hunter's, and to overturn two empty tin cups in her fright.

"Sir," said Martha, recovering herself, and casting a mischievous glance at Danforth, which was reciprocated with interest.

Mr. Arthur Jones felt that he was making himself ridiculous, and suppressing his wrath, he finished his magnificent commencement: "Will you give me a drink of water?" At which Martha pointed with her little embrowned hand to the pitcher, saying:

"There it is;" then, turning her back to her lover, she cast another arch glance at Danforth, and taking his cap from the table, began to blow upon the yellow fur, and put it to her cheek, as if it had been a pet kitten she was caressing, and all for the laudable purpose of tormenting the man who loved her, and whom she loved better than any thing in existence. Jones turned on her a bitter contemptuous look, and raising the pitcher to his lips, left the room. In a few minutes the other hunters entered, and Jason Fellows, father to Martha, announced it as decided by the hunters, who had been holding a kind of council without, that Arthur Jones and William Danforth, as the two youngest members of the community, should be dispatched to the nearest settlement to request aid to protect them from the Indians, whose immediate attack they had good reason to fear.

Martha, on hearing the names of the emissaries mentioned, dropped the cup she had been filling.

"Oh, not him—not them, I mean—they will be overtaken and tomahawked by the way!" she exclaimed, turning to her father with a look of affright.

"Let Mr. Danforth remain," said Jones, advancing to the table; "I will undertake the mission alone."

Tears came into Martha's eyes, and she turned them reproachfully to her lover; but, full of his heroic resolution to be tomahawked and comfortably scalped on his own responsibility, he turned majestically, without deigning to meet the tearful glance which was well calculated to mitigate his jealous wrath.

Danforth, on being applied to, requested permission to defer his answer till the morning, and the hunters left the house to divide the game, which had been forgotten in the general excitement.

Danforth, who had lingered to the last, took up his cap, and whispering good-night to Martha, left the house. The poor girl scarcely heeded his departure. Her eyes filled with tears, and seating herself on a settee which ran along one end of the room, she folded her arms on a board which served as a back, and burying her face upon them, wept violently.

As she remained in this position, she heard a familiar step on the floor. Her heart beat quick, fluttered a moment, and then settled to its regular pulsations again, for her lover had seated himself beside her. Martha wiped the tears from her eyes and remained quiet, for she knew that he had returned, and with that knowledge, the spirit of coquetry had revived; and when Jones, softened by her apparent sorrow—for he had seen her parting with Danforth—put his hand softly under her forehead and raised her face, the creature was laughing— laughing at his folly, as he thought.

"Martha, you are doing wrong—wrong to yourself and to me," said the disappointed lover, rising indignantly and taking his hat, with which he advanced to the door.

"Don't go," said Martha, turning her head till one cheek only rested on her arm, and casting a glance, half-repentant, half-comic, on her retreating lover; "don't go off so; if you do, you'll be very sorry for it."

Jones hesitated—she became very serious—the tears sprang to her eyes, and she looked exceedingly penitent. He returned to her side. Had he appealed to her feelings then—had he spoken of the pain she had given him in her encouragement of another, she would have acknowledged the fault with all proper humility; but he did no such thing—he was a common-sense man, and he resolved to end his first love-quarrel in a common-sense manner, as if common-sense ever had any thing to do with lovers' quarrels. "I will reason with her," he thought. "He will say I have made him very wretched, and I will tell him I am very sorry," *she* thought.

"Martha," he said, very deliberately, "why do I find you on terms of such familiarity with this Manhattan fellow?"

Martha was disappointed. He spoke quite too calmly, and there was a sarcastic emphasis in the word "fellow," that roused her pride. The lips, which had just begun to quiver with repentance, worked themselves into a pouting fullness, till they resembled the rose-bud just as it bursts into leaves. Her rounded shoulder was turned pettishly toward her lover, with the air of a spoiled child, and she replied that "he was always finding fault."

Jones took her hand, and was proceeding in his sensible manner to convince her that she was wrong, and acted wildly, foolishly, and with a careless disregard to her own happiness.

As might be expected, the beautiful rustic snatched her hand away, turned her shoulder more decidedly on her lover, and bursting into tears, declared that she would thank him if he would stop scolding, and that she did not care if she never set eyes on him again.

He would have remonstrated; "Do listen to common-sense," he said, extending his hand to take hers.

"I hate common-sense!" she exclaimed, dashing away his hand; "I won't hear any more of your lecturing,—leave the house, and never speak to me again as long as you live."

Mr. Arthur Jones took up his hat, placed it deliberately on his head, and walked out of the house. With a heavy heart Martha watched his slender form as it disappeared in the darkness, and then stole away to her bed in the garret.

"He will call in the morning before he starts; he won't have the heart to go away without saying one word,—I am sure he won't," she repeated to herself over and over again, as she lay sobbing and weeping penitent tears on her pillow that night.

When William left the log tavern, he struck into the woods, and took his course toward the Pond. There was a moon, but the sky was clouded, and the little light which struggled to the earth, was too faint to penetrate the thick fo-

26

liage of the wilderness. Danforth must have been familiar with the track, for he found his way without difficulty through the wilderness, and never stopped till he came out on the northern brink of the Pond. He looked anxiously over the face of the little lake. The fitful moon had broken from a cloud, and was touching the tiny waves with beauty, while the broken, rocky shore encompassed it with shadow, like a frame-work of ebony. No speck was on its bosom; no sound was abroad, but the evening breeze as it rippled on the waters, and made a sweet whispering melody in the tree-tops.

Suddenly a light, as from a pine torch, was seen on a point of land jutting out from the opposite shore. Another and another flashed out, each bearing to a particular direction, and then a myriad of flames rose high and bright, illuminating the whole point, and shooting its fiery reflection, like a meteor, almost across the bosom of the waters.

"Yes, they are preparing for work," muttered Danforth, as he saw a crowd of painted warriors arrange themselves around the camp-fire, each with his firelock[6] in his hand. There was a general movement. Dark faces flittered in quick succession between him and the blaze, as the warriors performed the heavy march, or war-dance, which usually preceded the going out of a hostile party.

Danforth left the shore, and striking out in an oblique direction, arrived, after half an hour of quick walking, at the Indian encampment. He threaded his way through the cluster of bark wigwams, till he came to one standing on the verge of the inclosure. It was of logs, and erected with a regard to comfort which the others wanted. The young hunter drew aside the mat which hung over the entrance, and looked in. A young Indian girl was sitting on a pile of furs at the opposite extremity. She wore no paint—her cheek was round and smooth, and large gazelle-like eyes gave a soft brilliancy to her countenance, beautiful beyond expression. Her dress was a robe of dark chintz, open at the throat, and confined at the waist by a narrow belt of wampum, which, with the bead bracelets on her naked arms, and the embroidered moccasins laced over her feet, was the only Indian ornament about her. Even her hair, which all of her tribe wore laden with ornaments, and hanging down the back, was braided and wreathed in raven bands over her smooth forehead. An infant, almost naked, was lying in her lap, throwing its unfettered limbs about, and lifting his little hands to his mother's mouth, as she rocked back and forth on her seat of skins, chanting, in a sweet, mellow voice, the burden of an Indian lullaby. As the form of the hunter darkened the entrance, the Indian girl started up with a look of affectionate joy, and laying her child on the pile of skins, advanced to meet him.

"Why did the white man leave his woman so many nights?" she said, in her broken English, hanging fondly about him; "the boy and his mother have listened long for the sound of his moccasins."

Danforth passed his arm around the waist of his Indian wife, and drawing her to him, bent his cheek to hers, as if that slight caress was sufficient answer to her gentle greeting, and so it was; her untutored heart, rich in its natural affections, had no aim, no object, but what centered in the love she bore her white husband. The feelings which in civilized life are scattered over a thousand objects, were, in her bosom, centered in one single being; he supplied the place of

---

6 *firelock* flintlock musket.

all the high aspirations—of all the passions and sentiments which are fostered into strength by society, and as her husband bowed his head to hers, the blood darkened her cheek, and her large, liquid eyes were flooded with delight.

"And what has Malaeska been doing since the boy's father went to the wood?" inquired Danforth, as she drew him to the couch where the child was lying half buried in the rich fur.

"Malaeska has been alone in the wigwam, watching the shadow of the big pine. When her heart grew sick, she looked in the boy's eyes and was glad," replied the Indian mother, laying the infant in his father's arms.

Danforth kissed the child, whose eyes certainly bore a striking resemblance to his own; and parting the straight, black hair from a forehead which scarcely bore a tinge of its mother's blood, muttered, "It's a pity the little fellow is not quite white."

The Indian mother took the child, and with a look of proud anguish, laid her finger on its cheek, which was rosy with English blood.

"Malaeska's father is a great chief—the boy will be a chief in her father's tribe; but Malaeska never thinks of that when she sees the white man's blood come into the boy's face." She turned mournfully to her seat again.

"He will make a brave chief," said Danforth, anxious to soften the effects of his inadvertent speech; "but tell me, Malaeska, why have the warriors kindled the council fire? I saw it blaze by the pond as I came by."

Malaeska could only inform that the body of a dead Indian had been brought to the encampment about dusk, and that it was supposed he had been shot by some of the whites from the settlement. She said that the chief had immediately called a council to deliberate on the best means of revenging their brother's death.

Danforth had feared this movement in the savages, and it was to mitigate their wrath that he sought the encampment at so late an hour. He had married the daughter of their chief, and, consequently, was a man of considerable importance in the tribe. But he felt that his utmost exertion might fail to draw them from their meditated vengeance, now that one of their number had been slain by the whites. Feeling the necessity of his immediate presence at the council, he left the wigwam and proceeded at a brisk walk to the brink of the Pond. He came out of the thick forest which fringed it a little above the point on which the Indians were collected. Their dance was over, and from the few guttural tones which reached him, Danforth knew that they were planning the death of some particular individuals, which was probably to precede their attack on the settlement. The council fire still streamed high in the air, reddening the waters and lighting up the trees and foreground with a beautiful effect, while the rocky point seemed of emerald pebbles, so brilliant was the reflection cast over it, and so distinctly did it display the painted forms of the savages as they sat in a circle round the blaze, each with his weapon lying idly by his side. The light lay full on the glittering wampum and feathery crest of one who was addressing them with more energy than is common to the Indian warrior.

Danforth was too far off to collect a distinct hearing of the discourse, but with a feeling of perfect security, he left the deep shadow in which he stood, and approached the council fire. As the light fell upon him, the Indians leaped to their feet, and a savage yell rent the air, as if a company of fiends had been disturbed in their orgies. Again and again was the fierce cry reiterated, till the woods resounded with the wild echo rudely summoned from the caves. As the young hunter stood lost in astonishment at the strange commotion, he was seized by the savages, and dragged before their chief, while the group around furiously demanded vengeance, quick and terrible, for the death of their slain brother. The truth flashed across the hunter's mind. It was his death they had been planning. It was he they supposed to be the slayer of the Indian. He remonstrated and declared himself guiltless of the red man's death. It was in vain. He had been seen on the mountain by one of the tribe, not five minutes before the dead body of the Indian was found. Almost in despair the hunter turned to the chief.

"Am I not your son—the father of a young chief—one of your own tribe?" he said, with appealing energy.

The saturnine face of the chief never changed, as he answered in his own language: "The red man has taken a rattlesnake to warm in his wigwam—the warriors shall crush his head!" and with a fierce grin, he pointed to the pile of resinous wood which the savages were heaping on the council fire.

Danforth looked round on the group preparing for his destruction. Every dusky face was lighted up with a demoniac thirst for blood, the hot flames quivering into the air, their gorgeous tints amalgamating and shooting upward like a spire of living rainbows, while a thousand fiery tongues, hissing and darting onward like vipers eager for their prey, licked the fresh pine-knots heaped for his death-pyre. It was a fearful sight, and the heart of the brave hunter quailed within him as he looked. With another wild whoop, the Indians seized their victim, and were about to strip him for the sacrifice. In their blind fury they tore him from the grasp of those who held him, and were too intent on divesting him of his clothes to remark that his limbs were free. But he was not so forgetful. Collecting his strength for a last effort, he struck the nearest savage a blow in the chest, which sent him reeling among his followers, then taking advantage of the confusion, he tore off his cap, and springing forward with the bound of an uncaged tiger, plunged into the lake. A shout rent the air, and a score of dark heads broke the water in pursuit.

Fortunately, a cloud was over the moon, and the fugitive remained under the water till he reached the shadow thrown by the thickly-wooded bank, when, rising for a moment, he supported himself and hurled his cap out toward the center of the pond. The ruse succeeded, for the moon came out just at the instant, and with renewed shouts the savages turned in pursuit of the empty cap. Before they learned their mistake, Danforth had made considerable headway under the friendly bank, and took to the woods just as the shoal of Indians' heads entered the shadow in eager chase.

The fugitive stood for a moment on the brink of the forest, irresolute, for he knew not which course to take.

"I have it; they will never think of looking for me there," he exclaimed, dashing through the undergrowth and taking the direction toward "the Straka." The whoop of the pursuers smote his ear as they made the land. On, on he bounded with the swiftness of a hunted stag, through swamp and brushwood, and over rocks. He darted till he came in sight of his own wigwam. The sound of pursuit had died away, and he began to hope that the savages had taken the track which led to the settlement.

Breathless with exertion he entered the hut. The boy was asleep, but his mother was listening for the return of her husband.

"Malaeska," he said, catching her to his panting heart; "Malaeska, we must part; your tribe seek my life; the warriors are on my track now—now! Do you hear their shouts?" he added.

29

A wild whoop came from the woods below, and forcing back the arms she flung about him, he seized a war-club and stood ready for the attack.

Malaeska sprang to the door, and looked out with the air of a frightened doe. Darting back to the pile of furs, she laid the sleeping child on the bare earth, and motioning her husband to lie down, heaped the skins over his prostrate form; then taking the child in her arms, she stretched herself on the pile, and drawing a bear-skin over her, pretended to be asleep. She had scarcely composed herself, when three savages entered the wigwam. One bore a blazing pine-knot, with which he proceeded to search for the fugitive. While the others were busy among the scanty furniture, he approached the trembling wife, and after feeling about among the furs without effect, lifted the bear-skins which covered her; but her sweet face in apparent slumber, and the beautiful infant lying across her bosom, were all that rewarded his search. As if her beauty had power to tame the savage, he carefully replaced the covering over her person, and speaking to his companions, left the hut without attempting to disturb her further.

Malaeska remained in her feigned slumber till she heard the Indians take to the woods again. Then she arose and lifted the skins from off her husband, who was nearly suffocated under them. When he had regained his feet, she placed the war-club in his hand, and taking up the babe, led the way to the entrance of the hut. Danforth saw by the act, that she intended to desert her tribe and accompany him in his flight. He had never thought of introducing her as his wife among the whites, and now that circumstances made it necessary for him to part with her forever, or to take her among his people for shelter, a pang, such as he had never felt, came to his heart. His affections struggled powerfully with his pride. The picture of his disgrace—of the scorn with which his parents and sisters would receive the Indian wife and half-Indian child, presented itself before him, and he had not the moral courage to risk the degradation which her companionship would bring upon him. These conflicting thoughts flashed through his mind in an instant, and when his wife stopped at the door, and, looking anxiously in his face, beckoned him to follow, he said, sharply, for his conscience was ill at ease:

"Malaeska, I go alone; you and the boy must remain with your people."

His words had a withering effect on the poor Indian. Her form drooped, and she raised her eyes with a look so mingled with humiliation and reproach, that the hunter's heart thrilled painfully in his bosom. Slowly, and as if her soul and strength were paralyzed, she crept to her husband's feet, and sinking to her knees, held up the babe.

"Malaeska's breast will die, and the boy will have no one to feed him," she said.

That beautiful child—that young mother kneeling in her humiliation—those large dark eyes, dim with the intensity of her solicitude, and that voice so full of tender entreaty—the husband's heart could not withstand them. His bosom heaved, tears gathered in his eyes, and raising the Indian and her child of his bosom, he kissed them both again and again.

"Malaeska," he said, folding her close to his heart, "Malaeska, I must go now; but when seven suns have passed, I will come again; or, if the tribe still seek my life, take the child and come to the settlement. I shall be there."

The Indian woman bowed her head in humble submission.

"The white man is good. Malaeska will come," she said.

One more embrace, and the poor Indian wife was alone with her child.

Poor Martha Fellows arose early, and waited with nervous impatience for the appearance of her lover; but the morning passed, the hour of noon drew near, and he came not. The heart of the maiden grew heavy, and when her father came in to dine, her eyes were red with weeping, and a cloud of mingled sorrow and petulance darkened her handsome face. She longed to question her father about Jones, but he had twice replenished his brown earthen bowl with pudding and milk, before she could gather courage to speak.

"Have you seen Arthur Jones this morning?" she at length questioned, in a low, timid voice.

The answer she received, was quite sufficient punishment for all her coquettish folly of the previous night. Jones had left the settlement—left it in anger with her, without a word of explanation—without even saying farewell. It really was hard. The little coquette had the heart-ache terribly, till he frightened it away by telling her of the adventure which Danforth had met with among the Indians, and of his departure with Arthur Jones in search of aid from the nearest settlement. The old man gloomily added, that the savages would doubtless burn the houses over their heads, and massacre every living being within them, long before the two brave fellows would return with men. Such, indeed, were the terrible fears of almost every one in the little neighborhood. Their apprehensions, however, were premature. Part of the Indian tribe had gone out on a hunting-party among the hills, and were ignorant of the fatal shot with which Jones had aroused the animosity of their brethren; while those who remained, were dispersed in a fruitless pursuit after Danforth.

On the afternoon of the fifth day after the departure of their emissaries, the whites began to see unequivocal symptoms of an attack; and now their fears did not deceive them. The hunting-party had returned to their encampment, and the detached parties were gathering around "the Straka." About dark, an Indian appeared in the skirts of the clearing, as if to spy out the position of the whites. Soon after, a shot was fired at the Englishman, before mentioned, as he returned from his work, which passed through the crown of his hat. That hostilities were commencing, was now beyond a doubt, and the males of the settlement met in solemn conclave, to devise measures for the defence of their wives and children. Their slender preparations were soon made; all were gathered around one of the largest houses in gloomy apprehension; the women and children within, and the men standing in front, sternly resolving to die in the defence of their loved ones. Suddenly there came up a sound from the wood, the trampling of many feet, and the crackling of brushwood, as if some large body of men were forcing a way through the tangled forest. The women bowed their pallid faces, and gathering their children in their arms, waited appalled for the attack. The men stood ready, each grasping his weapon, their faces pallid, and their eyes kindled with stern courage, as they heard the stifled groans of the loved objects cowering behind them for protection. The sound became nearer and more distinct; dark forms were seen dimly moving among the trees, and then a file of men came out into the clearing. They were whites, led on by William Danforth and Arthur Jones. The settlers uttered a boisterous shout, threw down their arms, and ran in a body to meet the new-comers. The women sprang to their feet, some weeping, others laughing in hysterical joy, and all embracing their children with frantic energy.

Never were there more welcome guests than the score of weary men who refreshed themselves in the various houses of the settlement that night. Sentinels were placed, and each settler returned to his dwelling, accompanied by three or four guests; every heart beat high, save one—Martha Fellows; she, poor girl, was sad among the general rejoicing; her lover had not spoken to her, though she lingered near his side in the crowd, and had once almost touched him. Instead of going directly to her father's house, as had been his custom, he accepted the Englishman's invitation, and departed to sleep in his dwelling.

Now this same Englishman had a niece residing with him, who was considered by some to be more beautiful than Martha herself. The humble maiden thought of Jones, and of the bright blue eyes of the English girl, till her heart burned with the very same jealous feelings she had so ridiculed in her lover.

"I will see him! I will see them both!" she exclaimed, starting up from the settle[7] where she had remained, full of jealous anxiety, since the dispersing of the crowd; and unheeded by her father, who was relating his hunting exploits to the five strangers quartered on him, she dashed away her tears, threw a shawl over her head, and taking a cup, as an excuse for borrowing something, left the house.

The Englishman's dwelling stood on the outward verge of the clearing, just within the shadow of the forest. Martha had almost reached the entrance, when a dark form rushed from its covert in the brushwood, and rudely seizing her, darted back into the wilderness. The terrified girl uttered a fearful shriek; for the fierce eyes gazing down upon her, were those of a savage. She could not repeat the cry, for the wretch crushed her form to his naked chest with a grasp of iron, and winding his hand in her hair, was about to dash her to the ground. That moment a bullet whistled by her cheek. The Indian tightened his hold with spasmodic violence, staggered back, and fell to the ground, still girding her in his death-grasp; a moment he writhed in mortal agony—warm blood gushed over his victim—the heart under her struggled fiercely in its last throes; then the lifeless arms relaxed, and she lay fainting on a corpse.

CHAPTER 2

He lay upon the trampled ground,
　　She knelt beside him there,
While a crimson stream gush'd slowly
　　'Neath the parting of his hair.
His head was on her bosom thrown—
　　She sobb'd his Christian name—
He smiled, for still he knew her,
　　And strove to do the same.
　　　　　—Frank Lee Benedict.[1]

"OH, Arthur! dear Arthur, I am glad it was you that saved me," whispered Martha, about an hour after her rescue, as she lay on the settle[2] in her father's house, with Arthur Jones bending anxiously over her.

Jones dropped the hand he had been holding, and turned away with troubled features.

---

7 *settle*　high-backed wooden bench.
1 *Frank Lee Benedict*　American writer (1834–1910).

Martha looked at him, and her eyes were brimming with tears. "Jones," she said humbly and very affectionately, "Jones, I did wrong the other night, and I am sorry for it; will you forgive me?"

"I will—but never again—never, as I live," he replied, with a stern determination in his manner, accompanied by a look that humbled her to the heart. In after years, when Martha was Arthur Jones' wife, and when the stirrings of vanity would have led her to trifle with his feelings, she remembered that look, and dared not brave it a second time.

At sunrise, the next morning, an armed force went into the forest, composed of all who could be spared from the settlement, amounting to about thirty fighting-men. The Indians, encamped about "the Straka," more than doubled that number, yet the handful of brave whites resolved to offer them a decisive combat.

The little band was approaching the northeastern extremity of the Pond, when they halted for a moment to rest. The spot on which they stood was level, and thinly timbered. Some were sitting on the grass, and others leaning on their guns, consulting on their future movements, when a fiendish yell arose like the howl of a thousand wild beasts, and, as if the very earth had yawned to emit them, a band of warriors sprang up in appalling numbers, on the front and rear, and approaching them, three abreast, fired into the group with terrible slaughter.

The whites returned their fire, and the sounds of murderous strife were indeed horrible. Sternly arose the white man's shout amid the blazing of guns and the whizzing of tomahawks, as they flashed though the air on their message of blood. Above all burst out the war-whoop of the savages, sometimes rising hoarse, and like the growling of a thousand bears; then, as the barking of as many wolves, and again, sharpening to the shrill, unearthly cry of a tribe of wild-cats. Oh, it was fearful, that scene of slaughter. Heart to heart, and muzzle to muzzle, the white and red man battled in horrid strife. The trees above them drooped under a cloud of smoke, and their trunks were scarred with gashes, cut by the tomahawks which had missed their more deadly aim. The ground was burdened with the dead, and yet the strife raged fiercer and fiercer, till the going down of the sun.

In the midst of the fight was William Danforth. Many a dusky form bit the dust, and many a savage howl followed the discharge of his trusty gun. But at length it became foul with continued use, and he went to the brink of the Pond to wash it. He was stooping to the water, when the dark form of an Indian chief cast its shadow a few feet from him. He, too, had come down to clean his gun. The moment he had accomplished his purpose, he turned to the white man, who had been to him as a son, and drawing his muscular form up to its utmost height, uttered a defiance in the Indian tongue. Instantly the weapons of both were loaded and discharged. The tall form of the chief wavered unsteadily for a moment, and fell forward, half its length, into the Pond. He strove to rise. His hands dashed wildly on the crimson water, the blows grew fainter, and the chief was dead.

The setting sun fell brilliantly over the glittering raiment of the prostrate chief—his long, black hair streamed out upon the water, and the tiny waves rippled playfully among the gorgeous feathers which had been his savage crown. A little back on the green bank, lay Danforth, wounded unto death. He strove to creep to the battle-field, but the blood gushed afresh from his wounds, and he fell back upon the earth faint and in despair.

The savages retreated; the sounds of strife became more distant, and the poor youth was left alone with the body of the slain warrior. He made one more desperate effort, and secured the gun which had belonged to the chief; though faint with loss of blood, he loaded that as well as his own, and placing them beside him, resolved to defend the remnant of life, yet quivering at his heart, to the last moment. The sun went slowly down; the darkness fell like a veil over the lake, and there he lay, wounded and alone, in the solitude of the wilderness. Solemn and regretful were the thoughts of the forsaken man as that night of agony went by. Now his heart lingered with strange and terrible dread around the shadowy portals of eternity which were opening before him; again it turned with a strong feeling of self-condemnation to his Indian wife and the infant pledge of the great love, which had made him almost forsake kindred and people for their sakes.

The moon arose, and the dense shadow of a hemlock, beneath which he had fallen, lay within a few feet of him like the wing of a great bird, swayed slowly forward with an imperceptible and yet certain progress. The eyes of the dying man were fixed on the margin of the shadow with a keen, intense gaze. There was something terrible in its stealthy creeping and silent advance, and he strove to elude it as if it had been a living thing; but with every motion the blood gushed afresh from his heart, and he fell back upon the sod, his white teeth clenched with pain, and his hands clutched deep into the damp moss. Still his keen eyes glittered in the moonlight with the fevered workings of pain and imagination. The shadow on which they turned was to him no shadow, but now a nest of serpents, creeping with their insidious coils toward him; and again, a pall—a black funereal pall, dragged forward by invisible spirits, and about to shut him out from the light forever. Slowly and surely it crept across his damp forehead and over his glowing eyes. His teeth unclenched, his hands relaxed, and a gentle smile broke over his pale lips, when he felt with what a cool and spirit-like touch it visited him. Just then a human shadow mingled with that of the tree, and the wail of a child broke on the still night air. The dying hunter struggled and strove to cry out,—"Malaeska—Ma—Ma—Mala—"

The poor Indian girl heard the voice, and with a cry, half of frenzied joy and half of fear, sprang to his side. She flung her child on the grass and lifted her dying husband to her heart, and kissed his damp forehead in a wild, eager agony of sorrow.

"Malaeska," said the young man, striving to wind his arms about her, "my poor girl, what will become of you? O God! who will take care of my boy?"

The Indian girl pushed back the damp hair from his forehead, and looked wildly down into his face. A shiver ran through her frame when she saw the cold, gray shadows of death gathering there; then her black eyes kindled, her beautiful lip curved to an expression more lofty than a smile, her small hand pointed to the West, and the wild religion of her race gushed up from her heart, a stream of living poetry.

"The hunting-ground of the Indian is yonder, among the purple clouds of the evening. The stars are very thick there, and the red light is heaped together like mountains in the heart of a forest. The sugar-maple gives its waters all the year round, and the breath of the deer is sweet, for it feeds on the golden spirebush and the ripe berries. A lake of bright waters is there. The Indian's canoe flies over it like a bird high up in the morning. The West has rolled back its clouds, and a great chief has passed through. He will hold back the clouds that his white son may go up to the face of the Great Spirit. Malaeska and her boy

34

will follow. The blood of the red man is high in her heart, and the way is open. The lake is deep, and the arrow sharp; death will come when Malaeska calls him. Love will make her voice sweet in the land of the Great Spirit; the white man will hear it, and call her to his bosom again!"

A faint, sad smile flitted over the dying hunter's face, and his voice was choked with a pain which was not death. "My poor girl," he said, feebly drawing her kindling[2] face to his lips, "there is no great hunting-ground as you dream. The whites have another faith, and—O God! I have taken away her trust, and have none to give in return!"

The Indian's face drooped forward, the light of her wild, poetic faith had departed with the hunter's last words, and a feeling of cold desolation settled on her heart. He was dying on her bosom, and she knew not where he was going, nor that their parting might not be eternal.

The dying man's lips moved as if in prayer. "Forgive me, O Father of mercies! forgive me that I have left this poor girl in her heathen ignorance," he murmured, faintly, and his lips continued to move though there was no perceptible sound. After a few moments of exhaustion, he fixed his eyes on the Indian girl's face with a look of solemn and touching earnestness.

"Malaeska," he said, "talk not of putting yourself and the boy to death. That would be a sin, and God would punish it. To meet me in another world, Malaeska, you must learn to love the white man's God, and wait patiently till he shall send you to me. Go not back to your tribe when I am dead. Down at the mouth of the great river are many whites; among them are my father and mother. Find your way to them, tell them how their son died, and beseech them to cherish you and the boy for his sake. Tell them how much he loved you, my poor girl. Tell them—I can not talk more. There is a girl at the settlement, one Martha Fellows; go to her. She knows of you, and has papers—a letter to my father. I did not expect this, but had prepared for it. Go to her—you will do this—promise, while I can understand."

Malaeska had not wept till now, but her voice was choked, and tears fell like rain over the dying man's face as she made the promise.

He tried to thank her, but the effort died away in a faint smile and a tremulous motion of the white lips—"Kiss me, Malaeska."

The request was faint as a breath of air, but Malaeska heard it. She flung herself on his bosom with a passionate burst of grief, and her lips clung to his as if they would have drawn him back from the very grave. She felt the cold lips moving beneath the despairing pressure of hers, and lifted her head.

"The boy, Malaeska; let me look on my son."

The child had crept to his mother's side, and crouching on his hands and knees, sat with his large black eyes filled with a strange awe, gazing on the white face of his father. Malaeska drew him closer, and with instinctive feelings he wound his arms round the neck, and nestled his face close to the ashy cheek of the dying man. There was a faint motion of the hands as if the father would have embraced his child, and then all was still. After a time, the child felt the cheek beneath his waxing hard and cold. He lifted his head and pored with breathless wonder over the face of his father's corpse. He looked up at his mother. She, too, was bending intently over the face of the dead, and her eyes were full of a wild, melancholy light. The child was bewildered. He passed his

---

2 *kindling* glowing with emotion.

35

tiny hand once more over the cold face, and then crept away, buried his head in the folds of his mother's dress, and began to cry.

Morning dawned upon the little lake, quietly and still, as if nothing but the dews of heaven and the flowers of earth had ever tasted its freshness; yet all under the trees, the tender grass and the white blossoms, were crushed to the ground, stained and trampled in human blood. The delicious light broke, like a smile from heaven, over the still bosom of the waters, and flickered cheeringly through the dewy branches of the hemlock which shadowed the prostrate hunter. Bright dew-drops lay thickly on his dress, and gleamed, like a shower of seed pearls, in his rich, brown hair. The green moss on either side was soaked with a crimson stain, and the pale, leaden hue of dissolution had settled on his features. He was not alone; for on the same mossy couch lay the body of the slaughtered chief; the limbs were composed, as if on a bier—the hair wiped smooth, and the crescent of feathers, broken and wet, were arranged with care around his bronzed temples. A little way off, on a hillock, purple with flowers, lay a beautiful child, beckoning to the birds as they fluttered by—plucking up the flowers, and uttering his tiny shout of gladness, as if death and sorrow were not all around him. There, by the side of the dead hunter, sat Malaeska, the widow, her hands dropping nervously by her side, her long hair sweeping the moss, and her face bowed on her bosom, stupefied with the overwhelming poignancy of her grief. Thus she remained, motionless and lost in sorrow, till the day was at its noon. Her child, hungry and tired with play, had cried itself to sleep among the flowers; but the mother knew it not—her heart and all her faculties seemed closed as with a portal of ice.

That night when the moon was up, the Indian widow dug a grave, with her own hands, on the green margin of the lake. She laid her husband and her father side by side, and piled sods upon them. Then she lifted the wretched and hungry babe from the earth, and, with a heavy heart, bent her way to "the Straka."

CHAPTER 3

The sunset fell to the deep, deep stream,
    Ruddy as gold could be,
While russet brown and a crimson gleam
    Slept in each forest-tree;
But the heart of the Indian wife was sad
    As she urged her light canoe,
While her boy's young laugh rose high and glad
    When the wild birds o'er them flew.

MARTHA FELLOWS and her lover were alone in her father's cabin on the night after the Indian engagement. They were both paler than usual, and too anxious about the safety of their little village for any thing like happiness, or tranquil conversation. The old man had been stationed as sentinel on the verge of the clearing; and as the two sat together in silence, with hands interlocked, and gazing wistfully in each other's face, a rifle-shot cut sharply from the old man's station. They both started to their feet, and Martha clung shrieking to her lover. Jones forced her back to the settle—and, snatching his rifle, sprang to

36

the door. There was a sound of approaching footsteps, and with it was mingled the voice of old Fellows, and the sweeter and more imperfect tones of a female, with the sobbing breath of a child. As Jones stood wondering at the strange sound, a remarkable group darkened the light which streamed from the cabin door. It was Fellows partly supporting and partly dragging forward a pale and terrified Indian girl. The light glittered upon her picturesque raiment, and revealed the dark, bright eyes of a child which was fastened to her back, and which clung to her neck silent with terror and exhaustion.

"Come along, you young porcupine! You skulking copper-colored little squaw, you! We shan't kill you, nor the little pappoose, neither; so you needn't shake so. Come along! There's Martha Fellows, if you can find enough of your darnationed queer English to tell her what you want."

As he spoke, the rough, but kind-hearted old man entered the hut, pushing the wretched Malaeska and her child before him.

"Martha! why what in the name of nature makes you look so white about the mouth? You needn't be afraid of this little varmint, no how. She's as harmless as a gartersnake. Come, see if you can find out what she wants of you. She can talk the drollest you ever heard. But I've scared away her senses, and she only stares at me like a shot deer."

When the Indian heard the name of the astonished girl, into whose presence she had been dragged, she withdrew from the old man's grasp and stole timidly toward the settle.

"The white man left papers with the maiden—Malaeska only wants the papers," she pleaded, placing her small palms beseechingly together.

Martha turned still more pale, and started to her feet. "It is true then," she said, almost wildly. "Poor Danforth is dead, and these forlorn creatures, his widow and child, have come to me at last. Oh! Jones, he was telling me of this the night you got so angry. I could not tell you why we were talking so much together; but I knew all the time that he had an Indian wife—it seemed as if he had a forewarning of his death, and must tell some one. The last time I saw him, he gave me a letter, sealed with black, and bade me seek his wife, and persuade her to carry it to his father, if he was killed in the fight. It is that letter she has come after; but how will she find her way to Manhattan?"

"Malaeska knows which way the waters run: she can find a path down the big river. Give her the papers that she may go!" pleaded the sad voice of the Indian.

"Tell us first," said Jones, addressing her kindly, "have the Indians left our neighborhood? Is there no danger of an attack?"

"The white man need not fear. When the great chief died, the smoke of his wigwam went out; and his people have gone beyond the mountains. Malaeska is alone."

There was wretchedness and touching pathos in the poor girl's speech, that affected the little group even to tears.

"No you ain't, by gracious!" exclaimed Fellows, dashing his hand across his eyes. "You shall stay and live with me, and help Matt, you shall—and that's the end on't. I'll make a farmer of the little pappoose. I'll bet a beaver-skin that he'll larn to gee and haw the oxen and hold plow afore half the Dutch boys that are springing up here as thick as clover-tops in a third year's clearing."

Malaeska did not perfectly understand the kind settler's proposition; but the tone and manner were kindly, and she knew that he wished to help her.

"When the boy's father was dying, he told Malaeska to go to his people, and they would tell her how to find the white man's God. Give her the papers, and she will go. Her heart will be full when she thinks of the kind words and the soft looks which the white chiefs and the bright-haired maiden have given her."

"She goes to fulfill a promise to the dead—we ought not to prevent her," said Jones.

Malaeska turned her eyes eagerly and gratefully upon him as he spoke, and Martha went to her bed and drew the letter, which had been intrusted to her care, from beneath the pillow. The Indian took it between her trembling hands, and pressing it with a gesture almost of idolatry to her lips, thrust it into her bosom.

"The white maiden is good! Farewell!" she turned toward the door as she spoke.

"Stay! It will take many days to reach Manhattan—take something to eat, or you will starve on the way," said Martha, compassionately.

"Malaeska has her bow and arrow, and she can use them; but she thanks the white maiden. A piece of bread for the boy—he has cried to his mother many times for food; but her bosom was full of tears, and she had none to give him."

Martha ran to the cupboard and brought forth a large fragment of bread and a cup of milk. When the child saw the food, he uttered a soft, hungry murmur, and his little fingers began to work eagerly on his mother's neck. Martha held the cup to his lips, and smiled through her tears to see how hungrily he swallowed, and with what a satisfied and pleased look his large, black eyes were turned up to hers as he drank. When the cup was withdrawn, the boy breathed a deep sigh of satisfaction, and let his head fall sleepily on his mother's shoulder; her large eyes seemed full of moonlight, and a gleam of pleasure shot athwart her sad features; she unbound a bracelet of wampum from her arm and placed it in Martha's hand. The next instant she was lost in the darkness without. The kind settler rushed out, and hallooed for her to come back; but her step was like that of a fawn, and while he was wandering fruitlessly around the settlement, she reached the margin of the creek; and, unmooring a canoe, which lay concealed in the sedge, placed herself in it, and shot round the point to the broad bosom of the Hudson.

Night and morning, for many successive days, that frail canoe glided down the current, amid the wild and beautiful scenery of the Highlands, and along the park-like shades of a more level country. There was something in the sublime and lofty handiwork of God which fell soothingly on the sad heart of the Indian. Her thoughts were continually dwelling on the words of her dead husband, ever picturing to themselves the land of spirits where he had promised that she should join him. The perpetual change of scenery, the sunshine playing with the foliage, and the dark, heavy masses of shadow, flung from the forests and the rocks on either hand, were continually exciting her untamed imagination to comparison with the heaven of her wild fancy. It seemed, at times, as if she had but to close her eyes and open them again to be in the presence of her lost one. There was something heavenly in the solemn, perpetual flow of the river, and in the music of the leaves as they rippled to the wind, that went to the poor widow's heart like the soft voice of a friend. After a day or two, the gloom which hung about her young brow, partially departed. Her cheek again dimpled to the happy laugh of her child, and when he nestled down to sleep in the furs at the bottom of the canoe, her soft, plaintive lullaby would steal over the waters like the song of a wild bird seeking in vain for its mate.

Malaeska never went on shore, except to gather wild fruit, and occasionally to kill a bird, which her true arrow seldom failed to bring down. She would strike a fire and prepare her game in some shady nook by the river side, while the canoe swung at its mooring, and her child played on the fresh grass, shouting at the cloud of summer insects that flashed by, and clapping his tiny hands at the humming-birds that came to rifle honey from the flowers that surrounded him.

The voyage was one of strange happiness to the widowed Indian. Never did Christian believe in the pages of Divine Writ with more of trust, than she placed in the dying promise of her husband, that she should meet him again in another world. His spirit seemed forever about her, and to her wild, free imagination, the passage down the magnificent stream seemed a material and glorious path to the white man's heaven. Filled with strange, sweet thoughts, she looked abroad on the mountains looming up from the banks of the river—on the forest-trees so various in their tints, and so richly clothed, till she was inspired almost to forgetfulness of her affliction. She was young and healthy, and every thing about her was so lovely, so grand and changing, that her heart expanded to the sunshine like a flower which has been bowed down, but not crushed beneath the force of a storm. Part of each day she spent in a wild, dreamy state of imagination. Her mind was lulled to sweet musings by the gentle sounds that hovered in the air from morning till evening, and through the long night, when all was hushed save the deep flow of the river. Birds came out with their cheerful voices at dawn, and at midday she floated in the cool shadow of the hills, or shot into some cove for a few hours' rest. When the sunset shed its gorgeous dyes over the river—and the mountain ramparts, on either side, were crimson as with the track of contending armies—when the boy was asleep, and the silent stars came out to kindle up her night path, then a clear, bold melody gushed from the mother's lips like a song from the heart of a nightingale. Her eye kindled, her cheek grew warm, the dip of her paddle kept a liquid accompaniment to her rich, wild voice, as the canoe floated downward on waves that seemed rippling over a world of crushed blossoms, and were misty with the approach of evening.

Malaeska had been out many days, when the shady gables and the tall chimneys of Manhattan broke upon her view, surrounded by the sheen of its broad bay, and by the forest which covered the uninhabited part of the island. The poor Indian gazed upon it with an unstable but troublesome fear. She urged her canoe into a little cove on the Hoboken shore, and her heart grew heavy as the grave, as she pondered on the means of fulfilling her charge. She took the letter from her bosom; the tears started to her eyes, and she kissed it with a regretful sorrow, as if a friend were about to be rendered up from her affections forever. She took the child to her heart, and held him there till its throbbings grew audible, and the strength of her misgivings could not be restrained. After a time she became more calm. She lifted the child from her bosom, laved his hands and face in the stream, and brushed his black hair with her palm till it glowed like the neck of a raven. Then she girded his little crimson robe with a string of wampum, and after arranging her own attire, shot the canoe out of the cove and urged it slowly across the mouth of the river. Her eyes were full of tears all the way, and when the child murmured, and strove to comfort her with his infant caress, she sobbed aloud, and rowed steadily forward.

It was a strange sight to the phlegmatic inhabitants of Manhattan, when Malaeska passed through their streets in full costume, and with the proud, free tread of her race. Her hair hung in long braids down her back, each braid fastened at the end with a tuft of scarlet feathers. A coronet of the same bright plumage circled her small head, and her robe was gorgeous with beads, and fringed with porcupine quills. A bow of exquisite workmanship was in her hand, and a scarf of scarlet cloth bound the boy to her back. Nothing could be more strikingly beautiful than the child. His spirited head was continually turning from one strange object to another, and his bright, black eyes were brim-full of childish wonder. One little arm was flung around his young mother's neck, and its fellow rested on the feathered arrow-shafts which crowded the quiver slung against her left shoulder. The timid, anxious look of the mother, was in strong contrast with the eager gaze of the boy. She had caught much of the delicacy and refinement of civilized life from her husband, and her manner became startled and fawnlike beneath the rude gaze of the passers-by. The modest blood burned in her cheek, and the sweet, broken English trembled on her lips, when several persons, to whom she showed the letter passed by without answering her. She did not know that they were of another nation than her husband, and spoke another language than that which love had taught her. At length she accosted an aged man who could comprehend her imperfect language. He read the name on the letter, and saw that it was addressed to his master, John Danforth, the richest fur-trader in Manhattan. The old servingman led the way to a large, irregular building, in the vicinity of what is now Hanover Square. Malaeska followed with a lighter tread, and a heart relieved of its fear. She felt that she had found a friend in the kind old man who was conducting her to the home of her husband's father.

The servant entered this dwelling and led the way to a low parlor, paneled with oak and lighted with small panes of thick, greenish glass. A series of Dutch tiles[1]—some of them most exquisite in finish and design, surrounded the fire-place, and a coat-of-arms, elaborately carved in oak, stood out in strong relief from the paneling above. A carpet, at that time an uncommon luxury, covered a greater portion of the floor, and the furniture was rich in its material, and ponderous with heavy carved work. A tall, and rather hard-featured man sat in an arm-chair by one of the narrow windows, reading a file of papers which had just arrived in the last merchant-ship from London. A little distance from him, a slight and very thin lady of about fifty was occupied with household sewing; her work-box stood on a small table before her, and a book of common-prayer lay beside it. The servant had intended to announce his strange guests, but, fearful of losing sight of him, Malaeska followed close upon his footsteps, and before he was aware of it, stood within the room, holding her child by the hand.

"A woman, sir,—an Indian woman, with a letter," said the embarrassed servant, motioning his charge to draw back. But Malaeska had stepped close to the merchant, and was looking earnestly in his face when he raised his eyes from the papers. There was something cold in his severe gaze as he fixed it on her through his spectacles. The Indian felt chilled and repulsed; her heart was full, and she turned with a look of touching appeal to the lady. That face was one to which a child would have fled for comfort; it was tranquil and full of kindness. Malaeska's face brightened as she went up to her, and placed the letter in her hands without speaking a word; but the palpitation of her heart was visible through her heavy garments, and her hands shook as she relinquished the precious paper.

---

1 *Dutch tiles* traditionally in blue, depicting scenes from the Bible.

"The seal is black," said the lady, turning very pale as she gave the letter to her husband, "but it is *his* writing," she added, with a forced smile. "He could not have sent word himself, were he—ill." She hesitated at the last word, for, spite of herself, the thoughts of death lay heavily at her heart.

The merchant composed himself in his chair, settled his spectacles, and after another severe glance at the bearer, opened the letter. His wife kept her eyes fixed anxiously on his face as he read. She saw that his face grew pale, that his high, narrow forehead contracted, and that the stern mouth became still more rigid in its expression. She knew that some evil had befallen her son—her only son, and she grasped a chair for support; her lips were bloodless, and her eyes became keen with agonizing suspense. When her husband had read the letter through, she went close to him, but looked another way as she spoke.

"Tell me! has any harm befallen my son?" Her voice was low and gentle, but husky with suspense.

Her husband did not answer, but his hand fell heavily upon his knee, and the letter rattled in his unsteady grasp; his eyes were fixed on his trembling wife with a look that chilled her to the heart. She attempted to withdraw the letter from his hand, but he clenched it the firmer.

"Let it alone—he is dead—murdered by the savages—why should you know more?"

The poor woman staggered back, and the fire of anxiety went out from her eyes.

"Can there be any thing worse than death—the death of the first-born of our youth—cut off in his proud manhood?" she murmured, in a low, broken voice.

"Yes, woman!" said the husband, almost fiercely; "there is a thing worse than death—disgrace!"

"Disgrace coupled with my son? You are his father, John. Do not slander him now that he is dead—before his mother, too." There was a faint, red spot then upon that mild woman's face, and her mouth curved proudly as she spoke. All that was stern in her nature had been aroused by the implied charge against the departed.

"Read, woman, read! Look on that accursed wretch and her child! They have enticed him into their savage haunts, and murdered him. Now they come to claim protection and reward for the foul deed."

Malaeska drew her child closer to her as she listened to this vehement language, and shrank slowly back to a corner of the room, where she crouched, like a frightened hare, looking wildly about, as if seeking some means to evade the vengeance which seemed to threaten her.

After the first storm of feeling, the old man buried his face in his hands and remained motionless, while the sobs of his wife, as she read her son's letter, alone broke the stillness of the room.

Malaeska felt those tears as an encouragement, and her own deep feelings taught her how to reach those of another. She drew timidly to the mourner and sank at her feet.

"Will the white woman look upon Malaeska?" she said, in a voice full of humility and touching earnestness. "She loved the young white chief, and when the shadows fell upon his soul, he said that his mother's heart would grow soft to the poor Indian woman who had slept in his bosom while she was very young. He said that her love would open to his boy like a flower to the sunshine. Will the white woman look upon the boy? He is like his father."

"He is, poor child, he is!" murmured the bereaved mother, looking on the boy through her tears—"like him, as he was when we were both young, and he the blessing of our hearts. Oh, John, do you remember his smile?—how his cheek would dimple when we kissed it! Look upon this poor, fatherless creature; they are all here again; the sunny eye and the broad forehead. Look upon him, John, for my sake—for the sake of our dead son, who prayed us with his last breath to love *his* son. Look upon him!"

The kind woman led the child to her husband as she spoke, and resting her arm on his shoulder, pressed her lips upon his swollen temples. The pride of his nature was touched. His bosom heaved, and tears gushed through his rigid fingers. He felt a little form draw close to his knee, and a tiny, soft hand strive with its feeble might to uncover his face. The voice of nature was strong within him. His hands dropped, and he pored with a troubled face over the uplifted features of the child.

Tears were in those young, bright eyes as they returned his grandfather's gaze, but when a softer expression came into the old man's face, a smile broke through them, and the little fellow lifted both his arms and clasped them over the bowed neck of his grandfather. There was a momentary struggle, and then the merchant folded the boy to his heart with a burst of strong feeling such as his iron nature had seldom known.

"He *is* like his father. Let the woman go back to her tribe; we will keep the boy."

Malaeska sprang forward, clasped her hands, and turned with an air of wild, heart-thrilling appeal to the lady.

"You will not send Malaeska from her child. No—no, white woman. Your boy has slept against your heart, and you have felt his voice in your ear, like the song of a young mocking-bird. You would not send the poor Indian back to the woods without her child. She has come to you from the forest, that she may learn the path to the white man's heaven, and see her husband again, and you will not show it her. Give the Indian woman her boy; her heart is growing very strong; she will not go back to the woods alone!"

As she spoke these words, with an air more energetic even than her speech, she snatched the child from his grandfather's arms, and stood like a lioness guarding her young, her lips writhing and her black eyes flashing fire, for the savage blood kindled in her veins at the thought of being separated from her son.

"Be quiet, girl, be quiet. If you go, the child shall go with you," said the gentle Mrs. Danforth. "Do not give way to this fiery spirit; no one will wrong you."

Malaeska dropped her air of defiance, and placing the child humbly at his grandfather's feet, drew back, and stood with her eyes cast down, and her hands clasped deprecatingly together, a posture of supplication in strong contrast with her late wild demeanor.

"Let them stay. Do not separate the mother and the child!" entreated the kind lady, anxious to soothe away the effect of her husband's violence. "The thought of a separation drives her wild, poor thing. *He* loved her;—why should we send her back to her savage haunts? Read this letter once more, my husband. You can not refuse the dying request of our first-born."

With gentle and persuasive words like these, the kind lady prevailed. Malaeska was allowed to remain in the house of her husband's father, but it was only as the nurse of her own son. She was not permitted to acknowledge herself as his mother; and it was given out that young Danforth had married in one of

42

the new settlements—that the young couple had fallen victims to the savages, and that their infant son had been rescued by an Indian girl, who brought him to his grandfather. The story easily gained credit, and it was no matter of wonder that the old fur merchant soon became fondly attached to the little orphan, or that the preserver of his grandchild was made an object of grateful attention in his household.

CHAPTER 4

"Her heart is in the wild wood;
Her heart is not here.
Her heart is in the wild wood;
It was hunting the deer."

IT WOULD have been an unnatural thing, had that picturesque young mother abandoned the woods, and prisoned herself in a quaint old Dutch house, under the best circumstances. The wild bird, which has fluttered freely from its nest through a thousand forests, might as well be expected to love its cage, as this poor wild girl her new home, with its dreary stillness and its leaden regularity. But love was all-powerful in that wild heart. It had brought Malaeska from her forest home, separated her from her tribe in its hour of bitter defeat, and sent her a forlorn wanderer among strangers that regarded her almost with loathing.

The elder Danforth was a just man, but hard as granite in his prejudices. An only son had been murdered by the savages to whom this poor young creature belonged. His blood—all of his being that might descend to posterity—had been mingled with the accursed race who had sacrificed him. Gladly would he have rent the two races asunder, in the very person of his grandchild, could the pure half of his being been thus preserved.

But he was a proud, childless old man, and there was something in the boy's eyes, in the brave lift of his head, and in his caressing manner, which filled the void in his heart, half with love and half with pain. He could no more separate the two passions in his own soul, than he could drain the savage blood from the little boy's veins.

But the house-mother, the gentle wife, could see nothing but her son's smile in that young face, nothing but his look in the large eyes, which, black in color, still possessed something of the azure light that had distinguished those of the father.

The boy was more cheerful and bird-like than his mother, for all her youth had gone out on the banks of the pond where her husband died. Always submissive, always gentle, she was nevertheless a melancholy woman. A bird which had followed its young out into strange lands, and caged it there, could not have hovered around it more hopelessly.

Nothing but her husband's dying wish would have kept Malaeska in Manhattan. She thought of her own people incessantly—of her broken, harassed tribe, desolated by the death of her father, and whose young chief she had carried off and given to strangers.

But shame dyed Malaeska's cheek as she thought of these things. What right had she, an Indian of the pure blood, to bring the grandchild of her father under the roof of his enemies? Why had she not taken the child in her arms and joined her people as they sang the death-chant for her father, "who," she murmured to herself again and again, "was a great chief," and retreated with them deep into the wilderness, to which they were driven, giving them a chief in her son?

But no! passion had been too strong in Malaeska's heart. The woman conquered the patriot; and the refinement which affection had given her, enslaved the wild nature without returning a compensation of love for the sacrifice. She pined for her people—all the more that they were in peril and sorrow. She longed for the shaded forest-paths, and the pretty lodge, with its couches of fur and its floor of blossoming turf. To her the very winds seemed chained among the city houses; and when she heard them sighing through the gables, it seemed to her that they were moaning for freedom, as she was in the solitude of her lonely life.

They had taken the child from her. A white nurse was found, who stepped in between the young heir and his mother, thrusting her ruthlessly aside. In this the old man was obstinate. The wild blood of the boy must be quenched; he must know nothing of the race from which his disgrace sprang. If the Indian woman remained under his roof, it must be as a menial, and on condition that all natural affection lay crushed within her—unexpressed, unguessed at by the household.

But Mrs. Danforth had compassion on the poor mother. She remembered the time when her own child had made all the pulses of her being thrill with love, which now took the form of a thousand tender regrets. She could not watch the lone Indian stealing off to her solitary room under the gable roof—a mother, yet childless—without throbs of womanly sorrow. She was far too good a wife to brave her husband's authority, but, with the cowardliness of a kind heart, she frequently managed to evade it. Sometimes in the night she would creep out of her prim chamber, and steal the boy from the side of his nurse, whom she bore on her own motherly bosom to the solitary bed of Malaeska.

As if Malaeska had a premonition of the kindliness, she was sure to be wide awake, thinking of her child, and ready to gush forth in murmurs of thankfulness for the joy of clasping her own son a moment to that lonely heart.

Then the grandmother would steal to her husband's side again, charging it upon her memory to awake before daylight, and carry the boy back to the stranger's bed, making her gentle charity a secret as if it had been a sin.

It was pitiful to see Malaeska haunting the footsteps of her boy all the day long. If he was taken into the garden, she was sure to be hovering around the old pear-trees, where she could sometimes unseen lure him from his play, and lavish kisses on his mouth as he laughed recklessly, and strove to abandon her for some bright flower or butterfly that crossed his path. This snatch of affection, this stealthy way of appeasing a hungry nature, was enough to drive a well-tutored woman mad; as for Malaeska, it was a marvel that she could tame her erratic nature into the abject position allotted her in that family. She had neither the occupation of a servant, nor the interests of an equal.

Forbidden to associate with the people in the kitchen, yet never welcomed in the formal parlor when its master was at home, she hovered around the halls and corners of the house, or hid herself away in the gable chambers, embroidering beautiful trifles on scraps of silk and fragments of bright cloth, with which she strove to bribe the woman who controlled her child, into forbearance and kindness.

But alas, poor woman! submission to the wishes of the dead was a terrible duty; her poor heart was breaking all the time; she had no hope, no life; the very glance of her eye was an appeal for mercy; her step, as it fell on the turf, was leaden with despondency—she had nothing on earth to live for.

This state of things arose when the child was a little boy; but as he grew older the bitterness of Malaeska's lot became more intense. The nurse who had supplanted her went away; for he was becoming a fine lad, and far removed from the need of woman's care. But this brought her no nearer to his affections. The Indian blood was strong in his young veins; he loved such play as brought activity and danger with it, and broke from the Indian woman's caresses with a sort of scorn, and she knew that the old grandfather's prejudice was taking root in his heart, and dared not utter a protest. She was forbidden to lavish tenderness on her son, or to call forth his in return, lest it might create suspicion of the relationship.

In his early boyhood, she could steal to his chamber at night, and give free indulgence to the wild tenderness of her nature; but after a time even the privilege of watching him in his sleep was denied to her. Once, when she broke the tired boy's rest by her caresses, he became petulant, and chided her for her obtrusiveness. The repulse went to her heart like iron. She had no power to plead; for her life, she dared not tell him the secret of that aching love which she felt—too cruelly felt—oppressed his boyhood; for that would be to expose the disgrace of blood which embittered the old man's pride.

She was his mother; yet her very existence in that house was held as a reproach. Every look that she dared to cast on her child, was watched jealously as a fault. Poor Malaeska! hers was a sad, sad life.

She had borne every thing for years, dreaming, poor thing, that the eternal cry that went up from her heart would be answered, as the boy grew older; but when he began to shrink proudly from her caresses, and question the love that was killing her, the despair which smoldered at her heart broke forth, and the forest blood spoke out with a power that not even a sacred memory of the dead could oppose. A wild idea seized upon her. She would no longer remain in the white man's house, like a bird beating its wings against the wires of a cage. The forests were wide and green as ever. Her people might yet be found. She would seek them in the wilderness. The boy should go with her, and become the chief of his tribe, as her father had been. That old man should not forever trample down her heart. There was a free life which she would find or die.

The boy's childish petulance had created this wild wish in his mother's heart. The least sign of repulsion drove her frantic. She began to thirst eagerly for her old free existence in the woods; but for the blood of her husband, which ran in the old man's veins, she would have given way to the savage hate of her people, against the household in which she had been so unhappy. As it was, she only panted to be away with her child, who must love her when no white man stood by to rebuke him. With her aroused energies the native reticence of her tribe came to her aid. The stealthy art of warfare against an enemy awoke. They should not know how wretched she was. Her plans must be securely made. Every step toward freedom should be carefully considered. These thoughts occupied Malaeska for days and weeks. She became active in her little chamber. The bow and sheaf of arrows that had given her the appearance of a young Diana when she came to Manhattan in her canoe, was taken down from the wall, newly strung, and the stone arrow-heads patiently sharpened. Her dress, with its gorgeous embroidery of fringe and wampum, was examined with care.

45

She must return to her people as she had left them. The daughter of a chief—the mother of a chief—not a fragment of the white man's bounty should go with her to the forest.

Cautiously, and with something of native craft, Malaeska made her preparations. Down upon the shores of the Hudson, lived an old carpenter who made boats for a living. Malaeska had often seen him at his work, and her rude knowledge of his craft gave peculiar interest to the curiosity with which she regarded him. The Indian girl had long been an object of his especial interest, and the carpenter was flattered by her admiration of his work.

One day she came to his house with a look of eager watchfulness. Her step was hurried, her eye wild as a hawk's when its prey is near. The old man was finishing a fanciful little craft, of which he was proud beyond any thing. It was so light, so strong, so beautifully decorated with bands of red and white around the edge—no wonder the young woman's eyes brightened when she saw it.

"What would he take for the boat?" That was a droll question from her. Why he had built it to please his own fancy. A pair of oars would make it skim the water like a bird. He had built it with an eye to old Mr. Danforth, who had been down to look at his boats for that dark-eyed grandson, whom he seemed to worship. None of his boats were fanciful or light enough for the lad. So he had built this at a venture.

Malaeska's eyes kindled brighter and brighter. Yes, yes; she, too, was thinking of the young gentleman; she would bring him to look at the boat. Mrs. Danforth often trusted the boy out with her; if he would only tell the price, perhaps they might be able to bring the money, and give the boat a trial on the Hudson.

The old man laughed, glanced proudly at his handiwork, and named a price. It was not too much; Malaeska had double that amount in the embroidered pouch that hung in her little room at home—for the old gentleman had been liberal to her in every thing but kindness. She went home elated and eager; all was in readiness. The next day—oh, how her heart glowed as she thought of the next day!

CHAPTER 5

> Her boat is on the river,
> With the boy by her side;
> With her bow and her quiver
> She stands in her pride.

THE NEXT afternoon old Mr. Danforth was absent from home. A municipal meeting, or something of that kind, was to be attended, and he was always prompt in the performance of public duties. The good housewife had not been well for some days. Malaeska, always a gentle nurse, attended her with unusual assiduity. There was something evidently at work in the Indian woman's heart. Her lips were pale, her eyes full of pathetic trouble. After a time, when weariness made the old lady sleepy, Malaeska stole to the bedside, and kneeling down, kissed the withered hand that fell over the bed, with strange humility. This action was so light that the good lady did not heed it, but afterward it came to her like a dream, and as such she remembered this leave-taking of the poor mother.

William—for the lad was named after his father—was in a moody state that afternoon. He had no playfellows, for the indisposition of his grandmother had shut all strangers from the house, so he went into the garden, and began to draw the outlines of a rude fortification from the white pebbles that paved the principal walk. He was interrupted in the work by a pair of orioles, that came dashing through the leaves of an old apple-tree in a far end of the garden, in full chase and pursuit, making the very air vibrate with their rapid motion.

After chasing each other up and down, to and fro in the clear sunshine, they were attracted by something in the distance, and darted off like a couple of golden arrows, sending back wild gushes of music in the start.

The boy had been watching them with his great eyes full of envious delight. Their riotous freedom charmed him; he felt chained and caged even in that spacious garden, full of golden fruit and bright flowers as it was. The native fire kindled in his frame.

"Oh, if I were only a bird, that could fly home when I pleased, and away to the woods again—the bright, beautiful woods that I can see across the river, but never must play in. How the birds love it though!"

The boy stopped speaking, for, like any other child kept to himself, he was talking over his thoughts aloud. But a shadow fell across the white pebbles on which he sat, and this it was which disturbed him.

It was the Indian woman, Malaeska, with a forced smile on her face and looking wildly strange. She seemed larger and more stately than when he had seen her last. In her hand she held a light bow tufted with yellow and crimson feathers. When she saw his eyes brighten at the sight of the bow, Malaeska took an arrow from the sheaf which she carried under her cloak, and fitted it to the string.

"See, this is what we learn in the woods."

The two birds were wheeling to and fro across the garden and out into the open space; their plumage flashed in the sunshine and gushes of musical triumph floated back as one shot ahead of the other. Malaeska lifted her bow with something of her old forest gracefulness—a faint twang of the bowstring—a sharp whiz of the arrow, one of the birds fluttered downward, with a sad little cry, and fell upon the ground, trembling like a broken poplar flower.

The boy started up—his eye brightened and his thin nostrils dilated, the savage instincts of his nature broke out in all his features.

"And you learned how to do this in the woods, Malaeska?" he said, eagerly.

"Yes; will you learn too?"

"Oh, yes—give hold here—quick—quick!"

"Not here; we learn these things in the woods; come with me, and I will show you all about it." Malaeska grew pale as she spoke, and trembled in all her limbs. What if the boy refused to go with her?

"What! over the river to the woods that look so bright and so brown when the nuts fall? Will you take me there, Malaeska?"

"Yes, over the river where it shines like silver."

"You will? oh my!—but how?"

"Hush! not so loud. In a beautiful little boat."

"With white sails, Malaeska?"

"No—with paddles."

"Ah, me!—but I can't make them go in the water; once grandfather let me try, but I had to give it up."

"But I can make them go."

"You! why, that isn't a woman's work."

"No, but everybody learns it in the woods."

"Can I?"

"Yes!"

"Then come along before grandfather comes to say we shan't; come along, I say; I want to shoot and run and live in the woods—come along, Malaeska. Quick, or somebody will shut the gate."

Malaeska looked warily around—on the windows of the house, through the thickets, and along the gravel walks. No one was in sight. She and her boy were all alone. She breathed heavily and lingered, thinking of the poor lady within.

"Come!" cried the boy, eagerly; "I want to go—come along to the woods."

"Yes, yes," whispered Malaeska, "to the woods—it is our home. There I shall be a mother once more."

With the steps of a young deer, starting for its covert, she left the garden. The boy kept bravely on with her, bounding forward with a laugh when her step was too rapid for him to keep up with it. Thus, in breathless haste, they passed through the town into the open country and along the rough banks of the river.

A little inlet, worn by the constant action of the water, ran up into the shore, which is now broken with wharves and bristling with masts. A clump of old forest-hemlocks bent over the waters, casting cool, green shadows upon it till the sun was far in the west.

In these shadows, rocking sleepily on the ripples, lay the pretty boat which Malaeska had purchased. A painted basket, such as the peaceful Indians sometimes sent to market, stood in the stern stored with bread; a tiger-skin, edged with crimson cloth, according to the Indian woman's fancy, lay along the bottom of the boat, and cushions of scarlet cloth, edged with an embroidery of beads, lay on the seat.

William Danforth broke into a shout when he saw the boat and its appointments.

"Are we going in this? May I learn to row, now—now?" With a leap he sprang into the little craft, and seizing the oars, called for her to come on, for he was in a hurry to begin.

Malaeska loosened the cable, and holding the end in her hand, sprang to the side of her child.

"Not yet, my chief, not yet; give the oars to me a little while; when we can no longer see the steeples, you shall pull them," she said.

The boy gave up his place with an impatient toss of his head, which sent the black curls flying over his temples. But the boat shot out into the river with a velocity that took away his breath, and he sat down in the bow, laughing as the silver spray rained over him. With her face to the north, and her eyes flashing with the eager joy of escape, Malaeska dashed up the river; every plunge of the oars was a step toward freedom—every gleam of the sun struck her as a smile from the Great Spirit to whom her husband and father had gone.

When the sun went down, and the twilight came on, the little boat was far up the river. It had glided under the shadows of Weehawken, and was skirting the western shore toward the Highlands, at that time crowned by an unbroken forest, and savage in the grandeur of wild nature.

Now Malaeska listened to the entreaties of her boy, and gave the oars into his small hands. No matter though the boat receded under his brave but imperfect efforts; once out of sight of the town, Malaeska had less fear, and smiled securely at the energy with which the little fellow beat the waters. He was indignant if she attempted to help him, and the next moment was sure to send a storm of rain over her in some more desperate effort to prove how capable he was of taking the labor from her hands.

Thus the night came on, soft and calm, wrapping the mother and child in a world of silvery moonbeams. The shadows which lay along the hills bounded their watery path with gloom. This made the boy sad, and he began to feel mournfully weary; but scenes like this were familiar with Malaeska, and her old nature rose high and free in this solitude which included all that she had in the living world—her freedom and the son of her white husband.

"Malaeska," said the boy, creeping to her side, and laying his head on her lap, "Malaeska, I am tired—I want to go home."

"Home! but you have not seen the woods. Courage, my chief, and we will go on shore."

"But it is black—so black, and something is crying there—something that is sick or wants to get home like me."

"No, no,—It is only a whippowil singing to the night."

"A whippowil? Is that a little boy, Malaeska? Let us bring him into the boat."

"No, my child, it is only a bird."

"Poor bird!" sighed the boy; "how it wants to get home."

"No, it loves the woods. The bird would die if you took if from the shade of the trees," said Malaeska, striving to pacify the boy, who crept upward into her lap and laid his cheek against hers. She felt that he trembled, and that tears lay cold on his cheeks. "Don't, my William, but look up and see how many stars hang over us—the river is full of them."

"Oh, but grandfather will be missing me," pleaded the boy.

Malaeska felt herself chilled; she had taken the boy but not his memory; that went back to the opulent home he had left. With her at his side, and the beautiful universe around, he thought of the old man who had made her worse than a serf in his household—who had stolen away the human soul that God had given into her charge. The Indian woman grew sad to the very depths of her soul when the boy spoke of his grandfather.

"Come," she said, with mournful pathos, "now we will find an open place in the woods. You shall have a bed like the pretty flowers. I will build a fire, and you shall see it grow red among the branches."

The boy smiled in the moonlight.

"A fire out of doors! Yes, yes, let's go into the woods. Will the birds talk to us there?"

"The birds talk to us always when we get into the deep of the woods."

Malaeska urged her boat into a little inlet that ran up between two great rocks upon the shore, where it was sheltered and safe; then she took the tiger-skin and the cushions in her arms, and, cautioning the boy to hold on to her dress, began to mount a little elevation where the trees were thin and the grass abundant, as she could tell from the odor of wild-flowers that came with the wind. A rock lay embedded in this rich forest-grass, and over it a huge white poplar spread its branches like a tent.

Upon this rock Malaeska enthroned the boy, talking to him all the time, as she struck sparks from a flint which she took from her basket, and began to kindle a fire from the dry sticks which lay around in abundance. When William saw the flames rise up high and clear, illuminating the beautiful space around, and shooting gleams of gold through the poplar's branches he grew brave again, and coming down from his eminence, began to gather brushwood that the fire might keep bright. Then Malaeska took a bottle of water and some bread, with fragments of dried beef, from her basket, and the boy came smiling from his work. He was no longer depressed by the dark, and the sight of food made him hungry.

How proudly the Indian mother broke the food and surrendered it to his eager appetite. The bright beauty of her face was something wonderful to look upon as she watched him by the firelight. For the first time, since he was a little infant, he really seemed to belong to her.

When he was satisfied with food, and she saw that his eyelids began to droop, Malaeska went to some rocks at a little distance, and tearing up the moss in great green fleeces, brought it to the place she had chosen under the poplar-tree, and heaped a soft couch for the child. Over this she spread the tiger-skin with its red border, and laid the crimson pillows whose fringes glittered in the firelight like gems around the couch of a prince.

To this picturesque bed Malaeska took the boy, and seating herself by his side, began to sing as she had done years ago under the roof of her wigwam. The lad was very weary, and fell asleep while her plaintive voice filled the air and was answered mournfully back by a night-bird deep in the blackness of the forest.

When certain that the lad was asleep, Malaeska lay down on the hard rock by his side, softly stealing one arm over him and sighing out her troubled joy as she pressed his lips with her timid kisses.

Thus the poor Indian sunk to a broken rest, as she had done all her life, piling up soft couches for those she loved, and taking the cold stone for herself. It was her woman's destiny, not the more certain because of her savage origin. Civilization does not always reverse this mournful picture of womanly self-abnegation.

When the morning came, the boy was aroused by a full chorus of singing-birds that fairly made the air vibrate with their melody. In and out through the branches rang their wild minstrelsy, till the sunshine came laughing through the greenness, giving warmth and pleasant light to the music. William sat up, rubbing his eyes, and wondering at the strange noises. Then he remembered where he was, and called aloud for Malaeska. She came from behind a clump of trees, carrying a partridge in her hand, pierced through the heart with her arrow. She flung the bird on the rock at William's feet, and kneeling down before him, kissed his feet, his hands, and the folds of his tunic, smoothing his hair and his garments with pathetic fondness.

"When shall we go home, Malaeska?" cried the lad, a little anxiously. "Grandfather will want us."

"This is the home for a young chief," replied the mother, looking around upon the pleasant sky and the forest-turf, enameled with wild-flowers. "What white man has a tent like this?"

The boy looked up and saw a world of golden tulip-blossoms starring the branches above him.

"It lets in the cold and the rain," he said, shaking the dew from his glossy hair. "I don't like the woods, Malaeska."

"But you will—oh yes, you will," answered the mother, with anxious cheerfulness; "see, I have shot a bird for your breakfast."

"A bird? and I am so hungry."

"And see here, what I have brought from the shore."

She took a little leaf-basket from a recess in the rocks, and held it up full of black raspberries with the dew glittering upon them.

The boy clapped his hands, laughing merrily.

"Give me the raspberries—I will eat them all. Grandfather isn't here to stop me, so I will eat and eat till the basket is empty. After all, Malaeska, it is pleasant being in the woods—come, pour the berries on the moss, just here, and get another basketful while I eat these; but don't go far—I am afraid when you are out of sight. No, no, let me build the fire—see how I can make the sparks fly."

Down he came from the rock, forgetting his berries, and eager to distinguish himself among the brushwood, while Malaeska withdrew a little distance and prepared her game for roasting.

The boy was quick and full of intelligence; he had a fire blazing at once, and shouted back a challenge to the birds as its flames rose in the air, sending up wreaths of delicate blue smoke into the poplar branches, and curtaining the rocks with mist.

Directly the Indian woman came forward with her game, nicely dressed and pierced with a wooden skewer; to this she attached a piece of twine, which, being tied to a branch overhead, swung its burden gently to and fro before the fire.

While this rustic breakfast was in preparation, the boy went off in search of flowers or berries—any thing that he could find. He came back with a quantity of green wild cherries in his tunic, and a bird's nest, with three speckled eggs in it, which he had found under a tuft of fern leaves. A striped squirrel, that ran down a chestnut-limb, looked at him with such queer earnestness, that he shouted lustily to Malaeska, saying that he loved the beautiful woods and all the pretty things in it.

When he came back, Malaeska had thrown off her cloak, and crowned herself with a coronal of scarlet and green feathers, which rendered her savage dress complete, and made her an object of wondering admiration to the boy, as she moved in and out through the trees, with her face all aglow with proud love.

While the partridge was swaying to and fro before the fire, Malaeska gathered a handful of chestnut-leaves and wove them together in a sort of mat; upon this cool nest she laid the bird, and carved it with a pretty poniard which William's father had given her in his first wooing; then she made a leaf-cup, and, going to a little spring which she had discovered, filled it with crystal water. So, upon the flowering turf, with wild birds serenading them, and the winds floating softly by, the mother and boy took their first regular meal in the forest. William was delighted; every thing was fresh and beautiful to him. He could scarcely contain his eagerness to be in action long enough to eat the delicate repast which Malaeska diversified with smiles and caresses. He wanted to shoot the birds that sang so sweetly in the branches, all unconscious that the act would inflict pain on the poor little songsters; he could not satisfy himself with gazing on the gorgeous raiment of his mother—it was something wonderful in his eyes.

At last the rustic meal was ended, and with his lips reddened by the juicy fruit, he started up, pleading for the bow and arrow.

Proud as a queen and fond as a woman, Malaeska taught him how to place the arrow on the bowstring, and when to lift it gradually toward his face. He took to it naturally, the young rogue, and absolutely danced for joy when his which only brought tears into the child's eyes, for they reminded him of home and all its comforts.

"Malaeska," he said, "when shall we go back to grandfather and grandmother? I know they want to see us."

"No, no; we must not think about that," said Malaeska, anxiously.

"But I can't help it—how can I?" persisted the boy, mournfully.

"Don't—don't say you love them—I mean your grandfather—more than you love Malaeska. She would die for you."

"Yes; but I don't want you to die, only to go back home," he pleaded.

"We are going home—to our beautiful home in the woods, which I told you of."

"Dear me, I'm so tired of the woods."

"Tired of the woods?"

"Yes, I *am* tired. They are nice to play in, but it isn't home, no way. How far is it, Malaeska, to where grandfather lives?"

"I don't know—I don't want to know. We shall never—never go there again," said the Indian, passionately. "You are mine, all mine."

The boy struggled in her embrace restively.

"But I won't stay in the woods. I want to be in a real house, and sleep in a soft bed, and—and—there, now, it is going to rain; I hear it thunder. Oh, how I want to go home!"

There was in truth a storm mustering over them; the wind rose and moaned hoarsely through the pines. Malaeska was greatly distressed, and gathered the tired boy lovingly to her bosom for shelter.

"Have patience, William; nothing shall hurt you. Tomorrow we will row the boat all day. You shall pull the oars yourself."

"Shall I, though?" said the boy, brightening a little; "but will it be on the way home?"

"We shall go across the mountains where the Indians live. The brave warriors who will make William their king."

"But I don't want to be a king, Malaeska!"

"A chief—a great chief—who shall go to the war-path and fight battles."

"Ah, I should like that, with your pretty bow and arrow, Malaeska; wouldn't I shoot the wicked red-skins?"

"Ah, my boy, don't say that."

"Oh," said the child, shivering, "the wind is cold; how it sobs in the pine boughs. Don't you wish we were at home now?"

"Don't be afraid of the cold," said Malaeska, in a troubled voice; "see, I will wrap this cloak about you, and no rain can come through the fur blanket. We are brave, you and I—what do we care for a little thunder and rain—it makes me feel brave."

"But you don't care for home; you love the woods and the rain. The thunder and lightning makes your eyes bright, but I don't like it; so take me home, please, and then you may go to the woods; I won't tell."

"Oh, don't—don't. It breaks my heart," cried the poor mother. "Listen, William: the Indians—my people—the brave Indians want you for a chief. In a few years you shall lead them to war."

"But I hate the Indians."

"No, no."

"They are fierce and cruel."

"Not to you—not to you!"

"I won't live with the Indians!"

"They are a brave people—you shall be their chief."

"They killed my father."

"But I am of those people. I saved you and brought you among the white people."

"Yes, I know; grandmother told me that."

"And I belonged to the woods."

"Among the Indians?"

"Yes. Your father loved these Indians, William."

"Did he—but they killed him."

"But it was in battle."

"In fair battle; did you say that?"

"Yes, child. Your father was friendly with them, but they thought he had turned enemy. A great chief met him in the midst of the fight, and they killed each other. They fell and died together."

"Did you know this great chief, Malaeska?"

"He was my father," answered the Indian woman, hoarsely; "my own father."

"Your father and mine; how strange that they should hate each other," said the boy, thoughtfully.

"Not always," answered Malaeska, struggling against the tears that choked her words; "at one time they loved each other."

"Loved each other! that is strange; and did my father love you, Malaeska?"

White as death the poor woman turned; a hand was clenched under her deer-skin robe, and pressed hard against her heart; but she had promised to reveal nothing, and bravely kept her word.

The boy forgot his reckless question the moment it was asked, and did not heed her pale silence, for the storm was gathering darkly over them. Malaeska wrapped him in her cloak, and sheltered him with her person. The rain began to patter heavily overhead; but the pine-tree was thick with foliage, and no drops, as yet, could penetrate to the earth.

"See, my boy, we are safe from the rain; nothing can reach us here," she said, cheering his despondency. "I will heap piles of dry wood on the fire, and shelter you all night long."

She paused a moment, for flashes of blue lightning began to play fiercely through the thick foliage overhead, revealing depths of darkness that was enough to terrify a brave man. No wonder the boy shrank and trembled as it flashed and quivered over him.

Malaeska saw how frightened he was, and piled dry wood recklessly on the fire, hoping that its steady blaze would reassure him.

They were encamped on a spur of the Highlands that shot in a precipice over the stream, and the light of Malaeska's fire gleamed far and wide, casting a golden track far down the Hudson.

Four men, who were urging a boat bravely against the storm, saw the light, and shouted eagerly to each other.

"Here she is; nothing but an Indian would keep up a fire like that. Pull steadily, and we have them."

They did pull steadily, and defying the storm, the boat made harbor under the cliff where Malaeska's fire still burned. Four men stole away from the boat, and crept stealthily up the hill, guided by the lightning and the gleaming fire above. The rain, beating among the branches, drowned their footsteps; and they spoke only in hoarse whispers, which were lost on the wind.

William had dropped asleep with tears on his thick eyelashes, which the strong firelight revealed to Malaeska, who regarded him with mournful affection. The cold wind chilled her through and through, but she did not feel it. So long as the boy slept comfortably she had no want.

I have said that the storm muffled all other sounds; and the four men who had left their boat at the foot of the cliff stood close by Malaeska before she had the least idea of their approach. Then a blacker shadow than fell from the pine, darkened the space around her, and looking suddenly up, she saw the stern face of old Mr. Danforth between her and the firelight.

Malaeska did not speak or cry aloud, but snatching the sleeping boy close to her heart, lifted her pale face to his, half-defiant, half-terrified.

"Take my grandson from the woman and bring him down to the boat," said the old man, addressing those that came with him.

"No, no, he is mine!" cried Malaeska, fiercely. "Nothing but the Great Spirit shall take him from me again!"

The sharp anguish in her voice awoke the boy. He struggled in her arms, and looking around, saw the old man.

"Grandfather, oh! grandfather, take me home. I do want to go home," he cried, stretching out his arms.

"Oh!" I have not the power of words to express the bitter anguish of that single exclamation, when it broke from the mother's pale lips. It was the cry of a heart that snapped its strongest fiber there and then. The boy wished to leave her. She had no strength after that, but allowed them to force him from her arms without a struggle. The rattlesnake had not paralyzed her so completely.

So they took the boy ruthlessly from her embrace, and carried him away. She followed after without a word of protest, and saw them lift him into the boat and push off, leaving her to the pitiless night. It was a cruel thing—bitterly cruel—but the poor woman was stupefied with the blow, and watched the boat with heavy eyes. All at once she heard the boy calling after her:

"Malaeska, come too. Malaeska—Malaeska!"

She heard the cry, and her icy heart swelled passionately. With the leap of a panther she sprang to her own boat, and dashed after her tormenters, pulling fiercely through the storm. But with all her desperate energy, she was not able to overtake those four powerful men. They were out of sight directly, and she drifted after them alone—all alone.

Malaeska never went back to Mr. Danforth's house again, but she built a lodge on the Weehawken shore, and supported herself by selling painted baskets and such embroideries as the Indians excel in. It was a lonely life, but sometimes she met her son in the streets of Manhattan, or sailing on the river, and this poor happiness kept her alive.

After a few months, the lad came to her lodge. His grandmother consented to the visit, for she still had compassion on the lone Indian, and would not let the youth go beyond sea without bidding her farewell. In all the bitter anguish of that parting Malaeska kept her faith, and smothering the great want of her soul, saw her son depart without putting forth the holy claim of her motherhood. One day Malaeska stood upon the shore and saw a white-sailed ship veer from her moorings and pass away with cruel swiftness toward the ocean, the broad, boundless ocean, that seemed to her like eternity.

56

CHAPTER 7

Alone in the forest, alone,
When the night is dark and late—
Alone on the waters, alone,
She drifts to her woman's fate.

A GAIN Malaeska took to her boat and, all alone, began her mournful journey to the forest. After the fight at Catskill, her brethren had retreated into the interior. The great tribe, which gave its name[1] to the richest intervale[2] in New York State, was always munificent in its hospitality to less fortunate brethren, to whom its hunting-grounds were ever open. Malaeska knew that her people were mustered somewhere near the amber-colored falls of Genesee, and she began her mournful voyage with vague longings to see them again, now that she had nothing but memories to live upon.

With a blanket in the bow of her boat, a few loaves of bread, and some meal in a coarse linen bag, she started up the river. The boat was battered and beginning to look old—half the gorgeous paint was worn from its sides, and the interior had been often washed by the tempests that beat over the little cove near her lodge where she had kept it moored. She made no attempt to remedy its desolate look. The tigerskin was left behind in her lodge. No crimson cushions rendered the single seat tempting to sit upon. These fanciful comforts were intended for the boy—motherly love alone provided them; but now she had no care for things of this kind. A poor lone Indian woman, trampled on by the whites, deserted by her own child, was going back to her kinsfolk for shelter. Why should she attempt to appear less desolate than she was?

Thus, dreary and abandoned, Malaeska sat in her boat, heavily urging it up the stream. She had few wants, but pulled at the oars all day long, keeping time to the slow movement with her voice, from which a low funereal chant swelled continually.

Sometimes she went ashore, and building a fire in the loneliness, cooked the fish she had speared or the bird her arrow had brought down; but these meals always reminded her of the few happy days spent, after the sylvan fashion, with her boy, and she would sit moaning over the untasted food till the very birds that hovered near would pause in their singing to look askance at her. So she relaxed in her monotonous toil but seldom, and generally slept in her little craft, with the current rippling around her, wrapped only in a coarse, gray blanket.

No one cared about her movements, and no one attempted to bring her back, or she might have been traced at intervals by some rock close to the shore, blackened with embers, where she had baked her corn-bread, or by the feathers of a bird which she had dressed, without caring to eat it.

Day after day—day after day, Malaeska kept on her watery path till she came to the mouth of the Mohawk. There she rested a little, with a weary, heavy-hearted dread of pursuing her journey further. What if her people should reject her as a renegade? She had deserted them in their hour of deep trouble—fled from the grave of her father, their chief, and had carried his grandson away to his bitterest enemy, the white man.

---

1 *its name* Mohawk.
2 *intervale* lowland adjacent to a river; here, the Mohawk River.

limbs were so weary that she longed to call out and pray the chief to kill her then and there; but he kept on a little in advance, only turning now and then to be sure that she followed.

Once she ventured to ask him why he put off her death so long; but he pointed along the trail, and walked along without deigning a reply. During the day he took a handful of parched corn from his pouch and told her to eat; but for himself, through that long night and day, he never tasted a morsel.

Toward sunset they came out on the banks of the Mohawk, near the very spot where she had left her boat. The Indian paused here and looked steadily at his victim.

The blood grew cold in Malaeska's veins—death was terrible when it came so near. She cast one look of pathetic pleading on his face, then, folding her hands, stood before him, waiting for the moment.

"Malaeska!"

His voice was softened, his lips quivered as the name once so sweet to his heart passed through them.

"Malaeska, the river is broad and deep. The keel of your boat leaves no track. Go! the Great Spirit will light you with his stars. Here is corn and dried venison. Go in peace!"

She looked at him with her wild tender eyes; her lips began to tremble, her heart swelled with gentle sweetness, which was the grace of her civilization. She took the red hand of the savage and kissed it reverently.

"Farewell," she said; "Malaeska has no words; her heart is full."

The savage began to tremble; a glow of the old passion came over him.

"Malaeska, my wigwam is empty; will you go back? It is my right to save or kill."

"*He* is yonder, in the great hunting-ground, waiting for Malaeska to come. Could she go blushing from another chief's wigwam?"

For one instant those savage features were convulsed; then they settled down into the cold gravity of his former expression, and he pointed to the boat.

She went down to the edge of the water, while he took the blanket from his shoulders and placed it in the boat. Then he pushed the little craft from its mooring, and motioned her to jump in; he forbore to touch her hand, or even look on her face, but saw her take up the oars and leave the shore without a word; but when she was out of sight, his head fell forward on his bosom, and he gradually sank to an attitude of profound grief.

While he sat upon a fragment of rock, with a rich sunset crimsoning the water at his feet, a canoe came down the river, urged by a white man, the only one who ever visited his tribe. This man was a missionary among the Indians, who held him in reverence as a great medicine chief, whose power of good was something to marvel at.

The chief beckoned to the missionary, who seemed in haste, but he drew near the shore. In a few brief but eloquent words the warrior spoke of Malaeska, of the terrible fate from which she had just been rescued, and of the forlorn life to which she must henceforth be consigned. There was something grand in this compassion that touched a thousand generous impulses in the missionary's heart. He was on his course down the river—for his duties lay with the Indians of many tribes—so he promised to overtake the lonely woman, to comfort and protect her from harm till she reached some settlement.

The good man kept his word. An hour after, his canoe was attached to Malaeska's little craft by its slender cable, and he was conversing kindly with her of those things that interested his pure nature most.

Malaeska listened with meek and grateful attention. No flower ever opened to the sunshine more sweetly than her soul received the holy revelations of that good man. He had no time or place for teaching, but seized any opportunity that arose where a duty could be performed. His mission lay always where human souls required knowledge. So he never left the lonely woman till long after they had passed the mouth of the Mohawk, and were floating on the Hudson. When they came in sight of the Catskill range, Malaeska was seized with an irresistible longing to see the graves of her husband and father. What other place in the wide, wide world had she to look for? Where could she go, driven forth as she was by her own people, and by the father of her husband?

Surely among the inhabitants of the village she could sell such trifles as her inventive talent could create, and if any of the old lodges stood near "the Straka," that would be shelter enough.

With these thoughts in her mind, Malaeska took leave of the missionary with many a whispered blessing, and took her way to "the Straka." There she found an old lodge, through whose crevices the winds had whistled for years; but she went diligently to work, gathering moss and turf with which this old home, connected with so many sweet and bitter associations, was rendered habitable again. Then she took possession, and proceeded to invent many objects of comfort and even taste, with which to beautify the spot she had consecrated with memories of her passionate youth, and its early, only love.

The woods were full of game, and wild fruits were abundant; so that it was a long, long time before Malaeska's residence in the neighborhood was known. She shrank from approaching a people who had treated her so cruelly, and so kept in utter loneliness so long as solitude was possible.

In all her life Malaeska retained but one vague hope, and that was for the return of her son from that far-off country to which the cruel whites had sent him. She had questioned the missionary earnestly about these lands, and had now a settled idea of their extent and distance across the ocean. The great waters no longer seemed like eternity to her, or absence so much like death. Some time she might see her child again; till then she would wait and pray to the white man's God.

CHAPTER 8

Huzza, for the forests and hills!
  Huzza, for the berries so blue!
Our baskets we'll cheerily fill,
  While the thickets are sparkling with dew.

YEARS before the scene of our story returns to Catskill, Arthur Jones and the pretty Martha Fellows had married and settled down in life. The kind-hearted old man died soon after the union, and left the pair inheritors of his little shop and of a respectable landed property. Arthur made an indulgent, good husband, and Martha soon became too much confined by the cares of a rising family, for any practice of the teasing coquetry which had characterized her girlhood. She seconded her husband in all his money-making projects; was an economical and thrifty housekeeper; never allowed her children to go barefooted, except in the very warmest weather; and, to use her own words, made a point of holding her head as high as any woman in the settlement.

If an uninterrupted course of prosperity could entitle a person to this privilege, Mrs. Jones certainly made no false claim to it. Every year added something to her husband's possessions. Several hundred acres of cleared land were purchased beside that which he inherited from his father-in-law; the humble shop gradually increased to a respectable variety-store, and a handsome frame-house occupied the site of the old log-cabin.

Besides all this, Mr. Jones was a justice of the peace and a dignitary in the village; and his wife, though a great deal stouter than when a girl, and the mother of six children, had lost none of her healthy good looks, and at the age of thirty-eight continued to be a very handsome woman indeed.

Thus was the family situated at the period when our story returns to them. One warm afternoon, in the depth of summer, Mrs. Jones was sitting in the porch of her dwelling occupied in mending a garment of home-made linen, which, from its size, evidently belonged to some one of her younger children. A cheese-press, with a rich heavy mass of curd compressed between the screws, occupied one side of the porch; and against it stood a small double flax-wheel, unbanded, and with a day's work yet unreeled from the spools. A hatchel[1] and a pair of hand-cards,[2] with a bunch of spools tied together by a tow string, lay in a corner, and high above, on rude wooden pegs, hung several enormous bunches of tow and linen yarn, the products of many weeks' hard labor.

Her children had gone into the woods after whortleberries,[3] and the mother now and then laid down her work and stepped out to the green sward beyond the porch to watch their coming, not anxiously, but as one who feels restless and lost without her usual companions. After standing on the grass for awhile, shading her eyes with her hand and looking toward the woods, she at last returned to the porch, laid down her work, and entering the kitchen, filled the tea-kettle and began to make preparations for supper. She had drawn a long pine table to the middle of the floor, and was proceeding to spread it, when her eldest daughter came through the porch, with a basket of whortleberries on her arm. Her pretty face was flushed with walking, and a profusion of fair tresses flowed in some disorder from her pink sun bonnet, which was falling partly back from her head.

"Oh, mother, I have something so strange to tell you," she said, setting down the basket with its load of ripe, blue fruit, and fanning herself with a bunch of chestnut-leaves gathered from the woods. "You know the old wigwam by 'the Straka?' Well, when we went by it, the brush, which used to choke up the door, was all cleared off; the crevices were filled with green moss and leaves, and a cloud of smoke was curling beautifully up from the roof among the trees. We could not tell what to make of it, and were afraid to look in at first; but finally I peeped through an opening in the logs, and as true as you are here, mother, there sat an Indian woman reading—reading, mother! did you know that Indi-

---

1 *hatchel*   metal instrument used to split and comb flax fibers.
2 *hand-cards*   metal-toothed flax combs.
3 *whortleberries*   blue-black berries of a certain hardy dwarf shrub.

ans could read? The inside of the wigwam was hung with straw matting, and there was a chest in it, and some tools, and a little shelf of books, and another with some earthern dishes and a china cup and saucer, sprigged with gold, standing upon it. I did not see any bed, but there was a pile of fresh, sweet fern in one corner, with a pair of clean sheets spread on it, which I suppose she sleeps on, and there certainly was a feather pillow lying at the top.

"Well, the Indian woman looked kind and harmless; so I made an excuse to go in, and ask for a cup to drink out of.

"As I went round to the other side of the wigwam, I saw that the smoke came up from a fire on the outside; a kettle was hanging in the flame, and several other pots and kettles stood on a little bench by the trunk of an oak-tree, close by. I must have made some noise, for the Indian woman was looking toward the door when I opened it, as if she were a little afraid, but when she saw who it was, I never saw any one smile so pleasantly; she gave me the china cup, and went with me out to the spring where the boys were playing.

"As I was drinking, my sleeve fell back, and she saw the little wampum bracelet which you gave me, you know, mother. She started and took hold of my arm, and stared in my face, as if she would have looked me through; at last she sat down on the grass by the spring, and asked me to sit down by her and tell her my name. When I told her, she seemed ready to cry with joy; tears came into her eyes, and she kissed my hand two or three times, as if I had been the best friend she ever had on earth.

"I told her that a poor Indian girl had given the bracelet to you, before you were married to my father. She asked a great many questions about it, and you.

"When I began to describe the Indian fight, and the chief's grave down by the lake, she sat perfectly still till I had done; then I looked in her face: great tears were rolling one by one down her cheeks, her hands were locked in her lap, and her eyes were fixed upon my face with a strange stare, as if she did not know what she was gazing so hard at. She looked in my face, in this way, more than a minute after I had done speaking.

"The boys stopped their play, for they had begun to dam up the spring, and stood with their hands full of turf, huddled together, and staring at the poor woman as if they had never seen a person cry before. She did not seem to mind them, but went into the wigwam again without speaking a word."

"And was that the last you saw of her?" inquired Mrs. Jones, who had become interested in her daughter's narration.

"Oh, no; she came out again just as we were going away from the spring. Her voice was more sweet and mournful than it had been, and her eyes looked heavy and troubled. She thanked me for the story I had told her, and gave me this pair of beautiful moccasins."

Mrs. Jones took the moccasins from her daughter's hand. They were of neatly dressed deer-skin, covered with beads and delicate needle-work in silk.

"It is strange!" muttered Mrs. Jones; "one might almost think it possible. But nonsense; did not the old merchant send us word that the poor creature and her child were lost in the Highlands—that they died of hunger? Well, Sarah," she added, turning to her daughter, "is this all? What did the woman say when she gave you the moccasins? I don't wonder that you are pleased with them."

"She only told me to come again, and—"

Here Sarah was interrupted by a troop of noisy boys, who came in a body through the porch, flourishing their straw hats and swinging their whortleberry baskets heavy with fruit, back and forth at each step.

"Hurra! hurra! Sarah's fallen in love with an old squaw. How do you do, Miss Jones? Oh, mother, I wish you coulda-seen her hugging and kissing the copper-skin—it was beautiful!"

Here the boisterous rogues set up a laugh that rang through the house, like the breaking up of a military muster.

"Mother, do make them be still; they have done nothing but tease and make fun of me all the way home," said the annoyed girl, half crying.

"How did the old squaw's lips taste, hey?" persisted the eldest boy, pulling his sister's sleeve, and looking with eyes full of saucy mischief up into her face. "Sweet as maple-sugar, wasn't it? Come, tell."

"Arthur—Arthur! you had better be quiet, if you know when you're well off!" exclaimed the mother, with a slight motion of the hand, which had a great deal of significant meaning to the mischievous group.

"Oh, don't—please, don't!" exclaimed the spoiled urchin, clapping his hands to his ears and running off to a corner, where he stood laughing in his mother's face. "I say, Sarah, was it sweet?"

"Arthur, don't let me speak to you again, I say," cried Mrs. Jones, making a step forward and doing her utmost to get up a frown, while her hand gave additional demonstration of its hostile intent.

"Well, then, make her tell me; you ought to cuff *her* ears for not answering a civil question—hadn't she, boys?"

There was something altogether too ludicrous in this impudent appeal, and in the look of demure mischief put on by the culprit. Mrs. Jones bit her lips and turned away, leaving the boy, as usual, victor of the field. "He isn't worth minding, Sarah," she said, evidently ashamed of her want of resolution; "come into the 'out-room,' I've something to tell you."

When the mother and daughter were alone, Mrs. Jones sat down and drew the young girl into her lap.

"Well, Sarah," she said, smoothing down the rich hair that lay against her bosom, "your father and I have been talking about you to-day. You are almost sixteen, and can spin your day's work with any girl in the settlement. Your father says that after you have learned to weave and make cheese, he will send you down to Manhattan to school."

"Oh, mother, did he say so? in real, real earnest?" cried the delighted girl, flinging her arms round her mother's neck and kissing her yet handsome mouth with joy at the information it had just conveyed. "When will he let me go? I can learn to weave and make cheese in a week."

"If you learn all that he thinks best for you to know in two years, it will be as much as we expect. Eighteen is quite young enough. If you are very smart at home, you shall go when you are eighteen."

"Two years is a long, long time," said the girl, in a tone of disappointment; "but then father is kind to let me go at all. I will run down to the store and thank him. But, mother," she added, turning back from the door, "was there really any harm in talking with the Indian woman? There was nothing about her that did not seem like the whites but her skin, and that was not so *very* dark."

"Harm? No child; how silly you are to let the boys tease you so."

"I will go and see her again, then—may I?"

"Certainly—but see; your father is coming to supper; run out and cut the bread. You must be very smart, now; remember the school."

During the time which intervened between Sarah Jones' sixteenth and eighteenth year, she was almost a daily visitor at the wigwam. The little footpath which led from the village to "the Straka," though scarcely definable to others, became as familiar to her as the grounds about her father's house. If a day or two passed in which illness or some other cause prevented her usual visit, she was sure to receive some token of remembrance from the lone Indian woman. Now, it reached her in the form of a basket of ripe fruit, or a bunch of wild flowers, tied together with the taste of an artist; again, it was a cluster of grapes, with the purple bloom lying fresh upon them, or a young mocking-bird, with notes as sweet as the voice of a fountain, would reach her by the hands of some village boy.

These affectionate gifts could always be traced to the inhabitant of the wigwam, even though she did not, as was sometimes the case, present them in person.

There was something strange in the appearance of this Indian woman, which at first excited the wonder, and at length secured the respect of the settlers. Her language was pure and elegant, sometimes even poetical beyond their comprehension, and her sentiments were correct in principle, and full of simplicity. When she appeared in the village with moccasins or pretty painted baskets for sale, her manner was apprehensive and timid as that of a child. She never sat down, and seldom entered any dwelling, preferring to sell her merchandise in the open air, and using as few words as possible in the transaction. She was never seen to be angry, and a sweet patient smile always hovered about her lips when she spoke. In her face there was more than the remains of beauty; the poetry of intellect and of warm, deep feeling, shed a loveliness over it seldom witnessed on the brow of a savage. In truth, Malaeska was a strange and incomprehensible being to the settlers. But she was so quiet, so timid and gentle, that they all loved her, bought her little wares, and supplied her wants as if she had been one of themselves.

There was something beautiful in the companionship which sprang up between the strange woman and Sarah Jones. The young girl was benefited by it in a manner which was little to be expected from an intercourse so singular and, seemingly, so unnatural. The mother was a kind-hearted worldly woman, strongly attached to her family, but utterly devoid of those fine susceptibilities which make at once the happiness and the misery of so many human beings. But all the elements of an intellectual, delicate, and high-souled woman slumbered in the bosom of her child. They beamed in the depths of her large blue eyes, broke over her pure white forehead, like perfume from the leaves of a lily, and made her small mouth eloquent with smiles and the beauty of unpolished thoughts.

At sixteen the character of the young girl had scarcely begun to develop itself; but when the time arrived when she was to be sent away to school, there remained little except mere accomplishments for her to learn. Her mind had become vigorous by a constant intercourse with the beautiful things of nature. All the latent properties of a warm, youthful heart, and of a superior intellect, had been gently called into action by the strange being who had gained such an ascendency over her feelings.

The Indian woman, who in herself combined all that was strong, picturesque, and imaginative in savage life, with the delicacy, sweetness, and refinement which follows in the train of civilization, had trod with her the wild beautiful scenery of the neighborhood. They had breathed the pure air of the mountain together, and watched the crimson and amber clouds of sunset melt into evening, when pure sweet thoughts came to their hearts naturally, as light shines from the bosom of the star.

65

timid; she would have given the world to turn and run away any distance so that in the end she reached home.

The door opened, at least the upper half, and they were admitted into a hall paved with little Dutch tiles, spotlessly clean, through which they were led into a parlor barren and prim in all its appointments, but which was evidently the grand reception-room of the establishment. Nothing could have been more desolate than the room, save that it was redeemed by two narrow windows which overlooked the angle of the green inclosure in which the house stood. This angle was separated by a low wall from what seemed a broad and spacious garden, well filled with fruit-trees and flowering shrubbery.

The spring was just putting forth its first buds, and Sarah forgot the chilliness within as she saw the branches of a young apple-tree, flushed with the first tender green, drooping over the wall. It reminded her pleasantly of the orchard at home.

The door opened, and, with a nervous start, Sarah arose with her father to receive the little Frenchwoman who came in with a fluttering courtesy, eager to do the honors of her establishment.

Madame Monot took Sarah out of her father's hands with a graceful dash that left no room for appeal. "She knew it all—exactly what the young lady required—what would best please her very respectable parents—there was no need of explanations—the young lady was fresh as a rose—very charming—in a few months they should see—that was all—Monsieur Jones need have no care about his child—Madame would undertake to finish her education very soon—music, of course—an instrument had just come from Europe on purpose for the school—then French, nothing easier—Madame could promise that the young lady should speak French beautifully in one—two—three—four months, without doubt—Monsieur Jones might retire very satisfied—his daughter should come back different—perfect, in fact."

With all this volubility, poor Jones was half talked, half courtesied out of the house, without having uttered a single last word of farewell, or held his daughter one moment against the honest heart that yearned to carry her off again, despite his great ambition to see her a lady.

Poor Sarah gazed after him till her eyes were blinded with unshed tears; then she arose with a heavy heart and followed Madame to the room which was henceforth to be her refuge from the most dreary routine of duties that ever a poor girl was condemned to. It was a comfort that the windows overlooked that beautiful garden. That night, at a long, narrow table, set out with what the unsuspecting girl at first considered the preliminaries of a meal, Sarah met the score of young ladies who were to be her schoolmates. Fortunately she had no appetite and did not mind the scant fare. Fifteen or twenty girls, some furtively, others boldly, turning their eyes upon her, was enough to frighten away the appetite of a less timid person.

Poor Sarah! of all the homesick school-girls that ever lived, she was the most lonely. Madame's patronizing kindness only sufficed to bring the tears into her eyes which she was struggling so bravely to keep back.

But Sarah was courageous as well as sensitive. She came to Manhattan to study; no matter if her heart ached, the brain must work; her father had made great sacrifices to give her six months at this expensive school; his money and kindness must not be thrown away.

Thus the brave girl reasoned, and, smothering the haunting wish for home, she took up her tasks with energy.

Meantime Jones returned home with a heavy heart and a new assortment of spring goods, that threw every female heart in Catskill into a flutter of excitement. Every hen's nest in the neighborhood was robbed before the eggs were cold, and its contents transported to the store. As for butter, there was a universal complaint of its scarcity on the home table, while Jones began to think seriously of falling[4] a cent on the pound, it came in so abundantly.

CHAPTER 10

'Twas a dear, old-fashion'd garden,
  Half sunshine and half shade,
Where all day long the birds and breeze
  A pleasant music made;
And hosts of bright and glowing flowers
  Their perfume shed around,
Till it was like a fairy haunt
  That knew no human sound.
          —FRANK LEE BENEDICT.

IT WAS a bright spring morning, the sky full of great fleecy clouds that chased each other over the clear blue, and a light wind stirring the trees until their opening buds sent forth a delicious fragrance, that was like a perfumed breath from the approaching summer.

Sarah Jones stood by the window of her little room, looking wistfully out into the neighboring garden, oppressed by a feeling of loneliness and homesickness, which made her long to throw aside her books, relinquish her half-acquired accomplishments, and fly back to her quiet country home.

It seemed to her that one romp with her brothers through the old orchard, pelting each other with the falling buds, would be worth all the French and music she could learn in a score of years. The beat of her mother's lathe[1] in the old-fashioned loom, would have been pleasanter music to her ear, than that of the pianoforte, which she had once thought so grand an affair; but since then she had spent so many weary hours over it, shed so many tears upon the cold white keys, which made her fingers ache worse than ever the spinning-wheel had done, that, like any other school-girl, she was almost inclined to regard the vaunted piano as an instrument of torture, invented expressly for her annoyance.

She was tired of thinking and acting by rule, and though Madame Monot was kind enough in her way, the discipline to which Sarah was forced to submit, was very irksome to the untrained country girl. She was tired of having regular hours for study—tired of walking out for a stated time in procession with the other girls—nobody daring to move with any thing like naturalness or freedom—and very often she felt almost inclined to write home and ask them to send for her.

It was in a restive, unhappy mood, like the one we have been describing, that she stood that morning at the window, when she ought to have been hard at work over the pile of books which lay neglected upon her little table.

---

4 *falling* lowering the price.
1 *lathe* moveable swing-frame that beats the woof into the warp.

That pretty garden which she looked down upon, was a sore temptation to her; and had Madame Monot known how it distracted Sarah's attention, there is every reason to believe that she would have been removed in all haste to the opposite side of the house, where, if she chose to idle at her casement, there would be nothing more entertaining than a hard brick wall to look at. Just then, the garden was more attractive than at any other season of the year. The spring sunshine had made the shorn turf like a green carpet, the trim flower-beds were already full of early blossoms, the row of apple-trees was one great mass of flowers, and the tall pear-tree in the corner was just beginning to lose its delicate white leaves, sprinkling them daintily over the grass, where they fluttered about like a host of tiny butterflies.

The old-fashioned stoop that opened from the side of the house into the garden, was covered with a wild grape-vine, that clambered up to the pointed Dutch gables, hung down over the narrow windows, and twined and tangled itself about as freely and luxuriantly as it could have done in its native forest.

Sarah watched the gardener as he went soberly about his various duties, and she envied him the privilege of wandering at will among the graveled walks, pausing under the trees and bending over the flower-beds.

Perhaps in these days, when nothing but scentless japonicas and rare foreign plants are considered endurable, that garden would be an ordinary affair enough, at which no well-trained boarding-school miss would condescend to look for an instant; but to Sarah Jones it was a perfect little paradise.

The lilac bushes nodded in the wind, shaking their purple and white plumes, like groups of soldiers on duty; great masses of snow-balls stood up in the center of the beds; peonies, violets, lilies of the valley, tulips, syringas, and a host of other dear old-fashioned flowers, lined the walks; and, altogether, the garden was lovely enough to justify the poor girl's admiration. There she stood, quite forgetful of her duties; the clock in the hall struck its warning note—she did not even hear it; some one might at any moment enter and surprise her in the midst of her idleness and disobedience—she never once thought of it, so busily was she watching every thing in the garden.

The man finished his morning's work and went away, but Sarah did not move. A pair of robins had flown into the tall pear-tree, and were holding an animated conversation, interspersed with bursts and gushes of song. They flew from one tree to another, once hovering near the grape-vine, but returned to the pear-tree at last, sang, chirped, and danced about in frantic glee, and at last made it evident that they intended to build a nest in that very tree. Sarah could have clapped her hands with delight! It was just under her window—she could watch them constantly, study or no study. She worked herself into such a state of excitement at the thought, that Madame Monot would have been shocked out of her proprieties at seeing one of her pupils guilty of such folly.

The clock again struck—that time in such a sharp, reproving way, that it reached even Sarah's ear. She started, looked nervously round, and saw the heap of books upon the table.

"Oh, dear me," she sighed; "those tiresome lessons! I had forgotten all about them. Well, I will go to studying in a moment," she added, as if addressing her conscience or her fears. "Oh, that robin—how he does sing."

She forgot her books again, and just at that moment there was a new object of interest added to those which the garden already possessed.

The side door of the house opened, and an old gentleman stepped out upon the broad stoop, stood there for a few moments, evidently enjoying the morning air, then passed slowly down the steps into the garden, supporting himself by his stout cane, and walking with considerable care and difficulty, like any feeble old man.

Sarah had often seen him before, and she knew very well who he was. He was the owner of the house that the simple girl so coveted, and his name was Danforth.

She had learned every thing about him, as a school-girl is sure to do concerning any person or thing that strikes her fancy. He was very wealthy indeed, and had no family except his wife, the tidiest, darling old lady, who often walked in the garden herself, and always touched the flowers, as she passed, as if they had been pet children.

The venerable old pair had a grandson, but he was away in Europe, so they lived in their pleasant mansion quite alone, with the exception of a few domestics, who looked nearly as aged and respectable as their master and mistress.

Sarah had speculated a great deal about her neighbors. She did so long to know them, to be free to run around in their garden, and sit in the pleasant rooms that overlooked it, glimpses of which she had often obtained through the open windows, when the housemaid was putting things to rights.

Sarah thought that she might possibly be a little afraid of the old gentleman, he looked so stern; but his wife she longed to kiss and make friends with at once; she looked so gentle and kind, that even a bird could not have been afraid of her.

Sarah watched Mr. Danforth walk slowly down the principal garden-path, and seat himself in a little arbor overrun by a trumpet honeysuckle, which was not yet in blossom, although there were faint traces of red among the green leaves, which gave promise of an ample store of blossoms before many weeks.

He sat there some time, apparently enjoying the sunshine that stole in through the leaves. At length Sarah saw him rise, move toward the entrance, pause an instant, totter, then fall heavily upon the ground.

She did not wait even to think or cry out—every energy of her free, strong nature was aroused. She flew out of her room down the stairs, fortunately encountering neither teachers nor pupils, and hurried out of the street-door.

The garden was separated from Madame Monot's narrow yard by a low stone wall, along the top of which ran a picket fence. Sarah saw a step-ladder that had been used by a servant in washing windows; she seized it, dragged it to the wall, and sprang lightly from thence into the garden.

It seemed to her that she would never reach the spot where the poor gentleman was lying, although, in truth, scarcely three minutes had elapsed between the time that she saw him fall and reached the place where he lay.

Sarah stooped over him, raised his head, and knew at once what was the matter—he had been seized with apoplexy. She had seen her grandfather die with it, and recognized the symptoms at once. It was useless to think of carrying him; so she loosened his neckcloth, lifted his head upon the arbor seat, and darted toward the house, calling with all her might the name by which she had many times heard the gardener address the black cook.

"Eunice! Eunice!"

At her frantic summons, out from the kitchen rushed the old woman, followed by several of her satellites, all screaming at once to know what was the matter, and wild with astonishment at the sight of a stranger in the garden.

"Quick! quick!" cried Sarah. "Your master has been taken with a fit; come and carry him into the house. One of you run for a doctor."

"Oh, de laws! oh, dear! oh, dear!" resounded on every side; but Sarah directed them with so much energy that the women, aided by an old negro who had been roused by the disturbance, conveyed their master into the house, and laid him upon a bed in one of the lower rooms.

"Where is your mistress?" questioned Sarah.

"Oh, she's gwine out," sobbed the cook; "oh, my poor ole masser, my poor ole masser!"

"Have you sent for the doctor?"

"Yes, young miss, yes; he'll be here in a minit, bress yer pooty face."

Sarah busied herself over the insensible man, applying every remedy that she could remember of having seen her mother use when her grandfather was ill, and really did the very things that ought to have been done.

It was not long before the doctor arrived, bled his patient freely, praised Sarah's presence of mind, and very soon the old gentleman returned to consciousness.

Sarah heard one of the servants exclaim: "Oh, dar's missus! praise de Lord!"

A sudden feeling of shyness seized the girl, and she stole out of the room and went into the garden, determined to escape unseen. But before she reached the arbor she heard one of the servants calling after her.

"Young miss! young miss! Please to wait; ole missus wants to speak to you."

Sarah turned and walked toward the house, ready to burst into tears with timidity and excitement. But the lady whom she had so longed to know, came down the steps and moved toward her, holding out her hand. She was very pale, and shaking from head to foot; but she spoke with a certain calmness, which it was evident she would retain under the most trying circumstances.

"I can not thank you," she said; "if it had not been for you, I should never have seen my husband alive again."

Sarah began to sob, the old lady held out her arms, and the frightened girl actually fell into them. There they stood for a few moments, weeping in each other's embrace, and by those very tears establishing a closer intimacy than years of common intercourse would have done.

"How did you happen to see him fall?" asked the old lady.

"I was looking out of my window," replied Sarah, pointing to her open casement, "and when I saw it I ran over at once."

"You are a pupil of Madame Monot's, then?"

"Yes—and, oh my, I must go back! They will scold me dreadfully for being away so long."

"Do not be afraid," said Mrs. Danforth, keeping fast hold of her hand when she tried to break away. "I will make your excuses to Madame; come into the house. I can not let you go yet."

She led Sarah into the house, and seated her in an easy chair in the old-fashioned sitting-room.

"Wait here a few minutes, if you please, my dear. I must go to my husband."

She went away and left Sarah quite confused with the strangeness of the whole affair. Here she was, actually seated in the very apartment she had so desired to enter—the old lady she had so longed to know addressing her as if she had been a favorite child.

She peeped out of the window toward her late prison; every thing looked quiet there, as usual. She wondered what dreadful penance she would be made to undergo, and decided that even bread and water for two days would not be so great a hardship, when she had the incident of the morning to reflect upon.

She looked about the room, with its quaint furniture, every thing so tidy and elegant, looking as if a speck of dust had never by any accident settled in the apartment, and thinking it the prettiest place she had seen in her life.

Then she began thinking about the poor sick man, and worked herself into a fever of anxiety to hear tidings concerning him. Just then a servant entered with a tray of refreshments, and set it on the table near her, saying:

"Please, miss, my missus says you must be hungry, 'cause it's your dinner-time."

"And how is your master?" Sarah asked.

"Bery comferble now; missee'll be here in a minit. Now please to eat sumfin."

Sarah was by no means loth to comply with the invitation, for the old cook had piled the tray with all sorts of delicacies, that presented a pleasing contrast to the plain fare she had been accustomed to of late.

By the time she had finished her repast Mrs. Danforth returned, looking more composed and relieved.

"The doctor gives me a great deal of encouragement," she said; "my husband is able to speak; by to-morrow he will thank you better than I can."

"Oh, no," stammered Sarah; "I don't want any thanks, please. I didn't think—I—"

She fairly broke down, but Mrs. Danforth patted her hand and said, kindly:

"I understand. But at least you must let me love you very much."

Sarah felt her heart flutter and her cheeks glow. The blush and smile on that young face were a more fitting answer than words could have given.

"I have sent an explanation of your absence to Madame Monot," continued Mrs. Danforth, "and she has given you permission to spend the day with me; so you need have no fear of being blamed."

The thought of a whole day's freedom was exceedingly pleasant to Sarah, particularly when it was to be spent in that old house, which had always appeared as interesting to her as a story. It required but a short time for Mrs. Danforth and her to become well acquainted, and the old lady was charmed with her loveliness, and natural, graceful manners.

She insisted upon accompanying Mrs. Danforth into the sick room, and made herself so useful there, that the dear lady mentally wondered how she had ever got on without her.

When Sarah returned to her home that night, she felt that sense of relief which any one who has led a monotonous life for months must have experienced, when some sudden event has changed its whole current, and given a new coloring to things that before appeared tame and insignificant.

During the following days Sarah was a frequent visitor at Mr. Danforth's house, and after that, circumstances occurred which drew her into still more intimate companionship with her new friend.

One of Madame Monot's house-servants was taken ill with typhus fever, and most of the young ladies left the school for a few weeks. Mrs. Danforth insisted upon Sarah's making her home at their house during the interval, an invitation which she accepted with the utmost delight.

Mr. Danforth still lingered—could speak and move—but the favorable symptoms which at first presented themselves had entirely disappeared, and there was little hope given that he could do more than linger for a month or two longer. During that painful season Mrs. Danforth found in Sarah a sympathizing and consoling friend. The sick man himself became greatly attached to her, and could not bear that she should even leave his chamber.

The young girl was very happy in feeling herself thus prized and loved, and the quick weeks spent in that old house were perhaps among the happiest of her life, in spite of the saddening associations which surrounded her.

One morning while she was sitting with the old gentleman, who had grown so gentle and dependent that those who had known him in former years would scarcely have recognized him, Mrs. Danforth entered the room, bearing several letters in her hand.

"European letters, my dear," she said to her husband, and while she put on her glasses and seated herself to read them, Sarah stole out into the garden.

She had not been there long, enjoying the fresh loveliness of the day, before she heard Mrs. Danforth call her.

"Sarah, my dear; Sarah."

The girl went back to the door where the old lady stood.

"Share a little good news with me in the midst of all our trouble," she said; "my dear, my boy—my grandson—is coming home."

Sarah's first thought was one of regret—every thing would be so changed by the arrival of a stranger; but that was only a passing pang of selfishness; her next reflection was one of unalloyed delight, for the sake of that aged couple.

"I am very glad, dear madam; his coming will do his grandfather so much good."

"Yes, indeed; more than all the doctors in the world."

"When do you expect him?"

"Any day, now; he was to sail a few days after the ship that brought these letters, and as this vessel has been detained by an accident, he can not be far away."

"I am to go back to school to-day," said Sarah, regretfully.

"But you will be with us almost as much," replied Mrs. Danforth. "I have your mother's permission, and will go myself to speak with Madame. You will run over every day to your lessons, but you will live here; we can not lose our pet so soon."

"You are very kind—oh, so kind," Sarah said, quite radiant at the thought of not being confined any longer in the dark old school-building.

"It is you who are good to us. But come, we will go over now; I must tell Madame Monot at once."

The explanations were duly made, and Sarah returned to her old routine of lessons; but her study-room was now the garden, or any place in Mr. Danforth's house that she fancied.

The old gentleman was better again; able to be wheeled out of doors into the sunshine; and there was nothing he liked so much as sitting in the garden, his wife knitting by his side, Sarah studying at his feet, and the robins singing in the pear-trees overhead, as if feeling it a sacred duty to pay their rent by morning advances of melody.

CHAPTER 11

A welcome to the homestead—
The gables and the trees
And welcome to the true hearts,
As the sunshine and the breeze.

ONE bright morning, several weeks after Mr. Danforth's attack, the three were seated in their favorite nook in the garden.

It was a holiday with Sarah; there were no lessons to study; no exercises to practice; no duty more irksome than that of reading the newspaper aloud to the old gentleman, who particularly fancied her fresh, happy voice.

Mrs. Danforth was occupied with her knitting, and Sarah sat at their feet upon a low stool, looking so much like a favorite young relative that it was no wonder if the old pair forgot that she was unconnected with them, save by the bonds of affection, and regarded her as being, in reality, as much a part of their family as they considered her in their hearts.

While they sat there, some sudden noise attracted Mrs. Danforth's attention; she rose and went into the house so quietly that the others scarcely noticed her departure.

It was not long before she came out again, walking very hastily for her, and with such a tremulous flutter in her manner, that Sarah regarded her in surprise.

"William!" she said to her husband, "William!"

He roused himself from the partial doze into which he had fallen, and looked up.

"Did you speak to me?" he asked.

"I have good news for you. Don't be agitated—it is all pleasant."

He struggled up from his seat, steadying his trembling hands upon his staff.

"My boy has come!" he exclaimed, louder and more clearly than he had spoken for weeks; "William, my boy!"

At the summons, a young man came out of the house and ran toward them. The old gentleman flung his arms about his neck and strained him close to his heart.

"My boy!" was all he could say; "my William!"

When they had all grown somewhat calmer, Mrs. Danforth called Sarah, who was standing at a little distance.

"I want you to know and thank this young lady, William," she said; "your grandfather and I owe her a great deal."

She gave him a brief account of the old gentleman's fall, and Sarah's presence of mind; but the girl's crimson cheeks warned her to pause.

"No words can repay such kindness," said the young man, as he relinquished her hand, over which he had bowed with the ceremonious respect of the time.

"It is I who owe a great deal to your grandparents," Sarah replied, a little tremulously, but trying to shake off the timidity which she felt beneath his dark eyes. "I was a regular prisoner, like any other school-girl, and they had the goodness to open the door and let me out."

"Then fidgety old Madame Monot had you in charge?" young Danforth said, laughing; "I can easily understand that it must be a relief to get occasionally where you are not obliged to wait and think by rule."

"There—there!" said the old lady; "William is encouraging insubordination already; you will be a bad counselor for Sarah."

Both she and her husband betrayed the utmost satisfaction at the frank and cordial conversation which went on between the young pair; and in an hour Sarah was as much at ease as if she had been gathering wild-flowers in her native woods.

Danforth gave them long and amusing accounts of his adventures, talked naturally and well of the countries he had visited, the notable places he had seen, and never had man three more attentive auditors.

That was a delightful day to Sarah; and as William Danforth had not lost, in his foreign wanderings, the freshness and enthusiasm pleasant in youth, it was full of enjoyment to him likewise.

There was something so innocent in Sarah's loveliness—something so unstudied in her graceful manner, that the very contrast she presented to the

The poor wife attempted to shake her head, but she could not, even by a motion, force herself to an untruth. So, dropping both hands in her lap, she shrunk away from his glance, and the tears began to roll down her cheeks.

"Speak!" said the old man, hoarsely.

She answered, in a voice low and hoarse as his own, "Malaeska went to her tribe; but they have cruel laws, and looking upon her as a traitor in giving her son to us, sent her into the woods with one who was chosen to kill her."

The old man did not speak, but his eyes opened wildly and he fell forward upon his face.

William and Sarah were coquetting, with her lessons, under the old pear-tree, between the French phrases; he had been whispering something sweeter than words ever sounded to her before in any language, and her cheeks were one flush of roses as his breath floated over them.

"Tell me—look at me—any thing to say that you have known this all along," he said, bending his flashing eyes on her face with a glance that made her tremble.

She attempted to look up, but failed in the effort. Like a rose that feels the sunshine too warmly, she drooped under the glow of her own blushes.

"Do speak," he pleaded.

"Yes," she answered, lifting her face with modest firmness to his, "Yes, I do love you."

As the words left her lips, a cry made them both start.

"It is grandmother's voice; he is ill again," said the young man.

They moved away, shocked by a sudden recoil of feelings. A moment brought them in sight of the old man, who lay prostrate on the earth. His wife was bending over him, striving to loosen his dress with her withered little hands.

"Oh, come," she pleaded, with a look of helpless distress; "help me untie this, or he will never breathe again."

It was all useless; the old man never did breathe again. A single blow had smitten him down. They bore him into the house, but the leaden weight of his body, the limp fall of his limbs, all revealed the mournful truth too plainly. It was death—sudden and terrible death.

If there is an object on earth calculated to call forth the best sympathies of humanity, it is an "old widow"—a woman who has spent the spring, noon, and autumn of life, till it verges into winter, with one man, the first love of her youth, the last love of her age—the spring-time when love is a passionate sentiment, the winter-time when it is august.

In old age men or women seldom resist trouble—it comes, and they bow to it. So it was with this widow: she uttered no complaints, gave way to no wild outbreak of sorrow—"she was lonesome—very lonesome without him," that was all her moan; but the raven threads that lay in the snow of her hair, were lost in the general whiteness before the funeral was over, and after that she began to bend a little, using his staff to lean on. It was mournful to see how fondly her little wrinkled hands would cling around the head, and the way she had of resting her delicate chin upon it, exactly as he had done.

But even his staff, the stout prop of his waning manhood, was not strong enough to keep that gentle old woman from the grave. She carried it to the last, but one day it stood unused by the bed, which was white and cold as the snow-drift through which they dug many feet before they could lay her by her husband's side.

78

CHAPTER 12

Put blossoms on the mantle-piece,
Throw sand upon the floor,
A guest is coming to the house,
That never came before.

SARAH JONES had been absent several months, when a rumor got abroad in the village, that the school-girl had made a proud conquest in Manhattan. It was said that Squire Jones had received letters from a wealthy merchant of that place, and that he was going down the river to conduct his daughter home, when a wedding would soon follow, and Sarah Jones be made a lady.

This report gained much of its probability from the demeanor of Mrs. Jones. Her port became more lofty when she appeared in the street, and she was continually throwing out insinuations and half-uttered hints, as if her heart were panting to unburden itself of some proud secret, which she was not yet at liberty to reveal.

When Jones actually started for Manhattan, and it was whispered about that his wife had taken a dress-pattern of rich chintz from the store, for herself, and had bought each of the boys a new wool hat, conjecture became almost certainty; and it was asserted boldly, that Sarah Jones was coming home to be married to a man as rich as all outdoors, and that her mother was beginning to hold her head above common folks on the strength of it.

About three weeks after this report was known, Mrs. Jones, whose motions were watched with true village scrutiny, gave demonstrations of a thorough house-cleaning. An old woman, who went out to days' work, was called in to help, and there were symptoms of slaughter observable in the barn-yard one night after the turkeys and chickens had gone to roost; all of which kept the public mind in a state of pleasant excitement.

Early the next morning, after the barn-yard massacre, Mrs. Jones was certainly a very busy woman. All the morning was occupied in sprinkling white sand on the nicely-scoured floor of the outroom, or parlor, which she swept very expertly into a series of angular figures called herring-bones, with a new splint broom. After this, she filled the fire-place with branches of hemlock and white pine, wreathed a garland of asparagus, crimson with berries, around the little looking-glass, and, dropping on one knee, was filling a large pitcher on the hearth from an armful of wild-flowers, which the boys had brought her from the woods, when the youngest son came hurrying up from the Point, to inform her that a sloop had just hove in sight and was making full sail up the river.

"Oh, dear, I shan't be half ready!" exclaimed the alarmed housekeeper, snatching up a handful of meadow-lilies, mottled so heavily with dark-crimson spots, that the golden bells seemed drooping beneath a weight of rubies and small garnet stones, and crowding them down into the pitcher amid the rosy spray of wild honeysuckle-blossoms, and branches of flowering dogwood.

"Here, Ned, give me the broom, quick! and don't shuffle over the sand so. There, now," she continued, gathering up the fragments of leaves and flowers from the hearth, and glancing hastily around the room, "I wonder if any thing else is wanting?"

Every thing seemed in order, even to her critical eye. The tea-table stood in one corner, its round top turned down and its polished surface reflecting the herring-bones drawn in the sand, with the distinctness of a mirror. The chairs were in their exact places, and the new crimson moreen[1] cushions and valance decorated the settee, in all the brilliancy of their first gloss. Yes, nothing more was to be done, still the good woman passed her apron over the speckless table and flirted it across a chair or two, before she went out, quite determined that no stray speck of dust should disgrace her child on coming home.

Mrs. Jones closed the door, and hurried up to the square bedroom, to be certain that all was right there also. A patch-work quilt, pieced in what old ladies call "a rising sun," radiated in tints of red, green, and yellow, from the center of the bed down to the snow-white valances. A portion of the spotless homespun sheet was carefully turned over the upper edge of the quilt, and the whole was surmounted by a pair of pillows, white as a pile of newly-drifted snow-flakes. A pot of roses, on the window-sill, shed a delicate reflection over the muslin curtains looped up on either side of the sash; and the fresh wind, as it swept through, scattered their fragrant breath deliciously through the little room.

Mrs. Jones gave a satisfied look and then hurried to the chamber prepared for her daughter, and began to array her comely person in the chintz dress, which had created such a sensation in the village. She had just encased her arms in the sleeves, when the door partly opened, and the old woman, who had been hired for a few days as "help," put her head through the opening. "I say, Miss Jones, I can't find nothin' to make the stuffin' out on."

"My goodness! isn't that turkey in the oven yet? I do believe, if I could be cut into a hundred pieces, it wouldn't be enough for this house. What do you come to me for?—don't you know enough to make a little stuffing, without my help?"

"Only give me enough to do it with, and if I don't, why, there don't nobody, that's all; but I've been a looking all over for some sausengers, and can't find none, nowhere."

"Sausages? Why, Mrs. Bates, you don't think that I would allow that fine turkey to be stuffed with sausages?"

"I don't know nothin' about it, but I tell you just what it is, Miss Jones, if you are a-growing so mighty partic'lar about your victuals, just cause your darter's a-coming home with a rich beau, you'd better cook 'em yourself; nobody craves the job," retorted the old woman, in her shrillest voice, shutting the door with a jar that shook the whole apartment.

"Now the cross old thing will go off just to spite me," muttered Mrs. Jones, trying to smother her vexation, and, opening the door, she called to the angry "help:"

"Why, Mrs. Bates, do come back, you did not stay to hear me out. Save the chickens' livers and chop them up with bread and butter; season it nicely, and, I dare say, you will be as well pleased with it as can be."

"Well, and if I du, what shall I season with—sage or summer-savory? I'm sure I'm willing to du my best," answered the partially mollified old woman.

"A little of both, Mrs. Bates—oh, dear! won't you come back and see if you can make my gown meet? There—do I look fit to be seen?"

"Now, what do you ask that for, Miss Jones? you know you look as neat as a new pin. This is a mighty purty calerco, ain't it, though?"

---

1 *moreen*   a heavy woollen or woollen and cotton material.

The squire's lady had not forgotten all the feelings of her younger days, and the old woman's compliment had its effect.

"I will send down to the store for some tea and molasses for you to take home to-night, Mrs. Bates, and—"

"Mother! mother!" shouted young Ned, bolting into the room, "the sloop has tacked, and is making for the creek. I see three people on the deck, and I'm almost sure father was one of them—they will be here in no time."

"Gracious me!" muttered the old woman, hurrying away to the kitchen.

Mrs. Jones smoothed down the folds of her new dress with both hands, as she ran down to the "out-room." She took her station in a stiff, high-backed chair by the window, with a look of consequential gentility, as if she had done nothing but sit still and receive company all her life.

After a few minutes' anxious watching, she saw her husband and daughter coming up from the creek, accompanied by a slight, dark, and remarkably graceful young man, elaborately, but not gayly dressed, for the fashion of the time, and betraying even in his air and walk peculiar traits of high-breeding and refinement. His head was slightly bent, and he seemed to be addressing the young lady who leaned on his arm.

The mother's heart beat high with mingled pride and affection, as she gazed on her beautiful daughter thus proudly escorted home. There was triumph in the thought, that almost every person in the village might witness the air of gallantry and homage with which she was regarded by the handsomest and richest merchant of Manhattan. She saw that her child looked eagerly toward the house as they approached, and that her step was rapid, as if impatient of the quiet progress of her companions. Pride was lost in the sweet thrill of maternal affection which shot through the mother's heart. She forgot all her plans, in the dear wish to hold her first-born once more to her bosom; and ran to the door, her face beaming with joy, her arms outstretched, and her lips trembling with the warmth of their own welcome.

The next moment her child was clinging about her, lavishing kisses on her handsome mouth, and checking her caresses to gaze up through the mist of tears and smiles which deluged her own sweet face, to the glad eyes that looked down so fondly upon her.

"Oh, mother! dear, dear mother, how glad I am to get home! Where are the boys? where is little Ned?" inquired the happy girl, rising from her mother's arms, and looking eagerly round for other objects of affectionate regard.

"Sarah, don't you intend to let me speak to your mother?" inquired the father, in a voice which told how truly his heart was in the scene.

Sarah withdrew from her mother's arms, blushing and smiling through her tears; the husband and wife shook hands half a dozen times over; Mrs. Jones asked him how he had been, what kind of a voyage he had made, how he liked Manhattan, and a dozen other questions, all in a breath; and then the stranger was introduced. Mrs. Jones forgot the dignified courtesy which she had intended to perpetrate on the entrance of her guest, and shook him heartily by the hand, as if she had been acquainted with him from his cradle.

When the happy group entered the parlor, they found Arthur, who had been raised to the dignity of storekeeper in the father's absence, ready to greet his parent and sister; and the younger children huddled together at the door which led to the kitchen, brimful of eager joy at the father's return, and yet too much afraid of the stranger to enter the room.

thing I abhor on earth, it is a savage—a fierce, blood-thirsty wild beast in human form!"

There was something in the stern expression of his face which pained and startled the young girl who gazed on it; a brilliancy of the eye, and an expansion of the thin nostrils, which bespoke terrible passions when once excited to the full.

"This is a strange prejudice," she murmured, unconsciously, while her eyes sank from their gaze on his face.

"It is no prejudice, but a part of my nature," he retorted, sternly, pacing up and down the room. "An antipathy rooted in the cradle, which grew stronger and deeper with my manhood. I loved my grandfather, and from him I imbibed this early hate. His soul loathed the very name of Indian. When he met one of the prowling creatures in the highway, I have seen his lips writhe, his chest heave, and his face grow white, as if a wild beast had started up in his path. There was one in our family, an affectionate, timid creature, as the sun ever shone upon. I can remember loving her very dearly when I was a mere child, but my grandfather recoiled at the very sound of her name, and seemed to regard her presence as a curse, which for some reason he was compelled to endure. I could never imagine why he kept her. She was very kind to me, and I tried to find her out after my return from Europe, but you remember that my grandparents died suddenly during my absence,[2] and no one could give me any information about her. Save that one being, there is not a savage, male or female, whom I should not rejoice to see exterminated from the face of the earth. Do not, I pray you, look so terribly shocked, my sweet girl; I acknowledge the feeling to be a prejudice too violent for adequate foundation; but it was grounded in my nature by one whom I respected and loved as my own life, and it will cling to my heart as long as there is a pulse left in it."

"I have no predilection for savages as a race," said Sarah, after a few moments' silence, gratified to find some shadow of reason for her lover's violence; "but you make one exception, may I not also be allowed a favorite especially as she is a white in education, feeling, every thing but color? You would not have me neglect one of the kindest, best friends I ever had on earth, because the tint of her skin is a shade darker than my own?"

Her voice was sweet and persuasive, a smile trembled on her lips, and she laid a hand gently on his arm as she spoke. He must have been a savage indeed, had he resisted her winning ways.

"I would have you forgive my violence and follow your own sweet impulses," he said, putting back the curls from her uplifted forehead, and drawing her to his bosom; "say you have forgiven me, dear, and then go where you will."

It was with gentle words like these, that he had won the love of that fair being; they fell upon her heart, after his late harshness, like dew to a thirsty violet. She raised her glistening eyes to his with a language more eloquent than words, and disengaging herself from his arms, glided softly out of the room.

These words could hardly be called a lovers' quarrel, and yet they parted with all the sweet feelings of reconciliation, warm at the heart of each.

---

2 *grandparents died suddenly during my absence* inconsistent with earlier narrative, perhaps resulting from author's revisions of serial version.

> By that forest-grave she mournful stood,
> While her soul went forth in prayer;
> Her life was one long solitude,
> Which she offer'd, meekly, there.

S ARAH pursued the foot-path, which she had so often trod through the forest, with a fawn-like lightness of step, and a heart that beat quicker at the sight of each familiar bush or forest-tree, which had formerly been the waymark of her route.

"Poor woman, she must have been very lonely," she murmured, more than once, when the golden blossoms of a spice-bush, or the tendrils of a vine trailing over the path, told how seldom it had been traveled of late, and her heart imperceptibly became saddened by the thoughts of her friend; spite of this, she stopped occasionally to witness the gambols of a gray squirrel among the tall branches, that swayed and rustled in the sunshine overhead, and smiled at her usual timidity, when, thus employed, a slender grass-snake crept across her foot and coiled itself up in the path like a chain of living emeralds; his small eyes glittering like sparks of fire, his tiny jaw open, and a sharp little tongue playing within like a red-hot needle cleft at the point. She forced herself to look upon the harmless reptile, without a fear which she knew to be childish, and turning aside, pursued her way to "the Straka."

To her disappointment, she found the wigwam empty, but a path was beaten along the edge of the woods, leading toward the Pond, which she had never observed before. She turned into it with a sort of indefinite expectation of meeting her friend; and after winding through the depths of the forest for nearly a mile, the notes of a wild, plaintive song rose and fell—a sad, sweet melody—on the still air.

A few steps onward brought the young girl to a small open space surrounded by young saplings and flowering shrubs; tall grass swept from a little mound which swelled up from the center, to the margin of the inclosure, and a magnificent hemlock shadowed the whole space with its drooping boughs.

A sensation of awe fell upon the heart of the young girl, for, as she gazed, the mound took the form of a grave. A large rose-tree, heavy with blossoms, drooped over the head, and the sheen of rippling waters broke through a clump of sweetbrier, which hedged it in from the lake.

Sarah remembered that the Indian chief's grave was on the very brink of the water, and that she had given a young rose-tree to Malaeska years ago, which must have shot up into the solitary bush standing before her, lavishing fragrance from its pure white flowers over the place of the dead.

This would have been enough to convince her that she stood by the warrior's grave, had the place been solitary, but at the foot of the hemlock, with her arms folded on her bosom and her calm face uplifted toward heaven, sat Malaeska. Her lips were slightly parted, and the song which Sarah had listened to afar off broke from them—a sad pleasant strain, that blended in harmony with the rippling waters and the gentle sway of the hemlock branches overhead.

Sarah remained motionless till the last note of the song died away on the lake, then she stepped forward into the inclosure. The Indian woman saw her and arose, while a beautiful expression of joy beamed over her face.

"The bird does not feel more joyful at the return of spring, when snows have covered the earth all winter, than does the poor Indian's heart at the sight of her child again," she said, taking the maiden's hand and kissing it with a graceful movement of mingled respect and affection. "Sit down, that I may hear the sound of your voice once more."

They sat down together at the foot of the hemlock.

"You have been lonely, my poor friend, and ill, I fear; how thin you have become during my absence," said Sarah, gazing on the changed features of her companion.

"I shall be happy again now," replied the Indian, with a faint sweet smile, "you will come to see me every day."

"Yes, while I remain at home, but—but—I'm going back again soon."

"You need not tell me more in words, I can read it in the tone of your voice, in the light of that modest eye, though the silken lash does droop over it like leaves around a wet violet—in the color coming and going on those cheeks; another is coming to take you from home," said the Indian, with a playful smile. "Did you think the lone woman could not read the signs of love—that she has never loved herself?"

"You?"

"Do not look so wild, but tell me of yourself. Are you to be married so *very* soon?"

"In four days."

"Then where will your home be?"

"In Manhattan."

There were a few moments of silence. Sarah sat gazing on the turf, with the warm blood mantling to her cheek, ashamed and yet eager to converse more fully on the subject which flooded her young heart with supreme content. The Indian continued motionless, lost in a train of sad thoughts conjured up by the last word uttered; at length she laid her hand on that of her companion, and spoke; her voice was sad, and tears stood in her eyes.

"In a few days you go from me again—oh, it is very wearisome to be always alone; the heart pines for something to love. I have been petting a little wren, that has built his nest under the eaves of my wigwam, since you went away; it was company for me, and will be again. Do not look so pitiful, but tell me who is he that calls the red blood to your cheek? What are his qualities? Does he love you as one like you should be loved? Is he good, brave?"

"He says that he loves me," replied the young girl, blushing more deeply, and a beautiful smile broke into her eyes as she raised them for a moment to the Indian's face.

"And you?"

"I have neither experience nor standard to judge love by. If to think of one from morning to night, be love—to feel his presence color each thought even when he is far away—to know that he is haunting your beautiful day-dreams, wandering with you through the lovely places which fancy is continually presenting to one in solitude, filling up each space and thought of your life, and yet in no way diminishing the affection which the heart bears to others, but increasing it rather—if to be made happy with the slightest trait of noble feeling, proud in his virtues, and yet quick-sighted and doubly sensitive to all his faults, clinging to him in spite of those faults—if this be love, then I do love with the whole strength of my being. They tell me it is but a dream, which will pass

86

away, but I do not believe it; for in my bosom the first sweet flutter of awakened affection, has already settled down to a deep feeling of contentment. My heart is full of tranquillity, and, like that white rose which lies motionless in the sunshine burdened with the wealth of its own sweetness, it unfolds itself day by day to a more pure and subdued state of enjoyment. This feeling may not be the love which men talk so freely of, but it can not change—never—not even in death, unless William Danforth should prove utterly unworthy!"

"William Danforth! Did I hear aright? Is William Danforth the name of your affianced husband?" inquired the Indian, in a voice of overwhelming surprise, starting up with sudden impetuosity and then slowly sinking back to her seat again. "Tell me," she added, faintly, and yet in a tone that thrilled to the heart, "has this boy—this young gentleman, I mean—come of late from across the big waters?"

"He came from Europe a year since, on the death of his grandparents," was the reply.

"A year, a whole year!" murmured the Indian, clasping her hands over her eyes with sudden energy. Her head sunk forward upon her knees, and her whole frame shivered with a rush of strong feeling, which was perfectly unaccountable to the almost terrified girl who gazed upon her. "Father of Heaven, I thank thee! my eyes shall behold him once more. O God, make me grateful!" These words, uttered so fervently, were muffled by the locked hands of the Indian woman, and Sarah could only distinguish that she was strongly excited by the mention of her lover's name.

"Have you ever known Mr. Danforth!" she inquired, when the agitation of the strange woman had a little subsided. The Indian did not answer, but raising her head, and brushing the tears from her eyes, she looked in the maiden's face with an expression of pathetic tenderness that touched her to the heart.

"And *you* are to be *his* wife? You, my bird of birds."

She fell upon the young girl's neck as she spoke, and wept like an infant; then, as if conscious of betraying too deep emotion, she lifted her head, and tried to compose herself; while Sarah sat gazing on her, agitated, bewildered, and utterly at a loss to account for this sudden outbreak of feeling, in one habitually so subdued and calm in her demeanor. After sitting musingly and in silence several moments, the Indian again lifted her eyes; they were full of sorrowful meaning, yet there was an eager look about them which showed a degree of excitement yet unsubdued.

"Dead—are they both dead? his grandparents, I mean?" she said, earnestly.

"Yes, they are both dead; he told me so."

"And he—the young man—where is he now?"

"I left him at my father's house, not three hours since."

"Come, let us go."

The two arose, passed through the inclosure, and threaded the path toward the wigwam slowly and in silence. The maiden was lost in conjecture, and her companion seemed pondering in some hidden thought of deep moment. Now her face was sad and regretful in its look, again it lighted up a thrilling expression of eager and yearning tenderness.

The afternoon shadows were gathering over the forest, and being anxious to reach home before dark, Sarah refused to enter the wigwam when they reached it. The Indian went in for a moment, and returned with a slip of birch bark, on which a few words were lightly traced in pencil.

"Give this to the young man," she said, placing the bark in Sarah's hand; "and now good-night—good-night."

Sarah took the bark and turned with a hurried step to the forest track. She felt agitated, and as if something painful were about to happen. With a curiosity aroused by the Indian's strange manner, she examined the writing on the slip of bark in her hand; it was only a request that William Danforth would meet the writer at a place appointed, on the bank of the Catskill Creek, that evening. The scroll was signed, "Malaeska."

Malaeska! It was singular, but Sarah Jones had never learned the Indian's name before.

CHAPTER 14

"Wild was her look, wild was her air,
Back from her shoulders stream'd the hair—
The locks, that wont her brow to shade,
Started erectly from her head;
Her figure seem'd to rise more high—
From her pale lips a frantic cry
Rang sharply through the moon's pale light—
And life to her was endless night."

THE point of land, which we have described in the early part of this story, as hedging in the outlet of Catskill Creek, gently ascends from the juncture of the two streams and rolls upward into a broad and beautiful hill, which again sweeps off toward the mountains and down the margin of the Hudson in a vast plain, at the present day cut up into highly cultivated farms, and diversified by little eminences, groves, and one large tract of swamp-land. Along the southern margin of the creek the hill forms a lofty and picturesque bank, in some places dropping to the water in a sheer descent of forty or fifty feet, and others, sloping down in a more gradual but still abrupt fall, broken into little ravines, and thickly covered with a fine growth of young timber.

A foot-path winds up from the stone dwelling, which we have already described, along the upper verge of this bank to the level of the plain, terminating in a singular projection of earth which shoots out from the face of the bank some feet over the stream, taking the form of a huge serpent's head. This projection commands a fine view of the village, and is known to the inhabitants by the title of "Hoppy Nose,"[1] from a tradition attached to it. The foot-path, which terminates at this point, receives a melancholy interest from the constant presence of a singular being who has trod it regularly for years. Hour after hour, and day after day, through sunshine and storm, he is to be seen winding among the trees, or moving with a slow monotonous walk along this track, where it verges into the rich sward. Speechless he has been for years, not from inability, but from a settled unbroken habit of silence. He is perfectly gentle and inoffensive, and from his quiet bearing a slight observer might mistake him for a meditative philosopher, rather than a man slightly and harmlessly insane as a peculiar expression in his clear, blue eyes and his resolute silence must surely proclaim him to be.

---

1 *"Hoppy Nose"*   generally refers to odor or fragrance of hops.

But we are describing subsequent things, rather than the scenery as it existed at the time of our story. Then, the hillside and all the broad plain was a forest of heavy timbered land, but the bank of the creek was much in its present condition. The undergrowth throve a little more luxuriantly, and the "Hoppy Nose" shot out from it covered with a thick coating of grass, but shrubless, with the exception of two or three saplings and a few clumps of wild-flowers.

As the moon arose on the night after Sarah Jones' interview with the Indian woman, that singular being stood upon the "Hoppy Nose," waiting the appearance of young Danforth. More than once she went out to the extreme verge of the projection, looked eagerly up and down the stream, then back into the shadow again, with folded arms, continued her watch as before.

At length a slight sound came from the opposite side; she sprang forward, and supporting herself by a sapling, bent over the stream, with one foot just touching the verge of the projection, her lips slightly parted, and her left hand holding back the hair from her temples, eager to ascertain the nature of the sound. The sapling bent and almost snapped beneath her hold, but she remained motionless, her eyes shining in the moonlight with a strange, uncertain luster, and fixed keenly on the place whence the sound proceeded.

A canoe cut out into the river, and made toward the spot where she was standing.

"It is he!" broke from her parted lips, as the moonlight fell on the clear forehead and graceful form of a young man, who stood upright in the little shallop,[2] and drawing a deep breath, she settled back, folded her arms, and waited his approach.

The sapling had scarcely swayed back to its position, when the youth curved his canoe round to a hollow in the bank, and climbing along the ascent, he drew himself up the steep side of the "Hoppy Nose" by the brushwood, and sprang to the Indian woman's side.

"Malaeska," he said, extending his hand with a manner and voice of friendly recognition; "my good, kind nurse, believe me, I am rejoiced to have found you again."

Malaeska did not take his hand, but after an intense and eager gaze into his face, flung herself on his bosom, sobbing aloud, murmuring soft, broken words of endearment, and trembling all over with a rush of unconquerable tenderness.

The youth started back, and a frown gathered on his haughty forehead. His prejudices were offended, and he strove to put her from his bosom; even gratitude for all her goodness could not conquer the disgust with which he recoiled from the embrace of a savage.

"Malaeska," he said, almost sternly, attempting to unclasp her arms from his neck, "You forget—I am no longer a boy—be composed, and say what I can do for you?"

But she only clung to him the more passionately, and answered with an appeal that thrilled to his very heart.

"Put not your mother away—she has waited long—my son! my son!"

The youth did not comprehend the whole meaning of her words. They were more energetic and full of pathos than he had ever witnessed before; but she had been his nurse, and he had been long absent from her, and the strength of

---

2 *shallop*   term, derived from "sloop," referring to a small, open boat oared or sailed in shallow waters.

Divinity degree in 1860, becoming a Unitarian minister like his father. During the Civil War, he supported the Union. Though he was exempt from military service, it was at this time that he began to write juvenile fiction as well as adult fiction, in an effort to persuade young readers that the War was necessary.

His need for funds prompted him to accept a call to the Unitarian pulpit in Brewster, Massachusetts, in 1864. There, he completed two novels, one for boys and one for older girls, and carried out his religious and social duties as a pastor, to the satisfaction of his congregation. But, in early 1866, rumors began to surface about Alger's relationship with some of the boys in the church, who claimed he had molested them. Confronted by members of the congregation who had substantiated the rumors, Alger admitted that he had been "imprudent" and left town immediately amid threats of violence from some of the townspeople. He was 34 years old.

Alger's father interceded for him with the Brewster church, vowing that his son would never again enter a pulpit. Alger too appealed for mercy, for his family's sake rather than his own, and the church agreed to take no further action as long as Alger never again allied himself with the Unitarian church or called himself Reverend. Alger kept his part of the bargain, never publicly referring to his stay in Brewster, always correcting anyone who addressed him as a minister, and protecting his family even into his grave by instructing that all his papers be destroyed.

Alger had to begin a new life. He headed for New York and, in the pattern that was to typify the rest of his life, he immediately applied himself to writing as much and as quickly as he could, carefully saving the little money he was able to make. In what must surely be an expression of his ambiguous feelings about the Brewster incident, he also began to visit some of New York's charitable institutions devoted to caring for orphaned boys. He had always been an advocate for charity toward the homeless; now he began to contribute his own meager funds to this cause and during his life arranged to support several such boys and make sure they received an education.

In touring such places as the Newsboys' Lodging House, which cared for more than 8,000 homeless boys during 1866 alone, he struck the vein of literary gold that was to create his reputation as a writer. There he saw orphaned boys surviving in the street thanks to a combination of cleverness, luck, and hard work. These boys—known as "street Arabs" in the slang of the day—were the inspiration for Alger's next writing project, *Ragged Dick; Or, Street Life in New York with the Boot-blacks*, which first appeared in 1867 as a serial in a youth magazine called *Student and Schoolmate*. He wrote twelve installments, and the magazine's readers liked it so well that its publisher contracted with Alger to produce more of the same, advertising him as "at the head of successful writers for the young." Alger soon signed a contract with another publisher who wanted to produce *Ragged Dick* as a novel. In this form, in 1868, it sold out the first edition in a matter of weeks, a bona fide success.

For the remainder of his career as a writer of juveniles, Alger would seek similar success but never find it. In a sense, he continued to write *Ragged Dick*, recycling the same plot and characters, changing only the settings and names. He serialized, borrowed from himself, revised previously published material, and sometimes wrote under a pseudonym, so that it is difficult to come up with exact figures about his output, but it was certainly prolific.

He did not become rich. At best, he was comfortable for a while, and for a while he was a celebrity. But, even as early as 1869, he needed to augment his income and took a position tutoring the five sons of Joseph Seligman, a wealthy New York banker. He remained in this apparently happy situation for eight years, then lived in boarding houses until near the end of his life. He continued to produce fiction for adults as well as young adults, though with little critical notice or success. He began to suffer depression and eye problems, and by 1896, he retired to the Massachusetts home of his sister to rest. Recognizing that he could not complete his work, he contacted the young New York editor and writer Edward Stratemeyer offering a contract to finish his last juvenile, *Out for Business*. He perceived rightly that Stratemeyer was going to have a "book reputation." Stratemeyer did complete the work, but Alger never saw it. He died in 1899.

Alger's reputation experienced two more surges. When his books were reissued in the early part of the twentieth century, several completed by Stratemeyer, they sold extremely well. They seemed to express the mood of Progressivism that dominated the nation. After 1920, the sales of the books declined sharply, but the *idea* of them began to fill the need for hopeful fantasies of success. Public figures such as writer Thomas Wolfe and governor of New York Herbert Lehman, recalled Alger's books with praise for their dedication to the American values of hard work and honesty. By the 1940s he had become "A Monument to Free Enterprise," as one magazine called him, and "Horatio Alger stories" of the poor and disadvantaged rising to success were legion. Some of these encomiums confuse the writer Horatio Alger, Jr. with the characters in his stories, an error that has persisted, and some inaccurately suggest that Alger's protagonists rise to great wealth. But, in 1947, the American Schools and Colleges Association instituted the Horatio Alger Awards, honoring those who represent the perceived Alger virtues: triumph over adversity, and political and economic conservatism. Billy Graham, Dwight Eisenhower, and Ronald Reagan are among those who have won this award.

Ragged Dick bridges nineteenth- and twentieth-century Young Adult fiction. Its own literary ancestors are the dime novel, with its rapid pace, sensational events, and shady characters, and the moral tales which had been standard fare for young American readers since the Puritans. Its plucky protagonist looks forward to such Golden Age works as *Treasure Island*, *The Adventures of Huckleberry Finn*, and *The Jungle Books*, and even more directly, to series mystery/adventures such as *The Rover Boys*, *The Hardy Boys*, and *Nancy Drew*. But it also foreshadows quite a different sort of Young Adult novel: Virginia Hamilton's *The Planet of Junior Brown* (1971) also treats New York City homeless boys who take care of each other physically and morally. Like Dick, Hamilton's Buddy is a shrewd, courageous survivor, but in a darker, more dangerous world, a modern counterpoint to Alger's comparatively sunny city.

The themes of the Alger's novel are money and appearance. Alger never misses an opportunity to tell what things cost, how much Dick makes, how much he needs, and how much he saves. Dick's calculations, especially as he begins to accumulate money, lie at the heart of the plot. But from the beginning, Alger stresses that Dick is "good-looking" in both senses—physical and moral—even in his rags. His poor situation at the beginning of the novel is the result more of carelessness about the future than the innate worthlessness that Alger wants us to recognize in Micky Maguire or Jim Travis. After Dick gains a new suit of clothes, others see him as the fine fellow he really is. Throughout the book, he says he wants to be "respectable," a word that means, at its root, the ability to be *looked at* with approval. In Alger's ledger book, Dick has that quality from the beginning; like Cinderella, his rags were his disguise.

97

Dick is an engaging character as well as a symbolic one. Despite Alger's often self-conscious style, he has, in the first three-quarters of the book, some of the same qualities that make us love Huckleberry Finn: an original wit, a street-wise cleverness, the ability to spot a phony, a sense of honest bewilderment at some of the trappings and behaviors of his social betters, a sincere loyalty to his friends, and a measure of comfort with himself that most of us would envy. Like Huck, he seems to have sprung from his creator fully alive and talking. Twain, the artist, was able to let Huck be his insurgent self all the way. Alger, the writer for hire, needed to write a moral book—for himself, for his young audience, and for a publisher's contract. So, unlike Huck, after Dick is introduced to respectability, he finds himself attracted to it. When at the end of the novel his rags are stolen by another street boy, he is glad. But the reader is sorry, for by then Dick is not nearly as lively a character as he was at first.

Alger's tale, contrary to his twentieth-century reputation, is not a rags to riches story, nor does it praise the kind of business schemes that made money only for such men as Andrew Carnegie and Jay Gould. *Ragged Dick* takes place before stock market manipulations and strike-breaking became the business of business. In an implicit criticism of the overvaluation of individual effort, he shows that a helping hand is ultimately the one which receives the true rewards. Readers of his day, and those readers who devoured his novels in the early 1900s, were looking back nostalgically to a time when, they believed, the free enterprise system really did work to the advantage of the honest, hardworking poor.

RAGGED DICK
OR, STREET LIFE IN NEW YORK
WITH THE BOOT-BLACKS

PREFACE

"RAGGED DICK" was contributed as a serial story to the pages of the *Schoolmate*, a well-known juvenile magazine, during the year 1867. While in course of publication, it was received with so many evidences of favor that it has been rewritten and considerably enlarged, and is now presented to the public as the first volume of a series intended to illustrate the life and experiences of the friendless and vagrant children who are now numbered by thousands in New York and other cities.

Several characters in the story are sketched from life. The necessary information has been gathered mainly from personal observation and conversations with the boys themselves. The author is indebted also to the excellent Superintendent of the Newsboys' Lodging House, in Fulton Street, for some facts of which he has been able to make use. Some anachronisms may be noted. Wherever they occur, they have been admitted, as aiding in the development of the story, and will probably be considered as of little importance in an unpretending volume, which does not aspire to strict historical accuracy.

The author hopes that, while the volumes in this series may prove interesting as stories, they may also have the effect of enlisting the sympathies of his readers in behalf of the unfortunate children whose life is described, and of leading them to co-operate with the praiseworthy efforts now making [sic] by the Children's Aid Society and other organizations to ameliorate their condition.

New York, April, 1868

CHAPTER 1

Ragged Dick is Introduced to the Reader

"WAKE up there, youngster," said a rough voice.

Ragged Dick opened his eyes slowly, and stared stupidly in the face of the speaker, but did not offer to get up.

"Wake up, you young vagabond!" said the man a little impatiently; "I suppose you'd lay there all day, if I hadn't called you."

"What time is it?" asked Dick.

"Seven o'clock."

"Seven o'clock! I oughter 've been up an hour ago. I know what 'twas made me so precious sleepy. I went to the Old Bowery last night, and didn't turn in till past twelve."

"You went to the Old Bowery? Where'd you get your money?" asked the man, who was a porter in the employ of a firm doing business on Spruce Street.

"Made it by shines, in course. My guardian don't allow me no money for theatres, so I have to earn it."

"Some boys get it easier than that," said the porter significantly.

"You don't catch me stealin', if that's what you mean," said Dick.

"Don't you ever steal, then?"

"No, and I wouldn't. Lots of boys does it, but I wouldn't."

"Well, I'm glad to hear you say that. I believe there's some good in you, Dick, after all."

"Oh, I'm a rough customer!" said Dick. "But I wouldn't steal. It's mean."

"I'm glad you think so, Dick," and the rough voice sounded gentler than at first. "Have you got any money to buy your breakfast?"

"No, but I'll soon get some."

While this conversation has been going on, Dick had got up. His bedchamber had been a wooden box half full of straw, on which the young boot-black had reposed his weary limbs, and slept as soundly as if it had been a bed of down. He dumped down into the straw without taking the trouble of undressing. Getting up too was an equally short process. He jumped out of the box, shook himself, picked out one or two straws that had found their way into rents in his clothes, and, drawing a well-worn cap over his uncombed locks, he was all ready for the business of the day.

Dick's appearance as he stood beside the box was rather peculiar. His pants were torn in several places, and had apparently belonged in the first instance to a boy two sizes larger than himself. He wore a vest, all the buttons of which were gone except two, out of which peeped a shirt which looked as if it had been worn a month. To complete his costume he wore a coat too long for him, dating back, if one might judge from its general appearance, to a remote antiquity.

Washing the face and hands is usually considered proper in commencing the day, but Dick was above such refinement. He had no particular dislike to dirt, and did not think it necessary to remove several dark streaks on his face and hands. But in spite of his dirt and rags there was something about Dick that was attractive. It was easy to see that if he had been clean and well dressed he would have been decidedly good-looking. Some of his companions were sly, and their faces inspired distrust; but Dick had a frank, straight-forward manner that made him a favorite.

Dick's business hours had commenced. He had no office to open. His little blacking-box was ready for use, and he looked sharply in the faces of all who passed, addressing each with, "Shine yer boots, sir?"

"How much?" asked a gentleman on his way to his office.

"Ten cents," said Dick, dropping his box, and sinking upon his knees on the sidewalk, flourishing his brush with the air of one skilled in his profession.

"Ten cents! Isn't that a little steep?"

"Well, you know 'taint all clear profit," said Dick, who had already set to work. "There's the *blacking* costs something, and I have to get a new brush pretty often."

"And you have a large rent too," said the gentleman quizzically, with a glance at a large hole in Dick's coat.

"Yes, sir," said Dick, always ready to joke; "I have to pay such a big rent for my manshun up on Fifth Avenoo, that I can't afford to take less than ten cents a shine. I'll give you a bully shine, sir."

"Be quick about it, for I am in a hurry. So your house is on Fifth Avenue, is it?"

"It isn't anywhere else," said Dick, and Dick spoke the truth there.

"What tailor do you patronize?" asked the gentleman, surveying Dick's attire.

"Would you like to go to the same one?" asked Dick, shrewdly.

"Well, no; it strikes me that he didn't give you a very good fit."

"This coat once belonged to General Washington," said Dick, comically. "He wore it all through the Revolution, and it got torn some, 'cause he fit so hard. When he died he told his widder to give it to some smart young feller that hadn't got none of his own; so she gave it to me. But if you'd like it, sir, to remember General Washington by, I'll let you have it reasonable."

"Thank you, but I wouldn't want to deprive you of it. And did your pants come from General Washington too?"

"No, they was a gift from Lewis Napoleon.[1] Lewis had outgrown 'em and sent 'em to me,—he's bigger than me, and that's why they don't fit."

"It seems you have distinguished friends. Now, my lad, I suppose you would like your money."

"I shouldn't have any objection," said Dick.

"I believe," said the gentleman, examining his pocket-book, "I haven't got anything short of twenty-five cents. Have you got any change?"

"Not a cent," said Dick. "All my money's invested in the Erie Railroad."

"That's unfortunate."

"Shall I get the money changed, sir?"

"I can't wait; I've got to meet an appointment immediately. I'll hand you twenty-five cents, and you can leave the change at my office any time during the day."

"All right, sir. Where is it?"

"No. 125 Fulton Street. Shall you remember?"

"Yes, sir. What name?"

"Greyson—office on second floor."

"All right, sir; I'll bring it."

---

1 *Lewis Napoleon* Dick's joking pronunciation (cf. p. 118 of Louis Napoleon (1808–1873), ruler of France 1852–1870.

"I wonder whether the little scamp will prove honest," said Mr. Greyson to himself, as he walked away. "If he does, I'll give him my custom regularly. If he don't, as is most likely, I shan't mind the loss of fifteen cents."

Mr. Greyson didn't understand Dick. Our ragged hero wasn't a model boy in all respects. I am afraid he swore sometimes, and now and then he played tricks upon unsophisticated boys from the country, or gave a wrong direction to honest old gentlemen unused to the city. A clergyman in search of the Cooper Institute he once directed to the Tombs Prison, and, following him unobserved, was highly delighted when the unsuspicious stranger walked up the front steps of the great stone building on Centre Street, and tried to obtain admission.

"I guess he wouldn't want to stay long if he did get in," thought Ragged Dick, hitching up his pants. "Leastways I shouldn't. They're so precious glad to see you that they won't let you go, but board you gratooitous, and never send in no bills."

Another of Dick's faults was his extravagance. Being always wide-awake and ready for business, he earned enough to have supported him comfortably and respectably. There were not a few young clerks who employed Dick from time to time in his professional capacity, who scarcely earned as much as he, greatly as their style and dress exceeded his. But Dick was careless of his earnings. Where they went he could hardly have told himself. However much he managed to earn during the day, all was generally spent before morning. He was fond of going to the Old Bowery Theatre, and to Tony Pastor's,[2] and if he had any money left afterwards, he would invite some of his friends in somewhere to have an oyster stew; so it seldom happened that he commenced the day with a penny.

Then I am sorry to add that Dick had formed the habit of smoking. This cost him considerable, for Dick was rather fastidious about his cigars, and wouldn't smoke the cheapest. Besides, having a liberal nature, he was generally ready to treat his companions. But of course the expense was the smallest objection. No boy of fourteen can smoke without being affected injuriously. Men are frequently injured by smoking, and boys always. But large numbers of the newsboys and boot-blacks form the habit. Exposed to the cold and wet they find that it warms them up, and the self-indulgence grows upon them. It is not uncommon to see a little boy, too young to be out of his mother's sight, smoking with all the apparent satisfaction of a veteran smoker.

There was another way in which Dick sometimes lost money. There was a noted gambling-house on Baxter Street, which in the evening was sometimes crowded with these juvenile gamesters, who staked their hard earnings, generally losing of course, and refreshing themselves from time to time with a vile mixture of liquor at two cents a glass. Sometimes Dick strayed in here, and played with the rest.

I have mentioned Dick's faults and defects, because I want it understood, to begin with, that I don't consider him a model boy. But there were some good points about him nevertheless. He was above doing anything mean or dishonorable. He would not steal, or cheat, or impose upon younger boys, but was frank and straight-forward, manly and self-reliant. His nature was a noble one, and had saved him from all mean faults. I hope my young readers will like him as I do, without being blind to his faults. Perhaps, although he was only a bootblack, they may find something in him to imitate.

---

2 *Tony Pastor's*   a Manhattan restaurant.

And now, having fairly introduced Ragged Dick to my young readers, I must refer them to the next chapter for his further adventures.

CHAPTER 2

Johnny Nolan

AFTER Dick had finished polishing Mr. Greyson's boots he was fortunate enough to secure three other customers, two of them reporters in the Tribune establishment, which occupies the corner of Spruce Street and Printing House Square.

When Dick had got through with his last customer the City Hall clock indicated eight o'clock. He had been up an hour, and hard at work, and naturally began to think of breakfast. He went up to the head of Spruce Street, and turned into Nassau. Two blocks further, and he reached Ann Street. On this street was a small, cheap restaurant, where for five cents Dick could get a cup of coffee, and for ten cents more, a plate of beef-steak with a plate of bread thrown in. These Dick ordered, and sat down at a table.

It was a small apartment with a few plain tables unprovided with cloths, for the class of customers who patronized it were not very particular. Our hero's breakfast was soon before him. Neither the coffee nor the steak were as good as can be bought at Delmonico's; but then it is very doubtful whether, in the present state of his wardrobe, Dick would have been received at that aristocratic restaurant, even if his means had admitted of paying the high prices there charged.

Dick had scarcely been served when he espied a boy about his own size standing at the door, looking wistfully into the restaurant. This was Johnny Nolan, a boy of fourteen, who was engaged in the same profession as Ragged Dick. His wardrobe was in very much the same condition as Dick's.

"Had your breakfast, Johnny?" inquired Dick, cutting off a piece of steak.

"No."

"Come in, then. Here's room for you."

"I ain't got no money," said Johnny, looking a little enviously at his more fortunate friend.

"Haven't you had any shines?"

"Yes, I had one, but I shan't get any pay till to-morrow."

"Are you hungry?"

"Try me, and see."

"Come in. I'll stand treat this morning."

Johnny Nolan was nowise slow to accept this invitation, and was soon seated beside Dick.

"What'll you have, Johnny?"

"Same as you."

"Cup o' coffee and beefsteak," ordered Dick.

These were promptly brought, and Johnny attacked them vigorously.

Now, in the boot-blacking business, as well as in higher avocations, the same rule prevails, that energy and industry are rewarded, and indolence suffers. Dick was energetic and on the alert for business, but Johnny the reverse. The consequence was that Dick earned probably three times as much as the other.

"How do you like it?" asked Dick, surveying Johnny's attacks upon the steak with evident complacency.

"It's hunky."

I don't believe "hunky" is to be found in either Webster's or Worcester's big dictionary; but boys will readily understand what it means.

"Do you come here often?" asked Johnny.

"Most every day. You'd better come too."

"I can't afford it."

"Well, you'd ought to, then," said Dick. "What do you do with your money, I'd like to know?"

"I don't get near as much as you, Dick."

"Well, you might if you tried. I keep my eyes open—that's the way I get jobs. You're lazy, that's what's the matter."

Johnny did not see fit to reply to this charge. Probably he felt the justice of it, and preferred to proceed with the breakfast, which he enjoyed the more as it cost him nothing.

Breakfast over, Dick walked up to the desk, and settled the bill. Then, followed by Johnny, he went out into the street.

"Where are you going, Johnny?"

"Up to Mr. Taylor's, on Spruce Street, to see if he don't want a shine."

"Do you work for him reg'lar?"

"Yes. Him and his partner wants a shine most every day. Where are you goin'?"

"Down front of the Astor House. I guess I'll find some customers there."

At this moment Johnny started, and, dodging into an entry way, hid behind the door, considerably to Dick's surprise.

"What's the matter now?" asked our hero.

"Has he gone?" asked Johnny, his voice betraying anxiety.

"Who gone, I'd like to know?"

"That man in the brown coat."

"What of him. You ain't scared of him, are you?"

"Yes, he got me a place once."

"Where?"

"Ever so far off."

"What if he did?"

"I ran away."

"Didn't you like?"

"No, I had to get up too early. It was on a farm, and I had to get up at five to take care of the cows. I like New York best."

"Didn't they give you enough to eat?"

"Oh, yes, plenty."

"And you had a good bed?"

"Yes."

"Then you'd better have stayed. You don't get either of them here. Where'd you sleep last night?"

"Up an alley in an old wagon."

"You had a better bed than that in the country, didn't you?"

"Yes, it was as soft as—as cotton."

Johnny had once slept on a bale of cotton, the recollection supplying him with a comparison.

"Why didn't you stay?"

"I felt lonely," said Johnny.

Johnny could not exactly explain his feelings, but it is often the case that the young vagabond of the streets, though his food is uncertain, and his bed may be any old wagon or barrel that he is lucky enough to find unoccupied when night sets in, gets so attached to his precarious but independent mode of life, that he feels discontented in any other. He is accustomed to the noise and bustle and ever-varied life of the streets, and in the quiet scenes of the country misses the excitement in the midst of which he has always dwelt.

Johnny had but one tie to bind him to the city. He had a father living, but he might as well have been without one. Mr. Nolan was a confirmed drunkard, and spent the greater part of his wages for liquor. His potations made him ugly, and inflamed a temper never very sweet, working him up sometimes to such a pitch of rage that Johnny's life was in danger. Some months before, he had thrown a flat-iron at his son's head with such terrific force that unless Johnny had dodged he would not have lived long enough to obtain a place in our story. He fled the house, and from that time had not dared to re-enter it. Somebody had given him a brush and box of blacking, and he had set up in business on his own account. But he had not energy enough to succeed, as has already been stated, and I am afraid the poor boy had met with many hardships, and suffered more than once from cold and hunger. Dick had befriended him more than once, and often given him a breakfast or dinner, as the case might be.

"How'd you get away?" asked Dick, with some curiosity. "Did you walk?"

"No, I rode on the cars."

"Where'd you get your money? I hope you didn't steal it."

"I didn't have none."

"What did you do, then?"

"I got up about three o'clock, and walked to Albany."

"Where's that?" asked Dick, whose ideas on the subject of geography were rather vague.

"Up the river."

"How far?"

"About a thousand miles," said Johnny, whose conceptions of distance were equally vague.

"Go ahead. What did you do then?"

"I hid on top of a freight car, and came all the way without their seeing me.* That man in the brown coat was the man that got me the place, and I'm afraid he'd want to send me back."

"Well," said Dick, reflectively, "I dunno as I'd like to live in the country. I couldn't go to Tony Pastor's, or the Old Bowery. There wouldn't be no place to spend my evenings. But I say, it's tough in winter, Johnny, 'specially when your overcoat's at the tailor's, an' likely to stay there."

"That's so, Dick. But I must be goin', or Mr. Taylor'll get somebody else to shine his boots."

Johnny walked back to Nassau Street, while Dick kept on his way to Broadway.

"That boy," soliloquized Dick, as Johnny took his departure, "ain't got no ambition. I'll bet he won't get five shines to-day. I'm glad I ain't like him. I couldn't go to the theatre, nor buy no cigars, nor get half as much as I wanted to eat.—Shine yer boots, sir?"

---

*A fact.

"I must have made a mistake," faltered the clerk.

"I shall not give you a chance to make such another mistake in my employ," said the merchant sternly. "You may go up to the desk and ask for what wages are due you. I shall have no further occasion for your services."

"Now, youngster," said Dick's patron, as they went out of the store, after he had finally got the bill changed. "I must pay you something extra for your trouble. Here's fifty cents."

"Thank you, sir," said Dick. "You're very kind. Don't you want some more bills changed?"

"Not to-day," said he with a smile. "It's too expensive."

"I'm in luck," thought our hero complacently. "I guess I'll go to Barnum's tonight, and see the bearded lady, the eight-foot giant, the two-foot dwarf, and the other curiosities, too numerous to mention."

Dick shouldered his box and walked up as far as the Astor House. He took his station on the side-walk, and began to look about him.

Just behind him were two persons,—one, a gentleman of fifty; the other, a boy of thirteen or fourteen. They were speaking together, and Dick had no difficulty in hearing what was said.

"I am sorry, Frank, that I can't go about, and show you some of the sights of New York, but I shall be full of business to-day. It is your first visit to the city too."

"Yes, sir."

"There's a good deal worth seeing here. But I'm afraid you'll have to wait till next time. You can go out and walk by yourself, but don't venture too far, or you may get lost."

Frank looked disappointed.

"I wish Tom Miles knew I was here," he said. "He would go around with me."

"Where does he live?"

"Somewhere up town, I believe."

"Then, unfortunately, he is not available. If you would rather go with me than stay here, you can, but as I shall be most of the time in merchants' counting-rooms, I am afraid it would not be very interesting."

"I think," said Frank, after a little hesitation, "that I will go off by myself. I won't go very far, and if I lose my way, I will inquire for the Astor House."

"Yes, anybody will direct you here."

"Very well, Frank, I am sorry I can't do better for you."

"Oh, never mind, uncle, I shall be amused in walking around, and looking at the shop-windows. There will be a great deal to see."

Now Dick had listened to all this conversation. Being an enterprising young man, he thought he saw a chance for a speculation, and determined to avail himself of it.

Accordingly he stepped up to the two just as Frank's uncle was about leaving, and said, "I know all about the city, sir; I'll show him around, if you want me too."

The gentleman looked a little curiously at the ragged figure before him.

"So you are a city boy, are you?"

"Yes, sir," said Dick, "I've lived here ever since I was a baby."

"And you know all about the public buildings, I suppose?"

"Yes, sir."

"And the Central Park?"

"Yes, sir. I know my way all round."

The gentleman looked thoughtful.

"I don't know what to say, Frank," he remarked after a while. "It is rather a novel proposal. He isn't exactly the sort of guide I would have picked out for you. Still he looks honest. He has an open face, and I think can be depended upon."

"I wish he wasn't so ragged and dirty," said Frank, who felt a little shy about being seen with such a companion.

"I'm afraid you haven't washed your face this morning," said Mr. Whitney, for that was the gentleman's name.

"They didn't have no wash-bowls at the hotel where I stopped," said Dick.

"What hotel did you stop at?"

"The Box Hotel."

"The Box Hotel?"

"Yes, sir, I slept in a box on Spruce Street."

Frank surveyed Dick curiously.

"How did you like it?" he asked.

"I slept bully."

"Suppose it had rained."

"Then I'd have wet my best clothes," said Dick.

"Are these all the clothes you have?"

"Yes, sir."

Mr. Whitney spoke a few words to Frank, who seemed pleased with the suggestion.

"Follow me, my lad," he said.

Dick in some surprise obeyed orders, following Mr. Whitney and Frank into the hotel, past the office, to the foot of the staircase. Here a servant of the hotel stopped Dick, but Mr. Whitney explained that he had something for him to do, and he was allowed to proceed.

They entered a long entry, and finally paused before a door. This being opened a pleasant chamber was disclosed.

"Come in, my lad," said Mr. Whitney.

Dick and Frank entered.

CHAPTER 4

Dick's New Suit

"Now," said Mr. Whitney to Dick, "my nephew here is on his way to a boarding-school. He had a suit of clothes in his trunk about half worn. He is willing to give them to you. I think they will look better than those you have on."

Dick was so astonished that he hardly knew what to say. Presents were something that he knew very little about, never having received any to his knowledge. That so large a gift should be made to him by a stranger seemed very wonderful.

The clothes were brought out, and turned out to be a neat gray suit.

"Before you put them on, my lad, you must wash yourself. Clean clothes and a dirty skin don't go very well together. Frank, you may attend to him. I am obliged to go at once. Have you got as much money as you require?"

"Yes, uncle."

"One more word, my lad," said Mr. Whitney, addressing Dick; "I may be rash in trusting a boy of whom I know nothing, but I like your looks, and I think you will prove a proper guide for my nephew."

"Yes, I will, sir," said Dick, earnestly. "Honor bright!"

"Very well. A pleasant time to you."

The process of cleansing commenced. To tell the truth Dick needed it, and the sensation of cleanliness he found both new and pleasant. Frank added to his gift a shirt, stockings, and an old pair of shoes. "I am sorry I haven't any cap," said he.

"I've got one," said Dick.

"It isn't so new as it might be," said Frank, surveying an old felt hat, which had once been black, but was now dingy, with a large hole in the top and a portion of the rim torn off.

"No," said Dick; "my grandfather used to wear it when he was a boy, and I've kep' it ever since out of respect for his memory. But I'll get a new one now. I can buy one cheap on Chatham Street."

"Is that near here?"

"Only five minutes' walk."

"Then we can get on the way."

When Dick was dressed in his new attire, with his face and hands clean, and his hair brushed, it was difficult to imagine that he was the same boy.

He now looked quite handsome, and might readily have been taken for a young gentleman, except that his hands were red and grimy.

"Look at yourself," said Frank, leading him before the mirror.

"By gracious!" said Dick, starting back in astonishment, "that isn't me, is it?"

"Don't you know yourself?" asked Frank, smiling.

"It reminds me of Cinderella," said Dick, "when she was changed into a fairy princess. I see it one night at Barnum's. What'll Johnny Nolan say when he sees me? He won't dare to speak to such a young swell as I be now. Ain't it rich?" and Dick burst into a loud laugh. His fancy was tickled by the anticipation of his friend's surprise. Then the thought of the valuable gifts he had received occurred to him, and he looked gratefully at Frank.

"You're a brick," he said.

"A what?"

"A brick! You're a jolly good fellow to give me such a present."

"You're quite welcome, Dick," said Frank, kindly. "I'm better off than you are, and I can spare the clothes just as well as not. You must have a new hat though. But that we can get when we go out. The old clothes you can make into a bundle."

"Wait a minute till I get my handkercher," and Dick pulled from the pocket of the pants a dirty rag, which might have been white once, though it did not look like it, and had apparently once formed a part of a sheet or shirt.

"You mustn't carry that," said Frank.

"But I've got a cold," said Dick.

"Oh, I don't mean you to go without a handkerchief. I'll give you one."

Frank opened his trunk and pulled out two, which he gave to Dick.

"I wonder if I ain't dreamin'," said Dick, once more surveying himself doubtfully in the glass. "I'm afraid I'm dreamin', and shall wake up in a barrel, as I did night afore last."

"Shall I pinch you so you can wake here?" asked Frank, playfully.

"Yes," said Dick, seriously, "I wish you would."

He pulled up the sleeve of his jacket, and Frank pinched him pretty hard, so that Dick winced.

"Yes, I guess I'm awake," said Dick; "you've got a pair of nippers, you have."

"But what shall I do with my brush and blacking?" he asked.

"You can leave them here till we come back," said Frank. "They will be safe."

"Hold on a minute," said Dick, surveying Frank's boots with a professional eye, "you ain't got a good shine on them boots. I'll make 'em shine so you can see your face in 'em."

And he was as good as his word.

"Thank you," said Frank; "now you had better brush your own shoes."

This had not occurred to Dick, for in general the professional boot-black considers his blacking too valuable to expend on his own shoes or boots, if he is fortunate enough to possess a pair.

The two boys now went downstairs together. They met the same servant who had spoken to Dick a few minutes before, but there was no recognition.

"He don't know me," said Dick. "He thinks I'm a young swell like you."

"What's a swell?"

"Oh, a feller that wears nobby clothes like you."

"And you, too, Dick."

"Yes," said Dick, "who'd ever have thought as I should have turned into a swell?"

They had now got out on Broadway, and were slowly walking along the west side by the Park, when who should Dick see in front of him, but Johnny Nolan?

Instantly Dick was seized with a fancy for witnessing Johnny's amazement at his change in appearance. He stole up behind him, and struck him on the back.

"Hallo, Johnny, how many shines have you had?"

Johnny turned round expecting to see Dick, whose voice he recognized, but his astonished eyes rested on a nicely dressed boy (the hat alone excepted) who looked indeed like Dick, but so transformed in dress that it was difficult to be sure of his identity.

"What luck, Johnny?" repeated Dick.

Johnny surveyed him from head to foot in great bewilderment.

"Who be you?" he said.

"Well, that's a good one," laughed Dick; "so you don't know Dick?"

"Where'd you get all them clothes?" asked Johnny. "Have you been stealin'?"

"Say that again, and I'll lick you. No, I've lent my clothes to a young feller as was goin' to a party, and didn't have none fit to wear, and so I put on my second-best for a change."

Without deigning any further explanation, Dick went off, followed by the astonished gaze of Johnny Nolan, who could not quite make up his mind whether the neat-looking boy he had been talking with was really Ragged Dick or not.

In order to reach Chatham Street it was necessary to cross Broadway. This was easier proposed than done. There is always such a throng of omnibuses, drays, carriages, and vehicles of all kinds in the neighborhood of the Astor House, that the crossing is formidable to one who is not used to it. Dick made nothing of it, dodging in and out among the horses and wagons with perfect self-possession. Reaching the opposite sidewalk, he looked back, and found that Frank had retreated in dismay, and that the width of the street was between them.

"Come across!" called out Dick.

"I don't see any chance," said Frank, looking anxiously at the prospect before him. "I'm afraid of being run over."

"If you are, you can sue 'em for damages," said Dick.

Finally Frank got safely over after several narrow escapes, as he considered them.

"Is it always so crowded?" he asked.

"A good deal worse sometimes," said Dick. "I knowed a young man once who waited six hours for a chance to cross, and at last got run over by an omnibus, leaving a widder and a large family of orphan children. His widder, a beautiful young woman, was obliged to start a peanut and apple stand. There she is now."

"Where?"

Dick pointed to a hideous old woman, of large proportions, wearing a bonnet of immense size, who presided over an apple-stand close by.

Frank laughed.

"If that is the case," he said, "I think I will patronize her."

"Leave it to me," said Dick, winking.

He advanced gravely to the apple-stand, and said, 'Old lady, have you paid your taxes?"

The astonished woman opened her eyes.

"I'm a gov'ment officer," said Dick, "sent by the mayor to collect your taxes. I'll take it in apples just to oblige. That big red one will about pay what you're owin' to the gov'ment."

"I don't know nothing about no taxes," said the old woman, in bewilderment.

"Then," said Dick, "I'll let you off this time. Give us two of your best apples, and my friend here, the President of the Common Council, will pay you."

Frank smiling, paid three cents apiece for the apples, and they sauntered on, Dick remarking, "If these apples ain't good, old lady, we'll return 'em, and get our money back." This would have been rather difficult in his case, as the apple was already half consumed.

Chatham Street, where they wished to go, being on the East side, the two boys crossed the Park. This is an enclosure of about ten acres, which years ago was covered with a green sward,[1] but is now a great thoroughfare for pedestrians and contains several important public buildings. Dick pointed out the City Hall, the Hall of Records, and the Rotunda. The former is a white building of large size, and surmounted by a cupola.

"That's where the mayor's office is," said Dick. "Him and me are very good friends. I once blacked his boots by partic'lar appointment. That's the way I pay my city taxes."

CHAPTER 5

Chatham Street and Broadway

THEY were soon in Chatham Street, walking between rows of ready-made clothing shops, many of which had half their stock in trade exposed on the sidewalk. The proprietors of these establishments stood at the doors, watching attentively the passersby, extending urgent invitations to any who even glanced at the goods, to enter.

"Walk in, young gentlemen," said a stout man, at the entrance of one shop.

---

1 *a green sward*   greensward, an area of grassy turf.

"No, I thank you," replied Dick, "as the fly said to the spider."

"We're selling off at less than cost."

"Of course you be. That's where you makes your money," said Dick. "There ain't nobody of any enterprise that pretends to make any profit on his goods."

The Chatham Street trader looked after our hero as if he didn't quite comprehend him; but Dick, without waiting for a reply, passed on with his companion.

In some of the shops auctions seemed to be going on.

"I am only offered two dollars, gentlemen, for this elegant pair of doeskin pants, made of the very best of cloth. It's a frightful sacrifice. Who'll give an eighth? Thank you, sir. Only seventeen shillings! Why the cloth cost more by the yard!"

This speaker was standing on a little platform haranguing to three men, holding in his hand meanwhile a pair of pants very loose in the legs, and presenting a cheap Bowery look.

Frank and Dick paused before the shop door, and finally saw them knocked down to rather a verdant-looking individual[1] at three dollars.

"Clothes seem to be pretty cheap here," said Frank.

"Yes, but Baxter Street is the cheapest place."

"Is it?"

"Yes. Johnny Nolan got a whole rig-out there last week, for a dollar—coat, cap, vest, pants, and shoes. They was very good measure, too, like my best clothes that I took off to oblige you."

"I shall know where to come for clothes next time," said Frank, laughing. "I had no idea the city was so much cheaper than the country. I suppose the Baxter Street tailors are fashionable?"

"In course they are. Me and Horace Greeley[2] always go there for clothes. When Horace gets a new suit, I always have one made just like it; but I can't go the white hat. It ain't becomin' to my style of beauty."

A little farther on a man was standing out on the sidewalk, distributing small printed handbills. One was handed to Frank, which he read as follows—

"GRAND CLOSING-OUT SALE!—A variety of Beautiful and Costly Articles for Sale, at a Dollar apiece. Unparalleled Inducements! Walk in, Gentlemen!"

"Whereabouts is this sale?" asked Frank.

"In here, young gentlemen," said a black-whiskered individual, who appeared suddenly on the scene. "Walk in."

"Shall we go in, Dick?"

"It's a swindlin' shop," said Dick, in a low voice. "I've been there. That man's a reg'lar cheat. He's seen me before, but he don't know me coz of my clothes."

"Step in and see the articles," said the man, persuasively. "You needn't buy, you know."

"Are all the articles worth more'n a dollar?" asked Dick.

"Yes," said the other, "and some worth a great deal more."

"Such as what?"

"Well, there's a silver pitcher worth twenty dollars."

"And you sell it for a dollar. That's very kind of you," said Dick, innocently.

"Walk in, and you'll understand it."

---

1 *knocked down to a rather verdant-looking individual* sold to a "green" or inexperienced-looking person.

2 *Horace Greeley* (1811–1872) American journalist and politician.

"No, I guess not," said Dick. "My servants is so dishonest that I wouldn't like to trust 'em with a silver pitcher. Come along, Frank. I hope you'll succeed in your charitable enterprise of supplyin' the public with silver pitchers at nineteen dollars less than they are worth."

"How does he manage, Dick?" asked Frank, as they went on.

"All his articles are numbered, and he makes you pay a dollar, and then shakes some dice, and whatever the figgers come to, is the number of the article you draw. Most of 'em ain't worth sixpence."

A hat and cap store being close at hand, Dick and Frank went in. For seventy-five cents, which Frank insisted on paying, Dick succeeded in getting quite a neat-looking cap, which corresponded much better with his appearance than the one he had on. The last, not being considered worth keeping, Dick dropped on the sidewalk, from which, on looking back, he saw it picked up by a brother boot-black who appeared to consider it better than his own.

They retraced their steps and went up Chambers Street to Broadway. At the corner of Broadway and Chambers Street is a large white marble warehouse, which attracted Frank's attention.

"What building is that?" he asked, with interest.

"That belongs to my friend. A. T. Stewart," said Dick. "It's the biggest store on Broadway.* If I ever retire from boot-blackin', and go into mercantile pursuits, I may buy him out, or build another store that'll take the shine off this one."

"Were you ever in the store?" asked Frank.

"No," said Dick; "but I'm intimate with one of Stewart's partners. He is a cash boy, and does nothing but take money all day."

"A very agreeable employment," said Frank, laughing.

"Yes," said Dick, "I'd like to be in it."

The boys crossed to the West side of Broadway, and walked slowly up the street. To Frank it was a very interesting spectacle. Accustomed to the quiet of the country, there was something fascinating in the crowds of people thronging the sidewalks, and the great variety of vehicles constantly passing and repassing in the street. Then again the shop-windows with their multifarious contents interested and amused him, and he was constantly checking Dick to look in at some well-stocked window.

"I don't see how so many shopkeepers can find people enough to buy of them," he said. "We haven't got but two stores in our village, and Broadway seems to be full of them."

"Yes," said Dick; "and it's pretty much the same in the avenoos, 'specially the Third, Sixth, and Eighth avenoos. The Bowery, too, is a great place for shoppin'. There everybody sells cheaper'n anybody else, and nobody pretends to make no profit on their goods."

"Where's Barnum's Museum?" asked Frank.

"Oh, that's down nearly opposite the Astor House," said Dick. "Didn't you see a great building with lots of flags?"

"Yes."

"Well, that's Barnum's.** That's where the Happy Family live, and the lions, and bears, and curiosities generally. It's a tip-top place. Haven't you ever been there? It's most as good as the Old Bowery, only the plays isn't quite so excitin'."

---

*Mr. Stewart's Tenth Street store was not open at the time Dick spoke.
**Since destroyed by fire, and rebuilt farther up Broadway, and again burned down in February.

"I'll go if I get time," said Frank. "There is a boy at home who came to New York a month ago, and went to Barnum's, and has been talking about it ever since, so I suppose it must be worth seeing."

"They've got a great play at the Old Bowery now," pursued Dick. " 'Tis called the 'Demon of the Danube.' The Demon falls in love with a young woman, and drags her by the hair up to the top of a steep rock where his castle stands."

"That's a queer way of showing his love," said Frank, laughing.

"She didn't want to go with him, you know, but was in love with another chap. When he heard about his girl bein' carried off, he felt awful, and swore an oath not to rest till he had got her free. Well, at last he got into the castle by some underground passage, and he and the Demon had a fight. Oh, it was bully seein' 'em roll round on the stage, cuttin' and slashin' at each other."

"And which got the best of it?"

"At first the Demon seemed to be ahead, but at last the young Baron got him down, and struck a dagger into his heart, sayin', 'Die, false and perjured villain! The dogs shall feast upon thy carcass!' and then the Demon give an awful howl and died. Then the Baron seized his body, and threw it over the precipice."

"It seems to me the actor who plays the Demon ought to get extra pay, if he has to be treated that way."

"That's so," said Dick; "but I guess he's used to it. It seems to agree with his constitution."

"What building is that?" asked Frank, pointing to a structure several rods back from the street, with a large yard in front. It was an unusual sight for Broadway, all the other buildings in that neighborhood being even with the street.

"That is the New York Hospital," said Dick. "They're a rich institution, and take care of sick people on very reasonable terms."

"Did you ever go in there?"

"Yes," said Dick; "there was a friend of mine, Johnny Mullen, he was a news-boy, got run over by a omnibus as he was crossin' Broadway down near Park Place. He was carried to the Hospital, and me and some of his friends paid his board while he was there. It was only three dollars a week, which was very cheap, considerin' all the care they took of him. I got leave to come and see him while he was here. Everything looked so nice and comfortable, that I thought a little of coaxin' a omnibus driver to run over me, so I might go there too."

"Did your friend have to have his leg cut off?" asked Frank, interested.

"No," said Dick; "though there was a young student there that was very anxious to have it cut off; but it wasn't done, and Johnny is around the streets as well as ever."

While this conversation was going on they reached No. 365, at the corner of Franklin Street.*

"That's Taylor's Saloon," said Dick. "When I come into a fortun' I shall take my meals there reg'lar."

"I have heard of it very often," said Frank. "It is said to be very elegant. Suppose we go in and take an ice-cream. It will give us a chance to see it to better advantage."

"Thank you," said Dick; "I think that's the most agreeable way of seein' the place myself."

---

*Now the office of the Merchants' Union Express Company.

The boys entered, and found themselves in a spacious and elegant saloon, resplendent with gilding, and adorned on all sides by costly mirrors. They sat down to a small table with a marble top, and Frank gave the order.

"It reminds me of Aladdin's palace," said Frank, looking about him.

"Does it?" said Dick; "he must have had plenty of money."

"He had an old lamp, which he had only to rub, when the Slave of the Lamp would appear, and do whatever he wanted."

"That must have been a valooable lamp. I'd be willin' to give all my Erie shares for it."

There was a tall, gaunt individual at the next table, who apparently heard this last remark of Dick's. Turning towards our hero, he said, "May I inquire, young man, whether you are largely interested in this Erie Railroad?"

"I haven't got no property except what's invested in Erie," said Dick, with a comical side-glance at Frank.

"Indeed! I suppose the investment was made by your guardian."

"No," said Dick; "I manage my property myself."

"And I presume your dividends have not been large?"

"Why, no," said Dick; "you're about right there. They haven't."

"As I supposed. It's poor stock. Now, my young friend, I can recommend a much better investment, which will yield you a large annual income. I am agent of the Excelsior Copper Mining Company, which possesses one of the most productive mines in the world. It's sure to yield fifty per cent. on the investment. Now, all you have to do is to sell out your Erie shares, and invest in our stock, and I'll insure you a fortune in three years. How many shares did you say you had?"

"I didn't say, that I remember," said Dick. "Your offer is very kind and obligin', and as soon as I get time I'll see about it."

"I hope you will," said the stranger. "Permit me to give you my card. 'Samuel Snap, No.—Wall Street.' I shall be most happy to receive a call from you, and exhibit the maps of our mine. I should be glad to have you mention the matter also to your friends. I am confident you could do no greater service than to induce them to embark in our enterprise."

"Very good," said Dick.

Here the stranger left the table, and walked up to the desk to settle his bill.

"You see what it is to be a man of fortun', Frank," said Dick, "and wear good clothes. I wonder what that chap'll say when he sees me blackin' boots to-morrow in the street?"

"Perhaps you earn your money more honorably than he does, after all," said Frank. "Some of these mining companies are nothing but swindles, got up to cheat people out of their money."

"He's welcome to all he gets out of me," said Dick.

CHAPTER 6

Up Broadway to Madison Square

As the boys pursued their way up Broadway, Dick pointed out the prominent hotels and places of amusement. Frank was particularly struck with the imposing fronts of the St. Nicholas and Metropolitan Hotels, the former of white marble, the latter of a subdued brown hue, but not less elegant in its internal appointments. He was not surprised to be informed that each of these splendid structures cost with the furnishing not far from a million dollars.

At Eighth Street Dick turned to the right, and pointed out the Clinton Hall Building now occupied by the Mercantile Library, comprising at that time over fifty thousand volumes.*

A little farther on they came to a large building standing by itself just at the opening of Third and Fourth Avenues, and with one side on each.

"What is that building?" asked Frank.

"That's the Cooper Institute," said Dick; "built by Mr. Cooper, a particular friend of mine. Me and Peter Cooper used to go to school together."

"What is there inside?" asked Frank.

"There's a hall for public meetins' and lectures in the basement, and a readin' room and a picture gallery up above," said Dick.

Directly opposite Cooper Institute, Frank saw a very large building of brick, covering about an acre of ground.

"Is that a hotel?" he asked.

"No," said Dick; "that's the Bible House. It's the place where they make Bibles. I was in there once,—saw a big pile of 'em."

"Did you ever read the Bible?" asked Frank, who had some idea of the neglected state of Dick's education.

"No," said Dick; "I've heard it's a good book, but I never read one. I ain't much on readin'. It makes my head ache."

"I suppose you can't read very fast."

"I can read the little words pretty well, but the big ones is what stick me."

"If I lived in the city, you might come every evening to me, and I would teach you."

"Would you take so much trouble about me?" asked Dick, earnestly.

"Certainly; I should like to see you getting on. There isn't much chance of that if you don't know how to read and write."

"You're a good feller," said Dick, gratefully. "I wish you did live in New York. I'd like to know somethin'. Whereabouts do you live?"

"About fifty miles off, in a town on the left bank of the Hudson. I wish you'd come up and see me sometime. I would like to have you come and stop two or three days."

"Honor bright?"

"I don't understand."

"Do you mean it?" asked Dick, incredulously.

"Of course I do. Why shouldn't I?"

"What would your folks say if they knowed you asked a boot-black to visit you?"

"You are none the worse for being a boot-black, Dick."

"I ain't used to genteel society," said Dick. "I shouldn't know how to behave."

"Then I could show you. You won't be a boot-black all your life, you know."

"No," said Dick; "I'm goin' to knock off when I get to be ninety."

"Before that, I hope," said Frank, smiling.

"I really wish I could get somethin' else to do," said Dick, soberly. "I'd like to be a office boy, and learn business, and grow up 'spectable."

"Why don't you try, and see if you can't get a place, Dick?"

---

*Now not far from one hundred thousand.

"Who'd take Ragged Dick?"

"But you ain't ragged now, Dick."

"No," said Dick; "I look a little better than I did in my Washington coat and Louis Napoleon pants. But if I got in a office, they wouldn't give me more'n three dollars a week, and I couldn't live 'spectable on that."

"No, I suppose not," said Frank, thoughtfully. "But you would get more at the end of the first year."

"Yes," said Dick; "but by that time I'd be nothin' but skin and bones."

Frank laughed. "That reminds me," he said, "of the story of an Irishman, who, out of economy, thought he would teach his horse to feed on shavings. So he provided the horse with a pair of green spectacles which made the shavings look eatable. But unfortunately, just as the horse got learned, he up and died."

"The hoss must have been a fine specimen of architectur' by the time he got through," remarked Dick.

"Whereabouts are we now?" asked Frank, as they emerged from Fourth Avenue into Union Square.

"That is Union Park," said Dick, pointing to a beautiful enclosure, in the centre of which was a pond, with a fountain playing.

"Is that the statue of General Washington?" asked Frank, pointing to a bronze equestrian statue on a granite pedestal.

"Yes," said Dick; "he's growed some since he was President. If he'd been as tall as that when he fit in the Revolution, he'd have walloped the Britishers some, I reckon."

Frank looked up at the statue, which is fourteen and a half feet high, and acknowledged the justice of Dick's remark.

"How about the coat, Dick?" he asked. "Would it fit you?"

"Well, it might be rather loose," said Dick, "I ain't much more'n ten feet high with my boots off."

"No, I should think not," said Frank, smiling. "You're a queer boy, Dick."

"Well, I've been brought up queer. Some boys is born with a silver spoon in their mouth. Victoria's boys is born with a gold spoon, set with di'monds; but gold and silver was scarce when I was born, and mine was pewter."

"Perhaps the gold and silver will come by and by, Dick. Did you ever hear of Dick Whittington?"

"Never did. Was he a Ragged Dick?"

"I shouldn't wonder if he was. At any rate he was very poor when he was a boy, but he didn't stay so. Before he died, he became Lord Mayor of London."

"Did he?" asked Dick, looking interested. "How did he do it?"

"Why, you see, a rich merchant took pity on him, and gave him a home in his own house, where he used to stay with the servants, being employed in little errands. One day the merchant noticed Dick picking up pins and needles that had been dropped, and asked him why he did it. Dick told him he was going to sell them when he got enough. The merchant was pleased with his saving disposition, and when soon after, he was going to send a vessel to foreign parts, he told Dick he might send anything he pleased in it, and it should be sold to his advantage. Now Dick had nothing in the world but a kitten which had been given him a short time before."

"How much taxes did he have to pay on it?" asked Dick.

"Not very high, probably. But having only the kitten, he concluded to send it along. After sailing a good many months, during which the kitten grew up to be a strong cat, the ship touched at an island never before known, which happened to be infested with rats and mice to such an extent that they worried everybody's life out, and even ransacked the king's palace. To make a long story short, the captain, seeing how matters stood, brought Dick's cat ashore, and she soon made the rats and mice scatter. The king was highly delighted when he saw what havoc she made among the rats and mice, and resolved to have her at any price. So he offered a great quantity of gold for her, which, of course, the captain was glad to accept. It was faithfully carried back to Dick, and laid the foundation of his fortune. He prospered as he grew up, and in time became a very rich merchant, respected by all, and before he died was elected Lord Mayor of London."

"That's a pretty good story," said Dick; "but I don't believe all the cats in New York will ever make me mayor."

"No, probably not, but you may rise in some other way. A good many distinguished men have once been poor boys. There's hope for you, Dick, if you'll try."

"Nobody ever talked to me so before," said Dick. "They just called me Ragged Dick, and told me I'd grow up to be a vagabone (boys who are better educated need not be surprised at Dick's blunders) and come to the gallows."

"Telling you so won't make it turn out so, Dick. If you'll try to be somebody, and grow up into a respectable member of society, you will. You may not become rich—it isn't everybody that becomes rich, you know—but you can obtain a good position, and be respected."

"I'll try," said Dick, earnestly. "I needn't have been Ragged Dick so long if I hadn't spent my money in goin' to the theatre, and treatin' boys to oysterstews, and bettin' money on cards, and such like."

"Have you lost money that way?"

"Lots of it. One time I saved up five dollars to buy me a new rig-out, cos my best suit was all in rags, when Limpy Jim wanted me to play a game with him."

"Limpy Jim?" said Frank, interrogatively.

"Yes, he's lame; that's what makes us call him Limpy Jim."

"I suppose you lost?"

"Yes, I lost every penny, and had to sleep out, cos I hadn't a cent to pay for lodgin'. 'Twas a awful cold night, and I got most froze."

"Wouldn't Jim let you have any of the money he had won to pay for a lodging?"

"No; I axed him for five cents, but he wouldn't let me have it."

"Can you get lodging for five cents?" asked Frank, in surprise.

"Yes," said Dick, "but not at the Fifth Avenue Hotel. That's it right out there."

CHAPTER 7

The Pocket-book

THEY had reached the junction of Broadway and of Fifth Avenue. Before them was a beautiful park of ten acres. On the left-hand side was a large marble building, presenting a fine appearance with its extensive white front. This was the building at which Dick pointed.

"Is that the Fifth Avenue Hotel?" asked Frank. "I've heard of it often. My Uncle William always stops there when he comes to New York."

"I once slept on the outside of it," said Dick. "They was very reasonable in their charges, and told me I might come again."

"Perhaps sometime you'll be able to sleep inside," said Frank.

"I guess that'll be when Queen Victoria goes to the Five Points[1] to live."

"It looks like a palace," said Frank. "The queen needn't be ashamed to live in such a beautiful building as that."

Though Frank did not know it, one of the queen's palaces is far from being as fine a looking building as the Fifth Avenue Hotel. St. James' Palace is a very ugly-looking brick structure, and appears much more like a factory than like the home of royalty. There are few hotels in the world as fine-looking as this democratic institution.

At that moment a gentleman passed them on the sidewalk, who looked back at Dick, as if his face seemed familiar.

"I know that man," said Dick, after he had passed. "He's one of my customers."

"What is his name?"

"I don't know."

"He looked back as if he thought he knew you."

"He would have knowed me at once if it hadn't been for my new clothes," said Dick. "I don't look much like Ragged Dick now."

"I suppose your face looked familiar."

"All but the dirt," said Dick, laughing. "I don't always have the chance of washing my face and hands in the Astor House."

"You told me," said Frank, "that there was a place where you could get lodging for five cents. Where's that?"

"It's the News-boys' Lodgin' House, on Fulton Street," said Dick, "up over the 'Sun' office. It's a good place. I don't know what us boys would do without it. They give you supper for six cents, and a bed for five cents more."

"I suppose some boys don't even have the five cents to pay,—do they?"

"They'll trust the boys," said Dick. "But I don't like to get trusted. I'd be ashamed to get trusted for five cents, or ten either. One night I was comin' down Chatham Street, with fifty cents in my pocket. I was goin' to get a good oyster-stew, and then go to the lodgin' house; but somehow it slipped through a hole in my trowses-pocket, and I hadn't a cent left. If it had been summer I shouldn't have cared, but it's rather tough stayin' out winter nights."

Frank, who had always possessed a good home of his own, found it hard to realize that the boy who was walking at his side had actually walked the streets in the cold without a home, or money to procure the common comfort of a bed.

"What did you do?" he asked, his voice full of sympathy.

"I went to the 'Times' office. I knowed one of the pressmen, and he let me set down in a corner, where I was warm, and I soon got fast asleep."

"Why don't you get a room somewhere, and so always have a home to go to?"

"I dunno," said Dick. "I never thought of it. P'rhaps I may hire a furnished house on Madison Square."

"That's where Flora McFlimsey lived."

"I don't know her," said Dick, who had never read the popular poem of which she is the heroine.

---

1 *the Five Points*   a rough section of New York City.

While this conversation was going on, they had turned into Twenty-fifth Street, and had by this time reached Third Avenue.

Just before entering it, their attention was drawn to the rather singular conduct of an individual in front of them. Stopping suddenly, he appeared to pick up something from the sidewalk, and then looked about him in rather a confused way.

"I know his game," whispered Dick. "Come along and you'll see what it is."

He hurried Frank forward until they overtook the man, who had come to a stand-still.

"Have you found anything?" asked Dick.

"Yes," said the man, "I've found this."

He exhibited a wallet which seemed stuffed with bills, to judge from its plethoric appearance.

"Whew!" exclaimed Dick; "you're in luck."

"I suppose somebody has lost it," said the man, "and will offer a handsome reward."

"Which you'll get."

"Unfortunately I am obliged to take the next train to Boston. That's where I live. I haven't time to hunt up the owner."

"Then I suppose you'll take the pocket-book with you," said Dick, with assumed simplicity.

"I should like to leave it with some honest fellow who would see it returned to the owner," said the man, glancing at the boys.

"I'm honest," said Dick.

"I've no doubt of it," said the other. "Well, young man, I'll make you an offer. You take the pocket-book—"

"All right. Hand it over, then."

"Wait a minute. There must be a large sum inside. I shouldn't wonder if there might be a thousand dollars. The owner will probably give you a hundred dollars reward."

"Why don't you stay and get it?" asked Frank.

"I would, only there is sickness in my family, and I must get home as soon as possible. Just give me twenty dollars, and I'll hand you the pocket-book, and let you make whatever you can out of it. Come, that's a good offer. What do you say?"

Dick was well dressed, so that the other did not regard it as at all improbable that he might possess that sum. He was prepared, however, to let him have it for less, if necessary.

"Twenty dollars is a good deal of money," said Dick, appearing to hesitate.

"You'll get it back, and a good deal more," said the stranger, persuasively.

"I don't know but I shall. What would you do, Frank?"

"I don't know but I would," said Frank, "if you've got the money." He was not a little surprised to think that Dick had so much by him.

"I don't know but I will," said Dick, after some irresolution. "I guess I won't lose much."

"You can't lose anything," said the stranger briskly. "Only be quick, for I must be on my way to the cars. I am afraid I shall miss them now."

Dick pulled out a bill from his pocket, and handed it to the stranger, receiving the pocket-book in return. At that moment a policeman turned the corner, and the stranger, hurriedly thrusting the bill into his pocket, without looking at it, made off with rapid steps.

"What is th...er it's Stewart
"I hope there'st."

Dick laughe...ok, in order to
"I'll risk tha...l by Dick's re-
"But you ga...nake one more
"If I had giv...
"But you di...
"He though...it ain't conve-
"What was ...and stop with
"It was noth...he measles, and
Frank looke...nbs, in gineral,
"You ought
"Didn't he ...at Frank could
"I don't kno...at the dropper
"What do y...
Frank surve...
"Money, and a...lars as a reward
"There ain'...e to go back to
don't believe it...
So saying he...de away with a
out with pieces...
who was unuse...
looked amazed...all my life for
"I knowed h...
there. This wall...
in, and all my o...
"That's the k...
"That's so!" ...
"By hokey!" ...
ag'in. He looks...
By this time ...
Approaching...fter a pause.
pocket-book, yo...
"Beg your pa...t any father or
"Yes, I was."
" 'Cause you...s old. My father
ain't the honor ...as ever heard of
He looked si...
man's temper. A...
upon in return. ...s poor, and they
"Give me bac...r husband went
"Couldn't do...
contents is so va...
likely to come d...but," he contin-
"You gave me...
"It's what I us...
"You've swind...
"I thought it ...
"None of you...e owner; John Jacob
pocket-book, I'll...

...her," said Dick. "I changed my
...a newsboy, and diffused intelli-
...y once in a big speech he made
...e Greeley and James Gordon
...

...in their papers, and people
...e mornin' I was stuck on a lot
...I called out 'GREAT NEWS!
...ent off like hot cakes, and I
...ld remembered me, and said
...ge my business."

..., 'specially about one poor
...lp cryin' to think the queen
...money for the paper."

...was small sales and small
...stock, and didn't want to
...n to pay for a lodgin', I
...But it cost too much to

...onately.

...hungry and cold, with
...ver could do," he added

...lo it."

...day, and hadn't sold any
...n'. With that I bought an
...hen evenin' come I was
...e bread. It made me feel
...nd I thought maybe they
...e me a loaf, and take their
...tches to last three months;
...tandin' at the stove warmin'
...hungry I thought I would
...a big pile I don't think he'd

...man came in ag'in, he said he
...St. Mark's Place. His boy was
...ne he'd give me ten cents if I

would go. My business wasn't very pressin' just then, so I went, and when I come back, I took my pay in bread and cakes. Didn't they taste good, though?"

"So you didn't stay long in the match business Dick?"

"No, I couldn't sell enough to make it pay. Then there was some folks that wanted me to sell cheaper to them; so I couldn't make any profit. There was one old lady—she was rich, too, for she lived in a big brick house—beat me down so, that I didn't make no profit at all; but she wouldn't buy without, and I hadn't sold none that day; so I let her have them. I don't see why rich folks should be so hard upon a poor boy that wants to make a livin'."

"There's a good deal of meanness in the world, I'm afraid, Dick."

"If everybody was like you and your uncle," said Dick, "there would be some chance for poor people. If I was rich I'd try to help 'em along."

"Perhaps you will be rich sometime, Dick."

Dick shook his head.

"I'm afraid all my wallets will be like this," said Dick, indicating the one he had received from the dropper, "and will be full of papers what ain't of no use to anybody except the owner."

"That depends very much on yourself, Dick," said Frank. "Stewart wasn't always rich, you know."

"Wasn't he?"

"When he first came to New York as a young man he was a teacher, and teachers are not generally very rich. At last he went into business, starting in a small way, and worked his way up by degrees. But there was one thing he determined in the beginning; that he would be strictly honorable in all his dealings, and never overreach any one for the sake of making money. If there was a chance for him, Dick, there is a chance for you."

"He knowed enough to be a teacher, and I'm awful ignorant," said Dick.

"But you needn't stay so."

"How can I help it?"

"Can't you learn at school?"

"I can't go to school 'cause I've got my livin' to earn. It wouldn't do me much good if I learned to read and write, and just as I'd got learned I starved to death."

"But are there no night-schools?"

"Yes."

"Why don't you go? I suppose you don't work in the evenings."

"I never cared much about it," said Dick, "and that's the truth. But since I've got to talkin' with you, I think more about it. I guess I'll begin to go."

"I wish you would, Dick. You'll make a smart man if you only get a little education."

"Do you think so?" asked Dick, doubtfully.

"I know so. A boy who has earned his own living ever since he was seven years old must have something in him. I feel very much interested in you, Dick. You've had a hard time of it so far in life, but I think better times are in store. I want you to do well, and I feel sure you can if you only try."

"You're a good fellow," said Dick, gratefully. "I'm afraid I'm a pretty rough customer, but I ain't as bad as some. I mean to turn over a new leaf, and try to grow up 'spectable."

"There've been a great many boys begin as low down as you, Dick, that have grown up respectable and honored. But they had to work pretty hard for it."

"I'm willin' to work hard," said Dick.

"That's a lie!" exclaimed Dick, indignantly.

"Oh, you're in league with him, I dare say," said the woman spitefully. "You're as bad as he is, I'll be bound."

"You're a nice female, you be!" said Dick, ironically.

"Don't you dare to call me a female, sir," said the lady, furiously.

"Why, you ain't a man in disguise, be you?" said Dick.

"You are very much mistaken, madam," said Frank, quietly. "The conductor may search me, if you desire it."

A charge of theft, made in a crowded car, of course made quite a sensation. Cautious passengers instinctively put their hands on their pockets, to make sure that they, too, had not been robbed. As for Frank, his face flushed, and he felt very indignant that he should even be suspected of so mean a crime. He had been carefully brought up, and been taught to regard stealing as low and wicked.

Dick, on the contrary, thought it a capital joke that such a charge should have been made against his companion. Though he had brought himself up, and known plenty of boys and men, too, who would steal, he had never done so himself. He thought it mean. But he could not be expected to regard it as Frank did. He had been too familiar with it in others to look upon it with horror.

Meanwhile the passengers rather sided with the boys. Appearances go a great ways, and Frank did not look like a thief.

"I think you must be mistaken, madam," said a gentleman sitting opposite. "The lad does not look as if he would steal."

"You can't tell by looks," said the lady, sourly. "They're deceitful; villains are generally well dressed."

"Be they?" said Dick. "You'd ought to see me with my Washington coat on. You'd think I was the biggest villain ever you saw."

"I've no doubt you are," said the lady, scowling in the direction of our hero.

"Thank you, ma'am," said Dick. " 'Tisn't often I get such fine compliments."

"None of your impudence," said the lady, wrathfully. "I believe you're the worst of the two."

Meanwhile the car had been stopped.

"How long are we going to stop here?" demanded a passenger, impatiently. "I'm in a hurry, if none of the rest of you are."

"I want my pocket-book," said the lady, defiantly.

"Well, ma'am, I haven't got it, and I don't see as it's doing you any good detaining us all here."

"Conductor, will you call a policeman to search that young scamp?" continued the aggrieved lady. "You don't expect I'm going to lose my money, and do nothing about it."

"I'll turn my pockets inside out if you want me to," said Frank, proudly. "There's no need of a policeman. The conductor, or any one else, may search me."

"Well, youngster," said the conductor, "if the lady agrees, I'll search you."

The lady signified her assent.

Frank accordingly turned his pockets inside out; but nothing was revealed except his own porte-monnaie and a penknife.

"Well, ma'am, are you satisfied?" asked the conductor.

"No, I ain't," said she, decidedly.

"You don't think he's got it still?"

"No, but he's passed it over to his confederate, that boy there that's so full of impudence."

"That's me," said Dick, comically.

"He confesses it," said the lady; "I want him searched."

"All right," said Dick, "I'm ready for the operation, only as I've got valooable property about me be careful not to drop any of my Erie Bonds."

The conductor's hand forthwith dove into Dick's pocket, and drew out a rusty jack-knife, a battered cent, about fifty cents in change, and the capacious pocket-book which he had received from the swindler who was anxious to get back to his sick family in Boston.

"Is that yours, ma'am?" asked the conductor, holding up the wallet which excited some amazement, by its size, among the other passengers.

"It seems to me you carry a large pocket-book for a young man of your age," said the conductor.

"That's what I carry my cash and valooable papers in," said Dick.

"I suppose that isn't yours, ma'am," said the conductor, turning to the lady.

"No," said she, scornfully. "I wouldn't carry round such a great wallet at that. Most likely he's stolen it from somebody else."

"What a prime detective you'd be!" said Dick. "P'rhaps you know who I took it from."

"I don't know but my money's in it," said the lady, sharply. "Conductor, will you open that wallet, and see what there is in it?"

"Don't disturb the valooable papers," said Dick, in a tone of pretended anxiety.

The contents of the wallet excited some amusement among the passengers.

"There don't seem to be much money here," said the conductor, taking out a roll of tissue paper cut out in the shape of bills, and rolled up.

"No," said Dick. "Didn't I tell you them were papers of no valoo to anybody but the owner? If the lady'd like to borrow, I won't charge no interest."

"Where is my money, then?" said the lady, in some discomfiture. "I shouldn't wonder if one of the young scamps had thrown it out of the window."

"You'd better search your pocket once more," said the gentleman opposite. "I don't believe either of the boys is in fault. They don't look to me as if they would steal."

"Thank you, sir," said Frank.

The lady followed out the suggestion, and, plunging her hand once more into her pocket, drew out a small porte-monnaie. She hardly knew whether to be glad or sorry at this discovery. It placed her in rather an awkward position after the fuss she had made, and the detention to which she had subjected the passengers, now, as it proved, for nothing.

"Is that the pocket-book you thought stolen?" asked the conductor.

"Yes," said she, rather confusedly.

"Then you've been keeping me waiting all this time for nothing," he said, sharply. "I wish you'd take care to be sure next time before you make such a disturbance for nothing. I've lost five minutes, and shall not be on time."

"I can't help it," was the cross reply; "I didn't know it was in my pocket."

"It seems to me you owe an apology to the boys you accused of a theft which they have not committed," said the gentleman opposite.

"I shan't apologize to anybody," said the lady, whose temper was not of the best; "least of all to such whipper-snappers as they are."

"Thank you, ma'am," said Dick, comically, "your handsome apology is accepted. It ain't of no consequence, only I didn't like to expose the contents of my valooable pocket-book, for fear it might excite the envy of some of my poor neighbors."

"You're a character," said the gentleman who had already spoken, with a smile.

"A bad character!" muttered the lady.

But it was quite evident that the sympathies of those present were against the lady, and on the side of the boys who had been falsely accused, while Dick's drollery had created considerable amusement.

The cars had now reached Fifty-ninth Street, the southern boundary of the Park, and here our hero and his companion got off.

"You'd better look out for pickpockets, my lad," said the conductor, pleasantly. "That big wallet of yours might prove a great temptation."

"That's so," said Dick. "That's the misfortin' of being rich. Astor and me don't sleep much for fear of burglars breakin' in and robbin' us of our valooable treasures. Sometimes I think I'll give all my money to an Orphan Asylum, and take it out in board. I guess I'd make money by the operation."

While Dick was speaking, the car rolled away, and the boys turned up Fifty-ninth Street, for two long blocks yet separated them from the Park.

CHAPTER 10

Introduces a Victim of Misplaced Confidence

"WHAT a queer chap you are, Dick!" said Frank laughing. "You always seem to be in good spirits."

"No, I ain't always. Sometimes I have the blues."

"When?"

"Well, once last winter it was awful cold, and there was big holes in my shoes, and my gloves and all my warm clothes was at the tailor's. I felt as if life was sort of tough, and I'd like it if some rich man would adopt me, and give me plenty to eat and drink and wear, without my havin' to look so sharp after it. Then agin' when I've seen boys with good homes, and fathers, and mothers, I've thought I'd like to have somebody to care for me."

Dick's tone changed as he said this, from his usual levity, and there was a touch of sadness in it. Frank, blessed with a good home and indulgent parents, could not help pitying the friendless boy who had found life such up-hill work.

"Don't say you have no one to care for you, Dick," he said, lightly laying his hand on Dick's shoulder. "I will care for you."

"Will you?"

"If you will let me."

"I wish you would," said Dick, earnestly. "I'd like to feel that I have one friend who cares for me."

Central Park was now before them, but it was far from presenting the appearance which it now exhibits. It had not been long since work had been commenced upon it, and it was still very rough and unfinished. A rough tract of land, two miles and a half from north to south, and a half a mile broad, very rocky in parts, was the material from which the Park Commissioners have made the present beautiful enclosure. There were no houses of good appearance near it, buildings being limited mainly to rude temporary huts used by the workmen who were employed in improving it. The time will undoubtedly come when the Park will be surrounded by elegant residences, and compare favorably in this respect with the most attractive parts of any city in the world. But at the time when Frank and Dick visited it, not much could be said in favor either of the Park or its neighborhood.

"If this is Central Park," said Frank, who naturally felt disappointed, "I don't think much of it. My father's got a large pasture that is much nicer."

"It'll look better some time," said Dick. "There ain't much to see now but rocks. We will take a walk over it if you want to."

"No," said Frank, "I've seen as much of it as I want to. Besides, I feel tired."

"Then we'll go back. We can take the Sixth Avenue cars. They will bring us out at Vesey Street, just beside the Astor House."

"All right," said Frank. "That will be the best course. I hope," he added, laughing, "our agreeable lady friend won't be there. I don't care about being accused of *stealing* again."

"She was a tough one," said Dick. "Wouldn't she make a nice wife for a man that likes to live in hot water, and didn't mind bein' scalded two or three times a day?"

"Yes, I think she'd just suit him. Is that the right car, Dick?"

"Yes, jump in, and I'll follow."

The Sixth Avenue is lined with stores, many of them of very good appearance, and would make a very respectable principal street for a good-sized city. But it is only one of several long business streets which run up the island, and illustrate the extent and importance of the city to which they belong.

No incidents worth mentioning took place during their ride down town. In about three-quarters of an hour the boys got out of the car beside the Astor House.

"Are you goin' in now, Frank?" asked Dick.

"That depends upon whether you have anything else to show me."

"Wouldn't you like to go to Wall Street?"

"That's the street where there are so many bankers and brokers,—isn't it?"

"Yes, I s'pose you ain't afraid of bulls and bears,—are you?"

"Bulls and bears?" repeated Frank, puzzled.

"Yes."

"What are they?"

"The bulls is what tries to make the stocks go up, and the bears is what try to growl 'em down."

"Oh, I see. Yes, I'd like to go."

Accordingly they walked down on the west side of Broadway as far as Trinity Church, and then, crossing, entered a street not very wide or very long, but of very great importance. The reader would be astonished if he could know the amount of money involved in the transactions which take place in a single day in this street. It would be found that although Broadway is much greater in length, and lined with stores, it stands second to Wall Street in this respect.

"What is that large marble building?" asked Frank, pointing to a massive structure on the corner of Wall and Nassau Streets. It was in the form of a parallelogram, two hundred feet long by ninety wide, and about eighty feet in height, the ascent to the entrance being by eighteen granite steps.

"That's the Custom House," said Dick.

"It looks like pictures I've seen of the Parthenon at Athens," said Frank, meditatively.

"Where's Athens?" asked Dick. "It ain't in York State,—is it?"

"Not the Athens I mean, at any rate. It is in Greece, and was a famous city two thousand years ago."

"I believe your name is Ephraim Smith," continued Dick.

"You're mistaken," said the man, and was about to move off.

"Stop a minute," said Dick. "Don't you keep your money in the Washington Bank?"

"I don't know any such bank. I'm in a hurry, young man, and I can't stop to answer any foolish questions."

The boat had by this time reached the Brooklyn pier, and Mr. Ephraim Smith seemed in a hurry to land.

"Look here," said Dick, significantly; "you'd better not go on shore unless you want to jump into the arms of a policeman."

"What do you mean?" asked the man, startled.

"That little affair of yours is known to the police," said Dick; "about how you got fifty dollars out of a greenhorn on a false check, and it mayn't be safe for you to go ashore."

"I don't know what you're talking about," said the swindler with affected boldness, though Dick could see that he was ill at ease.

"Yes you do," said Dick. "There isn't but one thing to do. Just give me back that money, and I'll see that you're not touched. If you don't, I'll give you up to the first p'liceman we meet."

Dick looked so determined, and spoke so confidently, that the other, overcome by his fears, no longer hesitated, but passed a roll of bills to Dick and hastily left the boat.

All this Frank witnessed with great amazement, not understanding what influence Dick could have obtained over the swindler sufficient to compel restitution.

"How did you do it?" he asked eagerly.

"I told him I'd exert my influence with the president to have him tried by *habeas corpus*,"[1] said Dick.

"And of course that frightened him. But tell me, without joking, how you managed."

Dick gave a truthful account of what occurred, and then said, "Now we'll go back and carry the money."

"Suppose we don't find the poor countryman?"

"Then the p'lice will take care of it."

They remained on board the boat, and in five minutes were again in New York. Going up Wall Street, they met the countryman a little distance from the Custom House. His face was marked with the traces of deep anguish; but in his case even grief could not subdue the cravings of appetite. He had purchased some cakes of one of the old women who spread out for the benefit of passers-by an array of apples and seed-cakes, and was munching them with melancholy satisfaction.

"Hilloa!" said Dick. "Have you found your money?"

"No," ejaculated the young man, with a convulsive gasp. "I shan't ever see it again. The mean skunk's cheated me out of it. Consarn his picter!"[2] It took me most six months to save it up. I was workin' for Deacon Pinkham in our place. Oh, I wish I'd never come to New York! The deacon, he told me he'd keep it for me; but I wanted to put it in the bank, and now it's all gone, boo hoo!"

---

1 *habeas corpus*   Latin for "you should have the body"; refers to a legal document used to release someone from unlawful restraint and bring him before a judge. Dick uses the term jokingly.

2 *consarn his picter*   "curse his false appearance."

And the miserable youth, having despatched his cakes, was so overcome by the thought of his loss that he burst into tears.

"I say," said Dick, "dry up, and see what I've got here."

The youth no sooner saw the roll of bills, and comprehended that it was indeed his lost treasure, than from the depths of anguish he was exalted to the most ecstatic joy. He seized Dick's hand, and shook it with so much energy that our hero began to feel rather alarmed for its safety.

" 'Pears to me you take my arm for a pump-handle," said he. "Couldn't you show your gratitood some other way? It's just possible I may want to use my arm ag'in some time."

The young man desisted, but invited Dick most cordially to come up and stop a week with him at his country home, assuring him that he wouldn't charge him anything for board.

"All right!" said Dick. "If you don't mind I'll bring my wife along, too. She's delicate, and the country air might do her good."

Jonathan stared at him in amazement, uncertain whether to credit the fact of his marriage. Dick walked on with Frank, leaving him in an apparent state of stupefaction, and it is possible that he has not yet settled the affair to his satisfaction.

"Now," said Frank, "I think I'll go back to the Astor House. Uncle has probably got through his business and returned."

"All right," said Dick.

The two boys walked up to Broadway, just where the tall steeple of Trinity faces the street of bankers and brokers, and walked leisurely to the hotel. When they arrived at the Astor House, Dick said, "Good-by, Frank."

"Not yet," said Frank; "I want you to come in with me."

Dick followed his young patron up the steps. Frank went to the reading-room, where, as he had thought probable, he found his uncle already arrived, and reading a copy of "The Evening Post," which he had just purchased outside.

"Well, boys," he said, looking up, "have you had a pleasant jaunt?"

"Yes, sir," said Frank. "Dick's a capital guide."

"So this is Dick," said Mr. Whitney, surveying him with a smile. "Upon my word, I should hardly have known him. I must congratulate him on his improved appearance."

"Frank's been very kind to me," said Dick, who, rough street-boy as he was, had a heart easily touched by kindness, of which he had never experienced much. "He's a tip-top fellow."

"I believe he is a good boy," said Mr. Whitney. "I hope, my lad, you will prosper and rise in the world. You know in this free country poverty in early life is no bar to a man's advancement. I haven't risen very high myself," he added, with a smile, "but have met with moderate success in life; yet there was a time when I was as poor as you."

"Were you, sir?" asked Dick, eagerly.

"Yes, my boy, I have known the time when I have been obliged to go without my dinner because I didn't have enough money to pay for it."

"How did you get up in the world?" asked Dick, anxiously.

"I entered a printing-office as an apprentice, and worked for some years. Then my eyes gave out and I was obliged to give that up. Not knowing what else to do, I went into the country, and worked on a farm. After a while I was lucky enough to invent a machine, which has brought me in a great deal of money. But there was one thing I got while I was in the printing-office which I value more than money."

"What was that, sir?"

"A taste for reading and study. During my leisure hours I improved myself by study, and acquired a large part of the knowledge which I now possess. Indeed, it was one of my books that first put me on the track of the invention, which I afterwards made. So you see, my lad, that my studious habits paid me in money, as well as in another way."

"I'm awful ignorant," said Dick, soberly.

"But you are young, and, I judge, a smart boy. If you try to learn, you can, and if you ever expect to do anything in the world, you must know something of books."

"I will," said Dick, resolutely. "I ain't always goin' to black boots for a livin'."

"All labor is respectable, my lad, and you have no cause to be ashamed of any honest business; yet when you can get something to do that promises better for your future prospects, I advise you to do so. Till then earn your living in the way you are accustomed to, avoid extravagance, and save up a little money if you can."

"Thank you for your advice," said our hero. "There ain't many that takes an interest in Ragged Dick."

"So that's your name," said Mr. Whitney. "If I judge you rightly, it won't be long before you change it. Save your money, my lad, buy books, and determine to be somebody, and you may yet fill an honorable position."

"I'll try," said Dick. "Good-night, sir."

"Wait a minute, Dick," said Frank. "Your blacking-box and old clothes are upstairs. You may want them."

"In course," said Dick. "I couldn't get along without my best clothes, and my stock in trade."

"You may go up to the room with him, Frank," said Mr. Whitney. "The clerk will give you the key. I want to see you, Dick, before you go."

"Yes, sir," said Dick.

"Where are you going to sleep to-night, Dick?" asked Frank, as they went upstairs together.

"P'r'aps at the Fifth Avenue Hotel—on the outside," said Dick.

"Haven't you any place to sleep, then?"

"I slept in a box, last night."

"In a box?"

"Yes, on Spruce Street."

"Poor fellow!" said Frank, compassionately.

"Oh, 'twas a bully bed—full of straw! I slept like a top."

"Don't you earn enough to pay for a room, Dick?"

"Yes," said Dick; "only I spend my money foolish, goin' to the Old Bowery, and Tony Pastor's, and sometimes gamblin' in Baxter Street."

"You won't gamble any more,—will you, Dick?" said Frank, laying his hand persuasively on his companion's shoulder.

"No, I won't," said Dick.

"You'll promise?"

"Yes, and I'll keep it. You're a good feller. I wish you was goin' to be in New York."

"I am going to a boarding-school in Connecticut. The name of the town is Barnton. Will you write to me, Dick?"

"My writing would look like hens' tracks," said our hero.

"Never mind. I want you to write. When you write you can tell me how to direct, and I will send you a letter."

"I wish you would," said Dick. "I wish I was more like you."

"I hope you will make a much better boy, Dick. Now we'll go in to my uncle. He wishes to see you before you go."

They went into the reading-room. Dick had wrapped up his blacking-brush in a newspaper with which Frank had supplied him, feeling that a guest of the Astor House should hardly be seen coming out of the hotel displaying such a professional sign.

"Uncle, Dick's ready to go," said Frank.

"Good-by, my lad," said Mr. Whitney. "I hope to hear good accounts of you sometime. Don't forget what I have told you. Remember that your future position depends mainly upon yourself, and that it will be high or low as you choose to make it."

He held out his hand, in which was a five-dollar bill. Dick shrunk back.

"I don't like to take it," he said. "I haven't earned it."

"Perhaps not," said Mr. Whitney; "but I give it to you because I remember my own friendless youth. I hope it may be of service to you. Sometime when you are a prosperous man, you can repay it in the form of aid to some poor boy, who is struggling upward as you are now."

"I will, sir," said Dick, manfully.

He no longer refused the money, but took it gratefully, and, bidding Frank and his uncle good-by, went out into the street. A feeling of loneliness came over him as he left the presence of Frank, for whom he had formed a strong attachment in the few hours he had known him.

CHAPTER 12

Dick Hires a Room on Mott Street

GOING out into the fresh air Dick felt the pangs of hunger. He accordingly went to a restaurant and got a substantial supper. Perhaps it was the new clothes he wore, which made him feel a little more aristocratic. At all events, instead of patronizing the cheap restaurant where he usually procured his meals, he went into the refectory attached to Lovejoy's Hotel, where the prices were higher and the company more select. In his ordinary dress, Dick would have been excluded, but now he had the appearance of a very respectable, gentlemanly boy, whose presence would not discredit any establishment. His orders were therefore received with attention by the waiter and in due time a good supper was placed before him.

"I wish I could come here every day," thought Dick. "It seems kind o' nice and 'spectable, side of the other place. There's a gent at that other table that I've shined boots for more'n once. He don't know me in my new clothes. Guess he don't know his boot-black patronizes the same establishment."

His supper over, Dick went up to the desk, and, presenting his check, tendered in payment his five-dollar bill, as if it were one of a large number which he possessed. Receiving back his change he went out into the street.

Two questions now arose: How should he spend the evening, and where should he pass the night? Yesterday, with such a sum of money in his possession, he would have answered both questions readily. For the evening, he would have passed it at the Old Bowery, and gone to sleep in any out-of-the-way place that offered. But he had turned over a new leaf, or resolved to do so. He meant to save his money for some useful purpose,—to aid his advancement in the world. So he could not afford the theatre. Besides, with his new clothes, he was unwilling to pass the night out of doors.

"I should spile 'em," he thought, "and that wouldn't pay."

So he determined to hunt up a room which he could occupy regularly, and consider as his own, where he could sleep nights, instead of depending on boxes and old wagons for a chance shelter. This would be the first step towards respectability, and Dick determined to take it.

He accordingly passed through the City Hall Park, and walked leisurely up Centre Street.

He decided that it would hardly be advisable for him to seek lodgings in Fifth Avenue, although his present cash capital consisted of nearly five dollars in money, besides the valuable papers contained in his wallet. Besides, he had reason to doubt whether any in his line of business lived on that aristocratic street. He took his way to Mott Street, which is considerably less pretentious, and halted in front of a shabby brick lodging-house kept by a Mrs. Mooney, with whose son Tom, Dick was acquainted.

Dick rang the bell, which sent back a shrill metallic response.

The door was opened by a slatternly servant, who looked at him inquiringly, and not without curiosity. It must be remembered that Dick was well dressed, and that nothing in his appearance bespoke his occupation. Being naturally a good-looking boy, he might readily be mistaken for a gentleman's son.

"Well, Queen Victoria," said Dick, "is your missus at home?"

"My name's Bridget," said the girl.

"Oh, indeed!" said Dick. "You looked so much like the queen's picter what she gave me last Christmas in exchange for mine, that I couldn't help calling you by her name."

"Oh, go along wid ye!" said Bridget. "It's makin' fun ye are."

"If you don't believe me," said Dick, gravely, "all you've got to do is to ask my partic'lar friend, the Duke of Newcastle."

"Bridget!" called a shrill voice from the basement.

"The missus is calling me," said Bridget, hurriedly. "I'll tell her ye want her."

"All right!" said Dick.

The servant descended into the lower regions, and in a short time a stout, red-faced woman appeared on the scene.

"Well, sir, what's your wish?" she asked.

"Have you got a room to let?" asked Dick.

"Is it for yourself you ask?" questioned the woman, in some surprise.

Dick answered in the affirmative.

"I haven't got any very good rooms vacant. There's a small room in the third story."

"I'd like to see it," said Dick.

"I don't know as it would be good enough for you," said the woman, with a glance at Dick's clothes.

"I ain't very partic'lar about accommodations," said our hero. "I guess I'll look at it."

Dick followed the landlady up two narrow staircases, uncarpeted and dirty, to the third landing, where he was ushered into a room about ten feet square. It could not be considered a very desirable apartment. It had once been covered with an oilcloth carpet, but this was now very ragged, and looked worse than none. There was a single bed in the corner, covered with an indiscriminate heap of bed-clothing, rumpled and not over-clean. There was a bureau, with the veneering scratched and in some parts stripped off, and a small glass, eight inches by ten, cracked across the middle; also two chairs in rather a disjointed condition. Judging from Dick's appearance, Mrs. Mooney thought he would turn from it in disdain.

But it must be remembered that Dick's past experience had not been of a character to make him fastidious. In comparison with a box, or an empty wagon, even this little room seemed comfortable. He decided to hire it if the rent proved reasonable.

"Well, what's the tax?" asked Dick.

"I ought to have a dollar a week," said Mrs. Mooney, hesitatingly.

"Say seventy-five cents, and I'll take it," said Dick.

"Every week in advance?"

"Yes."

"Well, as times is hard, and I can't afford to keep it empty, you may have it. When will you come?"

"To-night," said Dick.

"It ain't lookin' very neat. I don't know as I can fix it up to-night."

"Well, I'll sleep here to-night, and you can fix it up to-morrow."

"I hope you'll excuse the looks. I'm a lone woman, and my help is so shiftless, I have to look after everything myself; so I can't keep things as straight as I want to."

"All right!" said Dick.

"Can you pay me the first week in advance?" asked the landlady, cautiously.

Dick responded by drawing seventy-five cents from his pocket, and placing it in her hand.

"What's your business, sir, if I may inquire?" said Mrs. Mooney.

"Oh, I'm professional!" said Dick.

"Indeed!" said the landlady, who did not feel much enlightened by this answer.

"How's Tom?" asked Dick.

"Do you know my Tom?" said Mrs. Mooney in surprise. "He's gone to sea,—to Californy. He went last week."

"Did he?" said Dick. "Yes, I knew him."

Mrs. Mooney looked upon her new lodger with increased favor, on finding that he was acquainted with her son, who, by the way, was one of the worst young scamps in Mott Street, which is saying considerable.

"I'll bring over my baggage from the Astor House this evening," said Dick in a tone of importance.

"From the Astor House!" repeated Mrs. Mooney, in fresh amazement.

"Yes, I've been stoppin' there a short time with some friends," said Dick.

Mrs. Mooney might be excused for a little amazement at finding that a guest from the Astor House was about to become one of her lodgers—such transfers not being common.

"Did you say you was purfessional?" she asked.

"Yes, ma'am," said Dick, politely.

"You ain't a—a—" Mrs. Mooney paused, uncertain what conjecture to hazard.

"Oh, no, nothing of the sort," said Dick, promptly. "How could you think so, Mrs. Mooney?"

"No offense, sir," said the landlady, more perplexed than ever.

"Certainly not," said our hero. "But you must excuse me now, Mrs. Mooney, as I have business of great importance to attend to."

"You'll come round this evening?"

Dick answered in the affirmative, and turned away.

"I wonder what he is!" thought the landlady, following him with her eyes as he crossed the street. "He's got good clothes on, but he don't seem very particular about his room. Well; I've got all my rooms full now. That's one comfort."

Dick felt more comfortable now that he had taken the decisive step of hiring a lodging, and paying a week's rent in advance. For seven nights he was sure of a shelter and a bed to sleep in. The thought was a pleasant one to our young vagrant, who hitherto had seldom known when he rose in the morning where he should find a resting-place at night.

"I must bring my traps[1] round," said Dick to himself. "I guess I'll go to bed early to-night. It'll feel kinder good to sleep in a reg'lar bed. Boxes is rather hard to the back, and ain't comfortable in case of rain. I wonder what Johnny Nolan would say if he knew I'd got a room of my own."

CHAPTER 13

Micky Maguire

ABOUT nine o'clock Dick sought his new lodgings. In his hands he carried his professional wardrobe, namely, the clothes which he had worn at the commencement of the day, and the implements of his business. These he stowed away in the bureau drawers, and by the light of a flickering candle took off his clothes and went to bed. Dick had a good digestion and a reasonably good conscience; consequently he was a good sleeper. Perhaps, too, the soft feather bed conduced to slumber. At any rate his eyes were soon closed, and he did not awake until half-past six the next morning.

He lifted himself on his elbow, and stared around him in transient bewilderment.

"Blest if I hadn't forgot where I was," he said to himself. "So this is my room, is it? Well, it seems kind of 'spectable to have a room and a bed to sleep in. I'd orter be able to afford seventy-five cents a week. I've throwed away more money than that in one evenin'. There ain't no reason why I shouldn't live 'spectable. I wish I knowed as much as Frank. He's a tip-top feller. Nobody ever cared enough for me before to give me good advice. It was kicks, and cuffs, and swearin' at me all the time. I'd like to show him I can do something."

While Dick was indulging in these reflections, he had risen from bed, and, finding an accession to the furniture of his room, in the shape of an ancient wash-stand bearing a cracked bowl and broken pitcher, indulged himself in the rather unusual ceremony of a good wash. On the whole, Dick preferred to be clean, but it was not always easy to gratify his desire. Lodging in the street as he had been accustomed to do, he had had no opportunity to perform his toilet in the customary manner. Even now he found himself unable to arrange his dishevelled locks, having neither comb nor brush. He determined to purchase a comb, at least, as soon as possible, and a brush too, if he could get one cheap. Meanwhile he combed his hair with his fingers as well as he could, though the result was not quite so satisfactory as it might have been.

---

1 *traps* personal belongings.

A question now came up for consideration. For the first time in his life Dick possessed two suits of clothes. Should he put on the clothes Frank had given him, or resume his old rags?

Now, twenty-four hours before, at the time Dick was introduced to the reader's notice, no one could have been less fastidious as to his clothing than he. Indeed, he had rather a contempt for good clothes, or at least he thought so. But now, as he surveyed the ragged and dirty coat and the patched pants, Dick felt ashamed of them. He was unwilling to appear in the streets with them. Yet, if he went to work in his new suit, he was in danger of spoiling it, and he might not have it in his power to purchase a new one. Economy dictated a return to the old garments. Dick tried them on, and surveyed himself in the cracked glass; but the reflection did not please him.

"They don't look 'spectable," he decided; and forthwith taking them off again, he put on the new suit of the day before.

"I must try to earn a little more," he thought, "to pay for my room, and to buy some new clo'es when these is wore out."

He opened the door of his chamber, and went downstairs and into the street, carrying his blacking-box with him.

It was Dick's custom to commence his business before breakfast; generally it must be owned, because he began the day penniless, and must earn his meal before he ate it. To-day it was different. He had four dollars left in his pocket-book; but this he had previously determined not to touch. In fact he had formed the ambitious design of starting an account at a savings' bank, in order to have something to fall back upon in case of sickness or any other emergency, or at any rate as a reserve fund to expend in clothing or other necessary articles when he required them. Hitherto he had been content to live on from day to day without a penny ahead; but the new vision of respectability which now floated before Dick's mind, owing to his recent acquaintance with Frank, was beginning to exercise a powerful effect upon him.

In Dick's profession as in others there are lucky days, when everything seems to flow prosperously. As if to encourage him in his new-born resolution, our hero obtained no less than six jobs in the course of an hour and a half. This gave him sixty cents, quite abundant to purchase his breakfast, and a comb besides. His exertions made him hungry, and, entering a small eating-house he ordered a cup of coffee and a beefsteak. To this he added a couple of rolls. This was quite a luxurious breakfast for Dick, and more expensive than he was accustomed to indulge himself with. To gratify the curiosity of my young readers, I will put down the items with their cost—

Coffee, ... 5 cts.
Beefsteak, ... 15
A couple of rolls, ... 5
_____25 cts.

It will thus be seen that our hero had expended nearly one-half of his morning's earnings. Some days he had been compelled to breakfast on five cents, and then he was forced to content himself with a couple of apples, or cakes. But a good breakfast is a good preparation for a busy day, and Dick sallied forth from the restaurant lively and alert, ready to do a good stroke of business.

Dick's change of costume was liable to lead to one result of which he had not thought. His brother boot-blacks might think he had grown aristocratic, and was putting on airs,—that, in fact, he was getting above his business, and desirous to outshine his associates. Dick had not dreamed of this, because in fact, in spite of his new-born ambition, he entertained no such feelings. There was nothing of what boys call "big-feeling" about him. He was a thorough democrat, using the word not politically, but in its proper sense, and was disposed to fraternize with all whom he styled "good fellows," without regard to their position. It may seem a little unnecessary to some of my readers to make this explanation; but they must remember that pride and "big-feeling" are confined to no age or class, but may be found in boys as well as men, and in boot-blacks as well as those of a higher rank.

The morning being a busy time with the boot-blacks, Dick's changed appearance had not as yet attracted much attention. But when business slackened a little, our hero was destined to be reminded of it.

Among the down-town boot-blacks was one hailing from the Five Points,—a stout, red-haired, freckled-faced boy of fourteen, bearing the name of Micky Maguire. This boy, by his boldness and recklessness, as well as by his personal strength, which was considerable, had acquired an ascendency among his fellow professionals, and had a gang of subservient followers, whom he led on to acts of ruffianism, not unfrequently terminating in a month or two at Blackwell's Island. Micky himself had served two terms there; but the confinement appeared to have had very little effect in amending his conduct, except, perhaps, in making him a little more cautious about an encounter with the "copps," as the members of the city police are, for some unknown reason, styled among the Five-Point boys.

Now Micky was proud of his strength, and of the position of leader which it had secured him. Moreover he was democratic in his tastes, and had a jealous hatred of those who wore good clothes and kept their faces clean. He called it putting on airs, and resented the implied superiority. If he had been fifteen years older, and had a trifle more education, he would have interested himself in politics, and been prominent at ward meetings, and a terror to respectable voters on election day. As it was, he contented himself with being the leader of a gang of young ruffians, over whom he wielded a despotic power.

Now it is only justice to Dick to say that, so far as wearing good clothes was concerned, he had never hitherto offended the eyes of Micky Maguire. Indeed, they generally looked as if they patronized the same clothing establishment. On this particular morning it chanced that Micky had not been very fortunate in a business way, and, as a natural consequence, his temper, never very amiable, was somewhat ruffled by the fact. He had had a very frugal breakfast,—not because he felt abstemious, but owing to the low state of his finances. He was walking along with one of his particular friends, a boy nick-named Limpy Jim, so called from a slight peculiarity in his walk, when all at once he espied our friend Dick in his new suit.

"My eyes!" he exclaimed, in astonishment; "Jim, just look at Ragged Dick. He's come into a fortun', and turned gentleman. See his new clothes."

"So he has," said Jim. "Where'd he get 'em, I wonder?"

"Hooked 'em, p'r'aps. Let's go and stir him up a little. We don't want no gentlemen on our beat. So he's puttin' on airs,—is he? I'll give him a lesson."

So saying the two boys walked up to our hero, who had not observed them, his back being turned, and Micky Maguire gave him a smart slap on the shoulder.

Dick turned round quickly.

CHAPTER 14

A Battle and a Victory

"WHAT'S that for?" demanded Dick, turning round to see who had struck him.

"You're gettin' mighty fine!" said Micky Maguire, surveying Dick's new clothes with a scornful air.

There was something in his words and tone, which Dick, who was disposed to stand up for his dignity, did not at all relish.

"Well, what's the odds if I am?" he retorted. "Does it hurt you any?"

"See him put on airs, Jim," said Micky, turning to his companion. "Where'd you get them clo'es?"

"Never mind where I got 'em. Maybe the Prince of Wales gave 'em to me."

"Hear him, now, Jim," said Micky. "Most likely he stole 'em."

"Stealin' ain't in *my* line."

It might have been unconscious the emphasis which Dick placed on the word "my." At any rate Micky chose to take offence.

"Do you mean to say *I* steal?" he demanded, doubling up his fist, and advancing towards Dick in a threatening manner.

"I don't say anything about it," answered Dick, by no means alarmed at this hostile demonstration. "I know you've been to the island twice. P'r'aps 'twas to make a visit along of the Mayor and Aldermen. Maybe you was a innocent victim of oppression. I ain't a goin' to say."

Mickey's freckled face grew red with wrath, for Dick had only stated the truth.

"Do you mean to insult me?" he demanded shaking the fist already doubled up in Dick's face. "Maybe you want a lickin'?"

"I ain't partic'larly anxious to get one," said Dick, coolly. "They don't agree with my constitution which is nat'rally delicate. I'd rather have a good dinner than a lickin' any time."

"You're afraid," sneered Micky. "Isn't he, Jim?"

"In course he is."

"P'r'aps I am," said Dick, composedly, "but it don't trouble me much."

"Do you want to fight?" demanded Micky, encouraged by Dick's quietness, fancying he was afraid to encounter him.

"No, I don't" said Dick. "I ain't fond of fightin'. It's a very good amusement, and very bad for the complexion, 'specially for the eyes and nose, which is apt to run red, white, and blue."

Micky misunderstood Dick, and judged from the tenor of his speech that he would be an easy victim. As he knew, Dick very seldom was concerned in any street fight,—not from cowardice, as he imagined—but because he had too much good sense to do so. Being quarrelsome, like all bullies, and supposing that he was more than a match for our hero, being about two inches taller, he could no longer resist an inclination to assault him, and tried to plant a blow in Dick's face which would have hurt him considerably if he had not drawn back just in time.

Now, though Dick was far from quarrelsome, he was ready to defend himself on all occasions, and it was too much to expect that he would stand quiet and allow himself to be beaten.

He dropped his blacking-box on the instant, and returned Micky's blow with such good effect that the young bully staggered back, and would have fallen, if he had not been propped up by his confederate, Limpy Jim.

"Go in, Micky!" shouted the latter, who was rather a coward on his own account, but liked to see others fight. "Polish him off, that's a good feller."

Micky was now boiling over with rage and fury, and required no urging. He was fully determined to make a terrible example of poor Dick. He threw himself upon him, and strove to bear him to the ground; but Dick, avoiding a close hug, in which he might possibly have got the worst of it, by an adroit movement, tripped up his antagonist, and stretched him on the sidewalk.

"Hit him, Jim!" exclaimed Micky, furiously.

Limpy Jim did not seem inclined to obey orders. There was a quiet strength and coolness about Dick, which alarmed him. He preferred that Micky should incur all the risks of battle, and accordingly set himself to raising his fallen comrade.

"Come, Micky," said Dick, quietly, "you'd better give it up. I wouldn't have touched you if you hadn't hit me first. I don't want to fight. It's low business."

"You're afraid of hurtin' your clo'es," said Micky, with a sneer.

"Maybe I am," said Dick. "I hope I haven't hurt yours."

Micky's answer to this was another attack, as violent and impetuous as the first. But his fury was in the way. He struck wildly, not measuring his blows, and Dick had no difficulty in turning aside, so that his antagonist's blow fell upon the empty air, and his momentum was such that he nearly fell forward headlong. Dick might readily have taken advantage of his unsteadiness, and knocked him down; but he was not vindictive, and chose to act on the defensive, except when he could not avoid it.

Recovering himself, Micky saw that Dick was a more formidable antagonist than he had supposed, and was meditating another assault, better planned, which by its impetuosity might bear our hero to the ground. But there was an unlooked-for interference.

"Look out for the 'copp,' " said Jim, in a low voice.

Micky turned round and saw a tall policeman heading towards him, and thought it might be prudent to suspend hostilities. He accordingly picked up his blacking-box, and hitching up his pants, walked off, attended by Limpy Jim.

"What's that chap been doing?" asked the policeman of Dick.

"He was amoosin' himself by pitchin' into me," replied Dick.

"What for?"

"He didn't like it 'cause I patronized a different tailor from him."

"Well, it seems to me you *are* dressed pretty smart for a boot-black," said the policeman.

"I wish I wasn't a boot-black," said Dick.

"Never mind, my lad. It's an honest business," said the policeman, who was a sensible man and a worthy citizen. "It's an honest business. Stick to it till you get something better."

"I mean to," said Dick. "It ain't easy to get out of it, as the prisoner remarked, when he was asked how he liked his residence."

"I hope you don't speak from experience."

"No," said Dick; "I don't mean to get into prison if I can help it."

"Do you see that gentleman over there?" asked the officer, pointing to a well-dressed man who was walking on the other side of the street.

"Yes."

"Well, he was once a newsboy."

"And what is he now?"

"He keeps a bookstore, and is quite prosperous."

Dick looked at the gentleman with interest, wondering if he should look as respectable when he was a grown man.

It will be seen that Dick was getting ambitious. Hitherto he had thought very little of the future, but was content to get along as he could, dining as well as his means would allow, and spending the evenings in the pit of the Old Bowery, eating peanuts between the acts if he was prosperous, and if unlucky supping on dry bread or an apple, and sleeping in an old box or a wagon. Now, for the first time, he began to reflect that he could not black boots all his life. In seven years he would be a man, and, since his meeting with Frank, he felt he would like to be a respectable man. He could see and appreciate the difference between Frank and such a boy as Micky Maguire, and it was not strange that he preferred the society of the former.

In the course of the next morning, in pursuance of his new resolutions for the future, he called at a savings bank, and held out four dollars in bills besides another dollar in change. There was a high railing, and a number of clerks busily writing at desks behind it. Dick, never having been in a bank before, did not know where to go. He went, by mistake, to the desk where money was paid out.

"Where's your book?" asked the clerk.

"I haven't got any."

"Have you any money deposited here?"

"No, sir, I want to leave some here."

"Then go to the next desk."

Dick followed directions, and presented himself before an elderly man with gray hair, who looked at him over the rims of his spectacles.

"I want you to keep that for me," said Dick, awkwardly emptying his money out on the desk.

"How much is there?"

"Five dollars."

"Have you got an account here?"

"No, sir."

"Of course you can write?"

The "of course" was said on account of Dick's neat dress.

"Have I got to do any writing?" asked our hero, a little embarrassed.

"We want you to sign your name in this book," and the old gentleman shoved round a large folio volume containing the names of depositors.

Dick surveyed the book with some awe.

"I ain't much on writin'," he said.

"Very well, write as well as you can."

The pen was put into Dick's hand, and, after dipping it in the inkstand, he succeeded after a hard effort, accompanied by many contortions of the face, in inscribing upon the book of the bank the name

Dick Hunter.

"Dick!—that means Richard, I suppose," said the bank officer, who had some difficulty in making out the signature.

"No; Ragged Dick is what folks call me."

"You don't look very ragged."

"No, I've left my rags to home. They might get wore out if I used 'em too common."

"Well, my lad, I'll make out a book in the name of Dick Hunter, since you seem to prefer Dick to Richard. I hope you will save up your money and deposit more with us."

Our hero took his bank-book, and gazed on the entry "Five Dollars" with a new sense of importance. He had been accustomed to joke about Erie shares, but now, for the first time, he felt himself a capitalist; on a small scale, to be sure, but still it was no small thing for Dick to have five dollars which he could call his own. He firmly determined that he would lay by every cent he could spare from his earnings towards the fund he hoped to accumulate.

But Dick was too sensible not to know that there was something more than money needed to win a respectable position in the world. He felt that he was very ignorant. Of reading and writing he only knew the rudiments, and that, with a slight acquaintance with arithmetic, was all he did know of books. Dick knew he must study hard, and he dreaded it. He looked upon learning as attended with greater difficulties than it really possesses. But Dick had good pluck. He meant to learn, nevertheless, and resolved to buy a book with his first spare earnings.

When Dick went home at night he locked up his bank-book in one of the drawers of the bureau. It was wonderful how much more independent he felt whenever he reflected upon the contents of that drawer, and with what an important air of joint ownership he regarded the bank building in which his small savings were deposited.

CHAPTER 15

Dick Secures a Tutor

THE next morning Dick was unusually successful, having plenty to do, and receiving for one job twenty-five cents,—the gentleman refusing to take change. Then flashed upon Dick's mind the thought that he had not yet returned the change due to the gentleman whose boots he had blacked on the morning of his introduction to the reader.

"What'll he think of me?" said Dick to himself. "I hope he won't think I'm mean enough to keep the money."

Now Dick was scrupulously honest, and though the temptation to be otherwise had often been strong, he had always resisted it. He was not willing on any account to keep money which did not belong to him, and he immediately started for 125 Fulton Street (the address which had been given him) where he found Mr. Greyson's name on the door of an office on the first floor.

The door being open, Dick walked in.

"Is Mr. Greyson in?" he asked of a clerk who sat on a high stool before a desk.

"Not just now. He'll be in soon. Will you wait?"

"Yes," said Dick.

"Very well; take a seat then."

Dick sat down and took up the morning "Tribune," but presently came to a word of four syllables, which he pronounced to himself a "sticker," and laid it down. But he had not long to wait, for five minutes later Mr. Greyson entered.

"Did you wish to speak to me, my lad?" said he to Dick, whom in his new clothes he did not recognize.

"Yes, sir," said Dick. "I owe you some money."

"Indeed!" said Mr. Greyson, pleasantly; "that's an agreeable surprise. I didn't know but you had come for some. So you are a debtor of mine, and not a creditor?"

"I believe that's right," said Dick, drawing fifteen cents from his pocket, and placing in Mr. Greyson's hand.

"Fifteen cents!" repeated he, in some surprise. "How do you happen to be indebted to me in that amount?"

"You gave me a quarter for a-shinin' your boots, yesterday mornin', and couldn't wait for the change. I meant to have brought it before, but I forgot all about it till this mornin'."

"It had quite slipped my mind also. But you don't look like the boy I employed. If I remember rightly he wasn't as well dressed as you."

"No," said Dick. "I was dressed for a party, then, but the clo'es was too well ventilated to be comfortable in cold weather."

"You're an honest boy," said Mr. Greyson. "Who taught you to be honest?"

"Nobody," said Dick. "But it's mean to cheat and steal. I've always knowed that."

"Then you've got ahead of some of our business men. Do you read the Bible?"

"No," said Dick. "I've heard it's a good book, but I don't know much about it."

"You ought to go to some Sunday School. Would you be willing?"

"Yes," said Dick, promptly. "I want to grow up 'spectable. But I don't know where to go."

"Then I'll tell you. The church I attend is at the corner of Fifth Avenue and Twenty-first Street."

"I've seen it," said Dick.

"I have a class in the Sunday School there. If you'll come next Sunday, I'll take you into my class, and do what I can to help you."

"Thank you," said Dick, "but p'r'aps you'll get tired of teaching me. I'm awful ignorant."

"No, my lad," said Mr. Greyson, kindly. "You evidently have some good principles to start with, as you have shown by your scorn of dishonesty. I shall hope good things of you in the future."

"Well, Dick," said our hero, apostrophizing himself, as he left the office; "you're gettin' up in the world. You've got money invested, and are goin' to attend church, by particular invitation, on Fifth Avenue. I shouldn't wonder much if you should find cards, when you get home, from the Mayor, requestin' the honor of your company to dinner, along with other distinguished guests."

Dick felt in very good spirits. He seemed to be emerging from the world in which he had hitherto lived, into a new atmosphere of respectability, and the change seemed very pleasant to him.

At six o'clock Dick went into a restaurant on Chatham Street, and got a comfortable supper. He had been so successful during the day that, after paying for this, he still had ninety cents left. While he was despatching his supper, another boy came in, smaller and slighter than Dick, and sat down beside him. Dick recognized him as a boy who three months before had entered the ranks of the boot-blacks, but who, from a natural timidity, had not been able to earn much. He was ill-fitted for the coarse companionship of the street boys, and shrank from the rude jokes of his present associates. Dick had never troubled him; for our hero had a certain chivalrous feeling which would not allow him to bully or disturb a younger and weaker boy than himself.

"How are you, Fosdick?" said Dick, as the other seated himself.

"Pretty well," said Fosdick. "I suppose you're all right."

"Oh, yes, I'm right side up with care. I've been havin' a bully supper. What are you goin' to have?"

"Some bread and butter."

"Why don't you get a cup o' coffee?"

"Why," said Fosdick, reluctantly, "I haven't got money enough to-night."

"Never mind," said Dick; "I'm in luck to-day. I'll stand treat."

"That's kind in you," said Fosdick, gratefully.

"Oh, never mind that," said Dick.

Accordingly he ordered a cup of coffee, and a plate of beef-steak, and was gratified to see that his young companion partook of both with evident relish. When the repast was over, the boys went out into the street together, Dick passing at the desk to settle for both suppers.

"Where are you going to sleep to-night, Fosdick?" asked Dick, as they stood on the sidewalk.

"I don't know," said Fosdick, a little sadly. "In some door-way, I expect. But I'm afraid the police will find me out, and make me move on."

"I'll tell you what," said Dick, "you must go home with me. I guess my bed will hold two."

"Have you got a room?" asked the other, in surprise.

"Yes," said Dick, rather proudly, and with a little excusable exultation. "I've got a room over on Mott Street; there I can receive my friends. That'll be better than sleepin' in a door-way,—won't it?"

"Yes, indeed it will," said Fosdick. "How lucky I was to come across you! It comes hard to me living as I do. When my father was alive I had every comfort."

"That's more'n I ever had," said Dick. "But I'm goin' to try to live comfortable now. Is your father dead?"

"Yes," said Fosdick, sadly. "He was a printer; but he was drowned one dark night from a Fulton ferry-boat, and, as I had no relations in the city, and no money, I was obliged to go to work as quick as I could. But I don't get on very well."

"Didn't you have no brothers nor sisters?" asked Dick.

"No," said Fosdick; "father and I used to live alone. He was always so much company to me that I feel very lonesome without him. There's a man out West somewhere that owes him two thousand dollars. He used to live in the city, and father lent him all his money to help him go into business; but he failed, or pretended to, and went off. If father hadn't lost that money he would have left me well off; but no money would have made up his loss to me."

"What's the man's name that went off with your father's money?"

"His name is Hiram Bates."

"P'r'aps you'll get the money again, sometime."

"There isn't much chance of it," said Fosdick. "I'd sell out my chances of that for five dollars."

"Maybe I'll buy you out some time," said Dick. "Now, come round and see what sort of a room I've got. I used to go to the theatre evenings, when I had money; but now I'd rather go to bed early, and have a good sleep."

"I don't care much about theatres," said Fosdick. "Father didn't use to let me go very often. He said it wasn't good for boys."

"I like to go to the Old Bowery sometimes. They have tip-top plays there. Can you read and write well?" he asked, as a sudden thought came to him.

"Yes," said Fosdick. "Father always kept me at school when he was alive, and I stood pretty well in my classes. I was expecting to enter at the Free Academy* next year."

"Then I'll tell you what," said Dick; "I'll make a bargain with you. I can't read much more'n a pig; and my writin' looks like hens' tracks. I don't want to grow up knowin' no more'n a four-year-old boy. If you'll teach me readin' and writin' evenin's, you shall sleep in my room every night. That'll be better'n door-steps or old boxes, where I've slept many a time."

"Are you in earnest?" said Fosdick, his face lighting up hopefully.

"In course I am," said Dick. "It's fashionable for young gentlemen to have private tootors to introduce 'em into the flower-beds of literatoor and science, and why should't I foller the fashion? You shall be my perfessor; only you must promise not to be very hard if my writin' looks like a rail-fence or a bender."

"I'll try not to be too severe," said Fosdick, laughing. "I shall be thankful for such a chance to get a place to sleep. Have you got anything to read out of?"

"No," said Dick. "My extensive and well-selected library was lost overboard in a storm, when I was sailin' from the Sandwich Islands to the desert of Sahara. But I'll buy a paper. That'll do me a long time."

Accordingly Dick stopped at a paper-stand, and bought a copy of a weekly paper, filled with the usual variety of reading matter,—stories, sketches, poems, etc.

They soon arrived at Dick's lodging-house. Our hero, procuring a lamp from the landlady, led the way into his apartment, which he entered with the proud air of a proprietor.

"Well, how do you like it, Fosdick?" he asked, complacently.

The time was when Fosdick would have thought it untidy and not particularly attractive. But he had served a severe apprenticeship in the streets, and it was pleasant to feel himself under shelter, and he was not disposed to be critical.

"It looks very comfortable, Dick," he said.

"The bed ain't very large," said Dick; "but I guess we can get along."

"Oh, yes," said Fosdick, cheerfully. "I don't take up much room."

"Then that's all right. There's two chairs, you see, one for you and one for me. In case the mayor comes in to spend the evenin' socially, he can sit on the bed."

The boys seated themselves, and five minutes later, under the guidance of his young tutor, Dick had commenced his studies.

CHAPTER 16

The First Lesson

FORTUNATELY for Dick, his young tutor was well qualified to instruct him. Henry Fosdick, though only twelve years old, knew as much as many boys of fourteen. He had always been studious and ambitious to excel. His father, being a printer, employed in an office where books were printed, often brought home new books in sheets, which Henry was always glad to read. Mr. Fosdick had been, besides, a subscriber to the Mechanics' Apprentices' Library, which

---

*Now the college of the city of New York.

contains many thousands of well-selected and instructive books. Thus Henry had acquired an amount of general information, unusual in a boy of his age. Perhaps he had devoted too much time to study, for he was not naturally robust. All this, however, fitted him admirably for the office to which Dick had appointed him,—that of his private instructor.

The two boys drew up their chairs to the rickety table, and spread out the paper before them.

"The exercises generally commence with ringing the bell," said Dick; "but as I ain't got none, we'll have to do without."

"And the teacher is generally provided with a rod," said Fosdick. "Isn't there a poker handy, that I can use in case my scholar doesn't behave well?"

"'Taint lawful to use fire-arms," said Dick.

"Now, Dick," said Fosdick, "before we begin, I must find out how much you already know. Can you read any?"

"Not enough to hurt me," said Dick. "All I know about readin' you could put in a nutshell, and there'd be room left for a small family."

"I suppose you know your letters?"

"Yes," said Dick, "I know 'em all, but not intimately. I guess I can call 'em all by name."

"Where did you learn them? Did you ever go to school?"

"Yes; I went two days."

"Why did you stop?"

"It didn't agree with my constitution."

"You don't look very delicate," said Fosdick.

"No," said Dick, "I ain't troubled much that way; but I found lickins didn't agree with me."

"Did you get punished?"

"Awful," said Dick.

"What for?"

"For indulgin' in a little harmless amoosement," said Dick. "You see the boy that was sittin' next to me fell asleep, which I considered improper in school-time; so I thought I'd help the teacher a little by wakin' him up. So I took a pin and stuck into him; but I guess it went a little too far, for he screeched awful. The teacher found out what it was that made him holler, and whipped me with a ruler till I was black and blue. I thought 'twas about time to take a vacation; so that's the last time I went to school."

"You didn't learn to read in that time, of course?"

"No," said Dick; "but I was a newsboy a little while; so I learned a little, just so's to find out what the news was. Sometimes I didn't read straight and called the wrong news. One mornin' I asked another boy what the paper said, and he told me the King of Africa was dead. I thought it was all right till folks began to laugh."

"Well, Dick, if you'll only study well, you won't be liable to make such mistakes."

"I hope so," said Dick. "My friend Horace Greeley told me the other day that he'd get me to take his place now and then when he was off makin' speeches if my edication hadn't been neglected."

"I must find a good piece for you to begin on," said Fosdick, looking over the paper.

"Find an easy one," said Dick, "with words of one story."

Fosdick at length found a piece which he thought would answer. He discovered on trial that Dick had not exaggerated his deficiencies. Words of two syllables he seldom pronounced right, and was much surprised when he was told how "through" was sounded.

"Seems to me it's throwin' away letters to use all them," he said.

"How would you spell it?" asked his young teacher.

"T-h-r-u," said Dick.

"Well," said Fosdick, "there's a good many other words that are spelt with more letters than they need to have. But it's the fashion, and we must follow it."

But if Dick was ignorant, he was quick, and had an excellent capacity. Moreover he had a perseverance, and was not easily discouraged. He had made up his mind he must know more, and was not disposed to complain of the difficulty of his task. Fosdick had occasion to laugh more than once at his ludicrous mistakes; but Dick laughed too, and on the whole both were quite interested in the lesson.

At the end of an hour and a half the boys stopped for the evening

"You're learning fast, Dick," said Fosdick. "At this rate you will soon learn to read well."

"Will I?" asked Dick with an expression of satisfaction. "I'm glad of that. I don't want to be ignorant. I didn't use to care, but I do now. I want to grow up 'spectable."

"So do I, Dick. We will both help each other, and I am sure we can accomplish something. But I am beginning to feel sleepy."

"So am I," said Dick. "Them hard words make my head ache. I wonder who made 'em all?"

"That's more than I can tell. I suppose you've seen a dictionary."

"That's another of 'em. No, I can't say I have, though I may have seen him in the street without knowin' him."

"A dictionary is a book containing all the words in the language."

"How many are there?"

"I don't rightly know; but I think there are about fifty thousand."

"It's a pretty large family," said Dick. "Have I got to learn 'em all?"

"That will not be necessary. There are a large number which you would never find occasion to use."

"I'm glad of that," said Dick; "for I don't expect to live to be more'n a hundred, and by that time I wouldn't be more'n half through."

By this time the flickering lamp gave a decided hint to the boys that unless they made haste they would have to undress in the dark. They accordingly drew off their clothes, and Dick jumped into bed. But Fosdick, before doing so, knelt down by the side of the bed, and said a short prayer.

"What's that for?" asked Dick, curiously.

"I was saying my prayers," said Fosdick, as he rose from his knees. "Don't you ever do it?"

"No," said Dick. "Nobody ever taught me."

"Then I'll teach you. Shall I?"

"I don't know," said Dick, dubiously. "What's the good?"

Fosdick explained as well as he could, and perhaps his simple explanation was better adapted to Dick's comprehension than one from an older person would have been. Dick felt more free to ask questions, and the example of his new friend, for whom he was beginning to feel a warm attachment, had considerable effect upon him. When, therefore, Fosdick asked again if he should teach him a prayer, Dick consented, and his young bedfellow did so. Dick was not naturally irreligious. If he had lived without a knowledge of God and of religious things, it was scarcely to be wondered at in a lad who, from an early age, had been thrown upon his own exertions for the means of living, with no one to care for him or give him good advice. But he was so far good that he could appreciate goodness in others, and this it was that had drawn him to Frank in the first place, and now to Henry Fosdick. He did not, therefore, attempt to ridicule his companion, as some boys better brought up might have done, but was willing to follow his example in what something told him was right. Our young hero had taken an important step towards securing that genuine respectability which he was ambitious to attain.

Weary with the day's work, and Dick perhaps still more fatigued by the unusual mental effort he had made, the boys soon sank into a deep and peaceful slumber, from which they did not awaken till six o'clock the next morning. Before going out Dick sought Mrs. Mooney, and spoke to her on the subject of taking Fosdick as a room-mate. He found that she had no objection, provided he would allow her twenty-five cents a week extra, in consideration of the extra trouble which his companion might be expected to make. To this Dick assented, and the arrangement was definitely concluded.

This over, the two boys went out and took stations near each other. Dick had more of a business turn than Henry, and less shrinking from publicity, so that his earnings were greater. But he had undertaken to pay the entire expenses of the room, and needed to earn more. Sometimes, when two customers presented themselves at the same time, he was able to direct one to his friend. So at the end of the week both boys found themselves with surplus earnings. Dick had the satisfaction of adding two dollars and a half to his deposits in the Savings Bank, and Fosdick commenced an account by depositing seventy-five cents.

On Sunday morning Dick bethought himself of his promise to Mr. Greyson to come to the church on Fifth Avenue. To tell the truth, Dick recalled it with some regret. He had never been inside a church since he could remember, and he was not much attracted by the invitation he had received. But Henry, finding him wavering, urged him to go, and offered to go with him. Dick gladly accepted the offer, feeling that he required some one to lend him countenance under such unusual circumstances.

Dick dressed himself with scrupulous care, giving his shoes a "shine" so brilliant that it did him great credit in a professional point of view, and endeavored to clean his hands thoroughly; but, in spite of all he could do, they were not so white as if his business had been of a different character.

Having fully completed his preparations, he descended into the street, and, with Henry by his side, crossed over to Broadway.

The boys pursued their way up Broadway, which on Sunday presents a striking contrast in its quietness to the noise and confusion of ordinary weekdays, as far as Union Square then turned down Fourteenth Street, which brought them to Fifth Avenue.

"Suppose we dine at Delmonico's," said Fosdick, looking towards that famous restaurant.

"I'd have to sell some of my Erie shares," said Dick.

A short walk now brought them to the church of which mention has already been made. They stood outside, a little abashed, watching the fashionably attired people who were entering, and were feeling a little undecided as to whether they had better enter also, when Dick felt a light touch upon his shoulder.

Turning round, he met the smiling glance of Mr. Greyson.

"So, my young friend, you have kept your promise," he said. "And whom have you brought with you?"

"A friend of mine," said Dick. "His name is Henry Fosdick."

"I am glad you have brought him. Now follow me, and I will give you seats."

CHAPTER 17

Dick's First Appearance in Society

IT WAS the hour for morning service. The boys followed Mr. Greyson into the handsome church, and were assigned seats in his own pew.

There were two persons already seated in it,—a good-looking lady of middle age, and a pretty little girl of nine. They were Mrs. Greyson and her only daughter Ida. They looked pleasantly at the boys as they entered, smiling a welcome to them.

The morning service commenced. It must be acknowledged that Dick felt rather awkward. It was an unusual place for him, and it need not be wondered at that he felt like a cat in a strange garret. He would not have known when to rise if he had not taken notice of what the rest of the audience did, and followed their example. He was sitting next to Ida and as it was the first time he had ever been near so well-dressed a young lady, he naturally felt bashful. When the hymns were announced, Ida found the place, and offered a hymn-book to our hero. Dick took it awkwardly, but his studies had not yet been pursued far enough for him to read the words readily. However, he resolved to keep up appearances, and kept his eyes fixed steadily on the hymn-book.

At length the service was over. The people began to file slowly out of church, and among them, of course, Mr. Greyson's family and the two boys. It seemed very strange to Dick to find himself in such different companionship from what he had been accustomed, and he could not help thinking, "Wonder what Johnny Nolan 'ould say if he could see me now!"

But Johnny's business engagements did not often summon him to Fifth Avenue, and Dick was not likely to be seen by any of his friends in the lower part of the city.

"We have our Sunday school in the afternoon," said Mr. Greyson. "I suppose you live at some distance from here?"

"In Mott Street, sir," answered Dick.

"That is too far to go and return. Suppose you and your friend come and dine with us, and then we can come here together in the afternoon."

Dick was as much astonished at this invitation as if he had really been invited by the Mayor to dine with him and the Board of Aldermen. Mr. Greyson was evidently a rich man, and yet he had actually invited two boot-blacks to dine with him.

"I guess we'd better go home, sir," said Dick, hesitating.

"I don't think you can have any very pressing engagements to interfere with your accepting my invitation," said Mr. Greyson, good-humoredly, for he understood the reasons of Dick's hesitation. "So I take it for granted that you both accept."

Before Dick fairly knew what he intended to do, he was walking down Fifth Avenue with his new friends.

Now, our young hero was not naturally bashful; but he certainly felt so now, especially as Miss Ida Greyson chose to walk by his side, leaving Henry Fosdick to walk with her father and mother.

"What is your name?" asked Ida, pleasantly.

Our hero was about to answer "Ragged Dick," when it occurred to him that in the present company he had better forget his old nickname.

"Dick Hunter," he answered.

"Dick!" repeated Ida. "That means Richard doesn't it?"

"Everybody calls me Dick."

"I have a cousin Dick," said the young lady, sociably. "His name is Dick Wilson. I suppose you don't know him?"

"No," said Dick.

"I like the name of Dick," said the young lady, with charming frankness.

Without being able to tell why, Dick felt rather glad she did. He plucked up courage to ask her name.

"My name is Ida," answered the young lady. "Do you like it?"

"Yes," said Dick. "It's a bully name."

Dick turned red as soon as he had said it, for he felt that he had not used the right expression.

The little girl broke into a silvery laugh.

"What a funny boy you are!" she said.

"I didn't mean, it," said Dick, stammering. "I meant it's a tip-top name."

Here Ida laughed again, and Dick wished himself back in Mott Street.

"How old are you?" inquired Ida, continuing her examination.

"I'm fourteen,—goin' on fifteen," said Dick.

"You're a big boy of your age," said Ida. "My cousin Dick is a year older than you, but he isn't as large."

Dick looked pleased. Boys generally like to be told that they are large of their age.

"How old be you?" asked Dick, beginning to feel more at his ease.

"I'm nine years old," said Ida. "I go to Miss Jarvis's school. I've just begun to learn French. Do you know French?"

"Not enough to hurt me," said Dick.

Ida laughed again, and told him that he was a droll boy.

"Do you like it?" asked Dick.

"I like it pretty well, except the verbs. I can't remember them well. Do you go to school?"

"I'm studying with a private tutor," said Dick.

"Are you? So is my cousin Dick. He's going to college this year. Are you going to college?"

"Not this year."

"Because, if you did, you know you'd be in the same class with my cousin. It would be funny to have two Dicks in one class."

They turned down Twenty-fourth Street, passing the Fifth Avenue Hotel on the left, and stopped before an elegant house with a brown stone front. The bell was rung, and the door being opened, the boys, somewhat abashed, followed Mr. Greyson into a handsome hall. They were told where to hang their hats, and a moment afterwards were ushered into a comfortable dining-room, where a table was spread for dinner.

Dick took his seat on the edge of a sofa, and was tempted to rub his eyes to make sure that he was really awake. He could hardly believe that he was a guest in so fine a mansion.

Ida helped to put the boys at their ease.

"Do you like pictures?" she asked.

"Very much," answered Henry.

The little girl brought a book of handsome engravings, and, seating herself beside Dick, to whom she seemed to have taken a decided fancy, commenced showing them to him.

"There are the Pyramids of Egypt," she said, pointing to one engraving.

"What are they for?" asked Dick, puzzled. "I don't see any winders."

"No," said Ida, "I don't believe anybody lives there. Do they, papa?"

"No, my dear. They are used for the burial of the dead. The largest of them is said to be the loftiest building in the world with one exception. The spire of the Cathedral of Strasburg is twenty-four feet higher, if I remember rightly."

"Is Egypt near here?" asked Dick.

"Oh, no, it's ever so many miles off; about four or five hundred. Didn't you know?"

"No," said Dick. "I never heard."

"You don't appear to be very accurate in your information, Ida," said her mother. "Four or five thousand miles would be considerably nearer the truth."

After a little more conversation they sat down to dinner. Dick seated himself in an embarrassed way. He was very much afraid of doing or saying something which would be considered an impropriety, and had the uncomfortable feeling that everybody was looking at him, and watching his behavior.

"Where do you live, Dick?" asked Ida, familiarly.

"In Mott Street."

"Where is that?"

"More than a mile off."

"Is it a nice street?"

"Not very," said Dick. "Only poor folks live there."

"Are you poor?"

"Little girls should be seen and not heard," said her mother, gently.

"If you are," said Ida, "I'll give you the five-dollar gold-piece aunt gave me for a birthday present."

"Dick cannot be called poor, my child," said Mrs. Greyson, "since he earns his living by his own exertions."

"Do you earn your living?" asked Ida, who was a very inquisitive young lady, and not easily silenced. "What do you do?"

Dick blushed violently. At such a table, and in presence of the servant who was standing at that moment behind his chair, he did not like to say that he was a shoe-black, although he well knew that there was nothing dishonorable in the occupation.

Mr. Greyson perceived his feelings, and to spare them said, "You are too inquisitive, Ida. Some time Dick may tell you, but you know we don't talk of business on Sundays."

Dick in his embarrassment had swallowed a large spoonful of hot soup, which made him turn red in the face. For the second time, in spite of the prospect of the best dinner he had ever eaten, he wished himself back in Mott Street. Henry Fosdick was more easy and unembarrassed than Dick, not having led such a vagabond and neglected life. But it was to Dick that Ida chiefly directed her conversation, having apparently taken a fancy to his frank and handsome face. I believe I have already said that Dick was a very good-looking boy, especially now since he kept his face clean. He had a frank, honest expression, which generally won its way to the favor of those with whom he came in contact.

Dick got along pretty well at the table by dint of noticing how the rest acted, but there was one thing he could not manage, eating with his fork, which, by the way, he thought a very singular arrangement.

At length they arose from the table, somewhat to Dick's relief. Again Ida devoted herself to the boys, and exhibited a profusely illustrated Bible for their entertainment. Dick was interested in looking at the pictures, though he knew very little of their subjects. Henry Fosdick was much better informed; as might have been expected.

When the boys were about to leave the house with Mr. Greyson for the Sunday school, Ida placed her hand on Dick's, and said persuasively, "You'll come again, Dick, won't you?"

"Thank you," said Dick, "I'd like to," and he could not help thinking Ida the nicest girl he had ever seen.

"Yes," said Mrs. Greyson, hospitably, "we shall be glad to see you both here again."

"Thank you very much," said Henry Fosdick, gratefully. "We shall like very much to come."

I will not dwell upon the hour spent in Sunday school, nor upon the remarks of Mr. Greyson to his class. He found Dick's ignorance of religious subjects so great that he was obliged to begin at the beginning with him. Dick was interested in hearing the children sing, and readily promised to come again the next Sunday.

When the service was over Dick and Henry walked homewards. Dick could not help letting his thoughts rest on the sweet little girl who had given him so cordial a welcome, and hoping that he might meet her again.

"Mr. Greyson is a nice man,—isn't he, Dick?" asked Henry, as they were turning into Mott Street, and were already in sight of their lodging-house.

"Ain't he, though?" said Dick. "He treated us just as if we were young gentlemen."

"Ida seemed to take a great fancy to you."

"She's a tip-top girl," said Dick, "but she asked so many questions that I didn't know what to say."

He had scarcely finished speaking, when a stone whizzed by his head, and, turning quickly, he saw Micky Maguire running round the corner of the street which they had just passed.

CHAPTER 18

Micky Maguire's Second Defeat

DICK was no coward. Nor was he in the habit of submitting passively to an insult. When, therefore, he recognized Micky Maguire as his assailant, he instantly turned and gave chase. Micky anticipated pursuit, and ran at his utmost speed. It is doubtful if Dick would have overtaken him, but Micky had the ill luck to trip just as he had entered a narrow alley, and, falling with some violence, received a sharp blow from the hard stones, which made him scream with pain.

"Ow!" he whined. "Don't you hit a feller when he's down."

"What made you fire that stone at me?" demanded our hero, looking down at the fallen bully.

"Just for fun," said Micky.

"It would have been a very agreeable s'prise if it had hit me," said Dick. "S'posin' I fire a rock at you jest for fun."

"Don't!" exclaimed Micky, in alarm.

"It seems you don't like agreeable s'prises," said Dick, "any more'n the man did what got hooked by a cow one mornin, before breakfast. It didn't improve his appetite much."

"I've most broke my arm," said Micky, ruefully, rubbing the affected limb.

"If it's broke you can't fire no more stones, which is a very cheerin' reflection," said Dick. "Ef you haven't money enough to buy a wooden one I'll lend you a quarter. There's one good thing about wooden ones, they ain't liable to get cold in winter, which is another cheerin' reflection."

"I don't want none of yer cheerin' reflections," said Micky, sullenly. "Yer company ain't wanted here."

"Thank you for your polite invitation to leave," said Dick, bowing ceremoniously. "I'm willin' to go, but ef you throw any more stones at me, Micky Maguire, I'll hurt you worse than the stones did."

The only answer made to this warning was a scowl from his fallen opponent. It was quite evident that Dick had the best of it, and he thought it prudent to say nothing.

"As I've got a friend waitin' outside, I shall have to tear myself away," said Dick. "You'd better not throw any more stones, Micky Maguire, for it don't seem to agree with your constitution."

Micky muttered something which Dick did not stay to hear. He backed out of the alley, keeping watchful eye on his fallen foe, and rejoined Henry Fosdick, who was waiting his return.

"Who was it, Dick?" he asked.

"A partic'lar friend of mine, Micky Maguire," said Dick. "He playfully fired a rock at my head as a mark of his 'fection. He loves me like a brother, Micky does."

"Rather a dangerous kind of a friend, I should think," said Fosdick. "He might have killed you."

"I've warned him not to be so 'fectionate another time," said Dick.

"I know him," said Henry Fosdick. "He's at the head of a gang of boys living at the Five-Points. He threatened to whip me once because a gentleman employed me to black his boots instead of him."

"He's been at the Island two or three times for stealing," said Dick. "I guess he won't touch me again. He'd rather get hold of small boys. If he ever does anything to you, Fosdick, just let me know, and I'll give him a thrashing."

Dick was right. Micky Maguire was a bully, and like most bullies did not fancy tackling boys whose strength was equal or superior to his own. Although he hated Dick more than ever, because he thought our hero was putting on airs, he had too lively a remembrance of his strength and courage to venture upon another open attack. He contented himself, therefore, whenever he met Dick, with scowling at him. Dick took this very philosophically, remarking that, "if it was soothin' to Micky's feelings, he might go ahead, as it didn't hurt him much."

It will not be necessary to chronicle the events of the next few weeks. A new life had commenced for Dick. He no longer haunted the gallery of the Old

Bowery; and even Tony Pastor's hospitable doors had lost their old attractions. He spent two hours every evening in study. His progress was astonishingly rapid. He was gifted with a natural quickness; and he was stimulated by the desire to acquire a fair education as a means of "growin' up 'spectable," as he termed it. Much was due also to the patience and perseverance of Henry Fosdick, who made a capital teacher.

"You're improving wonderfully, Dick," said his friend, one evening, when Dick had read an entire paragraph without a mistake.

"Am I?" said Dick, with satisfaction.

"Yes. If you'll buy a writing-book to-morrow, we can begin writing to-morrow evening."

"What else do you know, Henry?" asked Dick.

"Arithmetic, and geography, and grammar."

"What a lot you know!" said Dick, admiringly.

"I don't *know* any of them," said Fosdick. "I've only studied them. I wish I knew a great deal more."

"I'll be satisfied when I know as much as you," said Dick.

"It seems a great deal to you now, Dick, but in a few months you'll think differently. The more you know, the more you'll want to know."

"Then there ain't any end to learnin'?" said Dick.

"No."

"Well," said Dick, "I guess I'll be as much as sixty before I know everything."

"Yes; as old as that, probably," said Fosdick, laughing.

"Anyway, you know too much to be blackin' boots. Leave that to ignorant chaps like me."

"You won't be ignorant long, Dick."

"You'd ought to get into some office or countin'-room."

"I wish I could," said Fosdick, earnestly. "I don't succeed very well at blacking boots. You make a great deal more than I do."

"That's cause I ain't troubled with bashfulness," said Dick. "Bashfulness ain't as natural to me as it is to you. I'm always on hand, as the cat said to the milk. You'd better give up shines, Fosdick, and give your 'tention to mercantile pursuits."

"I've thought of trying to get a place," said Fosdick; "but no one would take me with these clothes;" and he directed his glance to his well-worn suit, which he kept as neat as he could, but which, in spite of all his care, began to show decided marks of use. There was also here and there a stain of blacking upon it, which, though an advertisement of his profession, scarcely added to its good appearance.

"I almost wanted to stay at home from Sunday school last Sunday," he continued, "because I thought everybody would notice how dirty and worn my clothes had got to be."

"If my clothes wasn't two sizes too big for you," said Dick, generously, "I'd change. You'd look as if you'd got into your great-uncle's suit by mistake."

"You're very kind, Dick, to think of changing," said Fosdick, "for your suit is much better than mine; but I don't think that mine would suit you very well. The pants would show a little more of your ankles than is the fashion, and you couldn't eat a very hearty dinner without bursting the buttons off the vest."

"That wouldn't be very convenient," said Dick. "I ain't fond of lacin' to show my elegant figger. But I say," he added with a sudden thought, "how much money have we got in the savings' bank?"

Fosdick took a key from his pocket, and went to the drawer in which the bank-books were kept, and, opening it, brought them out for inspection.

It was found that Dick had the sum of eighteen dollars and ninety cents placed to his credit, while Fosdick had six dollars and forty-five cents. To explain the large difference, it must be remembered that Dick had deposited five dollars before Henry deposited anything, being the amount he had received as a gift from Mr. Whitney.

"How much does that make, the lot of it?" asked Dick. "I ain't much on figgers yet, you know."

"It makes twenty-five dollars and thirty-five cents, Dick," said his companion, who did not understand the thought which suggested the question.

"Take it, and buy some clothes, Henry," said Dick, shortly.

"What, your money too?"

"In course."

"No, Dick, you are too generous. I couldn't think of it. Almost three-quarters of the money is yours. You must spend it on yourself."

"I don't need it," said Dick.

"You may not need it now, but you will some time."

"I shall have some more then."

"That may be; but it wouldn't be fair for me to use your money, Dick. I thank you all the same for your kindness."

"Well, I'll lend it to you, then," persisted Dick, "and you can pay me when you get to be a rich merchant."

"But it isn't likely I ever shall be one."

"How d'you know? I went to a fortun' teller once, and she told me I was born under a lucky star with a hard name, and I should have a rich man for my particular friend, who would make my fortun'. I guess you are going to be the rich man."

Fosdick laughed, and steadily refused for some time to avail himself of Dick's generous proposal; but at length, perceiving that our hero seemed much disappointed, and would be really glad if his offer were accepted, he agreed to use as much as might be needful.

This at once brought back Dick's good-humor, and he entered with great enthusiasm into his friend's plans.

The next day they withdrew the money from the bank, and, when business got a little slack, in the afternoon, set out in search of a clothing store. Dick knew enough of the city to be able to find a place where a good bargain could be obtained. He was determined that Fosdick should have a good serviceable suit, even if it took all the money they had. The result of their search was that for twenty three dollars Fosdick obtained a very neat outfit, including a couple of shirts, a hat, and a pair of shoes, besides a dark mixed suit, which appeared stout and of good quality.

"Shall I send the bundle home?" asked the salesman, impressed by the off-hand manner in which Dick drew out the money in payment for the clothes.

"Thank you," said Dick, "you're very kind, but I'll take it home myself, and you can allow me something for my trouble."

"All right," said the clerk, laughing: "I'll allow it on your next purchase."

Proceeding to their apartment in Mott Street, Fosdick at once tried on his new suit, and it was found to be an excellent fit. Dick surveyed his new friend with much satisfaction.

"You look like a young gentleman of fortun'," he said, "and do credit to your governor."

"I suppose that means you, Dick," said Fosdick, laughing.

"In course it does."

"You should say *of* course," said Fosdick, who, in virtue of his position as Dick's tutor, ventured to correct his language from time to time.

"How dare you correct your gov'nor?" said Dick, with comic indignation. "'I'll cut you off with a shillin', you young dog,' as the Markis says to his nephew in the play at the Old Bowery."

CHAPTER 19

Fosdick Changes His Business

FOSDICK did not venture to wear his new clothes while engaged in his business. This he felt would have been wasteful extravagance. About ten o'clock in the morning, when business slackened, he went home, and dressing himself went to a hotel where he could see copies of the *Morning Herald* and *Sun*, and, noting down the places where a boy was wanted, went on a round of applications. But he found it no easy thing to obtain a place. Swarms of boys seemed to be out of employment, and it was not unusual to find from fifty to a hundred applicants for a single place.

There was another difficulty. It was generally desired that the boy wanted should reside with his parents. When Fosdick, on being questioned, revealed the fact of his having no parents, and being a boy of the street, this was generally sufficient of itself to insure a refusal. Merchants were afraid to trust one who had led such a vagabond life. Dick, who was always ready for an emergency, suggested borrowing a white wig, and passing himself off for Fosdick's father or grandfather. But Henry thought this might be rather a difficult character for our hero to sustain. After fifty applications and as many failures, Fosdick began to get discouraged. There seemed to be no way out of his present business, for which he felt unfitted.

"I don't know but I shall have to black boots all my life," he said, one day, despondently, to Dick.

"Keep a stiff upper lip," said Dick. "By the time you get to be a gray-headed veteran, you may get a chance to run errands for some big firm on the Bowery, which is a very cheerin' reflection."

So Dick by his drollery and perpetual good spirits kept up Fosdick's courage.

"As for me," said Dick, "I expect by that time to lay up a colossal fortun' out of shines, but live in princely style on the Avenoo."

But one morning, Fosdick, straying into French's Hotel, discovered the following advertisement in the columns of "The Herald,"—

"WANTED—A smart, capable boy to run of errands, and make himself generally useful in a hat and cap store. Salary three dollars a week at first. Inquire at No.—Broadway, after ten o'clock, A.M."

He determined to make application, and, as the City Hall clock just then struck the hour indicated, lost no time in proceeding to the store, which was only a few blocks distant from the Astor House. It was easy to find the store, as from a dozen to twenty boys were already assembled in front of it. They surveyed each other askance, feeling that they were rivals, and mentally calculating each other's chances.

"There isn't much chance for me," said Fosdick to Dick, who had accompanied him. "Look at all these boys. Most of them have good homes, I suppose, and good recommendations, while I have nobody to refer to."

"Go ahead," said Dick. "Your chance is as good as anybody's."

While this was passing between Dick and his companion, one of the boys, a rather supercilious-looking young gentleman, genteelly dressed, and evidently having a very high opinion of his dress and himself turned suddenly to Dick, and remarked,—

"I've seen you before."

"Oh, have you?" said Dick, whirling round; "then p'r'aps you'd like to see me behind."

At this unexpected answer all the boys burst into a laugh with the exception of the questioner, who, evidently considered that Dick had been disrespectful.

"I've seen you somewhere," he said, in a surly tone, correcting himself.

"Most likely you have," said Dick. "That's where I generally keep myself."

There was another laugh at the expense of Roswell Crawford, for that was the name of the young aristocrat. But he had his revenge ready. No boy relishes being an object of ridicule, and it was with a feeling of satisfaction that he retorted,—

"I know you for all your impudence. You're nothing but a boot-black."

This information took the boys who were standing around by surprise, for Dick was well-dressed, and had none of the implements of his profession with him.

"S'pose I be," said Dick. "Have you got any objection?"

"Not at all," said Roswell, curling his lip; "only you'd better stick to blacking boots, and not try to get into a store."

"Thank you for your kind advice," said Dick. "Is it gratooitous, or do you expect to be paid for it?"

"You're an impudent fellow."

"That's a very cheerin' reflection," said Dick, good-naturedly.

"Do you expect to get this place when there's gentlemen's sons applying for it? A boot-black in a store! That would be a good joke."

Boys as well as men are selfish, and, looking upon Dick as a possible rival, the boys who listened seemed disposed to take the same view of the situation.

"That's what I say," said one of them, taking sides with Roswell.

"Don't trouble yourselves," said Dick. "I ain't agoin' to cut you out. I can't afford to give up a independent and loocrative profession for a salary of three dollars a week."

"Hear him talk!" said Roswell Crawford, with an unpleasant sneer. "If you are not trying to get the place, what are you here for?"

"I came with a friend of mine," said Dick, indicating Fosdick, "who's goin' in for the situation."

"Is he a boot-black, too?" demanded Roswell, superciliously.

"He!" retorted Dick, loftily. "Didn't you know his father was a member of Congress, and intimately acquainted with all the biggest men in the State?"

The boys surveyed Fosdick as if they did not quite know whether to credit this statement, which, for the credit of Dick's veracity, it will be observed he did not assert, but only propounded in the form of a question. There was no time for comment, however, as just then the proprietor of the store came to the door, and, casting his eyes over the waiting group, singled out Roswell Crawford, and asked him to enter.

"Well, my lad, how old are you?"

"Fourteen years old," said Roswell, consequentially.

"Are your parents living?"

"Only my mother. My father is dead. He was a gentleman," he added complacently.

"Oh, was he?' said the shop-keeper. "Do you live in the city?"

"Yes, sir. In Clinton Place."

"Have you ever been in a situation before?"

"Yes, sir," said Roswell, a little reluctantly.

"Where was it?"

"In an office on Dey Street."

"How long were you there?"

"A week."

"It seems to me that was a short time. Why did you not stay longer?"

"Because," said Rosewell, loftily, "the man wanted me to get to the office at eight o'clock, and make the fire. I'm a gentleman's son, and am not used to such dirty work."

"Indeed!" said the shop-keeper. "Well young gentleman, you may step aside a few minutes. I will speak with some of the other boys before making my selection."

Several other boys were called in and questioned. Roswell stood by and listened with an air of complacency. He could not help thinking his chances the best. "The man can see I'm a gentleman, and will do credit to his store," he thought.

At length it came to Fosdick's turn. He entered with no very sanguine anticipations of success. Unlike Roswell, he set a very low estimate upon his qualifications when compared with those of other applicants. But his modest bearing, and quiet, gentlemanly manner, entirely free from pretension, prepossessed the shop-keeper, who was a sensible man, in his favor.

"Do you reside in the city?" he asked.

"Yes, sir," said Henry.

"What is your age?"

"Twelve."

"Have you ever been in any situation?"

"No, sir."

"I should like to see a specimen of your hand writing. Here, take the pen and write your name."

Henry Fosdick had a very handsome handwriting for a boy of his age, while Roswell, who had submitted to the same test, could do little more than scrawl.

"Do you reside with your parents?"

"No, sir, they are dead."

"Where do you live, then?"

"In Mott Street."

Roswell curled his lip when this name was pronounced, for Mott Street, as my New York readers know, is in the immediate neighborhood of the Five-Points, and very far from a fashionable locality.

"Have you any testimonials to present?" asked Mr. Henderson, for that was his name.

Fosdick hesitated. This was the question which he had foreseen would give him trouble.

But at this moment it happened most opportunely that Mr. Greyson entered the shop with the intention of buying a hat.

"Yes," said Fosdick, promptly; "I will refer to this gentleman."

"How do you do, Fosdick?" asked Mr. Greyson, noticing him for the first time. "How do you happen to be here?"

"I am applying for a place, sir," said Fosdick. "May I refer the gentleman to you?"

"Certainly, I shall be glad to speak a good word for you. Mr. Henderson, this is a member of my Sunday-school class, for whose good qualities and good abilities I can speak confidently."

"That will be sufficient," said the shop-keeper, who knew Mr. Greyson's high character and position. "He could have no better recommendation. You may come to the store to-morrow morning at half-past seven o'clock. The pay will be three dollars a week for the first six months. If I am satisfied with you, I shall then raise it to five dollars."

The other boys looked disappointed, but none more so than Roswell Crawford. He would have cared less if any one else had obtained the situation; but for a boy who lived in Mott Street to be preferred to him, a gentleman's son, he considered indeed humiliating. In a spirit of petty spite, he was tempted to say, "He's a boot-black. Ask him if he isn't."

"He's an honest and intelligent lad," said Mr. Greyson. "As for you, young man, I only hope you have one-half his good qualities."

Roswell Crawford left the store in disgust, and the other unsuccessful applicants with him.

"What luck, Fosdick?" asked Dick, eagerly, as his friend came out of the store.

"I've got the place," said Fosdick, in accents of satisfaction; "but it was only because Mr. Greyson spoke up for me."

"He's a trump," said Dick, enthusiastically.

The gentleman, so denominated, came out before the boys went away, and spoke with them kindly.

Both Dick and Henry were highly pleased at the success of the application. The pay would indeed be small, but, expended economically, Fosdick thought he could get along on it, receiving his room rent, as before, in return for his services as Dick's private tutor. Dick determined, as soon as his education would permit, to follow his companion's example.

"I don't know as you'll be willin' to room with a boot-black," he said, to Henry, "now you're goin' into business."

"I couldn't room with a better friend, Dick," said Fosdick, affectionately, throwing his arm round our hero. "When we part, it'll be because you wish it."

So Fosdick entered upon a new career.

CHAPTER 20

Nine Months Later

THE next morning Fosdick rose early, put on his new suit, and, after getting breakfast, set out for the Broadway store in which he had obtained a position. He left his little blacking-box in the room.

"It'll do to brush my own shoes," he said. "Who knows but I may have to come back to it again?"

"No danger," said Dick; "I'll take care of the feet, and you'll have to look after the heads, now you're in a hat-store."

"I wish you had a place too," said Fosdick.

"I don't know enough yet," said Dick. "Wait till I've gradooated."

"And can put A. B. after your name."

"What's that?"

"It stands for Bachelor of Arts. It's a degree that students get when they graduate from college."

"Oh," said Dick, "I didn't know but it meant A Boot-black. I can put that after my name now. Wouldn't Dick Hunter, A. B., sound tip-top?"

"I must be going," said Fosdick. "It won't do for me to be late the very first morning."

"That's the difference between you and me," said Dick. "I'm my own boss, and there ain't no one to find fault with me if I'm late. But I might as well be goin' too. There's a gent as comes down to his store pretty early that generally wants a shine."

The two boys parted at the Park. Fosdick crossed it, and proceeded to the hat-store, while Dick, hitching up his pants, began to look about him for a customer. It was seldom that Dick had to wait long. He was always on the alert, and if there was any business to do he was always sure to get his share of it. He had now a stronger inducement than ever to attend strictly to business; his little stock of money in the savings bank having been nearly exhausted by his liberality to his room-mate. He determined to be as economical as possible, and moreover to study as hard as he could, that he might be able to follow Fosdick's example, and obtain a place in a store or counting-room. As there were no striking incidents occurring in our hero's history within the next nine months, I propose to pass over that period, and recount the progress he made in that time.

Fosdick was still at the hat-store, having succeeded in giving perfect satisfaction to Mr. Henderson. His wages had just been raised to five dollars a week. He and Dick still kept house together at Mrs. Mooney's lodging-house, and lived very frugally, so that both were able to save up money. Dick had been unusually successful in business. He had several regular patrons, who had been drawn to him by his ready wit, and quick humor, and from two of them he had received presents of clothing, which had saved him any expense on that score. His income had averaged quite seven dollars a week in addition to this. Of this amount he was now obliged to pay one dollar weekly for the room which he and Fosdick occupied, but he was still able to save one half the remainder. At the end of nine months therefore, or thirty-nine weeks, it will be seen that he had accumulated no less a sum than one hundred and seventeen dollars. Dick may be excused for feeling like a capitalist when he looked at the long row of deposits in his little bank-book. There were other boys in the same business who had earned as much money, but they had had little care for the future, and spent as they went along, so that few could boast a bank-account, however small.

"You'll be a rich man some time, Dick," said Henry Fosdick, one evening.

"And live on Fifth Avenoo," said Dick.

"Perhaps so. Stranger things have happened."

"Well," said Dick, "if such a misfortin' should come upon me I should bear it like a man. When you see a Fifth Avenoo manshun for sale for a hundred and seventeen dollars, just let me know and I'll buy it as an investment."

"Two hundred and fifty years ago you might have bought one for that price, probably. Real estate wasn't very high among the Indians."

"Just my luck," said Dick; "I was born too late. I'd orter have been an Indian, and lived in splendor on my present capital."

"I'm afraid you'd have found your present business rather unprofitable at that time."

But Dick had gained something more valuable than money. He had studied regularly every evening, and his improvement had been marvellous. He could now read well, write a fair hand, and had studied arithmetic as far as Interest. Besides this he had obtained some knowledge of grammar and geography. If some of my boy readers, who have been studying for years, and got no farther than this, should think it incredible that Dick, in less than a year, and studying evenings only, should have accomplished it, they must remember that our hero was very much in earnest in his desire to improve. He knew that, in order to grow up respectable, he must be well advanced, and he was willing to work. But then the reader must not forget that Dick was naturally a smart boy. His street education had sharpened his faculties, and taught him to rely upon himself. He knew that it would take him a long time to reach the goal which he had set before him, and he had patience to keep on trying. He knew that he had only himself to depend upon, and he determined to make the most of himself,—a resolution which is the secret of success in nine cases out of ten.

"Dick," said Fosdick, one evening, after they had completed their studies, "I think you'll have to get another teacher soon."

"Why?" asked Dick, in some surprise. "Have you been offered a more loocrative position?"

"No," said Fosdick, "but I find I have taught you all I know myself. You are now as good a scholar as I am."

"Is that true?" said Dick, eagerly, a flush of gratification coloring his brown cheek.

"Yes," said Fosdick. "You've made wonderful progress. I propose, now that evening schools have begun, that we join one, and study together through the winter."

"All right," said Dick. "I'd be willin' to go now; but when I first began to study I was ashamed to have anybody know that I was so ignorant. Do you really mean, Fosdick, that I know as much as you?"

"Yes, Dick, it's true."

"Then I've got you to thank for it," said Dick, earnestly. "You've made me what I am."

"And haven't you paid me, Dick?"

"By payin' the room rent," said Dick, impulsively. "What's that? It isn't half enough. I wish you'd take half my money; you deserve it."

"Thank you, Dick, but you're too generous. You've more than paid me. Who was it took my part when all the other boys imposed upon me? And who gave me money to buy clothes, and so got me my situation?"

"Oh, that's nothing!" said Dick.

"It's a great deal, Dick. I shall never forget it. But now it seems to me you might try to get a situation yourself."

"Do I know enough?"

"You know as much as I do."

"Then I'll try," said Dick, decidedly.

"I wish there was a place in our store," said Fosdick. "It would be pleasant for us to be together."

"Never mind," said Dick; "there'll be plenty of other chances. P'r'aps A. T. Stewart might like a partner. I wouldn't ask more'n a quarter of the profits."

"Which would be a very liberal proposal on your part," said Fosdick, smiling. "But perhaps Mr. Stewart might object to a partner living on Mott Street."

"I'd just as lieves move to Fifth Avenoo," said Dick. "I ain't got no prejudices in favor of Mott Street."

"Nor I," said Fosdick, "and in fact I have been thinking it might be a good plan for us to move as soon as we could afford. Mrs. Mooney doesn't keep the room quite so neat as she might."

"No," said Dick. "She ain't got no prejudices against dirt. Look at that towel."

Dick held up the article indicated, which had now seen service nearly a week, and hard service at that,—Dick's avocation causing him to be rather hard on towels.

"Yes," said Fosdick, "I've got about tired of it. I guess we can find some better place without having to pay much more. When we move, you must let me pay my share of the rent."

"We'll see about that," said Dick. "Do you propose to move to Fifth Avenoo?"

"Not just at present, but to some more agreeable neighborhood than this. We'll wait till you get a situation, and then we can decide."

A few days later, as Dick was looking about for customers in the neighborhood of the Park, his attention was drawn to a fellow boot-black, a boy about a year younger than himself, who appeared to have been crying.

"What's the matter, Tom?" asked Dick. "Haven't you had luck to-day?"

"Pretty good," said the boy; "but we're havin' hard times at home. Mother fell last week and broke her arm, and to-morrow we've got to pay the rent, and if we don't the landlord says he'll turn us out."

"Haven't you got anything except what you earn?" asked Dick.

"No," said Tom, "not now. Mother used to earn three or four dollars a week; but she can't do nothin' now, and my little sister and brother are too young."

Dick had quick sympathies. He had been so poor himself, and obliged to submit to so many privations that he knew from personal experience how hard it was. Tom Wilkins he knew as an excellent boy who never squandered his money, but faithfully carried it home to his mother. In the days of his own extravagance and shiftlessness he had once or twice asked Tom to accompany him to the Old Bowery or Tony Pastor's, but Tom had always steadily refused.

"I am sorry for you, Tom," he said. "How much do you owe for rent?"

"Two weeks now," said Tom.

"How much is it a week?"

"Two dollars a week—that makes four."

"Have you got anything towards it?"

"No; I've had to spend all my money for food for mother and the rest of us. I've had pretty hard work to do that. I don't know what we'll do. I haven't any place to go to, and I'm afraid mother'll get cold in her arm."

"Can't you borrow the money somewhere?" asked Dick.

Tom shook his head despondingly.

"All the people I know are as poor as I am," said he. "They'd help me if they could, but it's hard work for them to get along themselves."

"I'll tell you what, Tom," said Dick, impulsively, "I'll stand your friend."

"Have you got any money?" asked Tom, doubtfully.

"Got any money!" repeated Dick. "Don't you know that I run a bank on my own account? How much is it you need?"

"Four dollars," said Tom. "If we don't pay that before to-morrow night, out we go. You haven't got as much as that, have you?"

"Here are three dollars," said Dick, drawing out his pocket-book. "I'll let you have the rest to-morrow, and maybe a little more."

"You're a right down good fellow, Dick," said Tom; "but won't you want it yourself?"

"Oh, I've got some more," said Dick.

"Maybe I'll never be able to pay you."

" 'Spose you don't," said Dick; "I guess I won't fail."

"I won't forget it, Dick. I hope I'll be able to do somethin' for you some-time."

"All right," said Dick. "I'd ought to help you. I haven't got no mother to look out for. I wish I had."

There was a tinge of sadness in his tone, as he pronounced the last four words; but Dick's temperament was sanguine, and he never gave way to unavailing sadness. Accordingly he began to whistle as he turned away, only adding, "I'll see you to-morrow, Tom."

The three dollars which Dick had handed to Tom Wilkins were his savings for the present week. It was now Thursday afternoon. His rent, which amounted to a dollar, he expected to save out of the earnings of Friday and Saturday. In order to give Tom the additional assistance he had promised, Dick would be obliged to have recourse to his bank-savings. He would not have ventured to trench upon it for any other reason but this. But he felt that it would be selfish to allow Tom and his mother to suffer when he had it in his power to relieve them. But Dick was destined to be surprised, and that in a disagreeable manner, when he reached home.

CHAPTER 21

Dick Loses His Bank-book

IT WAS hinted at the close of the last chapter that Dick was destined to be disagreeably surprised on reaching home.

Having agreed to give further assistance to Tom Wilkins, he was naturally led to go to the drawer where he and Fosdick kept their bank-books. To his surprise and uneasiness *the drawer proved to be empty.*

"Come here a minute, Fosdick," he said.

"What's the matter, Dick?"

"I can't find my bank-book, nor yours either. What's 'come of them?"

"I took mine with me this morning, thinking I might want to put in a little more money. I've got it in my pocket, now."

"But where's mine?" asked Dick, perplexed.

"I don't know. I saw it in the drawer when I took mine this morning."

"Are you sure?"

"Yes, positive, for I looked into it to see how much you had got."

Besides this, there was another thought that troubled him. When he obtained a place he could not expect to receive as much as he was now making from blacking boots,—probably not more than three dollars a week,—while his expenses without clothing would amount to four dollars. To make up the deficiency he had confidently relied upon his savings, which would be sufficient to carry him along for a year, if necessary. If he should not recover his money, he would be compelled to continue a boot-black for at least six months longer; and this was rather a discouraging reflection. On the whole it is not to be wondered at that Dick felt unusually sober this evening, and that neither of the boys felt much like studying.

The two boys consulted as to whether it would be best to speak to Travis about it. It was not altogether easy to decide. Fosdick was opposed to it.

"It will only put him on his guard," said he, "and I don't see it will do any good. Of course he will deny it. We'd better keep quiet, and watch him, and, by giving notice at the bank, we can make sure that he doesn't get any money on it. If he does present himself at the bank, they will know at once that he is a thief, and he can be arrested."

This view seemed reasonable, and Dick resolved to adopt it. On the whole, he began to think prospects were brighter than he had at first supposed, and his spirits rose a little.

"How'd he know I had any bank-book? That's what I can't make out," he said.

"Don't you remember?" said Fosdick, after a moment's thought, "we were speaking of our savings, two or three evenings since?"

"Yes," said Dick.

"Our door was a little open at the time, and I heard somebody come upstairs, and stop a minute in front of it. It must have been Jim Travis. In that way he probably found out about your money, and took the opportunity to-day to get hold of it."

This might or might not be the correct explanation. At all events it seemed probable.

The boys were just on the point of going to bed, later in the evening, when a knock was heard at the door, and, to their no little surprise, their neighbor, Jim Travis, proved to be the caller. He was a sallow-complexioned young man, with dark hair and blood-shot eyes.

He darted a quick glance from one to the other as he entered, which did not escape the boys' notice.

"How are ye, to-night?" he said, sinking into one of the two chairs with which the room was scantily furnished.

"Jolly," said Dick. "How are you?"

"Tired as a dog," was the reply. "Hard work and poor pay; that's the way with me. I wanted to go to the theatre, to-night, but I was hard up, and couldn't raise the cash."

Here he darted another quick glance at the boys; but neither betrayed anything.

"You don't go out much, do you?" he said.

"Not much," said Fosdick. "We spend our evenings in study."

"That's precious slow," said Travis, rather contemptuously. "What's the use of studying so much? You don't expect to be a lawyer, do you, or anything of that sort?"

"Maybe," said Dick. "I haven't made up my mind yet. If my feller-citizens should want me to go to Congress some time, I shouldn't want to disapp'int 'em; and then readin' and writin' might come handy."

"Well," said Travis, rather abruptly, "I'm tired, and I guess I'll turn in."

"Good-night," said Fosdick.

The boys looked at each other as their visitor left the room.

"He came in to see if we'd missed the bank-book," said Dick.

"And to turn off suspicion from himself, by letting us know he had no money," added Fosdick.

"That's so," said Dick. "I'd like to have searched them pockets of his."

CHAPTER 22

Tracking the Thief

FOSDICK was right in supposing that Jim Travis had stolen his bank-book. He was also right in supposing that that worthy young man had come to the knowledge of Dick's savings by what he had accidentally overheard. Now, Travis, like a very large number of young men of his class, was able to dispose of a larger amount of money than he was able to earn. Moreover, he had no great fancy for work at all, and would have been glad to find some other way of obtaining money enough to pay his expenses. He had recently received a letter from an old companion, who had strayed out to California, and going at once to the mines had been lucky enough to get possession of a very remunerative claim. He wrote to Travis that he had already realized two thousand dollars from it, and expected to make his fortune within six months.

Two thousand dollars! This seemed to Travis a very large sum, and quite dazzled his imagination. He was at once inflamed with the desire to go out to California and try his luck. In his present situation he only received thirty dollars a month, which was probably all that his services were worth, but went a very little way towards gratifying his expensive tastes. Accordingly he determined to take the next steamer to the land of gold, if he could possibly manage to get money enough to pay the passage.

The price of a steerage passage at that time was seventy-five dollars,—not a large sum, certainly,—but it might as well have been seventy-five hundred for any chance James Travis had of raising the amount at present. His available funds consisted of precisely two dollars and a quarter; of which sum, one dollar and a half was due to his washerwoman. This, however, would not have troubled Travis much, and he would conveniently have forgotten all about it; but, even leaving this debt unpaid, the sum at his command would not help him materially towards paying his passage money.

Travis applied for help to two or three of his companions; but they were all of that kind who never keep an account with savings banks, but carry all their spare cash about with them. One of these friends offered to lend him thirty-seven cents, and another a dollar; but neither of these offers seemed to encourage him much. He was about giving up his project in despair, when he learned, accidentally, as we have already said, the extent of Dick's savings.

One hundred and seventeen dollars! Why, that would not only pay his passage, but carry him up to the mines, after he had arrived in San Francisco. He could not help thinking it over, and the result of this thinking was that he determined to borrow it of Dick without leave. Knowing that neither of the boys were in their rooms in the daytime, he came back in the course of the morning, and, being admitted by Mrs. Mooney herself, said, by way of accounting for his presence, that he had a cold, and had come back for a handkerchief. The landlady suspected nothing, and, returning at once to her work in the kitchen, left the coast clear.

Travis at once entered Dick's room, and, as there seemed to be no other place for depositing money, tried the bureau-drawers. They were all readily opened, except one, which proved to be locked. This he naturally concluded must contain the money, and going back to his own chamber for the key of the bureau, tried it on his return, and found to his satisfaction that it would fit. When he discovered the bank-book, his joy was mingled with disappointment. He had expected to find bank-bills instead. This would have saved all further trouble, and would have been immediately available. Obtaining money at the savings bank would involve fresh risk. Travis hesitated whether to take it or not; but finally decided that it would be worth the trouble and hazard.

He accordingly slipped the book into his pocket, locked the drawer again, and, forgetting all about the handkerchief for which he had come home, went downstairs, and into the street.

There would have been time to go to the savings bank that day, but Travis had already been absent from his place of business some time, and did not venture to take the additional time required. Besides, not being very much used to savings banks, never having had occasion to use them, he thought it would be more prudent to look over the rules and regulations, and see if he could not get some information as to the way he ought to proceed. So the day passed, and Dick's money was left in safety at the bank.

In the evening, it occurred to Travis that it might be well to find out whether Dick had discovered his loss. This reflection it was that induced the visit which is recorded at the close of the last chapter. The result was that he was misled by the boys' silence on the subject, and concluded that nothing had yet been discovered.

"Good!" thought Travis, with satisfaction. "If they don't find out for twenty-four hours, it'll be too late, then, and I shall be all right."

There being a possibility of the loss being discovered before the boys went out in the morning, Travis determined to see them at that time, and judge whether such was the case. He waited, therefore, until he heard the boys come out, and then opened his own door.

"Morning, gents," said he, sociably. "Going to business?"

"Yes," said Dick. "I'm afraid my clerks'll be lazy if I ain't on hand."

"Good joke!" said Travis. "If you pay good wages, I'd like to speak for a place."

"I pay all I get myself," said Dick. "How's business with you?"

"So so. Why don't you call round, some time?"

"All my evenin's is devoted to literatoor and science," said Dick. "Thank you all the same."

"Where do you hang out?" inquired Travis, in choice language, addressing Fosdick.

"At Henderson's hat and cap store, on Broadway."

"I'll look in upon you some time when I want a title," said Travis. "I suppose you sell cheaper to your friends."

"I'll be as reasonable as I can," said Fosdick, not very cordially; for he did not much fancy having it supposed by his employer that such a disreputable-looking person as Travis was a friend of his.

However, only said this social.

"You haven't any ⸺ of showing himself at th⸺

"No," said Fosdick; ⸺

"Yes," said Travis, with ⸺versation, and encoura⸺ore, and two since. I've missed one or ⸺ earl-handled knife, hav⸺s to be any too honest. Likely she's got 'e⸺"

"What are you goin' to do about ⸺od. "I left it on my bureed.

"I'll keep mum unless I lose somethin⸺atters. Bridget don't l⸺ haul her over the coals. Have you missed an⸺

"No," said Fosdick, answering for himself, ⸺en I'll kick up a row, ⸺ the truth.

There was a gleam of satisfaction in the eyes of Tra⸺do without violating

"They haven't found it out yet," he thought. "I'll bag ⸺ then they may whistle for it." ⸺eard this.

Having no further object to serve in accompanying the boys, to-day, and good-morning, and turned down another street. ⸺de them

"He's mighty friendly all of a sudden," said Dick.

"Yes," said Fosdick; "it's very evident what it all means. He wants to find ⸺ whether you have discovered your loss or not."

"But he didn't find out."

"No; we've put him on the wrong track. He means to get his money to-day, no doubt."

"My money," suggested Dick.

"I accept the correction," said Fosdick.

"Of course, Dick, you'll be on hand as soon as the bank opens."

"In course I shall. Jim Travis'll find he's walked into the wrong shop."

"The bank opens at ten o'clock, you know."

"I'll be there on time."

The two boys separated.

"Good luck, Dick," said Fosdick, as he parted from him. "It'll all come out right, I think."

"I hope 'twill," said Dick.

He had recovered from his temporary depression, and made up his mind that the money would be recovered. He had no idea of allowing himself to be out-witted by Jim Travis, and enjoyed already, in anticipation, the pleasure of de-feating his rascality.

It wanted two hours and a half yet to ten o'clock, and this time to Dick was too precious to be wasted. It was the time of his greatest harvest. He accord-ingly repaired to his usual place of business, succeeded in obtaining six cus-tomers, which yielded him sixty cents. He then went to a restaurant, and got some breakfast. It was now half-past nine, and Dick, feeling that it wouldn't do to be late, left his box in charge of Johnny Nolan, and made his way to the bank.

The officers had not yet arrived, and Dick lingered on the outside, waiting till they should come. He was not without a little uneasiness, fearing that Travis might be as prompt as himself, and finding him there, might suspect something, and so escape the snare. But, though looking cautiously up and down the street, he could discover no traces of the supposed thief. In due time ten o'clock struck, and immediately afterwards the doors of the bank were thrown open, and our hero entered.

visit for the last nine

asantly. "Have you got some

habit ...oon."

...ne to k... bank-book's been stole."

As Dick ha... ning, ...fortunate. Not so bad as it might be,

months, the... t? You'll...y."

"You're ...ut that," said Dick. "I was afraid he might have got

more mo...ed the cas...

"I d...ef can't ...en if he had, I remember you, and should have

"S...at I came...

tho...

...aken?"

...hasn't been "I missed it in the evenin' when I got home."

...ed him. W...cion as to the person who took it?" asked the cashier.

"Yesterday," told all he knew as to the general character and suspicious

"Have yo...ravis, and the cashier agreed with him that he was probably the

Dick th...o gave his reason for thinking that he would visit the bank that

conduct...o withdraw the funds.

thief. ...good," said the cashier. "We'll be ready for him. What is the number

mor... ur book?"

"No. 5,678," said Dick.

"Now give me a little description of this Travis whom you suspect."

Dick accordingly furnished a brief outline sketch of Travis, not particularly complimentary to the latter.

"That will answer. I think I shall know him," said the cashier. "You may depend upon it that he shall receive no money on your account."

"Thank you," said Dick.

Considerably relieved in mind, our hero turned towards the door, thinking that there would be nothing gained by his remaining longer, while he would of course lose time.

He had just reached the doors, which were of glass, when through them he perceived James Travis himself just crossing the street, and apparently coming towards the bank. It would not do, of course, for him to be seen.

"Here he is," he exclaimed, hurrying back. "Can't you hide me somewhere? I don't want to be seen."

The cashier understood at once how the land lay. He quickly opened a little door, and admitted Dick behind the counter.

"Stoop down," he said, "so as not to be seen."

Dick had hardly done so when Jim Travis opened the outer door, and, looking about him in a little uncertainty, walked up to the cashier's desk.

CHAPTER 23

Travis Is Arrested

JIM TRAVIS advanced into the bank with a doubtful step, knowing well that he was on a dishonest errand, and heartily wishing that he were well out of it. After a little hesitation, he approached the paying-teller, and, exhibiting the bank-book, said, "I want to get my money out."

The bank-officer took the book, and, after looking at it a moment, said, "How much do you want?"

"The whole of it," said Travis.

"You can draw out any part of it, but to draw out the whole requires a week's notice."

"Then I'll take a hundred dollars."

"Are you the person to whom the book belongs?"

"Yes, sir," said Travis, without hesitation.

"Your name is—"

"Hunter."

The bank-clerk went to a large folio volume, containing the names of depositors, and began to turn over the leaves. While he was doing this, he managed to send out a young man connected with the bank for a policeman. Travis did not perceive this, or did not suspect that it had anything to do with himself. Not being used to savings banks, he supposed the delay only what was usual. After a search, which was only intended to gain time that a policeman might be summoned, the cashier came back, and, sliding out a piece of paper to Travis, said, "It will be necessary for you to write an order for the money."

Travis took a pen, which he found on the ledge outside, and wrote the order, signing his name "Dick Hunter," having observed that name on the outside of the book.

"Your name is Dick Hunter, then?" said the cashier, taking the paper, and looking at the thief over his spectacles.

"Yes," said Travis, promptly.

"But," continued the cashier, "I find Hunter's age is put down on the bankbook as fourteen. Surely you must be more than that."

Travis would gladly have declared that he was only fourteen; but, being in reality twenty-three, and possessing a luxuriant pair of whiskers, this was not to be thought of. He began to feel uneasy.

"Dick Hunter's my younger brother," he said. "I'm getting out the money for him."

"I thought you said your own name was Dick Hunter," said the cashier.

"I said my name was Hunter," said Travis, ingeniously. "I didn't understand you."

"But you've signed the name of Dick Hunter to this order. How is that?" questioned the troublesome cashier.

Travis saw that he was getting himself into a tight place; but his self-possession did not desert him.

"I thought I must give my brother's name," he answered.

"What is your own name?"

"Henry Hunter."

"Can you bring any one to testify that the statement you are making is correct?"

"Yes, a dozen if you like," said Travis, boldly. "Give me the book, and I'll come back this afternoon. I didn't think there'd be such a fuss about getting out a little money."

"Wait a moment. Why don't your brother come himself?"

"Because he's sick. He's down with the measles," said Travis.

Here the cashier signed to Dick to rise and show himself. Our hero accordingly did so.

175

"You will be glad to find that he has recovered," said the cashier, pointing to Dick.

With an exclamation of anger and dismay, Travis, who saw the game was up, started for the door, feeling that safety made such a course prudent. But he was too late. He found himself confronted by a burly policeman, who seized him by the arm, saying, "Not so fast, my man. I want you."

"Let me go," exclaimed Travis, struggling to free himself.

"I'm sorry I can't oblige you," said the officer. "You'd better not make a fuss, or I may have to hurt you a little."

Travis sullenly resigned himself to his fate, darting a look of rage at Dick, whom he considered the author of his present misfortune.

"This is your book," said the cashier, handing back his rightful property to our hero. "Do you wish to draw out any money?"

"Two dollars," said Dick.

"Very well. Write an order for that amount."

Before doing so, Dick, who now that he saw Travis in the power of the law began to pity him, went up to the officer, and said,—

"Won't you let him go? I've got my bank-book back, and I don't want anything done to him."

"Sorry I can't oblige you," said the officer; "but I'm not allowed to do it. He'll have to stand his trial."

"I'm sorry for you, Travis," said Dick. "I didn't want you arrested. I only wanted my bank-book back."

"Curse you!" said Travis, scowling vindictively. "Wait till I get free. See if I don't fix you."

"You needn't pity him too much," said the officer. "I know him now. He's been on the Island before."

"It's a lie," said Travis, violently.

"Don't be too noisy, my friend," said the officer. "If you've got no more business here, we'll be going."

He withdrew with the prisoner in charge, and Dick, having drawn his two dollars, left the bank. Notwithstanding the violent words the prisoner had used towards himself, and his attempted robbery, he could not help feeling sorry that he had been instrumental in causing his arrest.

"I'll keep my book a little safer hereafter," thought Dick. "Now I must go and see Tom Wilkins."

Before dismissing the subject of Travis and his theft, it may be remarked that he was duly tried, and, his guilt being clear, was sent to Blackwell's Island for nine months. At the end of that time, on his release, he got a chance to work his passage on a ship to San Francisco, where he probably arrived in due time. At any rate, nothing more has been heard of him, and probably his threat of vengeance against Dick will never be carried into effect.

Returning to the City Hall Park, Dick soon fell in with Tom Wilkins.

"How are you, Tom?" he said. "How's your mother?"

"She's better, Dick, thank you. She felt worried about bein' turned out into the street; but I gave her that money from you, and now she feels a good deal easier."

"I've got some more for you, Tom," said Dick, producing a two-dollar bill from his pocket.

"I ought not to take it from you, Dick."

"Oh, it's all right, Tom. Don't be afraid."

"But you may need it yourself."

"There's plenty more where that came from."

"Any way, one dollar will be enough. With that we can pay the rent."

"You'll want the other to buy something to eat."

"You're very kind, Dick."

"I'd ought to be. I've only got myself to take care of."

"Well, I'll take it for my mother's sake. When you want anything done just call on Tom Wilkins."

"All right. Next week, if your mother doesn't get better, I'll give you some more."

Tom thanked our hero very gratefully, and Dick walked away, feeling the self-approval which always accompanies a generous and disinterested action. He was generous by nature, and, before the period at which he is introduced to the reader's notice, he frequently treated his friends to cigars and oyster-stews. Sometimes he invited them to accompany him to the theatre at his expense. But he never derived from these acts of liberality the same degree of satisfaction as from this timely gift to Tom Wilkins. He felt that his money was well bestowed, and would save an entire family from privation and discomfort. Five dollars would, to be sure, make something of a difference in the amount of his savings. It was more than he was able to save up in a week. But Dick felt fully repaid for what he had done, and he felt prepared to give as much more, if Tom's mother should continue to be sick, and should appear to him to need it.

Besides all this, Dick felt a justifiable pride in his financial ability to afford so handsome a gift. A year before, however much he might have desired to give, it would have been quite out of his power to give five dollars. His cash balance never reached that amount. It was seldom, indeed, that it equalled one dollar. In more ways than one Dick was beginning to reap the advantage of his self-denial and judicious economy.

It will be remembered that when Mr. Whitney at parting with Dick presented him with five dollars, he told him that he might repay it to some other boy who was struggling upward. Dick thought of this, and it occurred to him that after all he was only paying up an old debt.

When Fosdick came home in the evening, Dick announced his success in recovering his lost money, and described the manner in which it had been brought about.

"You're in luck, Dick," said Fosdick. "I guess we'd better not trust the bureau-drawer again."

"I mean to carry my book round with me," said Dick.

"So shall I, as long as we stay at Mrs. Mooney's. I wish we were in a better place."

"I must go down and tell her she needn't expect Travis back. Poor chap, I pity him!"

Travis was never more seen in Mrs. Mooney's establishment. He was owing that lady for a fortnight's rent of his room, which prevented her feeling much compassion for him. The room was soon after let to a more creditable tenant, who proved a less troublesome neighbor than his predecessor.

CHAPTER 24

Dick Receives a Letter

IT WAS about a week after Dick's recovery of his bank-book, that Fosdick brought home with him in the evening a copy of the "Daily Sun."

"Would you like to see your name in print, Dick?" he asked.

"Yes," said Dick, who was busy at the washstand, endeavoring to efface the marks which his day's work had left upon his hands. "They haven't put me up for mayor, have they? 'Cause if they have, I shan't accept. It would interfere too much with my private business."

"No," said Fosdick, "they haven't put you up for office yet, though that may happen sometime. But if you want to see your name in print, here it is."

Dick was rather incredulous, but, having dried his hands on the towel, took the paper, and following the directions of Fosdick's finger, observed in the list of advertised letters the name of "RAGGED DICK."

"By gracious, so it is," said he. "Do you s'pose it means me?"

"I don't know of any other Ragged Dick,—do you?"

"No," said Dick, reflectively; "it must be me. But I don't know of anybody that would be likely to write to me."

"Perhaps it is Frank Whitney," suggested Fosdick, after a little reflection. "Didn't he promise to write to you?"

"Yes," said Dick, "and he wanted me to write to him."

"Where is he now?"

"He was going to a boarding-school in Connecticut, he said. The name of the town was Barnton."

"Very likely the letter is from him."

"I hope it is. Frank was a tip-top boy, and he was the first that made me ashamed of bein' so ignorant and dirty."

"You had better go to the post-office to-morrow morning, and ask for the letter."

"P'r'aps they won't give it to me."

"Suppose you wear the old clothes you used to a year ago, when Frank first saw you? They won't have any doubt of your being Ragged Dick then."

"I guess I will. I'll be sort of ashamed to be seen in 'em though," said Dick, who had considerable more pride in a neat personal appearance than when we were first introduced to him.

"It will be only for one day, or one morning," said Fosdick.

"I'd do more'n that for the sake of gettin' a letter from Frank. I'd like to see him."

The next morning, in accordance with the suggestion of Fosdick, Dick arrayed himself in the long disused Washington coat and Napoleon pants, which he had carefully preserved, for what reason he could hardly explain.

When fairly equipped, Dick surveyed himself in the mirror,—if the little seven-by-nine-inch looking-glass, with which the room was furnished, deserved the name. The result of the survey was not on the whole a pleasing one. To tell the truth, Dick was quite ashamed of his appearance, and, on opening the chamber-door, looked around to see that the coast was clear, not being willing to have any of his fellow-boarders see him in his present attire.

He managed to slip out into the street unobserved, and, after attending to two or three regular customers who came down-town early in the morning, he made his way down Nassau Street to the post-office. He passed along until he came to a compartment on which he read ADVERTISED LETTERS, and, stepping up to the little window, said,—

"There's a letter for me. I saw it advertised in the 'Sun' yesterday."

"What name?" demanded the clerk.

"Ragged Dick," answered our hero.

"That's a queer name," said the clerk, surveying him a little curiously. "Are you Ragged Dick?"

"If you don't believe me, look at my clo'es," said Dick.

"That's pretty good proof, certainly," said the clerk, laughing. "If that isn't your name, it deserves to be."

"I believe in dressin' up to your name," said Dick.

"Do you know any one in Barnton, Connecticut?" asked the clerk, who had by this time found the letter.

"Yes," said Dick. "I know a chap that's at boardin'-school there."

"It appears to be in a boy's hand. I think it must be yours."

The letter was handed to Dick through the window. He received it eagerly, and drawing back so as not to be in the way of the throng who were constantly applying for letters, or slipping them into the boxes provided for them, hastily opened it, and began to read. As the reader may be interested in the contents of the letter as well as Dick, we transcribe it below.

It was dated Barnton, Conn., and commenced thus—

"Dear Dick—You must excuse my addressing this letter to 'Ragged Dick'; but the fact is, I don't know what your last name is, nor where you live. I am afraid there is not much chance of your getting this letter; but I hope you will. I have thought of you very often, and wondered how you were getting along, and I should have written to you before if I had known where to direct.

"Let me tell you a little about myself. Barnton is a very pretty country town, only about six miles from Hartford. The boarding-school which I attend is under the charge of Ezekiel Munroe, A.M. He is a man of about fifty, a graduate of Yale College, and has always been a teacher. It is a large two-story house, with an addition containing a good many small bed-chambers for the boys. There are about twenty of us, and there is one assistant teacher who teaches the English branches. Mr. Munroe, or Old Zeke, as we call him behind his back, teaches Latin and Greek. I am studying both these languages, because father wants me to go to college.

"But you won't be interested in hearing about our studies. I will tell you how we amuse ourselves. There are about fifty acres of land belonging to Mr. Munroe; so that we have plenty of room for play. About a quarter of a mile from the house there is a good-sized pond. There is a large, round-bottomed boat, which is stout and strong. Every Wednesday and Saturday afternoon, when the weather is good, we go out rowing on the pond. Mr. Barton, the assistant teacher, goes with us, to look after us. In the summer we are allowed to go in bathing. In the winter there is splendid skating on the pond.

"Besides this, we play ball a good deal, and we have various other plays. So we have a pretty good time, although we study pretty hard too. I am getting on very well in my studies. Father has not decided yet where he will send me to college.

"I wish you were here, Dick. I should enjoy your company, and besides I should like to feel that you were getting an education. I think you are naturally a pretty smart boy; but I suppose, as you have to earn your own living, you don't get much chance to learn. I only wish I had a few hundred dollars of my own. I would have you come up

179

here, and attend school with us. If I ever have a chance to help you in any way, you may be sure that I will.

"I shall have to wind up my letter now, as I have to hand in a composition to-morrow, on the life and character of Washington. I might say that I have a friend who wears a coat that once belonged to the general. But I suppose that coat must be worn out by this time. I don't much like writing compositions. I would a good deal rather write letters.

"I have written a longer letter than I meant to. I hope you will get it, though I am afraid not. If you do, you must be sure to answer it, as soon as possible. You needn't mind if your writing does look like 'hens-tracks,' as you told me once.

"Good-by, Dick. You must always think of me, as your very true friend,

"Frank Whitney"

Dick read this letter with much satisfaction. It is always pleasant to be remembered, and Dick had so few friends that it was more to him than to boys who are better provided. Again, he felt a new sense of importance in having a letter addressed to him. It was the first letter he had ever received. If it had been sent to him a year before, he would not have been able to read it. But now, thanks to Fosdick's instructions, he could not only read writing, but he could write a very good hand himself.

There was one passage in the letter which pleased Dick. It was where Frank said that if he had the money he would pay for his education himself.

"He's a tip-top feller," said Dick. "I wish I could see him ag'in."

There were two reasons why Dick would like to have seen Frank. One was, the natural pleasure he would have in meeting a friend; but he felt also that he would like to have Frank witness the improvement he had made in his studies and mode of life.

"He'd find me a little more 'spectable than when he first saw me," thought Dick.

Dick had by this time got up to Printing House Square. Standing on Spruce Street, near the "Tribune" office, was his old enemy, Micky Maguire.

It has already been said that Micky felt a natural enmity towards those in his own condition in life who wore better clothes than himself. For the last nine months, Dick's neat appearance had excited the ire of the young Philistine.[1] To appear in neat attire and with a clean face Micky felt was a piece of presumption, and an assumption of superiority on the part of our hero, and he termed it "tryin' to be a swell."

Now his astonished eyes rested on Dick in his ancient attire, which was very similar to his own. It was a moment of triumph to him. He felt that "pride had had a fall," and he could not forbear reminding Dick of it.

"Them's nice clo'es you've got on," said he, sarcastically, as Dick came up.

"Yes," said Dick, promptly. "I've been employin' your tailor. If my face was only dirty we'd be taken for twin brothers."

"So you've give up tryin' to be a swell?"

"Only for this partic'lar occasion," said Dick. "I wanted to make a fashionable call, so I put on my regimentals."[2]

"I don't b'lieve you've got any better clo'es," said Micky.

"All right," said Dick, "I won't charge you nothin' for what you believe."

---

1 *young Philistine* ignorant youth.
2 *regimentals* formal military dress uniform.

Here a customer presented himself for Micky, and Dick went back to his
room to change his clothes, before resuming business.

CHAPTER 25

Dick Writes His First Letter

WHEN Fosdick reached home in the evening, Dick displayed his letter with
some pride.

"It's a nice letter," said Fosdick, after reading it. "I should like to know
Frank."

"I'll bet you would," said Dick. "He's a trump."[1]

"When are you going to answer it?"

"I don't know," said Dick dubiously. "I never writ a letter."

"There's no reason why you shouldn't. There's always a first time, you
know."

"I don't know what to say," said Dick.

"Get some paper and sit down to it, and you'll find enough to say. You can do
that this evening instead of studying."

"If you'll look it over afterwards, and shine it up a little."

"Yes, if it needs it; but I rather think Frank would like it best just as you
wrote it."

Dick decided to adopt Fosdick's suggestion. He had very serious doubts as to
his ability to write a letter. Like a good many other boys, he looked upon it as a
very serious job, not reflecting that, after all, letter-writing is nothing but talking upon paper. Still, in spite of his misgivings, he felt that the letter ought to
be answered, and he wished Frank to hear from him. After various preparations,
he at last got settled down to his task, and, before the evening was over, a letter
was written. As the first letter which Dick had ever produced, and because it
was characteristic of him, my readers may like to read it.

Here it is—

*"Dear Frank—I got your letter this mornin', and was very glad to hear you hadn't
forgotten Ragged Dick. I ain't so ragged as I was. Openwork coats and trousers has
gone out of fashion. I put on the Washington coat and Napoleon pants to go to the
post-office, for fear they wouldn't think I was the boy that was meant. On my way
back I received the congratulations of my intimate friend, Micky Maguire, on my
improved appearance.*

*"I've give up sleepin' in boxes, and old wagons, findin' it didn't agree with my
constitution. I've hired a room in Mott Street, and have got a private tooter, who
rooms with me and looks after my studies in the evenin'. Mott Street ain't very fashionable; but my manshun on Fifth Avenoo isn't finished yet, and I'm afraid it won't
be till I'm a gray-haired veteran. I've got a hundred dollars towards it, which I've
saved from my earnin's. I haven't forgot what you and your uncle said to me, and
I'm trying to grow up 'spectable. I haven't been to Tony Pastor's, or the Old Bowery,
for ever so long. I'd rather save up my money to support me in my old age. When my*

---

1 *trump* admirable fellow.

hair gets gray, I'm goin' to knock off blackin' boots, and go into some light, genteel employment, such as keepin' an apple-stand, or disseminatin' pea-nuts among the people.

"I've got so as to read pretty well, so my tooter says. I've been studyin' geography and grammar also. I've made such astonishin' progress that I can tell a noun from a conjunction as far away as I can see 'em. Tell Mr. Munroe that if he wants an accomplished teacher in his school, he can send for me, and I'll come on by the very next train. Or, if he wants to sell out for a hundred dollars, I'll buy the whole concern, and agree to teach the scholars all I know myself in less than six months. Is teachin' as good business, generally speakin', as blackin' boots? My private tooter combines both, and is makin' a fortun' with great rapidity. He'll be as rich as Astor some time, if he only lives long enough.

"I should think you'd have a bully time at your school. I should like to go out in the boat, or play ball with you. When are you comin' to the city? I wish you'd write and let me know when you do, and I'll call and see you. I'll leave my business in the hands of my numerous clerks, and go round with you. There's lots of things you didn't see when you was here before. They're getting on fast at the Central Park. It looks better than it did a year ago.

"I ain't much used to writin' letters. As this is the first one I ever wrote, I hope you'll excuse the mistakes. I hope you'll write to me again soon. I can't write so good a letter as you; but I'll do my best, as the man said when he was asked if he could swim over to Brooklyn backwards. Good-by, Frank. Thank you for all your kindness. Direct your next letter to No.—Mott Street.

"Your true friend,

"Dick Hunter"

When Dick had written the last word, he leaned back in his chair, and surveyed the letter with much satisfaction.

"I didn't think I could have wrote such a long letter, Fosdick," said he.

"Written would be more grammatical, Dick," suggested his friend.

"I guess there's plenty of mistakes in it," said Dick. "Just look at it, and see."

Fosdick took the letter, and read it over carefully.

"Yes, there are some mistakes," he said; "but it sounds so much like you that I think it would be better to let it go just as it is. It will be more likely to remind Frank of what you were when he first saw you."

"Is it good enough to send?" asked Dick, anxiously.

"Yes, it seems to me to be quite a good letter. It is written just as you talk. Nobody but you could have written such a letter, Dick. I think Frank will be amused at your proposal to come up there as teacher."

"P'r'aps it would be a good idea for us to open a seleck school here in Mott Street," said Dick, humorously. "We could call it 'Professor Fosdick and Hunter's Mott Street Seminary.' Boot-blackin' taught by Professor Hunter."

The evening was so far advanced that Dick decided to postpone copying his letter till the next evening. By this time he had come to have a very fair handwriting, so that when the letter was complete it really looked quite creditable, and no one would have suspected that it was Dick's first attempt in this line. Our hero surveyed it with no little complacency. In fact, he felt rather proud of it, since it reminded him of the great progress he had made. He carried it down to the post-office, and deposited it with his own hands in the proper box. Just on the steps of the building, as he was coming out, he met Johnny Nolan, who

had been sent on an errand to Wall Street by some gentleman, and was just returning.

"What are you doin' down here, Dick?" asked Johnny.

"I've been mailin' a letter."

"Who sent you?"

"Nobody."

"I mean, who writ the letter?"

"I wrote it myself."

"Can you write letters?" asked Johnny, in amazement.

"Why shouldn't I?"

"I didn't know you could write. I can't."

"Then you ought to learn."

"I went to school once; but it was too hard work, so I give it up."

"You're lazy, Johnny,—that's what's the matter. How'd you ever expect to
know anything, if you don't try?"

"I can't learn."

"You can, if you want to."

Johnny Nolan was evidently of a different opinion. He was a good-natured
boy, large of his age, with nothing particularly bad about him, but utterly lacking in that energy, ambition, and natural sharpness, for which Dick was distinguished. He was not adapted to succeed in the life which circumstances had
forced upon him; for in the street-life of the metropolis a boy needs to be on
the alert, and have all his wits about him, or he will find himself wholly distanced by his more enterprising competitors for popular favor. To succeed in
his profession, humble as it is, a boot-black must depend upon the same qualities which gain success in higher walks in life. It was easy to see that Johnny, unless very much favored by circumstances, would never rise much above his
present level. For Dick, we cannot help hoping much better things.

CHAPTER 26

An Exciting Adventure

DICK now began to look about for a position in a store or counting-room.
Until he should obtain one he determined to devote half the day to blacking boots, not being willing to break in upon his small capital. He found that he
could earn enough in half a day to pay all his necessary expenses, including the
entire rent of the room. Fosdick desired to pay his half; but Dick steadily refused, insisting upon paying so much as compensation for his friend's services as
instructor.

It should be added that Dick's peculiar way of speaking and use of slang
terms had been somewhat modified by his education and his intimacy with
Henry Fosdick. Still he continued to indulge in them to some extent, especially
when he felt like joking, and it was natural to Dick to joke, as my readers have
probably found out by this time. Still his manners were considerably improved,
so that he was more likely to obtain a situation than when first introduced to
our notice.

Just now, however, business was very dull, and merchants, instead of hiring
new assistants, were disposed to part with those already in their employ. After

making several ineffectual applications, Dick began to think he should be obliged to stick to his profession until the next season. But about this time something occurred which considerably improved his chances of preferment.

This is the way it happened.

As Dick, with a balance of more than a hundred dollars in the savings bank, might fairly consider himself a young man of property, he thought himself justified in occasionally taking a half holiday from business, and going on an excursion. On Wednesday afternoon Henry Fosdick was sent by his employer on an errand to that part of Brooklyn near Greenwood Cemetery. Dick hastily dressed himself in his best, and determined to accompany him.

The two boys walked down to the South Ferry, and, paying their two cents each, entered the ferry boat. They remained at the stern, and stood by the railing, watching the great city, with its crowded wharves, receding from view. Beside them was a gentleman with two children—a girl of eight and a little boy of six. The children were talking gayly to their father. While he was pointing out some object of interest to the little girl, the boy managed to creep, unobserved, beneath the chain that extends across the boat, for the protection of passengers, and, stepping incautiously to the edge of the boat, fell over into the foaming water.

At the child's scream, the father looked up, and, with a cry of horror, sprang to the edge of the boat. He would have plunged in, but, being unable to swim, would only have endangered his own life, without being able to save his child.

"My child!" he exclaimed in anguish,—"who will save my child? A thousand—ten thousand dollars to any one who will save him!"

There chanced to be but few passengers on board at the time, and nearly all those were either in the cabins or standing forward. Among the few who saw the child fall was our hero.

Now Dick was an expert swimmer. It was an accomplishment which he had possessed for years, and he no sooner saw the boy fall than he resolved to rescue him. His determination was formed before he heard the liberal offer made by the boy's father. Indeed, I must do Dick the justice to say that, in the excitement of the moment, he did not hear it at all, nor would it have stimulated the alacrity with which he sprang to the rescue of the little boy.

Little Johnny had already risen once, and gone under for the second time, when our hero plunged in. He was obliged to strike out for the boy, and this took time. He reached him none too soon. Just as he was sinking for the third and last time, he caught him by the jacket. Dick was stout and strong, but Johnny clung to him so tightly, that it was with great difficulty he was able to sustain himself.

"Put your arms round my neck," said Dick.

The little boy mechanically obeyed, and clung with a grasp strengthened by his terror. In this position Dick could bear his weight better. But the ferry-boat was receding fast. It was quite impossible to reach it. The father, his face pale with terror and anguish, and his hands clasped in suspense, saw the brave boy's struggles, and prayed with agonizing fervor that he might be successful. But it is probable, for they were now midway of the river, that both Dick and the little boy whom he had bravely undertaken to rescue would have been drowned, had not a row-boat been fortunately near. The two men who were in it witnessed the accident, and hastened to the rescue of our hero.

"Keep up a little longer," they shouted, bending to their oars, "and we will save you."

Dick heard the shout, and it put fresh strength into him. He battled manfully with the treacherous sea, his eyes fixed longingly upon the approaching boat.

"Hold on tight, little boy," he said. "There's a boat coming."

The little boy did not see the boat. His eyes were closed to shut out the fearful water, but he clung the closer to his young preserver. Six long, steady strokes, and the boat dashed along side. Strong hands seized Dick and his youthful burden, and drew them into the boat, both dripping with water.

"God be thanked!" exclaimed the father, as from the steamer he saw the child's rescue. "That brave boy shall be rewarded, if I sacrifice my whole fortune to compass it."

"You've had a pretty narrow escape, young chap," said one of the boatman to Dick. "It was a pretty tough job you undertook."

"Yes," said Dick. "That's what I thought when I was in the water. If it hadn't been for you, I don't know what would have 'come of us."

"Anyhow you're a plucky boy, or you wouldn't have dared to jump into the water after this little chap. It was a risky thing to do."

"I'm used to the water," said Dick, modestly. "I didn't stop to think of the danger, but I wasn't going to let that little fellow drown without tryin' to save him."

The boat at once headed for the ferry wharf on the Brooklyn side. The captain of the ferry-boat, seeing the rescue, did not think it necessary to stop his boat, but kept on his way. The whole occurrence took place in less time than I have occupied in telling it.

The father was waiting on the wharf to receive his little boy, with what feelings of gratitude and joy can be easily understood. With a burst of happy tears he clasped him to his arms. Dick was about to withdraw modestly, but the gentleman perceived the movement, and, putting down the child, came forward, and, clasping his hand, said with emotion, "My brave boy, I owe you a debt I can never repay. But for your timely service I should now be plunged into an anguish which I cannot think of without a shudder."

Our hero was ready enough to speak on most occasions, but always felt awkward when he was praised.

"It wasn't any trouble," he said, modestly. "I can swim like a top."

"But not many boys would have risked their lives for a stranger," said the gentleman. "But," he added with a sudden thought, as his glance rested on Dick's dripping garments, "both you and my little boy will take cold in wet clothes. Fortunately I have a friend living close at hand, at whose house you will have an opportunity of taking off your clothes, and having them dried."

Dick protested that he never took cold; but Fosdick, who had now joined them, and who, it is needless to say, had been greatly alarmed at Dick's danger, joined in urging compliance with the gentleman's proposal, and in the end our hero had to yield. His new friend secured a hack, the driver of which agreed for extra recompense to receive the dripping boys into his carriage, and they were whirled rapidly to a pleasant house in a side street, where matters were quickly explained, and both boys were put to bed.

"I ain't used to goin' to bed quite so early," thought Dick. "This is the queerest excursion I ever took."

Like most active boys Dick did not enjoy the prospect of spending half a day in bed; but his confinement did not last as long as he anticipated.

In about an hour the door of his chamber was opened, and a servant appeared, bringing a new and handsome suit of clothes throughout.

"You are to put on these," said the servant to Dick; "but you needn't get up till you feel like it."

"Whose clothes are they?" asked Dick.

"They are yours."

"Mine! Where did they come from?"

"Mr. Rockwell sent out and bought them for you. They are the same size as your wet ones."

"Is he here now?"

"No. He bought another suit for the little boy, and has gone back to New York. Here's a note he asked me to give you."

Dick opened the paper, and read as follows—

"Please accept this outfit of clothes as the first instalment of a debt which I can never repay. I have asked to have your wet suit dried, when you can reclaim it. Will you oblige me by calling to-morrow at my counting room, No.—, Pearl Street.
"Your friend,

"James Rockwell"

CHAPTER 27

Conclusion

WHEN Dick was dressed in his new suit, he surveyed his figure with pardonable complacency. It was the best he had ever worn, and fitted him as well as if it had been made expressly for him.

"He's done the handsome thing," said Dick to himself; "but there wasn't no 'casin for his givin' me these clothes. My lucky stars are shinin' pretty bright now. Jumpin' into the water pays better than shinin' boots; but I don't think I'd like to try it more'n once a week."

About eleven o'clock the next morning Dick repaired to Mr. Rockwell's counting-room on Pearl Street. He found himself in front of a large and handsome warehouse. The counting-room was on the lower floor. Our hero entered, and found Mr. Rockwell sitting at a desk. No sooner did that gentleman see him than he arose, and, advancing, shook Dick by the hand in the most friendly manner.

"My young friend," he said, "you have done me so great service that I wish to be of some service to you in return. Tell me about yourself, and what plans or wishes you have formed for the future."

Dick frankly related his past history, and told Mr. Rockwell of his desire to get into a store or counting room, and of the failure of all his applications thus far. The merchant listened attentively to Dick's statement, and, when he had finished, placed a sheet of paper before him, and, handing him a pen, said, "Will you write your name on this piece of paper?"

Dick wrote in a free, bold hand, the name Richard Hunter. He had very much improved in his penmanship, as has already been mentioned, and now had no cause to be ashamed of it.

Mr. Rockwell surveyed it approvingly.

"How would you like to enter my counting-room as clerk, Richard?" he asked.

Dick was about to say "Bully," when he recollected himself, and answered, "Very much."

"I suppose you know something of arithmetic, do you not?"

"Yes, sir."

"Then you may consider yourself engaged at a salary of ten dollars a week. You may come next Monday morning."

"Ten dollars!" repeated Dick, thinking he must have misunderstood.

"Yes; will that be sufficient?"

"It's more than I can earn," said Dick, honestly.

"Perhaps it is at first," said Mr. Rockwell, smiling; "but I am willing to pay you that. I will besides advance you as fast as your progress will justify it."

Dick was so elated than he hardly restrained himself from some demonstration which would have astonished the merchant; but he exercised self-control, and only said, "I'll try to serve you so faithfully, sir, that you won't repent having taken me into your service."

"And I think you will succeed," said Mr. Rockwell, encouragingly. "I will not detain you any longer, for I have some important business to attend to. I shall expect to see you on Monday morning."

Dick left the counting-room, hardly knowing whether he stood on his head or his heels, so overjoyed was he at the sudden change in his fortunes. Ten dollars a week was to him a fortune, and three times as much as he had expected to obtain at first. Indeed he would have been glad, only the day before, to get a place at three dollars a week. He reflected that with the stock of clothes which he had now on hand, he could save up at least half of it, and even then live better than he had been accustomed to do; so that his little fund in the savings bank, instead of being diminished, would be steadily increasing. Then he was to be advanced if he deserved it. It was indeed a bright prospect for a boy who, only a year before, could neither read nor write, and depended for a night's lodging upon the chance hospitality of an alley-way or old wagon. Dick's great ambition to "grow up 'spectable" seemed likely to be accomplished after all.

"I wish Fosdick was as well off as I am," he thought generously. But he determined to help his less fortunate friend, and assist him up the ladder as he advanced himself.

When Dick entered his room on Mott Street, he discovered that some one else had been there before him, and two articles of wearing apparel had disappeared.

"By gracious!" he exclaimed; "somebody's stole my Washington coat and Napoleon pants. Maybe it's an agent of Barnum's, who expects to make a fortun' by exhibitin' the valooable wardrobe of a gentleman of fashion."

Dick did not shed many tears over his loss, as, in his present circumstances, he never expected to have any further use for the well-worn garments. It may be stated that he afterwards saw them adorning the figure of Micky Maguire; but whether that estimable young man stole them himself, he never ascertained. As to the loss, Dick was rather pleased that it had occurred. It seemed to cut him off from the old vagabond life which he hoped never to resume. Henceforward he meant to press onward, and rise as high as possible.

Although it was yet only noon, Dick did not go out again with his brush. He felt that it was time to retire from business. He would leave his share of the public patronage to other boys less fortunate than himself. That evening Dick and Fosdick had a long conversation. Fosdick rejoiced heartily in his friend's success, and on his side had the pleasant news to communicate that his pay had been advanced to six dollars a week.

"I think we can afford to leave Mott Street now," he continued. "This house isn't as neat as it might be, and I should like to live in a nicer quarter of the city."

"All right," said Dick. "We'll hunt up a new room to-morrow. I shall have plenty of time, having retired from business. I'll try to get my reg'lar customers to take Johnny Nolan in my place. That boy hasn't any enterprise. He needs somebody to look out for him."

"You might give him your box and brush, too, Dick."

"No," said Dick; "I'll give him some new ones, but mine I want to keep, to remind me of the hard times I've had, when I was an ignorant boot-black, and never expected to be anything better."

"When, in short, you were 'Ragged Dick.' You must drop that name, and think of yourself now as—"

"Richard Hunter. Esq.," said our hero, smiling.

"A young gentleman on the way to fame and fortune," added Fosdick.

Here ends the story of Ragged Dick. As Fosdick said, he is Ragged Dick no longer. He has taken a step upward, and is determined to mount still higher. There are fresh adventures in store for him, and for others who have been introduced in these pages. Those who have felt interested in his early life will find his history continued in a new volume, forming the second of the series, to be called—

FAME AND FORTUNE

or,

THE PROGRESS OF RICHARD HUNTER.

L. M. Montgomery
1874–1942

WHEN read to children aged, say seven to ten, *Anne of Green Gables* may seem to emphasize its innocence and delight. When read by young adults, *Anne* may seem a somewhat less innocent book. Perhaps it is fair to say that the child in all of us will always respond delightedly to Anne's pixy qualities; her sensitivity to her own moods, feelings, and bodily sensations; her animation and energy; her romantic imagination and closeness to nature; her touching need for a loving home and parental care; her daily connection to beauty and joy. Still, even from the outset of her story, even at the age of eleven, Anne, in the fashion of many young adult heroines, fairly flings challenges to those around her. As she progresses through middle adolescence, moreover, she encounters many of the predictable, and sobering, experiences patterned in novels for youth.

Not only does Anne's behavior often exasperate the daylights out of her adoptive parents, the brother-sister team of Matthew and Marilla Cuthbert, and not only does she hurl the dreaded h-word at their neighbor, Mrs. Rachel Lynde, but also Anne challenges some of the most basic principles and beliefs held by those adults and by the wider community. Marilla describes Anne as "a freckled witch of a girl who knew and cared nothing about God's love." Anne finds the Scots Presbyterian minister's God "way too far off to make it worth while." What Anne worships is the divine beauty of the natural, palpable world, a beauty of this life in the here and now and not an afterlife in a hoped-for heaven. Anne, who would "rather be pretty than clever," informs the "aesthetic sense" of Marilla and the empathic "imagination" of Miss Barry. She peoples the landscape with "pagan" nature spirits. Like the heroines of Shakespeare's *Twelfth Night* and of such films as "Babette's Feast" and "Like Water for Chocolate," Anne enters a world already made sour and colorless by forced pieties. By sheer counterforce of personal example, these heroines restore their too often puritanical communities to life. In so doing, they remind us all that the young may renew the old, if they will only listen. Still, in the fashion of many stories chronicling young adulthood, Anne finds that to restore some of the innocent pleasure in life within her peers and elders she must, at the same time, lose some innocence of her own.

Anne's maturation from play toward duty reflects her author's own experience. Born on Canada's Prince Edward Island in 1874, Lucy Maud Montgomery was raised by grandparents. Combining school and solitude in her childhood, Maud's reverence for nature stemmed from both her countryside wanderings and her reading. Steeped in the romantic and sentimental literature of her day, she aspired to write poems and stories. She submitted her early efforts to contests and journals and slowly found acceptance. After teaching schoolchildren for several years, and then working briefly for a Halifax newspaper, she returned, at 28, to the farm of her now widowed grandmother. There she provided companionship but also continued her writings for publication. It was during her nine years spent with her grandmother that she penned and published *Anne*, an instant success. At thirty-seven, Maud married the Presbyterian minister, Ewan Macdonald, and entered a new life of demanding community service, interspersed with continued writing of the *Anne* series and other books.

Maud found many of the duties of a minister's wife to be toilsome and irksome, and, in her private journal, she specifically critiqued a Protestant strain of mistrust for sensory delights and of disdain for the natural world as fallen and sinful rather than gloriously reflecting God's handiwork. Still, she persevered in her community service, and her own accommodation matches, to some extent, the one she devised for Anne.

Around her wooded homestead, Anne is all green and golden, seized with the fire of romantic imagination. At school, she must be more restrained and practical, compete on exams, and contend with boys such as Gilbert Blythe. As the teenaged Sarah Jones, in *Malaeska*, left her rural home to shape a new self at school in Manhattan and as Ragged Dick sought to merge his street-smart trickster role with one of more sober respectability, so Anne endures the classic young adult search for a workable and true identity. "There's such a lot of different Annes in me," she declares to her best friend, Diana. How are the different Annes to be harmonized? The answer, as usual, involves compromise. Trying, more and more, "not to imagine anything but to keep [her] thoughts on facts," Anne learns not to imagine the wood haunted by ghosts and goblins. She will "grow up to be sensible," accept her "besetting sin" of imagining too much, and conclude, even, that "it's no use trying to be romantic in Avonlea." Adolescent Anne now faces "the worst of growing up . . . The things you wanted so much when you were a child don't seem half so wonderful to you when you get them." Here is that darkening of reality, that scent of disillusion, that has grown ever stronger through the long history of young adult literature.

In *Malaeska* and in *Ragged Dick*, the schools attended by Sarah Jones and by Frank Whitney are private boarding schools, one for girls the other for boys. By the time of Anne, a half century after the era of Dick and Frank, the majority school is public and coeducational. Public high school for Anne, living at the turn of the century, involves, moreover, not merely teachers and subjects but also boys and potential mating. For a while, Anne can hold Gilbert at arm's length. She tells Marilla: "Young men are all very well in their place, but it doesn't do to drag them into everything, does it? Diana and I are thinking seriously of promising each other that we will never marry but be nice old maids and live together for ever." As young adult literature works ceaselessly over the great liminal transitions of youth from family to same-sex chumships to cross-sex pairings, this very tentative "solution" of Anne's—simply to keep the other sex at bay—seems (perhaps wistfully) naïve. It is, however, a strategy that Maud Montgomery pursued for a very long time, and, no doubt contrary to the expectations of many first-time readers, in *Anne*, Maud allows her heroine to emulate her. Anne puts off Gilbert Blythe, though "she had a vague consciousness that masculine friendship might also be a good thing to round out one's conceptions of companionship." In many later young adult novels, male-female friendship, and even love, will gradually edge toward center stage.

Also kept at bay in *Anne* is any serious consideration of ethnic and similar diversities at school or in the community. Anne and her young adult friends seem to be all white, Protestant, and more or less allied in social standing. There are, to be sure, some glancing jibes at French-Canadian (Catholic) Jerry Buote, and at Italians, and Jews, just as in *Ragged Dick* the English-descended Whitneys, Greysons, Fosdicks, and Hunters hold in easy contempt the Irish-named land-lady, Mrs. Mooney, and bully, Mickey Maguire. Three or four decades after *Anne*, however, in John R. Tunis' YA classic, All-American, with its Abraham Lincoln High, the melting pot will be boiling for certain.

As young adult literature matured toward its golden decades of realism in the second half of the twentieth century, it took on ever greater, and darker, problems of youth's real life: racial and religious bigotry, sex, parental divorce and abuse, drugs, violence. All this may make *Anne*, when viewed retrospectively, seem hopelessly naïve, seem literature for children. Nonetheless, when read carefully, *Anne* tells the story of a girl's far journey into womanhood, a journey with its own real and sobering consequences. Shrewd Miss Barry recognizes that teenaged Anne can never be as funny as before: "I don't know that she is as amusing as she was when she was a child." A woman now, who has left child-hood behind, Anne must endure the death of Matthew and the "horrible dull ache of misery" it brings on. To assist the aging and weakening Marilla, Anne delays, or forgoes, her higher education at Redmond. Even as she has Anne conclude that, still, "all's right with the world," the author concedes: "Anne's horizons had closed in." This is, then, the bittersweet ending reached by so many narratives of adolescence awaking to the losses, as well as gains, experi-enced in any true entrance to adulthood. In *Anne*, at least, if not in all such coming-of-age stories, the sweet still outweighs the bitter, for Anne has brought too much joy to too many hearts for her to remain, in memory, anything other than the veritable angel of Avonlea.

ANNE OF GREEN
GABLES

"The good stars met in your horoscope,
Made you of spirit and fire and dew."
—BROWNING.[1]

---

1 *Browning* These are lines 19–20 from "Evelyn Hope" (1855) by Robert Browning
(1812–1889), a dramatic monologue telling of the speaker's love for Evelyn Hope who was "sixteen
years old when she died" and whose "soul was pure and true" (9, 18).

CHAPTER 1

Mrs. Rachel Lynde Is Surprised

M RS. RACHEL LYNDE lived just where the Avonlea main road dipped down into a little hollow, fringed with alders and ladies' eardrops and traversed by a brook that had its source away back in the woods of the old Cuthbert place; it was reputed to be an intricate, headlong brook in its earlier course through those woods, with dark secrets of pool and cascade; but by the time it reached Lynde's Hollow it was a quiet, well-conducted little stream, for not even a brook could run past Mrs. Rachel Lynde's door without due regard for decency and decorum; it probably was conscious that Mrs. Rachel was sitting at her window, keeping a sharp eye on everything that passed, from brooks and children up, and that if she noticed anything odd or out of place she would never rest until she had ferreted out the whys and wherefores thereof.

There are plenty of people, in Avonlea and out of it, who can attend closely to their neighbours' business by dint of neglecting their own; but Mrs. Rachel Lynde was one of those capable creatures who can manage their own concerns and those of other folks into the bargain. She was a notable housewife; her work was always done and well done; she "ran" the Sewing Circle, helped run the Sunday-school, and was the strongest prop of the Church Aid Society and Foreign Missions Auxiliary. Yet with all this Mrs. Rachel found abundant time to sit for hours at her kitchen window, knitting "cotton warp" quilts[1]—she had knitted sixteen of them, as Avonlea housekeepers were wont to tell in awed voices—and keeping a sharp eye on the main road that crossed the hollow and wound up the steep red hill beyond. Since Avonlea occupied a little triangular peninsula jutting out into the Gulf of St. Lawrence, with water on two sides of it, anybody who went out of it or into it had to pass over that hill road and so run the unseen gauntlet of Mrs. Rachel's all-seeing eye.

She was sitting there one afternoon in early June. The sun was coming in at the window warm and bright; the orchard on the slope below the house was in a bridal flush of pinky-white bloom, hummed over by a myriad of bees. Thomas Lynde—a meek little man whom Avonlea people called "Rachel Lynde's husband"—was sowing his late turnip seed on the hill field beyond the barn; and Matthew Cuthbert ought to have been sowing his on the big red brook field away over by Green Gables. Mrs. Rachel knew that he ought because she had heard him tell Peter Morrison the evening before in William J. Blair's store over at Carmody that he meant to sow his turnip seed the next afternoon. Peter had asked him, of course, for Matthew Cuthbert had never been known to volunteer information about anything in his whole life.

And yet here was Matthew Cuthbert, at half-past three on the afternoon of a busy day, placidly driving over the hollow and up the hill; moreover, he wore a white collar and his best suit of clothes, which was plain proof that he was going out of Avonlea; and he had the buggy and the sorrel mare, which betokened that he was going a considerable distance. Now, where was Matthew Cuthbert going and why was he going there?

Had it been any other man in Avonlea Mrs. Rachel, deftly putting this and that together, might have given a pretty good guess as to both questions. But

---

1 *"cotton warp" quilts*   quilts or bedspreads made soft from cotton thread; the "warp" is the heavier thread running lengthwise in the fabric.

Matthew so rarely went from home that it must be something pressing and un-usual which was taking him; he was the shyest man alive and hated to have to go among strangers or to any place where he might have to talk. Matthew, dressed up with a white collar and driving in a buggy, was something that didn't happen often. Mrs. Rachel, ponder as she might, could make nothing of it and her afternoon's enjoyment was spoiled.

"I'll just step over to Green Gables after tea and find out from Marilla where he's gone and why," the worthy woman finally concluded. "He doesn't generally go to town this time of year and he *never* visits; if he'd run out of turnip seed he wouldn't dress up and take the buggy to go for more; he wasn't driving fast enough to be going for a doctor. Yet something must have happened since last night to start him off. I'm clean puzzled, that's what, and I won't know a minute's peace of mind or conscience until I know what has taken Matthew Cuthbert out of Avonlea to-day."

Accordingly after tea Mrs. Rachel set out; she had not far to go; the big, rambling, orchard-embowered house where the Cuthberts lived was a scant quarter of a mile up the road from Lynde's Hollow. To be sure, the long lane made it a good deal further. Matthew Cuthbert's father, as shy and silent as his son after him, had got as far away as he possibly could from his fellow men without actually retreating into the woods when he founded his homestead. Green Gables was built at the furthest edge of his cleared land and there it was to this day, barely visible from the main road along which all the other Avonlea houses were so sociably situated. Mrs. Rachel Lynde did not call living in such a place *living* at all.

"It's just *staying*, that's what," she said as she stepped along the deep-rutted, grassy lane bordered with wild rose bushes. "It's no wonder Matthew and Marilla are both a little odd, living away back here by themselves. Trees aren't much company, though dear knows if they were there'd be enough of them. I'd ruther look at people. To be sure, they seem contented enough; but then, I suppose, they're used to it. A body can get used to anything, even to being hanged, as the Irishman said."[2]

With this Mrs. Rachel stepped out of the lane into the backyard of Green Gables. Very green and neat and precise was that yard, set about on one side with great patriarchal willows and on the other with prim Lombardies.[3] Not a stray stick nor stone was to be seen, for Mrs. Rachel would have seen it if there had been. Privately she was of the opinion that Marilla Cuthbert swept that yard over as often as she swept her house. One could have eaten a meal off the ground without overbrimming the proverbial peck of dirt.

Mrs. Rachel rapped smartly at the kitchen door and stepped in when bidden to do so. The kitchen at Green Gables was a cheerful apartment—or would have been cheerful if it had not been so painfully clean as to give it something of the appearance of an unused parlour. Its windows looked east and west; through the west one, looking out on the back yard, came a flood of mellow June sunlight; but the east one, whence you got a glimpse of the bloom of white cherry-trees in the left orchard and nodding, slender birches down in the hollow by the brook, was greened over by a tangle of vines. Here sat Marilla Cuthbert, when she sat at

---

2 *A body . . . Irishman said*   proverbial slur against the Irish as more "used to" hanging than were other groups.

3 *patriarchal willows . . . Lombardies*   the willows are ancient and perhaps of imposing spread with their downward-hanging branches while the Lombardy poplars are relatively slender (with upward-pointing branches).

all, always slightly distrustful of sunshine, which seemed to her too dancing and irresponsible a thing for a world which was meant to be taken seriously; and here she sat now, knitting, and the table behind her was laid for supper.

Mrs. Rachel, before she had fairly closed the door, had taken mental note of everything that was on that table. There were three plates laid, so that Marilla must be expecting some one home with Matthew to tea;[4] but the dishes were every-day dishes and there was only crab-apple preserves and one kind of cake, so that the expected company could not be any particular company. Yet what of Matthew's white collar and the sorrel mare? Mrs. Rachel was getting fairly dizzy with this unusual mystery about quiet, unmysterious Green Gables.

"Good evening, Rachel," Marilla said briskly. "This is a real find evening, isn't it? Won't you sit down? How are all your folks?"

Something that for lack of any other name might be called friendship existed and always had existed between Marilla Cuthbert and Mrs. Rachel, in spite of—or perhaps because of—their dissimilarity.

Marilla was a tall, thin woman, with angles and without curves; her dark hair showed some gray streaks and was always twisted up in a hard little knot behind with two wire hairpins stuck aggressively through it. She looked like a woman of narrow experience and rigid conscience, which she was; but there was a saving something about her mouth which, if it had been ever so slightly developed, might have been considered indicative of a sense of humour.

"We're all pretty well," said Mrs. Rachel. "I was kind of afraid *you* weren't, though, when I saw Matthew starting off to-day. I thought maybe he was going to the doctor's."

Marilla's lips twitched understandingly. She had expected Mrs. Rachel up; she had known that the sight of Matthew jaunting off so unaccountably would be too much for her neighbour's curiosity.

"Oh, no, I'm quite well although I had a bad headache yesterday," she said. "Matthew went to Bright River. We're getting a little boy from an orphan asylum in Nova Scotia and he's coming on the train to-night."

If Marilla had said that Matthew had gone to Bright River to meet a kangaroo from Australia Mrs. Rachel could not have been more astonished. She was actually stricken dumb for five seconds. It was unsupposable that Marilla was making fun of her, but Mrs. Rachel was almost forced to suppose it.

"Are you in earnest, Marilla?" she demanded when voice returned to her.

"Yes, of course," said Marilla, as if getting boys from orphan asylums in Nova Scotia were part of the usual spring work on any well-regulated Avonlea farm instead of being an unheard of innovation.

Mrs. Rachel felt that she had received a severe mental jolt. She thought in exclamation points. A boy! Marilla and Matthew Cuthbert of all people adopting a boy! From an orphan asylum! Well, the world was certainly turning upside down! She would be surprised at nothing after this! Nothing!

"What on earth put such a notion into your head?" she demanded disapprovingly.

This had been done without her advice being asked, and must perforce be disapproved.

"Well, we've been thinking about it for some time—all winter in fact," returned Marilla. "Mrs. Alexander Spencer was up here one day before Christmas and she

---

4 *tea* here, meaning supper.

said she was going to get a little girl from the asylum over in Hopetown in the spring. Her cousin lives there and Mrs. Spencer has visited her and knows all about it. So Matthew and I have talked it over off and on ever since. We thought we'd get a boy. Matthew is getting up in years, you know—he's sixty—and he isn't so spry as he once was. His heart troubles him a good deal. And you know how desperate hard it's got to be to get hired help. There's never anybody to be had but those stupid, half-grown little French boys; and as soon as you do get one broke into your ways and taught something he's up and off to the lobster canneries or the States. At first Matthew suggested getting a Barnardo boy.[5] But I said 'no' flat to that. 'They may be all right—I'm not saying they're not—but no London street Arabs[6] for me,' I said. 'Give me a native born at least. There'll be a risk, no matter who we get. But I'll feel easier in my mind and sleep sounder at nights if we get a born Canadian' So in the end we decided to ask Mrs. Spencer to pick us out one when she went over to get her little girl. We heard last week she was going, so we sent her word by Richard Spencer's folks at Carmody to bring us a smart, likely boy of about ten or eleven. We decided that would be the best age—old enough to be of some use in doing chores right off and young enough to be trained up proper. We mean to give him a good home and schooling. We had a telegram from Mrs. Alexander Spencer to-day—the mail-man brought it from the station—saying they were coming on the five-thirty train tonight. So Matthew went to Bright River to meet him. Mrs. Spencer will drop him off there. Of course she goes on to White Sands station herself."

Mrs. Rachel prided herself on always speaking her mind; she proceeded to speak it now, having adjusted her mental attitude to this amazing piece of news.

"Well, Marilla, I'll just tell you plain that I think you're doing a mighty foolish thing—a risky thing, that's what. You don't know what you're getting. You're bringing a strange child into your house and home and you don't know a single thing about him nor what his disposition is like nor what sort of parents he had nor how he's likely to turn out. Why, it was only last week I read in the paper how a man and his wife up west of the Island took a boy out of an orphan asylum and he set fire to the house at night—set it *on purpose*, Marilla—and nearly burnt them to a crisp in their beds. And I know another case where an adopted boy used to suck the eggs—they couldn't break him of it. If you had asked my advice in the matter—which you didn't do, Marilla—I'd have said for mercy's sake not to think of such a thing, that's what."

This Job's comforting[7] seemed neither to offend nor alarm Marilla. She knitted steadily on.

"I don't deny there's something in what you say, Rachel. I've had some qualms myself. But Matthew was terrible set on it. I could see that, so I gave in. It's so seldom Matthew sets his mind on anything that when he does I always feel it's my duty to give in. And as for the risk, there's risks in pretty near everything a body does in this world. There's risks in people's having children of their own if it comes to that—they don't always turn out well. And then Nova Scotia is right close to the Island. It isn't as if we were getting him from England or the States. He can't be much different from ourselves."

---

5 *Barnardo boy*   orphan immigrant from Britain to North America. In the 1860s Dr. Thomas Barnardo, advocating such child immigration, began to establish housing for poor orphans who often were taken from the Barnardo homes to serve as domestics and farm workers.

6 *street Arabs*   homeless children (thought of as wandering or nomadic, hence "Arabs").

7 *Job's comforting*   In the Biblical book of Job, Job's friends lecture the suffering Job instead of comforting him.

"Well, I hope it will turn out all right," said Mrs. Rachel in a tone that plainly indicated her painful doubts. "Only don't say I didn't warn you if he burns Green Gables down or puts strychnine in the well—I heard of a case over in New Brunswick where an orphan asylum child did that and the whole family died in fearful agonies. Only, it was a girl in that instance."

"Well, we're not getting a girl," said Marilla, as if poisoning wells were a purely feminine accomplishment and not to be dreaded in the case of a boy. "I'd never dream of taking a girl to bring up. I wonder at Mrs. Alexander Spencer for doing it. But there, *she* wouldn't shrink from adopting a whole orphan asylum if she took it into her head."

Mrs. Rachel would have liked to stay until Matthew came home with his imported orphan. But reflecting that it would be a good two hours at least before his arrival she concluded to go up the road to Robert Bell's and tell them the news. It would certainly make a sensation second to none, and Mrs. Rachel dearly loved to make a sensation. So she took herself away, somewhat to Marilla's relief, for the latter felt her doubts and fears reviving under the influence of Mrs. Rachel's pessimism.

"Well, of all things that ever were or will be!" ejaculated Mrs. Rachel when she was safely out in the lane. "It does really seem as if I must be dreaming. Well, I'm sorry for that poor young one and no mistake. Matthew and Marilla don't know anything about children and they'll expect him to be wiser and steadier than his own grandfather, if so be's he ever had a grandfather, which is doubtful. It seems uncanny to think of a child at Green Gables somehow; there's never been one there, for Matthew and Marilla were grown up when the new house was built—if they ever *were* children, which is hard to believe when one looks at them. I wouldn't be in that orphan's shoes for anything. My, but I pity him, that's what."

So said Mrs. Rachel to the wild rose bushes out of the fulness of her heart; but if she could have seen the child who was waiting patiently at the Bright River station at that very moment her pity would have been still deeper and more profound.

CHAPTER 2

Matthew Cuthbert Is Surprised

MATTHEW Cuthbert and the sorrel mare jogged comfortably over the eight miles to Bright River. It was a pretty road, running along between snug farmsteads, with now and again a bit of balsamy fir wood to drive through or a hollow where wild plums hung out their filmy bloom. The air was sweet with the breath of many apple orchards and the meadows sloped away in the distance to horizon mists of pearl and purple; while

> "The little birds sang as if it were
> The one day of summer in all the year."[1]

---

1 *The little birds . . . year*   from "The Vision of Sir Launfal" (1.2.3-4) by James Russell Lowell (1819–1891).

Matthew enjoyed the drive after his own fashion, except during the moments when he met women and had to nod to them—for in Prince Edward Island you are supposed to nod to all and sundry you meet on the road whether you know them or not.

Matthew dreaded all women except Marilla and Mrs. Rachel; he had an uncomfortable feeling that the mysterious creatures were secretly laughing at him. He may have been quite right in thinking so, for he was an odd-looking personage, with an ungainly figure and long iron-gray hair that touched his stooping shoulders, and a full, soft brown beard which he had worn ever since he was twenty. In fact, he had looked at twenty very much as he looked at sixty, lacking a little of the grayness.

When he reached Bright River there was no sign of any train; he thought he was too early, so he tied his horse in the yard of the small Bright River hotel and went over to the station-house. The long platform was almost deserted; the only living creature in sight being a girl who was sitting on a pile of shingles at the extreme end. Matthew, barely noting that it *was* a girl, sidled past her as quickly as possible without looking at her. Had he looked he could hardly have failed to notice the tense rigidity and expectation of her attitude and expression. She was sitting there waiting for something or somebody and, since sitting and waiting was the only thing to do just then, she sat and waited with all her might and main.

Matthew encountered the station-master locking up the ticket-office preparatory to going home for supper, and asked him if the five-thirty train would soon be along.

"The five-thirty train has been in and gone half an hour ago," answered that brisk official. "But there was a passenger dropped off for you—a little girl. She's sitting out there on the shingles. I asked her to go into the ladies' waiting-room, but she informed me gravely that she preferred to stay outside. 'There was more scope for imagination,' she said. She's a case, I should say."

"I'm not expecting a girl," said Matthew blankly. "It's a boy I've come for. He should be here. Mrs. Alexander Spencer was to bring him over from Nova Scotia for me."

The station-master whistled.

"Guess there's some mistake," he said. "Mrs. Spencer came off the train with that girl and gave her into my charge. Said you and your sister were adopting her from an orphan asylum and that you would be along for her presently. That's all *I* know about it—and I haven't got any more orphans concealed hereabouts."

"I don't understand," said Matthew helplessly, wishing that Marilla was at hand to cope with the situation.

"Well, you'd better question the girl," said the station-master carelessly. "I dare say she'll be able to explain—she's got a tongue of her own, that's certain. Maybe they were out of boys of the brand you wanted."

He walked jauntily away, being hungry, and the unfortunate Matthew was left to do that which was harder for him than bearding a lion in its den—walk up to a girl—a strange girl—an orphan girl—and demand of her why she wasn't a boy. Matthew groaned in spirit as he turned about and shuffled gently down the platform towards her.

She had been watching him ever since he had passed her and she had her eyes on him now. Matthew was not looking at her and would not have seen what she was really like if he had been, but an ordinary observer would have seen this:

A child of about eleven, garbed in a very short, very tight, very ugly dress of yellowish gray wincey.[2] She wore a faded brown sailor hat and beneath the hat, extending down her back, were two braids of very thick, decidedly red hair. Her face was small, white and thin, also much freckled; her mouth was large and so were her eyes, that looked green in some lights and moods and gray in others.

So far, the ordinary observer; an extraordinary observer might have seen that the chin was very pointed and pronounced; that the big eyes were full of spirit and vivacity; that the mouth was sweet-lipped and expressive; that the forehead was broad and full; in short, our discerning extraordinary observer might have concluded that no commonplace soul inhabited the body of this stray woman-child of whom shy Matthew Cuthbert was so ludicrously afraid.

Matthew, however, was spared the ordeal of speaking first, for as soon as she concluded that he was coming to her she stood up, grasping with one thin brown hand the handle of a shabby, old-fashioned carpet-bag; the other she held out to him.

"I suppose you are Mr. Matthew Cuthbert of Green Gables?" she said in a peculiarly clear, sweet voice. "I'm very glad to see you. I was beginning to be afraid you weren't coming for me and I was imagining all the things that might have happened to prevent you. I had made up my mind that if you didn't come for me to-night I'd go down the track to that big wild cherry-tree at the bend, and climb up into it to stay all night. I wouldn't be a bit afraid, and it would be lovely to sleep in a wild cherry-tree all white with bloom in the moonshine, don't you think? You could imagine you were dwelling in marble halls, couldn't you? And I was quite sure you would come for me in the morning, if you didn't tonight."

Matthew had taken the scrawny little hand awkwardly in his; then and there he decided what to do. He could not tell this child with the glowing eyes that there had been a mistake; he would take her home and let Marilla do that. She couldn't be left at Bright River anyhow, no matter what mistake had been made, so all questions and explanations might as well be deferred until he was safely back at Green Gables.

"I'm sorry I was late," he said shyly. "Come along. The horse is over in the yard. Give me your bag."

"Oh, I can carry it," the child responded cheerfully. "It isn't heavy. I've got all my worldly goods in it, but it isn't heavy. And if it isn't carried in just a certain way the handle pulls out—so I'd better keep it because I know the exact knack of it. It's an extremely old carpet-bag. Oh, I'm very glad you've come, even if it would have been nice to sleep in a wild cherry-tree. We've got to drive a long piece, haven't we? Mrs. Spencer said it was eight miles. I'm glad because I love driving. Oh, it seems so wonderful that I'm going to live with you and belong to you. I've never belonged to anybody—not really. But the asylum was the worst. I've only been in it four months, but that was enough. I don't suppose you ever were an orphan in an asylum, so you can't possibly understand what it is like. It's worse than anything you could imagine. Mrs. Spencer said it was wicked of me

---

2 *wincey* linsey-woolsey, plain cloth weaving linen (or cotton) with wool.

to talk like that, but I didn't mean to be wicked. It's so easy to be wicked without knowing it, isn't it? They were good, you know—the asylum people. But there is so little scope for the imagination in an asylum—only just in the other orphans. It *was* pretty interesting to imagine things about them—to imagine that perhaps the girl who sat next to you was really the daughter of a belted earl, who had been stolen away from her parents in her infancy by a cruel nurse who died before she could confess. I used to lie awake at nights and imagine things like that, because I didn't have time in the day. I guess that's why I'm so thin—I *am* dreadful thin, ain't I? There isn't a pick[3] on my bones. I do love to imagine I'm nice and plump, with dimples in my elbows."

With this Matthew's companion stopped talking, partly because she was out of breath and partly because they had reached the buggy. Not another word did she say until they had left the village and were driving down a steep little hill, the road part of which had been cut so deeply into the soft soil that the banks, fringed with blooming wild cherry-trees and slim white birches, were several feet above their heads.

The child put out her hand and broke off a branch of wild plum that brushed against the side of the buggy.

"Isn't that beautiful? What did that tree, leaning out from the bank, all white and lacy, make you think of?" she asked.

"Well now, I dunno," said Matthew.

"Why, a bride, of course—a bride all in white with a lovely misty veil. I've never seen one, but I can imagine what she would look like. I don't ever expect to be a bride myself. I'm so homely nobody will ever want to marry me—unless it might be a foreign missionary. I suppose a foreign missionary mightn't be very particular. But I do hope that some day I shall have a white dress. That is my highest ideal of earthly bliss. I just love pretty clothes. And I've never had a pretty dress in my life that I can remember—but of course it's all the more to look forward to, isn't it? And then I can imagine that I'm dressed gorgeously. This morning when I left the asylum I felt so ashamed because I had to wear this horrid old wincey dress. All the orphans had to wear them, you know. A merchant in Hopeton last winter donated three hundred yards of wincey to the asylum. Some people said it was because he couldn't sell it, but I'd rather believe that it was out of the kindness of his heart, wouldn't you? When we got on the train I felt as if everybody must be looking at me and pitying me. But I just went to work and imagined that I had on the most beautiful pale blue silk dress—because when you *are* imagining you might as well imagine something worth while—and a big hat all flowers and nodding plumes, and a gold watch, and kid gloves and boots. I felt cheered up right away and I enjoyed my trip to the Island with all my might. I wasn't a bit sick coming over in the boat. Neither was Mrs. Spencer, although she generally is. She said she hadn't time to get sick, watching to see that I didn't fall overboard. She said she never saw the beat of me for prowling about. But if it kept her from being seasick it's a mercy I did prowl, isn't it? And I wanted to see everything that was to be seen on that boat, because I didn't know whether I'd ever have another opportunity. Oh, there are a lot more cherry-trees all in bloom! This Island is the bloomiest place. I just love it already, and I'm so glad I'm going to live here. I've always heard that Prince Edward Island was the prettiest place in the world, and I used to imagine

---

3 *pick*   edible bit, mouthful, morsel.

I was living here, but I never really expected I would. It's delightful when your imaginations come true, isn't it? But those red roads are so funny. When we got into the train at Charlottetown and the red roads began to flash past I asked Mrs. Spencer what made them red[4] and she said she didn't know and for pity's sake not to ask her any more questions. She said I must have asked her a thousand already. I suppose I had, too, but how are you going to find out about things if you don't ask questions? And what *does* make the roads red?"

"Well now, I dunno," said Matthew.

"Well, that is one of the things to find out sometime. Isn't it splendid to think of all the things there are to find out about? It just makes me feel glad to be alive—it's such an interesting world. It wouldn't be half so interesting if we knew all about everything, would it? There'd be no scope for imagination then, would there? But am I talking too much? People are always telling me I do. Would you rather I didn't talk? If you say so I'll stop. I *can* stop when I make up my mind to it, although it's difficult."

Matthew, much to his own surprise, was enjoying himself. Like most quiet folks he liked talkative people when they were willing to do the talking themselves and did not expect him to keep up his end of it. But he had never expected to enjoy the society of a little girl. Women were bad enough in all conscience, but little girls were worse. He detested the way they had of sidling past him timidly, with sidewise glances, as if they expected him to gobble them up at a mouthful if they ventured to say a word. This was the Avonlea type of well-bred little girl. But this freckled witch was very different, and although he found it rather difficult for his slower intelligence to keep up with her brisk mental processes he thought that he "kind of liked her chatter." So he said as shyly as usual:

"Oh, you can talk as much as you like. I don't mind."

"Oh, I'm so glad. I know you and I are going to get along together fine. It's such a relief to talk when one wants to and not be told that children should be seen and not heard. I've had that said to me a million times if I have once. And people laugh at me because I use big words. But if you have big ideas you have to use big words to express them, haven't you?"

"Well now, that seems reasonable," said Matthew.

"Mrs. Spencer said that my tongue must be hung in the middle. But it isn't—it's firmly fastened at one end. Mrs. Spencer said your place was named Green Gables. I asked her all about it. And she said there were trees all around it. I was gladder than ever. I just love trees. And there weren't any at all about the asylum, only a few poor weeny-teeny things out in front with little whitewashed cagey things about them. They just looked like orphans themselves, those trees did. It used to make me want to cry to look at them. I used to say to them, 'Oh, you *poor* little things! If you were out in a great big woods with other trees all around you and little mosses and Junebells growing over your roots and a brook not far away and birds singing in your branches, you could grow, couldn't you? But you can't where you are. I know just exactly how you feel, little trees.' I felt sorry to leave them behind this morning. You do get so attached to things like that, don't you? Is there a brook anywhere near Green Gables? I forgot to ask Mrs. Spencer that."

"Well now, yes, there's one right below the house."

---

4 *what made them red* iron particles in the earth.

"Fancy! It's always been one of my dreams to live near a brook. I never expected I would, though. Dreams don't often come true, do they? Wouldn't it be nice if they did? But just now I feel pretty nearly perfectly happy. I can't feel exactly perfectly happy because—well, what colour would you call this?"

She twitched one of her long glossy braids over her thin shoulder and held it up before Matthew's eyes. Matthew was not used to deciding on the tints of ladies' tresses, but in this case there couldn't be much doubt.

"It's red, ain't it?" he said.

The girl let the braid drop back with a sigh that seemed to come from her very toes and to exhale forth all the sorrows of the ages.

"Yes, it's red," she said resignedly. "Now you see why I can't be perfectly happy. Nobody could who had red hair. I don't mind the other things so much—the freckles and the green eyes and my skinniness. I can imagine them away. I can imagine that I have a beautiful rose-leaf complexion and lovely starry violet eyes. But I *cannot* imagine that red hair away. I do my best. I think to myself, 'Now my hair is a glorious black, black as the raven's wing.' But all the time I *know* it is just plain red, and it breaks my heart. It will be my lifelong sorrow. I read of a girl once in a novel who had a lifelong sorrow, but it wasn't red hair. Her hair was pure gold rippling back from her alabaster brow. What is an alabaster brow? I never could find out. Can you tell me?"

"Well now, I'm afraid I can't," said Matthew, who was getting a little dizzy. He felt as he had once felt in his rash youth when another boy had enticed him on the merry-go-round at a picnic.

"Well, whatever it was it must have been something nice because she was divinely beautiful. Have you ever imagined what it must feel like to be divinely beautiful?"

"Well now, no, I haven't," confessed Matthew ingenuously.

"I have, often. Which would you rather be if you had the choice—divinely beautiful or dazzlingly clever or angelically good?"

"Well now, I—I don't know exactly."

"Neither do I. I can never decide. But it doesn't make much real difference for it isn't likely I'll ever be either. It's certain I'll never be angelically good, Mrs. Spencer says—oh, Mr. Cuthbert! Oh, Mr. Cuthbert!! Oh, Mr. Cuthbert!!!"

That was not what Mrs. Spencer had said; neither had the child tumbled out of the buggy nor had Matthew done anything astonishing. They had simply rounded a curve in the road and found themselves in the "Avenue."

The "Avenue," so called by the Newbridge people, was a stretch of road four or five hundred yards long, completely arched over with huge, wide-spreading apple-trees, planted years ago by an eccentric old farmer. Overhead was one long canopy of snowy fragrant bloom. Below the boughs the air was full of a purple twilight and far ahead a glimpse of painted sunset sky shone like a great rose window at the end of a cathedral aisle.

Its beauty seemed to strike the child dumb. She leaned back in the buggy, her thin hands clasped before her, her face lifted rapturously to the white splendour above. Even when they had passed out and were driving down the long slope to Newbridge she never moved or spoke. Still with rapt face she gazed afar into the sunset west, with eyes that saw visions trooping splendidly across that glowing background. Through Newbridge, a bustling little village where dogs barked at them and small boys hooted and curious faces peered from the windows, they drove, still in silence. When three more miles had dropped away behind them the child had not spoken. She could keep silence, it was evident, as energetically as she could talk.

"I guess you're feeling pretty tired and hungry," Matthew ventured at last, accounting for her long visitation of dumbness with the only reason he could think of. "But we haven't very far to go now—only another mile."

She came out of her reverie with a deep sigh and looked at him with the dreamy gaze of a soul that had been wondering afar, star-led.

"Oh, Mr. Cuthbert," she whispered, "that place we came through—that white place—what was it?"

"Well now, you must mean the Avenue," said Matthew after a few moments' profound reflection. "It is a kind of pretty place."

"Pretty? Oh, *pretty* doesn't seem the right word to use. Nor beautiful, either. They don't go far enough. Oh, it was wonderful—wonderful. It's the first thing I ever saw that couldn't be improved upon by imagination. It just satisfied me here"—she put one hand on her breast—"it made a queer funny ache and yet it was a pleasant ache. Did you ever have an ache like that, Mr. Cuthbert?"

"Well now, I just can't recollect that I ever had."

"I have it lots of times, whenever I see anything royally beautiful. But they shouldn't call that lovely place the Avenue. There is no meaning in a name like that. They should call it—let me see—the White Way of Delight. Isn't that a nice imaginative name? When I don't like the name of a place or a person I always imagine a new one and always think of them so. There was a girl at the asylum whose name was Hepzibah Jenkins, but I always imagined her as Rosalia DeVere. Other people may call that place the Avenue, but I shall always call it the White Way of Delight. Have we really only another mile to go before we get home? I'm glad and I'm sorry. I'm sorry because this drive has been so pleasant and I'm always sorry when pleasant things end. Something still pleasanter may come after, but you can never be sure. And it's so often the case that it isn't pleasanter. That has been my experience anyhow. But I'm glad to think of getting home. You see, I've never had a real home since I can remember. It gives me that pleasant ache again just to think of coming to a really truly home. Oh, isn't that pretty!"

They had driven over the crest of a hill. Below them was a pond, looking almost like a river so long and winding was it. A bridge spanned it midway and from there to its lower end, where an amber-hued belt of sand-hills shut it in from the dark blue gulf beyond, the water was a glory of many shifting hues— the most spiritual shadings of crocus and rose and ethereal green, with other elusive tintings for which no name has ever been found. Above the bridge the pond ran up into fringing groves of fir and maple and lay all darkly translucent in their wavering shadows. Here and there a wild plum leaned out from the bank like a whiteclad girl tip-toeing to her own reflection. From the marsh at the head of the pond came the clear, mournfully-sweet chorus of the frogs. There was a little gray house peering around a white apple orchard on a slope beyond and, although it was not yet quite dark, a light was shining from one of its windows.

"That's Barry's pond," said Matthew.

"Oh, I don't like that name, either. I shall call it—let me see—the Lake of Shining Waters. Yes, that is the right name for it. I know because of the thrill. When I hit on a name that suits exactly it gives me a thrill. Do things ever give you a thrill?"

Matthew ruminated.

"Well now, yes. It always kind of gives me a thrill to see them ugly white grubs that spade up in the cucumber beds. I hate the look of them."

"Oh, I don't think that can be exactly the same kind of a thrill. Do you think it can? There doesn't seem to be much connection between grubs and lakes of shining waters, does there? But why do other people call it Barry's pond?"

"I reckon because Mr. Barry lives up there in that house. Orchard Slope's the name of his place. If it wasn't for that big bush[5] behind it you could see Green Gables from here. But we have to go over the bridge and round by the road, so it's near half a mile further."

"Has Mr. Barry any little girls? Well, not so very little either—about my size."

"He's got one about eleven. Her name is Diana."

"Oh!" with a long indrawing of breath. "What a perfectly lovely name!"

"Well now, I dunno. There's something dreadful heathenish about it, seems to me. I'd ruther Jane or Mary or some sensible name like that. But when Diana was born there was a schoolmaster boarding there and they gave him the naming of her and he called her Diana."

"I wish there had been a schoolmaster like that around when *I* was born, then. Oh, here we are at the bridge. I'm going to shut my eyes tight. I'm always afraid going over bridges. I can't help imagining that perhaps, just as we get to the middle, they'll crumple up like a jack-knife and nip us. So I shut my eyes. But I always have to open them for all when I think we're getting near the middle. Because, you see, if the bridge *did* crumple up I'd want to *see* it crumple. What a jolly rumble it makes! I always like the rumble part of it. Isn't it splendid there are so many things to like in this world? There, we're over. Now I'll look back. Good night, dear Lake of Shining Waters. I always say good night to the things I love, just as I would to people. I think they like it. That water looks as if it was smiling at me."

When they had driven up the further hill and around a corner Matthew said:

"We're pretty near home now. That's Green Gables over—"

"Oh, don't tell me," she interrupted breathlessly, catching at his partially raised arm and shutting her eyes that she might not see his gesture. "Let me guess. I'm sure I'll guess right."

She opened her eyes and looked about her. They were on the crest of a hill. The sun had set some time since, but the landscape was still clear in the mellow afterlight. To the west a dark church spire rose up against a marigold sky. Below was a little valley and beyond a long, gently-rising slope with snug farm-steads scattered along it. From one to another the child's eyes darted, eager and wistful. At last they lingered on one away to the left, far back from the road, dimly white with blossoming trees in the twilight of the surrounding woods. Over it, in the stainless southwest sky, a great crystal-white star was shining like a lamp of guidance and promise.

"That's it, isn't it?" she said, pointing.

Matthew slapped the reins on the sorrel's back delightedly.

"Well now, you've guessed it! But I reckon Mrs. Spencer described it so's you could tell."

"No, she didn't—really she didn't. All she said might just as well have been about most of those other places. I hadn't any real idea what it looked like. But just as soon as I saw it I felt it was home. Oh, it seems as if I must be in a dream.

---

5 *that big bush*   clump of trees or other substantial foliage.

Do you know, my arm must be black and blue from the elbow up, for I've pinched myself so many times to-day. Every little while a horrible sickening feeling would come over me and I'd be so afraid it was all a dream. Then I'd pinch myself to see if it was real—until suddenly I remembered that even supposing it was only a dream I'd better go on dreaming as long as I could; so I stopped pinching. But it is real and we're nearly home."

With a sigh of rapture she relapsed into silence. Matthew stirred uneasily. He felt glad that it would be Marilla and not he who would have to tell this waif of the world that the home she longed for was not to be hers after all. They drove over Lynde's Hollow, where it was already quite dark, but not so dark that Mrs. Rachel could not see them from her window vantage, and up the hill and into the long lane of Green Gables. By the time they arrived at the house Matthew was shrinking from the approaching revelation with an energy he did not understand. It was not of Marilla or himself he was thinking or of the trouble this mistake was probably going to make for them, but of the child's disappointment. When he thought of that rapt light being quenched in her eyes he had an uncomfortable feeling that he was going to assist at murdering something—much the same feeling that came over him when he had to kill a lamb or calf or any other innocent little creature.

The yard was quite dark as they turned into it and the poplar leaves were rustling silkily all round it.

"Listen to the trees talking in their sleep," she whispered, as he lifted her to the ground. "What nice dreams they must have!"

Then, holding tightly to the carpet-bag which contained "all her worldly goods," she followed him into the house.

CHAPTER 3

Marilla Cuthbert Is Surprised

MARILLA came briskly forward as Matthew opened the door. But when her eyes fell on the odd little figure in the stiff, ugly dress, with the long braids of red hair and the eager, luminous eyes, she stopped short in amazement.

"Matthew Cuthbert, who's that?" she ejaculated. "Where is the boy?"

"There wasn't any boy," said Matthew wretchedly. "There was only *her*."

He nodded at the child, remembering that he had never even asked her name.

"No boy! But there *must* have been a boy," insisted Marilla. "We sent word to Mrs. Spencer to bring a boy."

"Well, she didn't. She brought *her*. I asked the station-master. And I had to bring her home. She couldn't be left there, no matter where the mistake had come in."

"Well, this is a pretty piece of business!" ejaculated Marilla.

During this dialogue the child had remained silent, her eyes roving from one to the other, all the animation fading out of her face. Suddenly she seemed to grasp the full meaning of what had been said. Dropping her precious carpet-bag she sprang forward a step and clasped her hands.

"You don't want me!" she cried. "You don't want me because I'm not a boy! I might have expected it. Nobody ever did want me. I might have known it was all too beautiful to last. I might have known nobody really did want me. Oh, what shall I do? I'm going to burst into tears!"

Burst into tears she did. Sitting down on a chair by the table, flinging her arms out upon it, and burying her face in them, she proceeded to cry stormily. Marilla and Matthew looked at each other deprecatingly across the stove. Neither of them knew what to say or do. Finally Marilla stepped lamely into the breach.

"Well, well, there's no need to cry so about it."

"Yes, there *is* need!" The child raised her head quickly, revealing a tear-stained face and trembling lips. "*You* would cry, too, if you were an orphan and had come to a place you thought was going to be home and found that they didn't want you because you weren't a boy. Oh, this is the most *tragical* thing that ever happened to me!"

Something like a reluctant smile, rather rusty from long disuse, mellowed Marilla's grim expression.

"Well, don't cry any more. We're not going to turn you out-of-doors to-night. You'll have to stay here until we investigate this affair. What's your name?"

The child hesitated for a moment.

"Will you please call me Cordelia?" she said eagerly.

"*Call* you Cordelia! Is that your name?"

"No-o-o, it's not exactly my name, but I would love to be called Cordelia. It's such a perfectly elegant name."

"I don't know what on earth you mean. If Cordelia isn't your name, what is?"

"Anne Shirley," reluctantly faltered forth the owner of that name, "but oh, please do call me Cordelia. It can't matter much to you what you call me if I'm only going to be here a little while, can it? And Anne is such an unromantic name."

"Unromantic fiddlesticks!" said the unsympathetic Marilla. "Anne is a real good plain sensible name. You've no need to be ashamed of it."

"Oh, I'm not ashamed of it," explained Anne, "only I like Cordelia better. I've always imagined that my name was Cordelia—at least, I always have of late years. When I was young I used to imagine it was Geraldine, but I like Cordelia better now. But if you call me Anne please call me Anne spelled with an *e*."

"What difference does it make how it's spelled?" asked Marilla with another rusty smile as she picked up the teapot.

"Oh, it makes *such* a difference. It *looks* so much nicer. When you hear a name pronounced can't you always see it in your mind, just as if it was printed A-n-n-e out? I can; and A-n-n looks dreadful, but A-n-n-e looks so much more distinguished. If you'll only call me Anne spelled with an *e* I shall try to reconcile myself to not being called Cordelia."

"Very well, then, Anne spelled with an *e*, can you tell us how this mistake came to be made? We sent word to Mrs. Spencer to bring us a boy. Were there no boys at the asylum?"

"Oh, yes, there was an abundance of them. But Mrs. Spencer said *distinctly* that you wanted a girl about eleven years old. And the matron said she thought I would do. You don't know how delighted I was. I couldn't sleep all last night for joy. Oh," she added reproachfully, turning to Matthew, "why didn't you tell me at the station that you didn't want me and leave me there? If I hadn't seen the White Way of Delight and the Lake of Shining Waters it wouldn't be so hard."

"What on earth does she mean?" demanded Marilla, staring at Matthew.

"She—she's just referring to some conversation we had on the road," said Matthew hastily. "I'm going out to put the mare in, Marilla. Have tea ready when I come back."

"Did Mrs. Spencer bring anybody over besides you?" continued Marilla when Matthew had gone out.

"She brought Lily Jones for herself. Lily is only five years old and she is very beautiful. She has nut-brown hair.[1] If I was very beautiful and had nut-brown hair would you keep me?"

"No. We want a boy to help Matthew on the farm. A girl would be of no use to us. Take off your hat. I'll lay it and your bag on the hall table."

Anne took off her hat meekly. Matthew came back presently and they sat down to supper. But Anne could not eat. In vain she nibbled at the bread and butter and pecked at the crab-apple preserve out of the little scalloped glass dish by her plate. She did not really make any headway at all.

"You're not eating anything," said Marilla sharply, eying her as if it were a serious shortcoming.

Anne sighed.

"I can't. I'm in the depths of despair. Can you eat when you are in the depths of despair?"

"I've never been in the depths of despair, so I can't say," responded Marilla.

"Weren't you? Well, did you ever try to *imagine* you were in the depths of despair?"

"No, I didn't."

"Then I don't think you can understand what it's like. It's a very uncomfortable feeling indeed. When you try to eat a lump comes right up in your throat and you can't swallow anything, not even if it was a chocolate caramel. I had one chocolate caramel once two years ago and it was simply delicious. I've often dreamed since then that I had a lot of chocolate caramels, but I always wake up just when I'm going to eat them. I do hope you won't be offended because I can't eat. Everything is extremely nice, but still I cannot eat."

"I guess she's tired," said Matthew, who hadn't spoken since his return from the barn. "Best put her to bed, Marilla."

Marilla had been wondering where Anne should be put to bed. She had prepared a couch in the kitchen chamber for the desired and expected boy. But, although it was neat and clean, it did not seem quite the thing to put a girl there somehow. But the spare room was out of the question for such a stray waif, so there remained only the east gable room. Marilla lighted a candle and told Anne to follow her, which Anne spiritlessly did, taking her hat and carpet-bag from the hall table as she passed. The hall was fearsomely clean; the little gable chamber in which she presently found herself seemed still cleaner.

Marilla set the candle on a three-legged, three-cornered table and turned down the bedclothes.

"I suppose you have a nightgown?" she questioned.

Anne nodded.

"Yes, I have two. The matron of the asylum made them for me. They're fearfully skimpy. There is never enough to go around in an asylum, so things are

---

1 *nut-brown hair*   proverbially beautiful, as in the anonymous ballad of "The Nut-Brown Maid" (who, like Anne, endures a testing of her character but is cherished thereafter).

always skimpy—at least in a poor asylum like ours. I hate skimpy night-dresses. But one can dream just as well in them as in lovely trailing ones, with frills around the neck, that's one consolation."

"Well, undress as quick as you can and go to bed. I'll come back in a few minutes for the candle. I daren't trust you to put it out yourself. You'd likely set the place on fire."

When Marilla had gone Anne looked around her wistfully. The whitewashed walls were so painfully bare and staring that she thought they must ache over their own bareness. The floor was bare, too, except for a round braided mat in the middle such as Anne had never seen before. In one corner was the bed, a high, old-fashioned one, with four dark, low-turned posts.[2] In the other corner was the aforesaid three-cornered table adorned with a fat, red velvet pincushion hard enough to turn the point of the most adventurous pin. Above it hung a little six by eight mirror. Midway between table and bed was the window, with an icy white muslin frill over it, and opposite it was the wash-stand. The whole apartment was of a rigidity not to be described in words, but which sent a shiver to the very marrow of Anne's bones. With a sob she hastily discarded her garments, put on the skimpy nightgown and sprang into bed where she burrowed face downward into the pillow and pulled the clothes over her head. When Marilla came up for the light various skimpy articles of raiment scattered most untidily over the floor and a certain tempestuous appearance of the bed were the only indications of any presence save her own.

She deliberately picked up Anne's clothes, placed them neatly on a prim yellow chair, and then, taking up the candle, went over to the bed.

"Good night," she said, a little awkwardly, but not unkindly.

Anne's white face and big eyes appeared over the bedclothes with a startling suddenness.

"How can you call it a *good* night when you know it must be the very worst night I've ever had?" she said reproachfully.

Then she dived down into invisibility again.

Marilla went slowly down to the kitchen and proceeded to wash the supper dishes. Matthew was smoking—a sure sign of perturbation of mind. He seldom smoked, for Marilla set her face against it as a filthy habit; but at certain times and seasons he felt driven to it and then Marilla winked at the practice, realizing that a mere man must have some vent for his emotions.

"Well, this is a pretty kettle of fish," she said wrathfully. "This is what comes of sending word instead of going ourselves. Robert Spencer's folks have twisted that message somehow. One of us will have to drive over and see Mrs. Spencer to-morrow, that's certain. This girl will have to be sent back to the asylum."

"Yes, I suppose so," said Matthew reluctantly.

"You *suppose* so! Don't you know it?"

"Well now, she's a real nice little thing, Marilla. It's kind of a pity to send her back when she's so set on staying here."

"Matthew Cuthbert, you don't mean to say you think we ought to keep her!"

Marilla's astonishment could not have been greater if Matthew had expressed a predilection for standing on his head.

---

2 *low-turned posts* perhaps, rounded on a lathe but lacking much variation in diameter from top to bottom. Montgomery's manuscript read "low, turned posts," but there is no record of her objecting to the editing of this for the 1908 edition.

"Well now, no, I suppose not—not exactly," stammered Matthew, uncomfortably driven into a corner for his precise meaning. "I suppose—we could hardly be expected to keep her."

"I should say not. What good would she be to us?"

"We might be some good to her," said Matthew suddenly and unexpectedly.

"Matthew Cuthbert, I believe that child has bewitched you! I can see as plain as plain that you want to keep her."

"Well now, she's a real interesting little thing," persisted Matthew. "You should have heard her talk coming from the station."

"Oh, she can talk fast enough. I saw that at once. It's nothing in her favour, either. I don't like children who have so much to say. I don't want an orphan girl and if I did she isn't the style I'd pick out. There's something I don't understand about her. No, she's got to be despatched straightway back to where she came from."

"I could hire a French boy to help me," said Matthew, "and she'd be company for you."

"I'm not suffering for company," said Marilla shortly. "And I'm not going to keep her."

"Well now, it's just as you say, of course, Marilla," said Matthew rising and putting his pipe away. "I'm going to bed."

To bed went Matthew. And to bed, when she had put her dishes away, went Marilla, frowning most resolutely. And up-stairs, in the east gable, a lonely, heart-hungry, friendless child cried herself to sleep.

CHAPTER 4

Morning at Green Gables

IT WAS broad daylight when Anne awoke and sat up in bed, staring confusedly at the window through which a flood of cheery sunshine was pouring and outside of which something white and feathery waved across glimpses of blue sky.

For a moment she could not remember where she was. First came a delightful thrill, as of something very pleasant; then a horrible remembrance. This was Green Gables and they didn't want her because she wasn't a boy!

But it was morning and, yes, it was a cherry-tree in full bloom outside of her window. With a bound she was out of bed and across the floor. She pushed up the sash—it went up stiffly and creakily, as if it hadn't been opened for a long time, which was the case: and it stuck so tight that nothing was needed to hold it up.

Anne dropped on her knees and gazed out into the June morning, her eyes glistening with delight. Oh, wasn't it beautiful? Wasn't it a lovely place? Suppose she wasn't really going to stay here! She would imagine she was. There was scope for imagination here.

A huge cherry-tree grew outside, so close that its boughs tapped against the house, and it was so thick-set with blossoms that hardly a leaf was to be seen. On both sides of the house was a big orchard, one of apple-trees and one of cherry-trees, also showered over with blossoms; and their grass was all sprinkled with dandelions. In the garden below were lilac-trees purple with flowers, and their dizzily sweet fragrance drifted up to the window on the morning wind.

Below the garden a green field lush with clover sloped down to the hollow where the brook ran and where scores of white birches grew, upspringing airily out of an undergrowth suggestive of delightful possibilities in ferns and mosses and woodsy things generally. Beyond it was a hill, green and feathery with spruce and fir; there was a gap in it where the gray gable end of the little house she had seen from the other side of the Lake of Shining Waters was visible.

Off to the left were the big barns and beyond them, away down over green, low-sloping fields, was a sparkling blue glimpse of sea.

Anne's beauty-loving eyes lingered on it all, taking everything greedily in; she had looked on so many unlovely places in her life, poor child; but this was as lovely as anything she had ever dreamed.

She knelt there, lost to everything but the loveliness around her, until she was startled by a hand on her shoulder. Marilla had come in unheard by the small dreamer.

"It's time you were dressed," she said curtly.

Marilla really did not know how to talk to the child, and her uncomfortable ignorance made her crisp and curt when she did not mean to be.

Anne stood up and drew a long breath.

"Oh, isn't it wonderful?" she said, waving her hand comprehensively at the good world outside.

"It's a big tree," said Marilla, "and it blooms great, but the fruit don't amount to much never—small and wormy."

"Oh, I don't mean just the tree; of course it's lovely—yes, it's *radiantly* lovely—it blooms as if it meant it—but I meant everything, the garden and the orchard and the brook and the woods, the whole big dear world. Don't you feel as if you just loved the world on a morning like this? And I can hear the brook laughing all the way up here. Have you ever noticed what cheerful things brooks are? They're always laughing. Even in winter-time I've heard them under the ice. I'm so glad there's brook near Green Gables. Perhaps you think it doesn't make any difference to me when you're not going to keep me, but it does. I shall always like to remember that there is a brook at Green Gables even if I never see it again. If there wasn't a brook I'd be *haunted* by the uncomfortable feeling that there ought to be one. I'm not in the depths of despair this morning. I never can be in the morning. Isn't it a splendid thing that there are mornings? But I feel very sad. I've just been imagining that it was really me you wanted after all and that I was to stay here for ever and ever. It was a great comfort while it lasted. But the worst of imagining things is that the time comes when you have to stop and that hurts."

"You'd better get dressed and come down-stairs and never mind your imaginings," said Marilla as soon as she could get a word in edgewise. "Breakfast is waiting. Wash your face and comb your hair. Leave the window up and turn your bedclothes back over the foot of the bed. Be as smart as you can."

Anne could evidently be smart to some purpose for she was down-stairs in ten minutes' time, with her clothes neatly on, her hair brushed and braided, her face washed, and a comfortable consciousness pervading her soul that she had fulfilled all Marilla's requirements. As a matter of fact, however, she had forgotten to turn back the bedclothes.

"I'm pretty hungry this morning," she announced, as she slipped into the chair Marilla placed for her. "The world doesn't seem such a howling wilderness as it did last night. I'm so glad it's a sunshiny morning. But I like rainy mornings real well, too. All sorts of mornings are interesting, don't you think? You don't know what's going to happen through the day, and there's so much scope for imagination. But I'm glad it's not rainy to-day because it's easier to be cheerful and bear up under affliction on a sunshiny day. I feel that I have a good deal to bear up under. It's all very well to read about sorrows and imagine yourself living through them heroically, but it's not so nice when you really come to have them, is it?"

"For pity's sake hold your tongue," said Marilla. "You talk entirely too much for a little girl."

Thereupon Anne held her tongue so obediently and thoroughly that her continued silence made Marilla rather nervous, as if in the presence of something not exactly natural. Matthew also held his tongue—but this at least was natural—so that the meal was a very silent one.

As it progressed Anne became more and more abstracted, eating mechanically, with her big eyes fixed unswervingly and unseeingly on the sky outside the window. This made Marilla more nervous than ever; she had an uncomfortable feeling that while this odd child's body might be there at the table her spirit was far away in some remote airy cloudland, borne aloft on the wings of imagination. Who would want such a child about the place?

Yet Matthew wished to keep her, of all unaccountable things! Marilla felt that he wanted it just as much this morning as he had the night before, and that he would go on wanting it. That was Matthew's way—take a whim into his head and cling to it with the most amazing silent persistency—a persistency ten times more potent and effectual in its very silence than if he had talked it out.

When the meal was ended Anne came out of her reverie and offered to wash the dishes.

"Can you wash dishes right?" asked Marilla distrustfully.

"Pretty well. I'm better at looking after children, though. I've had so much experience at that. It's such a pity you haven't any here for me to look after."

"I don't feel as if I wanted any more children to look after than I've got at present. *You're* problem enough in all conscience. What's to be done with you I don't know. Matthew is a most ridiculous man."

"I think he's lovely," said Anne reproachfully. "He is so very sympathetic. He didn't mind how much I talked—he seemed to like it. I felt that he was a kindred spirit[1] as soon as ever I saw him."

"You're both queer enough, if that's what you mean by kindred spirits," said Marilla with a sniff. "Yes, you may wash the dishes. Take plenty of hot water, and be sure you dry them well. I've got enough to attend to this morning for I'll have to drive over to White Sands in the afternoon and see Mrs. Spencer. You'll come with me and we'll settle what's to be done with you. After you've finished the dishes go up-stairs and make your bed."

Anne washed the dishes deftly enough, as Marilla, who kept a sharp eye on the process, discerned. Later on she made her bed less successfully, for she had never learned the art of wrestling with a feather tick. But it was done somehow and smoothed down; and then Marilla, to get rid of her, told her she might go out-of-doors and amuse herself until dinner-time.[2]

---

1 *kindred spirit* person of like character and temperament (a common literary cliché).
2 *dinner-time* midday, when the main meal was served.

Anne flew to the door, face alight, eyes glowing. On the very threshold she stopped short, wheeled about, came back and sat down by the table, light and glow as effectually blotted out as if some one had clapped an extinguisher on her.

"What's the matter now?" demanded Marilla.

"I don't dare go out," said Anne, in the tone of a martyr relinquishing all earthly joys. "If I can't stay here there is no use in my loving Green Gables. And if I go out there and get acquainted with all those trees and flowers and the orchard and the brook I'll not be able to help loving it. It's hard enough now, so I won't make it any harder. I want to go out so much—everything seems to be calling to me, 'Anne, Anne, come out to us. Anne, Anne, we want a playmate'—but it's better not. There is no use in loving things if you have to be torn from them, is there? And it's *so* hard to keep from loving things, isn't it? That was why I was so glad when I thought I was going to live here. I thought I'd have so many things to love and nothing to hinder me. But that brief dream is over. I am resigned to my fate now, so I don't think I'll go out for fear I'll get unresigned again. What is the name of that geranium on the window-sill, please?"

"That's the apple-scented geranium."

"Oh, I don't mean that sort of a name. I mean just a name you gave it yourself. Didn't you give it a name? May I give it one then? May I call it—let me see—Bonny would do—may I call it Bonny while I'm here? Oh, do let me!"

"Goodness, I don't care. But where on earth is the sense of naming a geranium?"

"Oh, I like things to have handles even if they are only geraniums. It makes them seem more like people. How do you know but that it hurts a geranium's feelings just to be called a geranium and nothing else? You wouldn't like to be called nothing but a woman all the time. Yes, I shall call it Bonny. I named that cherry-tree outside my bedroom window this morning. I called it Snow Queen because it was so white. Of course, it won't always be in blossom, but one can imagine that it is, can't one?"

"I never in all my life saw or heard anything to equal her," muttered Marilla, beating a retreat down cellar after potatoes. "She *is* kind of interesting, as Matthew says. I can feel already that I'm wondering what on earth she'll say next. She'll be casting a spell over me, too. She's cast it over Matthew. That look he gave me when he went out said everything he said or hinted last night over again. I wish he was like other men and would talk things out. A body could answer back then and argue him into reason. But what's to be done with a man who just *looks*?"

Anne had relapsed into reverie, with her chin in her hands and her eyes on the sky, when Marilla returned from her cellar pilgrimage. There Marilla left her until the early dinner was on the table.

"I suppose I can have the mare and buggy this afternoon, Matthew?" said Marilla.

Matthew nodded and looked wistfully at Anne. Marilla intercepted the look and said grimly:

"I'm going to drive over to White Sands and settle this thing. I'll take Anne with me and Mrs. Spencer will probably make arrangements to send her back to Nova Scotia at once. I'll set your tea out for you and I'll be home in time to milk the cows."

Still Matthew said nothing and Marilla had a sense of having wasted words and breath. There is nothing more aggravating than a man who won't talk back—unless it is a woman who won't.

Matthew hitched the sorrel into the buggy in due time and Marilla and Anne set off. Matthew opened the yard gate for them, and as they drove slowly through, he said, to nobody in particular as it seemed:

"Little Jerry Buote from the Creek was here this morning, and I told him I guessed I'd hire him for the summer."

Marilla made no reply, but she hit the unlucky sorrel such a vicious clip with the whip that the fat mare, unused to such treatment, whizzed indignantly down the lane at an alarming pace. Marilla looked back once as the buggy bounced along and saw that aggravating Matthew leaning over the gate, looking wistfully after them.

CHAPTER 5

Anne's History

"DO YOU know," said Anne confidentially, "I've made up my mind to enjoy this drive. It's been my experience that you can nearly always enjoy things if you make up your mind firmly that you will. Of course, you must make it up *firmly*. I am not going to think about going back to the asylum while we're having our drive. I'm just going to think about the drive. Oh, look, there's one little early wild rose out! Isn't it lovely? Don't you think it must be glad to be a rose? Wouldn't it be nice if roses could talk? I'm sure they could tell us such lovely things. And isn't pink the most bewitching colour in the world? I love it, but I can't wear it. Red-headed people can't wear pink, not even in imagination. Did you ever know of anybody whose hair was red when she was young, but got to be another colour when she grew up?"

"No, I don't know as I ever did," said Marilla mercilessly, "and I shouldn't think it likely to happen in your case, either."

Anne sighed.

"Well, that is another hope gone. My life is a perfect graveyard of buried hopes.[1] That's a sentence I read in a book once, and I say it over to comfort myself whenever I'm disappointed in anything."

"I don't see where the comforting comes in myself," said Marilla.

"Why, because it sounds so nice and romantic, just as if I were a heroine in a book, you know. I am so fond of romantic things, and a graveyard full of buried hopes is about as romantic a thing as one can imagine, isn't it? I'm rather glad I have one. Are we going across the Lake of Shining Waters to-day?"

"We're not going over Barry's pond, if that's what you mean by your Lake of Shining Waters. We're going by the shore road."

"Shore road sounds nice," said Anne dreamily. "Is it as nice as it sounds? Just when you said 'shore road' I saw it in a picture in my mind, as quick as that! And White Sands is a pretty name, too; but I don't like it as well as Avonlea. Avonlea is a lovely name. It just sounds like music. How far is it to White Sands?"

---

1 *buried hopes*   common phrase in poems of the romantic era, as, for example, in "A timid grace sits trembling in her eye" by Charles Lamb (1775–1834) or in "Sarah II" by Rebekah Hyneman (1816–1875): "And earth, so long the grave of buried hopes."

"It's five miles; and as you're evidently bent on talking you might as well talk to some purpose by telling me what you know about yourself."

"Oh, what I *know* about myself isn't really worth telling," said Anne eagerly. "If you'll only let me tell you what I *imagine* about myself you'll think it ever so much more interesting."

"No, I don't want any of your imaginings. Just you stick to bald facts. Begin at the beginning. Where were you born and how old are you?"

"I was eleven last March," said Anne, resigning herself to bald facts with a little sigh. "And I was born in Bolingbroke, Nova Scotia. My father's name was Walter Shirley, and he was a teacher in the Bolingbroke High School. My mother's name was Bertha Shirley. Aren't Walter and Bertha lovely names? I'm so glad my parents had nice names. It would be a real disgrace to have a father named—well, say Jedediah, wouldn't it?"

"I guess it doesn't matter what a person's name is as long as he behaves himself," said Marilla, feeling herself called upon to inculcate a good and useful moral.

"Well, I don't know." Anne looked thoughtful. "I read in a book once that a rose by any other name would smell as sweet[2] but I've never been able to believe it. I don't believe a rose *would* be as nice if it was called a thistle or a skunk cabbage. I suppose my father could have been a good man even if he had been called Jedediah; but I'm sure it would have been a cross. Well, my mother was a teacher in the High School, too, but when she married father she gave up teaching, of course. A husband was enough responsibility. Mrs. Thomas said that they were a pair of babies and as poor as church mice. They went to live in a weeny-teeny little yellow house in Bolingbroke. I've never seen that house, but I've imagined it thousands of times. I think it must have had honeysuckle over the parlour window and lilacs in the front yard and lilies of the valley just inside the gate. Yes, and muslin curtains in all the windows. Muslin curtains give a house such an air. I was born in that house. Mrs. Thomas said I was the homeliest baby she ever saw, I was so scrawny and tiny and nothing but eyes, but that mother thought I was perfectly beautiful. I should think a mother would be a better judge than a poor woman who came in to scrub, wouldn't you? I'm glad she was satisfied with me anyhow; I would feel so sad if I thought I was a disappointment to her—because she didn't live very long after that, you see. She died of fever when I was just three months old. I do wish she'd lived long enough for me to remember calling her mother. I think it would be so sweet to say 'mother,' don't you? And father died four days afterwards from fever, too. That left me an orphan and folks were at their wits' end, so Mrs. Thomas said, what to do with me. You see, nobody wanted me even then. It seems to be my fate. Father and mother had both come from places far away and it was well known they hadn't any relatives living. Finally Mrs. Thomas said she'd take me, though she was poor and had a drunken husband. She brought me up by hand.[3] Do you know if there is anything in being brought up by hand that ought to make people who are brought up that way better than other people? Because whenever I was naughty Mrs. Thomas would ask me how I could be such a bad girl when she had brought me up by hand—reproachful-like.

---

2 *rose . . . sweet*   See William Shakespeare's *Romeo and Juliet*, 2.2.43–44.

3 *brought me up by hand*   with her own hands, perhaps including hand-feeding or, in this context, spanking. Compare Charles Dickens' *Great Expectations*: "She had brought me up 'by hand'" (1881, Chapter 2).

"Mr. and Mrs. Thomas moved away from Bolingbroke to Marysville, and I lived with them until I was eight years old. I helped look after the Thomas children—there were four of them younger than me—and I can tell you they took a lot of looking after. Then Mr. Thomas was killed falling under a train and his mother offered to take Mrs. Thomas and the children, but she didn't want me. Mrs. Thomas was at *her* wits' end, so she said, what to do with me. Then Mrs. Hammond from up the river came down and said she'd take me, seeing I was handy with children, and I went up the river to live with her in a little clearing among the stumps. It was a very lonesome place. I'm sure I could never have lived there if I hadn't had an imagination. Mr. Hammond worked a little sawmill up there, and Mrs. Hammond had eight children. She had twins three times. I like babies in moderation, but twins three times in succession is *too much*. I told Mrs. Hammond so firmly, when the last pair came. I used to get so dreadfully tired carrying them about.

"I lived up river with Mrs. Hammond over two years, and then Mr. Hammond died and Mrs. Hammond broke up housekeeping. She divided her children among her relatives and went to the States. I had to go to the asylum at Hopeton, because nobody would take me. They didn't want me at the asylum, either; they said they were overcrowded as it was. But they had to take me and I was there four months until Mrs. Spencer came."

Anne finished up with another sigh, of relief this time. Evidently she did not like talking about her experiences in a world that had not wanted her.

"Did you ever go to school?" demanded Marilla, turning the sorrel mare down the shore road.

"Not a great deal. I went a little the last year I stayed with Mrs. Thomas. When I went up river we were so far from a school that I couldn't walk it in winter and there was vacation in summer, so I could only go in the spring and fall. But of course I went while I was at the asylum. I can read pretty well and I know ever so many pieces of poetry off by heart—'The Battle of Hohenlinden' and 'Edinburgh after Flodden,' and 'Bingen on the Rhine,' and lots of the 'Lady of the Lake' and most of 'The Seasons,' by James Thompson. Don't you just love poetry that gives you a crinkly feeling up and down your back? There is a piece in the Fifth Reader—'The Downfall of Poland'—that is just full of thrills. Of course, I wasn't in the Fifth Reader—I was only in the Fourth—but the big girls used to lend me theirs to read."[4]

"Were those women—Mrs. Thomas and Mrs. Hammond—good to you?" asked Marilla, looking at Anne out of the corner of her eye.

"O-o-o-h," faltered Anne. Her sensitive little face suddenly flushed scarlet and embarrassment sat on her brow. "Oh, they *meant* to be—I know they meant to be just as good and kind as possible. And when people mean to be good to you, you don't mind very much when they're not quite—always. They had a good deal to worry them, you know. It's very trying to have a drunken husband,

---

4 *The Battle of Hohenlinden . . . theirs to read*   Scottish poet Thomas Campbell (1777–1844) authored "Hohenlinden" and "On the Downfall of Poland" (the latter from his longer poem "The Pleasures of Hope" 1799); Scottish poet William Edmonston Aytoun (1813–1865) wrote "Edinburgh after Flodden"; English author Caroline Elizabeth Sarah Norton (1808–1877) wrote "Bingen on the Rhine"; Scottish author Sir Walter Scott (1771–1832) wrote *The Lady of the Lake*; James Thomson (1700–1748), a Scottish-born English writer, was a preromantic who introduced, in *The Season*, many themes of nature worship taken up by later poets. Several of the poems appeared in the *Royal Reader* series of graded reading instruction, widely taught in the provincial public schools.

you see; and it must be very trying to have twins three times in succession, don't you think? But I feel sure they meant to be good to me."

Marilla asked no more questions. Anne gave herself up to a silent rapture over the shore road and Marilla guided the sorrel abstractedly while she pondered deeply. Pity was suddenly stirring in her heart for the child. What a starved, unloved life she had had—a life of drudgery and poverty and neglect; for Marilla was shrewd enough to read between the lines of Anne's history and divine the truth. No wonder she had been so delighted at the prospect of a real home. It was a pity she had to be sent back. What if she, Marilla, should indulge Matthew's unaccountable whim and let her stay? He was set on it; and the child seemed a nice, teachable little thing.

"She's got too much to say," thought Marilla, "but she might be trained out of that. And there's nothing rude or slangy in what she does say. She's ladylike. It's likely her people were nice folks."

The shore road was "woodsy and wild and lonesome."[5] On the right hand, scrub firs, their spirits quite unbroken by long years of tussle with the gulf winds, grew thickly. On the left were the steep red sandstone cliffs, so near the track in places that a mare of less steadiness than the sorrel might have tried the nerves of the people behind her. Down at the base of the cliffs were heaps of surf-worn rocks or little sandy coves inlaid with pebbles as with ocean jewels; beyond lay the sea, shimmering and blue, and over it soared the gulls, their pinions flashing silvery in the sunlight.

"Isn't the sea wonderful?" said Anne, rousing from a long, wide-eyed silence. "Once, when I lived in Marysville, Mr. Thomas hired an express-wagon and took us all to spend the day at the shore ten miles away. I enjoyed every moment of that day, even if I had to look after the children all the time. I lived it over in happy dreams for years. But this shore is nicer than the Marysville shore. Aren't those gulls splendid? Would you like to be a gull? I think I would—that is, if I couldn't be a human girl. Don't you think it would be nice to wake up at sunrise and swoop down over the water and away out over that lovely blue all day; and then at night to fly back to one's nest? Oh, I can just imagine myself doing it. What big house is that just ahead, please?"

"That's the White Sands Hotel. Mr. Kirke runs it, but the season hasn't begun yet. There are heaps of Americans come there for the summer. They think this shore is just about right."

"I was afraid it might be Mrs. Spencer's place," said Anne mournfully. "I don't want to get there. Somehow, it will seem like the end of everything."

CHAPTER 6

Marilla Makes Up Her Mind

GET there they did, however, in due season. Mrs. Spencer lived in a big yellow house at White Sands Cove, and she came to the door with surprise and welcome mingled on her benevolent face.

---

5 *woodsy and wild and lonesome* from "Cobbler Keezar's Vision" by John Greenleaf Whittier (1807–92).

"Dear, dear," she exclaimed, "you're the last folks I was looking for to-day, but I'm real glad to see you. You'll put your horse in? And how are you, Anne?"

"I'm as well as can be expected, thank you," said Anne smilelessly. A blight seemed to have descended on her.

"I suppose we'll stay a little while to rest the mare," said Marilla, "but I promised Matthew I'd be home early. The fact is, Mrs. Spencer, there's been a queer mistake somewhere, and I've come over to see where it is. We sent word, Matthew and I, for you to bring us a boy from the asylum. We told your brother Robert to tell you we wanted a boy ten or eleven years old."

"Marilla Cuthbert, you don't say so!" said Mrs. Spencer in distress. "Why, Robert sent the word down by his daughter Nancy and she said you wanted a girl—didn't she, Flora Jane?" appealing to her daughter who had come out to the steps.

"She certainly did, Miss Cuthbert," corroborated Flora Jane earnestly.

"I'm dreadful sorry," said Mrs. Spencer. "It is too bad; but it certainly wasn't my fault, you see, Miss Cuthbert. I did the best I could and I thought I was following your instructions. Nancy is a terrible flighty thing. I've often had to scold her well for her heedlessness."

"It was our own fault," said Marilla resignedly. "We should have come to you ourselves and not left an important message to be passed along by word of mouth in that fashion. Anyhow, the mistake has been made and the only thing to do now is to set it right. Can we send the child back to the asylum? I suppose they'll take her back, won't they?"

"I suppose so," said Mrs. Spencer thoughtfully, "but I don't think it will be necessary to send her back. Mrs. Peter Blewett was up here yesterday, and she was saying to me how much she wished she'd sent by me for a little girl to help her. Mrs. Peter has a large family, you know, and she finds it hard to get help. Anne will be the very girl for her. I call it positively providential."

Marilla did not look as if she thought Providence had much to do with the matter. Here was an unexpectedly good chance to get this unwelcome orphan off her hands, and she did not even feel grateful for it.

She knew Mrs. Peter Blewett only by sight as a small, shrewish-faced woman without an ounce of superfluous flesh on her bones. But she had heard of her. "A terrible worker and driver," Mrs. Peter was said to be; and discharged servant girls told fearsome tales of her temper and stinginess, and her family of pert, quarrelsome children. Marilla felt a qualm of conscience at the thought of handing Anne over to her tender mercies.[1]

"Well, I'll go in and we'll talk the matter over," she said.

"And if there isn't Mrs. Peter coming up the lane this blessed minute!" exclaimed Mrs. Spencer, bustling her guests through the hall into the parlour, where a deadly chill struck on them as if the air had been strained so long through dark green, closely drawn blinds that it had lost every particle of warmth it had ever possessed. "That is real lucky, for we can settle the matter right away. Take the armchair, Miss Cuthbert. Anne, you sit here on the ottoman and don't wriggle. Let me take your hats. Flora Jane, go out and put the kettle on. Good afternoon, Mrs. Blewett. We were just saying how fortunate it

---

1 *tender mercies* "A righteous man regardeth the life of his beast; but the tender mercies of the wicked are cruel" (Proverbs 12.10).

was you happened along. Let me introduce you two ladies. Mrs. Blewett, Miss Cuthbert. Please excuse me for just a moment. I forgot to tell Flora Jane to take the buns out of the oven."

Mrs. Spencer whisked away, after pulling up the blinds. Anne, sitting mutely on the ottoman, with her hands clasped tightly in her lap, stared at Mrs. Blewett as one fascinated. Was she to be given into the keeping of this sharp-faced, sharp-eyed woman? She felt a lump coming up in her throat and her eyes smarted painfully. She was beginning to be afraid she couldn't keep the tears back when Mrs. Spencer returned, flushed and beaming, quite capable of taking any and every difficulty, physical, mental or spiritual, into consideration and settling it out of hand.

"It seems there's been a mistake about this little girl, Mrs. Blewett," she said. "I was under the impression that Mr. and Miss Cuthbert wanted a little girl to adopt. I was certainly told so. But it seems it was a boy they wanted. So if you're still of the same mind you were yesterday, I think she'll be just the thing for you."

Mrs. Blewett darted her eyes over Anne from head to foot.

"How old are you and what's your name?" she demanded.

"Anne Shirley," faltered the shrinking child, not daring to make any stipulations regarding the spelling thereof, "and I'm eleven years old."

"Humph! You don't look as if there was much to you. But you're wiry. I don't know but the wiry ones are the best after all. Well, if I take you you'll have to be a good girl, you know—good and smart and respectful. I'll expect you to earn your keep, and no mistake about that. Yes, I suppose I might as well take her off your hands, Miss Cuthbert. The baby's awful fractious, and I'm clean worn out attending to him. If you like I can take her right home now."

Marilla looked at Anne and softened at sight of the child's pale face with its look of mute misery—the misery of a helpless little creature who finds itself once more caught in the trap from which it had escaped. Marilla felt an uncomfortable conviction that, if she denied the appeal of that look, it would haunt her to her dying day. Moreover, she did not fancy Mrs. Blewett. To hand a sensitive, "high-strung" child over to such a woman! No, she could not take the responsibility of doing that!

"Well, I don't know," she said slowly. "I didn't say that Matthew and I had absolutely decided that we wouldn't keep her. In fact, I may say that Matthew is disposed to keep her. I just came over to find out how the mistake had occurred. I think I'd better take her home again and talk it over with Matthew. I feel that I oughtn't to decide on anything without consulting him. If we make up our mind not to keep her we'll bring or send her over to you to-morrow night. If we don't you may know that she is going to stay with us. Will that suit you, Mrs. Blewett?"

"I suppose it'll have to," said Mrs. Blewett ungraciously.

During Marilla's speech a sunrise had been dawning on Anne's face. First the look of despair faded out; then came a faint flush of hope; her eyes grew deep and bright as morning stars. The child was quite transfigured; and, a moment later, when Mrs. Spencer and Mrs. Blewett went out in quest of a recipe the latter had come to borrow, she sprang up and flew across the room to Marilla.

"Oh, Miss Cuthbert, did you really say that perhaps you would let me stay at Green Gables?" she said, in a breathless whisper, as if speaking aloud might shatter the glorious possibility. "Did you really say it? Or did I only imagine that you did?"

"I think you'd better learn to control that imagination of yours, Anne, if you can't distinguish between what is real and what isn't," said Marilla crossly. "Yes, you did hear me say just that and no more. It isn't decided yet and perhaps we will conclude to let Mrs. Blewett take you after all. She certainly needs you much more than I do."

"I'd rather go back to the asylum than go to live with her," said Anne passionately. "She looks exactly like a—like a gimlet."

Marilla smothered a smile under the conviction that Anne must be reproved for such a speech.

"A little girl like you should be ashamed of talking so about a lady and a stranger," she said severely. "Go back and sit down quietly and hold your tongue and behave as a good girl should."

"I'll try to do and be anything you want me, if you'll only keep me," said Anne, returning meekly to her ottoman.

When they arrived back at Green Gables that evening Matthew met them in the lane. Marilla from afar had noted him prowling along it and guessed his motive. She was prepared for the relief she read in his face when he saw that she had at least brought Anne back with her. But she said nothing to him, relative to the affair, until they were both out in the yard behind the barn milking the cows. Then she briefly told him Anne's history and the result of the interview with Mrs. Spencer.

"I wouldn't give a dog I liked to that Blewett woman," said Matthew with unusual vim.

"I don't fancy her style myself," admitted Marilla, "but it's that or keeping her ourselves, Matthew. And, since you seem to want her, I suppose I'm willing—or have to be. I've been thinking over the idea until I've got kind of used to it. It seems a sort of duty. I've never brought up a child, especially a girl, and I dare say I'll make a terrible mess of it. But I'll do my best. So far as I'm concerned, Matthew, she may stay."

Matthew's shy face was a glow of delight.

"Well now, I reckoned you'd come to see it in that light, Marilla," he said. "She's such an interesting little thing."

"It'd be more to the point if you could say she was a useful little thing," retorted Marilla, "but I'll make it my business to see she's trained to be that. And mind, Matthew, you're not to go interfering with my methods. Perhaps an old maid doesn't know much about bringing up a child, but I guess she knows more than an old bachelor. So you just leave me to manage her. When I fail it'll be time enough to put your oar in."

"There, there, Marilla, you can have your own way," said Matthew reassuringly. "Only be as good and kind to her as you can be without spoiling her. I kind of think she's one of the sort you can do anything with if you only get her to love you."

Marilla sniffed, to express her contempt for Matthew's opinions concerning anything feminine, and walked off to the dairy with the pails.

"I won't tell her tonight that she can stay," she reflected, as she strained the milk into the creamers. "She'd be so excited that she wouldn't sleep a wink. Marilla Cuthbert, you're fairly in for it. Did you ever suppose you'd see the day when you'd be adopting an orphan girl? It's surprising enough; but not so surprising as that Matthew should be at the bottom of it, him that always seemed to have such a mortal dread of little girls. Anyhow, we've decided on the experiment and goodness only knows what will come of it."

CHAPTER 7

Anne Says Her Prayers

WHEN Marilla took Anne up to bed that night she said stiffly: "Now, Anne, I noticed last night that you threw your clothes all about the floor when you took them off. That is a very untidy habit, and I can't allow it at all. As soon as you take off any article of clothing fold it neatly and place it on the chair. I haven't any use at all for little girls who aren't neat."

"I was so harrowed up in my mind last night that I didn't think about my clothes at all," said Anne. "I'll fold them nicely tonight. They always made us do that at the asylum. Half the time, though, I'd forget, I'd be in such a hurry to get into bed nice and quiet and imagine things."

"You'll have to remember a little better if you stay here," admonished Marilla. "There, that looks something like. Say your prayers now and get into bed."

"I never say any prayers," announced Anne.

Marilla looked horrified astonishment.

"Why, Anne, what do you mean? Were you never taught to say your prayers? God always wants little girls to say their prayers. Don't you know who God is, Anne?"

"'God is a spirit, infinite, eternal and unchangeable, in His being, wisdom, power, holiness, justice, goodness, and truth,'" responded Anne promptly and glibly.

Marilla looked rather relieved.

"So you do know something then, thank goodness! You're not quite a heathen. Where did you learn that?"

"Oh, at the asylum Sunday-school. They made us learn the whole catechism. I liked it pretty well. There's something splendid about some of the words. 'Infinite, eternal and unchangeable.' Isn't that grand? It has such a roll to it—just like a big organ playing. You couldn't quite call it poetry, I suppose, but it sounds a lot like it, doesn't it?"

"We're not talking about poetry, Anne—we are talking about saying your prayers. Don't you know it's a terrible wicked thing not to say your prayers every night? I'm afraid you are a very bad little girl."

"You'd find it easier to be bad than good if you had red hair," said Anne reproachfully. "People who haven't red hair don't know what trouble is. Mrs. Thomas told me that God made my hair red *on purpose*, and I've never cared about Him since. And anyhow I'd always be too tired at night to bother saying prayers. People who have to look after twins can't be expected to say their prayers. Now, do you honestly think they can?"

Marilla decided that Anne's religious training must be begun at once. Plainly there was no time to be lost.

"You must say your prayers while you are under my roof, Anne."

"Why, of course, if you want me to," assented Anne cheerfully. "I'd do anything to oblige you. But you'll have to tell me what to say for this once. After I get into bed I'll imagine out a real nice prayer to say always. I believe that it will be quite interesting, now that I come to think of it."

"You must kneel down," said Marilla in embarrassment.

Anne knelt at Marilla's knee and looked up gravely.

"Why must people kneel down to pray? If I really wanted to pray I'll tell you what I'd do. I'd go out into a great big field all alone or into the deep, deep woods, and I'd look up into the sky—up—up—up into that lovely blue sky that looks as if there was no end to its blueness. And then I'd just *feel* a prayer. Well, I'm ready. What am I to say?"

Marilla felt more embarrassed than ever. She had intended to teach Anne the childish classic, "Now I lay me down to sleep."[1] But she had, as I have told you, the glimmerings of a sense of humour—which is simply another name for a sense of the fitness of things; and it suddenly occurred to her that that simple little prayer, sacred to white-robed childhood lisping at motherly knees, was entirely unsuited to this freckled witch of a girl who knew and cared nothing about God's love, since she had never had it translated to her through the medium of human love.

"You're old enough to pray for yourself, Anne," she said finally. "Just thank God for your blessings and ask Him humbly for the things you want."

"Well, I'll do my best," promised Anne, burying her face in Marilla's lap. "Gracious heavenly Father—that's the way the ministers say it in church, so I suppose it's all right in a private prayer, isn't it?" she interjected, lifting her head for a moment. "Gracious heavenly Father, I thank Thee for the White Way of Delight and the Lake of Shining Waters and Bonny and the Snow Queen. I'm really extremely grateful for them. And that's all the blessings I can think of just now to thank Thee for. As for the things I want, they're so numerous that it would take a great deal of time to name them all, so I will only mention the two most important. Please let me stay at Green Gables; and please let me be good-looking when I grow up. I remain,

"Yours respectfully,
"Anne Shirley."

"There, did I do it all right?" she asked eagerly, getting up. "I could have made it much more flowery if I'd had a little more time to think it over."

Poor Marilla was only preserved from complete collapse by remembering that it was not irreverence, but simply spiritual ignorance on the part of Anne that was responsible for this extraordinary petition. She tucked the child up in bed, mentally vowing that she should be taught a prayer the very next day, and was leaving the room with the light when Anne called her back.

"I've just thought of it now. I should have said 'Amen' in place of 'yours respectfully,' shouldn't I?—the way the ministers do. I'd forgotten it, but I felt a prayer should be finished off in some way, so I put in the other. Do you suppose it will make any difference?"

"I—I don't suppose it will," said Marilla. "Go to sleep now like a good child. Good night."

"I can say good night to-night with a clear conscience," said Anne, cuddling luxuriously down among her pillows.

Marilla retreated to the kitchen, set the candle firmly on the table, and glared at Matthew.

"Matthew Cuthbert, it's about time somebody adopted that child and taught her something. She's next door to a perfect heathen. Will you believe that she never said a prayer in her life till to-night? I'll send to the manse to-morrow and borrow the Peep of Day series;[2] that's what I'll do. And she shall go to

---

1 *childish classic . . . sleep*" "childish" in the sense of being often taught to children and printed first in *The New England Primer*, a popular reading guide.

2 *Peep of Day series* religious instruction for children presented by Favell Lee Mortimer (1802–1878) in the 1830s and 1840s.

Sunday-school just as soon as I can get some suitable clothes made for her. I foresee that I shall have my hands full. Well, well, we can't get through this world without our share of trouble. I've had a pretty easy life of it so far, but my time has come at last and I suppose I'll just have to make the best of it."

CHAPTER 8

Anne's Bringing-Up Is Begun

FOR reasons best known to herself, Marilla did not tell Anne that she was to stay at Green Gables until the next afternoon. During the forenoon she kept the child busy with various tasks and watched over her with a keen eye while she did them. By noon she had concluded that Anne was smart and obedient, willing to work and quick to learn; her most serious shortcoming seemed to be a tendency to fall into day-dreams in the middle of a task and forget all about it until such time as she was sharply recalled to earth by a reprimand or a catastrophe.

When Anne had finished washing the dinner dishes she suddenly confronted Marilla with the air and expression of one desperately determined to learn the worst. Her thin little body trembled from head to foot; her face flushed and her eyes dilated until they were almost black; she clasped her hands tightly and said in an imploring voice:

"Oh, please, Miss Cuthbert, won't you tell me if you are going to send me away or not? I've tried to be patient all the morning, but I really feel that I cannot bear not knowing any longer. It's a dreadful feeling. Please tell me."

"You haven't scalded the dish-cloth in clean hot water as I told you to do," said Marilla immovably. "Just go and do it before you ask any more questions, Anne."

Anne went and attended to the dish-cloth. Then she returned to Marilla and fastened imploring eyes on the latter's face.

"Well," said Marilla, unable to find any excuse for deferring her explanation longer, "I suppose I might as well tell you. Matthew and I have decided to keep you—that is, if you will try to be a good little girl and show yourself grateful. Why, child, whatever is the matter?"

"I'm crying," said Anne in a tone of bewilderment. "I can't think why. I'm glad as glad can be. Oh, *glad* doesn't seem the right word at all. I was glad about the White Way and the cherry blossoms—but this! Oh, it's something more than glad. I'm so happy. I'll try to be so good. It will be up-hill work, I expect, for Mrs. Thomas often told me I was desperately wicked. However, I'll do my very best. But can you tell me why I'm crying?"

"I suppose it's because you're all excited and worked up," said Marilla disapprovingly. "Sit down on that chair and try to calm yourself. I'm afraid you both cry and laugh far too easily. Yes, you can stay here and we will try to do right by you. You must go to school; but it's only a fortnight till vacation so it isn't worth while for you to start before it opens again in September."

"What am I to call you?" asked Anne. "Shall I always say Miss Cuthbert? Can I call you Aunt Marilla?"

"No; you'll call me just plain Marilla. I'm not used to being called Miss Cuthbert and it would make me nervous."

"It sounds awfully disrespectful to say just Marilla," protested Anne.

"I guess there'll be nothing disrespectful in it if you're careful to speak respectfully. Everybody, young and old, in Avonlea calls me Marilla except the minister. He says Miss Cuthbert—when he thinks of it."

"I'd love to call you Aunt Marilla," said Anne wistfully. "I've never had an aunt or any relation at all—not even a grandmother. It would make me feel as if I really belonged to you. Can't I call you Aunt Marilla?"

"No. I'm not your aunt and I don't believe in calling people names that don't belong to them."

"But we could imagine you were my aunt."

"I couldn't," said Marilla grimly.

"Do you never imagine things different from what they really are?" asked Anne wide-eyed.

"No."

"Oh!" Anne drew a long breath. "Oh, Miss—Marilla, how much you miss!"

"I don't believe in imagining things different from what they really are," retorted Marilla. "When the Lord puts us in certain circumstances He doesn't mean for us to imagine them away. And that reminds me. Go into the sitting-room, Anne—be sure your feet are clean and don't let any flies in—and bring me out the illustrated card that's on the mantelpiece. The Lord's Prayer is on it and you'll devote your spare time this afternoon to learning it off by heart. There's to be no more of such praying as I heard last night."

"I suppose I was very awkward," said Anne apologetically, "but then, you see, I'd never had any practice. You couldn't really expect a person to pray very well the first time she tried, could you? I thought out a splendid prayer after I went to bed, just as I promised you I would. It was nearly as long as a minister's and so poetical. But would you believe it? I couldn't remember one word when I woke up this morning. And I'm afraid I'll never be able to think out another one as good. Somehow, things never are so good when they're thought out a second time. Have you ever noticed that?"

"Here is something for you to notice, Anne. When I tell you to do a thing I want you to obey me at once and not stand stock-still and discourse about it. Just you go and do as I bid you."

Anne promptly departed for the sitting-room across the hall; she failed to return; after waiting ten minutes Marilla laid down her knitting and marched after her with a grim expression. She found Anne standing motionless before a picture hanging on the wall between the two windows, with her hands clasped behind her, her face uplifted, and her eyes astar with dreams. The white and green light strained through apple-trees and clustering vines outside fell over the rapt little figure with a half-unearthly radiance.

"Anne, whatever are you thinking of?" demanded Marilla sharply.

Anne came back to earth with a start.

"That," she said, pointing to the picture—a rather vivid chromo[1] entitled, "Christ Blessing Little Children"—"and I was just imagining I was one of them—that I was the little girl in the blue dress, standing off by herself in the corner as if she didn't belong to anybody, like me. She looks lonely and sad, don't you think? I guess she hadn't any father or mother of her own. But she wanted to be blessed, too, so she just crept shyly up on the outside of the crowd,

---

1 *chromo*   chromolithograph: colored picture printed from stone or from zinc plates.

hoping nobody would notice her—except Him. I'm sure I know just how she felt. Her heart must have beat and her hands must have got cold, like mine did when I asked you if I could stay. She was afraid He mightn't notice her. But it's likely He did, don't you think? I've been trying to imagine it all out—her edging a little nearer all the time until she was quite close to Him; and then He would look at her and put His hand on her hair and oh, such a thrill of joy as would run over her! But I wish the artist hadn't painted Him so sorrowful-looking. All His pictures are like that, if you've noticed. But I don't believe He could really have looked so sad or the children would have been afraid of Him."

"Anne," said Marilla, wondering why she had not broken into this speech long before, "you shouldn't talk that way. It's irreverent—positively irreverent."

Anne's eyes marvelled.

"Why, I felt just as reverent as could be. I'm sure I didn't mean to be irreverent."

"Well, I don't suppose you did—but it doesn't sound right to talk so familiarly about such things. And another thing, Anne, when I send you after something you're to bring it at once and not fall into mooning and imagining before pictures. Remember that. Take that card and come right to the kitchen. Now, sit down in the corner and learn that prayer off by heart."

Anne set the card up against the jugful of apple blossoms she had brought in to decorate the dinner-table—Marilla had eyed that decoration askance, but had said nothing—propped her chin on her hands, and fell to studying it intently for several silent minutes.

"I like this," she announced at length. "It's beautiful. I've heard it before—I heard the superintendent of the asylum Sunday-school say it over once. But I didn't like it then. He had such a cracked voice and he prayed it so mournfully. I really felt sure he thought praying was a disagreeable duty. This isn't poetry, but it makes me feel just the same way poetry does. 'Our Father who art in heaven, hallowed be Thy name.' That is just like a line of music. Oh, I'm so glad you thought of making me learn this, Miss—Marilla."

"Well, learn it and hold your tongue," said Marilla shortly.

Anne tipped the vase of apple blossoms near enough to bestow a soft kiss on a pink-cupped bud, and then studied diligently for some moments longer.

"Marilla," she demanded presently, "do you think that I shall ever have a bosom friend in Avonlea?"

"A—a what kind of a friend?"

"A bosom friend—an intimate friend, you know—a really kindred spirit to whom I can confide my inmost soul. I've dreamed of meeting her all my life. I never really supposed I would, but so many of my loveliest dreams have come true all at once that perhaps this one will, too. Do you think it's possible?"

"Diana Barry lives over at Orchard Slope and she's about your age. She's a very nice little girl, and perhaps she will be a playmate for you when she comes home. She's visiting her aunt over at Carmody just now. You'll have to be careful how you behave yourself, though. Mrs. Barry is a very particular woman. She won't let Diana play with any little girl who isn't nice and good."

Anne looked at Marilla through the apple blossoms, her eyes aglow with interest.

"What is Diana like? Her hair isn't red, is it? Oh, I hope not. It's bad enough to have red hair myself, but I positively couldn't endure it in a bosom friend."

"Diana is a very pretty little girl. She has black eyes and hair and rosy cheeks. And she is good and smart, which is better than being pretty."

Marilla was as fond of morals as the Duchess in Wonderland,[2] and was firmly convinced that one should be tacked on to every remark made to a child who was being brought up.

But Anne waved the moral inconsequently aside and seized only on the delightful possibilities before it.

"Oh, I'm so glad she's pretty. Next to being beautiful oneself—and that's impossible in my case—it would be best to have a beautiful bosom friend. When I lived with Mrs. Thomas she had a bookcase in her sitting-room with glass doors. There weren't any books in it; Mrs. Thomas kept her best china and her preserves there—when she had any preserves to keep. One of the doors was broken. Mr. Thomas smashed it one night when he was slightly intoxicated. But the other was whole and I used to pretend that my reflection in it was another little girl who lived in it. I called her Katie Maurice and we were very intimate. I used to talk to her by the hour, especially on Sunday and tell her everything. Katie was the comfort and consolation of my life. We used to pretend that the bookcase was enchanted and that if I only knew the spell I could open the door and step right into the room where Katie Maurice lived, instead of into Mrs. Thomas' shelves of preserves and china. And then Katie Maurice would have taken me by the hand and led me out into a wonderful place, all flowers and sunshine and fairies, and we would have lived there happy for ever after. When I went to live with Mrs. Hammond it just broke my heart to leave Katie Maurice. She felt it dreadfully, too, I know she did, for she was crying when she kissed me good-bye through the bookcase door. There was no bookcase at Mrs. Hammond's. But just up the river a little way from the house there was a long green little valley, and the loveliest echo lived there. It echoed back every word you said, even if you didn't talk a bit loud. So I imagined that it was a little girl called Violetta and we were great friends and I loved her almost as well as I loved Katie Maurice—not quite, but almost, you know. The night before I went to the asylum I said good-bye to Violetta, and oh, her good-bye came back to me in such sad, sad tones. I had become so attached to her that I hadn't the heart to imagine a bosom friend at the asylum, even if there had been any scope for imagination there."

"I think it's just as well there wasn't," said Marilla drily. "I don't approve of such goings-on. You seem to half believe your own imaginations. It will be well for you to have a real live friend to put such nonsense out of your head. But don't let Mrs. Barry hear you talking about your Katie Maurices and your Violettas or she'll think you tell stories."

"Oh, I won't. I couldn't talk of them to everybody—their memories are too sacred for that. But I thought I'd like to have you know about them. Oh, look, here's a big bee just tumbled out of an apple blossom. Just think what a lovely place to live—in an apple blossom! Fancy going to sleep in it when the wind was rocking it. If I wasn't a human girl I think I'd like to be a bee and live among the flowers."

"Yesterday you wanted to be a sea-gull," sniffed Marilla. "I think you are very fickle-minded. I told you to learn that prayer and not talk. But it seems impossible for you to stop talking if you've got anybody that will listen to you. So go up to your room and learn it."

"Oh, I know it pretty nearly all now—all but just the last line."

---

2 *as fond of morals as the Duchess in Wonderland* See *Alice's Adventures in Wonderland* by Lewis Carroll (Charles Lutwidge Dodgson 1832–1898), Chapter 9.

"Well, never mind, do as I tell you. Go to your room and finish learning it well, and stay there until I call you down to help me get tea."

"Can I take the apple blossoms with me for company?" pleaded Anne.

"No; you don't want your room cluttered up with flowers. You should have left them on the tree in the first place."

"I did feel a little that way, too," said Anne. "I kind of felt I shouldn't shorten their lovely lives by picking them—I wouldn't want to be picked if I were an apple blossom. But the temptation was *irresistible*. What do you do when you meet with an irresistible temptation?"

"Anne, did you hear me tell you to go to your room?"

Anne sighed, retreated to the east gable, and sat down in a chair by the window.

"There—I know this prayer. I learned that last sentence coming up-stairs. Now I'm going to imagine things into this room so that they'll always stay imagined. The floor is covered with a white velvet carpet with pink roses all over it and there are pink silk curtains at the windows. The walls are hung with gold and silver brocade tapestry. The furniture is mahogany. I never saw any mahogany, but it does sound *so* luxurious. This is a couch all heaped with gorgeous silken cushions, pink and blue and crimson and gold, and I am reclining gracefully on it. I can see my reflection in that splendid big mirror hanging on the wall. I am tall and regal, clad in a gown of trailing white lace, with a pearl cross on my breast and pearls in my hair. My hair is of midnight darkness and my skin is a clear ivory pallor. My name is the Lady Cordelia Fitzgerald. No, it isn't—I can't make *that* seem real."

She danced up to the little looking-glass and peered into it. Her pointed freckled face and solemn gray eyes peered back at her.

"You're only Anne of Green Gables," she said earnestly, "and I see you, just as you are looking now, whenever I try to imagine I'm the Lady Cordelia. But it's a million times nicer to be Anne of Green Gables than Anne of nowhere in particular, isn't it?"

She bent forward, kissed her reflection affectionately, and betook herself to the open window.

"Dear Snow Queen, good afternoon. And good afternoon, dear birches down in the hollow. And good afternoon, dear gray house up on the hill. I wonder if Diana is to be my bosom friend. I hope she will, and I shall love her very much. But I must never quite forget Katie Maurice and Violetta. They would feel so hurt if I did and I'd hate to hurt anybody's feelings, even a little bookcase girl's or a little echo girl's. I must be careful to remember them and send them a kiss every day."

Anne blew a couple of airy kisses from her finger tips past the cherry blossoms and then, with her chin in her hands, drifted luxuriously out on a sea of daydreams.

CHAPTER 9

Mrs. Rachel Lynde Is Properly Horrified

ANNE had been a fortnight at Green Gables before Mrs. Lynde arrived to inspect her. Mrs. Rachel, to do her justice, was not to blame for this. A severe and unseasonable attack of grippe had confined that good lady to her house ever since the occasion of her last visit to Green Gables. Mrs. Rachel was not often sick and had a well-defined contempt for people who were; but grippe, she asserted, was like no other illness on earth and could only be interpreted as one of the special visitations of Providence. As soon as her doctor allowed her to put her foot out of doors she hurried up to Green Gables, bursting with curiosity to see Matthew and Marilla's orphan, concerning whom all sorts of stories and suppositions had gone abroad in Avonlea.

Anne had made good use of every waking moment of that fortnight. Already she was acquainted with every tree and shrub about the place. She had discovered that a lane opened out below the apple orchard and ran up through a belt of woodland; and she had explored it to its furthest end in all its delicious vagaries of brook and bridge, fir coppice and wild cherry arch, corners thick with fern, and branching byways of maple and mountain ash.

She had made friends with the spring down in the hollow—that wonderful deep, clear icy-cold spring; it was set about with smooth red sandstones and rimmed in by great palmlike clumps of water fern; and beyond it was a log bridge over the brook.

That bridge led Anne's dancing feet up over a wooded hill beyond, where perpetual twilight reigned under the straight, thick-growing firs and spruces; the only flowers there were myriads of delicate "June bells," those shyest and sweetest of woodland blooms, and a few pale, aerial starflowers, like the spirits of last year's blossoms. Gossamers glimmered like threads of silver among the trees and the fir boughs and tassels[1] seemed to utter friendly speech.

All these raptured voyages of exploration were made in the odd half hours which she was allowed for play, and Anne talked Matthew and Marilla half deaf over her discoveries. Not that Matthew complained, to be sure; he listened to it all with a wordless smile of enjoyment on his face; Marilla permitted the "chatter" until she found herself becoming too interested in it, whereupon she always promptly quenched Anne by a curt command to hold her tongue.

Anne was out in the orchard when Mrs. Rachel came, wandering at her own sweet will through the lush, tremulous grasses splashed with ruddy evening sunshine; so that good lady had an excellent chance to talk her illness fully over, describing every ache and pulse beat with such evident enjoyment that Marilla thought even grippe must bring its compensations. When details were exhausted Mrs. Rachel introduced the real reason of her call.

"I've been hearing some surprising things about you and Matthew."

"I don't suppose you are any more surprised than I am myself," said Marilla. "I'm getting over my surprise now."

"It was too bad there was such a mistake," said Mrs. Rachel sympathetically. "Couldn't you have sent her back?"

"I suppose we could, but we decided not to. Matthew took a fancy to her. And I must say I like her myself—although I admit she has her faults. The house seems a different place already. She's a real bright little thing."

Marilla said more than she had intended to say when she began, for she read disapproval in Mrs. Rachel's expression.

"It's a great responsibility you've taken on yourself," said that lady gloomily, "especially when you've never had any experience with children. You don't know much about her or her real disposition, I suppose, and there's no guessing how a child like that will turn out. But I don't want to discourage you, I'm sure, Marilla."

---

1 *tassels*   hanging blossoms.

"I'm not feeling discouraged" was Marilla's dry response. "When I make up my mind to do a thing it stays made up. I suppose you'd like to see Anne. I'll call her in."

Anne came running in presently, her face sparkling with the delight of her orchard rovings; but, abashed at finding herself in the unexpected presence of a stranger, she halted confusedly inside the door. She certainly was an odd-looking little creature in the short tight wincey dress she had worn from the asylum, below which her thin legs seemed ungracefully long. Her freckles were more numerous and obtrusive than ever; the wind had ruffled her hatless hair into over-brilliant disorder; it had never looked redder than at that moment.

"Well, they didn't pick you for your looks, that's sure and certain," was Mrs. Rachel Lynde's emphatic comment. Mrs. Rachel was one of those delightful and popular people who pride themselves on speaking their mind without fear or favour. "She's terrible skinny and homely, Marilla. Come here, child, and let me have a look at you. Lawful heart, did any one ever see such freckles? And hair as red as carrots! Come here, child, I say."

Anne "came there," but not exactly as Mrs. Rachel expected. With one bound she crossed the kitchen floor and stood before Mrs. Rachel, her face scarlet with anger, her lips quivering, and her whole slender form trembling from head to foot.

"I hate you," she cried in a choked voice, stamping her foot on the floor. "I hate you—I hate you—I hate you—" a louder stamp with each assertion of hatred. "How dare you call me skinny and ugly? How dare you say I'm freckled and red-headed? You are a rude, impolite, unfeeling woman!"

"Anne!" exclaimed Marilla in consternation.

But Anne continued to face Mrs. Rachel undauntedly, head up, eyes blazing, hands clenched, passionate indignation exhaling from her like an atmosphere.

"How dare you say such things about me?" she repeated vehemently. "How would you like to have such things said about you? How would you like to be told that you are fat and clumsy and probably hadn't a spark of imagination in you? I don't care if I do hurt your feelings by saying so! I hope I hurt them. You have hurt mine worse than they were ever hurt before even by Mrs. Thomas' intoxicated husband. And I'll *never* forgive you for it, never, never!"

Stamp! Stamp!

"Did anybody ever see such a temper!" exclaimed the horrified Mrs. Rachel.

"Anne, go to your room and stay there until I come up," said Marilla, recovering her powers of speech with difficulty.

Anne, bursting into tears, rushed to the hall door, slammed it until the tins on the porch wall outside rattled in sympathy, and fled through the hall and up the stairs like a whirlwind. A subdued slam above told that the door of the east gable had been shut with equal vehemence.

"Well, I don't envy you your job bringing *that* up, Marilla," said Mrs. Rachel with unspeakable solemnity.

Marilla opened her lips to say she knew not what of apology or deprecation. What she did say was a surprise to herself then and ever afterwards.

"You shouldn't have twitted her about her looks, Rachel."

"Marilla Cuthbert, you don't mean to say that you are upholding her in such a terrible display of temper as we've just seen?" demanded Mrs. Rachel indignantly.

"No," said Marilla slowly, "I'm not trying to excuse her. She's been very naughty and I'll have to give her a talking to about it. But we must make allowances for her. She's never been taught what is right. And you *were* too hard on her, Rachel."

Marilla could not help tacking on that last sentence, although she was again surprised at herself for doing it. Mrs. Rachel got up with an air of offended dignity.

"Well, I see that I'll have to be very careful what I say after this, Marilla, since the fine feelings of orphans, brought from goodness knows where, have to be considered before anything else. Oh, no, I'm not vexed—don't worry yourself. I'm too sorry for you to leave any room for anger in my mind. You'll have your own troubles with that child. But if you'll take my advice—which I suppose you won't do, although I've brought up ten children and buried two—you'll do that 'talking to' you mention with a fair-sized birch switch. I should think *that* would be the most effective language for that kind of a child. Her temper matches her hair I guess. Well, good evening, Marilla. I hope you'll come down to see me often as usual. But you can't expect me to visit here again in a hurry, if I'm liable to be flown at and insulted in such a fashion. It's something new in *my* experience."

Whereat Mrs. Rachel swept out and away—if a fat woman who always waddled *could* be said to sweep away—and Marilla with a very solemn face betook herself to the east gable.

On the way up-stairs she pondered uneasily as to what she ought to do. She felt no little dismay over the scene that had just been enacted. How unfortunate that Anne should have displayed such temper before Mrs. Rachel Lynde, of all people! Then Marilla suddenly became aware of an uncomfortable and rebuking consciousness that she felt more humiliation over this than sorrow over the discovery of such a serious defect in Anne's disposition. And how was she to punish her? The amiable suggestion of the birch switch—to the efficiency of which all of Mrs. Rachel's own children could have borne smarting testimony—did not appeal to Marilla. She did not believe she could whip a child. No, some other method of punishment must be found to bring Anne to a proper realization of the enormity of her offence.

Marilla found Anne face downward on her bed, crying bitterly, quite oblivious of muddy boots on a clean counterpane.

"Anne," she said, not ungently.

No answer.

"Anne," with greater severity, "get off that bed this minute and listen to what I have to say to you."

Anne squirmed off the bed and sat rigidly on a chair beside it, her face swollen and tear-stained and her eyes fixed stubbornly on the floor.

"This is a nice way for you to behave, Anne! Aren't you ashamed of yourself?"

"She hadn't any right to call me ugly and red-headed," retorted Anne, evasive and defiant.

"You hadn't any right to fly into such a fury and talk the way you did to her, Anne. I was ashamed of you—thoroughly ashamed of you. I wanted you to behave nicely to Mrs. Lynde, and instead of that you have disgraced me. I'm sure I don't know why you should lose your temper like that just because Mrs. Lynde said you were red-haired and homely. You say it yourself often enough."

"Oh, but there's such a difference between saying a thing yourself and hearing other people say it," wailed Anne. "You may know a thing is so, but you can't help hoping other people don't quite think it is. I suppose you think I have an awful temper, but I couldn't help it. When she said those things something just rose right up in me and choked me. I *had* to fly out at her."

"Well, you made a fine exhibition of yourself I must say. Mrs. Lynde will have a nice story to tell about you everywhere—and she'll tell it, too. It was a dreadful thing for you to lose your temper like that, Anne."

"Just imagine how you would feel if somebody told you to your face that you were skinny and ugly," pleaded Anne tearfully.

An old remembrance suddenly rose up before Marilla. She had been a very small child when she had heard one aunt say of her to another, "What a pity she is such a dark, homely little thing." Marilla was every day of fifty before the sting had gone out of that memory.

"I don't say that I think Mrs. Lynde was exactly right in saying what she did to you, Anne," she admitted in a softer tone. "Rachel is too outspoken. But that is no excuse for such behaviour on your part. She was a stranger and an elderly person and my visitor—all three very good reasons why you should have been respectful to her. You were rude and saucy and"—Marilla had a saving inspiration of punishment—"you must go to her and tell her you are very sorry for your bad temper and ask her to forgive you."

"I can never do that," said Anne determinedly and darkly. "You can punish me in any way you like, Marilla. You can shut me up in a dark, damp dungeon inhabited by snakes and toads and feed me only on bread and water and I shall not complain. But I cannot ask Mrs. Lynde to forgive me."

"We're not in the habit of shutting people up in dark, damp dungeons," said Marilla, drily, "especially as they're rather scarce in Avonlea. But apologize to Mrs. Lynde you must and shall and you'll stay here in your room until you can tell me you're willing to do it."

"I shall have to stay here for ever then," said Anne mournfully, "because I can't tell Mrs. Lynde I'm sorry I said those things to her. How can I? I'm *not* sorry. I'm sorry I've vexed you; but I'm *glad* I told her just what I did. It was a great satisfaction. I can't say I'm sorry when I'm not, can I? I can't even *imagine* I'm sorry."

"Perhaps your imagination will be in better working order by the morning," said Marilla, rising to depart. "You'll have the night to think over your conduct in and come to a better frame of mind. You said you would try to be a very good girl if we kept you at Green Gables, but I must say it hasn't seemed very much like it this evening."

Leaving this Parthian shaft[2] to rankle in Anne's stormy bosom, Marilla descended to the kitchen, grievously troubled in mind and vexed in soul. She was as angry with herself as with Anne, because, whenever she recalled Mrs. Rachel's dumbfounded countenance her lips twitched with amusement and she felt a most reprehensible desire to laugh.

CHAPTER 10

Anne's Apology

MARILLA said nothing to Matthew about the affair that evening; but when Anne proved still refractory the next morning an explanation had to be made to account for her absence from the breakfast-table. Marilla told Matthew

---

2 *Parthian shaft* remark made while leaving, in the reputed manner of Parthian horsemen who in retreat still shot at their enemies.

the whole story, taking pains to impress him with a due sense of the enormity of Anne's behaviour.

"It's a good thing Rachel Lynde got a calling down; she's a meddlesome old gossip," was Matthew's consolatory rejoinder.

"Matthew Cuthbert, I'm astonished at you. You know that Anne's behaviour was dreadful, and yet you take her part! I suppose you'll be saying next thing that she oughtn't to be punished at all."

"Well now—no—not exactly," said Matthew uneasily. "I reckon she ought to be punished a little. But don't be too hard on her, Marilla. Recollect she hasn't ever had any one to teach her right. You're—you're going to give her something to eat, aren't you?"

"When did you ever hear of me starving people into good behaviour?" demanded Marilla indignantly. "She'll have her meals regular, and I'll carry them up to her myself. But she'll stay up there until she's willing to apologize to Mrs. Lynde, and that's final, Matthew."

Breakfast, dinner, and supper were very silent meals—for Anne still remained obdurate. After each meal Marilla carried a well-filled tray to the east gable and brought it down later on not noticeably depleted. Matthew eyed its last descent with a troubled eye. Had Anne eaten anything at all?

When Marilla went out that evening to bring the cows from the back pasture, Matthew, who had been hanging about the barns and watching, slipped into the house with the air of a burglar and crept upstairs. As a general thing Matthew gravitated between the kitchen and the little bedroom off the hall where he slept; once in a while he ventured uncomfortably into the parlour or sitting-room when the minister came to tea. But he had never been upstairs in his own house since the spring he helped Marilla paper the spare bedroom, and that was four years ago.

He tiptoed along the hall and stood for several minutes outside the door of the east gable before he summoned courage to tap on it with his fingers and then open the door to peep in.

Anne was sitting on the yellow chair by the window, gazing mournfully out into the garden. Very small and unhappy she looked, and Matthew's heart smote him. He softly closed the door and tiptoed over to her.

"Anne," he whispered, as if afraid of being overheard, "how are you making it, Anne?"

Anne smiled wanly.

"Pretty well. I imagine a good deal, and that helps to pass the time. Of course, it's rather lonesome. But then, I may as well get used to that."

Anne smiled again, bravely facing the long years of solitary imprisonment before her.

Matthew recollected that he must say what he had come to say without loss of time, lest Marilla return prematurely.

"Well now, Anne, don't you think you'd better do it and have it over with?" he whispered. "It'll have to be done sooner or later, you know, for Marilla's a dreadful determined woman—dreadful determined, Anne. Do it right off, I say, and have it over."

"Do you mean apologize to Mrs. Lynde?"

"Yes—apologize—that's the very word," said Matthew eagerly. "Just smooth it over so to speak. That's what I was trying to get at."

"I suppose I could do it to oblige you," said Anne thoughtfully. "It would be true enough to say I am sorry, because I *am* sorry now. I wasn't a bit sorry last

night. I was mad clear through, and I stayed mad all night. I know I did because
I woke up three times and I was just furious every time. But this morning it was
all over. I wasn't in a temper any more—and it left a dreadful sort of goneness,
too. I felt so ashamed of myself. But I just couldn't think of going and telling
Mrs. Lynde so. It would be so humiliating. I made up my mind I'd stay shut up
here for ever rather than do that. But still—I'd do anything for you—if you
really want me to—"

"Well now, of course I do. It's terrible lonesome down-stairs without you.
Just go and smooth it over—that's a good girl."

"Very well," said Anne resignedly. "I'll tell Marilla as soon as she comes in
that I've repented."

"That's right—that's right, Anne. But don't tell Marilla I said anything about
it. She might think I was putting my oar in and I promised not to do that."

"Wild horses won't drag the secret from me," promised Anne solemnly.
"How would wild horses drag a secret from a person anyhow?"

But Matthew was gone, scared at his own success. He fled hastily to the re-
motest corner of the horse pasture lest Marilla should suspect what he had been
up to. Marilla herself, upon her return to the house, was agreeably surprised to
hear a plaintive voice calling, "Marilla," over the banisters.

"Well?" she said, going into the hall.

"I'm sorry I lost my temper and said rude things, and I'm willing to go and
tell Mrs. Lynde so."

"Very well." Marilla's crispness gave no sign of her relief. She had been wondering what under the canopy[1] she should do if Anne did not give in. "I'll take
you down after milking."

Accordingly, after milking, behold Marilla and Anne walking down the lane,
the former erect and triumphant, the latter drooping and dejected. But half-way
down Anne's dejection vanished as if by enchantment. She lifted her head and
stepped lightly along, her eyes fixed on the sunset sky and an air of subdued exhilaration about her. Marilla beheld the change disapprovingly. This was no
meek penitent such as it behooved her to take into the presence of the offended
Mrs. Lynde.

"What are you thinking of, Anne?" she asked sharply.

"I'm imagining out what I must say to Mrs. Lynde," answered Anne dreamily.

This was satisfactory—or should have been so. But Marilla could not rid herself of the notion that something in her scheme of punishment was going askew.
Anne had no business to look so rapt and radiant.

Rapt and radiant Anne continued until they were in the very presence of
Mrs. Lynde, who was sitting knitting by her kitchen window. Then the radiance
vanished. Mournful penitence appeared on every feature. Before a word was
spoken Anne suddenly went down on her knees before the astonished Mrs.
Rachel and held out her hands beseechingly.

"Oh, Mrs. Lynde, I am so extremely sorry," she said with a quiver in her
voice. "I could never express all my sorrow, no, not if I used up a whole dictionary. You must just imagine it. I behaved terribly to you—and I've disgraced the
dear friends, Matthew and Marilla, who have let me stay at Green Gables although I'm not a boy. I'm a dreadfully wicked and ungrateful girl, and I deserve

---

1 *what under the canopy*   that is, what under the overhanging firmament, or what in heaven's
name.

to be punished and cast out by respectable people for ever. It was very wicked of me to fly into a temper because you told me the truth. It *was* the truth; every word you said was true. My hair is red and I'm freckled and skinny and ugly. What I said to you was true, too, but I shouldn't have said it. Oh, Mrs. Lynde, please, please, forgive me. If you refuse it will be a lifelong sorrow to me. You wouldn't like to inflict a lifelong sorrow on a poor little orphan girl, would you, even if she had a dreadful temper? Oh, I am sure you wouldn't. Please say you forgive me, Mrs. Lynde."

Anne clasped her hands together, bowed her head, and waited for the word of judgment.

There was no mistaking her sincerity—it breathed in every tone of her voice. Both Marilla and Mrs. Lynde recognized its unmistakable ring. But the former understood in dismay that Anne was actually enjoying her valley of humiliation—was revelling in the thoroughness of her abasement. Where was the wholesome punishment upon which she, Marilla, had plumed herself? Anne had turned it into a species of positive pleasure.

Good Mrs. Lynde, not being overburdened with perception, did not see this. She only perceived that Anne had made a very thorough apology and all resentment vanished from her kindly, if somewhat officious, heart.

"There, there, get up, child," she said heartily. "Of course I forgive you. I guess I was a little too hard on you, anyway. But I'm such an outspoken person. You just mustn't mind me, that's what. It can't be denied your hair is terrible red; but I knew a girl once—went to school with her, in fact—whose hair was every mite as red as yours when she was young, but when she grew up it darkened to a real handsome auburn. I wouldn't be a mite surprised if yours did, too—not a mite."

"Oh, Mrs. Lynde!" Anne drew a long breath as she rose to her feet. "You have given me a hope. I shall always feel that you are a benefactor. Oh, I could endure anything if I only thought my hair would be a handsome auburn when I grew up. It would be so much easier to be good if one's hair was a handsome auburn, don't you think? And now may I go out into your garden and sit on that bench under the apple-trees while you and Marilla are talking? There is so much more scope for imagination out there."

"Laws, yes, run along, child. And you can pick a bouquet of them white June lilies over in the corner if you like."

As the door closed behind Anne Mrs. Lynde got briskly up to light a lamp.

"She's a real odd little thing. Take this chair, Marilla; it's easier than the one you've got; I just keep that for the hired boy to sit on. Yes, she certainly is an odd child, but there is something kind of taking about her after all. I don't feel so surprised at you and Matthew keeping her as I did—nor so sorry for you, either. She may turn out all right. Of course, she has a queer way of expressing herself—a little too—well, too kind of forcible, you know; but she'll likely get over that now that she's come to live among civilized folks. And then, her temper's pretty quick, I guess; but there's one comfort, a child that has a quick temper, just blaze up and cool down, ain't never likely to be sly or deceitful. Preserve me from a sly child, that's what. On the whole, Marilla, I kind of like her."

When Marilla went home Anne came out of the fragrant twilight of the orchard with a sheaf of white narcissi in her hands.

"I apologized pretty well, didn't I?" she said proudly as they went down the lane. "I thought since I had to do it I might as well do it thoroughly."

"You did it thoroughly, all right enough," was Marilla's comment. Marilla was dismayed at finding herself inclined to laugh over the recollection. She had also an uneasy feeling that she ought to scold Anne for apologizing so well; but then, that was ridiculous! She compromised with her conscience by saying severely:

"I hope you won't have occasion to make many more such apologies. I hope you'll try to control your temper now, Anne."

"That wouldn't be so hard if people wouldn't twit me about my looks," said Anne with a sigh. "I don't get cross about other things; but I'm *so* tired of being twitted about my hair and it just makes me boil right over. Do you suppose my hair will really be a handsome auburn when I grow up?"

"You shouldn't think so much about your looks, Anne. I'm afraid you are a very vain little girl."

"How can I be vain when I know I'm homely?" protested Anne. "I love pretty things; and I hate to look in the glass and see something that isn't pretty. It makes me feel so sorrowful—just as I feel when I look at any ugly thing. I pity it because it isn't beautiful."

"Handsome is as handsome does," quoted Marilla.[2]

"I've had that said to me before, but I have my doubts about it," remarked sceptical Anne, sniffing at her narcissi. "Oh, aren't these flowers sweet! It was lovely of Mrs. Lynde to give them to me. I have no hard feelings against Mrs. Lynde now. It gives you a lovely, comfortable feeling to apologize and be forgiven, doesn't it? Aren't the stars bright to-night? If you could live in a star, which one would you pick? I'd like that lovely clear big one away over there above that dark hill."

"Anne, do hold your tongue," said Marilla, thoroughly worn out trying to follow the gyrations of Anne's thoughts.

Anne said no more until they turned into their own lane. A little gypsy wind came down it to meet them, laden with the spicy perfume of young dew-wet ferns. Far up in the shadows a cheerful light gleamed out through the trees from the kitchen at Green Gables. Anne suddenly came close to Marilla and slipped her hand into the older woman's hard palm.

"It's lovely to be going home and know it's home," she said. "I love Green Gables already, and I never loved any place before. No place ever seemed like home. Oh, Marilla, I'm so happy. I could pray right now and not find it a bit hard."

Something warm and pleasant welled up in Marilla's heart at touch of that thin little hand in her own—a throb of the maternity she had missed, perhaps. Its very unaccustomedness and sweetness disturbed her. She hastened to restore her sensations to their normal calm by inculcating a moral.

"If you'll be a good girl you'll always be happy, Anne. And you should never find it hard to say your prayers."

"Saying one's prayers isn't exactly the same thing as praying," said Anne meditatively. "But I'm going to imagine that I'm the wind that is blowing up there in those tree-tops. When I get tired of the trees I'll imagine I'm gently waving down here in the ferns—and then I'll fly over to Mrs. Lynde's garden and set the flowers dancing—and then I'll go with one great swoop over the clover field—and then I'll blow over the Lake of Shining Waters and ripple it

---

2 *Handsome . . . Marilla*   See *The Vicar of Wakefield* by Oliver Goldsmith (1731–1774), Chapter 1.

all up into little sparkling waves. Oh, there's so much scope for imagination in a wind! So I'll not talk any more just now, Marilla."

"Thanks be to goodness for that," breathed Marilla in devout relief.

CHAPTER 11

Anne's Impressions of Sunday-School

"WELL, how do you like them?" said Marilla.

Anne was standing in the gable-room, looking solemnly at three new dresses spread out on the bed. One was of snuffy coloured[1] gingham which Marilla had been tempted to buy from a peddler the preceding summer because it looked so serviceable; one was of black-and-white checked sateen which she had picked up at a bargain counter in the winter; and one was a stiff print of an ugly blue shade which she had purchased that week at a Carmody store.

She had made them up herself, and they were all made alike—plain skirts fulled[2] tightly to plain waists, with sleeves as plain as waist and skirt and tight as sleeves could be.

"I'll imagine that I like them," said Anne soberly.

"I don't want you to imagine it," said Marilla offended. "Oh, I can see you don't like the dresses! What is the matter with them? Aren't they neat and clean and new?"

"Yes."

"Then why don't you like them?"

"They're—they're not—pretty," said Anne reluctantly.

"Pretty!" Marilla sniffed. "I didn't trouble my head about getting pretty dresses for you. I don't believe in pampering vanity, Anne, I'll tell you that right off. Those dresses are good, sensible, serviceable dresses, without any frills or furbelows about them, and they're all you'll get this summer. The brown gingham and the blue print will do you for school when you begin to go. The sateen is for church and Sunday-school. I'll expect you to keep them neat and clean and not to tear them. I should think you'd be grateful to get most anything after those skimpy wincey things you've been wearing."

"Oh, I *am* grateful," protested Anne. "But I'd be ever so much gratefuller if—if you'd made just one of them with puffed sleeves. Puffed sleeves are so fashionable now. It would give me such a thrill, Marilla, just to wear a dress with puffed sleeves."

"Well, you'll have to do without your thrill. I hadn't any material to waste on puffed sleeves. I think they are ridiculous-looking things anyhow. I prefer the plain, sensible ones."

"But I'd rather look ridiculous when everybody else does than plain and sensible all by myself," persisted Anne mournfully.

"Trust you for that! Well, hang those dresses carefully up in your closet, and then sit down and learn the Sunday-school lesson. I got a quarterly[3] from

---

1 *snuffy coloured* tobacco-colored, brown.
2 *fulled* gathered or pleated.
3 *quarterly* Sunday-school lessons, distributed every three months.

Mr. Bell for you and you'll go to Sunday-school to-morrow," said Marilla, disappearing downstairs in high dudgeon.

Anne clasped her hands and looked at the dresses.

"I did hope there would be a white one with puffed sleeves," she whispered disconsolately. "I prayed for one, but I didn't much expect it on that account. I didn't suppose God would have time to bother about a little orphan girl's dress. I knew I'd just have to depend on Marilla for it. Well, fortunately I can imagine that one of them is of snow-white muslin with lovely lace frills and three-puffed sleeves."

The next morning warnings of a sick headache prevented Marilla from going to Sunday-school with Anne.

"You'll have to go down and call for Mrs. Lynde, Anne," she said. "She'll see that you get into the right class. Now, mind you behave yourself properly. Stay to preaching afterwards and ask Mrs. Lynde to show you our pew. Here's a cent for collection. Don't stare at people and don't fidget. I shall expect you to tell me the text when you come home."

Anne started off irreproachably, arrayed in the stiff black-and-white sateen, which, while decent as regards length and certainly not open to the charge of skimpiness, contrived to emphasize every corner and angle of her thin figure. Her hat was a little, flat, glossy, new sailor, the extreme plainness of which had like-wise much disappointed Anne, who had permitted herself secret visions of ribbon and flowers. The latter, however, were supplied before Anne reached the main road, for, being confronted half-way down the lane with a golden frenzy of wind-stirred buttercups and a glory of wild roses, Anne promptly and liberally garlanded her hat with a heavy wreath of them. Whatever other people might have thought of the result it satisfied Anne, and she tripped gaily down the road, holding her ruddy head with its decoration of pink and yellow very proudly.

When she reached Mrs. Lynde's house she found that lady gone. Nothing daunted Anne proceeded onward to the church alone. In the porch she found a crowd of little girls, all more or less gaily attired in whites and blues and pinks, and all staring with curious eyes at this stranger in their midst, with her extraordinary head adornment. Avonlea little girls had already heard queer stories about Anne; Mrs. Lynde said she had an awful temper; Jerry Buote, the hired boy at Green Gables, said she talked all the time to herself or to the trees and flowers like a crazy girl. They looked at her and whispered to each other behind their quarterlies. Nobody made any friendly advances, then or later on when the opening exercises were over and Anne found herself in Miss Rogerson's class.

Miss Rogerson was a middle-aged lady who had taught a Sunday-school class for twenty years. Her method of teaching was to ask the printed questions from the quarterly and look sternly over its edge at the particular little girl she thought ought to answer the question. She looked very often at Anne, and Anne, thanks to Marilla's drilling, answered promptly; but it may be questioned if she understood very much about either question or answer.

She did not think she liked Miss Rogerson, and she felt very miserable; every other little girl in the class had puffed sleeves. Anne felt that life was really not worth living without puffed sleeves.

"Well, how did you like Sunday-school?" Marilla wanted to know when Anne came home. Her wreath having faded, Anne had discarded it in the lane, so Marilla was spared the knowledge of that for a time.

"I didn't like it a bit. It was horrid."

"Anne Shirley!" said Marilla rebukingly.

Anne sat down on the rocker with a long sigh, kissed one of Bonny's leaves, and waved her hand to a blossoming fuchsia.

"They might have been lonesome while I was away," she explained. "And now about the Sunday-school. I behaved well, just as you told me. Mrs. Lynde was gone, but I went right on myself. I went into the church, with a lot of other little girls, and I sat in the corner of a pew by the window while the opening exercises went on. Mr. Bell made an awfully long prayer. I would have been dreadfully tired before he got through if I hadn't been sitting by that window. But it looked right out on the Lake of Shining Waters, so I just gazed at that and imagined all sorts of splendid things."

"You shouldn't have done anything of the sort. You should have listened to Mr. Bell."

"But he wasn't talking to me," protested Anne. "He was talking to God and he didn't seem to be very much interested in it, either. I think he thought God was too far off to make it worth while. I said a little prayer myself, though. There was a long row of white birches hanging over the lake and the sunshine fell down through them, 'way, 'way down, deep into the water. Oh, Marilla, it was like a beautiful dream! It gave me a thrill and I just said, 'Thank you for it, God,' two or three times."

"Not out loud, I hope," said Marilla anxiously.

"Oh, no, just under my breath. Well, Mr. Bell did get through at last and they told me to go into the class-room with Miss Rogerson's class. There were nine other girls in it. They all had puffed sleeves. I tried to imagine mine were puffed, too, but I couldn't. Why couldn't I? It was as easy as could be to imagine they were puffed when I was alone in the east gable, but it was awfully hard there among the others who had really truly puffs."

"You shouldn't have been thinking about your sleeves in Sunday-school. You should have been attending to the lesson. I hope you knew it."

"Oh, yes; and I answered a lot of questions. Miss Rogerson asked ever so many. I don't think it was fair for her to do all the asking. There were lots I wanted to ask her, but I didn't like to because I didn't think she was a kindred spirit. Then all the other little girls recited a paraphrase.[4] She asked me if I knew any. I told her I didn't, but I could recite, 'The Dog at His Master's Grave'[5] if she liked. That's in the Third Royal Reader. It isn't a really truly religious piece of poetry, but it's so sad and melancholy that it might as well be. She said it wouldn't do and she told me to learn the nineteenth paraphrase[6] for next Sunday. I read it over in church afterwards and it's splendid. There are two lines in particular that just thrill me.

> "'Quick as the slaughtered squadrons fell
> In Midian's evil day'[7]

I don't know what 'squadrons' means nor 'Midian,' either, but it sounds *so* tragical. I can hardly wait until next Sunday to recite it. I'll practise it all the week. After Sunday-school I asked Miss Rogerson—because Mrs. Lynde was

---

4 *paraphrase*   verse rendition of sacred scripture, prepared by Scots Presbyterian churches.
5 *The Dog at His Master's Grave*   pious, sentimental poem by Lydia Sigourney (1791–1865).
6 *nineteenth paraphrase*   from the Presbyterian hymnbook.
7 *Quick . . . day*   There are several wars with Midian mentioned in the Old Testament; the defeat of the Midianites by Gideon's host is described in Judges 7–8.

too far away—to show me your pew. I sat just as still as I could and the text was Revelations, third chapter, second and third verses. It was a very long text. If I was a minister I'd pick the short, snappy ones. The sermon was awfully long, too. I suppose the minister had to match it to the text. I didn't think he was a bit interesting. The trouble with him seems to be that he hasn't enough imagination. I didn't listen to him very much. I just let my thoughts run and I thought of the most surprising things."

Marilla felt helplessly that all this should be sternly reproved, but she was hampered by the undeniable fact that some of the things Anne had said, especially about the minister's sermons and Mr. Bell's prayers, were what she herself had really thought deep down in her heart for years, but had never given expression to. It almost seemed to her that those secret, unuttered, critical thoughts had suddenly taken visible and accusing shape and form in the person of this outspoken morsel of neglected humanity.

CHAPTER 12

A Solemn Vow and Promise

IT WAS not until the next Friday that Marilla heard the story of the flower-wreathed hat. She came home from Mrs. Lynde's and called Anne to account.

"Anne, Mrs. Rachel says you went to church last Sunday with your hat rigged out ridiculous with roses and buttercups. What on earth put you up to such a caper? A pretty-looking object you must have been!"

"Oh, I know pink and yellow aren't becoming to me," began Anne.

"Becoming fiddlesticks! It was putting flowers on your hat at all, no matter what colour they were, that was ridiculous. You are the most aggravating child!"

"I don't see why it's any more ridiculous to wear flowers on your hat than on your dress," protested Anne. "Lots of little girls there had bouquets pinned on their dresses. What was the difference?"

Marilla was not to be drawn from the safe concrete into dubious paths of the abstract.

"Don't answer me back like that, Anne. It was very silly of you to do such a thing. Never let me catch you at such a trick again. Mrs. Rachel says she thought she would sink through the floor when she saw you come in all rigged out like that. She couldn't get near enough to tell you to take them off till it was too late. She says people talked about it something dreadful. Of course they would think I had no better sense than to let you go decked out like that."

"Oh, I'm so sorry," said Anne, tears welling into her eyes. "I never thought you'd mind. The roses and buttercups were so sweet and pretty I thought they'd look lovely on my hat. Lots of the little girls had artificial flowers on their hats. I'm afraid I'm going to be a dreadful trial to you. Maybe you'd better send me back to the asylum. That would be terrible; I don't think I could endure it; most likely I would go into consumption; I'm so thin as it is, you see. But that would be better than being a trial to you."

"Nonsense," said Marilla, vexed at herself for having made the child cry. "I don't want to send you back to the asylum, I'm sure. All I want is that you should behave like other little girls and not make yourself ridiculous. Don't cry any more. I've got some news for you. Diana Barry came home this afternoon.

I'm going up to see if I can borrow a skirt pattern from Mrs. Barry, and if you like you can come with me and get acquainted with Diana."

Anne rose to her feet, with clasped hands, the tears still glistening on her cheeks; the dish-towel she had been hemming slipped unheeded to the floor.

"Oh, Marilla, I'm frightened—now that it has come I'm actually frightened. What if she shouldn't like me! It would be the most tragical disappointment of my life."

"Now, don't get into a fluster. And I do wish you wouldn't use such long words. It sounds so funny in a little girl. I guess Diana'll like you well enough. It's her mother you've got to reckon with. If she doesn't like you it won't matter how much Diana does. If she has heard about your outburst to Mrs. Lynde and going to church with buttercups round your hat I don't know what she'll think of you. You must be polite and well-behaved, and don't make any of your startling speeches. For pity's sake, if the child isn't actually trembling!"

Anne *was* trembling. Her face was pale and tense.

"Oh, Marilla, you'd be excited, too, if you were going to meet a little girl you hoped to be your bosom friend and whose mother mightn't like you," she said as she hastened to get her hat.

They went over to Orchard Slope by the short cut across the brook and up the firry hill grove. Mrs. Barry came to the kitchen door in answer to Marilla's knock. She was a tall, black-eyed, black-haired woman, with a very resolute mouth. She had the reputation of being very strict with her children.

"How do you do, Marilla?" she said cordially. "Come in. And this is the little girl you have adopted, I suppose?"

"Yes, this is Anne Shirley," said Marilla.

"Spelled with an *e*," gasped Anne, who, tremulous and excited as she was, was determined there should be no misunderstanding on that important point.

Mrs. Barry, not hearing or not comprehending, merely shook hands and said kindly:

"How are you?"

"I am well in body although considerably rumpled up in spirit, thank you, ma'am," said Anne gravely. Then aside to Marilla in an audible whisper, "There wasn't anything startling in that, was there, Marilla?"

Diana was sitting on the sofa, reading a book which she dropped when the callers entered. She was a very pretty little girl, with her mother's black eyes and hair, and rosy cheeks, and the merry expression which was her inheritance from her father.

"This is my little girl, Diana," said Mrs. Barry. "Diana, you might take Anne out into the garden and show her your flowers. It will be better for you than straining your eyes over that book. She reads entirely too much—" this to Marilla as the little girls went out—"and I can't prevent her, for her father aids and abets her. She's always poring over a book. I'm glad she has the prospect of a playmate—perhaps it will take her more out-of-doors."

Outside in the garden, which was full of mellow sunset light streaming through the dark old firs to the west of it, stood Anne and Diana, gazing bashfully at one another over a clump of gorgeous tiger lilies.

The Barry garden was a bowery wilderness of flowers which would have delighted Anne's heart at any time less fraught with destiny. It was encircled by huge old willows and tall firs, beneath which flourished flowers that loved the shade. Prim, right-angled paths, neatly bordered with clam-shells, intersected it like moist red ribbons and in the beds between old-fashioned flowers ran riot.

There were rosy bleeding-hearts and great splendid crimson peonies; white, fragrant narcissi and thorny, sweet Scotch roses; pink and blue and white columbines and lilac-tinted Bouncing Bets; clumps of southern-wood and ribbon grass and mint; purple Adam-and-Eve, daffodils, and masses of sweet clover white with its delicate, fragrant, feathery sprays; scarlet lightening that shot its fiery lances over prim white musk-flowers; a garden it was where sunshine lingered and bees hummed, and winds, beguiled into loitering, purred and rustled.

"Oh, Diana," said Anne at last, clasping her hands and speaking almost in a whisper, "do you think—oh, do you think you can like me a little—enough to be my bosom friend?"

Diana laughed. Diana always laughed before she spoke.

"Why, I guess so," she said frankly. "I'm awfully glad you've come to live at Green Gables. It will be jolly to have somebody to play with. There isn't any other girl who lives near enough to play with, and I've no sisters big enough."

"Will you swear to be my friend for ever and ever?" demanded Anne eagerly.

Diana looked shocked.

"Why, it's dreadfully wicked to swear," she said rebukingly.

"Oh no, not my kind of swearing. There are two kinds, you know."

"I never heard of but one kind," said Diana doubtfully.

"There really is another. Oh, it isn't wicked at all. It just means vowing and promising solemnly."

"Well, I don't mind doing that," agreed Diana, relieved. "How do you do it?"

"We must join hands—so," said Anne gravely. "It ought to be over running water. We'll just imagine this path is running water. I'll repeat the oath first. I solemnly swear to be faithful to my bosom friend, Diana Barry, as long as the sun and moon shall endure. Now you say it and put my name in."

Diana repeated the "oath" with a laugh fore and aft. Then she said:

"You're a queer girl, Anne. I heard before that you were queer. But I believe I'm going to like you real well."

When Marilla and Anne went home Diana went with them as far as the log bridge. The two little girls walked with their arms about each other. At the brook they parted with many promises to spend the next afternoon together.

"Well, did you find Diana a kindred spirit?" asked Marilla as they went up through the garden of Green Gables.

"Oh, yes," sighed Anne, blissfully unconscious of any sarcasm on Marilla's part. "Oh, Marilla, I'm the happiest girl on Prince Edward Island this very moment. I assure you I'll say my prayers with a right good-will to-night. Diana and I are going to build a playhouse in Mr. William Bell's birch grove to-morrow. Can I have those broken pieces of china that are out in the wood-shed? Diana's birthday is in February and mine is in March. Don't you think that is a very strange coincidence? Diana is going to lend me a book to read. She says it's perfectly splendid and tremendously exciting. She's going to show me a place back in the woods where rice lilies grow. Don't you think Diana has got very soulful eyes? I wish I had soulful eyes. Diana is going to teach me to sing a song called 'Nelly in the Hazel Dell.'[1] She's going to give me a picture to put up in my room; it's a perfectly beautiful picture, she says—a lovely lady in a pale blue silk

---

1 *Nelly in the Hazel Dell*   popular song by George Frederick Root (1820–1895) about a lover's watch over his dead beloved's grave.

dress. A sewing-machine agent gave it to her. I wish I had something to give Diana. I'm an inch taller than Diana, but she is ever so much fatter; she says she'd like to be thin because it's so much more graceful, but I'm afraid she only said it to soothe my feelings. We're going to the shore some day to gather shells. We have agreed to call the spring down by the log bridge the Dryad's Bubble. Isn't that a perfectly elegant name? I read a story once about a spring called that. A dryad is a sort of grown-up fairy, I think."

"Well, all I hope is you won't talk Diana to death," said Marilla. "But remember this in all your planning, Anne. You're not going to play all the time nor most of it. You'll have your work to do and it'll have to be done first."

Anne's cup of happiness was full, and Matthew caused it to overflow. He had just got home from a trip to the store at Carmody, and he sheepishly produced a small parcel from his pocket and handed it to Anne, with a deprecatory look at Marilla.

"I heard you say you liked chocolate sweeties, so I got you some," he said.

"Humph," sniffed Marilla. "It'll ruin her teeth and stomach. There, there, child, don't look so dismal. You can eat those, since Matthew has gone and got them. He'd better have brought you peppermints. They're wholesomer. Don't sicken yourself eating them all at once now."

"Oh, no, indeed, I won't," said Anne eagerly. "I'll just eat one to-night, Marilla. And I can give Diana half of them, can't I? The other half will taste twice as sweet to me if I give some to her. It's delightful to think I have something to give her."

"I will say it for the child," said Marilla when Anne had gone to her gable, "she isn't stingy. I'm glad, for of all faults I detest stinginess in a child. Dear me, it's only three weeks since she came, and it seems as if she'd been here always. I can't imagine the place without her. Now, don't be looking I-told-you-so, Matthew. That's bad enough in a woman, but it isn't to be endured in a man. I'm perfectly willing to own up that I'm glad I consented to keep the child and that I'm getting fond of her, but don't you rub it in, Matthew Cuthbert."

CHAPTER 13

The Delights of Anticipation

"I'T'S TIME Anne was in to do her sewing," said Marilla, glancing at the clock and then out into the yellow August afternoon where everything drowsed in the heat. "She stayed playing with Diana more than half an hour more'n I gave her leave to; and now she's perched out there on the woodpile talking to Matthew, nineteen to the dozen,[1] when she knows perfectly well that she ought to be at her work. And of course he's listening to her like a perfect ninny. I never saw such an infatuated man. The more she talks and the odder the things she says, the more he's delighted evidently. Anne Shirley, you come right in here this minute, do you hear me!"

A series of staccato taps on the west window brought Anne flying in from the yard, eyes shining, cheeks faintly flushed with pink, unbraided hair streaming behind her in a torrent of brightness.

---

1 *talking to Matthew, nineteen to the dozen*   running on in her talk very fast or extensively.

"Oh, Marilla," she exclaimed breathlessly, "there's going to be a Sunday-school picnic next week—in Mr. Harmon Andrews' field, right near the Lake of Shining Waters. And Mrs. Superintendent Bell and Mrs. Rachel Lynde are going to make ice-cream—think of it, Marilla—*ice-cream!* And oh, Marilla, can I go to it?"

"Just look at the clock, if you please, Anne. What time did I tell you to come in?"

"Two o'clock—but isn't it splendid about the picnic, Marilla? Please can I go? Oh, I've never been to a picnic—I've dreamed of picnics, but I've never—"

"Yes, I told you to come at two o'clock. And it's a quarter to three. I'd like to know why you didn't obey me, Anne."

"Why, I meant to, Marilla, as much as could be. But you have no idea how fascinating Idlewild is. And then, of course, I had to tell Matthew about the picnic. Matthew is such a sympathetic listener. Please can I go?"

"You'll have to learn to resist the fascination of Idle-whatever-you-call-it. When I tell you to come in at a certain time I mean that time and not half an hour later. And you needn't stop to discourse with sympathetic listeners on your way, either. As for the picnic, of course you can go. You're a Sunday-school scholar, and it's not likely I'd refuse to let you go when all the other little girls are going."

"But—but," faltered Anne, "Diana says that everybody must take a basket of things to eat. I can't cook, as you know, Marilla, and—and—I don't mind going to a picnic without puffed sleeves much, but I'd feel terribly humiliated if I had to go without a basket. It's been preying on my mind ever since Diana told me."

"Well, it needn't prey any longer. I'll bake you a basket."

"Oh, you dear good Marilla. Oh, you are so kind to me. Oh, I'm so much obliged to you."

Getting through with her "ohs" Anne cast herself into Marilla's arms and rapturously kissed her sallow cheek. It was the first time in her whole life that childish lips had voluntarily touched Marilla's face. Again that sudden sensation of startling sweetness thrilled her. She was secretly vastly pleased at Anne's impulsive caress, which was probably the reason why she said brusquely:

"There, there, never mind your kissing nonsense. I'd sooner see you doing strictly as you're told. As for cooking, I mean to begin giving you lessons in that some of these days. But you're so feather-brained, Anne, I've been waiting to see if you'd sober down a little and learn to be steady before I begin. You've got to keep your wits about you in cooking and not stop in the middle of things to let your thoughts rove over all creation. Now, get out your patchwork and have your square done before tea-time."

"I do *not* like patchwork," said Anne dolefully, hunting out her workbasket and sitting down before a little heap of red and white diamonds with a sigh. "I think some kinds of sewing would be nice; but there's no scope for imagination in patchwork. It's just one little seam after another and you never seem to be getting anywhere. But of course I'd rather be Anne of Green Gables sewing patchwork than Anne of any other place with nothing to do but play. I wish time went as quick sewing patches as it does when I'm playing with Diana, though. Oh, we do have such elegant times, Marilla. I have to furnish most of the imagination, but I'm well able to do that. Diana is simply perfect in every other way. You know that little piece of land across the brook that runs up between our farm and Mr. Barry's. It belongs to Mr. William Bell, and right in the corner there is a little ring of white birch trees—the most romantic spot, Marilla. Diana and I have our playhouse there. We call it Idlewild. Isn't that a poeti-cal name? I assure you it took me some time to think it out. I stayed awake nearly a whole night before I invented it. Then, just as I was dropping off to sleep, it came like an inspiration. Diana was *enraptured* when she heard it. We have got our house fixed up elegantly. You must come and see it, Marilla—won't you? We have great big stones, all covered with moss, for seats, and boards from tree to tree for shelves. And we have all our dishes on them. Of course, they're all broken but it's the easiest thing in the world to imagine that they are whole. There's a piece of a plate with a spray of red and yellow ivy on it that is especially beautiful. We keep it in the parlour and we have the fairy glass there, too. The fairy glass is as lovely as a dream. Diana found it out in the woods behind their chicken house. It's all full of rainbows—just little young rainbows that haven't grown big yet—and Diana's mother told her it was bro-ken off a hanging lamp they once had. But it's nicer to imagine the fairies lost it one night when they had a ball, so we call it the fairy glass. Matthew is going to make us a table. Oh, we have named that little round pool over in Mr. Barry's field Willowmere. I got that name out of the book Diana lent me. That was a thrilling book, Marilla. The heroine had five lovers. I'd be satisfied with one, wouldn't you? She was very handsome and she went through great tribulations. She could faint as easy as anything. I'd love to be able to faint, wouldn't you, Marilla? It's so romantic. But I'm really very healthy for all I'm so thin. I believe I'm getting fatter, though. Don't you think I am? I look at my elbows every morning when I get up to see if any dimples are coming. Diana is having a new dress made with elbow sleeves. She is going to wear it to the picnic. Oh, I do hope it will be fine next Wednesday. I don't feel that I could endure the disap-pointment if anything happened to prevent me from getting to the picnic. I suppose I'd live through it, but I'm certain it would be a lifelong sorrow. It wouldn't matter if I got to a hundred picnics in after years; they wouldn't make up for missing this one. They're going to have boats on the Lake of Shining Waters—and ice-cream as I told you. I have never tasted ice-cream. Diana tried to explain what it was like, but I guess ice-cream is one of those things that are beyond imagination."

"Anne, you have talked even on for ten minutes by the clock," said Marilla. "Now, just for curiosity's sake, see if you can hold your tongue for the same length of time."

Anne held her tongue as desired. But for the rest of the week she talked pic-nic and thought picnic and dreamed picnic. On Saturday it rained and she worked herself up into such a frantic state lest it should keep on raining until and over Wednesday, that Marilla made her sew an extra patchwork square by way of steadying her nerves.

On Sunday Anne confided to Marilla on the way home from church that she grew actually cold all over with excitement when the minister announced the picnic from the pulpit.

"Such a thrill as went up and down my back, Marilla! I don't think I'd ever really believed until then that there was honestly going to be a picnic. I couldn't help fearing I'd only imagined it. But when a minister says a thing in the pulpit you just have to believe it."

"You set your heart too much on things, Anne," said Marilla with a sigh. "I'm afraid there'll be a great many disappointments in store for you through life."

"Oh, Marilla, looking forward to things is half the pleasure of them," ex-claimed Anne. "You mayn't get the things themselves; but nothing can prevent you from having the fun of looking forward to them. Mrs. Lynde says, 'Blessed are they who expect nothing for they shall not be disappointed.' But I think it would be worse to expect nothing than to be disappointed."

Marilla wore her amethyst brooch to church that day as usual. Marilla always wore her amethyst brooch to church. She would have thought it rather sacrilegious to leave it off—as bad as forgetting her Bible or her collection dime. That amethyst brooch was Marilla's most treasured possession. A sea-faring uncle had given it to her mother who in turn had bequeathed it to Marilla. It was an old-fashioned oval, containing a braid of her mother's hair, surrounded by a border of very fine amethysts. Marilla knew too little about precious stones to realize how fine the amethysts actually were; but she thought them very beautiful and was always pleasantly conscious of their violet shimmer at her throat, above her good brown satin dress, even although she could not see it.

Anne had been smitten with delighted admiration when she first saw that brooch.

"Oh, Marilla, it's a perfectly elegant brooch. I don't know how you can pay attention to the sermon or the prayers when you have it on. *I* couldn't, I know. I think amethysts are just sweet. They are what I used to think diamonds were like. Long ago, before I had ever seen a diamond, I read about them and I tried to imagine what they would be like. I thought they would be lovely glimmering purple stones. When I saw a real diamond in a lady's ring one day I was so disappointed I cried. Of course, it was very lovely but it wasn't my idea of a diamond. Will you let me hold the brooch for one minute, Marilla? Do you think amethysts can be the souls of good violets?"

CHAPTER 14

Anne's Confession

O N THE Monday evening before the picnic Marilla came down from her room with a troubled face.

"Anne," she said to that small personage, who was shelling peas by the spotless table and singing "Nelly of the Hazel Dell" with a vigour and expression that did credit to Diana's teaching, "did you see anything of my amethyst brooch? I thought I stuck it in my pincushion when I came home from church yesterday evening, but I can't find it anywhere."

"I—I saw it this afternoon when you were away at the Aid Society," said Anne, a little slowly. "I was passing your door when I saw it on the cushion, so I went in to look at it."

"Did you touch it?" said Marilla sternly.

"Y-e-e-s," admitted Anne, "I took it up and I pinned it on my breast just to see how it would look."

"You had no business to do anything of the sort. It's very wrong in a little girl to meddle. You shouldn't have gone into my room in the first place and you shouldn't have touched a brooch that didn't belong to you in the second. Where did you put it?"

"Oh, I put it back on the bureau. I hadn't it on a minute. Truly, I didn't mean to meddle, Marilla. I didn't think about its being wrong to go in and try on the brooch; but I see now that it was and I'll never do it again. That's one good thing about me. I never do the same naughty thing twice."

"You didn't put it back," said Marilla. "That brooch isn't anywhere on the bureau. You've taken it out or something, Anne."

"I *did* put it back," said Anne quickly—pertly, Marilla thought. "I don't just remember whether I stuck it on the pincushion or laid it in the china tray. But I'm perfectly certain I put it back."

"I'll go and have another look," said Marilla, determining to be just. "If you put that brooch back it's there still. If it isn't I'll know you didn't, that's all!"

Marilla went to her room and made a thorough search, not only over the bureau but in every other place she thought the brooch might possibly be. It was not to be found and she returned to the kitchen.

"Anne, the brooch is gone. By your own admission you were the last person to handle it. Now, what have you done with it? Tell me the truth at once. Did you take it out and lose it?"

"No, I didn't," said Anne solemnly, meeting Marilla's angry gaze squarely. "I never took the brooch out of your room and that is the truth, if I was to be led to the block for it—although I'm not very certain what a block is. So there, Marilla."

Anne's "so there" was only intended to emphasize her assertion, but Marilla took it as a display of defiance.

"I believe you are telling me a falsehood, Anne," she said sharply. "I know you are. There now, don't say anything more unless you are prepared to tell the whole truth. Go to your room and stay there until you are ready to confess."

"Will I take the peas with me?" said Anne meekly.

"No, I'll finish shelling them myself. Do as I bid you."

When Anne had gone Marilla went about her evening tasks in a very disturbed state of mind. She was worried about her valuable brooch. What if Anne had lost it? And how wicked of the child to deny having taken it, when anybody could see she must have! With such an innocent face, too!

"I don't know what I wouldn't sooner have had happen," thought Marilla, as she nervously shelled the peas. "Of course, I don't suppose she meant to steal it or anything like that. She's just taken it to play with or help along that imagination of hers. She must have taken it, that's clear, for there hasn't been a soul in that room since she was in it, by her own story, until I went up to-night. And the brooch is gone, there's nothing surer. I suppose she has lost it and is afraid to own up for fear she'll be punished. It's a dreadful thing to think she tells falsehoods. It's a far worse thing than her fit of temper. It's a fearful responsibility to have a child in your house you can't trust. Slyness and untruthfulness—that's what she has displayed. I declare I feel worse about that than about the brooch. If she'd only have told the truth about it I wouldn't mind so much."

Marilla went to her room at intervals all through the evening and searched for the brooch, without finding it. A bed-time visit to the east gable produced no result. Anne persisted in denying that she knew anything about the brooch but Marilla was only the more firmly convinced that she did.

She told Matthew the story the next morning. Matthew was confounded and puzzled; he could not so quickly lose faith in Anne but he had to admit that circumstances were against her.

"You're sure it hasn't fell down behind the bureau?" was the only suggestion he could offer.

"I've moved the bureau and I've taken out the drawers and I've looked in every crack and cranny," was Marilla's positive answer. "The brooch is gone and that child has taken it and lied about it. That's the plain, ugly truth, Matthew Cuthbert, and we might as well look it in the face."

"Well now, what are you going to do about it?" Matthew asked forlornly, feeling secretly thankful that Marilla and not he had to deal with the situation. He felt no desire to put his oar in this time.

"She'll stay in her room until she confesses," said Marilla grimly, remembering the success of this method in the former case. "Then we'll see. Perhaps we'll be able to find the brooch if she'll only tell where she took it; but in any case she'll have to be severely punished, Matthew."

"Well now, you'll have to punish her," said Matthew, reaching for his hat. "I've nothing to do with it, remember. You warned me off yourself."

Marilla felt descrted by every one. She could not even go to Mrs. Lynde for advice. She went up to the east gable with a very serious face and left it with a face more serious still. Anne steadfastly refused to confess. She persisted in asserting that she had not taken the brooch. The child had evidently been crying and Marilla felt a pang of pity which she sternly repressed. By night she was, as she expressed it, "beat out."

"You'll stay in this room until you confess, Anne. You can make up your mind to that," she said firmly.

"But the picnic is to-morrow, Marilla," cried Anne. "You won't keep me from going to that, will you? You'll just let me out for the afternoon, won't you? Then I'll stay here as long as you like afterwards *cheerfully*. But I *must* go to the picnic."

"You'll not go to picnics nor anywhere else until you've confessed, Anne."

"Oh, Marilla," gasped Anne.

But Marilla had gone out and shut the door.

Wednesday morning dawned as bright and fair as if expressly made to order for the picnic. Birds sang around Green Gables; the Madonna lilies in the garden sent out whiffs of perfume that entered in on viewless winds at every door and window, and wandered through halls and rooms like spirits of benediction. The birches in the hollow waved joyful hands as if watching for Anne's usual morning greeting from the east gable. But Anne was not at her window. When Marilla took her breakfast up to her she found the child sitting primly on her bed, pale and resolute, with tight-shut lips and gleaming eyes.

"Marilla, I'm ready to confess."

"Ah!" Marilla laid down her tray. Once again her method had succeeded; but her success was very bitter to her. "Let me hear what you have to say then, Anne."

"I took the amethyst brooch," said Anne, as if repeating a lesson she had learned. "I took it just as you said. I didn't mean to take it when I went in. But it did look so beautiful, Marilla, when I pinned on my breast that I was overcome by an irresistible temptation. I imagined how perfectly thrilling it would be to take it to Idlewild and play I was the Lady Cordelia Fitzgerald. It would be so much easier to imagine I was the Lady Cordelia if I had a real amethyst brooch on. Diana and I made necklaces of roseberries but what are roseberries compared to amethysts? So I took the brooch. I thought I could put it back before you came home. I went all the way around by the road to lengthen out the time. When I was going over the bridge across the Lake of Shining Waters I took the brooch off to have another look at it. Oh, how it did shine in the sunlight! And then, when I was leaning over the bridge, it just slipped through my fingers— so—and went down—down—down, all purply-sparkling, and sank forevermore beneath the Lake of Shining Waters. And that's the best I can do at confessing, Marilla."

Marilla felt hot anger surge up into her heart again. This child had taken and lost her treasured amethyst brooch and now sat there calmly reciting the details thereof without the least apparent compunction or repentance.

"Anne, this is terrible," she said, trying to speak calmly. "You are the very wickedest girl I ever heard of."

"Yes, I suppose I am," agreed Anne tranquilly. "And I know I'll have to be punished. It'll be your duty to punish me, Marilla. Won't you please get it over right off because I'd like to go to the picnic with nothing on my mind."

"Picnic, indeed! You'll go to no picnic to-day, Anne Shirley. That shall be your punishment. And it isn't half severe enough either for what you've done!"

"Not go to the picnic!" Anne sprang to her feet and clutched Marilla's hand. "But you *promised* me I might! Oh, Marilla, I must go to the picnic. That was why I confessed. Punish me any way you like but that. Oh, Marilla, please, please, let me go to the picnic. Think of the ice-cream! For anything you know I may never have a chance to taste ice-cream again."

Marilla disengaged Anne's clinging hands stonily.

"You needn't plead, Anne. You are not going to the picnic and that's final. No, not a word."

Anne realized that Marilla was not to be moved. She clasped her hands together, gave a piercing shriek, and then flung herself face downwards on the bed, crying and writhing in an utter abandonment of disappointment and despair.

"For the land's sake!" gasped Marilla, hastening from the room. "I believe the child is crazy. No child in her senses would behave as she does. If she isn't she's utterly bad. Oh dear, I'm afraid Rachel was right from the first. But I've put my hand to the plough and I won't look back."

That was a dismal morning. Marilla worked fiercely and scrubbed the porch floor and the dairy shelves when she could find nothing else to do. Neither the shelves nor the porch needed it—but Marilla did. Then she went out and raked the yard.

When dinner was ready she went to the stairs and called Anne. A tear-stained face appeared, looking tragically over the banisters.

"Come down to your dinner, Anne."

"I don't want any dinner, Marilla," said Anne sobbingly. "I couldn't eat anything. My heart is broken. You'll feel remorse of conscience some day, I expect, for breaking it, Marilla, but I forgive you. Remember when the time comes that I forgive you. But please don't ask me to eat anything, especially boiled pork and greens. Boiled pork and greens are so unromantic when one is in affliction."

Exasperated Marilla returned to the kitchen and poured out her tale of woe to Matthew, who, between his sense of justice and his unlawful sympathy with Anne, was a miserable man.

"Well now, she shouldn't have taken the brooch, Marilla, or told stories about it," he admitted, mournfully surveying his plateful of unromantic pork and greens as if he, like Anne, thought it a food unsuited to crises of feeling, "but she's such a little thing—such an interesting little thing. Don't you think it's pretty rough not to let her go to the picnic when she's so set on it?"

"Matthew Cuthbert, I'm amazed at you. I think I've let her off entirely too easy. And she doesn't appear to realize how wicked she's been at all—that's what worries me most. If she'd really felt sorry it wouldn't be so bad. And you don't seem to realize it, neither; you're making excuses for her all the time to yourself—I can see that."

"Well now, she's such a little thing," feebly reiterated Matthew. "And there should be allowances made, Marilla. You know she's never had any bringing up."

"Well, she's having it now," retorted Marilla.

The retort silenced Matthew if it did not convince him. That dinner was a very dismal meal. The only cheerful thing about it was Jerry Buote, the hired boy, and Marilla resented his cheerfulness as a personal insult.

When her dishes were washed and her bread sponge set and her hens fed Marilla remembered that she had noticed a small rent in her best black lace shawl when she had taken it off on Monday afternoon on returning from the Ladies' Aid. She would go and mend it.

The shawl was in a box in her trunk. As Marilla lifted it out, the sunlight, falling through the vines that clustered thickly about the window, struck upon something caught in the shawl—something that glittered and sparkled in facets of violet light. Marilla snatched at it with a gasp. It was the amethyst brooch, hanging to a thread of the lace by its catch!

"Dear life and heart," said Marilla blankly, "what does this mean? Here's my brooch safe and sound that I thought was at the bottom of Barry's pond. Whatever did that girl mean by saying she took it and lost it? I declare I believe Green Gables is bewitched. I remember now that when I took off my shawl Monday afternoon I laid it on the bureau for a minute. I suppose the brooch got caught in it somehow. Well!"

Marilla betook herself to the east gable, brooch in hand. Anne had cried herself out and was sitting dejectedly by the window.

"Anne Shirley," said Marilla solemnly, "I've just found my brooch hanging to my black lace shawl. Now I want to know what that rigmarole you told me this morning meant."

"Why, you said you'd keep me here until I confessed," returned Anne wearily, "and so I decided to confess because I was bound to get to the picnic. I thought out a confession last night after I went to bed and made it as interesting as I could. And I said it over and over so that I wouldn't forget it. But you wouldn't let me go to the picnic after all, so all my trouble was wasted."

Marilla had to laugh in spite of herself. But her conscience pricked her.

"Anne, you do beat all! But I was wrong—I see that now. I shouldn't have doubted your word when I'd never known you to tell a story. Of course, it wasn't right for you to confess to a thing you hadn't done—it was very wrong to do so. But I drove you to it. So if you'll forgive me, Anne, I'll forgive you and we'll start square again. And now get yourself ready for the picnic."

Anne flew up like a rocket.

"Oh, Marilla, isn't it too late?"

"No, it's only two o'clock. They won't be more than well gathered yet and it'll be an hour before they have tea. Wash your face and comb your hair and put on your gingham. I'll fill a basket for you. There's plenty of stuff baked in the house. And I'll get Jerry to hitch up the sorrel and drive you down to the picnic ground."

"Oh, Marilla," exclaimed Anne, flying to the washstand. "Five minutes ago I was so miserable I was wishing I'd never been born and now I wouldn't change places with an angel!"

That night a thoroughly happy, completely tired out Anne returned to Green Gables in a state of beatification impossible to describe.

"Oh, Marilla, I've had a perfectly scrumptious time. Scrumptious is a new word I learned to-day. I heard Mary Alice Bell use it. Isn't it very expressive? Everything was lovely. We had a splendid tea and then Mr. Harmon Andrews took us all for a row on the Lake of Shining Waters—six of us at a time. And Jane Andrews nearly fell overboard. She was leaning out to pick water lilies and if Mr. Andrews hadn't caught her by her sash just in the nick of time she'd have fallen in and prob'ly been drowned. I wish it had been me. It would have been such a romantic experience to have been nearly drowned. It would be such a thrilling tale to tell. And we had the ice-cream. Words fail me to describe that ice-cream. Marilla, I assure you it was sublime."

That evening Marilla told the whole story to Matthew over her stocking basket.

"I'm willing to own up that I made a mistake," she concluded candidly, "but I've learned a lesson. I have to laugh when I think of Anne's 'confession,' although I suppose I shouldn't for it really was a falsehood. But it doesn't seem as bad as the other would have been, somehow, and anyhow I'm responsible for it. That child is hard to understand in some respects. But I believe she'll turn out all right yet. And there's one thing certain, no house will ever be dull that she's in."

CHAPTER 15

A Tempest in the School Teapot

"WHAT a splendid day!" said Anne, drawing a long breath. "Isn't it good just to be alive on a day like this? I pity the people who aren't born yet for missing it. They may have good days, of course, but they can never have this one. And it's splendider still to have such a lovely way to go to school by, isn't it?"

"It's a lot nicer than going round by the road; that is so dusty and hot," said Diana practically, peeping into her dinner basket and mentally calculating if the three juicy, toothsome, raspberry tarts reposing there were divided among ten girls how many bites each girl would have.

The little girls of Avonlea school always pooled their lunches, and to eat three raspberry tarts all alone or even to share them only with one's best chum would have forever and ever branded as "awful mean" the girl who did it. And yet, when the tarts were divided among ten girls you just got enough to tantalize you.

The way Anne and Diana went to school *was* a pretty one. Anne thought those walks to and from school with Diana couldn't be improved upon even by imagination. Going around by the main road would have been so unromantic; but to go by Lover's Lane and Willowmere and Violet Vale and the Birch Path was romantic, if ever anything was.

Lover's Lane opened out below the orchard at Green Gables and stretched far up into the woods to the end of the Cuthbert farm. It was the way by which the cows were taken to the back pasture and the wood hauled home in winter. Anne had named it Lover's Lane before she had been a month at Green Gables.

"Not that lovers ever really walk there," she explained to Marilla, "but Diana and I are reading a perfectly magnificent book and there's a Lover's Lane in it. So we want to have one, too. And it's a very pretty name, don't you think? So romantic! We can imagine the lovers into it, you know. I like that lane because you can think out loud there without people calling you crazy."

Anne, starting out alone in the morning, went down Lover's Lane as far as the brook. Here Diana met her, and the two little girls went on up the lane under the leafy arch of maples—"maples are such sociable trees," said Anne; "they're always rustling and whispering to you,"—until they came to a rustic bridge. Then they left the lane and walked through Mr. Barry's back field and past Willowmere. Beyond Willowmere came Violet Vale—a little green dimple in the shadow of Mr. Andrew Bell's big woods. "Of course there are no violets there now," Anne told Marilla, "but Diana says there are millions of them in spring. Oh, Marilla, can't you just imagine you see them? It actually takes away my breath. I named it Violet Vale. Diana says she never saw the beat of me for hitting on fancy names for places. It's nice to be clever at something, isn't it? But Diana named the Birch Path. She wanted to, so I let her; but I'm sure I could have found something more poetical than plain Birch Path. Anybody can think of a name like that. But the Birch Path is one of the prettiest places in the world, Marilla."

It was. Other people besides Anne thought so when they stumbled on it. It was a little narrow, twisting path, winding down over a long hill straight through Mr. Bell's woods, where the light came down sifted through so many emerald screens that it was as flawless as the heart of a diamond. It was fringed in all its length with slim young birches, white-stemmed and lissom boughed;[1] ferns and starflowers and wild lilies-of-the-valley and scarlet tufts of pigeon berries grew thickly along it; and always there was a delightful spiciness in the air and music of bird calls and the murmur and laugh of wood winds in the trees overhead. Now and then you might see a rabbit skipping across the road if you were quiet—which, with Anne and Diana, happened about once in a blue moon. Down in the valley the path came out to the main road and then it was just up the spruce hill to the school.

The Avonlea school was a whitewashed building, low in the eaves and wide in the windows, furnished inside with comfortable substantial old-fashioned desks that opened and shut, and were carved all over their lids with the initials and hieroglyphics of three generations of school-children. The schoolhouse was set back from the road and behind it was a dusky fir wood and a brook where all the children put their bottles of milk in the morning to keep cool and sweet until dinner hour.

Marilla had seen Anne start off to school on the first day of September with many secret misgivings. Anne was such an odd girl. How would she get on with the other children? And how on earth would she ever manage to hold her tongue during school hours?

Things went better than Marilla feared, however. Anne came home that evening in high spirits.

---

1 *lissom boughed*   that is, with lithesome or supple branches.

"I think I'm going to like school here," she announced. "I don't think much of the master, though. He's all the time curling his moustache and making eyes at Prissy Andrews. Prissy is grown-up, you know. She's sixteen and she's studying for the entrance examination into Queen's Academy at Charlottetown next year. Tillie Boulter says the master is *dead gone* on her. She's got a beautiful complexion and curly brown hair and she does it up so elegantly. She sits in the long seat at the back and he sits there, too, most of the time—to explain her lessons, he says. But Ruby Gillis says she saw him writing something on her slate and when Prissy read it she blushed as red as a beet and giggled; and Ruby Gillis says she doesn't believe it had anything to do with the lesson."

"Anne Shirley, don't let me hear you talking about your teacher in that way again," said Marilla sharply. "You don't go to school to criticize the master. I guess he can teach *you* something and it's your business to learn. And I want you to understand right off that you are not to come home telling tales about him. That is something I won't encourage. I hope you were a good girl."

"Indeed I was," said Anne comfortably. "It wasn't so hard as you might imagine, either. I sit with Diana. Our seat is right by the window and we can look down to the Lake of Shining Waters. There are a lot of nice girls in school and we had scrumptious fun playing at dinner time. It's so nice to have a lot of little girls to play with. But of course I like Diana best and always will. I *adore* Diana. I'm dreadfully far behind the others. They're all in the fifth book and I'm only in the fourth. I feel that it's kind of a disgrace. But there's not one of them has such an imagination as I have and I soon found that out. We had reading and geography and Canadian History and dictation to-day. Mr. Phillips said my spelling was disgraceful and he held up my slate so that everybody could see it, all marked over. I felt so mortified, Marilla; he might have been politer to a stranger, I think. Ruby Gillis gave me an apple and Sophia Sloane lent me a lovely pink card with 'May I see you home?' on it. I'm to give it back to her to-morrow. And Tillie Boulter let me wear her bead ring all the afternoon. Can I have some of those pearl beads off the old pincushion in the garret to make myself a ring? And oh Marilla, Jane Andrews told me that Minnie MacPherson told her that she heard Prissy Andrews tell Sara Gillis that I had a very pretty nose. Marilla, that is the first compliment I have ever had in my life and you can't imagine what a strange feeling it gave me. Marilla, have I really a pretty nose? I know you'll tell me the truth."

"Your nose is well enough," said Marilla shortly. Secretly she thought Anne's nose was a remarkably pretty one; but she had no intention of telling her so.

That was three weeks ago and all had gone smoothly so far. And now, this crisp September morning, Anne and Diana were tripping blithely down the Birch Path, two of the happiest little girls in Avonlea.

"I guess Gilbert Blythe will be in school to-day," said Diana. "He's been visiting his cousins over in New Brunswick all summer and he only came home Saturday night. He's *aw'fly* handsome, Anne. And he teases the girls something terrible. He just torments our lives out."

Diana's voice indicated that she rather liked having her life tormented out than not.

"Gilbert Blythe?" said Anne. "Isn't it his name that's written up on the porch wall with Julia Bell's and a big 'Take Notice' over them?"

"Yes," said Diana, tossing her head, "but I'm sure he doesn't like Julia Bell so very much. I've heard him say he studied the multiplication table by her freckles."

"Oh, don't speak about freckles to me," implored Anne. "It isn't delicate when I've got so many. But I do think that writing take-notices up on the wall about the boys and girls is the silliest ever. I should just like to see anybody dare to write my name up with a boy's. Not, of course," she hastened to add, "that anybody would."

Anne sighed. She didn't want her name written up. But it was a little humiliating to know that there was no danger of it.

"Nonsense," said Diana, whose black eyes and glossy tresses had played such havoc with the hearts of Avonlea schoolboys that her name figured on the porch walls in half a dozen take-notices. "It's only meant as a joke. And don't you be too sure your name won't ever be written up. Charlie Sloane is *dead gone* on you. He told his mother—his *mother*, mind you—that you were the smartest girl in school. That's better than being good-looking."

"No, it isn't," said Anne, feminine to the core. "I'd rather be pretty than clever. And I hate Charlie Sloane. I can't bear a boy with goggle eyes. If any one wrote my name up with his I'd *never* get over it, Diana Barry. But it *is* nice to keep head of your class."

"You'll have Gilbert in your class after this," said Diana, "and he's used to being head of his class, I can tell you. He's only in the fourth book although he's nearly fourteen. Four years ago his father was sick and had to go out to Alberta for his health and Gilbert went with him. They were there three years and Gil didn't go to school hardly any until they came back. You won't find it so easy to keep head after this, Anne."

"I'm glad," said Anne quickly. "I couldn't really feel proud of keeping head of little boys and girls of just nine or ten. I got up yesterday spelling 'ebullition.' Josie Pye was head and, mind you, she peeped in her book. Mr. Phillips didn't see her—he was looking at Prissy Andrews—but I did. I just swept her a look of freezing scorn and she got as red as a beet and spelled it wrong after all."

"Those Pye girls are cheats all round," said Diana indignantly, as they climbed the fence of the main road. "Gertie Pye actually went and put her milk bottle in my place in the brook yesterday. Did you ever? I don't speak to her now."

When Mr. Phillips was in the back of the room hearing Prissy Andrews' Latin Diana whispered to Anne,

"That's Gilbert Blythe sitting right across the aisle from you, Anne. Just look at him and see if you don't think he's handsome."

Anne looked accordingly. She had a good chance to do so, for the said Gilbert Blythe was absorbed in stealthily pinning the long yellow braid of Ruby Gillis, who sat in front of him, to the back of her seat. He was a tall boy, with curly brown hair, roguish hazel eyes and a mouth twisted into a teasing smile. Presently Ruby Gillis started up to take a sum to the master; she fell back into her seat with a little shriek, believing that her hair was pulled out by the roots. Everybody looked at her and Mr. Phillips glared so sternly that Ruby began to cry. Gilbert had whisked the pin out of sight and was studying his history with the soberest face in the world; but when the commotion subsided he looked at Anne and winked with inexpressible drollery.

"I think your Gilbert Blythe *is* handsome," confided Anne to Diana, "but I think he's very bold. It isn't good manners to wink at a strange girl."

But it was not until the afternoon that things really began to happen.

Mr. Phillips was back in the corner explaining a problem in algebra to Prissy Andrews and the rest of the scholars were doing pretty much as they pleased, eating green apples, whispering, drawing pictures on their slates, and driving crickets, harnessed to strings, up and down the aisle. Gilbert Blythe was trying to make Anne Shirley look at him and failing utterly, because Anne was at that moment totally oblivious, not only of the very existence of Gilbert Blythe, but of every other scholar in Avonlea school and of Avonlea school itself. With her chin propped on her hands and her eyes fixed on the blue glimpse of the Lake of Shining Waters that the west window afforded, she was far away in a gorgeous dreamland, hearing and seeing nothing save her own wonderful visions.

Gilbert Blythe wasn't used to putting himself out to make a girl look at him and meeting with failure. She *should* look at him, that red-haired Shirley girl with the little pointed chin and the big eyes that weren't like the eyes of any other girl in Avonlea school.

Gilbert reached across the aisle, picked up the end of Anne's long red braid, held it out at arm's length and said in a piercing whisper,

"Carrots! Carrots!"

Then Anne looked at him with a vengeance!

She did more than look. She sprang to her feet, her bright fancies fallen into cureless ruin. She flashed one indignant glance at Gilbert from eyes whose angry sparkle was swiftly quenched in equally angry tears.

"You mean, hateful boy!" she exclaimed passionately. "How dare you!"

And then—Thwack! Anne had brought her slate down on Gilbert's head and cracked it—slate, not head—clear across.

Avonlea school always enjoyed a scene. This was an especially enjoyable one. Everybody said, "Oh" in horrified delight. Diana gasped. Ruby Gillis who was inclined to be hysterical, began to cry. Tommy Sloane let his team of crickets escape him altogether while he stared open-mouthed at the tableau.

Mr. Phillips stalked down the aisle and laid his hand heavily on Anne's shoulder.

"Anne Shirley, what does this mean?" he said angrily.

Anne returned no answer. It was asking too much of flesh and blood to expect her to tell before the whole school that she had been called "carrots." Gilbert it was who spoke up stoutly.

"It was my fault, Mr. Phillips. I teased her."

Mr. Phillips paid no heed to Gilbert.

"I am sorry to see a pupil of mine displaying such a temper and such a vindictive spirit," he said in a solemn tone, as if the mere fact of being a pupil of his ought to root out all evil passions from the hearts of small imperfect mortals. "Anne, go and stand on the platform in front of the blackboard for the rest of the afternoon."

Anne would have infinitely preferred a whipping to this punishment, under which her sensitive spirit quivered as from a whiplash. With a white, set face she obeyed. Mr. Phillips took a chalk crayon and wrote on the blackboard above her head.

"Ann Shirley has a very bad temper. Ann Shirley must learn to control her temper," and then read it out loud so that even the primer class, who couldn't read writing, should understand it.

Anne stood there the rest of the afternoon with that legend above her. She did not cry or hang her head. Anger was still too hot in her heart for that and it sustained her amid all her agony of humiliation. With resentful eyes and passionred cheeks she confronted alike Diana's sympathetic gaze and Charlie Sloane's indignant nods and Josie Pye's malicious smiles. As for Gilbert Blythe, she would not even look at him. She would *never* look at him again! She would never speak to him!!

When school was dismissed Anne marched out with her red head held high. Gilbert Blythe tried to intercept her at the porch door.

"I'm awful sorry I made fun of your hair, Anne," he whispered contritely. "Honest I am. Don't be mad for keeps, now."

Anne swept by disdainfully, without look or sign of hearing. "Oh, how could you, Anne?" breathed Diana as they went down the road, half reproachfully, half admiringly. Diana felt that *she* could never have resisted Gilbert's plea.

"I shall never forgive Gilbert Blythe," said Anne firmly. "And Mr. Phillips spelled my name without an *e*, too. The iron has entered into my soul, Diana."

Diana hadn't the least idea what Anne meant but she understood it was something terrible.

"You mustn't mind Gilbert making fun of your hair," she said soothingly. "Why, he makes fun of all the girls. He laughs at mine because it's so black. He's called me a crow a dozen times; and I never heard him apologize for anything before, either."

"There's a great deal of difference between being called a crow and being called carrots," said Anne with dignity. "Gilbert Blythe has hurt my feelings *excruciatingly*, Diana."

It is possible the matter might have blown over without more excruciation if nothing else had happened. But when things begin to happen they are apt to keep on.

Avonlea scholars often spent noon hour picking gum in Mr. Bell's spruce grove over the hill and across his big pasture field. From there they could keep an eye on Eben Wright's house, where the master boarded. When they saw Mr. Phillips emerging therefrom they ran for the schoolhouse; but the distance being about three times longer than Mr. Wright's lane they were very apt to arrive there, breathless and gasping, some three minutes too late.

On the following day Mr. Phillips was seized with one of his spasmodic fits of reform and announced, before going home to dinner, that he should expect to find all the scholars in their seats when he returned. Any one who came in late would be punished.

All the boys and some of the girls went to Mr. Bell's spruce grove as usual, fully intending to stay only long enough to "pick a chew." But spruce groves are seductive and yellow nuts of gum beguiling; they picked and loitered and strayed; and as usual the first thing that recalled them to a sense of the flight of time was Jimmy Glover shouting from the top of a patriarchal old spruce, "Master's coming."

The girls, who were on the ground, started first and managed to reach the schoolhouse in time but without a second to spare. The boys, who had to wriggle hastily down from the trees, were later; and Anne, who had not been picking gum at all but was wandering happily in the far end of the grove, waist deep among the bracken, singing softly to herself, with a wreath of rice lilies on her hair as if she were some wild divinity of the shadowy places, was latest of all. Anne could run like a deer, however; run she did with the impish result that she overtook the boys at the door and was swept into the schoolhouse among them just as Mr. Phillips was in the act of hanging up his hat.

Mr. Phillips' brief reforming energy was over; he didn't want the bother of punishing a dozen pupils; but it was necessary to do something to save his word, so he looked about for a scapegoat and found it in Anne, who had dropped into her seat, gasping for breath, with her forgotten lily wreath hanging askew over one ear and giving her a particularly rakish and dishevelled appearance.

"Anne Shirley, since you seem to be so fond of the boys' company we shall indulge your taste for it this afternoon," he said sarcastically. "Take those flowers out of your hair and sit with Gilbert Blythe."

The other boys snickered. Diana, turning pale with pity, plucked the wreath from Anne's hair and squeezed her hand. Anne stared at the master as if turned to stone.

"Did you hear what I said, Anne?" queried Mr. Phillips sternly.

"Yes, sir," said Anne slowly, "but I didn't suppose you really meant it."

"I assure you I did,"—still with the sarcastic inflection which all the children, and Anne especially, hated. It flicked on the raw.[2] "Obey me at once."

For a moment Anne looked as if she meant to disobey. Then, realizing that there was no help for it, she rose haughtily; stepped across the aisle, sat down beside Gilbert Blythe, and buried her face in her arm on the desk. Ruby Gillis, who got a glimpse of it as it went down, told the others going home from school that she'd "acksually never seen anything like it—it was so white, with awful little red spots in it."

To Anne, this was the end of all things. It was bad enough to be singled out for punishment from among a dozen equally guilty ones; it was worse still to be sent to sit with a boy; but that that boy should be Gilbert Blythe was heaping insult on injury to a degree utterly unbearable. Anne felt that she could *not* bear it and it would be of no use to try. Her whole being seethed with shame and anger and humiliation.

At first the other scholars looked and whispered and giggled and nudged. But as Anne never lifted her head and as Gilbert worked fractions as if his whole soul was absorbed in them and them only, they soon returned to their own tasks and Anne was forgotten. When Mr. Phillips called the history class out Anne should have gone; but Anne did not move, and Mr. Phillips, who had been writing some verses "To Priscilla" before he called the class, was thinking about an obstinate rhyme still and never missed her. Once, when nobody was looking, Gilbert took from his desk a little pink candy heart with a gold motto on it, "You are sweet," and slipped it under the curve of Anne's arm. Whereupon Anne arose, took the pink heart gingerly between the tips of her fingers, dropped it on the floor, ground it to powder beneath her heel, and resumed her position without deigning to bestow a glance on Gilbert.

When school went out Anne marched to her desk, ostentatiously took out everything therein, books and writing tablet, pen and ink, testament and arithmetic, and piled them neatly on her cracked slate.

"What are you taking all those things home for, Anne?" Diana wanted to know, as soon as they were out on the road. She had not dared to ask the question before.

"I am not coming back to school any more," said Anne.

Diana gasped and stared at Anne to see if she meant it.

"Will Marilla let you stay home?" she asked.

"She'll have to," said Anne. "I'll *never* go to school to that man again."

---

2 *It flicked on the raw*   It hurt her most exposed and vulnerable feelings.

"Oh, Anne!" Diana looked as if she were ready to cry. "I do think you're mean. What shall I do? Mr. Phillips will make me sit with that horrid Gertie Pye—I know he will because she is sitting alone. Do come back, Anne."

"I'd do almost anything in the world for you, Diana," said Anne sadly. "I'd let myself be torn limb from limb if it would do you any good. But I can't do this, so please don't ask it. You harrow up my very soul."

"Just think of all the fun you will miss," mourned Diana. "We are going to build the loveliest new house down by the brook; and we'll be playing ball next week and you've never played ball, Anne. It's tremenjusly exciting. And we're going to learn a new song—Jane Andrews is practising it up now; and Alice Andrews is going to bring a new Pansy book[3] next week and we're all going to read it out loud, chapter about, down by the brook. And you know you are so fond of reading out loud, Anne."

Nothing moved Anne in the least. Her mind was made up. She would not go to school to Mr. Phillips again; she told Marilla so when she got home.

"Nonsense," said Marilla.

"It isn't nonsense at all," said Anne, gazing at Marilla with solemn, reproachful eyes. "Don't you understand, Marilla? I've been insulted."

"Insulted fiddlesticks! You'll go to school to-morrow as usual."

"Oh, no." Anne shook her head gently. "I'm not going back, Marilla. I'll learn my lessons at home and I'll be as good as I can be and hold my tongue all the time if it's possible at all. But I will not go back to school I assure you."

Marilla saw something remarkably like unyielding stubbornness looking out of Anne's small face. She understood that she would have trouble in overcoming it; but she resolved wisely to say nothing more just then.

"I'll run down and see Rachel about it this evening," she thought. "There's no use reasoning with Anne now. She's too worked up and I've an idea she can be awful stubborn if she takes the notion. Far as I can make out from her story, Mr. Phillips has been carrying matters with a rather high hand. But it would never do to say so to her. I'll just talk it over with Rachel. She's sent ten children to school and she ought to know something about it. She'll have heard the whole story, too, by this time."

Marilla found Mrs. Lynde knitting quilts as industriously and cheerfully as usual.

"I suppose you know what I've come about," she said, a little shamefacedly.

Mrs. Rachel nodded.

"About Anne's fuss in school, I reckon," she said. "Tillie Boulter was in on her way home from school and told me about it."

"I don't know what to do with her," said Marilla. "She declares she won't go back to school. I never saw a child so worked up. I've been expecting trouble ever since she started to school. I knew things were going too smooth to last. She's so high-strung. What would you advise, Rachel?"

"Well, since you've asked my advice, Marilla," said Mrs. Lynde amiably—Mrs. Lynde dearly loved to be asked for advice—"I'd just humour her a little at first, that's what I'd do. It's my belief that Mr. Phillips was in the wrong. Of course, it

---

3 *a new Pansy book* books series of stories for girls, with heroines whom Montgomery satirizes in her journals. The series was authored by Isabella Alden (1841–1930) whose pseudonym was "Pansy."

doesn't do to say so to the children, you know. And of course he did right to punish her yesterday for giving way to temper. But to-day it was different. The others who were late should have been punished as well as Anne, that's what. And I don't believe in making the girls sit with the boys for punishment. It isn't modest. Tillie Boulter was real indignant. She took Anne's part right through and said all the scholars did, too. Anne seems real popular among them, somehow. I never thought she'd take with them so well."

"Then you really think I'd better let her stay home," said Marilla in amazement.

"Yes. That is, I wouldn't say school to her again until she said it herself. Depend upon it, Marilla, she'll cool off in a week or so and be ready enough to go back of her own accord, that's what, while, if you were to make her go back right off, dear knows what freak or tantrum she'd take next and make more trouble than ever. The less fuss made the better, in my opinion. She won't miss much by not going to school, as far as *that* goes. Mr. Phillips isn't any good at all as a teacher. The order he keeps is scandalous, that's what, and he neglects the young fry and puts all his time on those big scholars he's getting ready for Queen's. He'd never have got the school for another year if his uncle hadn't been a trustee—*the* trustee, for he just leads the other two around by the nose, that's what. I declare, I don't know what education in this Island is coming to."

Mrs. Rachel shook her head, as much as to say if she were only at the head of the educational system of the Province things would be much better managed.

Marilla took Mrs. Rachel's advice and not another word was said to Anne about going back to school. She learned her lessons at home, did her chores, and played with Diana in the chilly purple autumn twilights; but when she met Gilbert Blythe on the road or encountered him in Sunday-school she passed him by with an icy contempt that was no whit thawed by his evident desire to appease her. Even Diana's efforts as a peacemaker were of no avail. Anne had evidently made up her mind to hate Gilbert Blythe to the end of life.

As much as she hated Gilbert, however, did she love Diana, with all the love of her passionate little heart, equally intense in its likes and dislikes. One evening Marilla, coming in from the orchard with a basket of apples, found Anne sitting alone by the east window in the twilight, crying bitterly.

"Whatever's the matter now, Anne?" she asked.

"It's about Diana," sobbed Anne luxuriously. "I love Diana so, Marilla. I cannot ever live without her. But I know very well when we grow up that Diana will get married and go away and leave me. And oh, what shall I do? I hate her husband—I just hate him furiously. I've been imagining it all out—the wedding and everything—Diana dressed in snowy garments, with a veil, and looking as beautiful and regal as a queen; and me the bridesmaid, with a lovely dress, too, and puffed sleeves, but with a breaking heart hid beneath my smiling face. And then bidding Diana good-bye-e-e—" Here Anne broke down entirely and wept with increasing bitterness.

Marilla turned quickly away to hide her twitching face; but it was no use; she collapsed on the nearest chair and burst into such a hearty and unusual peal of laughter that Matthew, crossing the yard outside, halted in amazement. When had he heard Marilla laugh like that before?

"Well, Anne Shirley," said Marilla as soon as she could speak, "if you must borrow trouble, for pity's sake borrow it handier home. I should think you had an imagination, sure enough."

CHAPTER 16

Diana Is Invited to Tea with Tragic Results

OCTOBER was a beautiful month at Green Gables, when the birches in the hollow turned as golden as sunshine and the maples behind the orchard were royal crimson and the wild cherry-trees along the lane put on the loveliest shades of dark red and bronzy green, while the fields sunned themselves in aftermaths.[1]

Anne revelled in the world of colour about her.

"Oh, Marilla," she exclaimed one Saturday morning, coming dancing in with her arms full of gorgeous boughs, "I'm so glad I live in a world where there are Octobers. It would be terrible if we just skipped from September to November, wouldn't it? Look at these maple branches. Don't they give you a thrill—several thrills? I'm going to decorate my room with them."

"Messy things," said Marilla, whose aesthetic sense was not noticeably developed. "You clutter up your room entirely too much with out-of-doors stuff, Anne. Bedrooms were made to sleep in."

"Oh, and dream in too, Marilla. And you know one can dream so much better in a room where there are pretty things. I'm going to put these boughs in the old blue jug and set them on my table."

"Mind you don't drop leaves all over the stairs then. I'm going to a meeting of the Aid Society at Carmody this afternoon, Anne, and I won't likely be home before dark. You'll have to get Matthew and Jerry their supper, so mind you don't forget to put the tea to draw until you sit down at the table as you did last time."

"It was dreadful of me to forget," said Anne apologetically, "but that was the afternoon I was trying to think of a name for Violet Vale and it crowded other things out. Matthew was so good. He never scolded a bit. He put the tea down himself and said we could wait awhile as well as not. And I told him a lovely fairy story while we were waiting, so he didn't find the time long at all. It was a beautiful fairy story, Marilla. I forgot the end of it, so I made up an end for it myself and Matthew said he couldn't tell where the join came in."

"Matthew would think it all right, Anne, if you took a notion to get up and have dinner in the middle of the night. But you keep your wits about you this time. And—I don't really know if I'm doing right—it may make you more addlepated than ever—but you can ask Diana to come over and spend the afternoon with you and have tea here."

"Oh, Marilla!" Anne clasped her hands. "How perfectly lovely! You *are* able to imagine things after all or else you'd never have understood how I've longed for that very thing. It will seem so nice and grown-uppish. No fear of my forgetting to put the tea to draw when I have company. Oh Marilla, can I use the rosebud spray tea-set?"

"No, indeed! The rosebud tea-set! Well, what next? You know I never use that except for the minister or the Aids. You'll put down the old brown tea-set. But you can open the little yellow crock of cherry preserves. It's time it was being used anyhow—I believe it's beginning to work.[2] And you can cut some fruit-cake and have some of the cookies and snaps."

---

1 *aftermaths*   stubble after mowing or second growth of crops in same season.

2 *work*   ferment. Montgomery's manuscript and the 1925 edition contain the variant, "go."

"I can just imagine myself sitting down at the head of the table and pouring out the tea," said Anne, shutting her eyes ecstatically. "And asking Diana if she takes sugar! I know she doesn't but of course I'll ask her just as if I didn't know. And then pressing her to take another piece of fruit-cake and another helping of preserves. Oh, Marilla, it's a wonderful sensation just to think of it. Can I take her into the spare room to lay off her hat when she comes? And then into the parlour to sit?"

"No. The sitting-room will do for you and your company. But there's a bottle half full of raspberry cordial that was left over from the church social the other night. It's on the second shelf of the sitting-room closet and you and Diana can have it if you I like, and a cooky to eat with it along in the afternoon, for I dare-say Matthew'll be late coming in to tea since he's hauling potatoes to the vessel."

Anne flew down to the hollow, past the Dryad's Bubble and up the spruce path to Orchard Slope, to ask Diana to tea. As a result, just after Marilla had driven off to Carmody, Diana came over, dressed in her second best dress and looking exactly as it is proper to look when asked out to tea. At other times she was wont to run into the kitchen without knocking; but now she knocked primly at the front door. And when Anne, dressed in *her* second best, as primly opened it, both little girls shook hands as gravely as if they had never met before. This unnatural solemnity lasted until after Diana had been taken to the east gable to lay off her hat and then had sat for ten minutes in the sitting-room, toes in position.

"How is your mother?" inquired Anne politely, just as if she had not seen Mrs. Barry picking apples that morning in excellent health and spirits.

"She is very well, thank you. I suppose Mr. Cuthbert is hauling potatoes to the *Lily Sands* this afternoon, is he?" said Diana, who had ridden down to Mr. Harmon Andrews' that morning in Matthew's cart.

"Yes. Our potato crop is very good this year. I hope your father's potato crop is good, too."

"It is fairly good, thank you. Have you picked many of your apples yet?"

"Oh, ever so many," said Anne, forgetting to be dignified and jumping up quickly. "Let's go out to the orchard and get some of the Red Sweetings, Diana. Marilla says we can have all that are left on the tree. Marilla is a very generous woman. She said we could have fruit-cake and cherry preserves for tea. But it isn't good manners to tell your company what you are going to give them to eat, so I won't tell you what she said we could have to drink. Only it begins with an *r* and a *c* and it's a bright red colour. I love bright red drinks, don't you? They taste twice as good as any other colour."

The orchard, with its great sweeping boughs that bent to the ground with fruit, proved so delightful that the little girls spent most of the afternoon in it, sitting in a grassy corner where the frost had spared the green and the mellow autumn sunshine lingered warmly, eating apples and talking as hard as they could. Diana had much to tell Anne of what went on in school. She had to sit with Gertie Pye and she hated it; Gertie squeaked her pencil all the time and it just made her—Diana's—blood run cold; Ruby Gillis had charmed all her warts away, true's you live, with a magic pebble that old Mary Joe from the Creek gave her. You had to rub the warts with the pebble and then throw it away over your left shoulder at the time of the new moon and the warts would all go. Charlie Sloane's name was written up with Em White's on the porch wall and Em White was *awful mad* about it; Sam Boulter had "sassed" Mr. Phillips in

259

class and Mr. Phillips whipped him and Sam's father came down to the school and dared Mr. Phillips to lay a hand on one of his children again; and Mattie Andrews had a new red hood and a blue crossover[3] with tassels on it and the airs she put on about it were perfectly sickening; and Lizzie Wright didn't speak to Mamie Wilson because Mamie Wilson's grown-up sister had cut out Lizzie Wright's grown-up sister with her beau; and everybody missed Anne so and wished she'd come to school again; and Gilbert Blythe—

But Anne didn't want to hear about Gilbert Blythe. She jumped up hurriedly and said suppose they go in and have some raspberry cordial.

Anne looked on the second shelf of the room pantry but there was no bottle of raspberry cordial there. Search revealed it away back on the top shelf. Anne put it on a tray and set it on the table with a tumbler.

"Now, please help yourself, Diana," she said politely. "I don't believe I'll have any just now. I don't feel as if I wanted any after all those apples."

Diana poured herself out a tumblerful, looked at its bright red hue admiringly, and then sipped it daintily.

"That's awfully nice raspberry cordial, Anne," she said. "I didn't know raspberry cordial was so nice."

"I'm real glad you like it. Take as much as you want. I'm going to run out and stir the fire up. There are so many responsibilities on a person's mind when they're keeping house, isn't there?"

When Anne came back from the kitchen Diana was drinking her second glassful of cordial; and, being entreated thereto by Anne, she offered no particular objection to the drinking of a third. The tumblerfuls were generous ones and the raspberry cordial was certainly very nice.

"The nicest I ever drank," said Diana. "It's ever so much nicer than Mrs. Lynde's although she brags of hers so much. It doesn't taste a bit like hers."

"I should think Marilla's raspberry cordial would prob'ly be much nicer than Mrs. Lynde's," said Anne loyally. "Marilla is a famous cook. She is trying to teach me to cook but I assure you, Diana, it is uphill work. There's so little scope for imagination in cookery. You just have to go by rules. The last time I made a cake I forgot to put the flour in. I was thinking the loveliest story about you and me, Diana. I thought you were desperately ill with smallpox and everybody deserted you, but I went boldly to your bedside and nursed you back to life; and then I took the smallpox and died and I was buried under those poplar trees in the graveyard and you planted a rosebush by my grave and watered it with your tears; and you never, never forgot the friend of your youth who sacrificed her life for you. Oh, it was such a pathetic tale, Diana. The tears just rained down over my cheeks while I mixed the cake. But I forgot the flour and the cake was a dismal failure. Flour is so essential to cakes, you know. Marilla was very cross and I don't wonder. I'm a great trial to her. She was terribly mortified about the pudding sauce last week. We had a plum pudding for dinner on Tuesday and there was half the pudding and a pitcherful of sauce left over. Marilla said there was enough for another dinner and told me to set it on the pantry shelf and cover it. I meant to cover it just as much as could be, Diana, but when I carried it in I was imagining I was a nun—of course I'm a Protestant but I imagined I was a Catholic—taking the veil to bury a broken heart in cloistered seclusion; and I forgot all about covering the pudding sauce. I thought of it next

---

3 *crossover*   knit or crochet wrap worn over the shoulders and crossed in front.

morning and ran to the pantry. Diana, fancy if you can my extreme horror at finding a mouse drowned in that pudding sauce! I lifted the mouse out with a spoon and threw it out in the yard and then I washed the spoon in three waters. Marilla was out milking and I fully intended to ask her when she came in if I'd give the sauce to the pigs; but when she did come in I was imagining that I was a frost fairy going through the woods turning the trees red and yellow, whichever they wanted to be, so I never thought about the pudding sauce again and Marilla sent me out to pick apples. Well, Mr. and Mrs. Chester Ross from Spencervale came here that morning. You know they are very stylish people, especially Mrs. Chester Ross. When Marilla called me in dinner was all ready and everybody was at the table. I tried to be as polite and dignified as I could be, for I wanted Mrs. Chester Ross to think I was a ladylike little girl even if I wasn't pretty. Everything went right until I saw Marilla coming with the plum pudding in one hand and the pitcher of pudding sauce, *warmed up*, in the other. Diana, that was a terrible moment. I remembered everything and I just stood up in my place and shrieked out, 'Marilla, you mustn't use that pudding sauce. There was a mouse drowned in it. I forgot to tell you before.' Oh, Diana, I shall never forget that awful moment if I live to be a hundred. Mrs. Chester Ross just *looked* at me and I thought I would sink through the floor with mortification. She is such a perfect housekeeper and fancy what she must have thought of us. Marilla turned red as fire but she never said a word—then. She just carried that sauce and pudding out and brought in some strawberry preserves. She even offered me some, but I couldn't swallow a mouthful. It was like heaping coals of fire on my head. After Mrs. Chester Ross went away Marilla gave me a dreadful scolding. Why, Diana, what is the matter?"

Diana had stood up very unsteadily; then she sat down again, putting her hands to her head.

"I'm—I'm awful sick," she said, a little thickly. "I—I—must go right home."

"Oh, you mustn't dream of going home without your tea," cried Anne in distress. "I'll get it right off—I'll go and put the tea down this very minute."

"I must go home," repeated Diana, stupidly but determinedly.

"Let me get you a lunch anyhow," implored Anne. "Let me give you a bit of fruit-cake and some of the cherry preserves. Lie down on the sofa for a little while and you'll be better. Where do you feel bad?"

"I must go home," said Diana, and that was all she would say. In vain Anne pleaded.

"I never heard of company going home without tea," she mourned. "Oh, Diana, do you suppose that it's possible you're really taking the smallpox? If you are I'll go and nurse you, you can depend on that. I'll never forsake you. But I do wish you'd stay till after tea. Where do you feel bad?"

"I'm awful dizzy," said Diana.

And indeed, she walked very dizzily. Anne, with tears of disappointment in her eyes, got Diana's hat and went with her as far as the Barry yard fence. Then she wept all the way back to Green Gables, where she sorrowfully put the remainder of the raspberry cordial back into the pantry and got tea ready for Matthew and Jerry, with all the zest gone out of the performance.

The next day was Sunday and as the rain poured down in torrents from dawn till dusk Anne did not stir abroad from Green Gables. Monday afternoon Marilla sent her down to Mrs. Lynde's on an errand. In a very short space of time Anne came flying back up the lane, with tears rolling down her cheeks. Into the kitchen she dashed and flung herself face downward on the sofa in an agony.

"Whatever has gone wrong now, Anne?" queried Marilla in doubt and dismay. "I do hope you haven't gone and been saucy to Mrs. Lynde again."

No answer from Anne save more tears and stormier sobs!

"Anne Shirley, when I ask you a question I want to be answered. Sit right up this very minute and tell me what you are crying about."

Anne sat up, tragedy personified.

"Mrs. Lynde was up to see Mrs. Barry to-day and Mrs. Barry was in an awful state," she wailed. "She says that I set[4] Diana *drunk* Saturday and sent her home in a disgraceful condition. And she says I must be a thoroughly bad, wicked little girl and she's never, never going to let Diana play with me again. Oh, Marilla, I'm just overcome with woe."

Marilla stared in blank amazement.

"Set Diana drunk!" she said when she found her voice. "Anne, are you or Mrs. Barry crazy? What on earth did you give her?"

"Not a thing but raspberry cordial," sobbed Anne. "I never thought raspberry cordial would set people drunk, Marilla—not even if they drank three big tumblerfuls as Diana did. Oh, it sounds so—so—like Mrs. Thomas' husband! But I didn't mean to set her drunk."

"Drunk fiddlesticks!" said Marilla, marching to the sitting-room pantry. There on the shelf was a bottle which she at once recognized as one containing some of her three year old homemade currant wine for which she was celebrated in Avonlea, although certain of the stricter sort, Mrs. Barry among them, disapproved strongly of it. And at the same time Marilla recollected that she had put the bottle of raspberry cordial down in the cellar instead of in the pantry as she had told Anne.

She went back to the kitchen with the wine bottle in her hand. Her face was twitching in spite of herself.

"Anne, you certainly have a genius for getting into trouble. You went and gave Diana currant wine instead of raspberry cordial. Didn't you know the difference yourself?"

"I never tasted it," said Anne. "I thought it was the cordial. I meant to be so—so—hospitable. Diana got awfully sick and had to go home. Mrs. Barry told Mrs. Lynde she was simply dead drunk. She just laughed silly like when her mother asked her what was the matter and went to sleep and slept for hours. Her mother smelled her breath and knew she was drunk. She had a fearful headache all day yesterday. Mrs. Barry is so indignant. She will never believe but what I did it on purpose."

"I should think she would better punish Diana for being so greedy as to drink three glassfuls of anything," said Marilla shortly. "Why, three of those big glasses would have made her sick even if it had only been cordial. Well, this story will be a nice handle for those folks who are so down on me for making currant wine, although I haven't made any for three years ever since I found out that the minister didn't approve. I just kept that bottle for sickness. There, there, child, don't cry. I can't see as you were to blame although I'm sorry it happened so."

"I must cry," said Anne. "My heart is broken. The stars in their courses fight against me,[5] Marilla. Diana and I are parted forever. Oh, Marilla, I little dreamed of this when first we swore our vows of friendship."

---

4 *set*   made, became the cause for, or knowingly encouraged.
5 *the stars in their courses fight against me*   See Judges 5.20.

"Don't be foolish, Anne. Mrs. Barry will think better of it when she finds you're not really to blame. I suppose she thinks you've done it for a silly joke or something of that sort. You'd best go up this evening and tell her how it was."

"My courage fails me at the thought of facing Diana's injured mother," sighed Anne. "I wish you'd go, Marilla. You're so much more dignified than I am. Likely she'd listen to you quicker than to me."

"Well, I will," said Marilla, reflecting that it would probably be the wiser course. "Don't cry any more, Anne. It will be all right."

Marilla had changed her mind about its being all right by the time she got back from Orchard Slope. Anne was watching for her coming and flew to the porch door to meet her.

"Oh, Marilla, I know by your face that it's been no use," she said sorrowfully. "Mrs. Barry won't forgive me?"

"Mrs. Barry, indeed!" snapped Marilla. "Of all the unreasonable women I ever saw she's the worst. I told her it was all a mistake and you weren't to blame, but she just simply didn't believe me. And she rubbed it well in about my currant wine and how I'd always said it couldn't have the least effect on anybody. I just told her plainly that currant wine wasn't meant to be drunk three tumblerfuls at a time and that if a child I had to do with was so greedy I'd sober her up with a right good spanking."

Marilla whisked into the kitchen, grievously disturbed, leaving a very much distracted little soul in the porch behind her. Presently Anne stepped out bareheaded into the chill autumn dusk; very determinedly and steadily she took her way down through the sere clover field over the log bridge and up through the spruce grove, lighted by a pale little moon hanging low over the western woods. Mrs. Barry, coming to the door in answer to a timid knock, found a white-lipped, eager-eyed suppliant on the doorstep.

Her face hardened. Mrs. Barry was a woman of strong prejudices and dislikes, and her anger was of the cold, sullen sort which is always hardest to overcome. To do her justice, she really believed Anne had made Diana drunk out of sheer malice prepense, and she was honestly anxious to preserve her little daughter from the contamination of further intimacy with such a child.

"What do you want?" she said stiffly.

Anne clasped her hands.

"Oh, Mrs. Barry, please forgive me. I did not mean to—to—intoxicate Diana. How could I? Just imagine if you were a poor little orphan girl that kind people had adopted and you had just one bosom friend in all the world. Do you think you would intoxicate her on purpose? I thought it was only raspberry cordial. I was firmly convinced it was raspberry cordial. Oh, please don't say that you won't let Diana play with me any more. If you do you will cover my life with a dark cloud of woe."

This speech, which would have softened good Mrs. Lynde's heart in a twinkling, had no effect on Mrs. Barry except to irritate her still more. She was suspicious of Anne's big words and dramatic gestures and imagined that the child was making fun of her. So she said, coldly and cruelly:

"I don't think you are a fit little girl for Diana to associate with. You'd better go home and behave yourself."

Anne's lip quivered.

"Won't you let me see Diana just once to say farewell?" she implored.

"Diana has gone over to Carmody with her father," said Mrs. Barry, going in and shutting the door.

Anne went back to Green Gables calm with despair.

"My last hope is gone," she told Marilla. "I went up and saw Mrs. Barry myself and she treated me very insultingly. Marilla, I do *not* think she is a well-bred woman. There is nothing more to do except to pray and I haven't much hope that that'll do much good because, Marilla, I do not believe that God Himself can do very much with such an obstinate person as Mrs. Barry."

"Anne, you shouldn't say such things," rebuked Marilla, striving to overcome that unholy tendency to laughter which she was dismayed to find growing upon her. And indeed, when she told the whole story to Matthew that night, she did laugh heartily over Anne's tribulations.

But when she slipped into the east gable before going to bed and found that Anne had cried herself to sleep an unaccustomed softness crept into her face.

"Poor little soul," she murmured, lifting a loose curl of hair from the child's tear-stained face. Then she bent down and kissed the flushed cheek on the pillow.

CHAPTER 17

A New Interest in Life

THE next afternoon Anne, bending over her patchwork at the kitchen window, happened to glance out and beheld Diana down by the Dryad's Bubble beckoning mysteriously. In a trice Anne was out of the house and flying down to the hollow, astonishment and hope struggling in her expressive eyes. But the hope faded when she saw Diana's dejected countenance.

"Your mother hasn't relented?" she gasped.

Diana shook her head mournfully.

"No; and oh, Anne, she says I'm never to play with you again. I've cried and cried and I told her it wasn't your fault, but it wasn't any use. I had ever such a time coaxing her to let me come down and say good-bye to you. She said I was only to stay ten minutes and she's timing me by the clock."

"Ten minutes isn't very long to say an eternal farewell in," said Anne tearfully. "Oh, Diana, will you promise faithfully never to forget me, the friend of your youth, no matter what dearer friends may caress thee?"

"Indeed I will," sobbed Diana, "and I'll never have another bosom friend—I don't want to have. I couldn't love anybody as I love you."

"Oh, Diana," cried Anne, clasping her hands, "do you *love* me?"

"Why, of course I do. Didn't you know that?"

"No." Anne drew a long breath. "I thought you *liked* me of course, but I never hoped you *loved* me. Why, Diana, I didn't think anybody could love me. Nobody ever has loved me since I can remember. Oh, this is wonderful! It's a ray of light which will forever shine on the darkness of a path severed from thee, Diana. Oh, just say it once again."

"I love you devotedly, Anne," said Diana stanchly, "and I always will, you may be sure of that."

"And I will always love thee, Diana," said Anne, solemnly extending her hand. "In the years to come thy memory will shine like a star over my lonely life, as that last story we read together says. Diana, wilt thou give me a lock of thy jet-black tresses in parting to treasure forevermore?"

"Have you got anything to cut it with?" queried Diana, wiping away the tears which Anne's affecting accents had caused to flow afresh, and returning to practicalities.

"Yes. I've got my patchwork scissors in my apron pocket fortunately," said Anne. She solemnly clipped one of Diana's curls. "Fare thee well, my beloved friend. Henceforth we must be as strangers though living side by side. But my heart will ever be faithful to thee."

Anne stood and watched Diana out of sight, mournfully waving her hand to the latter whenever she turned to look back. Then she returned to the house, not a little consoled for the time being by this romantic parting.

"It is all over," she informed Marilla. "I shall never have another friend. I'm really worse off than ever before, for I haven't Katie Maurice and Violetta now. And even if I had it wouldn't be the same. Somehow, little dream girls are not satisfying after a real friend. Diana and I had such an affecting farewell down by the spring. It will be sacred in my memory forever. I used the most pathetic language[1] I could think of and said 'thou' and 'thee.' 'Thou' and 'thee' seem so much more romantic than 'you.' Diana gave me a lock of her hair and I'm going to sew it up in a little bag and wear it around my neck all my life. Please see that it is buried with me, for I don't believe I'll live very long. Perhaps when she sees me lying cold and dead before her Mrs. Barry may feel remorse for what she has done and will let Diana come to my funeral."

"I don't think there is much fear of your dying of grief as long as you can talk, Anne," said Marilla unsympathetically.

The following Monday Anne surprised Marilla by coming down from her room with her basket of books on her arm and her lips primmed up into a line of determination.

"I'm going back to school," she announced. "That is all there is left in life for me, now that my friend has been ruthlessly torn from me. In school I can look at her and muse over days departed."

"You'd better muse over your lessons and sums," said Marilla, concealing her delight at this development of the situation. "If you're going back to school I hope we'll hear no more of breaking slates over people's heads and such carryings-on. Behave yourself and do just what your teacher tells you."

"I'll try to be a model pupil," agreed Anne dolefully. "There won't be much fun in it, I expect. Mr. Phillips said Minnie Andrews was a model pupil and there isn't a spark of imagination or life in her. She is just dull and poky and never seems to have a good time. But I feel so depressed that perhaps it will come easy to me now. I'm going round by the road. I couldn't bear to go by the Birch Path all alone. I should weep bitter tears if I did."

Anne was welcomed back to school with open arms. Her imagination had been sorely missed in games, her voice in the singing, and her dramatic ability in the perusal aloud of books at dinner hour. Ruby Gillis smuggled three blue plums over to her during testament reading; Ella May Macpherson gave her an enormous yellow pansy cut from the covers of a floral catalogue—a species of desk decoration much prized in Avonlea school. Sophia Sloane offered to teach

---

1 *pathetic language*   expressing and arousing tenderness and pity.

her a perfectly elegant new pattern of knit lace, *so* nice for trimming aprons. Katie Boulter gave her a perfume bottle to keep slate-water in and Julia Bell copied carefully on a piece of pale pink paper, scalloped on the edges, the following effusion:

"TO ANNE
"When twilight drops her curtain down
And pins it with a star
Remember that you have a friend
Though she may wander far."

"It's so nice to he appreciated," sighed Anne rapturously to Marilla that night.

The girls were not the only scholars who "appreciated" her. When Anne went to her seat after dinner hour—she had been told by Mr. Phillips to sit with the model Minnie Andrews—she found on her desk a big luscious "strawberry apple." Anne caught it up all ready to take a bite, when she remembered that the only place in Avonlea where strawberry apples grew was in the old Blythe orchard on the other side of the Lake of Shining Waters. Anne dropped the apple as if it were a red-hot coal and ostentatiously wiped her fingers on her handkerchief. The apple lay untouched on her desk until the next morning, when little Timothy Andrews, who swept the school and kindled the fire, annexed it as one of his perquisites. Charlie Sloane's slate pencil, gorgeously bedizened with striped red and yellow paper, costing two cents where ordinary pencils cost only one, which he sent up to her after dinner hour, met with a more favourable reception. Anne was graciously pleased to accept it and rewarded the donor with a smile which exalted that infatuated youth straightway into the seventh heaven of delight and caused him to make such fearful errors in his dictation that Mr. Phillips kept him in after school to rewrite it.

But as,

"The Caesar's pageant shorn of Brutus' bust
Did but of Rome's best son remind her more,"[2]

so the marked absence of any tribute or recognition from Diana Barry, who was sitting with Gertie Pye, embittered Anne's little triumph.

"Diana might just have smiled at me once, I think," she mourned to Marilla that night. But the next morning a note, most fearfully and wonderfully twisted and folded, and a small parcel, were passed across to Anne.

"Dear Anne," ran the former, "Mother says I'm not to play with you or talk to you even in school. It isn't my fault and don't be cross at me, because I love you as much as ever. I miss you awfully to tell all my secrets to and I don't like Gertie Pye one bit. I made you one of the new bookmarkers out of red tissue

---

2 *The Caesar's pageant . . . more* from *Childe Harold's Pilgrimage* by George Gordon Byron (1788–1824), 3.21.

paper. They are awfully fashionable now and only three girls in school know how to make them. When you look at it remember

"Your true friend,
"DIANA BARRY."

Anne read the note, kissed the bookmark, and despatched a prompt reply back to the other side of the school.

"MY OWN DARLING DIANA:—

"Of course I am not cross at you because you have to obey your mother. Our spirits can commune. I shall keep your lovely present forever. Minnie Andrews is a very nice little girl—although she has no imagination—but after having been Diana's busum friend I cannot be Minnie's. Please excuse mistakes because my spelling isn't very good yet, although much improoved.

"Yours until death us do part,
"ANNE or CORDELIA SHIRLEY.

"P. S. I shall sleep with your letter under my pillow to-night.

"A. or C. S."

Marilla pessimistically expected more trouble since Anne had again begun to go to school. But none developed. Perhaps Anne caught something of the "model" spirit from Minnie Andrews; at least she got on very well with Mr. Phillips thenceforth. She flung herself into her studies heart and soul, determined not to be outdone in any class by Gilbert Blythe. The rivalry between them was soon apparent; it was entirely good-natured on Gilbert's side; but it is much to be feared that the same thing cannot be said of Anne, who had certainly an unpraiseworthy tenacity for holding grudges. She was as intense in her hatreds as in her loves. She would not stoop to admit that she meant to rival Gilbert in school work, because that would have been to acknowledge his existence which Anne persistently ignored; but the rivalry was there and honours fluctuated between them. Now Gilbert was head of the spelling class; now Anne, with a toss of her long red braids, spelled him down. One morning Gilbert had all his sums done correctly and had his name written on the blackboard on the roll of honour; the next morning Anne, having wrestled wildly with decimals the entire evening before, would be first. One awful day they were ties and their names were written up together. It was almost as bad as a "take-notice" and Anne's mortification was as evident as Gilbert's satisfaction. When the written examinations at the end of each month were held the suspense was terrible. The first month Gilbert came out three marks ahead. The second Anne beat him by five. But her triumph was marred by the fact that Gilbert congratulated her heartily before the whole school. It would have been ever so much sweeter to her if he had felt the sting of his defeat.

Mr. Phillips might not be a very good teacher; but a pupil so inflexibly determined on learning as Anne was could hardly escape making progress under any kind of a teacher. By the end of the term Anne and Gilbert were both promoted into the fifth class and allowed to begin studying the elements of "the branches"—by which Latin, geometry, French and algebra were meant. In geometry Anne met her Waterloo.

"It's perfectly awful stuff, Marilla," she groaned. "I'm sure I'll never be able to make head or tail of it. There is no scope for imagination in it at all. Mr.

Phillips says I'm the worst dunce he ever saw at it. And Gil—I mean some of the others are so smart at it. It is extremely mortifying, Marilla. Even Diana gets along better than I do. But I don't mind being beaten by Diana. Even although we meet as strangers now I still love her with an *inextinguishable* love. It makes me very sad at times to think about her. But really, Marilla, one can't stay sad very long in such an interesting world, can one?"

CHAPTER 18

Anne to the Rescue

ALL things great are wound up with all things little. At first glance it might not seem that the decision of a certain Canadian Premier to include Prince Edward Island in a political tour could have much or anything to do with the fortunes of little Anne Shirley at Green Gables. But it had.

It was in January the Premier came, to address his loyal supporters and such of his non-supporters as chose to be present at the monster mass meeting held in Charlottetown. Most of the Avonlea people were on the Premier's side of politics; hence, on the night of the meeting nearly all the men and a goodly proportion of the women had gone to town, thirty miles away. Mrs. Rachel Lynde had gone too. Mrs. Rachel Lynde was a red-hot politician and couldn't have believed that the political rally could be carried through without her, although she was on the opposite side of politics. So she went to town and took her husband— Thomas would be useful in looking after the horse—and Marilla Cuthbert with her. Marilla had a sneaking interest in politics herself, and as she thought it might be her only chance to see a real live Premier, she promptly took it, leaving Anne and Matthew to keep house until her return the following day.

Hence, while Marilla and Mrs. Rachel were enjoying themselves hugely at the mass meeting, Anne and Matthew had the cheerful kitchen at Green Gables all to themselves. A bright fire was glowing in the old-fashioned Waterloo stove and blue-white frost crystals were shining on the window-panes. Matthew nodded over a *Farmers' Advocate* on the sofa and Anne at the table studied her lessons with grim determination, despite sundry wistful glances at the clock shelf, where lay a new book that Jane Andrews had lent her that day. Jane had assured her that it was warranted to produce any number of thrills, or words to that effect, and Anne's fingers tingled to reach out for it. But that would mean Gilbert Blythe's triumph on the morrow. Anne turned her back on the clock shelf and tried to imagine it wasn't there.

"Matthew, did you ever study geometry when you went to school?"

"Well now, no, I didn't," said Matthew, coming out of his doze with a start.

"I wish you had," sighed Anne, "because then you'd be able to sympathize with me. You can't sympathize properly if you've never studied it. It is casting a cloud over my whole life. I'm such a dunce at it, Matthew."

"Well now, I dunno," said Matthew soothingly. "I guess you're all right at anything. Mr. Phillips told me last week in Blair's store at Carmody that you was the smartest scholar in school and was making rapid progress. 'Rapid progress' was his very words. There's them as runs down Teddy Phillips and says he ain't much of a teacher; but I guess he's all right."

Matthew would have thought any one who praised Anne was "all right."

"I'm sure I'd get on better with geometry if only he wouldn't change the letters," complained Anne. "I learn the proposition off by heart, and then he draws it on the blackboard and puts different letters from what are in the book and I get all mixed up. I don't think a teacher should take such a mean advantage, do you? We're studying agriculture now and I've found out at last what makes the roads red. It's a great comfort. I wonder how Marilla and Mrs. Lynde are enjoying themselves. Mrs. Lynde says Canada is going to the dogs the way things are being run at Ottawa, and that it's an awful warning to the electors. She says if women were allowed to vote we would soon see a blessed change. What way do you vote, Matthew?"

"Conservative," said Matthew promptly. To vote Conservative was part of Matthew's religion.

"Then I'm Conservative too," said Anne decidedly. "I'm glad, because Gil— because some of the boys in school are Grits. I guess Mr. Phillips is a Grit[1] too, because Prissy Andrews' father is one, and Ruby Gillis says that when a man is courting he always has to agree with the girl's mother in religion and her father in politics. Is that true, Matthew?,"

"Well now, I dunno," said Matthew.

"Did you ever go courting, Matthew?"

"Well now, no, I dunno's I ever did," said Matthew, who had certainly never thought of such a thing in his whole existence.

Anne reflected with her chin in her hands.

"It must be rather interesting, don't you think, Matthew? Ruby Gillis says when she grows up she's going to have ever so many beaus on the string and have them all crazy about her; but I think that would be too exciting. I'd rather have just one in his right mind. But Ruby Gillis knows a great deal about such matters because she has so many big sisters, and Mrs. Lynde says the Gillis girls have gone off like hot cakes. Mr. Phillips goes up to see Prissy Andrews nearly every evening. He says it is to help her with her lessons, but Miranda Sloane is studying for Queen's, too, and I should think she needed help a lot more than Prissy because she's ever so much stupider, but he never goes to help her in the evenings at all. There are a great many things in this world that I can't understand very well, Matthew."

"Well now, I dunno as I comprehend them all myself," acknowledged Matthew.

"Well, I suppose I must finish up my lessons. I won't allow myself to open that new book Jane lent me until I'm through. But it's a terrible temptation, Matthew. Even when I turn my back on it I can see it there just as plain. Jane said she cried herself sick over it. I love a book that makes me cry. But I think I'll carry that book into the sitting-room and lock it in the jam closet and give you the key. And you must *not* give it to me, Matthew, until my lessons are done, not even if I implore you on my bended knees. It's all very well to say resist temptation, but it's ever so much easier to resist it if you can't get the key. And then shall I run down the cellar and get some russets, Matthew? Wouldn't you like some russets?"

"Well now, I dunno but what I would," said Matthew, who never ate russets but knew Anne's weakness for them.

Just as Anne emerged triumphantly from the cellar with her plateful of russets came the sound of flying footsteps on the icy board walk outside and the next moment the kitchen door was flung open and in rushed Diana Barry,

---

1 *Grit*   a Liberal in Canadian politics, a Clear-Grit (as in solid, hard, firm, genuine).

white-faced and breathless, with a shawl wrapped hastily around her head. Anne promptly let go of her candle and plate in her surprise, and plate, candle, and apples crashed together down the cellar ladder and were found at the bottom embedded in melted grease, the next day, by Marilla, who gathered them up and thanked mercy the house hadn't been set on fire.

"Whatever is the matter, Diana?" cried Anne. "Has your mother relented at last?"

"Oh, Anne, do come quick," implored Diana nervously. "Minnie May is awful sick—she's got croup, Young Mary Joe says—and father and mother are away to town and there's nobody to go for the doctor. Minnie May is awful bad and Young Mary Joe doesn't know what to do—and oh, Anne, I'm so scared!"

Matthew, without a word, reached out for cap and coat, slipped past Diana and away into the darkness of the yard.

"He's gone to harness the sorrel mare to go to Carmody for the doctor," said Anne, who was hurrying on hood and jacket. "I know it as well as if he'd said so. Matthew and I are such kindred spirits I can read his thoughts without words at all."

"I don't believe he'll find the doctor at Carmody," sobbed Diana. "I know that Doctor Blair went to town and I guess Doctor Spencer would go too, Young Mary Joe never saw anybody with croup and Mrs. Lynde is away. Oh, Anne!"

"Don't cry, Di," said Anne cheerily. "I know exactly what to do for croup. You forget that Mrs. Hammond had twins three times. When you look after three pairs of twins you naturally get a lot of experience. They all had croup regularly. Just wait till I get the ipecac bottle—you mayn't have any at your house. Come on now."

The two little girls hastened out hand in hand and hurried through Lovers' Lane and across the crusted field beyond, for the snow was too deep to go by the shorter wood way. Anne, although sincerely sorry for Minnie May, was far from being insensible to the romance of the situation and to the sweetness of once more sharing that romance with a kindred spirit.

The night was clear and frosty, all ebony of shadow and silver of snowy slope; big stars were shining over the silent fields; here and there the dark pointed firs stood up with snow powdering their branches and the wind whistling through them. Anne thought it was truly delightful to go skimming through all this mystery and loveliness with your bosom friend who had been so long estranged.

Minnie May, aged three, was really very sick. She lay on the kitchen sofa, feverish and restless, while her hoarse breathing could be heard all over the house. Young Mary Joe, a buxom, broad-faced French girl from the Creek, whom Mrs. Barry had engaged to stay with the children during her absence, was helpless and bewildered, quite incapable of thinking what to do, or doing it if she thought of it.

Anne went to work with skill and promptness.

"Minnie May has croup all right; she's pretty bad, but I've seen them worse. First we must have lots of hot water. I declare, Diana, there isn't more than a cupful in the kettle! There, I've filled it up, and, Mary Joe, you may put some wood in the stove. I don't want to hurt your feelings, but it seems to me you might have thought of this before if you'd any imagination. Now, I'll undress Minnie May and put her to bed, and you try to find some soft flannel cloths, Diana. I'm going to give her a dose of ipecac first of all."

Minnie May did not take kindly to the ipecac, but Anne had not brought up three pairs of twins for nothing. Down that ipecac went, not only once, but many times during the long, anxious night when the two little girls worked patiently over the suffering Minnie May, and Young Mary Joe, honestly anxious to do all she could, kept on a roaring fire and heated more water than would have been needed for a hospital of croupy babies.

It was three o'clock when Matthew came with the doctor, for he had been obliged to go all the way to Spencervale for one. But the pressing need for assistance was past. Minnie May was much better and was sleeping soundly.

"I was awfully near giving up in despair," explained Anne. "She got worse and worse until she was sicker than ever the Hammond twins were, even the last pair. I actually thought she was going to choke to death. I gave her every drop of ipecac in that bottle, and when the last dose went down I said to myself—not to Diana or Young Mary Joe, because I didn't want to worry them any more than they were worried, but I had to say it to myself just to relieve my feelings—'This is the last lingering hope and I fear 'tis a vain one.' But in about three minutes she coughed up the phlegm and began to get better right away. You must just imagine my relief, doctor, because I can't express it in words. You know there are some things that cannot be expressed in words."

"Yes, I know," nodded the doctor. He looked at Anne as if he were thinking some things about her that couldn't be expressed in words. Later on, however, he expressed them to Mr. and Mrs. Barry.

"That little red-headed girl they have over at Cuthbert's is as smart as they make 'em. I tell you she saved that baby's life, for it would have been too late by the time I got here. She seems to have a skill and presence of mind perfectly wonderful in a child of her age. I never saw anything like the eyes of her when she was explaining the case out to me."

Anne had gone home in the wonderful, white-frosted winter morning, heavy-eyed from loss of sleep, but still talking unweariedly to Matthew as they crossed the long white field and walked under the glittering fairy arch of the Lovers' Lane maples.

"Oh, Matthew, isn't it a wonderful morning? The world looks like something God had just imagined for His own pleasure, doesn't it? Those trees look as if I could blow them away with a breath—pouf! I'm so glad I live in a world where there are white frosts, aren't you? And I'm so glad Mrs. Hammond had three pairs of twins after all. If she hadn't I mightn't have known what to do for Minnie May. I'm real sorry I was ever cross with Mrs. Hammond for having twins. But, oh, Matthew, I'm so sleepy. I can't go to school. I just know I couldn't keep my eyes open and I'd be so stupid. But I hate to stay home for Gil—some of the others will get head of the class, and it's so hard to get up again—although of course the harder it is the more satisfaction you have when you do get up, haven't you?"

"Well now, I guess you'll manage all right," said Matthew, looking at Anne's white little face and the dark shadows under her eyes. "You just go right to bed and have a good sleep. I'll do all the chores."

Anne accordingly went to bed and slept so long and soundly that it was well on in the white and rosy winter afternoon when she awoke and descended to the kitchen where Marilla, who had arrived home in the meantime, was sitting knitting.

"Oh, did you see the Premier?" exclaimed Anne at once. "What did he look like, Marilla?"

"Well, he never got to be Premier on account of his looks," said Marilla. "Such a nose as that man had! But he can speak. I was proud of being a Conservative. Rachel Lynde, of course, being a Liberal, had no use for him. Your dinner is in the oven, Anne; and you can get yourself some blue plum preserve out of the pantry. I guess you're hungry. Matthew has been telling me about last night. I must say it was fortunate you knew what to do. I wouldn't have had any idea myself, for I never saw a case of croup. There now, never mind talking till you've had your dinner. I can tell by the look of you that you're just full up with speeches, but they'll keep."

Marilla had something to tell Anne, but she did not tell it just then, for she knew if she did Anne's consequent excitement would lift her clear out of the region of such material matters as appetite or dinner. Not until Anne had finished her saucer of blue plums did Marilla say:

"Mrs. Barry was here this afternoon, Anne. She wanted to see you, but I wouldn't wake you up. She says you saved Minnie May's life, and she is very sorry she acted as she did in that affair of the current wine. She says she knows now you didn't mean to set Diana drunk, and she hopes you'll forgive her and be good friends with Diana again. You're to go over this evening if you like, for Diana can't stir outside the door on account of a bad cold she caught last night. Now, Anne Shirley, for pity's sake don't fly clean up into the air."

The warning seemed not unnecessary, so uplifted and aerial was Anne's expression and attitude as she sprang to her feet, her face irradiated with the flame of her spirit.

"Oh, Marilla, can I go right now—without washing my dishes? I'll wash them when I come back, but I cannot tie myself down to anything so unromantic as dish-washing at this thrilling moment."

"Yes, yes, run along," said Marilla indulgently. "Anne Shirley—are you crazy? Come back this instant and put something on you. I might as well call to the wind. She's gone without a cap or wrap. Look at her tearing through the orchard with her hair streaming. It'll be a mercy if she doesn't catch her death of cold."

Anne came dancing home in the purple winter twilight across the snowy places. Afar in the south-west was the great shimmering, pearl-like sparkle of an evening star in a sky that was pale golden and ethereal rose over gleaming white spaces and dark glens of spruce. The tinkles of sleigh-bells among the snowy hills came like elfin chimes through the frosty air, but their music was not sweeter than the song in Anne's heart and on her lips.

"You see before you a perfectly happy person, Marilla," she announced. "I'm perfectly happy—yes, in spite of my red hair. Just at present I have a soul above red hair. Mrs. Barry kissed me and cried and said she was so sorry and she could never repay me. I felt fearfully embarrassed, Marilla, but I just said as politely as I could, 'I have no hard feelings for you, Mrs. Barry. I assure you once for all that I did not mean to intoxicate Diana and henceforth I shall cover the past with the mantle of oblivion.' That was a pretty dignified way of speaking, wasn't it, Marilla? I felt that I was heaping coals of fire on Mrs. Barry's head. And Diana and I had a lovely afternoon. Diana showed me a new fancy crochet stitch her aunt over at Carmody taught her. Not a soul in Avonlea knows it but us, and we pledged a solemn vow never to reveal it to any one else. Diana gave me a beautiful card with a wreath of roses on it and a verse of poetry:

" 'If you love me as I love you
Nothing but death can part us two.'

"And that is true, Marilla. We're going to ask Mr. Phillips to let us sit together in school again, and Gertie Pye can go with Minnie Andrews. We had an elegant tea. Mrs. Barry had the very best china set out, Marilla, just as if I was real company. I can't tell you what a thrill it gave me. Nobody ever used their very best china on my account before. And we had fruit-cake and pound-cake and doughnuts and two kinds of preserves, Marilla. And Mrs. Barry asked me if I took tea and said, 'Pa, why don't you pass the biscuits to Anne?' It must be lovely to be grown up, Marilla, when just being treated as if you were is so nice."

"I don't know about that," said Marilla with a brief sigh.

"Well, anyway, when I am grown up," said Anne decidedly, "I'm always going to talk to little girls as if they were, too, and I'll never laugh when they use big words. I know from sorrowful experience how that hurts one's feelings. After tea Diana and I made taffy. The taffy wasn't very good, I suppose because neither Diana nor I had ever made any before. Diana left me to stir it while she buttered the plates and I forgot and let it burn; and then when we set it out on the platform[2] to cool the cat walked over one plate and that had to be thrown away. But the making of it was splendid fun. Then when I came home Mrs. Barry asked me to come over as often as I could and Diana stood at the window and threw kisses to me all the way down to Lovers' Lane. I assure you, Marilla, that I feel like praying to-night and I'm going to think out a special brand-new prayer in honour of the occasion."

CHAPTER 19

A Concert, a Catastrophe, and a Confession

"MARILLA, can I go over to see Diana just for a minute?" asked Anne, running breathlessly down from the east gable one February evening.

"I don't see what you want to be traipsing about after dark for," said Marilla shortly. "You and Diana walked home from school together and then stood down there in the snow for half an hour more, your tongues going the whole blessed time, clickety-clack. So I don't think you're very badly off to see her again."

"But she wants to see me," pleaded Anne. "She has something very important to tell me."

"How do you know she has?"

"Because she just signalled to me from her window. We have arranged a way to signal with our candles and cardboard. We set the candle on the window-sill and make flashes by passing the cardboard back and forth. So many flashes mean a certain thing. It was my idea, Marilla."

"I'll warrant you it was," said Marilla emphatically. "And the next thing you'll be setting fire to the curtains with your signalling nonsense."

"Oh, we're very careful, Marilla. And it's so interesting. Two flashes mean, 'Are you there?' Three mean 'yes' and four 'no.' Five mean, 'Come over as soon as possible, because I have something important to reveal.' Diana has just signalled five flashes, and I'm really suffering to know what it is."

---

2 *platform*   counter, stand, or storage rack.

"Well, you needn't suffer any longer," said Marilla sarcastically. "You can go, but you're to be back here in just ten minutes, remember that."

Anne did remember it and was back in the stipulated time, although probably no mortal will ever know just what it cost her to confine the discussion of Diana's important communication within the limits of ten minutes. But at least she had made good use of them.

"Oh, Marilla, what do you think? You know tomorrow is Diana's birthday. Well, her mother told her she could ask me to go home with her from school and stay all night with her. And her cousins are coming over from Newbridge in a big pung sleigh[1] to go to the Debating Club concert at the hall to-morrow night. And they are going to take Diana and me to the concert—if you'll let me go, that is. You will, won't you, Marilla? Oh, I feel so excited."

"You can calm down then, because you're not going. You're better at home in your own bed, and as for that Club concert, it's all nonsense, and little girls should not be allowed to go out to such places at all."

"I'm sure the Debating Club is a most respectable affair," pleaded Anne.

"I'm not saying it isn't. But you're not going to begin gadding about to concerts and staying out all hours of the night. Pretty doings for children. I'm surprised at Mrs. Barry's letting Diana go."

"But it's such a very special occasion," mourned Anne, on the verge of tears. "Diana has only one birthday in a year. It isn't as if birthdays were common things, Marilla. Prissy Andrews is going to recite 'Curfew Must Not Ring To-night.'[2] That is such a good moral piece, Marilla, I'm sure it would do me lots of good to hear it. And the choir are going to sing four lovely pathetic songs that are pretty near as good as hymns. And oh, Marilla, the minister is going to take part; yes, indeed, he is; he's going to give an address. That will be just about the same thing as a sermon. Please, mayn't I go, Marilla?"

"You heard what I said, Anne, didn't you? Take off your boots now and go to bed. It's past eight."

"There's just one more thing, Marilla," said Anne, with the air of producing the last shot in her locker. "Mrs. Barry told Diana that we might sleep in the spare-room bed. Think of the honour of your little Anne being put in the spare-room bed."

"It's an honour you'll have to get along without. Go to bed, Anne, and don't let me hear another word out of you."

When Anne, with tears rolling over her cheeks, had gone sorrowfully upstairs, Matthew, who had been apparently sound asleep on the lounge during the whole dialogue, opened his eyes and said decidedly:

"Well now, Marilla, I think you ought to let Anne go."

"I don't then," retorted Marilla. "Who's bringing this child up, Matthew, you or me?"

"Well now, you," admitted Matthew.

"Don't interfere then."

---

1 *pung sleigh*   one- or two-horse sleigh with box-shaped body.

2 *Curfew Must Not Ring Tonight*   a 60-line poem by Rosa Hartwick Thorpe (1850–1939) about a maid in England, during the wars of Oliver Cromwell, whose sweetheart is doomed to die at the ringing of the curfew bell: she contrives to trick the blind and deaf sexton bell-ringer by climbing a ladder to hold the bell's clapper with her hands, thus muffling the sound and, with the arrival of Cromwell's troops, saving her lover.

"Well now, I ain't interfering. It ain't interfering to have your own opinion. And my opinion is that you ought to let Anne go."

"You'd think I ought to let Anne go to the moon if she took the notion, I've no doubt," was Marilla's amiable rejoinder. "I might have let her spend the night with Diana, if that was all. But I don't approve of this concert plan. She'd go there and catch cold like as not, and have her head filled up with nonsense and excitement. It would unsettle her for a week. I understand that child's disposition and what's good for it better than you, Matthew."

"I think you ought to let Anne go," repeated Matthew firmly. Argument was not his strong point, but holding fast to his opinion certainly was. Marilla gave a gasp of helplessness and took refuge in silence. The next morning, when Anne was washing the breakfast dishes in the pantry, Matthew paused on his way out to the barn to say to Marilla again:

"I think you ought to let Anne go, Marilla."

For a moment Marilla looked things not lawful to be uttered. Then she yielded to the inevitable and said tartly:

"Very well, she can go, since nothing else'll please you."

Anne flew out of the pantry, dripping dish-cloth in hand.

"Oh, Marilla, Marilla, say those blessed words again."

"I guess once is enough to say them. This is Matthew's doings and I wash my hands of it. If you catch pneumonia sleeping in a strange bed or coming out of that hot hall in the middle of the night, don't blame me, blame Matthew. Anne Shirley, you're dripping greasy water all over the floor. I never saw such a careless child."

"Oh, I know I'm a great trial to you, Marilla," said Anne repentantly. "I make so many mistakes. But then just think of all the mistakes I don't make, although I might. I'll get some sand and scrub up the spots before I go to school. Oh, Marilla, my heart was just set on going to that concert. I never was to a concert in my life, and when the other girls talk about them in school I feel so out of it. You didn't know just how I felt about it, but you see Matthew did. Matthew understands me, and it's so nice to be understood, Marilla."

Anne was too excited to do herself justice as to lessons that morning in school. Gilbert Blythe spelled her down in class and left her clear out of sight in mental arithmetic. Anne's consequent humiliation was less than it might have been, however, in view of the concert and the spare-room bed. She and Diana talked so constantly about it all day that with a stricter teacher than Mr. Phillips dire disgrace must inevitably have been their portion.

Anne felt that she could not have borne it if she had not been going to the concert, for nothing else was discussed that day in school. The Avonlea Debating Club, which met fortnightly all winter, had had several smaller free entertainments; but this was to be a big affair, admission ten cents, in aid of the library. The Avonlea young people had been practising for weeks, and all the scholars were especially interested in it by reason of older brothers and sisters who were going to take part. Everybody in school over nine years of age expected to go, except Carrie Sloane, whose father shared Marilla's opinions about small girls going out to night concerts. Carrie Sloane cried into her grammar all the afternoon and felt that life was not worth living.

For Anne the real excitement began with the dismissal of school and increased therefrom in crescendo until it reached to a crash of positive ecstasy in the concert itself. They had a "perfectly elegant tea;" and then came the delicious occupation of dressing in Diana's little room up-stairs. Diana did Anne's front hair in the new pompadour style and Anne tied Diana's bows with the especial knack she possessed; and they experimented with at least half a dozen different ways of arranging their back hair. At last they were ready, cheeks scarlet and eyes glowing with excitement.

True, Anne could not help a little pang when she contrasted her plain black tam and shapeless, tight-sleeved, home-made gray cloth coat with Diana's jaunty fur cap and smart little jacket. But she remembered in time that she had an imagination and could use it.

Then Diana's cousins, the Murrays from Newbridge, came; they all crowded into the big pung sleigh, among straw and furry robes. Anne revelled in the drive to the hall, slipping along over the satin-smooth roads with the snow crisping under the runners. There was a magnificent sunset, and the snowy hills and deep blue water of the St. Lawrence Gulf seemed to rim in the splendour like a huge bowl of pearl and sapphire brimmed with wine and fire. Tinkles of sleigh-bells and distant laughter, that seemed like the mirth of wood elves, came from every quarter.

"Oh, Diana," breathed Anne, squeezing Diana's mittened hand under the fur robe, "isn't it all like a beautiful dream? Do I really look the same as usual? I feel so different that it seems to me it must show in my looks."

"You look awfully nice," said Diana, who having just received a compliment from one of her cousins, felt that she ought to pass it on. "You've got the loveliest colour."

The programme that night was a series of "thrills" for at least one listener in the audience, and, as Anne assured Diana, every succeeding thrill was thrillier than the last. When Prissy Andrews, attired in a new pink silk waist with a string of pearls about her smooth white throat and real carnations in her hair—rumour whispered that the master had sent all the way to town for them for her— "climbed the slimy ladder, dark without one ray of light," Anne shivered in luxurious sympathy; when the choir sang "Far Above the Gentle Daisies"[3] Anne gazed at the ceiling as if it were frescoed with angels; when Sam Sloane proceeded to explain and illustrate "How Sockery Set a Hen"[4] Anne laughed until people sitting near her laughed too, more out of sympathy with her than with amusement at a selection that was rather threadbare even in Avonlea; and when Mr. Phillips gave Mark Antony's oration over the dead body of Caesar[5] in the most heart-stirring tones—looking at Prissy Andrews at the end of every sentence—Anne felt that she could rise and mutiny on the spot if but one Roman citizen led the way.

Only one number on the programme failed to interest her. When Gilbert Blythe recited "Bingen on the Rhine"[6] Anne picked up Rhoda Murray's library book and read it until he had finished, when she sat rigidly stiff and motionless while Diana clapped her hands until they tingled.

---

3 *Far Above the Gentle Daisies* hymn-form song by George Cooper and Harrison Millard (1869) in which the singer imagines being reunited with dead beloved in heaven's "love and rapture."

4 *How Sockery Set a Hen* prose "joke" in phonetically spelled "German" dialect of English; farmer Sockery tells how he tried to get a hen to sit on some eggs but ended up stuck in a barrel.

5 *Mark Antony's oration . . . Caesar* in Shakespeare's *Julius Caesar* 3.2.

6 *Bingen on the Rhine* by Caroline Elizabeth Sarah Norton (1808–1877) and mentioned above in Chapter 5 (see Note 4): a dying soldier's lament. It contains the passage: "There's another—not a sister: in the happy days gone by, / You'd have known her by the merriment that sparkled in her eye; / Too innocent for coquetry, too fond for idle scorning, / O friend, I fear the lightest heart makes sometimes heaviest mourning."

It was eleven when they got home, sated with dissipation, but with the exceeding sweet pleasure of talking it all over still to come. Everybody seemed asleep and the house was dark and silent. Anne and Diana tiptoed into the parlour, a long narrow room out of which the spare room opened. It was pleasantly warm and dimly lighted by the embers of a fire in the grate.

"Let's undress here," said Diana. "It's so nice and warm."

"Hasn't it been a delightful time?" sighed Anne rapturously. "It must be splendid to get up and recite there. Do you suppose we will ever be asked to do it, Diana?"

"Yes, of course, some day. They're always wanting the big scholars to recite. Gilbert Blythe does often and he's only two years older than us. Oh, Anne, how could you pretend not to listen to him? When he came to the line,

"'There's another, *not* a sister,'

he looked right down at you."

"Diana," said Anne with dignity, "you are my bosom friend, but I cannot allow even you to speak to me of that person. Are you ready for bed? Let's run a race and see who'll get to the bed first."

The suggestion appealed to Diana. The two little white-clad figures flew down the long room, through the spare-room door, and bounded on the bed at the same moment. And then—something—moved beneath them, there was a gasp and a cry—and somebody said in muffled accents:

"Merciful goodness!"

Anne and Diana were never able to tell just how they got off that bed and out of the room. They only knew that after one frantic rush they found themselves tiptoeing shiveringly up-stairs.

"Oh, who was it—*what* was it?" whispered Anne, her teeth chattering with cold and fright.

"It was Aunt Josephine," said Diana, gasping with laughter. "Oh, Anne, it was Aunt Josephine, however she came to be there. Oh, and I know she will be furious. It's dreadful—it's really dreadful—but did you ever know anything so funny, Anne?"

"Who is your Aunt Josephine?"

"She's father's aunt and she lives in Charlottetown. She's awfully old—seventy anyhow—and I don't believe she was *ever* a little girl. We were expecting her out for a visit, but not so soon. She's awfully prim and proper and she'll scold dreadfully about this, I know. Well, we'll have to sleep with Minnie May—and you can't think how she kicks."

Miss Josephine Barry did not appear at the early breakfast the next morning. Mrs. Barry smiled kindly at the two little girls.

"Did you have a good time last night? I tried to stay awake until you came home, for I wanted to tell you Aunt Josephine had come and that you would have to go up-stairs after all, but I was so tired I fell asleep. I hope you didn't disturb your aunt, Diana."

Diana preserved a discreet silence, but she and Anne exchanged furtive smiles of guilty amusement across the table. Anne hurried home after breakfast and so remained in blissful ignorance of the disturbance which presently resulted in the Barry household until the late afternoon, when she went down to Mrs. Lynde's on an errand for Marilla.

"So you and Diana nearly frightened poor old Miss Barry to death last night?" said Mrs. Lynde severely, but with a twinkle in her eye. "Mrs. Barry was here a few minutes ago on her way to Carmody. She's feeling real worried over it. Old Miss Barry was in a terrible temper when she got up this morning—and Josephine Barry's temper is no joke, I can tell you that. She wouldn't speak to Diana at all."

"It wasn't Diana's fault," said Anne contritely. "It was mine. I suggested racing to see who would get into bed first."

"I knew it!" said Mrs. Lynde with the exultation of a correct guesser. "I knew that idea came out of your head. Well, it's made a nice lot of trouble, that's what. Old Miss Barry came out to stay for a month, but she declares she won't stay another day and is going right back to town to-morrow, Sunday and all as it is. She'd have gone to-day if they could have taken her. She had promised to pay for a quarter's music lessons for Diana, but now she is determined to do nothing at all for such a tomboy. Oh, I guess they had a lively time of it there this morning. The Barrys must feel cut up. Old Miss Barry is rich and they'd like to keep on the good side of her. Of course, Mrs. Barry didn't say just that to me, but I'm a pretty good judge of human nature, that's what."

"I'm such an unlucky girl," mourned Anne. "I'm always getting into scrapes myself and getting my best friends—people I'd shed my heart's blood for—into them, too. Can you tell me why it is so, Mrs. Lynde?"

"It's because you're too heedless and impulsive, child, that's what. You never stop to think—whatever comes into your head to say or do you say or do it without a moment's reflection."

"Oh, but that's the best of it," protested Anne. "Something just flashes into your mind, so exciting, and you must out with it. If you stop to think it over you spoil it all. Haven't you never felt that yourself, Mrs. Lynde?"

No, Mrs. Lynde had not. She shook her head sagely.

"You must learn to think a little, Anne, that's what. The proverb you need to go by is 'Look before you leap'—especially into spare-room beds."

Mrs. Lynde laughed comfortably over her mild joke, but Anne remained pensive. She saw nothing to laugh at in the situation, which to her eyes appeared very serious. When she left Mrs. Lynde's she took her way across the crusted fields to Orchard Slope. Diana met her at the kitchen door.

"Your Aunt Josephine was very cross about it, wasn't she?" whispered Anne.

"Yes," answered Diana, stifling a giggle with an apprehensive glance over her shoulder at the closed sitting-room door. "She was fairly dancing with rage, Anne. Oh, how she scolded. She said I was the worst-behaved girl she ever saw and that my parents ought to be ashamed of the way they had brought me up. She says she won't stay and I'm sure I don't care. But father and mother do."

"Why didn't you tell them it was my fault?" demanded Anne.

"It's likely I'd do such a thing, isn't it?" said Diana with just scorn. "I'm no telltale, Anne Shirley, and anyhow I was just as much to blame as you."

"Well, I'm going in to tell her myself," said Anne resolutely.

Diana stared.

"Anne Shirley, you'd never! why—she'll eat you alive!"

"Don't frighten me any more than I am frightened," implored Anne. "I'd rather walk up to a cannon's mouth. But I've got to do it, Diana. It was my fault and I've got to confess. I've had practice in confessing fortunately."

"Well, she's in the room," said Diana. "You can go in if you want to. I wouldn't dare. And I don't believe you'll do a bit of good."

278

With this encouragement Anne bearded the lion in its den—that is to say, walked resolutely up to the sitting-room door and knocked faintly. A sharp "Come in" followed.

Miss Josephine Barry, thin, prim and rigid, was knitting fiercely by the fire, her wrath quite unappeased and her eyes snapping through her gold-rimmed glasses. She wheeled around in her chair, expecting to see Diana, and beheld a white-faced girl whose great eyes were brimmed up with a mixture of desperate courage and shrinking terror.

"Who are you?" demanded Miss Josephine Barry without ceremony.

"I'm Anne of Green Gables," said the small visitor tremulously, clasping her hands with her characteristic gesture, "and I've come to confess, if you please."

"Confess what?"

"That it was all my fault about jumping into bed on you last night. I suggested it. Diana would never have thought of such a thing, I am sure. Diana is a very lady-like girl, Miss Barry. So you must see how unjust it is to blame her."

"Oh, I must, hey? I rather think Diana did her share of the jumping at least. Such carryings-on in a respectable house!"

"But we were only in fun," persisted Anne. "I think you ought to forgive us, Miss Barry, now that we've apologized. And anyhow, please forgive Diana and let her have her music lessons. Diana's heart is set on her music lessons, Miss Barry, and I know too well what it is to set your heart on a thing and not get it. If you must be cross with any one, be cross with me. I've been so used in my early days to having people cross at me that I can endure it much better than Diana can."

Much of the snap had gone out of the old lady's eyes by this time and was replaced by a twinkle of amused interest. But she still said severely:

"I don't think it is any excuse for you that you were only in fun. Little girls never indulged in that kind of fun when I was young. You don't know what it is to be awakened out of a sound sleep, after a long and arduous journey, by two great girls coming bounce down on you."

"I don't *know*, but I can *imagine*," said Anne eagerly. "I'm sure it must have been very disturbing. But then, there is our side of it too. Have you any imagination, Miss Barry? If you have, just put yourself in our place. We didn't know there was anybody in that bed and you nearly scared us to death. It was simply awful the way we felt. And then we couldn't sleep in the spare room after being promised. I suppose you are used to sleeping in spare rooms. But just imagine what you would feel like if you were a little orphan girl who had never had such an honour."

All the snap had gone by this time. Miss Barry actually laughed—a sound which caused Diana, waiting in speechless anxiety in the kitchen outside, to give a great gasp of relief.

"I'm afraid my imagination is a little rusty—it's so long since I used it," she said. "I dare say your claim to sympathy is just as strong as mine. It all depends on the way we look at it. Sit down here and tell me about yourself."

"I am very sorry I can't," said Anne firmly. "I would like to, because you seem like an interesting lady, and you might even be a kindred spirit although you don't look very much like it. But it is my duty to go home to Miss Marilla Cuthbert. Miss Marilla Cuthbert is a very kind lady who has taken me to bring up properly. She is doing her best, but it is very discouraging work. You must not blame her because I jumped on the bed. But before I go I do wish you would tell me if you will forgive Diana and stay just as long as you meant to in Avonlea."

"I think perhaps I will if you will come over and talk to me occasionally," said Miss Barry.

That evening Miss Barry gave Diana a silver bangle bracelet and told the senior members of the household that she had unpacked her valise.

"I've made up my mind to stay simply for the sake of getting better acquainted with that Anne-girl," she said frankly. "She amuses me, and at my time of life an amusing person is a rarity."

Marilla's only comment when she heard the story was, "I told you so." This was for Matthew's benefit.

Miss Barry stayed her month out and over. She was a more agreeable guest than usual, for Anne kept her in good humour. They became firm friends.

When Miss Barry went away she said:

"Remember, you Anne-girl, when you come to town you're to visit me and I'll put you in my very sparest spare-room bed to sleep."

"Miss Barry was a kindred spirit, after all," Anne confided to Marilla. "You wouldn't think so to look at her, but she is. You don't find it right out at first, as in Matthew's case, but after awhile you come to see it. Kindred spirits are not so scarce as I used to think. It's splendid to find out there are so many of them in the world."

CHAPTER 20

A Good Imagination Gone Wrong

SPRING had come once more to Green Gables—the beautiful, capricious, reluctant Canadian spring, lingering along through April and May in a succession of sweet, fresh, chilly days, with pink sunsets and miracles of resurrection and growth. The maples in Lovers' Lane were red-budded and little curly ferns pushed up around the Dryad's Bubble. Away up in the barrens, behind Mr. Silas Sloane's place, the Mayflowers blossomed out, pink and white stars of sweetness under their brown leaves. All the school girls and boys had one golden afternoon gathering them, coming home in the clear, echoing twilight with arms and baskets full of flowery spoil.

"I'm so sorry for people who live in lands where there are no Mayflowers," said Anne. "Diana says perhaps they have something better, but there couldn't be anything better than Mayflowers, could there, Marilla? And Diana says if they don't know what they are like they don't miss them. But I think that is the saddest thing of all. I think it would be *tragic*, Marilla, not to know what Mayflowers are like and *not* to miss them. Do you know what I think Mayflowers are, Marilla? I think they must be the souls of the flowers that died last summer and this is their heaven. But we had a splendid time to-day, Marilla. We had our lunch down in a big mossy hollow by an old well—such a *romantic* spot. Charlie Sloane dared Arty Gillis to jump over it, and Arty did because he wouldn't take a dare. Nobody would in school. It is very *fashionable* to dare. Mr. Phillips gave all the Mayflowers he found to Prissy Andrews and I heard him say 'sweets to the sweet.' He got that out of a book, I know; but it shows he has some imagination.[1] I was offered some Mayflowers too, but I rejected them with scorn. I can't tell you the person's name because I have vowed never to let it cross my lips. We

---

[1] *sweets . . . imagination* In Shakespeare's *Hamlet*, (5.1.243) Queen Gertrude says "Sweets to the sweet" as she throws flowers upon the corpse of Ophelia.

made wreaths of the Mayflowers and put them on our hats; and when the time came to go home we marched in procession down the road, two by two, with our bouquets and wreaths, singing 'My Home on the Hill.'[2] Oh, it was so thrilling, Marilla. All Mr. Silas Sloane's folks rushed out to see us and everybody we met on the road stopped and stared after us. We made a real sensation."

"Not much wonder! Such silly doings!" was Marilla's response.

After the Mayflowers came the violets, and Violet Vale was empurpled with them. Anne walked through it on her way to school with reverent steps and worshipping eyes, as if she trod on holy ground.

"Somehow," she told Diana, "when I'm going through here I don't really care whether Gil—whether anybody gets ahead of me in class or not. But when I'm up in school it's all different and I care as much as ever. There's such a lot of different Annes in me. I sometimes think that is why I'm such a troublesome person. If I was just the one Anne it would be ever so much more comfortable, but then it wouldn't be half so interesting."

One June evening, when the orchards were pink-blossomed again, when the frogs were singing silverly sweet in the marshes about the head of the Lake of Shining Waters, and the air was full of the savour of clover fields and balsamic fir woods, Anne was sitting by her gable window. She had been studying her lessons, but it had grown too dark to see the book, so she had fallen into wide-eyed reverie, looking out past the boughs of the Snow Queen, once more bestarred with its tufts of blossom.

In all essential respects the little gable chamber was unchanged. The walls were as white, the pincushion as hard, the chairs as stiffly and yellowly upright as ever. Yet the whole character of the room was altered. It was full of a new vital, pulsing personality that seemed to pervade it and to be quite independent of schoolgirl books and dresses and ribbons, and even of the cracked blue jug full of apple blossoms on the table. It was as if all the dreams, sleeping and waking, of its vivid occupant had taken a visible although immaterial form and had tapestried the bare room with splendid filmy tissues of rainbow and moonshine. Presently Marilla came briskly in with some of Anne's freshly ironed school aprons. She hung them over a chair and sat down with a short sigh. She had had one of her headaches that afternoon, and although the pain had gone she felt weak and "tuckered out," as she expressed it. Anne looked at her with eyes limpid with sympathy.

"I do truly wish I could have had the headache in your place, Marilla. I would have endured it joyfully for your sake."

"I guess you did your part in attending to the work and letting me rest," said Marilla. "You seem to have got on fairly well and made fewer mistakes than usual. Of course it wasn't exactly necessary to starch Matthew's handkerchiefs! And most people when they put a pie in the oven to warm up for dinner take it out and eat it when it gets hot instead of leaving it to be burned to a crisp. But that doesn't seem to be your way evidently."

Headaches always left Marilla somewhat sarcastic.

"Oh, I'm so sorry," said Anne penitently. "I never thought about that pie from the moment I put it in the oven till now, although I felt *instinctively* that there was something missing on the dinner table. I was firmly resolved, when you left me in charge this morning, not to imagine anything, but keep my thoughts on facts. I did pretty well until I put the pie in, and then an irresistible

2 *My Home on the Hill* song by W. C. Baker (1866).

temptation came to me to imagine I was an enchanted princess shut up in a lonely tower with a handsome knight riding to my rescue on a coal-black steed. So that is how I came to forget the pie. I didn't know I starched the handkerchiefs. All the time I was ironing I was trying to think of a name for a new island Diana and I have discovered up the brook. It's the most ravishing spot, Marilla. There are two maple-trees on it and the brook flows right around it. At last it struck me that it would be splendid to call it Victoria Island because we found it on the Queen's birthday. Both Diana and I are very loyal. But I'm very sorry about that pie and the handkerchiefs. I wanted to be extra good to-day because it's an anniversary. Do you remember what happened this day last year, Marilla?"

"No, I can't think of anything special."

"Oh, Marilla, it was the day I came to Green Gables. I shall never forget it. It was the turning-point in my life. Of course it wouldn't seem so important to you. I've been here for a year and I've been so happy. Of course, I've had my troubles, but one can live down troubles. Are you sorry you kept me, Marilla?"

"No, I can't say I'm sorry," said Marilla, who sometimes wondered how she could have lived before Anne came to Green Gables, "no, not exactly sorry. If you've finished your lessons, Anne, I want you to run over and ask Mrs. Barry if she'll lend me Diana's apron pattern."

"Oh—it's—it's too dark," cried Anne.

"Too dark? Why, it's only twilight. And goodness knows you've gone over often enough after dark."

"I'll go over early in the morning," said Anne eagerly. "I'll get up at sunrise and go over, Marilla."

"What has got into your head now, Anne Shirley? I want that pattern to cut out your new apron this evening. Go at once and be smart, too."

"I'll have to go around by the road, then," said Anne, taking up her hat reluctantly.

"Go by the road and waste half an hour! I'd like to catch you!"

"I can't go through the Haunted Wood, Marilla," cried Anne desperately. Marilla stared.

"The Haunted Wood! Are you crazy? What under the canopy is the Haunted Wood?"

"The spruce wood over the brook," said Anne in a whisper.

"Fiddlesticks! There is no such thing as a haunted wood anywhere. Who has been telling you such stuff?"

"Nobody," confessed Anne. "Diana and I just imagined the wood was haunted. All the places around here are so—so—*commonplace*. We just got this up for our own amusement. We began it in April. A haunted wood is so very romantic, Marilla. We chose the spruce grove because it's so gloomy. Oh, we have imagined the most harrowing things. There's a white lady walks along the brook just about this time of the night and wrings her hands and utters wailing cries. She appears when there is to be a death in the family. And the ghost of a little murdered child haunts the corner up by Idlewild; it creeps up behind you and lays its cold fingers on your hand—so. Oh, Marilla, it gives me a shudder to think of it. And there's a headless man stalks up and down the path and skeletons glower at you between the boughs. Oh, Marilla, I wouldn't go through the Haunted Wood after dark now for anything. I'd be sure that white things would reach out from behind the trees and grab me."

"Did ever any one hear the like!" ejaculated Marilla, who had listened in dumb amazement. "Anne Shirley, do you mean to tell me you believe all that wicked nonsense of your own imagination?"

"Not believe *exactly*," faltered Anne "At least, I don't believe it in daylight. But after dark, Marilla, it's different. That is when ghosts walk."

"There are no such things as ghosts, Anne."

"Oh, but there are, Marilla," cried Anne eagerly. "I know people who have seen them. And they are respectable people. Charlie Sloane says that his grandmother saw his grandfather driving home the cows one night after he'd been buried for a year. You know Charlie Sloane's grandmother wouldn't tell a story for anything. She's a very religious woman. And Mrs. Thomas' father was pursued home one night by a lamb of fire with its head cut off hanging by a strip of skin. He said he knew it was the spirit of his brother and that it was a warning he would die within nine days. He didn't, but died two years after, so you see it was really true. And Ruby Gillis says—".

"Anne Shirley," interrupted Marilla firmly, "I never want to hear you talking in this fashion again. I've had my doubts about that imagination of yours right along, and if this is going to be the outcome of it, I won't countenance any such doings. You'll go right over to Barry's, and you'll go through that spruce grove, just for a lesson and a warning to you. And never let me hear a word out of your head about haunted woods again."

Anne might plead and cry as she liked—and did, for her terror was very real. Her imagination had run away with her and she held the spruce grove in mortal dread after nightfall. But Marilla was inexorable. She marched the shrinking ghostseer down to the spring and ordered her to proceed straightway over the bridge and into the dusky retreats of wailing ladies and headless spectres beyond.

"Oh, Marilla, how can you be so cruel?" sobbed Anne. "What would you feel like if a white thing did snatch me up and carry me off?"

"I'll risk it," said Marilla unfeelingly. "You know I always mean what I say. I'll cure you of imagining ghosts into places. March, now."

Anne marched. That is, she stumbled over the bridge and went shuddering up the horrible dim path beyond. Anne never forgot that walk. Bitterly did she resent the license she had given to her imagination. The goblins of her fancy lurked in every shadow about her, reaching out their cold, fleshless hands to grasp the terrified small girl who had called them into being. A white strip of birch bark blowing up from the hollow over the brown floor of the grove made her heart stand still. The long-drawn wail of two old boughs rubbing against each other brought out the perspiration in beads on her forehead. The swoop of bats in the darkness over her was as the wings of unearthly creatures. When she reached Mr. William Bell's field she fled across it as if pursued by an army of white things, and arrived at the Barry kitchen door so out of breath that she could hardly gasp out her request for the apron pattern. Diana was away so that she had no excuse to linger. The dreadful return journey had to be faced. Anne went back over it with shut eyes, preferring to take the risk of dashing her brains out among the boughs to that of seeing a white thing. When she finally stumbled over the log bridge she drew one long shivering breath of relief.

"Well, so nothing caught you?" said Marilla unsympathetically.

"Oh, Mar—Marilla," chattered Anne, "I'll b-b-be cont-t-tented with c-c-commonplace places after this."

CHAPTER 21

A New Departure in Flavourings

"DEAR me, there is nothing but meetings and partings in this world, as Mrs. Lynde says," remarked Anne plaintively, putting her slate and books down on the kitchen table on the last day of June and wiping her red eyes with a very damp handkerchief. "Wasn't it fortunate, Marilla, that I took an extra handkerchief to school to-day? I had a presentiment that it would be needed."

"I never thought you were so fond of Mr. Phillips that you'd require two handkerchiefs to dry your tears just because he was going away," said Marilla.

"I don't think I was crying because I was really so very fond of him," reflected Anne. "I just cried because all the others did. It was Ruby Gillis started it. Ruby Gillis has always declared she hated Mr. Phillips, but just as soon as he got up to make his farewell speech she burst into tears. Then all the girls began to cry, one after the other. I tried to hold out, Marilla. I tried to remember the time Mr. Phillips made me sit with Gil—with a boy; and the time he spelled my name without an *e* on the blackboard; and how he said I was the worst dunce he ever saw at geometry and laughed at my spelling; and all the times he had been so horrid and sarcastic; but somehow I couldn't, Marilla, and I just had to cry too. Jane Andrews has been talking for a month about how glad she'd be when Mr. Phillips went away and she declared she'd never shed a tear. Well, she was worse than any of us and had to borrow a handkerchief from her brother—of course the boys didn't cry—because she hadn't brought one of her own, not expecting to need it. Oh, Marilla, it was heartrending. Mr. Phillips made such a beautiful farewell speech beginning, 'The time has come for us to part.' It was very affecting. And he had tears in his eyes too, Marilla. Oh, I felt dreadfully sorry and remorseful for all the times I'd talked in school and drawn pictures of him on my slate and made fun of him and Prissy. I can tell you I wished I'd been a model pupil like Minnie Andrews. *She* hadn't anything on her conscience. The girls cried all the way home from school. Carrie Sloane kept saying every few minutes, 'The time has come for us to part,' and that would start us off again whenever we were in any danger of cheering up. I do feel dreadfully sad, Marilla. But one can't feel quite in the depths of despair with two months vacation before them, can they, Marilla? And besides, we met the new minister and his wife coming from the station. For all I was feeling so bad about Mr. Phillips going away I couldn't help taking a little interest in a new minister, could I? His wife is very pretty. Not exactly regally lovely, of course—it wouldn't do, I suppose, for a minister to have a regally lovely wife, because it might set a bad example. Mrs. Lynde says the minister's wife over at Newbridge sets a very bad example because she dresses so fashionably. Our new minister's wife was dressed in blue muslin with lovely puffed sleeves and a hat trimmed with roses. Jane Andrews said she thought puffed sleeves were too worldly for a minister's wife, but I didn't make any such uncharitable remark, Marilla, because I know what it is to long for puffed sleeves. Besides, she's only been a minister's wife for a little while, so one should make allowances, shouldn't they? They are going to board with Mrs. Lynde until the manse is ready."

If Marilla, in going down to Mrs. Lynde's that evening, was actuated by any motive save her avowed one of returning the quilting-frames she had borrowed the preceding winter, it was an amiable weakness shared by most of the Avonlea people. Many a thing Mrs. Lynde had lent, sometimes never expecting to see it again, came home that night in charge of the borrowers thereof. A new minister, and moreover a minister with a wife, was a lawful object of curiosity in a quiet little country settlement where sensations were few and far between.

Old Mr. Bentley, the minister whom Anne had found lacking in imagination, had been pastor of Avonlea for eighteen years. He was a widower when he came, and a widower he remained, despite the fact that gossip regularly married him to this, that or the other one, every year of his sojourn. In the preceding February he had resigned his charge and departed amid the regrets of his people, most of whom had the affection born of long intercourse for their good old minister in spite of his shortcomings as an orator. Since then the Avonlea church had enjoyed a variety of religious dissipation in listening to the many and various candidates and "supplies" who came Sunday after Sunday to preach on trial. These stood or fell by the judgment of the fathers and mothers in Israel;[1] but a certain small, red-haired girl who sat meekly in the corner of the old Cuthbert pew also had her opinions about them and discussed the same in full with Matthew, Marilla always declining from principle to criticize ministers in any shape or form.

"I don't think Mr. Smith would have done, Matthew," was Anne's final summing up. "Mrs. Lynde says his delivery was so poor, but I think his worst fault was just like Mr. Bentley's—he had no imagination. And Mr. Terry had too much; he let it run away with him just as I did mine in the matter of the Haunted Wood. Besides, Mrs. Lynde says his theology wasn't sound. Mr. Gresham was a very good man and a very religious man, but he told too many funny stories and made the people laugh in church; he was undignified, and you must have some dignity about a minister, mustn't you, Matthew? I thought Mr. Marshall was decidedly attractive; but Mrs. Lynde says he isn't married, or even engaged, because she made special inquiries about him, and she says it would never do to have a young unmarried minister in Avonlea, because he might marry in the congregation and that would make trouble. Mrs. Lynde is a very far-seeing woman, isn't she, Matthew? I'm very glad they've called Mr. Allan. I liked him because his sermon was interesting and he prayed as if he meant it and not just as if he did it because he was in the habit of it. Mrs. Lynde says he isn't perfect, but she says she supposes we couldn't expect a perfect minister for seven hundred and fifty dollars a year, and anyhow his theology is sound because she questioned him thoroughly on all the points of doctrine. And she knows his wife's people and they are most respectable and the women are all good housekeepers. Mrs. Lynde says that sound doctrine in the man and good housekeeping in the woman make an ideal combination for a minister's family."

The new minister and his wife were a young, pleasant-faced couple, still in their honeymoon, and full of all good and beautiful enthusiasms for their chosen life-work. Avonlea opened its heart to them from the start. Old and young liked the frank, cheerful young man with his high ideals, and the bright, gentle little lady who assumed the mistress-ship of the manse. With Mrs. Allan Anne fell promptly and whole-heartedly in love. She had discovered another kindred spirit.

"Mrs. Allan is perfectly lovely," she announced one Sunday afternoon. "She's taken our class and she's a splendid teacher. She said right away she didn't think it was fair for the teacher to ask all the questions, and you know, Marilla, that is

---

1 *fathers and mothers in Israel*   that is, those in highest standing in the church community.

exactly what I've always thought. She said we could ask her any question we liked, and I asked ever so many. I'm good at asking questions, Marilla."

"I believe you," was Marilla's emphatic comment.

"Nobody else asked any except Ruby Gillis, and she asked if there was to be a Sunday-school picnic this summer. I didn't think that was a very proper question to ask because it hadn't any connection with the lesson—the lesson was about Daniel in the lions' den—but Mrs. Allan just smiled and said she thought there would be. Mrs. Allan has a lovely smile; she has such *exquisite* dimples in her cheeks. I wish I had dimples in my cheeks, Marilla. I'm not half so skinny as I was when I came here, but I have no dimples yet. If I had perhaps I could influence people for good. Mrs. Allan said we ought always to try to influence other people for good. She talked so nice about everything. I never knew before that religion was such a cheerful thing. I always thought it was kind of melancholy, but Mrs. Allan's isn't, and I'd like to be a Christian if I could be one like her. I wouldn't want to be one like Mr. Superintendent Bell."

"It's very naughty of you to speak so about Mr. Bell," said Marilla severely. "Mr. Bell is a real good man."

"Oh, of course he's good," agreed Anne, "but he doesn't seem to get any comfort out of it. If I could be good I'd dance and sing all day because I was glad of it. I suppose Mrs. Allan is too old to dance and sing and of course it wouldn't be dignified in a minister's wife. But I can just feel she's glad she's a Christian and that she'd be one even if she could get to heaven without it."

"I suppose we must have Mr. and Mrs. Allan up to tea some day soon," said Marilla reflectively. "They've been most everywhere but here. Let me see. Next Wednesday would be a good time to have them. But don't say a word to Matthew about it, for if he knew they were coming he'd find some excuse to be away that day. He'd got so used to Mr. Bentley he didn't mind him, but he's going to find it hard to get acquainted with a new minister, and a new minister's wife will frighten him to death."

"I'll be as secret as the dead," assured Anne. "But oh, Marilla, will you let me make a cake for the occasion? I'd love to do something for Mrs. Allan, and you know I can make a pretty good cake by this time."

"You can make a layer cake," promised Marilla.

Monday and Tuesday great preparations went on at Green Gables. Having the minister and his wife to tea was a serious and important undertaking, and Marilla was determined not to be eclipsed by any of the Avonlea housekeepers. Anne was wild with excitement and delight. She talked it all over with Diana Tuesday night in the twilight, as they sat on the big red stones by the Dryad's Bubble and made rainbows in the water with little twigs dipped in fir balsam.

"Everything is ready, Diana, except my cake which I'm to make in the morning, and the baking-powder biscuits which Marilla will make just before tea-time. I assure you, Diana, that Marilla and I have had a busy two days of it. It's such a responsibility having a minister's family to tea. I never went through such an experience before. You should just see our pantry. It's a sight to behold. We're going to have jellied chicken and cold tongue. We're to have two kinds of jelly, red and yellow, and whipped cream and lemon pie, and cherry pie, and three kinds of cookies, and fruit-cake, and Marilla's famous yellow plum preserves that she keeps especially for ministers, and pound cake and layer cake, and biscuits as aforesaid; and new bread and old both, in case the minister is dyspeptic and can't eat new. Mrs. Lynde says ministers mostly are dyspeptic, but

I don't think Mr. Allan has been a minister long enough for it to have had a bad effect on him. I just grow cold when I think of my layer cake. Oh, Diana, what if it shouldn't be good! I dreamed last night that I was chased all around by a fearful goblin with a big layer cake for a head."

"It'll be good, all right," assured Diana, who was a very comfortable sort of friend. "I'm sure that piece of the one you made that we had for lunch in Idlewild two weeks ago was perfectly elegant."

"Yes; but cakes have such a terrible habit of turning out bad just when you especially want them to be good," sighed Anne, setting a particularly well-balsamed twig afloat. "However, I suppose I shall just have to trust to Providence and be careful to put in the flour. Oh, look, Diana, what a lovely rainbow! Do you suppose the dryad will come out after we go away and take it for a scarf?"

"You know there is no such thing as a dryad," said Diana. Diana's mother had found out about the Haunted Wood and had been decidedly angry over it. As a result Diana had abstained from any further imitative flights of imagination and did not think it prudent to cultivate a spirit of belief even in harmless dryads.

"But it's so easy to imagine there is," said Anne. "Every night, before I go to bed, I look out of my window and wonder if the dryad is really sitting here, combing her locks with the spring for a mirror. Sometimes I look for her footprints in the dew in the morning. Oh, Diana, don't give up your faith in the dryad!"

Wednesday morning came. Anne got up at sunrise because she was too excited to sleep. She had caught a severe cold in the head by reason of her dabbling in the spring on the preceding evening; but nothing short of absolute pneumonia could have quenched her interest in culinary matters that morning. After breakfast she proceeded to make her cake. When she finally shut the oven door upon it she drew a long breath.

"I'm sure I haven't forgotten anything this time, Marilla. But do you think it will rise? Just suppose perhaps the baking-powder isn't good? I used it out of the new can. And Mrs. Lynde says you can never be sure of getting good baking-powder nowadays when everything is so adulterated. Mrs. Lynde says the Government ought to take the matter up, but she says we'll never see the day when a Tory Government will do it. Marilla, what if that cake doesn't rise?"

"We'll have plenty without it," was Marilla's unimpassioned way of looking at the subject.

The cake did rise, however, and came out of the oven as light and feathery as golden foam. Anne, flushed with delight, clapped it together with layers of ruby jelly and, in imagination, saw Mrs. Allan eating it and possibly asking for another piece!

"You'll be using the best tea-set, of course, Marilla," she said. "Can I fix up the table with ferns and wild roses?"

"I think that's all nonsense," sniffed Marilla. "In my opinion it's the eatables that matter and not flummery decorations."

"Mrs. Barry had *her* table decorated," said Anne, who was not entirely guiltless of the wisdom of the serpent[2] "and the minister paid her an elegant compliment. He said it was a feast for the eye as well as the palate."

---

2 *wisdom of the serpent*　as depicted, for example, in Genesis 3.1, Matthew 10.16, Milton's *Paradise Lost*, and elsewhere.

"Well, do as you like," said Marilla, who was quite determined not to be surpassed by Mrs. Barry or anybody else. "Only mind you leave enough room for the dishes and the food."

Anne laid herself out to decorate in a manner and after a fashion that should leave Mrs. Barry's nowhere. Having abundance of roses and ferns and a very artistic taste of her own, she made that tea-table such a thing of beauty that when the minister and his wife sat down to it they exclaimed in chorus over its loveliness.

"It's Anne's doings," said Marilla, grimly just; and Anne felt that Mrs. Allan's approving smile was almost too much happiness for this world.

Matthew was there, having been inveigled into the party only goodness and Anne knew how. He had been in such a state of shyness and nervousness that Marilla had given him up in despair, but Anne took him in hand so successfully that he now sat at the table in his best clothes and white collar and talked to the minister not uninterestingly. He never said a word to Mrs. Allan, but that perhaps was not to be expected.

All went merry as a marriage bell until Anne's layer cake was passed. Mrs. Allan, having already been helped to a bewildering variety, declined it. But Marilla, seeing the disappointment on Anne's face, said smilingly:

"Oh, you must take a piece of this, Mrs. Allan. Anne made it on purpose for you."

"In that case I must sample it," laughed Mrs. Allan, helping herself to a plump triangle, as did also the minister and Marilla.

Mrs. Allan took a mouthful of hers and a most peculiar expression crossed her face; not a word did she say, however, but steadily ate away at it. Marilla saw the expression and hastened to taste the cake.

"Anne Shirley!" she exclaimed, "what on earth did you put into that cake?"

"Nothing but what the recipe said, Marilla," cried Anne with a look of anguish. "Oh, isn't it all right?"

"All right! It's simply horrible. Mrs. Allan, don't try to eat it. Anne, taste it yourself. What flavouring did you use?"

"Vanilla," said Anne, her face scarlet with mortification after tasting the cake. "Only vanilla. Oh, Marilla, it must have been the baking-powder. I had my suspicions of that bak—"

"Baking-powder fiddlesticks! Go and bring me the bottle of vanilla you used."

Anne fled to the pantry and returned with a small bottle partially filled with a brown liquid and labelled yellowly, "Best Vanilla."

Marilla took it, uncorked it, smelled it.

"Mercy on us, Anne, you've flavoured that cake with *anodyne liniment*. I broke the liniment bottle last week and poured what was left into an old empty vanilla bottle. I suppose it's partly my fault—I should have warned you—but for pity's sake why couldn't you have smelled it?"

Anne dissolved into tears under this double disgrace.

"I couldn't—I had such a cold!" and with this she fairly fled to the gable chamber, where she cast herself on the bed and wept as one who refuses to be comforted.

Presently a light step sounded on the stairs and somebody entered the room.

"Oh, Marilla," sobbed Anne without looking up, "I'm disgraced for ever. I shall never be able to live this down. It will get out—things always do get out in

Avonlea. Diana will ask me how my cake turned out and I shall have to tell her the truth. I shall always be pointed at as the girl who flavoured a cake with ano- dyne liniment. Gil—the boys in school will never get over laughing at it. Oh, Marilla, if you have a spark of Christian pity don't tell me that I must go down and wash the dishes after this. I'll wash them when the minister and his wife are gone, but I cannot ever look Mrs. Allan in the face again. Perhaps she'll think I tried to poison her. Mrs. Lynde says she knows an orphan girl who tried to poi- son her benefactor. But the liniment isn't poisonous. It's meant to be taken in- ternally—although not in cakes. Won't you tell Mrs. Allan so, Marilla?"

"Suppose you jump up and tell her so yourself," said a merry voice.

Anne flew up, to find Mrs. Allan standing by her bed, surveying her with laughing eyes.

"My dear little girl, you mustn't cry like this," she said, genuinely disturbed by Anne's tragic face. "Why, it's all just a funny mistake that anybody might make."

"Oh, no, it takes me to make such a mistake," said Anne forlornly. "And I wanted to have that cake so nice for you, Mrs. Allan."

"Yes, I know, dear. And I assure you I appreciate your kindness and thought- fulness just as much as if it had turned out all right. Now, you mustn't cry any more, but come down with me and show me your flower garden. Miss Cuthbert tells me you have a little plot all your own. I want to see it, for I'm very much interested in flowers."

Anne permitted herself to be led down and comforted, reflecting that it was really providential that Mrs. Allan was a kindred spirit. Nothing more was said about the liniment cake, and when the guests went away Anne found that she had enjoyed the evening more than could have been expected, considering that terrible incident. Nevertheless she sighed deeply.

"Marilla, isn't it nice to think that to-morrow is a new day with no mistakes in it yet?"

"I'll warrant you'll make plenty in it," said Marilla. "I never saw your beat for making mistakes, Anne."

"Yes, and well I know it," admitted Anne mournfully. "But have you ever no- ticed one encouraging thing about me, Marilla? I never make the same mistake twice."

"I don't know as that's much benefit when you're always making new ones."

"Oh, don't you see, Marilla? There *must* be a limit to the mistakes one per- son can make, and when I get to the end of them, then I'll be through with them. That's a very comforting thought."

"Well, you'd better go and give that cake to the pigs," said Marilla. "It isn't fit for any human to eat, not even Jerry Buote."

CHAPTER 22

Anne Is Invited Out to Tea

"AND what are your eyes popping out of your head about now?" asked Ma- rilla, when Anne had just come in from a run to the post-office. "Have you discovered another kindred spirit?"

Excitement hung around Anne like a garment, shone in her eyes, kindled in every feature. She had come dancing up the lane, like a wind-blown sprite, through the mellow sunshine and lazy shadows of the August evening.

"No, Marilla, but oh, what do you think? I am invited to tea at the manse to-morrow afternoon! Mrs. Allan left the letter for me at the post-office. Just look at it, Marilla. 'Miss Anne Shirley, Green Gables.' That is the first time I was ever called 'Miss.' Such a thrill as it gave me! I shall cherish it for ever among my choicest treasures."

"Mrs. Allan told me she meant to have all the members of her Sunday-school class to tea in turn," said Marilla, regarding the wonderful event very coolly. "You needn't get in such a fever over it. Do learn to take things calmly, child."

For Anne to take things calmly would have been to change her nature. All "spirit and fire and dew," as she was, the pleasures and pains of life came to her with trebled intensity. Marilla felt this and was vaguely troubled over it, realizing that the ups and downs of existence would probably bear hardly on this impulsive soul and not sufficiently understanding that the equally great capacity for delight might more than compensate. Therefore Marilla conceived it to be her duty to drill Anne into a tranquil uniformity of disposition as impossible and alien to her as to a dancing sunbeam in one of the brook shallows. She did not make much headway, as she sorrowfully admitted to herself. The downfall of some dear hope or plan plunged Anne into "deeps of affliction." The fulfilment thereof exalted her to dizzy realms of delight. Marilla had almost begun to despair of ever fashioning this waif of the world into her model little girl of demure manners and prim deportment. Neither would she have believed that she really liked Anne much better as she was.

Anne went to bed that night speechless with misery because Matthew had said the wind was round northeast and he feared it would be a rainy day to-morrow. The rustle of the poplar leaves about the house worried her, it sounded so like pattering rain-drops, and the dull, faraway roar of the gulf, to which she listened delightedly at other times, loving its strange, sonorous, haunting rhythm, now seemed like a prophecy of storm and disaster to a small maiden who particularly wanted a fine day. Anne thought that the morning would never come.

But all things have an end, even nights before the day on which you are invited to take tea at the manse. The morning, in spite of Matthew's predictions, was fine and Anne's spirits soared to their highest.

"Oh, Marilla, there is something in me to-day that makes me just love everybody I see," she exclaimed as she washed the breakfast dishes. "You don't know how good I feel! Wouldn't it be nice if it could last? I believe I could be a model child if I were just invited out to tea every day. But oh, Marilla, it's a solemn occasion, too. I feel so anxious. What if I shouldn't behave properly? You know I never had tea at a manse before, and I'm not sure that I know all the rules of etiquette, although I've been studying the rules given in the Etiquette Department of the *Family Herald* ever since I came here. I'm so afraid I'll do something silly or forget to do something I should do. Would it be good manners to take a second helping of anything if you wanted to *very* much?"

"The trouble with you, Anne, is that you're thinking too much about yourself. You should just think of Mrs. Allan and what would be nicest and most agreeable for her," said Marilla, hitting for once in her life on a very sound and pithy piece of advice. Anne instantly realized this.

"You are right, Marilla. I'll try not to think about myself at all."

Anne evidently got through her visit without any serious breach of "eti-quette" for she came home through the twilight, under a great, high-sprung sky gloried over with trails of saffron and rosy cloud, in a beatified state of mind and told Marilla all about it happily, sitting on the big red sandstone slab at the kitchen door with her tired curly head in Marilla's gingham lap.

A cool wind was blowing down over the long harvest fields from the rims of firry western hills and whistling through the poplars. One clear star hung above the orchard and the fireflies were flitting over in Lovers' Lane, in and out among the ferns and rustling boughs. Anne watched them as she talked and somehow felt that wind and stars and fireflies were all tangled up together into something unutterably sweet and enchanting.

"Oh, Marilla, I've had a most *fascinating* time. I feel that I have not lived in vain and I shall always feel like that even if I should never be invited to tea at a manse again. When I got there Mrs. Allan met me at the door. She was dressed in the sweetest dress of pale pink organdy, with dozens of frills and elbow sleeves, and she looked just like a seraph. I really think I'd like to be a minister's wife when I grow up, Marilla. A minister mightn't mind my red hair because he wouldn't be thinking of such worldly things. But then of course one would have to be naturally good and I'll never be that, so I suppose there's no use in think-ing about it. Some people are naturally good, you know, and others are not. I'm one of the others. Mrs. Lynde says I'm full of original sin. No matter how hard I try to be good I can never make such a success of it as those who are naturally good. It's a good deal like geometry, I expect. But don't you think the trying so hard ought to count for something? Mrs. Allan is one of the naturally good people. I love her passionately. You know there are some people, like Matthew and Mrs. Allan, that you can love right off without any trouble. And there are others, like Mrs. Lynde, that you have to try very hard to love. You know you *ought* to love them because they know so much and are such active workers in the church, but you have to keep reminding yourself of it all the time or else you forget. There was another little girl at the manse to tea, from the White Sands Sunday-school. Her name was Lauretta Bradley, and she was a very nice little girl. Not exactly a kindred spirit, you know, but still very nice. We had an elegant tea, and I think I kept all the rules of etiquette pretty well. After tea Mrs. Allan played and sang and she got Lauretta and me to sing, too. Mrs. Allan says I have a good voice and she says I must sing in the Sunday-school choir after this. You can't think how I was thrilled at the mere thought. I've longed so to sing in the Sunday-school choir, as Diana does, but I feared it was an honour I could never aspire to. Lauretta had to go home early because there is a big concert in the White Sands hotel to-night and her sister is to recite at it. Lau-retta says that the Americans at the hotel give a concert every fortnight in aid of the Charlottetown hospital, and they ask lots of the White Sands people to re-cite. Lauretta said she expected to be asked herself some day. I just gazed at her in awe. After she had gone Mrs. Allan and I had a heart to heart talk. I told her everything—about Mrs. Thomas and the twins and Katie Maurice and Violetta and coming to Green Gables and my troubles over geometry. And would you believe it, Marilla? Mrs. Allan told me she was a dunce at geometry, too. You don't know how that encouraged me. Mrs. Lynde came to the manse just before I left, and what do you think, Marilla? The trustees have hired a new teacher and it's a lady. Her name is Miss Muriel Stacy. Isn't that a romantic name? Mrs. Lynde says they've never had a female teacher in Avonlea before and she thinks it is a dangerous innovation. But I think it will be splendid to have a lady

teacher, and I really don't see how I'm going to live through the two weeks before school begins, I'm so impatient to see her."

CHAPTER 23

Anne Comes to Grief in an Affair of Honour

ANNE had to live through more than two weeks, as it happened. Almost a
month having elapsed since the liniment cake episode, it was high time for
her to get into fresh trouble of some sort, little mistakes, such as absent-mindedly
emptying a pan of skim milk into a basket of yarn balls in the pantry instead of into
the pigs' bucket, and walking clean over the edge of the log bridge into the brook
while wrapped in imaginative reverie, not really being worth counting.

A week after the tea at the manse Diana Barry gave a party.

"Small and select," Anne assured Marilla. "Just the girls in our class."

They had a very good time and nothing untoward happened until after tea,
when they found themselves in the Barry garden, a little tired of all their games
and ripe for any enticing form of mischief which might present itself. This
presently took the form of "daring."

Daring was the fashionable amusement among the Avonlea small fry just
then. It had begun among the boys, but soon spread to the girls, and all the silly
things that were done in Avonlea that summer because the doers thereof were
"dared" to do them would fill a book by themselves.

First of all Carrie Sloane dared Ruby Gillis to climb to a certain point in the
huge old willow-tree before the front door; which Ruby Gillis, albeit in mortal
dread of the fat green caterpillars with which said tree was infested and with the
fear of her mother before her eyes if she should tear her new muslin dress, nimbly did, to the discomfiture of the aforesaid Carrie Sloane.

Then Josie Pye dared Jane Andrews to hop on her left leg around the garden
without stopping once or putting her right foot to the ground; which Jane Andrews gamely tried to do, but gave out at the third corner and had to confess
herself defeated.

Josie's triumph being rather more pronounced than good taste permitted,
Anne Shirley dared her to walk along the top of the board fence which bounded
the garden to the east. Now, to "walk" board fences requires more skill and
steadiness of head and heel than one might suppose who has never tried it. But
Josie Pye, if deficient in some qualities that make for popularity, had at least a
natural and inborn gift, duly cultivated, for walking board fences. Josie walked
the Barry fence with an airy unconcern which seemed to imply that a little thing
like that wasn't worth a "dare." Reluctant admiration greeted her exploit, for
most of the other girls could appreciate it, having suffered many things themselves in their efforts to walk fences. Josie descended from her perch, flushed
with victory, and darted a defiant glance at Anne.

Anne tossed her red braids.

"I don't think it's such a very wonderful thing to walk a little, low, board
fence," she said. "I knew a girl in Marysville who could walk the ridge-pole of a
roof."

"I don't believe it," said Josie flatly. "I don't believe anybody could walk a
ridge-pole. *You* couldn't, anyhow."

"Couldn't I?" cried Anne rashly.

"Then I dare you to do it," said Josie defiantly. "I dare you to climb up there and walk the ridge-pole of Mr. Barry's kitchen roof."

Anne turned pale, but there was clearly only one thing to be done. She walked towards the house, where a ladder was leaning against the kitchen roof. All the fifth-class girls said, "Oh!" partly in excitement, partly in dismay.

"Don't you do it, Anne," entreated Diana. "You'll fall off and be killed. Never mind Josie Pye. It isn't fair to dare anybody to do anything so dangerous."

"I must do it. My honour is at stake," said Anne solemnly. "I shall walk that ridge-pole, Diana, or perish in the attempt. If I am killed you are to have my pearl bead ring."

Anne climbed the ladder amid breathless silence, gained the ridge-pole, balanced herself uprightly on that precarious footing, and started to walk along it, dizzily conscious that she was uncomfortably high up in the world and that walking ridge-poles was not a thing in which your imagination helped you out much. Nevertheless, she managed to take several steps before the catastrophe came. Then she swayed, lost her balance, stumbled, staggered and fell, sliding down over the sun-baked roof and crashing off it through the tangle of Virginia creeper beneath—all before the dismayed circle below could give a simultaneous, terrified shriek.

If Anne had tumbled off the roof on the side up which she ascended Diana would probably have fallen heir to the pearl bead ring then and there. Fortunately she fell on the other side, where the roof extended down over the porch so nearly to the ground that a fall therefrom was a much less serious thing. Nevertheless, when Diana and the other girls had rushed frantically around the house—except Ruby Gillis, who remained as if rooted to the ground and went into hysterics—they found Anne lying all white and limp among the wreck and ruin of the Virginia creeper.

"Anne, are you killed?" shrieked Diana, throwing herself on her knees beside her friend. "Oh, Anne, dear Anne, speak just one word to me and tell me if you're killed."

To the immense relief of all the girls, and especially of Josie Pye, who, in spite of lack of imagination, had been seized with horrible visions of a future branded as the girl who was the cause of Anne Shirley's early and tragic death, Anne sat dizzily up and answered uncertainly:

"No, Diana, I am not killed, but I think I am rendered unconscious."

"Where?" sobbed Carrie Sloane. "Oh, where, Anne?"

Before Anne could answer Mrs. Barry appeared on the scene. At sight of her Anne tried to scramble to her feet, but sank back again with a sharp little cry of pain.

"What's the matter? Where have you hurt yourself?" demanded Mrs. Barry.

"My ankle," gasped Anne. "Oh, Diana, please find your father and ask him to take me home. I know I can never walk there. And I'm sure I couldn't hop so far on one foot when Jane couldn't even hop around the garden."

Marilla was out in the orchard picking a panful of summer apples when she saw Mr. Barry coming over the log bridge and up the slope, with Mrs. Barry beside him and a whole procession of little girls trailing after him. In his arms he carried Anne, whose head lay limply against his shoulder.

At that moment Marilla had a revelation. In the sudden stab of fear that pierced to her very heart she realized what Anne had come to mean to her. She would have admitted that she liked Anne—nay, that she was very fond of Anne.

But now she knew as she hurried wildly down the slope that Anne was dearer to her than anything on earth.

"Mr. Barry, what has happened to her?" she gasped, more white and shaken than the self-contained, sensible Marilla had been for many years.

Anne herself answered, lifting her head.

"Don't be very frightened, Marilla. I was walking the ridge-pole and I fell off. I expect I have sprained my ankle. But, Marilla, I might have broken my neck. Let us look on the bright side of things."

"I might have known you'd go and do something of the sort when I let you go to that party," said Marilla, sharp and shrewish in her very relief. "Bring her in here, Mr. Barry, and lay her on the sofa. Mercy me, the child has gone and fainted!"

It was quite true. Overcome by the pain of her injury, Anne had one more of her wishes granted to her. She had fainted dead away.

Matthew, hastily summoned from the harvest field, was straightway despatched for the doctor, who in due time came, to discover that the injury was more serious than they had supposed. Anne's ankle was broken.

That night, when Marilla went up to the east gable, where a white-faced girl was lying, a plaintive voice greeted her from the bed.

"Aren't you very sorry for me, Marilla?"

"It was your own fault," said Marilla, twitching down the blind and lighting a lamp.

"And that is just why you should be sorry for me," said Anne, "because the thought that it *is* all my own fault is what makes it so hard. If I could blame it on anybody I would feel so much better. But what would you have done, Marilla, if you had been dared to walk a ridge-pole?"

"I'd have stayed on good firm ground and let them dare away. Such absurdity!" said Marilla.

Anne sighed.

"But you have such strength of mind, Marilla. I haven't. I just felt that I couldn't bear Josie Pye's scorn. She would have crowed over me all my life. And I think I have been punished so much that you needn't be very cross with me, Marilla. It's not a bit nice to faint, after all. And the doctor hurt me dreadfully when he was setting my ankle. I won't be able to go around for six or seven weeks and I'll miss the new lady teacher. She won't be new any more by the time I'm able to go to school. And Gil—everybody will get ahead of me in class. Oh, I am an afflicted mortal. But I'll try to bear it all bravely if only you won't be cross with me, Marilla."

"There, there, I'm not cross," said Marilla. "You're an unlucky child, there's no doubt about that; but, as you say, you'll have the suffering of it. Here now, try and eat some supper."

"Isn't it fortunate I've got such an imagination?" said Anne. "It will help me through splendidly, I expect. What do people who haven't any imagination do when they break their bones, do you suppose, Marilla?"

Anne had good reason to bless her imagination many a time and oft during the tedious seven weeks that followed. But she was not solely dependent on it. She had many visitors and not a day passed without one or more of the school-girls dropping in to bring her flowers and books and tell her all the happenings in the juvenile world of Avonlea.

"Everybody has been so good and kind, Marilla," sighed Anne happily, on the day when she could first limp across the floor. "It isn't very pleasant to be laid up; but there *is* a bright side to it, Marilla. You find out how many friends you have. Why, even Superintendent Bell came to see me, and he's really a very fine man. Not a kindred spirit, of course; but still I like him and I'm awfully sorry I ever criticized his prayers. I believe now he really does mean them, only he has got into the habit of saying them as if he didn't. He could get over that if he'd take a little trouble. I gave him a good broad hint. I told him how hard I tried to make my own little private prayers interesting. He told me all about the time he broke his ankle when he was a boy. It does seem so strange to think of Superintendent Bell ever being a boy. Even my imagination has its limits for I can't imagine *that*. When I try to imagine him as a boy I see him with gray whiskers and spectacles, just as he looks in Sunday-school, only small. Now, it's so easy to imagine Mrs. Allan as a little girl. Mrs. Allan has been to see me fourteen times. Isn't that something to be proud of, Marilla? When a minister's wife has so many claims on her time! She is such a cheerful person to have visit you, too. She never tells you it's your own fault and she hopes you'll be a better girl on account of it. Mrs. Lynde always told me that when she came to see me; and she said it in a kind of way that made me feel she might hope I'd be a better girl, but didn't really believe I would. Even Josie Pye came to see me. I received her as politely as I could, because I think she was sorry she dared me to walk a ridge-pole. If I had been killed she would have had to carry a dark burden of remorse all her life. Diana has been a faithful friend. She's been over every day to cheer my lonely pillow. But oh, I shall be so glad when I can go to school for I've heard such exciting things about the new teacher. The girls all think she is perfectly sweet. Diana says she has the loveliest fair curly hair and such fascinating eyes. She dresses beautifully, and her sleeve puffs are bigger than anybody else's in Avonlea. Every other Friday afternoon she has recitations and everybody has to say a piece or take part in a dialogue. Oh, it's just glorious to think of it. Josie Pye says she hates it, but that is just because Josie has so little imagination. Diana and Ruby Gillis and Jane Andrews are preparing a dialogue, called 'A Morning Visit,' for next Friday. And the Friday afternoons they don't have recitations Miss Stacy takes them all to the woods for a 'field' day and they study ferns and flowers and birds. And they have physical culture exercises every morning and evening. Mrs. Lynde says she never heard of such goings-on and it all comes of having a lady teacher. But I think it must be splendid and I believe I shall find that Miss Stacy is a kindred spirit."

"There's one thing plain to be seen, Anne," said Marilla, "and that is that your fall off the Barry roof hasn't injured your tongue at all."

CHAPTER 24

Miss Stacy and Her Pupils Get Up a Concert

I T WAS October again when Anne was ready to go back to school—a glorious October, all red and gold, with mellow mornings when the valleys were filled with delicate mists as if the spirit of autumn had poured them in for the sun to drain—amethyst, pearl, silver, rose, and smoke-blue. The dews were so heavy that the fields glistened like cloth of silver and there were such heaps of rustling leaves in the hollows of many-stemmed woods to run crisply through. The Birch Path was a canopy of yellow and the ferns were sear and brown all along it. There was a tang in the very air that inspired the hearts of small maidens tripping, unlike snails, swiftly and willingly to school,[1] and it *was* jolly to be back again at the little brown desk beside Diana, with Ruby Gillis nodding across the aisle and Carrie Sloane sending up notes and Julia Bell passing a "chew" of gum down from the back seat. Anne drew a long breath of happiness as she sharpened her pencil and arranged her picture cards in her desk. Life was certainly very interesting.

In the new teacher she found another true and helpful friend. Miss Stacy was a bright, sympathetic young woman with the happy gift of winning and holding the affections of her pupils and bringing out the best that was in them mentally and morally. Anne expanded like a flower under this wholesome influence and carried home to the admiring Matthew and the critical Marilla glowing accounts of school work and aims.

"I love Miss Stacy with my whole heart, Marilla. She is so ladylike and she has such a sweet voice. When she pronounces my name I feel *instinctively* that she's spelling it with an *e*. We had recitations this afternoon. I just wish you could have been there to hear me recite 'Mary, Queen of Scots.'[2] I just put my whole soul into it. Ruby Gillis told me coming home that the way I said the line, 'Now for my father's arm, she said, my woman's heart farewell,' just made her blood run cold."

"Well now, you might recite it for me some of these days, out in the barn," suggested Matthew.

"Of course I will," said Anne meditatively, "but I won't be able to do it so well, I know. It won't be so exciting as it is when you have a whole schoolful before you hanging breathlessly on your words. I know I won't be able to make your blood run cold."

"Mrs. Lynde says it made *her* blood run cold to see the boys climbing to the very tops of those big trees on Bell's hill after crows' nests last Friday," said Marilla. "I wonder at Miss Stacy for encouraging it."

"But we wanted a crow's nest for nature study," explained Anne. "That was on our field afternoon. Field afternoons are splendid, Marilla. And Miss Stacy explains everything so beautifully. We have to write compositions on our field afternoons and I write the best ones."

"It's very vain of you to say so then. You'd better let your teacher say it."

"But she *did* say it, Marilla. And indeed I'm not vain about it. How can I be, when I'm such a dunce at geometry? Although I'm really beginning to see through it a little, too. Miss Stacy makes it so clear. Still, I'll never be good at it and I assure you it is a humbling reflection. But I love writing compositions. Mostly Miss Stacy lets us choose our own subjects; but next week we are to write a composition on some remarkable person. It's hard to choose among so many remarkable people who have lived. Mustn't it be splendid to be remarkable and have compositions written about you after you're dead? Oh, I would dearly love to be remarkable. I think when I grow up I'll be a trained nurse and go with the Red Crosses to the field of battle as a messenger of mercy. That is, if I don't go out as a foreign missionary. That would be very romantic, but one would have to be very good to be a missionary, and that would be a stumbling-block. We have physical culture exercises every day, too. They make you graceful and promote digestion."

---

1 *maidens tripping . . . to school*   See Shakespeare's *As You Like It* (2.7.144–46).
2 *Mary, Queen of Scots*   by Henry Glassford Bell (1803–1874).

"Promote fiddlesticks!" said Marilla, who honestly thought it was all non-sense.

But all the field afternoons and recitation Fridays and physical culture contortions paled before a project which Miss Stacy brought forward in November. This was that the scholars of Avonlea school should get up a concert and hold it in the hall on Christmas night, for the laudable purpose of helping to pay for a schoolhouse flag. The pupils one and all taking graciously to this plan, the preparations for a programme were begun at once. And of all the excited performers-elect none was so excited as Anne Shirley, who threw herself into the undertaking heart and soul, hampered as she was by Marilla's disapproval. Marilla thought it all rank foolishness.

"It's just filling your heads up with nonsense and taking time that ought to be put on your lessons," she grumbled. "I don't approve of children's getting up concerts and racing about to practices. It makes them vain and forward and fond of gadding."

"But think of the worthy object," pleaded Anne. "A flag will cultivate a spirit of patriotism, Marilla."

"Fudge! There's precious little patriotism in the thoughts of any of you. All you want is a good time."

"Well, when you can combine patriotism and fun, isn't it all right? Of course it's real nice to be getting up a concert. We're going to have six choruses and Diana is to sing a solo. I'm in two dialogues—'The Society for the Suppression of Gossip' and 'The Fairy Queen.'[3] The boys are going to have a dialogue, too. And I'm to have two recitations, Marilla. I just tremble when I think of it, but it's a nice thrilly kind of tremble. And we're to have a tableau at the last—'Faith, Hope and Charity.' Diana and Ruby and I are to be in it, all draped in white with flowing hair. I'm to be Hope, with my hands clasped—so—and my eyes uplifted. I'm going to practise my recitations in the garret. Don't be alarmed if you hear me groaning. I have to groan heartrendingly in one of them, and it's really hard to get up a good artistic groan, Marilla. Josie Pye is sulky because she didn't get the part she wanted in the dialogue. She wanted to be the fairy queen. That would have been ridiculous, for who ever heard of a fairy queen as fat as Josie? Fairy queens must be slender. Jane Andrews is to be the queen and I am to be one of her maids of honour. Josie says she thinks a red-haired fairy is just as ridiculous as a fat one, but I do not let myself mind what Josie says. I'm to have a wreath of white roses on my hair and Ruby Gillis is going to lend me her slippers because I haven't any of my own. It's necessary for fairies to have slippers, you know. You couldn't imagine a fairy wearing boots, could you? Especially with copper toes? We are going to decorate the hall with creeping spruce and fir mottoes with pink tissue-paper roses in them. And we are all to march in two by two after the audience is seated, while Emma White plays a march on the organ. Oh, Marilla, I know you are not so enthusiastic about it as I am, but don't you hope your little Anne will distinguish herself?"

"All I hope is that you'll behave yourself. I'll be heartily glad when all this fuss is over and you'll be able to settle down. You are simply good for nothing

---

3 *two dialogues . . . Fairy Queen* T. S. Denison's *Friday Afternoon Series of Dialogues . . . Suitable for Boys and Girls in School Entertainments* (1879) contains "The Society for the Suppression of Gossip," a one-act comedy in which the Society members vainly try to suppress their inclinations to gossip. "The Fairy Queen" by Thomas Percy (1729–1811) is a poetic monologue of fairy queen Mab derivative from speeches in Shakespeare's *Romeo and Juliet* and *A Midsummer Night's Dream.*

just now with your head stuffed full of dialogues and groans and tableaus. As for your tongue, it's a marvel it's not clean worn out."

Anne sighed and betook herself to the back yard, over which a young new moon was shining through the leafless poplar boughs from an apple-green western sky, and where Matthew was splitting wood. Anne perched herself on a block and talked the concert over with him, sure of an appreciative and sympathetic listener in this instance at least.

"Well now, I reckon it's going to be a pretty good concert. And I expect you'll do your part fine," he said, smiling down into her eager, vivacious little face. Anne smiled back at him. Those two were the best of friends and Matthew thanked his stars many a time and oft that he had nothing to do with bringing her up. That was Marilla's exclusive duty; if it had been his he would have been worried over frequent conflicts between inclination and said duty. As it was, he was free to "spoil Anne"—Marilla's phrasing—as much as he liked. But it was not such a bad arrangement after all; a little "appreciation" sometimes does quite as much good as all the conscientious "bringing up" in the world.

CHAPTER 25

Matthew Insists on Puffed Sleeves

MATTHEW was having a bad ten minutes of it. He had come into the kitchen, in the twilight of a cold, gray December evening, and had sat down in the wood-box corner to take off his heavy boots, unconscious of the fact that Anne and a bevy of her schoolmates were having a practice of "The Fairy Queen" in the sitting-room. Presently they came trooping through the hall and out into the kitchen, laughing and chattering gaily. They did not see Matthew, who shrank bashfully back into the shadows beyond the wood-box with a boot in one hand and a bootjack in the other, and he watched them shyly for the aforesaid ten minutes as they put on caps and jackets and talked about the dialogue and the concert. Anne stood among them, bright-eyed and animated as they; but Matthew suddenly became conscious that there was something about her different from her mates. And what worried Matthew was that the difference impressed him as being something that should not exist. Anne had a brighter face, and bigger, starrier eyes, and more delicate features than the others; even shy, unobservant Matthew had learned to take note of these things; but the difference that disturbed him did not consist in any of these respects. Then in what did it consist?

Matthew was haunted by this question long after the girls had gone, arm in arm, down the long, hard-frozen lane and Anne had betaken herself to her books. He could not refer it to Marilla, who, he felt, would be quite sure to sniff scornfully and remark that the only difference she saw between Anne and the other girls was that they sometimes kept their tongues quiet while Anne never did. This, Matthew felt, would be no great help.

He had recourse to his pipe that evening to help him study it out, much to Marilla's disgust. After two hours of smoking and hard reflection Matthew arrived at a solution of his problem. Anne was not dressed like the other girls!

The more Matthew thought about the matter the more he was convinced that Anne never had been dressed like the other girls—never since she had come to Green Gables. Marilla kept her clothed in plain, dark dresses, all made after the same unvarying pattern. If Matthew knew there was such a thing as fashion in dress it is much as he did; but he was quite sure that Anne's sleeves did not look at all like the sleeves the other girls wore. He recalled the cluster of little girls he had seen around her that evening—all gay in waists of red and blue and pink and white—and he wondered why Marilla always kept her so plainly and soberly gowned.

Of course, it must be all right. Marilla knew best and Marilla was bringing her up. Probably some wise, inscrutable motive was to be served thereby. But surely it would do no harm to let the child have one pretty dress—something like Diana Barry always wore. Matthew decided that he would give her one; that surely could not be objected to as an unwarranted putting in of his oar. Christmas was only a fortnight off. A nice new dress would be the very thing for a present. Matthew, with a sigh of satisfaction, put away his pipe and went to bed, while Marilla opened all the doors and aired the house.

The very next evening Matthew betook himself to Carmody to buy the dress, determined to get the worst over and have done with it. It would be, he felt assured, no trifling ordeal. There were some things Matthew could buy and prove himself no mean bargainer; but he knew he would be at the mercy of shopkeepers when it came to buying a girl's dress.

After much cogitation Matthew resolved to go to Samuel Lawson's store instead of William Blair's. To be sure, the Cuthberts always had gone to William Blair's; it was almost as much a matter of conscience with them as to attend the Presbyterian church and vote Conservative. But William Blair's two daughters frequently waited on customers there and Matthew held them in absolute dread. He could contrive to deal with them when he knew exactly what he wanted and could point it out; but in such a matter as this, requiring explanation and consultation, Matthew felt that he must be sure of a man behind the counter. So he would go to Lawson's, where Samuel or his son would wait on him.

Alas! Matthew did not know that Samuel, in the recent expansion of his business, had set up a lady clerk also; she was a niece of his wife's and a very dashing young person indeed, with a huge, drooping pompadour, big, rolling brown eyes, and a most extensive and bewildering smile. She was dressed with exceeding smartness and wore several bangle bracelets that glittered and rattled and tinkled with every movement of her hands. Matthew was covered with confusion at finding her there at all; and those bangles completely wrecked his wits at one fell swoop.

"What can I do for you this evening, Mr. Cuthbert?" Miss Lucilla Harris inquired, briskly and ingratiatingly, tapping the counter with both hands.

"Have you any—any—any—well now, say any garden rakes?" stammered Matthew.

Miss Harris looked somewhat surprised, as well she might, to hear a man inquiring for garden rakes in the middle of December.

"I believe we have one or two left over," she said, "but they're up-stairs in the lumber-room. I'll go and see."

During her absence Matthew collected his scattered senses for another effort.

When Miss Harris returned with the rake and cheerfully inquired: "Anything else to-night, Mr. Cuthbert?" Matthew took his courage in both hands and replied: "Well now, since you suggest it, I might as well—take—that is—look at—buy some—some hayseed."

Miss Harris had heard Matthew Cuthbert called odd. She now concluded that he was entirely crazy.

"We only keep hayseed in the spring," she explained loftily. "We've none on hand just now."

"Oh, certainly—certainly—just as you say," stammered unhappy Matthew, seizing the rake and making for the door. At the threshold he recollected that he had not paid for it and he turned miserably back. While Miss Harris was counting out his change he rallied his powers for a final desperate attempt.

"Well now—if it isn't too much trouble—I might as well—that is—I'd like to look at—at—some sugar."

"White or brown?" queried Miss Harris patiently.

"Oh—well now—brown," said Matthew feebly.

"There's a barrel of it over there," said Miss Harris, shaking her bangles at it. "It's the only kind we have."

"I'll—I'll take twenty pounds of it," said Matthew, with beads of perspiration standing on his forehead.

Matthew had driven half-way home before he was his own man again. It had been a gruesome experience but it served him right, he thought, for committing the heresy of going to a strange store. When he reached home he hid the rake in the tool-house, but the sugar he carried in to Marilla.

"Brown sugar!" exclaimed Marilla. "Whatever possessed you to get so much? You know I never use it except for the hired man's porridge or black fruit-cake. Jerry's gone and I've made my cake long ago. It's not good sugar, either—it's coarse and dark—William Blair doesn't usually keep sugar like that."

"I—I thought it might come in handy sometime," said Matthew, making good his escape.

When Matthew came to think the matter over he decided that a woman was required to cope with the situation. Marilla was out of the question. Matthew felt sure she would throw cold water on his project at once. Remained only Mrs. Lynde; for of no other woman in Avonlea would Matthew have dared to ask advice. To Mrs. Lynde he went accordingly, and that good lady promptly took the matter out of the harassed man's hands.

"Pick out a dress for you to give Anne? To be sure I will. I'm going to Carmody to-morrow and I'll attend to it. Have you something particular in mind? No? Well, I'll just go by my own judgment then. I believe a nice rich brown would just suit Anne, and William Blair has some new gloria[1] in that's real pretty. Perhaps you'd like me to make it up for her, too, seeing that if Marilla was to make it Anne would probably get wind of it before the time and spoil the surprise? Well, I'll do it. No, it isn't a mite of trouble. I like sewing. I'll make it to fit my niece, Jenny Gillis, for she and Anne are as like as two peas as far as figure goes."

"Well now, I'm much obliged," said Matthew, "and—and—I dunno—but I'd like—I think they make the sleeves different nowadays to what they used to be. If it wouldn't be asking too much I—I'd like them made in the new way."

"Puffs? Of course. You needn't worry a speck more about it, Matthew. I'll make it up in the very latest fashion," said Mrs. Lynde. To herself she added when Matthew had gone:

---

1 *gloria*   silk and cotton or wool in a close weave.

"It'll be a real satisfaction to see that poor child wearing something decent for once. The way Marilla dresses her is positively ridiculous, that's what, and I've ached to tell her so plainly a dozen times. I've held my tongue though, for I can see Marilla doesn't want advice and she thinks she knows more about bringing children up than I do for all she's an old maid. But that's always the way. Folks that has brought up children know that there's no hard and fast method in the world that'll suit every child. But them as never have think it's all as plain and easy as Rule of Three[2]—just set your three terms down so fashion, and the sum'll work out correct. But flesh and blood don't come under the head of arithmetic and that's where Marilla Cuthbert makes her mistake. I suppose she's trying to cultivate a spirit of humility in Anne by dressing her as she does; but it's more likely to cultivate envy and discontent. I'm sure the child must feel the difference between her clothes and the other girls'. But to think of Matthew taking notice of it! That man is waking up after being asleep for over sixty years."

Marilla knew all the following fortnight that Matthew had something on his mind, but what it was she could not guess, until Christmas Eve, when Mrs. Lynde brought up the new dress. Marilla behaved pretty well on the whole, although it is very likely she distrusted Mrs. Lynde's diplomatic explanation that she had made the dress because Matthew was afraid Anne would find out about it too soon if Marilla made it.

"So this is what Matthew has been looking so mysterious over and grinning about to himself for two weeks, is it?" she said a little stiffly but tolerantly. "I knew he was up to some foolishness. Well, I must say I don't think Anne needed any more dresses. I made her three good, warm, serviceable ones this fall, and anything more is sheer extravagance. There's enough material in those sleeves alone to make a waist, I declare there is. You'll just pamper Anne's vanity, Matthew, and she's as vain as a peacock now. Well, I hope she'll be satisfied at last, for I know she's been hankering after those silly sleeves ever since they came in, although she never said a word after the first. The puffs have been getting bigger and more ridiculous right along; they're as big as balloons now. Next year anybody who wears them will have to go through a door sideways."

Christmas morning broke on a beautiful white world. It had been a very mild December and people had looked forward to a green Christmas; but just enough snow fell softly in the night to transfigure Avonlea. Anne peeped out from her frosted gable window with delighted eyes. The firs in the Haunted Wood were all feathery and wonderful; the birches and wild cherry-trees were outlined in pearl; the ploughed fields were stretches of snowy dimples; and there was a crisp tang in the air that was glorious. Anne ran down-stairs singing until her voice reechoed through Green Gables.

"Merry Christmas, Marilla! Merry Christmas, Matthew! Isn't it a lovely Christmas? I'm so glad it's white. Any other kind of Christmas doesn't seem real, does it? I don't like green Christmases. They're *not* green—they're just nasty faded browns and grays. What makes people call them green? Why— why—Matthew, is that for me? Oh, Matthew!"

---

2 *Rule of Three*   "rule of three, a method of finding a fourth number from three given numbers, of which the first is in the same proportion to the second as the third is to the unknown fourth": *Oxford English Dictionary*, "rule" sb. 8. b. That is, a method of finding an unknown value in an equation of fractions.

Matthew had sheepishly unfolded the dress from its paper swathings and held it out with a deprecatory glance at Marilla, who feigned to be contemptuously filling the teapot, but nevertheless watched the scene out of the corner of her eye with a rather interested air.

Anne took the dress and looked at it in reverent silence. Oh, how pretty it was—a lovely soft brown gloria with all the gloss of silk; a skirt with dainty frills and shirrings;[3] a waist elaborately pintucked in the most fashionable way, with a little ruffle of filmy lace at the neck. But the sleeves—they were the crowning glory! Long elbow cuffs, and above them two beautiful puffs divided by rows of shirring and bows of brown silk ribbon.

"That's a Christmas present for you, Anne," said Matthew shyly. "Why—why—Anne, don't you like it? Well now—well now."

For Anne's eyes had suddenly filled with tears.

"*Like* it! Oh, Matthew!" Anne laid the dress over a chair and clasped her hands. "Matthew, it's perfectly exquisite. Oh, I can never thank you enough. Look at those sleeves! Oh, it seems to me this must be a happy dream."

"Well, well, let us have breakfast," interrupted Marilla. "I must say, Anne, I don't think you needed the dress; but since Matthew has got it for you, see that you take good care of it. There's a hair ribbon Mrs. Lynde left for you. It's brown, to match the dress. Come now, sit in."

"I don't see how I'm going to eat breakfast," said Anne rapturously. "Breakfast seems so commonplace at such an exciting moment. I'd rather feast my eyes on that dress. I'm so glad that puffed sleeves are still fashionable. It did seem to me that I'd never get over it if they went out before I had a dress with them. I'd never have felt quite satisfied, you see. It was lovely of Mrs. Lynde to give me the ribbon, too. I feel that I ought to be a very good girl indeed. It's at times like this I'm sorry I'm not a model little girl; and I always resolve that I will be in future. But somehow it's hard to carry out your resolutions when irresistible temptations come. Still, I really will make an extra effort after this."

When the commonplace breakfast was over Diana appeared, crossing the white log bridge in the hollow, a gay little figure in her crimson ulster. Anne flew down the slope to meet her.

"Merry Christmas, Diana! And oh, it's a wonderful Christmas. I've something splendid to show you. Matthew has given me the loveliest dress, with *such* sleeves. I couldn't even imagine any nicer."

"I've got something more for you," said Diana breathlessly. "Here—this box. Aunt Josephine sent us out a big box with ever so many things in it—and this is for you. I'd have brought it over last night, but it didn't come until after dark, and I never feel very comfortable coming through the Haunted Wood in the dark now."

Anne opened the box and peeped in. First a card with "For the Anne-girl and Merry Christmas," written on it; and then, a pair of the daintiest little kid slippers, with beaded toes and satin bows and glistening buckles.

"Oh," said Anne, "Diana, this is too much. I must be dreaming."

"*I* call it providential," said Diana. "You won't have to borrow Ruby's slippers now, and that's a blessing, for they're two sizes too big for you, and it would be awful to hear a fairy shuffling. Josie Pye would be delighted. Mind you, Rob Wright went home with Gertie Pye from the practice night before last. Did you ever hear anything equal to that?"

---

3 *shirrings*   in dressmaking, a series of stitchings running closely parallel to gather the material.

All the Avonlea scholars were in a fever of excitement that day, for the hall had to be decorated and a last grand rehearsal held.

The concert came off in the evening and was a pronounced success. The little hall was crowded; all the performers did excellently well, but Anne was the bright particular star of the occasion, as even envy, in the shape of Josie Pye, dared not deny.

"Oh, hasn't it been a brilliant evening?" sighed Anne, when it was all over and she and Diana were walking home together under a dark, starry sky.

"Everything went off very well," said Diana practically. "I guess we must have made as much as ten dollars. Mind you, Mr. Allan is going to send an account of it to the Charlottetown papers."

"Oh, Diana, will we really see our names in print? It makes me thrill to think of it. Your solo was perfectly elegant, Diana. I felt prouder than you did when it was encored. I just said to myself, 'It is my dear bosom friend who is so honoured.'"

"Well, your recitations just brought down the house, Anne. That sad one was simply splendid."

"Oh, I was so nervous, Diana. When Mr. Allan called out my name I really cannot tell how I ever got up on that platform. I felt as if a million eyes were looking at me and through me, and for one dreadful moment I was sure I couldn't begin at all. Then I thought of my lovely puffed sleeves and took courage. I knew that I must live up to those sleeves, Diana. So I started in, and my voice seemed to be coming from ever so far away. I just felt like a parrot. It's providential that I practised those recitations so often up in the garret, or I'd never have been able to get through. Did I groan all right?"

"Yes, indeed, you groaned lovely," assured Diana.

"I saw old Mrs. Sloane wiping away tears when I sat down. It was splendid to think I had touched somebody's heart. It's so romantic to take part in a concert, isn't it? Oh, it's been a very memorable occasion indeed."

"Wasn't the boys' dialogue fine?" said Diana. "Gilbert Blythe was just splendid. Anne, I do think it's awful mean the way you treat Gil. Wait till I tell you. When you ran off the platform after the fairy dialogue one of your roses fell out of your hair. I saw Gil pick it up and put it in his breast-pocket. There now. You're so romantic that I'm sure you ought to be pleased at that."

"It's nothing to me what that person does," said Anne loftily. "I simply never waste a thought on him, Diana."

That night Marilla and Matthew, who had been out to a concert for the first time in twenty years, sat for awhile by the kitchen fire after Anne had gone to bed.

"Well now, I guess our Anne did as well as any of them," said Matthew proudly.

"Yes, she did," admitted Marilla. "She's a bright child, Matthew. And she looked real nice, too. I've been kind of opposed to this concert scheme, but I suppose there's no real harm in it after all. Anyhow, I was proud of Anne tonight, although I'm not going to tell her so."

"Well now, I was proud of her and I did tell her so 'fore she went up-stairs," said Matthew. "We must see what we can do for her some of these days, Marilla. I guess she'll need something more than Avonlea school by and by."

"There's time enough to think of that," said Marilla. "She's only thirteen in March. Though to-night it struck me she was growing quite a big girl. Mrs. Lynde made that dress a mite too long, and it makes Anne look so tall. She's quick to learn and I guess the best thing we can do for her will be to send her to Queen's after a spell. But nothing need be said about that for a year or two yet."

"Well now, it'll do no harm to be thinking it over off and on," said Matthew. "Things like that are all the better for lots of thinking over."

CHAPTER 26

The Story Club Is Formed

JUNIOR Avonlea found it hard to settle down to humdrum existence again. To Anne in particular things seemed fearfully flat, stale, and unprofitable after the goblet of excitement she had been sipping for weeks. Could she go back to the former quiet pleasures of those far-away days before the concert? At first, as she told Diana, she did not really think she could.

"I'm positively certain, Diana, that life can never be quite the same again as it was in those olden days," she said mournfully, as if referring to a period of at least fifty years back. "Perhaps after awhile I'll get used to it, but I'm afraid concerts spoil people for every-day life. I suppose that is why Marilla disapproves of them. Marilla is such a sensible woman. It must be a great deal better to be sensible; but still, I don't believe I'd really want to be a sensible person, because they are so unromantic. Mrs. Lynde says there is no danger of my ever being one, but you can never tell. I feel just now that I may grow up to be sensible yet. But perhaps that is only because I'm tired. I simply couldn't sleep last night for ever so long. I just lay awake and imagined the concert over and over again. That's one splendid thing about such affairs—it's so lovely to look back to them."

Eventually, however, Avonlea school slipped back into its old groove and took up its old interests. To be sure, the concert left traces. Ruby Gillis and Emma White, who had quarrelled over a point of precedence in their platform seats, no longer sat at the same desk, and a promising friendship of three years was broken up. Josie Pye and Julia Bell did not "speak" for three months, because Josie Pye had told Bessie Wright that Julia Bell's bow when she got up to recite made her think of a chicken jerking its head, and Bessie told Julia. None of the Sloanes would have any dealings with the Bells, because the Bells had declared that the Sloanes had too much to do in the programme, and the Sloanes had retorted that the Bells were not capable of doing the little they had to do properly. Finally, Charlie Sloane fought Moody Spurgeon MacPherson, because Moody Spurgeon had said that Anne Shirley put on airs about her recitations, and Moody Spurgeon was "licked;" consequently Moody Spurgeon's sister, Ella May, would not "speak" to Anne Shirley all the rest of the winter. With the exception of these trifling frictions, work in Miss Stacy's little kingdom went on with regularity and smoothness.

The winter weeks slipped by. It was an unusually mild winter, with so little snow that Anne and Diana could go to school nearly every day by way of the Birch Path. On Anne's birthday they were tripping lightly down it, keeping eyes and ears alert amid all their chatter, for Miss Stacy had told them that they must soon write a composition on "A Winter's Walk in the Woods," and it behooved them to be observant.

"Just think, Diana, I'm thirteen years old to-day," remarked Anne in an awed voice. "I can scarcely realize that I'm in my teens. When I woke this morning it seemed to me that everything must be different. You've been thirteen for a month, so I suppose it doesn't seem such a novelty to you as it does to me. It makes life seem so much more interesting. In two more years I'll be really grown up. It's a great comfort to think that I'll be able to use big words then without being laughed at."

"Ruby Gillis says she means to have a beau as soon as she's fifteen," said Diana.

"Ruby Gillis thinks of nothing but beaus," said Anne disdainfully. "She's actually delighted when any one writes her name up in a take-notice for all she pretends to be so mad. But I'm afraid that is an uncharitable speech. Mrs. Allan says we should never make uncharitable speeches; but they do slip out so often before you think, don't they? I simply can't talk about Josie Pye without making an uncharitable speech, so I never mention her at all. You may have noticed that. I'm trying to be as much like Mrs. Allan as I possibly can, for I think she's perfect. Mr. Allan thinks so too. Mrs. Lynde says he just worships the ground she treads on and she doesn't really think it right for a minister to set his affections so much on a mortal being. But then, Diana, even ministers are human and have their besetting sins just like everybody else. I had such an interesting talk with Mrs. Allan about besetting sins last Sunday afternoon. There are just a few things it's proper to talk about on Sundays and that is one of them. My besetting sin is imagining too much and forgetting my duties. I'm striving very hard to overcome it and now that I'm really thirteen perhaps I'll get on better."

"In four more years we'll be able to put our hair up," said Diana. "Alice Bell is only sixteen and she is wearing hers up, but I think that's ridiculous. I shall wait until I'm seventeen."

"If I had Alice Bell's crooked nose," said Anne decidedly, "I wouldn't—but there! I won't say what I was going to because it was extremely uncharitable. Besides, I was comparing it with my own nose and that's vanity. I'm afraid I think too much about my nose ever since I heard that compliment about it long ago. It really is a great comfort to me. Oh, Diana, look, there's a rabbit. That's something to remember for our woods composition. I really think the woods are just as lovely in winter as in summer. They're so white and still, as if they were asleep and dreaming pretty dreams."

"I won't mind writing that composition when its time comes," sighed Diana. "I can manage to write about the woods, but the one we're to hand in Monday is terrible. The idea of Miss Stacy telling us to write a story out of our own heads!"

"Why, it's as easy as wink," said Anne.

"It's easy for you because you have an imagination," retorted Diana, "but what would you do if you had been born without one? I suppose you have your composition all done?"

Anne nodded, trying hard not to look virtuously complacent and failing miserably.

"I wrote it last Monday evening. It's called 'The Jealous Rival; or, in Death Not Divided.' I read it to Marilla and she said it was stuff and nonsense. Then I read it to Matthew and he said it was fine. That is the kind of critic I like. It's a sad, sweet story. I just cried like a child while I was writing it. It's about two beautiful maidens called Cordelia Montmorency and Geraldine Seymour who lived in the same village and were devotedly attached to each other. Cordelia was a regal brunette with a coronet of midnight hair and duskly flashing eyes. Geraldine was a queenly blonde with hair like spun gold and velvety purple eyes."

"I never saw anybody with purple eyes," said Diana dubiously.

"Neither did I. I just imagined them. I wanted something out of the common. Geraldine had an alabaster brow, too. I've found out what an alabaster brow is. That is one of the advantages of being thirteen. You know so much more than you did when you were only twelve."

"Well, what became of Cordelia and Geraldine?" asked Diana, who was beginning to feel rather interested in their fate.

"They grew in beauty side by side until they were sixteen. Then Bertram De-Vere came to their native village and fell in love with the fair Geraldine. He saved her life when her horse ran away with her in a carriage, and she fainted in his arms and he carried her home three miles; because, you understand, the carriage was all smashed up. I found it rather hard to imagine the proposal because I had no experience to go by. I asked Ruby Gillis if she knew anything about how men proposed because I thought she'd likely be an authority on the subject, having so many sisters married. Ruby told me she was hid in the hall pantry when Malcolm Andrews proposed to her sister Susan. She said Malcolm told Susan that his dad had given him the farm in his own name and then said, 'What do you say, darling pet, if we get hitched this fall?' And Susan said, 'Yes—no—I don't know—let me see,'—and there they were, engaged as quick as that. But I didn't think that sort of a proposal was a very romantic one, so in the end I had to imagine it out as well as I could. I made it very flowery and poetical and Bertram went on his knees, although Ruby Gillis says it isn't done nowadays. Geraldine accepted him in a speech a page long. I can tell you I took a lot of trouble with that speech. I rewrote it five times and I look upon it as my masterpiece. Bertram gave her a diamond ring and a ruby necklace and told her they would go to Europe for a wedding tour, for he was immensely wealthy. But then, alas, shadows began to darken over their path. Cordelia was secretly in love with Bertram herself and when Geraldine told her about the engagement she was simply furious, especially when she saw the necklace and the diamond ring. All her affection for Geraldine turned to bitter hate and she vowed that she should never marry Bertram. But she pretended to be Geraldine's friend the same as ever. One evening they were standing on the bridge over a rushing turbulent stream and Cordelia, thinking they were alone, pushed Geraldine over the brink with a wild, mocking, 'Ha, ha, ha.' But Bertram saw it all and he at once plunged into the current, exclaiming, 'I will save thee, my peerless Geraldine.' But alas, he had forgotten he couldn't swim, and they were both drowned, clasped in each other's arms. Their bodies were washed ashore soon afterwards. They were buried in the one grave and their funeral was most imposing, Diana. It's so much more romantic to end a story up with a funeral than a wedding. As for Cordelia, she went insane with remorse and was shut up in a lunatic asylum. I thought that was a poetical retribution for her crime."

"How perfectly lovely!" sighed Diana, who belonged to Matthew's school of critics. "I don't see how you can make up such thrilling things out of your own head, Anne. I wish my imagination was as good as yours."

"It would be if you'd only cultivate it," said Anne cheeringly. "I've just thought of a plan, Diana. Let's you and I have a story club all our own and write stories for practice. I'll help you along until you can do them by yourself. You ought to cultivate your imagination, you know. Miss Stacy says so. Only we must take the right way. I told her about the Haunted Wood, but she said we went the wrong way about it in that."

This was how the story club came into existence. It was limited to Diana and Anne at first, but soon it was extended to include Jane Andrews and Ruby Gillis and one or two others who felt that their imaginations needed cultivating. No boys were allowed in it—although Ruby Gillis opined that their admission would make it more exciting—and each member had to produce one story a week.

"It's extremely interesting," Anne told Marilla. "Each girl has to read her story out loud and then we talk it over. We are going to keep them all sacredly and have them to read to our descendants. We each write under a nom-de-plume. Mine is Rosamond Montmorency. All the girls do pretty well. Ruby Gillis is rather sentimental. She puts too much love-making into her stories and you know too much is worse than too little. Jane never puts any because she says it makes her feel so silly when she has to read it out loud. Jane's stories are extremely sensible. Then Diana puts too many murders into hers. She says most of the time she doesn't know what to do with the people so she kills them off to get rid of them. I mostly always have to tell them what to write about, but that isn't hard for I've millions of ideas."

"I think this story-writing business is the foolishest yet," scoffed Marilla. "You'll get a pack of nonsense into your heads and waste time that should be put on your lessons. Reading stories is bad enough but writing them is worse."

"But we're so careful to put a moral into them all, Marilla," explained Anne. "I insist upon that. All the good people are rewarded and all the bad ones are suitably punished. I'm sure that must have a wholesome effect. The moral is the great thing. Mr. Allan says so. I read one of my stories to him and Mrs. Allan and they both agreed that the moral was excellent. Only they laughed in the wrong places. I like it better when people cry. Jane and Ruby almost always cry when I come to the pathetic parts. Diana wrote her Aunt Josephine about our club and her Aunt Josephine wrote back that we were to send her some of our stories. So we copied out four of our very best and sent them. Miss Josephine Barry wrote back that she had never read anything so amusing in her life. That kind of puzzled us because the stories were all very pathetic and almost everybody died. But I'm glad Miss Barry liked them. It shows our club is doing some good in the world. Mrs. Allan says that ought to be our object in everything. I do really try to make it my object but I forget so often when I'm having fun. I hope I shall be a little like Mrs. Allan when I grow up. Do you think there is any prospect of it, Marilla?"

"I shouldn't say there was a great deal," was Marilla's encouraging answer. "I'm sure Mrs. Allan was never such a silly, forgetful little girl as you are."

"No; but she wasn't always so good as she is now either," said Anne seriously. "She told me so herself—that is, she said she was a dreadful mischief when she was a girl and was always getting into scrapes. I felt so encouraged when I heard that. Is it very wicked of me, Marilla, to feel encouraged when I hear that other people have been bad and mischievous? Mrs. Lynde says it is. Mrs. Lynde says she always feels shocked when she hears of any one ever having been naughty, no matter how small they were. Mrs. Lynde says she once heard a minister confess that when he was a boy he stole a strawberry tart out of his aunt's pantry and she never had any respect for that minister again. Now, I wouldn't have felt that way. I'd have thought that it was real noble of him to confess it, and I'd have thought what an encouraging thing it would be for small boys nowadays who do naughty things and are sorry for them to know that perhaps they may grow up to be ministers in spite of it. That's how I'd feel, Marilla."

"The way I feel, at present, Anne," said Marilla, "is that it's high time you had those dishes washed. You've taken half an hour longer than you should with all your chattering. Learn to work first and talk afterwards."

CHAPTER 27

Vanity and Vexation of Spirit[1]

MARILLA, walking home one late April evening from an Aid meeting, real-ized that the winter was over and gone with the thrill of delight that spring never fails to bring to the oldest and saddest as well as to the youngest and merriest. Marilla was not given to subjective analysis of her thoughts and feelings. She probably imagined that she was thinking about the Aids and their missionary box and the new carpet for the vestry-room, but under these reflec-tions was a harmonious consciousness of red fields smoking into pale-purply mists in the declining sun, of long, sharp-pointed fir shadows falling over the meadow beyond the brook, of still, crimson-budded maples around a mirror-like wood-pool, of a wakening in the world and a stir of hidden pulses under the gray sod. The spring was abroad in the land and Marilla's sober, middle-aged step was lighter and swifter because of its deep, primal gladness.

Her eyes dwelt affectionately on Green Gables, peering through its network of trees and reflecting the sunlight back from its windows in several little corus-cations of glory. Marilla, as she picked her steps along the damp lane, thought that it was really a satisfaction to know that she was going home to a briskly snapping wood fire and a table nicely spread for tea, instead of to the cold com-fort of old Aid meeting evenings before Anne had come to Green Gables.

Consequently, when Marilla entered her kitchen and found the fire black out, with no sign of Anne anywhere, she felt justly disappointed and irritated. She had told Anne to be sure and have tea ready at five o'clock, but now she must hurry to take off her second-best dress and prepare the meal herself against Matthew's return from ploughing.

"I'll settle Miss Anne when she comes home," said Marilla grimly, as she shaved up kindlings with a carving knife and more vim than was strictly neces-sary. Matthew had come in and was waiting patiently for his tea in his corner. "She's gadding off somewhere with Diana, writing stories or practising dia-logues or some such tomfoolery, and never thinking once about the time or her duties. She's just got to be pulled up short and sudden on this sort of thing. I don't care if Mrs. Allan does say she's the brightest and sweetest child she ever knew. She may be bright and sweet enough, but her head is full of nonsense and there's never any knowing what shape it'll break out in next. Just as soon as she grows out of one freak she takes up with another. But there! Here I am saying the very thing I was so riled with Rachel Lynde for saying at the Aid to-day. I was real glad when Mrs. Allan spoke up for Anne, for if she hadn't I know I'd have said something too sharp to Rachel before everybody. Anne's got plenty of faults, goodness knows, and far be it from me to deny it. But I'm bringing her up and not Rachel Lynde, who'd pick faults in the Angel Gabriel himself if he lived in Avonlea. Just the same, Anne has no business to leave the house like this when I told her she was to stay home this afternoon and look after things. I must say, with all her faults, I never found her disobedient or untrustworthy be-fore and I'm real sorry to find her so now."

"Well now, I dunno," said Matthew, who, being patient and wise and, above all, hungry, had deemed it best to let Marilla talk her wrath out unhindered, having

---

1 *Vanity and Vexation of Spirit*   See Ecclesiastes 1.14.

learned by experience that she got through with whatever work was on hand much quicker if not delayed by untimely argument. "Perhaps you're judging her too hasty, Marilla. Don't call her untrustworthy until you're sure she has disobeyed you. Mebbe it can all be explained—Anne's a great hand at explaining."

"She's not here when I told her to stay," retorted Marilla. "I reckon she'll find it hard to explain *that* to my satisfaction. Of course I knew you'd take her part, Matthew. But I'm bringing her up, not you."

It was dark when supper was ready, and still no sign of Anne, coming hurriedly over the log bridge or up Lovers' Lane, breathless and repentant with a sense of neglected duties. Marilla washed and put away the dishes grimly. Then, wanting a candle to light her down cellar, she went up to the east gable for the one that generally stood on Anne's table. Lighting it, she turned around to see Anne herself lying on the bed, face downward among the pillows.

"Mercy on us," said astonished Marilla, "have you been asleep, Anne?"

"No," was the muffled reply.

"Are you sick then?" demanded Marilla anxiously, going over to the bed.

Anne cowered deeper into her pillows as if desirous of hiding herself for ever from mortal eyes.

"No. But please, Marilla, go away and don't look at me. I'm in the depths of despair and I don't care who gets head in class or writes the best composition or sings in the Sunday-school choir any more. Little things like that are of no importance now because I don't suppose I'll ever be able to go anywhere again. My career is closed. Please, Marilla, go away and don't look at me."

"Did any one ever hear the like?" the mystified Marilla wanted to know. "Anne Shirley, whatever is the matter with you? What have you done? Get right up this minute and tell me. This minute, I say. There now, what is it?"

Anne had slid to the floor in despairing obedience.

"Look at my hair, Marilla," she whispered.

Accordingly, Marilla lifted her candle and looked scrutinizingly at Anne's hair, flowing in heavy masses down her back. It certainly had a very strange appearance.

"Anne Shirley, what have you done to your hair? Why, it's *green!*"

Green it might be called, if it were any earthly colour—a queer, dull, bronzy green, with streaks here there of the original red to heighten the ghastly effect. Never in all her life had Marilla seen anything so grotesque as Anne's hair at that moment.

"Yes, it's green," moaned Anne. "I thought nothing could be as bad as red hair. But now I know it's ten times worse to have green hair. Oh, Marilla, you little know how utterly wretched I am."

"I little know how you got into this fix, but I mean to find out," said Marilla. "Come right down to the kitchen—it's too cold up here—and tell me just what you've done. I've been expecting something queer for some time. You haven't got into any scrape for over two months, and I was sure another one was due. Now, then, what did you do to your hair?"

"I dyed it."

"Dyed it! Dyed your hair! Anne Shirley, didn't you know it was a wicked thing to do?"

"Yes, I knew it was a little wicked," admitted Anne. "But I thought it was worth while to be a little wicked to get rid of red hair. I counted the cost, Marilla. Besides, I meant to be extra good in other ways to make up for it."

"Well," said Marilla sarcastically, "if I'd decided it was worth while to dye my hair I'd have dyed it a decent colour at least. I wouldn't have dyed it green."

"But I didn't mean to dye it green, Marilla," protested Anne dejectedly. "If I was wicked I meant to be wicked to some purpose. He said it would turn my hair a beautiful raven black—he positively assured me that it would. How could I doubt his word, Marilla? I know what it feels like to have your word doubted. And Mrs. Allan says we should never suspect any one of not telling us the truth unless we have proof that they're not. I have proof now—green hair is proof enough for anybody. But I hadn't then and I believed every word he said *implicitly.*"

"Who said? Who are you talking about?"

"The pedlar that was here this afternoon. I bought the dye from him."

"Anne Shirley, how often have I told you never to let one of those Italians in the house! I don't believe in encouraging them to come around at all."

"Oh, I didn't let him in the house. I remembered what you told me, and I went out, carefully shut the door, and looked at his things on the step. Besides, he wasn't an Italian—he was a German Jew. He had a big box full of very interesting things and he told me he was working hard to make enough money to bring his wife and children out from Germany. He spoke so feelingly about them that it touched my heart. I wanted to buy something from him to help him in such a worthy object. Then all at once I saw the bottle of hair dye. The pedlar said it was warranted to dye any hair a beautiful raven black and wouldn't wash off. In a trice I saw myself with beautiful raven black hair and the temptation was irresistible. But the price of the bottle was seventy-five cents and I had only fifty cents left out of my chicken money. I think the pedlar had a very kind heart, for he said that, seeing it was me, he'd sell it for fifty cents and that was just giving it away. So I bought it, and as soon as he had gone I came up here and applied it with an old hair-brush as the directions said. I used up the whole bottle, and oh, Marilla, when I saw the dreadful colour it turned my hair I repented of being wicked, I can tell you. And I've been repenting ever since."

"Well, I hope you'll repent to good purpose," said Marilla severely, "and that you've got your eyes opened to where your vanity has led you, Anne. Goodness knows what's to be done. I suppose the first thing is to give your hair a good washing and see if that will do any good."

Accordingly, Anne washed her hair, scrubbing it vigorously with soap and water, but for all the difference it made she might as well have been scouring its original red. The pedlar had certainly spoken the truth when he declared that the dye wouldn't wash off, however his veracity might be impeached in other respects.

"Oh, Marilla, what shall I do?" questioned Anne in tears. "I can never live this down. People have pretty well forgotten my other mistakes—the liniment cake and setting Diana drunk and flying into a temper with Mrs. Lynde. But they'll never forget this. They will think I am not respectable. Oh, Marilla, 'what a tangled web we weave when first we practise to deceive.'[2] That is poetry, but it is true. And oh, how Josie Pye will laugh! Marilla, I *cannot* face Josie Pye. I am the unhappiest girl in Prince Edward Island."

Anne's unhappiness continued for a week. During that time she went nowhere and shampooed her hair every day. Diana alone of outsiders knew the fatal secret, but she promised solemnly never to tell, and it may be stated here and now that she kept her word. At the end of the week Marilla said decidedly:

"It's no use, Anne. That is fast dye if ever there was any. Your hair must be cut off; there is no other way. You can't go out with it looking like that."

---

2 *what ... deceive* See *Marmion*, 6.17.27–28, by Walter Scott (1771–1832).

Anne's lips quivered, but she realized the bitter truth of Marilla's remarks. With a dismal sigh she went for the scissors.

"Please cut it off at once, Marilla, and have it over. Oh, I feel that my heart is broken. This is such an unromantic affliction. The girls in books lose their hair in fevers or sell it to get money for some good deed, and I'm sure I wouldn't mind losing my hair in some such fashion half so much. But there is nothing comforting in having your hair cut off because you've dyed it a dreadful colour, is there? I'm going to weep all the time you're cutting it off, if it won't interfere. It seems such a tragic thing."

Anne wept then, but later on, when she went upstairs and looked in the glass, she was calm with despair. Marilla had done her work thoroughly and it had been necessary to shingle the hair as closely as possible. The result was not becoming, to state the case as mildly as may be. Anne promptly turned her glass to the wall.

"I'll never, never look at myself again until my hair grows," she exclaimed passionately.

Then she suddenly righted the glass.

"Yes, I will, too. I'd do penance for being wicked that way. I'll look at myself every time I come to my room and see how ugly I am. And I won't try to imagine it away, either. I never thought I was vain about my hair, of all things, but now I know I was, in spite of its being red, because it was so long and thick and curly. I expect something will happen to my nose next."

Anne's clipped head made a sensation in school on the following Monday, but to her relief nobody guessed the real reason for it, not even Josie Pye, who, however, did not fail to inform Anne that she looked like a perfect scarecrow.

"I didn't say anything when Josie said that to me," Anne confided that evening to Marilla, who was lying on the sofa after one of her headaches, "because I thought it was part of my punishment and I ought to bear it patiently. It's hard to be told you look like a scarecrow and I wanted to say something back. But I didn't. I just swept her one scornful look and then I forgave her. It makes you feel very virtuous when you forgive people, doesn't it? I mean to devote all my energies to being good after this and I shall never try to be beautiful again. Of course it's better to be good. I know it is, but it's sometimes so hard to believe a thing even when you know it. I do really want to be good, Marilla, like you and Mrs. Allan and Miss Stacy, and grow up to be a credit to you. Diana says when my hair begins to grow to tie a black velvet ribbon around my head with a bow at one side. She says she thinks it will be very becoming. I will call it a snood—that sounds so romantic. But am I talking too much, Marilla? Does it hurt your head?"

"My head is better now. It was terrible bad this afternoon, though. These headaches of mine are getting worse and worse. I'll have to see a doctor about them. As for your chatter, I don't know that I mind it—I've got so used to it."

Which was Marilla's way of saying that she liked to hear it.

CHAPTER 28

An Unfortunate Lily Maid

"OF COURSE you must be Elaine, Anne," said Diana. "I could never have the courage to float down there."

"Nor I," said Ruby Gillis with a shiver. "I don't mind floating down when there's two or three of us in the flat and we can sit up. It's fun then. But to lie down and pretend I was dead—I just couldn't. I'd die really of fright."

"Of course it would be romantic," conceded Jane Andrews. "But I know I couldn't keep still. I'd be popping up every minute or so to see where I was and if I wasn't drifting too far out. And you know, Anne, that would spoil the effect."

"But it's so ridiculous to have a red-headed Elaine," mourned Anne. "I'm not afraid to float down and I'd *love* to be Elaine. But it's ridiculous just the same. Ruby ought to be Elaine because she is so fair and has such lovely long golden hair—Elaine had 'all her bright hair streaming down,' you know. And Elaine was the lily maid.[1] Now, a red-haired person cannot be a lily maid."

"Your complexion is just as fair as Ruby's," said Diana earnestly, "and your hair is ever so much darker than it used to be before you cut it."

"Oh, do you really think so?" exclaimed Anne, flushing sensitively with delight. "I've sometimes thought it was myself—but I never dared to ask any one for fear she would tell me it wasn't. Do you think it could be called auburn now, Diana?"

"Yes, and I think it is real pretty," said Diana, looking admiringly at the short, silky curls that clustered over Anne's head and were held in place by a very jaunty black velvet ribbon and bow.

They were standing on the bank of the pond, below Orchard Slope, where a little headland fringed with birches ran out from the bank; at its tip was a small wooden platform built out into the water for the convenience of fishermen and duck hunters. Ruby and Jane were spending the midsummer afternoon with Diana, and Anne had come over to play with them.

Anne and Diana had spent most of their playtime that summer on and about the pond. Idlewild was a thing of the past, Mr. Bell having ruthlessly cut down the little circle of trees in his back pasture in the spring. Anne had sat among the stumps and wept, not without an eye to the romance of it; but she was speedily consoled, for, after all, as she and Diana said, big girls of thirteen, going on fourteen, were too old for such childish amusements as playhouses, and there were more fascinating sports to be found about the pond. It was splendid to fish for trout over the bridge and the two girls learned to row themselves about in the little flat-bottomed dory Mr. Barry kept for duck shooting.

It was Anne's idea that they dramatize Elaine. They had studied Tennyson's poem in school the preceding winter, the Superintendent of Education having prescribed it in the English course for the Prince Edward Island schools. They had analyzed and parsed it and torn it to pieces in general until it was a wonder there was any meaning at all left in it for them, but at least the fair lily maid and Lancelot and Guinevere and King Arthur had become very real people to them, and Anne was devoured by secret regret that she had not been born in Camelot. Those days, she said, were so much more romantic than the present.

Anne's plan was hailed with enthusiasm. The girls had discovered that if the flat were pushed off from the landing-place it would drift down with the current under the bridge and finally strand itself on another headland lower down which ran out at a curve in the pond. They had often gone down like this and nothing could be more convenient for playing Elaine.

"Well, I'll be Elaine," said Anne, yielding reluctantly, for, although she would have been delighted to play the principal character, yet her artistic sense de-

---

1 *all her bright hair . . . lily maid* In *Idylls of the King*, by Alfred Tennyson (1809–1892), Elaine, "the lily maid of Astolat," dies for love of Sir Launcelot. Her body is placed in a boat and is oared by a deaf and dumb servitor downstream to Camelot.

manded fitness for it and this, she felt, her limitations made impossible. "Ruby, you must be King Arthur and Jane will be Guinevere and Diana must be Lancelot. But first you must be the brothers and the father. We can't have the old dumb servitor because there isn't room for two in the flat when one is lying down. We must pall the barge all its length in blackest samite. That old black shawl of your mother's will be just the thing, Diana."

The black shawl having been procured, Anne spread it over the flat and then lay down on the bottom, with closed eyes and hands folded over her breast.

"Oh, she does look really dead," whispered Ruby Gillis nervously, watching the still, white little face under the flickering shadows of the birches. "It makes me feel frightened, girls. Do you suppose it's really right to act like this? Mrs. Lynde says that all play-acting is abominably wicked."

"Ruby, you shouldn't talk about Mrs. Lynde," said Anne severely. "It spoils the effect because this is hundreds of years before Mrs. Lynde was born. Jane, you arrange this. It's silly for Elaine to be talking when she's dead."

Jane rose to the occasion. Cloth of gold for coverlet there was none, but an old piano scarf of yellow Japanese crepe was an excellent substitute. A white lily was not obtainable just then, but the effect of a tall blue iris placed in one of Anne's folded hands was all that could be desired.

"Now, she's all ready," said Jane. "We must kiss her quiet brows and, Diana, you say, 'Sister, farewell for ever,' and Ruby, you say, 'Farewell, sweet sister,' both of you as sorrowfully as you possibly can. Anne, for goodness sake smile a little. You know Elaine 'lay as though she smiled.' That's better. Now push the flat off."

The flat was accordingly pushed off, scraping roughly over an old embedded stake in the process. Diana and Jane and Ruby only waited long enough to see it caught in the current and headed for the bridge before scampering up through the woods, across the road, and down to the lower headland where, as Lancelot and Guinevere and the King, they were to be in readiness to receive the lily maid.

For a few minutes Anne, drifting slowly down, enjoyed the romance of her situation to the full. Then something happened not at all romantic. The flat began to leak. In a very few moments it was necessary for Elaine to scramble to her feet, pick up her cloth of gold coverlet and pall of blackest samite and gaze blankly at a big crack in the bottom of her barge through which the water was literally pouring. That sharp stake at the landing had torn off the strip of batting nailed on the flat. Anne did not know this, but it did not take her long to realize that she was in a dangerous plight. At this rate the flat would fill and sink long before it could drift to the lower headland. Where were the oars? Left behind at the landing!

Anne gave one gasping little scream which nobody ever heard; she was white to the lips, but she did not lose her self-possession. There was one chance—just one.

"I was horribly frightened," she told Mrs. Allan the next day, "and it seemed like years while the flat was drifting down to the bridge and the water rising in it every moment. I prayed, Mrs. Allan, most earnestly, but I didn't shut my eyes to pray, for I knew the only way God could save me was to let the flat float close enough to one of the bridge piles for me to climb up on it. You know the piles are just old tree trunks and there are lots of knots and old branch stubs on them. It was proper to pray, but I had to do my part by watching out and right well I knew it. I just said, 'Dear God, please take the flat close to a pile and I'll do the rest,' over and over again. Under such circumstances you don't think

313

much about making a flowery prayer. But mine was answered, for the flat bumped right into a pile for a minute and I flung the scarf and the shawl over my shoulder and scrambled up on a big providential stub. And there I was, Mrs. Allan, clinging to that slippery old pile with no way of getting up or down. It was a very unromantic position, but I didn't think about that at the time. You don't think much about romance when you have just escaped from a watery grave. I said a grateful prayer at once and then I gave all my attention to holding on tight, for I knew I should probably have to depend on human aid to get back to dry land."

The flat drifted under the bridge and then promptly sank in midstream. Ruby, Jane, and Diana, already awaiting it on the lower headland, saw it disappear before their very eyes and had not a doubt but that Anne had gone down with it. For a moment they stood still, white as sheets, frozen with horror at the tragedy; then, shrieking at the tops of their voices, they started on a frantic run up through the woods, never pausing as they crossed the main road to glance the way of the bridge. Anne, clinging desperately to her precarious foothold, saw their flying forms and heard their shrieks. Help would soon come, but meanwhile her position was a very uncomfortable one.

The minutes passed by, each seeming an hour to the unfortunate lily maid. Why didn't somebody come? Where had the girls gone? Suppose they had fainted, one and all! Suppose nobody ever came! Suppose she grew so tired and cramped that she could hold on no longer! Anne looked at the wicked green depths below her, wavering with long, oily shadows, and shivered. Her imagination began to suggest all manner of gruesome possibilities to her.

Then, just as she thought she really could not endure the ache in her arms and wrists another moment, Gilbert Blythe came rowing under the bridge in Harmon Andrews' dory!

Gilbert glanced up and, much to his amazement, beheld a little white scornful face looking down upon him with big, frightened but also scornful gray eyes.

"Anne Shirley! How on earth did you get there?" he exclaimed.

Without waiting for an answer he pulled close to the pile and extended his hand. There was no help for it; Anne, clinging to Gilbert Blythe's hand, scrambled down into the dory, where she sat, drabbled and furious, in the stern with her arms full of dripping shawl and wet crepe. It was certainly extremely difficult to be dignified under the circumstances!

"What has happened, Anne?" asked Gilbert, taking up his oars.

"We were playing Elaine," explained Anne frigidly, without even looking at her rescuer, "and I had to drift down to Camelot in the barge—I mean the flat. The flat began to leak and I climbed out on the pile. The girls went for help. Will you be kind enough to row me to the landing?"

Gilbert obligingly rowed to the landing and Anne, disdaining assistance, sprang nimbly on shore.

"I'm very much obliged to you," she said haughtily as she turned away. But Gilbert had also sprung from the boat and now laid a detaining hand on her arm.

"Anne," he said hurriedly, "look here. Can't we be good friends? I'm awfully sorry I made fun of your hair that time. I didn't mean to vex you and I only meant it for a joke. Besides, it's so long ago. I think your hair is awfully pretty now—honest I do. Let's be friends."

For a moment Anne hesitated. She had an odd, newly awakened consciousness under all her outraged dignity that the half-shy, half-eager expression in Gilbert's hazel eyes was something that was very good to see. Her heart gave a

314

quick, queer little beat. But the bitterness of her old grievance promptly stiffened up her wavering determination. That scene of two years before flashed back into her recollection as vividly as if it had taken place yesterday. Gilbert had called her "carrots" and had brought about her disgrace before the whole school. Her resentment, which to other and older people might be as laughable as its cause, was in no whit allayed and softened by time seemingly. She hated Gilbert Blythe! She would never forgive him!

"No," she said coldly, "I shall never be friends with you, Gilbert Blythe; and I don't want to be!"

"All right!" Gilbert sprang into his skiff with an angry colour in his cheeks. "I'll never ask you to be friends again, Anne Shirley. And I don't care either!"

He pulled away with swift defiant strokes, and Anne went up the steep, ferny little path under the maples. She held her head very high, but she was conscious of an odd feeling of regret. She almost wished she had answered Gilbert differently. Of course, he had insulted her terribly, but still—! Altogether, Anne rather thought it would be a relief to sit down and have a good cry. She was really quite unstrung, for the reaction from her fright and cramped clinging was making itself felt.

Half-way up the path she met Jane and Diana rushing back to the pond in a state narrowly removed from positive frenzy. They had found nobody at Orchard Slope, both Mr. and Mrs. Barry being away. Here Ruby Gillis had succumbed to hysterics, and was left to recover from them as best she might, while Jane and Diana flew through the Haunted Wood and across the brook to Green Gables. There they had found nobody either, for Marilla had gone to Carmody and Matthew was making hay in the back field.

"Oh, Anne," gasped Diana, fairly falling on the former's neck and weeping with relief and delight, "Oh, Anne—we thought—you were—drowned—and we felt like murderers—because we had made—you be—Elaine. And Ruby is in hysterics—oh, Anne, how did you escape?"

"I climbed up on one of the piles," explained Anne wearily, "and Gilbert Blythe came along in Mr. Andrews' dory and brought me to land."

"Oh, Anne, how splendid of him! Why, it's so romantic!" said Jane, finding breath enough for utterance at last. "Of course you'll speak to him after this."

"Of course I won't," flashed Anne with a momentary return of her old spirit. "And I don't want ever to hear the word romantic again, Jane Andrews. I'm awfully sorry you were so frightened, girls. It is all my fault. I feel sure I was born under an unlucky star. Everything I do gets me or my dearest friends into a scrape. We've gone and lost your father's flat, Diana, and I have a presentiment that we'll not be allowed to row on the pond any more."

Anne's presentiment proved more trustworthy than presentiments are apt to do. Great was the consternation in the Barry and Cuthbert households when the events of the afternoon became known.

"Will you *ever* have any sense, Anne?" groaned Marilla.

"Oh, yes, I think I will, Marilla," returned Anne optimistically. A good cry, indulged in the grateful solitude of the east gable, had soothed her nerves and restored her to her wonted cheerfulness. "I think my prospects of becoming sensible are brighter now than ever."

"I don't see how," said Marilla.

"Well," explained Anne, "I've learned a new and valuable lesson to-day. Ever since I came to Green Gables I've been making mistakes, and each mistake has helped to cure me of some great shortcoming. The affair of the amethyst brooch cured me of meddling with things that didn't belong to me. The Haunted Wood mistake cured me of letting my imagination run away with me. The liniment cake mistake cured me of carelessness in cooking. Dyeing my hair cured me of vanity. I never think about my hair and nose now—at least, very seldom. And today's mistake is going to cure me of being too romantic. I have come to the conclusion that it is no use trying to be romantic in Avonlea. It was probably easy enough in towered Camelot hundreds of years ago, but romance is not appreciated now. I feel quite sure that you will soon see a great improvement in me in this respect, Marilla."

"I'm sure I hope so," said Marilla skeptically.

But Matthew, who had been sitting mutely in his corner, laid a hand on Anne's shoulder when Marilla had gone out.

"Don't give up all your romance, Anne," he whispered shyly, "a little of it is a good thing—not too much, of course—but keep a little of it, Anne, keep a little of it."

CHAPTER 29

An Epoch in Anne's Life

Anne was bringing the cows home from the back pasture by way of Lovers' Lane. It was a September evening and all the gaps and clearings in the woods were brimmed up with ruby sunset light. Here and there the lane was splashed with it, but for the most part it was already quite shadowy beneath the maples, and the spaces under the firs were filled with a clear violet dusk like airy wine. The winds were out in their tops, and there is no sweeter music on earth than that which the wind makes in the fir-trees at evening.

The cows swung placidly down the lane, and Anne followed them dreamily, repeating aloud the battle canto from "Marmion"—which had also been part of their English course the preceding winter and which Miss Stacy had made them learn off by heart—and exulting in its rushing lines and the clash of spears in its imagery. When she came to the lines:

> "The stubborn spearsmen still made good
> Their dark impenetrable wood,"[1]

she stopped in ecstasy to shut her eyes that she might the better fancy herself one of that heroic ring. When she opened them again it was to behold Diana coming through the gate that led into the Barry field and looking so important that Anne instantly divined there was news to be told. But betray too eager curiosity she would not.

"Isn't this evening just like a purple dream, Diana? It makes me so glad to be alive. In the mornings I always think the mornings are best; but when evening comes I think it's lovelier still."

"It's a very fine evening," said Diana, "but oh, I have such news, Anne. Guess. You can have three guesses."

---

1 *The stubborn spearsmen . . . wood*   from Scott's *Marmion* (see Chapter 27, Note 2), 6.34.12–13.

"Charlotte Gillis is going to be married in the church after all and Mrs. Allan wants us to decorate it," cried Anne.

"No. Charlotte's beau won't agree to that, because nobody ever has been married in the church yet, and he thinks it would seem too much like a funeral. It's too mean, because it would be such fun. Guess again."

"Jane's mother is going to let her have a birthday party?"

Diana shook her head, her black eyes dancing with merriment.

"I can't think what it can be," said Anne in despair, "unless it's that Moody Spurgeon MacPherson saw you home from prayer-meeting last night. Did he?"

"I should think not," exclaimed Diana indignantly. "I wouldn't be likely to boast of it if he did, the horrid creature! I knew you couldn't guess it. Mother had a letter from Aunt Josephine to-day, and Aunt Josephine wants you and me to go to town next Tuesday and stop with her for the Exhibition. There!"

"Oh, Diana," whispered Anne, finding it necessary to lean up against a maple-tree for support, "do you really mean it? But I'm afraid Marilla won't let me go. She will say that she can't encourage gadding about. That was what she said last week when Jane invited me to go with them in their double-seated buggy to the American concert at the White Sands Hotel. I wanted to go, but Marilla said I'd be better at home learning my lessons and so would Jane. I was bitterly disappointed, Diana. I felt so heart-broken that I wouldn't say my prayers when I went to bed. But I repented of that and got up in the middle of the night and said them."

"I'll tell you," said Diana, "we'll get mother to ask Marilla. She'll be more likely to let you go then; and if she does we'll have the time of our lives, Anne. I've never been to an Exhibition, and it's so aggravating to hear the other girls talking about their trips. Jane and Ruby have been twice, and they're going this year again."

"I'm not going to think about it at all until I know whether I can go or not," said Anne resolutely. "If I did and then was disappointed, it would be more than I could bear. But in case I do go I'm very glad my new coat will be ready by that time. Marilla didn't think I needed a new coat. She said my old one would do very well for another winter and that I ought to be satisfied with having a new dress. The dress is very pretty, Diana—navy blue and made so fashionably. Marilla always makes my dresses fashionably now, because she says she doesn't intend to have Matthew going to Mrs. Lynde to make them. I'm so glad. It is ever so much easier to be good if your clothes are fashionable. At least, it is easier for me. I suppose it doesn't make such a difference to naturally good people. But Matthew said I must have a new coat, so Marilla bought a lovely piece of blue broadcloth, and it's being made by a real dressmaker over at Carmody. It's to be done Saturday night, and I'm trying not to imagine myself walking up the church aisle on Sunday in my new suit and cap, because I'm afraid it isn't right to imagine such things. But it just slips into my mind in spite of me. My cap is so pretty. Matthew bought it for me the day we were over at Carmody. It is one of those little blue velvet ones that are all the rage, with gold cord and tassels. Your new hat is elegant, Diana, and so becoming. When I saw you come into church last Sunday my heart swelled with pride to think you were my dearest friend. Do you suppose it's wrong for us to think so much about our clothes? Marilla says it is very sinful. But it *is* such an interesting subject, isn't it?"

Marilla agreed to let Anne go to town, and it was arranged that Mr. Barry should take the girls in on the following Tuesday. As Charlottetown was thirty miles away and Mr. Barry wished to go and return the same day, it was necessary to make a very early start. But Anne counted it all joy, and was up before sunrise on Tuesday morning. A glance from her window assured her that the day would be fine, for the eastern sky behind the firs of the Haunted Wood was all silvery and cloudless. Through the gap in the trees a light was shining in the western gable of Orchard Slope, a token that Diana was also up.

Anne was dressed by the time Matthew had the fire on and had the breakfast ready when Marilla came down, but for her own part was much too excited to eat. After breakfast the jaunty new cap and jacket were donned, and Anne hastened over the brook and up through the firs to Orchard Slope. Mr. Barry and Diana were waiting for her, and they were soon on the road.

It was a long drive, but Anne and Diana enjoyed every minute of it. It was delightful to rattle along over the moist roads in the early red sunlight that was creeping across the shorn harvest fields. The air was fresh and crisp, and little smoke-blue mists curled through the valleys and floated off from the hills. Sometimes the road went through woods where maples were beginning to hang out scarlet banners; sometimes it crossed rivers on bridges that made Anne's flesh cringe with the old, half-delightful fear; sometimes it wound along a harbour shore and passed by a little cluster of weather-gray fishing huts; again it mounted to hills whence a far sweep of curving upland or misty blue sky could be seen; but wherever it went there was much of interest to discuss. It was almost noon when they reached town and found their way to "Beechwood." It was quite a fine old mansion, set back from the street in a seclusion of green elms and branching beeches. Miss Barry met them at the door with a twinkle in her sharp black eyes.

"So you've come to see me at last, you Anne-girl," she said. "Mercy, child, how you have grown! You're taller than I am, I declare. And you're ever so much better-looking than you used to be, too. But I dare say you know that without being told."

"Indeed I didn't," said Anne radiantly. "I know I'm not so freckled as I used to be, so I've much to be thankful for, but I really hadn't dared to hope there was any other improvement. I'm so glad you think there is, Miss Barry."

Miss Barry's house was furnished with "great magnificence," as Anne told Marilla afterwards. The two little country girls were rather abashed by the splendour of the parlour where Miss Barry left them when she went to see about dinner.

"Isn't it just like a palace?" whispered Diana. "I never was in Aunt Josephine's house before, and I'd no idea it was so grand. I just wish Julia Bell could see this—she puts on such airs about her mother's parlour."

"Velvet carpet," sighed Anne luxuriously, "*and* silk curtains! I've dreamed of such things, Diana. But do you know I don't believe I feel very comfortable with them after all. There are so many things in this room and all so splendid that there is no scope for imagination. That is one consolation when you are poor—there are so many more things you can imagine about."

Their sojourn in town was something that Anne and Diana dated from for years. From first to last it was crowded with delights.

On Wednesday Miss Barry took them to the Exhibition grounds and kept them there all day.

"It was splendid," Anne related to Marilla later on. "I never imagined anything so interesting. I don't really know which department was the most interesting. I think I liked the horses and the flowers and the fancy work best. Josie Pye took first prize for knitted lace. I was real glad she did. And I was glad that I felt glad, for it shows I'm improving, don't you think Marilla, when I can rejoice in Josie's success? Mr. Harmon Andrews took second prize for Gravenstein apples and Mr. Bell took first prize for a pig. Diana said she thought it was ridiculous for a Sunday-school superintendent to take a prize in pigs, but I don't see why. Do you? She said she would always think of it after this when he was praying so solemnly. Clara Louise MacPherson took a prize for painting, and Mrs. Lynde got first prize for home-made butter and cheese. So Avonlea was pretty well represented, wasn't it? Mrs. Lynde was there that day, and I never knew how much I really liked her until I saw her familiar face among all those strangers. There were thousands of people there, Marilla. It made me feel dreadfully insignificant. And Miss Barry took us up to the grand stand to see the horse-races. Mrs. Lynde wouldn't go; she said horse-racing was an abomination, and she being a church-member, thought it her bounden duty to set a good example by staying away. But there were so many there I don't believe Mrs. Lynde's absence would ever be noticed. I don't think, though, that I ought to go very often to horse-races, because they *are* awfully fascinating. Diana got so excited that she offered to bet me ten cents that the red horse would win. I didn't believe he would, but I refused to bet, because I wanted to tell Mrs. Allan all about everything, and I felt sure it wouldn't do to tell her that. It's always wrong to do anything you can't tell the minister's wife. It's as good as an extra conscience to have a minister's wife for your friend. And I was very glad I didn't bet, because the red horse *did* win, and I would have lost ten cents. So you see that virtue was its own reward. We saw a man go up in a balloon. I'd love to go up in a balloon, Marilla; it would be simply thrilling; and we saw a man selling fortunes. You paid him ten cents and a little bird picked out your fortune for you. Miss Barry gave Diana and me ten cents each to have our fortunes told. Mine was that I would marry a dark-complected man who was very wealthy, and I would go across water to live. I looked carefully at all the dark men I saw after that, but I didn't care much for any of them, and anyhow I suppose it's too early to be looking out for him yet. Oh, it was a never-to-be-forgotten day, Marilla. I was so tired I couldn't sleep at night. Miss Barry put us in the spare room, according to promise. It was an elegant room, Marilla, but somehow sleeping in a spare room isn't what I used to think it was. That's the worst of growing up, and I'm beginning to realize it. The things you wanted so much when you were a child don't seem half so wonderful to you when you get them."

Thursday the girls had a drive in the park, and in the evening Miss Barry took them to a concert in the Academy of Music, where a noted prima donna was to sing. To Anne the evening was a glittering vision of delight.

"Oh, Marilla, it was beyond description. I was so excited I couldn't even talk, so you may know what it was like. I just sat in enraptured silence. Madame Selitsky was perfectly beautiful, and wore white satin and diamonds. But when she began to sing I never thought about anything else. Oh, I can't tell you how I felt. But it seemed to me that it could never be hard to be good any more. I felt like I do when I look up to the stars. Tears came into my eyes, but, oh, they were such happy tears. I was so sorry when it was all over, and I told Miss Barry I didn't see how I was ever to return to common life again. She said she thought if we went over to the restaurant across the street and had an ice-cream it might help me. That sounded so prosaic; but to my surprise I found it true. The ice-cream was delicious, Marilla, and it was so lovely and dissipated to be sitting there eating it at eleven o'clock at night. Diana said she believed she was born for city life. Miss Barry asked me what my opinion was, but I said I would have to think it over very seriously before I could tell her what I really thought. So I thought it over after I went to bed. That is the best time to think things out. And I came to the conclusion, Marilla, that I wasn't born for city life and that I was glad of it. It's nice to be eating ice-cream at brilliant restaurants at eleven o'clock at night once in awhile; but as a regular thing I'd rather be in the east gable at eleven, sound asleep, but kind of knowing even in my sleep that the stars were shining outside and that the wind was blowing in the firs across the brook. I told Miss Barry so at breakfast the next morning and she laughed. Miss Barry generally laughed at anything I said, even when I said the most solemn things. I don't think I liked it, Marilla, because I wasn't trying to be funny. But she is a most hospitable lady and treated us royally."

Friday brought going-home time, and Mr. Barry drove in for the girls.

"Well, I hope you've enjoyed yourselves," said Miss Barry, as she bade them good-bye.

"Indeed we have," said Diana.

"And you, Anne-girl?"

"I've enjoyed every minute of the time," said Anne, throwing her arms impulsively about the old woman's neck and kissing her wrinkled cheek. Diana would never have dared to do such a thing, and felt rather aghast at Anne's freedom. But Miss Barry was pleased, and she stood on her veranda and watched the buggy out of sight. Then she went back into her big house with a sigh. It seemed very lonely, lacking those fresh young lives. Miss Barry was a rather selfish old lady, if the truth must be told, and had never cared much for anybody but herself. She valued people only as they were of service to her or amused her. Anne had amused her, and consequently stood high in the old lady's good graces. But Miss Barry found herself thinking less about Anne's quaint speeches than of her fresh enthusiasms, her transparent emotions, her little winning ways, and the sweetness of her eyes and lips.

"I thought Marilla Cuthbert was an old fool when I heard she'd adopted a girl out of an orphan asylum," she said to herself, "but I guess she didn't make much of a mistake after all. If I'd a child like Anne in the house all the time I'd be a better and happier woman."

Anne and Diana found the drive home as pleasant as the drive in—pleasanter, indeed, since there was the delightful consciousness of home waiting at the end of it. It was sunset when they passed through White Sands and turned into the shore road. Beyond, the Avonlea hills came out darkly against the saffron sky. Behind them the moon was rising out of the sea that grew all radiant and transfigured in her light. Every little cove along the curving road was a marvel of dancing ripples. The waves broke with a soft swish on the rocks below them, and the tang of the sea was in the strong, fresh air.

"Oh, but it's good to be alive and to be going home," breathed Anne.

When she crossed the log bridge over the brook the kitchen light of Green Gables winked her a friendly welcome back, and through the open door shone the hearth fire, sending out its warm red glow athwart the chilly autumn night. Anne ran blithely up the hill and into the kitchen, where a hot supper was waiting on the table.

"So you've got back?" said Marilla, folding up her knitting.

"Yes, and, oh, it's so good to be back," said Anne joyously. "I could kiss everything, even to the clock. Marilla, a broiled chicken! You don't mean to say you cooked that for me!"

"Yes, I did," said Marilla. "I thought you'd be hungry after such a drive and need something real appetizing. Hurry and take off your things, and we'll have supper as soon as Matthew comes in. I'm glad you've got back, I must say. It's been fearful lonesome here without you, and I never put in four longer days."

After supper Anne sat before the fire between Matthew and Marilla, and gave them a full account of her visit.

"I've had a splendid time," she concluded happily, "and I feel that it marks an epoch in my life. But the best of it all was the coming home."

CHAPTER 30

The Queen's Class[1] Is Organized

MARILLA laid her knitting on her lap and leaned back in her chair. Her eyes were tired, and she thought vaguely that she must see about having her glasses changed the next time she went to town, for her eyes had grown tired very often of late.

It was nearly dark, for the dull November twilight had fallen around Green Gables, and the only light in the kitchen came from the dancing red flames in the stove.

Anne was curled up Turk-fashion[2] on the hearth-rug, gazing into that joyous glow where the sunshine of a hundred summers was being distilled from the maple cord-wood. She had been reading, but her book had slipped to the floor, and now she was dreaming, with a smile on her parted lips. Glittering castles in Spain were shaping themselves out of the mists and rainbows of her lively fancy; adventures wonderful and enthralling were happening to her in cloudland—adventures that always turned out triumphantly and never involved her in scrapes like those of actual life.

Marilla looked at her with a tenderness that would never have been suffered to reveal itself in any clearer light than that soft mingling of fireshine and shadow. The lesson of a love that should display itself easily in spoken word and open look was one Marilla could never learn. But she had learned to love this slim, gray-eyed girl with an affection all the deeper and stronger from its very undemonstrativeness. Her love made her afraid of being unduly indulgent, indeed. She had an uneasy feeling that it was rather sinful to set one's heart so intensely on any human creature as she had set hers on Anne, and perhaps she performed a sort of unconscious penance for this by being stricter and more critical than if the girl had been less dear to her. Certainly Anne herself had no idea how Marilla loved her. She sometimes thought wistfully that Marilla was very hard to please and distinctly lacking in sympathy and understanding. But she always checked the thought reproachfully, remembering what she owed to Marilla.

"Anne," said Marilla abruptly, "Miss Stacy was here this afternoon when you were out with Diana."

---

1 *Queen's Class*   the group of students at Anne's school who will study together to pass the entrance examination to Queen's College or Academy, first mentioned in Chapter 15.

2 *Turk-fashion*   with her legs bent and ankles crossed.

Anne came back from her other world with a start and a sigh.

"Was she? Oh, I'm so sorry I wasn't in. Why didn't you call me, Marilla? Diana and I were only over in the Haunted Wood. It's lovely in the woods now. All the little wood things—the ferns and the satin leaves and the crackerberries—have gone to sleep, just as if somebody had tucked them away until spring under a blanket of leaves. I think it was a little gray fairy with a rainbow scarf that came tiptoeing along the last moonlight night and did it. Diana wouldn't say much about that, though. Diana has never forgotten the scolding her mother gave her about imagining ghosts into the Haunted Wood. It had a very bad effect on Diana's imagination. It blighted it. Mrs. Lynde says Myrtle Bell is a blighted being. I asked Ruby Gillis why Myrtle was blighted, and Ruby said she guessed it was because her young man had gone back on her. Ruby Gillis thinks of nothing but young men, and the older she gets the worse she is. Young men are all very well in their place, but it doesn't do to drag them into everything, does it? Diana and I are thinking seriously of promising each other that we will never marry but be nice old maids and live together for ever. Diana hasn't quite made up her mind though, because she thinks perhaps it would be nobler to marry some wild, dashing, wicked young man and reform him. Diana and I talk a great deal about serious subjects now, you know. We feel that we are so much older than we used to be that it isn't becoming to talk of childish matters. It's such a solemn thing to be almost fourteen, Marilla. Miss Stacy took all us girls who are in our teens down to the brook last Wednesday, and talked to us about it. She said we couldn't be too careful what habits we formed and what ideals we acquired in our teens, because by the time we were twenty our characters would be developed and the foundation laid for our whole future life. And she said if the foundation was shaky we could never build anything really worth while on it. Diana and I talked the matter over coming home from school. We felt extremely solemn, Marilla. And we decided that we would try to be very careful indeed and form respectable habits and learn all we could and be as sensible as possible, so that by the time we were twenty our characters would be properly developed. It's perfectly appalling to think of being twenty, Marilla. It sounds so fearfully old and grown up. But why was Miss Stacy here this afternoon?"

"That is what I want to tell you, Anne, if you'll ever give me a chance to get a word in edgewise. She was talking about you."

"About me?" Anne looked rather scared. Then she flushed and exclaimed:

"Oh, I know what she was saying. I meant to tell you, Marilla, honestly I did, but I forgot. Miss Stacy caught me reading 'Ben Hur' in school yesterday afternoon when I should have been studying my Canadian history. Jane Andrews lent it to me. I was reading it at dinner-hour, and I had just got to the chariot-race when school went in. I was simply wild to know how it turned out—although I felt sure 'Ben Hur' must win because it wouldn't be poetical justice if he didn't—so I spread the history open on my desk-lid and then tucked 'Ben Hur' between the desk and my knee. It just looked as if I were studying Canadian history, you know, while all the while I was revelling in 'Ben Hur.' I was so interested in it that I never noticed Miss Stacy coming down the aisle until all at once I just looked up and there she was looking down at me, so reproachful like. I can't tell you how ashamed I felt, Marilla, especially when I heard Josie Pye giggling. Miss Stacy took 'Ben Hur' away, but she never said a word then. She kept me in at recess and talked to me. She said I had done very wrong in two respects. First, I was wasting the time I ought to have put on my studies; and secondly I was deceiving my teacher in trying to make it appear I was reading a history when it was a story-book instead. I had never realized until that moment, Marilla, that what I was doing was deceitful. I was shocked. I cried bitterly, and asked Miss Stacy to forgive me and I'd never do such a thing again; and I offered to do penance by never so much as looking at 'Ben Hur' for a whole week, not even to see how the chariot-race turned out. But Miss Stacy said she wouldn't require that, and she forgave me freely. So I think it wasn't very kind of her to come up here to you about it after all."

"Miss Stacy never mentioned such a thing to me, Anne, and it's only your guilty conscience that's the matter with you. You have no business to be taking story-books to school. You read too many novels anyhow. When I was a girl I wasn't so much as allowed to look at a novel."

"Oh, how can you call 'Ben Hur' a novel when it's really such a religious book?" protested Anne. "Of course it's a little too exciting to be proper reading for Sunday, and I only read it on week-days. And I never read *any* book now unless either Miss Stacy or Mrs. Allan thinks it is a proper book for a girl thirteen and three-quarters to read. Miss Stacy made me promise that. She found me reading a book one day called, 'The Lurid Mystery of the Haunted Hall.' It was one Ruby Gillis had lent me, and, oh, Marilla, it was so fascinating and creepy. It just curdled the blood in my veins. But Miss Stacy said it was a very silly, unwholesome book, and she asked me not to read any more of it or any like it. I didn't mind promising not to read any more like it, but it was *agonizing* to give back that book without knowing how it turned out. But my love for Miss Stacy stood the test and I did. It's really wonderful, Marilla, what you can do when you're truly anxious to please a certain person."

"Well, I guess I'll light the lamp and get to work," said Marilla. "I see plainly that you don't want to hear what Miss Stacy had to say. You're more interested in the sound of your own tongue than in anything else."

"Oh, indeed, Marilla, I do want to hear it," cried Anne contritely. "I won't say another word—not one. I know I talk too much, but I am really trying to overcome it, and although I say far too much, yet if you only knew how many things I want to say and don't, you'd give me some credit for it. Please tell me, Marilla."

"Well, Miss Stacy wants to organize a class among her advanced students who mean to study for the entrance examination into Queen's. She intends to give them extra lessons for an hour after school. And she came to ask Matthew and me if we would like to have you join it. What do you think about it yourself, Anne? Would you like to go to Queen's and pass for a teacher?"

"Oh, Marilla!" Anne straightened to her knees and clasped her hands. "It's been the dream of my life—that is, for the last six months, ever since Ruby and Jane began to talk of studying for the entrance. But I didn't say anything about it, because I supposed it would be perfectly useless. I'd love to be a teacher. But won't it be dreadfully expensive? Mr. Andrews says it cost him one hundred and fifty dollars to put Prissy through, and Prissy wasn't a dunce in geometry."

"I guess you needn't worry about that part of it. When Matthew and I took you to bring up we resolved we would do the best we could for you and give you a good education. I believe in a girl being fitted to earn her own living whether she ever has to or not. You'll always have a home at Green Gables as long as Matthew and I are here, but nobody knows what is going to happen in this uncertain. world, and it's just as well to be prepared. So you can join the Queen's class if you like, Anne."

"Oh, Marilla, thank you." Anne flung her arms about Marilla's waist and looked up earnestly into her face. "I'm extremely grateful to you and Matthew. And I'll study as hard as I can and do my very best to be a credit to you. I warn you not to expect much in geometry, but I think I can hold my own in anything else if I work hard."

"I dare say you'll get along well enough. Miss Stacy says you are bright and diligent." Not for worlds would Marilla have told Anne just what Miss Stacy had said about her; that would have been to pamper vanity. "You needn't rush to any extreme of killing yourself over your books. There is no hurry. You won't be ready to try the entrance for a year and a half yet. But it's well to begin in time and be thoroughly grounded, Miss Stacy says."

"I shall take more interest than ever in my studies now," said Anne blissfully, "because I have a purpose in life. Mr. Allan says everybody should have a purpose in life and pursue it faithfully. Only he says we must first make sure that it is a worthy purpose. I would call it a worthy purpose to want to be a teacher like Miss Stacy, wouldn't you, Marilla? I think it's a very noble profession."

The Queen's class was organized in due time. Gilbert Blythe, Anne Shirley, Ruby Gillis, Jane Andrews, Josie Pye, Charlie Sloane, and Moody Spurgeon MacPherson joined it. Diana Barry did not, as her parents did not intend to send her to Queen's. This seemed nothing short of a calamity to Anne. Never, since the night on which Minnie May had had the croup, had she and Diana been separated in any thing. On the evening when the Queen's class first remained in school for the extra lessons and Anne saw Diana go slowly out with the others, to walk home alone through the Birch Path and Violet Vale, it was all the former could do to keep her seat and refrain from rushing impulsively after her chum. A lump came into her throat, and she hastily retired behind the pages of her uplifted Latin grammar to hide the tears in her eyes. Not for worlds would Anne have had Gilbert Blythe or Josie Pye see those tears.

"But, oh, Marilla, I really felt that I had tasted the bitterness of death,[3] as Mr. Allan said in his sermon last Sunday, when I saw Diana go out alone," she said mournfully that night. "I thought how splendid it would have been if Diana had only been going to study for the Entrance, too. But we can't have things perfect in this imperfect world, as Mrs. Lynde says. Mrs. Lynde isn't exactly a comforting person sometimes, but there's no doubt she says a great many very true things. And I think the Queen's class is going to be extremely interesting. Jane and Ruby are just going to study to be teachers. That is the height of their ambition. Ruby says she will only teach for two years after she gets through, and then she intends to be married. Jane says she will devote her whole life to teaching, and never, never marry, because you are paid a salary for teaching, but a husband won't pay you anything, and growls if you ask for a share in the egg and butter money. I expect Jane speaks from mournful experience, for Mrs. Lynde says that her father is a perfect old crank, and meaner than second skimmings.[4] Josie Pye says she is just going to college for education's sake, because she won't have to earn her own living; she says of course it is different with orphans who are living on charity—*they* have to hustle. Moody Spurgeon is going

---

3 *bitterness of death*   1 Samuel 15.32.

4 *meaner than second skimmings*   That is, the second time one skims milk for cream (or skims any liquid for tasty or useful matter), one gets very little, but Jane's stingy father gives even less than that. Possibly the reference is to the meager remainder (such as skimmed milk) after the second skimming.

to be a minister. Mrs. Lynde says he couldn't be anything else with a name like that to live up to. I hope it isn't wicked of me, Marilla, but really the thought of Moody Spurgeon being a minister makes me laugh. He's such a funny-looking boy with that big fat face, and his little blue eyes, and his ears sticking out like flaps. But perhaps he will be more intellectual-looking when he grows up. Charlie Sloane says he's going to go into politics and be a member of Parliament, but Mrs. Lynde says he'll never succeed at that, because the Sloanes are all honest people, and it's only rascals that get on in politics nowadays."

"What is Gilbert Blythe going to be?" queried Marilla, seeing that Anne was opening her Caesar.

"I don't happen to know what Gilbert Blythe's ambition in life is—if he has any," said Anne scornfully.

There was open rivalry between Gilbert and Anne now. Previously the rivalry had been rather one-sided, but there was no longer any doubt that Gilbert was as determined to be first in class as Anne was. He was a foeman worthy of her steel. The other members of the class tacitly acknowledged their superiority, and never dreamed of trying to compete with them.

Since the day by the pond when she had refused to listen to his plea for forgiveness, Gilbert, save for the aforesaid determined rivalry, had evinced no recognition whatever of the existence of Anne Shirley. He talked and jested with the other girls, exchanged books and puzzles with them, discussed lessons and plans, sometimes walked home with one or the other of them from prayer-meeting or Debating Club. But Anne Shirley he simply ignored, and Anne found out that it is not pleasant to be ignored. It was in vain that she told herself with a toss of her head that she did not care. Deep down in her wayward, feminine little heart she knew that she did care, and that if she had that chance of the Lake of Shining Waters again she would answer very differently. All at once, as it seemed, and to her secret dismay, she found that the old resentment she had cherished against him was gone—gone just when she most needed its sustaining power. It was in vain that she recalled every incident and emotion of that memorable occasion and tried to feel the old satisfying anger. That day by the pond had witnessed its last spasmodic flicker. Anne realized that she had forgiven and forgotten without knowing it. But it was too late.

And at least neither Gilbert nor anybody else, not even Diana, should ever suspect how sorry she was and how much she wished she hadn't been so proud and horrid! She determined to "shroud her feelings in deepest oblivion," and it may be stated here and now that she did it, so successfully that Gilbert, who possibly was not quite so indifferent as he seemed, could not console himself with any belief that Anne felt his retaliatory scorn. The only poor comfort he had was that she snubbed Charlie Sloane, unmercifully, continually and undeservedly.

Otherwise the winter passed away in a round of pleasant duties and studies. For Anne the days slipped by like golden beads on the necklace of the year. She was happy, eager, interested; there were lessons to be learned and honours to be won; delightful books to read; new pieces to be practised for the Sunday-school choir; pleasant Saturday afternoons at the manse with Mrs. Allan; and then, almost before Anne realized it, spring had come again to Green Gables and all the world was abloom once more.

Studies palled just a wee bit then; the Queen's class, left behind in school while the others scattered to green lanes and leafy wood-cuts and meadow byways, looked wistfully out of the windows and discovered that Latin verbs and

French exercises had somehow lost the tang and zest they had possessed in the crisp winter months. Even Anne and Gilbert lagged and grew indifferent. Teacher and taught were alike glad when the term was ended and the glad vacation days stretched rosily before them.

"But you've done good work this past year," Miss Stacy told them on the last evening, "and you deserve a good, jolly vacation. Have the best time you can in the out-of-door world and lay in a good stock of health and vitality and ambition to carry you through next year. It will be the tug of war, you know—the last year before the Entrance."

"Are you going to be back next year, Miss Stacy?" asked Josie Pye.

Josie Pye never scrupled to ask questions; in this instance the rest of the class felt grateful to her; none of them would have dared to ask it of Miss Stacy, but all wanted to, for there had been alarming rumours running at large through the school for some time that Miss Stacy was not coming back the next year—that she had been offered a position in the graded school of her own home district and meant to accept. The Queen's class listened in breathless suspense for her answer.

"Yes, I think I will," said Miss Stacy. "I thought of taking another school, but I have decided to come back to Avonlea. To tell the truth, I've grown so interested in my pupils here that I found I couldn't leave them. So I'll stay and see you through."

"Hurrah!" said Moody Spurgeon. Moody Spurgeon had never been so carried away by his feelings before, and he blushed uncomfortably every time he thought about it for a week.

"Oh, I'm so glad," said Anne with shining eyes. "Dear Miss Stacy, it would be perfectly dreadful if you didn't come back. I don't believe I could have the heart to go on with my studies at all if another teacher came here."

When Anne got home that night she stacked all her text-books away in an old trunk in the attic, locked it, and threw the key into the blanket box.

"I'm not even going to look at a school book in vacation," she told Marilla. "I've studied as hard all the term as I possibly could and I've pored over that geometry until I know every proposition in the first book off by heart, even when the letters *are* changed. I just feel tired of everything sensible and I'm going to let my imagination run riot for the summer. Oh, you needn't be alarmed, Marilla. I'll only let it run riot within reasonable limits. But I want to have a real good jolly time this summer, for maybe it's the last summer I'll be a little girl. Mrs. Lynde says that if I keep stretching out next year as I've done this I'll have to put on longer skirts. She says I'm all running to legs and eyes. And when I put on longer skirts I shall feel that I have to live up to them and be very dignified. It won't even do to believe in fairies then, I'm afraid; so I'm going to believe in them with all my whole heart this summer. I think we're going to have a very gay vacation. Ruby Gillis is going to have a birthday party soon and there's the Sunday-school picnic and the missionary concert next month. And Mr. Barry says that some evening he'll take Diana and me over to the White Sands Hotel and have dinner there. They have dinner there in the evening, you know. Jane Andrews was over once last summer and she says it was a dazzling sight to see the electric lights and the flowers and all the lady guests in such beautiful dresses. Jane says it was her first glimpse into high life and she'll never forget it to her dying day."

Mrs. Lynde came up the next afternoon to find out why Marilla had not been at the Aid meeting on Thursday. When Marilla was not at Aid meeting people knew there was something wrong at Green Gables.

"Matthew had a bad spell with his heart Thursday," Marilla explained, "and I didn't feel like leaving him. Oh, yes, he's all right again now, but he takes them spells oftener than he used to and I'm anxious about him. The doctor says he must be careful to avoid excitement. That's easy enough, for Matthew doesn't go about looking for excitement by any means and never did, but he's not to do any very heavy work either and you might as well tell Matthew not to breathe as not to work. Come and lay off your things, Rachel. You'll stay to tea?"

"Well, seeing you're so pressing, perhaps I might as well stay," said Mrs. Rachel, who had not the slightest intention of doing anything else.

Mrs. Rachel and Marilla sat comfortably in the parlour while Anne got the tea and made hot biscuits that were light and white enough to defy even Mrs. Rachel's criticism.

"I must say Anne has turned out a real smart girl," admitted Mrs. Rachel, as Marilla accompanied her to the end of the lane at sunset. "She must be a great help to you."

"She is," said Marilla, "and she's real steady and reliable now. I used to be afraid she'd never get over her feather-brained ways, but she has and I wouldn't be afraid to trust her in anything now."

"I never would have thought she'd have turned out so well that first day I was here three years ago," said Mrs. Rachel. "Lawful heart, shall I ever forget that tantrum of hers! When I went home that night I says to Thomas, says I, 'Mark my words Thomas, Marilla Cuthbert'll live to rue the step she's took.' But I was mistaken and I'm real glad of it. I ain't one of those kind of people, Marilla, as can never be brought to own up that they've made a mistake. No, that never was my way, thank goodness. I did make a mistake in judging Anne, but it weren't no wonder, for an odder, unexpecteder witch of a child there never was in this world, that's what. There was no ciphering her out by the rules that worked with other children. It's nothing short of wonderful how she's improved these three years, but especially in looks. She's a real pretty girl got to be, though I can't say I'm overly partial to that pale, big-eyed style myself. I like more snap and colour, like Diana Barry has or Ruby Gillis. Ruby Gillis' looks are real showy. But somehow—I don't know how it is but when Anne and them are together, though she ain't half as handsome, she makes them look kind of common and overdone—something like them white June lilies she calls narcissus alongside of the big, red peonies, that's what."

CHAPTER 31

Where the Brook and River Meet[1]

Anne had her "good" summer and enjoyed it whole-heartedly. She and Diana fairly lived outdoors, revelling in all the delights that Lovers' Lane and the Dryad's Bubble and Willowmere and Victoria Island afforded. Marilla offered no objections to Anne's gipsyings. The Spencervale doctor who had come the night Minnie May had the croup met Anne at the house of a patient

---

1 *Where the Brook and River Meet* See Henry Wadsworth Longfellow's (1807–1882) poem "Maidenhood" in which he imagines the brook of girlhood flowing into the river of womanhood and the maiden "Standing with reluctant feet/Where the brook and river meet."

one afternoon early in vacation, looked her over sharply, screwed up his mouth, shook his head, and sent a message to Marilla Cuthbert by another person. It was:

"Keep that red-headed girl of yours in the open air all summer and don't let her read books until she gets more spring into her step."

This message frightened Marilla wholesomely. She read Anne's death warrant by consumption in it unless it was scrupulously obeyed. As a result, Anne had the golden summer of her life as far as freedom and frolic went. She walked, rowed, berried and dreamed to her heart's content; and when September came she was bright-eyed and alert, with a step that would have satisfied the Spencervale doctor and a heart full of ambition and zest once more.

"I feel just like studying with might and main," she declared as she brought her books down from the attic. "Oh, you good old friends, I'm glad to see your honest faces once more—yes, even you, geometry. I've had a perfectly beautiful summer, Marilla, and now I'm rejoicing as a strong man to run a race,[2] as Mr. Allan said last Sunday. Doesn't Mr. Allan preach magnificent sermons? Mrs. Lynde says he is improving every day and the first thing we know some city church will gobble him up and then we'll be left and have to turn to and break in another green preacher. But I don't see the use of meeting trouble half-way, do you, Marilla? I think it would be better just to enjoy Mr. Allan while we have him. If I were a man I think I'd be a minister. They can have such an influence for good, if their theology is sound; and it must be thrilling to preach splendid sermons and stir your hearers' hearts. Why can't women be ministers, Marilla? I asked Mrs. Lynde that and she was shocked and said it would be a scandalous thing. She said there might be female ministers in the States and she believed there was, but thank goodness we hadn't got to that stage in Canada yet and she hoped we never would. But I don't see why. I think women would make splendid ministers. When there is a social to be got up or a church tea or anything else to raise money the women have to turn to and do the work. I'm sure Mrs. Lynde can pray every bit as well as Superintendent Bell and I've no doubt she could preach too with a little practice."

"Yes, I believe she could," said Marilla drily. "She does plenty of unofficial preaching as it is. Nobody has much of a chance to go wrong in Avonlea with Rachel to oversee them."

"Marilla," said Anne in a burst of confidence,[3] "I want to tell you something and ask you what you think about it. It has worried me terribly—on Sunday afternoons, that is, when I think specially about such matters. I do really want to be good; and when I'm with you or Mrs. Allan or Miss Stacy I want it more than ever and I want to do just what would please you and what you would approve of. But mostly when I'm with Mrs. Lynde I feel desperately wicked and as if I wanted to go and do the very thing she tells me I oughtn't to do. I feel irresistibly tempted to do it. Now, what do you think is the reason I feel like that? Do you think it's because I'm really bad and unregenerate?"

Marilla looked dubious for a moment. Then she laughed.

"If you are I guess I am too, Anne, for Rachel often has that very effect on me. I sometimes think she'd have more of an influence for good, as you say yourself, if she didn't keep nagging people to do right. There should have been

2 *rejoicing as a strong man to run a race*   Psalm 19.5.
3 *confidence*   confidential trust or intimacy.

a special commandment against nagging. But there, I shouldn't talk so. Rachel is a good Christian woman and she means well. There isn't a kinder soul in Avonlea and she never shirks her share of work."

"I'm very glad you feel the same," said Anne decidedly. "It's so encouraging. I sha'n't worry so much over that after this. But I dare say there'll be other things to worry me. They keep coming up new all the time—things to perplex you, you know. You settle one question and there's another right after. There are so many things to be thought over and decided when you're beginning to grow up. It keeps me busy all the time thinking them over and deciding what is right. It's a serious thing to grow up, isn't it, Marilla? But when I have such good friends as you and Matthew and Mrs. Allan and Miss Stacy I ought to grow up successfully, and I'm sure it will be my own fault if I don't. I feel it's a great responsibility because I have only the one chance. If I don't grow up right I can't go back and begin over again. I've grown two inches this summer, Marilla. Mr. Gillis measured me at Ruby's party. I'm so glad you made my new dresses longer. That dark green one is so pretty and it was sweet of you to put on the flounce. Of course I know it wasn't really necessary, but flounces are so stylish this fall and Josie Pye has flounces on all her dresses. I know I'll be able to study better because of mine. I shall have such a comfortable feeling deep down in my mind about that flounce."

"It's worth something to have that," admitted Marilla.

Miss Stacy came back to Avonlea school and found all her pupils eager for work once more. Especially did the Queen's class gird up their loins for the fray, for at the end of the coming year, dimly shadowing their pathway already, loomed up that fateful thing known as "the Entrance," at the thought of which one and all felt their hearts sink into their very shoes. Suppose they did not pass! That thought was doomed to haunt Anne through the waking hours of that winter, Sunday afternoons inclusive, to the almost entire exclusion of moral and theological problems. When Anne had bad dreams she found herself staring miserably at pass lists of the Entrance exams, where Gilbert Blythe's name was blazoned at the top and in which hers did not appear at all.

But it was a jolly, busy, happy swift-flying winter. School work was as interesting, class rivalry absorbing, as of yore. New worlds of thought, feeling, and ambition, fresh, fascinating fields of unexplored knowledge seemed to be opening out before Anne's eager eyes.

"Hills peeped o'er hills and Alps on Alps arose."[4]

Much of all this was due to Miss Stacy's tactful, careful, broad-minded guidance. She led her class to think and explore and discover for themselves and encouraged straying from the old beaten paths to a degree that quite shocked Mrs. Lynde and the school trustees, who viewed all innovations on established methods rather dubiously.

Apart from her studies Anne expanded socially, for Marilla, mindful of the Spencervale doctor's dictum, no longer vetoed occasional outings. The Debating Club flourished and gave several concerts; there were one or two parties almost verging on grown-up affairs; there were sleigh drives and skating frolics galore.

4 *Hills . . . arose* from Alexander Pope's (1688–1744) *An Essay on Criticism* (1711), line 232: "Hills peep o'er Hills, and Alps on Alps arise!"

Between times Anne grew, shooting up so rapidly that Marilla was astonished one day, when they were standing side by side, to find the girl was taller than herself.

"Why, Anne, how you've grown!" she said, almost unbelievingly. A sigh followed on the words. Marilla felt a queer regret over Anne's inches. The child she had learned to love had vanished somehow and here was this tall, serious-eyed girl of fifteen, with the thoughtful brows and the proudly poised little head, in her place. Marilla loved the girl as much as she had loved the child, but she was conscious of a queer sorrowful sense of loss. And that night when Anne had gone to prayer-meeting with Diana, Marilla sat alone in the wintry twilight and indulged in the weakness of a cry. Matthew, coming in with a lantern, caught her at it and gazed at her in such consternation that Marilla had to laugh through her tears.

"I was thinking about Anne," she explained, "She's got to be such a big girl—and she'll probably be away from us next winter. I'll miss her terrible."

"She'll be able to come home often," comforted Matthew, to whom Anne was as yet and always would be the little, eager girl he had brought home from Bright River on that June evening four years before. "The branch railroad will be built to Carmody by that time."

"It won't be the same thing as having her here all the time," sighed Marilla gloomily, determined to enjoy her luxury of grief uncomforted. "But there—men can't understand these things!"

There were other changes in Anne no less real than the physical change. For one thing, she became much quieter. Perhaps she thought all the more and dreamed as much as ever, but she certainly talked less. Marilla noticed and commented on this also.

"You don't chatter half as much as you used to, Anne, nor use half as many big words. What has come over you?"

Anne coloured and laughed a little, as she dropped her book and looked dreamily out of the window, where big fat red buds were bursting out on the creeper in response to the lure of the spring sunshine.

"I don't know—I don't want to talk as much," she said, denting her chin thoughtfully with her forefinger. "It's nicer to think dear, pretty thoughts and keep them in one's heart, like treasures. I don't like to have them laughed at or wondered over. And somehow I don't want to use big words any more. It's almost a pity, isn't it, now that I'm really growing big enough to say them if I did want to. It's fun to be almost grown up in some ways, but it's not the kind of fun I expected, Marilla. There's so much to learn and do and think that there isn't time for big words. Besides, Miss Stacy says the short ones are much stronger and better. She makes us write all our essays as simply as possible. It was hard at first. I was so used to crowding in all the fine big words I could think of—and I thought of any number of them. But I've got used to it now and I see it's so much better."

"What has become of your story club? I haven't heard you speak of it for a long time."

"The story club isn't in existence any longer. We hadn't time for it—and anyhow I think we had got tired of it. It was silly to be writing about love and murder and elopements and mysteries. Miss Stacy sometimes has us write a story for training in composition, but she won't let us write anything but what might happen in Avonlea in our own lives, and she criticizes it very sharply and makes us criticize our own too. I never thought my compositions had so many faults until I began to look for them myself. I felt so ashamed I wanted to give up altogether, but Miss Stacy said I could learn to write well if I only trained myself to be my own severest critic. And so I am trying to."

"You've only two more months before the Entrance," said Marilla. "Do you think you'll be able to get through?"

Anne shivered.

"I don't know. Sometimes I think I'll be all right—and then I get horribly afraid. We've studied hard and Miss Stacy has drilled us thoroughly, but we mayn't get through for all that. We've each got a stumbling-block. Mine is geometry of course, and Jane's is Latin and Ruby's and Charlie's is algebra and Josie's is arithmetic. Moody Spurgeon says he feels it in his bones that he is going to fail in English history. Miss Stacy is going to give us examinations in June just as hard as we'll have at the Entrance and mark us just as strictly, so we'll have some idea. I wish it was all over, Marilla. It haunts me. Sometimes I wake up in the night and wonder what I'll do if I don't pass."

"Why, go to school next year and try again," said Marilla unconcernedly.

"Oh, I don't believe I'd have the heart for it. It would be such a disgrace to fail, especially if Gil—if the others passed. And I get so nervous in an examination that I'm likely to make a mess of it. I wish I had nerves like Jane Andrews. Nothing rattles her."

Anne sighed and, dragging her eyes from the witcheries of the spring world, the beckoning day of breeze and blue, and the green things upspringing in the garden, buried herself resolutely in her book. There would be other springs, but if she did not succeed in passing the Entrance Anne felt convinced that she would never recover sufficiently to enjoy them.

CHAPTER 32

The Pass List Is Out

WITH the end of June came the close of the term and the close of Miss Stacy's rule in Avonlea school. Anne and Diana walked home that evening feeling very sober indeed. Red eyes and damp handkerchiefs bore convincing testimony to the fact that Miss Stacy's farewell words must have been quite as touching as Mr. Phillips' had been under similar circumstances three years before. Diana looked back at the schoolhouse from the foot of the spruce hill and sighed deeply.

"It does seem as if it was the end of everything, doesn't it?" she said dismally.

"You oughtn't to feel half as badly as I do," said Anne, hunting vainly for a dry spot on her handkerchief. "You'll be back again next winter, but I suppose I've left the dear old school for ever—if I have good luck, that is."

"It won't be a bit the same. Miss Stacy won't be there, nor you nor Jane nor Ruby probably. I shall have to sit all alone, for I couldn't bear to have another deskmate after you. Oh, we have had jolly times, haven't we, Anne? It's dreadful to think they're all over."

Two big tears rolled down by Diana's nose.

"If you would stop crying I could," said Anne imploringly. "Just as soon as I put away my hanky I see you brimming up and that starts me off again. As Mrs. Lynde says, 'If you can't be cheerful, be as cheerful as you can. After all, I dare say I'll be back next year. This is one of the times I *know* I'm not going to pass. They're getting alarmingly frequent."

"Why, you came out splendidly in the exams Miss Stacy gave."

"Yes, but those exams didn't make me nervous. When I think of the real thing you can't imagine what a horrid cold fluttery feeling comes round my heart. And then my number is thirteen and Josie Pye says it's so unlucky. I am *not* superstitious and I know it can make no difference. But still I wish it wasn't thirteen."

"I do wish I were going in with you," said Diana. "Wouldn't we have a perfectly elegant time? But I suppose you'll have to cram in the evenings."

"No; Miss Stacy has made us promise not to open a book at all. She says it would only tire and confuse us and we are to go out walking and not think about the exams at all and go to bed early. It's good advice, but I expect it will be hard to follow; good advice is apt to be, I think. Prissy Andrews told me that she sat up half the night every night of her Entrance week and crammed for dear life; and I had determined to sit up *at least* as long as she did. It was so kind of your Aunt Josephine to ask me to stay at Beechwood while I'm in town."

"You'll write to me while you're in, won't you?"

"I'll write Tuesday night and tell you how the first day goes," promised Anne.

"I'll be haunting the post-office Wednesday," vowed Diana.

Anne went to town the following Monday and on Wednesday Diana haunted the post-office, as agreed, and got her letter.

"Dearest Diana," wrote Anne, "here it is Tuesday night and I'm writing this in the library at Beechwood. Last night I was horribly lonesome all alone in my room and wished so much you were with me. I couldn't 'cram' because I'd promised Miss Stacy not to, but it was as hard to keep from opening my history as it used to be to keep from reading a story before my lessons were learned.

"This morning Miss Stacy came for me and we went to the Academy, calling for Jane and Ruby and Josie on our way. Ruby asked me to feel her hands and they were as cold as ice. Josie said I looked as if I hadn't slept a wink and she didn't believe I was strong enough to stand the grind of the teacher's course even if I did get through. There are times and seasons even yet when I don't feel that I've made any great headway in learning to like Josie Pye!

"When we reached the Academy there were scores of students there from all over the Island. The first person we saw was Moody Spurgeon sitting on the steps and muttering away to himself. Jane asked him what on earth he was doing and he said he was repeating the multiplication table over and over to steady his nerves and for pity's sake not to interrupt him, because if he stopped for a moment he got frightened and forgot everything he ever knew, but the multiplication table kept all his facts firmly in their proper place!

"When we were assigned to our rooms Miss Stacy had to leave us. Jane and I sat together and Jane was so composed that I envied her. No need of the multiplication table for good, steady, sensible Jane! I wondered if I looked as I felt and if they could hear my heart thumping clear across the room. Then a man came in and began distributing the English examination sheets. My hands grew cold then and my head fairly whirled around as I picked it up. Just one awful moment,—Diana, I felt exactly as I did four years ago when I asked Marilla if I might stay at Green Gables—and then everything cleared up in my mind and my heart began beating again—I forgot to say that it had stopped altogether!— for I knew I could do something with *that* paper anyhow.

"At noon we went home for dinner and then back again for history in the afternoon. The history was a pretty hard paper and I got dreadfully mixed up in
the dates. Still, I think I did fairly well to-day. But oh, Diana, to-morrow the
geometry exam comes off and when I think of it it takes every bit of determination I possess to keep from opening my Euclid. If I thought the multiplication
table would help me any I would recite it from now till to-morrow morning.

"I went down to see the other girls this evening. On my way I met Moody
Spurgeon wandering distractedly around. He said he knew he had failed in history
and he was born to be a disappointment to his parents and he was going home on
the morning train; and it would be easier to be a carpenter than a minister, anyhow. I cheered him up and persuaded him to stay to the end because it would be
unfair to Miss Stacy if he didn't. Sometimes I have wished I was born a boy, but
when I see Moody Spurgeon I'm always glad I'm a girl and not his sister.

"Ruby was in hysterics when I reached their boarding-house; she had just discovered a fearful mistake she had made in her English paper. When she recovered
we went up-town and had an ice-cream. How we wished you had been with us.

"Oh, Diana, if only the geometry examination were over! But there, as Mrs.
Lynde would say, the sun will go on rising and setting whether I fail in geometry or not. That is true but not especially comforting. I think I'd rather it *didn't*
go on if I failed!

"Yours devotedly,
"ANNE."

The geometry examination and all the others were over in due time and Anne
arrived home on Friday evening, rather tired but with an air of chastened triumph about her. Diana was over at Green Gables when she arrived and they
met as if they had been parted for years.

"You old darling, it's perfectly splendid to see you back again. It seems like an
age since you went to town and oh, Anne, how did you get along?"

"Pretty well, I think, in everything but the geometry. I don't know whether I
passed in it or not and I have a creepy, crawly presentiment that I didn't. Oh, how
good it is to be back! Green Gables is the dearest, loveliest spot in the world."

"How did the others do?"

"The girls say they know they didn't pass, but I think they did pretty well.
Josie says the geometry was so easy a child of ten could do it! Moody Spurgeon
still thinks he failed in history and Charlie says he failed in algebra. But we
don't really know anything about it and won't until the pass list is out. That
won't be for a fortnight. Fancy living a fortnight in such suspense! I wish I
could go to sleep and never wake up until it is over."

Diana knew it would be useless to ask how Gilbert Blythe had fared, so she
merely said:

"Oh, you'll pass all right. Don't worry."

"I'd rather not pass at all than not come out pretty well up on the list,"
flashed Anne, by which she meant—and Diana knew she meant—that success
would be incomplete and bitter if she did not come out ahead of Gilbert Blythe.

"With this end in view Anne had strained every nerve during the examinations. So had Gilbert. They had met and passed each other on the street a
dozen times without any sign of recognition and every time Anne had held her
head a little higher and wished a little more earnestly that she had made friends
with Gilbert when he asked her, and vowed a little more determinedly to

surpass him in the examination. She knew that all Avonlea junior was wondering which would come out first; she even knew that Jimmy Glover and Ned Wright had a bet on the question and that Josie Pye had said there was no doubt in the world that Gilbert would be first; and she felt that her humiliation would be unbearable if she failed.

But she had another and nobler motive for wishing to do well. She wanted to "pass high" for the sake of Matthew and Marilla—especially Matthew. Matthew had declared to her his conviction that she "would beat the whole Island." That, Anne felt, was something it would be foolish to hope for even in the wildest dreams. But she did hope fervently that she would be among the first ten at least, so that she might see Matthew's kindly brown eyes gleam with pride in her achievement. That, she felt, would be a sweet reward indeed for all her hard work and patient grubbing among unimaginative equations and conjugations.

At the end of the fortnight Anne took to "haunting" the post-office also, in the distracted company of Jane, Ruby and Josie, opening the Charlottetown dailies with shaking hands and cold, sinkaway feelings as bad as any experienced during the Entrance week. Charlie and Gilbert were not above doing this too, but Moody Spurgeon stayed resolutely away.

"I haven't got the grit to go there and look at a paper in cold blood," he told Anne. "I'm just going to wait until somebody comes and tells me suddenly whether I've passed or not."

When three weeks had gone by without the pass list appearing Anne began to feel that she really couldn't stand the strain much longer. Her appetite failed and her interest in Avonlea doings languished. Mrs. Lynde wanted to know what else you could expect with a Tory superintendent of education at the head of affairs, and Matthew, noting Anne's paleness and indifference and the lagging steps that bore her home from the post-office every afternoon, began seriously to wonder if he hadn't better vote Grit at the next election.

But one evening the news came. Anne was sitting at her open window, for the time forgetful of the woes of examinations and the cares of the world, as she drank in the beauty of the summer dusk, sweet-scented with flower-breaths from the garden below and sibilant and rustling from the stir of poplars. The eastern sky above the firs was flushed faintly pink from the reflection of the west, and Anne was wondering dreamily if the spirit of colour looked like that, when she saw Diana come flying down through the firs, over the log bridge, and up the slope, with a fluttering newspaper in her hand.

Anne sprang to her feet, knowing at once what that paper contained. The pass list was out! Her head whirled and her heart beat until it hurt her. She could not move a step. It seemed an hour to her before Diana came rushing along the hall and burst into the room without even knocking, so great was her excitement.

"Anne, you've passed," she cried, "passed the *very first*—you and Gilbert both—you're ties—but your name is first. Oh, I'm so proud!"

Diana flung the paper on the table and herself on Anne's bed, utterly breathless and incapable of further speech. Anne lighted the lamp, oversetting the match-safe and using up half a dozen matches before her shaking hands could accomplish the task. Then she snatched up the paper. Yes, she had passed—there was her name at the very top of a list of two hundred! That moment was worth living for.

"You did just splendidly, Anne," puffed Diana, recovering sufficiently to sit up and speak, for Anne, starry-eyed and rapt, had not uttered a word. "Father brought the paper home from Bright River not ten minutes ago—it came out on the afternoon train, you know, and won't be here till to-morrow by mail— and when I saw the pass list I just rushed over like a wild thing. You've all passed, every one of you, Moody Spurgeon and all, although he's conditioned in history. Jane and Ruby did pretty well—they're half-way up—and so did Charlie. Josie just scraped through with three marks to spare, but you'll see she'll put on as many airs as if she'd led. Won't Miss Stacy be delighted? Oh, Anne, what does it feel like to see your name at the head of a pass list like that? If it were me I know I'd go crazy with joy. I am pretty near crazy as it is, but you're as calm and cool as a spring evening."

"I'm just dazzled inside," said Anne. "I want to say a hundred things, and I can't find words to say them in. I never dreamed of this—yes, I did, too, just once! I let myself think *once*, 'What if I should come out first?' quakingly, you know, for it seemed so vain and presumptuous to think I could lead the Island. Excuse me a minute, Diana. I must run right out to the field to tell Matthew. Then we'll go up the road and tell the good news to the others."

They hurried to the hayfield below the barn where Matthew was coiling hay, and, as luck would have it, Mrs. Lynde was talking to Marilla at the lane fence.

"Oh, Matthew," exclaimed Anne, "I've passed and I'm first—or one of the first! I'm not vain, but I'm thankful."

"Well now, I always said it," said Matthew, gazing at the pass list delightedly. "I knew you could beat them all easy."

"You've done pretty well, I must say, Anne," said Marilla, trying to hide her extreme pride in Anne from Mrs. Rachel's critical eye. But that good soul said heartily:

"I just guess she has done well, and far be it from me to be backward in saying it. You're a credit to your friends, Anne, that's what, and we're all proud of you."

That night Anne, who had wound up a delightful evening by a serious little talk with Mrs. Allan at the manse, knelt sweetly by her open window in a great sheen of moonshine and murmured a prayer of gratitude and aspiration that came straight from her heart. There was in it thankfulness for the past and reverent petition for the future; and when she slept on her white pillow her dreams were as fair and bright and beautiful as maidenhood might desire.

CHAPTER 33

The Hotel Concert

"PUT on your white organdy, by all means, Anne," advised Diana decidedly. They were together in the east gable chamber; outside it was only twilight—a lovely yellowish-green twilight with a clear blue cloudless sky. A big round moon, slowly deepening from her pallid lustre into burnished silver, hung over the Haunted Wood; the air was full of sweet summer sounds—sleepy birds twittering, freakish breezes, far-away voices and laughter. But in Anne's room the blind was drawn and the lamp lighted, for an important toilet was being made.

The east gable was a very different place from what it had been on that night four years before, when Anne had felt its bareness penetrate to the marrow of her spirit with its inhospitable chill. Changes had crept in, Marilla conniving at them resignedly, until it was as sweet and dainty a nest as a young girl could desire.

The velvet carpet with the pink roses and the pink silk curtains of Anne's early visions had certainly never materialized; but her dreams had kept pace with her growth, and it is not probable she lamented them. The floor was covered with a pretty matting, and the curtains that softened the high window and fluttered in the vagrant breezes were of pale green art muslin. The walls, hung not with gold and silver brocade tapestry, but with a dainty apple-blossom paper, were adorned with a few good pictures given Anne by Mrs. Allan. Miss Stacy's photograph occupied the place of honour, and Anne made a sentimental point of keeping fresh flowers on the bracket under it. To-night a spike of white lilies faintly perfumed the room like the dream of a fragrance. There was no "mahogany furniture," but there was a white-painted bookcase filled with books, a cushioned wicker rocker, a toilet-table befrilled with white muslin, a quaint, gilt-framed mirror with chubby pink cupids and purple grapes painted over its arched top, that used to hang in the spare room, and a low white bed.

Anne was dressing for a concert at the White Sands Hotel. The guests had got it up in aid of the Charlottetown hospital, and had hunted out all the available amateur talent in the surrounding districts to help it along. Bertha Sampson and Pearl Clay of the White Sands Baptist choir had been asked to sing a duet; Milton Clark of Newbridge was to give a violin solo; Winnie Adella Blair of Carmody was to sing a Scotch ballad; and Laura Spencer of Spencervale and Anne Shirley of Avonlea were to recite.

As Anne would have said at one time, it was "an epoch in her life," and she was deliciously athrill with the excitement of it. Matthew was in the seventh heaven of gratified pride over the honour conferred on his Anne, and Marilla was not far behind, although she would have died rather than admit it, and said she didn't think it was very proper for a lot of young folks to be gadding over to the hotel without any responsible person with them.

Anne and Diana were to drive over with Jane Andrews and her brother Billy in their double-seated buggy; and several other Avonlea girls and boys were going, too. There was a party of visitors expected out from town, and after the concert a supper was to be given to the performers.

"Do you really think the organdy will be best?" queried Anne anxiously. "I don't think it's as pretty as my blue-flowered muslin—and it certainly isn't so fashionable."

"But it suits you ever so much better," said Diana. "It's so soft and frilly and clinging. The muslin is stiff, and makes you look too dressed up. But the organdy seems as if it grew on you."

Anne sighed and yielded. Diana was beginning to have a reputation for notable taste in dressing, and her advice on such subjects was much sought after. She was looking very pretty herself on this particular night in a dress of the lovely wild-rose pink, from which Anne was for ever debarred; but she was not to take any part in the concert, so her appearance was of minor importance. All her pains were bestowed upon Anne, who, she vowed, must, for the credit of Avonlea, be dressed and combed and adorned to the queen's taste.

"Pull out that frill a little more—so; here, let me tie your sash; now for your slippers. I'm going to braid your hair in two thick braids, and tie them half-way up with big white bows—no, don't pull out a single curl over your forehead—just have the soft part. There is no way you do your hair suits you so well, Anne, and Mrs. Allan says you look like a Madonna when you part it so. I shall fasten this little white house rose just behind your ear. There was just one on my bush, and I saved it for you."

"Shall I put my pearl beads on?" asked Anne. "Matthew brought me a string from town last week, and I know he'd like to see them on me."

Diana pursed up her lips, put her black head on one side critically, and finally pronounced in favour of the beads, which were thereupon tied around Anne's slim milk-white throat.

"There's something so stylish about you, Anne," said Diana, with unenvious admiration. "You hold your head with such an air. I suppose it's your figure. I am just a dumpling. I've always been afraid of it, and now I know it is so. Well, I suppose I shall just have to resign myself to it."

"But you have such dimples," said Anne, smiling affectionately into the pretty, vivacious face so near her own. "Lovely dimples, like little dents in cream. I have given up all hope of dimples. My dimple-dream will never come true; but so many of my dreams have that I mustn't complain. Am I all ready now?"

"All ready," assured Diana, as Marilla appeared in the doorway, a gaunt figure with grayer hair than of yore and no fewer angles, but with a much softer face. "Come right in and look at our elocutionist, Marilla. Doesn't she look lovely?"

Marilla emitted a sound between a sniff and a grunt.

"She looks neat and proper. I like that way of fixing her hair. But I expect she'll ruin that dress driving over there in the dust and dew with it, and it looks most too thin for these damp nights. Organdy's the most unserviceable stuff in the world anyhow, and I told Matthew so when he got it. But there is no use in saying anything to Matthew nowadays. Time was when he would take my advice, but now he just buys things for Anne regardless, and the clerks at Carmody know they can palm anything off on him. Just let them tell him a thing is pretty and fashionable, and Matthew plunks his money down for it. Mind you keep your skirt clear of the wheel, Anne, and put your warm jacket on."

Then Marilla stalked down-stairs, thinking proudly how sweet Anne looked, with that

"One moonbeam from the forehead to the crown"[1]

and regretting that she could not go to the concert herself to hear her girl recite.

"I wonder if it *is* too damp for my dress," said Anne anxiously.

"Not a bit of it," said Diana, pulling up the window blind. "It's a perfect night, and there won't be any dew. Look at the moonlight."

"I'm so glad my window looks east into the sun-rising," said Anne, going over to Diana. "It's so splendid to see the morning coming up over those long hills and glowing through those sharp fir tops. It's new every morning, and I feel as if I washed my very soul in that bath of earliest sunshine. Oh, Diana, I love this little room so dearly. I don't know how I'll get along without it when I go to town next month."

"Don't speak of your going away to-night," begged Diana. "I don't want to think of it, it makes me so miserable, and I do want to have a good time this evening. What are you going to recite, Anne? And are you nervous?"

---

1 *One moonbeam . . . crown*   It appears that Marilla has been reading, or remembering, Elizabeth Barrett Browning's (1806–1861) *Aurora Lee* 4.1013.

"Not a bit. I've recited so often in public I don't mind at all now. I've decided to give "The Maiden's Vow."[2] It's so pathetic. Laura Spencer is going to give a comic recitation, but I'd rather make people cry than laugh."

"What will you recite if they encore you?"

"They won't dream of encoring me," scoffed Anne, who was not without her own secret hopes that they would, and already visioned herself telling Matthew all about it at the next morning's breakfast-table. "There are Billy and Jane now—I hear the wheels. Come on."

Billy Andrews insisted that Anne should ride on the front seat with him, so she unwillingly climbed up. She would have much preferred to sit back with the girls, where she could have laughed and chattered to her heart's content. There was not much of either laughter or chatter in Billy. He was a big, fat, stolid youth of twenty, with a round, expressionless face, and a painful lack of conversational gifts. But he admired Anne immensely, and was puffed up with pride over the prospect of driving to White Sands with that slim, upright figure beside him.

Anne, by dint of talking over her shoulder to the girls and occasionally passing a sop of civility to Billy—who grinned and chuckled and never could think of any reply until it was too late—contrived to enjoy the drive in spite of all. It was a night for enjoyment. The road was full of buggies, all bound for the hotel, and laughter, silver-clear, echoed and re-echoed along it. When they reached the hotel it was a blaze of light from top to bottom. They were met by the ladies of the concert committee, one of whom took Anne off to the performers' dressing-room, which was filled with the members of a Charlottetown Symphony Club, among whom Anne felt suddenly shy and frightened and countrified. Her dress, which, in the east gable, had seemed so dainty and pretty, now seemed simple and plain—too simple and plain, she thought, among all the silks and laces that glistened and rustled around her. What were her pearl beads compared to the diamonds of the big, handsome lady near her? And how poor her one wee white rose must look beside all the hothouse flowers the others wore! Anne laid her hat and jacket away, and shrank miserably into a corner. She wished herself back in the white room at Green Gables.

It was still worse on the platform of the big concert hall of the hotel, where she presently found herself. The electric lights dazzled her eyes, the perfume and hum bewildered her. She wished she were sitting down in the audience with Diana and Jane, who seemed to be having a splendid time away at the back. She was wedged in between a stout lady in pink silk and a tall, scornful looking girl in a white lace dress. The stout lady occasionally turned her head squarely around and surveyed Anne through her eyeglasses until Anne, acutely sensitive of being so scrutinized, felt that she must scream aloud; and the white lace girl kept talking audibly to her next neighbour about the "country bumpkins" and "rustic belles" in the audience, languidly anticipating "such fun" from the displays of local talent on the programme. Anne believed that she would hate that white lace girl to the end of life.

Unfortunately for Anne, a professional elocutionist was staying at the hotel and had consented to recite. She was a lithe, dark-eyed woman in a wonderful gown of shimmering gray stuff like woven moonbeams, with gems on her neck

---

2 *The Maiden's Vow* possibly the poem of that title by Caroline Oliphant (1766–1845) in which the maiden vows to remain true to her lost lover.

and in her dark hair. She had a marvellously flexible voice and wonderful power of expression; the audience went wild over her selection. Anne, for getting all about herself and her troubles for the time, listened with rapt and shining eyes; but when the recitation ended she suddenly put her hands over her face. She could never get up and recite after that—never. Had she ever thought she could recite? Oh, if she were only back at Green Gables!

At this unpropitious moment her name was called. Somehow, Anne—who did not notice the rather guilty little start of surprise the white lace girl gave, and would not have understood the subtle compliment implied therein if she had—got on her feet, and moved dizzily out to the front. She was so pale that Diana and Jane, down in the audience, clasped each other's hands in nervous sympathy.

Anne was the victim of an overwhelming attack of stage fright. Often as she had recited in public, she had never before faced such an audience as this, and the sight of it paralyzed her energies completely. Everything was so strange, so brilliant, so bewildering—the rows of ladies in evening dress, the critical faces, the whole atmosphere of wealth and culture about her. Very different this from the plain benches at the Debating Club, filled with the homely, sympathetic faces of friends and neighbours. These people, she thought, would be merciless critics. Perhaps, like the white lace girl, they anticipated amusement from her "rustic" efforts. She felt hopelessly, helplessly ashamed and miserable. Her knees trembled, her heart fluttered, a horrible faintness came over her; not a word could she utter, and the next moment she would have fled from the platform despite the humiliation which, she felt, must ever after be her portion if she did so.

But suddenly, as her dilated, frightened eyes gazed out over the audience, she saw Gilbert Blythe away at the back of the room, bending forward with a smile on his face—a smile which seemed to Anne at once triumphant and taunting. In reality it was nothing of the kind. Gilbert was merely smiling with appreciation of the whole affair in general and of the effect produced by Anne's slender white form and spiritual face against a background of palms in particular. Josie Pye, whom he had driven over, sat beside him, and her face certainly was both triumphant and taunting. But Anne did not see Josie, and would not have cared if she had. She drew a long breath and flung her head up proudly, courage and determination tingling over her like an electric shock. She *would not* fail before Gilbert Blythe—he should never be able to laugh at her, never, never! Her fright and nervousness vanished; and she began her recitation, her clear, sweet voice reaching to the farthest corner of the room without a tremor or a break. Self-possession was fully restored to her, and in the reaction from that horrible moment of powerlessness she recited as she had never done before. When she finished there were bursts of honest applause. Anne, stepping back to her seat, blushing with shyness and delight, found her hand vigorously clasped and shaken by the stout lady in pink silk.

"My dear, you did splendidly," she puffed. "I've been crying like a baby, actually I have. There, they're encoring you—they're bound to have you back!"

"Oh, I can't go," said Anne confusedly. "But yet I must, or Matthew will be disappointed. He said they would encore me."

"Then don't disappoint Matthew," said the pink lady, laughing.

Smiling, blushing, limpid-eyed, Anne tripped back and gave a quaint, funny little selection that captivated her audience still further. The rest of the evening was quite a little triumph for her.

When the concert was over, the stout, pink lady—who was the wife of an American millionaire—took her under her wing, and introduced her to everybody; and everybody was very nice to her. The professional elocutionist, Mrs. Evans, came and chatted with her, telling her that she had a charming voice and "interpreted" her selections beautifully. Even the white lace girl paid her a languid little compliment. They had supper in the big, beautifully decorated dining-room; Diana and Jane were invited to partake of this, also, since they had come with Anne, but Billy was nowhere to be found, having decamped in mortal fear of some such invitation. He was in waiting for them, with the team, however, when it was all over, and the three girls came merrily out into the calm, white moonshine radiance. Anne breathed deeply, and looked into the clear sky beyond the dark boughs of the firs.

Oh, it was good to be out again in the purity and silence of the night! How great and still and wonderful everything was, with the murmur of the sea sounding through it and the darkling cliffs beyond like grim giants guarding enchanted coasts.

"Hasn't it been a perfectly splendid time?" sighed Jane, as they drove away. "I just wish I was a rich American and could spend my summer at a hotel and wear jewels and low-necked dresses and have ice-cream and chicken salad every blessed day. I'm sure it would be ever so much more fun than teaching school. Anne, your recitation was simply great, although I thought at first you were never going to begin. I think it was better than Mrs. Evans'."

"Oh, no, don't say things like that, Jane," said Anne quickly, "because it sounds silly. It couldn't be better than Mrs. Evans', you know, for she is a professional, and I'm only a schoolgirl, with a little knack of reciting. I'm quite satisfied if the people just liked mine pretty well."

"I've a compliment for you, Anne," said Diana. "At least I think it must be a compliment because of the tone he said it in. Part of it was anyhow. There was an American sitting behind Jane and me—such a romantic-looking man, with coal-black hair and eyes. Josie Pye says he is a distinguished artist, and that her mother's cousin in Boston is married to a man that used to go to school with him. Well, we heard him say—didn't we, Jane?—'Who is that girl on the platform with the splendid Titian hair? She has a face I should like to paint.' There now, Anne. But what does Titian hair mean?"

"Being interpreted it means plain red, I guess," laughed Anne. "Titian was a very famous artist who liked to paint red-haired women."

"*Did* you see all the diamonds those ladies wore?" sighed Jane. "They were simply dazzling. Wouldn't you just love to be rich, girls?"

"We *are* rich," said Anne stanchly. "Why, we have sixteen years to our credit, and we're happy as queens, and we've all got imaginations, more or less. Look at that sea, girls—all silver and shadow and vision of things not seen. We couldn't enjoy its loveliness any more if we had millions of dollars and ropes of diamonds. You wouldn't change into any of those women if you could. Would you want to be that white lace girl and wear a sour look all your life, as if you'd been born turning up your nose at the world? Or the pink lady, kind and nice as she is, so stout and short that you'd really no figure at all? Or even Mrs. Evans, with that sad, sad look in her eyes? She must have been dreadfully unhappy sometime to have such a look. You *know* you wouldn't, Jane Andrews!"

"I *don't* know—exactly," said Jane unconvinced. "I think diamonds would comfort a person for a good deal."

"Well, I don't want to be any one but myself, even if I go uncomforted by diamonds all my life," declared Anne. "I'm quite content to be Anne of Green Gables, with my string of pearl beads. I know Matthew gave me as much love with them as ever went with Madame the Pink Lady's jewels."

CHAPTER 34

A Queen's Girl

THE next three weeks were busy ones at Green Gables, for Anne was getting ready to go to Queen's, and there was much sewing to be done, and many things to be talked over and arranged. Anne's outfit was ample and pretty, for Matthew saw to that, and Marilla for once made no objections whatever to anything he purchased or suggested. More—one evening she went up to the east gable with her arms full of a delicate pale green material.

"Anne, here's something for a nice light dress for you. I don't suppose you really need it; you've plenty of pretty waists; but I thought maybe you'd like something real dressy to wear if you were asked out anywhere of an evening in town, to a party or anything like that. I hear that Jane and Ruby and Josie have got 'evening dresses,' as they call them, and I don't mean you shall be behind them. I got Mrs. Allan to help me pick it in town last week, and we'll get Emily Gillis to make it for you. Emily has got taste, and her fits aren't to be equalled."

"Oh, Marilla, it's just lovely," said Anne. "Thank you so much. I don't believe you ought to be so kind to me—it's making it harder every day for me to go away."

The green dress was made up with as many tucks and frills and shirrings as Emily's taste permitted. Anne put it on one evening for Matthew's and Marilla's benefit, and recited "The Maiden's Vow" for them in the kitchen. As Marilla watched the bright, animated face and graceful motions her thoughts went back to the evening Anne had arrived at Green Gables, and memory recalled a vivid picture of the odd, frightened child in her preposterous yellowish-brown wincey dress, the heartbreak looking out of her tearful eyes. Something in the memory brought tears to Marilla's own eyes.

"I declare, my recitation has made you cry, Marilla," said Anne gaily, stooping over Marilla's chair to drop a butterfly kiss on that lady's cheek. "Now, I call that a positive triumph."

"No, I wasn't crying over your piece," said Marilla, who would have scorned to be betrayed into such weakness by any "poetry stuff." "I just couldn't help thinking of the little girl you used to be, Anne. And I was wishing you could have stayed a little girl, even with all your queer ways. You're grown up now and you're going away; and you look so tall and stylish and so—so—different altogether in that dress—as if you didn't belong in Avonlea at all—and I just got lonesome thinking it all over."

"Marilla!" Anne sat down on Marilla's gingham lap, took Marilla's lined face between her hands, and looked gravely and tenderly into Marilla's eyes. "I'm not a bit changed—not really. I'm only just pruned down and branched out. The real *me*—back here—is just the same. It won't make a bit of difference where I go or how much I change outwardly; at heart I shall always be your little Anne, who will love you and Matthew and dear Green Gables more and better every day of her life."

Anne laid her fresh young cheek against Marilla's faded one, and reached out a hand to pat Matthew's shoulder. Marilla would have given much just then to have possessed Anne's power of putting her feelings into words; but nature and habit had willed it otherwise, and she could only put her arms close about her girl and hold her tenderly to her heart, wishing that she need never let her go.

Matthew, with a suspicious moisture in his eyes, got up and went out-of-doors. Under the stars of the blue summer night he walked agitatedly across the yard to the gate under the poplars.

"Well now, I guess she ain't been much spoiled," he muttered, proudly. "I guess my putting in my oar occasional never did much harm after all. She's smart and pretty, and loving, too, which is better than all the rest. She's been a blessing to us, and there never was a luckier mistake than what Mrs. Spencer made—if it *was* luck. I don't believe it was any such thing. It was Providence, because the Almighty saw we needed her, I reckon."

The day finally came when Anne must go to town. She and Matthew drove in one fine September morning, after a tearful parting with Diana and an untearful, practical one—on Marilla's side at least—with Marilla. But when Anne had gone Diana dried her tears and went to a beach picnic at White Sands with some of her Carmody cousins, where she contrived to enjoy herself tolerably well; while Marilla plunged fiercely into unnecessary work and kept at it all day long with the bitterest kind of a heartache—the ache that burns and gnaws and cannot wash itself away in ready tears. But that night, when Marilla went to bed, acutely and miserably conscious that the little gable room at the end of the hall was untenanted by any vivid young life and unstirred by any soft breathing, she buried her face in her pillow, and wept for her girl in a passion of sobs that appalled her when she grew calm enough to reflect how very wicked it must be to take on so about a sinful fellow creature.

Anne and the rest of the Avonlea scholars reached town just in time to hurry off to the Academy. That first day passed pleasantly enough in a whirl of excitement, meeting all the new students, learning to know the professors by sight and being assorted and organized into classes. Anne intended taking up the Second Year work, being advised to do so by Miss Stacy; Gilbert Blythe elected to do the same. This meant getting a First Class teacher's license in one year instead of two, if they were successful; but it also meant much more and harder work. Jane, Ruby, Josie, Charlie, and Moody Spurgeon, not being troubled with the stirrings of ambition, were content to take up the Second Class work. Anne was conscious of a pang of loneliness when she found herself in a room with fifty other students, not one of whom she knew, except the tall, brown-haired boy across the room; and knowing him in the fashion she did, did not help her much, as she reflected pessimistically. Yet she was undeniably glad that they were in the same class; the old rivalry could still be carried on, and Anne would hardly have known what to do if it had been lacking.

"I wouldn't feel comfortable without it," she thought. "Gilbert looks awfully determined. I suppose he's making up his mind, here and now, to win the medal. What a splendid chin he has! I never noticed it before. I do wish Jane and Ruby had gone in for First Class, too. I suppose I won't feel so much like a cat in a strange garret when I get acquainted, though. I wonder which of the girls here are going to be my friends. It's really an interesting speculation. Of course I promised Diana that no Queen's girl, no matter now much I liked her, should ever be as dear to me as she is; but I've lots of second-best affections to bestow. I like the look of that girl with the brown eyes and the crimson waist. She looks vivid and red-rosy; and there's that pale, fair one gazing out of the window. She has lovely hair, and looks as if she knew a thing or two about dreams. I'd like to know them both—know them well—well enough to walk with my arm about their waists, and call them nicknames. But just now I don't know them and they don't know me, and probably don't want to know me particularly. Oh, it's lonesome!"

It was lonesomer still when Anne found herself alone in her hall bedroom that night at twilight. She was not to board with the other girls, who all had relatives in town to take pity on them. Miss Josephine Barry would have liked to board her, but Beechwood was so far from the Academy that it was out of the question; so Miss Barry hunted up a boarding-house, assuring Matthew and Marilla that it was the very place for Anne.

"The lady who keeps it is a reduced gentlewoman," explained Miss Barry. "Her husband was a British officer, and she is very careful what sort of boarders she takes. Anne will not meet with any objectionable persons under her roof. The table is good, and the house is near the Academy, in a quiet neighbourhood."

All this might be quite true, and, indeed, proved to be so, but it did not materially help Anne in the first agony of homesickness that seized upon her. She looked dismally about her narrow little room, with its dull-papered, pictureless walls, its small iron bedstead and empty bookcase; and a horrible choke came into her throat as she thought of her own white room at Green Gables, where she would have the pleasant consciousness of a great green still outdoors, of sweet peas growing in the garden, and moonlight falling on the orchard, of the brook below the slope and the spruce boughs tossing in the night wind beyond it, of a vast starry sky, and the light from Diana's window shining out through the gap in the trees. Here there was nothing of this; Anne knew that outside of her window was a hard street, with a network of telephone wires shutting out the sky, the tramp of alien feet, and a thousand lights gleaming on stranger faces. She knew that she was going to cry, and fought against it.

"I *won't* cry. It's silly—and weak—there's the third tear splashing down by my nose. There are more coming! I must think of something funny to stop them. But there's nothing funny except what is connected with Avonlea, and that only makes things worse—four—five—I'm going home next Friday, but that seems a hundred years away. Oh, Matthew is nearly home by now—and Marilla is at the gate, looking down the lane for him—six—seven—eight—oh, there's no use in counting them! They're coming in a flood presently. I can't cheer up—I don't *want* to cheer up. It's nicer to be miserable!"

The flood of tears would have come, no doubt, had not Josie Pye appeared at that moment. In the joy of seeing a familiar face Anne forgot that there had never been much love lost between her and Josie. As a part of Avonlea life even a Pye was welcome.

"I'm so glad you came up," Anne said sincerely.

"You've been crying," remarked Josie, with aggravating pity. "I suppose you're homesick—some people have so little self-control in that respect. I've no intention of being homesick, I can tell you. Town's too jolly after that poky old Avonlea. I wonder how I ever existed there so long. You shouldn't cry, Anne; it isn't becoming, for your nose and eyes get red, and then you seem *all* red. I'd a perfectly scrumptious time in the Academy today. Our French professor is simply a duck. His moustache would give you kerwollops of the heart. Have you anything eatable around, Anne? I'm literally starving. Ah, I guessed likely Marilla'd load you up with cake. That's why I called round. Otherwise I'd have gone to the park to hear the band play with Frank Stockley. He boards same place as I do, and he's a sport. He noticed you in class today, and asked me who the red-headed girl was. I told him you were an orphan that the Cuthberts had adopted, and nobody knew very much about what you'd been before that."

Anne was wondering if, after all, solitude and tears were not more satisfactory than Josie Pye's companionship when Jane and Ruby appeared, each with an inch of Queen's colour ribbon—purple and scarlet—pinned proudly to her coat. As Josie was not "speaking" to Jane just then she had to subside into comparative harmlessness.

"Well," said Jane with a sigh, "I feel as if I'd lived many moons since the morning. I ought to be home studying my Virgil—that horrid old professor gave us twenty lines to start in on to-morrow. But I simply couldn't settle down to study to-night. Anne, methinks I see the traces of tears. If you've been crying do own up. It will restore my self-respect, for I was shedding tears freely before Ruby came along. I don't mind being a goose so much if somebody else is goosey, too. Cake? You'll give me a teeny piece, won't you? Thank you. It has the real Avonlea flavour."

Ruby, perceiving the Queen's calendar lying on the table, wanted to know if Anne meant to try for the gold medal.

Anne blushed and admitted she was thinking of it.

"Oh, that reminds me," said Josie, "Queen's is to get one of the Avery scholarships after all. The word came to-day. Frank Stockley told me—his uncle is one of the board of governors, you know. It will be announced in the Academy to-morrow."

An Avery scholarship! Anne felt her heart beat more quickly, and the horizons of her ambition shifted and broadened as if by magic. Before Josie had told the news Anne's highest pinnacle of aspiration had been a teacher's provincial license, Class First, at the end of the year, and perhaps the medal! But now in one moment Anne saw herself winning the Avery scholarship, taking an Arts course at Redmond College, and graduating in a gown and mortar-board, all before the echo of Josie's words had died away. For the Avery scholarship was in English, and Anne felt that here her foot was on her native heath.

A wealthy manufacturer of New Brunswick had died and left part of his fortune to endow a large number of scholarships to be distributed among the various high schools and academies of the Maritime Provinces, according to their respective standings. There had been much doubt whether one would be allotted to Queen's, but the matter was settled at last, and at the end of the year the graduate who made the highest mark in English and English Literature would win the scholarship—two hundred and fifty dollars a year for four years at Redmond College. No wonder that Anne went to bed that night with tingling cheeks!

"I'll win that scholarship if hard work can do it," she resolved. "Wouldn't Matthew be proud if I got to be a B.A.? Oh, it's delightful to have ambitions. I'm so glad I have such a lot. And there never seems to be any end to them—

that's the best of it. Just as soon as you attain to one ambition you see another one glittering higher up still. It does make life so interesting."

CHAPTER 35

The Winter at Queen's

ANNE'S homesickness wore off, greatly helped in the wearing by her week-end visits home. As long as the open weather lasted the Avonlea students went out to Carmody on the new branch railway every Friday night. Diana and several other Avonlea young folks were generally on hand to meet them and they all walked over to Avonlea in a merry party. Anne thought those Friday evening gipsyings over the autumnal hills in the crisp golden air, with the home-lights of Avonlea twinkling beyond, were the best and dearest hours in the whole week.

Gilbert Blythe nearly always walked with Ruby Gillis and carried her satchel for her. Ruby was a very handsome young lady, now thinking herself quite as grown up as she really was; she wore her skirts as long as her mother would let her and did her hair up in town, though she had to take it down when she went home. She had large, bright-blue eyes, a brilliant complexion, and a plump showy figure. She laughed a great deal, was cheerful and good-tempered, and enjoyed the pleasant things of life frankly.

"But I shouldn't think she was the sort of girl Gilbert would like," whispered Jane to Anne. Anne did not think so either, but she would not have said so for the Avery scholarship. She could not help thinking, too, that it would be very pleasant to have such a friend as Gilbert to jest and chatter with and exchange ideas about books and studies and ambitions. Gilbert had ambitions, she knew, and Ruby Gillis did not seem the sort of person with whom such could be profitably discussed.

There was no silly sentiment in Anne's ideas concerning Gilbert. Boys were to her, when she thought about them at all, merely possible good comrades. If she and Gilbert had been friends she would not have cared how many other friends he had nor with whom he walked. She had a genius for friendship; girl friends she had in plenty; but she had a vague consciousness that masculine friendship might also be a good thing to round out one's conceptions of companionship and furnish broader standpoints of judgment and comparison. Not that Anne could have put her feelings on the matter into just such clear definition. But she thought that if Gilbert had ever walked home with her from the train, over the crisp fields and along the ferny byways, they might have had many and merry and interesting conversations about the new world that was opening around them and their hopes and ambitions therein. Gilbert was a clever young fellow, with his own thoughts about things and a determination to get the best out of life and put the best into it. Ruby Gillis told Jane Andrews that she didn't understand half the things Gilbert Blythe said; he talked just like Anne Shirley did when she had a thoughtful fit on and for her part she didn't think it any fun to be bothering about books and that sort of thing when you didn't have to. Frank Stockley had lots more dash and go, but then he wasn't half as good-looking as Gilbert and she really couldn't decide which she liked best!

In the Academy Anne gradually drew a little circle of friends about her, thoughtful, imaginative, ambitious students like herself. With the "rose-red" girl, Stella Maynard, and the "dream girl," Priscilla Grant, she soon became intimate, finding the latter pale spiritual-looking maiden to be full to the brim of mischief and pranks and fun, while the vivid, black-eyed Stella had a heartful of wistful dreams and fancies, as aerial and rainbow-like as Anne's own.

After the Christmas holidays the Avonlea students gave up going home on Fridays and settled down to hard work. By this time all the Queen's scholars had gravitated into their own places in the ranks and the various classes had assumed distinct and settled shadings of individuality. Certain facts had become generally accepted. It was admitted that the medal contestants had practically narrowed down to three—Gilbert Blythe, Anne Shirley, and Lewis Wilson; the Avery scholarship was more doubtful, any one of a certain six being a possible winner. The bronze medal for mathematics was considered as good as won by a fat, funny little up-country boy with a bumpy forehead and a patched coat.

Ruby Gillis was the handsomest girl of the year at the Academy; in the Second Year classes Stella Maynard carried off the palm for beauty, with a small but critical minority in favour of Anne Shirley. Ethel Marr was admitted by all competent judges to have the most stylish modes of hair-dressing, and Jane Andrews—plain, plodding, conscientious Jane—carried off the honours in the domestic science course. Even Josie Pye attained a certain preeminence as the sharpest-tongued young lady in attendance at Queen's. So it may be fairly stated that Miss Stacy's old pupils held their own in the wider arena of the academical course.

Anne worked hard and steadily. Her rivalry with Gilbert was as intense as it had ever been in Avonlea school, although it was not known in the class at large, but somehow the bitterness had gone out of it. Anne no longer wished to win for the sake of defeating Gilbert; rather, for the proud consciousness of a well-won victory over a worthy foeman. It would be worth while to win, but she no longer thought life would be insupportable if she did not.

In spite of lessons the students found opportunities for pleasant times. Anne spent many of her spare hours at Beechwood and generally ate her Sunday dinners there and went to church with Miss Barry. The latter was, as she admitted, growing old, but her black eyes were not dim nor the vigour of her tongue in the least abated. But she never sharpened the latter on Anne, who continued to be a prime favourite with the critical old lady.

"That Anne-girl improves all the time," she said. "I get tired of other girls—there is such a provoking and eternal sameness about them. Anne has as many shades as a rainbow and every shade is the prettiest while it lasts. I don't know that she is as amusing as she was when she was a child, but she makes me love her and I like people who make me love them. It saves me so much trouble in making myself love them."

Then, almost before anybody realized it, spring had come; out in Avonlea the Mayflowers were peeping pinkly out on the sere barrens where snow-wreaths lingered; and the "mist of green"[1] was on the woods and in the valleys. But in Charlottetown harassed Queen's students thought and talked only of examinations.

---

1 *mist of green*   perhaps from Tennyson's poem, "The Brook" 14.

"It doesn't seem possible that the term is nearly over," said Anne. "Why, last fall it seemed so long to look forward to—a whole winter of studies and classes. And here we are, with the exams looming up next week. Girls, sometimes I feel as if those exams meant everything, but when I look at the big buds swelling on those chestnut trees and the misty blue air at the end of the streets they don't seem half so important."

Jane and Ruby and Josie, who had dropped in, did not take this view of it. To them the coming examinations were constantly very important indeed—far more important than chestnut buds or May-time hazes. It was all very well for Anne, who was sure of passing at least, to have her moments of belittling them, but when your whole future depended on them—as the girls truly thought theirs did—you could not regard them philosophically.

"I've lost seven pounds in the last two weeks," sighed Jane. "It's no use to say don't worry. I *will* worry. Worrying helps you some—it seems as if you were doing something when you're worrying. It would be dreadful if I failed to get my license after going to Queen's all winter and spending so much money."

"*I* don't care," said Josie Pye. "If I don't pass this year I'm coming back next. My father can afford to send me. Anne, Frank Stockley says that Professor Tremaine said Gilbert Blythe was sure to get the medal and that Emily Clay would likely win the Avery scholarship."

"That may make me feel badly to-morrow, Josie," laughed Anne, "but just now I honestly feel that as long as I know the violets are coming out all purple down in the hollow below Green Gables and that little ferns are poking their heads up in Lovers' Lane, it's not a great deal of difference whether I win the Avery or not. I've done my best and I begin to understand what is meant by the 'joy of the strife.' Next to trying and winning, the best thing is trying and failing. Girls, don't talk about exams! Look at that arch of pale green sky over those houses and picture to yourselves what it must look like over the purply-dark beechwoods back of Avonlea."

"What are you going to wear for commencement, Jane?" asked Ruby practically.

Jane and Josie both answered at once and the chatter drifted into a side eddy of fashions. But Anne, with her elbows on the window sill, her soft cheek laid against her clasped hands, and her eyes filled with visions, looked out unheedingly across city roof and spire to that glorious dome of sunset sky and wove her dreams of a possible future from the golden tissue of youth's own optimism. All the Beyond was hers with its possibilities lurking rosily in the oncoming years— each year a rose of promise to be woven into an immortal chaplet.

CHAPTER 36

The Glory and the Dream[1]

O N THE morning when the final results of all the examinations were to be posted on the bulletin board at Queen's, Anne and Jane walked down the street together. Jane was smiling and happy; examinations were over and she

---

1 *The Glory and the Dream*   Compare, in William Wordsword's (1770–1850) "Intimations Ode" 57–58, "Whither is fled the visionary gleam? / Where is it now, the glory and the dream?"

was comfortably sure she had made a pass at least; further considerations troubled Jane not at all; she had no soaring ambitions and consequently was not affected with the unrest attendant thereon. For we pay a price for everything we get or take in this world; and although ambitions are well worth having, they are not to be cheaply won, but exact their dues of work and self-denial, anxiety and discouragement. Anne was pale and quiet; in ten more minutes she would know who had won the medal and who the Avery. Beyond those ten minutes there did not seem, just then, to be anything worth being called Time.

"Of course you'll win one of them anyhow," said Jane, who couldn't understand how the faculty could be so unfair as to order it otherwise.

"I have no hope of the Avery," said Anne. "Everybody says Emily Clay will win it. And I'm not going to march up to that bulletin board and look at it before everybody. I haven't the moral courage. I'm going straight to the girls' dressing-room. You must read the announcements and then come and tell me, Jane. And I implore you in the name of our old friendship to do it as quickly as possible. If I have failed just say so, without trying to break it gently; and whatever you do *don't* sympathize with me. Promise me this, Jane."

Jane promised solemnly; but, as it happened, there was no necessity for such a promise. When they went up the entrance steps of Queen's they found the hall full of boys who were carrying Gilbert Blythe around on their shoulders and yelling at the tops of their voices, "Hurrah for Blythe, Medallist!"

For a moment Anne felt one sickening pang of defeat and disappointment. So she had failed and Gilbert had won! Well, Matthew would be sorry—he had been so sure she would win.

And then!

Somebody called out:

"Three cheers for Miss Shirley, winner of the Avery!"

"Oh, Anne," gasped Jane, as they fled to the girls' dressing-room amid hearty cheers. "Oh, Anne, I'm so proud! Isn't it splendid?"

And then the girls were around them and Anne was the centre of a laughing, congratulating group. Her shoulders were thumped and her hands shaken vigorously. She was pushed and pulled and hugged and among it all she managed to whisper to Jane:

"Oh, won't Matthew and Marilla be pleased! I must write the news home right away."

Commencement was the next important happening. The exercises were held in the big assembly hall of the Academy. Addresses were given, essays read, songs sung, the public award of diplomas, prizes and medals made.

Matthew and Marilla were there, with eyes and ears for only one student on the platform—a tall girl in pale green, with faintly flushed cheeks and starry eyes, who read the best essay and was pointed out and whispered about as the Avery winner.

"Reckon you're glad we kept her, Marilla?" whispered Matthew, speaking for the first time since he had entered the hall, when Anne had finished her essay.

"It's not the first time I've been glad," retorted Marilla. "You do like to rub things in, Matthew Cuthbert."

Miss Barry, who was sitting behind them, leaned forward and poked Marilla in the back with her parasol.

"Aren't you proud of that Anne-girl? I am," she said.

Anne went home to Avonlea with Matthew and Marilla that evening. She had not been home since April and she felt that she could not wait another day. The apple-blossoms were out and the world was fresh and young. Diana was at Green Gables to meet her. In her own white room, where Marilla had set a flowering house rose on the window sill, Anne looked about her and drew a long breath of happiness.

"Oh, Diana, it's so good to be back again. It's so good to see those pointed firs coming out against the pink sky—and that white orchard and the old Snow Queen. Isn't the breath of the mint delicious? And that tea rose—why, it's a song and a hope and a prayer all in one. And it's *good* to see you again, Diana!"

"I thought you liked that Stella Maynard better than me," said Diana reproachfully. "Josie Pye told me you did. Josie said you were *infatuated* with her."

Anne laughed and pelted Diana with the faded "June lilies" of her bouquet.

"Stella Maynard is the dearest girl in the world except one and you are that one, Diana," she said. "I love you more than ever—and I've so many things to tell you. But just now I feel as if it were joy enough to sit here and look at you. I'm tired, I think—tired of being studious and ambitious. I mean to spend at least two hours to-morrow lying out in the orchard grass, thinking of absolutely nothing."

"You've done splendidly, Anne. I suppose you won't be teaching now that you've won the Avery?"

"No. I'm going to Redmond in September. Doesn't it seem wonderful? I'll have a brand-new stock of ambition laid in by that time after three glorious, golden months of vacation. Jane and Ruby are going to teach. Isn't it splendid to think we all got through even to Moody Spurgeon and Josie Pye?"

"The Newbridge trustees have offered Jane their school already," said Diana. "Gilbert Blythe is going to teach, too. He has to. His father can't afford to send him to college next year, after all, so he means to earn his own way through. I expect he'll get the school here if Miss Ames decides to leave."

Anne felt a queer little sensation of dismayed surprise. She had not known this; she had expected that Gilbert would be going to Redmond also. What would she do without their inspiring rivalry? Would not work, even at a co-educational college with a real degree in prospect, be rather flat without her friend the enemy?

The next morning at breakfast it suddenly struck Anne that Matthew was not looking well. Surely he was much grayer than he had been a year before.

"Marilla," she said hesitatingly when he had gone out, "is Matthew quite well?"

"No, he isn't," said Marilla in a troubled tone. "He's had some real bad spells with his heart this spring and he won't spare himself a mite. I've been real worried about him, but he's some better this while back and we've got a good hired man, so I'm hoping he'll kind of rest and pick up. Maybe he will now you're home. You always cheer him up."

Anne leaned across the table and took Marilla's face in her hands.

"You are not looking as well yourself as I'd like to see you, Marilla. You look tired. I'm afraid you've been working too hard. You must take a rest, now that I'm home. I'm just going to take this one day off to visit all the dear old spots and hunt up my old dreams, and then it will be your turn to be lazy while I do the work."

Marilla smiled affectionately at her girl.

"It's not the work—it's my head. I've a pain so often now—behind my eyes. Doctor Spencer's been fussing with glasses, but they don't do me any good. There is a distinguished oculist coming to the Island the last of June and the doctor says I must see him. I guess I'll have to. I can't read or sew with any comfort now. Well, Anne, you've done real well at Queen's I must say. To take First Class License in one year and win the Avery scholarship—well, well, Mrs. Lynde says pride goes before a fall and she doesn't believe in the higher education of women at all; she says it unfits them for woman's true sphere. I don't believe a word of it. Speaking of Rachel reminds me—did you hear anything about the Abbey Bank lately, Anne?"

"I heard that it was shaky," answered Anne. "Why?"

"That is what Rachel said. She was up here one day last week and said there was some talk about it. Matthew felt real worried. All we have saved is in that bank—every penny. I wanted Matthew to put it in the Savings Bank in the first place, but old Mr. Abbey was a great friend of father's and he'd always banked with him. Matthew said any bank with him at the head of it was good enough for anybody."

"I think he has only been its nominal head for many years," said Anne. "He is a very old man; his nephews are really at the head of the institution."

"Well, when Rachel told us that, I wanted Matthew to draw our money right out and he said he'd think of it. But Mr. Russell told him yesterday that the bank was all right."

Anne had her good day in the companionship of the outdoor world. She never forgot that day; it was so bright and golden and fair, so free from shadow and so lavish of blossom. Anne spent some of its rich hours in the orchard; she went to the Dryad's Bubble and Willowmere and Violet Vale; she called at the manse and had a satisfying talk with Mrs. Allan; and finally in the evening she went with Matthew for the cows, through Lovers' Lane to the back pasture. The woods were all gloried through with sunset and the warm splendour of it streamed down through the hill gaps in the west. Matthew walked slowly with bent head; Anne, tall and erect, suited her springing step to his.

"You've been working too hard to-day, Matthew," she said reproachfully. "Why won't you take things easier?"

"Well now, I can't seem to," said Matthew, as he opened the yard gate to let the cows through. "It's only that I'm getting old, Anne, and keep forgetting it. Well, well, I've always worked pretty hard and I'd rather drop in harness."

"If I had been the boy you sent for," said Anne wistfully, "I'd be able to help you so much now and spare you in a hundred ways. I could find it in my heart to wish I had been, just for that."

"Well now, I'd rather have you than a dozen boys, Anne," said Matthew patting her hand. "Just mind you that—rather than a dozen boys. Well now, I guess it wasn't a boy that took the Avery scholarship, was it? It was a girl—my girl—my girl that I'm proud of."

He smiled his shy smile at her as he went into the yard. Anne took the memory of it with her when she went to her room that night and sat for a long while at her open window, thinking of the past and dreaming of the future. Outside the Snow Queen was mistily white in the moonshine; the frogs were singing in the marsh beyond Orchard Slope. Anne always remembered the silvery, peaceful beauty and fragrant calm of that night. It was the last night before sorrow touched her life; and no life is ever quite the same again when once that cold, sanctifying touch has been laid upon it.

CHAPTER 37

The Reaper Whose Name Is Death

MONT-
GOMERY

*Anne of
Green Gables*
Chap. 37

"MATTHEW—Matthew—what is the matter? Matthew, are you sick?" It was Marilla who spoke, alarm in every jerky word. Anne came through the hall, her hands full of white narcissus—it was long before Anne could love the sight or odour of white narcissus again—in time to hear her and to see Matthew standing in the porch doorway, a folded paper in his hand, and his face strangely drawn and gray. Anne dropped her flowers and sprang across the kitchen to him at the same moment as Marilla. They were both too late; before they could reach him Matthew had fallen across the threshold.

"He's fainted," gasped Marilla. "Anne, run for Martin—quick, quick! He's at the barn."

Martin, the hired man, who had just driven home from the post-office, started at once for the doctor, calling at Orchard Slope on his way to send Mr. and Mrs. Barry over. Mrs. Lynde, who was there on an errand, came too. They found Anne and Marilla distractedly trying to restore Matthew to consciousness.

Mrs. Lynde pushed them gently aside, tried his pulse, and then laid her ear over his heart. She looked at their anxious faces sorrowfully and the tears came into her eyes.

"Oh, Marilla," she said gravely. "I don't think—we can do anything for him."

"Mrs. Lynde, you don't think—you can't think Matthew is—is—" Anne could not say the dreadful word; she turned sick and pallid.

"Child, yes, I'm afraid of it. Look at his face. When you've seen that look as often as I have you'll know what it means."

Anne looked at the still face and there beheld the seal of the Great Presence.

When the doctor came he said that death had been instantaneous and probably painless, caused in all likelihood by some sudden shock. The secret of the shock was discovered to be in the paper Matthew had held and which Martin had brought from the office that morning. It contained an account of the failure of the Abbey Bank.

The news spread quickly through Avonlea, and all day friends and neighbours thronged Green Gables and came and went on errands of kindness for the dead and living. For the first time shy, quiet Matthew Cuthbert was a person of central importance; the white majesty of death had fallen on him and set him apart as one crowned.

When the calm night came softly down over Green Gables the old house was hushed and tranquil. In the parlour lay Matthew Cuthbert in his coffin, his long gray hair framing his placid face on which there was a little kindly smile as if he but slept, dreaming pleasant dreams. There were flowers about him—sweet old-fashioned flowers which his mother had planted in the homestead garden in her bridal days and for which Matthew had always had a secret, wordless love. Anne had gathered them and brought them to him, her anguished, tearless eyes burning in her white face. It was the last thing she could do for him.

The Barrys and Mrs. Lynde stayed with them that night. Diana, going to the east gable, where Anne was standing at her window, said gently:

"Anne dear, would you like to have me sleep with you to-night?"

"Thank you, Diana." Anne looked earnestly into her friend's face. "I think you won't misunderstand me when I say that I want to be alone. I'm not afraid.

I haven't been alone one minute since it happened—and I want to be. I want to be quite silent and quiet and try to realize it. I *can't* realize it. Half the time it seems to me that Matthew can't be dead; and the other half it seems as if he must have been dead for a long time and I've had this horrible dull ache ever since."

Diana did not quite understand. Marilla's impassioned grief breaking all the bounds of natural reserve and lifelong habit in its stormy rush, she could comprehend better than Anne's tearless agony. But she went away kindly, leaving Anne alone to keep her first vigil with sorrow.

Anne hoped that tears would come in solitude. It seemed to her a terrible thing that she could not shed a tear for Matthew, whom she had loved so much and who had been so kind to her, Matthew, who had walked with her last evening at sunset and was now lying in the dim room below with that awful peace on his brow. But no tears came at first, even when she knelt by her window in the darkness and prayed, looking up to the stars beyond the hills—no tears, only the same horrible dull ache of misery that kept on aching until she fell asleep, worn out with the day's pain and excitement.

In the night she awakened, with the stillness and the darkness about her, and the recollection of the day came over her like a wave of sorrow. She could see Matthew's face smiling at her as he had smiled when they parted at the gate that last evening—she could hear his voice saying, "My girl—my girl that I'm proud of." Then the tears came and Anne wept her heart out. Marilla heard her and crept in to comfort her.

"There—there—don't cry so, Anne. It can't bring him back. It—it—isn't right to cry so. I knew that to-day, but I couldn't help it then. He'd always been such a good, kind brother to me—but God knows best."

"Oh, just let me cry, Marilla," sobbed Anne. "The tears don't hurt me like that ache did. Stay here for a little while with me and keep your arm round me—so. I couldn't have Diana stay, she's good and kind and sweet—but it's not her sorrow—she's outside of it and she couldn't come close enough to my heart to help me. It's our sorrow—yours and mine. Oh, Marilla, what will we do without him?"

"We've got each other, Anne. I don't know what I'd do if you weren't here—if you'd never come. Oh, Anne, I know I've been kind of strict and harsh with you maybe—but you mustn't think I didn't love you as well as Matthew did, for all that. I want to tell you now when I can. It's never been easy for me to say things out of my heart, but at times like this it's easier. I love you as dear as if you were my own flesh and blood and you've been my joy and comfort ever since you came to Green Gables."

Two days afterwards they carried Matthew Cuthbert over his homestead threshold and away from the fields he had tilled and the orchards he had loved and the trees he had planted; and then Avonlea settled back to its usual placidity and even at Green Gables affairs slipped into their old groove and work was done and duties fulfilled with regularity as before, although always with the aching sense of "loss in all familiar things."[1] Anne, new to grief, thought it almost sad that it could be so—that they *could* go on in the old way without Matthew. She felt something like shame and remorse when she discovered that the sunrises behind the firs and the pale pink buds opening in the garden gave

---

1 *loss in all familiar things*   from Whittier's "Snowbound" 20.

her the old inrush of gladness when she saw them—that Diana's visits were pleasant to her and that Diana's merry words and ways moved her to laughter and smiles—that, in brief, the beautiful world of blossom and love and friendship had lost none of its power to please her fancy and thrill her heart, that life still called to her with many insistent voices.

"It seems like disloyalty to Matthew, somehow, to find pleasure in these things now that he has gone," she said wistfully to Mrs. Allan one evening when they were together in the manse garden. "I miss him so much—all the time— and yet, Mrs. Allan, the world and life seem very beautiful and interesting to me for all. To-day Diana said something funny and I found myself laughing. I thought when it happened I could never laugh again. And it somehow seems as if I oughtn't to."

"When Matthew was here he liked to hear you laugh and he liked to know that you found pleasure in the pleasant things around you," said Mrs. Allan gently. "He is just away now; and he likes to know it just the same. I am sure we should not shut our hearts against the healing influences that nature offers us. But I understand your feeling. I think we all experience the same thing. We resent the thought that anything can please us when some one we love is no longer here to share the pleasure with us, and we almost feel as if we were unfaithful to our sorrow when we find our interest in life returning to us."

"I was down to the graveyard to plant a rose-bush on Matthew's grave this afternoon," said Anne dreamily. "I took a slip of the little white Scotch rose-bush his mother brought out from Scotland long ago; Matthew always liked those roses the best—they were so small and sweet on their thorny stems. It made me feel glad that I could plant it by his grave—as if I were doing something that must please him in taking it there to be near him. I hope he has roses like them in heaven. Perhaps the souls of all those little white roses that he has loved so many summers were all there to meet him. I must go home now. Marilla is all alone and she gets lonely at twilight."

"She will be lonelier still, I fear, when you go away again to college," said Mrs. Allan.

Anne did not reply; she said good night and went slowly back to Green Gables. Marilla was sitting on the front door-steps and Anne sat down beside her. The door was open behind them, held back by a big pink conch shell with hints of sea sunsets in its smooth inner convolutions.

Anne gathered some sprays of pale yellow honeysuckle and put them in her hair. She liked the delicious hint of fragrance, as of some aerial benediction, above her every time she moved.

"Doctor Spencer was here while you were away," Marilla said. "He says that the specialist will be in town to-morrow and he insists that I must go in and have my eyes examined. I suppose I'd better go and have it over. I'll be more than thankful if the man can give me the right kind of glasses to suit my eyes. You won't mind staying here alone while I'm away, will you? Martin will have to drive me in and there's ironing and baking to do."

"I shall be all right. Diana will come over for company for me. I shall attend to the ironing and baking beautifully—you needn't fear that I'll starch the handkerchiefs or flavour the cake with liniment."

Marilla laughed.

"What a girl you were for making mistakes in them days, Anne. You were always getting into scrapes. I did use to think you were possessed. Do you mind the time you dyed your hair?"

353

"Yes, indeed. I shall never forget it," smiled Anne, touching the heavy braid of hair that was wound about her shapely head. "I laugh a little now sometimes when I think what a worry my hair used to be to me—but I don't laugh *much* because it was a very real trouble then. I did suffer terribly over my hair and my freckles. My freckles are really gone; and people are nice enough to tell me my hair is auburn now—all but Josie Pye. She informed me yesterday that she really thought it was redder than ever, or at least my black dress made it look redder, and she asked me if people who had red hair ever got used to having it. Marilla, I've almost decided to give up trying to like Josie Pye. I've made what I would once have called a heroic effort to like her, but Josie Pye won't *be* liked."

"Josie is a Pye," said Marilla sharply, "so she can't help being disagreeable. I suppose people of that kind serve some useful purpose in society, but I must say I don't know what it is any more than I know the use of thistles. Is Josie going to teach?"

"No, she is going back to Queen's next year. So are Moody Spurgeon and Charlie Sloane. Jane and Ruby are going to teach and they have both got schools—Jane at Newbridge and Ruby at some place up west."

"Gilbert Blythe is going to teach too, isn't he?"

"Yes"—briefly.

"What a nice-looking young fellow he is," said Marilla absently. "I saw him in church last Sunday and he seemed so tall and manly. He looks a lot like his father did at the same age. John Blythe was a nice boy. We used to be real good friends, he and I. People called him my beau."

Anne looked up with swift interest:

"Oh, Marilla—and what happened?—why didn't you—"

"We had a quarrel. I wouldn't forgive him when he asked me to. I meant to, after awhile—but I was sulky and angry and I wanted to punish him first. He never came back—the Blythes were all mighty independent. But I always felt—rather sorry. I've always kind of wished I'd forgiven him when I had the chance."

"So you've had a bit of romance in your life, too," said Anne softly.

"Yes, I suppose you might call it that. You wouldn't think so to look at me, would you? But you never can tell about people from their outsides. Everybody has forgot about me and John. I'd forgotten myself. But it all came back to me when I saw Gilbert last Sunday."

CHAPTER 38

The Bend in the Road

MARILLA went to town the next day and returned in the evening. Anne had gone over to Orchard Slope with Diana and came back to find Marilla in the kitchen, sitting by the table with her head leaning on her hand. Something in her dejected attitude struck a chill to Anne's heart. She had never seen Marilla sit limply inert like that.

"Are you very tired, Marilla?"

"Yes—no—I don't know," said Marilla wearily, looking up. "I suppose I am tired but I haven't thought about it. It's not that."

"Did you see the oculist? What did he say?" asked Anne anxiously.

"Yes, I saw him. He examined my eyes. He says that if I give up all reading and sewing entirely and any kind of work that strains the eyes, and if I'm careful not to cry, and if I wear the glasses he's given me he thinks my eyes may not get any worse and my headaches will be cured. But if I don't he says I'll certainly be stone blind in six months. Blind! Anne, just think of it!"

For a minute Anne, after her first quick exclamation of dismay, was silent. It seemed to her that she could *not* speak. Then she said bravely, but with a catch in her voice:

"Marilla, *don't* think of it. You know he has given you hope. If you are careful you won't lose your sight altogether; and if his glasses cure your headaches it will be a great thing."

"I don't call it much hope," said Marilla bitterly. "What am I to live for if I can't read or sew or do anything like that? I might as well be blind—or dead. And as for crying, I can't help that when I get lonesome. But there, it's no good talking about it. If you'll get me a cup of tea I'll be thankful. I'm about done out. Don't say anything about this to any one for a spell yet, anyway. I can't bear that folks should come here to question and sympathize and talk about it."

When Marilla had eaten her lunch Anne persuaded her to go to bed. Then Anne went herself to the east gable and sat down by her window in the darkness alone with her tears and her heaviness of heart. How sadly things had changed since she had sat there the night after coming home! Then she had been full of hope and joy and the future had looked rosy with promise. Anne felt as if she had lived years since then, but before she went to bed there was a smile on her lips and peace in her heart. She had looked her duty courageously in the face and found it a friend—as duty ever is when we meet it frankly.

One afternoon a few days later Marilla came slowly in from the yard when she had been talking to a caller—a man whom Anne knew by sight as John Sadler from Carmody. Anne wondered what he could have been saying to bring that look to Marilla's face.

"What did Mr. Sadler want, Marilla?"

Marilla sat down by the window and looked at Anne. There were tears in her eyes in defiance of the oculist's prohibition and her voice broke as she said:

"He heard that I was going to sell Green Gables and he wants to buy it."

"Buy it! Buy Green Gables?" Anne wondered if she had heard aright. "Oh, Marilla, you don't mean to sell Green Gables!"

"Anne, I don't know what else is to be done. I've thought it all over. If my eyes were strong I could stay here and make out to look after things and manage, with a good hired man. But as it is I can't. I may lose my sight altogether; and anyway I'll not be fit to run things. Oh, I never thought I'd live to see the day when I'd have to sell my home. But things would only go behind worse and worse all the time, till nobody would want to buy it. Every cent of our money went in that bank; and there's some notes Matthew gave last fall to pay. Mrs. Lynde advises me to sell the farm and board somewhere—with her I suppose. It won't bring much—it's small and the buildings are old. But it'll be enough for me to live on I reckon. I'm thankful you're provided for with that scholarship, Anne. I'm sorry you won't have a home to come to in your vacations, that's all, but I suppose you'll manage somehow."

Marilla broke down and wept bitterly.

"You mustn't sell Green Gables," said Anne resolutely.

"Oh, Anne, I wish I didn't have to. But you can see for yourself. I can't stay here alone. I'd go crazy with trouble and loneliness. And my sight would go—I know it would."

355

"You won't have to stay here alone, Marilla. I'll be with you. I'm not going to Redmond."

"Not going to Redmond!" Marilla lifted her worn face from her hands and looked at Anne. "Why, what do you mean?"

"Just what I say. I'm not going to take the scholarship. I decided so the night after you came home from town. You surely don't think I could leave you alone in your trouble, Marilla, after all you've done for me. I've been thinking and planning. Let me tell you my plans. Mr. Barry wants to rent the farm for next year. So you won't have any bother over that. And I'm going to teach. I've applied for the school here—but I don't expect to get it for I understand the trustees have promised it to Gilbert Blythe. But I can have the Carmody school—Mr. Blair told me so last night at the store. Of course that won't be quite as nice or convenient as if I had the Avonlea school. But I can board home and drive myself over to Carmody and back, in the warm weather at least. And even in winter I can come home Fridays. We'll keep a horse for that. Oh, I have it all planned out, Marilla. And I'll read to you and keep you cheered up. You sha'n't be dull or lonesome. And we'll be real cosy and happy here together, you and I."

Marilla had listened like a woman in a dream.

"Oh, Anne, I could get on real well if you were here, I know. But I can't let you sacrifice yourself so for me. It would be terrible."

"Nonsense!" Anne laughed merrily. "There is no sacrifice. Nothing could be worse than giving up Green Gables—nothing could hurt me more. We must keep the dear old place. My mind is quite made up, Marilla. I'm *not* going to Redmond; and I *am* going to stay here and teach. Don't you worry about me a bit."

"But your ambitions—and—"

"I'm just as ambitious as ever. Only, I've changed the object of my ambitions. I'm going to be a good teacher—and I'm going to save your eyesight. Besides, I mean to study at home here and take a little college course all by myself. Oh, I've dozens of plans, Marilla. I've been thinking them out for a week. I shall give life here my best, and I believe it will give its best to me in return. When I left Queen's my future seemed to stretch out before me like a straight road. I thought I could see along it for many a milestone. Now there is a bend in it. I don't know what lies around the bend, but I'm going to believe that the best does. It has a fascination of its own, that bend, Marilla. I wonder how the road beyond it goes—what there is of green glory and soft, checkered light and shadows—what new landscapes—what new beauties—what curves and hills and valleys further on."

"I don't feel as if I ought to let you give it up," said Marilla, referring to the scholarship.

"But you can't prevent me. I'm sixteen and a half, 'obstinate as a mule,' as Mrs. Lynde once told me," laughed Anne. "Oh, Marilla, don't you go pitying me. I don't like to be pitied, and there is no need for it. I'm heart glad over the very thought of staying at dear Green Gables. Nobody could love it as you and I do—so we must keep it."

"You blessed girl!" said Marilla, yielding. "I feel as if you'd given me new life. I guess I ought to stick out and make you go to college—but I know I can't, so I ain't going to try. I'll make it up to you though, Anne."

When it became noised abroad in Avonlea that Anne Shirley had given up the idea of going to college and intended to stay home and teach there was a good deal of discussion over it. Most of the good folks, not knowing about Marilla's eyes, thought she was foolish. Mrs. Allan did not. She told Anne so in approving words that brought tears of pleasure to the girl's eyes. Neither did good Mrs. Lynde. She came up one evening and found Anne and Marilla sitting at the front door in the warm, scented summer dusk. They liked to sit there when the twilight came down and the white moths flew about in the garden and the odour of mint filled the dewy air.

Mrs. Rachel deposited her substantial person upon the stone bench by the door, behind which grew a row of tall pink and yellow hollyhocks, with a long breath of mingled weariness and relief.

"I declare I'm glad to sit down. I've been on my feet all day, and two hundred pounds is a good bit for two feet to carry round. It's a great blessing not to be fat, Marilla. I hope you appreciate it. Well, Anne, I hear you've given up your notion of going to college. I was real glad to hear it. You've got as much education now as a woman can be comfortable with. I don't believe in girls going to college with the men and cramming their heads full of Latin and Greek and all that nonsense."

"But I'm going to study Latin and Greek just the same, Mrs. Lynde," said Anne laughing. "I'm going to take my Arts course right here at Green Gables, and study everything that I would at college."

Mrs. Lynde lifted her hands in holy horror.

"Anne Shirley, you'll kill yourself."

"Not a bit of it. I shall thrive on it. Oh, I'm not going to overdo things. As 'Josiah Allen's wife' says, I shall be 'mejum.'[1] But I'll have lots of spare time in the long winter evenings, and I've no vocation for fancy work. I'm going to teach over at Carmody, you know."

"I don't know it. I guess you're going to teach right here in Avonlea. The trustees have decided to give you the school."

"Mrs. Lynde!" cried Anne, springing to her feet in her surprise. "Why, I thought they had promised it to Gilbert Blythe!"

"So they did. But as soon as Gilbert heard that you had applied for it he went to them—they had a business meeting at the school last night you know—and told them that he withdrew his application, and suggested that they accept yours. He said he was going to teach at White Sands. Of course he gave up the school just to oblige you, because he knew how much you wanted to stay with Marilla, and I must say I think it was real kind and thoughtful in him, that's what. Real self-sacrificing, too, for he'll have his board to pay at White Sands, and everybody knows he's got to earn his own way through college. So the trustees decided to take you. I was tickled to death when Thomas came home and told me."

"I don't feel that I ought to take it," murmured Anne. "I mean—I don't think I ought to let Gilbert make such a sacrifice for—for me."

"I guess you can't prevent him now. He's signed papers with the White Sands trustees. So it wouldn't do him any good now if you were to refuse. Of course you'll take the school. You'll get along all right, now that there are no Pyes going. Josie was the last of them, and a good thing she was, that's what. There's been some Pye or other going to Avonlea school for the last twenty years, and I

---

1 *As Josiah Allen's wife . . . mejum* Marietta Holley (1836–1926) used "Josiah Allen's Wife" as her persona in books of humorous dialogue written in dialect spellings such as "mejum" for "medium."

guess their mission in life was to keep school-teachers reminded that earth isn't their home. Bless my heart! What does all that winking and blinking at the Barry gable mean?"

"Diana is signalling for me to go over," laughed Anne. "You know we keep up the old custom. Excuse me while I run over and see what she wants."

Anne ran down the clover slope like a deer, and disappeared in the firry shadows of the Haunted Wood. Mrs. Lynde looked after her indulgently.

"There's a good deal of the child about her yet in some ways."

"There's a good deal more of the woman about her in others," retorted Marilla, with a momentary return of her old crispness.

But crispness was no longer Marilla's distinguishing characteristic. As Mrs. Lynde told her Thomas that night.

"Marilla Cuthbert has got *mellow*. That's what."

Anne went to the little Avonlea graveyard the next evening to put fresh flowers on Matthew's grave and water the Scotch rose-bush. She lingered there until dusk, liking the peace and calm of the little place, with its poplars whose rustle was like low, friendly speech, and its whispering grasses growing at will among the graves. When she finally left it and walked down the long hill that sloped to the Lake of Shining Waters it was past sunset and all Avonlea lay before her in a dream-like afterlight—"a haunt of ancient peace."[2] There was a freshness in the air as of a wind that had blown over honey-sweet fields of clover. Home lights twinkled out here and there among the homestead trees. Beyond lay the sea, misty and purple, with its haunting, unceasing murmur. The west was a glory of soft mingled hues, and the pond reflected them all in still softer shadings. The beauty of it all thrilled Anne's heart, and she gratefully opened the gates of her soul to it.

"Dear old world," she murmured, "you are very lovely, and I am glad to be alive in you."

Half-way down the hill a tall lad came whistling out of a gate before the Blythe homestead. It was Gilbert, and the whistle died on his lips as he recognized Anne. He lifted his cap courteously, but he would have passed on in silence, if Anne had not stopped and held out her hand.

"Gilbert," she said, with scarlet cheeks," I want to thank you for giving up the school for me. It was very good of you—and I want you to know that I appreciate it."

Gilbert took the offered hand eagerly.

"It wasn't particularly good of me at all, Anne. I was pleased to be able to do you some small service. Are we going to be friends after this? Have you really forgiven me my old fault?"

Anne laughed and tried unsuccessfully to withdraw her hand.

"I forgave you that day by the pond landing, although I didn't know it. What a stubborn little goose I was. I've been—I may as well make a complete confession—I've been sorry ever since."

"We are going to be the best of friends," said Gilbert, jubilantly. "We were born to be good friends, Anne. You've thwarted destiny long enough. I know we can help each other in many ways. You are going to keep up your studies, aren't you? So am I. Come, I'm going to walk home with you."

Marilla looked curiously at Anne when the latter entered the kitchen.

---

2 *haunt of ancient peace*   Tennyson, "The Palace of Art" 88.

"Who was that came up the lane with you, Anne?"

"Gilbert Blythe," answered Anne, vexed to find herself blushing. "I met him on Barry's hill."

"I didn't think you and Gilbert Blythe were such good friends that you'd stand for half an hour at the gate talking to him," said Marilla, with a dry smile.

"We haven't been—we've been good enemies. But we have decided that it will be much more sensible to be good friends in future. Were we really there half an hour? It seemed just a few minutes. But, you see, we have five years' lost conversations to catch up with, Marilla."

Anne sat long at her window that night companioned by a glad content. The wind purred softly in the cherry boughs, and the mint breaths came up to her. The stars twinkled over the pointed firs in the hollow and Diana's light gleamed through the old gap.

Anne's horizons had closed in since the night she had sat there after coming home from Queen's; but if the path set before her feet was to be narrow she knew that flowers of quiet happiness would bloom along it. The joys of sincere work and worthy aspiration and congenial friendship were to be hers; nothing could rob her of her birthright of fancy or her ideal world of dreams. And there was always the bend in the road!

"'God's in his heaven, all's right with the world,'"[3] whispered Anne softly.

---

3 *God's in his heaven, all's right with the world*   These are the last lines of Part 1 to Browning's dramatic poem "Pippa Passes" (1841). Pippa, an orphan, walks about, seeing the best in life despite grim realities that lurk nearby; her happy songs inspire changes of heart in those who listen and who most need to change their hearts.

Maureen Daly

1921–

WHEN she began writing *Seventeenth Summer*, Maureen Daly was only seventeen herself. Its publication and subsequent success made her a literary celebrity by the time she was in her early twenties. Although it was published as a novel for adults, *Seventeenth Summer* soon became the watershed romance novel for teen girls and still stands above the majority of teen romances for its emotional honesty and literary complexity.

Daly was born in Ireland and came to America with her parents and two older sisters when she was two years old. The family took up residence in Fond du Lac, Wisconsin, because it was as green as the Ireland they had left behind. Another sister was born in Fond du Lac, and there the family remained until the girls were grown. Like the mother in *Seventeenth Summer*, also about a family with four daughters in Fond du Lac, Daly's mother ran a careful household, taking pride in her sewing and her table settings. But Daly's father was not as distant as his fictional counterpart. He shook the house with his Irish jigs and entertained his daughters by telling them Irish tales and letting them style his hair. The sense of financial security that pervades the novel is also fictional, for like all who lived in America during the thirties, the Dalys felt the strain of the Depression. The girls' leisure activities focused mostly on nearby Lake Winnebago and regular trips to the public library; they were all ardent readers whose choices were never censored.

Daly attended a Catholic high school where she did cleaning chores to help pay her tuition. One of her teachers especially encouraged her writing, and by 1938 she had won first prize in *Scholastic Magazine*'s short story contest for her story "Sixteen," about a girl's hurt feelings when a boy doesn't call her—feelings that came straight from Daly's experience. Inspired by this success, she decided to write a novel. Her parents cleaned out the coal house in the basement for her use and got her an old typewriter, and she began *Seventeenth Summer*. She continued to write while she attended Rosary College in River Forest, Illinois, doing housecleaning to pay tuition. Her efforts paid off when she entered her budding novel in the Intercollegiate Novel Contest sponsored by Dodd, Mead publishers, and won. The novel was published the year she graduated, 1942; Daly's interviews and autographings kept her in the public eye for several years thereafter.

After graduation she headed to Chicago where she found work at the *Tribune* writing a column for teens. Later she also covered police beats for the paper, where she learned the importance of accurate detail. During this time she met the man she would marry, William McGivern, who courted her long distance when he was sent overseas in the Army. He too wanted to write, so after their marriage in 1946, Daly, believing that there was room in their household for only one fiction writer, continued her journalism work and wrote a few children's books, while Bill tackled the fiction. They traveled abroad for several years, then moved to a Pennsylvania farmhouse when their two children,

Megan and Patrick, began to attend college. They also collaborated on a few scripts for television.

Daly's later life is marked by sadness and loss. Her husband died of cancer in 1983; not long afterward, her daughter Megan also died of cancer. Her grief sent her to a psychologist, but it also sent her back to fiction. Unable to write directly of Megan's death, she began to construct a story based on Megan's first love affair, which became *Acts of Love* (1986). Later she wrote a sequel, *First a Dream* (1990). As in *Seventeenth Summer*, she based her characters on people she knew and places she felt connected to, creating in her stories tributes to her husband and child. She has lived alone since her husband's death, in Palm Desert, California, where she continues a disciplined writing life.

In the post-war forties, teen-agers were becoming big news and a lucrative market. It was the era of swing music, jive talk, and increasing economic power for teens; for businesses, teens represented money. Publishers of magazines began producing articles on cars and cosmetics for teen readers; Hollywood turned out superficial films about happy, wealthy, suburban teens—all white, of course—whose chief problems were their bumbling parents or getting a date for the prom. When teen girls discovered Daly's novel, they recognized something more honest. *Seventeenth Summer* quickly moved to the top of library lists of books most requested by teen readers, while other forties writers like Sally Benson, Rosamond du Jardin, and Betty Cavanna, turned out teen romances that were similar in some ways but less subtle, and less inclined to take seriously the emotions of teen girls. Teen life changed even more dramatically during the fifties and sixties, but surveys of libraries continued to rank Daly's novel among the books teen girls read most. By 1990, although by then it appealed to younger girls, it had sold more than seven million copies.

Seventeenth Summer's plot is classically simple: three summer months in seventeen-year-old Angie Morrow's life, during the liminal period between high school and college. She meets Jack in June; their romance blossoms through July; during August they face misunderstandings and disillusionments; they part as autumn arrives. Nature provides the accompaniment to Angie's emotions: the freshness and promise of spring, the heat of high summer, the dryness and approaching cold of late August in Wisconsin represent the complete naturalness of her feelings. The novel's pace lets the reader experience the leisure of the 1940s small-town summer, with its boat rides, picnics, Cokes at the local hangout, and a quiet home where life is orderly and calm.

The interior action is what counts, and what has made the novel transcend sixty years of evolving teen life. Angie is a complex protagonist, by turns shy and strong, immature and thoughtful. Her awareness of fashion, her efforts to appear at ease on a date, her sense that friends and schoolmates are much more sophisticated and attractive than she, her discomfort both at home and with friends—all are shared by every adolescent. Yet Angie is an individual. She takes such pride in her mother's clean, orderly home that we see a little incipient snobbery in her; she treats her younger sister Kitty with kindness; she loves the natural beauty around her, describing it in such poetic detail that we sense the emerging writer in her; she finds Jack's table manners irritating; she is naïve about a "fast" boy, necking customs, and her sister Lorraine's apparent sex life, but her own sensuality brings her pleasure. When she must say good-bye to Jack, she does so with dignity, and with joy at having experienced this love. The novel works by detailing the emotional nuances of this girl who is both completely ordinary and completely individual.

The novel's other characters, while less rounded, are nonetheless fully individual as we see them through Angie's observant eyes. Slight details convey suggestions of tension in the family: the father's travel; the mother's headaches; Lorraine's overeagerness for her dates, subsequent unhappiness, and rapid exit from the town. Jack is well dressed and polite, yet obviously uncomfortable in Angie's home; Martin, Lorraine's traveling salesman boyfriend, gives Angie a glimpse into a life of bars where he talks to girls in short skirts and thin blouses. Even Tony Becker, the "fast" boy Angie dates once, emerges as an interesting character, not stereotyped. This subtle treatment of character is one of the chief differences between Daly's novel and Judy Blume's *Forever*.

Although Angie today may appear amusingly innocent to teen readers who have grown up with Judy Blume novels and the sexual frankness of television and movies, those who read *Seventeenth Summer* sensitively will notice a controlled but definite sensuality that was certainly unusual in books for girls in the forties and is still rare in most teen romances. Angie is newly aware of her own lips and legs. She likes dancing with Tony Becker because of the way he holds her. Lying in bed at night she thinks only of Jack. During their first kiss, she keeps her eyes open to take in the full pleasure of the moment. At the height of their romance, "all flowed together into a stream of pleasantness like warm, thick honey." On warm days she feels "the strange new urge that was beating through me . . . Touching things sent a new pleasure through my hands that filled my whole body with satisfaction." On a boatride, "I had a sudden impulse to reach out and run my finger lightly over the even, dark arch of his eyebrows as he stood looking at me. But there was an odd look in his eyes, an odd, warm look that made my lips tingle as his eyes met mine." After a swim with Jack, "Something in me was suddenly alive. It was something new . . . It was warm, strange, and beating . . . My lips felt hot and my cheeks were tense with waiting." After a quarrel, they park in Jack's truck: "And the thought in my mind was as warm and mellow as the sunlight. How odd, I thought. How wonderfully, wonderfully odd to be kissed in the middle of the afternoon." The sensual climax comes at the end of the book, when, in late August, Angie and Jack accompany their friends on a picnic. There, in a moment of bacchanalian excess, Jack urges Angie into the woods where Angie experiences fear and excitement and desperation as they pick wild grapes in the dark: "They were bitter in our mouths as we ate them, with a strange, wild taste, and the seeds were hard against my teeth. But I plucked them and plucked them till both my hands were full and they fell to the earth and purple stains were dark on my arms . . . I wanted to speak but the words were dry in my throat." In the next moment, Jack begs Angie to marry him. Although Angie does seem to want to remain innocent, acknowledging that she is not ready for real passion ("Love is such a big word," she thinks), these suggestions of emerging desire and sexual contact provided an undercurrent of seriousness—and offered a freedom to the imagination—new in literature for young adults in the 1940s and still powerful today.

Seventeenth Summer's seriousness is established in the opening paragraph, when Angie insists that her love for Jack "wasn't silly, like sometimes, when girls sit in school and write a fellow's name all over the margin of their papers . . . and it wasn't puppy love or infatuation or love at first sight or anything that people always talk about and laugh." This tone is carried throughout, lending weight and dignity to Angie's musings and experiences as a teen girl. The novel offered new respect to this readership in other ways too. It acknowledges that teens smoke and drink and neck and pet, without passing any negative judgments on these activities—something still rare in Young Adult Literature. Angie gets a little drunk on her first and only beer, but it is just something that happened, not a moral issue. And there are other sexual undercurrents besides Angie's sensuality. Although the novel is more subtle than frank, there are clues that Lorraine is pregnant by Martin when she decides to leave town. The black pianist at the bar where Angie and Jack go on a date is apparently homosexual though Jack is too embarrassed to explain it to Angie.

The novel accurately depicts the double standard that controlled dating and sex in the 1930s, 1940s, and 1950s. The boy does the asking while the girl waits to be asked, and there are good girls and bad girls. A girl will find her identity in the peer group depending on the boy who likes her: "It's funny what a boy can do. One day you're nobody and the next day you're the girl that some fellow goes with and the other fellows look at you harder ... and the girls say hello and want you to walk down to the drugstore to have Cokes with them." Angie's peer group hangs out at McKnight's drugstore, where they keep tabs on each other: "It's almost like a secret police system—no one escapes being checked on. At least no one who counts ... They can start or stop any of the younger girls in town just by passing the word around." Angie accepts this system, yet she is also absolutely sure she is going to college—not the usual plan for girls of the late thirties, when the Depression was just lifting, or the early forties, when World War II needed young people in the work force. She loves Jack and she loves love and she certainly has sexual feelings, but she has a larger sense of her identity. She does not waver from her purpose. She is not ultimately dependent on males for her happiness. Here too, Daly's novel is both a part of and ahead of its time. Critic Virginia Schaefer Carroll has identified it as an "inherently feminist text": "a novel that focuses on the politics of the internal, the ways that an ordinary individual goes through the process of discovering and articulating her position" (*Children's Literature Association Quarterly* 21:1, 18).

In the rapidity of today's daily life and the ubiquitous sexuality in the media, *Seventeenth Summer* still offers the classic tale of romantic and physical love coping with social constraints, told in graceful, allusive prose that dignifies teen emotions. Maureen Daly opened her private emotions to a degree just shy of autobiography; this novel, she has said, was the only way she had to express the ecstasy she herself discovered in first love and sexual contact. *Seventeenth Summer* is anchored in a specific time and place and person. Yet like all good art, it has transformed that intensely personal experience into a universal one that many generations of girls have shared.

JUNE

I DON'T know just why I'm telling you all this. Maybe you'll think I'm being silly. But I'm not, really, because this is *important*. You see, it was different! It wasn't just because it was Jack and I either—it was something much more than that. It wasn't as it's written in magazine stories or as in morning radio serials where the boy's family always tease him about liking a girl and he gets embarrassed and stutters. And it wasn't silly, like sometimes, when girls sit in school and write a fellow's name all over the margin of their papers. I never even wrote Jack's name at all till I sent him a postcard that weekend I went up to Minaqua. And it wasn't puppy love or infatuation or love at first sight or anything that people always talk about and laugh. Maybe you don't know just what I mean. I can't really explain it—it's so hard to put in words but—well, it was just something I'd never felt before. Something I'd never even known. People can't tell you about things like that, you have to find them out for yourself. That's why it is so important. It was something I'll always remember because I just couldn't forget—it's a thing like that.

It happened this way. At the very beginning of the summer I met Jack—right after graduation. He had gone to the public high school and I went to the Academy just outside of town which is for girls only. I had heard of him often because he played guard on the high school basketball team and he sometimes dated Jane Rady who sat next to me in history class. That night (the night when things first began) I drove down to the post office with my father to mail a letter and because it was rather late Dad pulled up in front of McKnight's drugstore and said, "I'll just stop here and keep the motor running while you run in and get a stamp." McKnight's is where all the fellows and girls in Fond du Lac get together and I really would rather not have gone in alone—especially on a Friday night when most girls have dates—but I didn't want to tell my father that.

I remember just how it was. I was standing by the drug counter waiting for the clerk. The sides of the booths in McKnight's are rather high and in one, near the back, I could just see the top of someone's head with a short crew cut sticking up. He must have been having a Coke, for he tore the wrapping off the end of his straws and blew in them so that the paper covering shot over the side of the booth. Then he stood up to see where it had landed. It was Jack. He looked over at me, smiled, and then sat down again.

Of course I didn't know him yet, he just smiled to be friendly, but I waited for a few minutes looking at magazines in the rack near the front door, hoping he might stand up again or walk up to the soda fountain or something, but he didn't. So I just left. "You certainly took long enough," my father said gruffly, "I might have been arrested for parking double like this."

The next night my sister Lorraine came in from Chicago on the 2:40 a.m. train. She has been going to college for two years and wears her hair long, almost to her shoulders, and puts her lipstick on with a brush. We drove to meet her, Dad and I. It was raining a little then and the lights from the station shone on the wet bricks. The two-wheeled baggage carts were standing in a line, their long handles tipped up into the air. We waited while the train came out of the darkness, feeling its way with the long, yellow headlight beam. When it stopped, a man jumped out and ran into the station with a package under his arm. A conductor swung onto the platform and stood waving a lantern while the train waited, the engine panting out steam from between its wheels. Dad and I walked along, peering up at the windows. A boy at one of them woke up and waved to me sleepily.

Then we saw Lorraine half stumble down the steps with two suitcases and a black wool ram under her arm. "I fell asleep and almost forgot to get off," she said. Her hair was mussed up and her cheek was all crisscrossed red where she had been leaning on the rough upholstery. "One of the girls had this goat in her room and didn't want to pack it so I brought it home for Kitty. (Kitty is my sister who is ten but still likes toys.) You've got to hold it up straight or the rubber horns fall out." Lorraine laughed. "I'm glad I'm home—this should be a good summer, don't you think, Angie?" Dad kissed her gingerly—because of so much lipstick—and I took one bag to the car and he took the other and we went home.

That was Saturday. Monday was the day summer vacation really began.

It was just after nine o'clock and I was in the garden picking small round radishes and pulling the new green onions for dinner at noon. I remember it was a warm day with a blue and white sky. The garden was still wet with last night's rain and the black earth was steaming in the sun, while between my toes the ground was soft and squishy—I had taken off my shoes and left them on the garden path so they wouldn't get caked with mud—and I remember thinking how much fun it would be to go barefoot all the time. The little tomato plants were laid flat against the ground from last night's downfall and there were puddles like blue glass in the hollows. A breeze, soft with a damp, fishy smell, blew in from Lake Winnebago about three blocks away. I was so busy thinking about the weather, the warm sun, and the sleek little onions that I didn't even hear Jack come up the back sidewalk.

"Any baked goods today?" he called.

"I don't know," I answered, turning. "You'd better ring the back doorbell and ask my mother." I sidled over a little and stood in the thick quack grass beside the garden path. I don't like to have people see me in my bare feet.

"Why don't you ask her for me?" he called. "You know her better than I do." I stood still for a moment hoping he wouldn't notice my feet. "Come on, hurry," he said. "I don't care if you haven't any shoes on."

Now, it wasn't that I was shy or anything, but it's awkward when a boy has on a clean shirt and his hair combed and your hands are all muddy and you're in your bare feet. I tried to wipe off the mud on the quack grass before I went down the garden path.

"What were you doing." he asked, "picking radishes?" (I still had the bunch of radishes in my hand.) "That's kind of silly, isn't it?" he added laughing. "It's just my salesman's personality coming out—anything to start a conversation. Twice already this morning I caught myself saying to customers, 'What's it going to do—rain?' I've got to be careful not to get into a rut." He laughed again and I laughed too. It was such a warm, bright morning.

We talked together for a while and I told him I didn't know he worked for a bakery, and he said he hadn't until school let out and that he was going to drive one of the trucks for his father during the summer, and when I remarked that I didn't even know his father owned a bakery, he said, "You don't know much about me at all, do you?"

"I know your name," I answered.

366

"What?" he asked.

"Jack Duluth. I remember reading it in the paper when you made that long shot from the center of the floor in the basketball game with Oshkosh this winter."

"Good for you—just another one of my fans." He laughed. "What's your name—as if I didn't find out after I saw you in McKnight's the other night. Angie Morrow, short for Angeline, isn't it?"

I was glad he had asked about me, but for some reason it was embarrassing and I tried to change the subject. "I remember when you used to go with Jane Rady," I ventured. "She used to sit next to me in history class. She talked about you a lot. She told me about the time you drove to the city dump—"

"Forget it," Jack said sharply. "Forget all about it, see. All that is down the drain by now." For a moment I thought he was angry. "Go ask your mother if she needs any bread or doughnuts or anything, will you?" He sat down on the cement doorstep and I opened the door to go inside. All of a sudden he turned and said slowly, with a thought in his voice, "Say, Angie, you don't go steady or anything, do you?"

My heart jumped a little. "No, I don't," I answered and then added quickly, "My mother doesn't like me to go out much." It wouldn't do to say that I wasn't often asked, either. I waited a moment. "Do you, Jack?"

He laughed. "Of course not. None of the fellows I go around with do. Silly to tie yourself down to one girl. But, say, seeing you don't—how about going sailboating with me tonight? Me and Swede Vincent have got a little boat we bought last fall. Do you know Swede? He's a good guy. He'll come with us and sail it and you and I can just—ah—well, just sit. How about it?"

I didn't know, I told him. I would have to ask my mother first.

"Go ask her now," he urged, "when you ask her if she needs any bread. I'll wait."

"Oh, I can't do that!" I could hear my mother upstairs running the vacuum cleaner noisily over the rugs and I remembered I hadn't tidied up my bedroom yet. "Now's not such a good time to ask but I'll tell you by one o'clock," I promised, trying not to be too eager. "I'll try to fix it and if you'll call me then I can let you know."

"I'll call you at one then and let's skip the bakery goods for today. Please try to go," he added. "No girl has ever been out in our boat before so you'll be the first one. Something kind of special."

That was the first time I ever really talked to Jack. When I went back into the garden to get my shoes I noticed how the little tomato plants seemed to be straightening in the sun. And there were small paper-thin blossoms on the new pea plants.

My mother always lies down in the afternoon—at least, she has for the past three years, anyway. Right after lunch she went upstairs as always, turned down the chenille bedspread and drew the shades. Out on the side lawn in the shade of the house Kitty was sewing doll clothes and talking to herself in a quiet, little-girl singsong. From Callahan's, across the back garden, I could hear the drone of the baseball game on the radio. All the little children were in taking their naps and already our street had settled into the quiet of afternoon. I'd have to ask my mother soon for I knew that in a few moments she would be asleep.

Outside her bedroom door I paused. "Maybe I'd better count up to seventeen first," I thought. "Seventeen and then I'll ask her." So I counted slowly, deliberately, being careful not to skip. When I was younger I used to count up to fifteen while trying to decide things, then it was sixteen, and now it was seventeen—one count for each year. But when I got to seventeen I still hadn't figured out in my mind how I should say it. "Better count up to eighteen," I decided. "Eighteen because that's how old Jack is. After that I'll go in for sure."

My mother was almost asleep when I pushed open the door gently, lying on top of the blankets with my old blue flannel bathrobe thrown over her. Sunlight filtered through the drawn shades in a brownish-yellow glow and the crocheted circle used to pull them down twirled in the breeze. I swallowed hard and it made a noise in the quietness of the room.

"Mom," I ventured, "a boy asked me for a date tonight." She opened her eyes. "It will be all right and I'll be home early," I assured her hastily. "He'll come over first and you can meet him and make sure it's all right. They're nice people—he plays basketball and his father owns the DeLuxe bakery." I rushed the words after each other without stopping, before she could say no.

Rolling over toward the wall and nuzzling her head into the pillow she asked sleepily, "What's his name? I don't think I ever heard you mention him, did I?"

"Jack Duluth," I answered and waited. The room was quiet except for the sound of the window shade flapping in the breeze.

"Duluth as in Minnesota?" Lorraine called out. She was in her own room down the hall taking the curlers out of her hair. She keeps them in all the time except when she's going out. Lorraine wears her hair very long with just a little fluffy curl on the end like they all do in college. But already my mother was breathing lightly as if she were asleep.

"Mom," I said quietly, trying to keep the impatience out of my voice—my mother doesn't like it if we tease, "can I go or can't I? It will be all right—really it will."

"See what your sister thinks," she answered. "I suppose it's all right if you're home early. And see if you can fix that window shade so it doesn't flap so—put a book on the cord or something."

It had been as easy as that and my heart was beating fast as I closed the door softly behind me while downstairs the telephone rang. It was Jack.

We walked out to the lake, he and I. It was about half-past seven in the evening and the summer sky was still brushed red with the sun. "Looks like ostrich feathers on fire," Jack had said. We had cut through our back garden and through two empty lots and then crossed the highway between our house and the lake. Jack had held the barbed wire of the fence apart for me to crawl through and we went into the field behind the boathouses. "This is my own special short cut," I remembered him saying. "I like it better this way than walking through the park."

Along the path by the fence was a row of wild plum trees with hard green knobs of fruit hidden in the leaves. Little sparrows twittered excitedly and fluttered among the branches as we passed. Not many people came by this way. Just past the last fence was a row of whispering willow trees lined along the ditch by the railroad track. Water from the spring rains still gurgled and ran in ribbons between the swamp grass. "You'll have to jump," said Jack. "It's marshy here. Step first on that flat stone and then over onto the sewer top." There was a round cement sewer with a heavy, knobbed iron lid padlocked shut and almost hidden in the weeds. "Let me go first," he said, "then I'll catch your hand and help you across." The ground was marshy beneath my feet and I almost lost my balance on the smooth stone. Jack caught me and I remember his hand was tight and warm.

We hit a flat grassy spot a little farther on—just on this side of the tracks. "This is Hobo's Hollow," Jack told me. "Lots of times I come through here and see the fellows who have jumped the trains lying here sleeping. Sometimes there are four or five of them and they make a fire and cook things. I saw a man dead drunk here one day lying right in the sun with flies on him and a bottle in his hand and the next day he was gone. They never talk to me when I go by at all. Just sit and look."

I shivered a little. It was weird there with the air half gray-green from the thick trees and lush weeds and the coming night. There were bits of charred wood and old rusted cans sticking up in the grass. The wind sighed a little as it wove its way through the long line of willows. Jack pulled my hand suddenly and we scrambled up the cinder embankment of the railroad track. Directly beyond was a broad gravel drive and then the gray and white boathouses.

It was early in the season and many of the houses were still padlocked shut from the winter. Between them the little waves slop-slopped against the heavy wooden piles. "Swede said he'd have the boat out by the steps of the Big Hole," Jack told me. "He came out to clean her up a bit before you came. We had a sort of picnic in it last week and it's still all full of old sandwiches and stuff." The Big Hole was built by the city a few years ago to harbor small boats against the sudden vicious squalls that come up so quickly on Lake Winnebago. It's bordered on one side by the boathouses, on the other by a shrub-edged drive and on a third by the Point with a tall, white lighthouse on the end. Over on the right the water sloshes into a mass of treacherous water reeds and thick seaweeds. Beyond this is bare red clay scattered with water pipes and heaps of black dirt—an uncompleted WPA project.[1]

I saw Swede bending over in the boat arranging canvas. Jack whistled at him shrilly through his teeth and Swede straightened and waved. "You'll like Swede," Jack told me. "Some girls think he's kind of fast but I told him to be nice to you." Swede was rather fat with kinky blond hair and had on a very tight, very clean white sweat shirt.

"Hello," he called. And when we got up to the boat, "You're Angie Morrow, aren't you. I thought maybe at the last minute you wouldn't be able to come. Jack said he thought maybe your mother might not want you to go sailing," and he grinned at me.

"Everything's all right so long as we get her home by eleven," Jack told him. "Any time after that's no good. We won't go out far—just until we find the moon." He squeezed my hand. I couldn't help shivering a little—it was such a beautiful night.

In the Big Hole the wind barely wrinkled the water with waves. We moved slowly at first—Swede up in the bow and Jack and I sitting in the stern, until we had passed through the narrow space between the light-house and the breakwater. Already cars were parked along the Point with their headlight beams poking out into the thickening dusk. Almost everyone in Fond du Lac goes out for a drive in the evening and then stops for a while to look at the lake. Someone honked a horn and leaned out a car window to wave at us. "People do that just to be friendly," said Jack. "I don't know who it is."

"Are you comfortable?" he asked. "If you get chilly say so and you can put my sweater on." I just nodded. It was too lovely to talk. The boat rose and fell gently as it topped the waves. Swede was letting out the sail and the loose canvas flapped in the wind. Occasionally the greenish water slapped hard against the side of the boat and sent spray over the edge. "Here," said Jack. "We'll put this canvas over your legs—no sense in your getting wet. You're a good scout, do you know that? Lots of girls are scared to go out in boats."

---

1 *WPA project*   project sponsored by the Work Projects Administration (1935–43).

"I love it," I told him. He was sitting almost on the point of the stern with his red and white basketball sweater tied around his neck by the sleeves and a light wind was ruffling his hair from behind.

I sighed and he said to me, "You're not cold, are you? Remember, just say the word and the sweater's yours. I really brought it along for you—I never get cold myself." Leaning over, he put it around my shoulders and I remember thinking when he was so close how much he smelled like Ivory soap.

We were sailing in silence for a long time and way up in the sky, past the boathouses, was pasted a thin tissue-paper curve of moon. Swede had hung a lantern that swung in the darkness on his end of the boat and it licked red light over the tops of the waves. Just then he finished a cigarette and flipped it out over the water. We were far out by that time and the car lights were only star dots along the pier. It was very still. I looked back at Jack and he was sitting with his head thrown back, gazing at the sky. Far beyond him was only the darkness of the lake. The wind blew lightly, brushing through my hair. Jack moved forward suddenly and slipped up beside me on the narrow seat. "Angie Morrow," he said quietly. "You look nice with the wind in your hair."

And I remember just how he said it.

"That's one thing about the lake at night," he whispered. "No other place is so beautiful or so quiet. Sometimes Swede and I come out here and just drift for hours and don't talk at all. We just sit and watch the sky and think. You should see the water when the moon's out—I mean a big yellow summer moon. Swede mostly just thinks about girls when he's out here, but I like to think about clouds and God and things." He sat silent for a moment, watching the water. The sweater had slipped from my shoulders and he put his arm around me to hold it in place.

"I didn't know," I told him, "that boys thought much about *pretty* things. The fellows around McKnight's never act like they think about anything much."

"Most of them don't, but some of them do. We talk together a lot about girls and life and things. It's funny what some of those fellows think. Some of them have got big plans for what they want to do and who they want to marry and some of them never think at all."

"I just want to read a lot and learn everything I can," I told him. And then thinking that sounded rather dull I added, "I'd like to know about everything beautiful."

Jack sat up suddenly and looked at me. "Do you?" he said. "Do you really think that, Angie? You know, all my life I've wanted to know about beautiful things—to be cultured. Maybe that sounds funny to you. I haven't any background or anything. My mother and dad are swell, but I could never talk about a family tree or my grandfather who had whole stables full of horses . . . see what I mean? I've got to find out about all that sort of thing—my father's father was a farmer and my mother's father had a meat market out in Rosendale. Do you know," he said, "that until a couple of months ago I didn't even know what side a salad plate goes on?"

I wanted to tell him then about the silver fish service my mother has with the mother-of-pearl handles and the big curved-blade serving knife to match that looks like a Turkish dagger. I thought he might like to know about it because it was different and beautiful, but I couldn't think how to tell it so it didn't sound like bragging so I just said, "Salad plates go on the left, Jack, with the forks."

"And another thing I want to do is to go to an opera someday. I'd like to have a big black cape and a cane and a folding silk hat and I'd come in the door and

370

slap those old white gloves in the hat and walk right down the aisle. I don't know much about music," he said. "I don't even like it a lot but I could learn."

I wanted to tell *him* something too. There were so many things I had always thought about to myself and never wanted to tell anyone before. I almost told him about how I used to lie in bed at night and imagine that I was married to Nelson Eddy[2] just so I could pretend he took me places—night clubs and dances and things. "You know, Jack," I ventured, "once last winter when I went down to Chicago to see my sister Lorraine—the one that was sitting in the living room with curlers in her hair when you called for me—we went to see a play. It was called *Kiss the Boys Good-bye.* It wasn't a good play or anything. I mean, it wasn't like Shakespeare but it was a big hit and had a run on Broadway. A lot of it I didn't understand very well—I think it wasn't nice."

"We read *The Merchant of Venice* in English class," Jack answered. "Parts of that I didn't understand very well either—maybe that's because it's too nice." He laughed a little. His arm was on my shoulder and I relaxed and leaned back. He leaned over closer saying. "That's right. Just sit comfortable. Lean way back if you want." We were drifting then and Swede was sitting with his head resting on the side of the boat, half asleep. It was darker by that time and the moon was half hidden, cushioned in cloud. The boat rose and fell gently with the waves. "All I know is that I just want to be happy and turn out good, that's all," Jack mused, half to himself. Somehow it made me shiver a little.

For a long time no one spoke, I remember. Once Swede raised himself on his elbow and looked toward shore and then put his head down again. We were far out, drifting slowly, and the silence over the water seemed soft and thick. It was then I got that queer feeling. Maybe you won't understand what I mean. You see, I was just sitting there thinking of nothing in particular when suddenly I felt a warm tingling and then an almost guilty feeling—almost as if I were doing something I shouldn't. And I remember the wind blowing very cool on my cheeks. No one had even moved or said a word. I could see the glow of Swede's cigarette in the stern of the boat. It was then I felt that strange urge to turn my head and look at Jack to see what he was thinking, and an odd fear that if I did he might be looking at me. I could feel my thoughts loud in my brain as if they were hoarse whispers. A panicky, excited pulsing started in my throat. My cheeks were hot. I knew Jack was looking at me and I turned my head just a little so I could see his face. His arm tightened suddenly around my shoulders and a warm, contented feeling went me like when you drink hot milk.

Jack straightened just then and said quietly, "I think I'll light my pipe," and reached into his back pocket. I was strangely hurt he should want to move just at that moment, so I pulled the sweater tighter round my shoulders and sat up very straight, away from him. Jack filled his pipe, cupped in the hollow of his hand, pressing down the tobacco with his thumb, and then hunched over to light it. The first match guttered out. The wind snuffed out the second before he even got it near his pipe. He turned in the seat, pulled up his knees, and bent almost double with his shoulders pulled up to shelter it from the wind. The third match went out. "I'll tell you what, Angie," he said. "Give me that piece of canvas from round your legs. You hold it over my head and keep the wind out and I'll light my pipe." I unfolded the canvas and he ducked under. A moment later he pulled his head out explaining. "That doesn't seem to work either. I

---

2 *Nelson Eddy* (1901–67) popular light-opera singer who starred in a series of musical film romances in the 1930s.

can't hold the canvas off my face and keep the match lit at the same time. I'll tell you what. You put your head under, too, and strike the match and I'll light my pipe and keep the canvas up. Two heads ought to be able to hold it."

So we put the canvas over our heads and it seemed suddenly quiet and hushed, in out of the wind. The first match I struck broke and its head flipped off onto the bottom of the boat. "Try again," Jack said. He shifted toward me. It was very dark under the canvas. The second match flared.

My hand shook a little and Jack held it to steady it as he brought it over the pipe, drawing in deeply till the tobacco glowed, then puffing out the smoke. He took the pipe from his mouth, blew out the match, and dropped the burnt end to the bottom of the boat. I could see the glowing bowl of the pipe in his hand. Neither of us moved. And I remember wondering why it was so silent, so very silent, and why I didn't seem to be even breathing. I knew then that we were both thinking the same thing. I sensed the very warmth of his nearness.

It was only a moment, a long, silent moment, and then suddenly I pulled the canvas off my head and it brushed my hair forward over my face. I pushed it back and against my cheek the night air was damp and cool.

Swede was sitting up straight. "Hey, you," he said to Jack, "what were you doing with your heads under that canvas?"

"Lighting my pipe," Jack answered.

Swede smiled and winked. "Yeh?" he said, knowingly. "That's a new name for it."

I tucked the canvas tightly in around my legs, looking out over the lake, and said nothing. Jack was leaning back, slowly puffing at his pipe, watching me and not saying anything. After a long while he leaned over and knocked the ashes from his pipe into the water. Then looking at me, he said quietly, "We might as well have, you know."

About half-past nine it began to get rough. The wind changed and the lake grew dark and choppy. "We'd better turn her around," Jack called. The wind whipped the words out of his mouth and he waved his arms and pointed toward shore. Swede nodded and pulled at the ropes. The sail billowed out and swooped down toward the waves as the boat swung around to face the light-house. Little waves lipped over the sides and sloshed under the crossboards on the bottom. "Don't get scared," Jack said, "it's a little rough but Swede can hold it." I pulled the canvas tighter around my legs and the wind blew my hair around my face. Off in the north thunder rumbled and sharp lightning slit the sky. It took us almost an hour to reach shore in the shifting wind and there were only a few cars parked along the drive when we swung into the Big Hole.

"If you kids want to start home before the rain it's all right with me," yelled Swede against the wind. "I'll put the boat up and see that everything's covered. It looks like we're going to have a real rain, but you two have just about time to make it home."

"Thanks," said Jack. "I'll stop round to see you on the route tomorrow. Put my sweater on again, Angie. It's still chilly," and he pulled it down over my head. "Come on, we'll take the park road home."

"Good night, Swede," I called back. "Thank you, and I'm very glad I met you. I hope I see you again sometime." Swede was running down the sail and it was flapping wetly in the wind. The waves were dashing against the boat and he didn't hear me.

372

"Don't worry, Angie," Jack said. "You'll see him again."

My dog Kinkee ran out to meet us as we came up the walk, giving her tail a brief wag for me and then nosing around Jack's trouser cuff with a low growl. Kinkee is a chow and doesn't like strangers. "Go 'way," I told her. "It's all right. Maybe, Jack, she thinks you're a strange man who followed me home." It wasn't really funny but we both laughed.

"You know," said Jack, "when I was younger I used to think that if a chow licked you that black stuff on their tongues would come off." We were by the front steps now. My mother had heard the thunder and set the two potted ferns from the living room out on the steps to catch the rain. There was one lamp lit on the corner table in the living room and the light shone out onto the walk. The trees on the lawn were bending in the wind and the air was full of the damp, fishy smell of water that always blows in from Lake Winnebago just before a storm.

"Here's your sweater, Jack," I said and pulled it off over my head. His hand touched mine as he took it and I kept my fingers there for a moment, thrilled by my own daring.

"I'm afraid I have to go too now," he said but I waited. He had flung his sweater around his shoulders and tied the sleeves in a knot and then we both just stood without saying anything. You can't ask a boy, "When will I see you again?" or "Will I *ever* see you again?" I had meant to find out from my sisters what fellows usually say when they leave. I thought maybe I should tell him I had liked the boat or that it had been a pleasant sail or something, but all those words seemed silly. Already the first drops of rain were spotting the cement sidewalk dark.

"It's raining," Jack said and held out his hand to see if he could feel the drops. "That will be good for the gardens."

You can't say to a boy "Have I been fun tonight?" or "Don't you like me more than other girls—wouldn't you like to go out with me again?" A girl just can't say that sort of thing to a boy—especially when he's talking about gardens. So I just stood there and all of a sudden the rain started coming down hard and the wind tossed the trees with quick gusts and blew my skirt around my legs.

"Good night, Angie," he said. "You'd better get in the house quick. I've got to run for it. Get in quick so you don't get wet." He turned and cut across the front lawn with his sweater over his head.

And he hadn't even said. I didn't even know if he would call me again.

Softly I tiptoed upstairs. Far out over the lake, thunder rumbled like a slow freight. As I passed by my older sisters' bedroom lightning lit the sky and in the yellow flash I could see the two of them sleeping quietly, their hair in metal curlers and cold cream shining on their faces.

And that was the first night.

I woke early the next morning—so early that the first flaming slashes of dawn were just beginning to be reflected pinkly on my bedroom wall. For a long time I lay in a warm, sleepy haze, looking at the alarm clock and knowing it was too early to get up and yet not wanting to go back to sleep again. It was so pleasant lying thinking comfortable, blurred thoughts about summer and about the night before.

My sister Kitty lay beside me sleeping soundly with her arms flung up over her head. She wears her hair in long pigtails and it was all fuzzy from tossing on the pillow. Once she turned over wearily, muttering something to herself, and then smiled contentedly in her sleep. Outside the window there were birds twittering excitedly about new plans for the day and inside I lay looking at the ceiling and thinking.

In the brightness of the morning last night didn't seem quite real—as if it had been a movie which I had sat and watched but of which I had not really been a part. It could hardly have been me who felt almost beautiful just because wind was fingering through my hair and the moon was thin like a piece of sheer yellow silk. I knew in a little while I would be getting up and putting on blue denim slacks and eating cereal at the table beside the kitchen window and dusting window sills and talking to my mother about garden flowers and what to have for dinner just as I had for so many summers. There would be no more of the exquisite uncertainty of last night, no queer, tingling awe at the newness of the feeling, and no strange, filling satisfaction out of just being alive. All that was last night because it *was* night and because it was the first boy I had really been out with. Not because it was a special boy—a boy different from other boys—but just because it was the first one. After a while, maybe after years when I had had so many dates that most of them were hazy, I would think of last night and remember it and that breathless loveliness, the same way and with the same amused pleasure that I think now about how I used to wait for the first look at the tree on Christmas morning or about the sweet pink froth of cotton candy at carnivals. Maybe, I thought to myself, if I were to see Jack this morning in the bright sunlight his eyebrows might be scraggly or his face might be pale and silly.

What if he tells every girl she looks pretty with her hair blowing around her face. And what if I didn't look pretty at all and it was just because there was no one else around and nothing else to say. What if Swede had sat in the bow of the boat laughing to himself because Jack was being smooth and I was being silly by listening. There is a crack over in one corner of the ceiling of my bedroom and I found myself unconsciously lining my thoughts up on either side—the good and the bad. The nice things to remember and the things that maybe in the sunlight wouldn't be the same at all.

It might be that he would never call me again and I would spend the rest of the summer evenings going for rides with my mother and father and lying in bed trying to repiece that night in the boat and wondering where I could have failed. Maybe when I went away to college in the fall I would have to write all my themes for English class about water spraying over the side of boats and wet sails flapping in the wind and thin moons that were hardly there, because that would be all I could remember, all I could think of. Maybe all my life my heart would jump a little when I saw a short crew cut or a boy with a basketball sweater knotted around his neck. Maybe every time I heard the name "Jack" I would hold my breath and be afraid to turn around to see who was there in case it might be he.

The sunrise flush was fading on the wall and I shut my eyes, trying to sleep again. But the darkness was like the soft, hushed darkness had been with the canvas over my head in the boat and the wind outside ruffling the water. I caught my breath a little, knowing I was being silly and not being able to help it every time I thought of his hand and mine holding the match . . . Maybe if I got up quickly everything would be all right and I would forget. It could be, I thought, that I am still sleeping a little and holding a nice dream by the tail so it won't get away. But I could hear Kitty breathing quietly beside me and I could see the long crack zigzagged on the ceiling and the early sun shining in the window and I knew that I was wide awake. And I knew that even getting up quickly wouldn't help, that it was something that had nothing to do with waking or sleeping. Something that would be there all the time. And if I looked at myself in the mirror that morning I would see something different. My face would be the same but yet something had changed, and I would try not to look straight at my family all day in case they might see it too, and smile at each other and say, "Angie's growing up." And somehow I was afraid to have anyone know because I wasn't sure myself. I couldn't be sure at all until I saw Jack again.

About seven o'clock I heard my mother's bed creak across the hall and I heard her open my door softly and look in. Quickly I shut my eyes and sighed as if I were asleep. I didn't want to get up just yet. I wanted just a few minutes more to lie there and think. Just a few minutes more. She went into the bathroom then to get washed, and soon the morning noises began. There was the water running in the kitchen sink and the sound of five plates, four coffee cups, and one glass of milk being set on the table. The smell of freshly made coffee drifted upstairs and made me start thinking wide-awake, daytime thoughts. I could see in my mind just how it would be. My sister Lorraine would be sitting at one side of the table and my sister Margaret on the other. Lorraine would be rushing to get to work and Margaret would be in her house coat, all ready except to put her make-up on. My mother would pour the coffee and say, perhaps, that it was strong or weak or should have percolated longer or something. Then one of them would remember last night and say, "Oh, Angie. Did you have fun?" or maybe, "Do you think he'll ask you out again?"

And I would put cream in my coffee and tell them all about the boat and how good Swede was at sailing it and how it had started to rain just when we got home. And they would ask a few more questions while I said yes or no or whatever the answer should be, but I would never mention the moon or the cool clean smell of the wind or that I had worn Jack's sweater all evening or all the other small, warm thoughts that kept nudging at my memory even as I lay awake watching the sun grow brighter on the ceiling. I would eat my breakfast like any other morning, clear the table like any other morning and do the housework like any other morning; but somehow inside myself I would be waiting for the phone to ring or listening for a bakery truck to pull up at the curb in front of the house.

I got out of bed then without waking Kitty, dressed, and went downstairs. Just before I went into the kitchen I stopped and pinched my cheeks to make the muscles relax. Somehow my face felt stiff and unnatural. I had a queer feeling that when I sat down at the breakfast table I might not be able to eat at all. I might just look at everyone drinking their morning coffee and then suddenly blurt out foolishly, "I like a boy. And I never knew it would be like this!"

But that wasn't quite what happened. Lorraine was standing by the kitchen stove in her house coat, curling her hair with the curling iron—she had just washed it the night before.

My mother was sitting now in a clean blue print dress at the table next to the window drinking her coffee, and her hair, where it is turning white on the sides, was brushed back high off her face. She used to get very bad headaches and would have to lie in a darkened bedroom with cool cloths soaked in vinegar on her forehead. The vinegar had bleached her hair snow-white at the temples. My mother is the only person I know who looks completely wide-awake and fresh when she wakes up in the morning.

375

"Your tomato juice is in the icebox," she said to me. "I didn't think you'd be down for a while."

Outside, the garden earth was dark from last night's rain and cobwebs, dew-sparkled, were stretched on the grass. Everything had a fresh, clean smell. "I think it's almost cool enough to wear a sweater and skirt," Lorraine said. "You know, after being used to collegiate clothes I just hate wearing summer dresses that wrinkle so easily."

She had a job for the summer at the Elite Canvas Company, just sitting all day folding and addressing circulars which were sent all over the country to advertise awnings, golf bags, and canvas laundry bags. Every summer the Elite took on about twenty extra girls. My father is a good friend of one of the men in the office—they had played some early golf together the weekend before and he had arranged it.

At first no one mentioned the night before. "We'll put the winter things in the attic this morning." I remember my mother's saying to me. "Just let Kitty sleep and you get the stepladder from the garage and I'll hand the things up to you." Ours is the old-fashioned kind of attic that you get into through a trap door in a bedroom ceiling. "We can get all Lorraine's school clothes put away so the closets won't be crowded all summer," she added.

My sister Margaret came down just then, all ready for work. You would like my sister. She is tall, thin, moves very quickly, and is engaged to a boy from Milwaukee who looks and acts just like a giant baby panda. Leaning over she kissed Mom, or rather brushed her with her cheek so she wouldn't rub off her lipstick. "No tomato juice this morning," she said and drank her coffee standing up by the stove—Margaret is always in a rush.

There was the usual breakfast talk: "Did you hear the rain last night?" "What would you children like me to get for supper?" (Mom always calls us children), and "We should have a big day at the store today." Little everyday things that could be said on any morning and I waited, just drinking my coffee and eating my toast, knowing that at any moment someone would remember. I could almost feel the words just hanging in midair. My mother reached over to snap off a loose thread hanging from the hem of Margaret's dress. I remember that so well because that was just before Margaret turned to me, remembering, "—Oh, Angie, how was last night?"

"Fun," I answered. Then I told them about the rain and how good Swede was at sailing and Jack used to date Jane Rady and how I remember her talking about him when she used to sit next to me in history class and about how many people had been out riding because it was such a nice night and all the cars with bright headlights that had been lined up along Lighthouse Point. Maybe, I thought, I'm talking too much; maybe I'm talking too fast. My voice seemed not to be coming from me at all, and I was surprised to hear it so calm and casual when inside my head the thoughts were all warm and shaky.

"I used to know Jack's cousin," Lorraine said. Her hair was curled in rows of shiny sausage-curls, and she was holding the curling iron as far away from her head as possible so she wouldn't burn her cheek, talking with a funny grimace as if any movement might bring the iron too close. "He was a drip though. He used to wear real baggy pants and always got to school late and had to be sent to the office for tardy slips."

I tried to think of something to counteract that slur. It wouldn't do to have the family think that Jack had dull connections before they even knew him—it's important that the family like a boy—but nothing came to my mind quickly enough.

376

In the green clumps of marguerite daisies along the garden path, round knobby heads stuck up with the green sheaths half open, showing the white silk petals underneath. Mom pushed back the kitchen curtains to look at them, commenting absently that next spring we would plant only a few rows of vegetables and have the rest of the garden all in flowers. Lorraine looked at Margaret and she looked at me and we all smiled, because every summer, for as long as we could remember, my mother had said that.

Then Margaret glanced at her wrist watch and gave a little gasp, though she had known all the time that it was late, gulped down the rest of her coffee, and rushed out, leaving the front door half open, calling back, "Be sure to have something good for supper because I'm going to be real hungry!" Lorraine went upstairs to get dressed and Mom finished her coffee and a last piece of toast before clearing the breakfast things away.

Though I don't know just what I expected, I was vaguely disappointed that this was just like any other morning. The sun was bright on the kitchen floor, the coffee was steaming as always, and my mother looked just as calm and shiny clean as she always did. Maybe, I thought, I was wrong about last night and maybe everything is just the same. Maybe it wasn't—well, what I thought it was.

But all morning, puttering with the housework, I was really waiting for Jack to stop round on his bakery route, and my mind was far from finger marks on the white woodwork and dustcloths that smelled of oily furniture polish. But by eleven o'clock he had not come. And by eleven o'clock, with the beds all made and the housework done, I knew this was not an ordinary day; I knew definitely that everything was not the same.

We had had scrambled eggs and toast and tea for lunch, just the three of us, my mother and little sister and I, sitting at the end of the kitchen table. "Just a pick-up snack," Mom had said. "Whatever you can find in the icebox." At twelve o'clock I began to get a queer restless feeling, as if I wanted to sit drumming my fingers on the table top, and I could hear the big clock in the dining room very plainly as it ticked.

Perhaps, I kept thinking, Jack will call me now, while he is home for lunch; but by one o'clock I had decided that probably he didn't like to call when his mother and father were around—some boys are like that—and maybe he would stop off at McKnight's on his way back to the bakery and call me from there. Or perhaps he would even come over for a few minutes—my mind made up a series of pleasant little excuses for him as the time went by.

But by the time two o'clock came and I had put away the lunch dishes, the house had grown quiet and the trees were beginning to turn their shadows eastward on the lawn; that excited feeling of waiting seemed to turn hard and make an aching throb in my throat. I had been so sure he would come.

Kitty was in the garage making bright, tinkering noises, trying to straighten out a dent in her bicycle fender with a claw hammer, and she said, "Sure, I'd like to walk to the lake with you," when I asked her. "Wasn't doing much anyhow."

There were men working on the road that goes along the wide breakwater with the lighthouse on the end. One of them was leaning his chest on a pneumatic drill, pressing it hard into the gravel road and it made a loud rut-ta-tutting that echoed in the stillness of the afternoon, spitting up dirt and sprays of gravel as it dug. We stood to watch for a while. The rest of the men were working slowly, swinging their pickaxes in wide, lazy arcs, or just leaning on the

377

yellow, wooden trestles with the red danger flags fluttering, put there to turn the slow afternoon traffic away from the shallow gap in the road. Beyond them the lake was very blue. You could just barely see the strip of green and the thin fingers of smoke that was Oshkosh on the opposite shore.

Just behind me, inside the breakwater, was the Big Hole where the smaller sailing boats were tied. I knew if I looked I could see it. But I didn't want to—not yet. There is that funny fascinating suspense in waiting, like wiggling a very loose tooth with your tongue. And besides it wouldn't do to have Kitty know what I really came out for. She is a good scout but—well, I just didn't want her to know, that's all.

So we went over to watch the children swimming and splashing first, and then I pushed Kitty in a swing until she said she was beginning to feel dizzy, and we walked all the way to the refreshment stand at the other end of the park for an ice-cream cone and a bag of popcorn. By the time we had walked back she had chocolate ice cream dribbled down the front of her shirt and her chin was shiny from the butter off my popcorn and both of us were ready to go home.

Just as I had planned we took the long way, back through the park, and we had to pass the Big Hole on our way.

The afternoon sun was sparkling and glinting on the tip of each small, quick wave so that the whole stretch of water in the harbor seemed to be giggling in the sunlight. There was a long row of small green and white sailboats tied to the shore, nodding up and down as the water licked the anchoring piles. They all had single, slim masts jabbing upward and gray canvas stretched neatly over their cockpits and, to me, they all looked exactly the same! I couldn't even tell which one was Jack's! I felt suddenly so relieved that I could have laughed out loud just standing there, looking at the boats dancing at the ends of their short ropes and the blue water shining in the sun. I don't know just what I *had* expected to see—one boat standing off by itself, looking different from the rest or a sign on one of them saying, "This is the boat that Angie Morrow fell in love in!" or something equally as silly. But whatever it was, it wasn't there at all!

Just then a horn honked close behind us and Kitty and I both jumped in fright and turned to look. There was Swede. He pulled up alongside us and leaning out the car window, said, "Hi-yah, Angie. Want a ride home?"

It was annoying that he should come along just then. In the first place I hadn't wanted him to see me standing staring at the boat, and besides I could just hear him saying later, "Hey, Jack, that Angie don't look so good in the daytime! I saw her this afternoon out looking at the boat and she didn't look so good as at night."

I had on old slacks and I knew my nose was shiny, but Swede was smiling at me with his funny warm grin so there was nothing to do but say, "Hello, there. You scared me, honking that way. This is my sister Kitty, Swede." They nodded to each other and she bent down in an embarrassed little-girl sort of way, pretending to take a stone out of her shoe and softly whistling a breathy tune with no particular melody.

"Been looking at the boat?" Swede asked. I nodded. "Nice little job, isn't she? Did you have fun last night, Angie?"

Now is my chance to find out, I thought. Swede is sure to know if anyone does! "Oh, I had a wonderful time," I told him, and then added casually, very offhand, "Did Jack have fun?"

"Yeh, I guess he did."

"Don't you *know?*"

"No, he didn't say nothing."

"Did you see him today?"

"Sure."

"Well, what did he say?"

"Nothing much. At least nothing—about you."

So he hadn't said anything! After last night and the way he'd looked and my wearing his sweater, and after what had happened while trying to light his pipe and everything—and he hadn't said anything. I couldn't believe it! Swede was sitting running his finger up and down, playing with the grooves in the steering wheel. I looked at him and I could feel a question forming on my lips, "But didn't he even—" and I checked myself just in time, saying instead, "Thanks anyway for the ride, Swede, but I guess Kitty and I will walk home. It isn't very far. Thanks anyway."

"Okay," he said. "Glad I met you, Kitty. See you later, Angie," and the car pulled away.

The sun didn't seem quite so bright on the water now. We passed two little boys coming home from swimming with their hair sleeked back and damp canvas knickers pulled on over their still-wet swimming suits. They had stopped at the public drinking fountain where the water comes out so cold that it hurts your teeth, and were squirting mouthfuls of water at each other, their cheeks puffed out like chipmunks'. One yelled hello to Kitty, sending the water out of his mouth in a spout. He was in her room at school, she explained with injured dignity.

Mom was sitting in a canvas lawn chair in the shade at the side of the house when we got home, reading the evening paper. It is an unwritten rule in our house never to ask for a piece of the paper until my mother has finished with it, so Kitty and I both sat down to wait. The short-clipped grass was cool and fresh and full of little clover, the kind whose heads flip off like small pink and white balls before the lawn mower.

"I see where Grace Mary Wuerst is going to be married," my mother said. I raised an eyebrow in acknowledgement and Kitty just sat chewing a clover stem. She turned a page and after a moment or two—"Remind me to tell Dad that there is a new hospital going up in Sheboygan. They are open for bids next Monday." I raised the other eyebrow. My mother leafed through the last few pages quickly and then, without saying a word, pulled out an inside sheet and handed it to me and gave Kitty the page with the comic strips. We sat reading together and before long it began to get cooler and the shade from the house stretched out over the side lawn on which we were sitting, over the neighbors' driveway and printed the crooked shadow of a chimney halfway up the side of the neighbors' house. "You two had better go in and set the supper," my mother said. "Margaret and Lorraine will be here soon and perhaps we might all like to walk up and see a movie tonight."

I thought it over as I spread the cloth on the diningroom table. Of course, I couldn't say I didn't *want* to go, but if he should call when we were at the movie I'd never know! It might be that he hadn't said anything to Swede because, like me, he wasn't sure. And maybe Swede was just teasing me. Probably he and Jack had talked it all over and he just didn't want to tell me, that was all. Outside, long shadows lay on the grass and I could hear robins in the trees on the front lawn singing that lilting question they always ask from tree to tree as the sun is going down.

In the kitchen Kitty had been opening two cans of pork and beans and she popped something quickly in her mouth and was wiping her fingers on her slacks with a guilty look when I came in for the silverware. I still couldn't believe that he hadn't even *mentioned* last night, hadn't said anything at all.

No matter what you tell her, Kitty always eats the little piece of fat pork off the top of a can of pork and beans like that.

Even when you say prayers for it, a thing almost never happens the way this did. In five minutes more we would have been halfway down the block and I'd never have heard the phone ring at all. It was just as if it had been planned. Kitty and my other two sisters were already on the front steps with their hair all brushed and ready to go to the movie, and I had just run back upstairs for a clean handkerchief for my mother when the phone rang. It was Jack calling.

He knew it was late, he said, and he would have called earlier, but his father hadn't decided to let him use the car until a few minutes ago and would I like to go out for a while? Probably drive to Pete's or something. . . .

"Of course *not*," my mother said firmly. "Tell him that you were just going to the movies with us. The idea of thinking that you can go out any night in the week! Does he think you have nothing else to do?"

"Oh, let her go, Mom. With school just out it's good to fool around."

"Sure. It's a wonderful night to go out and Pete's is on the lake—let her go, Mom. The show isn't very good anyway."

"It won't hurt, Mom. Let her go."

My sisters were talking. I said nothing.

She mused a moment. "Well, all right. You may go this time but don't let this boy—" she *knew* his name was Jack—"think that you can be running around all the time. You have better things to do. I thought this was the summer you were going to get so much reading done. But you may go this time."

Halfway down the front sidewalk she turned and called, "Angie, you'd better put on your blue linen. You don't look very dressed up for an evening."

And I hurried upstairs to get ready, trying to calm the crowded, fluttery thoughts in my head. "I'll see you in ten minutes then," Jack had said.

You would like Pete's, I know. There is no other place quite like it. When we were little we used to go for drives on warm summer evenings with my mother and father and stop there for ice-cream cones. Everyone did. And now that the children were grown up they still stopped—to dance now and have Cokes or beer instead of ice-cream cones. Mr. Mingle (everyone calls him Pete) is past eighty and can just barely shuffle around, but he remembers everyone and can call each by his own name. The building, old and square, is built right on the lake shore about three miles out of town and the inside hasn't been painted for years. Outside, the lawns and flower beds have all run into one and stretch to the water's edge in a tangle of weeds. On one side is a gravel parking lot, for Pete's is always jammed at night with the crowd from high school.

We went in the side door, Jack and I, and sat in one of the booths which are set back in latticework arches with little black painted tables, the tops rough with carved initials. The edges of the carving are worn smooth by hundreds of Coke bottles and glasses of beer and by hands that have held each other tight across those tables. Off in one corner is Pete's old and irritable parrot perched on a wicker stand, scrawking at anyone who comes too near, continually rolling its yellow eyes in anger, and pecking at the pumpkin seeds in its food dish with an ugly beak that is chipped in layers like an old fingernail.

I felt a little scared. It was almost like making my debut or something. I had never been out to Pete's on a date before, and in our town that is the crucial test. Everyone is there and everyone sees you. I knew of a girl once who went out to Pete's with her cousin and no one else asked her to dance or paid any attention to her, and so she went away to college in the fall and never had dates at home for any of the dances at Christmas or Easter. If you don't make the grade at Pete's, you just don't make it.

"What will you have, Angie?" Jack asked. He hadn't said much to me on the way out—not much *about* me, I mean. Halfway to Pete's he had asked if I heard anything funny in the motor of the car—like a faint knocking or something, so we drove almost two miles in silence, he with his head cocked to one side and a scowl on his face and I sitting very still trying to look as if I were listening hard. In the end, just as we got to Pete's, he decided it had been his imagination after all. So you see, when he said, "What will you have, Angie?" that's when my evening, the evening of my "coming out," really began.

At Pete's you choose from only four things—beer, root beer, Coke, and peanuts salted in the shell. No one ever wants anything else. I wanted a Coke and he wanted a glass of beer and we both wanted peanuts, so Jack went up to the bar to get them to save old Pete the trouble. The bar is in a smaller room in the front and the jukebox is there, too, and that's where all the boys who haven't dates sit and play cards and watch the other fellows and girls as they come in.

While he was gone I traced through the maze of initials on the table top, trying to make out someone's I knew. Maybe, I thought, his is here somewhere. There was a heart with a J and another letter in it, but the second initial had been carved over so I couldn't make it out. I thought of scratching my own A.M. in a small, smooth space—just so it would look as if I had been there before, as if someone had wanted to carve my initials like they did other girls'—but I couldn't find anything to do it with. If I took a hairpin out of my hair the curl on top would fall down and I would have to fix it all over again.

I took the little mirror out of my purse to look at myself—I didn't often wear my hair with that big curl on top, and because they had all gone to the movies there was no one at home to consult before I left. It looked all right to me, but then Pete's is so hazy-dark that everything looks different anyway.

Swede walked in from the bar just then with a glass of beer in his hand and slid into the booth across from me. "Hi-yah, Angie," he said. "Jack will be back in a minute. He's talking to some of the fellows." He paused to take a sip of his beer. "Well, what's the good word?"

I didn't know just what he meant by that so I smiled, telling him I hadn't known he was going to be out here, and we began to talk about little things— did I drink beer, and whether or not the kids would like Pete's as well if it was all fixed up, and how come a good girl like me had wasted my talents by not going up to high school? I liked Swede. His hair was blond and kinky and he looked so well-fed and healthy that it seemed as if his chest would burst right through his sweater. Besides, he made me feel like a pretty girl, talking as he did—"A good girl like me wasting my talents by not going up to high school." Maybe it wouldn't be so hard to talk to the other fellows after all.

When Jack came back with my Coke and peanuts he brought two of his friends, boys who had played basketball with him, and in the beginning I felt

381

quite at ease with them. After the introductions they didn't pay much attention to me, but just talked about school, and that they had heard "Old Baldy" wasn't going to be teaching Math next year after the way he had thrown that book at Chuck Wilkins that day, and who was the new girl from Ninth Street that Dick Fox had had out for the past three nights? I just listened and laughed and drank my Coke and didn't seem to be out of place in the least. I'm sure none of them thought that this was my first night out at Pete's on a date and that I'd never sat in a booth with four boys at once before. I tried to act very natural and casual and didn't say much.

I didn't know Jane Rady was there that night at all until she came over from one of the darker booths near the back to talk with us, saying, "Well, Angie Morrow, I didn't know *you* were here!" in a funny surprised sort of voice that really sounded as if she were saying, "Well, Angie Morrow, I really never thought I'd see you out on a date!"

Jane is much shorter than I am with fluffy blond hair that she lets hang loose with no hairpins or bow or anything. And for some reason when you look at Jane you always see her mouth before you see the rest of her face.

All four of the boys said, "Hi, there, Janie!" and one stood up to give her his place but she said, "Oh, don't bother, I'll just squeeze in." It was so crowded that Jack had to put his arm around the back of the booth to make room and she looked at him with a little smile and purred under her breath, "Uum, nice!" and everyone laughed and said, "What a girl, Janie!" and I laughed, too, but my face felt stiff and the laugh came out funny though I don't think anyone noticed it for they were all listening to her.

I sat and listened too. It wasn't because I hadn't gone up to high school then; Jane hadn't gone up there either but she knew the things to say. She knew what they were talking about when they said, "Remember the night after the Sheboygan game when there were seven of us coming home in the back seat?" and "Did you hear what happened to Bartie when he broke the drum at the graduation dance last week?" Jane did remember and she had heard and she added a few more things that made the boys laugh and look at each other and then back at her. And of course, I laughed too but I felt very uncomfortable and conspicuous; and though I drank my Coke in little sips it did not last long enough, and I had to sit sliding ice round and round in the empty glass and rack my brains for something to say, something that would make them remember that I was there or make them at least think that I thought what they were talking about was interesting too.

I thought of saying brightly, as if the thought had just come to me, "Did Jack and Swede and I ever have fun sailboating last night!" But they might all turn and look at me, saying with a questioning inflection, "Yeah?" and I wouldn't know how to go on from there. Maybe Jack wouldn't want them to know we had been sailboating—after all he hadn't mentioned it himself, had he? He was lighting a cigarette for Jane just then and she blew the smoke in his face in a playful puff as she said, "Thanks," and smiled a little half-smile with the side of her mouth that didn't have the cigarette in it.

Through my mind mulled all the things she used to tell me about Jack when she sat next to me in the history class. The evening dragged on and on. The Coke had left a sweetish, sickening taste in my mouth and my whole body ached with wretchedness.

Swede's beer glass was empty and he stood up saying, "Can I get anything for anybody?" and balancing the empty glasses in a pyramid, he went out to the bar. In the other room someone had put a nickel in the jukebox and music began to come through the round amplifier all hung with crepe paper above the door. Jane gave a little gasp and made her eyes and mouth very round. "Oh, that song—I love it! Jack, dance with me!" She stood up, holding out her hand.

Jack looked at me and said, " 'Scuse me, will you?" I didn't blame him. Anyone with a date as dull as I was would naturally want to dance with someone else. Out of the corner of my eye I watched him. I didn't care, I said to myself. I was all wrong about last night anyway. It didn't make any difference—he was just like any other boy, any boy at all. I was all wrong.

The music seemed to fill the whole room at Pete's with its poignant tilt, and the little liquid waves of music seemed to curl in and out the latticework that arched the booths. I sat staring at the table and slid my Coke glass so that it covered the carved heart with the initial J in it. Of course I was all wrong about last night.

There were other people dancing now but it didn't seem to matter; Jack and Jane weren't looking at anyone. She was much shorter than he and danced with her arm crooked around his neck and her head back so that her fluffy hair hung halfway down her back. Neither of them seemed to be saying anything, just dancing and letting the music float round them. I tried to keep from watching them too hard. One of the fellows in our booth became restless and muttering, " 'Scuse me," went out to the bar. "I don't care," I thought. "Let him go. I know I'm dull. I don't care if he wants to go—everyone can't be like Jane Rady." It seemed as if my whole face was stiff with scowling and my eyebrows must be growing straight across my nose, dark and heavy.

The full disappointment of the evening struck me all in a lump. It was the rollicking sadness of the music that made my heart feel sore. It was that and the thought of last night and all the silly, wonderful things I had been feeling all day and the way my heart had jumped when the phone rang and it was Jack. And it was because he was there now dancing with Jane Rady when he hadn't even danced with me once and I was his date. And the other fellows didn't like me either and I was awkward and didn't know anything to talk about. It was all that and the sudden, sickening realization that I couldn't fool myself. I did care! It wasn't because it was the first boy I had ever really been out with—this was something different. I had never felt this way before—and he didn't even care! Someone had put another nickel in the music box and they kept on dancing.

So I just waited, toying with my empty glass, and the corners of my mouth seemed suddenly tired and a peculiar lonesome ache went through me right down into my hands. I just sat, not thinking of anything in particular, feeling as useless, as emptied, and as hollowed as a sucked orange.

Lying in bed that night thinking it over, slowly and clearly, I decided it was *me* that was all wrong. Other girls knew what to do. Other girls could talk with fellows and laugh with them and say funny things. Jane Rady could do it. Jane knew how to dance with her head back so her hair fell long and smooth as silk thread. Mine was curly all over and no matter how much I brushed it there were always little wispy curls around my face, as if I had just come out of a steamy shower. I wasn't the kind of a girl who could ever go into McKnight's drugstore and have a crowd of boys come over to sit with me, wanting to buy me a Coke. And I know I'd look silly if I shook my finger as if I were trucking and clicked time with my tongue, swaying from side to side the way some girls can do, when good dance music came on the radio. None of the fellows at Pete's had even offered me a cigarette because they could tell just by looking at me that I was the kind of girl who wouldn't know how to smoke!

And of course I had acted all wrong too. It made me squirm inside to think of it. When Jack and Jane had finished dancing I should have smiled as if I hadn't cared at all and said something smart like "smooth stuff there," or "just like Veloz and Yolanda,"[3] as any other girl would have done. But I didn't. My face had been stiff with misery, and seeing everyone else laughing and having so much fun I couldn't help thinking how much better it would have been if I had just gone to the movies with my mother and sisters. You know, if you don't see all the fellows and girls out on dates you don't think about it and then you don't feel so unhappy. If I hadn't gone out to Pete's at all things could have gone on as they had before—"Angie Morrow doesn't go out on dates because her mother doesn't let her"—and no one would have known I was such a drip. But now even Jack knew.

Only once during the whole evening had there been a trace of that strange, warm feeling of last night when, just before we went home, we had gone outside and down to the water's edge behind Pete's. The lake was rough and the waves tossed up, white with spray, sucking at the shore, and the wind went soughing through the line of old willows, swaying them with a sonorous, restless rhythm. We stood quiet, listening to the night sounds and watching the pale moon, half hidden by the gray cotton cloud stretched across it. Inside, Pete's had been so full of music and laughing, but out here the whole stretch of dark water and the thick weeds and the swaying trees on the shore seemed tormented by a strange, aching lonesomeness, and the wind blew in cool and damp from the lake with the familiar, moist smell of fish. Out here something in me relaxed; all the awkward restraint that had haunted me through the evening was lifted and I felt like taking off my shoes and dancing in the grass.

As we were going back to our car I noticed all the silent, dark cars parked around the gravel lot and remarked to Jack, "There don't seem to be nearly as many people inside as there are cars parked out here."

He looked at me a moment, as if he thought I was joking, and then said with an odd laugh and an inflection which I didn't quite understand, "You're a good kid, Angie." That's all he said and it may have been just my imagination mingled with the mysterious spell of the lake but for a moment, for the only time during the whole evening, I thought he looked at me as he had last night.

But the feeling couldn't last when, during that short ride back to town, I realized again with doubled humiliation what a terrible date I'd been. Jack didn't look at me once all the way home, or try to talk and as soon as we got in front of my house he jumped out of the car and came round to open my door. It seemed so funny, walking up the sidewalk, that just this time the night before I had been doing the same thing and wondering if he would call me again; and now he *had* called and I *had* gone out with him and here I was, still wondering if there would be another time. But tonight it was tinged with a little hopelessness. After the way I had acted what would any boy do?

Standing on the front steps, I had an uncomfortable feeling that there was something I should say; yet a girl just can't blurt out an apology for not being like other girls! I could almost feel the right words on my tongue, but when I opened my mouth to speak there was nothing there at all. I broke off a bit of

---

3 *Veloz and Yolanda*   Fran Veloz and Yolanda Casazza, regarded as the world's greatest ballroom dancers in the 1930s and 1940s, performed specialty dances in films and nightclubs.

the tall spruce that grows beside our steps and smelled the pungent piny odor rising in the air. Jack was standing running his finger round and round one of the scrolls in our wrought-iron stair railing. "Angie," he said slowly, "Angie, I'm going to be out of town for a couple of days." My heart slipped down a little. This was his way of saying that he wouldn't see me for a couple of days—a couple of days that would probably merge into a week and then turn out to be the rest of the summer. "Going up to Green Bay," he explained, "to see a cousin of mine and I won't be back till Friday afternoon some time." That's all right, my mind said hurriedly. That's all right, Jack. You don't have to tell me anything. I know how I've acted tonight. "I wondered," he went on, "if you'd like to go to the dance at the Country Club with me on Friday night. It's the first one of the summer and I thought maybe you'd like to go!"

Lying in bed that night I thought it over. I had wanted an invitation to that dance more than anything else in the world, but now that I had been asked I hardly wanted to go because I could tell beforehand just what it would be like. My mother, who is always good about things like that, would buy me a new summer evening dress to wear; and my two older sisters, who would probably be going too, would arrange my hair and lend me perfume to dab behind my ears and on the hem of my dress so I would swish up a glamorous smell when I walked; and there would be Kitty, sitting on the edge of her bed in her pajamas, watching each step and saying over and over, "Oh, how nice you look!" When we were all dressed my mother would stand back to look at us with her eyes shining, thinking, probably, how short a time ago it seemed since we were just little girls. Of course, I would smile and pretend to be excited and so glad to be going, but all the time, inside, I'd keep remembering how it had been at Pete's when I hadn't been able to talk to the fellows at all and I would keep thinking of how I had watched the cross parrot, pretending to be very interested in his chipped beak and yellow eyes just because no one bothered to talk to me.

I had never been to a dance at the Country Club before but my sisters had told me about them. Almost anyone could go. The people divide into crowds and cliques when they get there, the older ones, when they're not dancing, sitting at the bar, and the younger crowd at little tables drinking Cokes or walking around outside on the flagstone terrace. It was easy to imagine the girls like Jane Rady out there with their soft formals fluttering in the night breezes, laughing up at fellows in white coats whose cigarettes made bright holes in the darkness. And it was easy to imagine me, too, not ever saying anything smooth, not knowing what to do with my hands and laughing too often in a stiff, self-conscious way, just because I wouldn't be able to think of the right things to say. Even with a new formal and perfume on my hair I wouldn't be any different. If I hadn't been able to do it at Pete's I wouldn't be able to do it at the dance. I knew it. Other girls could have fun and get along with boys but I wasn't *like* other girls.

I turned over, shutting my eyes, trying to sleep, and on my fingers I could still smell the pungent spice of the spruce tree.

It was odd to remember that just this time last night the thoughts in my head had been as pleasant and sweet as warm, thick honey.

Doing the supper dishes next evening. Lorraine and I discussed what kind of a formal I should get, though we knew very well that in the end it would be my mother who would decide. All of us had agreed at supper time that it should be "something young and not too sophisticated." Margaret had suggested a blue and white sprigged dimity[4]—very quaint and littlegirlish, which has just come in at the store—but Lorraine thought something "less ordinary" would be better.

"You know," Lorraine said to me later, "a girl should always choose something different so she stands out on the dance floor. If you really wanted to do something unusual you should take a very, very long piece of ribbon and tie it in a small bow on the top of your head and let the streamers hang right down to the hem of your skirt. One of the girls at school did that at our spring dance this year. And another had a black net formal so she got some black veiling and wore it on her head with a red rose like a Spanish mantilla—but that would be a little exotic for Fond du Lac." My sister always knows a lot of original, clever ideas about clothes and even if she wasn't going to the dance herself she didn't mind talking about it.

No one had mentioned it out loud, of course, but we had all been hoping someone would ask her. When the older and younger go it's hard for the middle one to stay home. Lorraine never dates much in Fond du Lac. When she was at college in Chicago she used to go out a lot—at least as much as the other girls. There wasn't a chance for meeting many boys when you went to a girls' college with no college for boys nearby. She used to write home about the smooth blind dates she had for school dances and they almost always asked her out again afterward. Somehow the boys around our town didn't seem to appreciate her— there weren't many fellows who knew about books and English literature and the things that Lorraine learned in college. Of course, she never said anything about it but in the summertime it is handy to have a boy.

Kitty was outside playing "One, Two, Three, O'Leary" on the driveway and the ball made a pleasant, rhythmic bounce-bounce on the pavement. The man next door was cutting his lawn and between the noise of the lawn mower we could hear Margaret and my mother talking in the back garden. "You know," my mother was saying, "if you're sure it isn't too old looking, I think that blue sprigged should be nice for Angie."

"You'll like it!" Margaret assured her. "You and Angie come down to the store tomorrow and she can try it on. It's the prettiest one we have in right now and we certainly don't want her in one of those aqua or rose taffeta things." And then the lawn mower drowned them out again.

A few moments later Lorraine was just shaking some soap chips into the dishpan for me when we caught the tail end of a sentence from the back lawn— "well, it's a little late but Art can probably get hold of *someone* who will go, though, you know, Mom, most fellows wouldn't want to drive all the way up from Milwaukee just on the chance of a blind date!"

My mother's voice was very maternal and concerned. "I know. It wouldn't be so bad if Angie weren't going, too, but—" and then came the whirring sound of the lawn mower.

This was something we hadn't been meant to hear and I hoped perhaps Lorraine hadn't, so I made a clatter with the dishes and tried to pretend nothing had happened. But suddenly she turned to me and said in a tight voice, "Why if that isn't absolutely silly, Angie. Honestly! If I really *wanted* to go I could always ask one of the fellows up from Chicago, couldn't I?"

I checked myself just in time with the logical question on my lips—"Why don't you, Lorraine?"

---

4 *sprigged dimity*   sheer cotton fabric with a tiny design in it.

A moment later she threw her dish towel over the back of a chair and without looking at me said quickly, "Got to go upstairs a minute. Be right back to finish." I dried the rest of the dishes, swept the kitchen floor, and hung the dish towel on the rack to dry. The bounce-bounce of Kitty's ball on the driveway was beginning to get monotonous so I turned on the living room radio to drown out the sound. The breeze coming in the window was fresh and clean with the smell of newly cut grass.

When Lorraine finally came down I pretended to be very busy with the evening paper and she leafed through an old magazine, neither of us saying anything. Her cheeks were very white with powder but around her eyes was still red. It was funny that I had never realized before that Lorraine *minded* not dating.

On Friday night before the dance I stood in the garden, wondering what it was all about. Just a short time ago Jack called to say he would pick me up at a quarter-past nine. I was all ready except to slip my evening dress on over my head. In the end we had decided on the sprigged dimity and my mother had pressed it so the full skirt hung in soft, billowy folds and the small sleeves stuck up stiff and puffed as it was spread out on my bed. I had come out to the garden to pick bachelor's buttons for my hair in my long white slip, holding it high to keep the hem above the cool dew on the grass. And as I stood in the garden with the soft air against my cheek and a night breeze fingering through my hair, I couldn't help wondering a little.

From the house came familiar sounds—the radio in the living room purring out soft dance music, the noise of Lorraine clicking down the stairs as the telephone rang, and Kitty in her own bedroom talking to someone excitedly in a high, small voice. When Jack had called I had thought it would make me excited, after not having heard him for three days, but it didn't. It was just a boy's voice. Just a low, friendly boy's voice that might have belonged to anyone. I hadn't felt any particular thrill at all—at least I believed I hadn't; but now out in the garden with the night air so still and soft, the thought of him came back to me and played through my mind till my lips felt warm and my heart beat fast with the wonder of it.

In the past few days something had changed. I had never felt things inside of me before and now I wasn't even sure if I really felt warm and eager because it was my first Country Club dance and my dress was new, or if it was really because in such a short time, such a very short time, Jack would be there—or was it only that the night was so beautiful that I just wanted to feel something? That evening at Pete's had left me with a cautious soreness, half in my mind and half in my heart. And yet, out in the garden, I realized that some of the strange feeling of the first night still lingered. But I couldn't tell, really—it was all still so puzzling and so new. And the night breeze blew till the thin silk of my slip licked against my legs, cool and clean.

Beside the garden path was a rose vine clinging to a rough lattice support, the tender trailers tied with bits of string. The heavy-headed red roses looked black in the darkness, their perfume floating upward, bewitching the air. Over the whole garden the crickets sang with a steady, rhythmical cheeping, keeping time to the music of the night. The air was soft and warm with the smell of damp earth and the lush darkness of summer. Somewhere, off where lights were bright and the night was moving, I heard a car's brakes screak. The echo waited a moment and then all was still. One thought in my mind sang a beating refrain with the crickets—"in just a few minutes Jack will be here." Far up in the

out to straighten it. It is all part of the contented, weekend ritual, and he puffed and blew as he worked, bustling with importance while he polished the windshield till his neck was red with exertion. Then he stood back with the chamois cloth in his hand to admire it. My mother sat by the living-room window watching and we all laughed to ourselves, for we knew that by next weekend the car would be as dusty and untidy as ever.

Lorraine and I made the beds together, and the house smelled of roast and cauliflower from the kitchen, and everything was so pleasant and Sundayish that I forgot to ask what she had done last night and whether or not she had had fun with Martin Keefe.

Margaret and Art had gone for a ride and didn't get back until just before dinner was served. Art went out to the kitchen with his hands behind his back, walking in his funny way like a Teddy bear. In one hand he had a jar of green olives and a can of black olives in the other. Each Sunday he stops at some grocery store that is open late and brings home a contribution.

My mother was just lifting the roast out with two forks, dripping with sputtering hot fat, and Art set the olives down on the table to hold the meat platter for her. She saw them and looked at him with a softness in her eyes. "What's that for—a bribe?" she laughed and patted his cheek.

Until she met Art, Margaret had always gone with a different kind of boy— tall fellows who moved fast and laughed deep down in their throats and showed square white teeth when they talked. But after she met Art she never went out with another boy. He was just a little taller than she with thick, dark hair and warm brown eyes that were as soft and mellow as his voice. We got used to his queer humor and odd gentleness till we liked him so well that to say "Margaret and Art" was as easy and natural as "bread and butter" or "dark and handsome."

Later, when dinner was over and we were sitting around the table in a contented, Sunday-afternoon apathy, Kitty pushed back her chair, excused herself, and went out to play on the front lawn. She walked about listlessly, flipping off clover heads with a short stick, humming to herself in dejection. Every now and then she stopped to stare down the street.

My mother looked out at her and shook her head. "Really, we're going to have to do something about that child," she said. "When you three girls were younger you had each other—but there is no one on this street for her to play with. Angie, you don't seem to have any more interest in her than the man in the moon. If she wants to play dolls, you're dusting; if she wants to go swimming, you're just washing your hair. It will be a good many years before she can go dancing!"

It's funny how, having nice thoughts in your head, it is so pleasant to pull them all out and think them all over again. And I wanted to think about Jack just then, so I said, "Mom, if you'll excuse me, I'll take Kitty for a walk in the field. We can pick violets or something . . ." and my conscience didn't even prick at the deception.

Our house is the second from the last on our street from the edge of town. Beyond the end house runs a gravel road and then a broad stretch of undeveloped real estate, run wild with weeds and low, scraggly bushes. We have always called it the Field.

That afternoon Kitty and I just wandered aimlessly through the long grass that was still lush and fresh with the last rains of spring, not going anywhere. It was early summer and the water was still puddled in the ditches along the grassy road and underfoot the ground had a soft, spongy feeling. The sky was dotted with cotton cloud-puffs and Kitty walked along, zigzagging with her head back and

394

watching it till she was tired, and then plumped down to rest. I sat beside her. The breeze was like a gentle breathing and the sun hot on our faces till both of us were mellowed with contentment, basking in the almost liquid warmth of the sunshine.

Kitty rolled over on her back. "Angie," she said, her voice slow with thought, "did you ever wonder where the butterflies go when it rains?" I had to admit that until that moment I hadn't even thought of it.

"Well, I was thinking about it the other day, Angie," she told me, "and I figured that seeing they don't have holes or nests or anything, they must hide under leaves. That's the only place they *could* be. Probably under big leaves like on the rhubarb plants. Next time it rains remind me, and I'll go to poke the leaves with a stick. I won't hurt anything. I just want to see if the butterflies come out. . . ." and she lay mulling the thought over carefully.

After a while we got up from the soft grass and walked out farther across the Field until we came to the creek. It is a muddy, fast-moving tributary of Lake Winnebago and at this time of the year it is swollen with the early summer rains. We leaned over the wood bridge to watch it, Kitty and I, and it rushed past beneath, eddying around the cement piles of the bridge and stirring up the red-brown clay. There was a small dead tree fallen part way across the stream, and the water churned around the trunk and ribboned its way through the bare branches. She picked some flat leaves from the roadside and dropped them over the rail, watching them float a moment and then rush on down the stream. Later in the summer the water would be green and sluggish and there would be fat bullfrogs squatting in the mud along the bank, loudly clearing their throats as they sat hidden among the river rushes.

Tired of just standing, we edged our way cautiously down the bank, feet heavy with damp clay, and stood on the cement ledge under the bridge near the water's edge. The stream is only a few feet deep here but it was whirling along in such full, angry haste that it gave me a queer fear at its strength, and I took Kitty's arm with one hand, gripping the rough cement wall with the other. A car came along the gravel road and thundered over the bridge above our heads, sending a few bits of gravel hurtling over the side into the water.

Besides enjoying the loveliness of the afternoon I was stalling for time and I knew it. The minute I got home I would be hoping and waiting for Jack to call, but here, not knowing if he had called or if he would call, even the suspense was pleasant.

We walked away from the creek slowly, pushing aside the grass with our feet as we went, looking for the meadowlarks' nests hidden in the grass. Often in the summertime we had run across four of the small eggs with the red-brown speckles, secure in a nest, while the mother bird would fly above us in wide swoops to distract our attention, singing desperately, her high breast feathers throbbing with song.

When we got home my bare legs were nipped with small grass cuts and from even that short time in the sun Kitty had new freckles on her nose. The family were sitting in the shade of the side lawn and Lorraine was lounged on a canvas lawn chair, putting polish on her nails right down to the tips and holding her hands straight out in front of her till it dried. She is always very careful to wear her nail polish and lipstick to match.

"Angie, that boy called," my mother said as I came up the walk.

"What boy?" I asked, careful to make my voice sound surprised. I felt an instinctive need for caution. Individually my mother likes them well enough, but as dates she regards all boys with a vague, general disapproval—just in case.

"That boy, Jack," she answered, never looking up from her knitting. "Margaret spoke with him."

"He said he would call later, Angie," Margaret explained. "That he thought maybe you would like to go to some party at somebody's cottage tonight with him and some other fellows and girls. I told him you probably could and he said he would call back sometime before supper. You can wear my yellow sweater if you want, Ang—but be careful of it. I'd like to see him when he comes to pick you up—he sounded cute over the phone. He talks as if he has brown eyes—has he?"

There was a hot tingling round my face and I waited to be sure my voice wouldn't sound too eager, for my mother was knitting with fast, jerky movements as if she were annoyed and her needles clicked. "Do you mind if I go, Mom?"

"I don't know," she shrugged. "Ask your father."

I turned to him. "May I, Dad?"

"Whatever your mother says," he answered lightly, dismissing all responsibility. If he takes time to reprimand us, my father is always very stern but otherwise he doesn't bother at all. He was sitting then in a loose golf shirt that he always wears on weekends, and his neck showed soft and white at the throat where it is usually covered with his weekday shirt and tie. I stood waiting as he leafed through the paper.

My mother cleared her throat crossly. "I would certainly like to know with *whom* you are going, *where* you are going, and at what *time* you will be home. I don't like the idea of you girls just going out any time with anybody!"

It isn't that my mother doesn't like boys, as I explained, but because we are girls and because we are the kind of family who always use top sheets on the beds and always eat our supper in the dining room and things like that—well, she just didn't want us to go out with *anybody*.

"That will be the third time this week that you've seen that boy!"

This was just what I had been shying away from. For all the warm glow in my thoughts, thinking about Friday night, I didn't want anyone else to know or to ask questions.

"But, Mom, I'll find out about it first," I assured her hastily. "When he calls I'll ask where the party is and everything and I promise we'll be home early. It will be all right."

Later that evening when I was sitting in my bedroom waiting for Jack to come, I heard the phone ring downstairs and went down to answer. But Margaret had got there before me and she was standing holding it, with her hand over the mouthpiece, saying, "Honestly, Lorraine, if he wants a date and you go I'll just be furious at you—anyone calling for a date at this time of night!"

Lorraine was absently shining her fingernails on the sleeve of her blouse. "I don't know," she said slowly, not looking up, "I can't quite see why I *shouldn't* go, after all. I'm the only girl Martin really knows in town—maybe he's been busy all afternoon and didn't have time to call before." She looked over at Art but he just shrugged his shoulders.

"If he thinks he can get a date with you any time he calls! Last night may have been all right at the last minute because you haven't been home from school so long yourself; but two nights in a row . . . " Margaret stood jiggling the phone impatiently. Even when she was only in high school she didn't have to worry about not having boys like her.

"Hurry up," she urged Lorraine, "and decide what you're going to say to him. But I certainly know what I'd tell him!"

"Just say that you're busy and then you and your mother and father can go to a late show so you won't just have to be sitting here," Art suggested in his quiet voice. "From what you told me about last night, he sounds like one of those 'big men on campus' who never quite got over going to college. Do what you like, Lorraine, but I know what I'd think if I could get a girl at the last minute."

Margaret held out the phone. "Here," she said, "tell him you're busy."

It was just beginning to get dark outside and the room was thickening with dusk. We could hear the drone of my mother's and father's voices as they sat on the side lawn, but the rest of the house was quiet.

"If you want to go out so badly," Margaret added, "you can come along with Art and me."

"I know, I know that," Lorraine said slowly. "But, Margaret, I can go out with you and Art *any* Sunday night—I want to go out with *him!*"

Just as Jack and I pulled out of our driveway, Martin Keefe swung up to the curb in a low green coupe, screeching the tires against the curbstone, and as we turned the corner I looked back to see him crossing the lawn with his long, insolent stride to shake hands with my father.

Another couple drove out with us, friends of Jack's from high school, a girl named Margie and a tall, thin boy called Fitz. He had a very bad complexion and a shiftiness about him, as if by not looking directly at me he could avoid my looking at him and seeing his ugly skin. Margie was a tall, slim girl with quick, bright eyes and she talked continually, laughing between the words. Her hair hung long in the back but was swooped up into curls on the sides and crisscrossed with hairpins. Nervously, she kept adjusting the pins as she talked to me.

Leaning over the front seat she commented affably, "You're the girl who knows Jane Rady, aren't you? Us girls have a bridge club that meets every couple of weeks and she happened to mention you. Jane said she might stop out tonight with that new boy from Oshkosh she has a date with."

"Say, this is going to be some party," Fitz said with significant enthusiasm. "Is Tony Becker going to be out?"

"Don't know," Jack answered, keeping his eyes on the road. "I was talking to him at Pete's this afternoon and he said he'd be over if he could get the car." He looked back at Fitz. "But if he gets the car I don't think he'll waste his time at the party—huh, Fitz?"

"No, sir, that boy don't waste no time," Fitz agreed and whistled shrilly through his teeth. Margie laughed and there was some giggled whispering in the back seat, but I couldn't understand what they were talking about.

The cottage was only a few miles out of town along the lake shore, set far in off the highway. I had a feeling of apprehension as Jack swung into the rutted mud road. The car lurched sideways and Margie squealed with delight in the back seat. There were three other cars pulled up in the cottage drive and inside someone was playing Viennese waltzes on an old victrola.[6] Already an early moon was showing through the lace of the trees.

It was a shabby cottage. Jack explained to me later that it belonged to Fitz's family but they used it only during the last month of summer, and the rest of the year it lay vacant except when some of the bunch came out to go swimming

---

6 *victrola*   old record player, usually wind-up, with a large horn.

or to have a party. The front of the house was flush with the lake so we went in the back way into a kitchen smelling damp and musty, like old wood, with layers of yellowed newspaper on the shelves and a big wooden table.

No one had lived in the cottage since the summer before and the front room had the same damp, close smell as the kitchen. One of the girls took me off into a side room to powder my nose. There was a mirror on the wall and a bare bulb hanging from the ceiling. She seemed younger than the rest and more talkative, and as she edged around her mouth carefully with bright lipstick she remarked with emphasis, "Honestly, I'm so glad we're not having anything but beer, 'cause after *last night* I couldn't stand to look another mixed drink in the face." Her name was Dollie, and Jack told me later that she was only fifteen and had been dating the fellows in his crowd for only about three weeks. She was what the boys called "a find."

Until she had mentioned beer I had never thought just what people did do at parties like this—we couldn't just sit around and listen to Viennese waltzes all night. I hadn't really gone to parties since the days when we were small enough to care about ice cream and cake with pink frosting, and play drop-the-clothes-pins-in-the-bottle or Going to Jerusalem. Some of the other girls had come in and I thought of saying very casually, "What are we going to do—just sit around and talk?" but I didn't want them to know that I'd never been at a party like this before. It was important to act as if you had been around. Maybe they would whisper to their dates later in the evening. "You know that girl that Jack Duluth is with? She doesn't even know the score. She asked me before what we were going to do. I'll bet she's never even been at a party before!"

One of the girls said to me casually, "How long have you been going with Jack, Angeline?" I explained that I hadn't known him quite a week and that I'd just been out with him a few times. "That's what I thought," she went on, "be-cause last thing *we* knew he was dating a couple of girls from high school and then Jane Rady off and on and then all of a sudden he turned up with you at the dance . . . We kind of wondered," she added slowly. She was sitting on the arm of an old stuffed chair smoking a cigarette with deep puffs and holding the smoke in her mouth for a long time before blowing it out. I could tell by the way she spoke that she was a friend of Jane Rady's.

When we went back to the living room two of the boys were rolling back the old grass rug—"just in case someone might want to dance," and Dollie and the other girls got down on their knees to help roll, laughing and talking loudly. I tried to help too, but gave up because I felt awkward and in the way. Dollie sat down backwards suddenly with her legs sprawled in front of her and cried with a petulantly accusing voice, "Johnnie, you pushed me on purpose!" and every-one laughed.

I went out to the kitchen then where the others were crowded around Swede who had just come in. He was trying to screw a spigot into a barrel of beer. We never had beer at our house and I had always felt that there was something dis-graceful about it. For a moment I wished I hadn't come. Jack was holding the barrel for Swede and when the first beer dribbled out onto the floor he yelled, "There she goes! Wash out some glasses, somebody!"

I was glad to have something to do rather than just stand watching, so I opened the cupboard and took out some glasses to wash and the other girls came to help. There were half a dozen pink glass tumblers and three tall, heavy glasses with thick edges that looked as if they must have once been peanut but-ter jars. The faucet made a choking sound far down in the pipes as I turned it on and then water spouted out very brown and muddy, for it had been standing in the pipes unused for so long. We waited till it ran clear and then rinsed the glasses, setting them upside down on the newspapered table top to drip dry.

Everyone crowded round the barrel holding out his glass to be filled. Jack came over with one for me and when I shook my head he said suddenly, "That's right! I forgot you didn't drink beer! We should have stopped and picked up some root beer for you but I never even thought of it. I can't give you a glass of water either because the water out here isn't very good for drinking, and besides these glasses look too dirty to drink out of unless there is beer in them."

It was all right, I told him. Really it was all right. I didn't mind the least bit and I wasn't thirsty anyway. I hoped he wouldn't say anything to anyone else, for the other girls were all drinking it and having fun. For a minute I was tempted to take a glass myself. But then I thought of having to walk up the stairs when I got home and perhaps my mother would call from her room, "Angeline, come in a minute and tell me if you had a nice time," and I would weave my way over to her dressing table, fumble for the lamp, knocking over the perfume bottles in a glassy-eyed stupor—I had seen people in the movies who had had too much to drink.

Later they moved the beer keg into the living room and we all sat around on the chairs and on the floor, laughing and singing. I couldn't make myself sing with the rest, for my voice sounded queer, but no one seemed to notice. Swede was next to me and Jack sat on the arm of the davenport, singing and winking at me at the same time. A lamp with a parchment shade was lit on a corner table and the room was in a half-glow as if by firelight. Large night moths fluttered low around the shade and made vague shadows on the circle of light on the ceiling. There were musty brown-and-cream print drapes on the windows, full and shadowy, and I noticed that high on one of them was pinned a large yellow butterfly of waxed crepe paper with bent wire feelers and wings edged with a dust of gilt paint—the kind unemployed women used to make to sell from door to door during the depression. The floor and chairs were scattered with cushions stiff with painted roses and bright sunsets, or made of soft leather with doeskin fringes printed with pictures of tall pines and low yellow moons—souvenirs of the north country and the Indian reservations.

The whole room was filled with the damp smell of the lake and it was even a little chilly—the sort of chill that makes you feel more comfortable because you can snuggle against cushions and be grateful for their warmth and comfort. Those sitting on the floor joined hands and sang low songs as they swayed from side to side, and Jack slid off the wicker arm of the davenport and sat beside me. I was so contented and happy I felt as if I would like to sit right there without moving until I fell asleep. It was odd to think that just last week I hadn't known anything about this—about Jack, about girls who really went out and drank beer, about parties like this—the sort of things I used to hear Jane Rady talk about and never thought I would be a part of. Tonight had been easy. Everyone else had been laughing and talking so much they didn't seem to notice or mind that I just watched and enjoyed the whole thing without saying anything. The first misgivings I had felt when I saw them fitting the spigot into the beer barrel were gone, for after all they were just sitting in a circle singing now and there was nothing wrong about that! But back in my mind I had a vague guilty feeling that I probably wouldn't mention to my mother that there had been no older person there and that they had had beer—even if I hadn't drunk any myself.

Suddenly Dollie jumped up and said in her round, baby voice, "Come on, fill my glass and let's play 'chug-a-lug!'" Everyone passed around his glass to be filled and then, holding them high, began to sing a loud song with words which I couldn't catch for everyone was laughing so hard as they sang. Someone called out, "Dollie!" and they all went on laughing and singing like deep-throated bullfrogs—"chug-a-lug, chug-a-lug, chug-a-lug"—while she stood up, tilted her glass of beer and drank to the bottom without stopping. Then the song was started again and someone else's name was called and he drained his glass while the others kept up the rhythmic chant. They kept it up till they had gone the round of the circle and everyone was laughing so hard they could hardly catch their breath and I found myself laughing, too, with my mouth open.

Finally they laughed themselves quiet and Dollie gathered some of the painted cushions into a heap and leaned against the victrola, sleepy-eyed and contented. Someone shuffled through the pile of old records again and put on an old scratchy recording of a dramatic baritone singing "In The Valley of Sunshine and Roses." Fitz looked over at Margie and they both got up, rinsed their glasses at the kitchen sink, and went out to sit on the front porch. Soon we heard the creak-creak of the glider. Fitz and Margie were "going steady," Jack told me later.

Swede gathered up some cushions and made himself comfortable beside Dollie, and some of the others got car robes[7] from their cars and went out to sit on the front lawn. I didn't quite understand how, as if at a given signal, the whole party broke up into couples and drifted off by themselves. Jack and I still sat where we were, not saying anything, mostly because I didn't quite know what to say or what I was supposed to do now. Dollie, snuggled against the cushions, was rubbing over Swede's short curly hair with the back of her hand, saying over to herself softly, "Just like a kitten. Swede feels just like a kitty."

One of the boys came over to us saying, "Mind if we sit on the davenport—if you kids aren't going to use it?"

"Sure, sure," Jack said. "Go ahead. We can sit on the porch. Do you want to sit on the porch, Angie?" I nodded.

The front porch was built across the full length of the cottage and was screened in with long, black screens that ran from the floor to the ceiling. Out there, the darkness was warm and thick, for the broad front lawn stretching down to the lake was covered with trees and their branches, heavy with the full, lush foliage of early summer almost hid the moon. On one side was the glider and on the other a lumpy couch covered with the same musty brown-and-cream chintz as the drapes inside. Jack and I sat there. Out on the lawn near the lake's edge someone was building a bonfire and we watched it grow, flickering at first till the fire dried out the damp wood and then suddenly bright and leaping against the darkness of the water. It was very quiet with just the steady lap-lap of the water, the hush of the wind through the trees, and the occasional creak of the glider on the other side of the porch. Attracted by the light of the dim lamp inside, heavybodied June bugs bumped clumsily against the screens and night moths kept up a dainty flutter. Out on the lawn there was a wink of light like a firefly as someone lit a cigarette.

"Angie," Jack said, "let's get a robe from the car and sit out on the grass. It smells so damp and musty here that I'll bet if we turned this couch over cen-

---

7 *car robe*   blanket.

tipedes would crawl out from under it like from under a rock." He spread out the robe on the lawn and lay flat with his chin in his hands, smoking his pipe, and I sat beside him with a funny, choked feeling in my throat because I suddenly felt self-conscious being alone with him. I was running the fringe on the edge of the robe through my fingers, wondering whether or not it would seem funny if I suggested that maybe Swede and Dollie would like to come out to sit with us, when Jack turned to me and said in a puzzled voice, "Angie, you didn't have fun tonight, did you?"

"But I did. I did," I told him. "I liked it very much. The girls were all nice and the boys were funny and I really liked it—what made you think I didn't?" I watched him puff-puffing at his pipe, making the tobacco glow as he drew in.

"You didn't talk much," he explained, "and I thought maybe you were mad because of the beer or because we made too much noise or something. You seemed different Friday night. I don't know. Just thought maybe you were mad," and he reached over and I felt his fingers on mine. "If you ever don't like anything, Angie, just say so."

For the first time in my life I felt that warm, possessive power that comes from knowing that you are able to worry a boy. It wasn't fair I know, but I left my hand flat on the robe, pretending that I didn't even know he was looking at me, pretending that I didn't even know his hand was on mine.

"Is it about Friday night then?" he urged in the same worried tone. "Tell me what's the matter." After a moment's hesitation he added slowly, "Are you sorry, Angie?"

"Friday night?" My voice sounded high and incredulous as if I had never even heard of such a thing as a Friday night before.

"I don't know," he said. "I just thought you might be mad about it later on. I was almost afraid to call you this afternoon."

"Why? I certainly don't see why you should be," I heard myself saying in the same high, surprised voice, while my thoughts went slowly, carefully through my head as if they were on a tightrope. I had never thought of being angry about Friday night, but it just made me feel shy to think of it now that I was with him again. I had kissed him once, but what are girls supposed to say the next time they go out with a boy after a thing like that; what are they supposed to do?

"It's just that you're different from other girls I've known," he went on. "Most of them wouldn't give it a second thought but I didn't know what you would think about it the next day." His pipe had burned out and he sat tapping the bowl on the palm of his hand. The thick leaves were whispering above, and behind us the wind made a thin whistle in the screens of the porch. "It wasn't *wrong*, Angie!"

How queer all this is, I thought. Here am I sitting in the dark with a boy I didn't even know a week ago and he's worrying about what is in my head and I'm so mixed up I can't even tell him. He's worried about whether I'm angry at him because I haven't been talking all evening, and I haven't talked because all the other girls were so much prettier than I was that I couldn't think of anything to say.

It made me feel older than he to have him talk to me that way. "Of course it isn't wrong," I told him. "Things like stealing or telling lies are wrong but kissing someone you . . . well, it isn't . . . you know what I mean, Jack." I couldn't quite see his face in the darkness but I could feel his hand on mine, so I added softly, "Kissing someone you *like* isn't wrong!" and the words felt warm on my lips.

And all within a week I, Angie Morrow, was sitting there saying things I'd never dreamed of saying, things that belonged in a movie.

We mused over the thought for a while and soon the quiet stretched into long minutes till our thoughts cleared and both of us were conscious of the silence with nothing but the hushed night noises going on in it.

A car pulled in to the gravel drive, the door slammed, and someone called out, "Hey, anybody home here?" and Fitz and Margie left the front porch to go inside and we heard Swede talking. "That's Tony Becker who just came," Jack said. "I can tell by his voice. He always gets places late because he finds so much to do on the way. I wonder who he's got for a date tonight?"

I suggested that we go in to find out and say hello to Tony, but Jack held my hand. "Let's not go in quite yet, Angie—unless you really want to see Tony . . ." His voice turned the end of the sentence up into a question. "He told me that you and he got along pretty well at the dance."

"What's the matter, don't you like him?" I asked.

"Sure, I *like* him," he hastened to explain, "but Tony's just one of those guys. . . ."

He sat with his hands locked around his knees and said, "Let's just sit here a little while longer and then we'll go in and round up Fitz and Margie—it's getting late and I'll have to be getting you home soon. I'd like to talk to you a little more and if we go in we'll have to talk to Tony and everyone and I won't have a chance."

Inside someone was winding up the victrola again and overhead the moon inched its way from behind a cloud and showed in glimpses as the wind swayed the thick trees. It seemed so natural for me to be lying there listening to the waves and it wasn't surprising at all to feel Jack's hand in mine. I wondered contentedly if my mother was still sitting knitting the yellow sweater she was making me for college, and I wondered with a troubled feeling if Lorraine and Martin were having a good time. My thoughts bobbed in my head as if they were floating, as if they were airy, impersonal ideas resting lightly above my more solid and serious thoughts beneath.

I wonder, I thought, what I am really thinking. Last week I would have known definitely but now everything seemed vague and evasive. Every time I tried to think clearly about Jack and especially about Friday night there was a warm feeling in my heart and a very pleasant confused jumble in my head. Lying there on the car robe, I tried to imagine what I would have thought last week if someone had told me about a girl who had kissed a boy the third night she had been out with him. I tried to turn my thoughts so they looked inward; so I could really find out what was going on inside my head. Lying very still, my forehead wrinkled with concentration, I wondered.

"What," I said to myself, "will I do if he should want to kiss me good night?"

Just then Jack leaned over and said with a laugh in his voice, "Angie, Angie, what are you doing? You look so funny that at first I thought you were looking cross-eyed!"

The door of the screened porch slammed and two people stepped out onto the lawn. Jack sat up and listened in the darkness. Their voices came toward us and then a low, deep laugh, and Jack turned to me, his words twisted with annoyance. "Well, we might as well go in the house now, Angie, here comes Becker. I don't know who the girl is with him but I'd rather be where the bright lights are when that boy's around."

The next week passed quickly. Each morning I woke with an eager, expectant feeling as if I had just had a good dream. The days were filled with the mellow warmth of sunshine and the air was fresh with the smell of green leaves and damp earth that comes with early summer. Jack called every noon at a little after twelve and his calls punctuated the day like periods. It surprised me that my mother never seemed to mind that I talked with him so often, though we might just be sitting down to lunch when the phone rang. Once after he called I happened to look at myself in the mirror and was surprised at the bright, wide-awake look in my eyes.

Even my thoughts seemed changed. When I woke in the morning and looked in the bathroom mirror as I was washing my face the thought might strike me, "What would Jack think if he could see me now with lathery soap all over my face?" or when I was puttering in the garden I might wonder, "Does Jack ever notice the queer, cool smell that comes from nasturtium leaves?" When I did leisurely things like ironing or peeling potatoes for dinner I found my mind making up little stories about Jack and me, pretending that he had walked into McKnight's while Jane Rady was there and that he looked at her and then came over to sit with me, or pretending that he had come to visit me for a dance at college and all the other Freshmen were so nice to me after that, thinking that I must have been a popular girl in my home town to have such a nice-looking boy come all the way down to see me.

One morning Kitty was out playing on the front sidewalk. She had taken her old box of half-used crayons left from school, laying them in a row in the sun until they melted to a pliable consistency, and then bending them into bright-colored rings or melting the ends with a match, sticking several together to make a bracelet. "Costume jewelry," she called it. Every few minutes she came running into the house with excited plans of how she could make a fortune with just a few boxes of crayons by getting one of the local department stores to sell the crayon jewelry. Each summer Kitty is full of schemes to make money in a hurry. Once she had a lemonade stand that served soda crackers with each drink, and another time she had a route mapped out for the children in the neighborhood to sell the vegetables from our garden, door to door. None of the projects lasted more than two days.

Jack drove up in the bakery truck and was standing listening to her chatter that morning when I glanced out the window and saw him. I hurried up to my room and carefully edged on lipstick with the tip of my finger before I went out to talk with him. That evening the two of us went out with his cousin from Oklahoma who was about twenty years old and drank more beer than any boy I have ever seen. He and Jack talked mostly about what they had done together before Jack had moved North—he and his family had lived in Oklahoma until five years ago and his cousin said something about the girl that lived in the white house with the pines in front whom Jack used to like. So Jack must have been going with girls, at least *liking* them, since he was thirteen! The cousin talked to me too, and said that any time I happened to pass through his state to be sure to look him up. I told him that since Wisconsin was almost walking distance from Oklahoma I would probably see him often and they both laughed and I felt almost pleased with myself.

Lorraine went out with Martin three nights in a row that week. I never knew when they made their plans for dates for he never called the house. She explained that she "ran into him" almost every day after work. He was rooming at a house not far from the Elite Canvas Company, and if she didn't bump into him in front of his house she usually saw him having a Coke at the drugstore on the next block. Lorraine always said there was nothing she liked so much as a Coke after a day's work and always stopped at the drugstore on her way home.

When I asked what they did when they went out, she explained that they didn't go any of the places that the younger crowd went like Pete's and McKnight's, but that Martin knew some nice places a little farther out of town—the kind of place he had been used to going to when he had been at the university. Each night she got in very late and I always woke with a start as the car pulled silently up to the curb with headlights switched off, so as not to rouse anyone. My room is at the front of the house and I would lie awake till I heard the car door close and Lorraine tiptoe upstairs and undress silently for bed. She always smelled of her own perfume and the heavy man-smell of cigarette smoke and went through the rituals of getting ready for bed in the dark, being careful not to waken my mother. That third night she sat in bed for a very long time with her hands around her knees, thinking. I said nothing, pretending I was asleep, and much later she got up again and I could hear the water trickling as she washed her face in the bathroom. The sky was already beginning to get light before she fell asleep that night.

Jack told me that Martin came into the bakery every morning at about seven-thirty for fresh rolls for his breakfast. He made morning coffee in his room at the rooming house but ate the other two meals out. "He gives you the impression that he's a city fellow," Jack had said. "He walks like he's got on silk underwear or has a ten-dollar bill in his pocket or something."

That week and the next were filled with such a new happiness that my whole mind sang with the sheer joy of it. One afternoon Kitty and I took our bicycles and rode out through the Field until we reached the creek bank, and then along the water's edge to the bridge on the gravel road, and I caught my breath at the loveliness of it. On the other bank a twisted cottonwood tree was shedding its white wool that caught in bushes as it fell, drifted with the creek or fluffed along the road, pushed by the breeze. Blue-bodied dragonflies hovered low over the stream, their gauze wings shimmering in the sun, and river plants laid their broad leaves flat on the surface of the water. Kitty leaned over the iron railing of the bridge trying to rouse frogs by dropping stones straight down into the water with the same full, plopping sound they make as they dive in. I leaned over the railing too, thinking of Jack with the warm, hushed feeling that came into my mind whenever I thought of him too hard. I felt the breeze brush my cheek like a soft hand and below me, under the water, I watched the seaweed ripple with the current like long, green hair.

We rode farther along the gravel road till we came to the stretch that is lined with slim, whispering willows. This is the place I had often heard girls talk about with giggles at school. Fellows like Swede or boys like Fitz who had steady girls always stopped at night to park on Willow Road. I felt almost sacrilegious riding along it on my bicycle in broad daylight. There were deep tire marks in the soft earth where cars had pulled in at the side of the road, and I had heard about how the police car used to ride up and down every hour at night with a powerful spotlight, scaring the parkers away. It gave me a queer feeling, as if we shouldn't talk too loudly even if there was no one there.

"Look," Kitty cried. "Look. There's a shoe in the ditch!" There was a high-heeled black pump half-stuck in the mud, the leather cracked and graying from the weather. What an odd place for a shoe, I thought, and all the way back I had a vague, guilty feeling, as if I should have known better than to go to a place like that—and as if I had let Kitty see something she shouldn't.

It was almost suppertime when we turned for home. The sky was still blue and the sun bright but the birds had already begun the usual contented rites of

404

evening, flying from hummock to hummock and then circling high into the air with bursts of song. A low breeze hushed through the long grass, and along the roadside wild dill raised its dull yellow flower clusters high on thick stems and weeds showed the silver-gray underside of their leaves, brushed forward by the summer wind. As we turned in our own sidewalk, we caught the smell of pork chops frying and strong, fresh coffee. My mother had already begun to make the supper.

Margie called a little later that evening and asked me to walk to McKnight's with her for a Coke—Fitz and Jack were going out with the fellows so she knew I wouldn't be busy, she said. We had got along well at the cottage party and driving back to town she had remarked coyly, "Angie, let's you and me get together some night when the fellows are taking out their *other* girls!"

Fitz made a muffled protest in the back seat, something that began, "Aw, Margie, you know that you're the only—" and I didn't hear the rest.

My mother doesn't usually approve of my sisters and me going downtown alone at night. "There's something so cheap about seeing girls just walking up and down as if they were looking for something," she always said, but in our town all the girls do it. They get as dressed up as if they were going on a date and walk slowly up on one side of Main Street looking in the shop windows, picking out what they would like to buy if they had the money, and then down the other side, and everyone ends up at McKnight's to have a Coke about nine o'clock.

I had never liked to do it because I didn't know any of the fellows and I could sit in McKnight's for an hour if I wanted and no one would come over to have a Coke with me. But it would be different being with Margie—she had dated so many of the fellows and everyone knew she was Fitz's girl now.

There was the usual crowd standing in front of the drugstore when we went in. The younger fellows in our town have a system. To an adult or to someone from out of town it would mean nothing to see a group of young boys standing in front of McKnight's or on the nearest street corner. But I knew what they were there for—Jane Rady had told me before I had even known Jack—and all the other girls knew too. These are the "checkers." They are the more popular crowd at high school and every evening about half-past seven they gather to stand talking together with elaborate unconcern, while in actuality they are sharply watching the cars going by to see what fellows and girls are out together; they watch to see who is having a Coke with whom and to report any violations on the part of the girls who are supposed to be going steady.

It is almost like a secret police system—no one escapes being checked on. At least no one who counts. The checkers also keep their eyes open for new prospects among the young sophomore girls who are growing up and show signs of datable promise. They only watch out for the very pretty or very popular girls, so it is the most serious catastrophe of all not even to be noticed by the checkers. They were the ones who had spotted Dollie—they can start or stop any of the younger girls in town just by passing the word around. Most of them didn't even know my name until I began to date Jack.

When Margie and I passed them that night she smiled very wide and said brightly, "Hi, there, fellows," and they all smiled back with approval but none of them seemed to notice me at all.

"Of course they know you," Margie exclaimed, when I mentioned it to her later. "Any girl that goes with Jack Duluth is checkers material from then on.

405

Just wait. First thing in the morning one of the boys will stop in the bakery and let Jack know that they happened to see you having a Coke with me last night."

Margie was using a very instructive motherly tone of voice, as if she were teaching me my catechism.[8] "I always tell Fitz exactly what I'm planning to do when I'm not with him," she went on. "He so hates to have the boys tell him what I've been doing before he knows it himself. You see," she added comfortably, "Fitz and I are very much in love."

We both sipped our Cokes slowly for a while, watching others who came and went. Margie knew almost everyone and said, "Hi, there!" to each in the same bright voice. Once two girls came in with a slow, hesitant air. They were palish girls, about my age, with their hair very carefully set in neat waves and very little lipstick. One of them had on flat black oxfords—and everyone knows that no high school girl should wear anything but saddle shoes or collegiate moccasins! All the booths were filled but they walked down the aisle between them, peering over the high sides, looking for a place to sit down. No one said hello or offered to move or to make room so the girls turned, talking to themselves very busily and giggling a little, and walked out. But their faces had a stiff, hurt look. I knew just how they felt for until I had met Jack it was the same way with me—except that I wouldn't be stupid enough to wear flat black oxfords. Any girl who does that almost deserves not to have fellows look at her.

Margie lit a cigarette and between short puffs said, "You know, Angie, I can't figure you out. Going with Jack Duluth is really something—because of his being such a good basketball player and being so cute and everything, but it doesn't seem to make any difference to you at all."

"Of course it does," I hastened to assure her. I knew anything I said would be relayed from Margie to Fitz and from Fitz on to Jack. "But what am I supposed to do, Margie? I am certainly nice enough to him and I'm glad to hear him every time he calls—"

"You're nice enough to him," she explained, "but you don't seem to *worry* about him at all. All the girls worry about their fellows." She said it in the same matter-of-fact tone that she might have said 'girls brush their teeth every day.' "When I first started dating Fitz," she went on, "I used to come here every day after school to find out what the girls knew. You know, the boys they were dating would tell them what Fitz thought of me and whether he liked me or not and then they would tell me. Of course, now that we're in love it's different."

While we were talking Martin Keefe came in and asked for a package of cigarettes. He stood up at the soda fountain near the front of the store and didn't see me. He looked at his wrist watch irritably and was holding it up to his ear when a little blond girl from the perfume counter at one of the department stores came in, said something to him, and they left together, laughing. I remembered Lorraine at supper saying that she had a date with him that evening and wondered.

Later when I got home she was sitting in the bedroom brushing her hair and I asked her about it. "Yes," she explained carefully, "I was supposed to go out with him but just after you left he called and said that he had a collection to make in Waupun and wouldn't be able to keep the date tonight. Of course," she said pointedly, "I could have driven over *with* him if I had wanted to.

"He has a very good job, you know, Angie. In college he majored in business law and this is just a filler-in until he gets into something bigger. This pays very well though—I can tell by his big car and the smooth clothes he wears."

---

8 *catechism*   a summary of the basic principles of a religion given in question and answer form.

I undressed for bed, opened both windows, and turned back the spread. As I reached to put out the light Lorraine added—just as if there had been no lapse in the conversation at all—"But I'll probably see him tomorrow night instead."

It was then that I decided I wouldn't say a word about having seen him and the other girl.

The next day passed like a bubble. In the afternoon there was a quick summer shower, the kind that blows up from nowhere in a blue sky and spatters the sidewalks with big drops and then spends itself in a brief torrent. My mother had just got up from her afternoon nap and I had put the water on for tea and was standing at the kitchen window watching the rain flatten the corn leaves to the ground. The last of the June roses on the bush drooped their heads and the rain pelted their petals to the wet ground.

Almost as soon as it started the storm stopped and there was a rift in the dark clouds, the blue sky showing through. My mother laid two clean napkins on the kitchen table and drew it close to the window so we could smell the damp, clean smell of the wet earth. The sun came out, glistening on the leaves and making the whole garden look brighter, like a sudden smile after a hard cry.

Along the block, children came out into the street, chattering like little birds after the rain and we watched them paddling about on the wet grass in their bare feet, pulling small sailboats along the water in the gutter. Why is it, I thought, that rain has never seemed so wonderful to me before? Each day since the beginning of summer something had seemed new and surprising, things I had never noticed before.

That was the first day I had ever seen Jack in the afternoon and I was surprised at how natural even that seemed. He knocked at the front door and explained that he had finished his route early and just thought he would stop in.

"We're glad to have you," my mother said. (I always liked the way she talked to boys.) "Won't you have a cup of tea with Angie and me?" I sliced lemon out in the kitchen and put the sugar and cream on the table, while Jack went out to the bakery truck and came in, all smiling, with six sugared doughnuts on a paper pie plate and a small chocolate cake with chocolate frosting, sprinkled with very dubious chopped nuts.

This was the first time, too, I had ever eaten with Jack and every mouthful I took seemed too big and the tea made a noise in my throat as I swallowed it. Jack seemed perfectly at ease, holding his doughnut carefully with two fingers and not getting sugar on his sweater while he ate, and he and my mother talked about bakers and pies and whether or not many people make their own bread any more.

I passed him the lemon and he dropped a slice in his cup and then unconsciously poured cream in after it, stirring the two together. I looked at my mother and she looked at me, raising her eyebrows in a signal not to laugh, and went on talking.

As I sat there I found myself being grateful for so many little things around the kitchen that I had hardly valued before. I liked the little red-and-white-checked hand towels hanging on the rail, and the way the afternoon sun glinted on the faucets and the clean, well-swept look of the linoleum. I was glad my mother's hair was in a neat bun instead of a fuzzy permanent, and that her eyes looked as blue as her dress, and that the dog Kinkee sat in the corner very politely, not drooling as some dogs do when they see people eating. I was glad that Jack could know what a nice kitchen we had and that we used quaint flowered napkins instead of oil cloth on the kitchen table.

407

When he left I walked out to the truck at the curb with him. He looked so strong and brown with his football sweater on and a white shirt open at the throat that I could hardly keep from touching him. When he looked at me I had a queer feeling that maybe I had chocolate frosting on my face or that maybe the freckles on my nose showed too much in the sunlight. A small wind shook raindrops from the trees onto the sidewalk, and on the lawn young robins with soft, speckled breasts hopped about, scolding for worms.

My whole head was singing with such a warm happiness that when the truck pulled away I felt that if the grass had not still been wet there was nothing in the world I would rather have done than lie flat on my back with my hands behind my head, watching the sky, clear and bright-blue in the sunshine, and just think.

It wasn't until the next Sunday that I noticed anything strange about Lorraine. The day went much the same as always. After the dinner dishes had been done my father got his briefcase out of the car and spread his papers all over the kitchen table, working away at his prospects and order blanks for the rest of the afternoon. Kitty and Art played catch with a baseball out in the empty lot next to our house, while my mother sat in a garden chair knitting a pair of yellow wool ankle socks to match the sweater she had finished earlier in the week.

Upstairs, Lorraine had been listlessly sorting out the things in her dresser drawers, arranging neat piles of hankies, cosmetics, and odd jewelry on the bed, and then putting them back in as great a disorder as before. She looked very pale because she had put no lipstick on and nothing I tried to talk about seemed to interest her. I knew she hadn't even heard from Martin since he broke the date with her, and each night when she got home from work she would say brightly, "Anyone call?"

About five o'clock I happened to be alone in the living room, leafing through the morning funnies, when she came downstairs and said, "Angie, I've just *got* to call Martin and see if he has my gold compact. I've hunted *everywhere* and the last place I remember having it was in his car. Honestly, I'd just *hate* to lose that." As she looked through the phone book she added, "He should be home about now. I really can't think how I didn't miss it sooner."

Carefully I folded the funny papers and put them in a neat pile on the davenport. That gold compact was in her purse. I had seen her use it when we went to church in the morning. But there was nothing I could say. She must have wanted to call him very much, for I knew the compact was there and I knew she knew.

"Hello?" Her voice was casually eager. "I'd like to speak to Martin Keefe—if he isn't busy." There was a short pause while someone on the other end of the line was talking. "Oh, I see," she said. "And when do you expect him in?" Her voice was high, cheerful. "Oh, I see. I see." The receiver clicked down and in a minute she came into the living room humming softly under her breath.

"When do they expect him in?" I asked, making my voice as casual, as non-committal as hers. There are unspoken ethics between sisters.

She was standing by the table at the foot of the stairs, absent-mindedly plucking the dead blossoms from the bowl of iris. With the same careful uncon-cern she answered, "They don't expect him. He's out for the evening." She looked up at me and then turned quickly to go upstairs. "Angie," she called back. "Angie, don't tell Margaret and Art I called him. "They don't—they don't quite see it the way I do!" and then I heard her go into her room, shutting the door after her.

How sad, I thought. How sad to have to cry about a boy on such a beautiful Sunday afternoon.

You know how it is sometimes when things go along so smoothly that you feel certain something unforeseen must happen. To me it happened that Sunday at suppertime.

With no preamble, with no warning at all, my father said suddenly, his lips set in determination, "Angeline, I don't know as I like your going out so much!"

We were sitting at the dining-room table eating cold pork sandwiches made from the noon roast and fresh sliced tomatoes. I hadn't talked about Jack all day so I was puzzled to know what had made my father think of him. We had planned to walk to a movie that evening and except for feeling sorry for Lorraine, my mind had been humming to itself all day with a contented, muted sort of happiness. And now to have my father say that! It was like a blow at the back of the knees. Always he had been occasionally strict with us but his approvals and disapprovals usually came through my mother. And because he was only home on weekends he wasn't really cross very often.

"In the first place, you are too young to be seeing so much of one boy, and besides it seems to me," he went on severely as he stirred his coffee, "that your sister and you have enough to keep you busy helping your mother and getting some worthwhile reading done for college without all this running about." My mother didn't say a word and I could tell by her silence that he had discussed this with her before.

Then he cleared his throat and I could almost tell what was coming next, he had said it so often before, "You'll have plenty of time for dating later on, Angeline. Your schooling is what is important now. Remember that. Education is one thing no one can ever take away from you!"

Lorraine went into the kitchen for hot coffee just then and the others ate in silence, not looking up or trying to put in a good word for me. Kitty was carefully taking her sandwich apart, cutting the white fat from the pork with frowning concentration and carefully putting the whole thing back together again.

Then that night seemed to me the most important night of the whole year. Here was I with a date with a boy that dozens of girls would like to go out with and I would have to call him up and say in a simpery voice, "I can't go out because my father doesn't want me to!" You wouldn't have to say a thing like that to a boy like Jack twice! Next time he wanted a date he'd know where to call. He'd get some girl like Jane Rady whose mother and father *understood* about her going out. I had such a lump in my throat that I couldn't swallow and had to keep staring at my plate so they wouldn't see the tears nipping at my eyes.

And Lorraine was eating quietly, talking to one or the other from time to time, not letting anyone know how *she* felt.

Later, when the dishes were done, the milk bottles set out on the back doorstep, and the floor carefully swept, I ventured into the living room. My father was reading an old paper and Kitty was lying on the rug with her feet in the air doing bicycling exercises. I stood for a moment trying not to look too eager, trying to work up the courage to ask.

"Dad," my voice didn't sound like my own. "Dad, may I go?"

"Eh?" he said, looking up from the paper, his eyebrows quizzical. "Go where? With that boy?"

My mind almost smiled inside of me. The mood had completely gone over. He had been having one of his temporary, fatherly spells and now he had forgotten all about it.

409

"You can go this time," he said, but added sternly, "I don't want you running about too often though, understand. Your mother has been speaking to me about it. It isn't good for a girl your age to go out with one boy so much," and he turned back to his paper.

The lump in my throat seemed to melt away as he spoke. "You'd better comb your hair, Angie. It's almost a quarter after seven!" Kitty piped up from the floor.

It was the sort of night near the end of June when everything is warm and hushed, steeped in summer. Jack and I walked along the side streets on our way to the movie and at each corner the air was filled with an indistinct murmur from the haze of insects circling round the bright street lights. We passed a garden hedged in with flowered shrubs and the fragrance from the white night blossoms hung heavy on the breeze. People were sitting on their front porches enjoying the cool of the evening and we could hear the creak of rocking chairs and the pleasant hum-hum of voices as we passed. It was then that I realized how much older I felt when I was away from my family. It wasn't that I felt taller or fatter but just more important. At home they cared about what I thought, of course, but in a different way. They cared whether I would rather have pork chops or steak for dinner or whether I would rather have a white collar on my dress or no collar at all, but they didn't seem to think much or care what was actually in my head.

When I was away from them it was different. In McKnight's, Margie had been interested in what I thought of Fitz; Jack had been interested to know if I liked Tony Becker—at home you are just part of a family, but away from them you really are somebody!

Before us the poles of the street lights laid thick shadows across the sidewalk and above us, above the houses and the trees, a high, lonesome moon was tilted against the sky like a half-slice of lemon. My mind was puttering with small thoughts as we walked, thoughts about the people rocking on the porches and the funny way the wind in the trees made restless shifting shadows on the road, when Jack said, "Angie, we don't have to meet Fitz and Margie at the movie till a quarter-past eight, and if we walk just a little faster we'll be in time to stop in at church for Benediction on the way." The first chapel bells for Sunday service had rung just as we left home about fifteen minutes ago and I remembered brushing the sound from my mind. It made me ashamed now that I hadn't had the courage to suggest going myself.

But there is something so final, something so husband- and wifelike about going to church with a boy. Religion is too personal a thing to share promiscuously and the thought of being there with Jack filled me with a kind of awe; made me feel as though I should tiptoe up the aisle and genuflect in careful silence.

The very air of a church inspires reverence, and that night the lower stained-glass windows were tilted half open and the breeze stirred the warm air that was thick with the scent of flowers, incense, and the damp smell of leather from the prayer books and kneeling-benches. Kneeling beside him I felt so self-conscious and ill at ease I almost giggled, but Jack just knelt with his hands folded properly and his eyes ahead.

On the altar the tapers raised their flames in bright tiers and the squat candles of the votive lights filled the red glass holders with a warm glow like cups of wine. The ceiling of the church was vaulted into high shadowed arches and the organ music rolled out in full, rich swells above us; while the candle glow, the music, and the fragrance of the altar flowers filled the church with a heady, moving perfection. Jack knelt twisting his class ring round and round on his finger in unconscious thought. It was the first night I had seen him wear it and I remember noticing then the quick, clean look of his hands.

A series of pictures flipped through my mind—the way the wind had ruffled his hair that night in the boat, Jane Rady dancing with him, her hair falling like silk, that night at Pete's, out on the golf course at the dance when the moon was pale and high above the trees. . . . The candle glow on the altar and the thoughts in my head blurred together into memories so pleasant I could almost taste them. With a jolt I realized Jack was staring at me. I had been smiling in church! He passed me a little black prayer book he pulled from his back pocket and I turned my face toward the altar with the same small, humiliated feelings as if I had been caught chewing gum in school.

I will show him, I thought, and knelt very straight, my hands folded with my eyes raised the way figures do in the stained-glass windows. I made my lips just barely move in dainty, inaudible prayers, feeling very good and maidenly but he never moved. With my eyes straight ahead I could still tell that he never turned to look at me. . . . And I never knew before that ordinary boys prayed.

Later, as we went down the broad stone steps of the church, Jack took my arm with a squeeze and said happily, "Come on, Angie. We'll have to step it up so we don't keep Fitz and Margie waiting."

I realized then with a half-proud, half-ashamed feeling, that Jack was a better boy than I was a girl.

Tony Becker called me the next morning just after I had cleared away the breakfast dishes. "Hi, there," he said over the phone. "Guess who's talking." I knew it wasn't Jack's voice and I didn't think Martin Keefe would call in the morning even if he did call at all. It might have been Swede but he was too good a friend of Jack's to call me.

"I just drove over from Oshkosh to deliver some stuff for my dad," he went on. "This is Tony talking." Even though he had liked me a little I hadn't expected him to call. It seemed too much luck to have two boys wanting to date me when just a few weeks ago there hadn't been any. He asked me if I would like to do something with him on Wednesday night and I told him I certainly would. When he hung up I went out into the garden and could hardly keep the elation out of my voice as I said to my mother, "Tony Becker just called me."

Later in the morning I phoned Margie and we talked about little things till I ventured casually, "Oh, by the way, Tony Becker asked for a date Wednesday night." I thought she sounded queer when she asked me if I were going, but attributed it to jealousy—even if a girl is going steady I guess she doesn't like other girls to be *too* popular.

At noon I made sandwiches and tea and we had lunch on the back lawn, my mother, Kitty, and I. The sky was dazzling blue, and white cabbage butterflies flitted here and there over the garden in an endless dance. We slipped our tea slowly, enjoying the brightness of the day, while Kitty plucked handfuls of the short grass and showered them down on Kinkee who was sleeping beside her. The grass tickled the dog's black nose till she sneezed and then walked away in abused dejection. I kept waiting for the phone to ring till the one o'clock whistle blew at the factories on the edge of town. That was the first day in over two weeks that Jack hadn't called at noon.

That evening Margaret and I put on slacks and played baseball in the side lot with Kitty till the sun went down, and after that we went inside and played three-handed bridge with Lorraine while my mother sat with her reading glasses on, letting down the hem of one of Kitty's last summer's dresses.

Later, when I opened my window before going to bed, last night's moon was out again, just showing through the trees on our lawn. I tried to go to sleep very quickly. It seemed better not to think about Jack that night.

Lorraine told us when she came home from work the next day that she had a date with Martin that night. She met him having a Coke in the drugstore, she explained all smiling. He was just as nice as anything, asked how she'd been, and then suggested that they do something that night. "Honestly," she said to Margaret with enthusiasm, "you should have Art find out subtly where he gets his things . . . Martin has the most superb taste in clothes!"

She went upstairs and put her hair in curlers and came to the supper table with apologies and a film of cold cream on her face. No one mentioned Jack's not having called. My mother had had a letter from my father who was working on a prospect down in southern Illinois and he had hopes of closing a big deal in the morning. Kitty had spent the afternoon catching bumblebees in a canning jar and was rushing through her supper so she could let them loose again before they suffocated. All day long one half of my mind had been thinking about Tony Becker and tomorrow evening, and the other half was cautiously waiting for Jack to call. He might be in Green Bay visiting his cousin again, of course. Either I would get a postcard tomorrow or he would be certain to call.

That night I tried to stay awake until Lorraine came home to ask if she had had a good time. It struck me that I had been so busy thinking about Jack for the past few weeks that I hadn't taken the time to be nice to Lorraine or to talk with her the way we used to. I lay for a long time remembering how it used to be when we were all little girls and there was nothing to do on Saturday night but take baths and play pillow games in bed. I wondered if Lorraine thought about things like that anymore.

The old clock on the courthouse tower in the center of town rings out every hour, and late at night, when the town is still, the chimes echo out even to the edge of town. Lying in bed, I heard the clock strike midnight and then one o'clock. Outside the night was quiet and only an occasional car went down the street. Even the wind in the trees was hushed. Before long I lost hold of my thoughts and they slipped into dreams. I didn't hear Lorraine come in after all. I don't even think I heard two o'clock ring.

We drove back to Oshkosh on Wednesday evening. It is a twenty-mile drive from Fond du Lac on a wide curve of highway that runs along the lake, almost touching the shore. My mother hadn't liked Tony very well—I could tell that. He had been polite and friendly but there was something in the way he had talked to her—as if he had known her a long time, instead of being a little shy the way boys are supposed to be. It was almost seven-thirty when we left and the sun was going down, with stretches of cloud like graying cotton against the faint rose of the sky. A cool, moist wind blew in from the lake. Farther on, the highway goes through a stretch of sodden marshland, thick with slim, green rushes and stagnant with green-scummed pools. Here and there were the dark mounds of beaver hills, half hidden in the tall grass.

From the very beginning I liked Tony. There was something different about him. He drove faster and didn't look straight ahead with his eyes on the road the way Jack did, but kept turning to look at me. In fact, he looked at me so much that I began to feel that I must be very nice to look at. He asked me what I'd been doing with my summer and what college I was going to in the fall and the sort of things that make easy conversation. One stretch of highway runs directly along the lake shore and the water there was restless and choppy. There is a small island a short distance out with two heavy-headed trees on it. "Sometimes in stormy weather," said Tony, pointing it out, "the waves wash right over that island so that the trees look as if they are growing out of the water. I tried to land on it from a motorboat one afternoon but you can't do it. It's too rocky and the island's nothing but a piece of high marshland anyway."

He smoked one cigarette after another and I had to open my window to clear out the smoke, and the night air was cool and smelled of rain. We passed a long straight row of ash trees, bending gently with the wind and restless as before a storm. There is something fascinatingly secure about riding in a car at that time of evening. Along the road the barns and silos were changing into dark silhouettes against the sky and fields were losing their fences in the dusk. The road to Oshkosh is dotted with taverns that thrust their bright neon beer signs out into the night. In a yard before one of them, an old white farmhouse converted into a roadhouse, early customers had already parked their cars, like a row of dark beetles. We passed an old billboard that sagged drunkenly on tired legs, its supports sunk into the marshy ground. The whole countryside seemed caught in the silence that comes over everything just as the sun goes down. First lights were just beginning to wink on in the farmhouses and trees stirred uneasily, apprehensive of the coming night. The wind had twisted the dark clouds into weird shapes and in the whole gray-green pall of half-darkness I felt as if I would like to sit closer to Tony, safe inside the car with the bright headlights before us, pushing aside the dusk.

Just on the outskirts of Oshkosh was a line of new white frame houses with warm lights in their shiny windows, the young evergreens beside the doors still squat and green and the lawn still grassless and fresh with red clay. Tony slowed up as we went by and said, "Look at that, Angie. Look at that, will you? All those people sitting reading the evening paper in their nice, clean white boxes. Looks nice, doesn't it? Just like playing house." It was good to hear a boy talk that way and Tony had talked like that all the way from Fond du Lac.

He *liked* things. It was he who had pointed out to me that the corn in the fields was higher than usual for this time of year; he had showed me a tavern where he usually stopped on Friday night for crisp, hot little fish fried in deep fat; and he had told me with pleasure to listen how clear the music came through on the car radio since he had had the aerial adjusted. He seemed to be *glad* about everything. Each cigarette he smoked seemed to taste good and he watched the smoke, blue in the air. There was something about his mouth that seemed different from other boys. When I looked at him I felt so conscious of it. His lips were full and red and when he talked the words sounded slow and warm, as if he enjoyed saying them. I had noticed, too, that when he came up our front sidewalk, though he came fast enough, he seemed to be doing it slowly, to the fullest, and when he looked at me I felt that my face must be warm and smooth. I didn't get the same breathless feeling of expectation I felt when I was with Jack but rather a lazy, luxurious consciousness of being alive.

We stopped at a place called Chet's just on the edge of town. Instead of going around to the other side of the car to open my door, Tony just leaned across from the driver's seat and turned the handle. It struck me then what a big boy

413

stretched between the tomato plants, and the tomatoes were hard, green balls with the small twist of dried yellow blossom still stuck to the smooth skin. Little bright-green grasshoppers skipped on the grass of the back lawn, and along the cracks in the cement sidewalk the ants were busy mounding up their black mud-grain houses.

One afternoon we walked to the movie and in the soft, cool darkness I sat trying to keep my mind on the screen and hearing Kitty beside me making noise with a bag of peanuts, while all the time my heart was beating with an aching throb and I kept remembering that the last time I had been here was the Sunday night with Jack. I could re-act in my memory the contented feeling of being so near to him and the warm, clean pressure of his fingers on mine.

And as each day changed into evening and Margaret came home from work full of talk about Art and the store, and the setting sun slid long shadows onto the lawn, a queer, tired feeling crept over me and through me until even my hands went limp. I didn't even feel like a girl anymore. And all my thoughts turned into little prayers which I meant so much that it made me ache all over. "Just once," I kept saying. "Let him call just once."

Lorraine asked me to go for a walk with her one evening. Martin hadn't called for several days and she had been sitting by the front window reading, leafing restlessly through the pages of a magazine and glancing up quickly every time a car went past.

I knew why she wanted to go for a walk and I didn't blame her. For the past few days I had wanted to do it myself. We closed the front door softly behind us and then walked down our street quiet and thick with summer shadows, till we came to Park Avenue. The night was different here. Any small town is the same on a summer evening and slow cars went by one after another with their windows open, sending out quick snatches of music from the radio and twice we passed fellows and girls walking hand in hand, going toward the park.

"Let's hurry," said Lorraine.

There is something almost disgraceful about two girls, especially sisters, even going out for a walk alone when other girls have dates, so we turned off the avenue as soon as we could onto a side street, a street with heavy trees and lamp-posts only twice in the block.

I wish now I could have said something to Lorraine. Something quick and bright with happiness in it. If I could have said the right things that night, her whole summer, her whole life might have been different. But there was a certain wordless pride that kept us both from talking. I couldn't admit, even though I knew it was true, that Martin had only been taking her out because he was new in town and didn't know any other girls. I had to pretend that I didn't know that every day after work she walked to the drugstore looking for him and that once I had heard her call his boardinghouse and then hang up gently when a strange voice answered. I had to pretend that I thought she wasn't going out with him just because she didn't care to and that it was *she* who was turning *him* down. I had to pretend all that, and go along in silence as if we were just out for an ordinary walk because we were sisters and because when we were younger we played tag together and never argued over paper dolls or tattletaled about each other and it was the same now.

She didn't mention where we were going but I knew where Martin roomed. Most of the houses on his street were already sound asleep but some still had low floor lamps shining through their eyes. "Let's cross over to the other side, Angie," she said quietly. "I wouldn't want him to see me if he should happen to be outside."

We walked softly on padded feet with the street lamps making heavy summer shadows from the old trees on the sidewalk. A quick cat jumped silently from the bushes and then, as suddenly, was nothing in the darkness. We went on until we were directly across the street from where Martin lived but the boarding-house was quiet, its window shades pulled down like eyelids, and there was no green coupe pulled up at the curb. Lorraine said nothing at all but we both knew he wasn't at home.

The night was thick about us and the tree leaves whispered and small gnats made a moving fuzz around the streetlights. At the next corner we turned back automatically toward the avenue and out of the quietness of our thoughts, my sister said suddenly, "Angie, tell me—do you and Jack ever *neck?*"

She startled me and I could feel my face flush warm in the darkness. Necking was one of those words that everyone knew about but never said. I was embarrassed into confusion—Lorraine and I never talked about things like that.

"Do you mean have I—have I ever *kissed* him?" I asked and the words felt slow and awkward on my lips. And the night silence was pregnant with thoughts.

"No, no," she answered, her voice impatient. I couldn't see her face in the darkness. "I mean—you know what I mean. Do you ever *neck?*"

I didn't really know, I told her, stumbling over the words. I wasn't sure just what she meant . . . and something inside of me, panicky, kept hoping frantically she wouldn't say the word again.

"Well, Angie, I've talked with girls at school, smooth girls, and they all . . . well, if you go out with a fellow a few times . . . it isn't as if you have to be . . . You know how it is, Angie!"

There was something in her voice that was asking me to answer but I didn't know what it was that she wanted me to say. There was something in her voice that was saying so much more than the words themselves, an odd pleading that didn't fit with the words at all.

"Things are different now from the way they used to be," she went on urgently. "People don't think anything of it anymore . . . I mean, if it's only one boy you're going with and that sort of thing. It isn't like it used to be when you had to be almost engaged . . . now *everybody* does it and nobody thinks . . . you know what I mean . . ."

Her voice trailed off and she was looking at me hard in the darkness, waiting and I had to say something. I had to say something to get that worried, twisted sound out of her voice. I knew how she felt. She was thinking just as I was. There were little warm thoughts in her mind like soft fur, just as in mine: there were thoughts that made her lips tremble and set a quiet, steady, beating in her throat when the gentleness of the summer night touched her cheek and the air was fragrant with the smell of flowers hidden in the darkness. I knew how she felt.

And suddenly I remembered how it was when we were still little girls and I wanted to reach out to touch her hand as we walked. "It's all right," I told her gently. "It's all right, Lorraine. If you really like a boy—it's all right to kiss him."

She went along in silence for a few moments, brushing close against the bushes, letting the cool, dark leaves touch her arm. "Angie, you don't under-

For the rest of the day the word resounded in my head. But he hadn't been when he was with me, so how was I to know that Tony was a fast boy!

My mother brought home some newly shelled peas they had bought up at a vinery on the highway coming from Sheboygan. I picked out the small, round thistleheads that are always mixed with vinery peas and put the peas on to cook. "We passed Jack in the bakery truck headed for the lake just as we turned into the street," my mother said conversationally, tying on a clean apron. "He must have been going out to look at his boat."

Since morning my thoughts were so numbed that now I could look at her and nod in answer without my face showing anything.

Late the next afternoon all the ominous, heavy gloom I felt inside of me seemed to come out in the weather. I had been in the kitchen most of the day ironing Kitty's dresses and the clothes had the clean, fresh smell of having blown in the sun, but the steam came up hot from the ironing board and the air was damp and muggy. My hair was sticking in fuzzy curls on my neck, and from the radio in the living room I could hear the monotonous, inarticulate drone of the baseball game. It was the sort of day that made you wish you could go to bed right away and not have to wake up till tomorrow.

The weather was bound to break and finally in the late afternoon a storm rode in from the lake on a low wind that smelled of fish and the dark, troubled water of Winnebago. Over to the north the sky grew heavy and sullen, a dark gray-green, the color of old bruises, and the wind snaked its way through the grass and pushed the bushes flat against the house. Outside, neighbor women came to their doors calling to the children to come in before the rain came, and in our living room my mother switched off the radio, grumbling with sudden static, and came into the kitchen.

"Angeline," she suggested, "let's have a cup of tea and finish those macaroons in the cookie jar." She set out the cups, but just as the steam began to whistle from the nose of the kettle she said, "Or perhaps it's too near suppertime," and put the cups and tea-pot away again.

The smell of the lake was so strong the waves might well have been licking the back door step and the trees on the lawn tossed fitfully, as if they were worried beyond bearing. Kitty came in with her hair blown about saying, "Got to close the upstairs windows. It's going to rain." The sky was so dark that the air was gray-green and birds swooped low from the trees, uneasy about the coming storm. As I went to shut the kitchen window the wind blew the first rain against the pane in spiteful gusts, and out in the north, over the lake, lightning crooked a long, bright finger across the sky. It was a storm that would last the night.

"What shall we have for supper?" my mother asked. "It's the sort of night the children will be hungry."

"Pancakes and cocoa with marshmallows?" Kitty suggested hopefully. That is her stock menu for anything from picnics to birthday parties.

"All right," Mom agreed. "And, Angie, if you'll melt up some butter with brown sugar it will save us having to go to the store for syrup in the rain." Kitty hovered close to the stove with comments and suggestions till the syrup was done and I gave her the sweet, sticky pan to scrape.

Later, at supper, she sat bobbing the marshmallow in her cocoa cup up and down, saying every few moments, "Isn't this good, children? Isn't this good?" She always calls my other sisters and me "children" because my mother does and usually I laugh but tonight I didn't care.

420

Lorraine's hair was damp and uncurled from the rain and hung limp around her face. Every few minutes the lights in the chandelier dimmed as outside the lightning crackled, and we all held our conversation poised for a moment, waiting for the thunder to pass. The house had the warm, oppressive stillness in the air that comes from the tension of a storm and not having the windows open. For a moment I thought I couldn't stand it—all the pleasant, protected smugness that kept making me pretend and pretend. They all sat around the table, enjoying the luxurious taste of syrup and melted butter, with their lips soft and smiling and their faces happy as if they were eating slices of contentment. I had a sudden stifled feeling, as if the house were too small and the cream-colored dining room walls were crowding in close, so close that it made my very ribs ache.

My mother filled Kitty's cocoa cup again, smiling to herself. "Isn't this a good night to be all home, cozy and inside?" she questioned, and her voice was quiet and warm with sheer satisfaction. Outside, the wind pelted the rain in sheets against the window and went keening through the trees, its sad wail trailing behind.

We spent the whole miserable evening in the living room with the radio off because the air was static-filled with storm. Lorraine had pinned her wet hair into a scraggly knot at the back of her head like a neat washwoman and sat leafing through a pile of old magazines. My mother had picked apart a worn tweed suit of Margaret's to make over for me for college, and I slipped it on, tacked together, over my slacks while she made rough calculations with pins. "There," she said with satisfaction, "look, children. If that won't look smart with a long yellow sweater!" I inched around slowly to give her the whole effect while she said with her head cocked, chewing a bit of thread, "But you must stand straighter, Angie," and she gave me a motherly poke between the shoulder blades with her thimbled finger. "You've been slumping for over a week."

Margaret sat with a magazine and note paper on her knee writing to Art and smiling to herself, while the pen made a steady scratch-scratch in the quietness of the room.

I took a book from the shelf and lay down on the rug to read. There is nothing like filling your mind with new thoughts to crowd the old ones out, but somehow it didn't work. It was like taking castor oil with orange juice. When you drink through the sweet juice floating on the top everything seems all right but you inevitably come to the thick, sickening castor oil, heavy at the bottom.

Lorraine was chipping the nail polish off the nails of one hand with the other hand as she read, making a small, insistent noise as irritating as the screak of chalk on the blackboard. Martin had called just before the rain began for the first time this week. I had answered.

"Hi, there, Angeline," he had said.

And I was so surprised to hear his voice I blurted out, "Hello, Martin! I'm so glad you called!" That was wrong. Martin always laughs at anyone who is glad about anything.

"Yeah?" His voice twisted into a question and I could almost see his face with one eyebrow raised and a half-smile making his mouth sarcastically amused. "Your sister 'round?" he asked.

"Why, no. No, she isn't home from work yet," I explained, "but she'll be here in just a little while—"

"All right," he answered abruptly. "Thanks, Angie."

"What shall I tell her?" I insisted. "Was there anything special you wanted?"

"No, just tell her I called."

"Shall I tell her you'll call back, Martin?"

"If you want. Yeah, tell her I'll call back later," and he hung up.

When Lorraine came home from work I told her and I had watched her waiting as we ate supper, but the phone never rang. She kept looking at the clock every few minutes till the hand ticked its way past seven. Then she didn't look anymore.

Now, in the living room, it made me feel worse to see her so I turned over and put my head on my arms on the rug. I know now how a balloon feels when it bursts. The rough scratch of the pile was almost comforting against my face and my head ached with the effort of trying to hold back my thoughts, so I just closed my eyes and let them come. One sharp thought needled into my brain till I felt like squirming. Maybe right now they're out there, Jack and Jane Rady, listening to the music from the nickel machine at Pete's and laughing together every time the storm dimmed the lights, while outside the lake is tossing its waves high up on the back lawn. Or maybe they're at the movie, in the darkness and quiet, not knowing there is a storm at all. Her hair would be shining and hanging soft and straight. Maybe he had even touched her hair.

I wanted so badly to cry. Not with big, loud sobs, but just to sit by myself without making any noise and let the tears trickle slowly and silently without my having to stop them. I tried to force my mind back, back to the time before I knew Jack; but it kept puttering with little memories on the way and I couldn't get past that first night in the boat. Pictures kept see-sawing before my eyes till I was sick with unhappiness and my heart felt sore as a bruise.

The worst of the storm was clearing now and a fork of lightning did one last quick dance across the sky while low thunder applauded in the distance. But the rain was still steady on the window panes and runneled noisily in the eaves trough, and the wind was still worrying the tired trees. My mother shifted her sewing on her knee and said again with warm contentment, "Isn't this the best night to be all home, cozy and inside?"

I can't even tell you quite how it happened. I mean, it was the sort of thing that happens so fast that you can't even piece it together again afterward. It was late Saturday afternoon and I had walked down to Paine's drugstore to buy some turpentine to take the paint off Kitty's new sailor slacks. She had spent the morning in the garage refinishing her bicycle.

Paine's is a very plain drugstore with a bare, shiny front window all neatly arranged with well-dusted boxes of tooth paste, a special milk of magnesia display, and a small barrel of horehound drops[10] spilled artistically in one corner. It is the reliable sort of drugstore which does a large prescription business and even the few Cokes they serve have a slightly medicinal tang. I was sitting in a front booth all by myself. The sides of those booths are high and the table tops of cold speckled marble give the back of the drugstore a dusky gloom even in the daytime. I was sitting not thinking of anything, just being glad that the Saturday housework was done and noticing distastefully how white and puffy my hands looked from having scrubbed the kitchen linoleum. My mind was so tired of wondering and worrying that I just let thoughts wander in and out as they wanted to.

---

10 *horehound drops* a candy flavored with extract of the horehound plant, used as a cough remedy.

And all of a sudden there was Jack. When I think it over now we must have looked very silly to anyone watching—as if we were in a play and both overacting. He came in the door, whistling to himself and was swinging onto a high stool before the soda fountain when he saw me. Something happened to me then—a funny tingling feeling started right at the top of my head and went down over me in a quick wave leaving me suddenly very cold and wide-awake. I remember putting my hand on the bottle of turpentine wrapped in green paper on the seat beside me, thinking vaguely that if he should come over to talk to me it would be nice to have something to hold on to.

"Hello," he said, gruffly, as though he were clearing his throat. "Didn't see you at first."

"Hello, Jack." My face had a tight feeling as if I had washed it with too much soap.

I had always thought it was something like voting, that you weren't really supposed to start feeling with your heart till you were at least twenty-one. And here I was looking at him so hard I could almost *feel* myself seeing the clean, wet look of his crew cut and the familiar coarse knit of his football sweater, while my heart was pounding till it made my voice sound quavery.

"How've you been, Angie?" he asked, sliding into the booth across from me.

"Fine," I said quickly. "Fine, Jack. How have you been?" and I tried to look past him till I could be more sure of myself, till I could put my thoughts out of my eyes.

"I've just been down at the Y," he told me. "Swede, too. We had a swim and a shower. I always take an hour off on Saturday afternoon. We're rushed down at the bakery on Saturday night."

And then suddenly we were all out of conversation. There was a long, awkward silence with our thoughts very busy in it and I looked at him with a small smile anxious on my lips. I had the feeling that I wasn't really I at all but another person sitting in the booth across the aisle, looking over and watching.

"What you been doing, Angie?" He urged his voice to sound interested and I caught the cue.

"Nothing. What have *you* been doing? I haven't even seen Swede around lately." It wasn't the right thing to say. He knew I hadn't seen Swede. It didn't mean anything. Here I was with just a few minutes and I wasn't saying anything; nothing that mattered. Jack's hand was on the table and I felt my own close tight on the turpentine bottle; I wanted so much to touch it. Sometimes my hands seem to have minds of their own. I wanted so much to touch him that for a moment there didn't even seem to be a table between us. He looked at me then, straight at me, and I felt my eyes go soft.

"I've got to go, Angie," he said quickly. "I've got to get back right away because Saturday's so busy at the bakery." He said it but he never moved and it was as if he had never spoken at all.

Something had to be said and the words were suddenly on my lips, without any thoughts behind them, tingling to be said. "Jack, Margie told me what Fitz said you thought about that night with Tony. . . ."

But he wouldn't look at me then. "Did she?" and his tone was dull and uninterested. "Yeah," he added. I didn't know how to go on. I couldn't say that what he thought wasn't true when I didn't even know what he thought.

"I guess I was kinda surprised," he said with a half-smile, never raising his eyes.

"Surprised at what?"

"To hear that you went out with Tony."

"Why?"

"Why!" He looked at me in an exasperated way, running his hand through his hair, only his hair was clipped so short he really just smoothed over it. His voice was tight and quick as if he were angry.

"Gee, Angie, I take you out. Everything goes like it did. That night at the dance and then at the cottage and everything. And I start feeling . . . well, how I did . . . and then one morning Tony walks into the bakery and says he's got a date with you!"

And there was nothing I could say.

"Just when I start thinking, well, maybe it's all right, Fitz calls up and tells me that Margie just called him to tell him that you'd called her and said that you've got a date with Becker and you're even *proud* of it!"

He looked at me in a puzzled, hurt sort of way and his voice was almost pleading. "Gee, Angie!"

"But, Jack," I said, "Jack, how was I to know? I didn't know a thing about it!" I sat twisting a curl of hair round and round my finger because I was trying so hard to find the right words that I couldn't even keep my hands still.

"Honestly, Jack, I didn't know a thing about it until Margie told me."

"Couldn't you *tell?*"

"No, no, how could I tell?"

"Just by the way he looks at you. And you even danced with him at the Country Club dance!"

"But you were the one that arranged to exchange dances. I thought he was a friend of yours."

"Sure, he's a friend of mine. And he's a good guy too, but he's just that way. And any girl that I go with that would go out with Tony and—"

"And what?"

He looked up at me and his voice was quiet. "Didn't you, Angie?"

"Well, Jack! Honestly!" It was my turn to sound exasperated, but inside my head words were bumping together so fast that I didn't know what to say.

"How was I to know, Angie? I didn't think so at first, but then I talked to Swede and we both know Becker, and well, when you called up Margie to tell her about it and everything . . . how was I to know, Angie?" For a moment neither of us moved or spoke; but when I am very, very old I hope I can look back and remember all the wonderful things that went on in that silence.

"I've got the truck outside," he said huskily, nodding toward the door, "if I can take you home."

We took the longest way, the way that goes through the park and along the edge of the lake where the small boats moored at the shore dip in rhythm with the waves and the blue water is spangled with sunlight. And down the long, thin highway toward the country, passing cars with their windows glinting with sun, to the curved gravel road with scum-covered water in its ditches, growing with tall heavy-headed cattails and slim purple iris. Farther on the air is honeyed with the clean, sweet smell of clover and the willow trees shake their varnished leaves till they glitter in the sunlight.

Jack drove with both hands tight on the wheel and I sat close beside him till we came to the place where the Virginia creeper stretches heavy on the fences and the trees beside the road grow thick and gnarled, reaching up muscled arms, and the fields, all wild with mustard plants, are yellow as sunshine. Jack slowed the car while we held our breath and listened to the whole air singing

424

with the sound of insects and wind in the grass and the warm steady hum that is summer. And along the ditches the weeds were gray with the dry dust that rose in a cloud from the gravel road as we stopped. Behind us lay the town, lost beyond the fences and ditches, and ahead the whole country lay stretching, yellow-green in the sunlight.

And the thought in my mind was as warm and mellow as the sunlight. How odd, I thought. How wonderfully, wonderfully odd to be kissed in the middle of the afternoon.

JULY

IT WAS hot. It was hot with the steady beating heat that comes from a bare sky and a high sun, still and glaring, that covers the whole ground without a shadow. It was the kind of weather in which high school girls go about with their long silk hair pinned in knots on the top of their heads like scrubwomen, and little children splash in tubs of shallow water in their back yards and older people drag mattresses out onto airing porches to wait for a breeze in the still, quiet heat of the evening.

We were all hot. All of us. The soil in the garden was parched and hard, crisscrossed with wide cracks, and big brown grasshoppers, their wings dusty, were heavy on the bean plants and bared the green stems with their nibblings. Kitty pinned her braids on top of her head so the little ends stuck up like horns and rolled her slacks above her knees while new brown-dot freckles popped out on her nose. All afternoon the dog lay panting under the basement stairs where the heat brought the moisture out of the cement in damp patches like sweat that ran in slow trickles down the stone walls.

"Tomorrow we'll just pack a lunch, shut the house, and go away for the day," my mother said at suppertime. It was so warm that her thin dress stuck to the back of her chair every time she moved. "In all this heat I don't know as I could stand the noise and the firecrackers for a whole day," she went on, fanning herself gently with a napkin.

Art was there too, having driven up from Milwaukee with my father earlier in the afternoon—neither of them wanted to get mixed up with the Fourth-of-July traffic. "If one of us goes we'll all go," my mother added. She was irritated with the heat and talked with her lips in a thin, strained line. Even Kitty had noticed it and was being carefully quiet and polite. "All this worry of accidents and death tolls in the paper takes all the fun out of holidays for me," and she went on buttering her bread with thoughtful annoyance.

"Angie," my mother said, turning to me, "after we finish supper I wish you would hard-boil some eggs and put them in the icebox for the potato salad tomorrow. I don't want to have a single thing to do in the heat of the day.

"And Kitty, run downstairs and bring up the picnic baskets from the canning cupboard and put the dishes in then tonight." She was fanning herself with her napkin again. "Dad," she said to my father, "I wish you would take me for a short ride in the car—this heat is almost too much for me tonight."

Lorraine had been eating quietly but now she put down her fork and ventured, "You know, I don't know as I'll be able to go with you tomorrow—"

"Why not?" my father demanded sharply.

425

shreds of wings off the radiator of the car and laying them out side by side on hollyhock leaves.

It was almost five-thirty by then and my mother sat down on a garden chair and balanced her paper picnic plate on her knee. The sun was still as warm as noon, but shadows were beginning to stretch their lengths on the ground and the leaves of the trees were restless with small breezes. "Wouldn't you think," she said, "that Lorraine would have the niceness to *call* and say that she wasn't coming home for supper either? I don't know why it is that no one can make plans here anymore."

Art was lying on a car robe with his full paper plate on the grass and a Coke bottle propped up beside it. It was at times like this that I was glad he was going to be part of our family. He would do anything at all to prevent friction or unpleasantness and he said now in his odd, warm voice that always reminded me of soft suede, "Oh, I don't know, Mom. You know how it is when you're out. You just forget what time it is." Margaret passed him a sandwich just then and brushed her hand with the long bright nails against his, very gently.

My father had never said anything about Martin. In the beginning we were all so glad, and a little surprised, that Lorraine had someone to go out with that no one thought of criticizing. It isn't that she couldn't get along with fellows if she wanted to, I guess, but because she has gone to college and everything she just doesn't like "ordinary" boys. Until now my mother had never criticized Martin, either. "But you would think," she said, "that a boy who has his meals in a restaurant three times a day would be glad to have a nice, home-made picnic!"

Sorrow over the dead butterflies had completely left Kitty by now and she piped up, "Ah, him! He's so old he doesn't like anything. He never wants to catch my baseball or play with Kinkee or anything. I'll bet he doesn't even like ice cream!" and the edges of her voice were curled with scorn.

After we had finished eating I gathered the leftover bits of sandwiches and the half-eaten curves of water-melon that looked like broad, empty grins onto a paper plate, and then we all sat on the lawn, relieved that the heat of the day was passing and the cool of the evening was creeping in low over the grass. Kitty brought out my mother's knitting from the house, all wrapped in a clean towel, but she left it untouched while birds twittered in the garden hedge and a light wind stirred in the trees. Everything was so pleasant that my thoughts just floated, light and elusive, in my head.

When Jack came up the sidewalk the dog gave a short, gruff bark almost as if it were clearing its throat. I was sitting with my back turned and I hadn't known he was coming but yet I knew it was Jack. Without even turning my head I knew it was he and I knew exactly how he looked. My mother smiled at him and asked him to sit down with us while she nodded to me to clear the picnic things away.

My hands felt awkward and unaccustomed as I shooed the flies from the uncovered watermelon rinds and gathered up the paper plates. I stood uncertain for a moment, wondering if I should bring the things into the kitchen or dump them vulgarly into the garbage can at the end of the garden right then. Kinkee nosed politely around my bare legs, sniffing anxiously for scraps, so I decided to take the sandwich leavings into the kitchen and fill her bowl. Jack jumped to his feet to hold open the back door for me and I mumbled a "thank you" that somehow didn't come out at all.

It all seemed too strange to me. Inside, scraping bits of sandwiches and potato salad into the dog's dish, my hands shook and my cheeks had a hot prickly feeling. It didn't seem right to go outside again and sit there on the cool grass, liking Jack so well, right in front of my family! This was the sort of thing that belonged at Pete's or out near the boathouses, but not on my own back lawn with Kitty and Kinkee and everyone watching! It just didn't seem right. The dog sat up on her hind legs, begging with petulant squeaks, till I set her bowl on the floor.

From the back lawn I could hear my father's deep voice, Art's soft one, and the boy-voice that was Jack's, with polite pauses when I knew my mother was speaking. In the half-darkness of the kitchen I curled a few strands of hair around my fingers and held my hands tight to my face, just for a moment, to get my thoughts straight and to wait for that fast, excited beating to stop in my heart. Then I filled the dog's empty bowl with water from the kitchen faucet, set it on the floor, and went outside.

My father was talking in a formal tone, a tone he saves and puts on like a necktie for just such special occasions as this.

"Of course," he was saying, "it depends on what you want to do with your life. But for the girls here, I always feel that college is the best way to start."

"You're right, sir," Jack answered. "I really think you're right but with me it's different. I'm the only one and my dad needs me 'round the bakery. I figure maybe I can get some extra education through extension courses and just reading by myself—but my dad needs me 'round right now." Jack was sprawled on the grass, talking very fast and earnestly, his eyebrows knit together.

"But it seems to me the thing to do would be to try to get the education first," my father explained and my mind quickly jumped to Jack's defense. Maybe there was a mortgage or something. Maybe there was a whole family of poor first cousins that had to be supported. There were dozens of reasons why some people can't afford to go to college. After all, my father shouldn't talk that way to a boy he had met only twice before!

"I understand what you mean, sir," insisted Jack, talking carefully so it wouldn't sound as if he were contradicting. "If I had a son I would want him to go to college. But you see, we had a pretty good bakery business down in Oklahoma, but my mother wanted to move back here to be near her folks and now we have to build it up all over again. And it isn't so good—too many people in this town still bake their own bread and things."

"Where is your mother from, Jack?" my mother asked, her voice pleasant.

"After they were married she and Dad lived in Oklahoma till just a couple years ago, but she is originally from out near Rosendale," he said, turning toward her. "I have an aunt out there who says she knows you because you did some work together at a church bazaar once—her name is Alberts."

So Jack had been talking about my family to his aunt! And he must have been talking about me too. Perhaps, to tease him, his father had said, "Jack's got a new girl," and his aunt had looked up in surprise, asked what her name was, where she lived, and what she looked like, or maybe she had heard him talking to me on the phone or maybe after the parade today his father had said to him casually, "Who was that girl I saw you with this morning, son?" To think of anyone calling him "son" made me shiver a little—it seemed such a daringly personal thought—and I looked up quickly to see if anyone had been watching me. But Jack was chewing a bit of grass, looking off toward the lake, and my mother had her eyes on her knitting.

We sat outside for a long time while the sky grew dark and small new stars popped out and a thin crescent of moon made a bright curve in the sky. We

431

talked of everyday things and my father and mother addressed most of their remarks to Jack because he was company, and when he didn't understand he would question them with a quizzical "Please?" instead of the "Pardon me?" that we always used, and even in the darkness I could imagine his eyebrows knitted together in thought. Art slapped at the mosquitoes that kept up a steady murmur around our heads, but after the heat of the day the coolness of the evening was so pleasant that no one wanted to go into the house.

I found my mind following the conversation with the same back-and-forth movement with which one's eyes follow the ball in watching a ping-pong game. Each time anyone spoke to Jack I waited a little breathless to hear what answer he would toss back. At Pete's and in McKnight's I was sure of him but with my family I had been anxious. After all, it is quite a test for a boy to have to talk with six people at once.

Later on, much later, when the sky was very dark and the stars were sprinkled across it, hard and bright, Kitty decided it was time to go through her Fourth-of-July ritual of lighting her box of sparklers. We all sat, watching and making the right, appreciative comments, while she stood with each sparkler at arm's length, shooting off a wraith[3] of quick stars. As each one burned near the end she tossed it over her head so it fell in a bright arc to the ground, lying in the grass till the hot wire had glowed itself out. Kitty's teeth chittered with excitement and ecstasy, and having Jack and Art as audience added to the thrill. She had taken off her shoes and short socks to enjoy the coolness of the grass, and my mother warned, "Be careful of those hot wires in the darkness with your bare feet, Kitty dear." After the last sparkler had arched through the air and sputtered out in the grass, she gave a breathy little sigh and sat down beside me, all tired from the happiness of it. After the brightness of the sparklers the sky seemed even darker than before.

Somewhere off in the distance an ambulance siren sounded, faint at first with an eerie questioning, the sound swelling as it passed the corner of our street, going down Park Avenue and headed out toward the highway that runs along the lake. It sped on its way, leaving a long, thin wail of sound trailing behind it, while my mother stopped in her conversation, listening. All of us sat with our minds snapped in alertness, knowing what she was thinking. If we are all away from home and hear a fire siren, my mother is certain it is our house that is burning; if one of us is away and we hear an ambulance, she is sure it is one of us stretched out somewhere on the highway. We knew now she was thinking of Lorraine and we all began talking very fast and very animatedly to drown out the weird tail of sound that still lingered in the night. With sudden enthusiasm Jack burst out, "Mrs. Morrow, have you ever been sailboating?" and then petered out in a less eager account of the fun he and Swede had had that afternoon. It made my lips feel soft just hearing him then. How quickly, without even a word said, he had understood and become one of us!

Out in the dark sky just a few blocks from us the annual fireworks display was being set off over the lake. Explosions, like dull thuds, preceded a thin whistle as the rockets shot into the air, bursting into a million bright-pointed stars, showering down into the night. Kitty let out little breathless exclamations of awe, and the dog, frightened by the light, whimpered and lay down close to Art with her head meekly on her paws. For a long time no one said anything.

---

3 *wraith* ghost.

Fireworks should be watched in silence. Above us some of the rockets exploded in circles, echoing outward in diminishing rings of color while others burst into showers, hanging in mid-air for a moment like bright flower sprays, and one shot high, high above the others, like a brilliant comet and then plummeted to the earth, dragging a long scarlet tail down the sky. Jack whistled between his teeth and Kitty gave a little gasp of wonder. Above us the whole darkness seemed shot through with light and shattered with bursts of color that sent out a melting rain of stars. It seemed as if one could almost hear the brightness. The whole night tingled with it.

"I hope Lorraine and Martin don't miss this—wherever they are," my mother said quietly.

Jack was sitting, propped on his hands, with his head back looking at the sky and he moved his hand just a little so it barely touched mine. A tingling ran up my arm and I felt my face flush in the darkness. As a finale a series of rockets was set off in rapid succession till everything was a dazzle of quick-tailed shooting stars, fiery comets, and huge chrysanthemums of colored light. Long after the display had ceased the spectacle was bright before our eyes and the night sky was suddenly gentle and demure with the coy twinkle of pale stars. All of us felt the strange, silent natural beauty of it. The hushed night seemed so real, so lovely that I felt almost ashamed of the gaudy efforts of the faded rockets.

I wondered for a moment what my mother would think if she knew that I was sitting there in the darkness with Jack's hand on mine. And all those strange thoughts. I wondered if it were just me or if they all felt this night so mysterious, so pulsing with something unspoken. My whole body felt uneasy with it. Suddenly I had an almost uncontrollable impulse to reach out and touch Jack's bare throat gently, lightly with one finger, at the V of his shirt. And it was just then that he said politely to my mother, "Well, if you don't mind, Mrs. Morrow, I think I'd better be going now. I've got to be out on the route early tomorrow." He stood for a moment not knowing what else to say.

My mother rose from her chair too, saying, "I'm glad you came, Jack, and come again any time. It's nice having you." Her words sang in my ears as I walked to the front sidewalk with him. Kitty walked with us.

It was late and we all went into the house then and the others went straight upstairs while my mother turned back to call to me, "Angeline, be sure to see that the front door is unlocked for Lorraine."

"I will," I called back.

In the living room the window shades were still drawn as they had been against the heat of the afternoon and a few tired flies buzzed behind them against the windowpane. The air was hot and still and had the oppressive weight of not being lived in all day. There was something heavily, depressingly quiet about the whole room, and outside, somewhere in the city, the sound of an occasional late firecracker echoed. On the corner table was a vase of yellow flowers, limp and wilted, and in the heat of the afternoon the broad, smooth petals had dropped to the floor like tired butterflies. The night seemed suddenly husked of its beauty.

Quietly I turned the key in the lock and tried the knob of the front door. It was open. Lorraine would have no trouble getting in.

Of the days that followed I remember almost nothing definitely. Nothing seemed to stand out by itself but all flowed together into a stream of pleasant-

433

ness like warm, thick honey. Every moment was full of it. Every night there was the lonely, ecstatic wonder of thinking about Jack while I lay in bed alone; outside, the stars just pin-pricked the sky and the wind was gentle in the trees, and in the morning there was the slow luxury of waking with the first sun on the wall and knowing that a whole long day of thinking lay ahead. It was the sort of happiness that almost makes you sad it is so wonderful. Everything seemed different to me—everything.

Sometimes after I had been with Jack, I would go upstairs into my own room and my thoughts seemed as clear and steady as crystal, and I would look at my wrists all traced with thin, blue veins and somehow I almost expected to see them pulsing, all throbbing with the strange new urge that was beating through me. Sometimes I went for walks by myself far out into the big field and my legs felt strong and thin and clean. Touching things sent a new pleasure through my hands that filled my whole body with satisfaction. The rough bark of trees was good, hard, and I thrilled to the soft, silken curve of the dog's head as I stroked it. Words came out of my mouth like bubbles. Standing in our garden, watching fat bumblebees blunder against the broad faces of the sunflowers, I almost laughed aloud, and there was a new fascination about yellow-furred caterpillars, tufted like toothbrushes, inching along the hollyhock stems in the bright morning sun.

Sometimes I felt that my feet just wouldn't stay on the ground. I wanted to pick the leaves from the raspberry bushes with their smooth surfaces and the greenish-white fuzz underneath, and touch the softness to my lips. The lake breeze blew in warm and soft, and black and yellow spiders rocked in webs that glinted in the sun and the whole air shimmered with July heat. Everything, everything was wonderful. Sometimes the world seemed so full of the luxurious lushness and warmth of summer that one could almost reach out and eat it with a spoon.

In the evenings we went for walks, Jack and I—long, silent walks—not talking at all, not having to talk. Or we would go out to Pete's with Fitz and Margie or to the movies by ourselves. Sometimes when we sat in the movies Jack would hold my hand. It wasn't silly. We did it because it was good to sit so close together in the darkness and, somehow, by holding hands you can carry on a conversation without talking.

When my mother and I were home alone in the morning, doing the housework, I found myself telling her little, noncommittal things about him, anything just so I could say his name aloud. "Mom, Jack says that his father says that more people are buying regular bakery bread and that the fad for sliced bread is going out..." Often when Kitty and I were together I talked to her about him—Kitty will listen to anything. I told her how he had been the star of the basketball team at high school, how well he drove a car, and I once asked her if she had noticed how clean his shirts always looked. I talked and talked about things that made no difference to Kitty at all but just gave me the chance to think of him and say his name.

One afternoon Margie and I walked down to McKnight's to meet him. It was wonderful sitting there. Fitz stopped in and other fellows and girls came in, together and alone, and called "Hi!" or came over to talk with Jack and Fitz while Margie talked steadily and smiled broad smiles at everyone. She smiled so broadly that I noticed she had got lipstick on her teeth and I thought to tell her about it—but Fitz wasn't looking at her anyway. Occasionally a woman who had been shopping would come in with a little boy or girl and they both would have a quick ice-cream cone or a pineapple soda, and the child would eat slowly, staring at the older fellows and girls making so much noise, while the ice cream dribbled down his chin. Older people and very young didn't seem to belong here. No one belonged here but the "crowd," those who were "in." Until I met Jack I hadn't belonged here, either. I remembered once in early spring having come in with Kitty and having had a small Coke with her, sitting at the fountain, while from the back booths came the sound of laughing and talking. But no one had talked to me. I wasn't one of the crowd then. I remember I had told Kitty to hurry up and made her leave before the Coke was half finished. I couldn't stand being so out of things. But it was different now.

Fitz was working in a fruit store for the summer and said that he had to get right back, for he had just sneaked out for a few minutes and he didn't want them to miss him. After a while Jack said that he really should get back to the bakery too, for his father didn't know he had gone, either. But I knew he wouldn't leave. After Fitz had gone out the door Jack still sat with Margie and me, fingering his bent straws and waiting, as if he wanted to say something.

"How's this hot weather affecting business, Jack?" Margie asked in a professionally conversational tone. She always talks with an up-and-down movement, as if she were chewing gum. And she likes to be a special friend to all the boys, even if she is going steady.

"It isn't so bad," he answered. "People have to eat no matter what the weather does." He looked at her and then at me and the three of us just sat saying nothing. "Doughnuts and things will *always* sell," he added lamely.

Margie craned her neck to look over the booth to see if anyone she knew might be coming in the front door. There was no one.

"Angie," Jack said, "unless you've got to get home right away, would you like to go for a little ride with me? I've got the truck and I don't have to be back to the bakery for about twenty minutes or so. . . ."

"Go right ahead," Margie said to me indulgently. "I'll just sit here and talk to the kids and wait till you get back. Some one of the fellows is bound to come in," and she gave me one of her "I know how it is" smiles. I almost resented her thinking she knew all about Jack and me—even if she did.

He had the bakery truck parked just around the corner; the afternoon sun glinted on the windshield and the black leather seats were hot to touch. Jack got in beside me, started the motor, and swung the truck around in the opposite direction, away from the bakery, just in case he might run into his father. He drove out from the heat of the town to the coolness of the lake and pulled the truck up at the water's edge. The breeze was moist and cool and the water was blue and rollicking, teased with sunlight. A sand dredge was laboring in the harbor, its engines making a steady grunt-grunt and the whistle on its bridge giving out short, periodic snorts, as if it were blowing through its nose. We laughed, both of us, hearing it.

Jack reached into the shelves in the back of the truck and picked out four sugar cookies with raisins for us to eat. We sat munching them and laughing at the noises of the sand dredge and feeling the sun coming through the windshield, falling warm on our arms and legs. After a long time we went back to town.

Margie was still waiting in McKnight's when I came back. She had ordered another Coke and was being dainty about lighting her cigarette when I came in. "Where did you leave Jack?" she asked.

"He let me off in front and went on back to work," I explained, trying hard not to look straight at her. "His father won't like it that he's been gone so long as it is."

She took a long, leisurely draw on her cigarette and we both watched the slow smoke curling. Then, leaning across the table, Margie said to me in a low, confidential voice, "You know, Angie, that shows when a boy really likes a girl—when he wants to kiss her in the daytime!"

The very next Sunday Jack's aunt from Oklahoma passed through Chicago and his mother and father drove down to see her. But he stayed home. I wish now he had gone. He stayed to attend to the bakery and to see that the restaurants in town got their orders of hot rolls at eleven o'clock on Sunday morning. I would never have dared to mention it myself—in fact, I never even thought of it—but it was my mother who suggested that Jack come over for Sunday dinner.

"If his mother is going to be away I'm sure he won't want to prepare anything for himself," she said.

So I called him on Saturday evening while he was still at the bakery. My heart was pounding as I talked to him. Even if I did know him well, it seemed such a forward step to ask a boy to have dinner with your family! I could hear the sound of people moving about and the ring of the cash register behind his voice as we talked.

"Jack, my mother would like to know if you would like to come over for dinner tomorrow, seeing your mother and dad won't be home. . . ."

"You'll have to talk louder, Angie," he said. "We're pretty busy here and I can't hear you."

"I said," I repeated, articulating carefully, "would you like to come over for dinner tomorrow?"

"Gee, Angie, that's swell. That's really swell!" and his voice dropped low. "What time?"

"What are you whispering for?" I could tell he was talking with his mouth close to the phone.

"I just don't want my dad to hear," he said.

"Why?" I made my voice sound very surprised and a little insulted, though I knew very well what he meant. I had thought of it myself before I called.

"It's all right, of course," he assured me, hastily. "It's just that I don't know if my dad would like it so well . . . me, having dinner with girls, I mean. You know how it is. . . ."

"Of course," I said abruptly. "We'll expect you about noon, Jack," and I hung up. It wasn't nice of me. It wasn't nice of me at all, for I knew just what my father would think if I had been asked to have dinner at *Jack's* house. But I knew that Jack would worry all night. He would want to call back and ask me if I was angry with him, but the bakery would be rushed with last-minute Saturday night customers and he wouldn't have time. After the bakery had closed it would be too late and he would be afraid my mother would be annoyed with him for calling at such an hour. So he wouldn't know until tomorrow if I were angry with him or not and would spend all the rest of the evening thinking about it, while he waited on customers, and making up ways of explaining to me why he couldn't tell his father. Of course, I *knew* why and I wasn't angry at all. Only sometimes, even if you like a boy so much, it is almost fun to know he is worrying about you.

Sunday morning in the summer is almost too good, almost sensuously pleasant. All the windows were wide open and the sun lay in bright patches on the living-room rug and the hollyhocks grew straight and high around the back door and everywhere there was a feeling of warmth and oneness—as if there was no difference between inside the house and outside. Everywhere it was summer. My father spent the morning in the garden, straightening out vegetable rows with a hoe and piling up a heap of pulled weeds in an empty bushel basket, stopping now and then to wipe the sweat from his forehead. In the kitchen my mother tied on a frilled Sunday apron and began cutting the string beans for dinner. She kept looking out the window at my father, humming as she worked.

Even if the day was hot we were having roast pork and mashed potatoes for dinner because, as my mother said, "If your father has to eat out all week he deserves a good dinner at the weekend."

Upstairs Margaret and Lorraine were making the bed together and Kitty was reading the funny papers on the back lawn. Everyone knew that Jack was coming. They had known ever since my mother had suggested asking him, but somehow I shied away from talking about it. It didn't seem quite safe to talk about him anymore. I knew they didn't quite understand about Jack and me and I had a vague, uneasy feeling that if they did they wouldn't like it at all. My mind was always on the alert for the first word of disapproval. After all, what would my mother say if she knew that I, who had just been out of high school six weeks, was feeling the way I was? Families just don't understand about such things.

Kitty came into the kitchen to help peel the apples for the applesauce and then gathered up the long curls of peelings and went out to eat them on the lawn, sitting in the sun. Kinkee came over, wagging her tail and wiggling her nose in anticipation. Kitty held out a curl of apple skin and the dog sniffed it gently and then let it drop to the ground untouched.

My heart felt lumped inside me, warm with satisfaction. Everything seemed too wonderful. I had set the table in the dining room on one of the best white tablecloths and the bright sunshine streamed in the windows and glinted through the tall glasses onto the silverware, sending off sprays of light. In the center Lorraine had put a low bowl of pink cosmos from the garden with their feathery, fernlike leaves. A small green bug dropped onto the tablecloth and began inching its way toward a plate. I lifted it carefully on the corner of the Sunday funny paper and shook it out the front door. Outside the whole world seemed yellow-green and sunny. Even the way the trees shook their leaves seemed different.

Later I went upstairs and put two little pink guest towels in the bathroom. It seemed impossible to think that Jack would even be seeing what our upstairs looked like! From the kitchen rose the pleasant Sunday smell of roast pork and fresh garden peas, and outside I could hear the sound of neighbors laughing together as they sat on their front porches, and just across the street a man stood in his shirt sleeves with a pail of water and a chamois, shining his car. Everything seemed suddenly too wonderful. The clean sunshine, the good dinner in the oven, and just a few minutes to wait until Jack would be here! It couldn't be that good! It seemed as if I were drinking in the almost tangible pleasure of the morning like a rich, heavy malted milk that comes slow and thick through the straws.

My whole head sang with warm, summer-Sunday thoughts, till my hands tingled with the sheer joy of it. "O God," I thought, "O God, O God—stop making me be so glad! I can't stand being so happy!"

I was still sitting at my bedroom window when he came up the front sidewalk, and I waited there until I heard my mother open the front door for him and then the mumble of voices as my father came in from the garden to get

437

cleaned for dinner. In the living room someone turned on the radio. I knew that Jack would be sitting in the chair near the front door where he always sat and I waited till I knew my face was calm enough to face him without looking too happy. Then I went downstairs.

I don't know just what went wrong at dinner. It wasn't Jack's fault. It wasn't his table manners that were poor—it wasn't that at all. He sat very straight just as he should; kept his left hand in his lap while he ate and broke his roll into four little pieces just like it says in etiquette books. So it wasn't that.

We had all sat down at the table, my mother and father at the heads and Jack across from me. My mother had passed him the butter and the cut-glass dish of applesauce with her usual cool care and talked with him while my father was carving the roast. Art and Lorraine added little comments here and there. Martin had called Lorraine right after church to ask her to go out with him that night and she was in a soft-mouthed, benevolent mood. I thought then that everything was going to be all right.

Jack was just saying to my mother, "This aunt of mine that's stopping in Chicago is the one who used to live next to us in Oklahoma." My father should have seen that Jack was busy talking. But he didn't. He had just finished carving the roast and wanted to make room for the serving plates so he passed him the salad, thrusting it right into his hands, and Jack was so startled that he knocked against his water glass, steadying it just in time with his free hand while the salad bowl wavered in the other. He was across the table from me and no one else offered to help. It was agonizing to watch. The salad bowl was large and the table crowded so he balanced it on one hand, trying to serve himself with the double servers with the other and keep up the conversation at the same time. Art kept talking, too, attempting to cover up his awkwardness and pretending not to notice. My own fingers were anxious for Jack's as they fumbled.

And after that everything that happened was Lorraine's fault. She knew Jack had only graduated from high school. She knew that I had never said he was a smart boy. She knew it and yet she kept talking to him as if he were one of the boys she had known at college. Lorraine is like that sometimes. If I had been sitting at the table at the beginning I might have stopped it but I was in the kitchen just then.

Kitty had been quietly toying with her glass and one long-stemmed cosmos that leaned out from the rest until she knocked pollen from it into her milk and I left the table to go to the kitchen for a fresh glass. Someone had mentioned that the flies weren't bad at all for this time of the summer. It was just a casual remark but when I came back with Kitty's milk Lorraine had begun. She was saying, in her schoolteacher voice, "Perhaps it's like in that book. About us being like flies that the gods crush—only this time they got the flies." She laughed pleasantly but no one knew quite what she was talking about.

Jack was buttering his roll, not even listening, but she turned to him abruptly, "You've read that book, of course, haven't you, Jack?"

"What book?" He was startled.

"*The Bridge of San Luis Rey*," she explained kindly. "By Thornton Wilder. . . you know, the same man who won the Pulitzer Prize with *Our Town* . . . ?"

Jack gave her a half-smile of acknowledgment but his face remained blank. Lorraine should have stopped there, right there. Art broke in heartily to ask if anyone would like to go for a good swim later in the afternoon but Lorraine went on with enthusiasm. "I hear," she said, looking first at my mother and then

438

sweeping her eyes around the table back to Jack, "that William Saroyan writes his short stories in only three hours! Imagine!"

"It seems to me that worthwhile things should take more time than that," my mother commented mildly.

"Of course," Lorraine went on with pointed condescension, "that depends on whether you're a genius or not. Have you read his *My Name is Aram*, Jack . . . ?" and her voice trailed off into a question.

Leave him alone, my mind snapped at her. Leave him alone, why don't you? You wouldn't have read it, either, if you hadn't been to college and if you weren't as old as you are! He's only young. You can't expect him to know everything about everything. . . .

Jack looked at her in embarrassment and his lips were awkward with his words. "I don't read much," he confessed and my heart slipped down a little. "I don't read at all as much as I'd like to," he went on, "but, gee, with school and everything . . ." He looked at her in apology and then at me, adding feebly, "I played a lot of basketball and things. . . ."

Lorraine gave him a bright, understanding smile and let him go back to his eating. It wasn't that Lorraine is a mean girl. She didn't talk like that just to make Jack seem like a dull boy, she just wanted to make herself seem smarter. But he didn't know that and from that moment on everything went wrong. Each forkful of food seemed to be a separate problem to him. I saw him look at each piece of roast pork, lift it a little from his plate as if he were wondering whether or not he could make it, and then raise it quickly to his mouth with a jerky, forward movement of his body. He was so scared that someone would start to talk to him again that he ate too fast and kept his eyes glued to his plate in apprehension. Once my mother asked if he would care to help himself to more buttered peas and he stopped eating suddenly and looked at her with a startled "Ma'am?"

The day was suddenly unbearably hot and the knife in my fingers was cold and slippery. When I moved, the cloth of my thin dress stuck to the back of my chair and I had to keep my eyes busy with the salt and pepper shakers and the empty cut-glass applesauce dish to avoid meeting Jack's across the table. It seemed even worse because my mother had tried to make everything as nice as she could. In front of my whole family he had to act like that!

How were they to know that out at Pete's he was different? How were they to know that he had been president of his class at school for two years in a row, or that he had come in second in the state in the basketball free-throw contest? How did they know that he could dance to any kind of music at all, fast or slow, and that any girl in town would be glad to wear his basketball sweater even for one night? All they would remember was that he hadn't even been able to serve himself with double salad servers and that he filled his mouth too full when he ate. In our house where we had never been allowed to eat untidily, even when we sat in high chairs! It all seemed so suddenly and sickeningly clear—I could just see his father in shirt sleeves, folding food onto his knife and never using napkins except when there was company. And probably they brought the coffee pot right in and set it on the table. My whole mind was filled with a growing disdain and loathing. His family probably didn't even own a butter knife! No girl has to stand all that. Never. If a boy gets red in the face, sputters salad dressing on the tablecloth, and hasn't even read a single book to talk about when you ask him over for dinner, you don't have to be nice to him—even if he has kissed you and said things to you that no one has ever said before!

Even now it is hard to talk about what happened next. It was too awful. It was the kind of thing you read about but can't believe could ever happen to you. It sent the tears nipping at my eyes and made a tight ache in my throat till I almost thought I would have to leave the table. You see, we were having ice cream for dessert. Everyone was eating nicely and quietly and Lorraine, just at the moment it happened, was being dainty about selecting a cookie from the plate. I have heard *old men* making noise eating soup and other things but that's different, and I don't care because they are *old* and they perhaps have something wrong with their teeth. But eating such a simple thing as ice cream and with my family sitting there and everything. Jack clicked his spoon against his teeth! He looked up in surprise, as if he was wondering who could have done it, and then went on eating hastily. Lorraine cleared her throat and gave a little ho-hum sound to herself. And then it happened again! Quite by mistake but a definite, neat click, like knocking two water tumblers together. No one said anything— my family are too polite to say anything with their mouths but I knew what they were saying in their heads.

I saw my mother raise her eyebrows just a little. Just a little, as if a quick thought had passed through her mind and my heart shrank up into a tight ball of loathing till I felt that my whole insides would rattle around like a hard, brown peanut in a shell. In my mouth was a bitter taste as if I had been sucking a penny and I couldn't even raise my eyes to look at anyone. Twice! Twice in a house where no one ever forgets to say "Pardon me," or gets indigestion, or neglects to have a clean handkerchief! The utter shame of it sucked the whole hot, bright afternoon dry of happiness and I felt myself slowly begin to hate Jack.

And later on it was the same. My mother suggested pleasantly that we leave the dishes till the cool of the evening and that Jack take our car and drive Kitty and her to the movies. My father had to work on his business reports for the week and the others had plans of their own.

Sitting beside him, I never said a word. There was nothing to say. We dropped my mother and Kitty at the theater and then Jack turned the car north on Main Street toward the park. Any other afternoon it would have been different. Ordinarily we would both have thought of Pete's where Swede and some of the fellows were bound to be playing poker in the dark coolness of a back booth, or we would have thought of having a Coke in McKnight's with its air-conditioned brightness, or even of looking for Margie and Fitz who were bound to be parked out along a country road somewhere. But today was different. I wasn't thinking that kind of thoughts anymore. I sat very still beside Jack but my mind squirmed with repulsion and my lips curled with distaste as I thought of it. Any boy who couldn't even eat ice cream without making noise! Along the street people were walking leisurely, men in their shirt sleeves with the cuffs turned back and girls in summer dresses. A strong tar smell rose from the sun-baked streets and little glints of light shot out from the chromium radiator cap on the car. But I didn't care anymore about anything . . . just sat with my eyes straight ahead.

My hand lay beside me on the plush of the car seat. I was conscious of its being there. I felt Jack turn his head to look at me. Then he looked down at my hand. One move would have done it. If I had turned my head or even moved my hand just a little his fingers would have been on mine and we would have held our hands tight while we drove out along the lake shore and then out toward Pete's and everything would have been as wonderful as before. I knew that but somehow I just didn't care. There was one, small breathless moment, as quick as a thought. But I didn't move and Jack swung the car off Main Street and headed straight home with the afternoon sun glinting on the windshield and the warm air soothing in through the window. We drove straight home and Jack pulled the car into the driveway and opened my door for me. We walked to the front steps and, being very careful to avert my eyes, "Good-bye, Jack," I said.

He said good-bye and then stood looking at me. "Well," he began again, pursing his lips, and then stopped. "Well . . . good-bye, I guess," and I turned to go into the house.

And he hadn't even touched my hand!

And it was foolish of me. I know that now, and I knew then that in the bottom of my mind I wasn't angry, it was only in the very top. It is self-pampering, a sensuous luxury, to let yourself pretend to be angry, if only for a little while, with someone you really like. With summer so short and with college looming up large in September, I don't know why I did it. It was foolish when each day went so fast and each night was only a quick, breathless moment with not nearly enough time for seeing and thinking and wishing.

The next morning as I hung the clean clothes that smelled of soap and hot starch on the rope line, I thought it all over carefully. In the freshness of the new morning with the air warm and shimmering with summer and singing with the sound of the children playing and laundry trucks and my mother busy in the kitchen, I felt oddly ashamed. Jack must have been thinking funny thoughts that morning. He probably hadn't even known what I was angry about!

Margaret, who had the last two weeks of July for her vacation, had left the night before to spend it in Milwaukee with Art and his family. Even though she was engaged, my mother had disapproved at first with halfhearted, habitual disapproval. But she had gone and now the house was very quiet, especially at mealtime, but it gave Lorraine and me a chance to talk together. Lorraine always has to talk to someone and when Margaret is gone she talks to me. Of course, she doesn't say quite the same things and skips a lot she would tell Margaret but we *do* talk some things over.

I didn't see Jack all day Monday, but on Tuesday he called to ask if I would go to the movies with him that night. All day I had a shy, expectant feeling—as if I were going to meet him for the first time all over again and I had to keep crowding the thought of kissing him out of my mind. It isn't good to keep thinking about things like that. You get to look starry-eyed even in the daytime. It was swelteringly hot and we kept the living-room shades drawn all day and Kitty left the kitchen wet and sticky with her several watery attempts at lemonade. My mother was in the basement canning a bushel of early peaches and I went down casually to tell her it was Jack who had just called. She was sitting on one of Kitty's little doll chairs, slipping the skins from the peaches dipped in boiling water, and the air was clammy with a sweet steam, and moisture ran oozing from the cement walls. Bits of the wet skins stuck to the floor where they had dropped and plastered against the side of the big aluminum canning kettle. There were shiny canning jars set in a row, collared with red rubber rings, waiting to be filled. I told my mother about Jack and she pushed her hair back wearily from her forehead and said noncommittally, "I'm glad he called, Angeline. Will you run upstairs and bring me down the sack of sugar from the third shelf in the kitchen?"

Late in the afternoon Kitty went to the store for a pint of ice cream and the three of us ate it off saucers, sitting on the back lawn in the slanting shade of the

441

house. Around us the afternoon was humming with the steady beat of the heat and the sonorous drone of the bees in the hollyhocks and the small, quick wasps with black and yellow bodies that zigzagged low over the short cloverheads. My mother sighed. "You know," she said, "I almost wish this summer was over with heat and rush, and you and Lorraine were packed off to school. There is still so much to do to your clothes and getting curtains and a bedspread for your room . . . Here it is almost the last week of July . . . " And she left the thought in midair.

She is a little sad sometimes. I think it is because we are growing up—my sisters and I. Things that used to be so important aren't the same anymore. We are all beginning to care about separate things now. My heart beat faster with a sense of caution. Perhaps my mother was going to mention Jack. I felt sure that any day someone would find out and begin to ask questions. I don't know just what they would find out or how they would know what was going on in my head but they would guess somehow. They would ask—Were Jack and I going steady? Why did I see him so much? Wasn't I a little young to be *liking* a boy? I didn't want to have to answer things like that.

The grass on the side lawn was parched brown with irregular scallops of green where the shade of the trees shadowed the ground. Kinkee lay stretched in the sun, watching the little mud-colored grasshoppers that skipped in the dry stubble. Out in the garden the flowers were heavy-headed and tired in the steady heat and even the sparrows in the hedge were quiet. "I think," my mother went on quietly, "that I'll just finish up the rest of those peaches tomorrow. I'm not up to canning them in this heat!"

A sudden thought struck me. Wouldn't it be odd if my mother got old! After so long. After so many summers of picnics and parades and long walks around the park in the peace of the afternoon, to be suddenly tired. It is only natural that when your children are big you must be older but somehow I had never thought of its happening to my mother. It made me feel queerly conscience-stricken and there was a strange stiffness around my lips. What a peculiar thing to think of in the bright sunshine of the afternoon!

We went swimming later in the afternoon, Jack and I. He came just after four o'clock and pulled the truck up to the curb, honking the horn sharply twice. He couldn't come in, he explained, for he was in his swimming trunks and a sweatshirt—just finished work and was going out to Pete's for a swim and wanted to know if I would like to go with him.

I hurried upstairs for my suit and a bath towel while he carried on a loud conversation with my mother who was sitting in the late afternoon shade of the side lawn. As I came out the front door, Kitty was sitting on the front steps, fresh from her bath with her braids pinned up and a clean blue playsuit on. She was being very nonchalant about picking the leaves off a bit of twig broken from the bushes, careful not to look at Jack or me. "She wants to go with us," I thought. "She's been so hot all day and she wants to go with us but doesn't want to ask." Her whole attitude was tense with hoping and I knew it but shut my mind against the thought.

"Please, God," I said quickly to myself. "I haven't seen Jack since Sunday and I have so much I want to say to him. Just this once let me be selfish. Kitty can go swimming tomorrow or any other time but not now. Not with us."

Jack and I pulled away from the curb and I waved back at them, but Kitty's face was puckered with disappointment and I knew she was trying not to cry and my conscience turned over within me. As we turned onto the highway toward Pete's, Jack said lightly, "Maybe your little sister might have liked to come along, huh, Angie?"

Someday, I thought to myself, when she is very much older—say eighteen or so—I will explain to her and she won't be angry with me at all.

For the first few minutes I kept my eyes straight ahead, busying myself with the yellow and green summer scenery. Jack was whistling softly through his teeth. Out of the corner of my eye I saw his legs, as tan and smooth as a girl's, and I imagined suddenly how strong and clean he must have looked playing basketball in short khaki trunks. When he pushed down on the clutch, the ligaments moved under the smooth brown skin of his leg. All the antagonism and disgust of Sunday afternoon melted when we were alone together. Jack reached over to my side of the car to get a package of cigarettes from the glove compartment. His arm was very close to me and the consciousness of it made both our thoughts stand still for a moment. I laughed, a little self-conscious laugh, and turned my face toward him. He looked at me, too, just then, and I felt my eyes go soft, and his face was so close that I could have touched it with my cheek; and suddenly everything was just as it had been and I didn't even remember what day it was—that just two days ago had been that Sunday.

Someday when Kitty is very much older I will explain to her and I know she won't be angry with me. She won't be angry at all.

The lake behind Pete's lay flat and glassy in the sunlight. The lawn was green and lush near the water's edge, but farther from the shore it was littered with cigarette stubs, small bits of bottle glass, and faded scraps of red and green firecracker paper left from the Fourth of July. Sometimes people have weiner roasts here and on one side there was a patch of burnt litter where someone had made a fire, and around it lay bits of charred wood and a blackened beer can and the grass was burnt short like curly black hair.

Jack had pulled the truck over into the shade and had gone into Pete's while I put on my swimming suit. Finally I stepped carefully out onto the grass and slammed the truck door loudly to let him know I was ready. His steps crunched across the gravel as he came out and I was almost afraid to look at him. I wasn't sure just what he would look like without his sweatshirt on. I put a big bath towel carefully around my own shoulders and went down to the water's edge, waiting while he pulled the white sweatshirt off over his head and came up beside me. Then he gave a little run to the end of the short pier and took a shallow surface dive that brought him up laughing and shaking the water from his hair while his teeth shone white in the sunlight. His shoulders above the water were smooth and brown, shiny with the wet, and when he moved the muscles in his arms made a barely perceptible ripple. He swam out a short distance and then signaled for me to jump in.

Why is it there is always that self-conscious feeling about looking at a boy in swimming trunks? I think I was afraid that because I had only seen him in clean white shirts or sweatshirts or in his heavy basketball sweater that he might suddenly be thin and scrawny underneath and I would never have known it. Or his skin might be pale and soft like the underside of a frog and I might want to turn away and not look at him till he had pulled on his clothes again. Or maybe it was because my mother had always been careful about things like hanging the underclothes on the inside of the clotheslines, away from the street, and had always told us to pull our window shades down before going to bed at night.

443

The little wooden pier was slippery from the constant wash of the waves that slipped over the old boards, rotting openfaced in the sun. A long, green slime clung to the piles and moved slowly with the water. The lake was warm near the surface and chill near the bottom from the shifting, underwater springs that make Lake Winnebago treacherous. Jack was far out now and the water between us was smooth and limpid. Very near the shore where the trees hung low, a school of quick-tailed minnows glinted in the sun and were gone.

I began to walk out with the easy, languid grace one has in water, and beneath my feet the sand was hard and cold, ridged into regular little ripples. The far Oshkosh shore lay opposite, almost lost in the shimmer of sunshine and a low haze of smoke. When I reached swimming depth the water was warm and caressing on my shoulders and my arms looked very white and shapeless through the water. Jack and I swam side by side, leisurely, until we hit the first sand bar. When we stood up the water was only up to our waists and Jack looked at me with a surprised laugh, "Gee, Angie, you look pretty in the sunlight. Your eyes look like water!"

All around us the lake was flat and motionless, reflecting the sun and the puffs of clouds in the sky, without a movement or a ripple, as if the fish were down, down close to the sand and we were the only moving things in it. We seemed all alone in the smooth, unspoiled loveliness of the water. The sun was warm on our backs and Jack stood with water drops running from his hair and glistening on his face. I had a sudden impulse to reach out and run my finger lightly over the even, dark arch of his eyebrows as he stood looking at me. But there was an odd look in his eyes, an odd, warm look that made my lips tingle as his eyes met mine, and I knew it would be better not to touch him, not even to talk to him, just then.

Instead I turned away from him just a little, trailing my arm gently, slowly through the warm, green water till the ripples made slim, silver bracelets round my wrist.

Later we pulled ourselves onto the slimy little pier and then lay on the grass in the late sun where the trees began to stretch their large shadows lengthwise on the ground. The air was warm and a slight breeze just stirred the surface of the sun-glazed water. Jack looked up at the sky and sighed with contentment.

"Say, Angie—your sister still hear from that Martin fellow?" he queried.

"She sees him sometimes three times a week," I answered, unconsciously coming to her defense. "Why?"

"No reason. Just wondered."

"But why did you ask then?"

"No reason, Angie. Really. I just happened to think of it."

"Does he still come into the bakery for rolls in the morning?"

"Sometimes he does. Sometimes he eats at Walgreen's drugstore when the weather is so hot."

"He's nice, I think," I ventured slowly. I always had a feeling that Jack knew something about Martin that he didn't want to mention.

"Yeah, he's a good guy," he answered laconically and rolled over on his back, covering his eyes against the sun.

"Jack," I persisted, not wanting to let the matter drop. "Do you think he is too *old* for Lorraine?"

"No, no," he said, reassuringly. "He dates lots, lots younger ones sometimes."

444

"What do you mean?"

Jack sat up suddenly and ran his hand over his hair in irritation. "Gee, Angie, don't keep asking me questions about a guy I don't even know. All I see him is when he buys rolls or maybe I might meet him out some night. How do I know what he does or who he dates or anything. . . ?" He pulled a long grass stem and sat chewing the end, looking out over the lake, pretending to squint at something on the opposite shore. I knew he didn't want to talk about it anymore so I didn't probe him further.

Pete's is very quiet in the afternoon. There was only the occasional sound of a delivery truck with beer or Coca-Cola as it swung off the highway onto the gravel parking lot. The sun was sinking low in the west, making hot glass of the water, and a dragonfly as large as a humming bird, with shiny gauze wings, darted toward us and then zigzagged back toward the sun. Here and there on the lawn late dandelions were yellow and bits of broken glass caught the light. I put the towel around my shoulders and lay in almost sensuous warmth with the sky bright and the grass rough on my bare arms. There was a long silence with thoughts going on in it.

Jack sat flicking bits of stick toward the water and without looking at me he said, "You know, Angie, I've known you over a month and a half now. . . ."

I lay still, not saying anything, pretending to be watching the sun that was turning to pink in the water.

"That's the longest I've ever gone with any girl . . . at one time."

Something below the lake moved, making wide, silent rings on the smooth surface. The silence of the afternoon seemed suddenly loud with the rustle of the trees and the soft, sucking sound that even calm water makes against the shore. Something in me was suddenly alive. It was something new, something I had felt only in the last few days. It was warm, strange, and beating, and I wasn't even sure what the feeling meant. And somehow I was afraid to know. My lips felt hot and my cheeks were tense with waiting. Without lifting my eyes to look at him I knew his hand was close to mine on the grass and I could sense his groping for the right words to say.

"We'd better go, Jack," I said quietly. "Please. We'd better go right away." And I tried to keep my thoughts out of my words as I said it.

I had been so happy myself for the past few weeks that I hadn't had time to notice. But that night I realized Lorraine had changed. I wasn't sure just how, but she was different. While she waited for Martin we sat in our bedroom talking. It was close and hot and the night air was like warm velvet. The fluffy curtains at the window puffed out slowly and rhythmically with the summer breeze as if they, too, were panting in the heat. Lorraine's hair was pinned up in a tight roll around her head and she carried a small powder puff in a hankie so she could powder her shiny nose without being noticed. Martin was late and she was restless.

She began cleaning out her purse, arranging the things on the bed. We aren't supposed to smoke in our house, but I knew she did for there were tobacco crumbs on everything. "You know," she said and her voice was tight with agitation, "I almost wish school would start right away. You and I are going to have so much fun, Angie. I'll see that you get started with the right crowd of freshmen from the beginning and we'll really have fun together this year."

"I'd like to get away from all this," she went on.

"From what?" I asked. "From what? Don't you *like* summer?"

"Oh, no, it isn't that . . . it's just . . . well, everything."

"I don't know what you mean," I told her. "I think this has been one of the most wonderful summers we've ever had," and my heart beat faster as I said it.

"It's the sameness of it," she explained. "It's the same every morning," and she then went on in a mock sing-song, "You get up and it's hot, you get dressed and it's hot, you go to work and it's hot . . . I'm so sick of potato salad and cold meat and silly old ice cream and flies coming in the hole in the backdoor screen and having to wash out my slips every night that I could just die! I don't know—" She broke off with a little laugh.

We were silent for a moment and outside I could hear the faint sound of cars going by on Park Avenue and the early evening noise of the summer crickets. "If you and Martin aren't doing anything special tonight, why don't you come to the show with Jack and me?" I ventured. "It will be cooler there and it's nice to have somewhere definite to go."

"No, I think we'd rather not," and her superior tone was back again. "Martin and I never *plan* what we are going to do. Besides, if you are with someone interesting you don't have to *go* any place. That's what I mean is wrong with people in this town. They always have to *go* somewhere and never think how it is to just sit and talk about worthwhile things. It isn't like in cities where . . . well, you know what I mean . . . " and she let the sentence trail off, not bothering to finish it.

She sat thinking hard, mulling over her thoughts. "Do you know," she said unexpectedly, "I think Martin really likes me. . . ."

"Did he *tell* you?" I asked cautiously. I wasn't sure if that was too private a question or not.

"No," she answered laconically.

"How do you know then?"

"I just know. There are ways . . . I can just tell." But somehow her voice sounded tired as she said it.

The last two weeks of July melted away like brown sugar into nothing but warm, crowded memories. I let the inevitable imminence of college ride on the top of my thoughts, never really admitting to myself that it was there. Fitz and Margie and Jack and I went swimming together twice on the hottest days and one night when there was a moon—full and lush with that overripe look—we went sailing with Swede. And one afternoon Jack brought over a quart of ice cream and we all sat eating it on the back lawn. Jane Rady called Jack and asked him to go to a weiner roast with her that night, but he told her that he had a date with me. Margie told me about it later and I couldn't help feeling contentedly smug inside.

I tried to keep myself from seeing that summer was slipping by though everything about me sang with it—the full, warm swell of the July breezes and the full-blown poppies that turned heavy-headed and scattered their petals to the ground. In the garden the corn was ripe and the leaves were satin-shiny in the sunlight, and when I broke open the ears, the rows of even kernels showed through like teeth, in a sudden yellow grin. The tomatoes lay open to the sun, ripe and tight in their skies and crickets burrowed into them from the ground side, nibbling ragged holes in the firm red fruit. The squash vine that trailed between the corn put out a yellow trumpet of a blossom and little green, warted cucumbers lay on the hot earth. There was no more small pink and white clover scattered on the lawn and no damp, hidden corners, close to the house, with fresh, new shoots coming through. The air was heavy and sultry and the earth rich and full with growing. Summer was in its heyday.

Late one afternoon Jack and I went out for a ride along the old creek road. On the bridge over the stream he parked the truck and we got out to lean over the rail and look at the water. The long, hot days had shrunk the creek into a narrow trickle, leaving the green water reeds high and dry in a muck of red clay. As we stood there a farmer with a team of horses clop-clopped over the bridge with a straggling load of alfalfa with tiny purple flowers, and he stared at us in silence as he passed. Long after he had gone, a low, yellow dust from the wagon wheels hung over the road.

"I guess he thinks we're crazy," Jack said.

"Uhuh. I guess he does."

In from the fields came the silken hush of the wind in the tall weeds and the air was honey-sweet with clover. Along the creek, small willows shuddered and showed the white side of their leaves to the breeze and an occasional fat frog plopped into the water, dislodging patches of green-brown scum that lazied along with the current to catch against water reeds farther down the stream. Jack kicked a sprinkle of gravel over the bridge with the toe of his shoe and it splashed with a tinkling sound like small bells. The sun was warm on our heads and shoulders.

"It's getting on so that summer's almost over," he said, musing. "And it seems just like yesterday that school let out."

"It isn't nearly over," I told him. "It isn't much more than half gone."

"Sure it is," he insisted. "About four more weeks and you'll be going away to school. After July is gone, summer is gone."

"Four weeks is a long time, though, Jack, and maybe you can come down to see me at school once in a while—and then I'll always come home for holidays and things. . . ." I tried to make my voice sound reassuring.

"Sure, I know it," he said. "But it's just that it won't be summer anymore and it won't be quite the same."

A bit of bleached wood floated slowly beneath us, bobbing gently, and we watched it till it passed under the bridge and was gone. The coffee-brown water was shot through with sunlight. Jack turned to look me full in the face, squinting a little against the sun. "Gee, Angie," he said in a puzzled voice, "I don't know what it's going to be like around here when you're gone!"

My father had some business in Minaqua in far northern Wisconsin and my mother, Kitty, and I drove with him and spent the weekend. We drove for miles over long, cool highways lined with silent pine woods, strange and dark. All Saturday my mother and I shopped. We bought a playsuit for Kitty with Swiss embroidery and some bright, striped chintz for drapes and a bedspread for my room at college. "Something cheery is good when you're away from home," my mother said.

That night I tried to write Jack a note on hotel stationery but tore it up because the pen scratched and I couldn't think of anything to say anyway. I bought a colored postcard in the lobby with a picture of a tall, stratified rock with an Indian standing on it and wrote, "Dear Jack—You wouldn't believe how beautiful it is up here. The pines are wonderful. Be good and I'll see you soon." The next morning I was sorry I had sent it. It didn't say what I meant. But you can't put on a postcard how much you miss a boy.

I never expected to meet Lorraine and Martin there that night. Except for the few moments at the Fourth-of-July parade I had never seen them out together.

447

Jack and I went down to the Rathskeller by ourselves and met Fitz and Margie there. The Rathskeller is a night club; a dark, down-a-flight-of-stairs sort of place where it is necessary to keep the lights on even in the daytime. There are imitation windows set with leaded-colored glass and arranged with a glow of light behind them to give a touch of reality, but they are really set in the wall below street level. The walls are paneled in heavy wood and the tables and chairs are thick and brown so that the whole room seems to be in a yellow-brown haze all the time. It gave me a dark, excited feeling just to be there.

It was a hot, muggy night and even the breeze was warm, but in here the floors and walls gave off a dusky coolness. The four of us sat at a small table in the corner and I let Margie take the chair on the outside—I felt uneasy to be seen in a place like this. There had been bars in Pete's and Chet's but this place was different. It had such a dark, nighttime look. A waiter in a short, white coat and a pencil stuck behind his ear came to take our order and they all asked for beer except me. Even Margie asked for beer and when it came she poured it herself, tapping the glass with the bottle to keep the white foam from topping the edge of the glass. Then Fitz filled his glass, raised it, and touched Jack's. Then he touched Margie's and they all said something in a chorus that sounded to me like "Roast it!"[4] and took the first swallow. I just sipped my Coke and pretended to know what they were doing. I meant to ask Jack about it later.

Over in one corner was an ornate jukebox with lights inside that made its decorated front shine like murky, colored water flowing upward in a steady stream, twisting and turning until the colors seemed to be braided together. It was a gaudy thing, like a woman with too much rouge on, and the glow it made in the corner of the room was almost warm and tangible enough to touch and the bright, twisting colors added a strange color to the music that came out of the box. There was something oddly sensuous about it. Even when I was talking to Jack I could see it out of the corner of my eye, the slow, blurred turnings of the lights, quietly insistent.

Fitz and Margie left the table to dance and we watched them. There were others dancing, people who were older than we were. Most of the fellows had slick, wet-looking hair that still showed the comb marks—the kind of boy who wears a navy-blue suit with a narrow stripe for Sundays and for best occasions even in the heat of summertime. I remember noticing two girls sitting together at one of the tables. They wore thin blue satin blouses that caught the colored shine of the light of the jukebox, making them seem to move beneath the shiny material even when they were sitting perfectly still. I seemed to remember vaguely having seen them somewhere before. When they danced they stood first very close to their partners and then far away, moving with short, jerky steps and flat, expressionless faces. They never talked when they danced. Fitz danced with his chin on Margie's head and held her hand down far, near her hip. She closed her eyes and they didn't talk when they danced either, but that was different. Jack and I watched them till the glow of the jukebox and the warm dusk of the room mingled together and swam before my eyes in a low-light murkiness as exciting as wine.

We had doubled with Fitz and Margie so often that I had learned not to seem surprised at anything they did. When they came back to the table both had an-

---

4 *"Roast it!"* "Prosit!" Latin for "may it benefit," a common drinking toast, or "Prost"—German for "cheers."

other bottle of beer and we talked together for a short while before Fitz glanced nervously at his wrist watch, saying, "I hate to break this up but we'd better leave you kids and shove off. Margie's mother don't want her going out so much lately so we got to be cautious."

Margie opened her purse and patted her hair in the mirror, remarking coyly, "I know you two aren't going to mind being left alone. . . ."

Fitz looked at his watch again and stammered apologetically, "It's just a little after nine o'clock now but she has to be in early and if you kids don't care . . . well . . . you know how it is. We want a little time."

"That's all right, fella," Jack answered. "Go ahead."

After they left we moved to a table near the big grand piano that was set in the middle of the floor. "They've got a wonderful colored pianist for the floor show," Jack told me. "He doesn't come on till ten o'clock but I want to sit where we can see him as well as hear him. I don't know much about music myself but they say that fellow's got magic fingers."

"He's from Chicago," he explained. "Used to play at the Three Deuces there."

I drew my eyebrows together, trying to look interested, but I couldn't remember ever having heard of the Three Deuces before. And I had only been in Chicago twice.

"You know, that 'home of swing' place that everyone used to talk about," he went on, explaining with his hands as if he were blowing on a trumpet. "That place where they had big jive sessions and stuff—regular Bix Beiderbecke.[5] It burned down a couple of New Year's Eves ago."

He sat thinking, making wet rings on the brown table top with his beer glass. "Used to play there before it burned down," he commented absently.

Just then Martin and Lorraine came in. She was squinting a little to get used to the duskiness of the place and didn't see me at first. I was as surprised to see her as she was to see me, though I had often wondered where she and Martin went at night. Jack stood up as they came over to our table. "Hello there, Angie," Martin said heartily and, "Hi there, fellow, long time no see!" to Jack, pumping his hand and slapping him on the back. Jack looked surprised.

"Won't you two pull up a couple of chairs and have a glass of beer with us?" he asked politely.

But Lorraine put in hastily. "Thanks anyway, Jack. I don't think we'll bother. We were on our way somewhere else and just stopped in for—"

"Sure. 'Course we will," Martin interrupted, and pulled over two chairs from the next table. "We got a little time to spare—especially when I haven't seen this cute young sister of yours for such a long time," and he gave me an exaggerated wink. I had never seen him act the way he did that night.

When the waiter came to our table he said benevolently, "We'll have the same as before for these two and a couple of Scotch and seltzers here," pointing to Lorraine and himself.

"No, thank you," Lorraine interrupted again. "I'll have a Coke if you don't mind."

Martin looked at her. "A Coke . . ." he began incredulously and then looked at me. "Oh, Oh, all right. Sure. Waiter, make that one Scotch here and one Coke."

---

5 *Bix Beiderbecke*   (1903–1931) American Jazz composer and cornetist.

We were sitting near the jukebox and had to talk above the music. "You know, I'm beginning to like this little town of yours." He looked at Jack and me as if expecting an answer. "Yes, sir, it's a pretty good little town when you get to know the people. It's not like the big city, of course, and you can't have the fun you can in some towns, but it's like I always say—if you want fun, you've got to make it yourself."

"You're right there," Jack assented. "I know I've always had a good time here."

"I met an old fraternity brother of mine the other day in Waupun and I said to him, 'You know, if I had a wife and six kids and nowhere else to go there is nowhere I would rather live than Fond du Lac,'" and Martin guffawed loudly. But Jack didn't laugh with him and neither did I. Talking about your home town is like talking about your own mother.

Lorraine was restless and excused herself, going into the powder room. Martin turned to me, "That sister of yours is the greatest one for fixing up. Everytime you look at her it's prink, prink.[6] I tell her sometimes she's going to wear her face right off with that powder puff. Another beer, Jack?" He was trying hard to be pleasant now. I almost liked him.

When Lorraine came back she was freshly lipsticked, with her hair fluffed out, and her heels clicked sharply on the floor. "Come on, Martin, let's go now."

He turned in his chair and looked her squarely in the face, saying very deliberately and a little too loudly, "Let's go! We just got here, didn't we? We've got about twenty minutes to wait until the floor show starts and you want to go already!"

"I know, Martie," she answered coyly, her lips pouted, "I know we just got here, but I want to go. Come on!" and she smiled at him. Sometimes Lorraine talks as if she were sucking sugar lumps.

He drank down the rest of his beer and looked at us, sighing in mock exasperation. "It's like that all the time. Just when we get where there is people and fun it's 'Let's go! Let's go!'" and he squeaked out an imitation of Lorraine. "To hear her talk you'd think she *had* somewhere to go!"

Jack and I sat in an uncomfortable silence after they had gone. I noticed that Martin had nodded to the two girls in the thin satin blouses as he went out the door. We both knew that he hadn't been trying to be funny, and it made me curl up inside because it had been my own sister he had been talking to. Jack lit a cigarette, trying to think of something to say.

"Say, why don't you try a bottle of beer with me, Angie?" he suggested.

"Oh, no! No, thank you, really. I never drink beer."

"Come on," he urged. "Just for fun. One bottle won't hurt you."

"It would look so awful, though—me sitting here with a beer bottle in front of me. I'd look like a witch or something."

"All right," he assented. "I wouldn't want you to have to have one if you didn't want to but I just thought you might like it—this once."

"I'll tell you what," I suggested. "You order me a bottle and if I don't like it you can finish it. Will that be all right?"

"Well, if you want to, Angie . . . but don't do it just on account of me."

"No, no, I really want it. It will be sort of fun, I think."

"Waiter," he called. "Make that two bottles of beer this time. And bring us some potato chips to go with it."

---

6 *prink* primp.

He put his hand very close to mine on the table and looked at me with a warm gratitude in his eyes. It made my cheeks tingling hot and for a moment I forgot what I had been saying. When the waiter brought the beer Jack poured both our glasses. I took a cautious sip and screwed up my face at the flat bitterness. Jack winked at me and I laughed back at him—so much fuss over one bottle of beer. But when he wasn't looking I pushed the bottle over a little toward his side of the table. A girl can't feel like a lady with a bottle of beer before her.

When it was time for the floor show even the dim wall lights were switched off and the spotlight tossed a bright lariat of light around the baby grand piano in the middle of the floor. There was a moment's pause and the pianist came out of the darkness while a spatter of applause from the tables greeted him as he slid onto the bench. I had never seen a colored pianist before.

He sat for a moment, very still, with his head back and his eyes closed, poised and waiting, and then began running his hands up and down the keyboard. His fingers were chocolate-brown against the white keys and his foot kept up a dull beat-beat on the floor; his head bobbed. Jack looked at me and winked approval. This wasn't small-town music at all. With his eyes still closed, the colored man leaned back on the bench, way back, one hand limp at his side and the other like a dark spider on the high notes at the end of the keyboard, quick and supple, tingling the keys in a rippling, tantalizing way until it made my scalp prickle to hear him. Suddenly he swung back into position, both hands playing the whole keyboard, and let out a queer, wild cry that sounded like "Oh, rock the baby!" A laugh went round the room, from table to table, and everyone relaxed. He played on and on, rocking back and forth on the piano bench, rolling his eyes and shaking his head till his white teeth shone like dice against the black of his face. He played "St. Louis Blues" and then "Honeysuckle Rose," singing as his fingers ran over the keys, with his eyes turning up wildly in his head, drawing out the first words of the song long, sweet, and high, with a sensuously slow half-smile on his lips, holding it till I felt myself looking at Jack and laughing uneasily and almost breathing with relief when he swung off the high note into the rest of the piece. He played on and on, sitting in the bright circle of light, his fingers flashing, and after each number he paused, wiping his forehead, while people at the surrounding tables tossed in their requests like pennies.

"Like it, Angie?" Jack asked.

I nodded, sipping my beer slowly, almost enjoying the bitter, unpleasant taste. Jack ordered another bottle for himself. All around us the room was dark and cool with the underground coolness of wet stone, but the piano, its dark wood shining in the spotlight glare, set the air warm and throbbing with its music. The glass of beer made me cozy inside.

Jack leaned over and said quietly, "Gee, this is fun, Angie. Each night seems to be more fun because it's getting near the end. We've only got a few more weeks before you go back to school. . . ."

I didn't notice Jack order again and I didn't notice the waiter come to our table, but soon there was another full bottle of beer before me. The pianist had launched out with a fast piece, singing as he played, his foot on the pedal of the piano and his shoulders keeping rapid time to the beat of the music. Jack put his hand on mine and together we drummed time. At other tables people were knocking their glasses together in a clinking rhythm. I don't know how long we sat there sipping beer. I can't remember that, either. The table top felt like a cushion under my hand. Before long the music of the piano and the sound of the clapping of the audience seemed to come to me as from another room, floating in soft, gentle waves, and the effect struck me as so funny that I giggled!

Jack leaned over to touch my cheek with the back of his hand and I think he was laughing at me. "You're a honey, Angie. I like you so much tonight!"

I said something to him then—I must have said something. But talking was a queer feeling. I felt as if the thoughts came out of my mouth in bright bubbles and floated over to Jack before they burst into words and the sound of them came back to me. Everything seemed to be at a distance. I looked at the beer in my glass, clear as amber, and even to look at it made me feel mellow.

The colored man was playing again with his head thrown back; quick, sharp notes that seemed to trip over each other. His fingers kept up a rapid sparkle over the keys.

"Look, Jack," I remember saying, and the thought first puzzled and then amazed me. "He has red nail polish on! Isn't that funny—for a man?"

"Yeh," he answered laconically, playing with his beer glass. "It's pretty funny." It struck me as so amazing that I wanted to talk about it but Jack looked the other way. And that was all he said.

The whole room was cool with the smell of beer and blue with cigarette smoke. The piano tinkled through my brain in a steady stream and my thoughts seemed to run out with the note sounds. There was a tingle in my head like the sparkle of ginger ale. I could hear myself talking and talking to Jack, the words all mixed up with laughing, and he smiled back at me and I hummed to the music and we laughed and laughed again and I don't remember all the funny things he said. My brain was in a sing-song. It was such a hot night outside that he had worn no necktie; just a white sport shirt, open at the throat, and I had a blurred thought about how much he looked like the picture of Lord Byron[7] that had hung on the wall of my English room at school.

In the corner the face of the jukebox still shone with light and the twisting of the colors made me giddy. My cheeks were too hot now and I thought how nice it would be to feel for a moment the coolness of the night wind off the lake. "You must drive me down to look at the water before you take me home, Jack," I murmured to him. At least I think I did.

He finished his beer and the pianist played one last piece, hunched over the piano, his forehead shining, while he fretted the lower keys in a grumbling boogie-woogie that rumbled out to the very corners of the room, and then slid his long, dark fingers up the keyboard in a flourishing finish. He slid off the piano bench, gave the audience a quick black-and-white grin, and disappeared into a back room.

The bright spotlight was snapped off and the dim wall lights glowed on. The room was filled with an almost pleasant gloom, very quiet and cool, with its damp-stone smell. "We'd better go," I said. "We'd really better go home because I'm so sleepy now."

After that I never drank beer again. It had really been a wonderful evening—but no evening can be that wonderful by itself. That's how I know. I didn't realize it then and I hate to admit it now, but I must have been a little tight that night!

After that evening at the Rathskeller, Lorraine talked and talked about Martin even more than before. She told me about the smooth girls whom he used to

---

7 *Lord Byron* (1788–1824) George Gordon, British poet of the Romantic era.

date when he was at the university—long-haired, pretty girls who belonged to the best sororities; she told my mother how particular he was about everything he ate—never touched salads and didn't like butter on anything but toast; she even asked my father if he knew some man who lived out near Campbellsport who owned a big garage and to whom Martin had sold insurance at the beginning of the summer. Anything just to say his name. I was surprised at her. In fact, she talked about him so much that my mother began to give my father alarmed, raised-eyebrow looks at the dinner table.

She even asked Jack what kind of rolls Martin bought for his breakfast each morning, and how many, and whether he came every morning or bought a two days' supply at once. Jack told me later that he had charged the rolls for two weeks now and owed a little over a dollar and a half at the bakery. Martin phoned for three nights in a row, just before supper, and one night he and Lorraine went out for a Coke together, coming home much later, when we had all gone to bed. She borrowed three university annuals from a fellow who lives down our street—she wasn't just sure what year he had graduated—and looked up his picture. We lay on the living-room rug one evening, she and I, to look at the books together. We found his graduation picture on a back page and under it a list of the activities in which he had participated and Lorraine pointed out with pride that he had as many as any other boy on the page. He looked much younger then than he did now, with a high, white collar and a shiny look—like a man in a brilliantine[8] ad. We found another picture of him standing before his fraternity house with the rest of the committee for arrangements for the Junior Prom, but only half his face showed for there was another boy standing almost directly in front of him. Quite by accident Lorraine found the picture of the girl he used to date and on whom he had hung his fraternity pin when he was a sophomore.

"Where is his pin now?" I asked her.

"I really don't know. Maybe that little blonde still has it," she said. "Some girls are like that, you know, Angie. Never want to give a fellow up even when he doesn't like her anymore."

Margaret and Art drove up from Milwaukee late that Saturday afternoon—Margaret had to be back at work the following Monday morning—and Lorraine showed Martin's picture to them. At suppertime she announced that maybe he was even going to come to Chicago to work in November; he was writing to the main offices to see about a transfer. "You know, he is the kind of man who would be good in any territory," she commented. "And then if he is down that way he can come to the dances at school next year and he probably will be able to get blind dates for Angie too. That would be good," she added significantly, "because it takes some girls a long time to get started." I wondered what had made her change so suddenly; what had made her so sure of herself.

She even said that Martin might drive her back to Chicago when college classes begin in the fall. Art looked at Margaret, winked and said, "Hey, hey, what goes on here? We've been away too long, Maggie."

Jack went out with Swede and Fitz and some of the other fellows that night and Lorraine asked me to walk up to McKnight's for a Coke with her. "It's all right for me to be seen without a date," she explained lightly, "when everyone knows I'm practically going steady anyway. . . ." Martin had called just after supper to say that he wouldn't see her that weekend—he was driving up to

---

8 *brilliantine* a perfumed hairdressing oil.

Eagle River and wouldn't be back until late on Tuesday. He asked her then to go out with him the following Sunday.

"That's his birthday," she told us happily when he had hung up. "I don't know just how old he will be, but it certainly is something to have him ask me out for that night when he knows other cuter girls in town and everything, isn't it? We'll probably do something very special and have dinner somewhere first. I don't know what I should wear. Either I will have to get something new or borrow something of Margaret's . . ." She was giddy with excitement.

Under his breath my father muttered, "Just lucky you're going back to school in a month, young lady!" and went huffily back to his paper.

I have never known a hotter July. There was a soft, hazy, constant heat that hung over everything and never let up—only seemed to turn dark with evening. In our garden the black earth dried and crumbled brown, shrinking away till the twisted tomato roots showed above the ground. Out in the country the fields were a parched patchwork and only the trees were still green against the dust-yellow roll of the hills.

One afternoon after work, Lorraine walked uptown to pick out a birthday present for Martin. She had thought of giving him a year's subscription to *Time* magazine but came home with a wallet instead. "I think he'll like this," she explained, "because it is such a 'mannish' sort of gift." It was brown pigskin with a long zipper in it and special compartments for driver's license and personal papers. On one inside corner she had had his initials "M. K." stamped in gilt. That was Tuesday night and after supper she wrapped it in white tissue paper and I held my finger on the red ribbon while she tied three small bows. "Maybe I should think of something clever to put on a little card to go with it," she suggested. "I won't give it to him till Sunday though."

Jack came over about nine o'clock and we went for a walk around the park that night. Even the wind off the water was warm. When we came home Lorraine was still up, curled in a chair by the front window. "I just thought I'd sit here and read a bit," she yawned, "in case Martin calls when he gets back to town. He is supposed to get in tonight. It's too hot to sleep anyway."

On Wednesday he didn't call either and Lorraine puzzled over it all evening. "He must have been delayed in Eagle River," she explained to me. "That must be it. There wasn't a postcard for me in the noon mail or anything, was there, Angie?" No, I told her. There hadn't been a postcard or a letter. Nothing at all.

Kitty and I went for a ride with Jack the next afternoon. It was so hot that he pulled up near the water's edge at the park and opened the doors of the truck to let the breeze blow through. The sand dredge in the harbor was still at work, its engines rhythmic in the stillness, and the lake was almost perfectly calm, greenish near the shore and deep blue farther out. Here and there ominous shadows lay on the surface where silent undercurrents shifted beneath. Along the break-water small waves lipped over the rocks, spreading their foam in quiet frills, then slipping back into the stiller water.

"Your sister and Martin figure out what they're going to do to celebrate Sunday?" Jack asked, casually making conversation.

"No," I told him. "He didn't get back yet."

"Oh, didn't he?" his voice pricked up in surprise. "I thought he was supposed to come back on Tuesday night."

"He was, but he evidently didn't make it," I explained. A quick suspicion shot through my brain. "Why, what made you ask?"

"Nothing. I just wondered what they were going to do, that's all."

454

"But I mean, what made you think that he was going to get back on Tuesday night?"

"Because you told me he was," he answered.

"I know that," I insisted. "But why did you use that tone of voice when you said you thought he was supposed to come back Tuesday?"

"Don't be silly, Angie," he said, looking down at his hands. "I didn't use any tone of voice."

"You sound so queer. Why don't you look at me?" I demanded. "You talk as if you saw him. You talk as if he *did* get back—did he?"

"You're the one who ought to know that," he answered and started the motor of the car. I was certain then that something was going to happen.

Thursday and Friday limped by. On Friday night my father came home for the weekend and Lorraine took Martin's birthday wallet from the corner of her dressing-table drawer, unwrapping it carefully to show to him. "Look, Dad," she said. "Tell me honestly, if you were a fellow would you like this?"

He turned it over and over in his hand, looking into all the special compartments and trying the zipper. Then he looked at my mother and winked, "I'm still a fellow," he answered, "and I *do* like it so I guess that makes it all right." My father is always in a good mood when he comes home from work. He must have been trying to sell an order at a new house under construction, for I noticed there was red clay on the soles of his shoes.

Lorraine stayed at home all Saturday afternoon and all Saturday evening in case Martin might call. On Sunday she sat out on the back lawn where she could hear the phone easily if it should ring. No one mentioned him to her. Once she said to me, as if I had been arguing with her, "But, Angie, he wouldn't have asked me if he hadn't wanted me to go!" I knew what an empty, aching feeling she must have inside her. If only she hadn't talked about Martin so much earlier in the week!

In the later afternoon I brought out a deck of cards and she and Mother and I tried to play bridge on the grass of the back lawn; but the wind kept flipping the cards about and Lorraine wasn't interested anyway. So we just sat, not talking at all, and let the late sun fall warm across our legs. The breeze was sweet with the hay smell of grass long burned by the sun. A flock of wild canaries had flown in from the fields, flitting quickly in and out of the trees, and bobbing like fat yellow blossoms on the topmost branches.

Each moment dragged by, trailing suspense behind it. I couldn't make myself believe that he really wasn't going to call at all! We had our supper on the back lawn as usual and Kitty had to close Kinkee in the garage because she kept sniffing at the plate of sandwiches on the grass. It had been a long, warm day and the sun went down slowly and shadows were low on the ground, while the clouds above were still light and the trees were silhouetted black against the soft pink of the sky. The seconds were as slow as minutes. There was still no word, and watching Lorraine sitting, waiting, my heart felt as raw as cubed steak.

In the last glow of early evening sphinx moths came out, with their soft, furred bodies like small birds, blundering from flower to flower with their wings whirring and setting the tall honeysuckle rocking in the dusk. Mosquitoes hummed in the garden hedge and a meadowlark called, perched on the handle of a spade stuck in the earth at the far end of the garden path. Art was lying on his back on the cool grass, his head in Margaret's lap, looking at the first new stars that were just twinking yellow in the pale of the evening sky. Lorraine gave a short sigh and then went into the house and up to her bedroom.

After a long time my mother said to me, "Angeline, you'd better go up and speak to her."

I waited for a moment in the living room, trying to decide what would be the best words to say. Lorraine was sitting on the rug in her bedroom with the little dresser lamp beside her, its pink shade off, and the bare bulb glaring bright. She was sitting with a long darning needle in her hand, carefully picking at the gilt initials inside Martin's wallet. Neither of us spoke.

"See, Angie!" she said triumphantly, holding it up. "Look, I've got it all off now but one little part of the M. Probably Dad can use it or something. . . ."

I looked at her closely. She hadn't even been crying. I took the wallet and turned it over in my hand, holding it to the light. "That's nice, Lorraine," I said quietly, "You'd hardly ever know." That's what I said but there were needle pricks in the leather and I could still see where the initials had been.

That night, lying in bed, I could not help wishing that there wasn't so much sadness in growing up. It was all so confused in my mind. There had been the long, long days of being young and not wondering about tomorrow at all and thinking in a strange, forgotten child's world. There were days when my thoughts were as mild as feathers and even an hour seemed like a long time. Then suddenly it was like turning a sharp corner—you were older and the things that counted when you were young didn't count anymore at all, and looking back, you couldn't even see them. Growing up crowds your mind with new thoughts and new feelings so that you forget how you used to think and feel.

When Lorraine was a little girl she didn't know about people like Martin—none of us did. Nothing she had ever done had prepared her to feel the way she felt that night. We had never known about anything unpleasant. Our whole lives had been little-girl lives, crowded first with thoughts of kindergarten and going for exciting walks with the class in the early gray of spring to gather pussy willows along the creek banks, and eating oranges on the school playground at recess, oranges with skins so thick that they gave off a fine spray of fragrant oil when they were peeled. Somewhere in the years, Kitty was born and we seemed bigger because she was so little. Quiet memories of her slid into my mind. I could remember putting her into her crib on warm summer nights, her skin cool and baby-soft through the thin cotton of her nightgown; and then before long she was sitting by herself on the living-room rug and the floor was always strewn with painted-eyed dolls and scribbled-up color books. On the piano stool there is still a white mark where she set her wet box of water colors. After Kitty the days went faster, merging into long Wisconsin winters with snowdrifts piled almost up to the living-room windows, and hot, still summers with the sunlight pouring through the trees like yellow honey. Lorraine and Margaret and I were changing. Things that had once been so important didn't matter anymore. Carnivals still came to town and set up their Ferris wheels in bright wheels of light against the night sky and pitched little striped tents all stained brown with rain, but we no longer felt the same ecstatic thrills. And we didn't go out barefoot in the wet grass hunting for tiny, green-brown toads that came out after the rain. Our thoughts were on different things.

When Margaret was seventeen she had her first date with a Western Union messenger boy, and then one day I found a tube of lipstick hidden in the pocket of Lorraine's coat and shortly after that my mother bought her special Castile soap to use because her complexion wasn't good. Finally Lorraine went away to college, Margaret met Art, and we all began to live our lives separately. And no one said anything or seemed to think it odd.

I had seen it happen to both of my sisters and here was I, letting it happen to me. Every moment I was awake I was thinking of Jack, letting him into my house and into my days. Everything had changed. Until this summer telephones had never been important to me and now, always, I was waiting for it to ring. Growing up is like taking down the sides of your house and letting strangers walk in.

Lorraine lay beside me in bed sleeping—I think she was sleeping. We had both gone to bed early and quietly, not mentioning Martin. I had lain awake, waiting for her to say something, but she didn't; she hadn't even moved or turned her head on the pillow once. The night air made a light whistle through the screens and blew warm over the thin top sheet, and the trees on the front lawn seemed to be crowding their leaves stifflingly close to the windows. Somewhere, far off in the sky, heat lightning winked.

And I lay there wondering sadly how long—how many days and nights—it would take Lorraine to forget about Martin. How long before she could listen to soft music on the radio, see cars shining in the sun, or blue smoke rings floating without some thought of him coming into her mind. It would take a very long time. And for her there would be no more summer.

In the morning the sky was a dazzling blue with clean, white puffs of clouds scattered high over it. There was something brightly expectant about the morning—as if the sun had been up for hours and hours just waiting for the rest of the world to wake. Even before breakfast the air was hot and sparrows were bobbing in the hedges and the plants in the garden were drooping. There were big, dry cracks in the earth as wide as my wrist. "Looks like another scorcher," my mother remarked cheerfully. "Fine weather for the last day of July!" The house was buzzing with hurried, Monday morning noises, with my father talking through his coffee and his paper and Kitty keeping up a steady excited chatter that no one bothered to listen to, while Margaret click-clacked about the kitchen in a pair of flat, wooden-soled sandals she had bought in Milwaukee. My mother had got up earlier than the rest of us and the sonorous hum-hum of the washing machine in the basement came up to us as we ate breakfast.

But the brightness of the morning didn't last long. We had just got the first clothes hung on the line when a light wind came up and a few dark clouds floated into the sky out of the west; and by noon they had gathered together, dark and sullen, heavy and sagging with rain. The hot, dry air changed to an oppressive mugginess but still the rain didn't fall. The clouds were lined up, gray and sulky, as if they were waiting for something and the day dragged sluggishly by in a tiresome, clammy heat. The clothes took a long time to dry and I spent the afternoon ironing while my mother sat at the kitchen table sewing on buttons and mending little tears in Kitty's playsuits. It was so quiet that all my thoughts seemed to have a yawn in them.

At five o'clock Jack came. I had seen the black truck pull up at the curb and had run to open the door even before he knocked. I was wide-awake again the minute I saw him and the house no longer seemed hot. The storm had finally broken and the first rain fell in slow, round drops that spotted the sidewalks dark, drying up almost at once on the warm cement.

"Hello there, Mrs. Morrow," Jack said to Mother. "They've got you pretty busy, I see!"

457

"I like to get these things put away mended right away," she explained, snapping off a bit of thread with her teeth. "Angie's been ironing all afternoon and we'll be all through in about half an hour."

"We send our washing out," he said, but added hastily, "but that's because my mother helps down at the bakery sometimes and just doesn't have time to do it herself." Jack is always very careful not to hurt people's feelings; very careful not to pretend about anything.

He was restless that afternoon, seemed worried about something. He was sitting on a kitchen chair opposite my mother while I finished the shirt I had been ironing. I noticed he hardly heard what I said when I spoke to him. He took a cigarette and lit it at the kitchen stove—we were out of matches—and I took a saucer from the dish cupboard for the ashes. He just nodded at me and in a moment crushed the cigarette out. I had never seen him nervous before and it puzzled me to know what he was thinking. He shouldn't even have been away from the bakery so early in the afternoon.

"Mrs. Morrow," he said suddenly, "mind if I take Angie for a short ride?"

"No, of course I don't," she answered, "but it's almost suppertime."

"Oh, I'm sorry," and his tone was crestfallen, "I didn't realize that. I wasn't even thinking what time of day it was."

He looked at me to say something and my mind worked quickly. "Mom," I asked hopefully, "we could be back almost right away?"

"You may go if you like, Angeline. I don't mind at all, only I don't want you to miss your supper. Just be back by six." She gathered up a pile of clean, ironed clothes in her arm. "I'll get these things put away before Lorraine and Margaret get home."

I pulled the iron cord out of the wall socket and fluffed my fingers through my hair. Just as we were going out the front door my mother called after us, "Bring home some lemons, will you, Angie? It won't take you a minute to stop at the store and I think the children might like iced tea for supper."

"We will," I called back.

The rain was coming down harder now and together we ran for the car. The storm seemed to be rolling toward us high above the dark clouds, rumbling like a bowling ball. In the trees the sparrows cheep-cheeped in excitement and fluttered among the leaves.

The moment we were in the car Jack said impatiently, "I've got to talk to you, Angie. Where shall we go?"

"Out to the park maybe?"

"No, not there," he said, shaking his head. "I don't want to run into Swede right now. I talked to him a little while ago and he said he was going out to put an extra rope on the boat. This looks like a pretty bad squall coming up and that water gets plenty choppy."

We both thought a moment. "How about down past the creek on Willow Road," he suggested.

But I didn't want to go there. "That's not a—a 'day-time' place," I explained.

He started the car. "Let's just make it Pete's then. I could stand a Coke anyway."

The rain was falling at an angle, blown by the wind and dashing slantwise against the car windows. As we turned onto the highway the storm wind swept low in from the lake, making furrows in the waving grass along the fields. We passed a farmyard where a little boy was driving a team of horses into the barn and the chickens ran across the yard squawking, the wind parachuting their tail feathers and pushing them from behind.

458

"Have a cigarette?" Jack said, pulling out his package. It was a standing joke between us for he knew I never smoked, but he took one himself and I held the steering wheel for him while he rummaged through his pockets for a match.

"The farmers can really use this rain," I remarked. "This has been the hottest, driest July I can ever remember." It was falling so hard that the drops splashed back off the highway and the bushes at the roadside bent beneath its weight.

There were already puddles in the gravel lot as we pulled in behind Pete's. Jack shut off the motor and was silent for a moment. "Aren't we going in?" I asked.

"No," he answered. "Let's just stay here." The rain made a noisy pit-pat on the car roof and with the wind-shield wipers shut off, the water ran down the windows in a steady sheet.

"I thought you said you wanted a Coke?"

"I do. But we'll get that later. I want to talk to you alone, Angie."

All the way out to Pete's I had been wondering what it was he had to tell me; what it was that made his forehead all wrinkled with thought. As often as I had seen Jack and as much as I liked him I still felt almost afraid to be alone with him. I still had the self-conscious feeling that I should have worn a better dress and that I should have brushed my hair again before I had gone out with him. When he looked at me directly I almost felt that I knew what he must be thinking—he had gone out with so many girls who were prettier than I.

Now he started the motor again and pulled the truck to the very edge of the gravel lot as far from Pete's as we could get, very close to the water. The sky hung low, dark, and forbidding, and the lake was gray-green, choppy with waves, angry in the wind and lashed by the gray rain. Lake and sky were storming at each other in almost visible argument.

Jack shifted toward me and sat for a moment, absently picking at the cracked leather of the car seat. His face was thoughtful. His hands were as brown as his face and there was a white ring on one finger where he had changed his class ring from the left hand to the right. He was as ill at ease as I was and kept moistening his lips as if he were trying to work up the courage to say something.

I looked back at the wooden shelves in the truck behind us. They were still lined with several boxes of doughnuts and a gooey lemon meringue left from the day's sales and the air was sickeningly sweet, smelling like melted marshmallows. The front seat of the truck was suddenly very small and close.

"Jack," I said, "It's awfully hot in here!" The still, hesitant tension of waiting made me giddy with excitement.

He rolled down the car window on his side. "There. That better?" With the window open the storm seemed even nearer. Cool, wet air blew across my face and the tall old trees on the lawn bent low, twisting and moaning, wrenching at their trunks and writhing in a strange sympathy with the tormented water. Gray waves rolled crashing toward the shore and thrashed against the wooden pier, slapping like bare hands against the flat rocks. High sprays of foam tossed into the air and the wind was heavy with the damp, suggestive smell of fish. It gave me a strange, wild feeling, restless and lonesome. From the gray-green tumult of the water and the weird twistings of the trees we might have been miles and miles away from everything. Long, sharp lightning tore at the clouds and angry thunder snarled after it, loud above the noise of the lake. I had almost forgotten about Jack for a moment.

"Angie, look at me, will you?"

I turned toward him, my heart pounding in my throat. And as always when I looked straight into his eyes my clear, practical thoughts began to slip away from me as if they were buttered.

"I wanted to come out here where there was no one else so I could talk to you, Angie. Something's happened that I want to tell you."

The thoughts in my head were beating with my heart and I found myself watching his lips for the next words rather than waiting to hear them. Outside the wilder waves were leaping the rock barrier of the shore, puddling the grass beyond, and occasionally far-flung foam dashed itself against the windshield of the car. Jack's hand on mine was warm and insistent but his voice was strangely stiff and scared. I had never seen him like this before.

"I don't know quite how to tell you this, Angie. I wasn't going to tell you at all—at least for a while. But last night I talked it over with Swede and we talked and talked and he said what else was there to do?"

He paused again, not knowing how to go on. Taking another cigarette from the package in the pocket of his shirt, he lit it and flipped the match out the window. The damp breeze ran clean, soft fingers through my hair and laid its cool touch on my neck.

Jack took my hand again and began in a hurried, determined voice, "See, Angie, I don't mean that I'm a fast boy or anything but—I've been around a little. Not like Swede and Fitz maybe—I mean, well. I've dated a lot of girls though . . . and I've kissed a lot of them." He wasn't looking at me now.

"I know that, Jack," I answered quietly.

"I even went steady with Jane Rady for about two weeks last year. And I let her wear my class ring for a while . . ."

I didn't know what he was going to say; or what he wanted to say. It might mean that after today I was just going to be one of the other girls with him, but somehow I couldn't believe that. Early in June I might have believed it. Even last week I could have imagined what it would be like not to see Jack anymore, but not now. Not after everything.

The inside of the car was suddenly very small and secret with the storm outside thrashing around us and the rain pelting on the car roof. The whole wildness of it was pounding inside of me and there was a throbbing ache in the palms of my hands. The suspense in Jack's words, the warm slowness of his voice, made my throat dry with anxiety.

At last the words broke from him so quickly that he sounded almost as if he were going to cry. His forehead was puckered up with earnestness. "Gee, Angie, honey," he said, "I don't know what goes on in your head or what you feel, but I like you so much I think about you all the time! Nothing like this ever happened to me before. All the time—at work, when I'm with the fellows, and when I'm alone at night—all the time I think about you and wonder what you're doing and what you're thinking. When I first went out with you I just liked you a little bit but now it's getting worse and worse. I like you so much that I don't know what to do about it!"

The car was so quiet that the drumming of the rain on the roof was deafening. Everything else was breathlessly still. I wanted to reach over to touch the smooth, pulsing brownness of Jack's wrist as it rested on the steering wheel and to feel the warmth of his cheek, but my hands stayed open and empty in my lap.

His voice was strangely low and calm now. "I've thought about this for a long time and I know what I'm saying . . . I'm in love with you, Angie!"

460

Words tingled at my lips and I felt my hands trembling but there was nothing I could say. I didn't even know what I was thinking. Love is such a big word. And no one had ever said it to me before.

After a long time Jack started the car, the wheels crunched on the wet gravel, and we turned back toward town. Along the highway, lights showed blurred through the rain and the storm sky was dark with the darkness of night. Turning down my own street I saw that the light was on in our dining room and that my family was sitting around the table at supper.

It wasn't until I was inside the front door and Jack had pulled away from the curb that I remembered we hadn't stopped to get lemons for the iced tea.

AUGUST

IN A MOVIE it might have ended there. In fact, I almost thought it would for I didn't know myself what could come next. I was so bewildered and mixed up in my head about the whole thing that my first thought was to call Jack on the phone in the morning, just to hear his voice and to make sure that I hadn't been dreaming.

But I didn't, for that morning my mother wasn't feeling well. She was still in bed when I woke, the pillow wrinkled and the top sheet rumpled from her tossing, so I went downstairs softly to make fresh coffee, bringing it up hot and steaming, but she couldn't touch it. I knew then that she was really ill. I woke Margaret and Lorraine and they got ready for work in careful quietness, opening and closing doors gently, their faces worried and their lips pursed in silence. Each tiptoed in cautiously to say good-bye before she left, easing the bedroom door shut behind her. The whole house was filled with soft, whispery stillness.

Kitty slept late while I straightened my mother's bed, drawing the window shades carefully to keep them from squeaking on the rollers and slipping a clean pillowcase on the pillow, cool and smooth beneath her head. It was alarming to have my mother ill. It was like having the clock stop. Her cheeks were flushed and she complained that her head was throbbing, like hammers beating at the back of her neck; so I brought a cloth wrung out in vinegar and an ice pack, setting it gently on her forehead. Then I waited a moment, helplessly. There seemed to be nothing more I could do. She looked so quiet lying there with her eyes shut and her hands palms upward on the sheet. Already the warm air of the room was sharp with vinegar.

"Mom," I whispered, "anything else you would like?" but her lips didn't move though her hand gestured wearily on the sheet. The door closed quietly behind me. I realized then with guilt that I had noticed her being tired often lately, in little, quiet ways. . . .

Kitty had just waked and, sensing from the stillness of the house that something was wrong, she came tiptoeing out in her nightgown, her eyes round with questions and her braids fuzzy with sleeping. I explained in whispers that Mom didn't feel well and that she should dress quietly and come downstairs quietly, without her shoes. And to be very careful about slamming doors. She nodded solemnly and padded back to her room on feather-soft feet, turning back to me with a cautious finger on her lips. Kitty can make a game out of anything.

Downstairs the sun lay in bright squares on the kitchen floor as I cleared away the earlier breakfast and set Kitty's toast and milk on a napkin on the end

461

of the table. Even running the hot water into the dish-pan made too much noise and I had to wash each piece of table silver separately, sliding each clean plate carefully onto the pile on the kitchen shelf. The vacuum cleaner raised such a quick banshee wail[1] that I shut it off at once and just dusted the front room, plumping up cushions with soft fists and straightening the pictures on the wall. After that there was nothing to do.

Kitty had to be kept quiet and away from the house so I brought out her old straw sun hat and a basket and sent her to pull weeds at the far end of the garden. I watched her as she inched along the rows, bent over so her playsuit pulled short, showing her small, round legs brown in the sun. Once I went upstairs softly, opening the door just a little. My mother was lying quiet, with the ice bag slipped down over her eyes. She was breathing as if she were asleep, evenly, with an odd weariness.

By noontime Kitty had grown long-faced and mournful from playing by herself, so I packed a quick lunch of bread and butter and three small round tomatoes and sent her out to the creek to have a picnic. The tomatoes were still warm-skinned from lying in the garden sun and she took salt and pepper in a twist of wax paper to sprinkle on them, skipping off toward the Field with the dog behind her.

Shadows squatted short in the noon sun, so I set a tray very carefully with a clean linen napkin—crisp toast and canned chicken soup, steaming hot. I carried it upstairs hoping that by now my mother would be feeling well enough to eat something, but she was still asleep and her breathing was tired and regular, so I tiptoed back to the kitchen with the tray. I had never known her to sleep so late into the day before.

The house was so still that every step I took seemed to make the floor creak and the clock in the dining room ticked loudly through the whole downstairs. It was as annoying and sharp as fingers snapping. During her lunch hour Margaret called to see how Mom was feeling and I hurried to the phone, picking up the receiver before it could ring twice.

I wasn't used to having so much quiet time to myself and somehow I didn't like it. With no one else's thoughts about, it was necessary to think my own—and yesterday afternoon at Pete's was too disturbing to mull over by myself. It only made me more restless, for each thought was like tickling my heart with a feather. Sitting in a chair by the living-room window, I tried to read; but the trees outside sent in mottled leaf shadows that moved restlessly on the square of sunlight on the rug and I couldn't keep my mind on the print. My mind was drumming its fingers. The afternoon lagged by in a low haze of heat and quiet till I began to think lazy, ho-hum thoughts that made my eyelids heavy. Then I realized suddenly what was wrong with me—I was lonesome. Between twelve o'clock noon when Kitty had gone on her picnic and four o'clock while the house was still quiet and noiseless, I had used up all my own thoughts, all the comfortable ones, and now I was just lonesome. And I realized, too, what an empty place our house would be if my mother weren't in it. Thinking of it, I felt uneasily as if I were going to cry. I almost wanted to go upstairs to turn the water faucet on loudly in the bathroom or rattle a window shade just to wake her up . . . A house is no use at all if there are no noises of living going on in it.

---

1 *banshee wail*   The banshee is a female spirit in Gaelic folklore; its wail was said to presage a death in the family.

My mind was so turned inward with thinking that I didn't hear the truck pull up at the curb; didn't even know Jack was there till I heard his footsteps pounding up the front steps.

Hurrying to the front door with my finger on my lips I whispered at him, "Shhhh, Jack. Not such big feet! My mother doesn't feel well!"

He whispered back a loud apology and stepped in, closing the door behind him. "Angie, I've got something to tell you!" His voice was different from yesterday, quick and eager, and there was a bright, excited look on his face. He stayed standing as he talked.

"We're going back to Oklahoma!"

His words snapped my mind into alertness. "Jack . . . ! Why?"

He went on in a hoarse whisper, as loud as his natural voice, "We're all going, my mother and Dad and me. I've known for a long time that we might, but I never mentioned it because I always thought the plans would fall through!"

My heart slipped down inside me. "When did you find out for sure?"

"Just at breakfast this morning—my mother and Dad decided. You remember that time when that aunt of mine was in Chicago and they went down to see her? That time I had dinner at your house?" I remembered, I told him. "Well, they all talked it over that day and yesterday my father had a letter from her and this morning my mother and he decided that we would go back—definitely."

The whole idea was so new, so unexpected, that I couldn't jar myself into comprehending. I had thought of college. I had thought of Jane Rady or of a new girl but never of something like this! "But why, Jack?" I asked in a small voice. "I thought your mother and father *liked* it here. All your friends are here."

"But it's just five years since we moved away, Angie. We have friends down there too, and my dad has two brothers and my mother has a sister there. It isn't as if we were going down to strangers."

"But why go at all?" I insisted. "You have your house here and everything. I don't see why . . ." It was such a radical step, moving hundreds and hundreds of miles. Our family had never moved at all ever since I was born. People who live in our town stay there. It might be all right to go away for a vacation or to move a few blocks, but hundreds of miles!

Jack's voice was very earnest as he explained, as if he wanted to convince me that it was necessary to move, that it wasn't his idea, but I could tell he was just repeating what he had heard at home. "You see," he said, frowning, "the bakery business isn't so good here. There is a lot of competition and we're just a small place. Down in Oklahoma my dad figures he can go in with his two brothers and really make a go of it. He's been thinking about this for a long time. They didn't want to while I was in school because that would break up things for me, but now I'm graduated there really is nothing to keep us here." His last words limped out lamely.

The significance of what he had said seeped into my mind slowly, word by word, each bursting like a bubble into an inkling of realization as I stood staring at him. We had never talked about things beyond Pete's or Chicago at the very farthest and now—Oklahoma! The idea was too big to fit into my head all at once.

He fumbled with the doorknob. "Well . . . I've got to get back," he said. "I just brought some things home to my mother from downtown and I was supposed to take the truck right back to the bakery but I just thought I'd stop over. We aren't going till next month though, Angie."

He waited. I knew he expected me to say something; that I was sorry he was going, that I hoped something would happen to change the plans, anything at all. But I couldn't. I couldn't break down the shyness that always kept me from saying what I really thought and felt. It was, somehow, too embarrassing to be affectionate in the daytime and I couldn't even make myself touch his hand.

His voice was hesitant. "I could have called you, Angie, but I wanted to see you anyway."

"I'm really glad you came, Jack, but it's just that I'm so surprised I can't talk for a minute." Upstairs the bedsprings creaked as if my mother had waked and was tossing. Jack heard it too, and whispered, "I'd better go, but is it all right if I see you tonight?" I nodded stiffly and he laughed. "Angie, don't look so scared! There are still trains and buses and besides I haven't gone yet." He shook me a little. "We'll talk about it tonight."

Upstairs my mother asked for a glass of ice water, and when I brought it I had to hold the glass with both hands to keep the ice from rattling. The bedroom was hotly stuffy and sour with the smell of vinegar, the bedclothes tossed and twisted. "I so hate to be a bother to you children, being ill this way," she fretted, half to herself. "But I do think I will feel better by tomorrow. It's just the heat, I think."

My lips trembled with soft words but we aren't the kind of a family who loves each other out loud. "Wouldn't you like to change rooms, Mom?" I suggested quietly. "The shade of the trees has been on Kitty's room all afternoon and it's so much cooler than this. I could put on clean sheets in a minute. . . ?"

"No," she answered weakly. "Perhaps before supper, but I just don't want to right now. I'm a little tired, Angie." Her hands lay limp on the sheet and her head was heavy on the pillow, as if her neck was too weary to hold it up.

"Perhaps I can sleep again for a little while."

"Are you sure there's nothing I can get," I urged, "nothing you would like to eat?"

"In a little while I'd like a cup of strong tea but not now . . . Did I hear someone downstairs a few minutes ago?" she asked, her eyes still shut.

"Yes, that was Jack."

"Did he want you to go out for a drive? Go if you like, Angie, I'll be all right lying here."

"He's gone now," I told her. "But that's all right—he didn't want anything—special." There was no need to talk about it now. Later, when she was feeling better, and when I had had time to realize it myself, there would be opportunity enough. Jack was going away and there would be weeks to talk about it.

"That shade could go down just a little lower and then I'll try to sleep again. Make whatever you like for the children's supper, will you?" and her voice trailed off. Quietly I fixed the window shade and smoothed the pillow under her head.

Downstairs again I kept hoping that Kitty would play out at the creek until suppertime. There was so much to think about, I wanted the quietness now. All I had ever known about Oklahoma was vague stories I had heard about people striking oil down there and a few scenes of desert, spiky cactus, and milling cattle that I remembered from Western movies. None that seemed to fit in with Jack. Certainly cowboys didn't want bakery goods! Jack belonged in drugstores, swimming behind Pete's, or playing basketball in a school gym somewhere. I couldn't imagine him anywhere else. It struck me then that he hadn't said *where* in Oklahoma he was going to live, but I felt sure it would be way down near the southern border; probably almost into Texas. There was an old geography book in Kitty's bedroom, I knew, but I didn't want to look the state up; I didn't want to know how many miles there were between Wisconsin and Oklahoma.

Jack came over early that night and dried the supper dishes for me. After that we sat out on the front steps. I needed to talk to him alone, even if I didn't know what I wanted to say. The night air was warm and filmy, hanging loose around us like thin, black chiffon. Beside the front steps the pine trees were fragrant with the same cool spicy smell that lingers over pine forests. Yet there was a quiet lonesomeness about that night, a poignant stillness that made my voice sound small and hushed, hardly like my own.

"Jack, I forgot to ask you where you are going to live in Oklahoma." He was sitting two steps below, resting on his elbows with his head back and his hair almost touching my hand.

"We're going right back to where we came from," he explained without turning. "It's a pretty big place called Shawnee—about third largest in the state next to Tulsa. I went all through grade school there."

I remembered then that earlier in the summer his cousin had mentioned a little girl in a white house who used to live near Jack; a little girl Jack had liked. It was a white house with pine trees in front of it, his cousin had said. And probably it had green shutters and a broad back lawn, the kind of house a pretty girl would live in. I wondered vaguely, not really caring, if she were still there.

It would be a different life without him: I could feel it already. Probably I would slip back and back into the old self-consciousness that made even walking into McKnight's an agony. But it wouldn't do to have him know what I was thinking. "What are you going to do down there?" I asked. After all, we still had almost a month left.

"Well, I'll still be with my dad, of course. My uncle has a bakery there and we'll all work together. Dad thinks he can make a go of it." And suddenly his tone was casually defensive. "I suppose you wish I were going to school some more, don't you, Angie?"

All summer long he had talked as if I were ashamed of his not going to college; as if he were ashamed of it himself. He went on now in the same half-apologetic voice, "I'd like to, Angie—you know that. But I've got to stick with my dad. I guess I'll have to get educated my own way."

. . . Without Jack there would be no more Swede or Fitz and no more nights at Pete's. All the summer days would slip by as they had in other years, not meaning anything. There would be no reason for sunshine or the tangy, fishy wind off the lake. It made my throat ache with lonesomeness even when he was sitting so close to me that I could smell the clean soapiness of him and could have touched his hair with my hand.

He lit a cigarette and I could smell the blue smoke I couldn't even see in the darkness.

"Angie," he said, turning to me, "I think I'm growing out of the bakery business. I can't tell my dad that—not yet—but it's not what I want to do all my life. He gets sort of a happiness out of it but I am tired of it already. I'm tired of sweet sugar smells." He pondered a moment, with his lips puckered in thought. "There's something . . . disgusting about eating anyway."

Just as he couldn't tell his dad, so I hadn't been able to mention it to him, but I had never liked it, either—his being a baker. It didn't seem right that a tall boy with such a fuzzy crew cut and smooth sunburned skin should wear a big white baker's hat and work with vanilla and powdered sugar all day.

465

"Have you decided what you would like to do instead, Jack?"

"I don't just know, Angie. But I like to do 'hard' things. Sometimes I think I would even like to be a farmer. I still have some relatives out in Rosendale who farm—it's good, clean work. Last summer I spent about two weeks with them and I loved it. I talked to the fellows about jobs to see what they wanted to be and that, but Swede doesn't care much what he does and Fitz thinks he'd like to work in a men's store—he *cares* a lot about neckties and things."

He puffed at his cigarette. "I wouldn't like that because I like to do things that make me feel big. I like to row a boat; I like to lift heavy boxes down at the bakery—things that make you feel as if you have muscles." His voice grew louder as he talked about it. "I don't know if you know what I mean, Angie."

"I do, I do," I exclaimed, surprised to realize I knew exactly what he meant. "I know what you mean, Jack—it's like shaking rugs out of an upstairs window on a spring day. You can *feel* things—the air is cool and it's good to have a grip on something. The feeling comes to you through your hands, you can feel it on your cheek—you can almost *see* what you feel, it is so wonderful. Is that what you mean, Jack?"

"That's just it, Angie! You've got it," he said in excitement. "I never knew that anyone else felt like that. I'd like to do work that made me feel all the time the way I feel when I'm in swimming—as if my legs are long and hard. I *feel* the way they *look* in the water." He was talking fast and holding my hand so tightly that my knuckles hurt. He realized what he was doing then and both of us laughed.

"Gee, Angie, it's a relief to talk to a girl who knows what a fellow's talking about."

He stuck his legs out in front of him, stretching and leaning back, looking up at the sky. The night was so pricked bright with stars, like a page from an astronomy book, it hardly looked real. His voice went on in a dream sing-song. "What I'd really like to be is a transport pilot, Angie. I'd like to take a ship up at night when it was as black as this and you wouldn't even be able to see me. The tail light and the wing lights would look like stars and no one would know there had even been a plane up there at all till they noticed there were three stars gone."

He was leaning back so that my hand touched the warm brownness of his neck and his crew cut felt fuzzy against my bare knees like the fur of a teddy bear. "Way, way up," he whispered to himself, "so the moon would shine on the wings."

After a little while Lorraine came out. She had spent all evening in the bathroom combing and recombing her hair, parting it first on one side and then the other, critically. Now it was twisted up in tight curlers and knotted in a big red kerchief. Her face looked very small and pinched with no soft hair fluffed around it.

"Hear you're going to Oklahoma, Jack," she commented sharply, as she sat down on the steps beside us. "You're lucky. Wish I were getting away from this town myself."

"He won't be going away for a month though," I told her. "He won't leave until I leave for school," and I felt suddenly reassured for having said it. If I could actually talk about it I mustn't care so much myself!

Jack didn't stay long after that—he and I couldn't really talk with Lorraine there—but after he had gone we stayed out on the steps, thinking in silence. It was a night for thinking. I sat with my hand around my knees trying to urge myself into a belief that everything I had heard that day was true. Lorraine was picking apart a sprig of fir tree with her sharp fingernails.

I don't know how long we stayed there, without saying a word, and I didn't even hear her speak until she repeated loudly, "Angie, did you or didn't you?"

"Did I or didn't I what, Lorraine?"

"I said," she repeated with slow sarcasm, "None of you ever liked Martin very well from the beginning, *did you?*"

His absence had been brooding silently over the whole house ever since the Sunday of his birthday when he had broken the date with Lorraine and I knew the tension would have to crack sometime. He was the kind of boy that a whole family remembers and, often, wholly unrelated things would make me think suddenly of his hands and the odd habit he had of slowly flexing and unflexing his fingers as he looked at them and the perpetual soft sarcasm around his mouth. But Lorraine was waiting for me to answer.

"We liked him—of course, we did, Lorraine. Mom asked him to come with us on the Fourth of July picnic, didn't she? And we always were nice to him when he came over. . . ."

She had been so quietly thoughtful all evening that I was almost afraid to hear what she was going to say next.

"You weren't nice to him, Angie. You weren't rude to him but you weren't nice to him, either, none of you. But none of you ever understood him, that was all." There was no resentment, no bitterness. It was just something she wanted to say and she was saying it.

"You know, you didn't like him because he was different from us. He cared about different things and thought that other things mattered. That's why I liked him. He is a big-city boy all the way through."

Her words were hurrying out now, one after another and I could tell it was almost a relief to her to be talking. "I learned things from him that I never knew about before," she went on. "Lots of things—I know what it means when people are really happy, when they are really alive. You all feel sorry for me—you and Margaret and Art—but I don't care. I saw him lots of times when none of you even knew I was out with him!" she added triumphantly. "I can't even count how many times I've been with him, it's been so many. You will never know all the things we talked about and all the things he said. I know everything about him. I know what he likes to drink and how he smokes a cigarette and what kind of clothes he likes a girl to wear and how he looks when he's angry—you all thought I just dated him like any other boy. You didn't know he *liked* me, did you?"

"And no matter what ever happens," she said defiantly, "no matter what ever, ever happens; no matter what anyone thinks and no matter whether I ever see him again—I'm not sorry!"

She was no longer talking to me. She was only saying out loud the things that had been pounding in her head for days and days and the words came out now, cold and calm, as if she knew very well what each one meant but didn't care anymore. Sitting there, I felt oddly that I had never even known the girl; that she wasn't my sister at all. Not now.

The moments were long and tense as if both of us were waiting for something, somewhere to answer, to make her take back what she had said. And suddenly her hands were limp on her knee and her voice was slow and heavy, "Angeline, I don't know why I'm pretending when it isn't true. This isn't how I meant to grow up. I've heard of other girls . . . but that isn't how I meant to be. I don't want to pretend . . . but nothing will ever be the same anymore!"

She sighed with a little tired sound and I kept looking up at the stars, not wanting to see her face just then. And when she spoke again her tone was as dull, as flat as milk of magnesia, "Oh well, Angie. I guess it doesn't make much difference anyway."

We stayed there a long, long time for there was a soothing kindness in the wind and in the restful silence of the night and it was I who moved to go into the house first. Lorraine followed. My mother had been asleep for hours and the house was quiet with the breathing quiet of sleeping people.

My heart felt so hard it hurt inside me and as we tiptoed upstairs Lorraine touched my arm, whispering, "Angie, don't tell anyone I mentioned him, will you? Everything will be all right. I guess the night just . . . got me." She laughed to herself. "Don't worry. I won't ever mention him again."

It seemed only moments until morning and I woke with the sound of my mother's voice calling. The fever flush was still in her cheeks as I brought her a drink of ice water and her voice was still incredibly tired. It gave me an odd chill in the early aloneness of the morning. The hem of the sky was just faintly pink as I pulled her shades against the rising sun and, shutting the door softly, I went down into the half-light of the living room. Sleepy-eyed and curious, the dog came up from the basement, her tail wagging slowly in a contented stupor.

Once up I hated to go back to bed, so I made fresh coffee in the kitchen, deciding to wait up until the others waked. Kinkee nosed companionably around my bare ankles and then, lying down in the corner, went back to sleep. Except for the intermittent hiccup of the coffee pot percolating on the stove the house was quiet, breathlessly quiet. I opened the window wide to look out at the garden, fresh, green, and awake in the early morning with the clean smell of growing things. The air was like crystal and slowly the sun came up, sending streaks of apricot light across the blue of the sky. The cool air seemed to go straight down to the tips of my fingers as I breathed.

It is odd how one can feel like someone else early in the morning—bigger, cleaner, so much more alive. The dew on the back lawn, caught with sunlight, the quick twittering of the sparrows in the hedges—all seemed to be happening especially for me. It was going to be another August day, mellowed with sun; another day for thinking and feeling everything. It was wonderful and even the thought of Oklahoma didn't seem so gray in the freshness of the morning. We still had a month between us.

The strong smell of the coffee, the wind coming in from the lake, and the very fact that it was morning, filled me with a new exhilaration so that I dared to let myself play with a thought that I had shooed from my mind for the last two days. Such adult boldness is almost sinful, but ever since Jack told me in the truck behind Pete's I had wondered. But no matter how hard I tried to imagine, my lips wouldn't say it. Love is such a big word.

Later that day I brought the stepladder from the garage into the house to get the two big trunks for school out of the attic. Carefully I eased them, one at a time, out of the trap door in the roof, while Kitty stood below holding the ladder and chattering directions up at me. Both locks had to be fixed and I cleaned the trunks out carefully before sending them away with the repairman. In one was an old blue gym suit and a pair of gray rubber tennis shoes that made the inside of the trunk smell like old balloons. In the other were some papers of Lorraine's from school—an incomplete chemistry notebook, a sheaf of English themes, and a dance program with a browned gardenia stuck between the covers. The gym suit I threw into the clothes hamper and put the tennis shoes into the garbage can, but the other things I saved for Lorraine.

When she came home that afternoon I asked her what should be done with them.

"What did you find, Angie?"

"Just some old papers, a dance program, and a withered gardenia that looked as if it might have been a souvenir," I explained. She looked them over curiously, leafing through the papers, and then picked up the dance program. "This is from the spring dance of my sophomore year. So is the flower," she mused, and then suddenly gathered them all together in a crumpled heap.

"Just burn them, Angie," she said. "I'm not going to save anything anymore."

By evening my mother was feeling well enough to sit on the back lawn in a garden chair, still weak and thin-voiced but her cheeks had cooled. I asked her if she would mind my going out for a little while that night and she answered, "Of course not, dear. You go. Lorraine and Margaret will be here with me, and besides I think I will only sit up for a little while anyway." It worried me to hear her, for I knew she was patient and soft-voiced like that only when she was very tired. She is more gentle then because she hates to bother anyone by being ill. There is almost a sadness about her.

Jack had asked me to go for a ride that evening and he and Swede came over together to pick me up. He came down the back sidewalk, his face flushed with embarrassment, Swede trailing behind. "I certainly hope you're feeling better, Mrs. Morrow," he faltered. "Angie told me you were in bed yesterday and I thought maybe you would like this." He had been balancing a pie very carefully between two cardboard pie plates and he held it out to her.

"I asked my mother," he explained, "and she said that even if you weren't feeling well this would be all right to eat because it's lemon and there's only simple things in the filling."

My mother was surprised into silence but Margaret, sitting beside her, spoke up quickly saying. "Why, Jack, you honey! If that isn't nice. I just hope there's enough for a piece for all of us."

He smiled sheepishly and Lorraine took the pie from his clumsy hands, bringing it into the house. I heard her open the icebox door to slip it in.

"Really, Jack I can't tell you when I've been so pleasantly surprised." My mother's voice quavered a little. I couldn't tell if she were going to laugh or cry—sometimes she cries at the most surprising things. "Are you sure you and your friend wouldn't like to have a piece with us now!"

"Oh, I'm sorry," I interrupted, "I didn't introduce you, did I? Mom, this is Swede Vincent, and Swede, these are my sisters, Lorraine and Margaret, and the little one, Kitty, is out playing along the block somewhere."

They exchanged hellos, Swede jerking his head forward to each in turn, and then there was an awkward silence. "Swede is the one who sails the boat so well," I ventured.

"Of course, I remember," and my mother took it up smoothly. "You graduated in June with Jack, didn't you?"

Swede answered with a few embarrassed nods and a few mumbled words, smiling as if his face were starched. No one would ever believe he had been one of the most popular boys in the senior class last year. He seemed so uncomfortable I suggested almost at once that we leave and he sighed audibly, bowing to my mother with a hasty, "Very glad to have met you, ma'am" as he backed down the sidewalk. Jack nudged me and laughed.

Safe in the car, with the motor running, he soon got his confidence back. "Which one of those sisters was which now, Angie," he asked.

469

I explained that the one who had taken the pie from Jack was Lorraine and that the other one was Margaret. "That's the one I meant," he exclaimed with relish. "The one with the long hair and the low voice. That's what I call cute," and he licked his lips in mock appreciation. "Boy, that's something!" All his old swagger was back now.

Jack nudged me again quietly and winked.

Swede had a date with Dollie that evening and we had to cross the railroad tracks and drive beyond the river to get to her street. The house was gray and shabby and across the front ran a low wooden porch that sagged down to a mud lawn, pounded hard and flat as if children played on it often. There was a little red wagon across the sidewalk.

"Just honk!" Swede said. "Dollie don't like me to come in after her."

Jack honked the horn sharply twice and someone swung open the front door, bawling, "She'll be right out!" and the door bounced back on its hinges. The top half was made of screening and the lower half was of brown cardboard, stuck in the wooden frame, and on one side of the porch was an old car seat, set up as a couch.

"Dollie's the oldest," Swede explained, half in apology. "There's four kids younger."

Just then an upstairs window screeched in its sash and Dollie stuck her head out and waved, "Be right with you, Swede," and the window slammed down again. A few moments later she ran out, banging the door behind her.

"Hi, there, kids," she said to Jack and me, and "Hello, you big thing" to Swede, snuggling up to him playfully. Her face is so round and her mouth so baby-soft that next to Swede she looked like a doll.

"Is Pete's all right with you?" Jack asked.

And from the back seat Swede shouted, "Don't know where else!"

Long hot days and sudden rains had given Pete's a stuffy, musty smell and shot new, crooked cracks through the plaster. There were still ribbons of red, white, and blue crepe paper twisted in the lattice around the booth, hangovers from the Fourth of July, and the jukebox was blaring out music that rocked to the ceiling. We took a back booth and Swede ordered a Coke for Dollie, lit her cigarette, and went out to the bar. "He always does that," she giggled.

The old parrot in the corner was scrawking to itself, irritated with the heat, and the floor around the cage was littered with broken peanut shells, and the old bird swayed on the perch, breast feathers ruffled. It was cross and so dirty that we always took a booth as far away from the cage as possible.

Jack and I danced together once and then Swede came back from the bar, crowding Dollie into the corner of the booth as he sat down, nudging her with his elbow till she giggled at him to stop. "You old meanie," she pouted. While we had been dancing she had printed her initials and Swede's on the wall with lipstick and was coyly waiting for him to notice. She looked at me and giggled again.

But he finished his cigarette, flipped the butt at the parrot who scrawked and fluttered on the perch, rolling its yellow eyes in anger, and said, rising. "Let's get out of this firetrap. This is the kind of night to be outside," and he winked at Dollie. She drank down the rest of her Coke quickly and followed him, fluffing out her short hair with her fingers, signaling to us to come on. I guess she forgot all about the initials.

"We might as well go too, Angie," Jack suggested. "We can take a ride and, if you like, we can come back here again later."

470

In the car we turned the four windows down and the night wind came in, gentle and cool as water. Dollie sang as we drove in a soft, round voice as if her lips were pouted, and Swede joined her with a low boy-voice, improvising bass notes and joining in on the chorus. It was a beautiful summer night.

Jack turned off the main highway onto a dry country road that spat up gravel against the sides of the car and sent bits of stone stinging at the windshield. The road twisted before us, taffy-colored in the moonlight, and the moon shifted first from the right side and then to the left as we turned, laying shadows all around us. Dollie's singing dropped off to a quiet hum and then, after a while, stopped altogether. We drove and drove and the landscape was weirdly melancholy in the moonlight, touched with a lonesomeness and mystery that eluded it in the daytime. The trees along the roadside showed a light side to the moon, but secretly shielded the quiet, black shadows that lurked behind them, while on either side the fields lay flat and open. Something about the whole night made me want to whisper.

We were far out in the heart of the country now, lonesome with single barns and dark silos. Jack turned into a narrow, muddy lane, and bushes reaching out along the ditch brushed the car. The wheels caught in the deep, dry ruts and swerved to one side. "Jack," I said, "let's stop here."

Without saying a word, without asking why, he pulled the car to one side and shut off the motor. Swede and Dollie were silent in the back seat. To the right was a broad field, spotted with dark bushes and rimmed with a line of dark trees. Behind them the moonlight was clear and mellow, sending long, lean shadows across the ground like thin fingers. "Jack, I'd like to go for a walk right now. Not far. Just out to where those bushes are," and I pointed.

Swede sat up straight in the back seat and shouted, "You kids *crazy?* If I'd known you wanted to go walking we could have left you in town to walk round the park!"

"I just want to go as far as those dark bushes, Swede," I explained, turning round to him. "It all looks so odd in the moonlight and I've never walked in a field like that at night before. Don't you and Dollie want to come?"

"No, thanks," he answered, his voice slurring. "Dollie and me can be more comfortable right here in the car!"

Jack leaned over to open my door and the thick roadside weeds brushed as high as the running board. I stepped through them carefully and he took my hand to jump the low ditch at the edge of the road. Puddles from the last rain lay in the hollows, glassy in the moonlight, and the ground on the other side was spongy beneath our feet.

As we ran across the field the ground was bumpy beneath our feet like pastureland and I could hear him breathing hard as we went. Night dew was on the grass, cool and wet about my ankles, and here and there grew clumps of wild field daisies, their petals still open and white in the moonlight. Jack let go my hand and ran ahead. I tried to keep up with him, laughing and panting, stumbling in the darkness while my feet slipped on the wet ground. He didn't stop till he had reached the trees and waited there till I came panting up to him, my shoes heavy with clay. The trees were farther apart than they had seemed at a distance, with broad, squat, half-stumps in between. I sat down on one of these to rest, and the sides were furred with layers of white fungus that crumbled like paper between my fingers, giving the air a damp, mossy smell like wet, brown leaves. Jack sat down beside me.

From where we sat we could just barely see the car, black and shadowy at the edge of the gravel road with a small red wink of a tail light. No one but Jack would have come out here with me, without even asking why. I guess he *knew* why. We were near the dark clump of bushes I had seen from the car and the leaves were cool against my arm, their undersides wet with dew. I was still panting from running and laughing at the same time, a delicious feeling. The trees around us were old and tall, with thin, straight trunks and leaves that rustled high above us. Something quick, probably a rabbit, moved in the bushes.

"I'm glad we came out here," Jack whispered to me. "You can't really see the moon from inside the car." I nodded.

A leaf from the bushes brushed my hand and I recognized the touch. Picking one of them I handed it to Jack. "Feel this," I urged. "Feel how fuzzy it is on the other side. These are probably wild raspberry bushes."

He rubbed it gently against his cheek. "Oh, yeah," and his voice was slow with awe. "It feels just how Dollie looks like *she* feels—from looking at her, I mean." I laughed to myself to hear him.

Between the trees thick weeds grew high, black and secret in the moonlight; everything a different shade of darkness. All around us were muted night sounds as if the trees and bushes were whispering among themselves. Both of us sat listening. "Angie," he said suddenly, "did you know there is no such thing as sound!"

"What do you mean—no such thing as 'sound'?"

"Well, I'm not sure if I can explain it to you," he went on, "but it's what our teacher told us in science last year. For instance, if you break a balloon or something there really is no sound. There are sound *waves* sent out but unless there are ears—on people, of course—to pick up the vibrations, there is no sound."

"That hardly sounds right to me," I puzzled . . . "I never heard anything like that before."

"Sure, Angie, and the teacher told us that long ago, in caveman times, if those big dinosaurs went crashing through the forest, if there was no one there to hear them, there was no noise at all! Do you see now what I mean?" he asked.

"Maybe I do," I told him. "But it still doesn't seem quite right. If the dinosaurs made noise and still it couldn't be heard, I wonder what happened to it?"

He put his arm around my shoulder. "Now look, Angie, it's like this. Listen. Say that right now we aren't here, you and I. Say we're back in the car with Swede and Dollie or that we're still out at Pete's. There's no one here. There isn't a single car on that whole stretch of road. All of a sudden one of these trees cracks in the trunk and falls over. There is vibration but there is no sound at all because there is no one to hear it. Now do you see?"

I tried to crowd my thoughts into one small space to concentrate. In my mind I could see the bare field in the moonlight with the dark row of trees standing. It was deadly silent. No sound. No one to hear. Suddenly one of the trees sways a little, its top branches heavy. It sways again and then suddenly it topples over and falls full length on the ground. But it made no noise at all. It was like a feather falling on feathers. But the thought of the tall tree so silent in the darkness was eerie, almost terrifying, and I shivered. Jack's arm tightened round my shoulder, "Cold?" he asked. I shook my head.

I knew Swede and Dollie would be wondering where we were, what was taking us so long, but there were things I wanted to talk to Jack about. I had wanted to talk to him for a long time. For months there had been something inside of me, a disturbed, excited feeling as if there was something I should do at once but I was never sure just what it was. I thought Jack would understand. It was such a quick, urgent feeling and yet all very bewildering. I felt that I should

472

learn to dance better; that I should know how to drive a car; that I should read more. It seemed suddenly as if I had never done anything in my life—that everything was still ahead—and I wanted to know if Jack felt some of the same eager restlessness. I wanted to know but I didn't know how to ask.

"Jack," I ventured, "tell me something. Don't you wish sometimes that you had studied more in school? That you hadn't wasted so much time?"

His answer was hesitant. "I don't know as I'd say that, Angie. I had a pretty good time."

He didn't understand what I meant so I tried again. "But, Jack, don't you feel sometimes that you should have read more—that you've wanted your mind to be bigger so you could understand what goes on? You know what I mean . . ." He was sitting looking out into the darkness, hardly listening.

I wanted him to understand so badly, I almost shook him. "Jack, Jack, listen to me. This is important. I got it figured that I could be a smart girl and a smooth girl if I wasn't scared of so many things—if I didn't spend so much time wondering why I'm not what I'm not. I could be as smooth as Jane Rady if I stopped thinking about myself, don't you know that, Jack?

"You and I could start now to work on ourselves so we would be, maybe, great people when we grow up. I could brush my hair every night and you could read a lot so we would really be something. Do you see what I mean, Jack? Everything can be so wonderful if you work at it. . . ."

Somehow I still hadn't said what I wanted to say and the words tripped over each other, trying to sort out the right ones. "It's just that I feel we are wasting time. I think we are different from Fitz and Margie and Dollie—and even from Swede. Jack, it seems sometimes that I can't ever do things 'enough.' When I eat, everything tastes so good I can't get all the taste out of it; when I look at something—say, the lake—the waves are so green and the foam so white that it seems I can't look at it hard enough; there seems to be something there that I can't get at. And even when I'm with you, I can't seem to be with you . . . enough." That wasn't quite what I had meant to say and I let the words trail off awkwardly.

The night was suddenly very quiet except for the wind in the trees and the sound of the crickets singing—a pulsing chant that hung low to the ground. It was a pregnant, breathing silence and the whole field was throbbing with the still mystery of shadows and moon-light. I realized then that Jack hadn't been listening to me at all. He was watching me and his hand was on mine and his face was very serious in the dim light. His hand was on mine and then I felt the light touch on my wrist that sent a vague stirring through me and then his fingers were warm on my arm. The night seemed to be waiting; too still. "Jack," I whispered. "Jack, whatever is the matter with you!"

His voice was low, almost husky. "You know darn well what's the matter," he said.

But I didn't. I really didn't, and in a few moments I took his hand and we crossed back over the field to the quiet car.

After a while I tried not to count the days. Each night when I went to bed I pretended that I was just going to bed and nothing more; that it didn't mean marking off another day. I tried not to let myself think, "This is Friday and after this weekend we will have three more and that will be all." I fixed my dreams so carefully that I woke each morning almost believing that this was the beginning of the summer and not the end.

But even if it was only August there were already signs of summer's dying everywhere. The poppies in the garden that had been tousled pink blossoms only a few weeks before were now full-blown and hung heavy with busting seed pods, scattering the seed like little black bugs to the earth. The corn leaves dried in the sunlight and rustled with wind, while the fine, silken hair that hung from the ears shriveled, tobacco-brown. And I knew by the tomatoes that summer was ending. The vines sprawled luxuriantly over the earth still, but the runt tomatoes ripened before they were full-grown, not trusting the sun to shine many weeks longer. Small, white-cocooned webs of spider eggs appeared on the undersides of the clapboards of the house. There was a new ripe lushness about everything; not a fresh, bright greenness as in early summer but a full, heavy maturity that made everything look overripe and basking in the sun.

Jack noticed the change, too, and drove me out to look at the lake one afternoon. Dog days had come and the lake was thick with sea grass, rolling toward us in full, lazy, green swells. Water birds, with white arcs of wings, swooped low, reveling in the warmth of the air. It was almost impossible to feel sad. There was too much hidden excitement in the weather itself.

And something had changed in me too. What in the beginning had been a quick, breathless thrill was now a warm, beating gratitude that bordered on contentment. A strange, bewildering contentment. My feelings toward Jack were different now, fuller, richer. I was no longer afraid to look into his eyes or to touch his hand when I talked to him. I felt much older than I had in June and just being with him made my lips feel softer, smoother.

One night we went to the Fond du Lac County Fair—Fitz, Margie, Jack, and I. The fair is an annual county event and stirs our town for days. Weeks before, black and white banners had been hung low over Main Street, announcing the coming horse races and stock show, and little boys stuck handbills on front porches, printed with splashy ads for the carnival features and sideshows. All the rest of the year the buildings at the fairgrounds stood drab and empty, but for the week of the fair they were sprayed with whitewash and little red and blue flags shot up along the roofs and around the doorways. For several days before, the rutted roads that led from the main highway into the fairgrounds were lined with truckloads of vegetables and noisy livestock, and farmers led in their prize horses, the tails braided stumpy with ribbon and the manes shiny. The whole fairgrounds reeked with an earthy, animal smell.

We went to the fair the third night after its opening and it was as crowded as a dance floor with people bumping and jostling, shoving along. Fitz and Margie were waiting for us just inside the gates. It was still early so we decided to leave the Ferris wheel till later and walk by the sideshow tents, looking at the gaudy-colored posters and watching the barkers and the come-on girls first. We saw people craning their necks in front of the Hawaiian tent show and we stopped too. It was advertised as the largest show on the grounds and the barker wore a bright-red shirt and a flower *lei* twisted around his neck. There was a bare wooden stage with two hairy-stemmed palm trees on each end and four girls in the center, swaying gently, disinterestedly. Fitz whistled loudly between his teeth and Margie nudged him in the ribs, giggling and whispering. Other people crowded around us, shoving and pushing until we four stood almost at the edge of the platform. The barker shouted and pounded on the ticket box till the crowd grew larger, pressing in a gaping semicircle all around the tent, while the four girls waited, talking among themselves and staring down at the faces staring up at them. When the crowd got large enough one of them brought a ukelele from the tent, plunking at it tunelessly, singing as she played while the others twisted and swayed in a loose-hipped hula, coarse grass skirts swishing noisily as they moved. They all wore flat tennis shoes and no stockings and their legs were red with welts of mosquito bites.

The blond dancer on the end was younger than the rest and she kept watching Jack with a slow, easy smile as she danced. "That one on the end's got a case on you," Fitz remarked, his hand over his mouth. The girl on the stage whispered something to the dancer next to her and they both looked at Jack, laughing and thinking with their eyes.

"Let's get out of here," he said suddenly, pushing his way through the crowd behind him.

But Fitz caught his arm. "Naw, wait, Jack," he urged. "This is good. I want to see what happens."

Just then the girl with the ukelele twanged out a weak finale and the dancers turned to troop in under the flap of the tent. "Only ten cents for each and every one of you. Women and children alike," the barker shouted, slamming down the tickets. "Ten cents for the biggest musical dancing show on the grounds! Show going on inside at once—only ten cents. Get your tickets here!"

Just as she turned to go in the tent, the blonde called back to Jack, "Come on in, boy. For kids like you it's free—all of it." She looked at him a moment with her queer, easy smile and followed the others inside.

"Wow!" Fitz exploded. "You've got it on the ball! I want to see the rest of this!"

"We're not going in," Jack said, tersely.

"Come on," Margie pleaded in a sugar voice. "This is the first thing we've run across tonight that's really been fun. Come on, Angie, tell him to come on in. This is good."

I looked at Jack but said nothing for I didn't want to go in, either—women like that frighten me. Around us people who had heard the girl call to Jack stood waiting, staring curiously to see what he would do.

His face was dark and angry and he muttered to Fitz, "Shut up and get out of here." Fitz looked at him open-mouthed and then followed us through the crowd.

"Gee, Jack," he said in a puzzled voice when he caught up to him, "I didn't want to get you mad. I didn't think—"

"Let's just forget it," Jack answered abruptly.

"But, gee, Jack, all I said was—"

"Skip it, Fitz, will you?" and Jack turned and walked the other way.

After that the evening was spoiled. Fitz kept trying to explain that he really hadn't meant anything and Jack kept saying that was all right he wasn't angry; and yet all the time he was scowling and walking along stiffly with his hands in his pockets, hardly looking even at me. Just to break the tension, I suggested we go up in the Ferris wheel. In the seat above us, Fitz kept rocking till Margie squealed in fright but Jack just sat beside me, looking down and saying nothing. Beneath us the people were only round, dark heads and the lights were strung in bright necklaces around the booths and tents. We could look out past the fairgrounds to the highway where the car headlights were creeping in a bright line and the whole scene below us looked like a needlework picture in black and yellow.

Back on the ground we walked past a fun house with ugly pasteboard faces stuck on the front of it that let out groans and weird music, while inside the people shrieked and laughed, muffled by the walls. We passed hot-dog stands,

475

and popcorn stands that smelled deliciously of hot butter, and a lemonade booth with lukewarm lemonade in a huge glass barrel, floating with lemon rings; and we stood watching the merry-go-round with bright, dappled horses, shrilling out its loud, up-and-down music. But the fair wasn't fun anymore. Jack wasn't enjoying it and he showed it. His hands were still jammed in his pockets and he hardly heard me when I spoke to him.

The crowds, jostling and pushing, were suddenly annoying, while earlier in the evening they had all been part of the fun of the fair. Sometimes large families brushed past, all the children holding hands and gaping, trailing along in a line, their faces solemn with awe. Jack tripped over a taut rope from one of the tents and swore under his breath. I had never heard him swear before.

We were swept with the crowd before a large, openfaced tent where the barker was yelling, "Three balls for a dime, ladies and gentlemen. Three balls for a dime, ten for a quarter. Step right up and try your luck!"

At the back of the tent white wooden milk bottles were pyramided on a box and along the sides of the tent were shelves lined with canes, dolls, and fancy candy boxes for prizes. A fat man was throwing balls when we came, puffing as he threw, and his wife stood beside him, holding his coat and laughing till she shook. She was as fat as he was with cheeks like pink marshmallows.

"Fitz, win me something," Margie cried, in her petulant, going-steady voice. "You used to play baseball a lot."

"All right, honey. You pick out what you want. Give me three balls," he said to the man. Margie and Jack and I stepped back to give him room.

With the first three balls he tried too hard and his aim was bad. He tipped over one bottle and the other two balls bounced off the canvas back of the tent. "Give me three more," he said, trying to be casual. "I didn't know those balls were so light. But I think I've got the hang now." He took three more and wound up carefully before he threw them. It looked so easy, watching, but this time none of the balls even hit the box. His neck was dull red.

"Gimme ten," he said, sullenly, fishing in his pocket for a quarter.

We all stood waiting while he rolled the ball around in the palm of his hand, winding up slowly, and threw. This time he knocked two of the end bottles down and his face relaxed and with four more balls he knocked down the other six bottles. He was grinning now and Margie was smiling in a sort of relief. "What do I get?" he asked the man.

"Eight bottles with five balls will entitle you to a genuine gold-headed cane," the barker answered pompously, taking a little wooden cane off the shelf and handing it to Margie. It was enameled red with a gilt top tied with a piece of braid and she stuck it under her arm like a drum major, beaming at Fitz.

"What are you going to do with the other five balls?" I asked him.

"Jack, why don't you try throwing," he offered generously. "Get a cane for Angie, too."

"No, thanks," he said. "Not in the mood."

"Go ahead, Jack," Margie urged. "If Fitz can do it you can. . . ."

He took the balls from the man and eyed the milk bottles carefully. His fingers were supple on the ball and he weighed it casually in the palm of his hand before he threw. His aim was sure and easy and three end bottles toppled and with the next ball the center bottle supporting the rear and the last four bottles rolled off the box.

"Well, good for you," Margie said, tonelessly. And Fitz slapped him on the back.

476

Even the barker looked surprised. "You just shouldn't throw so hard," Jack explained to Fitz. "Those balls are light and so are the bottles."

"I guess you win," the man said and took a doll from the top shelf. Jack handed it to me. It was a cupie doll with feathers glued on behind so they stuck out around its head like a peacock's tail.

"Maybe Kitty would like it," he said, and "Thanks for the balls," to Fitz. Margie was annoyed now and trying to smile through a pout. She was annoyed because Jack had thrown the balls better than Fitz and because he had won a doll for me with Fitz's balls, and her lower lip stuck out like a sulky baby's.

We turned away from the tent and Fitz went to take her hand but she pulled it away in irritation. "I can walk by myself," she said.

Everyone was so cross by now that I suggested we go home, but Fitz burst out, "We haven't had anything to eat yet! What's the matter with you, Angie? You don't want to eat or go into sideshows or anything."

"Leave her alone," Jack said. "You're in a worse mood than I am, Fitz," and they looked at each other crossly. Suddenly Fitz reached over and gave him a playful punch in the ribs and Jack poked him back and they laughed sheepishly.

"If you two boys don't mind, I wish you would excuse us for a few minutes," Margie said primly. "We'll meet you somewhere, in a little while."

"Sure," Jack assented. "And we'll meet you . . . where, Fitz?"

"Make it in front of that hot-dog stand by the main gate," he answered. "Don't get your faces too painted up," he added teasingly, trying to catch Margie's eye, but she wouldn't look at him.

"Come on, Angie," she said crossly.

I turned back as we went and saw the fellows walking toward the shooting range where little mechanical ducks floated by on a revolving belt as targets, and I wanted secretly to go back to watch to see if Jack was better at rifle shooting too. Margie turned toward the Fine Arts Building where the 4H[2] exhibits were on display. "I didn't really want anything," she explained. "Just wanted to get away for a few minutes." Her mouth was still twisted into a discontented pout and she tossed the gilt-topped cane away under one of the booths. "Too much bother to carry," she said.

We looked with mild interest at the sewing exhibits lined on the walls, pinned with yellow and blue prize ribbons. There were gingham aprons with carefully ironed frills, fancy square-legged pajamas, and gingham dresses with stiff puffed sleeves and sashes of the same material. Margie sniffed in derision. She reached over the railing to look at the ruching[3] around the neck of one of the dresses and a woman with a large, toothy smile came over, saying with elaborate politeness, "Mustn't touch, girls!"

"Who wants to touch her old stuff?" Margie said under her breath, as we walked away. "Let's get out of here."

We went into the Produce Building next door that was bright with the colors of curved yellow squash, scrubbed brown potatoes, and shiny jars of honey arranged on display. There were shelves lined with boxes of red and green apples arranged in designs and little early pumpkins with skins like orange wax, and the whole room had a sweet, clean smell like summer clover. But neither of us looked at the displays for Margie was thinking about something—I could tell

---

2 *4H*   a club for youth sponsored by the U.S. Department of Agriculture. Its name comes from its goal: the improvement of head, heart, hands, and health.

3 *ruching*   ruffles or pleats of fine fabric, used for trimming women's clothes.

by her restlessness—and she walked along listlessly, her thoughts far away. I had learned to know her so well during the summer that I knew something was wrong. And I knew if I waited patiently she would tell me when she was ready.

And just as I thought, she turned to me in a few moments. "Angie," she said, "I've been thinking about you all day. Fitz was telling me last night about Jack's going to Oklahoma and everything. I knew that you were going away to school, but doesn't this make things different?"

"It makes some difference, Margie, but what can we do? I have to go to school—in fact, I want to very much—and Jack naturally has to go where his family goes, so what *can* we do? I don't know just what you mean at all."

Her voice was irritated. "It's just like I said early this summer—you don't think like other girls and it makes me mad 'cause I can't figure you out. You never seem to 'worry' about Jack and try to do anything about it. . . . It seems to me that if you liked him like he likes you, you'd worry more about his going away."

I couldn't help laughing at her for she was so cross that her face was screwed up like a Pekingese. "Margie," I said, "why don't you worry about yourself? There's nothing Jack and I can do. How about you and Fitz—you've been going together a long time and this is the first fall that you haven't gone back to school. . . ."

"I'll work somewhere," she answered, feeling suddenly important again and fluffing out her hair with her finger tips. "My dad knows some man in town who's going to get me a job in one of the department stores . . . I'd tell you about it, but I don't know myself for sure."

"And how about Fitz?"

"He'll work too, I suppose," but her tone was disinterested, as if her thoughts were already on something else. "Maybe he'll just stay on at the fruit store where he is as regular help. I don't know."

There was a short silence before I ventured casually, "What's wrong, Margie?"

She turned on me suddenly, her eyes screwed up. "Honestly, Angie, I'm so mad tonight I could just cry! I should think you'd be able to see it—anyone could see it with any sense! I've been getting just a little tired of a lot of things lately and I think I'm just about through."

"I didn't notice anything," I fibbed politely. "Fitz always seemed to be such a nice boy to me."

She looked at me closely. "I suppose he is nice enough but do you think he has anything else. I mean—personality or ability? Sometimes he seems so dumb—like tonight, not even being able to throw baseballs—that I just hate him. Sometimes I wonder if I haven't spoiled my chances by going steady . . . I don't even think he's as nice looking as I used to . . ." She was watching me carefully, to catch any reaction. "What do you think, Angie?"

"The four of us have had so much fun together I thought you liked him real well," I told her, verbally sliding out from under.

"I haven't liked him since one night this July when we went for a walk and we stopped for a while to sit on the swings at a grade school playground. After a while we went on the little merry-go-round and he got so dizzy he had to get off. I don't know why," she said, "but every time I think of him getting dizzy I get so disgusted I can't stand to look at him."

The thought was topmost on my mind, "Why do you go with him then?" but before I could say a word she added, "But a girl has to go out with somebody!"

They had gone steady since the middle of their senior year and she had worn his class ring since March. And they had been out together every night all sum-

478

mer. To realize that the whole thing was a farce was depressing and I didn't know whether to be annoyed with Margie or sorry for her.

"Oh, well," she shrugged, "let's go back and find the fellows anyway," and her voice was brighter now. She is probably relieved now that she has told someone, I thought. She just wanted to get it off her mind.

"Of course," she added, in her old matter-of-fact tone. "You wouldn't mention what I told you to anyone, would you, Angie? I'm not ready to break up yet."

Jack and Fitz were waiting for us and we all sat down on the plain benches at the hot-dog stand and ordered wieners stuck in crisp buttered rolls, oozing with yellow mustard and tomato sauce. Margie ate three and seemed to feel better afterward. She and Fitz smoked a cigarette before we left and I noticed he was holding her hand under the counter. I thought then that everything was as it had been.

They had walked to the fair so we were all driving home in Jack's car. It was parked far over in the grass lot and when we had walked to it, Margie said unexpectedly, "Fitz, why don't you drive instead of Jack?"

"Instead of Jack!" he asked in surprise. "But why—Jack's a good driver!"

"Sure," said Jack. "Don't you trust me, Margie? I've never run you up a post yet!"

"I know it," she answered calmly. "But I want Fitz to drive this time," and she opened the door herself to get into the front seat. Fitz looked hurt but said nothing.

Jack just looked at me, shrugged his shoulders, and he and I got into the back seat. Fitz backed out carefully, then went forward so suddenly the gears shrieked. He was angry now but Margie didn't seem to care. "I'd like to go home first," she said quietly.

He drove into town and went straight down Main Street, turning left and then on toward Margie's street. His face was stiff and sullen. He pulled up at the curb without a word and went round the front of the car to open her door. She turned, said good night to us, and then they both walked up the front side-walk without saying anything.

"Hey, what goes on there?" Jack asked me, his voice puzzled.

We sat waiting. The porch was screened in and thick with Virginia creeper vines, and the low hum of voices floated out to us. And then the hum died out. We waited a long time and finally Fitz slammed the screen door and bounded down the steps and into the car.

He started the motor, turning toward us as if we had questioned him. "She said to call her tomorrow and she'll let me know. I guess everything will be all right . . . Gee, I don't know what gets into girls sometimes!"

No month of my life has ever gone so fast. Those last days seemed to slip through my fingers like egg white and I almost wished the end would come, for the waiting was so hopeless and so tantalizing. I did the housework each day as usual, sewed name tags on my clothing for school in the afternoon and tried not to think what would happen when those September days finally came.

Thoughts of September were on Jack's mind too. We had Cokes together in McKnight's one afternoon while my mother was shopping and he told me that his father had already made arrangements to sell most of the bakery equipment to a baker in Waupun. "My uncle has all the equipment we'll need in Oklahoma already."

"I'm going to give some of my things to Swede, too, before I go. I've got things in my room I won't want to pack and I won't be needing my ice skates, either."

It was a warm afternoon and quiet. The druggist was dusting the shelves, removing the boxes and bottles, and rearranging them carefully, humming softly to himself. Neither Jack nor I spoke for a few moments but we were both thinking the same kind of thoughts. He had finished his Coke and was sitting sideways, one foot on the bench, smoking. Even the smoke was slow and lazy that afternoon, curling upward quietly.

Jack turned to me unexpectedly and, as if I had spoken first, said, "But, Angie, I couldn't have seen you much when you were away at school anyway!"

He stopped then and grinned, realizing I hadn't said a word. "Just thinking out loud, I guess."

His voice was earnest now. "I just want you to know for sure, Angie, that I don't *really* want to go to Oklahoma. . . ."

"I know it, Jack. It's just . . . well, I don't know . . . something." "Fate" was the word I had been thinking of.

"I can always come up to see you any time and you can come down to see me," he lied pleasantly, laughing at me.

"And over weekends you come up as far as Kansas City and I'll come down to meet you every Saturday night," I answered.

"Yep," he said and his face was serious again. "Honestly, though, Angie, I've got four-fifty already that I started to save toward coming down to Chicago to see you."

I felt my heart beast faster. "Really, have you, Jack? Maybe you *could* come up sometime then!"

"Sure, I could!" and he made his voice bright and confident, so confident that I knew he didn't mean it himself.

"What would your mother and dad say," I asked, knowing in my heart that he was thinking exactly the same thing.

"What *could* they say, Angie? I'm pretty old now. I do mostly what I want."

"But they would want to know why you wanted to come back. It's so far. What could you ever tell them, Jack?"

"Maybe I could say I want to come back to see Swede and Fitz." He didn't laugh as he spoke and I didn't feel like laughing, either. With the end only two weeks away it was no laughing matter.

Jack crushed his cigarette out with a thoughtful sigh. "Don't worry, Angie. I may not make it right away but I'll get up here again sometime."

Kitty and I worked in the garden for a whole day with the sun hot on our backs, pulling up the rows of overgrown vegetables and piling them in a heap in one corner of the garden to dry. The radishes had blossomed with white flowers and gone to seed, the round red radishes grown into long, gnarled roots, coarse and reedy. The leaves were rough and scratchy. Even the onion stems were thick and bulbous, topped with purple flower clusters. In the late afternoon we were finished, hands scratched and legs muddy, and we cleaned ourselves while my mother set out tea for us on the back doorstep. While we sipped at our cups Kitty was lying on the lawn, chewing a bit of grass. "Too bad you have to go away, Angie," she piped up, "'cause we are really going to have a fine fire when those things are dried."

I tried to pretend I hadn't heard her, but everything I did and saw and heard seemed to bring the days nearer to the end. Along the side of the house, the earlier hollyhocks had dropped their last blossoms and the seeds in the seed pods were like round, green overcoat buttons. The first asters were out, smoky-purple and heavy on the stems.

Lorraine came home from work early, even before I had set the table for supper. "We didn't have much to do this afternoon, so they let us out ahead of time," she explained. "The summer business has slowed up so we aren't very busy anymore."

"I'm glad you came home," Mom said. "It seems as if I've hardly seen you this summer at all—with one thing and another."

"I know it," she answered. "The first part went so fast and this last part is just dragging. At first everything seemed so busy and now it doesn't seem as if it should be summer anymore at all." I was busy at the open kitchen window and heard their voices on the back lawn.

Lorraine spoke again and her tone was cautious. "This afternoon I was thinking, Mom, that if all of you don't mind . . . I'd like to go back to Chicago!"

My mother said something I couldn't hear but Lorraine objected, "But she won't have to come. Freshmen don't have to be there till the tenth of the month, but I just *want* to go back early. There are some girl friends I would like to visit—a couple of them asked me to stay with them if I ever got to the city. And besides," she added hastily, "I've got a lot of important reading to get finished before I take my English comprehensive exam this year and I would like to get a head start—before the regular homework gets too heavy."

At supper my mother told us that Lorraine had decided to go back. "Of course, I think you're crazy, but if you want to, go ahead," Margaret shrugged.

"Your father won't like it, either," my mother objected, "but I suppose it's all right."

"I'll get a lot of reading done and having worked all summer, this will be like a vacation before starting school again," Lorraine explained. "I'll just take a few things and you can send the rest with Angie when she comes."

"It really seems a little foolish to me . . ." My mother was still hesitant but it was decided. Lorraine would leave on Sunday.

That night in bed she nudged me, saying softly, "Asleep, Angie?"

"No. I'm wide awake," I whispered. "What do you want?"

She was lying staring up at the ceiling, her arms behind her head, and she had been silent for so long I had thought she was asleep. "Guess what, Angie—I saw Martin today."

I felt myself instinctively grow cautious and eased my voice into casualness. "Did you really? What did he say, Lorraine?" As far as I knew she hadn't seen him since the Sunday night he had failed to call, and except for the night on the front steps she hadn't mentioned him once.

"He didn't say anything," she answered. "I just saw him driving by in the car." She waited a moment.

"He looked so nice, Angie. He went by quite fast so I just got a quick look but he had on that brown tweed suit of his that I always liked and his hat pushed way back on his head. He looked just like he used to look. . . ."

"Did he see you, Lorraine?"

"Well," and her voice was careful, picking the words thoughtfully, "I was just standing on the corner waiting to cross Park Avenue and he came up a side street and then turned down the Avenue . . . It was during lunch hour and I think he was hurrying uptown to eat. Angeline, he didn't see me. . . ."

Her voice was very quiet now and very empty, tired with lonesomeness. "He didn't see me," she repeated. "I'm almost sure."

She caught a late afternoon train for Chicago on Sunday. We all went out for a ride right after dinner—so she could say "good-bye" to things for the summer. We took the lake highway out to Pete's and I noticed that already the swamp grass along the road was turning yellow and the glossy leaves of the willow trees were a fading yellow-green. There were birds everywhere, flying low in the bushes and bending the tall grasses with their weight. Lorraine looked out the car window as we drove, not saying anything.

We passed fields of wheat, ripe and heavy-headed, honey-colored in the sunshine, and already long yellow feathers of early goldenrod grew in the ditches. There was a lush heat over everything; a slow, simmering heat that made you warm from the inside out. "We'll go for a turn around the park road. Would you like that, Lorraine?" my father asked and she nodded. I secretly hoped we might see Swede and Jack down by the boats as we passed, but the boat was empty, bobbing quietly by the dock.

Farther out on the lake sails tipped the skyline, matching the white of the clouds. We pulled up along the bank of the lagoon to give Lorraine a last summer look at the park and the water. It was peacefully quiet and water lilies like white wax floated on broad green pads, rocking on the slow current. "I never knew a summer could go so fast," she mused. Near the edge of the lagoon floated a dead white fish, its sides shining like mother-of-pearl, almost beautiful in the sunlight. I heard Lorraine sigh a little.

"Dad, I think it's almost traintime now. Let's just drive down Main Street once more before you take me to the station," she said.

The shops were all closed and the street was calm with Sunday afternoon quiet, but there were a few cars lining the curbs and Lorraine kept looking from side to side, very casually. We went from one end of the street to the other and then my father turned toward the station saying cheerfully, "Well, Lorraine, there's your last look at Fond du Lac for a while anyway."

"Oh, well," she said.

I carried one bag and Kitty lugged the other with both hands, and we waited with Lorraine at the platform until the train came and stood waving after her as it disappeared smaller, smaller down the track.

Going home we drove down Main Street again and though I looked on both sides of the street, noticing each car, I didn't see Martin's long green coupe that time either.

Fall was coming early that year. There was a queer sadness in the fact that summer should die so quickly, this of all years. Each day the freshness in the garden and the fields faded a little. The morning dews lay chill and frosty and in the evening long, quiet dusks came early, growing dark around the treetops while the birds lingered longer, with a strange melancholy in their songs.

Jack came over every morning, stopping off on his bakery route, and he called me every afternoon just after lunch. Once he remarked, laughing, "Angie, I never knew being in love took so much time!"

Every night we went out somewhere. Once when I was rushing through the supper dishes my mother came into the kitchen, the evening paper in her hand, saying, "Angeline, I hardly think it's . . ." and she paused. "You shouldn't really be seeing . . ."

"What did you say, Mom?" I asked, my heart pounding.

She looked at me a moment and smiled an odd, soft smile. "Oh, well . . ." she said quietly and went back into the living room.

For the last week she had been mending my clothes, tightening snap fasteners on my skirts and sewing buttons on my pajamas for school. Newspapers were spread in one corner of her bedroom and she laid my clothes in neat, careful piles, ready to be packed. The drapes and spread were ready for my room and she was just knitting the last sleeve on a new pale-pink sweater.

"We'll have no last-minute worries at all," she remarked one afternoon and I realized suddenly that she meant what she said. She knew that Jack would be leaving just a few days after I had gone, but she wasn't worrying about that at all. And I realized suddenly, too, that she didn't know that that was the only thing on my mind through those last days. But how could she know? To me every moment passed with an awareness that it had slipped by and that time was coming to an end. But to her these last days really meant nothing.

When Jack and I were together neither of us talked about it much—it was a refusing to admit and a refusing to believe that September was only a few days away. But without saying a word, we began to do "last things" together. One night out at Pete's the whole realization swept over me, coming so suddenly, startlingly, that it made my cheeks feel numb. All the same crowd was there that we had seen every night all summer. The air was still full of the damp cool smell of beer and the musty pleasantness of old wood, and the jukebox in the corner was still blaring out its nickel's worth of music every few minutes. I seemed to see them all separately—the familiar town boys standing at the bar, laughing, and girls with long sweaters pulled over their summer dresses. For them everything was the same. Only one or two of them would be going away. All the rest would be here night after night for nights on end, till outside the lake would be frozen over and the snow white on the ground and the tall bare trees creaking in the wind of winter. This time two weeks from now they would still be here. Two months from now they would still be here when I had counted out my last nights and rationed out my last minutes.

There were memories in everything. They seemed to hover in the corners and hang wispy in the music that came from the jukebox. They were floating like dust motes everywhere I looked. Swede danced with me once and he said softly, under the music, "Jack's going to miss you, Angie. You're a good kid—I'm sorry we didn't get to know you sooner, that's all," and I had to keep my head against his shoulder so he couldn't see my face just then.

Later Jack and I sat in a back booth by ourselves in silence, just being glad to be together, and we could hear the sharp voices of the boys in the front room playing cards and the muffle of feet dancing on the wooden floor, mingled with the music and the ring of beer glasses on the table—all the old, familiar sounds that were part of Pete's. Sitting on its perch, the old parrot was sleeping quietly with its head lolling to one side and its tail feathers drooping.

Jack gave a little laugh, smiling at his own thoughts, and looking up at me, he said, "Remember that first night, Angie?"

I nodded and he laughed again, shaking his head. That's all he said.

We decided to go sailboating one of those last nights and Swede went with us, but when we got to the lake it was dark and choppy, beating angrily against the boat as it rocked against the pier and sending high foam up over the gravel walk. The sky was dark and threatening and there was no moon. "I'd rather be a dead Chinaman than go out on a night like that," Swede muttered, shuddering, so we all got back into the car and drove uptown instead.

The next evening the three of us went out again, going along Willow Road far into the country and then back down the highway that runs along the lake and finally through the rutted roads of the silent, empty fairgrounds with its buildings already shuttered closed, as if they were already asleep for the winter. We even drove out to the narrow gravel road, past the field where the field daisies were still blooming and the thin trees stood still and dark and there was the same breathless mystery; the same strange quiet.

I remember Jack's remarking, "To look at it at night you'd never know anything had changed, would you?"

But it couldn't end as soundlessly and as painlessly as it had begun—that I knew. All the days and nights and warm weeks of sunshine couldn't fade away into nothingness like breathy whispers as soon as they were spoken. They were too full for that. There was too much behind it. Even as I counted those last hours I knew that something had to happen. I didn't know what it would be but I knew it would come—somehow.

And it did. It was the third night before I left. We went on a wiener roast together, about ten of us, as a sort of farewell party for both Jack and me. Jack had his car and we stopped to pick up Swede and Dollie and then Fitz and Margie, crowding all four of them into the back seat with the kindling wood and a picnic basket, while the others went in another car. We drove out to a wooded ledge about five miles from town where the trees grew thick and the woods were as wild and overgrown as a forest preserve.

It was barely dark and the trails were easy to find between the trees as we trailed along in Indian file, each carrying something, while Jack came last with his arms heaped with kindling wood, dragging a car robe behind him. There were clearings in the trees along the path, scattered with bits of charred logs and the dark ashes of other picnic fires. As we went in deeper and deeper, the woods seemed filled with a quiet listening, as if it hadn't heard another human sound for long years.

Margie led us to a place she knew of where the ground was flat and there was a heap of blackened stones already arranged for a fireplace. Swede pulled some paper from his pockets, bunching it together and placing kindling sticks carefully over the stones, while the rest of us scattered to look for more wood. The trees grew close together here, thick-trunked box elders with occasional slim birches slipped in between, and the dead branches on the ground were tangled with vines and matted with damp leaves. We broke off what smaller branches we could and kicked at rotten stumps till they rooted out of the earth, sending up a damp, mossy smell. Margie was pushing along beside Jack and Fitz who went in another direction. It was the first time I had seen her for almost two weeks—since the night of the fair—and I was anxious to talk with her. Jack was a little distance away between the trees, breaking sticks sharply over his knees. He couldn't have heard us.

"Margie," I whispered cautiously, "I've meant to call you for almost a week but didn't get around to it. I wanted to ask you how things were going with Fitz and you."

I couldn't see her face clearly in the half-darkness but she shrugged. "We've been going out as always since two days after that night at the fair. I stayed home for one night and then decided I didn't like it so I called him up the next day. I guess he knew I would. Anyway, I'm almost glad I did."

"So am I," I told her. "Otherwise maybe you two wouldn't be here tonight and it wouldn't be the same at all."

"Yeah, you get kind of used to having a boy around," she answered. Jack returned then and we turned back through the woods toward the fire. It was shining through the trees, licking light around the dark trunks and up into the branches.

Margie caught up with me and whispered softly in my ear as we walked. "Thanks a lot for not telling, Angie. I could tell by the way he acted that he really didn't know what went on at all."

Back around the fire the others were sharpening green sticks for the wieners and Dollie was buttering rolls with the handle of a spoon—Jack had brought them from the bakery, fresh and hot. Fitz and I spread the blankets carefully on the ground, watching out for twigs and sharp stones, and then had to fold them up again to look for a jackknife someone had laid down somewhere. We each cooked for ourselves, putting the wieners on sticks and holding them over the flame, turning slowly, carefully, till the tight skin burst, sending juice sputtering into the fire. The fragrance was tantalizing and Swede jammed his impatiently between a roll and ate it half-roasted.

"You big, old pig," Dollie laughed at him across the fire. "No wonder you're so fat." The firelight dancing made dimples in her cheeks and a soft, dark fluff of her hair, thick and shiny.

Someone had brought along some bottles of Coke but no one had remembered to bring a bottle opener, so Jack twisted at the tops with the edge of his jackknife till he had to give up in desperation, muttering under his breath. No one wanted to go into town for an opener so the bottles lay untouched on the grass. "Maybe afterwards," Jack said.

At first the fire was so hot that it crackled and snapped, sending twigs sparking out onto the grass till we had to draw our blankets farther back, out of reach. I almost forgot that we were miles from town; miles from anyone else. While we ate, everyone chattered and laughed so loudly that the circle of brightness around the fire seemed to be a room by itself in the middle of the forest darkness, walled with light. I looked furtively behind me once, awed by the silent bushes, dark and lonely, changing shape in the flicker of the firelight. "Something the matter, Angie?" Jack asked, touching my arm. But I shook my head.

As the fire burned lower we toasted marshmallows over the flames and Dollie pulled off the first toasted skin, retoasting the soft white ball that was left on the stick, licking her sticky fingers like a baby. Margie lay back on the blanket, looking up into the darkness, and Fitz crawled over to sit down beside her. She asked him for a cigarette and held his hand to steady it as he brought a match to the tip. Then he tossed the match away and put his hand back in hers, looking into the firelight. I felt almost sorry for Fitz then, he seemed to want to be liked so badly. The others pulled their blankets closer to the fire and tossed the paper bags and bits of wax paper into it, watching them go up in a quick blaze.

One of the boys suggested we sing for a while but the suggestion died away without an answer. We talked quietly and Jack sat close beside me with his knees hunched up, staring at the flames. He had been silent all evening long, and several times I caught him looking at me strangely, as if he were just going to say something and had suddenly changed his mind. Swede came over to sit on our blanket, too, and Dollie curled up beside him with her head on his knee. He bent over to whisper something to her, laughing and tangling his fingers in her hair.

Someone had picked up an old wooden wagon wheel in the woods and laid it over the glowing embers of the fire, and we all sat watching till it burst into slow flame. "Looks like a big Fourth of July pin wheel, doesn't it?" Swede whispered down to Dollie.

The trees stirred restlessly and the night was filled with a sense of uneasiness that made me feel uneasy myself, almost afraid of the darkness around us. The firelight sent shifting shadows onto the bushes and tree trunks so that the whole forest seemed to be full of silent things, watching. I couldn't tell what was wrong with me. It sent a queer panicky beating in my throat and my hands were hot and dry. Above us the sky was a dark velvet with pale small stars. The trees hid the moon.

The night was torn between the comforting warmth of the fire and the weird, restless shadows beyond the circle of light, but the others didn't seem to notice it. Only Jack was moody. He sat breaking up bits of twig and flipping them into the fire, his eyebrows knit together in thought. Once he looked at me and then ran his hand over his hair with a tired, unhappy gesture. The fire was burning low now and the wooden wheel lay flat in the ashes, the spokes still glowing red. The burned wood crumbled and settled down into the embers with an eerie sound like a soft sigh. As the fire burned low, the darkness closed in silently around us and a night wind blew over the coals, turning the ashes gray. Jack flipped the last twig into the fire.

"Someone want to go look for more wood with me?" Swede suggested.

Jack jumped to his feet. "Let Angie and me go, will you? I feel like a little walk anyway."

"In the darkness?" Something inside me went suddenly alarmed, cautious, and sent a chill around my heart. I didn't know of what I was afraid but there was something there. It seemed almost as if the darkness beyond was listening, waiting. My mind warned again and again with quick, sure thoughts not to go out of the protective circle of the firelight, out past the bushes where the trees grew close. I wanted suddenly to stay very near Swede and the others, away from the gentle, dark sway of the bushes and the quiet shadows that lay beyond. But yet there was something about Jack's voice that made me go.

"You aren't afraid to go with me, Angie," he said insistently, his voice warm with persuasion as he took my hand to help me to my feet.

At the edge of the circle of firelight he turned to call back to the others, "Better put on what wood you have there. This may take us a long time . . . in the dark."

We went out of the clearing and the bushes brushed against me as we passed, stretching out and touching my legs with their cool, damp leaves. Dead leaves were silent beneath our feet and trees leaned together like tall dark pillars, the light between them thin and eerie. I held tight to Jack's hand and stumbled after him. "Jack," I said. "Jack, this is silly. Please, please let's not go!"

He pulled at my hand, almost pleading, "Come on, Angie," he urged. "Oh, come. . . I really want you to!"

So I hurried along with one hand in his and one hand before me to feel for the trees in the darkness, and the bark was dry and rough beneath my touch. Once I tripped over a vine and it coiled around my ankle like a wet rope. "Jack," I cried, "Jack!" I was really frightened now and I didn't know why but I couldn't keep the fear out of my voice.

486

"I'm with you, Angie," was all he said.

We walked on cautiously, feeling between trees, stubbing against stones and breaking through bushes that scratched against our legs and cracked under our feet. Over our heads was the almost soundless hush of the wind in the heavy foliage, uneasy with the secrets of darkness, and the rest of the night was so quiet we could hear ourselves as we breathed. The firelight was far behind by now and the darkness had closed in around.

Suddenly ahead of us the trees parted, and beyond I could see a flat, rolling field high with wheat. And ahead we could see the moon that had been hidden in the trees and it hung very low, yellow and solemn, as if it were too heavy for the sky. Along the edge of the field ran a low wooden fence and we broke through the woods, leaving the darkness behind us. Jack held apart the last bushes and I stepped through them into the little clearing. The woods behind us was like a black wall. My breath came short and quick from running and I sat down on a fallen fence rail while Jack stood beside me, lighting a cigarette, but neither of us spoke.

Around me the weeds grew tall, almost up to my knees and cool with a night dampness, and reaching down I felt the leaves of one, knowing by the hairy softness and the fine cluster of tiny blossoms that it was wild foxglove. All around the plants grew thick and lush, with a late-summer richness, and I crushed a dark leaf between my fingers. Almost instantly there rose in the air the cool, sharp smell of mint, its fragrance startlingly eerie in the darkness. Jack moved toward me and then stopped.

Along the fence rails vines grew heavy, covered with thick, flat leaves shining broad in the moonlight. "Look, Angie," Jack whispered. "Those are wild grapes." I walked toward him, brushing through the weeds, and we felt through the grape leaves, our fingers quick in the darkness, till we found the hidden grape bunches. They were hard to pluck, and cool dew from the leaves shook down around our legs as we pulled them. Curling vine tendrils touched my arm like cold fingers. Some of the grapes were still green and hard but the earlier ones were ripe and soft to touch, the purple bunches oddly black in the moonlight. They were bitter in our mouths as we ate them, with a strange, wild taste, and the seeds were hard against my teeth. But I plucked them and plucked them till both my hands were full and they fell to the earth and purple stains were dark on my arms. Jack was standing back from the fence now, near the trees, and suddenly I knew he was waiting for me. And all the strength seemed to run out of me and the grapes felt cold and heavy in my hands.

Very quietly I stood. Everything around us was waiting. I could feel the tenseness of the bushes, the hushed expectancy over the grass tops, and behind us the wheat field was still in the moonlight. Great webs of silence seemed to hang, dark and heavy, swung low from tree to tree. The great treetops above leaned together, waiting with hushed whispers. I wanted to speak but the words were dry in my throat.

I could feel Jack's thoughts straining toward me and then I heard his voice, so low, so tense that I wasn't sure for a moment if I heard it at all. "Angie," he said, "Angie, please! Let's get married. . . . I don't want you to go!"

Once it had been said, the night came suddenly alive, pulsing with it; catching up the words and echoing them over and over, singing like chimes in my head. For a moment, only a brief moment that slipped by so swiftly that it meant nothing at all, desire laid warm, tremulous fingers along my throat. But it was only a moment and then the whole night melted away around me.

487

Everything was so calmly and painfully clear. I could remember my mother standing in her bedroom looking at my clothes in neat piles, ready to be packed for school, and saying in her soft, confident mother-voice, "We'll have no last-minute worries at all, Angie," and again I realized how much she meant it.

And then Jack was standing beside me with his arms tight around me, pleading, "Don't, Angie. Oh, honey, don't do that now. I only asked you because . . . oh, Angie!"

And I was crying with my face tight against his shoulder, standing in the tall weeds that were cool and damp against my bare legs.

Back in the firelight the others had already gathered up their things and were ready to leave. Swede kicked at the heap of glowing embers till they were scattered in the grass in a shower of sparks like fire-flies; and when Jack leaned over to gather up his car robe Swede patted him on the shoulder saying quietly, "That's okay, fellow."

The cars were still parked at the roadside and we put the picnic basket in the back seat again and Fitz got in first so Margie could sit on his knee and Swede and Dollie got in next. Jack opened the door for me and I stepped in carefully, trying not to look at him. He swung round to his own side of the car and slammed his door shut. My breath was still short in my throat and my hands were trembling, so I had to fold them together to keep them still.

Jack waited a moment before starting the motor. Just sitting beside him made my heart pound again. He took a cigarette from his pocket and bent over to light it, striking a match. I noticed his hands were trembling. He held the match with both hands to steady it. In the small glow of light his face was very young and very sad and I saw that his lips were still stained purple from the wild grapes.

And the next morning the swallows were there. I came downstairs early with my eyes small and tired and my heart aching with a weariness that went through me right down to my hands, leaving them limp and heavy on my wrists. I wondered what Jack was thinking then. His thoughts must have dragged as slowly and listlessly as mine with the same painful dullness. The whole night through, lying in bed, memories had corkscrewed through my mind till my head throbbed with thinking and now, in the morning light, everything was still as drab and dismally hopeless as I had dreamed.

The kitchen was filled with the usual fresh smell of morning coffee and my mother was sitting by the window, looking over the garden. "It's the first day of real fall we've had," she said. "We could almost stand a bit of fire." I poured a cup of coffee for myself, hoping the warmth of it would really get inside of me. It was such a dull morning that the grayness of it spread over my thoughts like mold. For the first time I could see brown sticks bare in the hedges and there were a few stiff-petaled zinnias, dull, heavy red, standing alone in the corner of the flower bed, the leaves curling. I tried not to look at the swallows but they were there.

Year after year and every year, we had watched the first flowers drop their petals, the squash turn orange between the corn rows, and leaves thin in the trees, but no one would admit the summer was over until one morning we would wake and the swallows would be there. It never failed. The swallows would come, lining the telephone wires, and from that day on it was fall. The wind would have frost on its breath and the grape leaves would curl and fall from the vines and the dew would be white patches frosted on the grass in early

488

morning. Soon, lonely killdeers would be winging across the sky, their wistful cries hanging in the cool, misty air.

And that morning, sitting by the kitchen window with my cup of coffee, I saw the telephone wires across the foot of the garden dotted with swallows, perched on the black lines like long-tailed notes—a bar of music, stark and sad against the gray fall sky.

It seemed so incredible I couldn't keep the surprise of it out of my voice, "How could it happen, Mom?" I asked. "How could it *end* overnight?"

She looked at me oddly and said, "It's always been like that, Angie. You just haven't been old enough to notice before."

We spent a long time over our breakfast, talking about school, planning; just loitering because there were only two days left and we wouldn't have breakfast together again for a long time.

And then suddenly my mother brightened. "Run up and wake that lazy little sister of yours while I straighten the kitchen. She and I have to go downtown this morning. I keep forgetting that you aren't the only one who is going to school. Kitty needs new shoes!"

I was just waving good-bye to them from the front window when the phone rang. I let it ring twice and then again before I answered it, because I knew it was Jack and it takes a moment or two to get your thoughts in order and to make sure your voice is calm. His voice on the other end of the wire sounded as tired as I felt, as if he had just got out of bed and wished he hadn't risen at all.

"Hi there, Angie," he said glumly. "Just called up to see how things were going with you this morning."

"Fine, Jack. How about you?"

"Pretty good, I guess. But we're packing some stuff—that's why I called you. I'm home here with my mother wrapping gunny sacks around some of the up-stairs furniture and tying it with rope to ship down to Oklahoma. She wants to get as much of it out of the way as she can."

"Lot of work?" I asked lamely. There was a scratching on his end of the line as if he were scribbling with a pencil on a piece of paper—an aimless, annoying sound and I could tell he was thinking of something else as he talked.

"It's not so much work but I don't think I'll be able to get over to see you today."

"Why not, Jack?"

" 'Cause my mother wants me round to help her. She's got her hair tied up in a dust cap and is really going at it. I can tell by the way she's working herself that she wouldn't like it if I took time off. . . ."

"Does she know I'm going away the day after tomorrow, Jack?"

"Yeah, I told her about it, Angie. And she said to say good-bye to you for her—even if she has never met you."

The conversation was empty, meaningless—there are times when two people can't really talk together without seeing each other. I could just imagine Jack at the other end of the wire, tapping his pencil on the table, his eyes thoughtful, not wanting to hang up and still not knowing what to say next. "I'd better get back to my packing too," I suggested. "There are still little things that have to be sorted out. I want to bring so much but it won't all fit in the bags."

"Okay, Angie," he answered. "But I'll see you tonight, won't I? I may even get a chance to drop round this afternoon but I really don't think so. But we'll have a good time tonight. We'll make it fun, Angie." His voice was warm and almost happy again and after he had hung up I sat holding the phone, as if by

489

doing so I could still hold onto the sound. In two days, I thought, I won't be able to hear his voice anymore.

Margaret didn't come home for supper that night so my mother and Kitty and I were alone. The gray sky of the day was melted into the darkness of a night sky and outside there was a wind that rustled in the bushes.

"I heard downtown that they expect to have a frost tonight," my mother told me. "It's unusual to have it come so early but they say this is going to be a very cold winter for us. The man in the shoestore said that already there have been hunters out after the ducks over the lake."

Kitty was quiet and contented after the day of shopping and she was eating placidly, her eyes already soft with sleep. "This year when it snows I'm going to make Daddy help me with a snow hill in the garden for my sled," she remarked, half to herself. "We'll build it with boards and put snow over it."

My drawers had all been emptied and my trunks packed and now we were all just marking off minutes till it was time to go down to the train. Now that the day was almost here there was nothing left to say; almost nothing left to think. But we sat and sat at our supper until it was dark outside and the tea kettle had steamed the windows opaque and inside the house seemed very warm and bright. Outside, the wind blew high in the trees, swaying just topmost branches and sending a few leaves floating down to the gutter.

"Not even two days left," kept running through my mind, keeping pace with the other more commonplace thoughts, trying to crowd them out. I was still sitting comfortably in my own kitchen and already my throat ached with lonesomeness and there was a queer, soundless crying inside of me. My mother was just finishing her supper tea and her face was very calm and happy, with her hair brushed up high, just showing white at the temples. I felt there was something that I wanted very much to say; some little words that would come out warm and shaky because they had been shut up inside of me for so long. But they must have been shut up inside too long, for when I tried then to say that I was sorry that summer was over and that I was going away; when I tried to say that I would miss them—no words came out at all!

And then for the last time Jack came. He came in the front door rubbing his hands together and his cheeks were red with cold. "Did you ever see such a change in the weather, Mrs. Morrow? This is regular football weather." He clapped his hands together and his voice was loud, having come in out of the wind. He had his basketball sweater on, buttoned up tightly, and everything about him had a crisp, fresh-air look.

My mother laughed, just looking at him. You couldn't help laughing at someone so brown-skinned and healthy who brought fresh air in with him when he came. He seemed taller to me that night.

"You wouldn't believe that just this time last week Kitty was running around in playsuits. We'll probably have weeks of Indian summer yet but it feels like real fall tonight," she said. "I was telling Angie that I heard downtown that we may have a touch of frost."

"I heard that too," Jack told her. "My dad told me he heard a warning on the radio to farmers and there was a notice in the weather report in the paper tonight. From the feel of that wind there could be!" and he laid the palms of his hands against his tingling cheeks.

"You're red, Jack!" Kitty laughed up at him and he pulled one of her braids.

"You're a little red yourself," he said.

490

My mother was worrying away under her breath. "I certainly do hate to have them go to waste when I could can them just as easily as not. A good frost will spoil them for sure."

"You're worrying about the tomatoes, aren't you, Mom?" I asked. Having to gather in the tomatoes before a frost was a yearly occurrence with us. It was all part of having winter come. We were never prepared for that first frost, for we could never quite believe that summer was really over.

"Let Jack and me take them in—will you, Jack?" It will take only about an hour. . . ." I knew he would do anything I asked that night.

"Really, Angie," my mother protested, "if Jack has something else he'd rather do we can just let them go. . . ."

"No, let's get them picked," he said quickly. "I like to do things like that. There's something about tonight that makes you feel good to be outside even if . . . well, even if it's the end of summer."

Kitty brought my old heavy sweater from an upstairs closet and I carried up three clean bushel baskets from the basement. "Just pick the riper ones and don't bother with those that are too small," my mother said as we went out the back door.

The garden lay very square in the moonlight edged with sharp sticks of hedge. I took one basket and Jack the other two, one in each hand—that would be enough for the scattered few tomatoes that were left. Most of the green leaves were dead and the knobby vines were already wet with might dew. We worked side by side, not talking at first, feeling about in the half-darkness for the tomatoes, and soon our hands were wet to the wrists and the rough wool of my sweater chafed. Even my fingers felt stiff. But somehow it was so natural to be working beside Jack that I didn't want to stop, even for a moment.

Little patches of spider web shone white and filmy in the moonlight, stretched from one sprawling vine to another. Once our hands touched among the cold leaves and my breath came short for a moment. Jack looked at me and laughed. "Funny girl, Angie," he whispered. The tomatoes were cold to touch and the ripe, red ones looked black in the darkness and their skins were smooth and moist. There were green ones with tough stems that broke with a snap and sometimes a whole vine would pull out of the earth, trailing from my hands and sending a shower of cold drops onto the hard ground. Our ankles were wet with dew but my cheeks were tingling warm and Jack was humming a happy, jerky tune under his breath as he moved among the plants. Small, hard, green tomatoes with dried blossoms till stuck to them fell on the mud with soft little thuds. We didn't speak at all but just tossed the tomatoes into the baskets, our arms moving in an unconscious rhythm, stopping now and then to blow on our fingers and to wipe the dew off our hands.

I could feel it getting colder by minutes and the wind blew harder till the dew on the bare vines and little clods of earth began to turn white. There were storm circles round the moon and wisps of dark cloud brushed across it. Jack picked an overripe tomato and its tight skin burst between his fingers. He threw it over his shoulder into the darkness and a moment later it fell softly somewhere in the hedge. Above us the wind was wailing quietly and high up in the night the moon was racing with a cloud. The bare vines stretched like sinews in the pale light and Jack struck a match to see if we had missed any tomatoes, but the wind snuffed it out. He laughed to himself.

One by one we carried the full, heavy baskets into the garage, the cold wire handles cutting into our hands. The soft blackness of the garage seemed very

491

still after the sharp chill gusts outside—as if the wind were holding its breath. We set them side by side on the cement floor and when the third basket was in place we covered the tomatoes carefully with newspapers to keep out the cold. Jack found some funnies in a corner and, striking a match, he began to read a sheet of Dick Tracy funnies,[4] yellowed at the edges. The match sputtered and went out. In the darkness we tucked the newspapers in tightly and shoved the baskets into one corner.

"Jack," I said, "I won't be able to see you tomorrow night at all. That last night will be sort of family night. . . ."

"That's all right, Angie. I sort of figured that. I guess tonight's the last then." I nodded my head but somehow I didn't feel sad anymore.

Outside the wind was nosing around the garage windows and slipping in under the door. Jack kissed me and his hands were cold on my cheeks. This is how it should be, I thought. This is Jack. This is how it should be and his lips were warm on mine; soft and warm, and his cheek was cool and firm. It was only moments. A whole summer summed up in a few moments and then we went into the house by the back door.

My mother had made hot cocoa and set two cups on the corner of the kitchen table. Our hands were muddy and we washed them together under the cold water of the kitchen sink. "Angie," my mother laughed, "you should see yourself—you even have mud on your cheeks!" Jack was very busy with the soap and water but his own cheeks were flushed.

We drank the cocoa steaming hot, talking and laughing at each other while our faces still tingled from the wind. Jack's hand looked very brown against the white of the kitchen table. My mother sat with us, sewing buttons on a school dress of Kitty's, and he said to her suddenly, "Mrs. Morrow would you mind awfully if Angie and I walked out to the lake for a little while?"

"At this time of night, Jack? It's after nine o'clock now." Her tone was disapproving. "I hardly think it would be wise."

"I know it's late," he added hastily, "But I just happened to think that if the frost comes there might be water in the boat and if it froze in there it wouldn't be good!" Then as if to add strength to his statement he said, "In fact, I know there's water in it."

My mother bent over to snap off a white thread with her teeth and for a moment I thought she was smiling. "All right," she said quietly, "but don't be long. Angie, pull that old sweater of mine that's hanging by the back door on over your own. I'd hate to have you going to school with a cold."

I looked at Jack and he looked quickly at me and then I took the cocoa cups to rinse them at the sink while Jack got the old sweater for me. "We really won't be long, Mom," I told her.

He opened the back door for me and I noticed that in the little hollows where the garage eaves trough dripped the water was covered with a thin scum of ice. The storm circles were dark around the moon and the garden lay very square in the cold light. Our breath rose in vague, misty clouds above our heads.

"Come on," he said happily. "Let's run part of the way, Angie. I'm so glad you could go."

We turned off our street and as we hit the park road the wind swept in from the lake, clean and cold, and breathing the fresh air made my mind feel sharp

---

4 *funnies*   comic strips.

and clear. I was laughing as we ran. This is how it should be, I thought. The wind sent tears to my eyes and brushed clean through my hair.

The sailboat was rocking against the pier, its mast sticking up like a slim finger, and the white sail was rolled up tightly like a canvas cocoon. Jack pulled in the rope and brought the boat close up to the dock, stepping in. The water was like ink. "Angie," he called against the wind, "will you see if you can find a can lying around so I can bail this water out? There's about three inches in here."

Along the pier I searched and among the rocks that lined the road, kicking among the stones. Waves from the lake itself were crashing madly over the break-water at the mouth of the harbor, loud as the wind, and the air was damp. Suddenly I ran across an old coffee can, wedged between two stones, half full of old rain water, and I pulled it out.

"Here, Jack, will this do?" I held it up and then realized he couldn't see it in the darkness.

"Toss it over, will you?" he called and I went to the edge of the pier and pitched the can toward the boat. Jack reached out to catch it but missed and it clattered splashily onto the floor.

"This is just swell," he said, bending the can between the palms of his hands so it would scoop up the water better. I sat on a rock and hunched up my knees to protect myself from the wind while I watched him. He stood with feet apart on the crossbars of the boat and ladled the water out over the side. The sound of the can made a rhythmic scoop-scoop that was pleasant and friendly among the wild lake noises.

"Warm enough, honey?" Jack called.

"This is wonderful," I called back. And it was. Just being there with him in the night and the freshness of the wind was enough. The boat rocked as Jack moved back and forth, setting the mast waving gently. It was a little boat and bobbed with every movement, and the water slapped loudly against its sides, sending spray spitting high. It splashed wet against my legs and the wind was cold, playing with my hair and tunneling up my skirts.

A car went past on the road, the headlights nosing aside the darkness. "Almost through!" Jack shouted and I waved back. He bent again to scoop up the water, pouring it over the side of the boat into the darker water around him.

My hands were cold so I slid them up my sleeves and waited. My thoughts went back over the summer and suddenly it seemed inevitable that we should be here at the lake, Jack and I, where we had started. It was like a song that began and ended with the same refrain. Behind it all was the quiet music of the lake. That first night when the water had been calm and the small, bright reflections of the stars had almost tinkled on the ripples; and the afternoons when the lake was wash-water blue in the sunlight; and now tonight, it was dark and bottomless, crashing against the breakwater and rocking restlessly in the harbor. I felt an almost motherly affection for the little sailboat that had spent the summer tethered to this same dock on its short rope, patient as the waves that licked against its sides. The darkness of the sky, the sound of the water—all of it blended into memories of the summer as vivid as the present. But this night wind was chill and sharp with frost.

Just then Jack called, "Pull up that rope, will you, Angie? I'm finished here." I took the rope in both hands and drew the sailboat tight to the pier and he jumped onto the dock beside me.

"There," he said. "Let her freeze." He squeezed my arm. "I think I'll leave this can right here in case someone else wants to bail out." He let it clatter to

493

the rocks. On the end of the breakwater the tall white lighthouse was turning its beacon, slashing through the darkness with long, sharp-edged blades of light, cutting over the tops of the waves. The night was so void of human sounds that the wind was suddenly a roar in my ears. Jack was standing very close to me.

And then I made my mind say it to myself, pinning down the squirm of thoughts till they admitted precisely and finally, "This is the last night." And it was just as it should be. It was right that Jack should have on his basketball sweater and that his lips should be warm and moist and his cold hand rough against my cheek. Over and over again, mixed with wind and the night darkness and the damp, fishy smell of the lake, it was as it should be. This must last for a long time, I thought. I must remember and remember. Every moment of it. This is forever.

Jack's voice was low and husky and his hand was shaking a little. "Angie," he whispered, "I know that you don't want your family to know but I want you to have this. You know why . . . I want you to have it," and he slipped off his class ring and laid it in the palm of my hand.

I held it a moment and it was still warm from the warmth of his finger, and his hand closed over mine so tightly that my own fingers hurt. And then all so suddenly it was time to go home. For the last time, it was time to go home.

And we walked side by side with the wind behind us and a gray cloud over the moon. And the puddles in the road were skimmed white with the first frost of fall. I was somehow afraid to put it on and I had no pocket in my sweater. There was nowhere to put it. So I walked all the way home with the class ring clutched in my hand.

The next day meant nothing for I didn't see Jack at all. And the next evening I spent with my family sitting in our living room, talking quietly but not thinking about anything. And then, so quickly, it was morning and we were up in the early gray-pinkness of it getting ready to drive to the station. Kitty had begged to be allowed to go down to the train with us but she was sleeping so peacefully, her braids outspread on the pillow, that my mother whispered, "Don't wake her, Angie. We'll be there and back before she knows we've even gone."

In the kitchen we had coffee together and the sunlight had just begun to color the sky. "It's going to be a beautiful day," my father said thoughtfully. "It seems a shame to get you up so early, Angeline, but this train will get you to Chicago before noon and that's what Lorraine wanted. It's good to travel in the clean of the morning anyway."

That station yard was achingly empty with vacant baggage wagons pulled to one side and a solitary taxi cab waiting, with its motor still running. There was an early morning lonesomeness about everything and none of us said much. I kept watching for Jack for I knew he would come. He hadn't said so, but I knew he would.

He drove up in the black bakery truck and I knew from the sound of the car door as it slammed that it was he. "Just thought I'd like to say good-bye," he told my mother and father, and they smiled. Looking at him then I thought of dozens and dozens of things I had meant to say to him and hadn't remembered until now. Little words were eager on my lips but my mother and father stood close beside us, looking down the shining curve of track, waiting for the train to break through the gray mist of morning. Someday I will tell him, I promised myself. After everything else is over.

The sound of the train came riding toward us and its great wheels churned into the station, hissing out steam, and the conductor stepped off onto the platform, waving a lantern, blacked out now in the light of the morning.

494

"I guess this is for you, Angie," my father said and he kissed me.

"You take care of yourself, dear," my mother whispered, softly. "You will write and let us know everything, won't you?" and she kissed my hair.

Jack stood, silent, " 'Bye, Jack," I said to him.

"Good-bye, Angie. Be good," he answered and for only a moment his hand was on mine.

"Lorraine will meet you at the station in Chicago," my mother called after me. "She promised she would be there on time, so, Angie dear, you won't have to worry about anything at all."

No, I thought, I won't have to worry about anything, and I looked back out of the train window to wave to them and saw Jack in the half-light of morning, standing with his hands jammed in his pockets and his basketball sweater knotted loosely around his neck. I won't have to worry about anything at all.

Quiet, sleeping houses and gray clapboard taverns slid by the window, lined along the track. I could feel the chug-chug of the train beneath me as the wheels turned. The drab edges of the town straggled past, shabby, sad-eyed houses and sagging sheds, trailing bits of worn rail fence around them. Fond du Lac gathered her shoddy outskirts in about her. Bushes in the fields were russet-leaved, catching the glow of the first light of morning and the treetops rocked with the waking birds. And slowly, slowly out of the grayness, morning was coming.

And I saw it all glide past me, lopped off by fence-posts, and I felt myself ache inside with a quiet sadness. And now I knew suddenly that it could come and could come forever, slipping by in the breath of a moment, and yet never again would there ever be anything quite as wonderful as that seventeenth summer!

495

S. E. Hinton

1948–

WHEN grown-ups say things like "It's a pity youth is wasted on the young," they imply that youth truly should be a time filled with promise and joy, that, for some strange reason, the young aren't wise, or brave, enough to seize the full fair flower of their youthful time. Such grown-ups may forget their own, far less joyful youth. If they should remember it accurately, they might say instead: "Youth is a thing the young are lucky to survive."

In *The Outsiders*, some of the youth do not survive. Those who do are scarred, it seems, for life. The book closes taking note of a dying boy's impossible dream: that his best friend manage somehow to retain his innocence, to remain as golden as bright sunrise. "When you're a kid everything's new dawn. . . . Keep that way." Thus the dying Johnny pleads with the novel's protagonist, Ponyboy Curtis, to "stay gold," to remain forever "a kid." The reason for Johnny's plea is plain enough: maturation presents a bleak prospect. The world of older adolescence is filled with alienation, violence, and doubt. Who would want to go there? Thinking of his older friend, Dallas Winston, slain by police, Ponyboy seethes with anguish for all youth who will share his fate: "I could picture hundreds and hundreds of boys living on the wrong sides of cities, boys with black eyes who jumped at their own shadows. Hundreds of boys who maybe watched sunsets and looked at stars and ached for something better. I could see boys going down under street lights because they were mean and tough and hated the world, and it was too late to tell them that there was still good in it, and they wouldn't believe you if you did. It was too vast a problem to be just a personal thing."

Disillusion is of course a staple of novels that are true to adolescent experience. In *Malaeska*, young William Danforth, stripped of his illusory identity, commits suicide. Even the insouciant Ragged Dick admits more and more often to being "ashamed" of his appearance and behavior, and, even as he gains modest wealth, he is reduced by the threat of theft to carrying his bankbook on his person, a telling sign of how much "respectability" may eventually hedge in his earlier, unthinking freedom, fun, and largesse. The generally bonny, sunny Anne of Green Gables admits that growing up is not the fun she expected: "it's a serious thing to grow up" she says. Even Angie Morrow, who finds her seventeenth summer "wonderful," also finds her wonder mingled with sadness, "so much sadness in growing up . . . my heart aching with a weariness that went through me . . . my throat ached with lonesomeness and there was a queer, soundless crying inside of me . . . I felt myself ache inside with a quiet sadness."

In *The Outsiders*, part of the sadness comes from facing the "vast problem" of unfair death and of hate and cruelty inflicted in the larger society. Ponyboy learns the hard way, and in the most graphic terms that "things are tough all over." His world of mean streets and early death radically darkens the young adult view. True, there is death in the earlier classics presented in this anthology. But the death of William Danforth, Jr., was an anomaly, an isolated act of self-destruction under peculiar circumstances. And the death of Matthew was something Anne was given to expect in due course. In the other works, death may hover on the horizon of danger (danger to the boy Ragged Dick rescues or to Angie's ailing mother), but in *The Outsiders* death becomes the name of the game. In the course of the novel, three boys are killed, and the larger society remains hostile to the fragile survival of those not killed. A quarter century after *Seventeenth Summer*, we have moved in *The Outsiders* from the nearly pre-World War II innocence and idealism of Fond du Lac, Wisconsin (with its relatively safe, class-blending high schools and its friendly drug store meeting spots for youth) to the urban environment of a parched Oklahoma city where no high school or drugstore or even parent or social worker can provide enough safety to keep kids out of gang warfare.

Leaving behind, as if forever, the generally upbeat, hopeful view of adolescence fostered by preceding young adult novels, where disillusion, if admitted, was still manageable, *The Outsiders* took a quantum leap into the reality, or at least one significant reality, of teen-age violence and near-despair. It may be significant that this genuinely breakthrough book, whose popularity is still enormous, was written by a sixteen-year-old determined to tell it like it is, and then some, from a middle-teenager's perspective. Susan Eloise Hinton was born in Tulsa three years after the close of the Second World War. Her family was in the middle class. In her middle childhood years, she combined a love of reading and writing with a tomboy streak that meant most of her friends were boys. At Will Rogers High School, in Tulsa, she was something of an outsider herself, though not a loner. She observed the conflicts between the more economically advantaged "Socials" and the blue-collar "Greasers" and tended to side with the Greasers though she also had some rich friends. She proved she could fight, sometimes carried a switchblade, and had a tooth chipped by a thrown bottle. When a Greaser friend of hers was badly beaten by "Socs" (pronounced "SO-shez") who didn't like his hair style, she wanted to write a story that would defend the humanity of the Greasers. *The Outsiders*, actually her third novel (first one published), was the result.

Written in her sophomore and junior years, at a time when her father was dying from a brain tumor, Hinton's novel, after four redrafts, was published in 1967 by Viking in New York as a general book for readers of all ages. It was immediately popular, especially with adolescent readers, and came to be classed as a young adult novel, selling to date over eight million copies. Hinton went on to write several more novels, on similar themes: *That Was Then, This Is Now* (1971), *Rumble Fish* (1975), *Tex* (1979), and *Taming the Star Runner* (1988), and, later, stories for younger children. All four of her (then-published) young adult novels were made into films between 1982 and 1985, two of them directed by Francis Ford Coppola and starring such actors as Matt Dillon, Tom Cruise, Patrick Swayze, Emilio Estevez, Nicholas Cage, and Dennis Hopper.

Why is *The Outsiders* still a best seller? Some critics find suspicious reasons, suggesting that young readers like the way Hinton glamorizes the Greasers, making them handsome, virile, tough, supportive, compassionate, smart, appreciative of beauty, yet tragically doomed to semi-orphanage and unfair treatment by society. Young, especially male, readers, according to this account, fall for the romantic, idealizing myth of abandoned but heroically self-sufficient youth that Hinton provides. Complexities of life with parents or in school are conven-

498

iently sidestepped, so this argument goes, and ethical judgments are reduced to simplistic levels. Violence is often glorified, and petty hoodlums are seen as "gallant." Hinton is faulted as a writer, moreover, for unrealistic plotting, melodrama, over-emotionalism, cliché descriptions, and so on. It all amounts to an argument that Hinton's young readers prefer to escape rather than face the real world of complex adjustment to family, peers, and society.

Such arguments have some validity, no doubt, yet they tend to discount not only the youth of the book's author but also the youth of its protagonist. Should either be expected to display much linguistic or moral sophistication? At one month over 13, Ponyboy Curtis inhabits a useful age from which to view the all-male social groups around him. Some social psychologists identify the period of about 10–14 among males and females as a time of likely early or pre-adolescent "chumship" when youths very often seek out social support from same-sex friendships, support equal to or stronger than that provided by their families of origin. As children mature from the relative and generally mother-dominant security of early childhood, their world is often progressively masculinized as they enter the more competitive, motor-active, and sometimes violent environments of male groups in schools, on playing fields, and in gangs, not to mention the more or less patriarchal culture surrounding them. Same-sex chumships provide, for a while, the levels and kinds of protection, support, sharing, even intimacy that this age group can best employ. From the relative safety of this peer group, first steps can be taken toward the cross-sex relations that will complete the eventual transition of many or most from being parented to being parents. *The Outsiders* zeroes in, then, upon the feelings young men may experience during the turbulent progression from family and chumship toward cross-sex relations. As younger adolescents, Ponyboy and his special friend, Johnny Cade, share their feelings in a way that older adolescent males might not, and the fact that their author was a sixteen-year-old girl (who had a younger sister) may help account for their vulnerability and openness; they are not too older-male-tough to feel their feelings and to share them, even to cry.

The youth of Ponyboy also helps account for his often-fascinating ambivalence: he both admires and feels alienated from his older brother Darry; he admires "nice" Soc girls but is "half-scared of all nice girls"; he officially detests the Socs but also recognizes a "basic sameness" with them, they are "human too" like the Greasers; and Ponyboy insists upon joining the rumbles yet sees the futility of fighting. In part, Ponyboy resists, as well he might, growing further into the violent, unfair world that awaits him. In part, he wants to escape. He longs for his parents who were lost in a car wreck. He wants to go "someplace without greasers or Socs": "I loved the country. I wanted to be out of towns and away from excitement." Paradoxically, when he and Johnny do go out into the countryside, they end up in an abandoned church, "on top of the world," where he imagines "We ain't gonna cry no more," resurrection talk. Still, this is the place where he shares the poem with Johnny, the poem that tells how "Eden sank to grief" and "nothing gold can stay." That church becomes for them a place of heroic sacrifice (saving children from the burning church, "a red hell," and wondering "were we sent from heaven?"), and they end their ambivalent pastoral journey through the traditional return to the city and its unresolved contradictions.

Part anthem for doomed and idealized youth, part bitter satire against abusive parents, social workers, and police, and part celebration of what is "still good" in the world, a recognition that "you don't just stop living because you lose someone . . . You don't quit!," *The Outsiders* roils and soars with an emotional intensity, a caring for its characters, rarely matched in the history of young adult literature. Though easy to snipe at, this novel endures for reasons that are, both simply and not so simply, good.

THE OUTSIDERS

CHAPTER 1

WHEN I STEPPED out into the bright sunlight from the darkness of the movie house, I had only two things on my mind: Paul Newman and a ride home. I was wishing I looked like Paul Newman—he looks tough and I don't—but I guess my own looks aren't so bad. I have light-brown, almost-red hair and greenish-gray eyes. I wish they were more gray, because I hate most guys that have green eyes, but I have to be content with what I have. My hair is longer than a lot of boys wear theirs, squared off in back and long at the front and sides, but I am a greaser and most of my neighborhood rarely bothers to get a haircut. Besides, I look better with long hair.

I had a long walk home and no company, but I usually lone it anyway, for no reason except that I like to watch movies undisturbed so I can get into them and live them with the actors. When I see a movie with someone it's kind of uncomfortable, like having someone read your book over your shoulder. I'm different that way. I mean, my second-oldest brother, Soda, who is sixteen-going-on-seventeen, never cracks a book at all, and my oldest brother, Darrel, who we call Darry, works too long and hard to be interested in a story or drawing a picture, so I'm not like them. And nobody in our gang digs movies and books the way I do. For a while there, I thought I was the only person in the world that did. So I loned it.

Soda tries to understand, at least, which is more than Darry does. But then, Soda is different from anybody; he understands everything, almost. Like he's never hollering at me all the time the way Darry is, or treating me as if I was six instead of fourteen. I love Soda more than I've ever loved anyone, even Mom and Dad. He's always happy-go-lucky and grinning, while Darry's hard and firm and rarely grins at all. But then, Darry's gone through a lot in his twenty years, grown up too fast. Sodapop'll never grow up at all. I don't know which way's the best. I'll find out one of these days.

Anyway, I went on walking home, thinking about the movie, and then suddenly wishing I had some company. Greasers can't walk alone too much or they'll get jumped, or someone will come by and scream "Greaser!" at them, which doesn't make you feel too hot; if you know what I mean. We get jumped by the Socs. I'm not sure how you spell it, but it's the abbreviation for the Socials, the jet set, the West-side rich kids. It's like the term "greaser," which is used to class all us boys on the East Side.

We're poorer than the Socs and the middle class. I reckon we're wilder, too. Not like the Socs, who jump greasers and wreck houses and throw beer blasts for kicks, and get editorials in the paper for being a public disgrace one day and an asset to society the next. Greasers are almost like hoods; we steal things and drive old souped-up cars and hold up gas stations and have a gang fight once in a while. I don't mean I do things like that. Darry would kill me if I got into trouble with the police. Since Mom and Dad were killed in an auto wreck, the three of us get to stay together only as long as we behave. So Soda and I stay out of trouble as much as we can, and we're careful not to get caught when we can't. I only mean that most greasers do things like that, just like we wear our hair long and dress in blue jeans and T-shirts, or leave our shirttails out and wear leather jackets and tennis shoes or boots. I'm not saying that either Socs or greasers are better; that's just the way things are.

I could have waited to go to the movies until Darry or Sodapop got off work. They would have gone with me, or driven me there, or walked along, although Soda just can't sit still long enough to enjoy a movie and they bore Darry to death. Darry thinks his life is enough without inspecting other people's. Or I could have gotten one of the gang to come along, one of the four boys Darry and Soda and I have grown up with and consider family. We're almost as close as brothers; when you grow up in a tight-knit neighborhood like ours you get to know each other real well. If I had thought about it, I could have called Darry and he would have come by on his way home and picked me up, or Two-Bit Mathews—one of our gang—would have come to get me in his car if I had asked him, but sometimes I just don't use my head. It drives my brother Darry nuts when I do stuff like that, 'cause I'm supposed to be smart; I make good grades and have a high IQ and everything, but I don't use my head. Besides, I like walking.

I about decided I didn't like it so much, though, when I spotted that red Corvair trailing me. I was almost two blocks from home then, so I started walking a little faster. I had never been jumped, but I had seen Johnny after four Socs got hold of him, and it wasn't pretty. Johnny was scared of his own shadow after that. Johnny was sixteen then.

I knew it wasn't any use though—the fast walking. I mean—even before the Corvair pulled up beside me and five Socs got out. I got pretty scared—I'm kind of small for fourteen even though I have a good build, and those guys were bigger than me. I automatically hitched my thumbs in my jeans and slouched, wondering if I could get away if I made a break for it. I remembered Johnny— his face all cut up and bruised, and I remembered how he had cried when we found him, half-conscious, in the corner lot. Johnny had it awful rough at home—it took a lot to make him cry.

I was sweating something fierce, although I was cold. I could feel my palms getting clammy and the perspiration running down my back. I get like that when I'm real scared. I glanced around for a pop bottle or a stick or something—Steve Randle, Soda's best buddy, had once held off four guys with a busted pop bottle—but there was nothing. So I stood there like a bump on a log while they surrounded me. I don't use my head. They walked around slowly, silently, smiling.

"Hey, grease," one said in an over-friendly voice. "We're gonna do you a favor, greaser. We're gonna cut all that long greasy hair off."

He had on a madras shirt. I can still see it. Blue madras. One of them laughed, then cussed me out in a low voice. I couldn't think of anything to say. There just isn't a whole lot you can say while waiting to get mugged, so I kept my mouth shut.

"Need a haircut, greaser?" The medium-sized blond pulled a knife out of his back pocket and flipped the blade open.

I finally thought of something to say. "No." I was backing up, away from that knife. Of course I backed right into one of them. They had me down in a second. They had my arms and legs pinned down and one of them was sitting on my chest with his knees on my elbows, and if you don't think that hurts, you're crazy. I could smell English Leather shaving lotion and stale tobacco, and I wondered foolishly if I would suffocate before they did anything. I was scared so bad I was wishing I would. I fought to get loose, and almost did for a second; then they tightened up on me and the one on my chest slugged me a couple of times. So I lay still, swearing at them between gasps. A blade was held against my throat.

"How'd you like that haircut to begin just below the chin?"

It occurred to me then that they could kill me. I went wild. I started screaming for Soda, Darry, anyone. Someone put his hand over my mouth, and I bit it as hard as I could, tasting the blood running through my teeth. I heard a muttered curse and got slugged again, and they were stuffing a handkerchief in my mouth. One of them kept saying. "Shut him up, for Pete's sake, shut him up!"

Then there were shouts and the pounding of feet, and the Socs jumped up and left me lying there, gasping. I lay there and wondered what in the world was happening—people were jumping over me and running by me and I was too dazed to figure it out. Then someone had me under the armpits and was hauling me to my feet. It was Darry.

"Are you all right, Ponyboy?"

He was shaking me and I wished he'd stop. I was dizzy enough anyway. I could tell it was Darry though—partly because of the voice and partly because Darry's always rough with me without meaning to be.

"I'm okay. Quit shaking me, Darry, I'm okay."

He stopped instantly. "I'm sorry."

He wasn't really. Darry isn't ever sorry for anything he does. It seems funny to me that he should look just exactly like my father and act exactly the opposite from him. My father was only forty when he died and he looked twenty-five and a lot of people thought Darry and Dad were brothers instead of father and son. But they only looked alike—my father was never rough with anyone without meaning to be.

Darry is six-feet-two, and broad-shouldered and muscular. He has dark-brown hair that kicks out in front and a slight cowlick in the back—just like Dad's—but Darry's eyes are his own. He's got eyes that are like two pieces of pale blue-green ice. They've got a determined set to them, like the rest of him. He looks older than twenty—tough, cool, and smart. He would be real handsome if his eyes weren't so cold. He doesn't understand anything that is not plain hard fact. But he uses his head.

I sat down again, rubbing my cheek where I'd been slugged the most.

Darry jammed his fists in his pockets. "They didn't hurt you too bad, did they?"

They did. I was smarting and aching and my chest was sore and I was so nervous my hands were shaking and I wanted to start bawling, but you just don't say that to Darry.

"I'm okay."

Sodapop came loping back. By then I had figured that all the noise I had heard was the gang coming to rescue me. He dropped down beside me, examining my head.

"You got cut up a little, huh, Ponyboy?"

I only looked at him blankly. "I did?"

He pulled out a handkerchief, wet the end of it with his tongue, and pressed it gently against the side of my head. "You're bleedin' like a stuck pig."

"I am?"

"Look!" He showed me the handkerchief, reddened as if by magic. "Did they pull a blade on you?"

I remembered the voice: "Need a haircut, greaser?" The blade must have slipped while he was trying to shut me up. "Yeah."

Soda is handsomer than anyone else I know. Not like Darry—Soda's movie-star kind of handsome, the kind that people stop on the street to watch go by. He's not as tall as Darry, and he's a little slimmer, but he has a finely drawn, sensitive face that somehow manages to be reckless and thoughtful at the same time. He's got dark-gold hair that he combs back—long and silky and straight—and in the summer the sun bleaches it to a shining wheat-gold. His eyes are dark brown—lively, dancing, recklessly laughing eyes that can be gentle and sympathetic one moment and blazing with anger the next. He has Dad's eyes, but Soda is one of a kind. He can get drunk in a drag race or dancing without ever getting near alcohol. In our neighborhood it's rare to find a kid who doesn't drink once in a while. But Soda never touches a drop—he doesn't need to. He gets drunk on just plain living. And he understands everybody.

He looked at me more closely. I looked away hurriedly, because, if you want to know the truth, I was starting to bawl. I knew I was as white as I felt and I was shaking like a leaf.

Soda just put his hand on my shoulder. "Easy, Ponyboy. They ain't gonna hurt you no more."

"I know," I said, but the ground began to blur and I felt hot tears running down my cheeks. I brushed them away impatiently. "I'm just a little spooked, that's all." I drew a quivering breath and quit crying. You just don't cry in front of Darry. Not unless you're hurt like Johnny had been that day we found him in the vacant lot. Compared to Johnny I wasn't hurt at all.

Soda rubbed my hair. "You're an okay kid, Pony."

I had to grin at him—Soda can make you grin no matter what. I guess it's because he's always grinning so much himself. "You're crazy, Soda, out of your mind."

Darry looked as if he'd like to knock our heads together. "You're both nuts."

Soda merely cocked one eyebrow, a trick he'd picked up from Two-Bit. "It seems to run in this family."

Darry stared at him for a second, then cracked a grin. Sodapop isn't afraid of him like everyone else and enjoys teasing him. I'd just as soon tease a full-grown grizzly; but for some reason, Darry seems to like being teased by Soda.

Our gang had chased the Socs to their car and heaved rocks at them. They came running toward us now—four lean, hard guys. They were all as tough as nails and looked it. I had grown up with them, and they accepted me, even though I was younger, because I was Darry and Soda's kid brother and I kept my mouth shut good.

Steve Randle was seventeen, tall and lean, with thick greasy hair he kept combed in complicated swirls. He was cocky, smart, and Soda's best buddy since grade school. Steve's specialty was cars. He could lift a hubcap quicker and more quietly than anyone in the neighborhood, but he also knew cars upside-down and backward, and he could drive anything on wheels. He and Soda worked at the same gas station—Steve part time and Soda full time—and their station got more customers than any other in town. Whether that was because Steve was so good with cars or because Soda attracted girls like honey draws flies, I couldn't tell you. I liked Steve only because he was Soda's best friend. He didn't like me—he thought I was a tagalong and a kid; Soda always took me with them when they went places if they weren't taking girls, and that bugged Steve. It wasn't my fault; Soda always asked me, I didn't ask him. Soda doesn't think I'm a kid.

Two-Bit Mathews was the oldest of the gang and the wisecracker of the bunch. He was about six feet tall, stocky in build, and very proud of his long rusty-colored sideburns. He had gray eyes and a wide grin, and he couldn't stop making funny remarks to save his life. You couldn't shut up that guy; he always had to get his two-bits worth in. Hence his name. Even his teachers forgot his real name was Keith, and we hardly remembered he had one. Life was one big joke to Two-Bit. He was famous for shoplifting and his black-handled switch-blade (which he couldn't have acquired without his first talent), and he was always smarting off to the cops. He really couldn't help it. Everything he said was so irresistibly funny that he just had to let the police in on it to brighten up their dull lives. (That's the way he explained it to me.) He liked fights, blondes, and for some unfathomable reason, school. He was still a junior at eighteen and a half and he never learned anything. He just went for kicks. I liked him real well because he kept us laughing at ourselves as well as at other things. He reminded me of Will Rogers—maybe it was the grin.

If I had to pick the real character of the gang, it would be Dallas Winston—Dally. I used to like to draw his picture when he was in a dangerous mood, for then I could get his personality down in a few lines. He had an elfish face, with high cheekbones and a pointed chin, small, sharp animal teeth, and ears like a lynx. His hair was almost white it was so blond, and he didn't like haircuts, or hair oil either, so it fell over his forehead in wisps and kicked out in the back in tufts and curled behind his ears and along the nape of his neck. His eyes were blue, blazing ice, cold with a hatred of the whole world. Dally had spent three years on the wild side of New York and had been arrested at the age of ten. He was tougher than the rest of us—tougher, colder, meaner. The shade of difference that separates a greaser from a hood wasn't present in Dally. He was as wild as the boys in the downtown outfits, like Tim Shepard's gang.

In New York, Dally blew off steam in gang fights, but here, organized gangs arc rarities—there are just small bunches of friends who stick together, and the warfare is between the social classes. A rumble, when it's called, is usually born of a grudge fight, and the opponents just happen to bring their friends along. Oh, there are a few named gangs around, like the River Kings and the Tiber Street Tigers, but here in the Southwest there's no gang rivalry. So Dally, even though he could get into a good fight sometimes, had no specific thing to hate. No rival gang. Only Socs. And you can't win against them no matter how hard you try, because they've got all the breaks and even whipping them isn't going to change that fact. Maybe that was why Dallas was so bitter.

He had quite a reputation. They have a file on him down at the police station. He had been arrested, he got drunk, he rode in rodeos, lied, cheated, stole, rolled drunks, jumped small kids—he did everything. I didn't like him, but he was smart and you had to respect him.

Johnny Cade was last and least. If you can picture a little dark puppy that has been kicked too many times and is lost in a crowd of strangers, you'll have Johnny. He was the youngest, next to me, smaller than the rest, with a slight build. He had big black eyes in a dark tanned face; his hair was jet-black and heavily greased and combed to the side, but it was so long that it fell in shaggy bangs across his forehead. He had a nervous, suspicious look in his eyes, and that beating he got from the Socs didn't help matters. He was the gang's pet, everyone's kid brother. His father was always beating him up, and his mother ignored him, except when she was hacked off at something, and then you could hear her yelling at him clear down at our house. I think he hated that worse than getting whipped. He would have run away a million times if we hadn't been there. If it hadn't been for the gang, Johnny would never have known what love and affection are.

I wiped my eyes hurriedly. "Didya catch 'em?"

"Nup. They got away this time, the dirty . . ." Two-Bit went on cheerfully, calling the Socs every name he could think of or make up.

"The kid's okay?"

"I'm okay." I tried to think of something to say. I'm usually pretty quiet around people, even the gang. I changed the subject. "I didn't know you were out of the cooler yet, Dally."

"Good behavior. Got off early." Dallas lit a cigarette and handed it to Johnny. Everyone sat down to have a smoke and relax. A smoke always lessens the tension. I had quit trembling and my color was back. The cigarette was calming me down. Two-Bit cocked an eyebrow. "Nice-lookin' bruise you got there, kid."

I touched my cheek gingerly. "Really?"

Two-Bit nodded sagely. "Nice cut, too. Makes you look tough."

Tough and *tuff* are two different words. *Tough* is the same as rough; *tuff* means cool, sharp—like a tuff-looking Mustang or a tuff record. In our neighborhood both are compliments.

Steve flicked his ashes at me. "What were you doin', walkin' by your lonesome?" Leave it to good old Steve to bring up something like that.

"I was comin' home from the movies. I didn't think . . ."

"You don't ever think," Darry broke in, "not at home or anywhere when it counts. You must think at school, with all those good grades you bring home, and you've always got your nose in a book, but do you ever use your head for common sense? No sirree, bub. And if you did have to go by yourself, you should have carried a blade."

I just stared at the hole in the toe of my tennis shoe. Me and Darry just didn't dig each other. I never could please him. He would have hollered at me for carrying a blade if I *had* carried one. If I brought home *B*'s, he wanted *A*'s, and if I got *A*'s, he wanted to make sure they stayed *A*'s. If I was playing football, I should be in studying, and if I was reading, I should be out playing football. He never hollered at Sodapop—not even when Soda dropped out of school or got tickets for speeding. He just hollered at me.

Soda was glaring at him. "Leave my kid brother alone, you hear? It ain't his fault he likes to go to the movies, and it ain't his fault the Socs like to jump us, and if he had been carrying a blade it would have been a good excuse to cut him to ribbons."

Soda always takes up for me.

Darry said impatiently, "When I want my kid brother to tell me what to do with my other kid brother, I'll ask you—kid brother." But he laid off me. He always does when Sodapop tells him to. Most of the time.

"Next time get one of us to go with you, Ponyboy," Two-Bit said. "Any of us will."

"Speakin' of movies"—Dally yawned, flipping away his cigarette butt—"I'm walkin' over to the Nightly Double tomorrow night. Anybody want to come and hunt some action?"

Steve shook his head. "Me and Soda are pickin' up Evie and Sandy for the game."

He didn't need to look at me the way he did right then. I wasn't going to ask if I could come. I'd never tell Soda, because he really likes Steve a lot, but sometimes I can't stand Steve Randle. I mean it. Sometimes I hate him.

Darry sighed, just like I knew he would. Darry never had time to do anything anymore. "I'm working tomorrow night."

Dally looked at the rest of us. "How about y'all? Two-Bit? Johnnycake, you and Pony wanta come?"

"Me and Johnny'll come," I said. I knew Johnny wouldn't open his mouth unless he was forced to. "Okay, Darry?"

"Yeah, since it ain't a school night." Darry was real good about letting me go places on the weekends. On school nights I could hardly leave the house.

"I was plannin' on getting boozed up tomorrow night," Two-Bit said. "If I don't, I'll walk over and find y'all."

Steve was looking at Dally's hand. His ring, which he had rolled a drunk senior to get, was back on his finger. "You break up with Sylvia again?"

"Yeah, and this time it's for good. That little broad was two-timin' me again while I was in jail."

I thought of Sylvia and Evie and Sandy and Two-Bit's many blondes. They were the only kind of girls that would look at us, I thought. Tough, loud girls who wore too much eye makeup and giggled and swore too much. I liked Soda's girl Sandy just fine, though. Her hair was natural blond and her laugh was soft, like her china-blue eyes. She didn't have a real good home or anything and was our kind—greaser—but she was a real nice girl. Still, lots of times I wondered what other girls were like. The girls who were bright-eyed and had their dresses a decent length and acted as if they'd like to spit on us if given a chance. Some were afraid of us, and remembering Dallas Winston, I didn't blame them. But most looked at us like we were dirt—gave us the same kind of look that the Socs did when they came by in their Mustangs and Corvairs and yelled "Grease!" at us. I wondered about them. The girls, I mean . . . Did they cry when their boys were arrested, like Evie did when Steve got hauled in, or did they run out on them the way Sylvia did Dallas? But maybe their boys didn't get arrested or beaten up or busted up in rodeos.

I was still thinking about it while I was doing my homework that night. I had to read *Great Expectations* for English, and that kid Pip, he reminded me of us— the way he felt marked lousy because he wasn't a gentleman or anything, and the way that girl[1] kept looking down on him. That happened to me once. One time in biology I had to dissect a worm, and the razor wouldn't cut, so I used my switchblade. The minute I flicked it out—I forgot what I was doing or I would never have done it—this girl right beside me kind of gasped, and said, "They are right. You are a hood." That didn't make me feel so hot. There were a lot of Socs in that class—I get put into A classes because I'm supposed to be smart—and most of them thought it was pretty funny. I didn't, though. She was a cute girl. She looked real good in yellow.

We deserve a lot of our trouble, I thought. Dallas deserves everything he gets, and should get worse, if you want the truth. And Two-Bit—he doesn't really want or need half the things he swipes from stores. He just thinks it's fun to swipe everything that isn't nailed down. I can understand why Sodapop and Steve get into drag races and fights so much, though—both of them have too much energy, too much feeling, with no way to blow it off.

"Rub harder, Soda," I heard Darry mumbling. "You're gonna put me to sleep."

---

1 Great Expectations . . . *that girl* One of the finest novels of Charles Dickens (1812–70), *Great Expectations* (1861) tells of the orphan, Philip Pirrip ("Pip"), who wants to marry the disdainful Estella and rise above his humble origins.

I looked through the door. Sodapop was giving Darry a back-rub. Darry is always pulling muscles; he roofs houses and he's always trying to carry two bundles of roofing up the ladder. I knew Soda would put him to sleep, because Soda can put about anyone out when he sets his head to it. He thought Darry worked too hard anyway. I did, too.

Darry didn't deserve to work like an old man when he was only twenty. He had been a real popular guy in school; he was captain of the football team and he had been voted Boy of the Year. But we just didn't have the money for him to go to college, even with the athletic scholarship he won. And now he didn't have time between jobs to even think about college. So he never went anywhere and never did anything anymore, except work out at gyms and go skiing with some old friends of his sometimes.

I rubbed my cheek where it had turned purple. I had looked in the mirror, and it did make me look tough. But Darry had made me put a Band-Aid on the cut.

I remembered how awful Johnny had looked when he got beaten up. I had just as much right to use the streets as the Socs did, and Johnny had never hurt them. Why did the Socs hate us so much? We left them alone. I nearly went to sleep over my homework trying to figure it out.

Sodapop, who had jumped into bed by this time, yelled sleepily for me to turn off the light and get to bed. When I finished the chapter I was on, I did.

Lying beside Soda, staring at the wall, I kept remembering the faces of the Socs as they surrounded me, that blue madras shirt the blond was wearing, and I could still hear a thick voice: "Need a haircut, greaser?" I shivered.

"You cold, Ponyboy?"

"A little," I lied. Soda threw one arm across my neck. He mumbled something drowsily. "Listen, kiddo, when Darry hollers at you . . . he don't mean nothin'. He's just got more worries than somebody his age ought to. Don't take him serious . . . you dig, Pony? Don't let him bug you. He's really proud of you 'cause you're so brainy. It's just because you're the baby—I mean, he loves you a lot. Savvy?"

"Sure," I said, trying for Soda's sake to keep the sarcasm out of my voice.

"Soda?"

"Yeah?"

"How come you dropped out?" I never have gotten over that. I could hardly stand it when he left school.

"'Cause I'm dumb. The only things I was passing anyway were auto mechanics and gym."

"You're not dumb."

"Yeah, I am. Shut up and I'll tell you something. Don't tell Darry, though."

"Okay."

"I think I'm gonna marry Sandy. After she gets out of school and I get a better job and everything. I might wait till you get out of school, though. So I can still help Darry with the bills and stuff."

"Tuff enough. Wait till I get out, though, so you can keep Darry off my back."

"Don't be like that, kid. I told you he don't mean half of what he says . . ."

"You in love with Sandy? What's it like?"

"Hhhmmm." He sighed happily. "It's real nice."

In a moment his breathing was light and regular. I turned my head to look at him and in the moonlight he looked like some Greek god come to earth. I wondered how he could stand being so handsome. Then I sighed. I didn't quite get

508

what he meant about Darry. Darry thought I was just another mouth to feed and somebody to holler at. Darry love me? I thought of those hard, pale eyes. Soda was wrong for once, I thought. Darry doesn't love anyone or anything, except maybe Soda. I didn't hardly think of him as being human. I don't care, I lied to myself, I don't care about him either. Soda's enough, and I'd have him until I got out of school. I don't care about Darry. But I was still lying and I knew it. I lie to myself all the time. But I never believe me.

CHAPTER 2

DALLY WAS WAITING for Johnny and me under the street light at the corner of Pickett and Sutton, and since we got there early, we had time to go over the drugstore in the shopping center and goof around. We bought Cokes and blew the straws at the waitress, and walked around eyeing things that were lying out in the open until the manager got wise to us and suggested we leave. He was too late, though; Dally walked out with two packages of Kools under his jacket.

Then we went across the street and down Sutton a little way to The Dingo. There are lots of drive-ins in town—the Socs go to The Way Out and to Rusty's, and the greasers go to The Dingo and to Jay's. The Dingo is a pretty rough hangout; there's always a fight going on there and once a girl got shot. We walked around talking to all the greasers and hoods we knew, leaning in car windows or hopping into the back seats, and getting in on who was running away, and who was in jail, and who was going with who, and who could whip who, and who stole what and when and why. We knew about everybody there. There was a pretty good fight while we were there between a big twenty-three-year-old greaser and a Mexican hitchhiker. We left when the switchblades came out, because the cops would be coming soon and nobody in his right mind wants to be around when the fuzz show.

We crossed Sutton and cut around behind Spencer's Special, the discount house, and chased two junior-high kids across a field for a few minutes; by then it was dark enough to sneak in over the back fence of the Nightly Double drive-in movie. It was the biggest in town, and showed two movies every night, and on weekends four—you could say you were going to the Nightly Double and have time to go all over town.

We all had the money to get in—it only costs a quarter if you're not in a car—but Dally hated to do things the legal way. He liked to show that he didn't care whether there was a law or not. He went around *trying* to break laws. We went to the rows of seats in front of the concession stand to sit down. Nobody else was there except two girls who were sitting down front. Dally eyed them coolly, then walked down the aisle and sat right behind them. I had a sick feeling that Dally was up to his usual tricks, and I was right. He started talking, loud enough for the two girls to hear. He started out bad and got worse. Dallas could talk awful dirty if he wanted to and I guess he wanted to then. I felt my ears get hot. Two-Bit or Steve or even Soda would have gone right along with him, just to see if they could embarrass the girls, but that kind of kicks just doesn't appeal to me. I sat there, struck dumb, and Johnny left hastily to get a Coke.

I wouldn't have felt so embarrassed if they had been greasy girls—I might even have helped old Dallas. But those two girls weren't our kind. They were tuff-looking girls—dressed sharp and really good-looking. They looked about sixteen or seventeen. One had short dark hair, and the other had long red hair. The redhead was getting mad, or scared. She sat up straight and she was chewing hard on her gum. The other one pretended not to hear Dally. Dally was getting impatient. He put his feet up on the back of the redhead's chair, winked at me, and beat his own record for saying something dirty. She turned around and gave him a cool stare.

"Take your feet off my chair and shut your trap."

Boy, she was good-looking. I'd seen her before; she was a cheerleader at our school. I'd always thought she was stuck-up.

Dally merely looked at her and kept his feet where they were. "Who's gonna make me?"

The other one turned around and watched us. "That's the greaser that jockeys for the Slash J sometimes," she said, as if we couldn't hear her.

I had heard the same tone a million times: "Greaser . . . greaser . . . greaser." Oh yeah, I had heard that tone before too many times. What are they doing at a drive-in without a car? I thought, and Dallas said, "I know you two. I've seen you around rodeos."

"It's a shame you can't ride bull half as good as you can talk it," the redhead said coolly and turned back around.

That didn't bother Dally in the least. "You two barrel race, huh?"

"You'd better leave us alone," the redhead said in a biting voice, "or I'll call the cops."

"Oh, my, my"—Dally looked bored—"you've got me scared to death. You ought to see my record sometime, baby." He grinned slyly. "Guess what I've been in for?"

"*Please* leave us alone," she said. "Why don't you be nice and leave us alone?"

Dally grinned roguishly. "I'm never nice. Want a Coke?"

She was mad by then. "I wouldn't drink it if I was starving in the desert. Get lost, hood!"

Dally merely shrugged and strolled off.

The girl looked at me. I was half-scared of her. I'm half-scared of all nice girls, especially Socs. "Are *you* going to start in on us?"

I shook my head, wide-eyed. "No."

Suddenly she smiled. Gosh, she was pretty. "You don't look the type. What's your name?"

I wished she hadn't asked me that. I hate to tell people my name for the first time. "Ponyboy Curtis."

Then I waited for the "You're kidding!" or "That's your *real* name?" or one of the other remarks I usually get. Ponyboy's my real name and personally I like it.

The redhead just smiled. "That's an original and lovely name."

"My dad was an original person," I said. "I've got a brother named Sodapop, and it says so on his birth certificate."

"My name's Sherri, but I'm called Cherry because of my hair. Cherry Valance."

"I know," I said. "You're a cheerleader. We go to the same school."

"You don't look old enough to be going to high school," the dark-haired girl said.

"I'm not. I got put up a year in grade school."

Cherry was looking at me. "What's a nice, smart kid like you running around with trash like that for?"

I felt myself stiffen. "I'm a grease, same as Dally. He's my buddy."

"I'm sorry, Ponyboy," she said softly. Then she said briskly, "Your brother Sodapop, does he work at a gasoline station? A DX,[1] I think?"

"Yeah."

"Man, your brother is one doll. I might have guessed you were brothers—you look alike."

I grinned with pride—I don't think I look one bit like Soda, but it's not every day I hear Socs telling me they think my brother is a doll.

"Didn't he used to ride in rodeos? Saddle bronc?"

"Yeah. Dad made him quit after he tore a ligament, though. We still hang around rodeos a lot. I've seen you two barrel race. You're good."

"Thanks," Cherry said, and the other girl, who was named Marcia, said, "How come we don't see your brother at school? He's not any older than sixteen or seventeen, is he?"

I winced inside. I've told you I can't stand it that Soda dropped out. "He's a dropout," I said roughly. "Dropout" made me think of some poor dumb-looking hoodlum wandering the streets breaking out street lights—it didn't fit my happy-go-lucky brother at all. It fitted Dally perfectly, but you could hardly say it about Soda.

Johnny came back then and sat down beside me. He looked around for Dally, then managed a shy "Hi" to the girls and tried to watch the movie. He was nervous, though. Johnny was always nervous around strangers. Cherry looked at him, sizing him up as she had me. Then she smiled softly, and I knew she had him sized up right.

Dally came striding back with an armful of Cokes. He handed one to each of the girls and sat down beside Cherry. "This might cool you off."

She gave him an incredulous look; and then she threw her Coke in his face. "That might cool *you* off, greaser. After you wash your mouth and learn to talk and act decent, I might cool off, too."

Dally wiped the Coke off his face with his sleeve and smiled dangerously. If I had been Cherry I would have beat it out of there. I knew that smile.

"Fiery, huh? Well, that's the way I like 'em." He started to put his arm around her, but Johnny reached over and stopped him.

"Leave her alone, Dally."

"Huh?" Dally was taken off guard. He stared at Johnny in disbelief. Johnny couldn't say "Boo" to a goose. Johnny gulped and got a little pale, but he said, "You heard me. Leave her alone."

Dallas scowled for a second. If it had been me, or Two-Bit, or Soda or Steve, or anyone but Johnny, Dally would have flattened him without a moment's hesitation. You just didn't tell Dally Winston what to do. One time, in a dime store, a guy told him to move over at the candy counter. Dally had turned around and belted him so hard it knocked a tooth loose. A complete stranger, too. But Johnny was the gang's pet, and Dally just couldn't hit him. He was Dally's pet, too. Dally got up and stalked off, his fists jammed in his pockets and a frown on his face. He didn't come back.

Cherry sighed in relief. "Thanks. He had me scared to death."

Johnny managed an admiring grin. "You sure didn't show it. Nobody talks to Dally like that."

---

1 *DX* Tulsa-based Sunray DX Oil Company was acquired by Sunoco in 1968.

She smiled. "From what I saw, you do."

Johnny's ears got red. I was still staring at him. It had taken more than nerve for him to say what he'd said to Dally—Johnny worshiped the ground Dallas walked on, and I had never heard Johnny talk back to anyone, much less his hero.

Marcia grinned at us. She was a little smaller than Cherry. She was cute, but that Cherry Valance was a real looker. "Y'all sit up here with us. You can protect us."

Johnny and I looked at each other. He grinned suddenly, raising his eyebrows so that they disappeared under his bangs. Would we ever have something to tell the boys! his eyes said plainly. We had picked up two girls, and classy ones at that. Not any greasy broads for us, but real Socs. Soda would flip when I told him.

"Okay," I said nonchalantly, "might as well."

I sat between them, and Johnny sat next to Cherry.

"How old are y'all?" Marcia asked.

"Fourteen," I said.

"Sixteen," said Johnny.

"That's funny," Marcia said, "I thought you were both . . ."

"Sixteen," Cherry finished for her.

I was grateful. Johnny looked fourteen and he knew it and it bugged him something awful.

Johnny grinned. "How come y'all ain't scared of us like you were Dally?"

Cherry sighed. "You two are too sweet to scare anyone. First of all, you didn't join in Dallas's dirty talk, and you made him leave us alone. And when we asked you to sit up here with us, you didn't act like it was an invitation to make out for the night. Besides that, I've heard about Dallas Winston, and he looked as hard as nails and twice as tough. And you two don't look mean."

"Sure," I said tiredly, "we're young and innocent."

"No," Cherry said slowly, looking at me carefully, "not innocent. You've seen too much to be innocent. Just not . . . dirty."

"Dally's okay," Johnny said defensively, and I nodded. You take up for your buddies, no matter what they do. When you're a gang, you stick up for the members. If you don't stick up for them, stick together, make like brothers, it isn't a gang any more. It's a pack. A snarling, distrustful, bickering pack like the Socs in their social clubs or the street gangs in New York or the wolves in the timber. "He's tough, but he's a cool old guy."

"He'd leave you alone if he knew you," I said, and that was true. When Steve's cousin from Kansas came down, Dally was decent to her and watched his swearing. We all did around nice girls who were the cousinly type. I don't know how to explain it—we try to be nice to the girls we see once in a while, like cousins or the girls in class; but we still watch a nice girl go by on a street corner and say all kinds of lousy stuff about her. Don't ask me why. I don't know why.

"Well," Marcia said with finality, "I'm glad he doesn't know us."

"I kind of admire him," Cherry said softly, so only I heard, and then we settled down to watch the movie.

Oh, yeah, we found out why they were without a car. They'd come with their boyfriends, but walked out on them when they found out the boys had brought some booze along. The boys had gotten angry and left.

"I don't care if they did." Cherry sounded annoyed. "It's not my idea of a good time to sit in a drive-in and watch people get drunk."

You could tell by the way she said it that her idea of a good time was probably high-class, and probably expensive. They'd decided to stay and see the movie anyway. It was one of those beach-party movies with no plot and no acting but a lot of girls in bikinis and some swinging songs, so it was all right. We were all four sitting there in silence when suddenly a strong hand came down on Johnny's shoulder and another on mine and a deep voice said, "Okay, greasers, you've had it."

I almost jumped out of my skin. It was like having someone leap out from behind a door and yell "Boo!" at you.

I looked fearfully over my shoulder and there was Two-Bit, grinning like a Chessy cat.[2] Glory, Two-Bit, scare us to death!" He was good at voice imitations and had sounded for all the world like a snarling Soc. Then I looked at Johnny. His eyes were shut and he was as white as a ghost. His breath was coming in smothered gasps. Two-Bit knew better than to scare Johnny like that. I guess he'd forgotten. He's kind of scatterbrained. Johnny opened his eyes and said weakly, "Hey, Two-Bit."

Two-Bit messed up his hair, "Sorry, kid," he said, "I forgot."

He climbed over the chair and plopped down beside Marcia. "Who's this, your great-aunts?"

"Great-grandmothers, twice removed," Cherry said smoothly.

I couldn't tell if Two-Bit was drunk or not. It's kind of hard to tell with him— he acts boozed up sometimes even when he's sober. He cocked one eyebrow up and the other down, which he always does when something puzzles him, or bothers him, or when he feels like saying something smart. "Shoot, you're ninety-six if you're a day."

"I'm a night," Marcia said brightly.

Two-Bit stared at her admiringly. "Brother, you're a sharp one. Where'd you two ever get to be picked up by a couple of greasy hoods like Pony and Johnny?"

"We really picked them up," Marcia said. "We're really Arabian slave traders and we're thinking about shanghaiing them. They're worth ten camels apiece at least."

"Five," Two-Bit disagreed. "They don't talk Arabian, I don't think. Say somethin' in Arabian, Johnnycake."

"Aw, cut it out!" Johnny broke in. "Dally was bothering them and when he left they wanted us to sit with them to protect them. Against wisecracking greasers like you, probably."

Two-Bit grinned, because Johnny didn't usually get sassy like that. We thought we were doing good if we could get him to talk at all. Incidentally, we don't mind being called greaser by another greaser. It's kind of playful then.

"Hey, where is ol' Dally, anyways?"

"He went hunting some action—booze or dames or a fight. I hope he don't get jailed again. He just got out."

"He'll probably find the fight," Two-Bit stated cheerfully. "That's why I came over. Mr. Timothy Shepard and Co. are looking for whoever so kindly slashed their car's tires, and since Mr. Curly Shepard spotted Dallas doing it . . . well . . . Does Dally have a blade?"

"Not that I know of," I said. "I think he's got a piece of pipe, but he busted his blade this morning."

"Good. Tim'll fight fair if Dally don't pull a blade on him. Dally shouldn't have any trouble."

---

2 *grinning like a Chessy-cat*   proverbial phrase, of undetermined origin but appearing in print by 1840 (and later in *Alice in Wonderland*) and referring to cats of Cheshire county, England.

Cherry and Marcia were staring at us. "You don't believe in playing rough or anything, do you?"

"A fair fight isn't rough," Two-Bit said. "Blades are rough. So are chains and heaters and pool sticks and rumbles. Skin fighting isn't rough. It blows off steam better than anything. There's nothing wrong with throwing a few punches. Socs are rough. They gang up on one or two, or they rumble each other with their social clubs. Us greasers usually stick together, but when we do fight among ourselves, it's a fair fight between two. And Dally deserves whatever he gets, 'cause slashed tires ain't no joke when you've got to work to pay for them. He got spotted, too, and that was his fault. Our one rule, besides Stick together, is Don't get caught. He might get beat up, he might not. Either way there's not going to be any blood feud between our outfit and Shepard's. If we needed them tomorrow they'd show. If Tim beats Dally's head in, and then tomorrow asks us for help in a rumble, we'll show. Dally was getting kicks. He got caught. He pays up. No sweat."

"Yeah, boy," Cherry said sarcastically, "real simple."

"Sure," Marcia said, unconcerned. "If he gets killed or something, you just bury him. No sweat."

"You dig okay, baby." Two-Bit grinned and lit a cigarette. "Anyone want a weed?"

I looked at Two-Bit admiringly. He sure put things into words good. Maybe he was still a junior at eighteen and a half, and maybe his sideburns were too long, and maybe he did get boozed up too much, but he sure understood things.

Cherry and Marcia shook their heads at his offering of cigarettes, but Johnny and I reached for one. Johnny's color was back and his breathing was regular, but his hand was shaking ever so slightly. A cigarette would steady it.

"Ponyboy, will you come with me to get some popcorn?" Cherry asked.

I jumped up. "Sure. Y'all want some?"

"I do," said Marcia. She was finishing the Coke Dally had given her. I realized then that Marcia and Cherry weren't alike. Cherry had said she wouldn't drink Dally's Coke if she was starving, and she meant it. It was the principle of the thing. But Marcia saw no reason to throw away a perfectly good, free Coke.

"Me too," said Two-Bit. He flipped me a fifty-cent piece. "Get Johnny some, too. I'm buyin'," he added as Johnny started to reach into his jeans pocket.

We went to the concession stand and, as usual, there was a line a mile long, so we had to wait. Quite a few kids turned to look at us—you didn't see a kid grease and a Socy cheerleader together often. Cherry didn't seem to notice.

"Your friend—the one with the sideburns—he's okay?"

"He ain't dangerous like Dallas if that's what you mean. He's okay."

She smiled and her eyes showed that her mind was on something else. "Johnny . . . he's been hurt bad sometime, hasn't he?" It was more of a statement than a question. "Hurt and scared."

"It was the Socs," I said nervously, because there were plenty of Socs milling around and some of them were giving me funny looks, as if I shouldn't be with Cherry or something. And I don't like to talk about it either—Johnny getting beat up, I mean. But I started in, talking a little faster than I usually do because I don't like to think about it either.

It was almost four months ago. I had walked down to the DX station to get a bottle of pop and to see Steve and Soda, because they'll always buy me a couple of bottles and let me help work on the cars. I don't like to go on weekends because then there is usually a bunch of girls down there flirting with Soda—all kinds of girls, Socs too. I don't care too much for girls yet. Soda says I'll grow out of it. He did.

It was a warmish spring day with the sun shining bright, but it was getting chilly and dark by the time we started for home. We were walking because we had left Steve's car at the station. At the corner of our block there's a wide, open field where we play football and hang out, and it's often a site for rumbles and fist fights. We were passing it, kicking rocks down the street and finishing our last bottle of Pepsi, when Steve noticed something lying on the ground. He picked it up. It was Johnny's blue-jeans jacket—the only jacket he had.

"Looks like Johnny forgot his jacket," Steve said, slinging it over his shoulder to take it by Johnny's house. Suddenly he stopped and examined it more carefully. There was a stain the color of rust across the collar. He looked at the ground. There were some more stains on the grass. He looked up and across the field with a stricken expression on his face. I think we all heard the low moan and saw the dark motionless hump on the other side of the lot at the same time. Soda reached him first. Johnny was lying face down on the ground. Soda turned him over gently, and I nearly got sick. Someone had beaten him badly.

We were used to seeing Johnny banged up—his father clobbered him around a lot, and although it made us madder than heck, we couldn't do anything about it. But those beatings had been nothing like this. Johnny's face was cut up and bruised and swollen, and there was a wide gash from his temple to his cheekbone. He would carry that scar all his life. His white T-shirt was splattered with blood. I just stood there, trembling with sudden cold. I thought he might be dead; surely nobody could be beaten like that and live. Steve closed his eyes for a second and muffled a groan as he dropped on his knees beside Soda.

Somehow the gang sensed what had happened. Two-Bit was suddenly there beside me, and for once his comical grin was gone and his dancing gray eyes were stormy. Darry had seen us from our porch and ran toward us, suddenly skidding to a halt. Dally was there, too, swearing under his breath, and turning away with a sick expression on his face. I wondered about it vaguely. Dally had seen people killed on the streets of New York's West Side. Why did he look sick now?

"Johnny?" Soda lifted him up and held him against his shoulder. He gave the limp body a slight shake. "Hey, Johnnycake."

Johnny didn't open his eyes, but there came a soft question. "Soda?"

"Yeah, it's me," Sodapop said. "Don't talk. You're gonna be okay."

"There was a whole bunch of them," Johnny went on, swallowing, ignoring Soda's command. "A blue Mustang full . . . I got so scared . . ." He tried to swear, but suddenly started crying, fighting to control himself, then sobbing all the more because he couldn't. I had seen Johnny take a whipping with a two-by-four from his old man and never let out a whimper. That made it worse to see him break now. Soda just held him and pushed Johnny's hair back out of his eyes. "It's okay, Johnnycake, they're gone now. It's okay."

Finally, between sobs, Johnny managed to gasp out his story. He had been hunting our football to practice a few kicks when a blue Mustang had pulled up beside the lot. There were four Socs in it. They had caught him and one of them had a lot of rings on his hand—that's what had cut Johnny up so badly. It wasn't just that they had beaten him half to death—he could take that. They had scared him. They had threatened him with everything under the sun. Johnny was high-strung anyway, a nervous wreck from getting belted every

515

time he turned around and from hearing his parents fight all the time. Living in those conditions might have turned someone else rebellious and bitter; it was killing Johnny. He had never been a coward. He was a good man in a rumble. He stuck up for the gang and kept his mouth shut good around cops. But after the night of the beating, Johnny was jumpier than ever. I didn't think he'd ever get over it. Johnny never walked by himself after that. And Johnny, who was the most law-abiding of us, now carried in his back pocket a six-inch switchblade. He'd use it, too, if he ever got jumped again. They had scared him that much. He would kill the next person who jumped him. Nobody was ever going to beat him like that again. Not over his dead body . . .

I had nearly forgotten that Cherry was listening to me. But when I came back to reality and looked at her, I was startled to find her as white as a sheet.

"All Socs aren't like that," she said. "You have to believe me, Ponyboy. Not all of us are like that."

"Sure," I said.

"That's like saying all you greasers are like Dallas Winston. I'll bet he's jumped a few people."

I digested that. It was true. Dally had jumped people. He had told us stories about muggings in New York that made the hair on the back of my neck stand up. But not all of us were that bad.

Cherry no longer looked sick, only sad. "I'll bet you think the Socs have it made. The rich kids, the West-side Socs. I'll tell you something, Ponyboy, and it may come as a surprise. We have troubles you've never even heard of. You want to know something?" She looked me straight in the eye. "Things are rough all over."

"I believe you," I said. "We'd better get back out there with the popcorn or Two-Bit'll think I ran off with his money."

We went back and watched the movie through again. Marcia and Two-Bit were hitting it off fine. Both had the same scatterbrained sense of humor. But Cherry and Johnny and I just sat there, looking at the movie and not talking. I quit worrying about everything and thought about how nice it was to sit with a girl without having to listen to her swear or to beat her off with a club. I knew Johnny liked it, too. He didn't talk to girls much. Once, while Dallas was in reform school, Sylvia had started hanging on to Johnny and sweet-talking him and Steve got hold of her and told her if she tried any of her tricks with Johnny he'd personally beat the tar out of her. Then he gave Johnny a lecture on girls and how a sneaking little broad like Sylvia would get him into a lot of trouble. As a result, Johnny never spoke to girls much, but whether that was because he was scared of Steve or because he was shy, I couldn't tell.

I got the same lecture from Two-Bit after we'd picked up a couple of girls downtown one day. I thought it was funny, because girls are one subject even Darry thinks I use my head about. And it really had been funny, because Two-Bit was half-crocked when he gave me the lecture, and he told me some stories that about made me want to crawl under the floor or something. But he had been talking about girls like Sylvia and the girls he and Dally and the rest picked up at drive-ins and downtown; he never said anything about Socy girls. So I figured it was all right to be sitting there with them. Even if they did have their own troubles. I really couldn't see what Socs would have to sweat about— good grades, good cars, good girls, madras and Mustangs and Corvairs—Man, I thought, if I had worries like that I'd consider myself lucky.

I know better now.

AFTER the movie was over it suddenly came to us that Cherry and Marcia didn't have a way to get home. Two-Bit gallantly offered to walk them home—the west side of town was only about twenty miles away—but they wanted to call their parents and have them come and get them. Two-Bit finally talked them into letting us drive them home in his car. I think they were still half-scared of us. They were getting over it, though, as we walked to Two-Bit's house to pick up the car. It seemed funny to me that Socs—if these girls were any example— were just like us. They liked the Beatles and thought Elvis Presley was out, and we thought the Beatles were rank and that Elvis was tuff, but that seemed the only difference to me. Of course greasy girls would have acted a lot tougher, but there was a basic sameness. I thought maybe it was money that separated us.

"No," Cherry said slowly when I said this. "It's not just money. Part of it is, but not all. You greasers have a different set of values. You're more emotional. We're sophisticated—cool to the point of not feeling anything. Nothing is real with us. You know, sometimes I'll catch myself talking to a girl-friend, and realize I don't mean half of what I'm saying. I don't really think a beer blast on the river bottom is super-cool, but I'll rave about one to a girl-friend just to be saying something." She smiled at me. "I never told anyone that. I think you're the first person I've ever really gotten through to."

She was coming through to me all right, probably because I was a greaser, and younger; she didn't have to keep her guard up with me.

"Rat race is a perfect name for it," she said. "We're always going and going and going, and never asking where. Did you ever hear of having more than you wanted? So that you couldn't want anything else and then started looking for something else to want? It seems like we're always searching for something to satisfy us, and never finding it. Maybe if we could lose our cool we could."

That was the truth. Socs were always behind a wall of aloofness, careful not to let their real selves show through. I had seen a social-club rumble once. The Socs even fought coldly and practically and impersonally.

"That's why we're separated," I said. "It's not money, it's feeling—you don't feel anything and we feel too violently."

"And"—she was trying to hide a smile—"that's probably why we take turns getting our names in the paper."

Two-Bit and Marcia weren't even listening to us. They were engaged in some wild conversation that made no sense to anyone but themselves.

I have quite a rep for being quiet, almost as quiet as Johnny. Two-Bit always said he wondered why Johnny and I were such good buddies. "You must make such interestin' conversation," he'd say, cocking one eyebrow, "you keepin' your mouth shut and Johnny not sayin' anything." But Johnny and I understood each other without saying anything. Nobody but Soda could really get me talking. Till I met Cherry Valance.

I don't know why I could talk to her; maybe for the same reason she could talk to me. The first thing I knew I was telling her about Mickey Mouse, Soda's horse. I had never told anyone about Soda's horse. It was personal.

Soda had this buckskin horse, only it wasn't his. It belonged to a guy who kept it at the stables where Soda used to work. Mickey Mouse was Soda's horse, though. The first day Soda saw him he said, "There's my horse," and I never doubted it. I was about ten then. Sodapop is horsecrazy. I mean it. He's always hanging around stables and rodeos, hopping on a horse every time he gets a chance. When I was ten I thought that Mickey Mouse and Soda looked alike and were alike. Mickey Mouse was a dark-gold buckskin, sassy and ornery, not much more than a colt. He'd come when Soda called him. He wouldn't come for anyone else. That horse loved Soda. He'd stand there and chew on Soda's sleeve or collar. Gosh, but Sodapop was crazy about that horse. He went down to see him every day. Mickey Mouse was a mean horse. He kicked other horses and was always getting into trouble. "I've got me a ornery pony," Soda'd tell him, rubbing his neck. "How come you're so mean, Mickey Mouse?" Mickey Mouse would just chew on his sleeve and sometimes nip him. But not hard. He may have belonged to another guy, but he was Soda's horse.

"Does Soda still have him?" Cherry asked.

"He got sold," I said. "They came and got him one day and took him off. He was a real valuable horse. Pure quarter."

She didn't say anything else and I was glad. I couldn't tell her that Soda had bawled all night long after they came and got Mickey Mouse. I had cried, too, if you want to know the truth, because Soda never really wanted anything except a horse, and he'd lost his. Soda had been twelve then, going-on-thirteen. He never let on to Mom and Dad how he felt, though, because we never had enough money and usually we had a hard time making ends meet. When you're thirteen in our neighborhood you know the score. I kept saving my money for a year, thinking that someday I could buy Mickey Mouse back for Soda. You're not so smart at ten.

"You read a lot, don't you, Ponyboy?" Cherry asked.

I was startled. "Yeah. Why?"

She kind of shrugged. "I could just tell. I'll bet you watch sunsets, too." She was quiet for a minute after I nodded. "I used to watch them, too, before I got so busy . . ."

I pictured that, or tried to. Maybe Cherry stood still and watched the sun set while she was supposed to be taking the garbage out. Stood there and watched and forgot everything else until her big brother screamed at her to hurry up. I shook my head. It seemed funny to me that the sunset she saw from her patio and the one I saw from the back steps was the same one. Maybe the two different worlds we lived in weren't so different. We saw the same sunset.

Marcia suddenly gasped. "Cherry, look what's coming."

We all looked and saw a blue Mustang coming down the street. Johnny made a small noise in his throat and when I looked at him he was white.

Marcia was shifting nervously. "What are we going to do?"

Cherry bit a fingernail. "Stand here," she said. "There isn't much else we can do."

"Who is it?" Two-Bit asked. "The F.B.I.?"

"No," Cherry said bleakly, "it's Randy and Bob."

"And," Two-Bit added grimly, "a few other of the socially elite checkered-shirt set."

"Your boyfriends?" Johnny's voice was steady, but standing as close to him as I was, I could see he was trembling. I wondered why—Johnny was a nervous wreck, but he never was that jumpy.

Cherry started walking down the street. "Maybe they won't see us. Act normal."

"Who's acting?" Two-Bit grinned. "I'm a natural normal."

"Wish it was the other way around," I muttered, and Two-Bit said, "Don't get mouthy, Ponyboy."

The Mustang passed us slowly and went right on by. Marcia sighed in relief. "That was close."

Cherry turned to me. "Tell me about your oldest brother. You don't talk much about him."

I tried to think of something to say about Darry, and shrugged. "What's to talk about? He's big and handsome and likes to play football."

"I mean, what's he like? I feel like I know Soda from the way you talk about him; tell me about Darry." And when I was silent she urged me on. "Is he wild and reckless like Soda? Dreamy, like you?"

My face got hot as I bit my lip. Darry . . . what was Darry like? "He's . . ." I started to say he was a good ol' guy but I couldn't. I burst out bitterly: "He's not like Sodapop at all and he sure ain't like me. He's hard as a rock and about as human. He's got eyes exactly like frozen ice. He thinks I'm a pain in the neck. He likes Soda—everybody likes Soda—but he can't stand me. I bet he wishes he could stick me in a home somewhere, and he'd do it, too, if Soda'd let him."

Two-Bit and Johnny were staring at me now. "No . . ." Two-Bit said, dumfounded. "No, Ponyboy, that ain't right . . . you got it wrong . . ."

"Gee," Johnny said softly, "I thought you and Darry and Soda got along real well . . ."

"Well, we don't," I snapped, feeling silly. I knew my ears were red by the way they were burning, and I was thankful for the darkness. I felt stupid. Compared to Johnny's home, mine was heaven. At least Darry didn't get drunk and beat me up or run me out of the house, and I had Sodapop to talk things over with. That made me mad, I mean making a fool of myself in front of everyone. "An' you can shut your trap, Johnny Cade, 'cause we all know you ain't wanted at home, either. And you can't blame them."

Johnny's eyes went round and he winced as though I'd belted him. Two-Bit slapped me a good one across the side of the head, and hard.

"Shut your mouth, kid. If you wasn't Soda's kid brother I'd beat the tar out of you. You know better than to talk to Johnny like that." He put his hand on Johnny's shoulder. "He didn't mean it, Johnny."

"I'm sorry," I said miserably. Johnny was my buddy. "I was just mad."

"It's the truth," Johnny said with a bleak grin. "I don't care."

"Shut up talkin' like that," Two-Bit said fiercely, messing up Johnny's hair. "We couldn't get along without you, so you can just shut up!"

"It ain't fair!" I cried passionately. "It ain't fair that we have all the rough breaks!" I didn't know exactly what I meant, but I was thinking about Johnny's father being a drunk and his mother a selfish slob, and Two-Bit's mother being a barmaid to support him and his kid sister after their father ran out on them, and Dally—wild, cunning Dally—turning into a hoodlum because he'd die if he didn't, and Steve—his hatred for his father coming out in his soft, bitter voice and the violence of his temper. Sodapop . . . a dropout so he could get a job and keep me in school, and Darry, getting old before his time trying to run a family and hold on to two jobs and never having any fun—while the Socs had so much spare time and money that they jumped us and each other for kicks, had beer blasts and river-bottom parties because they didn't know what else to do. Things were rough all over, all right. All over the East Side. It just didn't seem right to me.

"I know," Two-Bit said with a good-natured grin, "the chips are always down when it's our turn, but that's the way things are. Like it or lump it."

Cherry and Marcia didn't say anything. I guess they didn't know what to say. We had forgotten they were there. Then the blue Mustang was coming down the street again, more slowly.

"Well," Cherry said resignedly, "they've spotted us."

The Mustang came to a halt beside us, and the two boys in the front seat got out. They were Socs all right. One had on a white shirt and a madras ski jacket, and the other a light-yellow shirt and a wine-colored sweater. I looked at their clothes and realized for the first time that evening that all I had was a pair of jeans and Soda's old navy sweat shirt with the sleeves cut short. I swallowed. Two-Bit started to tuck in his shirttail, but stopped himself in time; he just flipped up the collar of his black leather jacket and lit a cigarette. The Socs didn't even seem to see us.

"Cherry, Marcia, listen to us . . ." the handsome black-haired Soc with the dark sweater began.

Johnny was breathing heavily and I noticed he was staring at the Soc's hand. He was wearing three heavy rings. I looked quickly at Johnny, an idea dawning on me. I remembered that it was a blue Mustang that had pulled up beside the vacant lot and that Johnny's face had been cut up by someone wearing rings . . .

The Soc's voice broke into my thoughts: ". . . just because we got a little drunk last time . . ."

Cherry looked mad. "A little? You call reeling and passing out in the streets 'a little'? Bob, I told you, I'm never going out with you while you're drinking, and I mean it. Too many things could happen while you're drunk. It's me or the booze."

The other Soc, a tall guy with a semi-Beatle haircut, turned to Marcia. "Baby, you know we don't get drunk very often . . ." When she only gave him a cold stare he got angry. "And even if you are mad at us, that's no reason to go walking the streets with these bums."

Two-Bit took a long drag on his cigarette, Johnny slouched and hooked his thumbs in his pockets, and I stiffened. We can look meaner than anything when we want to—looking tough comes in handy. Two-Bit put his elbow on Johnny's shoulder. "Who you callin' bums?"

"Listen, greasers, we got four more of us in the back seat . . ."

"Then pity the back seat," Two-Bit said to the sky.

"If you're looking for a fight . . ."

Two-Bit cocked an eyebrow, but it only made him look more cool. "You mean if I'm looking for a good jumping, you outnumber us, so you'll give it to us? Well . . ." He snatched up an empty bottle, busted off the end, and gave it to me, then reached in his back pocket and flipped out his switchblade. "Try it, pal."

"No!" Cherry cried. "Stop it!" She looked at Bob. "We'll ride home with you. Just wait a minute."

"Why?" Two-Bit demanded. "We ain't scared of them."

Cherry shuddered. "I can't stand fights . . . I can't stand them . . ."

I pulled her to one side. "I couldn't use this," I said, dropping the pop bottle. "I couldn't ever cut anyone. . . ." I had to tell her that, because I'd seen her eyes when Two-Bit flicked out his switch.

"I know," she said quietly, "but we'd better go with them. Ponyboy . . . I mean . . . if I see you in the hall at school or someplace and don't say hi, well, it's not personal or anything, but . . ."

"I know," I said.

"We couldn't let our parents see us with you all. You're a nice boy and everything . . ."

"It's okay," I said, wishing I was dead and buried somewhere. Or at least that I had on a decent shirt. "We aren't in the same class. Just don't forget that some of us watch the sunset too."

She looked at me quickly. "I could fall in love with Dallas Winston," she said. "I hope I never see him again, or I will."

She left me standing there with my mouth dropped open, and the blue Mustang vroomed off.

We walked on home, mostly in silence. I wanted to ask Johnny if those were the same Socs that had beaten him up, but I didn't mention it. Johnny never talked about it and we never said anything.

"Well, those were two good-lookin' girls if I ever saw any." Two-Bit yawned as we sat down on the curb at the vacant lot. He took a piece of paper out of his pocket and tore it up.

"What was that?"

"Marcia's number. Probably a phony one, too. I must have been outa my mind to ask for it. I think I'm a little soused."

So he had been drinking. Two-Bit was smart. He knew the score. "Y'all goin' home?" he asked.

"Not right now," I said. I wanted to have another smoke and to watch the stars. I had to be in by twelve, but I thought I had plenty of time.

"I don't know why I handed you that busted bottle," Two-Bit said, getting to his feet. "You'd never use it."

"Maybe I would have," I said. "Where you headed?"

"Gonna go play a little snooker and hunt up a poker game. Maybe get rip-roarin' drunk. I dunno. See y'all tomorrow."

Johnny and I stretched out on our backs and looked at the stars. I was freezing—it was a cold night and all I had was that sweat shirt, but I could watch stars in subzero weather. I saw Johnny's cigarette glowing in the dark and wondered vaguely what it was like inside a burning ember . . .

"It was because we're greasers," Johnny said, and I knew he was talking about Cherry. "We could have hurt her reputation."

"I reckon," I said, wondering if I ought to tell Johnny what she had said about Dallas.

"Man, that was a tuff car. Mustangs are tuff."

"Big-time Socs, all right," I said, a nervous bitterness growing inside me. It wasn't fair for the Socs to have everything. We were as good as they were; it wasn't our fault we were greasers. I couldn't just take it or leave it, like Two-Bit, or ignore it and love life anyway, like Sodapop, or harden myself beyond caring, like Dally, or actually enjoy it, like Tim Shepard. I felt the tension growing inside of me and I knew something had to happen or I would explode.

"I can't take much more." Johnny spoke my own feelings. "I'll kill myself or something."

"Don't," I said, sitting up in alarm. "You can't kill yourself, Johnny."

"Well, I won't. But I gotta do something. It seems like there's gotta be someplace without greasers or Socs, with just people. Plain ordinary people."

"Out of the big towns," I said, lying back down. "In the country . . ."

In the country . . . I loved the country. I wanted to be out of towns and away from excitement. I only wanted to lie on my back under a tree and read a book or draw a picture, and not worry about being jumped or carrying a blade or ending up married to some scatterbrained broad with no sense. The country would be like that, I thought dreamily. I would have a yeller cur dog, like I used to, and Sodapop could get Mickey Mouse back and ride in all the rodeos he wanted to, and Darry would lose that cold, hard look and be like he used to be, eight months ago, before Mom and Dad were killed. Since I was dreaming I brought Mom and Dad back to life . . . Mom could bake some more chocolate cakes and Dad would drive the pickup out early to feed the cattle. He would slap Darry on the back and tell him he was getting to be a man, a regular chip off the block, and they would be as close as they used to be. Maybe Johnny could come and live with us, and the gang could come out on weekends, and maybe Dallas would see that there was some good in the world after all, and Mom would talk to him and make him grin in spite of himself. "You've got quite a mom," Dally used to say. "She knows the score." She could talk to Dallas and kept him from getting into a lot of trouble. My mother was golden and beautiful . . .

"Ponyboy"—Johnny was shaking me—"Hey, Pony, wake up."

I sat up, shivering. The stars had moved. "Glory, what time is it?"

"I don't know. I went to sleep, too, listening to you rattle on and on. You'd better get home. I think I'll stay all night out here." Johnny's parents didn't care if he came home or not.

"Okay." I yawned. Gosh, but it was cold. "If you get cold or something come on over to our house."

"Okay."

I ran home, trembling at the thought of facing Darry. The porch light was on. Maybe they were asleep and I could sneak in, I thought. I peeked in the window. Sodapop was stretched out on the sofa, sound asleep, but Darry was in the armchair under the lamp, reading the newspaper. I gulped, and opened the door softly. Darry looked up from his paper. He was on his feet in a second. I stood there, chewing on my fingernail.

"Where the heck have you been? Do you know what time it is?" He was madder than I'd seen him in a long time. I shook my head wordlessly.

"Well, it's two in the morning, kiddo. Another hour and I would have had the police out after you. Where were you, Ponyboy?"—his voice was rising— "Where in the almighty universe were you?"

It sounded dumb, even to me, when I stammered, "I . . . I went to sleep in the lot . . ."

"You what?" He was shouting, and Sodapop sat up and rubbed his eyes.

"Hey, Ponyboy," he said sleepily, "where ya been?"

"I didn't mean to." I pleaded with Darry. "I was talking to Johnny and we both dropped off . . ."

"I reckon it never occurred to you that your brothers might be worrying their heads off and afraid to call the police because something like that could get you two thrown in a boys' home so quick it'd make your head spin. And you were asleep in the lot? Ponyboy, what on earth is the matter with you? Can't you use your head? You haven't even got a coat on."

I felt hot tears of anger and frustration rising. "I said I didn't mean to . . ."

"I didn't mean to!" Darry shouted, and I almost shook "I didn't think! I forgot! That's all I hear out of you! Can't you think of anything?"

"Darry . . ." Sodapop began, but Darry turned on him. "You keep your trap shut! I'm sick and tired of hearin' you stick up for him."

He should never yell at Soda. Nobody should ever holler at my brother. I exploded. "You don't yell at him!" I shouted. Darry wheeled around and slapped me so hard that it knocked me against the door.

Suddenly it was deathly quiet. We had all frozen. Nobody in my family had ever hit me. Nobody. Soda was wide-eyed. Darry looked at the palm of his hand where it had turned red and then looked back at me. His eyes were huge. "Ponyboy . . ."

I turned and ran out the door and down the street as fast as I could. Darry screamed, "Pony, I didn't mean to!" but I was at the lot by then and pretended I couldn't hear. I was running away. It was plain to me that Darry didn't want me around. And I wouldn't stay if he did. He wasn't ever going to hit me again.

"Johnny?" I called, and started when he rolled over and jumped up almost under my feet. "Come on, Johnny, we're running away."

Johnny asked no questions. We ran for several blocks until we were out of breath. Then we walked. I was crying by then. I finally just sat down on the curb and cried, burying my face in my arms. Johnny sat down beside me, one hand on my shoulder. "Easy, Ponyboy," he said softly, "we'll be okay."

I finally calmed down and wiped my eyes on my bare arm. My breath was coming in quivering sobs. "Gotta cigarette?"

He handed me one and struck a match.

"Johnny, I'm scared."

"Well, don't be. You're scarin' me. What happened? I never seen you bawl like that."

"I don't very often. It was Darry. He hit me. I don't know what happened, but I couldn't take him hollering at me and hitting me too. I don't know . . . sometimes we get along okay, then all of a sudden he blows up on me or else is naggin' at me all the time. He didn't use to be like that . . . we used to get along okay . . . before Mom and Dad died. Now he just can't stand me."

"I think I like it better when the old man's hittin' me." Johnny sighed. "At least then I know he knows who I am. I walk in that house, and nobody says anything. I walk out, and nobody says anything. I stay away all night, and nobody notices. At least you got Soda. I ain't got nobody."

"Shoot," I said, startled out of my misery, "you got the whole gang. Dally didn't slug you tonight' cause you're the pet. I mean, golly, Johnny, you got the whole gang."

"It ain't the same as having your own folks care about you," Johnny said simply. "It just ain't the same."

I was beginning to relax and wonder if running away was such a great idea. I was sleepy and freezing to death and I wanted to be home in bed, safe and warm under the covers with Soda's arm across me. I decided I would go home and just not speak to Darry. It was my house as much as Darry's, and if he wanted to pretend I wasn't alive, that was just fine with me. He couldn't stop me from living in my own house.

"Let's walk to the park and back. Then maybe I'll be cooled off enough to go home."

"Okay," Johnny said easily. "Okay."

Things gotta get better, I figured. They couldn't get worse. I was wrong.

CHAPTER 4

T HE PARK WAS ABOUT two blocks square, with a fountain in the middle and a small swimming pool for the little kids. The pool was empty now in the fall, but the fountain was going merrily. Tall elm trees made the park shadowy and dark, and it would have been a good hangout, but we preferred our vacant lot, and the Shepard outfit liked the alleys down by the tracks, so the park was left to lovers and little kids.

Nobody was around at two-thirty in the morning, and it was a good place to relax and cool off. I couldn't have gotten much cooler without turning into a popsicle. Johnny snapped up his jeans jacket and flipped up the collar.

"Ain't you about to freeze to death, Pony?"

"You ain't a'woofin'," I said, rubbing my bare arms between drags on my cigarette. I started to say something about the film of ice developing on the outer edges of the fountain when a sudden blast from a car horn made us both jump. The blue Mustang was circling the park slowly.

Johnny swore under his breath, and I muttered, "What do they want? This is our territory. What are Socs doing this far east?"

Johnny shook his head. "I don't know. But I bet they're looking for us. We picked up their girls."

"Oh, glory," I said with a groan, "this is all I need to top off a perfect night." I took one last drag on my weed and ground the stub under my heel. "Want to run for it?"

"It's too late now," Johnny said. "Here they come."

Five Socs were coming straight at us, and from the way they were staggering I figured they were reeling pickled. That scared me. A cool deadly bluff could sometimes shake them off, but not if they outnumbered you five to two and were drunk. Johnny's hand went to his back pocket and I remembered his switchblade. I wished for that broken bottle. I'd sure show them I could use it if I had to. Johnny was scared to death. I mean it. He was as white as a ghost and his eyes were wild-looking, like the eyes of an animal in a trap. We backed against the fountain and the Socs surrounded us. They smelled so heavily of whiskey and English Leather that I almost choked. I wished desperately that Darry and Soda would come along hunting for me. The four of us could handle them easily. But no one was around, and I knew Johnny and I were going to have to fight it out alone. Johnny had a blank, tough look on his face—you'd have had to know him to see the panic in his eyes. I stared at the Socs coolly. Maybe they could scare us to death, but we'd never let them have the satisfaction of knowing it.

It was Randy and Bob and three other Socs, and they recognized us. I knew Johnny recognized them; he was watching the moonlight glint off Bob's rings with huge eyes.

"Hey, whatta ya know?" Bob said a little unsteadily, "here's the little greasers that picked up our girls. Hey, greasers."

"You're outa your territory," Johnny warned in a low voice. "You'd better watch it."

Randy swore at us and they stepped in closer. Bob was eyeing Johnny. "Nup, pal, yer the ones who'd better watch it. Next time you want a broad, pick up yer own kind—dirt."

I was getting mad. I was hating them enough to lose my head.

"You know what a greaser is?" Bob asked. "White trash with long hair."

I felt the blood draining from my face. I've been cussed out and sworn at, but nothing ever hit me like that did. Johnnycake made a kind of gasp and his eyes were smoldering.

"You know what a Soc is?" I said, my voice shaking with rage. "White trash with Mustangs and madras." And then, because I couldn't think of anything bad enough to call them, I spit at them.

Bob shook his head, smiling slowly. "You could use a bath, greaser. And a good working over. And we've got all night to do it. Give the kid a bath, David."

I ducked and tried to run for it, but the Soc caught my arm and twisted it behind my back, and shoved my face into the fountain. I fought, but the hand at the back of my neck was strong and I had to hold my breath. I'm dying, I thought, and wondered what was happening to Johnny. I couldn't hold my breath any longer. I fought again desperately but only sucked in water. I'm drowning, I thought, they've gone too far . . . A red haze filled my mind and I slowly relaxed.

The next thing I knew I was lying on the pavement beside the fountain, coughing water and gasping. I lay there weakly, breathing in air and spitting out water. The wind blasted through my soaked sweat shirt and dripping hair. My teeth chattered unceasingly and I couldn't stop them. I finally pushed myself up and leaned back against the fountain, the water running down my face. Then I saw Johnny.

He was sitting next to me, one elbow on his knee, and staring straight ahead. He was a strange greenish-white, and his eyes were huger than I'd ever seen them.

"I killed him," he said slowly. "I killed that boy."

Bob, the handsome Soc, was lying there in the moonlight, doubled up and still. A dark pool was growing from him, spreading slowly over the blue-white cement. I looked at Johnny's hand. He was clutching his switchblade, and it was dark to the hilt. My stomach gave a violent jump and my blood turned icy.

"Johnny," I managed to say, fighting the dizziness, "I think I'm gonna be sick."

"Go ahead," he said in the same steady voice. "I won't look at you."

I turned my head and was quietly sick for a minute. Then I leaned back and closed my eyes so I wouldn't see Bob lying there.

This can't be happening. This can't be happening. This can't be . . .

"You really killed him, huh, Johnny?"

"Yeah." His voice quavered slightly. "I had to. They were drowning you, Pony. They might have killed you. And they had a blade . . . they were gonna beat me up. . . ."

"Like . . ."—I swallowed—"like they did before?"

Johnny was quiet for a minute. "Yeah," he said, "like they did before."

Johnny told me what had happened: "They ran when I stabbed him. They all ran . . ."

A panic was rising in me as I listened to Johnny's quiet voice go on and on. "Johnny!" I nearly screamed. "What are we gonna do? They put you in the electric chair for killing people!" I was shaking. I want a cigarette. I want a cigarette. I want a cigarette. We had smoked our last pack. "I'm scared, Johnny. What are we gonna do?"

Johnny jumped up and dragged me up by my sweat shirt. He shook me. "Calm down, Ponyboy. Get ahold of yourself."

I hadn't realized I was screaming. I shook loose. "Okay," I said, "I'm okay now."

Johnny looked around, slapping his pockets nervously. "We gotta get outa here. Get somewhere. Run away. The police'll be here soon." I was trembling, and it wasn't all from cold. But Johnny, except for the fact that his hands were twitching, looked as cool as Darry ever had. "We'll need money. And maybe a gun. And a plan."

Money. Maybe a gun? A plan. Where in the world would we get these things?

"Dally," Johnny said with finality. "Dally'll get us outa here."

I heaved a sigh. Why hadn't I thought of that? But I never thought of any-thing. Dallas Winston could do anything.

"Where can we find him?"

"I think at Buck Merril's place. There's a party over there tonight. Dally said somethin' about it this afternoon."

Buck Merril was Dally's rodeo partner. He was the one who'd got Dally the job as a jockey for the Slash J. Buck raised a few quarter horses, and made most of his money on fixed races and a little bootlegging. I was under strict orders from both Darry and Soda not to get caught within ten miles of his place, which was dandy with me. I didn't like Buck Merril. He was a tall lanky cowboy with blond hair and buckteeth. Or he used to be bucktoothed before he had the front two knocked out in a fight. He was out of it. He dug Hank Williams—how gross can you get?

Buck answered the door when we knocked, and a roar of cheap music came with him. The clinking of glasses, loud, rough laughter and female giggles, and Hank Williams. It scraped on my raw nerves like sandpaper. A can of beer in one hand, Buck glared down at us. "Whatta ya want?"

"Dally!" Johnny gulped, looking back over his shoulder. "We gotta see Dally."

"He's busy," Buck snapped, and someone in his living room yelled "A-ha!" and then "Yee-ha," and the sound of it almost made my nerves snap.

"Tell him it's Pony and Johnny," I commanded. I knew Buck, and the only way you could get anything from him was to bully him. I guess that's why Dal-las could handle him so easily, although Buck was in his mid-twenties and Dally was seventeen. "He'll come."

Buck glared at me for a second, then stumbled off. He was pretty well crocked, which made me apprehensive. If Dally was drunk and in a dangerous mood. . . .

He appeared in a few minutes, clad only in a pair of lowcut blue jeans, scratching the hair on his chest. He was sober enough, and that surprised me. Maybe he hadn't been there long.

"Okay, kids, whatta ya need me for?"

As Johnny told him the story, I studied Dally, trying to figure out what there was about this tough-looking hood that a girl like Cherry Valance could love. Towheaded and shifty-eyed, Dally was anything but handsome. Yet in his hard face there was character, pride, and a savage defiance of the world. He could never love Cherry Valance back. It would be a miracle if Dally loved anything. The fight for self-preservation had hardened him beyond caring.

He didn't bat an eye when Johnny told him what had happened, only grinned and said "Good for you" when Johnny told how he had knifed the Soc. Finally Johnny finished. "We figured you could get us out if anyone could. I'm sorry we got you away from the party."

"Oh, shoot, kid"—Dally glanced contemptuously over his shoulder—"I was in the bedroom."

He suddenly stared at me. "Glory, but your ears can get red, Ponyboy."

I was remembering what usually went on in the bedrooms at Buck's parties. Then Dally grinned in amused realization. "It wasn't anything like that, kid. I was asleep, or tryin' to be, with all this racket. Hank Williams"—he rolled his eyes and added a few adjectives after 'Hank Williams.' "Me and Shepard had a run-in and I cracked some ribs. I just needed a place to lay over." He rubbed his side ruefully. "Ol' Tim sure can pack a punch. He won't be able to see outa one eye for a week." He looked us over and sighed. "Well, wait a sec and I'll see what I can do about this mess." Then he took a good look at me. "Ponyboy, are you wet?"

"Y-y-yes-s," I stammered through chattering teeth.

"Glory hallelujah!" He opened the screen door and pulled me in, motioning for Johnny to follow. "You'll die of pneumonia 'fore the cops ever get you."

He half-dragged me into an empty bedroom, swearing at me all the way. "Get that sweat shirt off." He threw a towel at me. "Dry off and wait here. At least Johnny's got his jeans jacket. You ought to know better than to run away in just a sweat shirt, and a wet one at that. Don't you ever use your head?" He sounded so much like Darry that I stared at him. He didn't notice, and left us sitting on the bed.

Johnny lay back on it. "Wish I had me a weed."

My knees were shaking as I finished drying off, sitting there in my jeans.

Dally appeared after a minute. He carefully shut the door. "Here"—he handed us a gun and a roll of bills—"the gun's loaded. For Pete's sake, Johnny, don't point the thing at me. Here's fifty bucks. That's all I could get out of Merril tonight. He's blowin' his loot from that last race."

You might have thought it was Dally who fixed those races for Buck, being a jockey and all, but it wasn't. The last guy to suggest it lost three teeth. It's the truth. Dally rode the ponies honestly and did his best to win. It was the only thing Dally did honestly.

"Pony, do Darry and Sodapop know about this?"

I shook my head. Dally sighed. "Boy howdy, I ain't itchin' to be the one to tell Darry and get my head busted."

"Then don't tell him," I said. I hated to worry Sodapop, and would have liked to let him know I had gotten this far okay, but I didn't care if Darry worried himself gray-headed. I was too tired to tell myself I was being mean and unreasonable. I convinced myself it wouldn't be fair to make Dally tell him. Darry would beat him to death for giving us the money and the gun and getting us out of town.

"Here!" Dally handed me a shirt about sixty-million sizes too big. "It's Buck's—you an' him ain't exactly the same size, but it's dry." He handed me his worn brown leather jacket with the yellow sheep's-wool lining. "It'll get cold where you're going, but you can't risk being loaded down with blankets."

I started buttoning up the shirt. It about swallowed me. "Hop the three-fifteen freight to Windrixville," Dally instructed. "There's an old abandoned church on top of Jay Mountain. There's a pump in back so don't worry about water. Buy a week's supply of food as soon as you get there—this morning, before the story gets out, and then don't so much as stick your noses out the door. I'll be up there as soon as I think it's clear. Man, I thought New York was the only place I could get mixed up in a murder rap."

At the word "murder," Johnny made a small noise in his throat and shuddered.

Dally walked us back to the door, turning off the porch light before we stepped out. "Git goin'!" He messed up Johnny's hair. "Take care, kid," he said softly.

"Sure, Dally, thanks." And we ran into the darkness.

We crouched in the weeds beside the railroad tracks, listening to the whistle grow louder. The train slowed to a screaming halt. "Now," whispered Johnny. We ran and pulled ourselves into an open boxcar. We pressed against the side, trying to hold our breath while we listened to the railroad workers walk up and down outside. One poked his head inside, and we froze. But he didn't see us, and the boxcar rattled as the train started up.

"The first stop'll be Windrixville," Johnny said, laying the gun down gingerly. He shook his head. "I don't see why he gave me this. I couldn't shoot anybody."

Then for the first time, really, I realized what we were in for. Johnny had killed someone. Quiet, soft-spoken little Johnny, who wouldn't hurt a living thing on purpose, had taken a human life. We were really running away, with the police after us for murder and a loaded gun by our side. I wished we'd asked Dally for a pack of cigarettes. . . .

I stretched out and used Johnny's legs for a pillow. Curling up, I was thankful for Dally's jacket. It was too big, but it was warm. Not even the rattling of the train could keep me awake, and I went to sleep in a hoodlum's jacket, with a gun lying next to my hand.

I was hardly awake when Johnny and I leaped off the train into a meadow. Not until I landed in the dew and got a wet shock did I realize what I was doing. Johnny must have woke me up and told me to jump, but I didn't remember it. We lay in the tall weeds and damp grass, breathing heavily. The dawn was coming. It was lightening the sky in the east and a ray of gold touched the hills. The clouds were pink and meadow larks were singing. This is the country, I thought, half asleep. My dream's come true and I'm in the country.

"Blast it, Ponyboy"—Johnny was rubbing his legs—"you must have put my legs to sleep. I can't even stand up. I barely got off that train."

"I'm sorry. Why didn't you wake me up?"

"That's okay. I didn't want to wake you up until I had to."

"Now how do we find Jay Mountain?" I asked Johnny. I was still groggy with sleep and wanted to sleep forever right there in the dew and the dawn.

"Go ask someone. The story won't be in the paper yet. Make like a farm boy taking a walk or something."

"I don't look like a farm boy," I said. I suddenly thought of my long hair, combed back, and the slouching stride I used from habit. I looked at Johnny. He didn't look like any farm boy to me. He still reminded me of a lost puppy who had been kicked too often, but for the first time I saw him as a stranger might see him. He looked hard and tough, because of his black T-shirt and his blue jeans and jacket, and because his hair was heavily greased and so long. I saw how his hair curled behind his ears and I thought: We both need a haircut and some decent clothes. I looked down at my worn, faded blue jeans, my too-big shirt, and Dally's worn-out jacket. They'll know we're hoods the minute they see us, I thought.

"I'll have to stay here," Johnny said, rubbing his legs. "You go down the road and ask the first person you see where Jay Mountain is." He winced at the pain in his legs. "Then come back. And for Pete's sake, run a comb through your hair and quit slouching down like a thug."

So Johnny had noticed it too. I pulled a comb from my back pocket and combed my hair carefully. "I guess I look okay now, huh, Johnny?"

He was studying me. "You know, you look an awful lot like Sodapop, the way you've got your hair and everything. I mean, except your eyes are green."

"They ain't green, they're gray," I said, reddening. "And I look about as much like Soda as you do." I got to my feet. "He's good-looking."

"Shoot," Johnny said with a grin, "you are, too."

I climbed over the barbed-wire fence without saying anything else. I could hear Johnny laughing at me, but I didn't care. I went strolling down the red dirt road, hoping my natural color would come back before I met anyone. I wonder what Darry and Sodapop are doing now, I thought, yawning. Soda had the whole bed to himself for once. I bet Darry's sorry he ever hit me. He'll really get worried when he finds out Johnny and I killed that Soc. Then, for a moment, I pictured Sodapop's face when he heard about it. I wish I was home, I thought absently, I wish I was home and still in bed. Maybe I am. Maybe I'm just dreaming . . .

It was only last night that Dally and I had sat down behind those girls at the Nightly Double. Glory, I thought with a bewildering feeling of being rushed, things are happening too quick. Too fast. I figured I couldn't get into any worse trouble than murder. Johnny and I would be hiding for the rest of our lives. Nobody but Dally would know where we were, and he couldn't tell anyone because he'd get jailed again for giving us that gun. If Johnny got caught, they'd give him the electric chair, and if they caught me, I'd be sent to a reformatory. I'd heard about reformatories from Curly Shepard and I didn't want to go to one at all. So we'd have to be hermits for the rest of our lives, and never see anyone but Dally. Maybe I'd never see Darry or Sodapop again. Or even Two-Bit or Steve. I was in the country, but I knew I wasn't going to like it as much as I'd thought I would. There are things worse than being a greaser.

I met a sunburned farmer driving a tractor down the road. I waved at him and he stopped.

"Could you tell me where Jay Mountain is?" I asked as politely as I could.

He pointed on down the road. "Follow this road to that big hill over there. That's it. Taking a walk?"

"Yessir." I managed to look sheepish. "We're playing army and I'm supposed to report to headquarters there."

I can lie so easily that it spooks me sometimes—Soda says it comes from reading so much. But then, Two-Bit lies all the time too, and he never opens a book.

"Boys will be boys," the farmer said with a grin, and I thought dully that he sounded as corn-poney as Hank Williams. He went on and I walked back to where Johnny was waiting.

We climbed up the road to the church, although it was a lot farther away than it looked. The road got steeper with every step. I was feeling kind of drunk—I always do when I get too sleepy—and my legs got heavier and heavier. I guess Johnny was sleepier than I was—he had stayed awake on the train to make sure we got off at the right place. It took us about forty-five minutes to get there. We climbed in a back window. It was a small church, real old and spooky and spiderwebby. It gave me the creeps.

I'd been in church before. I used to go all the time, even after Mom and Dad were gone. Then one Sunday I talked Soda into coming with Johnny and me. He didn't want to come unless Steve did, and Two-Bit decided he might as well come too. Dally was sleeping off a hangover, and Darry was working. When Johnny and I went, we sat in the back, trying to get something out of the sermon and avoiding the people, because we weren't dressed so sharp most of the time. Nobody seemed to mind, and Johnny and I really liked to go. But that day . . . well, Soda can't sit still long enough to enjoy a movie, much less a sermon.

It wasn't long before he and Steve and Two-Bit were throwing paper wads at each other and clowning around, and finally Steve dropped a hymn book with a bang—accidentally, of course. Everyone in the place turned around to look at us, and Johnny and I nearly crawled under the pews. And then Two-Bit *waved* at them.

I hadn't been to church since.

But this church gave me a kind of creepy feeling. What do you call it? Premonition? I flopped down on the floor—and immediately decided not to do any more flopping. That floor was stone, and hard. Johnny stretched out beside me, resting his head on his arm. I started to say something to him, but I went to sleep before I could get the words out of my mouth. But Johnny didn't notice. He was asleep, too.

CHAPTER 5

I WOKE UP LATE IN the afternoon. For a second I didn't know where I was. You know how it is, when you wake up in a strange place and wonder where in the world you are, until memory comes rushing over you like a wave. I half convinced myself that I had dreamed everything that had happened the night before. I'm really home in bed, I thought. It's late and both Darry and Sodapop are up. Darry's cooking breakfast, and in a minute he and Soda will come in and drag me out of bed and wrestle me down and tickle me until I think I'll die if they don't stop. It's me and Soda's turn to do the dishes after we eat, and then we'll all go outside and play football. Johnny and Two-Bit and I will get Darry on our side, since Johnny and I are so small and Darry's the best player. It'll go like the usual weekend morning. I tried telling myself that while I lay on the cold rock floor, wrapped up in Dally's jacket and listening to the wind rushing through the trees' dry leaves outside.

Finally I quit pretending and pushed myself up. I was stiff and sore from sleeping on that hard floor, but I had never slept so soundly. I was still groggy. I pushed off Johnny's jeans jacket, which had somehow got thrown across me, and blinked, scratching my head. It was awful quiet, with just the sound of rushing wind in the trees. Suddenly I realized that Johnny wasn't there.

"Johnny?" I called loudly, and that old wooden church echoed me, *onny onny* . . . I looked around wildly, almost panic-stricken, but then caught sight of some crooked lettering written in the dust of the floor. *Went to get supplies. Be back soon. J.C.*

I sighed, and went to the pump to get a drink. The water from it was like liquid ice and it tasted funny, but it was water. I splashed some on my face and that woke me up pretty quick. I wiped my face off on Johnny's jacket and sat down on the back steps. The hill the church was on dropped off suddenly about twenty feet from the back door, and you could see for miles and miles. It was like sitting on the top of the world.

When you haven't got anything to do, you remember things in spite of yourself. I could remember every detail of the whole night, but it had the unreal quality of a dream. It seemed much longer than twenty-four hours since Johnny and I had met Dally at the corner of Pickett and Sutton. Maybe it was. Maybe Johnny had been gone a whole week and I had just slept. Maybe he had already been worked over by the fuzz and was waiting to get the electric chair since he wouldn't tell where I was. Maybe Dally had been killed in a car wreck or something and no one would ever know where I was, and I'd just die up here, alone, and turn into a skeleton. My over-active imagination was running away with me again. Sweat ran down my face and back, and I was trembling. My head swam, and I leaned back and closed my eyes. I guess it was partly delayed shock. Finally my stomach calmed down and I relaxed a little, hoping that Johnny would remember cigarettes. I was scared, sitting there by myself.

I heard someone coming up through the dead leaves toward the back of the church, and I ducked inside the door. Then I heard a whistle, long and low, ending in a sudden high note. I knew that whistle well enough. It was used by us and the Shepard gang for "Who's there?" I returned it carefully, then darted out the door so fast that I fell off the steps and sprawled flat under Johnny's nose.

I propped myself on my elbows and grinned up at him. "Hey, Johnny. Fancy meetin' you here."

He looked down at me over a big package. "I swear, Ponyboy, you're gettin' to act more like Two-Bit every day."

I tried unsuccessfully to cock an eyebrow. "Who's acting?" I rolled over and sprang up, happy that someone was there. "What'd you get?"

"Come on inside. Dally told us to stay inside."

We went in. Johnny dusted off a table with his jacket and started taking things out of the sack and lining them up neatly. "A week's supply of baloney, two loaves of bread, a box of matches . . ." Johnny went on.

I got tired of watching him do it all, so I started digging into the sack myself. "Wheee!" I sat down on a dusty chair and stared. "A paperback copy of *Gone with the Wind*! How'd you know I always wanted one?"

Johnny reddened. "I remembered you sayin' something about it once. And me and you went to see that movie, 'member? I thought you could maybe read it out loud and help kill time or something."

"Gee, thanks." I put the book down reluctantly. I wanted to start it right then. "Peroxide? A deck of cards . . ." Suddenly I realized something. "Johnny, you ain't thinking of . . ."

Johnny sat down and pulled out his knife. "We're gonna cut our hair, and you're gonna bleach yours." He looked at the ground carefully. "They'll have our descriptions in the paper. We can't fit 'em."

"Oh, no!" My hand flew to my hair. "No, Johnny, not my hair!"

It was my pride. It was long and silky, just like Soda's, only a little redder. Our hair was tuff—we didn't have to use much grease on it. Our hair labeled us greasers, too—it was our trademark. The one thing we were proud of. Maybe we couldn't have Corvairs or madras shirts, but we could have hair.

"We'd have to anyway if we got caught. You know the first thing the judge does is make you get a haircut."

"I don't see why," I said sourly. "Dally could just as easily mug somebody with short hair."

"I don't know either—it's just a way of trying to break us. They can't really do anything to guys like Curly Shepard or Tim; they've had about everything done to them. And they can't take anything away from them because they don't have anything in the first place. So they cut their hair."

I looked at Johnny imploringly. Johnny sighed. "I'm gonna cut mine too, and wash the grease out, but I can't bleach it. I'm too dark-skinned to look okay blond. Oh, come on, Ponyboy," he pleaded. "It'll grow back."

531

"Okay," I said, wide-eyed. "Get it over with."

Johnny flipped out the razor-edge of his switch, took hold of my hair, and started sawing on it. I shuddered. "Not too short," I begged. "Johnny, please . . ."

Finally it was over with. My hair looked funny, scattered over the floor in tufts. "It's lighter than I thought it was," I said, examining it. "Can I see what I look like now?"

"No," Johnny said slowly, staring at me. "We gotta bleach it first."

After I'd sat in the sun for fifteen minutes to dry the bleach, Johnny let me look in the old cracked mirror we'd found in a closet. I did a double take. My hair was even lighter than Sodapop's. I'd never combed it to the side like that. It just didn't look like me. It made me look younger, and scareder, too. Boy howdy, I thought, this really makes me look tuff. I look like a blasted pansy. I was miserable.

Johnny handed me the knife. He looked scared, too. "Cut the front and thin out the rest. I'll comb it back after I wash it."

"Johnny," I said tiredly, "you can't wash your hair in that freezing water in this weather. You'll get a cold."

He only shrugged. "Go ahead and cut it."

I did the best I could. He went ahead and washed it anyway, using the bar of soap he'd bought. I was glad I had had to run away with him instead of with Two-Bit or Steve or Dally. That would be one thing they'd never think of—soap. I gave him Dally's jacket to wrap up in, and he sat shivering in the sunlight on the back steps, leaning against the door, combing his hair back. It was the first time I could see that he had eyebrows. He didn't look like Johnny. His forehead was whiter where his bangs had been; it would have been funny if we hadn't been so scared. He was still shivering with cold. "I guess," he said weakly, "I guess we're disguised."

I leaned back next to him sullenly. "I guess so."

"Oh, shoot," Johnny said with fake cheerfulness, "it's just hair."

"Shoot nothing," I snapped. "It took me a long time to get that hair just the way I wanted it. And besides, this just ain't us. It's like being in a Halloween costume we can't get out of."

"Well, we got to get used to it," Johnny said with finality. "We're in big trouble and it's our looks or us."

I started eating a candy bar. "I'm still tired," I said. To my surprise, the ground blurred and I felt tears running down my cheeks. I brushed them off hurriedly. Johnny looked as miserable as I felt.

"I'm sorry I cut your hair off, Ponyboy."

"Oh, it ain't that," I said between bites of chocolate. "I mean, not all of it. I'm just a little spooky. I really don't know what's the matter. I'm just mixed up."

"I know," Johnny said through chattering teeth as we went inside. "Things have been happening so fast . . ." I put my arm across his shoulders to warm him up.

"Two-Bit shoulda been in that little one-horse store. Man, we're in the middle of nowhere; the nearest house is two miles away. Things were layin' out wide open, just waitin' for somebody slick like Two-Bit to come and pick 'em up. He coulda walked out with half the store." He leaned back beside me, and I could feel him trembling. "Good ol' Two-Bit," he said in a quavering voice. He must have been as homesick as I was.

"Remember how he was wisecrackin' last night?" I said. "Last night . . . just last night we were walkin' Cherry and Marcia over to Two-Bit's. Just last night we were layin' in the lot, lookin' up at the stars and dreaming . . ."

"Stop it!" Johnny gasped from between clenched teeth. "Shut up about last night! I killed a kid last night. He couldn't of been over seventeen or eighteen, and I killed him. How'd you like to live with that?" He was crying. I held him like Soda had held him the day we found him lying in the lot.

"I didn't mean to," he finally blurted out, "but they were drownin' you, and I was so scared . . ." He was quiet for a minute. "There sure is a lot of blood in people."

He got up suddenly and began pacing back and forth, slapping his pockets.

"Whatta we gonna do?" I was crying by then. It was getting dark and I was cold and lonesome. I closed my eyes and leaned my head back, but the tears came anyway.

"This is my fault," Johnny said in a miserable voice. He had stopped crying when I started. "For bringin' a little thirteen-year-old kid along. You ought to go home. You can't get into any trouble. You didn't kill him."

"No!" I screamed at him. "I'm fourteen! I've been fourteen for a month! And I'm in it as much as you are. I'll stop crying in a minute . . . I can't help it."

He slumped down beside me. "I didn't mean it like that, Ponyboy. Don't cry, Pony, we'll be okay. Don't cry . . ." I leaned against him and bawled until I went to sleep.

I woke up late that night. Johnny was resting against the wall and I was asleep on his shoulder. "Johnny?" I yawned. "You awake?" I was warm and sleepy.

"Yeah," he said quietly.

"We ain't gonna cry no more,[1] are we?"

"Nope. We're all cried out now. We're gettin' used to the idea. We're gonna be okay now."

"That's what I thought," I said drowsily. Then for the first time since Dally and I had sat down behind those girls at the Nightly Double, I relaxed. We could take whatever was coming now.

The next four or five days were the longest days I've ever spent in my life. We killed time by reading *Gone with the Wind* and playing poker. Johnny sure did like that book, although he didn't know anything about the Civil War and even less about plantations, and I had to explain a lot of it to him. It amazed me how Johnny could get more meaning out of some of the stuff in there than I could— I was supposed to be the deep one. Johnny had failed a year in school and never made good grades—he couldn't grasp anything that was shoved at him too fast, and I guess his teachers thought he was just plain dumb. But he wasn't. He was just a little slow to get things, and he liked to explore things once he did get them. He was especially stuck on the Southern gentlemen—impressed with their manners and charm.

"I bet they were cool ol' guys," he said, his eyes glowing, after I had read the part about them riding into sure death because they were gallant. "They remind me of Dally."

"Dally?" I said, startled. "Shoot, he ain't got any more manners than I do. And you saw how he treated those girls the other night. Soda's more like them Southern boys."

"Yeah . . . in the manners bit, and the charm, too, I guess," Johnny said slowly, "but one night I saw Dally gettin' picked up by the fuzz, and he kept real cool and

---

1 *ain't gonna cry no more* phrase in countless poems and songs, often with resurrection themes.

calm the whole time. They was gettin' him for breakin' out the windows in the school building, and it was Two-Bit who did that. And Dally knew it. But he just took the sentence without battin' an eye or even denyin' it. That's gallant."

That was the first time I realized the extent of Johnny's hero-worship for Dally Winston. Of all of us, Dally was the one I liked least. He didn't have Soda's understanding or dash, or Two-Bit's humor, or even Darry's superman qualities. But I realized that these three appealed to me because they were like the heroes in the novels I read. Dally was real. I liked my books and clouds and sunsets. Dally was so real he scared me.

Johnny and I never went to the front of the church. You could see the front from the road, and sometimes farm kids rode their horses by on their way to the store. So we stayed in the very back, usually sitting on the steps and looking across the valley. We could see for miles; see the ribbon of highway and the small dots that were houses and cars. We couldn't watch the sunset, since the back faced east, but I loved to look at the colors of the fields and the soft shadings of the horizon.

One morning I woke up earlier than usual. Johnny and I slept huddled together for warmth—Dally had been right when he said it would get cold where we were going. Being careful not to wake Johnny up, I went to sit on the steps and smoke a cigarette. The dawn was coming then. All the lower valley was covered with mist, and sometimes little pieces of it broke off and floated away in small clouds. The sky was lighter in the east, and the horizon was a thin golden line. The clouds changed from gray to pink, and the mist was touched with gold. There was a silent moment when everything held its breath, and then the sun rose. It was beautiful.

"Golly"—Johnny's voice beside me made me jump—"that sure was pretty."

"Yeah." I sighed, wishing I had some paint to do a picture with while the sight was still fresh in my mind.

"The mist was what was pretty," Johnny said. "All gold and silver."

"Uhmmmm," I said, trying to blow a smoke ring.

"Too bad it couldn't stay like that all the time."

"Nothing gold can stay."[2] I was remembering a poem I'd read once.

"What?"

> "Nature's first green is gold,
> Her hardest hue to hold.
> Her early leaf's a flower;
> But only so an hour.
> Then leaf subsides to leaf.
> So Eden sank to grief,
> So dawn goes down to day.
> Nothing gold can stay."

Johnny was staring at me. "Where'd you learn that? That was what I meant."

"Robert Frost wrote it. He meant more to it than I'm gettin', though." I was trying to find the meaning the poet had in mind, but it eluded me. "I always remembered it because I never quite got what he meant by it."

---

2 *Nothing gold can stay*   poem (1923) by Robert Frost (1874–1963).

"You know," Johnny said slowly, "I never noticed colors and clouds and stuff until you kept reminding me about them. It seems like they were never there before." He thought for a minute. "Your family sure is funny."

"And what happens to be so funny about it?" I asked stiffly.

Johnny looked at me quickly. "I didn't mean nothing. I meant, well, Soda kinda looks like your mother did, but he acts just exactly like your father. And Darry is the spittin' image of your father, but he ain't wild and laughing all the time like he was. He acts like your mother. And you don't act like either one."

"I know," I said. "Well," I said, thinking this over, "you ain't like any of the gang. I mean, I couldn't tell Two-Bit or Steve or even Darry about the sunrise and clouds and stuff. I couldn't even remember that poem around them. I mean, they just don't dig. Just you and Sodapop. And maybe Cherry Valance."

Johnny shrugged. "Yeah," he said with a sigh. "I guess we're different."

"Shoot," I said, blowing a perfect smoke ring, "maybe *they* are."

By the fifth day I was so tired of baloney I nearly got sick every time I looked at it. We had eaten all our candy bars in the first two days. I was dying for a Pepsi. I'm what you might call a Pepsi addict. I drink them like a fiend, and going for five days without one was about to kill me. Johnny promised to get some if we ran out of supplies and had to get some more, but that didn't help me right then. I was smoking a lot more there than I usually did—I guess because it was something to do—although Johnny warned me that I would get sick smoking so much. We were careful with our cigarettes—if that old church ever caught fire there'd be no stopping it.

On the fifth day I had read up to Sherman's siege of Atlanta in *Gone with the Wind*, owed Johnny a hundred and fifty bucks from poker games, smoked two packs of Camels, and as Johnny had predicted, got sick. I hadn't eaten anything all day; and smoking on an empty stomach doesn't make you feel real great. I curled up in a corner to sleep off the smoke. I was just about asleep when I heard, as if from a great distance, a low long whistle that went off in a sudden high note. I was too sleepy to pay any attention, although Johnny didn't have any reason to be whistling like that. He was sitting on the back steps trying to read *Gone with the Wind*. I had almost decided that I had dreamed the outside world and there was nothing real but baloney sandwiches and the Civil War and the old church and the mist in the valley. It seemed to me that I had always lived in the church, or maybe lived during the Civil War and had somehow got transplanted. That shows you what a wild imagination I have.

A toe nudged me in the ribs. "Glory," said a rough but familiar voice, "he looks different with his hair like that."

I rolled over and sat up, rubbing the sleep out of my eyes and yawning. Suddenly I blinked.

"Hey, Dally!"

"Hey, Ponyboy!" He grinned down at me. "Or should I say Sleeping Beauty?"

I never thought I'd live to see the day when I would be so glad to see Dally Winston, but right then he meant one thing: contact with the outside world. And it suddenly became real and vital.

"How's Sodapop? Are the fuzz after us? Is Darry all right? Do the boys know where we are? What . . ."

"Hold on, kid," Dally broke in. "I can't answer everything at once. You two want to go get something to eat first? I skipped breakfast and I'm about starved."

"*You're* starved?" Johnny was so indignant he nearly squeaked. I remembered the baloney.

"Is it safe to go out?" I asked eagerly.

"Yep." Dally searched his shirt pocket for a cigarette, and finding none, said, "Gotta cancer stick, Johnnycake?"

Johnny tossed him a whole package.

"The fuzz won't be lookin' for you around here," Dally said, lighting up. "They think you've lit out for Texas. I've got Buck's T-bird parked down the road a little way. Goshamighty, boys, ain't you been eatin' anything?"

Johnny looked startled. "Yeah. Whatever gave you the idea we ain't?"

Dally shook his head. "You're both pale and you've lost weight. After this, get out in the sun more. You look like you've been through the mill."

I started to say "Look who's talking" but decided it would be safer not to. Dally needed a shave—a stubble of colorless beard covered his jaw—and he looked like he was the one who'd been sleeping in his clothes for a week instead of us; I knew he hadn't seen a barber in months. But it was safer not to get mouthy with Dally Winston.

"Hey, Ponyboy"—he fumbled with a piece of paper in his back pocket—"I gotta letter for you."

"A letter? Who from?"

"The President, of course, stupid. It's from Soda."

"Sodapop?" I said, bewildered. "But how did he know . . . ?"

"He came over to Buck's a couple of days ago for something and found that sweat shirt. I told him I didn't know where you were, but he didn't believe me. He gave me this letter and half his pay check to give you. Kid, you ought to see Darry. He's takin' this mighty hard . . ."

I wasn't listening. I leaned back against the side of the church and read:

Ponyboy,

Well I guess you got into some trouble, huh? Darry and me nearly went nuts when you ran out like that. Darry is awful sorry he hit you. You know he didn't mean it. And then you and Johnny turned up mising and what with that dead kid in the park and Dally getting hauled into the station, well it scared us something awful. The police came by to question us and we told them as much as we could. I can't believe little old Johnny could kill somebody. I know Dally knows where you are, but you know him. He keeps his trap shut and won't tell me nothing. Darry hasn't got the slightest notion where you're at and it is nearly killing him. I wish you'd come back and turn your selves in but I guess you can't since Johnny might get hurt. You sure are famous. You got a paragraph in the newspaper even. Take care and say hi to Johnny for us.

Sodapop Curtis

He could improve his spelling, I thought after reading it through three or four times. "How come you got hauled in?" I asked Dally.

"Shoot, kid"—he grinned wolfishly—"them boys at the station know me by now. I get hauled in for everything that happens in our turf. While I was there I kinda let it slip that y'all were headin' for Texas. So that's where they're lookin'."

He took a drag on his cigarette and cussed it good-naturedly for not being a Kool. Johnny listened in admiration. "You sure can cuss good, Dally."

536

"Sure can," Dally agreed wholeheartedly, proud of his vocabulary. "But don't you kids get to pickin' up my bad habits."

He gave me a hard rub on the head. "Kid, I swear it don't look like you with your hair all cut off. It used to look tuff. You and Soda had the coolest-lookin' hair in town."

"I know," I said sourly. "I look lousy, but don't rub it in."

"Do y'all want somethin' to eat or not?"

Johnny and I leaped up. "You'd better believe it."

"Gee," Johnny said wistfully, "it sure will be good to get into a car again."

"Well," Dally drawled, "I'll give you a ride for your money."

Dally always did like to drive fast, as if he didn't care whether he got where he was going or not, and we came down the red dirt road off Jay Mountain doing eighty-five. I like fast driving and Johnny was crazy about drag races, but we both got a little green around the gills when Dally took a corner on two wheels with the brakes screaming. Maybe it was because we hadn't been in a car for so long.

We stopped at a Dairy Queen and the first thing I got was a Pepsi. Johnny and I gorged on barbecue sandwiches and banana splits.

"Glory," Dallas said, amazed, watching us gulp the stuff down. "You don't need to make like every mouthful's your last. I got plenty of money. Take it easy, I don't want you gettin' sick on me. And I thought I was hungry!"

Johnny merely ate faster. I didn't slow down until I got a headache.

"I didn't tell y'all something," Dally said, finishing his third hamburger. "The Socs and us are having all-out warfare all over the city. That kid you killed had plenty of friends and all over town it's Soc against grease. We can't walk alone at all. I started carryin' a heater . . ."

"Dally!" I said, frightened. "You kill people with heaters!"

"Ya kill 'em with switchblades, too, don't ya, kid?" Dally said in a hard voice. Johnny gulped. "Don't worry," Dally went on, "it ain't loaded. I ain't aimin' to get picked up for murder. But it sure does help a bluff. Tim Shepard's gang and our outfit are havin' it out with the Socs tomorrow night at the vacant lot. We got hold of the president of one of their social clubs and had a war council. Yeah"—Dally sighed, and I knew he was remembering New York—"just like the good old days. If they win, things go on as usual. If we do, they stay outa our territory but good. Two-Bit got jumped a few days ago. Darry and me came along in time, but he wasn't havin' too much trouble. Two-Bit's a good fighter. Hey, I didn't tell you we got us a spy."

"A spy?" Johnny looked up from his banana split. "Who?"

"That good-lookin' broad I tried to pick up that night you killed the Soc. The redhead, Cherry what's-her-name."

CHAPTER 6

JOHNNY GAGGED AND I almost dropped my hot-fudge sundae. "Cherry?" we both said at the same time. "The Soc?"

"Yeah," Dally said. "She came over to the vacant lot the night Two-Bit was jumped. Shepard and some of his outfit and us were hanging around there when she drives up in her little ol' Sting Ray. That took a lot of nerve. Some of us was for jumping her then and there, her bein' the dead kid's girl and all, but Two-Bit stopped us. Man, next time I want a broad I'll pick up my own kind."

"Yeah," Johnny said slowly, and I wondered if, like me, he was remembering another voice, also tough and just deepened into manhood, saying: "Next time you want a broad, pick up your own kind . . ." It gave me the creeps.

Dally was going on: "She said she felt that the whole mess was her fault, which it is, and that she'd keep up with what was comin' off with the Socs in the rumble and would testify that the Socs were drunk and looking for a fight and that you fought back in self-defense." He gave a grim laugh. "That little gal sure does hate me. I offered to take her over to The Dingo for a Coke and she said 'No, thank you' and told me where I could go in very polite terms."

She was afraid of loving you, I thought. So Cherry Valance, the cheerleader, Bob's girl, the Soc, was trying to help us. No, it wasn't Cherry the Soc who was helping us, it was Cherry the dreamer who watched sunsets and couldn't stand fights. It was hard to believe a Soc would help us, even a Soc that dug sunsets. Dally didn't notice. He had forgotten about it already.

"Man, this place is out of it. What do they do for kicks around here, play checkers?" Dally surveyed the scene without interest. "I ain't never been in the country before. Have you two?"

Johnny shook his head but I said, "Dad used to take us all huntin'. I've been in the country before. How'd you know about the church?"

"I got a cousin that lives around here somewheres. Tipped me off that it'd make a tuff hide-out in case of something. Hey, Ponyboy, I heard you was the best shot in the family."

"Yeah," I said. "Darry always got the most ducks, though. Him and Dad. Soda and I goofed around too much, scared most of our game away." I couldn't tell Dally that I hated to shoot things. He'd think I was soft.

"That was a good idea, I mean cuttin' your hair and bleachin' it. They printed your descriptions in the paper but you sure wouldn't fit 'em now."

Johnny had been quietly finishing his fifth barbecue sandwich, but now he announced: "We're goin' back and turn ourselves in."

It was Dally's turn to gag. Then he swore awhile. Then he turned to Johnny and demanded: "What?"

"I said we're goin' back and turn ourselves in," Johnny repeated in a quiet voice. I was surprised but not shocked. I had thought about turning ourselves in lots of times, but apparently the whole idea was a jolt to Dallas.

"I got a good chance of bein' let off easy," Johnny said desperately, and I didn't know if it was Dally he was trying to convince or himself. "I ain't got no record with the fuzz and it was self-defense. Ponyboy and Cherry can testify to that. And I don't aim to stay in that church all my life."

That was quite a speech for Johnny. His big black eyes grew bigger than ever at the thought of going to the police station, for Johnny had a deathly fear of cops, but went on: "We won't tell that you helped us, Dally, and we'll give you back the gun and what's left of the money and say we hitchhiked back so you won't get into trouble. Okay?"

Dally was chewing the corner of his ID card, which gave his age as twenty-one so he could buy liquor. "You sure you want to go back? Us greasers get it worse than anyone else."

Johnny nodded. "I'm sure. It ain't fair for Ponyboy to have to stay up in that church with Darry and Soda worryin' about him all the time. I don't guess . . ."—he swallowed and tried not to look eager—"I don't guess my parents are worried about me or anything?"

"The boys are worried," Dally said in a matter-of-fact voice. "Two-Bit was going to Texas to hunt for you."

"My parents," Johnny repeated doggedly, "did they ask about me?"

"No," snapped Dally, "they didn't. Blast it, Johnny, what do they matter? Shoot, my old man don't give a hang whether I'm in jail or dead in a car wreck or drunk in the gutter. That don't bother me none."

Johnny didn't say anything. But he stared at the dashboard with such hurt bewilderment that I could have bawled.

Dally cussed under his breath and nearly tore out the transmission of the T-bird as we roared out of the Dairy Queen. I felt sorry for Dally. He meant it when he said he didn't care about his parents. But he and the rest of the gang knew Johnny cared and did everything they could to make it up to him. I don't know what it was about Johnny—maybe that lost-puppy look and those big scared eyes were what made everyone his big brother. But they couldn't, no matter how hard they tried, take the place of his parents. I thought about it for a minute—Darry and Sodapop were my brothers and I loved both of them, even if Darry did scare me; but not even Soda could take Mom and Dad's place. And they were my real brothers, not just sort of adopted ones. No wonder Johnny was hurt because his parents didn't want him. Dally could take it—Dally was of the breed that could take anything, because he was hard and tough, and when he wasn't, he could turn hard and tough. Johnny was a good fighter and could play it cool, but he was sensitive and that isn't a good way to be when you're a greaser.

"Blast it, Johnny," Dally growled as we flew along the red road, "why didn't you think of turning yourself in five days ago? It would have saved a lot of trouble."

"I was scared," Johnny said with conviction. "I still am." He ran his finger down one of his short black sideburns. "I guess we ruined our hair for nothing, Ponyboy."

"I guess so." I was glad we were going back. I was sick of that church. I didn't care if I was bald.

Dally was scowling, and from long and painful experience I knew better than to talk to him when his eyes were blazing like that. I'd likely as not get clobbered over the head. That had happened before, just as it had happened to all the gang at one time or another. We rarely fought among ourselves—Darry was the unofficial leader, since he kept his head best, Soda and Steve had been best friends since grade school and never fought, and Two-Bit was just too lazy to argue with anyone. Johnny kept his mouth shut too much to get into arguments, and nobody ever fought with Johnny. I kept my mouth shut, too. But Dally was a different matter. If something beefed him, he didn't keep quiet about it, and if you rubbed him the wrong way—look out. Not even Darry wanted to tangle with him. He was dangerous.

Johnny just sat there and stared at his feet. He hated for any one of us to be mad at him. He looked awful sad. Dally glanced at him out of the corner of his eye. I looked out the window.

"Johnny," Dally said in a a pleading, high voice, using a tone I had never heard from him before, "Johnny, I ain't mad at you. I just don't want you to get hurt. You don't know what a few months in jail can do to you. Oh, blast it, Johnny"—he pushed his white-blond hair back out of his eyes—"you get hardened in jail. I don't want that to happen to you. Like it happened to me . . ."

I kept staring out the window at the rapidly passing scenery, but I felt my eyes getting round. Dally never talked like that. Never. Dally didn't give a Yankee dime[1] about anyone but himself, and he was cold and hard and mean. He never talked about his past or being in jail that way—if he talked about it at all, it was to brag. And I suddenly thought of Dally . . . in jail at the age of ten . . . Dally growing up in the streets . . .

"Would you rather have me living in hide-outs for the rest of my life, always on the run?" Johnny asked seriously.

If Dally had said yes, Johnny would have gone back to the church without hesitation. He figured Dally knew more than he did, and Dally's word was law. But he never heard Dally's answer, for we had reached the top of Jay Mountain and Dally suddenly slammed on the brakes and stared. "Oh, glory!" he whispered. The church was on fire!

"Let's go see what the deal is," I said, hopping out.

"What for?" Dally sounded irritated. "Get back in here before I beat your head in."

I knew Dally would have to park the car and catch me before he could carry out his threat, and Johnny was already out and following me, so I figured I was safe. We could hear him cussing us out, but he wasn't mad enough to come after us. There was a crowd at the front of the church, mostly little kids, and I wondered how they'd gotten there so quickly. I tapped the nearest grownup. "What's going on?"

"Well, we don't know for sure," the man said with a good-natured grin. "We were having a school picnic up here and the first thing we knew, the place is burning up. Thank goodness this is a wet season and the old thing is worthless anyway." Then, to the kids, he shouted, "Stand back, children. The firemen will be coming soon."

"I bet we started it," I said to Johnny. "We must have dropped a lighted cigarette or something."

About that time a lady came running up. "Jerry, some of the kids are missing."

"They're probably around here somewhere. You can't tell with all this excitement where they might be."

"No." She shook her head. "They've been missing for at least a half an hour. I thought they were climbing the hill . . ."

Then we all froze. Faintly, just faintly, you could hear someone yelling. And it sounded like it was coming from inside the church.

The woman went white. "I told them not to play in the church . . . I told them . . ." She looked like she was going to start screaming, so Jerry shook her.

"I'll get them, don't worry!" I started at a dead run for the church, and the man caught my arm. "I'll get them. You kids stay out!"

I jerked loose and ran on. All I could think was: We started it. We started it. We started it!

I wasn't about to go through that flaming door, so I slammed a big rock through a window and pulled myself in. It was a wonder I didn't cut myself to death, now that I think about it.

"Hey, Ponyboy."

---

1 *Yankee dime*   common expression in the South: something worthless there in the Confederate era.

I looked around, startled. I hadn't realized Johnny had been right behind me all the way. I took a deep breath, and started coughing. The smoke filled my eyes and they started watering. "Is that guy coming?"

Johnny shook his head. "The window stopped him."

"Too scared?"

"Naw . . ." Johnny gave me a grin. "Too fat."

I couldn't laugh because I was scared I'd drown in the smoke. The roar and crackling was getting louder, and Johnny shouted the next question.

"Where's the kids?"

"In the back, I guess," I hollered, and we started stumbling through the church. I should be scared, I thought with an odd detached feeling, but I'm not. The cinders and embers began falling on us, stinging and smarting like ants. Suddenly, in the red glow and the haze, I remembered wondering what it was like in a burning ember, and I thought: Now I know, it's a red hell. Why aren't I scared?

We pushed open the door to the back room and found four or five little kids, about eight years old or younger, huddled in a corner. One was screaming his head off, and Johnny yelled, "Shut up! We're goin' to get you out!" The kid looked surprised and quit hollering. I blinked myself—Johnny wasn't behaving at all like his old self. He looked over his shoulder and saw that the door was blocked by flames, then pushed open the window and tossed out the nearest kid. I caught one quick look at his face; it was red-marked from falling embers and sweat-streaked, but he grinned at me. He wasn't scared either. That was the only time I can think of when I saw him without that defeated, suspicious look in his eyes. He looked like he was having the time of his life.

I picked up a kid, and he promptly bit me, but I leaned out the window and dropped him as gently as I could, being in a hurry like that. A crowd was there by that time. Dally was standing there, and when he saw me he screamed, "For Pete's sake, get outa there! That roof's gonna cave in any minute. Forget those blasted kids!"

I didn't pay any attention, although pieces of the old roof were crashing down too close for comfort. I snatched up another kid, hoping he didn't bite, and dropped him without waiting to see if he landed okay or not. I was coughing so hard I could hardly stand up, and I wished I had time to take off Dally's jacket. It was hot. We dropped the last of the kids out as the front of the church started to crumble. Johnny shoved me toward the window. "Get out!"

I leaped out the window and heard timber crashing and the flames roaring right behind me. I staggered, almost falling, coughing and sobbing for breath. Then I heard Johnny scream, and as I turned to go back for him, Dally swore at me and clubbed me across the back as hard as he could, and I went down into a peaceful darkness.

When I came to, I was being bounced around, and I ached and smarted, and wondered dimly where I was. I tried to think but there was a high-pitched screaming going on, and I couldn't tell whether it was inside my head or out. Then I realized it was a siren. The fuzz, I thought dully. The cops have come for us. I tried to swallow a groan and wished wildly for Soda. Someone with a cold wet rag was gently sponging off my face, and a voice said, "I think he's coming around."

I opened my eyes. It was dark. I'm moving, I thought. Are they taking me to jail?

"Where . . .?" I said hoarsely, not able to get anything else out of my mouth. My throat was sore. I blinked at the stranger sitting beside me. But he wasn't a stranger . . . I'd seen him before . . .

"Take it easy, kid. You're in an ambulance."

"Where's Johnny?" I cried, frightened at being in this car with strangers. "And Dallas?"

"They're in the other ambulance, right behind us. Just calm down. You're going to be okay. You just passed out."

"I didn't either," I said in the bored, tough voice we reserved for strangers and cops. "Dallas hit me. How come?"

"Because your back was in flames, that's why."

I was surprised. "It was? Golly, I didn't feel it. It don't hurt."

"We put it out before you got burned. That jacket saved you from a bad burning, maybe saved your life. You just keeled over from smoke inhalation and a little shock—of course, that slap on the back didn't help much."

I remembered who he was then—Jerry somebody-or-other who was too heavy to get in the window. He must be a school teacher, I thought. "Are you taking us to the police station?" I was still a little mixed up as to what was coming off.

"The police station?" It was his turn to be surprised. "What would we want to take you to the police station for? We're taking all three of you to the hospital."

I let his first remark slide by. "Are Johnny and Dally all right?"

"Which one's which?"

"Johnny has black hair. Dally's the mean-looking one."

He studied his wedding ring. Maybe he's thinking about his wife, I thought. I wished he'd say something.

"We think the towheaded kid is going to be all right. He burned one arm pretty badly, though, trying to drag the other kid out the window. Johnny, well, I don't know about him. A piece of timber caught him across the back—he might have a broken back, and he was burned pretty severely. He passed out before he got out the window. They're giving him plasma now." He must have seen the look on my face because he hurriedly changed the subject. "I swear, you three are the bravest kids I've seen in a long time. First you and the black-haired kid climbing in that window, and then the tough-looking kid going back in to save him. Mrs. O'Briant and I think you were sent straight from heaven. Or are you just professional heroes or something?"

Sent from heaven? Had he gotten a good look at Dallas? "No, we're greasers," I said. I was too worried and scared to appreciate the fact that he was trying to be funny.

"You're what?"

"Greasers. You know, like hoods, JD's. Johnny is wanted for murder, and Dallas has a record with the fuzz a mile long."

"Are you kidding me?" Jerry stared at me as if he thought I was still in shock or something.

"I am not. Take me to town and you'll find out pretty quick."

"We're taking you to a hospital there anyway. The address card in your bill-fold said that was where you lived. Your name's really Ponyboy?"

"Yeah. Even on my birth certificate. And don't bug me about it. Are . . ."—I felt weak—"are the little kids okay?"

"Just fine. A little frightened maybe. There were some short explosions right after you all got out. Sounded just exactly like gunfire."

Gunfire. There went our gun. And *Gone with the Wind*. Were we sent from heaven? I started to laugh weakly. I guess that guy knew how close to hysterics I really was, for he talked to me in a low soothing voice all the way to the hospital.

I was sitting in the waiting room, waiting to hear how Dally and Johnny were. I had been checked over, and except for a few burns and a big bruise across my back, I was all right. I had watched them bring Dally and Johnny in on stretchers. Dally's eyes were closed, but when I spoke he had tried to grin and had told me that if I ever did a stupid thing like that again he'd beat the tar out of me. He was still swearing at me when they took him on in. Johnny was unconscious. I had been afraid to look at him, but I was relieved to see that his face wasn't burned. He just looked very pale and still and sort of sick. I would have cried at the sight of him so still except I couldn't in front of people.

Jerry Wood had stayed with me all the time. He kept thanking me for getting the kids out. He didn't seem to mind our being hoods. I told him the whole story—starting when Dallas and Johnny and I had met at the corner of Pickett and Sutton. I left out the part about the gun and our hitching a ride in the freight car. He was real nice about it and said that being heroes would help get us out of trouble, especially since it was self-defense and all.

I was sitting there, smoking a cigarette, when Jerry came back in from making a phone call. He stared at me for a second. "You shouldn't be smoking."

I was startled. "How come?" I looked at my cigarette. It looked okay to me. I looked around for a "No Smoking" sign and couldn't find one. "How come?"

"Why, uh," Jerry stammered, "uh, you're too young."

"I am?" I had never thought about it. Everyone in our neighborhood, even the girls, smoked. Except for Darry, who was too proud of his athletic health to risk a cigarette, we had all started smoking at an early age. Johnny had been smoking since he was nine; Steve started at eleven. So no one thought it unusual when I started. I was the weed-fiend in my family—Soda smokes only to steady his nerves or when he wants to look tough.

Jerry simply sighed, then grinned. "There are some people here to see you. Claim to be your brothers or something."

I leaped up and ran for the door, but it was already open and Soda had me in a bear hug and was swinging me around. I was so glad to see him I could have bawled. Finally he set me down and looked at me. He pushed my hair back. "Oh, Ponyboy, your hair . . . your tuff, tuff hair . . ."

Then I saw Darry. He was leaning in the doorway, wearing his olive jeans and black T-shirt. He was still tall, broad-shouldered Darry; but his fists were jammed in his pockets and his eyes were pleading. I simply looked at him. He swallowed and said in a husky voice, "Ponyboy . . ."

I let go of Soda and stood there for a minute. Darry didn't like me . . . he had driven me away that night . . . he had hit me . . . Darry hollered at me all the time . . . he didn't give a hang about me. . . . Suddenly I realized, horrified, that Darry was crying. He didn't make a sound, but tears were running down his cheeks. I hadn't seen him cry in years, not even when Mom and Dad had been killed. (I remembered the funeral. I had sobbed in spite of myself; Soda had broken down and bawled like a baby; but Darry had only stood there, his fists in his pockets and that look on his face, the same helpless, pleading look that he was wearing now.)

In that second what Soda and Dally and Two-Bit had been trying to tell me came through. Darry did care about me, maybe as much as he cared about

543

"He's getting mighty big to be carried," Soda said. I wanted to tell him to shut up and let me sleep but I only yawned.

"He's sure lost a lot of weight," Darry said.

I thought sleepily that I should at least pull off my shoes, but I didn't. I went to sleep the minute Darry tossed me on the bed. I'd forgotten how soft a bed really was.

I was the first one up the next morning. Soda must have pulled my shoes and shirt off for me; I was still wearing my jeans. He must have been too sleepy to undress himself, though; he lay stretched out beside me fully clothed. I wiggled out from under his arm and pulled the blanket up over him, then went to take a shower. Asleep, he looked a lot younger than going-on-seventeen, but I had noticed that Johnny looked younger when he was asleep, too, so I figured everyone did. Maybe people are younger when they are asleep.

After my shower, I put on some clean clothes and spent five minutes or so hunting for a hint of beard on my face and mourning over my hair. That bum haircut made my ears stick out.

Darry was still asleep when I went into the kitchen to fix breakfast. The first one up has to fix breakfast and the other two do the dishes. That's the rule around our house, and usually it's Darry who fixes breakfast and me and Soda who are left with the dishes. I hunted through the icebox and found some eggs. We all like our eggs done differently. I like them hard, Darry likes them in a bacon-and-tomato sandwich, and Sodapop eats his with grape jelly. All three of us like chocolate cake for breakfast. Mom had never allowed it with ham and eggs, but Darry let Soda and me talk him into it. We really didn't have to twist his arm; Darry loves chocolate cake as much as we do. Sodapop always makes sure there's some in the icebox every night and if there isn't he cooks one up real quick. I like Darry's cakes better; Sodapop always puts too much sugar in the icing. I don't see how he stands jelly and eggs and chocolate cake all at once, but he seems to like it. Darry drinks black coffee, and Sodapop and I drink chocolate milk. We could have coffee if we wanted it, but we like chocolate milk. All three of us are crazy about chocolate stuff. Soda says if they ever make a chocolate cigarette I'll have it made.

"Anybody home?" a familiar voice called through the front screen, and Two-Bit and Steve came in. We always just stick our heads into each other's houses and holler "Hey" and walk in. Our front door is always unlocked in case one of the boys is hacked off at his parents and needs a place to lay over and cool off. We never could tell who we'd find stretched out on the sofa in the morning. It was usually Steve, whose father told him about once a week to get out and never come back. It kind of bugs Steve, even if his old man does give him five or six bucks the next day to make up for it. Or it might be Dally, who lived anywhere he could. Once we even found Tim Shepard, leader of the Shepard gang and far from his own turf, reading the morning paper in the armchair. He merely looked up, said "Hi," and strolled out without staying for breakfast. Two-Bit's mother warned us about burglars, but Darry, flexing his muscles so that they bulged like oversized baseballs, drawled that he wasn't afraid of any burglars, and that we didn't really have anything worth taking. He'd risk a robbery, he said, if it meant keeping one of the boys from blowing up and robbing a gas station or something. So the door was never locked.

"In here!" I yelled, forgetting that Darry and Sodapop were still asleep. "Don't slam the door."

They slammed the door, of course, and Two-Bit came running into the kitchen. He caught me by the upper arms and swung me around, ignoring the fact that I had two uncooked eggs in my hand.

"Hey, Ponyboy," he cried gleefully, "long time no see."

You would have thought it had been five years instead of five days since I'd seen him last, but I didn't mind. I like ol' Two-Bit; he's a good buddy to have. He spun me into Steve, who gave me a playful slap on my bruised back and shoved me across the room. One of the eggs went flying. It landed on the clock and I tightened my grip on the other one, so that it crushed and ran all over my hand.

"Now look what you did," I griped. "There went our breakfast. Can't you two wait till I set the eggs down before you go shovin' me all over the country?" I really was a little mad, because I had just realized how long it had been since I'd eaten anything. The last thing I'd eaten was a hot-fudge sundae at the Dairy Queen in Windrixville, and I was hungry.

Two-Bit was walking in a slow circle around me, and I sighed because I knew what was coming.

"Man, dig baldy here!" He was staring at my head as he circled me. "I wouldn't have believed it. I thought all the wild Indians in Oklahoma had been tamed. What little squaw's got that tuff-lookin' mop of yours, Ponyboy?"

"Aw, lay off," I said. I wasn't feeling too good in the first place, kind of like I was coming down with something. Two-Bit winked at Steve, and Steve said, "Why, he had to get a haircut to get his picture in the paper. They'd never believe a greasy-lookin' mug could be a hero. How do you like bein' a hero, big shot?"

"How do I like *what?*"

"Being a hero. You know"—he shoved the morning paper at me impatiently—"like a big shot, even."

I stared at the newspaper. On the front page of the second section was the headline: JUVENILE DELINQUENTS TURN HEROES.

"What I like is the 'turn' bit," Two-Bit said, cleaning the egg up off the floor. "Y'all were heroes from the beginning. You just didn't 'turn' all of a sudden."

I hardly heard him. I was reading the paper. That whole page was covered with stories about us—the fight, the murder, the church burning, the Socs being drunk, everything. My picture was there, with Darry and Sodapop. The article told how Johnny and I had risked our lives saving those little kids, and there was a comment from one of the parents, who said that they would all have burned to death if it hadn't been for us. It told the whole story of our fight with the Socs—only they didn't say "Socs," because most grownups don't know about the battles that go on between us. They had interviewed Cherry Valance, and she said Bob had been drunk and that the boys had been looking for a fight when they took her home. Bob had told her he'd fix us for picking up his girl. His buddy Randy Adderson, who had helped jump us, also said it was their fault and that we'd only fought back in self-defense. But they were charging Johnny with manslaughter. Then I discovered that I was supposed to appear at juvenile court for running away, and Johnny was too, if he recovered. (Not *if*, I thought again. Why do they keep saying *if?*) For once, there weren't any charges against Dally, and I knew he'd be mad because the paper made him out a hero for saving Johnny and didn't say much about his police record, which he was kind of proud of. He'd kill those reporters if he got hold of them. There was another column about just Darry and Soda and me: how Darry worked on two jobs at once and made good at both of them, and about his outstanding record at school; it mentioned Sodapop dropping out of school so we could stay together, and that I made the honor roll at school all the time and might be a future track star. (Oh, yeah, I forgot—I'm on the A-squad track team, the youngest one. I'm a good runner.) Then it said we shouldn't be separated after we had worked so hard to stay together.

The meaning of that last line finally hit me. "You mean . . ."—I swallowed hard—"that they're thinking about putting me and Soda in a boys' home or something?"

Steve was carefully combing back his hair in complicated swirls. "Somethin' like that."

I sat down in a daze. We couldn't get hauled off now. Not after me and Darry had finally got through to each other, and now that the big rumble was coming up and we would settle this Soc-greaser thing once and for all. Not now, when Johnny needed us and Dally was still in the hospital and wouldn't be out for the rumble.

"No," I said out loud, and Two-Bit, who was scraping the egg off the clock, turned to stare at me.

"No what?"

"No, they ain't goin' to put us in a boys' home."

"Don't worry about it," Steve said, cocksure that he and Sodapop could handle anything that came up. "They don't do things like that to heroes. Where're Soda and Superman?"

That was as far as he got, because Darry, shaved and dressed, came in behind Steve and lifted him up off the floor, then dropped him. We all call Darry "Superman" or "Muscles" at one time or another; but one time Steve made the mistake of referring to him as "all brawn and no brain," and Darry almost shattered Steve's jaw. Steve didn't call him that again, but Darry never forgave him; Darry has never really gotten over not going to college. That was the only time I've ever seen Soda mad at Steve, although Soda attaches no importance to education. School bored him. No action.

Soda came running in. "Where's that blue shirt I washed yesterday?" He took a swig of chocolate milk out of the container.

"Hate to tell you, buddy," Steve said, still flat on the floor, "but you have to wear clothes to work. There's a law or something."

"Oh, yeah," Soda said. "Where're those wheat jeans, too?"

"I ironed. They're in my closet," Darry said. "Hurry up, you're gonna be late."

Soda ran back, muttering, "I'm hurryin', I'm hurryin'."

Steve followed him and in a second there was the general racket of a pillow fight. I absent-mindedly watched Darry as he searched the icebox for chocolate cake.

"Darry," I said suddenly, "did you know about the juvenile court?"

Without turning to look at me he said evenly, "Yeah, the cops told me last night."

I knew then that he realized we might get separated. I didn't want to worry him any more, but I said, "I had one of those dreams last night. The one I can't ever remember."

Darry spun around to face me, genuine fear on his face. "What?"

I had a nightmare the night of Mom and Dad's funeral. I'd had nightmares and wild dreams every once in a while when I was little, but nothing like this one. I woke up screaming bloody murder. And I never could remember what it was that had scared me. It scared Sodapop and Darry almost as bad as it scared me; for night after night, for weeks on end, I would dream this dream and wake up in a cold sweat or screaming. And I never could remember exactly what happened in it. Soda began sleeping with me, and it stopped recurring so often, but it happened often enough for Darry to take me to a doctor. The doctor said I had too much imagination. He had a simple cure, too: Study harder, read more, draw more, and play football more. After a hard game of football and four or five hours of reading, I was too exhausted, mentally and physically, to dream anything. But Darry never got over it, and every once in a while he would ask me if I ever dreamed any more.

"Was it very bad?" Two-Bit questioned. He knew the whole story, and having never dreamed about anything but blondes, he was interested.

"No," I lied. I had awakened in a cold sweat and shivering, but Soda was dead to the world. I had just wiggled closer to him and stayed awake for a couple of hours, trembling under his arm. That dream always scared the heck out of me.

Darry started to say something, but before he could begin, Sodapop and Steve came in.

"You know what?" Sodapop said to no one in particular. "When we stomp the Socies good, me and Stevie here are gonna throw a big party and everybody can get stoned. Then we'll go chase the Socs clear to Mexico."

"Where you gonna get the dough, little man?" Darry had found the cake and was handing out pieces.

"I'll think of somethin'," Sodapop assured him between bites.

"You going to take Sandy to the party?" I asked, just to be saying something. Instant silence. I looked around. "What's the deal?"

Sodapop was staring at his feet, but his ears were reddening. "No. She went to live with her grandmother in Florida."

"How come?"

"Look," Steve said, surprisingly angry, "does he have to draw you a picture? It was either that or get married, and her parents almost hit the roof at the idea of her marryin' a sixteen-year-old kid."

"Seventeen," Soda said softly. "I'll be seventeen in a couple of weeks."

"Oh," I said, embarrassed. Soda was no innocent; I had been in on bull sessions and his bragging was as loud as anyone's. But never about Sandy. Not ever about Sandy. I remembered how her blue eyes had glowed when she looked at him, and I was sorry for her.

There was a heavy silence. Then Darry said, "We'd better get on to work, Pepsi-Cola." Darry rarely called Soda by Dad's pet nickname for him, but he did so then because he knew how miserable Sodapop was about Sandy.

"I hate to leave you here by yourself, Ponyboy," Darry said slowly. "Maybe I ought to take the day off."

"I've stayed by my lonesome before. You can't afford a day off."

"Yeah, but you just got back and I really ought to stay . . ."

"I'll baby-sit him," Two-Bit said, ducking as I took a swing at him. "I haven't got anything better to do."

"Why don't you get a job?" Steve said. "Ever consider working for a living?"

"Work?" Two-Bit was aghast. "And ruin my rep? I wouldn't be baby-sittin' the kid here if I knew of some good day-nursery open on Saturdays."

I pulled his chair over backward and jumped on him, but he had me down in a second. I was kind of short on wind. I've got to cut out smoking or I won't make track next year.

"Holler uncle."

"Nope," I said, struggling, but I didn't have my usual strength.

Darry was pulling on his jacket. "You two do up the dishes. You can go to the movies if you want to before you go see Dally and Johnny." He paused for a second, watching Two-Bit squash the heck out of me. "Two-Bit, lay off. He ain't lookin' so good. Ponyboy, you take a couple of aspirins and go easy. You smoke more than a pack today and I'll skin you. Understood?"

"Yeah," I said, getting to my feet. "You carry more than one bundle of roofing at a time today and me and Soda'll skin you. Understood?"

He grinned one of his rare grins. "Yeah. See y'all this afternoon."

"Bye," I said. I heard our Ford's *vvrrrrooooom* and thought: Soda's driving. And they left.

". . . anyway, I was walking around downtown and started to take this short cut through an alley"—Two-Bit was telling me about one of his many exploits while we did the dishes. I mean, while I did the dishes. He was sitting on the cabinet, sharpening that black-handled switchblade he was so proud of—". . . and I ran into three guys. I says 'Howdy' and they just look at each other. Then one says 'We would jump you but since you're as slick as us we figger you don't have nothin' worth takin'.' I says 'Buddy, that's the truth' and went right on. Moral: What's the safest thing to be when one is met by a gang of social outcasts in an alley?"

"A judo expert?" I suggested.

"No, another social outcast!" Two-Bit yelped, and nearly fell off the cabinet from laughing so hard. I had to grin, too. He saw things straight and made them into something funny.

"We're gonna clean up the house," I said. "The reporters or police or somebody might come by, and anyway, it's time for those guys from the state to come by and check up on us."

"This house ain't messy. You oughtta see my house."

"I have. And if you had the sense of a billy goat you'd try to help around your place instead of bumming around."

"Shoot, kid, if I ever did that my mom would die of shock."

I liked Two-Bit's mother. She had the same good humor and easygoing ways that he did. She wasn't lazy like him, but she let him get away with murder. I don't know, though—it's just about impossible to get mad at him.

When we had finished, I pulled on Dally's brown leather jacket—the back was burned black—and we started for Tenth Street.

"I would drive us," Two-Bit said as we walked up the street trying to thumb a ride, "but the brakes are out on my car. Almost killed me and Kathy the other night." He flipped the collar of his black leather jacket up to serve as a windbreak while he lit a cigarette. "You oughtta see Kathy's brother. Now there's a hood. He's so greasy he glides when he walks. He goes to the barber for an oil change, not a haircut."

I would have laughed, but I had a terrific headache. We stopped at the Tasty Freeze to buy Cokes and rest up, and the blue Mustang that had been trailing us for eight blocks pulled in. I almost decided to run, and Two-Bit must have guessed this, for he shook his head ever so slightly and tossed me a cigarette. As I lit up, the Socs who had jumped Johnny and me at the park hopped out of the Mustang. I recognized Randy Adderson, Marcia's boyfriend, and the tall guy that had almost drowned me. I hated them. It was their fault Bob was dead;

their fault Johnny was dying; their fault Soda and I might get put in a boys' home. I hated them as bitterly and as contemptuously as Dally Winston hated.

Two-Bit put an elbow on my shoulder and leaned against me, dragging on his cigarette. "You know the rules. No jazz before the rumble," he said to the Socs.

"We know," Randy said. He looked at me. "Come here. I want to talk to you."

I glanced at Two-Bit. He shrugged. I followed Randy over to his car, out of earshot of the rest. We sat there in his car for a second, silent. Golly, that was the tuffest car I've ever been in.

"I read about you in the paper," Randy said finally. "How come?"

"I don't know. Maybe I felt like playing hero."

"I wouldn't have. I would have let those kids burn to death."

"You might not have. You might have done the same thing."

Randy pulled out a cigarette and pressed in the car lighter. "I don't know. I don't know anything anymore. I would never have believed a greaser could pull something like that."

"'Greaser' didn't have anything to do with it. My buddy over there wouldn't have done it. Maybe you would have done the same thing, maybe a friend of yours wouldn't have. It's the individual."

"I'm not going to show at the rumble tonight," Randy said slowly.

I took a good look at him. He was seventeen or so, but he was already old. Like Dallas was old. Cherry had said her friends were too cool to feel anything, and yet she could remember watching sunsets. Randy was supposed to be too cool to feel anything, and yet there was pain in his eyes.

"I'm sick of all this. Sick and tired. Bob was a good guy. He was the best buddy a guy ever had. I mean, he was a good fighter and tuff and everything, but he was a real person too. You dig?"

I nodded.

"He's dead—his mother has had a nervous breakdown. They spoiled him rotten. I mean, most parents would be proud of a kid like that—good-lookin' and smart and everything, but they gave in to him all the time. He kept trying to make someone say 'No' and they never did. They never did. That was what he wanted. For somebody to tell him 'No.' To have somebody lay down the law, set the limits, give him something solid to stand on. That's what we all want, really. One time . . ."—Randy tried to grin, but I could tell he was close to tears—"one time he came home drunker than anything. He thought sure they were gonna raise the roof. You know what they did? They thought it was something *they'd* done. They thought it was their fault—that they'd failed him and driven him to it or something. They took all the blame and didn't do anything to him. If his old man had just belted him—just once, he might still be alive. I don't know why I'm telling you this. I couldn't tell anyone else. My friends—they'd think I was off my rocker or turning soft. Maybe I am. I just know that I'm sick of this whole mess. That kid—your buddy, the one that got burned—he might die?"

"Yeah," I said, trying not to think about Johnny.

"And tonight . . . people get hurt in rumbles, maybe killed. I'm sick of it because it doesn't do any good. You can't win, you know that, don't you?" And when I remained silent he went on: "You can't win, even if you whip us. You'll still be where you were before—at the bottom. And we'll still be the lucky ones with all the breaks. So it doesn't do any good, the fighting and the killing. It doesn't prove a thing. We'll forget it if you win, or if you don't. Greasers will still be greasers and Socs will still be Socs. Sometimes I think it's the ones in the middle that are really the lucky stiffs . . ." He took a deep breath. "So I'd fight if I thought it'd do any good. I think I'm going to leave town. Take my little old Mustang and all the dough I can carry and get out."

"Running away won't help."

"Oh, hell, I know it," Randy half-sobbed, "but what can I do? I'm marked chicken if I punk out at the rumble, and I'd hate myself if I didn't. I don't know what to do."

"I'd help you if I could," I said. I remembered Cherry's voice: *Things are rough all over*. I knew then what she meant.

He looked at me. "No, you wouldn't. I'm a Soc. You get a little money and the whole world hates you."

"No," I said, "you hate the whole world."

He just looked at me—from the way he looked he could have been ten years older than he was. I got out of the car. "You would have saved those kids if you had been there," I said. "You'd have saved them the same as we did."

"Thanks, grease," he said, trying to grin. Then he stopped. "I didn't mean that. I meant, thanks, kid."

"My name's Ponyboy," I said. "Nice talkin' to you, Randy."

I walked over to Two-Bit, and Randy honked for his friends to come and get into the car.

"What'd he want?" Two-Bit asked. "What'd Mr. Super-Soc have to say?"

"He ain't a Soc," I said, "he's just a guy. He just wanted to talk."

"You want to see a movie before we go see Johnny and Dallas?"

"Nope," I said, lighting up another weed. I still had a headache, but I felt better. Socs were just guys after all. Things were rough all over, but it was better that way. That way you could tell the other guy was human too.

CHAPTER 8

THE NURSES WOULDN'T let us see Johnny. He was in critical condition. No visitors. But Two-Bit wouldn't take no for an answer. That was his buddy in there and he aimed to see him. We both begged and pleaded, but we were getting nowhere until the doctor found out what was going on.

"Let them go in," he said to the nurse. "He's been asking for them. It can't hurt now."

Two-Bit didn't notice the expression in his voice. It's true, I thought numbly, he is dying. We went in, practically on tiptoe, because the quietness of the hospital scared us. Johnny was lying still, with his eyes closed, but when Two-Bit said, "Hey, Johnnykid," he opened them and looked at us, trying to grin. "Hey, y'all."

The nurse, who was pulling the shades open, smiled and said, "So he can talk after all."

Two-Bit looked around. "They treatin' you okay, kid?"

"Don't . . ."—Johnny gasped—"don't let me put enough grease on my hair."

"Don't talk," Two-Bit said, pulling up a chair, "just listen. We'll bring you some hair grease next time. We're havin' the big rumble tonight."

Johnny's huge black eyes widened a little, but he didn't say anything.

"It's too bad you and Dally can't be in it. It's the first big rumble we've had—not countin' the time we whipped Shepard's outfit."

"He came by," Johnny said.

"Tim Shepard?"

Johnny nodded. "Came to see Dally."

Tim and Dallas had always been buddies.

"Did you know you got your name in the paper for being a hero?"

Johnny almost grinned as he nodded. "Tuff enough," he managed, and by the way his eyes were glowing, I figured Southern gentlemen had nothing on Johnny Cade.

I could see that even a few words were tiring him out; he was as pale as the pillow and looked awful. Two-Bit pretended not to notice.

"You want anything besides hair grease, kid?"

Johnny barely nodded. "The book"—he looked at me—"can you get another one?"

Two-Bit looked at me too. I hadn't told him about *Gone with the Wind*.

"He wants a copy of *Gone with the Wind* so I can read it to him," I explained. "You want to run down to the drugstore and get one?"

"Okay," Two-Bit said cheerfully. "Don't y'all run off."

I sat down in Two-Bit's chair and tried to think of something to say. "Dally's gonna be okay," I said finally. "And Darry and me, we're okay now."

I knew Johnny understood what I meant. We had always been close buddies, and those lonely days in the church strengthened our friendship. He tried to smile again, and then suddenly went white and closed his eyes tight.

"Johnny!" I said, alarmed. "Are you okay?"

He nodded, keeping his eyes closed. "Yeah, it just hurts sometimes. It usually don't . . . I can't feel anything below the middle of my back . . ."

He lay breathing heavily for a moment. "I'm pretty bad off, ain't I, Pony?"

"You'll be okay," I said with fake cheerfulness. "You gotta be. We couldn't get along without you."

The truth of that last statement hit me. We couldn't get along without him. We needed Johnny as much as he needed the gang. And for the same reason.

"I won't be able to walk again," Johnny started, then faltered. "Not even on crutches. Busted my back."

"You'll be okay," I repeated firmly. Don't start crying, I commanded myself, don't start crying, you'll scare Johnny.

"You want to know something, Ponyboy? I'm scared stiff. I used to talk about killing myself . . ." He drew a quivering breath. "I don't want to die now. It ain't long enough. Sixteen years ain't long enough. I wouldn't mind it so much if there wasn't so much stuff I ain't done yet and so many things I ain't seen. It's not fair. You know what? That time we were in Windrixville was the only time I've been away from our neighborhood."

"You ain't gonna die," I said, trying to hold my voice down. "And don't get juiced up, because the doc won't let us see you no more if you do."

Sixteen years on the streets and you can learn a lot. But all the wrong things, not the things you want to learn. Sixteen years on the streets and you see a lot. But all the wrong sights, not the sights you want to see.

Johnny closed his eyes and rested quietly for a minute. Years of living on the East Side teaches you how to shut off your emotions. If you didn't, you would explode. You learn to cool it.

A nurse appeared in the doorway. "Johnny," she said quietly, "your mother's here to see you."

Johnny opened his eyes. At first they were wide with surprise, then they darkened. "I don't want to see her," he said firmly.

"She's your mother."

"I said I don't want to see her." His voice was rising. "She's probably come to tell me about all the trouble I'm causing her and about how glad her and the old man'll be when I'm dead. Well, tell her to leave me alone. For once"—his voice broke—"for once just to leave me alone." He was struggling to sit up, but he suddenly gasped, went whiter than the pillowcase, and passed out cold.

The nurse hurried me out the door. "I was afraid of something like this if he saw anyone."

I ran into Two-Bit, who was coming in.

"You can't see him now," the nurse said, so Two-Bit handed her the book. "Make sure he can see it when he comes around." She took it and closed the door behind her. Two-Bit stood and looked at the door a long time. "I wish it was any one of us except Johnny," he said, and his voice was serious for once. "We could get along without anyone but Johnny."

Turning abruptly, he said, "Let's go see Dallas."

As we walked out into the hall, we saw Johnny's mother. I knew her. She was a little woman, with straight black hair and big black eyes like Johnny's. But that was as far as the resemblance went. Johnnycake's eyes were fearful and sensitive; hers were cheap and hard. As we passed her she was saying, "But I have a right to see him. He's my son. After all the trouble his father and I've gone to to raise him, this is our reward! He'd rather see those no-count hoodlums than his own folks . . ." She saw us and gave us such a look of hatred that I almost backed up. "It was your fault. Always running around in the middle of the night getting jailed and heaven knows what else . . ." I thought she was going to cuss us out. I really did.

Two-Bit's eyes got narrow and I was afraid he was going to start something. I don't like to hear women get sworn at, even if they deserve it. "No wonder he hates your guts," Two-Bit snapped. He was going to tell her off real good, but I shoved him along. I felt sick. No wonder Johnny didn't want to see her. No wonder he stayed overnight at Two-Bit's or at our house, and slept in the vacant lot in good weather. I remembered my mother . . . beautiful and golden, like Soda, and wise and firm, like Darry.

"Oh, lordy!" There was a catch in Two-Bit's voice and he was closer to tears than I'd ever seen him. "He has to live with that."

We hurried to the elevator to get to the next floor. I hoped the nurse would have enough sense not to let Johnny's mother see him. It would kill him.

Dally was arguing with one of the nurses when we came in. He grinned at us. "Man, am I glad to see you! These—hospital people won't let me smoke, and I want out!"

We sat down, grinning at each other. Dally was his usual mean, ornery self. He was okay.

"Shepard came by to see me a while ago."

"That's what Johnny said. What'd he want?"

"Said he saw my picture in the paper and couldn't believe it didn't have 'Wanted Dead or Alive' under it. He mostly came to rub it in about the rumble. Man, I hate not bein' in that."

Only last week Tim Shepard had cracked three of Dally's ribs. But Dally and Tim Shepard had always been buddies; no matter how they fought, they were two of a kind, and they knew it.

Dally was grinning at me. "Kid, you scared the devil outa me the other day. I thought I'd killed you."

"Me?" I said, puzzled. "Why?"

"When you jumped out of the church. I meant to hit you just hard enough to knock you down and put out the fire, but when you dropped like a ton of lead I thought I'd aimed too high and broke your neck." He thought for a minute. "I'm glad I didn't, though."

"I'll bet," I said with a grin. I'd never liked Dally—but then, for the first time, I felt like he was my buddy. And all because he was glad he hadn't killed me.

Dally looked out the window. "Uh . . ."—he sounded very casual—"how's the kid?"

"We just left him," Two-Bit said, and I could tell that he was debating whether to tell Dally the truth or not. "I don't know about stuff like this . . . but . . . well, he seemed pretty bad to me. He passed out cold before we left him."

Dally's jaw line went white as he swore between clenched teeth.

"Two-Bit, you still got that fancy black-handled switch?"

"Yeah."

"Give it here."

Two-Bit reached into his back pocket for his prize possession. It was a jet-handled switchblade, ten inches long, that would flash open at a mere breath. It was the reward of two hours of walking aimlessly around a hardware store to divert suspicion. He kept it razor sharp. As far as I knew, he had never pulled it on anyone; he used his plain pocketknife when he needed a blade. But it was his showpiece, his pride and joy—every time he ran into a new hood he pulled it out and showed off with it. Dally knew how much that knife meant to Two-Bit, and if he needed a blade bad enough to ask for it, well, he needed a blade. That was all there was to it. Two-Bit handed it over to Dally without a moment's hesitation.

"We gotta win that fight tonight," Dally said. His voice was hard. "We gotta get even with the Socs. For Johnny."

He put the switch under his pillow and lay back, staring at the ceiling. We left. We knew better than to talk to Dally when his eyes were blazing and he was in a mood like that.

We decided to catch a bus home. I just didn't feel much like walking or trying to hitch a ride. Two-Bit left me sitting on the bench at the bus stop while he went to a gas station to buy some cigarettes. I was kind of sick to my stomach and sort of groggy. I was nearly asleep when I felt someone's hand on my forehead. I almost jumped out of my skin. Two-Bit was looking down at me worriedly. "You feel okay? You're awful hot."

"I'm all right," I said, and when he looked at me as if he didn't believe me, I got a little panicky. "Don't tell Darry, okay? Come on, Two-Bit, be a buddy. I'll be well by tonight. I'll take a bunch of aspirins."

"All right," Two-Bit said reluctantly. "But Darry'll kill me if you're really sick and go ahead and fight anyway."

"I'm okay," I said, getting a little angry. "And if you keep your mouth shut, Darry won't know a thing."

"You know somethin'?" Two-Bit said as we were riding home on the bus. "You'd think you could get away with murder, living with your big brother and all, but Darry's stricter with you than your folks were, ain't he?"

555

"Yeah," I said, "but they'd raised two boys before me. Darry hasn't."

"You know, the only thing that keeps Darry from bein' a Soc is us."

"I know," I said. I had known it for a long time. In spite of not having much money, the only reason Darry couldn't be a Soc was us. The gang. Me and Soda. Darry was too smart to be a greaser. I don't know how I knew, I just did. And I was kind of sorry.

I was silent most of the way home. I was thinking about the rumble. I had a sick feeling in my stomach and it wasn't from being ill. It was the same kind of helplessness I'd felt that night Darry yelled at me for going to sleep in the lot. I had the same deathly fear that something was going to happen that none of us could stop. As we got off the bus I finally said it. "Tonight—I don't like it one bit."

Two-Bit pretended not to understand. "I never knew you to play chicken in a rumble before. Not even when you was a little kid."

I knew he was trying to make me mad, but I took the bait anyway. "I ain't chicken, Two-Bit Mathews, and you know it," I said angrily. "Ain't I a Curtis, same as Soda and Darry?"

Two-Bit couldn't deny this, so I went on: "I mean, I got an awful feeling something's gonna happen."

"Somethin' *is* gonna happen. We're gonna stomp the Socs' guts, that's what."

Two-Bit knew what I meant, but doggedly pretended not to. He seemed to feel that if you said something was all right, it immediately was, no matter what. He's been that way all his life, and I don't expect he'll change. Sodapop would have understood, and we would have tried to figure it out together, but Two-Bit just ain't Soda. Not by a long shot.

Cherry Valance was sitting in her Corvette by the vacant lot when we came by. Her long hair was pinned up, and in daylight she was even better looking. That Sting Ray was one tuff car. A bright red one. It was cool.

"Hi, Ponyboy," she said. "Hi, Two-Bit."

Two-Bit stopped. Apparently Cherry had shown up there before during the week Johnny and I had spent in Windrixville.

"What's up with the big-times?"

She tightened the strings on her ski jacket. "They play your way. No weapons, fair deal. Your rules."

"You sure?"

She nodded. "Randy told me. He knows for sure."

Two-Bit turned and started home. "Thanks, Cherry."

"Ponyboy, stay a minute," Cherry said. I stopped and went back to her car. "Randy's not going to show up at the rumble."

"Yeah," I said, "I know."

"He's not scared. He's just sick of fighting. Bob . . ." She swallowed, then went on quietly. "Bob was his best buddy. Since grade school."

I thought of Soda and Steve. What if one of them saw the other killed? Would that make them stop fighting? No, I thought, maybe it would make Soda stop, but not Steve. He'd go on hating and fighting. Maybe that was what Bob would have done if it had been Randy instead of him.

"How's Johnny?"

"Not so good," I said. "Will you go up to see him?"

She shook her head. "No. I couldn't."

"Why not?" I demanded. It was the least she could do. It was her boyfriend who had caused it all . . . and then I stopped. Her boyfriend . . .

"I couldn't," she said in a quiet, desperate voice. "He killed Bob. Oh, maybe Bob asked for it. I know he did. But I couldn't ever look at the person who killed him. You only knew his bad side. He could be sweet sometimes, and friendly. But when he got drunk . . . it was that part of him that beat up Johnny. I knew it was Bob when you told me the story. He was so proud of his rings. Why do people sell liquor to boys? Why? I know there's a law against it, but kids get it anyway. I can't go see Johnny. I know I'm too young to be in love and all that, but Bob was something special. He wasn't just any boy. He had something that made people follow him, something that marked him different, maybe a little better, than the crowd. Do you know what I mean?"

I did. Cherry saw the same things in Dallas. That was why she was afraid to see him, afraid of loving him. I knew what she meant all right. But she also meant she wouldn't go see Johnny because he had killed Bob. "That's okay," I said sharply. It wasn't Johnny's fault Bob was a booze-hound and Cherry went for boys who were bound for trouble. "I wouldn't want you to see him. You're a traitor to your own kind and not loyal to us. Do you think your spying for us makes up for the fact that you're sitting there in a Corvette while my brother drops out of school to get a job? Don't you ever feel sorry for us. Don't you ever try to give us handouts and then feel high and mighty about it."

I started to turn and walk off, but something in Cherry's face made me stop. I was ashamed—I can't stand to see girls cry. She wasn't crying, but she was close to it.

"I wasn't trying to give you charity, Ponyboy. I only wanted to help. I liked you from the start . . . the way you talked. You're a nice kid, Ponyboy. Do you realize how scarce nice kids are nowadays? Wouldn't you try to help me if you could?"

I would. I'd help her and Randy both, if I could. "Hey," I said suddenly, "can you see the sunset real good from the West Side?"

She blinked, startled, then smiled. "Real good."

"You can see it good from the East Side, too," I said quietly.

"Thanks, Ponyboy." She smiled through her tears. "You dig okay."

She had green eyes. I went on, walking home slowly.

CHAPTER 9

I T WAS ALMOST SIX-thirty when I got home. The rumble was set for seven, so I was late for supper, as usual. I always come in late. I forget what time it is. Darry had cooked dinner: baked chicken and potatoes and corn—two chickens because all three of us eat like horses. Especially Darry. But although I love baked chicken, I could hardly swallow any. I swallowed five aspirins, though, when Darry and Soda weren't looking. I do that all the time because I can't sleep very well at night. Darry thinks I take just one, but I usually take four. I figured five would keep me going through the rumble and maybe get rid of my headache.

Then I hurried to take a shower and change clothes. Me and Soda and Darry always got spruced up before a rumble. And besides, we wanted to show those Socs we weren't trash, that we were just as good as they were.

"Soda," I called from the bathroom, "when did you start shaving?"

"When I was fifteen," he yelled back.

"When did Darry?"

"When he was thirteen. Why? You figgerin' on growing a beard for the rumble?"

"You're funny. We ought to send you in to the *Reader's Digest*. I hear they pay a lot for funny things."

Soda laughed and went right on playing poker with Steve in the living room. Darry had on a tight black T-shirt that showed every muscle on his chest and even the flat hard muscles of his stomach. I'd hate to be the Soc who takes a crack at him, I thought as I pulled on a clean T-shirt and a fresh pair of jeans. I wished my T-shirt was tighter—I have a pretty good build for my size, but I'd lost a lot of weight in Windrixville and it just didn't fit right. It was a chilly night and T-shirts aren't the warmest clothes in the world, but nobody ever gets cold in a rumble, and besides, jackets interfere with your swinging ability.

Soda and Steve and I had put on more hair oil than was necessary, but we wanted to show that we were greasers. Tonight we could be proud of it. Greasers may not have much, but they have a rep. That and long hair. (What kind of world is it where all I have to be proud of is a reputation for being a hood, and greasy hair? I don't want to be a hood, but even if I don't steal things and mug people and get boozed up, I'm marked lousy. Why should I be proud of it? Why should I even pretend to be proud of it?) Darry never went in for the long hair. His was short and clean all the time.

I sat in the armchair in the living room, waiting for the rest of the outfit to show up. But of course, tonight the only one coming would be Two-Bit; Johnny and Dallas wouldn't show. Soda and Steve were playing cards and arguing as usual. Soda was keeping up a steady stream of wisecracks and clowning, and Steve had turned up the radio so loud that it almost broke my eardrums. Of course everybody listens to it loud like that, but it wasn't just the best thing for a headache.

"You like fights, don't you, Soda?" I asked suddenly.

"Yeah, sure." He shrugged. "I like fights."

"How come?"

"I don't know." He looked at me, puzzled. "It's action. It's a contest. Like a drag race or a dance or something."

"Shoot," said Steve, "I want to beat those Socs' heads in. When I get in a fight I want to stomp the other guy good. I like it, too."

"How come you like fights, Darry?" I asked, looking up at him as he stood behind me, leaning in the kitchen doorway. He gave me one of those looks that hide what he's thinking, but Soda piped up: "He likes to show off his muscles."

"I'm gonna show 'em off on you, little buddy, if you get any mouthier."

I digested what Soda had said. It was the truth. Darry liked anything that took strength, like weight-lifting or playing football or roofing houses, even if he was proud of being smart too. Darry never said anything about it, but I knew he liked fights. I felt out of things. I'll fight anyone anytime, but I don't like to.

"I don't know if you ought to be in this rumble, Pony," Darry said slowly.

Oh, no, I thought in mortal fear, I've got to be in it. Right then the most important thing in my life was helping us whip the Socs. Don't let him make me stay home now. I've got to be in it.

"How come? I've always come through before, ain't I?"

"Yeah," Darry said with a proud grin. "You fight real good for a kid your size. But you were in shape before. You've lost weight and you don't look so great, kid. You're tensed up too much."

"Shoot," said Soda, trying to get the ace out of his shoe without Steve's seeing him, "we all get tensed up before a rumble. Let him fight tonight. Skin never hurt anyone—no weapons, no danger."

"I'll be okay," I pleaded. "I'll get hold of a little one, okay?"

558

"Well, Johnny won't be there this time . . ."—Johnny and I sometimes ganged up on one big guy—"but then, Curly Shepard won't be there either, or Dally, and we'll need every man we can get."

"What happened to Shepard?" I asked, remembering Tim Shepard's kid brother. Curly, who was a tough, cool, hard-as-nails Tim in miniature, and I had once played chicken by holding our cigarette ends against each other's fingers. We had stood there, clenching our teeth and grimacing, with sweat pouring down our faces and the smell of burning flesh making us sick, each refusing to holler, until Tim happened to stroll by. When he saw that we were really burning holes in each other he cracked our heads together, swearing to kill us both if we ever pulled a stunt like that again. I still have the scar on my forefinger. Curly was an average downtown hood, tough and not real bright, but I liked him. He could take anything.

"He's in the cooler," Steve said, kicking the ace out of Soda's shoe. "In the reformatory."

Again? I thought, and said, "Let me fight, Darry. If it was blades or chains or something it'd be different. Nobody ever gets really hurt in a skin rumble."

"Well"—Darry gave in—"I guess you can. But be careful, and if you get in a jam, holler and I'll get you out."

"I'll be okay," I said wearily. "How come you never worry about Sodapop as much? I don't see you lecturin' him."

"Man"—Darry grinned and put his arm across Soda's shoulders—"this is one kid brother I don't have to worry about."

Soda punched him in the ribs affectionately.

"This kiddo can use his head."

Sodapop looked down at me with mock superiority, but Darry went on: "You can see he uses it for one thing—to grow hair on." He ducked Soda's swing and took off for the door.

Two-Bit stuck his head in the door just as Darry went flying out of it. Leaping as he went off the steps, Darry turned a somersault in mid-air, hit the ground, and bounced up before Soda could catch him.

"Welup," Two-Bit said cheerfully, cocking an eyebrow, "I see we are in prime condition for a rumble. Is everybody happy?"

"Yeah!" screamed Soda as he too did a flying somersault off the steps. He flipped up to walk on his hands and then did a no-hands cartwheel across the yard to beat Darry's performance. The excitement was catching. Screeching like an Indian, Steve went running across the lawn in flying leaps, stopped suddenly, and flipped backward. We could all do acrobatics because Darry had taken a course at the Y and then spent a whole summer teaching us everything he'd learned on the grounds that it might come in handy in a fight. It did, but it also got Two-Bit and Soda jailed once. They were doing mid-air flips down a downtown sidewalk, walking on their hands, and otherwise disturbing the public and the police. Leave it to those two to pull something like that.

With a happy whoop I did a no-hands cartwheel off the porch steps, hit the ground, and rolled to my feet. Two-Bit followed me in a similar manner.

"I am a greaser," Sodapop chanted. "I am a JD and a hood. I blacken the name of our fair city. I beat up people. I rob gas stations. I am a menace to society. Man, do I have fun!"

"Greaser . . . greaser . . . greaser . . ." Steve singsonged. "O victim of environment, underprivileged, rotten, no-count hood!"

"Juvenile delinquent, you're no good!" Darry shouted.

559

"Get thee hence, white trash," Two-Bit said in a snobbish voice. "I am a Soc. I am the privileged and the well-dressed. I throw beer blasts, drive fancy cars, break windows at fancy parties."

"And what do you do for fun?" I inquired in a serious, awed voice.

"I jump greasers!" Two-Bit screamed, and did a cartwheel.

We settled down as we walked to the lot. Two-Bit was the only one wearing a jacket; he had a couple of cans of beer stuffed in it. He always gets high before a rumble. Before anything else, too, come to think of it. I shook my head. I'd hate to see the day when I had to get my nerve from a can. I'd tried drinking once before. The stuff tasted awful, I got sick, had a headache, and when Darry found out, he grounded me for two weeks. But that was the last time I'd ever drink. I'd seen too much of what drinking did for you at Johnny's house.

"Hey, Two-Bit," I said, deciding to complete my survey, "how come you like to fight?"

He looked at me as if I was off my nut. "Shoot, everybody fights."

If everybody jumped in the Arkansas River, ol' Two-Bit would be right on their heels. I had it then. Soda fought for fun, Steve for hatred, Darry for pride, and Two-Bit for conformity. Why do I fight? I thought, and couldn't think of any real good reason. There isn't any real good reason for fighting except self-defense.

"Listen, Soda, you and Ponyboy," Darry said as we strode down the street, "if the fuzz show, you two beat it out of there. The rest of us can only get jailed. You two can get sent to a boys' home."

"Nobody in this neighborhood's going to call the fuzz," Steve said grimly. "They know what'd happen if they did."

"All the same, you two blow at the first sign of trouble. You hear me?"

"You sure don't need an amplifier," Soda said, and stuck out his tongue at the back of Darry's head. I stifled a giggle. If you want to see something funny, it's a tough hood sticking his tongue out at his big brother.

Tim Shepard and company were already waiting when we arrived at the vacant lot, along with a gang from Brumly, one of the suburbs. Tim was a lean, catlike eighteen-year-old who looked like the model JD you see in movies and magazines. He had the right curly black hair, smoldering dark eyes, and a long scar from temple to chin where a tramp had belted him with a broken pop bottle. He had a tough, hard look to him, and his nose had been broken twice. Like Dally's, his smile was grim and bitter. He was one of those who enjoy being a hood. The rest of his bunch were the same way. The boys from Brumly, too. Young hoods—who would grow up to be old hoods. I'd never thought about it before, but they'd just get worse as they got older, not better. I looked at Darry. He wasn't going to be any hood when he got old. He was going to get somewhere. Living the way we do would only make him more determined to get somewhere. That's why he's better than the rest of us, I thought. He's going somewhere. And I was going to be like him. I wasn't going to live in a lousy neighborhood all my life.

Tim had the tense, hungry look of an alley cat—that's what he's always reminded me of, an alley cat—and he was constantly restless. His boys ranged from fifteen to nineteen, hard-looking characters who were used to the strict discipline Tim gave out. That was the difference between his gang and ours—they had a leader and were organized; we were just buddies who stuck together—each man was his own leader. Maybe that was why we could whip them.

560

Tim and the leader of the Brumly outfit moved forward to shake hands with each of us—proving that our gangs were on the same side in this fight, although most of the guys in those two outfits weren't exactly what I'd like to call my friends. When Tim got to me he studied me, maybe remembering how his kid brother and I had played chicken. "You and the quiet black-headed kid were the ones who killed that Soc?"

"Yeah," I said, pretending to be proud of it; then I thought of Cherry and Randy and got a sick feeling in my stomach.

"Good goin', kid. Curly always said you were a good kid. Curly's in the reformatory for the next six months." Tim grinned ruefully, probably thinking of his roughneck, hard-headed brother. "He got caught breakin' into a liquor store, the little . . ." He went on to call Curly every unprintable name under the sun—in Tim's way of thinking, terms of affection.

I surveyed the scene with pride. I was the youngest one there. Even Curly, if he had been there, had turned fifteen, so he was older than me. I could tell Darry realized this too, and although he was proud, I also knew he was worried. Shoot, I thought, I'll fight so good this time he won't ever worry about me again. I'll show him that someone besides Sodapop can use his head.

One of the Brumly guys waved me over. We mostly stuck with our own outfits, so I was a little leery of going over to him, but I shrugged. He asked to borrow a weed, then lit up. "That big guy with y'all, you know him pretty well?"

"I ought to, he's my brother," I said. I couldn't honestly say "Yes." I knew Darry as well as he knew me, and that isn't saying a whole lot.

"No kiddin'? I got a feelin' he's gonna be asked to start the fireworks around here. He a pretty good bopper?"

He meant rumbler. Those Brumly boys have weird vocabularies. I doubt if half of them can read a newspaper or spell much more than their names, and it comes out in their speech. I mean, you take a guy that calls a rumble "bop-action," and you can tell he isn't real educated.

"Yep," I said. "But why him?"

He shrugged. "Why anybody else?"

I looked our outfits over. Most greasers don't have real tuff builds or anything. They're mostly lean and kind of panther-looking in a slouchy way. This is partly because they don't eat much and partly because they're slouchy. Darry looked like he could whip anyone there. I think most of the guys were nervous because of the 'no weapons' rule. I didn't know about the Brumly boys, but I knew Shepard's gang were used to fighting with anything they could get their hands on—bicycle chains, blades, pop bottles, pieces of pipe, pool sticks, or sometimes even heaters. I mean guns. I have a kind of lousy vocabulary, too, even if I am educated. Our gang never went in for weapons. We're just not that rough. The only weapons we ever used were knives, and shoot, we carried them mostly just for looks. Like Two-Bit with his black-handled switch. None of us had ever really hurt anybody, or wanted to. Just Johnny. And he hadn't wanted to.

"Hey, Curtis!" Tim yelled. I jumped.

"Which one?" I heard Soda yell back.

"The big one. Come on over here."

The guy from Brumly looked at me. "What did I tell ya?"

I watched Darry going toward Tim and the leader of the Brumly boys. He shouldn't be here, I thought suddenly. I shouldn't be here and Steve shouldn't be here and Soda shouldn't be here and Two-Bit shouldn't be here. We're greasers, but not hoods, and we don't belong with this bunch of future convicts. We could end up like them, I thought. We could. And the thought didn't help my headache.

I went back to stand with Soda and Steve and Two-Bit then, because the Socs were arriving. Right on time. They came in four carloads, and filed out silently. I counted twenty-two of them. There were twenty of us, so I figured the odds were as even as we could get them. Darry always liked to take on two at a time anyway. They looked like they were all cut from the same piece of cloth: clean-shaven with semi-Beatle haircuts, wearing striped or checkered shirts with light-red or tan-colored jackets or madras ski jackets. They could just as easily have been going to the movies as to a rumble. That's why people don't ever think to blame the Socs and are always ready to jump on us. We look hoody and they look decent. It could be just the other way around—half of the hoods I know are pretty decent guys underneath all that grease, and from what I've heard, a lot of Socs are just cold-blooded mean—but people usually go by looks.

They lined up silently, facing us, and we lined up facing them. I looked for Randy but didn't see him. I hoped he wasn't there. A guy with a madras shirt stepped up. "Let's get the rules straight—nothing but our fists, and the first to run lose. Right?"

Tim flipped away his beer can. "You savvy real good."

There was an uneasy silence: Who was going to start it? Darry solved the problem. He stepped forward under the circle of light made by the street lamp. For a minute, everything looked unreal, like a scene out of a JD movie or something. Then Darry said, "I'll take on anyone."

He stood there, tall, broad-shouldered, his muscles taut under his T-shirt and his eyes glittering like ice. For a second it looked like there wasn't anyone brave enough to take him on. Then there was a slight stir in the faceless mob of Socs, and a husky blond guy stepped forward. He looked at Darry and said quietly, "Hello, Darrel."

Something flickered behind Darry's eyes and then they were ice again. "Hello, Paul."

I heard Soda give a kind of squeak and I realized that the blond was Paul Holden. He had been the best halfback on Darry's football team at high school and he and Darry used to buddy it around all the time. He must be a junior in college by now, I thought. He was looking at Darry with an expression I couldn't quite place, but disliked. Contempt? Pity? Hate? All three? Why? Because Darry was standing there representing all of us, and maybe Paul felt only contempt and pity and hate for greasers? Darry hadn't moved a muscle or changed expression, but you could see he hated Paul now. It wasn't only jealousy—Darry had a right to be jealous; he was ashamed to be on our side, ashamed to be seen with the Brumly boys, Shepard's gang, maybe even us. Nobody realized it but me and Soda. It didn't matter to anyone but me and Soda.

That's stupid, I thought swiftly, they've both come here to fight and they're both supposed to be smarter than that. What difference does the side make?

Then Paul said, "I'll take you," and something like a smile crossed Darry's face. I knew Darry had thought he could take Paul any time. But that was two or three years ago. What if Paul was better now? I swallowed. Neither one of my brothers had ever been beaten in a fight, but I wasn't exactly itching for someone to break the record.

They moved in a circle under the light, counterclockwise, eyeing each other, sizing each other up, maybe remembering old faults and wondering if they were still there. The rest of us waited with mounting tension. I was reminded of Jack London's books—you know, where the wolf pack waits in silence for one of two members to go down in a fight. But it was different here. The moment either one swung a punch, the rumble would be on.

The silence grew heavier, and I could hear the harsh heavy breathing of the boys around me. Still Darry and the Soc walked slowly in a circle. Even I could feel their hatred. They used to be buddies, I thought, they used to be friends, and now they hate each other because one has to work for a living and the other comes from the West Side. They shouldn't hate each other . . . I don't hate the Socs any more . . . they shouldn't hate . . .

"Hold up!" a familiar voice yelled. "Hold it!" Darry turned to see who it was, and Paul swung—a hard right to the jaw that would have felled anyone but Darry. The rumble was on. Dallas Winston ran to join us.

I couldn't find a Soc my size, so I took the next-best size and jumped on him. Dallas was right beside me, already on top of someone.

"I thought you were in the hospital," I yelled as the Soc knocked me to the ground and I rolled to avoid getting kicked.

"I was." Dally was having a hard time because his left arm was still in bad shape. "I ain't now."

"How?" I managed to ask as the Soc I was fighting leaped on me and we rolled near Dally.

"Talked the nurse into it with Two-Bit's switch. Don't you know a rumble ain't a rumble unless I'm in it?"

I couldn't answer because the Soc, who was heavier than I took him for, had me pinned and was slugging the sense out of me. I thought dizzily that he was going to knock some of my teeth loose or break my nose or something, and I knew I didn't have a chance. But Darry was keeping an eye out for me; he caught that guy by the shoulder and half lifted him up before knocking him three feet with a sledge-hammer blow. I decided it would be fair for me to help Dally since he could use only one arm.

They were slugging it out, but Dallas was getting the worst of it, so I jumped on his Soc's back, pulling his hair and pounding him. He reached back and caught me by the neck and threw me over his head to the ground. Tim Shepard, who was fighting two at once, accidentally stepped on me, knocking my breath out. I was up again as soon as I got my wind, and jumped right back on the Soc, trying my best to strangle him. While he was prying my fingers loose, Dally knocked him backward, so that all three of us rolled on the ground, gasping, cussing, and punching.

Somebody kicked me hard in the ribs and I yelped in spite of myself. Some Soc had knocked out one of our bunch and was kicking me as hard as he could. But I had both arms wrapped around the other Soc's neck and refused to let go. Dally was slugging him, and I hung on desperately, although that other Soc was kicking me and you'd better believe it hurt. Finally he kicked me in the head so hard it stunned me, and I lay limp, trying to clear my mind and keep from blacking out. I could hear the racket, but only dimly through the buzzing in my ears. Numerous bruises along my back and on my face were throbbing, but I felt detached from the pain, as if it wasn't really me feeling it.

"They're running!" I heard a voice yell joyfully. "Look at the dirty—run!"

It seemed to me that the voice belonged to Two-Bit, but I couldn't be sure. I tried to sit up, and saw that the Socs were getting into their cars and leaving. Tim Shepard was swearing blue and green because his nose was broken again, and the leader of the Brumly boys was working over one of his own men because he had broken the rules and used a piece of pipe in the fighting. Steve lay doubled up and groaning about ten feet from me. We found out later he had three broken ribs. Sodapop was beside him, talking in a low steady voice. I did a double take when I saw Two-Bit—blood was streaming down one side of his face and one hand was busted wide open; but he was grinning happily because the Socs were running.

"We won," Darry announced in a tired voice. He was going to have a black eye and there was a cut across his forehead. "We beat the Socs."

Dally stood beside me quietly for a minute, trying to grasp the fact that we had really beaten the Socs. Then, grabbing my shirt, he hauled me to my feet. "Come on!" He half dragged me down the street. "We're goin' to see Johnny."

I tried to run but stumbled, and Dally impatiently shoved me along. "Hurry! He was gettin' worse when I left. He wants to see you."

I don't know how Dallas could travel so fast and hard after being knocked around and having his sore arm hurt some more, but I tried to keep up with him. Track wasn't ever like the running I did that night. I was still dizzy and had only a dim realization of where I was going and why.

Dally had Buck Merril's T-bird parked in front of our house, and we hopped into it. I sat tight as Dally roared the car down the street. We were on Tenth when a siren came on behind us and I saw the reflection of the red light flashing in the windshield.

"Look sick," Dally commanded. "I'll say I'm taking you to the hospital, which'll be truth enough."

I leaned against the cold glass of the window and tried to look sick, which wasn't too hard, feeling the way I did right then.

The policeman looked disgusted. "All right, buddy, where's the fire?"

"The kid"—Dally jerked a thumb toward me—"he fell over on his motorcycle and I'm takin' him to the hospital."

I groaned, and it wasn't all fake-out. I guess I looked pretty bad, too, being cut and bruised like I was.

The fuzz changed his tone. "Is he real bad? Do you need an escort?"

"How would I know if he's bad or not? I ain't no doc. Yeah, we could use an escort." And as the policeman got back into his car I heard Dally hiss, "Sucker!"

With the siren ahead of us, we made record time getting to the hospital. All the way there Dally kept talking and talking about something, but I was too dizzy to make most of it out.

"I was crazy, you know that, kid? Crazy for wantin' Johnny to stay outa trouble, for not wantin' him to get hard. If he'd been like me he'd never have been in this mess. If he'd got smart like me he'd never have run into that church. That's what you get for helpin' people. Editorials in the paper and a lot of trouble. . . . You'd better wise up, Pony . . . you get tough like me and you don't get hurt. You look out for yourself and nothin' can touch you . . ."

He said a lot more stuff, but I didn't get it all. I had a stupid feeling that Dally was out of his mind, the way he kept raving on and on, because Dallas never talked like that, but I think now I would have understood if I hadn't been sick at the time.

The cop left us at the hospital as Dally pretended to help me out of the car. The minute the cop was gone, Dally let go of me so quick I almost fell. "Hurry!"

We ran through the lobby and crowded past people into the elevator. Several people yelled at us, I think because we were pretty racked-up looking, but Dally had nothing on his mind except Johnny, and I was too mixed up to know anything but that I had to follow Dally. When we finally got to Johnny's room, the doctor stopped us. "I'm sorry, boys, but he's dying."

"We gotta see him," Dally said, and flicked out Two-Bit's switchblade. His voice was shaking. "We're gonna see him and if you give me any static you'll end up on your own operatin' table."

The doctor didn't bat an eye. "You can see him, but it's because you're his friends, not because of that knife."

Dally looked at him for a second, then put the knife back in his pocket. We both went into Johnny's room, standing there for a second, getting our breath back in heavy gulps. It was awful quiet. It was scary quiet. I looked at Johnny. He was very still, and for a moment I thought in agony: He's dead already. We're too late.

Dally swallowed, wiping the sweat off his upper lip. "Johnnycake?" he said in a hoarse voice. "Johnny?"

Johnny stirred weakly, then opened his eyes. "Hey," he managed softly.

"We won," Dally panted. "We beat the Socs. We stomped them—chased them outa our territory."

Johnny didn't even try to grin at him. "Useless . . . fighting's no good. . . ." He was awful white.

Dally licked his lips nervously. "They're still writing editorials about you in the paper. For being a hero and all." He was talking too fast and too calmly. "Yeah, they're calling you a hero now and heroizin' all the greasers. We're all proud of you, buddy."

Johnny's eyes glowed. Dally was proud of him. That was all Johnny had ever wanted.

"Ponyboy."

I barely heard him. I came closer and leaned over to hear what he was going to say.

"Stay gold, Ponyboy. Stay gold . . ." The pillow seemed to sink a little, and Johnny died.

You read about people looking peacefully asleep when they're dead, but they don't. Johnny just looked dead. Like a candle with the flame gone. I tried to say something, but I couldn't make a sound.

Dally swallowed and reached over to push Johnny's hair back. "Never could keep that hair back . . . that's what you get for tryin' to help people, you little punk, that's what you get . . ."

Whirling suddenly, he slammed back against the wall. His face contracted in agony, and sweat streamed down his face.

"Damnit, Johnny . . ." he begged, slamming one fist against the wall, hammering it to make it obey his will. "Oh, damnit, Johnny, don't die, please don't die . . ."

He suddenly bolted through the door and down the hall.

CHAPTER 10

I WALKED DOWN the hall in a daze. Dally had taken the car and I started the long walk home in a stupor. Johnny was dead. But he wasn't. That still body back in the hospital wasn't Johnny. Johnny was somewhere else—maybe asleep in the lot, or playing the pinball machine in the bowling alley, or sitting on the

565

back steps of the church in Windrixville. I'd go home and walk by the lot, and Johnny would be sitting on the curb smoking a cigarette, and maybe we'd lie on our backs and watch the stars. He isn't dead, I said to myself. He isn't dead. And this time my dreaming worked. I convinced myself that he wasn't dead.

I must have wandered around for hours; sometimes even out into the street, getting honked at and cussed out. I might have stumbled around all night except for a man who asked me if I wanted a ride.

"Huh? Oh. Yeah, I guess so," I said. I got in. The man, who was in his mid-twenties, looked at me.

"Are you all right, kid? You look like you've been in a fight."

"I have been. A rumble. I'm okay." Johnny is *not* dead, I told myself, and I believed it.

"Hate to tell you this, kiddo," the guy said dryly, "but you're bleedin' all over my car seats."

I blinked. "I am?"

"Your head."

I reached up to scratch the side of my head where it'd been itching for a while, and when I looked at my hand it was smeared with blood.

"Gosh, mister, I'm sorry," I said, dumfounded.

"Don't worry about it. This wreck's been through worse. What's your address? I'm not about to dump a hurt kid out on the streets this time of night."

I told him. He drove me to my house, and I got out. "Thanks a lot."

What was left of our gang was in the living room. Steve was stretched out on the sofa, his shirt unbuttoned and his side bandaged. His eyes were closed, but when the door shut behind me he opened them, and I suddenly wondered if my own eyes looked as feverish and bewildered as his. Soda had a wide cut on his lip and a bruise across his cheek. There was a Band-Aid over Darry's forehead and he had a black eye. One side of Two-Bit's face was taped up—I found out later he had four stitches in his cheek and seven in his hand where he had busted his knuckles open over a Soc's head. They were lounging around, reading the paper and smoking.

Where's the party? I thought dully. Weren't Soda and Steve planning a party after the rumble? They all looked up when I walked in. Darry leaped to his feet.

"Where have you been?"

Oh, let's don't start that again, I thought. He stopped suddenly.

"Ponyboy, what's the matter?"

I looked at all of them, a little frightened. "Johnny . . . he's dead." My voice sounded strange, even to me. But he's not dead, a voice in my head said. "We told him about beatin' the Socs and . . . I don't know, he just died." He told me to stay gold, I remembered. What was he talking about?

There was a stricken silence. I don't think any of us had realized how bad off Johnny really had been. Soda made a funny noise and looked like he was going to start crying. Two-Bit's eyes were closed and his teeth were clenched, and I suddenly remembered Dally. . . . Dally pounding on the wall . . .

"Dallas is gone," I said. "He ran out like the devil was after him. He's gonna blow up. He couldn't take it."

How can I take it? I wondered. Dally is tougher than I am. Why can I take it when Dally can't? And then I knew. Johnny was the only thing Dally loved. And now Johnny was gone.

"So he finally broke." Two-Bit spoke everyone's feelings. "So even Dally has a breaking point."

566

I started shaking. Darry said something in a low voice to Soda.

"Ponyboy," Soda said softly, like he was talking to an injured animal, "you look sick. Sit down."

I backed up, just like a frightened animal, shaking my head. "I'm okay." I felt sick. I felt as if any minute I was going to fall flat on my face, but I shook my head. "I don't want to sit down."

Darry took a step toward me, but I backed away. "Don't touch me," I said. My heart was pounding in slow thumps, throbbing at the side of my head, and I wondered if everyone else could hear it. Maybe that's why they're all looking at me, I thought, they can hear my heart beating . . .

The phone rang, and after a moment's hesitation, Darry turned from me to it. He said "Hello" and then listened. He hung up quickly.

"It was Dally. He phoned from a booth. He's just robbed a grocery store and the cops are after him. We gotta hide him. He'll be at the lot in a minute."

We all left the house at a dead run, even Steve, and I wondered vaguely why no one was doing somersaults off the steps this time. Things were sliding in and out of focus, and it seemed funny to me that I couldn't run in a straight line.

We reached the vacant lot just as Dally came in, running as hard as he could, from the opposite direction. The wail of a siren grew louder and then a police car pulled up across the street from the lot. Doors slammed as the policemen leaped out. Dally had reached the circle of light under the street lamp, and skidding to a halt, he turned and jerked a black object from his waistband. I remembered his voice: *I been carryin' a heater. It ain't loaded, but it sure does help a bluff.*

It was only yesterday that Dally had told Johnny and me that. But yesterday was years ago. A lifetime ago.

Dally raised the gun, and I thought: You blasted fool. They don't know you're only bluffing. And even as the policemen's guns spit fire into the night I knew that was what Dally wanted. He was jerked half around by the impact of the bullets, then slowly crumpled with a look of grim triumph on his face. He was dead before he hit the ground. But I knew that was what he wanted, even as the lot echoed with the cracks of shots, even as I begged silently—Please, not him . . . not him and Johnny both—I knew he would be dead, because Dally Winston wanted to be dead and he always got what he wanted.

Nobody would write editorials praising Dally. Two friends of mine had died that night: one a hero, the other a hoodlum. But I remembered Dally pulling Johnny through the window of the burning church; Dally giving us his gun, although it could mean jail for him; Dally risking his life for us, trying to keep Johnny out of trouble. And now he was a dead juvenile delinquent and there wouldn't be any editorials in his favor. Dally didn't die a hero. He died violent and young and desperate, just like we all knew he'd die someday. Just like Tim Shepard and Curly Shepard and the Brumly boys and the other guys we knew would die someday. But Johnny was right. He died gallant.

Steve stumbled forward with a sob, but Soda caught him by the shoulders.

"Easy, buddy, easy," I heard him say softly, "there's nothing we can do now."

Nothing we can do . . . not for Dally or Johnny or Tim Shepard or any of us . . . My stomach gave a violent start and turned into a hunk of ice. The world was spinning around me, and blobs of faces and visions of things past were dancing in the red mist that covered the lot. It swirled into a mass of colors and I felt myself swaying on my feet. Someone cried, "Glory, look at the kid!"

And the ground rushed up to meet me very suddenly.

When I woke up it was light. It was awfully quiet. Too quiet. I mean, our house just isn't naturally quiet. The radio's usually going full blast and the TV is turned up loud and people are wrestling and knocking over lamps and tripping over the coffee table and yelling at each other. Something was wrong, but I couldn't quite figure it out. Something had happened . . . I couldn't remember what. I blinked at Soda bewilderedly. He was sitting on the edge of the bed watching me.

"Soda . . ."—my voice sounded weak and hoarse—"is somebody sick?"

"Yeah." His voice was oddly gentle. "Go back to sleep now."

An idea was slowly dawning on me. "Am *I* sick?"

He stroked my hair. "Yeah, you're sick. Now be quiet."

I had one more question. I was still kind of mixed up. "Is Darry sorry I'm sick?" I had a funny feeling that Darry was sad because I was sick. Everything seemed vague and hazy.

Soda gave me a funny look. He was quiet for a moment. "Yeah, he's sorry you're sick. Now please shut up, will ya, honey? Go back to sleep."

I closed my eyes. I was awful tired.

When I woke up next, it was daylight and I was hot under all the blankets on me. I was thirsty and hungry, but my stomach was so uneasy I knew I wouldn't be able to hold anything down. Darry had pulled the armchair into the bedroom and was asleep in it. He should be at work, I thought. Why is he asleep in the armchair?

"Hey, Darry," I said softly, shaking his knee. "Hey, Darry, wake up."

He opened his eyes. "Ponyboy, you okay?"

"Yeah," I said, "I think so."

Something had happened . . . but I still couldn't remember it, although I was thinking a lot clearer than I was the last time I'd waked up.

He sighed in relief and pushed my hair back. "Gosh, kid, you had us scared to death."

"What was the matter with me?"

He shook his head. "I told you you were in no condition for a rumble. Exhaustion, shock, minor concussion—and Two-Bit came blubberin' over here with some tale about how you were running a fever before the rumble and how it was all his fault you were sick. He was pretty torn up that night," Darry said. He was quiet for a minute. "We all were."

And then I remembered. Dallas and Johnny were dead. Don't think of them, I thought. (Don't remember how Johnny was your buddy, don't remember that he didn't want to die. Don't think of Dally breaking up in the hospital, crumpling under the street light. Try to think that Johnny is better off now, try to remember that Dally would have ended up like that sooner or later. Best of all, don't think. Blank your mind. Don't remember. Don't remember.)

"Where'd I get a concussion?" I said. My head itched, but I couldn't scratch it for the bandage. "How long have I been asleep?"

"You got a concussion from getting kicked in the head—Soda saw it. He landed all over that Soc. I've never seen him so mad. I think he could have whipped anyone, in the state he was in. Today's Tuesday, and you've been asleep and delirious since Saturday night. Don't you remember?"

"No," I said slowly. "Darry, I'm not ever going to be able to make up the school I've missed. And I've still got to go to court and talk to the police about Bob's getting killed. And now . . . with Dally . . ."—I took a deep breath—"Darry, do you think they'll split us up? Put me in a home or something?"

He was silent. "I don't know, baby. I just don't know."

I stared at the ceiling. What would it be like, I wondered, staring at a different ceiling? What would it be like in a different bed, in a different room? There was a hard painful lump in my throat that I couldn't swallow.

"Don't you even remember being in the hospital?" Darry asked. He was trying to change the subject.

I shook my head. "I don't remember."

"You kept asking for me and Soda. Sometimes for Mom and Dad, too. But mostly for Soda."

Something in his tone of voice made me look at him. Mostly for Soda. Did I ask for Darry at all, or was he just saying that?

"Darry . . ." I didn't know quite what I wanted to say. But I had a sick feeling that maybe I hadn't called for him while I was delirious, maybe I had only wanted Sodapop to be with me. What all had I said while I was sick? I couldn't remember. I didn't want to remember.

"Johnny left you his copy of *Gone with the Wind*. Told the nurse he wanted you to have it."

I looked at the paperback lying on the table. I didn't want to finish it. I'd never get past the part where the Southern gentlemen go riding into sure death because they are gallant. Southern gentlemen with big black eyes in blue jeans and T-shirts, Southern gentlemen crumpling under street lights. Don't remember. Don't try to decide which one died gallant. Don't remember.

"Where's Soda?" I asked, and then I could have kicked myself. Why can't you talk to Darry, you idiot? I said to myself. Why do you feel uncomfortable talking to Darry?

"Asleep, I hope. I thought he was going to go to sleep shaving this morning and cut his throat. I had to push him to bed, but he was out like a light in a second."

Darry's hopes that Soda was asleep were immediately ruined, because he came running in, clad only in a pair of blue jeans.

"Hey, Ponyboy!" he yelped, and leaped for me, but Darry caught him.

"No rough stuff, little buddy."

So Soda had to content himself with bouncing up and down on the bed and pounding on my shoulder.

"Gosh, but you were sick. You feel okay now?"

"I'm okay. Just a little hungry."

"I should think you would be," Darry said. "You wouldn't eat anything most of the time you were sick. How'd you like some mushroom soup?"

I suddenly realized just how empty I was. "Man, I'd like that just fine."

"I'll go make some. Sodapop, take it easy with him, okay?"

Soda looked back at him indignantly. "You'd think I was going to challenge him to a track meet or something right off the bat."

"Oh, no," I groaned. "Track meet. I guess this just about puts me out of every race. I won't be back in condition for the meets. And the coach was counting on me."

"Golly, there's always next year," Soda said. Soda never has grasped the importance Darry and I put on athletics. Like he never has understood why we went all-out for studying. "Don't sweat it about some track meet."

"Soda," I said suddenly. "What all did I say while I was delirious?"

"Oh, you thought you were in Windrixville most of the time. Then you kept saying that Johnny didn't mean to kill that Soc. Hey, I didn't know you didn't like baloney."

I went cold. "I don't like it. I never liked it."

Soda just looked at me. "You used to eat it. That's why you wouldn't eat anything while you were sick. You kept saying you didn't like baloney, no matter what it was we were trying to get you to eat."

"I don't like it," I repeated. "Soda, did I ask for Darry while I was sick?"

"Yeah, sure," he said, looking at me strangely. "You asked for him and me both. Sometimes Mom and Dad. And for Johnny."

"Oh. I thought maybe I didn't ask for Darry. It was bugging me."

Soda grinned. "Well, you did, so don't worry. We stayed with you so much that the doctor told us we were going to end up in the hospital ourselves if we didn't get some sleep. But we didn't get any anyway."

I took a good look at him. He looked completely worn out; there were circles under his eyes and he had a tense, tired look to him. Yet his dark eyes were still laughing and carefree and reckless.

"You look beat," I said frankly. "I bet you ain't had three hours sleep since Saturday night."

He grinned but didn't deny it. "Scoot over." He crawled over me and flopped down and before Darry came back in with the soup we were both asleep.

CHAPTER 11

I HAD TO STAY IN BED a whole week after that. That bugged me; I'm not the kind that can lie around looking at the ceiling all the time. I read most of the time, and drew pictures. One day I started flipping through one of Soda's old yearbooks and came across a picture that seemed vaguely familiar. Not even when I read the name Robert Sheldon did it hit me who it was. And then I finally realized it was Bob. I took a real good long look at it.

The picture didn't look a whole lot like the Bob I remembered, but nobody ever looks a whole lot like his picture in a yearbook anyway. He had been a sophomore that year—that would make him about eighteen when he died. Yeah, he was good-looking even then, with a grin that reminded me of Soda's, a kind of reckless grin. He had been a handsome black-haired boy with dark eyes—maybe brown, like Soda's, maybe dark-blue, like the Shepard boys'. Maybe he'd had black eyes. Like Johnny. I had never given Bob much thought—I hadn't had time to think. But that day I wondered about him. What was he like?

I knew he liked to pick fights, had the usual Soc belief that living on the West Side made you Mr. Super-Tuff, looked good in dark wine-colored sweaters, and was proud of his rings. But what about the Bob Sheldon that Cherry Valance knew? She was a smart girl; she didn't like him just because he was good-looking. Sweet and friendly, stands out from the crowd—that's what she had said. A real person, the best buddy a guy ever had, kept trying to make somebody stop him—Randy had told me that. Did he have a kid brother who idolized him? Maybe a big brother who kept bugging him not to be so wild? His parents let him run wild—because they loved him too much or too little? Did they hate us now? I hoped they hated us, that they weren't full of that pity-the-victims-of-environment junk the social workers kept handing Curly Shepard every time he got sent off to reform school. I'd rather have anybody's hate than their pity. But, then, maybe they understood, like Cherry Valance. I looked at Bob's picture and I could begin to see the person we had killed. A reckless, hot-tempered boy, cocky and scared stiff at the same time.

"Ponyboy."

"Yeah?" I didn't look up. I thought it was the doctor. He'd been coming over to see me almost every day, although he didn't do much except talk to me.

"There's a guy here to see you. Says he knows you." Something in Darry's voice made me look up, and his eyes were hard. "His name's Randy."

"Yeah, I know him," I said.

"You want to see him?"

"Yeah." I shrugged. "Sure, why not?"

A few guys from school had dropped by to see me; I have quite a few friends at school even if I am younger than most of them and don't talk much. But that's what they are—school friends, not buddies. I had been glad to see them, but it bothered me because we live in kind of a lousy neighborhood and our house isn't real great. It's run-down looking and everything, and the inside's kind of poor-looking, too, even though for a bunch of boys we do a pretty good job of house-cleaning. Most of my friends at school come from good homes, not filthy-rich like the Socs, but middle-class, anyway. It was a funny thing—it bugged me about my friends seeing our house. But I couldn't have cared less about what Randy thought.

"Hi, Ponyboy." Randy looked uncomfortable standing in the doorway.

"Hi, Randy," I said. "Have a seat if you can find one." Books were lying all over everything. He pushed a couple off a chair and sat down.

"How you feeling? Cherry told me your name was on the school bulletin."

"I'm okay. You can't really miss my name on any kind of bulletin."

He still looked uncomfortable, although he tried to grin.

"Wanna smoke?" I offered him a weed, but he shook his head. "No, thanks. Uh, Ponyboy, one reason I came here was to see if you were okay, but you— we—got to go see the judge tomorrow."

"Yeah," I said, lighting a cigarette. "I know. Hey, holler if you see one of my brothers coming. I'll catch it for smoking in bed."

"My dad says for me to tell the truth and nobody can get hurt. He's kind of upset about all this. I mean, my dad's a good guy and everything, better than most, and I kind of let him down, being mixed up in all this."

I just looked at him. That was the dumbest remark I ever heard anyone make. He thought *he* was mixed up in this? He didn't kill anyone, he didn't get his head busted in a rumble, it wasn't his buddy that was shot down under a street light. Besides, what did he have to lose? His old man was rich, he could pay whatever fine there was for being drunk and picking a fight.

"I wouldn't mind getting fined," Randy said, "but I feel lousy about the old man. And it's the first time I've felt anything in a long time."

The only thing I'd felt in a long time was being scared. Scared stiff. I'd put off thinking about the judge and the hearing for as long as I could. Soda and Darry didn't like to talk about it either, so we were all silently counting off the days while I was sick, counting the days that we had left together. But with Randy sticking solidly to the subject it was impossible to think about anything else. My cigarette started trembling.

"I guess your folks feel kind of awful about it, too."

"My parents are dead. I live here with just Darry and Soda, my brothers." I took a long drag on my cigarette. "That's what's worrying me. If the judge decides Darry isn't a good guardian or something, I'm liable to get stuck in a home somewhere. That's the rotten part of this deal. Darry *is* a good guardian; he makes me study and knows where I am and who I'm with all the time. I mean, we don't get along so great sometimes, but he keeps me out of trouble, or did. My father didn't yell at me as much as he does."

"I didn't know that." Randy looked worried, he really did. A Soc, even, worried because some kid greaser was on his way to a foster home or something. That was really funny. I don't mean funny. You know what I mean.

"Listen to me, Pony. You didn't do anything. It was your friend Johnny that had the knife . . ."

"I had it." I stopped him. He was looking at me strangely. "I had the knife. I killed Bob."

Randy shook his head. "I saw it. You were almost drowned. It was the black-headed guy that had the switchblade. Bob scared him into doing it. I saw it."

I was bewildered. "I killed him. I had a switchblade and I was scared they were going to beat me up."

"No, kid, it was your friend, the one who died in the hospital . . ."

"Johnny is not dead." My voice was shaking. "Johnny is not dead."

"Hey, Randy." Darry stuck his head in the door. "I think you'd better go now."

"Sure," Randy said. He was still looking at me kind of funny. "See you around, Pony."

"Don't ever say anything to him about Johnny," I heard Darry say in a low voice as they went out. "He's still pretty racked up mentally and emotionally. The doc said he'd get over it if we gave him time."

I swallowed hard and blinked. He was just like all the rest of the Socs. Cold-blooded mean. Johnny didn't have anything to do with Bob's getting killed.

"Ponyboy Curtis, put out that cigarette!"

"Okay, okay." I put it out. "I ain't going to go to sleep smoking, Darry. If you make me stay in bed there ain't anywhere else I can smoke."

"You're not going to die if you don't get a smoke. But if that bed catches on fire you will. You couldn't make it to the door through that mess."

"Well, golly, I can't pick it up and Soda doesn't, so I guess that leaves you."

He was giving me one of those looks. "All right, all right," I said, "that don't leave you. Maybe Soda'll straighten it up a little."

"Maybe you can be a little neater, huh, little buddy?"

He'd never called me that before. Soda was the only one he ever called "little buddy."

"Sure," I said, "I'll be more careful."

CHAPTER 12

THE HEARING WASN'T anything like I thought it would be. Besides Darry and Soda and me, nobody was there except Randy and his parents and Cherry Valance and her parents and a couple of the other guys that had jumped Johnny and me that night. I don't know what I expected the whole thing to be like—I guess I've been watching too many Perry Mason shows. Oh, yeah, the doctor was there and he had a long talk with the judge before the hearing. I didn't know what he had to do with it then, but I do now.

First Randy was questioned. He looked a little nervous, and I wished they'd let him have a cigarette. I wished they'd let *me* have a cigarette; I was more than a little shaky myself. Darry had told me to keep my mouth shut no matter what Randy and everybody said, that I'd get my turn. All the Socs told the same story and stuck mainly to the truth, except they said Johnny had killed Bob; but I figured I could straighten that point out when I got my turn. Cherry told them what had happened before and after Johnny and I had been jumped—I think I saw a couple of tears slide down her cheeks, but I'm not sure. Her voice was sure steady even if she was crying. The judge questioned everyone carefully, but nothing real emotional or exciting happened like it does on TV. He asked Darry and Soda a little bit about Dally, I think to check our background and find out what kind of guys we hung out with. Was he a real good buddy of ours? Darry said, "Yes, sir," looking straight at the judge, not flinching; but Soda looked at me like he was sentencing me to the electric chair before he gave the same answer. I was real proud of both of them. Dally had been one of our gang and we wouldn't desert him. I thought the judge would never get around to questioning me. Man, I was scared almost stiff by the time he did. And you know what? They didn't ask me a thing about Bob's getting killed. All the judge did was ask me if I liked living with Darry, if I liked school, what kind of grades I made, and stuff like that. I couldn't figure it out then, but later I found out what the doctor had been talking to the judge about. I guess I looked as scared as I really was, because the judge grinned at me and told me to quit chewing my fingernails. That's a habit I have. Then he said I was acquitted and the whole case was closed. Just like that. Didn't even give me a chance to talk much. But that didn't bother me a lot. I didn't feel like talking anyway.

I wish I could say that everything went back to normal, but it didn't. Especially me. I started running into things, like the door, and kept tripping over the coffee table and losing things. I always have been kind of absent-minded, but man, then, I was lucky if I got home from school with the right notebook and with both shoes on. I walked all the way home once in my stocking feet and didn't even notice it until Steve made some bright remark about it. I guess I'd left my shoes in the locker room at school, but I never did find them. And another thing, I quit eating. I used to eat like a horse, but all of a sudden I wasn't hungry. Everything tasted like baloney. I was lousing up my schoolwork, too. I didn't do too badly in math, because Darry checked over my homework in that and usually caught all my mistakes and made me do it again, but in English I really washed out. I used to make A's in English, mostly because my teacher made us do compositions all the time. I mean, I know I don't talk good English (have you ever seen a hood that did?), but I can write it good when I try. At least, I could before. Now I was lucky to get a *D* on a composition.

It bothered my English teacher, the way I was goofing up, I mean. He's a real good guy, who makes us think, and you can tell he's interested in you as a person, too. One day he told me to stay in after the rest of the class left.

"Ponyboy, I'd like to talk to you about your grades."

Man, I wished I could beat it out of there. I knew I was flunking out in that class, but golly, I couldn't help it.

"There's not much to talk about, judging from your scores. Pony, I'll give it to you straight. You're failing this class right now, but taking into consideration the circumstances, if you come up with a good semester theme, I'll pass you with a *C* grade."

"Taking into consideration the circumstances"—brother, was that ever a way to tell me he knew I was goofing up because I'd been in a lot of trouble. At least that was a roundabout way of putting it. The first week of school after the hearing had been awful. People I knew wouldn't talk to me, and people I didn't know would come right up and ask about the whole mess. Sometimes even teachers. And my history teacher—*she* acted as if she was scared of me, even though I'd never caused any trouble in her class. You can bet that made me feel real tuff.

"Yessir," I said, "I'll try. What's the theme supposed to be on?"

"Anything you think is important enough to write about. And it isn't a reference theme; I want your own ideas and your own experiences."

My first trip to the zoo. Oh, boy, oh, boy. "Yessir," I said, and got out of there as fast as I could.

At lunch hour I met Two-Bit and Steve out in the back parking lot and we drove over to a little neighborhood grocery store to buy cigarettes and Cokes and candy bars. The store was the grease hang-out and that was about all we ever had for lunch. The Socs were causing a lot of trouble in the school cafeteria—throwing silverware and stuff—and everybody tried to blame it on us greasers. We all got a big laugh out of that. Greasers rarely even eat in the cafeteria.

I was sitting on the fender of Steve's car, smoking and drinking a Pepsi while he and Two-Bit were inside talking to some girls, when a car drove up and three Socs got out. I just sat there and looked at them and took another swallow of the Pepsi. I wasn't scared. It was the oddest feeling in the world. I didn't feel *anything*—scared, mad, or anything. Just zero.

"You're the guy that killed Bob Sheldon," one of them said. "And he was a friend of ours. We don't like nobody killing our friends, especially greasers."

Big deal. I busted the end off my bottle and held on to the neck and tossed away my cigarette. "You get back into your car or you'll get split."

They looked kind of surprised, and one of them backed up.

"I mean it." I hopped off the car. "I've had about all I can take from you guys." I started toward them, holding the bottle the way Tim Shepard holds a switch—out and away from myself, in a loose but firm hold. I guess they knew I meant business, because they got into their car and drove off.

"You really would have used that bottle, wouldn't you?" Two-Bit had been watching from the store doorway. "Steve and me were backing you, but I guess we didn't need to. You'd have really cut them up, huh?"

"I guess so," I said with a sigh. I didn't see what Two-Bit was sweating about—anyone else could have done the same thing and Two-Bit wouldn't have thought about it twice.

"Ponyboy, listen, don't get tough. You're not like the rest of us and don't try to be . . ."

What was the matter with Two-Bit? I knew as well as he did that if you got tough you didn't get hurt. Get smart and nothing can touch you . . .

"What in the world are you doing?" Two-Bit's voice broke into my thoughts. I looked up at him. "Picking up the glass."

He stared at me for a second, then grinned. "You little sonofagun," he said in a relieved voice. I didn't know what he was talking about, so I just went on picking up the glass from the bottle end and put it in a trash can. I didn't want anyone to get a flat tire.

I tried to write that theme when I got home. I really did, mostly because Darry told me to or else. I thought about writing about Dad, but I couldn't. It's going to be a long time before I can even think about my parents. A long time. I tried writing about Soda's horse, Mickey Mouse, but I couldn't get it right; it always came out sounding corny. So I started writing names across the paper. Darrel Shaynne Curtis, Jr. Soda Patrick Curtis. Ponyboy Michael Curtis. Then I drew horses all over it. *That* was going to get a good grade like all git-out.

"Hey, did the mail come in yet?" Soda slammed the door and yelled for the mail, just the way he does every day when he comes home from work. I was in the bedroom, but I knew he would throw his jacket toward the sofa and miss it, take off his shoes, and go into the kitchen for a glass of chocolate milk, because that's what he does every day of his life. He always runs around in his stocking feet—he doesn't like shoes.

Then he did a funny thing. He came in and flopped down on the bed and started smoking a cigarette. He hardly ever smokes, except when something is really bugging him or when he wants to look tough. And he doesn't have to impress us; we know he's tough. So I figured something was bothering him. "How was work?"

"Okay."

"Something wrong?"

He shook his head. I shrugged and went back to drawing horses.

Soda cooked dinner that night, and everything came out right. That was unusual, because he's always trying something different. One time we had green pancakes. Green. I can tell you one thing: if you've got a brother like Sodapop, you're never bored.

All through supper Soda was quiet, and he didn't eat much. That was really unusual. Most of the time you can't shut him up or fill him up. Darry didn't seem to notice, so I didn't say anything.

Then after supper me and Darry got into a fuss, about the fourth one we'd had that week. This one started because I hadn't done anything on that theme, and I wanted to go for a ride. It used to be that I'd just stand there and let Darry yell at me, but lately I'd been yelling right back.

"What's the sweat about my schoolwork?" I finally shouted. "I'll have to get a job as soon as I get out of school anyway. Look at Soda. He's doing okay, and he dropped out. You can just lay off!"

"You're not going to drop out. Listen, with your brains and grades you could get a scholarship, and we could put you through college. But schoolwork's not the point. You're living in a vacuum, Pony, and you're going to have to cut it out. Johnny and Dallas were our buddies, too, but you don't just stop living because you lose someone. I thought you knew that by now. You don't quit! And anytime you don't like the way I'm running things you can get out."

I went tight and cold. We never talked about Dallas or Johnny. "You'd like that, wouldn't you? You'd like me just to get out. Well, it's not that easy, is it, Soda?" But when I looked at Soda I stopped. His face was white, and when he looked at me his eyes were wide with a pained expression. I suddenly remembered Curly Shepard's face when he slipped off a telephone pole and broke his arm.

"Don't . . . Oh, you guys, why can't you . . . ." He jumped up suddenly and bolted out the door. Darry and I were struck dumb. Darry picked up the envelope that Soda had dropped.

"It's the letter he wrote Sandy," Darry said without expression. "Returned unopened."

So that was what had been bugging Soda all afternoon. And I hadn't even bothered to find out. And while I was thinking about it, I realized that I never had paid much attention to Soda's problems. Darry and I just took it for granted that he didn't have any.

"When Sandy went to Florida . . . it wasn't Soda, Ponyboy. He told me he loved her, but I guess she didn't love him like he thought she did, because it wasn't him."

"You don't have to draw me a picture," I said.

"He wanted to marry her anyway, but she just left." Darry was looking at me with a puzzled expression. "Why didn't he tell you? I didn't think he'd tell Steve or Two-Bit, but I thought he told you everything."

"Maybe he tried," I said. How many times had Soda started to tell me something, only to find I was daydreaming or stuck in a book? He would always listen to me, no matter what he was doing.

"He cried every night that week you were gone," Darry said slowly. "Both you and Sandy in the same week." He put the envelope down. "Come on, let's go after him."

We chased him clear to the park. We were gaining on him, but he had a block's head start.

"Circle around and cut him off," Darry ordered. Even out of condition I was the best runner. "I'll stay right behind him."

I headed through the trees and cut him off halfway across the park. He veered off to the right, but I caught him in a flying tackle before he'd gone more than a couple of steps. It knocked the wind out of both of us. We lay there gasping for a minute or two, and then Soda sat up and brushed the grass off his shirt.

"You should have gone out for football instead of track."

"Where did you think you were going?" I lay flat on my back and looked at him. Darry came up and dropped down beside us.

Soda shrugged. "I don't know. It's just . . . I can't stand to hear y'all fight. Sometimes . . . I just have to get out or . . . it's like I'm the middleman in a tug o' war and I'm being split in half. You dig?"

Darry gave me a startled look. Neither of us had realized what it was doing to Soda to hear us fight. I was sick and cold with shame. What he said was the truth. Darry and I did play tug of war with him, with never a thought to how much it was hurting him.

Soda was fiddling with some dead grass. "I mean, I can't take sides. It'd be a lot easier if I could, but I see both sides. Darry yells too much and tries too hard and takes everything too serious, and Ponyboy, you don't think enough, you don't realize all Darry's giving up just to give you a chance he missed out on. He could have stuck you in a home somewhere and worked his way through college. Ponyboy, I'm telling you the truth. I dropped out because I'm dumb. I really did try in school, but you saw my grades. Look, I'm happy working in a gas station with cars. You'd never be happy doing something like that. And Darry, you ought to try to understand him more, and quit bugging him about every little mistake he makes. He feels things differently than you do." He gave us a pleading look. "Golly, you two, it's bad enough having to listen to it, but when you start trying to get me to take sides . . ." Tears welled up in his eyes. "We're all we've got left. We ought to be able to stick together against everything. If we don't have each other, we don't have anything. If you don't have anything, you end up like Dallas . . . and I don't mean dead, either. I mean like he was before. And that's worse than dead. Please"—he wiped his eyes on his arm—"don't fight anymore."

Darry looked real worried. I suddenly realized that Darry was only twenty, that he wasn't so much older that he couldn't feel scared or hurt and as lost as the rest of us. I saw that I had expected Darry to do all the understanding without even trying to understand him. And he *had* given up a lot for Soda and me.

"Sure, little buddy," Darry said softly. "We're not going to fight anymore."

"Hey, Ponyboy"—Soda gave me a tearful grin—"don't you start crying, too. One bawl-baby in the family's enough."

576

"I'm not crying," I said. Maybe I was. I don't remember. Soda gave me a playful punch on the shoulder.

"No more fights. Okay, Ponyboy?" Darry said.

"Okay," I said. And I meant it. Darry and I would probably still have misunderstandings—we were too different not to—but no more fights. We couldn't do anything to hurt Soda. Sodapop would always be the middleman, but that didn't mean he had to keep getting pulled apart. Instead of Darry and me pulling me apart, he'd be pulling us together.

"Well," Soda said, "I'm cold. How about going home?"

"Race you," I challenged, leaping up. It was a real nice night for a race. The air was clear and cold and so clean it almost sparkled. The moon wasn't out but the stars lit up everything. It was quiet except for the sound of our feet on the cement and the dry, scraping sound of leaves blowing across the street. It was a real nice night. I guess I was still out of shape, because we all three tied. No. I guess we all just wanted to stay together.

I still didn't want to do my homework that night, though. I hunted around for a book to read, but I'd read everything in the house about fifty million times, even Darry's copy of *The Carpetbaggers*, though he'd told me I wasn't old enough to read it. I thought so too after I finished it. Finally I picked up *Gone with the Wind* and looked at it for a long time. I knew Johnny was dead. I had known it all the time, even while I was sick and pretending he wasn't. It was Johnny, not me, who had killed Bob—I knew that too. I had just thought that maybe if I played like Johnny wasn't dead it wouldn't hurt so much. The way Two-Bit, after the police had taken Dally's body away, had griped because he had lost his switchblade when they searched Dallas.

"Is that all that's bothering you, that switchblade?" a red-eyed Steve had snapped at him.

"No," Two-Bit had said with a quivering sigh, "but that's what I'm wishing was all that's bothering me."

But it still hurt anyway. You know a guy a long time, and I mean really know him, you don't get used to the idea that he's dead just overnight. Johnny was something more than a buddy to all of us. I guess he had listened to more beefs and more problems from more people than any of us. A guy that'll really listen to you, listen and care about what you're saying, is something rare. And I couldn't forget him telling me that he hadn't done enough, hadn't been out of our neighborhood all his life—and then it was too late. I took a deep breath and opened the book. A slip of paper fell out on the floor and I picked it up.

Ponyboy, I asked the nurse to give you this book so you could finish it. It was Johnny's handwriting. I went on reading, almost hearing Johnny's quiet voice. *The doctor came in a while ago but I knew anyway. I keep getting tireder and tireder. Listen, I don't mind dying now. It's worth it. It's worth saving those kids. Their lives are worth more than mine, they have more to live for. Some of their parents came by to thank me and I know it was worth it. Tell Dally it's worth it. I'm just going to miss you guys. I've been thinking about it, and that poem, that guy that wrote it, he meant you're gold when you're a kid, like green. When you're a kid everything's new, dawn. It's just when you get used to everything that it's day. Like the way you dig sunsets, Pony. That's gold. Keep that way, it's a good way to be. I want you to tell Dally to look at one. He'll probably think you're crazy, but ask for me. I don't think he's ever really seen a sunset. And don't be so bugged over being a greaser. You still have a lot of time to make yourself be what you want. There's still lots of good in the world. Tell Dally. I don't think he knows. Your buddy, Johnny.*

Tell Dally. It was too late to tell Dally. Would he have listened? I doubted it. Suddenly it wasn't only a personal thing to me. I could picture hundreds and hundreds of boys living on the wrong sides of cities, boys with black eyes who jumped at their own shadows. Hundreds of boys who maybe watched sunsets and looked at stars and ached for something better. I could see boys going down under street lights because they were mean and tough and hated the world, and it was too late to tell them that there was still good in it, and they wouldn't believe you if you did. It was too vast a problem to be just a personal thing. There should be some help, someone should tell them before it was too late. Someone should tell their side of the story, and maybe people would understand then and wouldn't be so quick to judge a boy by the amount of hair oil he wore. It was important to me. I picked up the phone book and called my English teacher.

"Mr. Syme, this is Ponyboy. That theme—how long can it be?"

"Why, uh, not less than five pages." He sounded a little surprised. I'd forgotten it was late at night.

"Can it be longer?"

"Certainly, Ponyboy, as long as you want it."

"Thanks," I said and hung up.

I sat down and picked up my pen and thought for a minute. Remembering. Remembering a handsome, dark boy with a reckless grin and a hot temper. A tough, tow-headed boy with a cigarette in his mouth and a bitter grin on his hard face. Remembering—and this time it didn't hurt—a quiet, defeated-looking sixteen-year-old whose hair needed cutting badly and who had black eyes with a frightened expression to them. One week had taken all three of them. And I decided *I* could tell people, beginning with my English teacher. I wondered for a long time how to start that theme, how to start writing about something that was important to me. And I finally began like this: When I stepped out into the bright sunlight from the darkness of the movie house, I had only two things on my mind: Paul Newman and a ride home . . .

Alice Childress

1920–1994

T HE PATH to Alice Childress's success as a Young Adult author took her from Charleston, South Carolina, to Harlem, across the stages of many theatres, and even to Russia. Along the way she developed two extraordinary gifts: her ability to re-create on paper the voices of ordinary people, and her insight into the impact of racial prejudice on those people.

Childress was born in Charleston, South Carolina, in 1920. When she was five, her parents separated and she was sent to live in Harlem with her maternal grandmother. Here her education began. Her grandmother Eliza, with only a fifth-grade education herself, was intensely interested in people, art, and writing. She encouraged her granddaughter to observe people closely, to imagine their histories, and to write down what she saw and thought. Childress also appreciated her fifth grade teacher, who introduced her to the library; she became a passionate reader and later applied what she learned to her own writing. When both her grandmother and her mother died, she left high school after only two years of study, and began to support herself and her daughter Jean, who was born in 1935.

Attracted to theatre perhaps because of the strong oral tradition she felt through her grandmother's storytelling, she began an eleven-year association with the American Negro Theatre in Harlem. The members of this company drew no salaries and were expected to perform behind the scenes as directors, costume designers, set builders, and any other necessary jobs in addition to acting on stage. In addition to serving in these capacities, Childress gradually made a name for herself as an actress, playing Titania in *A Midsummer Night's Dream* and performing in the ANT production of *Anna Lucasta*. This production was so successful it moved to Broadway for 957 performances. Childress was nominated for a Tony Award for her role.

Her political and social consciousness was already strengthening. Among the many African American actors who moved successfully from the American Negro Theatre to the larger theatre world was Sidney Poitier, who remembered Childress well, saying that she helped him to see himself in a new way and encouraged his awareness of black history. But Childress needed to do more, especially for black women. Out of her frustration with what she saw as the subservient roles available to black actresses and with "a feeling that I was somewhat alone in my ideas," she wrote her first play, *Florence*, in 1949. A one-act play, it takes place in a train station where a black woman and a white woman converse through the grille that separates the races there. Though only a minor success, it established the theme for the rest of her plays and novels: the "genteel poor"—usually black but also white—become heroic through their pride in the face of poverty and racial prejudice. In *Trouble in Mind*, produced in 1955, she exposes the prejudice against black women in the theatre. The main character, Wiletta, a talented black actress, refuses to play her character as

579

written—a woman who knowingly sends her son out to a lynch mob. Childress's play *Wedding Band* was first produced professionally in 1966. Set in the South, the emotionally charged drama concerns an interracial couple: Julia, a black seamstress, and her white common-law husband Herman, a poor baker. The two genuinely love each other, but they cannot live together. *Mojo: A Black Love Story* and *String* are one-act plays that also depict the complexities of racial prejudice; her two plays for young people—*When the Rattlesnake Sounds* (about Harriet Tubman), and *Let's Hear It for the Queen*, a parody of the Queen of Hearts nursery rhyme—show brave, unstereotyped female characters.

One of Childress's most inspiring female characters is Mildred, a domestic worker whom she created for a popular series of newspaper sketches called "Here's Mildred." Childress had done domestic work to support herself and her daughter, and she knew plenty of African American women who sometimes had to choose between their white employer's needs and those of their own families. But her Mildred is no meek drudge. In her dramatic monologues, spoken as if to her friend Marge, we see her strength. She works hard, speaks her mind when she has to, attends political meetings, and confronts her employers when they are unjust. She is a true original who deserves an audience today as much as in the 1950s—perhaps more, because of her revelations of the subtle inequities of the employer/domestic relationship. Collected as a book in 1956 called *Like One of the Family . . . Conversations from a Domestic's Life*, these monologues were reissued in 1986 with an introductory essay by Trudier Harris.

During the 1960s and 1970s, travel opportunities took Childress to the Mac-Dowell Colony, to Fisk and Harvard Universities, to the Soviet Union, to mainland China, and to Ghana, West Africa; at these places, she wrote, gave interviews, participated in panel discussions, and observed different forms of theatre. In 1969, she accepted a commission to write a script for the public television series "On Being Black." Her teleplay *Wine in the Wilderness*, about an artist seeking a representation of black womanhood, has often been performed by amateur theatre groups. In 1977, her home state of South Carolina honored her with Alice Childress week, celebrated in Charleston and Columbia. For the occasion, she wrote *Gullah*, later titled *Sea Island Song*, an hour-long folk story in dramatic form, with music by Nathan Woodard, whom she had married in 1957.

At the suggestion of editor F. N. Monjo, she established herself as a powerful writer for young adults with *A Hero Ain't Nothin' but a Sandwich*, published in 1973. YA scholar Alleen Pace Nilsen has said that its power and excellence helped to shape YA literature during that crucial period, and to bring it new respect. The book also became famous as one of the books removed from the Island Trees (New York) School library in the 1976 censorship case that eventually went to the Supreme Court. It has remained controversial because of its profanity and references to drugs. Childress herself wrote the screenplay for the film version, released in 1978.

Childress wrote two other YA novels. *Rainbow Jordan*, published in 1981, deals with a fourteen-year-old girl whose mother periodically abandons her and who eventually finds a home with Josephine, an older woman struggling with her own losses. *Those Other People*, published in 1989, introduces readers to Jonathan, a young gay man trying to accept himself. In none of her three books for young adults does Childress tell them that their problems will be solved easily or completely. Her equivocal endings reinforce her conviction that personal courage may be all we have between us and the world's injustice.

580

Childress's only child, Jean, died of cancer in 1990. When Childress herself died, also of cancer, in 1994, she was beginning a project concerning her great-grandmother, a freed slave who became the mother of Eliza, the grandmother who had first encouraged Childress to write.

A Hero Ain't Nothin' but a Sandwich is one of the most uncompromising books in the Young Adult genre. Having honed her narrative techniques through playwriting, Childress dispenses with a narrator and with all third-person description of the setting. Nothing comes between the reader and the characters. All eleven of them speak directly to us in a series of short dramatic monologues, holding nothing back, in a style that resembles William Faulkner's in his 1930 novel *As I Lay Dying*. The action revolves about thirteen-year-old Benjie, whose drug addiction is affecting those around him: his friend Jimmy Lee, his mother Rose, her common-law husband Butler, her mother Mrs. Bell, and his teachers Nigeria Greene and Bernard Cohen. Butler is trying to be a father to Benjie, but the boy cannot feel anyone believes in him, nor does Benjie believe he has a drug problem: "I *take* something sometime, but I ain't no user." The tension rises when his teachers finally report Benjie to the school authorities and he is put in the hospital to detox. The love of his mother and grandmother, and Butler's desire to help him, are taxed to the fullest. The center of the novel explodes in the voice of Walter the pusher—blunt, profane, full of hate for himself and the world: "Alla these cryin-Emma social workers rap out lyin jive bout the 'poor addict.' Dig it, ain't nobody ever held down nobody else and shot him in the vein. . . I hate the nigga most much as I'm hatin myself; the both of us ain't had no more sense than to be born Black in the middle of some big white action." Childress said she and her editor had many conversations about whether to leave Walter in the novel, but he stayed, the voice of temptation and anger that should not be ignored.

The novel is all the more remarkable because of Childress's ability to reproduce not only the emotional complexity of all these characters but their distinctive Black English, including individual subtleties. Benjie's, Butler's, and Rose's voices are slightly different from each other; Nigeria Greene's differs from theirs in turn, reflecting his more middle-class status as a teacher. The speech rhythms, the sometimes humorous but always incisive descriptions of hypocrisy, the accurate drug and sexual slang from the streets, make this novel more a "heard" experience than a "read" one. One after the other, we hear the characters' problems, their pride, and their reasons for what they do; each is absolutely convinced of his point of view, and each is convincing to the reader. Seldom has a novel taken on a social problem and revealed its human voice and heart with such complexity. The equivocal ending, so typical of Childress's work, is the only one possible.

Though the novel shows its roots in the black-pride movement of the sixties, particularly in the character of Nigeria Greene, it transcends that era because the problems it addresses have not changed, and because Childress puts them in completely human terms. In 1986, the Virginia English Bulletin printed an essay by a student who urged teachers to make the novel available to students. She said, "As one who has lived with heroin addiction in my family, I would fight to keep this book in junior high school classrooms . . . [It] is one hundred percent realistic with just the correct amount of hope: almost none. But this book makes a strong impression which could influence a few lives. It can only change lives, however, if adolescents read it."

581

A HERO AIN'T NOTHIN'
BUT A SANDWICH

BENJIE JOHNSON

NOW I am thirteen, but when I was a chile, it was hard to be a chile because my block is a tough block and my school is a tough school. I'm not trying to cop out on what I do or don't do cause man is man and chile is chile, but I ain't a chile no more. Don't nobody wanta be no chile cause, for some reason, it just hold you back in a lotta ways; unless you be a rich chile like in some movin picture or like on TV—where everybody is livin it up and their room is perfect-lookin and their swimmin pool and their block and their house and they also ridin round in one them quiet rollin Cads with a tape deck playin cool music and with air condition goin.

My block ain't no place to be a chile in peace. Somebody gonna cop your money and might knock you down cause you walkin with short bread and didn't even make it worth their while to stop and frisk you over. Ain't no letrit light bulb in my hallway for two three floors and we livin up next to the top floor. You best get over bein seven or eight, right soon, cause seven and eight is too big for relatives to be holdin your hand like when you was three, four, and five. No, Jack, you on your own and they got they thing to do, like workin, or going to court, or seein after they gas and letrit bills, and they dispossess—or final notice, bout on-time payments—and like that, you dig?

Walkin through dark, stinky hallways can be hard on anybody, man or chile, but a chile can get snatch in the dark and get his behind parts messed up by some weirdo; I'm talkin bout them sexuals. Soon's you get up to leven, twelve and so—they might cool it cause they scared you know where to land a good up-punch, dig? I say alla this cause it's a fact. I don't go for folks cryin and bein sorry over me, cause I'm a man and if I can't take it, well, later!

Some cats moanin the blues, cryin bout how whitey does, and how the society does, and how they be poor and ain't got this and that. Answer me this: If somebody stomp you down and cuttin your air off so you can't even breathe your breath, you think they gonna let up just cause you cryin bout the stompin they puttin on you? Hell, no! Fuck the society! Thass what I say! Lass thing the society can do for me is to boo-hoo and come on with that sorry-for-you talk.

I hate for people to lie on me. No matter what they color or creed—I can't stand nobody lyin. Everybody can be wrong sometime, and when you wrong, you oughta stand up and *be* wrong right out, and not be hidin and lyin. When I'm wrong, I just be it. I ain't scared of a livin ass, not even if they kill me. Why folks got to lie and say I'm on skag[1] say I'm a junkie? My grandmother say, "You a dope fiend." I don't call her coffee fiend or church fiend. No, I don't do that.

---

1 *skag* heroin.

Childress

*A Hero Ain't
Nothin' but a
Sandwich*
Benjie
Johnson

They lyin! If you "on" somethin, that mean you *hooked* and can't give it up. I ain't hooked. What's draggin them is that I ain't gettin off of it yet.

I don't mind too much when parents and schoolteachers, social workers and head shrinkers tag names on me and go to generalizin. They ole and it's parta they nature to be saying things like they know facts and you don't know nothin! But, man, it can get to you when your best friend, least somebody you *thought* was your friend, talkin at you and sayin you on skag and how you better kick. When I hear that word "kick," I think bout somebody tremblin and shakin and vomitin and screamin and goin crazy. Thass not me. I *take* somethin sometime, but I ain't no user. Fact is, I used to skin-pop only on weekend cause I wanted to keep my mind on school and wasn't near ready to give up on the society. For a time I was even diggin bein a social worker, a block organizer or somethin like that. They got lotsa guys out here makin good money workin to turn the real addicts off and put em on the right track again. The ones who do that best are those who was once on theyself and then later shook it. They for real, cause they in on what the scene is all about. If I was a social worker, I'd know what is what and how to do cause I have dug the scene and didden have to be studyin it from a jive book.

It bugged me hard when Jimmy-Lee start layin them jive-ass heart-to-heart raps on me. Talkin like he already a social worker. "Man," he say, "straighten up cause you gonna kill yourself." Answer me this, if Jimmy-Lee is my friend and I'm his, then that make us equal, right? Then how come he talkin like he got it made and I'm lost? That ain't no way to be equal and reach somebody. He don't reach me a-tall!

One day I went all the whole day long with nothin cept a couple-a joints and a taste-a wine. I felt kinda strange, but I went the day and the night too. I went it, Jack! Comes mornin, and I'm pullin myself together to go it some more. My mother started in. "Why you so draggy?" she say. When I don't answer and tryin to show my respeck by iggin her, she keep it up. "I hope you not takin somethin you should not have." She say it real nasty, and slammin the fryin pan down on the stove, signifyin; then she bang the dishes on the table so hard till it's a wonder they didn't smash to bits.

All that kinda action is bad for my nerves. Fact is, alla my family is nervous. My grandmother is nervouser than anybody. She get up sometime and walk back and forth, up and down the hallway, between her room and the kitchen, sayin, "Lord, Lord, what is this! What is it all about?" She be rubbin her hands together, shakin her head, and stompin her feet. She little and skinny but stomp when she walk, like you would expeck some fat person to make so much noise.

Then my mother get nervous from hearin the stompin and Grandma talkin to the Lord and she say, "Mama, for God sake! For God sake! Keep still till Butler get his breakfast and get outta here."

Butler is kinda like my stepfather. I give him credick for bein the coolest one mosta the time. He talk just plain and easy, and he start off sayin to me, "I'm not your father, but I have a thing or two to say and gonna say it," then he would maybe give some advice, or tell you what he don't like, but not hollerin. The fact that he's "step" might be why he ain't so nervous as us that's blood kin: he also don't have much in the way of bad habits.

He like to have a bottle of Seagram Seven on hand so he can take a taste-a that in the evenin, while he sittin back listenin to a radio talk show bout prejudice and race, and like that. Sippin his Seven Crown, he says to me, "Listen and learn, Benjie, time is changin, there's gonna be more opportunity." But he gets to my soul nerve when he keep sayin that, cause I don't see him doin nothin but bein a janitor in one of whitey's downtown buildins. Hear *him* tell it, he ain't no janitor, he a *maintenance* man. Dig it, *maintenance* man ain't nothin but a jive-ass name for janitor.

One night I say, "When they gonna have a opportunity for you?"

He shake his head and say how everything they got goin is for youth. "It all youth program," he say. "If you ain't young no more, the government want you to drop dead and not be takin space and breathin air."

Then I decide to sound on him, so I say, "Nothin's goin for me but other people's mouth." He say, "You oughta be hit in yours!"

Grandma then holler out, "Do it in fronta me and you'll be in trouble!"

Then Mama say, "Butler is not really gonna hit him! You and Benjie are both evil-minded." Grandma went to slammin dishes, and Mama and Butler start to quarrelin bout me. I get up and went over to Tiger's place. Sometimes it's better to fix yourself than to mess with other people.

Only reason I ever mainlined was on accounta money, what you call economics. It take more skag to skin-pop, cause the jolt is weaker than mainlinin. Half as much mainlined will give a high like the whole dose skin-popped.

I don't dig stealin or gettin into dirty action just to get somethin for my nerves. It don't seem fair to anybody and I been fair-minded all my life. I had to take three bucks outta my grandmother's pocketbook, but I wasn't stealin it. Jimmy-Lee told me his uncle was givin him ten smackers for a birthday present. Jimmy-Lee bein my boon,[2] I knew he'd lend me three singles so I could slip back what was borrowed before anybody found out.

One time his father had give him five bucks for school supplies, and Jimmy-Lee gave me a single for myself; it wasn't even a loan, he just say, "Here you go, my man, that's yours." We used to do that kinda smooth action, look out for one nother. Many a time I lend him my skates and don't ask for em back, dig? But the one time I cop somethin, as a borrow, from my grandmother, his ole, lyin uncle didden give him the ten. Fact is, his uncle went away on a cruise to the West Indies and act like he ain't never promise nothin! If he could go to the Virgin Island, why couldn't he hand Jimmy-Lee the ten? Answer me that.

I been catchin hell bout that money. Most times, when I'm wrong. I say it right out, but for some reason I stood there lyin, "I didden take it." I kept sayin it over and over, lyin like a dog. I ain't no chicken; but it seem like unfair to have three of 'em on me accusin like I'm their enemy, and they mine.

The real trouble is school and a jive-ass Black teacher name Nigeria. He pretend to be a Black Nationalist, but done turn Uncle Tom and got together with Mista Cohen, who is a Jew. The two of them did me in. Nigeria got the nerve to wear a black, red, and green button on his jacket. Somebody oughta rip the nationalist button off that spensive, British, hand-tailor suit. Nigeria Greene tole us he bought it in London when he went there on a vacation. He say, "This is what the English call a bespoke suit, and that means it's made to order." He's another one I once thought was for real. Wow, it cut through you, like a double-edge blade, when who you thought was a friend turn out to be stone enemy. Never trust a jive-ass nigga in a bespoke suit, specially one wearin a nationalist button.

The real dirty part is him gettin my mother and grandmother upset; after all, they only women. Look like the nigga woulda said, "No need to go to no lady bout this, I'll just talk to Benjie and see if we can rap out some kinda under-

---

2 *boon* good buddy.

standin." Sometime people don't know what they mouth can do, Jack! He hipped Cohen and the principal, then they notify my Gramma and she blabbin it all to my mother and Butler, then they jumpin in it. I'm the only one cool, cause if I wassen, I woulda tole the principal, the teachers, the social worker and the whole world that my stepfather ain't married to my mother no kinda way and that Nigeria believe in makin a all-Black government outta the United States: bet the law would say somethin to em bout that. But I ain't dirty, thassa fact.

BUTLER CRAIG

Stepfather

I'VE seen a lot in my lifetime, but never anything like this. Bein strung out on junk wasn't invented yesterday, no indeed, been goin on a long time, but damn if it ain't gettin worse. This the first time I've seen a child junkie thirteen years of age. I have heard of it, everybody has, and even heard worse; but I've never lived with it. I don't know what to do, and nobody else seems to either, no matter how much they be tryin, because there's too much jive talk bout "program" and "understandin." Damn, I *understand* it. The kid got to hangin round those that's in a junk bag and then got in one himself. How he's to get out is what's to be dealt with.

We can't put down nothin we hope to pick up again, cause now he's into stealin. Naturally, his own relatives are the easiest to rip off, cause we won't throw his behind in jail like strangers would.

These head-shrinker doctors pryin at his mother, wearin her soul out, cause their main hype is to find where to hang blame. A fact! They want every junkie to find somebody in his own house to blame. Always runnin down some jive bout "the society" on your TV, but when it comes to dope traffic and these not-yet-dry-behind-the-ears kids, all they wanta hand you is jive questions bout do you understand the junky, or if he didn't get a red bicycle for Christmas, or if you took him to a baseball game lately, and a whole lotta shit like that. Yeah, it's shit, that's also what he's usin, and that's what authorities be shovelin at everybody. Social workers and head shrinks don't take kids home to their house after they get through plantin dumb ideas; they send them back home to rob their loved ones. Reason we can still find soap or a rolla toilet paper in the bathroom is cause he can't sell that for nothin.

Benjie is my stepson, more or less, and I have tried to take the *step* outta that and be as much father as he will allow. His real dad been gone for the last many years, ain't left no forwardin address, and ain't sent him no bread. Last Christmas he mailed a greetin card, with a damn, white-ass Santa Claus on it. He sign the card "Daddy" and put the date on it, but still ain't said where to find him; neither did he write a little note askin if the boy been eatin a meal lately or anything like that. All right, sometime you gotta forget and chalk it up to life experience. After all, maybe somebody didn't understand the boy's father. You can keep tracin down who didn't understand who, until you trace back to Adam and Eve. Damn, *nobody* ever understood me! I don't understand myself, and I been tryin to do that all my life. I damn, for sure, don't understand bein treated like a dog cause I got a dark complexion. Neither do I latch on to all this civil-rights-struggle jive. It ain't for real yet, dig?

Twenty years ago, down in Georgia, a white cat gave me a hard way to go, made me his target. That's how they will do; might be almost decent to some other Black, but if there's a look in your eye, or somethin in your walk, that brings out the deep-down cracker thing inside him, then you in for a streaka hard luck. I heard bout white folks havin a "favorite" nigga, but there's more stories to be told bout who happen to be their unfavorite. This particular white cat used to low rate me with off-the-wall remarks; of course he was always in the company of some white buddy cats when he'd have a go at me.

I'd be comin in or out this crummy nightclub where I worked. I had me a saxophone, in those days, and doin a gig once in a while, when I wasn't helpin my uncle haul coal and wood. One day this shambly-lookin dude tripped me up when I was goin past him on the sidewalk. His friends cracked their sides laughin when he say, even before I could get up, "Nigga, why don't you watch your step?"

I dusted myself off and moved on. Some Black cats, across the street, went to talkin bad and tough bout what all they would do if it was them that got tripped.

"Man," they say, "thass dyin time!"

Some church folk standin near the corner, they say, "Best thing is take him to court, do it through N double A. Make a case!"

I didn't die *or* go to the N double A.[1] Wasn't anybody left in our family but my uncle and me. He was a fairly young cat, single and solid in my corner. I took *his* advice, cause I dug it the most. We quietly bought us two plane tickets for New York City, and after a few days went by, we made our move. Caught that trippin-up cracker bastard one dark night and beat his ass almost inta the next world, then took our plane and got the hell out fore his mouth healed enough to report what happen. Yeah, my uncle say, "Let *him* go to court and make a case."

I don't bother a livin, but I am very direct in my ways when they bother me. I am how I am, and I don't understand me any more than somebody else might, you see?

Me and Sweets work for every crumb we get to eat. If I could give her what all she deserve, she'd have it made. It make me mad for anybody to give her a bad time. One time she bought herself a leather handbag, with gold initials on the outside—R. C. That stand for Rose Craig. Rose is Sweets' first name, and Craig is my last. She got a nosey cousin who say, "What's the 'C' for? I didn't know you married again." Cousin was meddlin and bein nasty.

I said, "Craig is *my* name and I gave it to Sweets to use, if she wants it. When papers get legalized, and all like that, we can then go down to the courthouse and ask the law to sell us a license just so you won't have to be wonderin who's who and what's the 'C' for."

Cousin laughin that sick laugh people pull when they outta line and got put back in place. She say, "Go on, Butler, you too much!"

I laugh back how we do when we get somebody offa us. I say, "Yeah, I'm wise."

Sweets shake her head and talk kindly, "Yall cut it out, now."

People will go outta their way to sound on you when you mindin your business. The cousin is a fine person and studyin to be stenographer even, but she got too much mouth.

---

1 *N double A* NAACP, the National Association for the Advancement of Colored People, founded in 1909.

One time Sweets came down to my job to give me my keys, cause I had left them home. She looked fine in her suit and hat, also wearin gloves. *Neat!* This greasy, white son-bitch who was fixin a steam pipe, say to me, "Who's your fine, roly-poly chick?"

"Watch your mouth, buster," I say, "that's *Mrs.* Craig, my wife."

Dude looked sick and started in to mumblin out a string of sorries. I mean, I do my best to keep down confusion bout the two of us. She looks right, she cooks right, and we suit each other in every other kinda way; so anybody don't dig the combination, tough luck! We satisfied.

Reason I work damn hard on a square job and hit the jam-crowded subway each and every mornin is cause I couldn't afford to support my habit of playin the saxophone, or the habit couldn't support me. One week you got a one-night gig, the next week nothin; then soon you find yourself jammin for free, just to keep your sound goin; and you be broke, broke, broke. Also I'm seein some best musicians, shootin up and drinkin rotgut, killin themselves like they not the greatest sounds in the world, a fact!

The rest of 'em out here hauntin whitey's footsteps, round recordin studios, beggin for a break in them casual, easygoin tones we put on when we gotta ask and ask and beg—for a break. They give you a break all right; will steal your music and pay themselves the profit. Other choices I had was to get out and find a hardworkin job, knock somebody in the head for their bread, or try to live off some chick and let her do the worryin and hustlin for me. So I work at somethin I don't like. I'm a home man. I dig a place where you can close the door and shut the people-eaters outta your life. Doesn't have to be fancy, a music box with a good sound, a name-brand bottle that can be tasted now and then, food in the box, and a glad rag or two to wear when you wanta make a extra-nice appearance.

I try not to tangle with Sweets' mama. Sometimes, just as I'm ready for a minute of peace, to listen to a Coltrane record, while havin a cold brew, that's the very minute the old lady starts singin hymns so loud till Coltrane ain't got a chance, no matter how high I'm turnin up the volume.

Sweets can't walk away, it's not her nature. That's her mother, and the boy is her son; she couldn't sleep nights if she left. But there's a distance growin between us. Poor folks ain't got many ways to solve problems. But if we had plenty money, her mother could go to a nursin home or have her own apartment, and the boy could be taken to a far place, like down South with some nice farmer people . . . where there's no city nearby, just trees, air, fishin, and like that. Could live with middle-aged farm people who'll love him, feed him, and beat his butt if necessary.

It bugs me to see any more young-ass social workers. They ask too many questions. I'm not the one in trouble. It's a drag to work every day and then have strangers questionin you on your day off.

JIMMY-LEE POWELL

Benjie's Friend

ME AND BENJIE use to be tight. You see me, you see him. He was my boon! No matter where I go, he had to folla. Sometime I say, "Benjie, what you taggin behind me for?" Be soundin evil, but he don't care, he grinnin and sayin,

CHILDRESS

*A Hero Ain't
Nothin' but a
Sandwich*
Jimmy-Lee
Powell

"Goin where you goin, that's where." He mean he don't have to ask no questions, that wherever I'm at is fine with him. Benjie used to make me feel good, like I was a movie star or a basketball player on some big, winnin team, like the Knicks. Nobody could make no bad cracks or be soundin on me round Benjie. It was the same with me. I dug Benjie not bein jealous and jivin and holdin it gainst me cause I'm smarter than he is in school subjects, and that I made the basketball team and he didn't. Could read in his face that he be wishin he was in on it with me, but still glad I'm there!

Now he's soundin like from another planet, snifflin snot back up his nose, and eyes runnin water while puttin the beg on for more bread. One minute lookin pitiful, next minute mean and evil enough to cut out your heart with a dull knife. Sometime a junkie get mad with *you* cause he got a jones[1] and you ain't. That's why Benjie come down on me so hard.

"One thing," he say, "I ain't no chicken! If I wanta shoot up, I shoot! If I wanta stop, I stop! You a chickenshit!"

"Watch your mouth, boy," I say, "I don't play that game, and don't try to strong-arm me for my bread. We'll see who's chicken if you don't back up!"

Damn right he backed up. I can whip him, but I don't wanta. I'm feelin bad cause I give him his first jointa pot. Now I don't even smoke it myself, a fact, cause I got somethin else for a dollar to do; also, smokin, for me, is not such a fine gas. A high might be *the* thing for some, but it's just somethin I did to pass little time, and I don't have too much time to be passin because my brain is now into a lotta things. I don't dig turnin my head off and on like a water faucet. Also I don't wanta get caught off guard in this bad-ass wilderness, it's rough, and I want my wits woke, so I can find a better slot than the one I'm in.

There's some baaaaaaaaad studs out here, not strung out on nothin but nerve power. They hard-hustlin and doin everybody in, Jack. Who do you think they rob more than anybody else? The hophead, that's who! They will knock on a junkie for every dime he's got, they will also take his bread, promise to go get him a fix, and then never come back; the junkie then got nothin but a cramp in the gut and cold shakes. I tole Benjie, "No matter how much skag a guy gets, he will still feel low when he comes down, cause he knows that everybody is kickin on his ass and gettin themselves a case of the weirdo jollies outta seein him sweat for his next fix." Fact is, I seen a pusher make a junkie *beg* for his dose, before he would even sell it to him. You ready for that? Not me. All that talk bout bein a chicken, if you don't let somebody use your veins for a horse racin track, goes on past my head and I'm feelin no pain, dig?

I don't be preachin a sermon on the subject cause everybody don't dig bein told how dumb-ass they actin. To a cat that digs bein stoned, I say, "Right on, *kill* yourself, man." He be thinkin that sound good and will give you a full grin, like you his main boon. But I hate to hit down too hard on some these little junk men, cause many are good cats. Didn't junk knock Benjie down?

One time a guy name Carwell sold me some joints. I looked up Benjie, so we could try us a pot high. We went up the steps leadin to the roof in a house on the next block, a beat-up, fallin-down place where we know ain't no super give a damn. We on the steps smokin, suckin in the smoke like we been seein and hearin bout. I'm little bit older than they are, makes me cooler than them. Carwell and Benjie takin off and goin on, "Uuuuuuu-weee, um high, man.

---

1 *jones*   drug habit.

CHILDRESS

*A Hero Ain't
Nothin' but a
Sandwich*
Jimmy-Lee
Powell

Groovin, this is it, man." I'm feelin kinda simple-ass cause all that ain't happenin for me. I feel sorta so-what—but no big thing. The roof door is open, and I could see blue sky and a white cloud straight up over my head, so it's there, dig? Remind me of the time I went in on a sixty-five-cent pinta wine— muscatel, it give me a headache hangover. Pot high, for me, is a dumb kinda don't-give-a-damn, but I know it's a high, and I'm sorta quietly lookin it over and tryin to figure it out. I got what you call a inquisitive mind. Benjie and Carwell, they makin talk.

"This it!"

"Live or die, make me no difference."

I'm layin back studyin sky and their voices . . . just waitin for the high to pass. Nothin left of me but one dumb, sad feelin. I don't dig bein lost, I'm better off found. Carwell say, "I know a stud who buys grass by the bag!" I don't like Carwell, his eyes ugly, hard brown buttons. You got to *stay* stoned to stand Carwell a-tall, I'm still not likin him even with the high on. Losin yourself is for some, but it ain't for others. It ain't for me.

Benjie had a long stringa spit hangin offa his bottom lip. I'm lookin at spit, seein sky through a roof door, and turnin my bread over to the button-eyed Carwell. It ain't for me, dig? I really don't need no knockin out. I'm sorry how Benjie is now gettin caught up and expandin on the program.

A social worker is somebody who makes they bread and fame offa other people's troubles. Lotta people plannin to make it as a social worker, cause the field is so wide-ass open, and trouble, accordin to Benjie's grandma, is somethin that's sure gonna last *always*. Hell, I could be a social worker myself! When a junkie gets real messed up, the thorities send them into talk groups to get talked to. What you think they talkin bout? Just tellin how they papa and mama don't understand, and they also be sayin "ghetto" and things like that. Benjie gonna be brainwash with that crap. Right now, he try to tell me how his daddy run off and how that make him a child from a broken home. Shit! Sometime I wish my home was broke. Benjie don't know how to dig good luck! He's got a stepfather who's bringin in a color TV and hi-fi record player and all kinda good things people need. True, Mr. Butler Craig gives him talkins to bout don't do this and don't do that, damn, the man titled to say somethin. But Benjie steady complainin bout havin a step and a broken home.

I got a real father, but Mama say Daddy surely been broke on the wheela life. She talkin bout the Freedom Rides that used to happen in the South. My father was into all kindsa action, picketin and breakin down segregation at food stands and in bus stations and like that. He went on a March to Washington way back in 1951. He say that was the *first* time Martin Luther King spoke in fronta the Lincoln Memorial. Daddy got a certificate that look like a ten-dollar bill; it say, "This is to show that James Lee Powell went on the March to Washington for Civil Rights." Papa say he went down with A. Philip Randolph leadin New York marchers. Mama say, "Your father has been a part of whatever he thought might make us free, and his head has been whipped more than once. One time they turned our car over and set it on fire. He's broke down from peaceful protest."

Daddy belong to the old school, thought they could make white folks feel shame bout how they did us. He been a left-winger, that means a Communist, a Socialist, a Liberal, a Nationalist, or a Democrat. He's now what you call a Independent, that means you can change your mind from time to time. He's forever ready to jump into a new bag if it's what he calls "a promisin-lookin thing." He ain't got much time for me and Mama. He reads his books and go to talk on the corner as a stepladder speaker, speech always question society and the law. He can solid preach! Old guys dig him. My father is forty-three years old and the old fellas still call him "Youngblood." He ain't gonna buy no color TV cause he don't hang onto one job long enough to buy nothin. Mama, by herself, is steady bringin in money for the bills. He always gonna kick somebody's ass . . . and has been known to do it. He wake up evil sometime and cuss and slam doors. Mama say he been through a lot, but I don't go for too much door slammin.

He got books bout Garvey, Malcolm, Karl Marx, Du Bois and Martin Luther King, history books and Africa maps. He say, "It make me mad to work for a dumb-ass white man who don't know nothin a-tall." He quit a laundry truck job, the post office, and many others. When he got money, he's free-handed but he hardly ever have any. He kicked a hole in the bathroom door one night—and ain't nobody done anything to him. Mama was stirrin some hominy grits, she never even look up, just keep stirrin.

A white teacher name Mr. Cohen is the one who taught me to read good and fast, but he didn't know, cause he doesn't notice what's goin on half the time. I never learned much bout readin in the lower grades, cause all we did in my P.S. was bring in and sneak-read what we please, like dirty comic-strip books where funny-book characters all screwin each other, and like that. Some teachers let girls bring in love story magazines and even let us all play cards. You could do anything if you kept your voice down and did it quiet. That was how third and fourth grade went by. Teachers would use the period to get their absent-present files straight. When Mr. Cohen got holda our class, he was mad cause our readin was not cool a-tall. Every day he made us get up, stand to one side of the room, in a line, and do nothin but take turns readin out loud. It was like ridin a bicycle; one day, after bumblin and stumblin, I started to read fast and easy. I just knew how and been goin on ever since.

The Cyrenian Promise Baptist Church

SENIOR CITIZENS!

Read your BULLETIN BOARD *before* asking questions!

SPECIAL ANNOUNCEMENT

Our pastor, Reverend Holsom, regretfully announces the cancellation of all midweek evening meetings, due to purse snatchings and holdups perpetrated against elderly members as they leave the premises. As many activities as possible will be rechanneled to fit into the daylight hours of Saturday and Sunday afternoons. This Monday Reverend Holsom and a committee of concerned citizens will visit our local precinct captain to demand—
1. More and better police protection in this area.
2. An end to drug traffic in this area.

CHILDRESS

*A Hero Ain't
Nothin' but a
Sandwich*
Mrs. Ran-
som Bell

Join us at 9 A.M. in front of the church.
Last week one of our elderly members was
robbed and beaten as she left a night meeting of the Scholarship Fund Society. This
is only one of many such shameful incidents
which have occurred in this community. Send
Get Well Greetings to Mrs. Ransom (Elizabeth) Bell and offer up prayers for her
continued fine recovery.

MRS. RANSOM BELL

Grandmother

THIS house is my jail, only I pay rent. I'm afraid to go out in the street
alone, day or night. Bad boys now hate old people and will beat them and
take away our little money. Bein old is strange to me, cause I'm not yet used to
it. I have sat in the narrowness of this room, my hands folded in my lap, lookin
at the knuckles and veins of my fingers; they seem larger, knotty-lookin, my
mind tell me that's old. But if old was only looks, then old could be better dealt
with. Old is also *ailin*, you get a sudden jab or pain in your shoulder or knee
joint, and that pain be so perfectly sharp, it's like somebody stabbed a long, hot
ice pick right down to the bone. That'll happen three, four times in a row;
then when I brace before it stabs me again, it'll lie low and not come back for a
while, or it'll hit in a new place, like the back of my knee or the hip joint.
That's how ailin goes, you can't depend on how or where it'll happen next. But
old is also more than pain, I guess. Maybe old is your mind goin one way
whilst you go another

All my life I been hearin bout old folks and, of course, old folks is always
somebody else and you can understand that much better than when you might
be the one. There's a part of bein old that's got nothin to do with aches and
pains, you get sudden thoughts that flash in from no place. Thoughts can hurt
like real pain. Thoughts will not hang together long enough for me to sort
them out and think a matter through, cause just as I'm handlin one thing it flies
away and another will pick up where the first left off, only it's different—and
that's how I get mixed up.

I'm so glad I got Jesus! My personal Saviour, the Son of God! Jesus Christ is
a waymaker! When your enemies press in on every hand, and they sit in the seat
of the scornful, and when there is no heat in the radiator of this top-floor
walkup, and when my onliest daughter is hummin and sighin past me like a express train passin a freight, when the man she's livin with, in sin, and callin her
husband, is drinking whiskey in the presence of the Crucifixion picture on the
livin-room wall, when my grandson is stealin from me to buy dope, when they
leadin me, gainst my will, to go make paper flowers at the old folks' club, when
others pickin my clothes out for me and I'm not likin what they buy, when
won't nobody take me to church, when all the nice people I know are dead and
gone, when bad boys rob me in the street and knock me down, when all these

things come to pass—as predicted in the Scripture; bless the Lord! Even in the midst of my heartache, light shines in on my soul, and I am truly lifted! The walls of this little room just roll back, and bright glory shines everywhere, in my heart, in the air; round the mirror glass on the wall turns glinty and sparkly, and a glassa water is a glassa diamonds!

Yes, they hit me and knocked me down, my own kind did it to me, but I'm still alive. Don'tcha see how good God has been? Who would I have if I didden have Jesus? Never did I know I'd live to see a time like this. I wake up in the night and hear the next-door jukebox playin that loud, bad-rollin music, kinda tunes make folks think bout sexin, drinkin, and stayin up all night and bout usin bad language on each other. They play the drum like they swingin the hammer of Satan, thumpin it up gainst a cement wall, nothin but thumpin and no music in it. I be layin here, tremblin in the dark, but just as confusion is bout to smother me off the face-a the earth, I suddenly feel and know that Jesus, the natural Christ, is here in this room. He is here remindin me that I have claimed Him as my *personal* redeemer. Jesus is *here*, promisin life everlastin! Then confusion takes flight on the wings of angels. I chase that evil jukebox sound outta my head by singin from one hymn to another—"How Great Thou Art" and "Precious Lord Take My Hand." Suppose I had not been saved by the Blood of the Lamb? I mighta been in the insane asylum because bad boys mugged me in the street. It is the object of sin to drive you right-straight-clean outta your natural mind!

When I was a girl, down in Mississippi, my folks was sharin crop, we was poor, but there was some little good to it, cause I had the lovin service of my father and sweet mother. My father was a strong, good man and not like these triflin ones who are signs of the end to come. My mother was a womanly woman and knew how to sew clothin and can peaches, if and when she had some to can. My father got kill in a argument with a man who wouldn't pay him money that was owed for his hard work. Some said, "Too bad he had to lose his life over collectin a little bitta money."

My Mama say, "Many die from the cancer, others die from the double pneumonia, and some go when they drop dead from the heart failure; but my husband died from a case-a righteousness, and he look a heap better in his casket than them that naturally shriveled away between the sheets." She was proud of my father.

The Lord puts things on us to see how much we can bear, sometimes we fail the test and don't bear too well. My Mama say, "Everybody ain't Job." Look like our family just went downhill after Papa was buried. Mama sent one child to this relative and the other to that, then went off workin in domestic service so she could send us money. Wasn't long fore she followed Papa to the grave. The way we chirrun was scatter around, the double death just cause us to scatter more, everybody had to hit out for theyself.

I saw one brother once when I was dancin in St. Louis, Missoura. He was railroadin through as a Pullman porter. Lord knows I'm sorry for my beginnins in young woman-hood, but if you don't know, you don't know. There was two ways I could choose, do housework for white folk or be wife for some man. Only man that brought up the subject of marryin, at that time, was one who lived out in the country, a sorta mud hole of a crop-sharin place, and he had a few hogs and chickens of his own. He was upstandin, everybody say, but I didn't wanta cover any ground that I had covered before. Sharecroppin killed my parents, so that was bout enough of it for me.

In my day there was a dance called the shimmy, some called it the shake, and all who did that dancin, for pay, was call shake dancers. That was what I did. I learned how to stand up, with my hands over my head, stiffen out and shiver every parta my body all at once, and also one part at a time; even could make my bosom tremble while the rest of me was still. So I got a job doin that in a after-hour place where people come to dance, sing, drink bootleg whiskey and listen to the jazz. After-hour places was illegal, but the colored couldn't work in fine legal places. I wore silk dresses and fancy underwear with fine lace, and I'd lift my skirt to show the lacy underwear and then go into the shake, shimmyin one part at a time, then all parts. It's a wonder I didn't hurt myself, cause I had to do it four or five times a night, then wait table servin whiskey and fried chicken dinners. I received lots of rude proposals and drunks used to try and feel me, but I had made up my mind to live better than was expected, so I didn't encourage them. The Lord was graciously guidin my footsteps, because I got to meet my husband, who was a bricklayer who happen to be layin brick for the after-hour front fence. I sure didden have any hard luck about him. Ransom was his name, we got on fine, was married and came on North.

Up here, he couldn't get no bricklayin to do cause it was a all-white union. But we managed, he promised never to let anybody starve us off the face-a the earth. We rented a big eight-room apartment on Seventh Avenue and took in roomers, workinmen who also took meals with us. Ransom learned how to write policy slips and collect bets people make on number playin.

We only had the one child, our Rosie. She was still little when Ransom died from TB. You never grow too old to miss love . . . I sure miss Ransom.

BERNARD COHEN

Teacher

I'M WHITEY, I'll be the goat, okay? You have no idea how things go down when you're whitey in a Black setup. I go out to work every morning, like a lamb to the slaughter.

I got to contend with the students, the school board, the parents, the teacher's union, the Board of Ed., the PTA, the principal, winos on the block, the pushers, the hall monitors, and in particular, this one Black teacher who is the local Gestapo, with Black Power, like crazy, all over the emm-eff community. His name is Nigeria. No joke. He didn't become a take-a-new-name Muslim or anything like that. His parents named him *Nigeria*, even before Black, Black, Black hit the country.

Nigeria Greene is a pain in the ass. He's built like an oversized football player and walks down the hall like he owns the U. S. of A. and all that's in it. He teaches the bottom of the seventh grade, and I have the top. Got the picture? He gives his students a workup just before they hit my class. They come to me, at the beginning of the term, with eyes narrowed down to slits, they loll back in their seats as if to say, "Okay, motha, unroll your program and see what it gets you." He turns out a mean-ass, cold-hearted crew. All over his classroom walls are pictures of Black people—Marcus Garvey, Du Bois, Robeson, Harriet Tubman, and also many slaves who knocked off whitey in order to get free, and so forth. Was *I* ever a slave master? Did *I* bring slaves over here? Did *I* ever lynch a Black? Am *I* the one?

CHILDRESS

*A Hero Ain't
Nothin' but a
Sandwich*
Bernard
Cohen

Of course they have special needs. I put up pictures too, Frederick Douglass, Booker T. Washington, Ralph Bunche, even a picture of Malcolm X, all different kinds, something for everybody. They walk in, look the pictures over, then slap hands together, laughing like they're in on the joke of the year. You can't know what it's like to feel their contempt. Nigeria Greene passes my classroom, pauses in the doorway, and says, "Right on!" The students call out in a casual way, "Hey Africa, whatcha know!" They never directly like to call anyone or anything exactly what it is because, in their minds, that would be "square." Because his name is really Nigeria, they call him Africa; that way they're not calling him by his first name, and they can avoid saying *Mister* Greene. They used to rudely call me "Mista Charley," I took offense at that and told them to stop. One boy said, "Take it to court and fight for your civil rights like everybody else gotta do."

From nine in the morning to three in the afternoon, feels like I'm wading my way through a pool of cold molasses. I've started to quit, but then I get to wondering if Nigeria and his kind are trying to make me run. What will this country be if the all-Black schools get all-Black teachers? If we give up our seniority by default, they will move on to the assistant and principal jobs like—like Grant went through Richmond. Is it healthy for kids to learn nothing but Black history, Black supremacy, and Black power?

True, it's wrong to treat them unfairly, and I definitely uphold their right to be taught *some* of their history. In the past, I have wholeheartedly signed petitions to have more Blacks integrated into jobs where they have previously been shut out, the building trades, electrical unions, and so forth. But, in all fairness, I must say that in education we have absorbed more than our share of Blacks, we really have. A few more Nigeria Greenes, and we will succeed in cutting our own throats. What about *my* right to work? Are we to eliminate ourselves? I hear many whites complain about supporting *them* on welfare, but I know for a fact that there are Blacks who would like to take all the best jobs and support *us* on welfare.

Let the know-it-alls talk about busing or not busing, but I wish they would start busing teachers and leave students alone. I could stand a change of scene once in a while, without having to quit my job.

Added to the general hostility are the pushers around here selling pills for a dime each, ups mostly. Kids can drop pills in a soda or a glass of milk right in the lunch room. Pot, horse, and cocaine are also a part of the scene, but acid seems to be a whitey habit. In all fairness, I must say, kid addicts don't bother a soul, they don't. A junkie nods on off and lets you alone, when he's fixed. But don't leave your money or wristwatch where he might get to it when that dose is wearing off.

Nigeria Greene called me to one side and raised hell about Benjie being on the nod.

"Hey, man," he says, "you gonna let him ride the horse? A boy is hangin off his desk and you ain't made move the first."

Nigeria likes to say "ain't" even though he knows better. That's *their* way of trying to invent a language because they don't have one. He's also trying to impress the kids, make them believe he's a swinger and one of the crowd. At the moment he's in a big hassle to get a Swahili class started. What in the hell do they need with Swahili? Well, maybe they can use it to ask for a welfare check in two languages. I don't really mean that. I'm just tired of catching hell from Monday to Friday. There are a few other white teachers on this floor, but they are buddy-buddy with Nigeria and seem not to know what to think until he gives them the word. There's another white guy down on the second floor, but he's a racist. Last year the parents drew up a petition to get him out, but somehow or other he couldn't be dropped. The other whites are women, a few bleeding hearts, some check collectors who don't give a damn how the school system is run, and a couple of zombies who have grown old in the obedient service of the Board of Ed. Zombies wear the ugliest shoes ever made. They drag through the hall to the teachers' dayroom, carrying tea bags and cardboard boxes—to brew tea and snack sesame crackers. Try to enlighten them about current conditions, they shake their heads and start talking about a sabbatical.

I've tried to relate to Nigeria, but we can't communicate without having an argument. When he gets angry, his eyes go bloodshot and that bushy Afro seems bushier. "What do you want from me?" I said. "Remember I'm whitey. Nobody needs to hear me call Benjie or any other Black kid a junkie." I had to sock it to him the same way it gets socked to me.

He said, "Benjie is one of the best kids we'll ever see. If I could save him, I would—"

There's nothing to do when people shut me out. Some of the more refined Black teachers are cooperative and kindly, but they're clannish, too, when it comes to race matters, afraid of taking the part of a white person when another Black is in the picture.

My wife is forever planning to move out of the city. She never suggests any definite place, but nightly keeps the subject going along with dinner and through the CBS late news. When I suggest a place, she thinks it too far away, too dull, or too anything she can imagine. What she'd really like is a ten-room colonial house on a tree-shaded acre of ground in the center of the city, with two armed guards patrolling on twenty-four-hour service. The constant topic is crime in the street, muggings, and Negroes, Negroes, Negroes. On the other hand, she looks at pictures of the ones in the New York *Times*, those who are advisers to the government or the UN, sighs and says, "You must admit a lot of them *have* something, three strikes against them, but they still have something."

I had hopes of ignoring the race business, functioning at full speed and forging the way for better education. But now the Puerto Ricans want Puerto Rican teachers, the Blacks want Black, I'm afraid to run and afraid to stay. Everyone is for sale on a new auction block, which is the ground underfoot, wherever we stand.

If mayors, governors, and Presidents can't put a stop to drugs, why should anyone ask me, especially Nigeria Greene? Benjie was a fine boy, one of the best, in disposition. When the others acted up in class, Benjie looked at them, looked at me, then ended up looking out of the window. He must have been determined to remove himself. At any rate, he has.

BENJIE JOHNSON

WHEN I was a chile, me and my mother was cool with each other, got along just fine, also got along with my grandmother, who was a classic dancer when she was young. My mother used to help go over my homework and we be watchin our TV too: Do little homework, then look up and dig TV when the chase go on, or the mystery bout to be solve and the bad guy caught. I had me a happy childhood. Mama and me used to go for a walk on Satday night, go to the newstand bout ten o'clock and buy the Sunday newspaper with funnies in it, then we go to the candy store and buy us two little boxes of hand-dip ice cream, one for her and one for me, each gonna have our own box to eat outta while we read our papers. Sometime Mama say, "Let's go all the way!" Then she laugh and we go to the bakery shop and buy coffee ring to have early Sunday mornin.

I never did dig coffee to drink, but it smell fine when it perkin on Sunday. We be eatin our coffee cake with the raisins inside and nuts on top, and I have cold milk with mine. Sometime we don't have coffee cake, and Grandma make a bacon pancake. First she fry your piece-a bacon till it's criss, then she pour pancake batter topa that, so your pancake gonna come out with a piece-a criss bacon stuck in the middle of it.

Back in them days, we used to know when we was happy and didden have to be talkin it out to *see* if we was. Mama used to have a happy look right on her face. Grandma used to sing a hymn call "Will There Be Any Stars in My Crown?"—sing it on Sunday mornin while makin our bacon pancakes. Mama say, "When you gonna dance for us? Benjie, your grandma ain't never danced for me in her life."

Then I tease Grandma, "I don't believe you can dance!"

My grandmother take hold the end of her skirt and say, "A-one, and a-two and a-three!" Then laugh and say, "Fooled you, didden I!" She really didden fool nobody cause we knew she wasn't gonna dance. Grandma say, "My dancin days over."

Christmas time we had a nice tree and plenty fruit and candy. I'd get games and new clothes. Only time Mama look sad is when she say, "It's terrible for a woman to be alone."

I look at her and ask, "How you alone if you got me? You got me, Mama!"

She smile and say, "Sure have. You mine and I'm yours."

All that was back when I was six, seven and eight, back before Butler took over and stole my mother. Back in days before Nigeria Greene pulled the big double cross. I'm sorry I ever had him for a teacher. He really ratted.

NIGERIA GREENE

Teacher

THIS guy across the hall from me is not to be believed. He is white, and in this school because the system makes damn sure to have white representation in every nook and corner of the country, the world, and, in particular, in every Black community. Look around your city and let me know if you see coloreds represented fifty-fifty in the white community. No, it doesn't go down that way. I'm sick of explainin and talkin race. Race is the story of my life and my father's life, and I guess, his father and all the other fathers before that. As a kid, I was in on "race" discussions in school, at home, in church, everywhere. It's a wonder every Black person in the U.S. of A. hasn't gone stark, ravin mad from racism . . . and the hurtin it's put on us.

CHILDRESS

*A Hero Ain't
Nothin' but a
Sandwich*
Nigeria
Greene

My grandfather was a Garveyite,[1] a dues-payin member of the UNIA—United Negro Improvement Association. He talked my mother into givin me the name Nigeria. People used to call me Gerry to get around the pure African sound, but my name comes on fine these days.

As I said, Bernard Cohen is not to be believed. His whole mission in teaching is to convince Black kids that most whites are great except for a "few" rotten apples in every barrel. It burns me to see white teachers bend kid's ears with the same tune, year in and year out. They'd rather ruin their lives by makin them think they're imaginin the game bein run on them than to save them with truth. You can face hardship if you realize it's not all your fault and you are dealin with some things that have been deliberately dropped on you.

Most of the kids don't talk anything but Harlemese, but have minds as sharp as a double-edge razor. They laugh at textbooks because most invite laughter. "Our" school is fulla white-face books written by white writers. Only two pictures on my wall when I came here . . . George Washington and Abraham Lincoln. Abe was, at least, involved with the Civil War and the Emancipation thing; but George was a slaveholder, and it is impossible to hang George over my front blackboard and not discuss him. When I discuss him, I don't go by what's in these history books or we'd be dealin in lies. George was a slaveholder, and he had it put in his will to free alla his slaves *after* his death. But he owned a slave woman whose cookin was so fine that he freed her while he was livin. She musta really known how to barbecue!

Well, that time slot is over and outta our hands. But now is now, and I don't need a slaveholder lookin down on thirty-seven Black students, while I'm teachin history and civics lessons.

From a kid on up I was good at history. I mean I was good at memorizin what was put before me and was a whiz at recitin it back. If the book said a lie was truth, that lie was the answer I put down on my test paper. I learned that from my father. He was slick as a greasy whistle and yessed his way into the post office. It was hard for a brother to get in durin Papa's early years. You had to know somebody. Fortunately, he knew books were full of lies and never minded tellin me so, but he would also say, "Tell the lie back, tell 'em what they wanta hear, cause it's their book and their school and they will fail you if you don't write it down the way it reads. They'll do you outta the chance to earn yourself a crust of bread." Then he'd tag on the clincher, "Furthermore, if you don't bring me a good report, you gonna get outta here and labor hard because I won't support no full-grown man." He meant it too.

He was sincere in a hemmed-in kinda way and dealt with life exactly the way it was laid out, playin the game according to old, tested rules. He was a trustee of the church and took up collection every Sunday mornin. I can see him now, standin at attention, holdin the mahogany plate, his brown face lit by sunlight shinin through a stained-glass window. One Sunday I noticed the window was a picture of a sword-carryin, golden-haired angel, with snowy, feathery wings. The other windows also showed whites as saints and angels, none looked like my father or any of our people; there and then I began to find Black Nationalism within me, to realize there was no integration in God's heaven, and that I must accept even the Christian rejection of me and mine. I felt hatred for that evil God who made us sing, beg, weep and pray for humble admittance into his white heaven.

---

1 *Garveyite*   a follower of Marcus Garvey (1877–1910), who advocated separation of the races, including the voluntary emigration of African Americans to Africa.

CHILDRESS

*A Hero Ain't
Nothin' but a
Sandwich*
Nigeria
Greene

I decided to correctly give back all the silly answers required of me. I promised myself to make a day when I'd teach what could not be found in my schoolbook, teach how to search for and find withheld truth. I had to have a piece of paper labeled diploma in order to enter this so-called house of learnin where Black children are shut off, shut out and shut up, forced to study the history of their white conquerors, this peculiar place of white facts, white questions, white answers, and white final exams. I couldn't explain it to my father, because Grandpa's Garveyism had skipped right over his head and landed on me. I left Dad to enjoy what he had, the Saturday night poker game, Sunday mornins with stained-glass angels, lodge meetins, all the rituals which kill time from one holiday to the next. We saw the New Year in by eatin peas and rice for good luck. If peas and rice were lucky, we'd be free! My folks had the Fourth of July at the beach, Thanksgivin Day with my aunt in the country. Misery was almost sweet, plenty of finger-poppin and dancin—in between folks bein killed, chased, shot at, segregated. I finger-popped along with the rest and ate my share of souse[2] and sweet potato pie. But I had me a plan, Nigeria Greene was gonna be the Black Messiah of the classroom, gonna light the way with Blackness. I try to do it. I try, like Nat Turner[3] said, "because it pleases me to try."

But, as I was sayin, Cohen, across the hall from me, is not to be believed. Give him his due, he teaches hard, when kids leave his room, they take somethin with them, even if it's a lie. He has a tough hide to take what some-a these roughs can put on you, but spends mosta his time tryin to undo what I taught the term before. Mainly, he wants to make it clear that he's "not the one" who's doin us in. I've heard him sing that chorus so many times.

"Yes, there were slave masters, but *I'm* not a slave master. Yes, there is exploitation, but *I'm* not an exploiter. There are good and bad in all races. Skin color has nothing to do with social wrongs, all groups have been enslaved...."

I have to get my class strong enough to weather his storm. I've confronted him about this time after time. "Hey," I'd say, "why you messin up minds? What you layin on my people? Sound like you teachin us to sing a new song... 'God bless segregation and all that it's done for me.'"

He gave me a lotta sass. "Why do you slang talk?" he says. "Are you trying to prove that you're one of the elite underprivileged?"

"Right on," I said. "I'm one of the underprivileged, and I dig Black talk, I smile Black, think Black, walk Black, and all the Black that's not yet discovered is out there waitin for me to find it. You get off my kids!"

We go on like that sorta half jokin but meanin to draw blood with every dig. The oldest white folks' strategy is to attack a person in a way that looks fair. Dig how the Indians got washed away and labeled "hostile." It shakes Cohen to his boots when he hears me ask, "What time is it?" And the class hollers out, "It's nation time!" I'm teachin that it's high time to straighten up and hold hands because my inner clock is tellin me that now is only half past slavery.

I'm only hopin they can *hear* me. The enemy has turned off so many eardrums till some of us now hear only through the bloodstream. No stuff, brains and ears are turned off for the duration! If somethin *feels* good or puts

---

2 *souse*   pork pickled in brine.
3 *Nat Turner*   (1800–1831) executed leader of a failed American slave rebellion.

CHILDRESS

*A Hero Ain't
Nothin' but a
Sandwich
Nigeria
Greene*

him to sleep, that's all the turned-off brother needs to keep him quiet as the grave until grave time comes.

When I use this segregation they have laid on us, use it to bring us closer and wiser in Blackness, Cohen screams about "segregation in reverse!" I held a two-period rap session on that accusation. "How come it is," I say, "that when whitey pushes us off to one side through law and mass muscle, that is segregation, but when we get to usin our enforced togetherness, they call it 'segregation in reverse'?" Then I go to cookin on the subject and clarify for them. "What they mean," I say, "is that when segregation works against us, that's what it's suppose to do, so it's in forward, but when it starts to work against *them*, it's in reverse, meanin that it's goin the wrong way. You see, whitey is not ever gonna say *he* is bein segregated against, that would be too much like what happens to *me*. That's how come it is he yells that it's goin into 'reverse.'" When the hurtin is on us, it's in forward; on him it's in reverse.

Three teachers, two *Negroes* and one white, made complaints to the principal, the gripe was that I am "creating an atmosphere" which breeds hostility. I told them there would be hostility in this school if I had never been born. Dig?

Cohen wasn't in on the complaint because he tries not to stick his head in an electric fan when it's turned on. He also remembers how we almost went to swingin fists when he complained about my givin spellin lessons instead of stickin to history and civics. I challenged all the "expert" opinion that "inner city" children can't read. I told my class, "Yall can read and write, so don't hand me no jive. When I go in the toilet and note the handwritin on the wall, I have yet to see 'fuck you' and 'shit' spelled wrong, nor have I had any hardship in understandin those lines scrawled bout who did what to who, so if you can read and write dirty words, you damn sure can read and write all the rest."

Cohen's complaint resulted in the principal givin me a talk about "decency and morality in teachin methods due to the vulnerability of the young. . ." and so forth and so on. I wasn't ready for that, not ready for any white principal from a suburban-split-level-livin-segregated-Anglo-Saxon neighborhood to question my morality values, specially when he's makin his daily bread in a dirt-poor, so-called Black Community and spends his pay in West Park Gardens Drive, or wherever the hell else he buses out to when the bell rings at three o'clock. I cooked on him, "It's middle-class suburbanites who have been makin all the immorality news here of late," I say, "the ones playin switch partners with one another's wives. We, in the ghetto, think it's not nice to do that kinda thing. You folks got slum minds."

I give Cohen lots of air and plenty good room except to keep him in line when he needs it. My wife tells me to cool it and don't try to change the world all at once. Maybe I need some criticism, but so in hell does she. Why does she go to fashion shows? The community is fulla these clubwomen givin fashion shows at downtown white hotels. Who cares what kinda lace somebody is wearin with their silver fox jacket? Too many hardworkin chicks spendin bread and time on white satin with ermine linin and all that crap. When I read the Black press, I almost choke. Constantly givin champagne sips and one-hundred-dollar-a-plate dinners and costume balls and comin-out parties. Comin out from where? Our folks holdin meets and dances down at the Bunny Club. Why would a woman wanta look like a fur tail is growin outta her butt?

CHILDRESS

*A Hero Ain't
Nothin' but a
Sandwich*
Nigeria
Greene

Oh, so much gets to me! I keep seein this kid, Benjie, noddin over his desk when I pass Cohen's room, justa-sleepin and hangin. I walk in, look him over, and walk out. Cohen is gettin hot under the collar; so am I. Finally, I take Cohen to one side and tell him the boy looks stoned. He gives me the TV line. "Kids sit up all night watching late TV, when they get to school they have to rest—"

I cut him off. "Don't run that game on me," I say. "Let's take him downstairs and turn him in."

Cohen pulls stubborn on me. "This is a class," he says. "I'm not turning in anybody. The parents get upset, the principal gets upset, the kid feels betrayed."

"Right," I say, "but let all that happen rather than see the boy dead, let's don't kill him outta the kindness of our hearts."

We look Benjie over and spot a couple of needle marks. I say, "You been into anything you shouldn't, little brother?"

Kid says, "I'm cool, Nigeria." But his cool is too stoned. Cohen and I take him down to Principal and request notification of parents. Benjie backs up ugly and says, "You a traitor, man! Yall pickin on me cause I'm Black." He really cut up, called me a Oreo Cookie, that's Black on the outside and white on the inside. I wanta knock him down, cause that's my nature, but instead I take his bad mouthin.

Newspaper item:

Fabulous Fashion Show and Dance

The La Paloma Femme de la Jours held their ninth annual ball, fashion show, and champagne sip downtown at the gorgeous Metropolitan-Cadrington Arms Hotel on Saturday last. The Royalty Room, of which there is no whicher, was decorated with amazingly lifelike silver and white doves, their feathered wings stretched in full flight. Each bird bore a white orchid in its golden beak. Ten silvery, gleaming, electric fountains spouted out the bubbly, to make a most magnificent merry for a very worthy cause.

The best-known names from political, social, literary and entertainment worlds were present as snowflakes in a blizzard. Three bands, rock, jazz, and calypso, played a variety of now and then sounds. Our illustrious mayor made a gracious, albeit belated, entrance to commend the La Paloma Femme de la Jours for their compassionate, humanitarian work. Finally, the president of the elite club presented a $250 check to Mrs. Nigeria Greene, the lovely treasurer of the Friends of Drug Fighters Alliance.

ROSE JOHNSON (CRAIG)

Benjie's Mother

I TRY to keep the neighbors out of my business because every friend has a friend, and if I can't keep a secret, how can I ask them not to tell what I told? When you're full of silent troubles, people sometimes think you're crazy or standoffish. They talkin to me bout two-for-one food sales at the supermarket, and I'm answerin, "Oh, that's too bad, you have my deepest sympathy." That's because another person just told me about a death in the family. My mind stays confused these days. Well, maybe troubles should not be kept secret, might be better if we shout from the housetop, but everybody is too ashamed and so we ha-ha at trouble . . . to keep from lettin on.

There's a woman downstairs from me whose husband beats on her like he's fightin for the heavyweight crown, but she tells people she tripped on the sidewalk. Cross the hall is a neighbor who's coughin up his lungs, but he keeps talkin bout his "asthma" and buyin cough syrup and nose spray. Top-floor apartment got a young daughter who's expectin, with no husband in sight, and they talkin bout him bein in the service. Then there's Emma Dudley, chasin after every man she sees while tellin us how many she has to turn down. All tryin not to see what's here to be seen. But each and every one is blessed beyond understandin, cause they don't have a child who's on drugs—like I got.

The school brought me the news, but I had been suspicious before, but the thing seemed to get by me because you hate for a child to believe you always thinkin somethin's wrong. Maybe I haven't been takin enough time with Benjie since meetin Butler, my common-law husband, but Butler's been takin time. He bought tickets for a ball game so they could go together like father and son; I'da gone too, but here lately my mother been turnin on the gas and for-gettin to light it with the matches, another time she left bath water runnin and flooded the downstairs apartment. Butler is not one of those men who can't stand the stepchild because it's not his. He'd be crazy about Benjie if only the boy would let himself be liked, but the child is contrary and actin like he can't stand anybody.

Benjie was on the way at the time Big Benny and I got married. My in-laws had a fit because, as they put it, "He's young and has the whole world before him." Wonder what they thought was in front of me . . . besides a baby? I've seen it time and time again . . . folks feelin like their sons are gettin bad deals when their girlfriends get pregnant. I bet that's why families don't wish for girl babies much, cause they can grow up and get pregnant. People like boy children cause they can carry on the family name and also cause they are not the ones who ever have to have babies. I have even seen folks put she-cats out cause they're gonna have kittens. When kittens and puppies do get born, everybody wants a male one, if they want to take any a-tall.

Mama made me haul Big Benny into court. I had to almost cry blood before they awarded me fifteen dollars a week. Ben would pay one week and skip two; finally, I stopped goin to court about it, and the payments went down from once in a while to never. Mama had to put most of her money in the house for rent and food. Truth be told, it was her apartment in the first place. I went out to the factory . . . sewin on a power machine, turnin out flags and pennants for base-ball games and political rallies.

CHILDRESS

*A Hero Ain't
Nothin' but a
Sandwich*
The
Principal

A few years back I took on a extra job helpin out a caterer on weekends, servin private dinner parties, weddings, anniversaries, and like that; that's how I met Butler. He was servin drinks so he could save up for a car. Poor fella never managed to get his car. He was a Godsend to me in more ways than one. He's who I shoulda met in the first place, but I never did do anything right the first time around. Butler was the one lucky break in my life. Mama likes him too except for one or two matters. Fact is, he's the only one I've met that she could stand a-tall. She was so mad bout the way Ben treated me till she feared for me to trust anybody again.

I love Butler, from when I met him four years ago, right on up to this very day. No matter how our troubles go, I shall love him right on for all that he has been and done for me. He is my dependable love through thick and thin. He is strong and dark like cigar tobacco, and always ready to put himself out to help another person, to try and see things from their point of view. He looks good. When he laughs, his eyes crinkle shut and he slaps his hands together because he's enjoyin that laugh like it's the best thing in the world. When we go to the beach, I like to sit under the beach umbrella so I can watch him take that first dip in the water by himself. His body is firm and tough from hard work. He gets up, stretches his arms in the air, then says, "Wellllllll, guess I'll get me some-a this water, try it out, see if it's too cold for you chickens." He goes runnin down to the water's edge and plunges in without toe testin, goes right in over his head, and comes up with a whoop, a holler, and a laugh, "Wow! Cooooold!" That's how he does bout everything. Butler says, "If you into somethin, *be* in it." Nobody has to sit up nights wonderin and guessin what he means.

Me without a divorce, last year we just did the best we could, made a life together without legal papers. He is standin by my side before these teachers, social workers, and doctors without anything legal to back him up. If you don't think that's doin a lot, try dealin with officials. They are legal crazy! The worst sin in the world is fine with them if it's legal.

I wish I knew how to talk to Benjie. I feel shy or ashamed when I want to speak my real feelins. Be fine to tell him that something nice can happen for *him* in life, something like how it is with me and Butler. One day I almost said it . . . after goin over the words in my mind, "Benjie, the greatest thing in the world is to love someone and they love you too." But when I opened my mouth, I said, "Benjie, brush the crumbs off your jacket."

A child thinks his mother should be a mother and nothin else. Trouble is they been taught, all of us been taught, that love is for squares. Guess me and Butler don't look very special in his eyes . . . just a plump lady and a hardworkin man goin along doin their best.

THE PRINCIPAL

WALKING through these corridors, I remind myself that in three years I'll be ready for retirement. I have done some good in my time and would like to leave with my sanity and pension. I look forward to peaceful moments in which to write the definitive book on better methods of education.

In this school we have Blacks, whites and Spanish-speaking students and teachers. Our assembly programs have been planned to cover them all and the topics of the day, civil rights, economics, Vietnam, the vote, the draft, racism,

CHILDRESS

*A Hero Ain't
Nothin' but a
Sandwich*
The
Principal

nationalism, Communism, Socialism, welfare, homosexualism, women's rights, transvestism, a free Puerto Rico, Pan Africanism, the UN, Black capitalism, Zionism, Cuba, China, the Soviet Union, the religions of mankind, and so forth and so on. There aren't enough weeks in the year to cover the subjects. There must also be time slots for holiday celebrations, Christmas, Chanukah, Lincoln's and Washington's birthdays, Easter and Passover, Mother's Day and Yom Kippur, Columbus Day, Thanksgiving Day, and Brotherhood Week. In this school we also observe the birthdays of Martin Luther King, Jr., and Malcolm X, Puerto Rican Heritage Week, and Afro-American Culture Week. This morning I received a delegation requesting assembly programs for the observation of Oriental and Eastern cultures.

We manage to have a track team, a school band, a student newspaper, a Parent-Teacher Association, a Committee of Concerned Parents, a karate class, and an adult-education evening program.

I have outlived two teachers' strikes, three student rebellions, and one community riot. In the past few years theft has become a deepening problem. We have suffered the loss of office equipment, sports equipment, and even our American flag was stolen from the assembly platform. Anything that can be sold is likely to be stolen. I keep wondering: Who would want to buy a "hot" flag?

Handling teachers requires much tact. Mr. Cohen regularly threatens to leave. He is not the most diplomatic person I've ever met, and yet, mysteriously, the highest percentage of good readers come out of Cohen's class.

Mr. Nigeria Greene is definitely a Black Nationalist problem. It's all I can do to restrain him from painting his classroom walls black, red, and green—according to him, "Black for our color, green for the land to which we must return, and red for the blood which must be spilled to attain it." He has fashioned a philosophy from equal parts of democratic socialism and Garveyism, both generously sprinkled with the sayings of Mao Tse-tung.

He has fewer dropouts and less absenteeism than any other class, the highest library attendance, and his boys are the backbone of our track team. Bernard Cohen and Nigeria Greene do not get along very well, but the kids fare a bit better because they're both here.

Drugs may be illegally purchased anywhere, but there is an immediate, negative reaction on the part of the public when any specific school is mentioned by press or television. In one school a boy died from an overdose of drugs, picket lines surrounded the block, and the public clamored for a change of principal and staff members. Then came protests from citizen committees and the churches. When it all blew over, everything became as it was before, nothing changed, nothing accomplished. Parents are afraid of the dealers who poison their children; parents are afraid of their children. I share the same fears.

Experience has taught me to avoid the subject, except for the occasions when we have a scheduled visiting speaker who gives us an assembly talk on drug abuse. Very often the speaker is an ex-addict. I get an uncomfortable feeling that he is being projected as a heroic figure, and I fear that some of our students may see drugs as something to use and then bravely give up. The speaker does not mention that he is one in a hundred who was able to kick the habit . . . after all, it is the nature of each human being to think of himself as a one-in-a-hundred person.

We think of poverty as a condition simply meaning a lack of funds, no money, but when one sees fifth, sixth, and seventh generation poor, it is clear

CHILDRESS

*A Hero Ain't
Nothin' but a
Sandwich*
The
Principal

that poverty is as complicated as high finance. One gradually learns begrudgingly to respect the poverty-stricken: They have endurance; they push their vitamin-starved bodies on and on from one day to another; they continue to stand up under humiliation and abuse. Some buy ridiculous, high-priced, impractical clothing . . . on the installment plan, hoping to hide poverty behind fake prosperity. The racketeers swagger; they strut; putting on a show of indifference, looking down on the rest. They exploit each other, bleeding the weakest to obtain gaudy consumer goods for themselves, "the Cadillac poor," trapped, caught fast here, forced to live side by side with their victims. Seeing these things, all I can do is push education while the pusher pushes heroin.

Cohen and Nigeria brought the boy to my office. Those two men who have never seen eye to eye on anything got together to bring one more straw to this poor camel's back. The boy's face told the story; he had turned us off, and now we had the job of turning him in. I did it smoothly. His grandmother came first, giving us a long lecture on the ways of God; his mother and stepfather took him to Harlem Hospital with my signed referral for detoxification.

Each day I remember to praise honor and dignity, celebrate worthy heroes . . . and bear in mind that I shall soon reach the haven of retirement. No matter what I do or don't do there are drug addicts.

Newspaper item:

Drugs Available in Local Schools!

It has come to the attention of this reporter that drugs are readily available in at least one local grade school. One child, age thirteen, was spirited out of the building while heavily under the influence of narcotics. The principal is obviously trying to avoid scandal and responsibility by hushing up the incident. When we tried to reach him by telephone, he was "not available" according to a woman who nervously identified herself as a "clerk" in the office.

Certainly all concerned parents should protest this state of affairs to city, state, and federal officials. Our children must not be further victimized by ruthless pushers and timid school officials. Those incapable of guarding youngsters within the school should resign or be removed regardless of tenure. Community organizations, what say you? It is time to strike out against death! It is time to . . .

WALTER

CHILDRESS

*A Hero Ain't
Nothin' but a
Sandwich*
Walter

The Pusher

THE pusher, the pusher, that's all you hear! They don't call no other sales-man a pusher, but that's what he natural is . . . a pusher, no matter what he's sellin. Your TV set is fulla pushers tellin you to run right out and buy cake, candy, cars, soft drinks, beer, pies, and whatever the hell else they can talk you into buyin. Dig it, *they're* the pushers, not me. I don't push cause I don't haveta! These early-risin junk men be lookin for me, dig? I ain't said for them to "run right out" and buy nothin! But they runnin, and if they can't find me, they gonna find somebody else fast. Push? You outta your head? I don't let em know where the hell I live else they'd be clawin and knockin at my door, or in the street scratchin theyself and callin up at my winda, "Hey, Walter!"

Alla these cryin-Emma social workers rap out lyin jive bout the "poor ad-dict." Dig it, ain't nobody ever held down nobody else and shot him in the vein. The damn law is fix to give a "user" less time for pushin than a "nonuser." Dig it, nonuser means clean, and that's what I am. I don't shoot no shit in my arm! I handle it, look at it, cut it, sell it, and risk having my ass thrown underneath some lonesome jail, but I don't shoot up in myself and don't sniff nothin either, cause I damn sure know it'll eat the linin outta my nose. Dig on, I have tole junkies how skag blows health and mind! Like the cigarette pushers print on the package how it can do you harm, that's how I tell what junk can do. Talk bout tracks on your arm—hell, man, tracks ain't nothin. Your vein will close up tight and then you gotta find another vein to hit. You oughta dig some ulcerated sores, them that's got runnin holes in they arms and legs!

If I quit pushin tomorrow; you think any junkie is gonna do without his poi-son cause I didn't show? You need a straitjacket if you do! From city to city, town to town, from block to block and house to house, there is someone who will get you anything you want, if you got money! Talk bout pushin, I'm pushin for cops, when you get right down to it. You heard me! When I pay off, what the hell you think I'm payin with? Payin him outta my sales. I got to hustle ten bags before I can pay the fuzz five singles, dig? So I'm pushin for the law. If he hands on a little taste to the next fuzz-on-high, who's collectin offa him, that means I'm out here pushin for both of em, dig it? Been days when I paid off in front, before sellin even one bag—that's how rough the game is played. No, I didn't say *all* cops; all I can tell bout is who I pay. But dig this, when you pay fuzz, you ain't spendin much time wonderin who's like this and who's like that; the cat you pay is where your mind's at. What I know is I got cops pimpin off me.

You may's well sell to kids cause if you don't, they get some grown junkie to get it for them, and he's gonna take a cut outta they bag for hisself. No pain, I feel no pain bout this soft-hearted song they singin bout the "kid" who's an ad-dict. If I had me a kid, his Black ass would be home in bed at night, in the day he'd be in school, and I'd trouble myself to see to it, dig? I wouldn't be shufflin no soft-shoe dance and callin for the thorities! Trouble is, these torn-ass parents want me to be lookin out for their children while they mama is out on the street playin the single action. Their papa, if they got one, is drummin up sixty-seven cent for a pinta wine! If you don't believe me, stand round and dig the scene. They want me to be the baby-sitter!

I don't feel sorry for a livin! If I was to get bumped or go to jail for life, these crackers who own the world and all what's in it would go right on doin like they been doin, just as if my ass had never been born. They haulin horse[1] into the States by the ton . . . ain't most of it gettin here in nobody's suitcase, or sewed up in a dollbaby . . . that's some dumb-ass idea yall done picked up from TV.

Sometime I feel sorry for a guy who's carryin a monkey, but I don't feel sorry long. Feelin sorry ain't good for business. Junkies be wearin out my feelins and gettin into me for a free fix. Oh, yeah, yall don't hear bout the times you trust the lyin-ass, knowin damn well that soon's he gets a buck, he's gonna deal with somebody else and duck you till he run outta shoe leather. It's like this, weak is weak, when some dude is weak and keep feedin his weakness, he's done for! Yeah, he is, I say it's all over but the service and the flowers. Most times ain't gonna be no wreath cause they gonna plant him in a pine box that don't cost no more than the price-a two fixes, the state give him that free on-the-house, then they dump him with the rest of the unknown dead, inna big hole, and plow em all down together. If the niggas stuck together that close when they was alive, they could move the world. Potter's field,[2] that's where they get together.

Yeah, some do *kick*, but ain't but so many can do it. Although they all can walk round leanin over, scratchin, noddin, and talkin bout what they *gonna* do, I give em encouragement. "Do it man!" I say. "Do your thing!" I be sayin that while I'm slidin their next fix outta my sham cigarette pack. But when I be callin them weak, I still don't mean dumb, even though they into a dumb action. Some junkies supersmart. They talkin baaaaaaaaad, they rap out the history of the world, and tell what it's gonna take to get whitey's foot offa your neck, and what is a revolution, and what mistakes was made by Garvey, King, and Malcolm . . . but they can't keep their veins closed, dig? So they be rappin and noddin and boostin and buyin and comin out here every mornin funkier and more raggedy than the day before. Yeah, they walk that fallin-forward walk, that slack-kneed shuffle, tippy-toein along, eyes searchin round to see if somebody put down somethin they can pick up and sell.

When a mainliner is high, he feelin biggety with nothin to feel biggety bout. His underarm might have a sore in there, or he got a abscess on his gum or his groin, or he got maybe a case-a the double syphilis, could be his bowel ain't moved in two-three weeks cause horse constipates . . . but he's grinnin and rappin bout his groove. What the hell you want from me? He killin himself in his own way. It's a free country, right? If the nigga ain't gonna be or do nothin, he may's well nod away. Let him hold up his mama to keep with his habit . . . so long he don't hold *me* up. If one lay his hand on me, I'll kill him quicker than skag. I hate the nigga most much as I'm hatin myself; the both of us ain't had no more sense than to be born Black in the middle of some big white action.

I ain't the only one hustlin! Woman down the street is writin small-time policy . . . that big, fat-ass Black sista sit there eatin a dozen pig feet and five poundsa greasy potata salad—man, that's just her lunch! Come dinner she send her kid to the corner to buy four ordersa ribs with the hot sauce and french fries. She got her number customers lookin up their dreams in a "dream" book . . . pawnin their weddin rings to play the daily single action . . . tryin to hit that digit. Children got nothin to eat in the house . . . they livin offa Kool-Aid and crackers, plus what they can lift . . . while moms is waitin for the big "hit." Kids meanwhile comin down with ringworm and pellagra. Everybody lookin for a quick miracle . . . some easy kinda way to make it without buggin whitey too much.

---

1 *horse* heroin.
2 *Potter's field* generic term for a public burial place for the indigent and unidentified.

CHILDRESS

*A Hero Ain't
Nothin' but a
Sandwich*
Benjie
Johnson

Don'tcha know that if a fix could fix things, I'd shoot skag myself? Nothin is for free . . . not even a *feelin.* Some-a these whiteys usin horse cause they feelin bad bout how good it's suppose to be for them but they seein how it ain't goin down that way. The parents done sent big brother's ass off to get murdered . . . smiled and waved "good-bye" to the boys. "Send him to the Army, that'll keep him outta trouble." They pushin war, dig it? Ain't no way to live without pushin somethin. They ain't stopped horse from ridin through the Army—or any-wheres else.

Me, I say screw the weak and screw the power. If it's call free enterprise, then let it be free. Nother thing, if I had my way bout it, I wouldn't be related to a Black-ass nigga on this earth. All them that wanta die let em put a five in my pocket, and I'll help em to slowly make it on outta here, with a smile on their face . . . and one on mine. Less of them makes more room for me! The hell with the junkie, the wino, the capitalist, the welfare checks, the world . . . yeah, and fuck you, too!

BENJIE JOHNSON

I T LIKE bein in jail. They askin questions and keep askin the same ones, then go on to somethin else, then final double back and ask the first question when they think you mixed up and forgot what you said. The mainest thing they wanta know is how and where I got skag. You can get it just bout anyplace, but I ain't gonna squeal . . . and even if I did, the connection might not be there when they go to check him out. Sometime he ain't there when *I* get there. Con-nections float and change their scene, if they don't they'll get washed away in a sudden clean-up action.

What I did, I did, I don't blame anybody. Anyway, only one I know who's a connection is a fella name Walter. I met him through a guy call Tiger. Me and a boy name Carwell, we cut school and went up to Tiger's pad to buy us a joint to smoke. It ain't really Tiger's pad all to hisself. Is his aunt's house. She be out workin a sleep-in job and come home only once-twice a week. Tiger's mother is in a hospital gettin over some kinda breakdown, so this place is just bout like al-most his own. Tiger is fifteen and a baaaaad cat. Tiger is makin hisself money. If you know somebody, like I know Carwell, they can get you into Tiger's place cause they known to Tiger. It's comfortable and pleasant if you need a place to be when you cut school. When you cut, you got to go someplace, and it's hard to sit in some abandon apartment buildin that's rattysmellin and cold. If you try to get into a pitcher show, they will turn you away if it's a weekday and before three o'clock, that's cause they can lose they license. If you go in the park and try to sit it out in the cold, the plainclothesmen might pick you up. They got plainclothes and uniform fuzz who do nothin but go round the park and see who they can catch that might be up to somethin. They will pick you up and ask how come you not in school. The Black ones do it just like the white. Carwell say a pig is a pig no matter what color. So you kinda lost if you cuttin and got no place to wait it out till after three.

We went up to Tiger's. He don't charge you nothin for comin in, and it's a nice, clean, warm place, with a good record player and a TV. Tiger got wall-to-wall on the floor and drapes at the window . . . also venetian blinds . . . the bathroom got pink shower curtains with green sailboats all over it. Is one fine-lookin place. Tiger don't allow no gamblin, or dancin, or girl action and like

CHILDRESS

*A Hero Ain't
Nothin' but a
Sandwich*
Benjie
Johnson

that. Tiger say he don't wanta wise the neighbors and turn them gainst him by havin noise goin on. Fellas just be sittin round havin a smoke, they buy the joints offa Tiger. You can also buy little cake and candy and bottle-a Pepsi. Tiger say he keep the operation small so he can quick clear the place when his aunt comin home for her time-off days. On them time-off days she be hangin more fine curtains, cleanin, and waxin everything neatly and makin pillows and slip covers. Carwell say she hopin to someday be home and joy her fine-lookin house for Christmas and other holidays. Tiger got special afternoons when he sell dogs with pickle and mustard. But whenever it's his aunt's time-off day, he puts a red sticker on the wall in the downstairs stairs vestibule. If you go to his apartment when the sticker is up, he open the door and say in a loud voice, "Man, you got the wrong place, ain't no Tiger live here!" His for-real name is Gerald, but nobody call him that except his aunt and teachers at the school. When he talks loud and winks his eye, you know not to stand round and give trouble.

So this time when we went up to Tiger's, there was boys sittin round on the floor with works, they cookin horse and shootin up. Tiger say all that's happenin is a little skin-poppin. "Say, my man," Tiger say to Carwell, "why don't yall pop a taste and stop wastin your bread on gage[1] Smoke don't do nothin but make me burn up my strawberry incense tryin to put down the smell."

Everybody laugh and Carwell say, "No man, I ain't ready for that, me and smoke is doin all right."

Slick-lookin, light-skin boy name Kenny who live over near my block, he say, "Fact is, Carwell, we gonna call you Chicken Little."

Nother fella say, "Don't be so hard on him, man, maybe he tryin to set a good zample for his little titty-fro[2] friend."

Since it was me they callin titty-fro, I thought I'd try they bluff. I was really hopin they wouldn't gimme none, but I say, "Kenny, I'd take a light hit, but I ain't got but seventy-five cents."

Tiger look me over and say, "Right on!" Then he tell the fella that's doin the shootin, "Give the little man a hit, don't make it but a touch, cause we don't want no amachures to overdose on us." I was out there then and had to go it on through or else look like a big mouth who had to back down. Kenny gave me a toucha the needle, and first it seem like nothin was goin on, then next I was hot and cold and my heart went to boppin fast and my head drew tight. They was all watchin and Tiger say, "Damn, man, you got nerve."

I say, "Shit, ain't nothin."

Kenny say, "It might make you puke, kid."

I laugh and wave my hand like I know the score. I say, "Well, sometime life be that way." They fallin out laughin and diggin me like crazy.

I like how they watchin me and payin their respeck, lookin at me like they know somebody fine when they see him—and not just sittin back like I'm nobody. I kept waitin to be sick, but I wasn't. My head got to feelin funny, and after while I went to the bathroom, just in case, but all I felt was queasy and strange. Guess shootin is for feelin nothin. I didn't care what and just sat there, my heart thumpin inside and me wonderin. Every time I thought bout home, my mama come to mind. She is really okay. Gotta admit I dig that Butler sometime too. But they don't need me round. On Satday when they be joyin their

---

1 *gage* marijuana.
2 *titty-fro* baby.

day off, they goin out to the movies and say to me, "Hey, you wanta go to the show, too?" They always say "too," and when they say it, I'm thinkin that me as the one more would be one too many. I always say, "No, I got me a TV thing I wanta see." But, dig it, who wanta be the extra one goin along to eyeball some picture bout Black people bein poor? I dig movies where people got high-rise hotels and where they be international spies wearin they fine suits and hoppin big planes from one airport to nother, cats walkin like they in a Western even though they livin in the city, they walk that walk and look like they ain't never gonna let nobody bug them . . . and they got them fine good-quality guns stuck down in they belts. That's what I call a movie, Jack!

Sometime my mama and Butler almost be like a real movie, they laugh and hurry out the door like they got some wild, crazy secret and like everybody else is out of it, you know? She wear them tight, pretty, silky dresses with sequins and beads on the neck and sleeve, and smellin so good with perfume. He fine and neat in his navy blues. When they hit the sidewalk, he's holding up his hand and whistlin for a taxi like he the King of New York; me and Grandma be lookin out the window all excited cause they done turn us on with their fine way of going out. Grandma say, "Oh, joy! That's what you call happy!" But all of a sudden I'm wonderin in my mind, what they need with me? What they need with Grandma? What they need with anybody? I feel like a accident that happen to people. My blood father cut out on Mama. Musta gone cause he didn't dig me. Mama look at me lotta times and say, "My God, you look just like Big Benny, just like him." Her eyes be sad when she say it. Other times she studyin my face lookin like bout to say somethin, she almost say it, then wave her hand and say, "Never mind." She sayin never mind cause it's me. She don't say that to Butler.

I ask Grandma, "How come Mama gotta be whisperin and talkin secrets in Butler's ear all the time?"

Grandma say, "That's man-woman, and you haven't grown to know bout that yet."

I know I got a real father somewhere, and I bet Butler feelin biggety cause he's here and my real father is gone. I look at Butler quick sometime so I can catch him lookin biggety, but he slick enough to stay cool-lookin.

Sittin in Tiger's pad, I'm latchin onto some heavy thoughts and diggin how smart I really am. I don't care nothin a-tall bout nobody's next move . . . not even mine!

After that, some days I went for a hit, other days I didden, was justa off-and-on thing. Sometime, after a score, I'd be wishin there was a school examination test gonna take place cause I felt like it'd be easy to pass—but soon I'd get sleepy and don't care to blow my wig on no questions. Just sittin, feelin nothin, no pain. One day I thought it would be a groove to go by Tiger's and do my second or third mainline, just for a way to pass some time, dig? He got the red stamp up on the downstairs wall, but I go on past that cause now my patience is gettin tired of all this jive bout his aunt and her sleep-in job and all. Either you in somethin or you ain't, right?

I ring the bell and feelin evil when he hassles me bout how I got the wrong place. I don't move a inch cause I ain't one-a his chickens. I say, "Man, gimme some action and no stories." He look at me like he gonna go up side my head, but somethin told him to cool it.

He slip me a name and address and tell me, "Just say 'Tiger and Kenny—they my boons.' Thass our secret, okay?"

CHILDRESS

*A Hero Ain't
Nothin' but a
Sandwich*
Benjie
Johnson

The address turn out to be a candy store, but ain't no fellow name Walter there, just a old guy wipin off the counter with a dirty rag. I say, "Where is Walter?" Old guy look mad when he hear me say that.

"Git out," old man say. "Walter might be on the sidewalk, but he ain't inside-a here. Got it?" I go outside and stand.

Then this skinny, lean cat come over from cross the street. "You lookin for somebody round here?" he ask.

I fall in with the high sign. "Tiger and Kenny, they my boons."

He laugh, "Where's your diaper?"

I flash the color of my money and say, "Cool me, that's what." He went in the candy store with me followin behind. Cooled me in the back room. The old guy still moppin the counter, but he lookin scared like the worst chicken in the world.

"You more man than Tiger and Kenny put together." Walter lookin satisfy with me, he say, "Bring me some cash-in-advance customers, and I'll treat you right bout whatever you need . . . bring cash and you'll get yours, plus you won't ever be broke."

So that gave me two places to go, and that's how it is, one place leads to another, and soon you can score anytime you wants. You can walk up to a stranger and say, "My old man gotta score, or he gonna kill me." If you picked the wrong cat, he don't know what you talkin bout or will say, "Get outta my face!" But if you picked the right one, he'll take your bills and leave your stuff on a garbage can cover or drop it behind a old box that might be sittin there. They don't wanta be seen layin nothin in your hand. Ain't no trouble to find skag. So how can I say who did what and who is sellin? Right is right, I got some honor. Not like my main boon who cut out on me after we first lighted up together.

One time I say to Jimmy-Lee, "Hey, my man, let's go somewhere and smoke us a joint."

He say, "Man, I got somethin else for a dollar to do." Sure, when he was smokin, I smoked with him; then after I start, he quit. But that's OK, later for phonies! Meanwhile, back at the ranch, what's my stepfather doin? He drinkin his mash and talkin civil rights trash, like what all he would do if he was President of the U.S. of A. The nigga ain't nothin but a maintenance man! My mama busy makin him ham and egg sandwiches serve with cold beer. Grandma stompin her feet, singin "Near-o My God." Act like God is her chum-buddy. If God dig her so hard, how come she havin a tough time like everybody else? She keep sayin, "Pray, Benjie, pray for what you want." Later for the phonies! They all do some fool thing but want me perfect.

Now I'm layin up in this hospital bed tryin to keep my wits sharp so's not to put the whole neighborhood in jail by rattin on em when I get ast questions. This Black doctor wearin a white coat like a short-order cook, he comin round with the nurse, servin medicine. They also givin vitamin pills and shots in the butt, and I'm drinkin down glasses of funny-tastin stuff. Doctor try to act like a boon soul. I say, "What is this I gotta take?"

And he say, "Do you question the street dealer when he sells you a deck of horse mix with talcum?"

I look him in the eye and drink the medicine. Fellas in other beds watchin, so I say, "My mama never had no chickens."

Doc laugh and pinch my cheek so hard he almost draw blood. He say, "That's trankalizer." He lookin at me like ready to cry. I can't stand nobody treatin me like pitiful, I rather be kill, thassa fact.

CHILDRESS

*A Hero Ain't
Nothin' but a
Sandwich*
Benjie
Johnson

I'm feelin sleepy. The nurse givin butt shots. She say it's iron and vitamins. I'm sleepy too much. Wakin up and seein folks laughin while layin in their beds. My stomach sickly from trankalizer and vitamins . . . I'm tired and sad, feelin sometime hot and sometime cold. I wish I had me one friend, one who dig me the most and don't put anybody else ahead of me. Guess I'm in this sad world all by myself. Nobody care, why should they if your own daddy run off? They don't mean no harm, they can't help it. Trouble is this, too many folks expeck other folks to be carin bout them when it ain't no-way possible. So I'm layin here learnin how to expeck nothin. My toes, ankles, and legs look skinny and ashy dark. A narrow-face, yaller-headed white boy is in the bed cross the way, lookin at me like he wanta say somethin, but he waitin for me to be the one to speak first. I ain't gonna ast him shit. He don't go to my school and don't live round here. Layin in our hospital, he oughta speak first. I been through the hot and cold shivers, the head shrinks, and the visitor hour, so damn if I'm gonna make over him and be astin things. How come he can't ast me? Everybody always waitin to see where I'm comin from. I don't feel like before skag and don't feel skagged . . . feel old and beat, feelin jumpy and scared. I don't know what I'm scared of. I don't like bein scared-a nothin. My mama didn't have no chickens, you know.

BENJIE JOHNSON

A T HOME now for a week. They got my room fix up with a new bedspread and curtains. Bedspread got green rabbits on it, curtains just plain blue with nothin. I'm too old for rabbits, but blue curtains look groovy. House now quieter than ever before. Everybody polite to each other and tiptoein round. We got two kindsa ice cream, also fruit and cookies in the house. All talkin to me like I'm some stranger from outer space. "You really lookin fine." They keep sayin it. Grandma look at me and wag her finger. "You a *good* boy, Benjie, just good as can be." I don't wanta talk. I'm tryin to think how to do better and do what the soul doctor say: "Start anew, son." He's not the worst person in the world, you know.

I told him, "I don't do nothin right in the first place much less doin it *anew*."

"The world ain't perfect," Soul doctor say. "But hard as it is, life is still sweet. Dig life. That's why I'm a doctor, because I dig life."

My so-call stepfather, Butler, come in the room to have one-a them draggy heart-to-hearts. He tellin me how buddies is suppose to stick close to each other and tell and confide. All of a sudden my mama standin in the doorway listenin to how it's all goin down, so I move in and take over and say, "Relax, pal, you just a maintenance man—and we livin in a time when a hero ain't nothin but a sandwich—so don't strain yourself tryin to prove nothin." Butler turn round and ast Mama, "You wanta go over to the Paradise Bar for a cold brew so I can clear this boy outta my head?"

She say, "I'll go with you." When she talk to him, her voice rise up higher like she gonna sing a song. Mama act like Butler's Uncle Tom.

When they gone, I come out in the livin room and Grandma sittin there. "Boy, you all right?" she ast. I try to think up a serious thing to say that might be interestin to a old person. "Why is it," I ast, "that yall got bunnies on my bedspread but the curtains just plain? I like plain the best."

She snap me up somethin terrible, "Because," she say, "material *with* bunnies was three for a dollar and plain cost seventy-five cents a yard!" You can't be sociable with her. Then she holler bout how God knows she did her best when she use her "poor old hands" to make me bedspread and curtains. Ran in her room and slam the door, then lock it. Yeah, got a lock put on her door while I was in the hospital.

They can have back the spread and curtains, I'm too old for them fuckin bunnies anyway. I went in the bathroom, got down on the cold tile floor and prayed like never before in life, didn't pray no "Now I lay me down" like when I was a chile. "Please, God," I prayed, "send me a friend, someone to be crazy bout *me*. Pleeeeease, God!" I wait for like how Grandma say she get a *sign*. Nothin happenin but the sounds the faucet leakin. God somewhere else. I hit the bathtub so hard almost broke my hand.

I search for money. Ain't nothin in Mama's drawer, or the kitchen, or the bathroom, or anyplace. I open the closet door, and there is Butler's best suit and overcoat. I'm not gonna go on skag again, but I'm gonna main it one more time . . . so I'll remember what I'm givin up. I kicked once and I can kick anytime I wanta. Butler deserve to be punish, and she do too. He *livin* with my mama and makin out like he care bout me. They ain't ast me what I think bout them livin together. If she wanta live with somebody, why I gotta live with em too? If she separate from somebody, why I gotta separate? Bein a chile is bein a slave, and that's why I'm glad I ain't a chile no more. I'm takin his clothes; after all, he's takin my mama. Somebody who need the coat can use it, it'll do em some sincere good, and they'll gimmie a few dollars for myself. Damn, I ain't the worse person in the world.

One time I deliver some skag for Walter, and when I bring his money back, he give me a light fix for free. I don't believe in stealin, but my mama would sure rather I take Butler's things than go round pushin for Walter. Anyway, whatever anybody rather, I ain't never comin back. My real daddy don't want me and I'm damn sick and tireda havin Butler strainin to make out like he digs me and I'm his boon. It ain't true! It phony everywhere!

MISS EMMA DUDLEY

Neighbor

DEAR SISTER CLARA,

Hope these few words find you well. How is North Carolina these days? This neighborhood is getting closer to hell by the minute. I would gladly move back down home like you asked, but there is something about all that quiet that just seems to get to me. I have put out the word to try and get me a reliable male roomer, for the sake of income and protection. Me and my dog ain't enough. Woofie makes noise but thieves no longer fear dogs. I can't advertise in the newspaper for a roomer. I read about a woman takin in a stranger who went basurp[1] in the middle of the night and whacked her with a hatchet. She didn't die, but she'll never be the same.

I have to be careful who comes in my house, I'm still an attractive woman looking twenty years younger than my neighbors, but most of them got some

---

1 *went basurp*   went berserk (crazy).

kind of man and I haven't. Men are blind and don't know beauty and virtue when they see it. There's a fine-looking man living upstairs in this same apartment house . . . nicely built, hardworking, and carries himself with a manly air. Name is Butler Craig. Wouldn't you know he let himself get attached to a dumpy, plain woman they call Sweets. She's got a son named Benjie who is a thirteen-year-old junkie. Butler Craig always asks me about North Carolina because I once told him we have a family farm. I'd move back down home if I had a husband to keep me from bein lonely. Pray I get a man like this Butler.

Love,
YOUR SISTER EMMA

BUTLER CRAIG

LIVIN in the same house, but had to move downstairs. Miss Emma Dudley was nice enough to rent me space, and I do appreciate it, because she usually doesn't rent to people and I don't blame her. If I had a fine, quiet apartment to myself, I wouldn't rent out a room to a livin. There's somethin to be said for wakin up in the mornin all by yourself. You hear lotta blues songs bout bein lonesome; bet they weren't written by somebody who had to live boxed up with other people. It's also nice to wake up knowin that if you hung your overcoat in the closet last night, then it gotta still be hangin there this mornin; at least if it's gone, it had to be taken by somebody who broke in, and not by somebody who's livin there.

Miss Emma Dudley's got a police dog that'll bark you outta your head when you come near the front door. I had to get used to that.

"Don't pay him no mind, Mr. Butler," she say. "He just showin off. His bark is worse than his bite."

When somebody ring the bell, that dog, Woofie, runs down the length of the hall and throws hisself against the door like as if to break right on through it. I really had to get used to that.

Miss Emma Dudley came to my room door wearin a long pink, silk dress, the front cut down so low till look like any minute her knockers was gonna pop out and sing Glory Hallelujah. She's bringin a bottle of scotch, two glasses, and some snacks on a tray.

"Like to calm your nerves?" she say.

I didn't know what to answer, and before I could think up somethin, she's sittin on the foota my bed pourin drinks.

"I got a lovely, thick T-bone steak, if you're up to it," she say.

She goes chattin on bout this and that and how good her job is and bout the pension it will someday pay, smoothin her hands over her bosoms and pattin them back down in place, so they won't tumble over the fronta her dress.

Truth be known, I do feel like eatin a T-bone steak, and also gettin a little interested in anything else she might think up, but warnin signals are goin through my mind. You hear women complainin how they hate to go to dinner with a guy who's expectin some immediate return on his investment, but you don't hear bout the men who have eaten some woman's home cookin, and she's sittin there expectin him to, at least, marry her. Of course, in this case, there's more than cookin bein offered and advertised. Her charms are definitely on display, she's crossed her legs and hiked the pink dress up to her thigh, showin

613

black stockins look like made out of lace. And I see she has long, furry eye-lashes on . . . and battin them up and down while talkin. When she's laughin, she hold her head back and her mouth wide open, the overhead light is throwin 75 watts on her back, gold teeth. Miss Emma Dudley is a fine, flashy-lookin woman.

Bein by myself has its drawbacks. I miss Sweets. I feel like a fool goin up to see her whenever Benjie is out of the way, but I can't trust myself to face him. After me goin to school, seein teachers, psychiatrists, the police; after havin heart-to-hearts with him, to think he would rob me of my suit and overcoat. When he was in the hospital for detox, he said, "Don't nobody believe in me, Butler. If somebody believe in me, I swear I could do just fine. But nobody in the world believe in me no kinda way, bout nothin."

He was lookin so downhearted and sad. I felt sorry for him, *more* than sorry because his Grandma was goin on through visitin hour like she never gonna stop.

"A criminal, a thirteen-year-old, dope-fiend criminal. He's headin for the jailhouse. He stole my three dollars, and yall upheld him in it. It was mine, so yall didn't care that much!"

Everybody gets so excited until each talk turns into a ruckus. The social worker said to "discuss" together, didn't say to shout and accuse. What makes me mad is how we all get excited while Benjie sits there the coolest one. He asked to have somebody believe in him, so I went for it. When he came home, first thing I said was, "We gonna believe in you, son, you and me gonna be bud-dies through this, gonna be close together and come out winners."

All shook hands with each other, and each pledged how much each would do. Sweets' mama promised not to be pickin and naggin, and I promised to spend my free time with him to help beat temptation. I also gave the little double crosser the telephone number on my job, so he could call me in case he needed somebody real fast. Benjie had got to me so until I was fightin back tears, al-most boo-hooin out loud. Even went in the kitchen and made the son-bitch a milk shake with a egg in it. Was a feelin in the air like we had it made and was on the right track. Sweets' mama busied around doin nice things, brushin off his school jacket and sprinklin his sport shirt to iron it. We had it made. Sweets' mama say, "This feel like a true Christian home this evenin, really do." Once in a while you can have a perfect minute, a hot spot of time when you can say . . . that went well, proud of myself. It was like that for us, and he blew it again.

How much understandin can you have? I ain't God. If it's Sweets' fault or mine, all we can do is try . . . and I did that. She's still doin it, but I've had it. I knew it was time to get my hat before I lost control and killed the hard-headed junkie. Thirteen and forty-three ain't no match for each other. If I lay my hands on him, he'll be dead. I'm wore out from dealin with Benjie and holdin down a hardworkin job at the same time. I punch a time clock at seven every mornin, so that means rise and shine by five. I can't be stayin up till one A.M. beggin a boy to behave. My head is so full of Benjie till my mouth runs off to Miss Emma Dudley.

"Miss Emma," I say, "would your family down South be interested in boardin Sweets' boy for a few months? I'd pay them fair and meet the payment regular so he could be away from the city and able to see sky and run and play where there's no concrete and crowds. Me and Sweets could breathe easy for a while and maybe patch differences the child has made between us . . ." I stop when I see Miss Emma Dudley's eyes turn cold and harder than the ice in her glass.

614

She smoothed her bosoms, then picked up her tray of scotch and goodies. "I'm confused, Mr. Butler," she say, "there must be some kind of misunderstanding. I'm looking for ways to improve *my* life, not Sweets'. Why should my relatives take in her trouble?" She lean over close to my face and whisper, "Think about it, Mr. Butler, maybe you need to burn a few bridges behind you and find yourself a woman who's more your kind. Somebody could make you a good wife." With that she flounces on out. Guess she told me.

JIMMY-LEE POWELL

Benjie's Friend

I'M PASSIN my test papers and goin ahead of everybody else in track and basketball. I also got me a Saturday job at the grocery store. One time Benjie say to me, "Man, you got it made!"

I rock back on my heels lookin wise, fakin like I know some secret thing he ain't in on, then I say, "Just hangin in there, man, that's all." People like you to be actin cool and powerful, like you a real heavy person, in charge of your situation at all times. I ain't really got it all together. But soon as my bread piles up, I'm gonna get me a set-a drums and learn how to play em, that's bout the only secret I got.

Fact is, if I was on skag or just out of jail, they would maybe buy me a set-a drums just to help me straighten up. Sure, if I was in a drug bag, they'd pay me money to go to school and give me a head shrinker too. Some cats come outta detention and soon have folks advisin and workin to help them make it big. I'd like a little help myself, but I don't wanta get in trouble to get it, not really. I wish there was some place to go to without bein in trouble.

I'd go to that place, ring the bell, and say, "Please let me stay here until I get myself together. I'm not in trouble and my parents doin the best they can, but I don't wanta be home." Grown people got this deal where they get divorced from each other. The father and mother explain to the kid how they gonna divorce, but that it has nothin to do with the kid because the parents respectin and lovin him right on. Well, why can't you divorce your relatives?

I wanta get out from home. I could go to a place called "skag" and shoot up till there's nothin on my mind a-tall, but that's a trip you soon gotta take every day and, somewhere long the line, I'd get sicka catchin the same old train, but then it might be too late to get off.

I dig a place where somebody will open the door when you knock. They'd say, "Come on in. How's everything? What can I do for you?"

I'd say, "Nobody did no big wrong to me, but I gotta get a divorce from my parents, my neighborhood, my school, and my old buddies, so I can think or not think for two-three weeks. Could I come in without a habit or bein in bad with the law?"

The one who answer say, "That's what this place is for. We dig." He would call my home telephone and then say, "Hey, yall, Jimmy-Lee is here with us. He sends his best and say tell you he's just takin a divorce for now. . . . So yall go on to sleep, Jimmy-Lee is fine."

He'd show me to my private room and say, "Rest yourself, maybe in a day-so you might wanta rap on somethin." I'd stay there till I was together enough to

615

CHILDRESS

*A Hero Ain't
Nothin' but a
Sandwich*
Benjie
Johnson

go home again, or go wherever. Sure, they'd help anybody even if they didden snatch a pocketbook or shoot up.

I'd tell Benjie bout it, and he could go divorce trouble steada divorcin me, who was his boon. Nigeria Greene would be a good one for the door opener in a place like that.

Benjie don't half bother to speak to me anymore. If I was in trouble, like him, we would still be buddies. Friendship begin to split when one is caught in a habit and the other not. I've seen it time and time, needles divide guys, because the user rather be round another junkie. He through with you because he thinkin you lookin down on him. You through with him because you get scared of him, he smells like trouble when the monkey rides his back. Soon he's got to hustle hard for the monkey, and he hangs out with nobody but other hard hustlers.

BENJIE JOHNSON

T HIS counselor think he slick. He actin cool and maybe talk bout baseball or bout how he dig jazz; he lookin up in the air or down at the ground, to sneak up on makin me talk bout myself. Is all right with me cause he's a social worker and thass how they taught to do, but it gets me in the gut how he be actin like he really care. They all belong to the same club—Nigeria, Cohen, counselor, Butler, all of 'em. You'd think they dig me more than they do theyself. They just puttin on this buddy stuff cause they don't want me givin them and the society a lotta bother. Nobody digs a junkie, not that I'm one but they be thinkin I am, so it's most the same thing. Nobody digs niggas either, not even other niggas. White folks don't want you livin near them, and Black always preachin at your ass bout how you got no pride in yourself and your history. One good thing Jimmy-Lee's father once said, "Our history is dead if all it got to show is how we once could speak another language. History is to be made every day, not just told from some long time ago."

This counselor, I know the only reason we goin for a walk and talk is cause he gets paid to do it. If not for cats like me, his behind would starve to death. Sometime I *wanta* talk to him, but I don't like to rap bout my mother and relatives and bout underprivilege. Not that Hank be sayin "low-socio" and words like that. He's white but also a little bit smart and too slick for that. I gotta watch real sharp to see he don't catch me off-base. If I'm not careful, I might spill my guts. If they wanta talk me outta fixin, they should just do that. But Hank be tryin to find out how I started. He say, "You're a guy with a good brain, how'd you get into this?" I do wanta at least get along with Hank's program, give him things to put down on his report paper, help him out so we both be lookin good and pleasin everybody. After all, the man gotta hold his job. I know I don't *have* to be usin, it's somethin I started, but not a habit. I'd be a fool not to dig when skag is gettin to me. If that happen, I'll really stop.

Hank be waitin to hear bout my discontent with life and droppin hints for me, dig? So I follow up on what he drop. I'm sayin how nobody understand me, my school work ain't comin long so hot, not got the clothes I want for school, and like that. He be actin understandin, puttin his arm round my shoulder like boons forever. I know he ain't my boon and I'm not his. He live as far off from me as his white ass can get. No matter how many stories he tell bout baseball players and boxers who come out the slums, I notice he ain't movin in here so his son can get the chance to be a great athlete. People think you a fool.

I do my rappin on the inside, I rap to myself. I have got high and done some rappin with Kenny, but even then I'm holdin back, dig? People always gotta prove how you wrong and not seein the true picture. They don't know *my* true picture. If you do tell your truth, they will work on you till you take it back and say you wrong.

I know what my picture is. I hate school, even feel bad walkin to the school, forcin my feet to move where they don't wanta go. Schoolteachers can be some hard-eyed people, with talkin eyes; they mouth sayin one thing and them eyes be screamin another. Teach will say, "Be seated and open your book to page one nine-teen and be prepared to read as I call your name." But them eyes be stonyin down on you, speakin the message: "Shits, sit your ass down, open the book, and make a fool outta your dumb self when I start callin on the ones who the poorest readers."

Thass the message comin at you from whiteys. Then you got the special look that comes by shortwave from Black . . . they lookin sad like they could bust inta tears and they be sighin and shakin heads while they eyes sayin, "My people, my people, yall some bad-luck, sad-ass niggas." Then there a few like Nigeria Greene, he lookin at you all bright-eyed-Black and tellin how we descend from kings and queens back in Africa, how we was great when whitey was still a cave-man in Europe. But like Jimmy-Lee's father say, "Trouble is, we got no kings and queens right this very minute, and we ain't found out how to deal with that." I iced on Nigeria when he teamed up with Cohen and turned me in. That don't sound like descend from kings and queens, do it? He oughta take that green, red, and black button off his bespoke suit. And that Bernard Cohen be sayin the wrong thing every time he open his mouth. He say, "You can be somebody if you want." How the shit he don't know I'm somebody right now? He think *he* some-body and I'm not. He sincere, and I say . . . Hooray for sincere! . . . but it don't buy no steaks or plcat-back suits. His face look like a stompin ground for sadness when he be talkin serious and usin words like "ghetto." Now, since he and Nige-ria got so close they can piss through a straw together, they sayin "inner city." Inner city ain't nothin but the place they useta call ghetto and slum, dig?

I hate cafeteria in school. They got a steam table that'll blow your cool. They cook shiny, big garbage cans fulla soup. Cafeteria help be ploppin long-handled dippers and spoons down in brown, muddy gallonsa soup, stirrin and diggin up beans and carrots, splashin it out in your bowl like you a dead-ass nuisance that keep on needin to eat all time. They be sayin, "Speak up, bread or roll!" and "Step lively, move on!" They oughta put that message on a eight-track tape so they can shut up and just dip.

If I was to pick out middle C on the piano and keep hittin it, thass how it sound when my jography teacher be teachin. I don't listen, just turn her off and stare out the window at sky and freedom, thinkin how it would be if I had finish servin my time and was gone from here with my diploma . . . or gone without it. Then I'm hearin middle C get louder on my ear, she astin me to repeat what she been sayin. I wanna say, "Bitch, I'm tryin not to hear you." But since I got a mother, I'm thinkin jography teacher might be somebody's mother too, so I say, "I didden hear the last part."

Look like she could be decent and repeat it, but she wanta outfox you, so she say, "Tell us what part you did hear." When you don't answer, she flippin through her report book to make another mark gainst your record. I hate school, and that's how come I got to cuttin class and hangin out with those who hate the same.

Maybe it's like Butler say before he moved out on us, "Boy, you hate every-body, the whole country and all what's in it." Now that Butler's downstairs to

Miss Emma Dudley's, I'm hatin him more than school or the society. He made my mother cry. "You got him!" he told her. "Can't be both me and your son. I can't live with a lyin, thievin junkie! He's your blood, so there's no way to ask you to give him up. You got him, he's all yours!"

Mama say, "Yes, he's mine, and I'm his." She really standin up for me but cryin so hard like she can never stop.

Grandma was the one who surprise me, she beg Butler not to go. Damn, more than one time I heard her say, "Sure hadn't counted on him makin this his full-time home." Now she turn round and say, "Please, Butler, don't leave us!" Grabbin at his jacket and tryin to pull him back.

Mama say, "*Let* him go!"

Butler look sheepy and say, "Hell, I ain't goin nowhere but downstairs to Miss Emma Dudley. Call if you need me." I hate him more than ever. He's gone, but Mama and Grandma still talkin bout him and wishin he was back.

Newspaper advertisement:

REMOVE ALL EVIL

Do you need help? Mme. Snowson is in town with African secrets from the Deep South. I am a reader and adviser with answers. You don't tell me, I tell you. There is a cure for every problem. Evil spells have been removed after one visit. I give you, free of charge, one capsule of anointing oil, a ceremonial African incense stick, and a trial package of South Carolina Herbal Tea. These gifts are yours to keep as a special blessing. Enemies can be vanquished while you wait. You can have peace of mind by tomorrow sunrise. Has your loved one gone? Divine power and know-how can bring about a return. Know this! When everything goes wrong . . . something evil is working against you! Study the following testimonials:

"I have been blessed with money, love, and a fine house."
J. Smith, Newark, N.J.

"God bless you, Mme. Snowson! I am well and have won $500."
B. Monroe, Baltimore, Md.

"Have just married the lady of my choice and own two cars. Every blessing is now ours. My health so improved that operation is no longer necessary. I am sending money for the large size oil and more Incense and tea. Thank you for being my way-shower."
R. Robinson, Los Angeles, Calif.

MADAM SNOWSON IS OPEN SEVEN DAYS A WEEK
NOON TO MIDNIGHT
CALL . . . 558–67 . . .

MRS. ROSE JOHNSON (CRAIG)

Benjie's Mother

CHILDRESS

*A Hero Ain't
Nothin' but a
Sandwich*
Mrs. Rose
Johnson
(Craig)

Mama talked me into goin for a readin and a blessin, but she couldn't have if there wasn't somethin inside drivin me on to do it. I don't believe in fortune-tellers, but I believe in Benjie, so that's what sent me to Madam Snowson's.

We had to wait our turn in a small room while the reader told fortune in what they call "the consultation parlor." There were two before us. An old woman who kept rockin back and forth, and another lady busy drummin her fingers on the arms of her chair.

Mama whispered, "Alla this is gettin to my nerves." My mind stayed on Benjie and Butler.

The place smelled like fried liver and onions. It wasn't a bad smell, just a perfumy odor like what comes from good, fresh food when somebody knows how to cook it, however . . . I don't too much care for onions myself.

When the assistant, a young, pretty girl with a fluffy Afro hairdo, opened the consultation parlor door, to let a customer out, a trail of incense floated in behind her. I felt kinda tight inside like when you visit the doctor or dentist. One time we heard a customer cry out from the inner room, "Yes, yes, indeed! That's right!" Some say women are not able to keep a secret, but this is one happenin Butler will never know bout from me. I'd never hear the end of it. Anyway, now that he's moved downstairs to Miss Emma Dudley's, he doesn't need to hear of each and every thing I do. If he was at home, maybe I wouldn't be here tryin to find another way to save Benjie.

The assistant did not want us both in at the same time. "It's gonna cost yall five apiece anyway, so each may's well get the full separate treatment." I handed her a ten-dollar bill and told her we weren't tryin to do the reader out of her rightful fee. We went in together. The parlor was dark, lit only by a dim lamp with a reddish shade and several candles throwin large, fluttery shadows on the wall. The incense smoke and smell was heavy. I felt dizzy.

The reader is a skinny, short dark lady. She wears a plain blue smock and a fancy silver cross hangin from a chain. She has a goiter or some kinda growth in her neck, her eyes are wide open and stary. The room is skimpy on furniture, but me and Mama sit down on the best piece, a gold brocade-satin couch which is protected by a see-through plastic cover. The reader is silent as a grave in her straight-back chair; a small table is next to it; on the table is a fishbowl filled with water.

Madam dips her hands in the bowl; the assistant gives her a lacy towel. She dries her drippin fingers. We can hear water drops hittin the floor . . . plip, plip, plip.

"Ohhhhhhhh," Madam leans back and groans, "yall comin to me with such a heavy burden, it takes two to bear it. Bringin trouble like that cross which Jesus dragged to the killin place. Ohhhhhh, what a weight to bear."

Mama starts cryin. I take her arm and squeeze hard so she'll get back control.

Madam whispers, "Lord, Lord, Lord, tell us how to untangle Satan's bloody, meddlin horns from these troubled heart strings!"

I hear the outside swish of city traffic, the faraway happy sound of children laughin and playin somewhere down the street. My fingernails clutch into the palms of my hands, I'm prayin hard for help. I whisper the word to Madam: "Dope, my sister, the trouble is dope. Dope is takin away my son and my man . . . I want both of 'em back."

619

CHILDRESS

*A Hero Ain't
Nothin' but a
Sandwich*
Nigeria
Greene

"Well, Lord," she says, "you hearin from us again. Ain't you gonna give us credit for faith? We the most faithful people you ever made and not even in your own likeness. I know you gonna lead us beside the still water and restore our soul . . . in the long run. But, we need you right now, Lord—let dope dealers die from the hurtin they puttin on us! Let our poor children seal their veins against the attack of Satan's needles! Wash us strong and healthy! Wash us on a foamy, clean tide which will safely float us up to higher ground. Give us joy in the promise of evil defeated! Let this woman again see your love shinin in her man's eyes. Remember your promise, Lord! Deliver us from evil!"

I gave the reader a extra three dollars for a bottle of Indigo Blue. Free of charge, she gave me holy water to sprinkle in the corners of my apartment, to chase away evil. I'm to take a warm bath colored with Indigo Blue. I'm gonna lay down in blue water and give magic power a chance to wash off my hard luck. I don't want my son to die.

NIGERIA GREENE

M E AND MY WIFE paid twenty-five dollars a ticket to honor a Negro writer-rascal last night. Yeah, he was a rascal, a rogue, a thief, and a forked-tongue put-downer of everything Black that ever lived and breathed bad air.

Every time he hits a lick at his typewriter he carries us one step further away from freedom. We sat there spell-bound, wearin painted-on grins . . . along with our tuxedos and dashikis, yeah, in uniform to honor a rascal.

The guest of honor read from his book, preachin how all that ever held us back was mama, sister, girlfriend and . . . "the vast majority of misguided sisters and brothers!" We were rockin with laughter, but in the middle of a big ha-ha, a sick feelin hits me in the gut . . . I realize my stomach resents what my brain is acceptin.

I look around and see nothin but Black fat cats, those of us who have recently resigned from the house and field nigga society . . . we're fulla eats and twelve-year-old likker, we're now shinier than a pre-Civil War slave used to get on cat-fish fried in saturated hog grease. When this rascal finishes tellin us how the race is nothin, the whole room rises and we give him a Black standin ovation. Dig it, I find myself makin hooray noise right along with the rest.

We so-called "high achievers"—doctors, lawyers, teachers, actors, painters, poets, dancers—most of us now makin a buck offa either "puttin down the nigga" or "upliftin the nigga" on some specially "funded" gigs . . . we're the upper-strata welfare recipients, dig? Old slave massa's computer-programmed son has figured out a new category for us. While we were busy evaluatin "the house and field nigga," he came up with "the funded nigga" . . . those of us run-nin round talkin trash and drinkin our mash outta long-stem champagne glasses handed to us by smirkin time-and-a-half white waiters.

We got some special type guest white folk, too, they laughin louder than any-one else at the whitey jokes, they also enjoyin their newfound freedom of callin us "nigga" out loud, to our face, which deed is suppose to show that ain't no-body sensitive anymore, specially us. Fact is, we have turned into the most *in*sensitive bunch you'll find anywhere west of hell. There's also a light smatterin of Blacks who work hard for a livin, from pushin dress racks to makin change in the subway. This is their night to "pass" as professionals, they are for the evening "in" dress designing, or business programming, counseling, "urban"

CHILDRESS

*A Hero Ain't
Nothin' but a
Sandwich*
Benjie
Greene

projects and a great many initialed endeavors whose initials spell out words . . . SCRAM, SCOOT, FITE, GONE, and so on.

The MC is glad-greetin everybody and handin out compliments two for a penny, as usual, givin his all no matter what the cause or the purpose. The cat next to me whispers, "Say he gets up every mornin and turns on the news to see which way the wind is blowin, before he answers his telephone. After all, gotta know which bag to jump in, right?"

The platform is full of funded celebrities and fund raisers, big-time little spenders . . . to keep the ghetto cool, as well as Black and beautiful. Within the past twelve months they have all taken positions against school busin and are comin on strong as the hallelujah chorus with a new name for segregation: "QUALITY EDUCATION" . . . which is where the struggle is safer and about to be funded and refunded for the next many years.

Here and there are a few wistful, bewildered, lost, lonely, let-down brothers and sisters who are now beginnin to feel somethin must be wrong with themselves because they have let this hustler's harvest pass. The intellectual poor, those who have never been met at an airport by an air-conditioned chauffeured limousine, those who never heard the mayor speak at a midday luncheon, those never called to a White House conference, those not on casual speakin terms with the State Department.

The evening drank itself to an end when the liquor ran out along with the salted peanuts. The upper crust "in" group went off to the Top of the Sevens for "gin and ginger" with their white boons, the fringe-benefit-almost-in group went off to a pot-smoke-and-chili party to rap the guest of honor over the righteous coals. The guest of honor, "they" say, went off to meet a once-was-an-almost-top-white-movie-star, to snuggle against her boobs and cuss all other niggas till the dawn of another new day.

Me and my socializin African queen cabbed back uptown, with a few other tolerated squares, tryin to talk ourselves into likin what we've been doin, but bein and feelin less like ourselves, less and less. Now, in the calm of the mornin after, I'm askin myself what else is there? With a splittin headache, I'm facin my fate as a plain, uninfluential grade school teacher . . . knowin there are some Black children to be met, knowin there's nothin heard last night that can be passed on to them with pride. If they are shootin shit in the arm, their elders are shootin shit in the head . . . but we *never* OD out. Benjie killers! Laughin Benjie on to early death; drinkin his blood from a champagne glass. We're in some terrible trouble, but the kids don't need any more tired, opportunistic advice.

I'm gonna stand up tomorrow and tell my class, "Under adult supervision you have become a breed of junkies and acid trippers, muggers, purse snatchers and trust-no-one-over-thirtyites. You right not to trust anyone over thirty, we're makin millions outta your slave bodies, makin big profit from openin your veins and makin small profit trying to close them shut again. Yall better learn to defend yourself."

Junkie, junkie, you pushin the horse to yourself. The latest war is goin on within the confines of your very own veins . . . and so far the nation is losin. . . .

BENJIE JOHNSON

I BEEN bathin my own self for years, for as long as I can recall, so I don't dig Mama givin me a bath in blue water. That's the most humiliatinest thing that

CHILDRESS

*A Hero Ain't
Nothin' but a
Sandwich*
Benjie
Greene

ever happen. She pour blue dye in the bath water and say, "Hop in there, I'm gonna sponge you all over."

"For what?" I ast.

"To wash all the devil and hell off you."

"Ain't no devil and hell on me."

She pullin at my shirt and unbucklin my belt. She strong, Jack! She strong like crazy and pullin at my clothes so bad, till I say, "Awright, I'll take 'em off by myself!" She stop and stand back with her hands on her hips, still fussin.

"You better! I don't believe in spells; but if you got one on you, we gonna wash it off tonight!"

When you thirteen, you ain't suppose to be buck naked before your mama. I'm holdin a towel in fronta me to cover my personals and try to show respeck; she snatchin the towel off and pushin me in the tub.

"I don't wanta get in it." I say, How I know what that blue water is? How I know it won't gimmie a infection?

Mama curse and say, "Goddammit, you put anything in your arm that some scroungy stranger hand you. You gonna sit the hell on down in this blue water and see what it can do for you."

Mama don't curse, she really don't, will say dammit and what-the-hell, but when she sayin goddammit, that's somethin else. I tried to run out the bathroom. Grabbin the brush she clean the toilet with, she say, "I'll bust your brains loose!" I jump on in the tub fore she lose her mind. She don't leave nothin to do but follow what she say or fight her, so I went sloshin inta the tub. When it splash, she say, "Don'tcha get my hair fulla water! Be still, dammit!"

She's all outta line, but I'm tryin to forgive, cause I know she mad cause Butler is gone and she be missin him. My mama is over thirty-three years old and goin on like this bout some man. Maybe she can't help bein old and lovin somebody, but look like a old woman would be satisfy just to be cool and be somebody's mother.

She grab the washcloth and scrub all over me with blue water, my head, neck, it's all in my eyes even, then washin under my arms. "Stand up!" she holler. She washin between my legs and backside, till tears most come to my eyes. Not cause it's hurtin, but cause she's makin me feel shame. She say, "You ain't got nothin down there that I ain't seen before, ain't enough to see noway." Grown people think they can do you like a dog cause they got a few years on you. Ain't no easy way to get along with your relatives. When she think we had a good talk, it's a time when I been sayin, yeah, yeah, yeah, like after the blue bath when she say, "Benjie, you oughta do some better."

"Yeah, I do try."

"You lyin. I don't like that."

"Yeah, yes'm."

"That's better. Somethin on your mind bout me and Butler?"

"I'm glad he's gone away."

"We had planned to be married, but everything is so distress now that I'm not sure it's for the best. Why'd you steal his clothes, Benjie?"

I feel sorry for her cause she ready to cry. She wearin a long housecoat with flowers on it, blue and pink. One thing, she always look nice and neat-lookin. Once, in school, I had to write a composition bout a member of my family, that was when I was young and in lower grade.

Composition went like . . . "My mother is plump but not fat. She is not tall or short, but just in between. She can sew, cook, and clean house nicely. Best

622

thing about her is her walk, goin along like she's on her way to somewhere fine. Thing I don't like the most is her temper. She smile sweet and say, 'Don't do that, honeybunch,' say it over and over many times real cool, then she snatch up a pillow, throw it at you and yell . . . 'I SAY STOP!' . . . She won't get mad little by little, but just all at once.

"She is very nice-lookin, but not so pretty as to make you feel shame. She has a round face and smooth cheeks with a dimple in one; when she smile, the dimple gets deep. Her color is reddish brown. My grandmother say it is because we got some Indian way back in our family. My mother laugh, show her dimple, and say, 'And a whole lotta African!'

"She is not cheap. She will give me show fare and has also paid for Jimmy-Lee to go with me when his father didden give him fare. She is cool at all times except when very mad."

That's the way the composition went. I won a box of colorin crayons by writin it. Seem a long time back. Now she cryin. I almost wish Butler would walk in the door . . . almost. Now she take the blue bottle of dye which a fortune-teller gave her, lookin at it, laughin and cryin because sometime she can be sad and tickled at the same time. She pours the blue down the toilet.

"I know it ain't nothin," she say, "not a damn-ass thing. Nothin but ignorance and backward as hell."

Jack, if I was a cryin person, I'd cry, too, but I can't. It would kill me dead for somebody to see me cry, dig? Tears be burnin and stingin behind my eyes and like a heavy knot be in my throat. Somethin gotta be done fast, or else I'll cry like a chicken. Look like my mother dyin of sadness. I say, "Mama, maybe this blue bath gonna do some good." She look at me real kind and seem to feel better. Maybe when I get to be a older man, I'll dig where she's comin from much better. If I was old, in Butler's shoes, I might like some nice-lookin woman myself, even if she did have a son and a husband who was off somewhere. Life and the society must look different to old people.

BUTLER CRAIG

I FEEL out of place roomin downstairs here with Miss Emma Dudley, yet wasn't anything to do but leave Sweets. She asked me to come up and have dinner with her last night. I went, but it wasn't the same. The old lady went to mumblin and grumblin, so I just flat-footed asked her what was the matter. She lit into me.

"You mean what the *hell's* the matter! First thing, you can stop callin me 'the old lady'! My name is Mrs. Ransom Bell or else Elizabeth. Always askin Sweets 'How's the old lady?' I'm somebody too, don'tcha know. And stop fixin your voice when you talk to me, fixin it like you talkin to a chile."

That seemed fair enough, to call people what they wanta be called, and in a tone they like. But after I agreed, she still went on.

"Furthermore," she says, "you ran out on Rose. Men are good for nothin but runnin. Some these colored men ain't nothin but breath, britches, and shoe leather! When trouble comes, you run! I told Rosey to keep a sharp eye on the kinda man who runs when trouble comes."

After that, I ran again, made my retreat back down here, and had a night's sleep with peace and quiet. This room is fair-sized and neat, nice curtains at the window. My portable hi-fi is bringin in cool sounds, but through every note all

I can think about is Benjie stealin my suit and overcoat. What the old lady—
Mrs. Ransom Bell—expect from me? I dead sure can't do a day's work in my
socks and underwear. I had to go to the credit place and buy another suit and
coat, just in time . . . it's snowin and blowin today, Hawkins is really out there.[1]
Snow look pretty stickin to the windowpane. This the first quiet day off in the
last six weeks, but my mind so tore up till I can't relax. Why should I feel guilty?
I didn't harm anybody. When I went upstairs, I put fifty dollars in Sweets' hand
so she'd know I'm not really runnin away, no matter what the old lady—Miss
Elizabeth—say.

I'm feelin terrible bout bein accused of runnin. If I get hold of Benjie, they'll
put me in jail for what they call child batterin. I'll batter on his ass till there's
nothin left to hit. How can the boy do somethin terrible, then get mad with me
cause I'm the one he did it to? Day before yesterday he crossed to the other side
of the street when he saw me comin, actin like he's lookin in store windows. I
made a move in his direction, he broke into a run and cut round the corner.
Shiiiiit! Boy so damn jealous and mean, he made up his mind not to like me the
first time we met.

Social workers, doctors, teachers, all doin what they can and Sweets almost
outta her mind! I'm missin her more and more. Damn Benjie Johnson! But a
man can't live in a house where he's got no authority! It's Sweets' house and her
mama's.

Teacher named Nigeria is okay. He and me went for a beer the time we got
Benjie in detox. We see eye to eye except seem like I'm knowin him but he can't
know me; however, I won't hold that gainst him because he ain't supposed to
know and understand everybody, not even Benjie. His job is to teach kids to
study and learn, not how to cut them loose from habits. He kept tellin me that
it's nation time, time for us to pull together and rise, work united and all that.
I'm agreein, but what good is that, I ain't the one on junk. While we at the bar,
drinkin our cold Buds, I pointed out a nodder sittin cross the way, guy half-
collapsed over a glassa Coke.

"Too mucha this nation is on the nod," I said.

Nigeria goes rappin on harder than ever. I'm tryin to listen but can't catch
hold of anything long enough to turn it over. Cat talks and words tumble outta
his mouth, mixed up and leapin from one subject to another, like he gotta tell
everything he knows in ten minutes. He keep sayin, "It's nation time!" The cat
is strainin so hard to get to me, till I just have to encourage him.

I throw in a "Right on!" when he looks to see what I got to say. I really got
nothin to say . . . cause I'm busy wonderin how Benjie is handlin the kickin
treatment. He was damn lucky to get his butt in that hospital bed. They got a
long waitin list, and your people must answer questions and fill out papers.
You'd think he wouldn't ever wanta see a fix again. Out less than a week and
ripped off my suit. Him bein so young, I thought the cure and our forgiveness
would do everything. I was wrong. This Nigeria cat hummed in my ear bout
how big-shot whitey gangsters and racketeers are the *real ones* bringin skag into
the Black community, and not the street pusher. I say to him, "Man, when they
bring it, why we gotta shove it in the nation's arm? Black cats pushin what
whitey moves in. If we don't touch it, it'll lay there, right? The Black Nation
wanta play blindman's buff and not see these young, hard-ass men out here

---

1 *Hawkins is really out there*   saxophonist Coleman Hawkins is playing great jazz (on Butler's
portable hi-fi—i.e., high fidelity phonograph).

624

knockin folks in the head, snatchin pocketbooks, rippin off apartments, shootin down, knifin and muggin. Talk bout pollution in the river and how the fish bein poisoned, dig it, pollution now is in the brain and bloodstream, the very river of life!" No, wasn't nothin he could say back at me, cause right is right.

So now I'm layin here rememberin the past and watchin a snowstorm, feelin the blues. The bell ringin and the mailman is out in the vestibule blowin his screechin whistle. Miss Emma Dudley calls out, "Mr. Butler, mailman got a special delivery letter for me, door is open, but I'll be right back."

"Okay," I say, then turn off the FM. The dog goes runnin out behind her, barkin like the mailman is public enemy number one. I just lay on and think, tryin to figure me and Sweets' problems. A creepy feelin comes over me that I'm not alone. I hear no particular sound that's distinct, but maybe the floor creaked or a draft blew me the message. I know somebody is movin down the long, dark, narrow hall between the front door and the livin room. I've heard bout second sight and how people can know somethin they've not seen or heard, this must be it. All down my spine, in the pit-a my stomach, and at the backa my throat, I'm knowin that Benjie is here. I'm in my pajamas and don't reach for slippers. Barefooted, I get to the door, quietly ease it open and sneak down the hall. The livin room is directly in front of me, and the kitchen is off to the right, just before you reach it.

"Benjie," I say, "you here?"

No answer. I feel kinda silly as I go in the next room. There's a noise behind me. I turn and see him flash outta the kitchen. He's beatin it down the hall, carryin somethin. I light out behind him. "Drop it!" I say. "Drop whatcha got!"

He goes out the front door and takes to the stairs. I'm runnin behind him. Each flight is divided in two, a half flight of steps, then a small landin with a window, a turn and the second part of the flight takes you to the next set of apartments. I think he's headin for home, to Sweets, but on and up he goes past home, to the roof door. I'm puffin and blowin, but gainin ground while he fumbles with the latch on the roof door. He gets the latch off, then has to slam hisself gainst the door. It's jammed. I'm thinkin . . . Hot damn! I got him now! All of a sudden he throws this big, shiny somethin at me. I catch it! The son-bitch stole Miss Emma Dudley's electric toaster. I pitch it back at him; but he's gone, and the toaster smashes against the tin door. Somebody on top floor screams. I step out on the roof, into ice and snow; it's wet, cold, and slippery, but I don't give a damn. I want my hands on Benjie. He hops the division leading to the next roof while looking behind to see if I'm closin distance between us.

"You little bastard," I holler, "I'm gonna kill you!"

He zigzags and heads toward the backa the second roof, headin for where the division leads to a back airshaft; the shaft is an open, straight drop clean down to ground floor. "No," I'm screamin, "not there! Don't do it!" He's on top of the ledge, gonna try to jump the shaft and land on the next roof. He's standin there, slippin, losin his balance. I'm behind him as he slides down and almost straddles the top. I got one arm, he hits and flails out the other and goes over the edge. My hand is grabbed tight around his right arm, just above the elbow. He's swingin down over empty space, lookin up at me, weighin a ton and cryin like crazy. With my other hand I grab his jacket. His face is scared and pinched in like a skinny little old man. The weight of him is growin heavier, feel like holdin a baby grand piano by one leg. He's pullin me down on the wet, icy edge. Can't feel my fingers, have to watch to make sure they don't let loose. Cold as I am, hot sweat breakin out all over. Hands beginnin to sweat, can't tell if it's

625

CHILDRESS

*A Hero Ain't
Nothin' but a
Sandwich*
Benjie
Johnson

from Benjie's hand or mine. Wet hands can't hold much longer. He looks down at the courtyard, then up at me, growin heavier and heavier. "Let go, Butler," he says, "let me die. Drop me, man!" He's flailin his legs, tryin to work loose my hold, hollerin and fightin to die. "Let me be dead!"

Feel like I'm standin in a bag-a ice, pullin the shoulder loose from my body. Across my back, behind my knees, shakin and tremblin, gotta let loose . . . or go down with him. He keeps sayin it, "Lemme go, man!" I'm scared I'll do it. He's gonna flail around till he solve the problem for me and Sweets. His eyes locked on mine, we lookin right into each other. . . . Then I know *I was runnin from him* . . . like Sweets' mama say. If this was my flesh-and-blood child, I wouldn't have run when he stole my suit. . . . I went off cause he wasn't mine.

Now I'm inchin him a bit closer, workin and pullin, tryin not to think anymore, but thoughts stay. Benjie has stopped talkin, just hangin, givin up . . . givin me a chance to kill him. I did want him out the way, but not dead. I'll die if I lose him! Can't lose him! My knees pressin hard gainst the brick wall, bracin and pullin. His jacket sleeve is tearin, the cheap-Charlie shoulder paddin hangin out. Another strong pull, my arm is twistin outta the raw socket, another pull, my knees gratin gainst bricks, down to the bone.

"Brace yourself," I say, "brace your foot to the wall and climb on up here! Come on! Let's make it!"

He's grabbin to the fronta my pajamas, cloth tearin . . . I'm leanin back hard, his head now showin over the edge . . . then his chest. . . . I say, "Come on, goddammit! It's nation time!"

He's squirmin over the top. We fall back on the roof, into the snow, there's blood in the snow, my knees . . . bloody from scrapin gainst brick. We sittin there in the cold wet. Benjie's cryin and holdin to me like never gonna let go, body tremblin with the shiverin shakes . . . he's cryin the meanness out.

People on the roof shoutin and talkin, Sweets, the man from top floor, Miss Emma Dudley and her big dog, Woofie. Dog runnin back and forth, barkin like Benjie and me make him madder than ever. Miss Emma Dudley holdin up her broke toaster and goin on worse than Woofie. "Don't worry bout no goddamn toaster," I say. "Everything is under control, gonna buy you a new toaster!"

I take Benjie's hand and limp my way down to Sweets' house. I say, "It's you and me from now on, hear?" He still shiverin with a death grip on my hand, his nose and eyes runnin water like Niagara Falls. Sweets look so glad to hear me talkin that way. To myself I'm wonderin what to do beside talk. I don't know what to do. It's a terrible thing not to know what to do.

BENJIE JOHNSON

B UTLER is cool. I dig how he walks down the street like he ain't to be meddled with; the kinda cat you can call a real man, dig? He might knock you down, or you him, but he'll shake hands when it's all over, that is . . . if handshakin is in order. I also dig him talkin straight to a social worker, a doctor, or even a police. Like when the social worker ast him, "Are you the child's father?" Butler look him in the eye and say, "Let's put it this-a-way. I am who he has *got* for a father, that is sufficient to make him mine and me his."

The social worker look down at his paper, don't know what to write. When he look back up, he figure it's best not to bug Butler, so he say, "I'm gonna put down that you're his stepfather." Butler don't smile or grin but just say, "That'll do."

Hangin by one hand from a roof edge ain't no joke. Lookin down six, seven stories over a concrete backyard will blow your mind if your brain ain't in strong condition. My grandmother ast me what I was thinkin while hangin like that. No way for me to say cause I can't clear remember any one thought comin behind another, thassa fact. Day by day I'm losin some more of what little I did remember. Night by night I be dreamin it over again, each time different. One night I dream Butler drop me and I was fallin straight down to get smattered on concrete. I woke up just in time, with such a jump till I fell outta bed.

When I was hangin from the roof, I do remember hearin a rock record playin on somebody's hi-fi, or else just playin in my head . . . group singin "Baby Don'tcha Leave Me." . . . Thassa blast! Like a movie, Jack! I could see the singin group every time I close my eyes, group poppin they fingers, doin fancy steps, dancin forward and back, makin circles. My mind had them guys wearin spensive lace shirts, gold pants, and green suede shoes; they was fine, real fine. When I open my eyes, I'm lookin up into Butler's face, veins in his face all swole out. I tried to think of my real father's face. Could remember a little bit of how he looked, but seem like real father's nose was narrower, keener than Butler's . . . also his eyes was some bigger . . . and the complexion brighter. Butler's face kept wipin out the real father. I believed that if I could see my real father's face, it could save my life.

Butler kept talkin, sayin mixed-up words, words, words . . . real father's face could not get through Butler's words, you dig? Butler keep sendin down them words, and they ain't nothin but sound goin like a-hunh-a-hunh-a-hunh like bees, insects hummin . . . and then it come to me that maybe I'm dyin and that's why faces and words meanin nothin. Then I feel my body beginnin to move up, up, up, sunshine hittin on Butler's face, makin a shiny light . . . light drawin tears to my eyes . . . like lookin straight into the sun. When light start dimmin down, Butler's face came through clear and plain . . . and I'm movin on up. Voice inside-a my head say, "Butler, you are my father." Thassa weird trip, Jack.

Yeah, I dig him. After all, the man save my life. People don't go round savin other people every day, you know, specially people they mad with. Sittin in that cold, wet snow felt good cause I was joyin bein alive. Ain't nothin wrong with alive . . . if you gonna be somethin, be that!

My folks didden go to yellin at me like they can do sometime, no, they didden. They was glad bout me bein alive and well, everybody drowndin me with smiles, they really was. Middle of the night I woke up from the fallin-down dream and was hearin the voice again in my head: "Butler, you are my father." I got up shakin all over and wishin I had just a light skin pop to steady down my nerves, but I didden make one false move. I figured me a way to keep busy till the shakin pass. I wrote on a piece-a paper like how the teacher once gave me a hundred times to write—I WILL NOT ANSWER BACK—but, since this was me punishin myself, I wrote my own thing . . . one hundred times: BUTLER IS MY FATHER . . . BUTLER IS MY FATHER . . . BUTLER IS MY FATHER . . . filled up both sides of my paper, two rows on each side, and had to sharpen the pencil two, three times. Was neat-lookin writin. Next thing I went out in the hall to where Butler's new coat is hangin on the rack . . . and I fold that paper, put it in his pocket, then went on back to bed.

Come mornin, I'm feelin like a fool in the daylight, so I go to get the paper back . . . but Butler wearin his coat, ready to go see a doctor bout his arm.

CHILDRESS

A Hero Ain't Nothin' but a Sandwich
Benjie Johnson

CHILDRESS

*A Hero Ain't
Nothin' but a
Sandwich*
Benjie
Johnson

Later, when he come back home, I say, "Butler, let me hang up your coat for you." That seem natural cause his arm in a sling now. He say, "Thank you, Benjie, my man." I go in both pockets while hangin the coat on the rack, but wassen no paper, paper gone. I kept lookin at Butler's face to see if he gonna laugh or go into a heart to heart or what. The man got a straight face and *cool*. I'm thinkin he crumple it up and threw it way cause it mighta seem like a old candy wrapper or waste paper. Whatever his faults, nobody can say the man ain't cool.

* * *

Butler told Mama off bout takin me to Kenny's funeral. Kenny's mama and mine both belong to the union you have to belong to in order to sew in a factory. Kenny's mother, by livin round the corner from our house, used to come by when they both had to be at union meetin, and like that.

Poor Kenny just turn fifteen and didden have nothin else to do but get hold of a hot shot and die of a overdose. Some tryin to say he was slipped a hot shot on purpose cause he was meddlin with a guy's sister, but that turn out to be a lie cause the girl didden even know Kenny, except to see him sometime walkin by. Fact is, I'm thinkin he had been buyin and shootin weak doses that been cut down to little or nothin, then he come cross a strong deck, and it knocked on his heart. Anyhow, whatever way it went, he's a dead cat now.

My mama made me go to Kenny's funeral with her. I *had* to go. I'm on parole. They don't call it that, but I gotta report to a social worker who's workin with the youth court. If I don't show, they will book me into a reform detention and charge my family with negleck of a minor.

They be havin some tough laws and you better ply yourself to givin up whatever you takin and joinin with a program, or else you gonna be in a jail. I gotta report to a caseworker what all I been doin since I last saw him.

A undertakin parlor is a weird place. Undertakin parlors have one kinda potted plant, palms like what you get on Palm Sunday in church, except undertakin palm is green and not yaller like church palm. People got to sign a book and put down they name and address fore they go up front to where the dead is laid out. I say to my mama, "I don't want to go look at him. I can see from back here."

"March," Mama say, "march up and look."

It seem impolite to stare at him when he's dead. No stuff, he helpless and he ain't able to look back at nobody who's lookin down at him. He look cold grayish brown, and hard as stone, and seem like his eyes and mouth glued together. He wearin a dumb square-lookin dark-blue suit, with a white carnation pinned to it. His hands folded cross his stomach, lookin pitiful, Jack. That casket is stone gray, and the inside part is white, shiny, satiny stuff like the linin of a lady's perfume box or like them Valentine chocolates. The whole scene look like it belong in a scary movie. Organ music playin, but you can't see no organ cause the man hidin behind a screen playin music that never come to a end; when you think it gonna end, it switch to another piece without stoppin.

Mama say, "Poor Kenny didn't get many flowers."

Look to me like enough, big fancy flowers standin up on wire legs. One was a wheel with a spoke missin, made outta red roses, a white ribbon bow with gold letters on it spell out TO OUR BELOVED KENNY . . . There was another piece with the face of a clock set in the middle, time showin three o'clock. Mama say, "Uh, huh, that's the hour of his passin." How they know the hour of passin? They found him dead. The top half of the casket open, a lotta red carnations on the bottom part. Mama say, "Uh-huh, that is a half blanket-a flowers, really puttin him away right." All I'm thinkin is how Kenny was alive and laughin at Tiger's house. Mama would flip if she knew he gave me my first fix.

A lady sang a couple-a pieces and made people cry. Lady fat and short, her hair slicked back too tight, but she sing and hit them high notes without anybody havin to wonder if she was gonna make it.

Kenny's mama hollered out, "Please God! Please help us!" I don't dig funerals. When people die, they oughta fade away so you can't see them no more, so they be gone without lettin folks do all this to 'em. Tell you this, what I see sure don't make me look forward to bein dead.

There are numbers up on the wall, numbers of hymns people gotta sing. Preacher call out the number, you find it in the hymnbook, then rise and sing. Songs got no tune, people singin any kinds way and just goin la-la-hoo-hoo until they get down to Ahhhhhhhh-men, which is the end. Everybody cough like they in church, clearin they throat in a holy whisper. The minister waitin for coughin to be over, pattin his forehead and mouth with a white hankacha.

Mama copyin down the hymn number while people coughin She say, "I have to put a quarter on this figure. Poor Kenny might bring me some luck." I wanta say, "He ain't brought himself no luck, what make you think he gonna bring you some?" But I say nothin cause she the boss on everything since I'm on parole. But she shouldn't be thinkin bout winnin money at a time like this. If I was dead, it would hurt my feelins to think folks wants play my hymn number.

I felt so glad when I step outta that undertaker parlor. Only disrespeck was three boys in the street, wearin purple jackets with green writin sayin "The Highest Eternal Avengers" . . . they holdin signs, DEATH TO PUSHERS! KILL PUSHERS! I don't dig them uglyin up a funeral with signs. A couple-a times I delivered a deck for Walter, but I was not the real pusher myself. Glad I wasn't the one gave Kenny the overdose.

Insteada comin on home from in fronta the funeral, Mama gotta greet old folks, hug and kiss people, shake hands, and make me talk to em.

All say the same thing. "Mind now, you be a good boy and stay outta trouble." I say, "Yes, sir, yes, mam." I was glad Mama did not tell them bout me.

Jimmy-Lee there with his father, the old guy lookin dead as Kenny, clothes rumpled, eyes like they don't see nothin. Jimmy-Lee seem shamed of his dad, tryin to pull him to go home. People lookin at both of 'em. I feel sorry for Jimmy-Lee, I walk up and say, "Hey, my man." He look happy as a wagtail puppy.

"Where you been!" he say. "What you know!" When I was walkin off with Mama, he gave me a closed fist high sign and say, "Right on!" Jimmy-Lee got his ways, but he ain't the worst person in the world, you know.

Back home, Butler is mad at Mama for takin me to the funeral. He say, "You can't scare nobody into bein well. If you could, jails and hospitals all be empty."

Mama got mad when she find out Grandma told Butler bout the funeral and bout her givin me a bath in blue water from a fortune-teller. Mama hollered at Grandma. "Why," she say, "why you have to tell your guts to Butler? You talk bout him like a dog and tell me not to tell him my business, but soon as I turn my back, you shoot off your mouth. You just a spoon stirrer in your old age, makin a I-say-you-say between people. After all, you the one asked me to go to the reader-adviser. Too bad she didn't read and advise you to keep your mouth shut."

629

Grandma stomp, drag her feet and start singin . . . "Precious Lord Take My Hand.". . . . She's goin to her room. When she get to the door, she turn and say, "I don't like how that fortune-teller talk bout the Lord and dwellin on race and color. She was sassy to Jesus! Even if Jesus is white, I'm made in His image! Oh, how I love Him! If I gotta love white, make mine Jesus!"

Butler, he too much. Butler laughin and say, "Well, now, Mrs. Ransom Bell, who tole you Jesus is white? Egypt, Jerusalem, all that parta the world is Africa, fulla dark, nappy-headed folks. . . ."

Grandma say, "Shut up, sinner!" Then slam her door shut.

Butler stop laughin and tole Mama, "Woman, I don't wanta hear anymore about you goin to fortune-tellers or dealin in voo-doo. You're not gonna be layin that out in fronta the social worker, so don't be tryin no shortcuts to straightenin Benjie."

Mama punchin on the couch pillows like fluffin them up, she's mad now. "Dammit," she say. "Kill me! Why don't you and Benjie buy guns and shoot me through the heart! His father could run, you can run, he can run, even my mother can slam her door; but I got to hold my ground and keep a roof over our heads, clean house, put food on the table, and also hit it on out here to work each and every day. Dammit, get offa me! My name ain't *'Woman!'* I'm the one carin for Benjie and Mama, for better or worse, and these days it's mostly worse. And my name is still Johnson, not Craig!"

Butler say, "Hold on. I'm a man and you a woman and he's a child. . . ."

Mama cut him off. "I be damn," she say. "We all *people* before anything else. I'm somebody, too! One these days women gonna learn to get up and move, walk, and run out on everybody. How bout that? Now I'm packin a bag and leavin all of you! I'm movin out on family, the social worker, the police and schoolteachers! Yall figure the best way to do everything!"

She flew in the bedroom and slam the french door so hard till a piece-a glass fell out and smash to the floor. She kickin things in the bedroom, arguin so evil. I say to Butler, "You think she packin her bag?"

Butler say, "No, but she wanta." He walk up and down on the throw rug, then say, "Son, you drivin the ladies crazy."

I say, "I'm sorry, Butler."

"Look here," he say. "Square your shoulders, admit you been a junkie, but now gonna stay clean and report to daytime center for your followups. If you don't do right, Butler gonna have to knock you down, you hear?"

"I can do it," I say, "long as somebody believe in me."

"Dammit, Benjie," he say, "you gotta do it even if *nobody* believe in you, gotta be your own man, the supervisor of your veins, the night watchman and day shift foreman in charge-a your own affairs."

Butler pull me over to the window, and we lookin down in the courtyard what's mixed up from people who throw garbage.

"Straighten up, Benjie," he say. "Do it even livin on the edge of ugly, cause we got nowhere else to go right now. Will you be sure and report to followup tomorrow?"

"Yeah," I say, "but you be there too."

"All right," he say, "I'll take off early, one more time."

"Right on, Butler," I say, "and I'll never ask you to promise me nothin else."

Butler throw back his head and laugh hearty, like he do, then say, "I promise you one thing more, Benjie, you not gonna be thirteen forever. You will some-day be twenty-one, thirty-five and so on. Have patience. Soul doctor told me you not really hooked, just on the brink, you can draw back, you got it made, if you say so. How that strike you?"

"That strike me fine, Dad." Callin him dad slip out without thinkin. Sometime people say "dad" like usin slang, so I know that's what he thought I was meanin. But I stop bein shame of what I say, so I say it again. "Fine, Dad. . . . Butler, you ain't the worst person in the world, you know."

He say, "Thank you." Butler lookin serious, and we standin at the window together, and he put his hand on my shoulder.

Mama is sweepin up busted glass from the floor. She say, "Who wants a piece-a pie and a glassa cold milk?" She smilin like nothin happen.

JIMMY-LEE'S FATHER

Street Corner Speaker

HEY, YALL! Don't run by my stepladder so hasty. Where you hurryin to, the graveyard? I got somethin to tell you! Just saw a newborn baby girl who got here with a monkey on her back. Born hooked! Yall ready for that? Go in the hospital and ask if I'm lyin! Yeah, doctors had to drain out the blood from new little sister, had to fill her with new blood, blood from a stranger, to detox the brand-new infant child! Go ask the doctor to tell bout the many more gaspin their way into the world cryin and dyin for a fix! Got no home sweet home! Gotta send the baby to a *foster* home cause mom and dad on the nod . . . and done messed up the seed!

Yall must don't mind! Yall think skag is prosperity. Heartbreak, five bucks a bag! Whitey chargin us money to off ourselves, niggas out here hustlin for him! Look at brothers and sisters bent low, knees knocked together to keep from fallin on their ass, hangin over with hands clenched into helpless fists. DIG HOW TO KILL A NIGGA WITHOUT FIRIN A GUN! Teach him to kill hisself! Teach him to latch a monkey on baby's back fore baby draws breath. Brothers, your *honor* got to be more than somethin you call a judge! Look at the gray-haired sisters fraid to walk home, scared the strong young men gonna jump em, knock em in the head, snatch pocketbooks, and cut throats. Look up at the sky; whitey has walked out on space while our noses pointin down, on the nod! They lookin for a new neighborhood, dig? They have so demoralized the world, till it ain't fit to live in . . . poisoned the air, the streams, rivers and oceans, the earth and all that's in it, and the mind and body of man! Bible say the meek shall inherit the earth! We meek ain't gonna be gettin very much if the earth keep on keepin on like it is!

The children now risin up, but not to call you blessed! Hear me! Hear me! Them that's tryin to kick the habit, now crawlin to the one who put it on em . . . sayin. "Please, Massa, hold my hand and help me shake off my monkey." Look at em walking to the detox center where they can get a little taste-a somethin else to ease off skag. Go to hell, man! You can't get angry, cause you *numb*, can't feel a-tall. Walk on, man, damn your coward soul! I gave yall my life . . . now I'm standin before you, a moneyless, broke down son of Nat Turner . . . I got nothin left but breath in my body . . . here it go . . . take all of me . . . all I got left to offer the race . . . breath, breath . . . Freeeeeeeedom now! Freeeeeeeeeeeeeeeedom now!

631

NOTHIN really works until the boy *wants* to kick and report to the center on his own free will. Well, Benjie sure wants to, so we ahead of the game so far. Here I am waitin out in the street for the second damn time, but, after all, a promise can't always be kept the first time around.

Had to get me another few days off from work. That's no big thing because the time can come offa my vacation. After all, I did get picked, by Benjie, to be his father one hundred times. A chosen man so to speak. Well, some might say that me and my circumstances ain't quite good enough for the job. But I know better. I can do what social worker, head shrink and blood kin can't—give a boy back to himself, so he can turn man. You better believe it.

We've had us a few days happier than any ever before, days that came out right and Sweets now startin her divorce action on groundsa desertion. Last night, after supper, me and Benjie went to playin records, laughin, and havin us a natural ball. Even Mrs. Ransom Bell got caught up when Benjie say, "Dance, Grandma! When you ever gonna do your dance?" Wow! Mrs. Ransom Bell snatches her dress right up to the knee and counts off, "A-one and a-two and a-three." Then damn if she didn't go into a quiverin shake that's not to be believed, shook and shivered bout half a minute, went into a time step, then did a off-to-Buffalo that took her right to her room. We standin there speechless till we start to applaudin, then she close her door and went to singin "Rock of Ages" in top voice. Mrs. Ransom Bell is too much, she really is, cracks me up.

It's gettin cold standin here waitin for Benjie. First I was in the entranceway, but it came to me that Benjie wouldn't be able to see me if he was comin from the corner; if he can't see, he might go away and not try again later. Out here on the steps he can see me from both ends of the street. No way he can mistake me for somebody else, cause my arm is still in the sling . . . and stiff as a board. Doctor say a sprain can be worse than a break. All that roof action is hard on the joints.

I better stand out near the curb edge so he can be sure it's me. Damn, I could haul off and hit some-a these head shrinks and social workers, hit them full on, fist against front teeth. We've been followin their say-so and advice the way the apostles followed Jesus. Day before yesterday a shrink told Sweets it was bad how we never let Benjie make any decisions or have responsibility, so I gave him money to go in a store alone to buy a suit. Dig, he came home yesterday *wearin* the new outfit, with his old clothes wrapped in a box. I cracked up! Sweets cussed him, but I laughed till tears rolled down my cheeks. He had bought a *orange* suit with brown velvet lapels. Look like he was dressed in rotten orange peelins. Blew fifty-seven fifty on that cheap-Charlie suit. The cloth wrinklin and bucklin at the knee . . . and he ain't had it on but half hour. Truth is, reason I didn't get mad like Sweets . . . I was glad he didn't buy skag with the money. I was proud to see him do what he promised to do, even if it was done wrong.

I wish I could see that orange suit turnin the corner right now. Some-a these head shrinks got brass-ass, cold nerve, they don't know how close to a word-whippin they get when talkin rehab with me. I been learnin to button my lip and take stuff offa them that I wouldn't even take from Mrs. Ransom Bell. Today the adviser told me Benjie needs "some male hero figure he can identify with," then goes to showin me a lista books bout Black History, also tellin bout "colored" movie stars and great sports figures and how I must take Benjie to movies and ball games so he can see more heroes.

I gave the adviser some advice. I say, "Some these big-time, celebrity-high-lifers can't take care-a themselves, they in as much trouble as you and Benjie. Yall gotta learn to identify with *me*, who gotta get up to face the world every damn mornin with a clear head and a heavy heart. Benjie once told me a hero ain't nothin but a sandwich—and you say a hero is a celebrity! Listen to *my* credentials; then maybe yall can pin me on a hero button. I'm supportin three adults, one child, and the United States government on my salary . . . and can't claim any of em for tax exemption. So, explain me no heroes. Yeah, and some-a our neighborhood success stories are livin offa Benjie's veins, while they ridin round in limousines and grandstandin to win everybody's admiration."

A half-ass *Negro* guard then takes my arm and walks me toward the door, sayin, "Hush now, brother."

I had somethin for him too. I say, "Don't ease me out the door with that brother talk. Get your hand off me, man."

This skag trouble and the rehab has open up a whole new look at life for me.

Yeah, I'm out here standin in fronta the addict center. This is me! Musician fella I know passed by and say, "Butler, man, what you doin?"

I say, "Standin, waitin for my son, that's what." Fella knew by my tone that he's to leave the subject *alone* and not ask anything else. So that's what he did. Yeah, I'm standin and waitin. It don't pay to get restless and leave cause a child is little bit late. Kids really don't have a good sense-a time. Benjie likes to look in store windows. Lotsa times I say, "Benjie, come on, stop lookin in windows or we'll be late." Bet that's what he's doin now . . . lookin in windows. I would take a walk up to the corner and see if he's lingerin on the avenue, but that'd be the time he'd come from the other way and think I didn't show up. But won't hurt to go to the other side-a the street so it'll give me a better view of the corners on this side, also be no way for me to miss him. I know that he'll be here, but I sure wish he'd come on.

The wind is blowing colder now, but if I go in—he might get this far, then lose courage. Come on, Benjie, I believe in you . . . Benjie, don't hold back, come on, I'm waitin for you . . . hurry up, I'm waitin, boy . . . I'm waitin right here . . . It's nation time . . . I'm waitin for you. . . .

Robert Cormier

1925–2000

ORN January 17, 1925, second of eight children, in Leominster in north-central Massachusetts, Robert Cormier grew up in a neighborhood of French-Canadian immigrants. His father was a factory worker. He lived most of his life within three miles of his birth home. In 1938, Cormier graduated from St. Cecilia's parochial school where, he recounted, he once had seen from the school his family house burning but was forced to say certain prayers before being allowed to leave. Graduating from Leominster High School in 1942, he was president of the senior class. Cormier described himself though as an outsider and a fear-filled "wreck" as a teenager. At Fitchburg State College, which he attended for a year, Cormier found a friendly English teacher, Florence Conlon, who submitted one of Cormier's stories, "The Little Things that Count," to a Catholic magazine, *The Sign*. It was accepted and Cormier received $75. He married Constance Senay in 1948 and they had four children: Bobbie, Peter, Chris, and Renee, and ten grandchildren. From 1946–66, Cormier worked as reporter and editor, first for the Worcester *Telegram* and then for the Fitchburg *Sentinel*. Even while he won various awards for his journalism, he also wrote adult novels, three by 1965, all published and favorably reviewed.

Cormier first conceived *The Chocolate War* (inspired by his son Peter refusing, successfully, to sell chocolates for his school) as a novel for adults, but he agreed with his editor to market it as a young adult novel. Published in 1974, it was immediately popular. Several novels for young adults followed: *I Am the Cheese* (1977), *After the First Death* (1979), *The Bumblebee Flies Anyway* (1983), *Beyond the Chocolate War* (1985), a sequel in which Obie plots to kill Archie, *Fade* (1988), *Other Bells for Us to Ring* (1990), *We All Fall Down* (1991), *Tunes for Bears to Dance To* (1992), *In the Middle of the Night* (1995), *Tenderness* (1997), *Heroes* (1998), *Frenchtown Summer* (1999), and *The Rag and Bone Shop* (2001). Cormier also published two collections of short stories and short journal pieces. The novels have been translated into over a dozen languages and three have been made into films.

Cormier loved writing, reading (among his favorite authors were Mark Twain, Graham Greene, Ernest Hemingway, William Saroyan, John O'Hara, and J. D. Salinger), travel, walking, jazz, and people. He often surprised interviewers, who expected the author of such grim books to be grim, by proving himself uncynical, modest, even genial. After a lifetime devoted to writing his widely-acclaimed books, Robert Cormier died on November 2, 2000.

From the outset, *The Chocolate War* aroused significant controversy. Some critics argued that youthful readers tend to be too impressionable and vulnerable to withstand the book's defeatist ending. Others applauded the book's honesty and realism, hailing *The Chocolate War* as a groundbreaking attempt to challenge conventional stereotypes of lonely but successful heroes and to write genuine tragedy for young adults considered wise enough to appreciate the values upheld, if indirectly, by the book. The book remains one of the young adult novels most frequently censored from school libraries.

The setting of *The Chocolate War* is a Catholic boys' day school somewhere in New England. At Cormier's Trinity school, the trouble begins with violence and cruelty on the football field. The school looks the other way, and the implications are clear: something is rotten in the state of institutional values upheld in the school. Cormier presents a thorough-going dystopia in which the Assistant Headmaster, Brother Leon, presides with gleeful malice over a corrupt and demoralizing system for inflicting pain, shame, and servitude from the top down. Brother Leon, blessed with a pervasive "smell of perspiration," "rancid breath," and "venomous," "menacing" voice, has misappropriated school funds to buy 20,000 boxes of chocolates he hopes to get the boys to sell at great profit so as to enhance his power and become Headmaster. His monetary obsession, grafted on the student sellers as "Trinity's spirit . . . true spirit, a wonderful display of spirit . . . a spirit of brotherhood," makes a mockery of any true spiritual value suggested by the best meaning of Trinity. In this setting, moreover, his example is easily followed.

Brother Leon's chief henchman is one Archie Costello, Assigner for the Vigils, a gang that assigns cruel tasks to other students and thus maintains a fear-ridden "order" in the school. Archie, whose name suggests both Satan, the Arch-Enemy, and gangster (after the infamous mobster, Frankie Costello) boasts of his atheism to his sidekick, Obie: "When you march down to the rail, you're receiving The Body, man. Me, I'm just chewing a wafer they buy by the pound in Worcester . . . and when you say 'Jesus,' you're talking about your leader. But when I say 'Jesus,' I'm talking about a guy who walked the earth for thirty-three years like any other guy but caught the imagination of some PR cats." And of course the name "Vigils" mocks the biblical sense of devout waiting in anticipation of resurrection or return, converting it to a nickname for vigilantes. Through their lust for power, at any cost, Leon and Archie bring the school, figuratively, and its hero, Jerry Renault, literally, to their knees.

Jerry is a hero because he questions not only the corrupt chocolate sale but also the larger society around it and the school. Jerry wonders about his unceasing grief for his mother who died recently of cancer, about the codes of cruelty and unallowed protest on the football field and in the classroom, about the shame and guilt tied to sexual expression, about his father's numbed-out existence, about "his own life stretching ahead of him . . . a long succession of days and nights . . . not good, not bad, not great, not lousy, not exciting, not anything." And so Jerry decides that he dares to "disturb the universe" by refusing to sell the chocolates. His decision proves nearly fatal to his life, more fully fatal to his spirit. Yet he has exposed, for all to see, the corruption of the school administration and the immorality it sponsors. Or has he?

Cormier, in all his books, explores the politics of justice and freedom. He shows, in particular, the folly of expecting justice but the heroism of seeking it, the difficulty of achieving freedom, of "doing your own thing," but the breathless daring of acting on its behalf. In Cormier's world, which may be the world of most of us, it is heroic to seek justice and freedom because it is unusual to do so. At Trinity and in its surrounding town, people are mired in passivity, stuck in "their useless lives." It is not only Archie who sees that "the world was made up of two kinds of people—those who were victims and those who victimized."

636

Other students find that "life was rotten, that there were no heroes, really, and that you couldn't trust anybody, not even yourself." The theme of "willing victims" echoes through the book, as if the basic stuff of humankind were deficient, tainted with an original sin of self-pollution. Even Jerry has to admit: "most of the kids didn't give a damn or have any respect for the rights of others." Not only do the boys steal from and torment each other but they also, Cormier suggests, pervert their sexual energies—getting "horny" during violence on each other and committing "rape by eyeball" on girls. Jerry is trapped, finally, by his own fear of being thought a homosexual. Responding to the taunt of "fairy," Jerry finds he enjoys punching his taunter's face, "getting revenge finally." That one blow leads, of course, to Jerry's devastation—"not disturbing the universe but damaging it"—and to his apparent capitulation—"to play ball . . . to do whatever they wanted you to do . . . don't disturb the universe . . . otherwise, they murder you." Whether Jerry should be seen, at the end, as another willing victim, or whether his extended resistance makes him qualitatively different from his classmates, remains an open question.

In Cormier's world, the only final heroism is like that of the Greek mythic hero, Sisyphus, who was condemned to roll a huge boulder up a hill, watch helplessly as it rolled back, and then to begin again, forever. This is a bleak, existential ethic. Cormier insisted, however, that his books championed right over wrong. "On the surface they may look dark, but a closer reading reveals moral values." Many readers have agreed.

The Chocolate War made a place for itself in the gradual darkening and sobering progress of realistic fiction about and for youth, fiction by writers such as J. D. Salinger, Hannah Green, Julia Cunningham, S. E. Hinton, Paul Zindel, M. E. Kerr, Judy Blume, Robert Peck, and Alice Childress. Enacting the book's wrenching intensity, Cormier's style and structure leave little to be desired. The tense plot moves forward in a series of brief, cinematically vivid scenes, each of which is viewed through the perspective of a boy. We are never allowed into the mind of a grown-up; the narrator's omniscience extends only to the boys, so that all is rendered from their point of view. We know what they think and feel, but we can only guess, with them, what the Brothers and parents and townsfolk think and feel. This creates a firm and poignant separation between the generations, and it shows the many similarities, as well as some differences, in attitudes, responses, even vocabularies of the boys who are welded into one vibrating community of viciousness and humiliation.

Cormier gave some interesting reasons for the generational gap and, in particular, the minimal attention to parents in his books. He said: "I believe that there is a chasm between young people and adults. . . . I don't dwell on the parents in my books because I like to have the characters judged for themselves on their own actions. I didn't want people to say, well Archie comes from a broken home or a too wealthy home or a dysfunctional family. I didn't want him to have any cop outs."

Cormier has written *The Chocolate War* with terrific sensory immediacy, depicting the bodily impact of sights, sounds, tastes, touch/kinesthesia, and, above all smells. Cormier's command of pacing, of scenic variety, contrast, compression, and tension, of crackling dialogue and emotive extremes, of withering irony (notice the repeated ironic use of words like "beautiful" and "sweet"), of escalating shocks, and broken taboos is remarkable. The rhythms of the phrases and sentences, the varied sentence and paragraph lengths and structures, all the tools of emphasis and of carefully prepared climaxes drive the reader toward tightening engagement with the story and its ever-fascinating if often-repulsive characters. Robert Cormier was a firmly successful journalist and writer of novels for adults *before* he took up the writing of young adult novels. That he saw his path into young adult literature as an avenue for the development of his craft and growth of his understanding showed his belief in the dignity and worth of this genre. Destined to be long-read, long-cherished, Cormier wrote genuine classics.

CHAPTER 1

THEY MURDERED HIM.

As he turned to take the ball, a dam burst against the side of his head and a hand grenade shattered his stomach. Engulfed by nausea, he pitched toward the grass. His mouth encountered gravel, and he spat frantically, afraid that some of his teeth had been knocked out. Rising to his feet, he saw the field through drifting gauze but held on until everything settled into place, like a lens focusing, making the world sharp again, with edges.

The second play called for a pass. Fading back, he picked up a decent block and cocked his arm, searching for a receiver—maybe the tall kid they called The Goober. Suddenly, he was caught from behind and whirled violently, a toy boat caught in a whirlpool. Landing on his knees, hugging the ball, he urged himself to ignore the pain that gripped his groin, knowing that it was important to betray no sign of distress, remembering The Goober's advice, "Coach is testing you, testing, and he's looking for guts."

I've got guts, Jerry murmured, getting up by degrees, careful not to displace any of his bones or sinews. A telephone rang in his ears. Hello, hello, I'm still here. When he moved his lips, he tasted the acid of dirt and grass and gravel. He was aware of the other players around him, helmeted and grotesque, creatures from an unknown world. He had never felt so lonely in his life, abandoned, defenseless.

On the third play, he was hit simultaneously by three of them: one, his knees; another, his stomach; a third, his head—the helmet no protection at all. His body seemed to telescope into itself but all the parts didn't fit, and he was stunned by the knowledge that pain isn't just one thing—it is cunning and various, sharp here and sickening there, burning here and clawing there. He clutched himself as he hit the ground. The ball squirted away. His breath went away, like the ball—a terrible stillness pervaded him—and then, at the onset of panic, his breath came back again. His lips sprayed wetness and he was grateful for the sweet cool air that filled his lungs. But when he tried to get up, his body mutinied against movement. He decided the hell with it. He'd go to sleep right here, right out on the fifty yard line, the hell with trying out for the team, screw everything, he was going to sleep, he didn't care anymore . . .

"Renault!"

Ridiculous, someone calling his name.

"Renault!"

The coach's voice scraped like sandpaper against his ears. He opened his eyes flutteringly. "I'm all right," he said to nobody in particular, or to his father maybe. Or the coach. He was unwilling to abandon this lovely lassitude but he had to, of course. He was sorry to leave the earth, and he was vaguely curious about how he was going to get up, with both legs smashed and his skull battered

639

in. He was astonished to find himself on his feet, intact, bobbing like one of those toy novelties dangling from car windows, but erect.

"For Christ's sake," the coach bellowed, his voice juicy with contempt. A spurt of saliva hit Jerry's cheek.

Hey, coach, you spit on me, Jerry protested. Stop the spitting, coach. What he said aloud was, "I'm all right, coach," because he was a coward about stuff like that, thinking one thing and saying another, planning one thing and doing another—he had been Peter a thousand times and a thousand cocks had crowed in his lifetime.[1]

"How tall are you, Renault?"

"Five nine," he gasped, still fighting for breath.

"Weight?"

"One forty-five," he said, looking the coach straight in the eye.

"Soaking wet, I'll bet," the coach said sourly. "What the hell you want to play football for? You need more meat on those bones. What the hell you trying to play quarterback for? You'd make a better end. Maybe."

The coach looked like an old gangster: broken nose, a scar on his cheek like a stitched shoe-string. He needed a shave, his stubble like slivers of ice. He growled and swore and was merciless. But a helluva coach, they said. The coach stared at him now, the dark eyes probing, pondering. Jerry hung in there, trying not to sway, trying not to faint.

"All right," the coach said in disgust. "Show up tomorrow. Three o'clock sharp or you're through before you start."

Inhaling the sweet sharp apple air through his nostrils—he was afraid to open his mouth wide, wary of any movement that was not absolutely essential—he walked tentatively toward the sidelines, listening to the coach barking at the other guys. Suddenly, he loved that voice, "Show up tomorrow."

He trudged away from the field, blinking against the afternoon sun, toward the locker room at the gym. His knees were liquid and his body light as air, suddenly.

Know what? he asked himself, a game he played sometimes.

What?

I'm going to make the team.

Dreamer, dreamer.

Not a dream: it's the truth.

As Jerry took another deep breath, a pain appeared, distant, small—a radar signal of distress. Bleep, I'm here. Pain. His feet scuffled through crazy corn-flake leaves. A strange happiness invaded him. He knew he'd been massacred by the oncoming players, capsized and dumped humiliatingly on the ground. But he'd survived—he'd gotten to his feet. "You'd make a better end." Was the coach thinking he might try him at end? Any position, as long as he made the team. The bleep grew larger, localized now, between his ribs on the right side. He thought of his mother and how drugged she was at the end, not recognizing anyone, neither Jerry nor his father. The exhilaration of the moment vanished and he sought it in vain, like seeking ecstasy's memory an instant after jacking off and encountering only shame and guilt.

Nausea began to spread through his stomach, warm and oozy and evil.

"Hey," he called weakly. To nobody. Nobody there to listen.

---

1 *Peter . . . lifetime* As reported in the New Testament (Matt. 26.74–75, John 18.27), as Christ predicted, his disciple, Peter, fearfully denied knowing him—just before the cock crowed.

He managed to make it back to the school. By the time he had sprawled himself on the floor of the lavatory, his head hanging over the lip of the toilet bowl and the smell of disinfectant stinging his eyeballs, the nausea had passed and the bleep of pain had faded. Sweat moved like small moist bugs on his forehead.

And then, without warning, he vomited.

CHAPTER 2

OBIE WAS BORED. Worse than bored. He was disgusted. He was also tired. It seemed he was always tired these days. He went to bed tired and he woke up tired. He found himself yawning constantly. Most of all, he was tired of Archie. Archie the bastard. The bastard that Obie alternately hated and admired. For instance, at this minute he hated Archie with a special burning hate that was part of the boredom and the weariness. Notebook in hand, pencil poised, Obie looked at Archie now with fierce anger, furious at the way Archie sat there in the bleachers, his blond hair tossing lightly in the breeze, enjoying himself, for crying out loud, even though he knew that Obie would be late for work and yet keeping him here, stalling, killing time.

"You're a real bastard," Obie said finally, his frustration erupting, like a Coke exploding from a bottle after you shake it. "You know that?"

Archie turned and smiled at him benevolently, like a goddam king passing out favors.

"Jesus," Obie said, exasperated.

"Don't swear, Obie," Archie chided. "You'll have to tell it in confession."

"Look who's talking. I don't know how you had the nerve to receive communion at chapel this morning."

"It doesn't take nerve, Obie. When you march down to the rail, you're receiving The Body, man. Me, I'm just chewing a wafer they buy by the pound in Worcester."

Obie looked away in disgust.

"And when you say 'Jesus,' you're talking about your leader. But when I say 'Jesus,' I'm talking about a guy who walked the earth for thirty-three years like any other guy but caught the imagination of some *PR* cats. *PR* for Public Relations, in case you don't know, Obie."

Obie didn't bother to answer. You couldn't ever win an argument with Archie. He was too quick with the words. Especially when he fell into one of his phony hip moods. Saying *man* and *cat*, like he was a swinger, cool, instead of a senior in a lousy little high school like Trinity.

"Come on, Archie, it's getting late," Obie said, trying to appeal to Archie's better nature. "I'm going to get fired one of these days."

"Don't whine, Obie. Besides, you hate the job. You have a subconscious wish to be fired. Then you wouldn't have to stock the shelves any more or take crap from customers or work late Saturday night instead of going to the—what is it you go to?—the Teen-Age Canteen to drool over all those broads."

Archie was uncanny. How did he know Obie hated the stupid job? How did he know that Obie hated especially those Saturday nights stalking the supermarket canyons while everybody else was at the canteen?

"See? I'm doing you a favor. Enough of these late afternoons and the boss'll say, 'You're all done, Obie baby. Set free.' And you'll have won, right in front of him."

"And where'll my money come from?" Obie asked.

Archie waved his hand, signaling that he was tired of the conversation. You could see him physically withdraw although he was only a foot or two away from Obie on the bleacher bench. The shouts of the fellows from the football field below echoed feebly in the air. Archie's lower lip dropped. That meant he was concentrating. Thinking. Obie waited in anticipation, hating the thing in him that made him look at Archie in admiration. The way Archie could turn people on. Or off. The way he could dazzle you with his brilliance—those Vigil assignments that had made him practically a legend at Trinity—and the way he could disgust you with his cruelties, those strange offbeat cruelties of his, that had nothing to do with pain or violence but were somehow even worse. It made Obie uncomfortable to think of that stuff and he shrugged the thoughts away, waiting for Archie to talk, to say the name.

"Stanton," Archie said finally, whispering the name, caressing the syllables. "I think his first name is Norman."

"Right," Obie said, scrawling the name. Only two more to go. Archie had to come up with ten names by four o'clock and eight were now listed on Obie's pad.

"The assignment?" Obie prodded.

"Sidewalk."

Obie grinned as he wrote the word. Sidewalk: such an innocent word. But what Archie could do with simple things like a sidewalk and a kid like Norman Stanton whom Obie recalled as a blustering bragging character with wild red hair and eyelids matted with yellow crap.

"Hey, Obie," Archie said.

"Yeah?" Obie asked, on guard.

"You really going to be late for work? I mean—would you really lose your job?" Archie's voice was soft with concern, his eyes gentle with compassion. That's what baffled everyone about Archie—his changes of mood, the way he could be a wise bastard one minute and a great guy the next.

"I don't think they'd actually fire me. The guy who owns the place, he's a friend of the family. But I mean getting there late doesn't, like, help the cause. I'm overdue for a raise but he's holding it back until I get on the ball."

Archie nodded, all businesslike. "All right, we'll wrap it up. We'll get you on the ball. Maybe I ought to assign someone to the store, and make life interesting for your boss."

"Jeez, no," Obie said quickly. He shivered with dread, realizing how awesome Archie's power really was. Which is why you had to stay on the good side of the bastard. Buy him Hersheys all the time to satisfy his craving for chocolate. Thank God Archie didn't go in for pot or that stuff—Obie would have had to become a pusher, for crying out loud, to supply him. Obie was officially the secretary of The Vigils but he knew what the job really demanded. Carter, the president who was almost as big a bastard as Archie, said, "Keep him happy, when Archie's happy, we're all happy."

"Two more names," Archie mused now. He rose and stretched. He was tall and not too heavy. He moved with a subtle rhythm, languidly, the walk of an athlete although he hated all sports and had nothing but contempt for athletes. Particularly football players and boxers, which happened to be Trinity's two major sports. Usually, Archie didn't pick athletes for assignments—he claimed they were too stupid to absorb the delicate shadings, the subtle intricacies involved. Archie disliked violence—most of his assignments were exercises in the psychological rather than the physical. That's why he got away with so much.

The Trinity brothers wanted peace at any price, quiet on the campus, no broken bones. Otherwise, the sky was the limit. Which was right up Archie's alley.

"The kid they call The Goober," Archie said now.

Obie wrote down "Roland Goubert."

"Brother Eugene's room."

Obie smiled in delicious malice. He liked it when Archie involved the brothers in the assignments. Those were the most daring, of course. And someday Archie would go too far and trip himself up. In the meantime, Brother Eugene would do. He was a peaceful sort, made to order for Archie, naturally.

The sun vanished behind floating clouds. Archie brooded, isolating himself again. The wind rose, kicking puffs of dust from the football field. The field needed seeding. The bleachers also needed attention—they sagged, peeling paint like leprosy on the benches. The shadows of the goal posts sprawled on the field like grotesque crosses. Obie shivered.

"What the hell do they think I am?" Archie asked.

Obie remained silent. The question didn't seem to require an answer. It was as if Archie was talking to himself.

"These goddam assignments," Archie said. "Do they think it's easy?" His voice dripped sadness. "And the black box . . ."

Obie yawned. He was tired. And uncomfortable. He always yawned and got tired and uncomfortable when he found himself in situations like this, not knowing how to proceed, surprised at the anguish in Archie's voice. Or was Archie putting him on? You never knew about Archie. Obie was grateful when Archie finally shook his head as if warding off an evil spell.

"You're not much help, Obie."

"I never thought you needed much help, Archie."

"Don't you think I'm human, too?"

I'm not sure. That's what Obie almost said.

"All right, all right. Let's finish the damn assignments. One more name."

Obie's pencil was poised.

"Who was that kid who left the field a few minutes ago? The one they wiped out?"

"Kid named Jerry Renault. Freshman," Obie said, flipping through his notebook. He searched the *R*'s for Renault. His notebook was more complete than the school's files. It contained information, carefully coded, about everyone at Trinity, the kind of stuff that couldn't be found in official records. "Here it is. Renault, Jerome E. Son of James R. Pharmacist at Blake's. The kid's a freshman, birthday—let's see, he just turned fourteen. Oh—his mother died last spring. Cancer." There was more information about courses and records in grammar school and extracurricular activities but Obie closed the notebook as if he were lowering a coffin lid.

"Poor kid," Archie said. "Mother's dead."

Again that concern, that compassion in his voice.

Obie nodded. One more name. Who else?

"Must be hard on the poor kid."

"Right," Obie agreed, impatient.

"Know what he needs, Obie?" His voice was soft, dreamy, caressing.

"What?"

"Therapy."

The terrible word shattered the tenderness in Archie's voice.

"Therapy?"

"Right. Put him down."

"For crying out loud, Archie. You saw him out there. He's just a skinny kid trying to make the Freshman team. Coach'll grind him up like hamburger. And his mother's barely cold in the grave. What the hell you putting him on the list for?"

"Don't let him fool you, Obie. He's a tough one. Didn't you see him get wiped out down there and still get to his feet? Tough. And stubborn. He should have stayed down on that turf, Obie. That would have been the smart thing to do. Besides, he probably needs something to keep his mind off his poor dead mother."

"You're a bastard, Archie. I said it before and I'll say it again."

"Put him down." Ice in the voice, cold as polar regions.

Obie wrote down the name. Hell, it wasn't his funeral. "Assignment?"

"I'll think of something."

"You've only got till four," Obie reminded.

"The assignment must fit the kid. That's the beauty of it, Obie."

Obie waited a minute or two and couldn't resist asking. "You running out of ideas, Archie?" The great Archie Costello running dry? The possibility was staggering to contemplate.

"Just being artistic, Obie. It's an art, you know. Take a kid like this Renault. Special circumstances." He fell silent. "Put him down for the chocolates."

Obie wrote down: *Renault—Chocolates.* Archie would never run dry. The chocolates, for instance, were good for a dozen assignments.

Obie looked down at the field where the guys were skirmishing in the shadow of the goal posts. Sadness seized him. I should have gone out for football, he thought. He had wanted to—he'd been hot stuff with Pop Warner at St. Joe's. Instead, he had ended up as Secretary of The Vigils. Cool. But, hell, he couldn't even tell his parents about it.

"Know what, Archie?"

"What?"

"Life is sad, sometimes."

That was one of the great things about Archie, you could say things like that.

"Life is shit," Archie said.

The shadows of the goal posts definitely resembled a network of crosses, empty crucifixes. That's enough symbolism for one day, Obie told himself. If he hurried he could make the four o'clock bus to work.

CHAPTER 3

THE GIRL was heart-wrenchingly, impossibly beautiful. Desire weakened his stomach. A waterfall of blond hair splashed on her bare shoulders. He studied the photograph surreptitiously and then closed the magazine and put it back where it belonged, on the top shelf. He glanced around to see if he'd been observed. The store owner positively prohibited the reading of magazines and a sign said NO BUY NO READ. But the owner was busy at the far end of the place.

Why did he always feel so guilty whenever he looked at *Playboy* and the other magazines? A lot of guys bought them, passed them around at school, hid them in the covers of notebooks, even resold them. He sometimes saw copies scattered casually on coffee tables in the homes of his friends. He had once bought a girlie magazine, paying for it with trembling fingers—a dollar and a quarter, his finances shot down in flames until his next allowance. And he didn't know what to do with the damn thing once it was in his possession. Sneaking it home on the bus, hiding it in the bottom drawer of his room, he was terrified of discovery. Finally, tired of smuggling it into the bathroom for swift perusals, and weary of his deceit, and haunted by the fear that his mother would find the magazine, Jerry had sneaked it out of the house and dropped it into a catch-basin. He listened to it splash dismally below, bidding a wistful farewell to the squandered buck and a quarter. A longing filled him. Would a girl ever love him? The one devastating sorrow he carried within him was the fear that he would die before holding a girl's breast in his hand.

Out at the bus stop, Jerry leaned against a telephone pole, body weary, echoing the assault of the football practices. For three days his body had absorbed punishment. But he was still on the roster, luckily. Idly, he watched the people on the Common across the street. He saw them every day. They were now part of the scenery like the Civil War Cannon and the World War Monuments, the flagpole. Hippies. Flower Children. Street People. Drifters. Drop-Outs. Everybody had a different name for them. They came out in the spring and stayed until October, hanging around, calling taunts to passersby occasionally but most of the time quiet, languid and peaceful. He was fascinated by them and sometimes envied their old clothes, their sloppiness, the way they didn't seem to give a damn about anything. Trinity was one of the last schools to retain a dress code—shirt and tie. He watched a cloud of smoke swirl around a girl in a floppy hat. Grass? He didn't know. A lot of things he didn't know.

Absorbed in his thoughts, he didn't notice that one of the street people had detached himself from the others and was crossing the street, dodging cars deftly.

"Hey, man."

Startled, Jerry realized the guy was addressing him. "Me?"

The fellow stood in the street, on the other side of a green Volkswagen, his chest resting on the car's roof. "Yes, you." He was about nineteen, long black hair brushing his shoulders, a curling mustache, like a limp black snake draped on his upper lip, the ends dangling near his chin. "You been staring at us, man, like every day. Standing here and staring."

They really say *man*, Jerry thought. He didn't think anybody said *man* any more except as a joke. But this guy wasn't joking.

"Hey, man, you think we're in a zoo? That why you stare?"

"No. Look, I don't stare." But he did stare, every day.

"Yes, you do, man. You stand here and look at us. With your homework books and your nice shirt and your blue-and-white tie."

Jerry looked around uneasily. He confronted only strangers, nobody from school.

"We're not sub-humans, man."

"I didn't say you were."

"But you look it."

"Look," Jerry said, "I've got to get my bus." Which was ridiculous, of course, because the bus wasn't in sight.

"You know who's sub-human, man? You. You are. Going to school every day. And back home on the bus. And do your homework." The guy's voice was contemptuous. "Square boy. Middleaged at fourteen, fifteen. Already caught in a routine. Wow."

A hiss and the stench of exhaust announced the arrival of the bus. Jerry swung away from the guy.

"Go get your bus, square boy," he called. "Don't miss the bus, boy. You're missing a lot of things in the world, better not miss that bus."

645

Jerry walked to the bus like a sleepwalker. He hated confrontations. His heart hammered. He climbed aboard, dropped his token in the coin box and lurched to his seat as the bus moved away from the curb.

He sat down, breathed deeply, closed his eyes.

Go get your bus, square boy.

He opened his eyes and slitted them against the invasion of the sun through the window.

You're missing a lot of things in the world, better not miss that bus.

A big put-on, of course. That was their specialty, people like that. Putting people on. Nothing else to do with their lives, piddling away their lives.

And yet . . .

Yet, what?

He didn't know. He thought of his life—going to school and coming home. Even though his tie was loose, dangling on his shirt, he yanked it off. He looked up at the advertising placards above the windows, wanting to turn his thoughts away from the confrontation.

Why? someone had scrawled in a blank space no advertiser had rented.

Why not? someone else had slashed in answer.

Jerry closed his eyes, exhausted suddenly, and it seemed like too much of an effort even to think.

CHAPTER 4

"HOW MANY BOXES?"

"Twenty thousand."

Archie whistled in astonishment. He usually didn't blow his cool that easily, particularly with someone like Brother Leon. But the image of twenty thousand boxes of chocolates being delivered here to Trinity was ridiculous. Then he saw the mustache of moistness on Brother Leon's upper lip, the watery eyes and the dampness on his forehead. Something clicked. This wasn't the calm and deadly Leon who could hold a class in the palm of his hand. This was someone riddled with cracks and crevices. Archie became absolutely still, afraid that the rapid beating of his heart might betray his sudden knowledge, the proof of what he'd always suspected, not only of Brother Leon but most grownups, most adults: they were vulnerable, running scared, open to invasion.

"I know that's a lot of chocolates," Brother Leon admitted, managing to keep his voice casual, for which Archie admired him. A smart one, Leon, hard to pin down. Even though he was sweating like a madman, his voice remained calm, reasoned. "But we have tradition working in our favor. The chocolate sale is an annual event. The boys have come to expect it. If they can sell ten thousand boxes of chocolates in other years, why not twenty thousand this year? And these are special chocolates, Archie. High profit. A special deal."

"How is it special?" Archie asked, pressing his advantage, none of that student-talking-to-teacher crap in his voice. He was here in Leon's office by special invitation. Let Leon talk to the real Archie, not the kid who sat in his algebra class.

"Actually, these are Mother's Day chocolates. We were—that is, I was—able to pick them up at a bargain price. Beautiful boxes, gift boxes, and in perfect condition. They've been stored under the best of conditions since last spring.

All we have to do is remove the purple ribbons that say *Mother* and we're in business. We can sell them for two dollars a box and make a profit of almost a dollar on each one."

"But twenty thousand boxes." Archie performed some quick calculations although he wasn't a whiz at math. "We're about four hundred guys in the school. That means everybody's got to sell fifty boxes. Usually, the guys have a quota of twenty-five boxes each to sell and the price is a dollar." He sighed. "Now, everything is doubled. That's a lot of selling for this school, Brother Leon. For any school."

"I know that, Archie. But Trinity is special, isn't it? If I didn't think the boys of Trinity could do it, do you think I would take a risk? Aren't we capable of what others aren't?"

Bullshit, was what Archie thought.

"I know what you're wondering, Archie—why am I burdening you with this problem?"

Archie, in fact, *was* wondering why Brother Leon had laid his plans before him. He had never been particularly friendly with Leon or any other Trinity teacher. And Leon was a special breed. On the surface, he was one of those pale, ingratiating kind of men who tiptoed through life on small, quick feet. He looked like a henpecked husband, a pushover, a sucker. He was the Assistant Headmaster of the school but actually served as a flunky for the Head. Like an errand boy. But all this was deceptive. In the classroom, Leon was another person altogether. Smirking, sarcastic. His thin, high voice venomous. He could hold your attention like a cobra. Instead of fangs, he used his teacher's pointer, flicking out here, there, everywhere. He watched the class like a hawk, suspicious, searching out cheaters or daydreamers, probing for weaknesses in the students and then exploiting those weaknesses. He had never taken on Archie. Not yet.

"Let me paint you the picture," Leon said, leaning forward in his chair. "All private schools, Catholic or otherwise, are struggling these days. Many are closing down. Prices are going up and we have only so many sources of income. As you know, Archie, we're not one of those exclusive boarding schools. And we don't have any wealthy alumni to draw on. We're a day school, dedicated to preparing young men from middle class homes for college. There are no rich men's sons here. Take yourself, for instance. Your father operates an insurance agency. He makes a good salary but he's hardly wealthy, is he? Take Tommy Desjardins. His father's a dentist—very well off, they have two cars, a summer home—and that's about tops for the parents of Trinity boys." He held up his hand. "I'm not trying to put down the parents." Archie winced. It irritated him when grownups resorted to student language like *put down*. "What I'm saying, Archie, is that the parents are mostly in modest circumstances and can't absorb any more tuition increases. We have to find revenue wherever possible. Football barely pays for itself—we haven't had a winning season for three years. The interest in boxing has fallen off now that television doesn't feature boxing anymore . . ."

Archie stifled a yawn—so what else was new? "I'm putting my cards on the table, Archie, to show you, to impress upon you, how we have to tap every source of income, how even a chocolate sale can be vital and important to us . . ."

Silence fell. The school was hushed around them, so hushed that Archie wondered whether the office was soundproof. Classes were over for the day, of course, but that was the time when a lot of other action got started. Particularly Vigil action.

"Another thing," Leon went on. "We've kept this quiet but the Head is ill, perhaps seriously so. He's scheduled to enter the hospital tomorrow. Tests and things. The outlook isn't good . . ."

Archie waited for Leon to get to the point. Was he going to make a ridiculous pitch for the chocolate sale to be a success in honor of the sick Headmaster? "Win one for the Gipper" like some pukey late-night movie?

"He may be incapacitated for weeks."

"That's rough." So what?

"Which means—the school will be in my charge. The school will be my responsibility."

The silence again. But this time Archie felt a waiting in the silence. He had a feeling that Leon was about to make his point.

"I need your help, Archie."

"My help?" Archie asked, feigning surprise, trying to keep any trace of mockery out of his voice. He knew now why he was here. Leon didn't mean Archie's help—he meant the help of The Vigils. And didn't dare put it into words. No one was allowed to breathe a word about The Vigils. Officially, The Vigils did not exist. How could a school condone an organization like The Vigils? The school allowed it to function by ignoring it completely, pretending it wasn't there. But it was there, all right, Archie thought bitterly. It was there because it served a purpose. The Vigils kept things under control. Without The Vigils, Trinity might have been torn apart like other schools had been, by demonstrations, protests, all that crap. Archie was surprised by Leon's audacity, knowing his connection with The Vigils and bringing him in here this way.

"But how can *I* help?" Archie asked, turning the screw, emphasizing the singular of himself and not the plural of The Vigils.

"By getting behind the sale. As you said, Archie—twenty thousand boxes, that's a lot of chocolates."

"The price is doubled, too," Archie reminded him, enjoying himself now. "Two dollars a box, instead of one."

"But we need that money desperately."

"How about the bonus? The school always gives the boys a bonus."

"As usual, Archie. A day off from school when every chocolate has been sold."

"No free trip this year? Last year we were taken to Boston to a stage show." Archie didn't care about the trip but he enjoyed this reverse position—himself asking the questions and Leon squirming, so different from the classroom.

"I'll think of something as a substitute," Leon said.

Archie let the silence stretch.

"Can I count on you, Archie?" Leon's forehead was damp again.

Archie decided to plunge. To see how far he could go. "But what can I do? I'm just one guy."

"You have influence, Archie."

"Influence?" Archie's voice was coming out loud and clear. He was cool. In command. Let Leon sweat. Archie was sweet and cool. "I'm not a class officer. I'm not a member of the Student Council." Christ, if only the guys were here to see him. "I don't even make the Honor Roll . . ."

Suddenly, Leon wasn't sweating anymore. The beads of perspiration still danced on his forehead but he had become stiff and cold. Archie could feel the coldness—more than cold, an icy hate coming across the desk like a deadly ray from some bleak and lethal planet. Have I gone too far, he wondered. I've got this guy for algebra, my weakest subject.

"You know what I mean," Leon said, his voice like a door slamming.

Their eyes met, held. A showdown now? At this moment? Would that be the smart thing to do? Archie believed in always doing the smart thing. Not the thing you ached to do, not the impulsive act, but the thing that would pay off later. That's why he was The Assigner. That's why The Vigils depended on him. Hell, The Vigils *were* the school. And he, Archie Costello, was The Vigils. That's why Leon had called him here, that's why Leon was practically begging for his help. Archie suddenly had a terrific craving for a Hershey.

"I know what you mean," Archie said, postponing the showdown. Leon could be like money in the bank, for future use.

"You'll help, then?"

"I'll check with them," Archie said, letting *them* hang in the air.

And it hung.

Leon didn't pick it up.

Neither did Archie.

They looked at each other for a long moment.

"The Vigils will help," Archie said, unable to contain himself any longer. He had never been able to use those words—The Vigils—aloud to a teacher, had had to deny the existence of the organization for so long that it was beautiful to use them, to see the surprise on Leon's pale perspiring face.

Then he pushed back his chair and left the office without waiting for the teacher's dismissal.

CHAPTER 5

"Y OUR NAME IS GOUBERT?"

"Yes."

"They call you The Goober?"

"Yes."

"Yes, what?"

Archie was disgusted with himself even as he said it. *Yes, what?* like a scene from out of an old World War Two movie. But the kid Goubert stammered and then said, "Yes, *sir.*" Like a raw recruit.

"Know why you're here, Goober?"

The Goober hesitated. Despite his height, he was easily six-one, he reminded Archie of a child, someone who didn't belong here, as if he'd been caught sneaking into an Adults Only movie. He was too skinny, of course. And he had the look of a loser. Vigil bait.

"Yes, sir," The Goober finally said.

Archie was always puzzled about whatever there was inside of him that enjoyed these performances—toying with kids, leading them on, humiliating them, finally. He'd earned the job of Assigner because of his quick mind, his swift intelligence, his fertile imagination, his ability to see two moves ahead as if life were a giant checker or chess game. But something more than that, something nobody could find words to describe. Archie knew what it was and recognized it, although it eluded a definition. One night while watching an old Marx Brothers movie on the Late Show, he was held entranced by a scene where the brothers were searching for a missing painting. Groucho said, "We'll search every room in the house." Chico asked, "But what if it ain't in the house?"

Groucho replied, "Then we'll search the house next door." "What if there ain't no house next door?" And Groucho, "Then we'll build one." And they immediately started to draw up plans for building the house. That's what Archie did—built the house nobody could anticipate a need for, except himself, a house that was invisible to everyone else.

"If you know, then tell me why you're here, Goober," Archie said now, his voice gentle. He always treated them with tenderness, as if a bond existed between them.

Someone snickered. Archie stiffened, shot a look at Carter, a withering look that said, tell them to cut the crap. Carter snapped his fingers, which sounded in the quiet storage room like the banging of a gavel. The Vigils were grouped as usual in a circle around Archie and the kid receiving the assignment. The small room behind the gym was windowless with only one door leading to the gymnasium itself: a perfect spot for Vigil meetings—private, the solitary entrance easily guarded, and dim, lit by a single bulb dangling from the ceiling, a 40-watt bulb that bestowed only a feeble light on the proceedings. The silence was deafening after the snap of Carter's fingers. Nobody fooled around with Carter. Carter was the president of The Vigils because the president was always a football player—the muscle someone like Archie needed. But everyone knew that the head of The Vigils was The Assigner, Archie Costello, who was always one step ahead of them all.

The Goober looked frightened. He was one of those kids who always wanted to please everybody. The guy who never got the girl but worshipped her in secret while the big shot hero rode off in the sunset with her in the end.

"Tell me," Archie said, "why you're here." He allowed a bit of impatience to appear in his voice.

"For . . . an assignment."

"Do you realize that there's nothing personal in the assignment?"

The Goober nodded.

"That this is tradition here at Trinity?"

"Yes."

"And that you must pledge silence?"

"Yes," The Goober said, swallowing, his Adam's apple doing a dance in that long thin neck.

Silence.

Archie let it gather. He could feel a heightening of interest in the room. It always happened this way when an assignment was about to be given. He knew what they were thinking—what's Archie come up with this time? Sometimes Archie resented them. The members of The Vigils did nothing but enforce the rules. Carter was muscle and Obie an errand boy. Archie alone was always under pressure, devising the assignments, working them out. As if he was some kind of machine. Press a button: out comes an assignment. What did they know about the agonies of it all? The nights he tossed and turned? The times he felt used up, empty? And yet he couldn't deny that he exulted in moments like this, the guys leaning forward in anticipation, the mystery that surrounded them all, the kid Goober white-faced and frightened, the place so quiet you could almost hear your own heartbeat. And all eyes on him: Archie.

"Goober."

"Yes, yes sir." Swallow.

"Know what a screwdriver is?"

"Yes."

"Can you put your hands on one?"

"Yes, yes sir. My father. He has a tool chest."

"Fine. Know what they use screwdrivers for, Goober?"

"Yes."

"What for?"

"To screw things . . . I mean, to put screws into things."

Someone laughed. And Archie let it pass. A relief to the tension.

"And also, Goober," Archie said, "a screwdriver takes screws out of things. Right?"

"Yes, sir."

"A screwdriver, then, can loosen as well as tighten, right?"

"Right," The Goober said, nodding his head, eager, his attention fastened on the thought of the screwdriver, almost as if he were hypnotized, and Archie was carried on marvelous waves of power and glory, leading The Goober toward the ultimate destination, feeding him the information little by little, the best part of the lousy job. Not really lousy, though. Great, in fact. Beautiful, in fact. Worth all the sweat.

"Now, do you know where Brother Eugene's homeroom is located?"

The anticipation in the air was almost visible at this moment, blazing, electric.

"Yes. Room nineteen. Second floor."

"Right!" Archie said, as if giving The Goober an *A* for recitation. "Next Thursday afternoon, you'll make arrangements to be free. Afternoon, evening, all night, if necessary."

The Goober stood there, spellbound.

"The school will be deserted. The brothers, most of them, the ones who count, will be off to a conference at Provincial headquarters in Maine. The janitor is taking a day off. There'll be no one in the building after three in the afternoon. No one but you, Goober. You and your screwdriver."

Now, the final moment, the climax, almost like coming—

"And here's what you do, Goober." Pause. "You loosen."

"Loosen?" The Adam's apple dancing.

"Loosen."

Archie waited a beat—in strict command of the room, the silence almost unbearable—and said, "Everything in Brother Eugene's room is held together by screws. The chairs, the desks, the blackboards. Now, with your little screwdriver—maybe you'd better bring along various and assorted sizes, just in case—you start to loosen. Don't take out the screws. Just loosen them until they reach that point where they're almost ready to fall out, everything hanging there by a thread . . ."

A howl of delight came from the guys—probably Obie, who had gotten the picture, who could see the house that Archie was building, the house that didn't exist until he built it in their minds. Then, others joined in the laughter as they envisioned the result of the assignment. Archie let himself be caressed by the laughter of admiration, knowing that he'd scored again. They were always waiting for him to fail, to fall flat on his face, but he'd scored once more.

"Jeez," The Goober said. "That's going to take a lot of work. There's a lot of desks and chairs in there."

"You'll have all night. We guarantee you won't be disturbed."

"Jeez." The Adam's apple was positively convulsive now.

"Thursday," Archie said, a command in his voice, no nonsense, final, irrevocable.

The Goober nodded, accepting the assignment like a sentence of doom, the way all the others did, knowing there was no way out, no reprieve, no appeal. The law of The Vigils was final, everyone at Trinity knew that.

Somebody whispered, "Wow."

Carter snapped his fingers again and tension quickly built up in the room once more. But a different kind of tension. Tension with teeth in it. For Archie. He braced himself.

Reaching under the abandoned teacher's desk he sat behind as presiding officer, Carter pulled out a small black box. He shook it and the sound of marbles could be heard clicking together inside. Obie came forward, holding a key in his hand. Was that a smile on Obie's face? Archie couldn't be sure. He wondered, does Obie really hate me? Do they all hate me? Not that it mattered. Not while Archie held the power. He would conquer all, even the black box.

Carter took the key from Obie and held it up.

"Ready?" he asked Archie.

"Ready," Archie said, keeping his face expressionless, inscrutable as usual, even though he felt a bead of perspiration trace a cold path from his armpit to his rib. The black box was his nemesis. It contained six marbles: five of them white and one of them black. It was an ingenious idea thought up by someone long before Archie's time, someone who was wise enough—or a bastard enough—to realize that an assigner could go off the deep end if there wasn't some kind of control. The box provided the control. After every assignment, it was presented to Archie. If Archie drew a white marble, the assignment stood as ordered. If Archie drew the black marble, it would be necessary for Archie himself to carry out the assignment, to perform the duty he had assigned for others.

He had beaten the black box for three years—could he do it again? Or was his luck running out? Would the law of averages catch up to him? A tremor ran along his arm as he extended his hand toward the box. He hoped no one had noticed. Reaching inside, he grabbed a marble, concealed it in the palm of his hand. He withdrew his hand, held the arm straight out, calmly now, without shiver or tremor. He opened his hand. The marble was white.

The corner of Archie's mouth twitched as the tension of his body relaxed. He had beaten them again. He had won again. I am Archie. I cannot lose.

Carter snapped his fingers and the meeting began to break up. Suddenly, Archie felt empty, used up, discarded. He looked at the kid Goober who stood there in bewilderment, looking as if he were going to cry. Archie almost felt sorry for the kid. Almost. But not quite.

CHAPTER 6

BROTHER LEON WAS GETTING READY to put on his show. Jerry knew the symptoms—all the guys knew them. Most of them were freshmen and had been in Leon's class only a month or so but the teacher's pattern had already emerged. First, Leon gave them a reading assignment. Then he'd pace up and down, up and down, restless, sighing, wandering through the aisles, the blackboard pointer poised in his hand, the pointer he used either like a conductor's baton or a musketeer's sword. He'd use the tip to push around a book on a desk or to flick a kid's necktie, scratching gently down some guy's back, poking the pointer as if he were a rubbish collector picking his way through the debris of the classroom. One day, the pointer had rested on Jerry's head for a moment, and then passed on. Unaccountably, Jerry had shivered, as if he had just escaped some terrible fate.

Now, aware of Leon prowling ceaselessly around the classroom, Jerry kept his eyes on paper although he didn't feel like reading. Two more periods. He looked forward to football practice. After days of calisthenics, the coach had said that probably he'd let them use the ball this afternoon.

"Enough of this crap."

That was Brother Leon—always trying to shock. Using words like crap and bull and slipping in a few damns and hells once in a while. Actually, he did shock. Maybe because the words were so startling as they issued from this pale and inoffensive looking little man. Later on, you found out that he wasn't inoffensive, of course. Now, everyone looked up at Leon as that word crap echoed in the room. Ten minutes left—time enough for Leon to perform, to play one of his games. The class looked at him in a kind of horrible fascination.

The brother's glance went slowly around the room, like the ray of a lighthouse sweeping a familiar coast, searching for hidden defects. Jerry felt a sense of dread and anticipation, both at the same time.

"Bailey," Leon said.

"Yes, Brother Leon." Leon *would* pick Bailey: one of the weak kids, high honor student, but shy, introverted, always reading, his eyes redrimmed behind the glasses.

"Up here," Leon said, finger beckoning.

Bailey went quietly to the front of the room. Jerry could see a vein throbbing in the boy's temple.

"As you know, gentlemen," Brother Leon began, addressing the class directly and ignoring Bailey completely although the boy was standing beside him, "as you know, a certain discipline must be maintained in a school. A line must be drawn between teachers and students. We teachers would love to be one of the boys, of course. But that line of separation must remain. An invisible line, perhaps, but still there." His moist eyes gleamed. "After all, you can't see the wind but it's there. You see its handiwork, bending the trees, stirring the leaves . . ."

As he spoke he gestured, his arm becoming the wind, the pointer in his hand following the direction of the wind and suddenly, without warning, striking Bailey on the cheek. The boy leaped backward in pain and surprise.

"Bailey, I'm sorry," Leon said, but his voice lacked apology. Had it been an accident? Or another of Leon's little cruelties?

Now all eyes were on the stricken Bailey. Brother Leon studied him, looking at him as if he were a specimen under a microscope, as if the specimen contained the germ of some deadly disease. You had to hand it to Leon—he was a superb actor. He loved to read short stories aloud, taking all the parts, providing all the sound effects. Nobody yawned or fell asleep in Leon's class. You had to be alert every minute, just as everyone was alert now, looking at Bailey, wondering what Leon's next move would be. Under Leon's steady gaze, Bailey had stopped stroking his cheek, even though a pink welt had appeared, like an evil stain spreading on his flesh. Somehow, the tables were turned. Now it seemed as if Bailey had been at fault all along, that Bailey had committed an error, had stood in the wrong place at the wrong time and had caused his own misfortune. Jerry squirmed in his chair. Leon gave him the creeps, the way he could change the atmosphere in a room without even speaking a word.

"Bailey," Leon said. But not looking at Bailey, looking at the class as if they were all in on a joke that Bailey knew nothing about. As if the class and Leon were banded together in a secret conspiracy.

"Yes, Brother Leon?" Bailey asked, his eyes magnified behind the glasses.

A pause.

"Bailey," Brother Leon said. "Why do you find it necessary to cheat?"

They say the hydrogen bomb makes no noise: there's only a blinding white flash that strikes cities dead. The noise comes after the flash, after the silence. That's the kind of silence that blazed in the classroom now.

Bailey stood speechless, his mouth an open wound.

"Is silence an admission of guilt, Bailey?" Brother Leon asked, turning to the boy at last.

Bailey shook his head frantically. Jerry felt his own head shaking, joining Bailey in silent denial.

"Ah, Bailey," Leon sighed, his voice fluttering with sadness. "What are we going to do about you?" Turning toward the class again, buddies with them— him and the class against the cheat.

"I don't cheat, Brother Leon," Bailey said, his voice a kind of squeak.

"But look at the evidence, Bailey. Your marks—all *A*'s, no less. Every test, every paper, every homework assignment. Only a genius is capable of that sort of performance. Do you claim to be a genius, Bailey?"

Toying with him. "I'll admit you look like one—those glasses, that pointed chin, that wild hair . . ."

Leon leaned toward the class, tossing his own chin, awaiting the approval of laughter, everything in his manner suggesting the response of laughter from the class. And it came. They laughed. Hey, what's going on here, Jerry wondered even as he laughed with them. Because Bailey did somehow look like a genius or at least a caricature of the mad scientists in old movies.

"Bailey," Brother Leon said, turning his full attention to the boy again as the laughter subsided.

"Yes," Bailey replied miserably.

"You haven't answered my question." He walked deliberately to the window and was suddenly absorbed in the street outside, the September leaves turning brown and crisp.

Bailey stood alone at the front of the class, as if he was facing a firing squad. Jerry felt his cheeks getting warm, throbbing with the warmth.

"Well, Bailey?" From Leon at the window, still intent on the world outside.

"I don't cheat, Brother Leon," Bailey said, a surge of strength in his voice, like he was taking a last stand.

"Then how do you account for all those *A*'s?"

"I don't know."

Brother Leon whirled around. "Are you perfect, Bailey? All those *A*'s—that implies perfection. Is that the answer, Bailey?"

For the first time, Bailey looked at the class itself, in mute appeal, like something wounded, lost, abandoned.

"Only God is perfect, Bailey."

Jerry's neck began to hurt. And his lungs burned. He realized he'd been holding his breath. He gulped air, carefully, not wanting to move a muscle. He wished he was invisible. He wished he wasn't here in the classroom. He wanted to be out on the football field, fading back, looking for a receiver.

"Do you compare yourself with God, Bailey?"

Cut it out, Brother, cut it out, Jerry cried silently.

"If God is perfect and you are perfect, Bailey, does that suggest something to you?"

Bailey didn't answer, eyes wide in disbelief. The class was utterly silent. Jerry could hear the hum of the electric clock—he'd never realized before that electric clocks hummed.

"The other alternative, Bailey, is that you are not perfect. And, of course, you're not." Leon's voice softened. "I know you wouldn't consider anything so sacrilegious."

"That's right, Brother Leon," Bailey said, relieved.

"Which leaves us with only one conclusion," Leon said, his voice bright and triumphant, as if he had made an important discovery. "You cheat!"

In that moment, Jerry hated Brother Leon. He could taste the hate in his stomach—it was acid, foul, burning.

"You're a cheat, Bailey. And a liar." The words like whips.

You rat, Jerry thought. You bastard.

A voice boomed from the rear of the classroom.

"Aw, let the kid alone."

Leon whipped around. "Who said that?" His moist eyes glistened.

The bell rang, ending the period. Feet scuffled as the boys pushed back their chairs, preparing to leave, to get out of that terrible place.

"Wait a minute," Brother Leon said. Softly—but heard by everyone. "Nobody moves."

The students settled in their chairs again.

Brother Leon regarded them pityingly, shaking his head, a sad and dismal smile on his lips. "You poor fools," he said. "You idiots. Do you know who's the best one here? The bravest of all?" He placed his hand on Bailey's shoulder. "Gregory Bailey, that's who. He denied cheating. He stood up to my accusations. He stood his ground! But you, gentlemen, you sat there and enjoyed yourselves. And those of you who didn't enjoy yourselves allowed it to happen, allowed me to proceed. You turned this classroom into Nazi Germany for a few moments. Yes, yes, someone finally protested. *Aw, let the kid alone.*" Mimicking the deep voice perfectly. "A feeble protest, too little and too late." There was scuffling in the corridors, students waiting to enter. Leon ignored the noise. He turned to Bailey, touched the top of his head with the pointer as if he were bestowing knighthood. "You did well, Bailey. I'm proud of you. You passed the biggest test of all—you were true to yourself." Bailey's chin was wobbling all over the place. "Of course you don't cheat, Bailey," his voice tender and paternal. He gestured toward the class—he was a great one for gestures. "Your classmates out there. They're the cheaters. They cheated you today. They're the ones who doubted you—I never did."

Leon went to his desk. "Dismissed," he said, his voice filled with contempt for all of them.

CHAPTER 7

"Wнат're you doing, Emile?" Archie asked, amusement in his voice. The amusement was there because it was obvious what Emile Janza was doing—he was siphoning gas from a car, watching it flow into a glass jug.

tears came for both of them. Jerry didn't know where his own tears began and his father's left off. They wept without shame, out of a nameless need, and walked together afterward, arm in arm, toward the waiting car. The fiery knot of anger had come undone, unraveled, and Jerry realized as they drove back from the cemetery that something worse had taken its place—emptiness, a yawning cavity like a hole in his chest.

That was the last moment of intimacy he and his father had shared. The routine of school for himself, and work for his father, had been taken up and they both threw themselves into it. His father sold the house and they moved to a garden apartment where no memories lurked around corners. Jerry spent most of the summer in Canada, on the farm of a distant cousin. He had fallen into the routine of the farm willingly, hoping to build up his body for Trinity and football in the fall. His mother had been born in that small Canadian town. There was a kind of comfort walking the narrow streets where she herself had walked as a girl. When he returned to New England in late August, he and his father fell into a simple routine. Work and school. And football. On the field, bruised and battered or grimy and dirty, Jerry felt as if he was part of something. And he sometimes wondered, what was his father part of?

He thought of that now as he looked at his father. He'd come from school to find his father napping on a sofa in the den, arms folded across his chest. Jerry moved soundlessly through the apartment, not wanting to awaken the sleeping figure. His father was a pharmacist and worked all kinds of staggered hours for a chain of drugstores in the area. His work often included night shifts which meant broken sleep. As a result, he'd developed the habit of falling off into naps whenever he found a moment to relax. Jerry's stomach was weak from hunger but he sat quietly down across from his father now, waiting for him to waken. He was weary from practice, the constant punishment his body took, the frustration of never getting a play off, never completing a pass, the coach's sarcasm, the lingering September heat.

Watching his father sleep, the face relaxed in slumber, all the harsh lines of age less defined, he remembered hearing that people who had been married a long time began to resemble each other. He squinted his eyes, the way one inspects a fine painting, searching for his mother there in the face of his father. And, without warning, the anguish of her loss returned, like a blow to his stomach, and he was afraid that he would faint. Through some nightmarish miracle, he was able to superimpose the image of his mother's face on his father's—and for a moment the echo of all her sweetness was there and he had to go through all the horror of visualizing her in the coffin again.

His father awakened, as if slapped from sleep by an invisible hand. The vision vanished and Jerry leaped to his feet.

"Hi, Jerry," his father said, rubbing his eyes, sitting up. His hair wasn't even mussed. But then how could a stiff crew cut get mussed up? "Have a good day, Jerry?"

His father's voice restored normalcy. "Okay, I guess. Another practice. One of these days, I'll get a pass off."

"Fine."

"How was your day, Dad?"

"Fine."

"That's good."

"Mrs. Hunter left us a casserole. Tuna fish. She said you liked it fine last time."

Mrs. Hunter was the housekeeper. She spent every afternoon cleaning up the place and preparing some kind of evening meal for them. She was a gray-haired woman who constantly embarrassed Jerry because she insisted on tousling his hair and murmuring, "Child, child . . ." like he was a third grader or something.

"Hungry, Jerry? I can get it ready in five or ten minutes. Heat the oven and there it is . . ."

"Fine."

He was throwing one of his father's *fines* back at him although his father didn't notice. That was his father's favorite word—fine.

"Hey, Dad."

"Yes, Jerry?"

"Were things really fine at the store today?"

His father paused near the kitchen doorway, puzzled. "What do you mean, Jerry?"

"I mean, every day I ask you how things are going and every day you say fine. Don't you have some *great* days? Or *rotten* days?"

"A drugstore's pretty much the same all the time, Jerry. The prescriptions come in and we fill them—and that's about it. You fill them carefully, taking all precautions, double-checking. It's true what they say about doctors' handwriting, but I've told you that before." He was frowning now, as if searching his memory, trying to find something that would please the boy. "There was that attempted holdup three years ago—the time that drug addict came in like a wild man."

Jerry made an effort to hide his shock and disappointment. Was that the most exciting thing that had ever happened to his father? That pathetic holdup try by a scared young kid brandishing a toy pistol? Was life that dull, that boring and humdrum for people? He hated to think of his own life stretching ahead of him that way, a long succession of days and nights that were fine, *fine*—not good, not bad, not great, not lousy, not exciting, not anything.

He followed his father into the kitchen. The casserole slid into the oven like a letter into a mailbox. Jerry wasn't hungry suddenly, all appetite gone. "How about a salad?" his father asked. "I think there's lettuce and stuff around."

Jerry nodded automatically. Was this all there was to life, after all? You finished school, found an occupation, got married, became a father, watched your wife die, and then lived through days and nights that seemed to have no sunrises, no dawns and no dusks, nothing but a gray drabness. Or was he being fair to his father? To himself? Wasn't each man different? Didn't a man have a choice? How much did he know about his father, really?

"Hey, Dad."

"Yes, Jerry?"

"Nothing."

What could he ask him without sounding crazy? And he doubted whether his father would level with him, anyway. Jerry recalled an incident that had taken place years ago when his father worked in a neighborhood pharmacy, the kind of place where customers came to consult the druggist as if he possessed a doctor's certificate. Jerry had been hanging around the store one afternoon when an old man entered, bent and gnarled with age. He had a pain in his right side. What should I do, Mister Druggist? What do you think it is? Look, press here, Mister Druggist, do you feel the swelling there? Is there a medicine to cure me? His father had been patient with the old man, listening sympathetically, nodding, stroking his cheek as if he were preparing a diagnosis. He finally convinced the old man to go see a doctor. But for a moment there, Jerry had seen his father acting the part of a physician—wise and professional and compassionate. A regular bedside manner, even there in a drugstore. After the old man's departure, Jerry had asked, "Hey, Dad, did you ever want to be a doctor?" His father glanced up quickly and hesitated, taken by surprise. "No, of course not," he said. But Jerry had caught something in his manner, in his tone of voice, that ran counter to his answer. When Jerry tried to pursue the subject, his father suddenly became very busy with prescriptions and stuff. And he never brought up the subject again.

Now, seeing his father presiding in the kitchen, getting supper, for crying out loud—such a far cry from being a doctor—and his wife dead and his only son full of doubts about him, his life so pale and gray, Jerry was plunged into sadness. The stove signaled—casserole ready.

Later, preparing for bed and sleep, Jerry looked at himself in the mirror, saw himself as that guy on the Common must have seen him the other day: Square Boy. Just as he had superimposed his mother's image on his father's face, now he could see his father's face reflected in his own features. He turned away. He didn't want to be a mirror of his father. The thought made him cringe. I want to do something, be somebody. But what? But what?

Football. He'd make the team. That was something. Or was it, really?

For no reason at all, he thought of Gregory Bailey.

CHAPTER 10

LATER, ARCHIE HAD TO CONCEDE that Brother Leon had dramatized the sale too vividly and therefore put himself and The Vigils and the entire school on the spot.

To begin with, he called a special assembly at chapel. Following prayers and a lot of other religious hoopla, he started talking about all that school spirit crap. But with a difference this time. Standing at the pulpit, he gave the signal to a few of his stooges to bring in ten big cardboard posters which listed in alphabetical order every student in school. A series of blank rectangles had been drawn beside each name which, Leon explained, would be filled in as each student sold his quota of chocolates.

The student body watched with glee as Leon's stooges tried to scotch-tape the posters to the wall at the rear of the stage. The posters kept slipping to the floor, resisting the tape. The walls were made of concrete blocks, and tacks couldn't be used, of course. Hoots filled the air. Brother Leon looked annoyed, which increased the hoots and catcalls. There was nothing more beautiful in the world than the sight of a teacher getting upset. Finally, the posters were secured and Brother Leon took charge.

Archie had to admit that the Brother turned in one of his great performances. Academy Award caliber. He poured it on like Niagara—school spirit, the traditional sale that had never failed, the Headmaster lying sick in the hospital, the brotherhood of Trinity, the need for funds to keep this magnificent edifice of education operating on all gears. He recalled past triumphs, the trophies in the display case in the main corridor, the do-or-die determination that made Trinity a place of triumph through the years. Etc. Crap, of course, but effective when a master like Leon was at work, casting a spell with words and gestures.

"Yes," Brother Leon intoned, "the quota is doubled this year because we have more at stake than ever before." His voice an organ, filling the air. "Each boy must sell fifty boxes, but I know that each boy is willing to do his share. More than his share." He gestured toward the posters. "I promise you, gentlemen, that before this sale is ended each one of you will have the number 'fifty' inscribed in that final box, signifying that you have done your part for Trinity . . ."

There was a lot more but Archie tuned him out. Talk, talk, talk—that's all anybody ever heard in school. Archie squirmed uncomfortably in his seat, thinking of the Vigil meeting at which he had announced that Brother Leon had asked support for the sale and how he'd pledged the backing of The Vigils. Archie had been surprised at the ripple of doubt and skepticism from the members of The Vigils. "Christ, Archie," Carter had said, "we never get mixed up in this stuff." But Archie had overcome them as usual, pointing out that Leon's need for an endorsement from The Vigils was a symbol of how powerful the organization had become. And it was only a crappy chocolate sale. But now, listening to Leon sounding as if the school was embarking on the Crusades, for crying out loud, Archie was doubtful.

Looking at the posters and seeing his own name there, Archie plotted how his own fifty boxes would be sold. He wouldn't dream of selling the chocolates himself. He hadn't touched a box since his freshman days. Usually he found some willing kid who'd gladly sell Archie's quota along with his own, figuring it was something special to be singled out by the assigner of The Vigils. This year, he'd probably spread the burden around, picking out five guys, say, and have them sell only ten boxes each. It was better than sticking one kid with the entire quota, wasn't it?

Sitting back in comfort, Archie sighed now, contented, gratified by the heights his sense of fairness and compassion could reach.

CHAPTER 11

IT WAS AS IF somebody had dropped The Bomb.

Brian Kelly started it all when he touched his chair. It collapsed.

Then, everything happened at once.

Albert LeBlanc brushed against a desk as he made his way down the aisle and it fell apart after trembling crazily for a moment. The impact sent out vibrations which shot down two other chairs and a desk.

John Lowe was about to sit down when he heard the noise of collapsing furniture. He turned and in doing so touched his own desk. The desk disintegrated before his astonished eyes. Leaping backward, he hit his chair. Nothing happened to his chair. But Henry Couture's desk behind it shivered violently and tumbled to the floor.

The racket was deafening.

"My God," Brother Eugene cried as he entered the classroom and beheld the bedlam. Desks and chairs were falling apart as if being demolished by mysterious unheard dynamite explosions.

Brother Eugene rushed to his desk, that haven of security behind which a teacher always found protection. At his touch, the desk swayed drunkenly, shifted gears into a lopsided position and—miracle of miracles—remained upright at that strange tipsy angle. But his chair collapsed.

663

Boys scrambled madly and merrily around the room. Once they realized what was happening they dashed around Room Nineteen testing all the desks and chairs, watching with glee as they fell apart, and toppling the stubborn pieces of furniture that refused to go down without help.

"Wow," somebody yelled.

"The Vigils," somebody else called out—giving credit where credit was due.

The destruction of Room Nineteen took exactly thirty-seven seconds. Archie timed it from the doorway. A sweetness gathered in his breast as he saw the room being turned into a shambles, a sweet moment of triumph that compensated for all the other lousy things, his terrible marks, the black box. Witnessing the pandemonium, he knew that this was one of his major triumphs, one of those long-shot assignments that paid off beautifully, certain to become legend. He could picture Trinity students of the future discussing in wonder the day Room Nineteen exploded. He found it hard to suppress a howl of delight as he surveyed the havoc—*I made this happen*—and saw Brother Eugene's trembling chin and horror-stricken expression.

Behind the brother, the huge blackboard suddenly tore loose from its moorings and slid majestically to the floor, like a final curtain dropping on the chaos.

"You!"

Archie heard the voice in all its fury at the same instant that he felt the hands spinning him around. He swiveled to encounter Brother Leon. Leon wasn't pale at this moment. Scarlet splotches glistened on his cheeks as if he had been made up for some grotesque stage show. A horror show maybe, because there was nothing funny about him at this moment.

"You!" Leon said again, a wicked whisper that spilled into Archie's face the foul aftertaste of Leon's breakfast—the smell of stale bacon and eggs. "You did this," Leon said, digging the fingernails of one hand into Archie's shoulder while pointing to the chaos of Room Nineteen with the other.

Curious students from other classes had now gathered around the two entrances to the room, drawn by the crash and clatter. Some of them regarded the rubble with awe. Others glanced curiously at Brother Leon and Archie. No matter where they looked, it was great—an interruption of school routine, a diversion in the deadly order of the day.

"Didn't I tell you I wanted everything to go smoothly? No incidents? No funny business?"

The worst part of Leon's fury was the way he whispered, this terrible tortured hissing from his mouth, giving his words a tone more deadly than a shout or a yell. At the same time his grip on Archie's shoulder got tighter and Archie winced with pain.

"I didn't do anything. I didn't promise anything." Archie said automatically. Always deny everything, never apologize, never admit anything.

Leon pushed Archie up against a wall as the boys began to fill the corridor, pouring into Room Nineteen to view the destruction, and milling around outside; talking and gesturing, shaking their heads in wonder—the legend had already begun.

"I'm in charge, don't you see? This entire school is now my responsibility. The chocolate sale is ready to start and you pull something like this." Leon released him without warning, and Archie hung there as if suspended in mid-air. He turned and saw some guys staring at Leon and him. Staring at him! Archie Costello humiliated by this sniveling bastard of a teacher. His sweet moment of triumph spoiled by this nut and his ridiculous chocolate sale!

He watched Leon storming away, pushing his way through the tumultuous corridor, disappearing into the swarming stream of boys. Archie massaged his shoulder, gingerly feeling the spot where Leon's fingernails had bitten deep. Then he thrust himself into the crowd, pushing aside the guys gathered near the doorway. He stood at the entrance, drinking in the beautiful debris of Room Nineteen—his masterpiece. He saw Brother Eugene still standing there in the midst of the shambles, tears actually running down his cheeks.

Beautiful, beautiful.

Screw Brother Leon.

CHAPTER 12

"T RY IT AGAIN," the coach bellowed, his voice hoarse. The danger point— his voice always got hoarse when he lost his patience, when he was in danger of blowing his top.

Jerry picked himself up. His mouth was dry and he tried to suck spit into it. His ribs hurt, his entire left side was on fire. He stalked back to his position behind Adamo who played center. The other guys were already lined up, tense, waiting, aware that the coach wasn't happy with them. Not happy? Hell, he was furious, disgusted. He had arranged this special practice giving his freshmen a chance to scrimmage against a few members of the varsity, to show off all he had taught them and they were doing lousy, rotten, terrible.

There was no huddle, the coach barked the number of the next play, a play designed to suck in Carter, the big beefy varsity guard who looked as if he could chew freshmen up and spit them out. But the coach had said. "We'll have some surprises for Carter." It was tradition at Trinity to toss star players against the Freshmen and to build plays designed to stop the stars. This was the only reward the Freshman team reaped because most of them were too young or too small to play varsity.

Jerry crouched behind Adamo. He was determined to make this play work. He knew that the previous play hadn't worked because his timing was off and because he hadn't seen Carter come crashing out of nowhere. He had expected Carter to blitz and instead the big guard had pulled back and skirted the line, annihilating Jerry from behind. What infuriated Jerry was that Carter toppled him gently, lowering him to the ground almost tenderly as if to prove his superiority. I don't have to murder you, kid, it's easy enough this way, Carter seemed to be saying. But this was the seventh consecutive play and the damage of being tackled play after play was taking its toll.

"All right, guys, this is it. Make or break."

"It's all over, fellas," Carter taunted.

Jerry called the signals, hoping his voice sounded confident. He didn't feel confident. And yet he hadn't given up hope. Every play was a new beginning and even though something always seemed to go wrong he felt that they were on the verge of clicking. He had confidence in guys like Goober and Adamo and Croteau. Sooner or later, they had to click, all the work had to pay off. That is, if the coach didn't cut them all off the squad first.

Jerry's hands were joined like a duck's bill waiting to swallow the ball. At his signal, Adamo slapped the ball into his palms and Jerry began to fade at the same instant, to the right, slanted, swift, his arm already coming up, ready to be

She was a sweet girl who loved him for himself alone. She walked along the sidewalk with him, her breast brushing his arm, setting him on fire. The first time she rubbed against him he thought it was an accident and he pulled away, apologetic, leaving a space between them. Then she brushed against him again—that was the night he'd bought her the earrings—and he knew it wasn't an accident. He'd felt himself hardening and was suddenly ashamed and embarrassed and deliriously happy all at the same time. Him—Tubs Casper, forty pounds overweight which his father never let him forget. Him—with this beautiful girl's breast pushed against him, not beautiful the way his mother thought a girl was beautiful but beautiful in a ripe wild way, faded blue jeans hugging her hips, those beautiful breasts bouncing under her jersey. She was only fourteen and he was barely fifteen but they were in love, love dammit, and it was only money that kept them apart, money to take the bus to her house because she lived on the other side of town and they'd made plans to meet tomorrow, her birthday, at Monument Park, a picnic sort of, she'd bring the sandwiches and he'd bring the bracelet—he knew the delights that awaited him but he also knew deep down inside that the bracelet was more important than anything else . . .

All of which rushed him along now, out of breath and out of shape, trying to raise money that he knew dimly would lead him eventually only to trouble. Where would he raise enough money to pay it all back when the returns were due at school? But what the hell—he'd worry about it later. Right now he needed to raise the money and Rita loved him—tomorrow she'd probably let him get under her sweater.

He rang the doorbell of a rich-looking house on Sterns Avenue and prepared his most innocent and sweetest smile for whoever opened the door.

The woman's hair was damp and askew, and a little kid, maybe two or three years old, was tugging at her skirt. "Chocolates?" she asked, laughing bitterly as if Paul Consalvo had suggested the most absurd thing in the world. "You want me to buy chocolates?"

The baby, wearing a soggy-looking droopy diaper, was calling, "Mommy . . . mommy . . ." And another kid was howling somewhere in the apartment.

"It's for a good cause," Paul said. "Trinity School!"

Paul's nose wrinkled at the smell of pee.

"Jesus," the woman said. "Chocolates!"

"Mommee, mommee . . ." the kid squalled.

Paul felt sorry for older people, stuck in their houses and tenements with kids to take care of and housework to do. He thought of his own parents and their useless lives—his father collapsing into his nap every night after supper and his mother looking tired and dragged-out all the time. What the hell were they living for? He couldn't wait to get out of the house. "Where're you going all the time?" his mother asked as he fled the place. How could he tell her that he hated the house, that his mother and father were dead and didn't know it, that if it wasn't for television the place would be like a tomb. He couldn't say that because he really loved them and if the house caught fire in the middle of the night he'd rescue them, he'd be willing to sacrifice his own life for them. But, jeez, it was so boring, so deadly at home—what did they have to live for? They were too old for sex even, although Paul turned away from the thought. He couldn't believe that his mother and father ever actually . . .

"Sorry," the woman said, shutting the door in his face, still shaking her head in wonder at his sales pitch.

Paul stood in the doorway, wondering what to do. He'd had rotten luck this afternoon, hadn't sold a single box. He hated selling them anyway, although it gave him an excuse to get out of the house. But he couldn't really put his heart in it. He was just going through the motions.

Outside the apartment house, Paul considered his choices: pressing on with the sale despite his luck today or going home. He crossed the street and rang the doorbell of another apartment building. In an apartment house, you could knock off five or six families at one time even though the places all seemed to smell of pee.

Brother Leon had "volunteered" Brian Cochran for the position of Treasurer of the Chocolate Sale. Which meant that he'd looked around the classroom, pinned those watery eyes on Brian, pointed his finger and, *voilà*, as Brother Aimé said in French class, Brian was treasurer. He hated the job because he lived in fear of Brother Leon. You never knew about Leon. Brian was a senior and he'd had Leon as either a classroom teacher or as homeroom supervisor for four years and he was still uncomfortable in his presence. The teacher was unpredictable and yet predictable at the same time, which reasoning confused Brian because he wasn't exactly a hotshot in the psychology department. It was this: you knew that Leon would always do the unexpected—wasn't that being both predictable and unpredictable? He loved to toss surprise exams at a class—and he also could suddenly be the nice guy, not giving a test for weeks or giving a test and then throwing away the results. Or concocting a pass-fail test—he was famous for that type—where he threaded together questions that could throw a guy for a loss, with what seemed like a million possible answers. He was also quite a man with the pointer although he usually confined that kind of stuff to freshmen. If he ever pulled the pointer antics with, say, somebody like Carter, there'd be hell to pay. But not everybody was John Carter, president of The Vigils, All-Star Guard on the football team, and president of the Boxing Club. How Brian Cochran would love to be like John Carter, with muscles instead of glasses, quick with boxing gloves instead of figures.

Speaking of figures, Brian Cochran began double-checking the sales totals. As usual, there was a discrepancy between the amount of chocolates reported as sold and the actual money received. The guys were notorious for holding back some of the money until the last minute. Ordinarily, nobody got excited about it—it was human nature. A lot of the guys sold chocolates, spent the money on a big date or a big night, and then put in the money when they got their allowance or their pay at their part-time jobs. But this year, Brother Leon acted as if every dollar was a matter of life and death. In fact, he was driving Brian Cochran up a wall.

The job of treasurer called for Brian to check every homeroom at the end of the day and write down the returns the boys had reported. How many boxes sold. How much money turned in. Brian then went to Brother Leon's office and totaled all the figures. Then Brother Leon would come along and check Brian's report. Simple, right? Wrong. The way Brother Leon was carrying on this year made every day's report seem like a major headline event. Brian had never seen the Brother so edgy, so nervous. At first he'd gotten a kick out of the teacher's apprehension, the way the sweat poured off him like he had a special pump inside producing all that perspiration. When he came into the office and took off the black suit coat he was required to wear in the classroom during all seasons, sweat stains darkened his armpits, and he smelled as if he'd just gone ten rounds in the ring. He fidgeted and fussed around, double-checking Brian's figures, chewing on a pencil, pacing the floor.

Today, Brian was more puzzled than ever. Leon had passed around a report to all the homerooms listing total sales thus far at 4,582. Which was wrong. The kids had sold exactly 3,961 boxes and had made returns on 2,871. Sales were definitely lagging behind last year and so was the money. He couldn't understand why Leon had issued a false report. Did he think he could hype them up that way?

Brian shrugged, tabulating his own totals once more to be sure that Brother Leon wouldn't blame him for any discrepancies. He'd hate to have Leon for an enemy, which is one reason he'd accepted the job of treasurer without making waves. Brian was a member of Leon's algebra class and he didn't want to take any chances with extra homework or sudden unexplained *F*'s on exams.

Looking at the summary once again, Brian saw the zero next to the name of Jerome Renault. He chuckled. That was the freshman who refused to sell any chocolates. Brian shook his head—who'd want to buck the system? Hell, who'd want to buck Brother Leon? The kid must be some kind of madman.

"LeBlanc?"

"Six."

"Malloran?"

"Three."

The pause. The intake of breath. It had gotten to be a game now—this roll call, this fascinating moment in Brother Leon's homeroom. Even Goober couldn't help but get caught up in the tension although the entire situation made him slightly sick to his stomach. Goober was a peaceful figure. He hated strain, contention. Peace, let's have peace. But there was no peace in Brother Leon's room in the morning as he called the roll of chocolate sales. He stood tense at the desk, those watery eyes blinking in the morning light, while Jerry Renault sat as usual at his desk, without emotion, frigid, elbows resting on the surface of the desk.

"Parmentier?"

"Two."

Now—

"Renault."

Inhale.

"No."

Exhale.

The color spreading on Leon's face, like his veins had turned into scarlet neon signs.

"Santucci?"

"Two."

The Goober couldn't wait for the bell to ring.

CHAPTER 15

"Hey, Archie," Emile Janza called.

"Yes, Emile."

"You still got the picture?"

"What picture?" Suppressing a smile.

"You know what picture."

"Oh, *that* picture. Yes, Emile, I still have it."

"I don't suppose it's for sale, Archie."

"Not for sale, Emile. What would you want with that picture, anyway? To tell the truth, Emile, it's not the greatest picture ever taken of you. I mean, you're not even smiling or anything. There's this funny look on your face. But you're not smiling, Emile."

There was a funny look on Emile Janza's face right at this moment and he wasn't smiling now either. Anyone else but Archie would have been intimidated by that look.

"Where do you keep the picture, Archie?"

"It's safe, Emile. Very safe."

"That's good."

Archie wondered, should I tell him the truth about the picture? He knew that Emile Janza could be a dangerous enemy. On the other hand, the photograph also could be used as a weapon.

"Tell you what, Emile," Archie said. "Someday you might be able to get the photograph all for yourself."

Janza flipped his cigarette against a tree and watched the butt ricochet into the gutter. He withdrew a package from his pocket, discovered it was empty and tossed it away, watching the breeze move it along on the sidewalk. Emile Janza didn't care about keeping America beautiful.

"How can I get the photograph, Archie?"

"Well, you won't have to buy it, Emile."

"You mean you'd give it to me? There must be a catch, Archie."

"There is, Emile. But nothing you can't handle when the time comes."

"You let me know when the time comes. Okay, Archie?" Emile asked, giggling his foolish giggle.

"You'll be the first to know," Archie said.

The tone of their conversation had been light, bantering, but Archie knew that Emile was deadly serious underneath. Archie also knew that Janza would be willing to practically murder him in his sleep to get his hot hands on the picture. And the terrible irony—there was no picture after all. Archie had merely taken advantage of a ridiculous situation. What happened was this: Archie had cut a class and glided through the corridor, evading the brothers. Moving past an open locker, he'd spotted a camera dangling from one of the coat hooks. Automatically, Archie had taken the camera. He wasn't a thief, of course. He figured he'd merely abandon it somewhere so that the owner, whoever he was, would have to chase around the school looking for it. Stepping into the men's room to grab a quick smoke, Archie had pulled open the door to one of the stalls and confronted Janza sitting there, pants dropping on the floor, one hand furiously at work between his legs. Archie lifted the camera and pretended to take a picture, yelling "Hold it."

"Beautiful," Archie had called.

Janza had been too shocked and surprised to react quickly. By the time he had recovered, Archie was at the doorway, poised to flee if Janza made a move.

"Better hand over that camera," Janza called.

"If you're going to jack off in a toilet, at least lock your door," Archie taunted.

"The lock's broken," Emile replied. "All the locks are broken."

Leon's hands, the way the teacher pressed it, rolled it, his fingers like the legs of pale spiders with a victim in their clutch.

"But it's all rewarding," Leon went on. How was it that his voice was so cool when the hand holding the chalk was so tense, the veins sticking out, as if threatening to burst through the flesh?

"Rewarding?" Caroni had lost the thread of Brother Leon's thought.

"The chocolate sale," Leon said.

And the chalk split in his hand.

"For instance," Leon said, dropping the pieces and opening the ledger that was so familiar to everyone at Trinity, the ledger in which the daily sales were recorded. "Let me see—you have done fine in the sale, David. Eighteen boxes sold. Fine. Fine. Not only are you an excellent scholar but you possess school spirit."

Caroni blushed with pleasure—it was impossible for him to resist a compliment, even when he was all mixed up as he certainly was at the moment. All this talk of exams and teachers getting tired and making mistakes and now the chocolate sale . . . and the two pieces of broken chalk abandoned on the desk, like white bones, dead men's bones.

"If everyone did his part like you, David, the sale would be an instant success. Of course, not everyone has your spirit, David . . ."

Caroni wasn't sure what tipped him off. Maybe the way Brother Leon paused at this point. Maybe the entire conversation, all of it off-key somehow. Or maybe the chalk in Brother Leon's hands, the way he had snapped it in two while his voice remained cool and easy—which was the phony thing: the hand holding the chalk, all tense and nervous, or the cool, easy voice?

"Take Renault, for instance," Brother Leon continued. "Funny thing about him, isn't it?"

And Caroni knew. He found himself staring into the moist watchful eyes of the teacher and in a blinding flash he knew what this was all about, what was happening, what Brother Leon was doing, the reason for this little conversation after school. A headache began to assert itself above his right eye, the pain digging into his flesh—migraine. His stomach lurched sickeningly. Were teachers like everyone else, then? Were teachers as corrupt as the villains you read about in books or saw in movies and television? He'd always worshiped his teachers, had thought of becoming a teacher himself someday if he could overcome his shyness. But now—this. The pain grew in intensity, throbbing in his forehead.

"Actually, I feel badly for Renault," Brother Leon was saying. "He must be a very troubled boy to act this way."

"I guess so," Caroni said, stalling, uncertain of himself and yet knowing really what Brother Leon wanted. He had seen Brother Leon every day in the classroom calling out the names and had watched him recoil as if from a blow when Jerry Renault continued to refuse the chocolates. It had become a kind of joke among the fellows. Actually, Caroni had felt badly for Jerry Renault. He knew that no kid was a match for Brother Leon. But now he realized that Brother Leon had been the victim. He must have been climbing the walls all this time, David thought.

"Well, David."

And the echo of his name here in the classroom startled him. He wondered if he still had aspirins left in his locker. Forget the aspirins, forget the headache.

He knew now what the score was, what Leon was waiting to hear. Yet, could he be sure?

"Speaking of Jerry Renault . . ." Caroni said—a safe beginning, a statement he could draw back from, depending on Brother Leon's reaction.

"Yes?"

The hand had picked up one of the pieces of chalk again, and that "Yes?" had been too quick, too sudden to allow any doubt. Caroni found himself hung up between choices and the headache didn't help matters. Could he erase that *F* by telling Brother Leon simply what he wanted to hear? What was so terrible about that? On the other hand, an *F* could ruin him. And how about all the other *F*'s it was possible that Leon could give him in the future?

"Funny thing about Jerry Renault," Caroni heard himself saying. And then instinct caused him to add, "But I'm sure you know what it's all about, Brother Leon. The Vigils. The assignment . . ."

"Of course, of course," Leon said, sitting back, letting the chalk fall gently from his hand.

"It's a Vigil stunt. He's supposed to refuse to sell chocolates for ten days—ten school days—and then accept them. Boy, those Vigils, they're really something, aren't they?" His head was killing him and his stomach was a sea of nausea.

"Boys will be boys," Leon was saying, nodding his head, his voice a whisper—it was hard to tell whether he was surprised or relieved. "Knowing Trinity's spirit, it was obvious, of course. Poor Renault. You remember, Caroni, that I said he must be troubled. Terrible, to force a boy into that kind of situation, against his will. But it's all over then, isn't it? The ten days—why they're up, let's see, tomorrow." He was smiling now, gayly, and talking as if the words themselves didn't matter but that it was important to talk, as if the words were safety valves. And then Caroni realized that Brother Leon had used his name but this time he hadn't said *David* . . .

"Well, I guess that's it then," Brother Leon said, rising, "I've detained you too long, Caroni."

"Brother Leon," Caroni said. He couldn't be dismissed at this point. "You said you wanted to discuss my mark . . ."

"Oh, yes, yes, that's right, my boy. That *F* of yours."

Caroni felt doom pressing upon him. But went on anyway. "You said teachers make mistakes, they get tired . . ."

Brother Leon was standing now. "Tell you what, Caroni. At the end of the term, when the marks close, I'll review that particular test. Perhaps I'll be fresher then. Perhaps I'll see merit that wasn't apparent before . . ."

Now it was Caroni's turn to feel relief from the tension, although his headache still pounded and his stomach was still upset. Worse than that, however, he had allowed Brother Leon to blackmail him. If teachers did this kind of thing, what kind of world could it be?

"On the other hand, Caroni, perhaps the *F* will stand," Brother Leon said. "It depends . . ."

"I see, Brother Leon," Caroni said.

And he did see—that life was rotten, that there were no heroes, really, and that you couldn't trust anybody, not even yourself.

He had to get out of there as fast as possible, before he vomited all over Brother Leon's desk.

"ADAMO?"

"Three."

"Beauvais?"

"Five."

The Goober was impatient for the roll call to be over. Or, rather, for the roll call to reach Jerry Renault. Like everyone else, the Goober had finally learned that Jerry was carrying out a Vigil assignment—that's why he had refused to take the chocolates day after day, that's why he didn't want to talk about it with Goober. Now, Jerry could become himself again, human again. His football had suffered. "What the hell is the matter with you, Renault?" the coach asked in disgust yesterday, "do you want to play ball or not?" And Jerry had answered, "I'm playing ball." All the kids knew the double meaning his answer conveyed because it was public knowledge now. He and Goober had had only one brief conversation about the assignment—in fact, it wasn't really a conversation. Leaving football practice yesterday, Goober had whispered, "When does the assignment end?" And Jerry had said, "Tomorrow I take the chocolates."

"Hartnett?"

"One."

"You can do better than that, Hartnett," Leon said, but there was no anger, not even disappointment in his voice. Brother Leon was buoyant today and his mood had spread throughout the class. That's the way Leon's classes were—he set the mood and the temperature. When Brother Leon was happy everybody was happy, when he was miserable everybody was miserable.

"Johnson?"

"Five."

"Good, good."

Killelea . . . LeBlanc . . . Malloran . . . the roll call went on, the voices shouting out their sales and the teacher checking the names off on the sheet. The names and the responses sounded almost like a song, a melody for a classroom, a tune for many voices. Then Brother Leon called out "Parmentier." And there was tension in the air. Parmentier could have called out any number and it wouldn't have mattered, it wouldn't have created any impact at all. Because the next name was Renault.

"Three," Parmentier called out.

"Right," Brother Leon answered, making the check against the name. Looking up, he called "Renault."

The pause. The damn pause.

"No!"

The Goober felt as if his eyes were the lens for a television camera in one of those documentaries. He swung around in Jerry's direction and saw his friend's face, white, mouth half-open, his arms dangling at his sides. And then he swiveled to look at Brother Leon and saw the shock on the teacher's face, his mouth forming an oval of astonishment. It seemed almost as if Jerry and the teacher were reflections in a mirror.

Finally Brother Leon looked down.

"Renault," he said again, his voice like a whip.

"No. I'm not going to sell the chocolates."

Cities fell. Earth opened. Planets tilted. Stars plummeted. And the awful silence.

CHAPTER 18

W HY DID YOU DO IT?
I don't know.
Have you gone crazy?
Maybe I have.
It was a crazy thing to do.
I know, I know.
The way that "No" popped out of your mouth—why?
I don't know.

It was like the third degree, only he was both interrogator and suspect, both tough cop and hounded prisoner, a cruel spotlight pinning him in a blinding circle of light. All of this in his mind, of course, as he tossed in his bed, the sheet twisted around him like a shroud, suffocatingly.

He fought the sheet, filled suddenly with the terror of claustrophobia, being buried alive. Aware of his mortality, he turned over again, entangled in the bed-clothes. His pillow fell off the bed, hitting the floor with a dull thud, like a small body landing there. He thought of his mother dead in the coffin. When did death arrive? He had read a magazine article about heart transplants—even the doctors couldn't agree on the exact moment that death occurred. Listen, he told himself, no one can be buried alive these days, not like in the olden times when there was no embalming fluid and stuff. Now they removed all your blood and pumped in chemicals and stuff. To make certain you were dead. But suppose, let's just suppose that some small spark in your brain remained alive, and knew what was going on. His mother. Himself, someday.

He leaped from the bed in terror, flinging the sheet away. His body was moist, oozing perspiration. He sat on the edge of the bed, trembling. Then his feet touched the floor and the cool kiss of the linoleum established reality. The specter of suffocation vanished. He made his way through the darkness to the window, and pulled back the drape. The wind came up, scattering October leaves which fluttered to the ground like doomed and crippled birds.

Why did you do it?
I don't know.
Like a broken record.
Was it because of what Brother Leon does to people, like Bailey, the way he tortures them, tries to make fools of them in front of everybody?
More than that, more than that.
Then what?

He allowed the drape to fall back into place and surveyed the bedroom, squinting into the half-darkness. He padded over to the bed, shivering in the kind of coolness that can only be found in the middle of the night. He listened for night sounds. His father snored in the next room. A car gunned along the street outside. He'd love to be gunning along the street, going someplace, any-where. *I'm not going to sell the chocolates.* Boy.

He hadn't planned to do any such thing of course. He'd been happy to have the terrible assignment all over with, the assignment completed and life normal once again. Every morning he dreaded the roll call, the necessity of facing Brother Leon, saying *No* and watching Leon's reaction—how the teacher tried to pass off Jerry's rebellion as if it didn't matter, putting on a pathetic pretense of indifference but a pretense that was so transparent, so phony. It had been funny and terrible at the same time, watching Leon call the roll and waiting for his name to be called, and finally his name blazing in the air and the defiant *No.* The teacher might have been able to carry off his act successfully, except for his eyes. His eyes gave him away. His face was always under control but his eyes showed his vulnerability, gave Jerry a glimpse into the hell that was burning inside the teacher. Those moist eyes, the white eyeballs and the diluted blue of his pupils, eyes that reflected everything that went on in the class, reacting to everything. After Jerry had learned that the secret of Brother Leon lurked in his eyes, he became watchful, seeing the way the eyes betrayed the teacher at every turn. And then there came a time when Jerry was tired of it all, tired of watching the teacher, disgusted with the contest of wills that wasn't really a contest because Jerry had no choice. Cruelty sickened Jerry— and the assignment, he realized after a few days, was cruel, even though Archie Costello had insisted that it was only a stunt that everyone would get a kick out of later. And so he had finally waited, impatient for the assignment to come to an end, eager for that silent battle between Brother Leon and himself to be over with. He wanted life to be normal again—football, even his homework, without that daily burden weighing him down. He had felt isolated from the other fellows, separated by the secret he was forced to carry. He'd been tempted once or twice to talk it over with The Goober. In fact, he'd almost done so once when Goob tried to start a conversation. Instead, he'd cautioned himself to hold on for the two weeks, to carry it off, secrecy and all, and be done with it for good. He had met Brother Leon in the corridor late one afternoon after football practice and had seen hate flashing in the teacher's eyes. More than hate: something sick. Jerry had felt soiled, dirty, as if he should run to confession and bare his soul. And he'd consoled himself: when I accept the chocolates and Brother Leon realizes I was only carrying out a Vigil assignment then everything will be fine again.

Then why had he called *No* this morning? He'd wanted to end the ordeal— and then that terrible *No* had issued from his mouth.

In bed once more, Jerry lay without moving, trying to summon sleep. Listening to his father's snores, he thought of how his father was actually sleeping his life away, sleeping even when he was awake, not really alive. And how about me? What was it the guy on the Common had said the other day, his chin resting on the Volkswagen like some grotesque John the Baptist? *You're missing a lot of things in the world.*

He turned over, dismissing his doubts and calling to mind the figure of a girl he'd seen downtown the other day. Her sweater had bulged beautifully, her schoolbooks pressed against her rounded breasts. If my hands were only those books, he'd thought longingly. His hand now curled between his legs, he concentrated on the girl. But for once, it was no good, no good.

CHAPTER 19

THE next morning Jerry found out how a hangover must feel. His eyes burned with fire, fueled by lack of sleep. His head throbbed with shooting pains. His stomach was sensitive to the slightest movement and the lurching of the bus caused strange reactions in his body. It reminded him of when he was a kid and got carsick sometimes on trips to the beach with his parents so that they'd have to stop the car by the side of the road while Jerry either vomited or waited for the storm in his stomach to subside. What added to his troubles this morning was the possibility of a test in geography and he hadn't studied at all last night so wrapped up had he been in the chocolate sale and what had happened in Leon's class. Now, he was paying the penalty for too little sleep and no study—trying to read a lousy geography lesson on a lumbering lurching bus, the morning light dazzling on the white page.

Somebody slipped into the seat beside him.

"Hey, Renault, you got guts, know that?"

Jerry looked up, blinded momentarily as his eyes shifted from the page to the face of the kid who'd spoken to him. He knew him vaguely from school—a junior, maybe. Lighting a cigarette the way all the smokers did despite the "No Smoking" signs, the kid shook his head. "Boy, you really let Leon that bastard have it. Beautiful." He blew out smoke. Jerry's eyes stung.

"Oh," he said, feeling stupid. And surprised. Funny, all this time he had thought of the situation as a private battle between Brother Leon and himself, as if the two of them were alone on the planet. Now, he realized that it had gone beyond that.

"I'm so sick of selling the frigging chocolates," the kid said. He had a terrible case of acne, his face like a relief map. And his fingers were stained with nicotine. "I've been at Trinity two years—I transferred from Monument High when I was a freshman—and Christ I'm getting tired of selling stuff." He tried to blow a smoke ring but failed. Worse than that—the smoke blew back in Jerry's face, stinging his eyes. "If it isn't chocolates, it's Christmas cards. If it isn't Christmas cards, it's soap. If it isn't soap, it's calendars. But you know what?"

"What?" Jerry asked, wanting to get back to his geography.

"I never thought of just saying no. Like you did."

"I've got some studying to do," Jerry said, not knowing what to say, really.

"Boy, you're cool, know that?" the kid said admiringly.

Jerry blushed with pleasure despite himself. Who didn't want to be admired? And yet he felt guilty, knowing that he was accepting the kid's admiration under false pretenses, that he wasn't cool at all, not at all. His head pounded and his stomach moved menacingly and he realized he had to face Brother Leon and the roll call again this morning. And all the mornings to come.

The Goober was waiting for him at the school's entrance, standing tense and troubled among the other fellows waiting for school to start, like prisoners resigned to execution, taking their final drags from cigarettes before the bells began to ring. The Goober motioned Jerry aside. Jerry followed him guiltily. He realized that Goober wasn't the cheerful happy-go-lucky kid he'd known when school first started. What had happened? He'd been so wrapped up in his own concerns that he hadn't bothered about Goob.

"Jeez, Jerry, what did you do it for?" Goober asked, drawing him away from the others.

"Do what?"

But he knew what Goober meant.

"The chocolates."

"I don't know, Goob," Jerry said. It was no use faking out Goober the way he had faked out that kid on the bus. "That's the truth—I don't know."

"You're asking for trouble, Jerry. Brother Leon spells trouble."

"Look, Goob," Jerry said, wanting to reassure his friend, wanting to wipe that look of concern from his face. "It's not the end of the world. Four hundred kids in this school are going to sell chocolates. What does it matter if I don't?"

"It's not that simple, Jerry. Brother Leon won't let you get away with it."

The warning bell sounded. Cigarettes were flipped into the gutter or mashed into the sand-filled receptacle near the door. Last drags were inhaled lingeringly. Guys who'd been sitting in cars listening to rock on the radio switched them off and slammed the doors behind them.

"Nice going, kid," somebody said, hurrying by, the pat on the ass Trinity's traditional gesture of friendship. Jerry didn't see who it was.

"Keep it up, Jerry." This, a corner-of-the-mouth whisper from Adamo who hated Leon with a vengeance.

"See how the word is spreading?" Goober hissed. "What's more important—football and your marks or the lousy chocolate sale?"

The bell rang again. It meant two minutes left to get to your locker and then to your homeroom.

A senior by the name of Benson approached them. Seniors were trouble for freshmen. It was better to be ignored by them than to be noticed. But Benson was clearly headed in their direction. He was a nut, known for his lack of inhibitions, his complete disregard of the rules.

As he neared Jerry and Goober, he began a Jimmy Cagney imitation, shooting his cuffs and hunching his shoulders. "Hey, there, guy. I wouldn't . . . I wouldn't be in your shoes . . . I wouldn't be in your shoes for a thou, boy, a mill . . ." He punched Jerry playfully on the arm.

"You couldn't fit those shoes anyway, Benson," somebody yelled. And Benson danced away, Sammy Davis now, wide grin, feet tapping, body whirling.

Walking up the stairs, Goober said, "Do me a favor, Jerry. Take the chocolates today."

"I can't, Goob."

"Why not?"

"I just can't. I'm committed now."

"The goddam Vigils," Goober said.

Jerry had never heard Goober swear before. He'd always been a mild kind of kid, rolling with the punches, loose and carefree, running around the track while the other kids sat uptight during practice sessions.

"It's not The Vigils, Goob. They're not in it anymore. It's me."

They stopped at Jerry's locker.

"All right," Goober said, resigned, knowing it was useless to pursue the subject any further at the moment. Jerry felt sad suddenly because Goober looked so troubled, like an old man heaped with all the sorrows of the world, his thin face drawn and haggard, his eyes haunted, as if he had awakened from a nightmare he couldn't forget.

Jerry opened his locker. He had thumbtacked a poster to the back wall of the locker on the first day of school. The poster showed a wide expanse of beach, a sweep of sky with a lone star glittering far away. A man walked on the beach, a small solitary figure in all that immensity. At the bottom of the poster, these words appeared—*Do I dare disturb the universe?* By Eliot, who wrote the Waste Land thing they were studying in English. Jerry wasn't sure of the poster's meaning. But it had moved him mysteriously.[1] It was traditional at Trinity for everyone to decorate the interior of his locker with a poster. Jerry chose this one.

---

1 *Do I dare disturb the universe . . . moved him mysteriously*   In "The Love Song of J. Alfred Prufrock" (1915) by T(homas) S(tearns) Eliot (1888–1965), the title character documents the bleak, anesthetized world he lives in but dares not challenge. In Eliot's long poem, "The Waste Land" (1922), redemptive hope battles spiritual aridity.

He had no time now to ponder the poster any longer. The final bell rang and he had thirty seconds to get to class.

"Adamo?"

"Two."

"Beauvais?"

"Three."

It was a different roll call this morning, a new melody, a new tempo, as if Brother Leon were the conductor and the class the members of a verbal orchestra, but something wrong with the beat, something wrong with the entire proceedings, as if the members of the orchestra were controlling the pace and not the conductor. No sooner would Brother Leon call out a name than the response came immediately, before Leon had time to make a notation in the ledger. It was the kind of spontaneous game that developed in classes without premeditation, everyone falling into a sudden conspiracy. The quickness of the responses kept Brother Leon busy at his desk, head bent, pencil furiously scribbling. Jerry was glad that he wouldn't have to look into those watery eyes.

"LeBlanc?"

"One."

"Malloran?"

"Two."

Names and numbers sizzled in the air and Jerry began to notice something curious about it. All the ones and twos, and an occasional three. But no fives, no tens. And Brother Leon's head still bent, concentrating on the ledger. And finally—

"Renault."

It would be so easy, really, to yell "Yes." To say, "Give me the chocolates to sell, Brother Leon." So easy to be like the others, not to have to confront those terrible eyes every morning. Brother Leon finally looked up. The tempo of the roll call had broken.

"No," Jerry said.

He was swept with sadness, a sadness deep and penetrating, leaving him desolate like someone washed up on a beach, a lone survivor in a world full of strangers.

CHAPTER 20

"AT THIS PERIOD OF HISTORY, man began to learn more about his environment—"

Suddenly, pandemonium reigned. The class exploded in frantic motion. Brother Jacques looked aghast. The boys leaped from their chairs, performed an insane jig, jumping up and down as if to the beat of unheard music, all of this in complete silence—although the sound of their jogging feet was noisy enough—and then sat down again, frozen-faced, as if nothing had happened.

Obie watched the teacher sourly. Brother Jacques was obviously bewildered. Bewildered? Hell, he was on the edge of panic. The ritual had been going on for a week now and it would continue until the cue was heard no more. In the meantime, the class would suddenly erupt into a confusion of waving arms and jogging legs, unsettling poor Brother. Of course, Brother Jacques was easy to unsettle—he was new and young and sensitive, raw meat

685

for Archie. And he evidently didn't know what to do about it and so he didn't do anything, figuring apparently that the thing would run its course and why risk a futile showdown when it was obviously a prank. What else could it be? Funny, Obie thought, how everybody—the kids as well as the teachers—knew these stunts were planned or carried out by The Vigils and yet they still maintained that air of mystery, refusing to acknowledge it all. He wondered why. Obie had been involved in so many Vigil assignments that he'd lost count of them and he was continually amazed at how they got away with it all the time. In fact, he'd been getting tired of the assignments, of playing nursemaid for Archie and his trigger man as well. He was tired of being the fixer, making certain the assignment went off on schedule in order to maintain Archie's big shot reputation. Like the Room Nineteen assignment when he'd had to creep in there and help the kid Goober take the place apart—all that work so that Archie and The Vigils would look good. Even this particular assignment involved him—if Brother Jacques failed to come up with the cue, then Obie had to find a way to feed it to him.

The cue was the word "environment." As Archie had said when he announced the assignment, "The world today is concerned with ecology, the environment, our natural resources. We at Trinity also ought to get involved in this environment thing. You guys," he said, indicating the fourteen students of Grade Twelve Class II, of whom Obie was a member, "will carry on our environmental campaign. Let's say Brother Jacques' U.S. History class—history should be concerned with environment, shouldn't it? Now, whenever Brother Jacques says the word 'environment,' here's what happens . . ." And Archie had outlined the instructions.

"Suppose he doesn't use the word?" someone asked.

Archie looked toward Obie. "Oh, Brother Jacques will use the word. I'm sure somebody—Obie, maybe—will ask a question that will produce the word. Won't you, Obie?"

Obie had nodded, disguising his disgust. What the hell was Archie involving him in an assignment at this stage of the game for? He was a senior, for crying out loud. He was secretary of the goddam Vigils, for crying out loud. Jesus, how he hated Archie, that bastard.

A new kid, a transfer from Monument High, asked, "What happens when Brother Jacques finds out we're putting him on? When he finds out that the key word is environment?"

"Then he stops using it," Archie said. "Which is the point of the whole damn thing. I'm getting sick and tired of all this environment crap—and at least we'll have one teacher in the frigging school who'll cross it off his vocabulary list."

For his part, Obie was getting sick and tired of Archie, of picking up the pieces behind him, of performing those little services—like Room Nineteen or cueing in Brother Jacques, feeding him a question that could only lead to the word "environment" in the answer. Anyway he was getting fed up with the entire deal. And he was also biding his time, waiting for Archie to over-reach himself, to make a mistake. The black box was always there and who could tell when Archie's luck would run out?

"In any discussion of the environment . . ."

Here we go again, Obie thought in disgust as he found himself leaping up and down like a madman, jogging his heart out, hating every minute of the damn thing. And his energy was wearing down.

686

Brother Jacques used the word "environment" five more times in the next fifteen minutes. Obie and the other guys were practically wiped out from all that jumping up and down, weary, out of breath, their legs beginning to ache.

When Brother Jacques used the word a sixth time and a weary battalion of students struggled to their feet to perform their task, Obie saw a small smile play on the lips of the teacher. And he knew immediately what had happened. Archie, that bastard, must have tipped Brother Jacques off, anonymously, of course, to what was going on. And the teacher had turned the tables. It was now the teacher who was in command, making the guys jump up and down until they almost collapsed in exhaustion.

When they left the classroom, there was Archie leaning against the wall, that smirk of triumph on his face. The other guys didn't realize what had happened. But Obie did. He gave Archie a look that would shrivel anybody else, but Archie just kept that silly smile on his face.

Obie stalked off, insulted, injured. You bastard, he thought, I owe you for that.

CHAPTER 21

KEVIN CHARTIER HAD GONE to seven houses after school and hadn't sold a box. Mrs. Connors next to the dry cleaners had told him to come back at the end of the month when her Social Security check came from the government but he didn't have the heart to tell her that it would probably be too late by then. A dog chased him halfway home. It was like one of those terrible dogs the Nazis used for hunting down concentration camp prisoners who escaped in those old TV pictures. At home, disgusted, he telephoned his best friend, Danny Arcangelo.

"How'd you make out, Danny?" Kevin asked, trying to ignore his mother who stood near the phone making sounds at him. Kevin had learned long ago to translate whatever she was saying into gibberish. She could talk her head off now and the words reached his ears without meaning. A wild trick.

"I made out terrible," Danny whined. He always sounded like he had to blow his nose. "I sold one box—to my aunt."

"The one with diabetes?"

Danny howled. One thing about Danny, he was a great audience. But not Kevin's mother. She was still chattering away. Kevin knew what was bugging her. She never wanted him to eat when he was on the telephone. His mother didn't realize that eating wasn't something you did *separately*. Eating went along with whatever you happened to be doing at the time. You could eat doing anything. Well, almost anything. It's not polite to be on the phone with your mouth full of food, she always said. But right this minute, Danny also had *his* mouth full of food at the other end of the line. So who the hell was being impolite to who? Or whom? Screw it.

"I think maybe that Renault kid's got the right idea, after all," Kevin said, his mouth thick with peanut butter which, he wished he could explain to his mother, gave his words more resonance, like a disc jockey's.

"The freshman who's giving Brother Leon a hard time?"

"Yeah. He came flat out and said he wasn't going to sell the junk."

"I thought it was a Vigils thing," Danny said tentatively.

"It *was*," Kevin said, leering in triumph as his mother gave up and went into the kitchen. "But now it's something else." He wondered whether he was saying too much. "He was supposed to take the chocolates a couple of days ago. The assignment was over. But he still refused to take them."

Kevin could hear Danny chewing like a madman.

"What're you eating, anyway? Sounds delicious."

Danny howled again. "Chocolates. I bought a box myself. The least I could do for good old Trinity."

An awkward silence fell between them. Kevin was in line to become a member of The Vigils next year when he became a junior. No one could be sure, of course, but there had been some hints from the guys. His best friend, Danny, knew about the possibility—and he also knew that there was a certain secrecy about The Vigils that had to be maintained. They usually avoided Vigil talk although Kevin often had inside information about assignments and stuff and he often fed it to Danny in bits and pieces, finding it hard not to show off a bit. Yet he was always afraid that Danny might say something about The Vigils to some other guys, strictly by accident, and screw up the whole situation. They had reached that point now in their conversation.

"What happens now?" Danny asked, still unsure about poking his nose in but made reckless by curiosity.

"I don't know," Kevin said truthfully. "Maybe The Vigils will take some action. Maybe they don't give a hell. But I'll tell you one thing."

"What?"

"I'm getting sick of selling stuff. Jeez, my father's starting to call me 'my son, the salesman.' "

Danny guffawed again. Kevin was a natural mimic. "Yeah, I know what you mean. I'm getting tired of this selling crap. The kid's probably got the right idea."

Kevin agreed.

"For two cents, I'd stop," Danny said.

"Got change for a nickel?" Kevin said, all in fun, of course, but thinking how beautiful—bee-yoo-tee-full—it would be not to have to sell anything anymore. He looked up to find his mother approaching him again, her mouth moving and sounds coming out, and he sighed, tuning her out, like shutting off the sound on television while the picture remained.

"Know what?" Howie Anderson asked.

"What?" Richy Rondell answered, lazily, dreamily. He was watching a girl approach. Fantastic looking. Tight sweater, clinging, low-slung jeans. Jesus.

"I think the Renault kid is right about the chocolates," Howie said. He'd seen the girl too, as she moved along the sidewalk in front of Crane's Drug Store. But it didn't break his train of thought. Watching girls and devouring them with your eyes—rape by eyeball—was something you did automatically. "I'm not going to sell them anymore, either."

The girl paused to look at newspapers in a metal rack outside the store. Richy gazed at her with wistful lust. Suddenly he realized what Howie had said. "You're not?" he asked. Without taking his eyes off the girl—her back was turned now and he feasted himself on her rounded jeans—he pondered the meaning of what Howie had said, sensing the importance of the moment. Howie Anderson wasn't just another Trinity student. He was president of the junior class, an unusual guy. High honor student and varsity guard on the football team. He could also hold his own in the ring and almost knocked out that monster Carter in the intramural matches last year. His hand could shoot up in class to show he had the answer to a tough question. But that same hand could also shoot out and floor you if you screwed around with him. An intellectual roughneck—that's what one teacher had called him a while back. A freshman—nobody like Renault not selling chocolates—that was nothing. But Howie Anderson—that was *something*.

"It's the principle of the thing," Howie went on.

Richy plunged his hand in his pocket, grabbing shamelessly, something he couldn't resist whenever he got excited, about a girl or anything else.

"What principle, Howie?"

"This is what I mean," Howie said. "We pay tuition to go to Trinity, don't we? Right. Hell, I'm not even a Catholic, a lot of guys aren't, but they sell us a bill of goods that Trinity is the best prep school for college you can find around here. There's a case full of trophies in the auditorium—debating, football, boxing. And what happens? They turn us into salesmen. I have to listen to all this religious crap and even go to chapel. And sell chocolates on top of it all." He spat and a beautiful spray hit a mailbox, dripping down like a teardrop. "And now along comes a freshman. A *child*. He says no. He says 'I'm not going to sell the chocolates.' Simple. Beautiful. Something I never thought of before—just stop selling them."

Richy watched the girl drifting away.

"I'm with you, Howie. As of this moment, no more selling of chocolates." The girl was almost out of sight now, blocked from view by other people walking by. "Want to make it official? I mean, call a meeting of the class?"

Howie pondered the question.

"No, Richy. This is the age of do your thing. Let everybody do his thing. If a kid wants to sell, let him. If he doesn't, the same thing applies."

Howie's voice rang with authority, as if he was delivering a pronouncement to the world. Richy listened with a kind of awe. He was glad that Howie let him hang around—maybe some of Howie's leadership qualities would rub off on him. His eyes went to the street again, looking for another girl to enjoy.

The odor of sweat filled the air—a gym's sour perfume. Even though the place was deserted, the aftermath of that final period of calisthenics lingered, the stink of boy sweat; armpits and feet. And the rotten smell of old sneakers. That was one of the reasons why Archie had never been attracted to sports—he hated the secretions of the human body, pee or perspiration. He hated athletics because it speeded up the process of sweat. He couldn't stand the sight of greasy, oozing athletes drenched in their own body fluids. At least football players wore uniforms, but boxers wore only the trunks. Take a guy like Carter, bulging with muscles, every pore oozing sweat. Put him in boxing trunks and the sight was almost obscene. That's why Archie avoided the gym. He was a legend in the school for dreaming up ways of avoiding Phys. Ed. But he was here now waiting for Obie. Obie had left a note in Archie's locker. *Meet me in the gym after last period.* Obie loved dramatics. He also knew that Archie despised the gym and yet asked to be met here. Oh, Obie, how you must hate me, Archie thought, undisturbed by the knowledge. It was good to have people hate you—it kept you sharp. And then when you put the needle in them, the way he did constantly to Obie, you felt justified, you didn't have to worry about your conscience.

But at this minute he was getting annoyed with Obie. Where the hell was he? Sitting down on one of the bleacher seats, Archie found a sudden and unexpected peace in the deserted gymnasium. His moments of peace were becoming less frequent all the time. The Vigils—those assignments, the constant pressure. More assignments due and everybody waiting for what Archie would come up with. And Archie hollow and empty sometimes, no ideas at all. And his lousy marks. He was certain to flunk English this term, simply because English was mostly reading and he didn't have time anymore to spend four or five hours every night reading a lousy book. Anyway, between The Vigils and worrying about his marks, he didn't seem to have any time to himself anymore, not even time for girls, no time to hang around Miss Jerome's, the girls' high school across town where, when school let out for the day, you could let your eyes devour some luscious sights and usually talk one of them into the car, for a ride home. With detours. Instead, here he was every day, involved with assignments and homework, juggling all this activity and then getting stupid notes from Obie. Meet me in the gym . . .

Finally, Obie made his entrance. He didn't just walk in. He had to make a production out of it. He had to peek around the door and sniff the air and act like he was the spy coming in from the cold, for Christ's sake.

"Hey, Obie, I'm over here," Archie called dryly.

"Hi, Archie," Obie said as his leather heels clicked on the gym floor. There was a rule in the school—only sneakers on the gym floor but everybody ignored it except when there was a brother around.

"What do you want, Obie?" Archie asked, getting down to business without preliminaries, keeping his voice flat and dry as the Sahara. The fact that he had showed up for the meeting had been an admission of curiosity. Archie didn't want to overdo it by acting too eager for Obie's company and whatever he had to say. "I haven't much time. Important things await."

"This is important too," Obie said. Obie had a thin sharp face with a permanent worried look. That's why he was such an obvious stooge, an errand boy. The kind of kid you couldn't help kicking when he was down. And you also knew this—that he would get up again and vow revenge and never have the nerve or the know-how to take that revenge. "Remember that kid Renault? The chocolate assignment?"

"What about him?"

"He's still not selling the chocolates."

"So?"

"So—remember? His orders were not to sell them for ten school days. Okay. So the ten days came and went and he's still saying no."

"So what?"

This is what infuriated Obie—the way Archie tried so hard not to be impressed, to always play it cool. You could tell him that The Bomb was going to be dropped and he'd probably say "So what?" It got under Obie's skin, mostly because he suspected that it was an act, that Archie wasn't as cool as he pretended to be. And Obie was awaiting his chance to find out.

"Well, there's all kinds of rumors around the school. First of all, a lot of kids think that The Vigils are in on the deal, that Renault still isn't selling them because he's still carrying out the assignment. Then there are some kids who know the assignment is over and think that Renault is leading some kind of revolt against the sale. They say Brother Leon is climbing the wall every day . . ."

"Beautiful," Archie said, showing reaction to Obie's news at last.

"Every morning Leon calls the roll and every day this kid, a freshman, sits there, and won't sell the goddam chocolates."

"Beautiful."

"You said that."

"Continue," Archie said, ignoring Obie's sarcasm.

"Well, I understand that the sale is going lousy. Nobody wants to sell the chocolates in the first place and it's turned into a kind of farce in some classes."

Obie sat down on the bleacher seat beside Archie, pausing to let the report sink in.

Archie sniffed the air and said, "This gymnasium stinks." Pretending indifference to Obie's report but his thoughts racing, pondering the possibilities.

Obie poured it on. "The eager beavers, the brownnosers are out selling chocolates like madmen. So are Leon's pets, his special boys. So are the kids who still believe in school spirit." He sighed. "Anyway, there's a lot going on."

Archie was busy contemplating the far side of the gym, as if something interesting was going on over there. Obie followed his gaze—nothing. "Well, what do you think, Archie?" he asked.

"What do you mean—what do I think?"

"The situation. Renault. Brother Leon. The chocolates. The kids out there taking sides . . ."

"We'll see, we'll see," Archie said. "I don't know whether The Vigils should get involved or not." He yawned.

That phony yawn irritated Obie. "Hey, look, Archie. The Vigils are involved whether you know it or not."

"What are you talking about?"

"Look, you told the kid to refuse the chocolates in the first place. That's what started all this stuff. But the kid went beyond that. He was supposed to start selling after the assignment was over. So, now he's defying The Vigils. And a lot of guys know that. We are involved, Archie, whether we want to be or not."

Obie could see that he had scored. He saw something flash in Archie's eyes, like looking at a blank window and observing a ghost peeking out.

"Nobody defies The Vigils, Obie . . ."

"That's what Renault's doing."

". . . and gets away with it."

Archie had that dreamy look again and his lower lip drooped. "Here's what to do. Arrange to have Renault appear before The Vigils. Check up on the sale—get the totals, facts and figures."

"Right," Obie said, writing in his notebook. As much as he hated Archie, he loved to see him when he was swinging into action. Obie decided to add more fuel to the flames. "Another thing, Archie. Didn't The Vigils promise Leon way back they'd back him in the chocolate sale?"

Obie had scored again. Archie turned to him, surprise scrawled on his face. But he recovered quickly. "Let me worry about Leon. You just run your errands, Obie."

God, how Obie hated the son of a bitch. He snapped his notebook shut and left Archie sitting there in the polluted atmosphere of the gymnasium.

BRIAN COCHRAN COULDN'T BELIEVE his eyes. He went through the totals again, double-checking, making sure he hadn't screwed up. Frowning, biting the pencil, he pondered the results of his arithmetic—sales were dropping at an alarming rate. For a week now, they'd been going steadily downward. But yesterday, the sharpest drop of all.

What would Brother Leon say? That was Brian's main concern. Brian hated the job of treasurer because it was such a drag but mostly because it brought him into personal contact with Brother Leon. Leon gave Brian the chills. The teacher was unpredictable, moody. He was never satisfied. Complaints, complaints—your sevens look like nines, Cochran. Or, you spelled Sulkey's name wrong—it's Sulkey with an *e*, Cochran.

Brian had been lucky recently. Brother Leon had stopped checking the totals on a daily basis, almost as if he anticipated the bad news the figures contained and wanted to avoid finding out about it definitely. Today was zero hour, however. He had told Brian to prepare the totals. Now Brian waited for the teacher to show up. He'd go ape when he saw the figures. Brian shivered, actually shivered! He'd read how in historic times they killed the bearer of bad news. He had the feeling that Brother Leon was that kind of character, that he would need a scapegoat and Brian would be closest at hand. Brian sighed, tired of it all, wishing he were outside on this beautiful October day, gunning around in the old Chevy his father had bought him when school started. He loved the car. "Me and my Chevy," Brian hummed to the tune of a song he'd heard on the radio.

"Well, Brian."

Brother Leon had a way of sneaking up on you. Brian leaped and almost came to attention. That's the kind of lousy effect the teacher had on him.

"Yes, Brother Leon."

"Sit, sit," Leon said, and took his place behind the desk. Leon was sweating, as usual. He had removed his black jacket and his shirt was stained with wetness at the armpits. A faint smell of perspiration reached Brian.

"The totals are bad," Brian said, plunging, wanting to get it over with, wanting to get out of the school, this office, Leon's suffocating presence. And feeling simultaneously a twist of triumph—Leon was such a rat, let him have some bad news for a change.

"Bad?"

"The sales are down. Below last year's. And last year, the quota was half of what has to be sold this year."

"I know, I know," Leon said sharply, swiveling away in his desk chair as if Brian weren't important enough to be addressed directly. "Are you sure of your figures? You're not exactly a whiz at adding and subtracting, Cochran."

Brian flushed with anger. He was tempted to throw the master sheet at the Brother but held back. Nobody defied Brother Leon. Not Brian Cochran, anyway, who only wanted to get out of here.

"I double-checked everything," Brian said, keeping his voice even.

Silence.

The floor vibrated under Brian's feet. The boxing club working out in the gym, maybe, doing calisthenics or the other stuff boxers did.

"Cochran. Read off the names of the boys who have reached or surpassed their quota."

Brian reached for the lists. A simple task because Brother Leon insisted that all kinds of cross-indexed lists be kept so that you could tell at a glance just where students stood.

"Sulkey, sixty-two. Maronia, fifty-eight. LeBlanc, fifty-two—"

"Slower, slower," Brother Leon said, still facing away from Brian. "Begin again and slower."

It was spooky but Brian began again, pronouncing the names more exactly, pausing between names and figures.

"Sulkey . . . sixty-two . . . Maronia . . . fifty-eight . . . LeBlanc . . . fifty-two . . . Caroni . . . fifty . . ."

Brother Leon was nodding his head, as if listening to a beautiful symphony, as if lovely sounds filled the air.

"Fontaine . . . fifty . . ." Brian paused. "Those are the only ones who either made the quota or topped it, Brother Leon."

"Read the others. There are many students who sold over forty. Read those names . . ." His face still turned away, his body slouched in the chair.

Brian shrugged and continued, calling out the names in singsong fashion, with measured pauses, letting his voice linger over the names and numbers, a weird litany here in the quiet office. When he ran out of the sales in the forties, he continued into the thirties and Brother Leon did not tell him to halt.

". . . Sullivan . . . thirty-three . . . Charlton . . . thirty-two . . . Kelly . . . thirty-two . . . Ambrose . . . thirty-one . . ."

Once in a while Brian looked up to see Brother Leon's head nodding, as if he were communicating with someone unseen or only himself. While the recitation went on—from the thirties into the twenties.

His eyes running ahead, Brian saw that he was in for trouble. After he was through with the twenties and the teens, there was a big leap. He wondered how Brother Leon would react to the small returns. Brian began to grow warm and his voice turned hoarse. He needed a drink of water, not only to relieve the dryness of his throat but to ease the tension of his neck muscles.

". . . Antonelli . . . fifteen . . . Lombard . . . thirteen . . ." He cleared his throat, breaking the rhythm, interrupting the flow of the report. A deep breath and then, "Cartier . . . six." He shot a look at Brother Leon but the teacher hadn't moved. His hands were clasped together, resting in his lap. "Cartier . . . he only sold six because he's been out of school. Appendicitis. He's been in the hospital . . ."

Brother Leon waved his hand, a gesture that said, "I understand, it doesn't matter." At least, that's what Brian figured it meant. And the gesture also seemed to mean "continue." He looked at the last name on the list.

"Renault . . . zero."

The pause. No names left.

"Renault . . . zero," Brother Leon said, his voice a sibilant whisper. "Can you imagine that, Cochran? A Trinity boy who has refused to sell the chocolates? Do you know what's happened, Cochran? Do you know why the sales have fallen off?"

"I don't know, Brother Leon," Brian said lamely.

"The boys have become infected, Cochran. Infected by a disease we could call apathy. A terrible disease. Difficult to cure."

What was he talking about?

"Before a cure can be found, the cause must be discovered. But in this case, Cochran, the cause is known. The carrier of the disease is known."

Brian knew what he was getting at now. Leon figured that Renault was the cause, the carrier of the disease. As if reading Brian's mind, Leon whispered "Renault . . . Renault . . ."

Like a mad scientist plotting revenge in an underground laboratory, for crying out loud.

CHAPTER 23

"I'M QUITTING THE TEAM, Jerry."

"Why, Goob? I thought you liked football. We're just starting to click. You made a sensational catch yesterday."

They were headed for the bus stop. Today was Wednesday—no practice on Wednesday. Jerry was looking forward to arriving at the bus stop. There was a girl, beautiful, with hair like maple syrup. He'd seen her there a few times and she'd smiled at him. One day he'd gotten close enough to read her name on one of the schoolbooks she held in her arms. Ellen Barrett. Someday he'd get up the courage to speak to her. *Hi, Ellen.* Or call her on the telephone. Today maybe.

"Let's run," Goober said.

Off they went on a mad and awkward sprint. Their books prevented them from running with grace and abandon. But the mere act of running cheered up The Goober.

"Are you serious about quitting the team?" Jerry asked, his voice higher than usual, strained from the running.

"I've got to quit, Jerry." He was glad that his own voice was normal, unaffected by the running.

They turned into Gate Street.

"Why?" Jerry asked, launching himself into Gate Street with a burst of speed.

Their feet pounded on the pavement.

How can I tell him, Goob wondered.

Jerry had shot ahead. He glanced back over his shoulder, his face crimson with effort. "Why, damn it?"

The Goober caught up to him with a slight acceleration of his pace. He could easily have slid past him.

"Did you hear what happened to Brother Eugene?" The Goober asked.

"He got transferred," Jerry answered, squeezing the words out of himself like toothpaste from a tube. He was in good shape because of football but he wasn't a runner and didn't know the tricks.

"I heard he's gone on sick leave," Goober said.

"What's the difference?" Jerry replied. He took a deep sweet breath. "Hey, my legs are okay but my arms are killing me." He carried two books in each hand.

"Keep running."

"You're some kind of nut," Jerry said, humoring him.

They were approaching the intersection of Green and Gate. Seeing Jerry's discomfort, The Goober slackened his pace. "They say Brother Eugene's never been the same since Room Nineteen. They say he's all broken up over it. Can't eat or sleep. The shock."

"Rumors," Jerry gasped, "Hey, Goob, my lungs are burning up. I'm in a state of collapse."

"I know how he feels, Jerry. I know how a thing like that can drive somebody up a wall." Shouting the words into the wind. They had never discussed the destruction of Room Nineteen although Jerry knew about Goober's involvement. "Some people can't stand cruelty, Jerry. And that was a cruel thing to do to a guy like Eugene . . ."

"What's Brother Eugene got to do with not playing football?" Jerry asked, really gasping now, really sweating, his lungs threatening to burst and his arms aching from the burden of the books.

Goober put on the brakes, slackening his pace, coming finally to a halt. Jerry blew air out of his mouth as he collapsed on the edge of someone's front lawn. His chest rose and fell like human bellows.

The Goober sat on the curbstone, his legs jack-knifed, his feet in the gutter. He studied the leaves clustered beneath his feet. He was trying to find a way to explain to Jerry the connection between Brother Eugene and Room Nineteen and not playing football anymore. He knew there was a connection but it was hard to put into words.

"Look, Jerry. There's something rotten in that school. More than rotten." He groped for the word and found it but didn't want to use it. The word didn't fit the surroundings, the sun and the bright October afternoon. It was a midnight word, a howling wind word.

"The Vigils?" Jerry asked. He'd lain back on the lawn and was looking at the blue sky, the hurrying autumn clouds.

"That's part of it," The Goober said. He wished they were still running. "Evil," he said.

"What did you say?"

Crazy. Jerry would think he'd flipped. "Nothing," Goober said. "Anyway, I'm not going to play football. It's a personal thing, Jerry." He took a deep breath. "And I'm not going out for track next spring."

They sat in silence.

"What's the matter, Goob?" Jerry finally asked, voice troubled and loaded with concern.

"It's what they do to us, Jerry." It was easier saying the words because they weren't looking at each other, both staring ahead. "What they did to me that night in the classroom—I was crying like a baby, something I never thought I'd do again in my life. And what they did to Brother Eugene, wrecking his room, wrecking *him* . . ."

"Aw, take it easy, Goob."

"And what they're doing to you—the chocolates."

"It's all a game, Goob. Think of it as fun and games. Let them have their fun. Brother Eugene must have been on the borderline, anyway . . ."

"It's more than fun and games, Jerry. Anything that can make you cry and send a teacher away—tip him over the borderline—that's more than just fun and games."

They sat there for a long time, Jerry on the lawn and Goober on the curb. Jerry knew he'd be too late now to see the girl—Ellen Barrett—but he felt that Goober needed his presence at this moment. Some of the guys from school passed by and called to them. A bus came along and halted. The driver was disgusted when The Goober shook his head that they didn't want a ride.

After a while, Goober said, "Sell the chocolates, Jerry, will you?"

Jerry said, "Play football."

Goober shook his head. "I'm not giving anything more to Trinity. Not football, not running, not anything."

They sat in sadness. Finally, they gathered their books, got up, and walked in silence to the bus stop.

The girl wasn't there.

CHAPTER 24

"Y OU'RE IN TROUBLE," Brother Leon said.

You're in trouble, not me, Archie wanted to answer. But didn't. He had never spoken to Leon on the telephone before and the disembodied voice at the other end of the line had caught him off balance.

"What's the matter?" Archie asked cautiously, but knowing, of course.

"The chocolates," Leon said. "They're not selling. The entire sale is in jeopardy." Leon's breath filled in the gaps between the words as if he'd been running a long distance. Was he on the edge of panic?

"How bad is it?" Archie asked, relaxing now, stalling. He knew how bad it was.

"It could hardly be worse. The sale is more than half finished. The initial push is over. There is no momentum. Half the chocolates haven't been sold yet. And the sales are virtually at a standstill." Leon paused in the recital. "You're not being very effective, Archie."

Archie shook his head in grudging admiration. Here was Leon with his back to the wall and still he was on the offensive. *You're not being very effective, Archie.*

"You mean the finances are bad?" Archie taunted, launching his own offensive. To Leon, it may have sounded like a shot in the dark but it wasn't. The question was based on information Archie had received that afternoon from Brian Cochran.

Cochran had stopped him in the second-floor corridor and motioned Archie into an empty classroom. Archie had been reluctant. The kid was Leon's bookkeeper and probably his stooge. But the information revealed that Cochran was no stooge for Leon.

"Listen, I think Leon's in deep trouble. There's more than chocolates involved here, Archie."

Archie resented Cochran's familiarity, the use of his name. But he didn't say anything, curious about what the kid had to say.

"I overheard Leon talking with Brother Jacques. Jacques was trying to back him into a corner. He kept mentioning something about Leon abusing his power of attorney. That he'd overextended the school's finances. That was his exact word, 'overextended.' The chocolates came into it. Something about twenty thousand boxes and Leon paying cash in advance. I didn't hear all of it . . . I got out of there before they could find out I was around . . ."

"So what do you think, Cochran?" Archie asked, although he knew. Leon needed at least twenty thousand dollars to draw even with the school.

"I think Leon bought the chocolates with money that he wasn't supposed to use. Now, the sale's going lousy and he's caught in the middle. And Brother Jacques smells a rat . . ."

"Jacques is sharp," Archie said, remembering how Jacques had acted on Archie's anonymous tip about the word "environment"—making the class look ridiculous, Obie among them. "Good job, Cochran."

Cochran beamed at the praise. Encouraged, he drew some sheets of paper out of a book he was carrying. "Take a look at this stuff sometime, Archie. It's facts and figures about this year's sale and last year's. And it's all bad. I think Leon's on the run . . ."

But Cochran really didn't know Leon, Archie realized now as the teacher's voice came vibrantly over the line. Leon had ignored Archie's taunt about finances and had resumed his offensive.

"I thought you had influence, Archie. You and your . . . friends."

"It's not my sale, Brother Leon."

"It's your sale in more ways than you realize, Archie," Leon said, sighing. It was his phony sigh, his usual act. "You played games at the beginning, Archie, with that freshman Renault and got yourself involved. Now, the game has backfired."

Renault. Archie thought of the kid's refusal to sell, his ridiculous defiance. He remembered the triumph in Obie's voice when he'd told him of Renault's action—it's your move, Archie baby. But it was always Archie's move anyway.

And he moved now. "Just a minute," he told Brother Leon. He put down the phone and went to the den where he removed Cochran's data from his U.S. History textbook. Returning to the phone, he said, "I've got some figures here about last year's sale. Do you know they barely sold all the chocolates last year? Kids are getting tired of selling stuff. Last year, it took a lot of prizes and bonuses to get the kids to sell only twenty-five boxes at one dollar a box. And this year they're stuck with fifty boxes at two dollars each. That's why the sale is falling apart—not because of games being played."

Brother Leon's breathing filled the line, as if he were some kind of obscene phone caller.

"Archie," he said, whispering, menace in the whisper, as if the information he had to impart was too terrible to be spoken aloud. "I don't care about fun and games. I don't care whether it's Renault or your precious organization or the state of the economy. All I know is that the chocolates aren't being sold. And I want them sold!"

"Any ideas about how?" Archie said, fighting for time again. Funny, he knew Leon was in a precarious position and yet there was always the danger of underestimating him. He still had the authority of the school behind him. Archie had only his wits and a bunch of guys who were all big zeroes without him.

"Perhaps you should begin with Renault," Leon said. "I think he should be made to say 'yes' instead of 'no.' I'm convinced, Archie, that he's become a symbol to those who would like to see the sale defeated. The malingerers, the malcontents—they always rally around a rebel. Renault must sell the chocolates. And you, The Vigils—yes, I'm saying the name aloud—The Vigils must throw their full weight behind the sale . . ."

"That's quite an order, Brother."

"You've spoken the correct word, Archie. Order—it is an order."

"I don't know what you mean, Brother."

"I'll make it clear, Archie. If the sale goes down the drain, you and The Vigils also go down the drain. Believe me . . ."

Archie was about to respond, tempted to let Leon know that he had learned about the financial trouble, but he didn't get the chance. Leon, that bastard, had already hung up and the dial tone exploded in Archie's ear.

T HE SUMMONS LOOKED like a ransom note—letters cut out of a newspaper or magazine. *vIgiL MeEtinG tWO-THirTy*. The wackiness of the note, those crazy letters, made it seem childish and ridiculous. But that same touch of the childish also gave it an air of something not quite rational, faintly threatening and mocking. That was the special quality of The Vigils, of course, and Archie Costello.

Thirty minutes later, Jerry stood before The Vigils in the storage room. The nearby gym was occupied by fellows either practicing basketball or boxing calisthenics and the walls echoed with thuddings, bouncings and whistles blowing, like a grotesque sound track. Nine or ten Vigil members were present, including Carter who was getting tired of this Vigil crap, especially when it meant he had to miss boxing, and Obie who looked forward to the meeting with pleasure, wondering how Archie would proceed. Archie sat behind the card table. The table was covered with a scarf of purple and gold—the school colors. In the exact center of the table: a box of chocolates.

"Renault," Archie said softly.

Instinctively, Jerry came to attention, squaring his shoulders, sucking in his stomach, and immediately disgusted with himself.

"Have a chocolate, Renault?"

Jerry shook his head, sighing. He thought wistfully of the guys out on the football field in the sweet fresh wind, tossing the ball around before practice began.

"They're good," Archie said, opening the box and taking out a chocolate. He inhaled its flavor and popped it into his mouth. He chewed slowly, deliberately, smacking his lips in exaggerated fashion. A second chocolate followed the first. And a third followed the second. His mouth was crammed with candy now and his throat rippled as he swallowed. "Delicious," he said. "And only two dollars a box—a bargain."

Somebody laughed. A short bark that was instantly cut off as if a needle had been lifted from a record.

"But you wouldn't know about the price, would you, Renault?"

Jerry shrugged. But his heart began to beat wildly. He knew there had to be a showdown. And this was it.

Archie reached for another chocolate. Into his mouth. "How many boxes have you sold, Renault?"

"None."

"None?" Archie's gentle voice curled in surprise and wonder. He swallowed, shaking his head in mock puzzlement. Without taking his eyes from Jerry, he called, "Hey, Porter, how many boxes have you sold?"

"Twenty-one."

"Twenty-one?" Archie's voice was now filled with awe. "Hey, Porter, you must be one of those hustling, eager-beaver freshmen, huh?"

"I'm a senior."

"A senior?" More awe. "You mean to tell me you're a big-shot senior and you've still got enough spirit left to get out there and sell all those chocolates? Beautiful, Porter." The voice full of mockery—or was it? "Anybody else here sell chocolates?"

A chorus of numbers filled the air as if The Vigil members were calling bids at a weird auction.

"Forty-two."

"Thirty-three."

"Twenty."

"Nineteen."

"Forty-five."

Archie raised his hands and silence fell. Someone in the gym fell against the wall and shouted an obscenity. Obie marveled at the way Archie ran the meetings and how The Vigils quickly took his cues. Porter hadn't sold ten boxes, if any at all. Obie himself had only sold sixteen but had called out forty-five.

"And you, Renault, a freshman, a new student who should be filled with the spirit of Trinity, you haven't sold any? Zero? Nothing?" His hand reached for another chocolate. Actually, he loved them. Not as good as Hershey with almonds but an acceptable substitute.

"That's right," Jerry said, his voice small, a wrong-end-of-the-telescope kind of voice.

"Do you mind if I ask why?"

Jerry pondered the question. What should he do? Play a game? Tell it straight? But he wasn't sure if it would make sense if he told it straight, especially to a roomful of strangers.

"It's personal," he said finally, feeling like a loser, knowing he couldn't win. It had all been going so beautifully. Football, school, a girl who had smiled at him at the bus stop. He had edged close to her and seen her name written on one of her books—Ellen Barrett. She had smiled at him two days in a row and he'd been too shy to speak to her but had looked up all the Barretts in the phone book. Five of them. Tonight he was planning to call them up, track her down. It seemed to him that he'd be able to talk to her on the phone. Now, for some reason, he had the feeling he would never talk to her, never play football again—a crazy feeling but one that he couldn't shake.

Archie had been licking his fingers, one at a time, letting the echo of Jerry's response linger in the air. It was so quiet that he heard someone's stomach growl intimately.

"Renault," Archie said, friendly, his voice conversational. "I'll tell you something. Nothing's personal here in The Vigils. No secrets here, understand." He took a final suck at his thumb. "Hey, Johnson."

"Right," a voice called behind Jerry.

"How many times you jack off every day?"

"Twice," Johnson replied quickly.

"See?" asked Archie. "No secrets here, Renault. Nothing personal. Not in The Vigils."

Jerry had taken a shower this morning before school but now he smelled his own perspiration.

"Come on," Archie said, a good friend now, encouraging, coaxing. "You can tell us."

Carter blew air out of his mouth in exasperation. He was losing patience with Archie's cat and mouse crap. He had sat here for two years watching Archie play his silly games with kids, having Archie act the big shot as if he ran the show. Carter carried the responsibility for the assignments on his shoulders. As president, he also had to keep the other guys in line, keep them psyched up, ready to help make Archie's assignments work. And Carter wasn't crazy about this chocolate stuff. It was something beyond the control of The Vigils. It involved Brother Leon and he didn't trust Leon as far as he could throw him. Now, he watched the kid Renault, looking as if he was ready to faint with fright, his face pale and eyes wide with dread, and Archie having fun with him. Jesus. Carter hated this psychological crap. He loved boxing where everything was visible—the jabs, the hooks, the roundhouse swings, the glove in the stomach.

"Okay, Renault, play time is over," Archie said. The gentleness was gone from his voice. No chocolates in his mouth. "Tell us—why aren't you selling chocolates?"

"Because I don't want to," Jerry said, still stalling. Because—what else could he do?

"You don't want to?" Archie asked, incredulous.

Jerry nodded. He'd bought time.

"Hey, Obie."

"Right," Obie answered, stung. Why the hell did Archie have to pick on him all the time? What the hell did he want now?

"Do you want to come to school every day, Obie?"

"Hell, no," Obie responded, knowing what Archie wanted and giving it to him but resentful as well, feeling like a stooge, as if Archie was the ventriloquist and Obie the dummy.

"But you *come* to school, don't you?"

"Hell, yes."

Laughter greeted the answer and Obie allowed himself a smile. But a quick look from Archie wiped the smile away. Archie was dead serious. He could tell that by the way his lips were tight and thin and his eyes flashing like neon signs.

"See?" Archie said, swiveling back to Renault. "Everybody has to do things in this world they don't want to."

A terrific sadness swept over Jerry. As if somebody had died. The way he felt standing in the cemetery that day they buried his mother. And nothing you could do about it.

"Okay, Renault," Archie said, a finality in his voice.

You could feel the room tense. Obie sucked in his breath. Here it comes, the Archie touch.

"Here's your assignment. Tomorrow at the roll call, you take the chocolates. You say, 'Brother Leon, I accept the chocolates.' "

Stunned, Jerry blurted out "What?"

"Something wrong with your hearing, Renault?" Turning aside, he called, "Hey, McGrath, did you hear me?"

"Hell, yes."

"What did I say?"

"You said the kid should start selling chocolates."

Archie returned his attention to Jerry. "You're getting off easy, Renault. You've disobeyed The Vigils. That calls for punishment. Although The Vigils don't believe in violence, we have found it necessary to have a punishment code. The punishment is usually worse than the assignment. But we're letting you off cheap, Renault. We're just asking you to take the chocolates tomorrow. And sell them."

Jesus, Obie thought in disbelief, The great Archie Costello is running scared. The word "asking" was the tipoff. A slip of the lip, maybe. But as if Archie was trying to bargain with the kid, *asking*, for crying out loud. I've got you, Archie, you bastard. Obie had never known such sweet victory. The goddam freshman was going to screw Archie up, at last. Not the Black Box. Not Brother Leon. Not his own cleverness. But a skinny freshman. Because Obie was certain of one thing as if it was a natural law, like gravity—Renault wasn't going to sell the chocolates. He could tell by looking at the kid, standing there scared, like he could shit his pants, but not backing down. While Archie was *asking* him to sell the chocolates. Asking.

"Dismissed," Archie called out.

Carter was surprised at the sudden dismissal and he banged the gavel too hard, almost splitting the crate he used as a desk. He had a feeling that he had missed a beat somewhere, had missed a crucial moment. Archie and all his subtle crap. What the kid Renault needed was a stiff jab to the jaw and another to the belly. That'd make him sell the frigging chocolates. Archie and his stupid *let's not have any violence.* Anyway, the meeting was over and Carter felt like working out, like working up a sweat with the gloves and the big bag.

He banged the gavel again.

CHAPTER 26

"Hello."

His mind went blank.

"Hello?"

Was it her? But it had to be—this was the last Barrett in the book and the voice was fresh and appealing, the kind of voice that went with all that beauty he had seen at the bus stop.

"Hello," he managed, his voice emerging as an ugly croak.

"Is this Danny?" she asked.

He was instantly, insanely jealous of Danny, whoever Danny was.

"No," he croaked again, miserably.

"Who is this?" she asked, annoyance now in her voice.

"Is this Ellen? Ellen Barrett?" The name was strange on his tongue. He had never said it aloud although he had whispered it silently a thousand times.

Silence.

"Look," he began, his heart beating desperately.

"Look, you don't know who I am but I see you every day . . ."

"Are you some kind of pervert?" she asked, not horrified at all but good-naturedly curious, like, "Hey Ma, I've got a pervert on the line."

"No. I'm the fellow at the bus stop."

"What fellow? What bus stop?" Her voice had lost all its demureness. It had become a wise-guy, show-me kind of voice.

He wanted to say you smiled at me yesterday, the day before that, last week. And I love you. But couldn't. He suddenly saw how futile, how ridiculous the situation was. A fellow didn't call up a girl on the evidence of a smile and introduce himself this way. She probably smiled at a hundred guys a day.

"I'm sorry for bothering you," he said.

"Are you sure this isn't Danny? Are you trying to put me on, Danny? Look, Danny, I'm getting tired of you and your crap . . ."

Jerry hung up. He didn't want to hear anymore. The word "crap," echoing now in his mind, had destroyed all illusion about her. Like meeting a lovely girl and having her smile reveal rotten teeth. But his heart was still beating wildly. *Are you some kind of pervert?* Maybe I am. Not a sexual pervert but another kind. Wasn't refusing to sell the chocolates a kind of perversion? Wasn't it crazy to go on refusing to sell the chocolates, particularly after that last warning yesterday by Archie Costello and The Vigils? And yet this morning, he had stood his ground and fired a level and positive *No* at Brother Leon. For the first time, the word brought exultancy to him, a lifting of the spirit.

With the latest *No* resounding in his ears, Jerry had expected the school building to fall or something dramatic to happen. Nothing. He had seen Goober shake his head in dismay. But Goober didn't know about this new feeling, the sense that his bridges were burning behind him and for once in his life he didn't care. He was still buoyant when he arrived home, otherwise, he wouldn't have had the courage to call all those Barretts and to actually talk to the girl. It had been a miserable failure, of course. But he had made the call, taken a step, broken the routine of his days and nights.

He went into the kitchen, suddenly ravenous, and dumped some ice cream from the freezer into a dish.

"My name is Jerry Renault and I'm not going to sell the chocolates," he said to the empty apartment.

The words and his voice sounded strong and noble.

CHAPTER 27

THEY SHOULDN'T HAVE PICKED Frankie Rollo for an assignment, of course. A junior, Rollo was insolent, a troublemaker. He was a non-participant, refusing to take part in athletics or extra-curricular activities that were so important in the Trinity scene. He seldom opened a book and never did any homework, but he managed to survive because he possessed a native and cunning intelligence. His major talent was cheating. He was also lucky. Under ordinary circumstances, he was the kind of guy Archie took pleasure in assigning, watching him bend or break. All these so-called rough characters melted into ninety-seven-pound weaklings when confronted by Archie and The Vigils. The scorn and the swagger evaporated as they stood ill-at-ease in the storage room. But not Frankie Rollo. He stood loose and easy, unintimidated.

"Your name?" Archie asked.

"Come on, Archie," Rollo replied, smiling at all this foolishness. "You know my name."

The silence was awesome. But before that silence, a gasp from someone in the room. Archie was careful to keep his poker face, intent on not betraying an emotion. But he was shaken inside. No one had ever reacted this way before. No one had ever challenged Archie or an assignment.

"Let's not have any crap, Rollo," growled Carter. "Let's hear your name."

A pause. Archie swore silently. It was irritating to have Carter step in that way, as if he was coming to Archie's rescue. Ordinarily, Archie ran the meetings his way, not anybody else's way.

Rollo shrugged. "My name is Frankie Rollo," he announced in singsong fashion.

"You think you're a big shot, don't you?" Archie asked.

Rollo didn't respond but the smirk on his face was an eloquent answer.

"A big shot," Archie repeated, as if savoring the word, but stalling, playing for time, shifting his thoughts, knowing it would be necessary to improvise, to turn this insolent bastard into a victim.

"You said it, not me," Rollo said smugly.

"We like big shots here," Archie said. "In fact, that's our specialty—turning big shots into little shots."

"Cut the shit, will you, Archie?" Rollo said. "You're not impressing anybody."

Again that terrible silence, like a shock wave, stunning the room, an invisible blow. Even Obie who had looked forward to the day when a victim would defy the great Archie Costello blinked in disbelief.

"What did you say?" Archie asked, biting off every word and spitting it at Rollo.

"Hey, you guys," Rollo said, swiveling away from Archie and addressing the entire assembly. "I'm not a scared kid who pees his pants because the big bad Vigils call him to a meeting. Hell, you guys can't even scare a punk freshman into selling a few lousy chocolates . . ."

"Look, Rollo," Archie began.

But he didn't have a chance to finish as Carter leaped to his feet. Carter had been waiting for a moment like this for months, his hands itching for action in the storage room instead of sitting there week by week as Archie played his little cat-and-mouse games.

"That's enough out of you, Rollo," Carter said. Simultaneously, his hand shot out and struck Rollo on the jaw. Rollo's head snapped back—*snap* like a knuckle cracking—and he bellowed with pain. As Rollo lifted his hands to his face in tardy defense, Carter's fist sank sickeningly into his stomach. Rollo groaned and retched, doubled over, clutching himself in disbelief, gasping for breath. He was shoved from behind, and dropped to the floor coughing and spitting, crawling on all fours.

A muffled roar of approval rose from The Vigils. At last, action, physical action, something you could see with your own eyes.

"Get him out of here," Carter said.

Rollo was picked up by two Vigil members and half-carried, half-dragged toward the doorway. Archie had watched Rollo's swift demolition in dismay. He resented Carter's quick move into the spotlight, the way the guys had cheered Carter on. It had placed Archie at a disadvantage for the first time as assigner because Rollo had only been the curtain raiser, a bit of amusement Obie had arranged to enliven the proceedings. Actually, the meeting had been called to discuss Renault and what could be done about the stubborn freshman who refused to fall into line.

Carter called for order, banging his gavel on the table. In the developing silence, they could hear Rollo being dumped onto the gymnasium floor outside and then the sound of vomiting like a toilet being flushed.

"Okay, quiet," Carter demanded, as if he were yelling at Rollo to quit throwing up. Then he turned to Archie. "Sit down," he said. Archie recognized the command in Carter's voice. For a moment, he was tempted to challenge him but he realized that The Vigils had approved Carter's action against Rollo. This was no time to have a showdown with Carter, it was time to play it cool, cool. Archie sat.

"We've arrived at the moment of truth, Archie," Carter said. "And here's how I read it—tell me if I'm wrong. When a gross creep like Rollo comes in here and challenges The Vigils, then there's something wrong. Very wrong. We can't afford to have guys like Rollo thinking they can screw around with us. The word will spread and The Vigils fall apart." Carter paused to let them imagine the dissolution of The Vigils. "Now, I said that something is very wrong. And I'll tell you who's wrong. We are."

His words were greeted with surprise.

"How come *we're* wrong?" Obie, the perennial straight man, called out.

"First of all, because we let our name get connected with the goddam chocolate sale. Like it's our baby or something. Second of all, like Rollo said, we let a punk freshman make fools out of us." He turned to Archie. "Right, Archie?" The question was loaded with malice.

Archie didn't say anything. He was suddenly in a roomful of strangers and he decided to do nothing at all. When in doubt, play the waiting game. Watch for an opening. It would be ridiculous to disagree with Carter, of course. Word had been spreading throughout the school—the kid had refused to sell the chocolates in direct defiance of The Vigils. That's why they had assembled here this afternoon.

"Obie, show us what you found this morning on the bulletin board," Carter said.

Obie was eager to comply. Reaching under his chair he withdrew a poster that he had folded in two. Unfolded, the poster was about the size of an ordinary kitchen window. Obie held it up for all to see. The poster proclaimed in scrawled, scarlet letters—

SCREW THE CHOCOLATES
AND
SCREW THE VIGILS

"I saw the poster because I was late for math," Obie explained. "It was on the bulletin board in the main corridor."

"Do you think many guys saw it?" Carter asked.

"No. I'd shot by the bulletin board a minute before on the way to my locker for my math book. And the poster wasn't there. Chances are hardly anybody saw it."

"You think Renault put it up?" someone asked.

"No," Carter snorted. "Renault doesn't have to go around putting up posters. He's been saying screw The Vigils and the chocolates for weeks now. But this shows what's happening. The word is spreading. If Renault can get away with defying us, other people are gonna try." Finally, he turned to Archie. "Okay, Archie. You're the brains of the outfit. And you also got us into this mess. Where do we go from here?"

"You're pushing panic buttons for nothing," Archie said, voice quiet and casual. He knew what he must do—regain his previous status, wipe away the memory of Rollo's defiance and prove that he, Archie Costello, was still in command. He had to show them that he could take care of both Renault and the chocolates. And he was ready for them. While Carter had been making speeches and Obie flashing his poster around, Archie's mind had been racing, probing, testing. He always worked better under pressure, anyway. "First of all, you can't go around beating up half the kids in the school. That's why I usually lay off the strong-arm stuff in the assignments. The brothers would close us down in no time and the kids would really start sabotaging if we started hurting people." Noticing Carter's frown, Archie decided to throw him a bone—Carter still ran the meetings and as Vigils president he could be a dangerous adversary. "All right, Carter, I'll admit you did a beautiful job on Rollo and he had it coming. But nobody gives a damn about Rollo. He can lay in his vomit till kingdom come and nobody'd care. But Rollo's an exception."

"Rollo's an example," Carter said. "Let the word spread about Rollo and we won't have to worry about other kids acting wise or putting up posters."

Anticipating a deadlock on that topic, Archie changed directions. "But that doesn't sell chocolates, Carter," Archie said. "You told us The Vigils are linked up with the sale. Then the solution is simple. Let's get the goddam sale over with as soon as possible. Let's sell the chocolates. If Renault's turning into some kind of rebel hero because he's not selling the chocolates, how the hell is he going to look when everybody in the school is selling, except him?"

Murmurs of assent came from the members, but Carter appeared doubtful. "And how do we get everybody in the school to start selling the chocolates, Archie?"

Archie allowed himself the indulgence of a quiet, confident laugh, but closed his fists to hide his moist palms. "Simple, Carter. Like all great schemes and plans, it has the beauty of simplicity." The guys waited, spellbound as always when Archie began to outline assignments and plans. "We make selling chocolates popular. We make it cool to sell the things. We spread the word. We organize. We bring in the class officers, the homeroom officers, the student council, the kids with influence. Do or die for good old Trinity! Everybody sells!"

"Not everybody will want to sell fifty boxes, Archie," Obie called out, disturbed because somehow Archie had taken charge again—he had them eating out of his hand.

"They will, Obie," Archie predicted, "they will. Do your thing, they say, Obie, do your thing. Well, we're going to make selling chocolates the thing to do. And The Vigils will come out on top as usual. The school will love us for it—getting rid of their chocolates. We'll be able to write our own ticket with Leon and the brothers. Why do you think I pledged support to Leon in the first place?" Archie's voice was gentle with assurance, the old gentleness they all recognized as Archie's hallmark when he was sailing high, wide and handsome. They admired the way Carter had employed his fists to demolish Rollo but they felt more secure with Archie in command, Archie who was capable of surprise after surprise.

"How about Renault?" Carter asked.

"Don't worry about Renault."

"But I do, I worry about him," Carter said, sarcastically. "He's making patsies out of us."

"The Renault thing will take care of itself," Archie said. Couldn't Carter and the others see? Were they so blind to human nature, to developing situations? "Let me put it this way, Carter. Before the sale is over, Renault will be wishing with all his heart that he had sold the chocolates. And the school will be glad he didn't."

"Okay," Carter said, banging the gavel. He always banged the gavel when he was unsure of himself. The gavel was an extension of his fist. But feeling that Archie had somehow eluded him, had somehow won a victory, Carter said, "Look, Archie, if this backfires, if the sale doesn't work, then you've screwed yourself up, do you understand? You'll be all done and it won't take the Black Box."

Blood stung Archie's cheeks and a pulse throbbed dangerously in his temple. No one had ever talked to him that way before, not in front of everyone like this. With an effort he made himself stay loose, kept that smile on his lips like a label on a bottle, hiding his humiliation.

"You'd better be right, Archie," Carter said. "As far as I'm concerned, you're on probation until the last chocolate's sold."

The final humiliation. Probation.

Archie kept that smile on his face until he felt his cheeks would crack.

CHAPTER 28

H E HANDED THE BALL off to Guilmet, slapping it into his belly, and then hung in there, waiting for Carter to lunge through the line. The play called for Jerry to hit Carter low and send him toppling, an assignment Jerry didn't relish. Carter was easily fifty pounds heavier and he was used by the coach to keep the freshmen squad on their toes. But the coach always said, "It doesn't matter how big the body, it's what you do with it." Now, Jerry waited for Carter to emerge from the jungle of skirmishing bodies as Guilmet plunged off tackle. And there he was like a freight train on the loose, out of control, rampaging wildly, trying to careen toward Guilmet but too late, too late. Jerry leaped toward him, low, aiming for that vulnerable territory of the knees, the target pinpointed by the coach. Carter and Jerry collided like a street accident. Colored lights whirled—Fourth of July on an October afternoon. Jerry felt himself lunging toward the ground, arms and legs askew, all mixed up with Carter's arms and legs. There was exhilaration in the collision, the honest contact of football, not as beautiful maybe as a completed pass or a fake that threw your opponents off balance but beautiful nevertheless and manly, prideful.

The good damp smell of the grass, the earth, rushed into Jerry's nostrils and he let himself be carried on the waves of the sweet moment, knowing he'd carried out his assignment: get Carter. He glanced up to see Carter raising himself in astonishment, shaking his head. Jerry grinned as he got to his feet. Suddenly, he was struck from behind, a vicious blow to his kidneys, sickening in its impact. His knees caved in and he sank to the ground again. As he attempted to turn around to find out who had attacked him, another blow landed, someplace, and Jerry felt himself hurtling off-balance to the ground. He felt his eyes watering, tears spilling onto his cheeks. He looked around and saw the fellows getting into position for the next play.

"Come on, Renault," the coach called.

He got to one knee, then managed to stand on both feet. The pain was subsiding, translated now into a dull spreading ache.

"Come on, come on," the coach urged, irritable as usual.

Jerry made his way tenderly toward the lineup. He thrust his head and shoulders into the huddle, considering what play he should call next, but a part of him was not concerned with the play or the game. He lifted his head and scanned the field, as if he were figuring out what to do next. Who had assaulted him that way? Who hated him so much that he'd racked him up so viciously?

Not Carter—Carter had been in full view. But who else? Anybody. It could have been anybody. From his own team, maybe.

"You okay?" somebody inquired.

Jerry plunged into the huddle again. Called his own number—a run-keep. At least if he carried the ball, he'd be in full view of everyone and not as vulnerable to a sneak attack.

"Let's go," he said, putting juice into the words, letting them all know that he was fine, great, ready for action. He found that his rib cage ached when he walked.

Lined up behind the center, Jerry raised his eyes again, sweeping the players. Somebody was trying to wipe him out.

Give me eyes behind my head, he prayed, as he barked the signals.

The telephone rang as he inserted the key in the front door. Turning the key swiftly, he flung the door open and tossed his books on the chair in the hallway. The ringing went on unendingly, a lonely sound in the empty apartment.

Finally, he grabbed it off the wall.

"Hello."

Silence. Not even a dial tone. Then out of the silence, a faint sound, from a distance, getting closer, like someone chuckling, privately, at a secret intimate joke.

"Hello," Jerry said again.

The chuckle was louder now. An obscene phone call? Only girls got those, didn't they? Again that chuckle, more defined and louder but still somehow intimate and suggestive, a chuckle that said, I know something you don't know.

"Who is this?" Jerry asked.

And then the dial tone, like a fart in his ear.

That night at eleven o'clock the telephone rang again. Jerry figured it was his father—he was working the late shift at the drug store.

He lifted the receiver and said hello.

No response.

No sound at all.

He wanted to hang up but something made him hold the instrument to his ear, waiting.

The chuckle again.

It was weirder than three o'clock this afternoon. The night, the darkness outside, the apartment riddled with lamplight shadows seemed more menacing. Forget it, Jerry told himself, it always seems worse at night.

"Hey, who is this?" he asked, the sound of his voice restoring normalcy.

Still the chuckle, almost evil in its quiet mockery.

"This some creep? Some flaky nut? Some stupid jerk?" Jerry asked. Draw him out, make him angry.

The chuckle turned into a hoot of derision.

Then the dial tone again.

He seldom kept anything of value in his locker. The school was notorious for "borrowers"—kids who weren't exactly thieves but walked off with anything that wasn't nailed down or locked up. No sense buying a lock—it would be busted the first day. Privacy was virtually non-existent at Trinity. Most of the kids didn't give a damn or have any respect for the rights of others. They rummaged desks, pried lockers open, sifted through books on a perennial search for loot—money, pot, books, watches, clothing—anything.

The morning after that first night phone call, Jerry opened his locker and shook his head in disbelief. His poster had been smeared with ink or some kind of blue paint. The message had been virtually obliterated. *Do I dare disturb the universe?* was now a grotesque jumble of unconnected letters. It was such a senseless, childish act of vandalism that Jerry was more awed than angered. Who'd do such a crazy thing? Looking down, he saw that his new gym sneakers had been slashed, the canvas now limp shreds, rag-like. He'd made the mistake of leaving them here overnight.

Ruining the poster was one thing, a gross act, the work of the animal—and all schools had animals, even Trinity. But there was nothing prankish about ruining the sneakers. That was deliberate, somebody sending him a message.

The telephone calls.

The attack on the football field.

Now this.

He closed the locker quickly so no one would see the damage. For some reason, he felt ashamed.

He'd been dreaming of a fire, flames eating unknown walls, and the siren sounded, and then it wasn't a siren but the telephone. Jerry scrambled from his bed. In the hallway, his father was slamming the receiver down on the hook. "Something funny's going on around here." The grandfather clock chimed twice.

Jerry didn't have to blink the sleep from his eyes. He was wide awake, chilled, the floor cold beneath his feet.

"Who was it?" he asked. Although he knew, of course.

"Nobody," his father answered, disgusted. "Same thing happened last night about this time. But it didn't wake you up. Some nut on the other end of the line, laughing away like it's the biggest joke in the world." He reached out and tousled Jerry's hair. "Go back to bed, Jerry. There are all kinds of nuts running around loose."

It was hours before Jerry fell into a strange dreamless sleep.

"Renault," Brother Andrew called.

Jerry looked up. He'd been immersed in his new art project—copying a two-story house in order to learn perspective. A simple exercise but he loved the ordered lines, the neatness, the stark beauty of planes and angles.

"Yes, Brother?"

"Your watercolor. The landscape assignment."

"Yes?" Puzzled. The watercolor which was a major project had taken a week of painstaking work, simply because Jerry was not at his best in free art. He was more at ease with formal or geometric designs where the composition was well-defined. But the watercolor would account for fifty percent of his mark this semester.

"Today's the final day for handing it in," the Brother said. "I don't find yours here."

"I put it on your desk yesterday," Jerry said.

"Yesterday?" Brother Andrew asked, as if he'd never heard of yesterday. He was a fastidious, precise man who ordinarily taught math but had been filling in for the regular art teacher.

"Yes, sir," Jerry said firmly.

Eyebrows arched, the Brother looked through the pile of drawings on the desk.

Jerry sighed quietly, in resignation. He knew that Brother Andrew wouldn't find the drawing there. He wanted to turn, to scan the faces of the kids in the class, to find that one kid who'd be gloating in satisfaction. Hey, you're getting paranoid, he told himself. Who'd sneak in here and remove your drawing? Who'd watch so close that they'd even know you submitted the drawing yesterday?

Brother Andrew looked up. "To use a cliché, Renault, we are locked on the horns of a dilemma. Your landscape is not here. Now, either I have lost it and I do not make a habit of losing landscapes . . ." the teacher paused here as if, incredibly, he expected a laugh, and incredibly, the laugh did come ". . . or your memory is faulty."

"I handed it in, Brother." Firmly. Without panic.

The teacher looked steadily into Jerry's eyes. Jerry saw the honest doubt there. "Well, Renault, perhaps I *do* make a habit of losing landscapes, after all," he said, and Jerry felt a rush of camaraderie for the teacher. "At any rate, let me check further. Perhaps I left it in the teacher's lounge."

For some reason, this remark also provoked laughter and even the teacher joined in. It was late in the period and late in the day and everyone needed to relax, let down, take it easy. Jerry wanted to look around, to see whose eyes gleamed with triumph over the missing watercolor.

"Of course, Renault, as sympathetic as I am, if I do not find the landscape, then I must fail you this semester."

Jerry opened his locker.

The mess was still there. He hadn't torn down the poster or removed the sneakers, letting them remain there as symbols. Symbols of what? He wasn't certain. Looking wistfully at the poster, he pondered the damaged words: *Do I dare disturb the universe?*

The usual corridor pandemonium surrounded him, slammed locker doors, wild yells and whistles, pounding feet as the guys hurried to the afterschool activities, football, boxing, debating.

Do I dare disturb the universe?

Yes, I do, I do. I think.

Jerry suddenly understood the poster—the solitary man on the beach standing upright and alone and unafraid, poised at the moment of making himself heard and known in the world, the universe.

CHAPTER 29

B EAUTIFUL.
Brian Cochran added the totals again and again, toying with them, playing with them, as if he were a juggler and they were fascinating figures of delight. He couldn't wait to report the totals to Brother Leon.

In the past few days, the volume of sales had risen staggeringly. Staggeringly was the correct word. Brian felt as if he were drunk on the statistics, the figures like liquor, making him light-headed, giddy and dizzy.

What had happened? He wasn't certain. There was no single reason for the sudden turnabout, the surprising upswing, the unexpected rash of sales. But the proof of the change was not only here in the figures before him but everywhere in the school itself. Brian had witnessed the feverish activity and how the chocolates had suddenly become a vogue, a fad, the way hula hoops had caught on when they were kids in the first or second grade, the way demonstrations had been the big thing a few years ago. Rumors indicated that The

Vigils had adopted the sale as a special crusade. And that was possible, although Brian hadn't made any inquiries—he always steered clear of The Vigils. However, he'd seen some of the more prominent Vigil members way-laying kids in the corridors, checking on their sales, whispering menacingly to those who had sold only a few boxes. Each afternoon, teams of fellows left the school, loaded down with chocolates. They piled into automobiles and drove off. Brian heard that the teams drove to various sections of town and invaded neighborhoods, ringing doorbells, banging on doors, a massive sales effort as if they were all encyclopedia salesmen on commission, for crying out loud. Brian heard reports that someone had gotten permission to solicit at one of the local factories—four guys had circulated through the place and sold three hundred boxes in a couple of hours. The feverish activity kept Brian hopping, main-taining the records and then rushing down to the big boards in the assembly to post the results. The hall had become the school's focal point. "Hey, look," a kid had yelled out during the last posting. "Jimmy Demers sold his fifty boxes."

That was the creepy aspect of the sale, the way the credit was being distrib-uted among all the students. Brian didn't know whether this was fair or not but he didn't argue about methods—Brother Leon was interested in results and so was Brian. And yet Brian was made uncomfortable by the situation. A few min-utes ago, Carter had walked into the office with a fistful of money. Brian treated Carter with utmost care—he was head of The Vigils.

"Okay, kid," Carter had said, flinging the money, bills and change, on the desk. "Here's the returns. Seventy-five boxes sold—one hundred fifty dollars. Count it."

"Right." Brian leaped to the task under Carter's watchful gaze. His fingers trembled and he cautioned himself to make no mistakes. Let it be one-fifty exactly.

"Right on the nose," Brian reported.

And then came the weird part.

"Let me see the roster," Carter said.

Brian handed over the list of names, each name with boxes beside it in which returns were noted as they arrived, corresponding to the master list on the big boards in the assembly hall. After studying the roster for a few minutes, Carter told Brian to credit various students with sales returns. Brian made the entries as Carter called them out: Huart, thirteen . . . DeLillo, nine . . . Lemoine . . . sixteen. And so on, until the entire seventy-five boxes had been distributed among seven or eight students.

"Those guys worked hard selling the chocolates," Carter said, a silly smile on his face. "I want to make sure they get credit."

"Right," Brian said, not making waves. He knew, of course, that none of the fellows chosen by Carter had sold the chocolates. But that was not his business.

"How many guys reached the fifty quota today?" Carter asked.

Brian consulted his figures. "Six, counting Huart and LeBlanc. Those sales they just made put them over the top." Brian actually was able to keep a straight face.

"Know what, Cochran? You're a bright boy. You're cool. You catch on fast."

Fast? Hell, they'd been juggling the sales all week long and Brian hadn't caught on for two entire days. He was tempted now to ask Carter if the cam-paign had turned into a Vigils project—like one of Archie Costello's assign-ments—but decided to hold down his curiosity.

Before the afternoon had ended, the sale of four hundred and seventy-five boxes had been received—cold, cold cash—as the teams returned to school with horns blowing, high with the hilarity of success.

When Brother Leon arrived, they totaled the sales together and discovered that fifteen thousand and ten boxes of chocolates had been sold thus far. Only five thousand to go—or four thousand, nine hundred and ninety to be exact, as Brother Leon pointed out in that fussy meticulous way of his. But Leon wasn't a problem today. He, too, seemed giddy, high, his wet eyes sparkling with the success of the sale.

He actually called Brian by his first name.

When Brian went to the assembly hall to post the latest figures, a cheering bunch of fellows applauded as he made the entries. No one had ever applauded Brian Cochran before and he felt like a football hero, of all things.

CHAPTER 30

T HERE WAS NO NECESSITY for the chocolate roll call now because most of the students were bringing their returns directly to Brian Cochran in the office. But Brother Leon persisted anyway. The Goober noticed that the teacher now took a delight in the process, making a big deal of it. He read off the latest sales as reported to Brian Cochran, reciting them to the class in detail, lingering over the names and the totals, wringing as much drama and satisfaction out of the situation as possible. And he had stooges or frightened kids like David Caroni who sang out their reports in the classroom as Leon basked in the totals.

"Let's see, Hartnett," Leon said, shaking his head in pleased surprise. "The report says you sold fifteen boxes yesterday, bringing your total to forty-three. Wonderful!" And he'd glanced slyly at Jerry.

It was all ridiculous, of course, because Hartnett hadn't sold any chocolates at all. The sales had been made by the teams of fellows who went out every afternoon. The school had become chocolate crazy. But not Goober. As a show of sympathy to Jerry, he had decided to stop selling the chocolates altogether and his total had remained unchanged for the past week at twenty-seven. It was little enough to do.

"Mallan," Leon was calling out.

"Seven."

"Let me see now, Mallan. Why, that brings your total to forty-seven. Congratulations, Mallan. I'm sure you'll be selling those three remaining boxes today."

Goober shriveled in his seat. Next would be Parmentier. And then Jerry. He glanced toward Jerry, saw him sitting erect in his chair as if he was looking forward to having his name called.

"Parmentier."

"Seven."

"Parmentier, Parmentier," Leon marveled. "That makes your total, yes, by George, fifty! You've made the quota, Parmentier. Good boy, good boy! A round of cheers, gentlemen."

Goober faked his cheer—little enough.

The pause. And then Leon's voice sang out, "Renault!" That was the exact description—sang. His voice exultant, lyrical. Goober realized Leon didn't care now whether Jerry sold chocolates or not.

711

"No," Jerry answered, his own voice clear and forceful, ringing with a triumph of its own.

Maybe both of them could win. Maybe a showdown could be averted, after all. The sale was winding down. It could end in a stalemate and eventually be forgotten, absorbed by other school activities.

"Brother Leon."

All eyes turned to Harold Darcy who had spoken.

"Yes, Harold."

"May I ask a question?"

A frown of annoyance from the teacher. He'd been having such a great time that he resented the interruption.

"Yes, yes, Darcy."

"Would you ask Renault why he isn't selling the chocolates like everybody else?"

The sound of a car horn could be heard from two or three blocks away. Brother Leon's face was guarded. "Why do you want to know?" he asked.

"I figure it's my right to know. The right of everybody to know." He looked around for support. Somebody called out, "Right on." Darcy said, "Everybody else is doing his part, why isn't Renault?"

"Would you care to answer that, Renault?" the teacher said, the moist eyes flashing, the malice unmistakable.

Jerry paused, face flushed. "It's a free country," he said, words which touched off a ripple of laughter. Someone snickered. Brother Leon looked positively joyous and Goober felt nauseous.

"I'm afraid you'll have to be more original than that, Renault," Brother Leon said, playing to his audience, as usual.

Goober could see the color rising to Jerry's cheeks. He was also aware of a change in the class, a subtle alteration of mood and atmosphere. Until this particular roll call, the class had been neutral, indifferent toward Jerry's position, maintaining a live-and-let-live attitude. Today however, the air was filled with resentment. More than resentment—hostility. Take Harold Darcy. Ordinarily he was a regular kid, minding his own business with no tinge of the crusader or fanatic about him. And suddenly here he was challenging Jerry.

"Did you say this sale was voluntary, Brother Leon?" Jerry asked.

"Yes," the teacher said, hanging back as if he were trying to fade into the background, letting Jerry betray himself with his own words.

"Then I don't feel that I have to sell the chocolates."

A ripple of resentment across the classroom.

"You think you're better than we are?" Darcy shot out.

"No."

"Then who do you think you are?" Phil Beauvais asked.

"I'm Jerry Renault and I'm not going to sell the chocolates."

Damn it, Goober thought. Why didn't he bend a little? Just a little.

The bell rang. For a moment, the boys sat there, waiting, knowing that the issue hadn't been settled, something ominous in the waiting. Then the moment broke and the boys began to push back their chairs, rising from the desks, shuffling as usual. No one looked at Jerry Renault. By the time Goober got to the door, Jerry was walking swiftly to his next class. A crowd of boys, Harold Darcy among them, stood sullenly in the corridor, watching Jerry's progress down the hallway.

Later that afternoon, The Goober wandered to the assembly hall, attracted by cheers and hoots. He stood in the rear of the hall, watching as Brian Cochran posted the latest returns. There were probably fifty or sixty guys in the place, unusual for that time of day. Every time Cochran wrote in new sales, the fellows burst forth in cheers, led by, of all people, big bruising Carter who probably hadn't sold any chocolates at all but had others do his dirty work.

Brian Cochran consulted a sheet of paper he held in his hand and then went to one of the three big boards. Beside the name Roland Goubert, he wrote down the number fifty.

For a moment, it didn't occur to The Goober who Roland Goubert was—he watched, fascinated, unbelieving. And then—hey, that's me!

"Goober sold his fifty boxes," someone called.

Cheers, applause and ear-splitting whistles.

The Goober started to step forward in protest. He had only sold twenty-seven boxes, damn it. He had stopped at twenty-seven to show that he was supporting Jerry, even though nobody knew, not even Jerry. And now the whole thing evaporated and he found himself sinking back in the shadows, as if he could shrivel into invisibility. He didn't want trouble. He'd had enough trouble, and he had held on. But he knew his days at Trinity would be numbered if he walked into that group of jubilant guys and told them to erase the fifty beside his name.

Out in the corridor, The Goober's breath came fast. But otherwise he felt nothing. He willed himself to feel nothing. He didn't feel rotten. He didn't feel like a traitor. He didn't feel small and cowardly. And if he didn't feel all these things, then why was he crying all the way to his locker?

CHAPTER 31

"WHAT'S YOUR HURRY, KID?"
It was a familiar voice—the voice of all the bullies in the world, Harvey Cranch who used to wait for Jerry outside the third grade at St. John's, and Eddie Herman at summer camp who delighted in the small tortures he inflicted on the younger kids and the complete stranger who knocked him down at the circus one summer and tore the ticket from his hand. That was the voice he heard now: the voice of all the bullies and troublemakers and wise guys in the world. Mocking, goading, cajoling and looking for trouble. *What's your hurry, kid?* The voice of the enemy.

Jerry looked at him. The kid stood before him in defiant posture, feet planted firmly on the ground, legs spread slightly apart, hands flat against the sides of his legs as if he wore two-gun holsters and was ready to draw, or as if he was a karate expert with hands waiting to chop and slice. Jerry didn't know a thing about karate, except in his wildest dreams when he demolished his foes without mercy.

"I asked you a question," the kid said.

Jerry recognized him now—a wise guy named Janza. A freshman-baiter, somebody to stay away from.

"I know you asked me a question," Jerry said, sighing. He knew what was coming.

"What question?"

And there it was. The taunt, the beginning of the old cat-and-mouse game.

"The question you asked me," Jerry countered but knowing the futility of it. It didn't matter what he said or how he said it. Janza was looking for an opening and he'd find it.

"And what was it?"

"You wanted to know what was my hurry."

Janza smiled, having won his point, gained his little victory. A smug superior smile spread across his face, a knowing smile, as if he knew all of Jerry's secrets, a lot of dirty things about him.

"Know what?" Janza asked.

Jerry waited.

"You look like a wise guy," Janza said.

Why did the wise guys always accuse other people of being wise guys?

"What makes you think I'm a wise guy?" Jerry asked, trying to stall, hoping someone would come along. He remembered how Mr. Phaneuf had rescued him once when Harvey Cranch had cornered him near the old man's barn. But there was nobody around now. The football practice had been miserable. He hadn't completed a pass and the coach had finally dismissed him. *This ain't your day, Renault, take an early shower.* Turning away from the coach, Jerry had seen the secret smirks, the quick smiles on the faces of the players and had realized the truth. They'd dropped his passes purposely, had refused to block. Now that Goober had quit the team, there was no one he could trust. More paranoia, he chided himself, trudging along the pathway that led from the football field to the gym. And had encountered Janza who should have been out there practicing but had been waiting for him.

"Why do I think you're a wise guy?" Janza asked now. "Because you put on a big act, kid. You try to get by with a sincerity act. But you're not kidding me. You live in the closet." Janza smiled, a knowing, this-is-just-between-us smile, intimate, creepy.

"What do you mean—closet?"

Janza laughed, delighted, and touched Jerry's cheek with his hand, a brief light touch, as if they were old friends engaged in friendly conversation on an October afternoon, leaves whirling around them like giant confetti as the wind rose. Jerry figured he knew the meaning of Janza's light tap—Janza was aching for action, contact, violence. And he was getting impatient. But he didn't want to start the fight himself. He wanted to provoke Jerry into beginning—that's the way bullies worked so they could be held blameless after the slaughter. *He started it*, they'd claim. Strangely enough, Jerry felt as though he could actually beat Janza in a fight. He could feel a gathering of outrage that promised strength and endurance. But he didn't want to fight. He didn't want to return to grammar school violence, the cherished honor of the schoolyard that wasn't honor at all, the necessity of proving yourself by bloody noses and black eyes and broken teeth. Mainly, he didn't want to fight for the same reason he wasn't selling the chocolates—he wanted to make his own decisions, do his own thing, like they said.

"This is what I mean by *closet*," Janza said, his hand flicking out again, touching Jerry's cheek, but lingering this time for the fraction of a second in faint caress. "That you're hiding in there."

"Hiding what? Hiding from who?"

"From everybody. From yourself, even. Hiding that deep dark secret."

"What secret?" Confused now.

"That you're a fairy. A queer. Living in the closet, hiding away."

Vomit threatened Jerry's throat, a nauseous geyser he could barely hold down.

"Hey, you're blushing," Janza said. "The fairy's blushing . . ."

"Listen . . ." Jerry began but not knowing, really, how to begin or where. The worst thing in the world—to be called queer.

"*You* listen," Janza said, cool now, knowing he had struck a vulnerable spot. "You're polluting Trinity. You won't sell the chocolates like everybody else and now we find out you're a fairy." He shook his head in mock, exaggerated admiration. "You're really something, know that? Trinity has tests and ways of weeding the homos out but you were smart enough to get by, weren't you? You must be creaming all over—wow, four hundred ripe young bodies to rub against . . ."

"I'm not a fairy," Jerry cried.

"Kiss me," Janza said, puckering his lips grotesquely.

"You son of a bitch," Jerry said.

The words hung on the air, verbal flags of battle. And Janza smiled, a radiant smile of triumph. This is what he'd wanted all along, of course. This had been the reason for the encounter, the insults.

"What did you call me?" Janza asked.

"A son of a bitch," Jerry said, measuring out the words, saying them deliberately, eager now for the fight.

Janza threw back his head and laughed. The laughter surprised Jerry—he'd expected retaliation. Instead, Janza stood there utterly relaxed, hands on his hips, amused.

And that was when Jerry saw them. Three or four of them emerging from bushes and shrubbery, running, crouched, keeping themselves low. They were small, pigmy-like, and they moved so swiftly toward him that he couldn't get a good look at them, saw only a smear of smiling faces, smiling evilly. More coming now, five or six others, slipping into view from behind a cluster of pine trees, and before Jerry could gird himself for a fight or even raise his arms in defense, they were swarming all over him, hitting him high and low, tumbling him to the ground as if he was some kind of helpless Gulliver. A dozen fists pummeled his body, fingernails tore at his cheek and a finger clawed at his eye. They wanted to blind him. They wanted to kill him. Pain arrowed in his groin—somebody had kicked him there. The blows rained upon him without mercy, with no let-up, and he tried to curl up and make himself small, hiding his face but somebody was pounding his head furiously, *stop, stop,* another kick in his groin and he couldn't hold down the vomit now, it was coming and he tried to open his mouth to let it spray forth. As he threw up, they let him go, someone yelled "Jesus" in disgust and they withdrew. He could hear their gasps, their running feet receding although somebody stayed behind to kick him again, this time in his lower back, the final sheet of pain that drew a black curtain over his eyes.

CHAPTER 32

S WEET, SWEET IN THE DARK, SAFE. Dark and safe and quiet. He dared not move. He was afraid that his body would come loose, all his bones spilling out like a building collapsing, like a picket fence clattering apart. A small sound reached his ears and he realized it was himself, crooning softly, as if he were singing himself a lullaby. Suddenly, he missed his mother. Her absence formed tears on his cheeks. He hadn't cried at all from the beating, had lain there on the ground for a few moments after the brief blackout, and then had dragged himself up and made it agonizingly to the locker room at school, walking as if on a tightrope and one misstep would send him hurtling into depths below: oblivion. He'd washed himself, cold water like liquid fingernails inflaming the scratches on his face. I won't sell their chocolates whether they beat me up or not. And I'm not a fairy, not a queer. He had stolen away from the school, not wanting anyone to witness his painful passage down the street to the bus stop. He kept his collar up, like a criminal, like those men in newscasts being herded into court. Funny, somebody does violence to you but you're the one who has to hide, as if you're the criminal. He shuffled to the back of the bus, grateful that it wasn't one of the crowded school buses but a maverick bus that appeared at odd hours. The bus was full of old people, old women with blue hair and big handbags and they pretended not to see him, sailing their eyes askew from him as he stalked to the rear of the bus, but their noses wrinkled as they caught the smell of vomit when he passed. Somehow, he'd made it home on the jolting bus, made it to this quiet room where he now sat, sun bleeding low in the sky and spurting its veins on the den window. Dusk moved in. After a while, he took a warm bath, soaking in the water. Then he sat in the dark, quiet, letting himself mend, not stirring, feeling a dull ache settle in his bones now that the first waves of pain had moved away. The clock struck six. He was glad that his father was on the evening shift, at work until eleven. He didn't want his father to see him with these fresh cuts on his face, the bruises. Make it to the bedroom, he urged himself, undress, curl into cool sheets, tell him I came home sick, must be a virus, twenty-four-hour flu, and keep my face hidden.

The telephone rang.
Oh no, he protested.
Let me alone.
The ringing continued, mocking him the way Janza had mocked him.
Let it be, let it be, like the Beatles sang.
Still ringing.
And he saw suddenly that he must answer. They didn't want him to answer this time. They wanted to think that he was incapacitated, injured, unable to make it to the phone.
Jerry lifted himself from the bed, surprised at his mobility, and made his way through the living room to the phone. Don't stop ringing now, he said, don't stop ringing. I want to show them.
"Hello." Forcing strength into his voice.
Silence.
"I'm here," he said, shouting the words.
Silence again. Then the lewd chuckle. And the dial tone.

"Jerry . . . oh Jerry . . ."
"Yoo hoo, Jerree . . ."
The apartment Jerry and his father occupied was three floors above street level and the voices calling Jerry's name reached him faintly, barely penetrating the closed windows. That distant quality also gave the voices a ghostly resonance, like someone calling from the grave. In fact, he hadn't been certain at first that his name was being called. Slouched at the kitchen table, forcing

himself to sip Campbell's Chicken Broth, he heard the voices and thought they were the sound of kids playing in the street. Then he heard distinctly—

"Hey, Jerry . . ."

"Whatcha doing, Jerry?"

"Come on out and play, Jerry."

Ghostly voices from the past recalling when he was a little boy and the kids in the neighborhood came to the back door after supper calling him to go out and play. That was in the sweet time when he and his parents lived together in the house with the big backyard and a front lawn his father never got tired of mowing and watering.

"Hey, Jerry . . ."

But these voices calling now were not friendly after-supper voices but night-time voices, taunting and teasing and threatening.

Jerry went into the living room and looked down cautiously, careful not to be seen. The street was deserted except for a couple of parked cars. And still the voices sang.

"Jerree . . ."

"Come out and play, Jerry . . ."

A parody of those long ago childhood pleadings.

Peering out again, Jerry saw a shooting star in reverse. It split the darkness and he heard the dull plunk as a stone, not a star at all, hit the wall of the building near the window.

"Yoo hoo, Jerree . . ."

He squinted at the street below but the boys were well hidden. Then he saw a spray of light sweeping the trees and shrubs across the street. A pale face flared in the darkness as the ray of a flashlight caught and held it for a moment. The face disappeared in the night. Jerry recognized the plodding gait of the building custodian who evidently had been drawn out of his basement apartment by the voices. His flashlight swept the street.

"Who's there?" he shouted. "I'm gonna get the police . . ."

"Bye, bye, Jerry," a voice called.

"See you later, Jerry." Fading into the dark.

The telephone ruptured the night. Jerry groped upward from sleep, reaching for the sound. Instantly awake, he glanced at the alarm clock's luminous face. Two-thirty.

Painfully, his muscles and bones protesting, he lifted himself from the mattress and poised, on one elbow, to thrust himself from the bed.

The ringing persisted, ridiculously loud in the stillness of the night. Jerry's feet touched the floor and he padded toward the sound.

But his father was already at the phone. He glanced toward Jerry and Jerry drew back into the shadows, keeping his face hidden.

"Madmen loose in the world," his father muttered, standing there with his hand on the phone. "If you let it ring, they get their kicks. If you answer, they hang up and still get their kicks. And then start all over again."

The harassment had taken its toll on his father's face, his hair disheveled, purple crescents under his eyes.

"Take the phone off the hook, Dad."

His father sighed, nodded assent. "That's giving in to them, Jerry. But what the hell. Who are *them*, anyway?" His father lifted the receiver, holding it to his ear for a moment, then turned to Jerry. "The same thing, that crazy laugh and

717

then the dial tone." He placed the receiver on the table. "I'll report it to the telephone company in the morning." Peering in at Jerry, he said, "You okay, Jerry?"

"Fine. I'm just fine, Dad."

His father rubbed his eyes, wearily.

"Get some sleep, Jerry. A football player needs his sleep." Trying to keep it light.

"Right, Dad."

Compassion for his father welled in Jerry. Should he tell his father what it was all about? But he didn't want to involve him. His father had given in, taken the receiver off the hook, and that was defeat enough. He didn't want him to risk more.

In bed once more, small in the dark, Jerry willed his body to loosen, to relax. After a while, sleep plucked at him with soft fingers, soothing away the ache. But the phone rang in his dreams all night long.

CHAPTER 33

"JANZA, can't you do anything right?"

"What the hell are you talking about? By the time we got through with him, he'd been willing to sell a million boxes of chocolates."

"I mean those kids. I didn't tell you to make it a gang bang."

"That was a stroke of genius, Archie. That's what I thought it was. Let him get beat up by a bunch of kids. Psychological—isn't that what you're always talking about?"

"Where'd you get them? I don't want outsiders involved in this."

"Some animals from my neighborhood. They'd beat up their own grandmothers for a quarter."

"Did you use the queer pitch on him?"

"You were right, Archie. You called it beautiful. That really spaced him out. Hey, Archie, he isn't queer, is he?"

"Of course not. That's why he blew up. If you want to get under a guy's skin, accuse him of being something he isn't. Otherwise, you're only telling him something he knows."

The silence on the phone indicated Emile's appreciation of Archie's genius.

"What's next, Archie?"

"Let's cool it, Emile. I want to keep you in reserve. We've got some other stuff going now."

"I was just starting to enjoy myself."

"You'll have other chances, Emile."

"Hey Archie."

"Yes, Emile."

"How about the picture?"

"Suppose I told you there was no picture, Emile? That there was no film in the camera that day . . ."

Wow, that Archie. Full of surprises. But was he kidding around? Or telling the truth?

"I don't know, Archie."

"Emile, stick with me. All the way. And you can't go wrong. We need men like you,"

Emile swelled with pride. Was Archie talking about The Vigils? And was there really no photograph after all? What a relief that would be!

"You can count on me, Archie."

"I know that, Emile."

But after he'd hung up, Emile thought: Archie, that bastard.

CHAPTER 34

SUDDENLY, HE WAS INVISIBLE, without body, without structure, a ghost passing transparently through the hours. He'd made the discovery on the bus going to school. Eyes avoiding his. Looking away. Kids giving him wide berth. Ignoring him, as if he wasn't there. And he realized that he really wasn't there, as far as they were concerned. It was as if he were the carrier of a terrible disease and nobody wanted to become contaminated. And so they rendered him invisible, eliminating him from their presence. All the way to school he sat alone, his wounded cheek pressed against the cool glass of the window.

The chill of morning hurried him up the walk to the school entrance. He spotted Tony Santucci. Purely from instinct, Jerry nodded hello. Tony's face was usually a mirror, reflecting back whatever greeted him—a smile for a smile, a frown for a frown. But now he stared at Jerry. Not really stared. Actually, he wasn't looking at Jerry but *through* him as if Jerry were a window, a doorway. And then Tony Santucci fled the scene, into the school.

Jerry's progress through the corridor was like the parting of the Red Sea. Nobody brushed against him. Guys stepped out of his path, giving him passage, as if reacting to some secret signal. Jerry felt as though he could walk through a wall and emerge untouched on the other side.

He opened his locker—the mess was gone. The desecrated poster had been removed and the wall scrubbed clean. The sneakers were gone. The locker had an air of absence, of being unoccupied. He thought, maybe I should look in a mirror, see if I'm still here. But he was still here, all right. His cheek still stung with pain. Staring at the inside of the locker, like looking into an upright coffin, he felt as though someone was trying to obliterate him, remove all traces of his existence, his presence in the school. Or was he becoming paranoid?

In the classrooms, the teachers also seemed to be part of the conspiracy. They let their eyes slide over him, looking elsewhere when Jerry tried to catch their attention. Once, he waved his hand frantically to answer a question but the teacher ignored him. And yet it was hard to tell about teachers—they were mysterious, they could sense when something unusual was going on. Like today. The kids are giving Renault the freeze so let's go along with it.

Resigning himself to the freeze, Jerry drifted through the day. After a while, he began to enjoy his invisibility. He was able to relax. There was no longer any need to be on his guard, or afraid of being attacked. He was tired of being afraid, tired of being intimidated.

Between classes, Jerry searched for The Goober but didn't find him. Goober would have established reality once again, planted Jerry solidly in the world once more. But Goober was absent from school and Jerry figured it was just as well. He didn't want anybody else getting involved in his trouble. It was enough that the phone calls had involved his father. He thought of his father standing at the phone last night, haunted by the persistent ringing, and he thought, I should have sold the chocolates, after all. He didn't want his father's universe to be disturbed and he wanted his own to be put in order again.

After the last class that morning, Jerry walked freely down the corridor, headed for the cafeteria, swinging along with the crowd, enjoying his absence of identity. Approaching the stairs, he felt himself pushed from behind and he pitched forward, off balance. He began to fall, the stairs slanting dangerously before him. Somehow, he managed to grab the railing. He held on, pressing his body against the wall. As the stream of guys thudded past, he heard someone snicker, someone else hiss.

He knew he wasn't invisible any longer.

Brother Leon entered the office at the moment Brian Cochran finished his final tabulation. The end. The last total of them all. He looked up at the teacher, delighted with the timing of his arrival.

"Brother Leon, it's all over," Brian announced, triumph in his voice.

The teacher blinked rapidly, his face like a cash register that wasn't working. "Over?"

"The sale." Brian slapped down the sheet of paper. "Finished. Done with."

Brian watched the information sinking in. Leon took a deep breath and lowered himself into his chair. For an instant, Brian observed relief sweeping the teacher's face, as if a huge burden had been lifted from him. But it was only a brief glimpse. He looked at Brian sharply. "Are you sure?" he asked.

"Positive. And listen, Brother Leon. The money—it's amazing. Ninety-eight per cent has been turned in."

Leon stood up. "Let's check the figures," he said.

Anger surged through Brian. Couldn't the teacher let down for one minute? Couldn't he say "good job"? Or "thank God"? Or something? Instead, "let's check the figures."

Leon's rancid breath—didn't he ever eat anything else but bacon, for crissakes—filled the air as he stood beside Brian looking over the tabulations.

"There's only one thing," Brian said, hesitating to bring the subject up.

Leon caught the boy's doubt. "What's the matter?" he asked, more angry than curious, as if he anticipated an error on Brian's part.

"It's the freshman, Brother Leon."

"Renault? What about him?"

"Well, he still hasn't sold his chocolates. And it's weird, really weird."

"What's so weird about it, Cochran? The boy's obviously a misfit. He tried in his small ineffectual way to damage the sale and he succeeded in doing the opposite. The school rallied against him."

"But it's still weird. Our sales total comes to exactly nineteen thousand, nine hundred fifty boxes. Right on the nose. And that's practically impossible. I mean, there's always some spoilage, some boxes get lost or stolen. It's impossible to account for every single box. But this comes out right on the dot. With exactly fifty boxes missing—Renault's fifty."

"If Renault didn't sell them, then obviously they are not sold. And that's why there are fifty missing boxes," Leon said, his voice slow and reasonable, as if Brian were five years old.

Brian realized that Brother Leon didn't want to see the truth. He was only interested in the results of the sale, knowing that his previous nineteen thousand, nine hundred fifty boxes had been sold and he was off the hook. He'd probably be promoted, become Headmaster. Brian was glad he wouldn't be here next year, particularly if Leon became permanent Headmaster.

"You see what's important here, Cochran?" Leon asked, assuming his classroom voice. "School spirit. We have disproven a law of nature—one rotten apple does not spoil the barrel. Not if we have determination, a noble cause, a spirit of brotherhood . . ."

Brian sighed, looking down at his fingers, tuning Leon out, letting the words fall meaninglessly on his ears. He thought of Renault, that strange stubborn kid. Was Leon right, after all? That the school was more important than any one kid? But weren't individuals important, too? He thought of Renault standing alone against the school, The Vigils, everybody.

Ah, the hell with it, Brian thought as Leon's voice droned on sanctimoniously. The sale was over and his job as treasurer was over. He wouldn't be involved with Leon or Archie or even Renault anymore. Thank God for little favors.

"You got the fifty boxes set aside, Obie?"

"Yes, Archie."

"Beautiful."

"What's it all about, Archie?"

"We're having an assembly, Obie. Tomorrow night. A special assembly. To report on the chocolate sale. At the athletic field."

"Why the athletic field, Archie? Why not the school?"

"Because this assembly is strictly for the student body, Obie. The brothers are not involved. But everybody else will be there."

"Everybody?"

"Everybody."

"Renault?"

"He'll be there, Obie, he'll be there."

"You're really something else, Archie, you know that?"

"I know that, Obie."

"Pardon me for asking, Archie . . ."

"Ask away, Obie."

"What do you want Renault there for?"

"To give him a chance. A chance to get rid of his chocolates, old buddy."

"I'm not your old buddy, Archie."

"I know that, Obie."

"And how's Renault going to get rid of his chocolates, Archie?"

"He's going to raffle them off."

"A raffle?"

"A raffle, Obie."

CHAPTER 35

A RAFFLE, for crying out loud.
But what a raffle!

A raffle like no other in Trinity's history, in any school's history.

Archie, the architect of the event, watched the proceedings—the stadium filling up, the kids streaming in, the slips of paper being sold, passed back and forth, the lights dispelling some of the cool of the autumn evening. He stood near the improvised stage that Carter and The Vigils had erected that afternoon under Archie's direction—an old boxing ring resurrected from the bowels of the bleachers and restored to its former use except for the absence of ropes. The platform stood directly at the fifty-yard line close to the stands so that each kid would see everything and wouldn't miss any of the action. That was Archie. Give them their money's worth.

The athletic field was at least a quarter of a mile from the school and the residence where the brothers lived. But Archie had taken no chances. He had disguised the event as a football rally, strictly for students, without the inhibition of the teachers being present. They had arranged for the sweet-faced kid, Caroni, to ask for permission—Caroni who looked like a choir boy. What teacher could refuse him? And now the moment was at hand, the kids arriving, the air crisp and cool, excitement shivering through the crowd—and Renault and Janza there in the ring, glancing uneasily at each other.

Archie always marveled at things like this, things he had arranged and manipulated. For instance, all these guys tonight would be doing something else except for Archie who had been able to alter their actions. And all it took was a little bit of Archie's imagination and two phone calls.

The first call had been to Renault, the second to Janza. But Janza's call had been simply routine. Archie knew he could shape Janza's actions the way he could shape a piece of clay. But the call to Renault had required the right moves, resourcefulness and a little touch of Archie in the night. Shakespeare[1] yet, Archie chuckled.

The phone must have rung, oh, fifty times and Archie hadn't blamed the kid for not rushing to lift the receiver. But persistence paid off and finally there was Renault on the line, the quiet *hello*, the calm voice but something else, something else. Archie had detected another quality in the voice—a deadly calm, determination. Beautiful. The kid was ready. Archie had soared with triumph. The kid wanted to come out and fight. He wanted action.

"Want to get even, Renault?" Archie goaded. "Strike back? Get revenge? Show them what you think of their goddam chocolates?"

"How do I do that?" The voice was guarded but interested. Definitely interested.

"Easy, easy," Archie responded, "if you're not chicken, that is." The needle, always the needle.

Renault was silent.

"There's a guy named Janza. He's really a rotten kid, no class at all. He's not much more than an animal. And word has gotten around that he needed the help of a bunch of kids to make you fall in line. So I figure we ought to settle the matter. At an assembly at the athletic field. Boxing gloves. Everything under control. Here's a way to get even with everybody, Renault."

"With you too, Archie?"

"Me?" The voice innocent and sweet. "Hell, why me? I was only carrying out my job. I gave you an assignment—don't sell the chocolates—and then I gave you another—sell them. You did the rest, kid. I didn't beat you up. I don't believe in violence. But you touched off the fireworks . . ."

---

1 *a little touch . . . Shakespeare*   In Shakespeare's history play, *Henry V* (c. 1599), King Henry encourages his troops before the battle of Agincourt, providing, according to the Chorus figure, "a little touch of Harry in the night" (4.0.47).

Silence on the line again. Archie pressed on, softening his voice, cajoling, leading him on "Look, kid, I'm giving you this choice because I believe in fair play. Here's a chance to end it all and get on with other things. Christ, there's more to life than a lousy chocolate sale. You and Janza alone in the ring, facing each other fair and square. And that's it, finished, the end, all done. I guarantee it. Archie guarantees it."

And the kid had fallen for it, hook, line and sinker, although the conversation had gone back and forth for a while. Archie had been patient. Patience always paid off. And he had won, of course.

Now, surveying his handiwork, the crowded bleachers, the frantic comings and goings as the raffle tickets were bought and sold and the directions scrawled on the tickets. Archie exulted quietly. He had successfully conned Renault and Leon and The Vigils and the whole damn school. I can con anybody. I am Archie.

Pretend you're a spotlight, Obie told himself, a spotlight sweeping the place, stopping here and there, and lingering at other places, picking up the highlights of the thing, this momentous occasion. Because, let's admit it, this *is* an important event and Archie, that bastard, that clever clever bastard, has done it again. Look at him down there near the fight ring, like he's king of all he surveys. And he is, of course. He's got Renault there, pale and tense as if he's facing a firing squad, and Janza, the animal, a chained animal waiting to spring loose.

Obie, the spotlight, concentrated on Renault. Poor dumb doomed kid. He can't win and he doesn't know it. Not from Archie. Nobody wins from Archie. Archie, who'd been going down to defeat—what a great scene that had been, the last Vigils meeting when he'd stood there humiliated—but now he was on top again, all the chocolate sold, in charge once more, the entire school in the palm of his hand. All of which proves that the meek don't inherit the earth. Not very original. Archie must have said it at one time or another.

Don't move. Not a muscle. Just wait. Wait it out, wait and see.
Jerry's left leg had fallen asleep.
How can your leg fall asleep when you're standing up?
I don't know. But it's asleep.
Nerves, maybe. Tension.
At any rate, small darts stung his legs and he had to fight to keep from moving. He didn't dare move, afraid he would fall apart if he moved.

He knew now that it had been a mistake coming here, that Archie had faked him out, tricked him. For a few moments while Archie's voice whispered enticingly of sweet revenge, suggesting the fight as a way of ending it all, Jerry had actually believed it was possible, possible to beat Janza and the school and even Archie. He had thought of his father and the terrible look of defeat when he had listened on the phone the other night and finally placed the receiver on the table, giving up. I'm not giving up, Jerry had pledged, listening to Archie's goading voice. He also ached for a chance to confront Janza. Janza who had called him a fairy.

So, he had agreed to meet Janza in a fight and already Archie had doublecrossed him. Had doublecrossed Janza as well. He'd allowed them to be led onto the platform, stripped to the waist, shivering slightly in the evening air, given boxing gloves. And then Archie, his eyes sparkling with triumph and malice, had explained the rules. Those rules!

Jerry had been about to protest when Janza opened his mouth. "It's okay with me. I can beat this kid any way you want."

And Jerry saw, to his dismay, that Archie had counted on Janza's reaction, had counted on the guys filing into the stadium. He had known that Jerry couldn't back away now—he had come too far. Archie had bestowed one of his sickly sweet smiles on Jerry. "What do you say, Renault? Do you accept the rules?"

What could he say? After the phone calls and the beating. After the desecration of his locker. The silent treatment. Pushed downstairs. What they did to Goober, to Brother Eugene. What guys like Archie and Janza did to the school. What they would do to the world when they left Trinity.

Jerry tightened his body in determination. At least this was his chance to strike back, to hit out. Despite the odds Archie had set up with the raffle tickets.

"Okay," Jerry had said.

Now, standing here, one leg half asleep, nausea threatening his stomach, the night chilling his flesh, Jerry wondered if he hadn't lost the moment he had said *okay.*

The raffle tickets were selling like dirty pictures.

Brian Cochran was amazed but he shouldn't have been—he was getting used to being amazed where Archie Costello was concerned. First the chocolate sale. And now this—this wacky raffle. Never anything like it at Trinity. Or anywhere. And he had to admit that he was kind of enjoying himself even though he had protested when Archie approached him this afternoon, asking him to take charge of the raffle. "You did great with the chocolates," Archie said. The compliment melted Brian's opposition. Besides, he was scared stiff of Archie and The Vigils. Personal survival, that's what Brian believed in.

He had been seized by doubt again when Archie explained how the fight and the raffle would work. How are you going to get Renault and Janza to do it? That's what Brian wanted to know. Easy, Archie assured him. Renault's looking for revenge and Janza's a beast. And they can't back down with the whole school looking on. Then Archie's voice had gone cold again and Brian had shriveled inside. "You just do your job, Cochran, sell the tickets. And leave the details to me." So Brian had lined up a bunch of kids to do the selling. And Archie had been right, of course, because there they were, Renault and Janza up there on the platform, and the tickets were selling like there was no tomorrow.

Emile Janza was tired of being treated like one of the bad guys. That's the way Archie made him feel. "Hey, animal," Archie would say. Emile wasn't an animal. He had feelings like everybody else. Like the guy in the Shakespeare thing in English I, "Cut me, do I not bleed?"[2] All right, so he liked to screw around a little, get under people's skin. That was human nature, wasn't it? A guy had to protect himself at all times. Get them before they get you. Keep people guessing—and afraid. Like Archie with his rotten picture that didn't even exist. Archie had convinced him that there was no picture, after all. How could there be a picture, Emile, Archie'd reasoned. Remember how dim it was in the john that day? And I didn't have a flash. And there wasn't any film in the camera. And

---

2 *Shakespeare . . . bleed* In *The Merchant of Venice* (c. 1596), the Jewish moneylender Shylock, argues that Jews are no different from Christians ("If you prick us, do we not bleed?" 3.1.60–61) who have, by example in Venice, taught the Jews (so Shylock claims) to take revenge rather than forgive.

if there had been, I didn't have time to focus. The truth had both relieved Emile and made him mad as hell. But Archie had pointed out that Emile should be mad at people like Renault. Hell, Emile, guys like Renault are your enemy, not guys like me. They're the squares, Emile, they're the ones who screw it up for us, who blow the whistle, who make the rules. Then Archie had provided the climax, the door-slammer—besides, the guys are starting to talk about how Renault was beaten up, how you needed the help of others and couldn't do it yourself . . .

Emile looked across the stage at Renault. He longed for combat. To prove himself in front of the whole school. The hell with that psychology crap Archie had made him use—telling Renault he was a fairy. He should have used his fists, not his mouth.

He was impatient to get started. To wreck Renault in front of everybody, no matter what was written down on the raffle tickets.

And in a corner of his mind, there still lurked the doubt—did Archie have that picture of him in the john, after all?

CHAPTER 36

THOSE RAFFLE TICKETS.
Wow! Terrific!

Archie hadn't seen any that had been filled out yet and he stopped one of the guys who'd been recruited as a salesman by Brian Cochran.

"Let's see," Archie said, holding out his hand.

The kid was quick to comply and Archie was pleased at his submissiveness. I am Archie. My wish becomes command.

The sound of the restless audience in his ears, Archie scrutinized the paper. Scrawled there, the words

Janza
Right To Jaw
Jimmy Demers

That was the simple, stunning beauty of the raffle, the unexpected twist that Archie Costello was famous for, what they always knew Archie could do—top himself. In one stroke, Archie had forced Renault to show up here, to become part of the chocolate sale, and he also placed Renault at the mercy of the school, the students. The fighters on the platform would have no will of their own. They would have to fight the way the guys in the bleachers directed them. Everybody who bought a ticket—and who could refuse?—had a chance to be involved in the fight, to watch two guys battering each other while they were at a safe distance, with no danger of getting hurt. The risky part had been getting Renault here tonight. Once he was on the platform Archie knew he could not refuse to go on, even when he heard about the tickets. And that's the way it worked out. Beautiful.

Carter approached. "They're really selling, Archie," he said. Carter appreciated the fight concept. He loved boxing. He had, in fact, bought two tickets and had gotten a kick out of deciding which blows he would call for. He'd finally decided on a right cross to the jaw and an uppercut. At the last moment, he'd almost assigned the blows to Renault—give the kid a break. But Obie was standing nearby, Obie who stuck his nose in everybody else's business. So Carter had written in Janza's name. Janza, the beast, always ready to jump when Archie said jump.

"Looks like a beautiful night," Archie said now, smugly, that know-it-all attitude Carter hated. "You see, Carter, I told you everybody was pushing panic buttons for nothing."

"I don't know how you do it, Archie," Carter was forced to admit.

"Simple, Carter, simple." Archie reveled in the moment, basking in Carter's admiration, Carter who had humiliated him at The Vigils meeting. Someday he'd get even with Carter but at the moment it was satisfying enough to have Carter regarding him with awe and envy. "You see, Carter, people are two things: greedy and cruel. So we have a perfect setup here. The greed part—a kid pays a buck for a chance to win a hundred. Plus fifty boxes of chocolates. The cruel part—watching two guys hitting each other, maybe hurting each other, while they're safe in the bleachers. That's why it works, Carter, because we're all bastards."

Carter disguised his disgust. Archie repelled him in many ways but most of all by the way he made everybody feel dirty, contaminated, polluted. As if there was no goodness at all in the world. And yet Carter had to admit that he was looking forward to the fight, that he himself had bought not one but two tickets. Did that make him like everybody else—greedy and cruel, as Archie said? The question surprised him. Hell, he'd always thought of himself as one of the good guys. He had often used his position as president of The Vigils to keep control of Archie, to prevent him from going overboard on assignments. But did that make him one of the good guys? The question bothered Carter. That's what he hated about Archie. He made you feel guilty all the time. Christ, the world couldn't be as bad as Archie said it was. But hearing the shouts of the kids in the bleachers, impatient for the fight to get underway, Carter wondered.

Archie watched Carter drift away, looking troubled and perplexed. Great. Burning with jealousy. And who wouldn't be jealous of someone like Archie who always came out on top?

Cochran reported. "All sold out, Archie."

Archie nodded, assuming the role of the silent hero.

The moment was here.

Archie lifted his head toward the bleachers and it seemed to be some kind of signal. A ripple went through the crowd, a quickening of tempo, a sweep of suspense. All eyes were directed to the platform where Renault and Janza stood at diagonal corners.

In front of the platform stood a pyramid of chocolates—the last fifty boxes. The stadium lights burned bright.

Carter, gavel in hand, walked to the center of the platform. There was nothing to bang the gavel on so he simply raised it in the air.

The audience responded with applause, impatient shoutings, catcalls. "Let's go," someone yelled.

Carter gestured for silence.

But the silence had already fallen.

Archie, walking toward the platform for a close view of the proceedings, sucked in his breath, as if he were sipping this sweetest of all events. But he exhaled in surprise and stopped in his tracks as he saw Obie walk on the platform carrying the black box in his hands.

Obie smiled maliciously when he caught Archie standing there in surprise, his mouth wide open in astonishment. No one ever surprised the great Archie that way, and Obie's moment of triumph was a thing of beauty. He nodded toward Carter who was on his way to escort Archie to the platform.

Carter had been doubtful about using the black box, pointing out that this was not a Vigils meeting. How can we make Archie try for the marbles?

Obie had the answer, the kind of answer Archie himself would have given. "Because there are four hundred kids out there yelling for blood. And they don't care whose blood it is anymore. Everybody in the school knows about the black box—how can Archie back down?"

Carter pointed out that there was no guarantee that Archie would pull out the black marble. The black would mean he'd have to take on the position of one of the fighters. But there were five white marbles and only one black marble in the box. Archie's luck had held up throughout his career as the assigner—he had never drawn the black one.

"The law of averages," Obie had said to Carter. "He's going to have to draw two marbles—one for Renault, the other for Janza."

Carter had gazed steadily at Obie. "We couldn't . . . ?" His voice curled into a question mark.

"We can't fix it, no way. Where could I find six black marbles, for crying out loud? Anyway, Archie is too smart—we could never con him. But we can throw one hell of a scare into him. And who knows? Maybe his luck has run out."

Thus, the agreement. Obie would emerge with the black box at the moment before the drawings and the fight began. And that's exactly what he was doing now, crossing to the center of the platform as Carter went down to meet Archie.

"You guys are really something else, aren't you?" Archie said, pulling away from Carter's grip. "I can walk up there alone, Carter. And I'll walk back again, too."

Archie's fury was a cold hard ball in his chest but he played it cool. As usual. He had a feeling nothing could go wrong. I am Archie.

The sight of the black box stunned the gathering into a silence more deep than before. Only members of The Vigils and their victims had seen it. In the garish stadium light, the box was revealed as worn and threadbare, a small wooden container that might have been a discarded jewelry box. And yet it was a legend in the school. For potential victims, it was possible deliverance, protection, a weapon to be used against the might of The Vigils. Others doubted its existence: Archie Costello would never allow that sort of thing. But here was the black box now. Out in the open. In front of the whole frigging school. And Archie Costello looking at it, reaching out his hand to draw the marble.

The ceremony took only a minute or so because Archie insisted on getting it over quickly before anyone knew what was going on. The less drama, the better. Don't let Obie and Carter build it up. Thus, before any protest could be made, Archie had shot his hand out and pulled a marble from the box. White. Obie's jaw dropped in surprise. Things were moving too fast. He'd wanted Archie to squirm; he'd wanted the audience to realize what was going on here. He'd wanted to prolong the ceremony, get as much of the drama and suspense out of the situation as possible.

Archie's hand shot out again and it was too late for Obie to prevent the action. He drew in his breath.

The marble was hidden in Archie's closed fist. He held the fist out, toward the audience. Archie held his back stiff. The marble had to be white. He hadn't come this far to be denied at the last moment. He let a smile play over his lips as he faced the audience, gambling everything in his show of confidence.

He opened his palm and held up the marble for all to see.

White.

CHAPTER 37

THE GOOBER ARRIVED at the last moment and made his way through the turmoil to the top of the bleachers. He'd been reluctant to come. He had washed his hands of the school and its cruelties and hadn't wanted to witness Jerry's daily humiliations. The school also reminded him of his own betrayals and defections. For three days, he'd been home in bed. Sick. He wasn't at all sure whether he'd really been sick or whether his conscience had revolted, infecting his body, leaving him weak and nauseous. At any rate, the bed had become his private world, a small safe place without people, without The Vigils, without Brother Leon, a world with no chocolates to sell, no rooms to destory, no people to destroy. But one of the guys called up and told him about the fight between Jerry and Janza. And how the raffle tickets would control the fight. The Goober had moaned in protest. The bed had become unbearable. He had tossed and turned all day, prowling the bed like an animal seeking sleep, oblivion. He didn't want to go to the fight—Jerry couldn't possibly win. But he couldn't stay in bed, either. Finally, desperate, he had gotten out of bed, and dressed hurriedly, ignoring the protests of his parents. He had taken the bus across town and walked half a mile to the stadium. Now, he huddled in the seat, looking down at the platform, listening to Carter explaining the rules of the crazy fight. Terrible.

". . . and the kid whose written blow is the one that ends the fight, either by knockout or surrender, receives the prize . . ."

But the crowd was impatient for the action to begin. Goober looked around. These fellows in the stands were known to him, they were classmates, but suddenly they'd become strangers. They stared feverishly down at the platform. Some of them were yelling. "Kill 'em, kill 'em . . ." The Goober shivered in the night.

Carter advanced to the center of the platform where Obie held a cardboard carton. Carter reached in and pulled out a piece of paper. "John Tussier," he called. "He's written down Renault's name." Murmurs of disappointment, a few scattered boos. "He wants Renault to hit Janza with a right to the jaw."

Silence fell. The moment of truth. Renault and Janza faced each other, an arm's reach away. They had been standing in the traditional pose of fighters, gloves raised, ready for battle but a pathetic parody of professional fighters. Now, Janza followed the rules. He lowered his arms, prepared to take Jerry's blow without resistance.

Jerry hunched his shoulders, cocked his fist. He had been waiting for this moment, ever since Archie's voice had taunted him on the telephone. But he hesitated now. How could he hit anyone, even an animal like Janza, in cold blood? I'm not a fighter, he protested silently. Then think of how Janza let those kids beat you up.

The crowd was restless. "Action, action," someone called. And the cry was taken up by others.

"What's the matter, fairy?" Janza taunted. "Afraid you might hurt your little hand hitting great big Emile?"

Jerry sent his fist sailing toward Janza's jaw, but he had swung too quickly, without sufficient aim. The blow almost missed its target, finally brushing Janza's jaw ineffectually. Janza grinned.

Boos filled the air. "Fix," someone called.

Carter motioned to Obie to bring the box out quickly. He sensed the impatience of the crowd. They had paid their money and they wanted action. He hoped Janza's name would be on this slip. And it was. A kid named Marty Heller had ordered Janza to hit Renault with a right uppercut to the jaw. Carter sang out the command.

Jerry planted himself, like a tree.

Janza got ready, insulted by the cries of *fix*. Just because Renault was chicken. I'm not chicken, I'll show them. He had to prove that this was a genuine contest. If Renault wouldn't fight, then at least Emile Janza would.

He struck Jerry with all the force he could summon, the impact of the blow coming from his feet, up through his legs and thighs, the trunk of his body, the power pulsing through his body like some elemental force until it erupted through his arm, exploding into his fist.

Jerry had girded himself for the blow but it took him by surprise with its savagery and viciousness. The entire planet was jarred for a moment, the stadium swaying, the lights dancing. The pain in his neck was excruciating—his head had snapped back from the impact of Janza's fist. Sent reeling backward, he fought to stay on his feet and he somehow managed not to fall. His jaw was on fire, he tasted acid. Blood, maybe. But he pressed his lips together. He shook his head, quick vision-clearing shakings and established himself in the world once more.

Before he could gather himself together again, Carter's voice cried out "*Janza, right to the stomach*" and Janza struck without warning, a short sharp blow that missed Jerry's stomach but caught him in the chest. His breath went away, like it did in football, and then came back again. But the blow had lacked the power of the uppercut. He crouched again, fists erect, waiting for the next instructions. Dimly, he heard the crowd both cheering and booing but he concentrated on Janza who stood before him, that idiot smile on his face.

The next raffle ticket gave Jerry his chance to strike back at Janza. A kid Jerry had never heard of—someone named Arthur Robilard—called for a right cross. Whatever that was. Jerry had only a vague idea but he wanted to hit Janza now, to repay him for that first vicious blow. He cocked his right arm. He tasted bile in his mouth. He let his arm go. The glove struck Janza full face and Janza staggered back. The result surprised Jerry. He had never struck anyone like that before, in fury, premeditated, and he'd enjoyed catapulting all his power toward the target, the release of all his frustrations, hitting back at last, lashing out, getting revenge finally, revenge not only against Janza but all that he represented.

Janza's eyes leaped with surprise at the strength behind Jerry's blow. His immediate reaction was to counterpunch but he held himself in control.

Carter's voice. "Janza. Left uppercut."

Again, the quick jolting neck-snapping pain as Janza, without pause or preparation, struck out. Jerry backpedaled weakly. Why should his knees give way when the blow struck his jaw?

729

"I'll let you know later." He smiled at me and I smiled back. "You have nice dimples," he said.

"Thanks . . . everyone in my family has them."

He parked the car and we got out. It was cold and windy but the sun was shining. We walked down to the lake. It was partly frozen. Michael picked up a handful of stones and tossed them across the water. "What are you doing next year?"

"Going to college."

"Where?"

"I don't know yet," I said. "I applied to Penn State, Michigan and Denver. I have to see where I'm accepted. What about you?"

"University of Vermont, I hope. Either there or Middlebury." Michael took my hand and pulled off my mitten, which he shoved into his pocket. Holding hands, we started walking around the lake.

"I wish it would snow," he said, squeezing my fingers.

"Me too."

"You ski?"

"No . . . I just like snow."

"I love to ski."

"I know how to water ski," I told him.

"That's different."

"Are you good . . . at skiing, I mean?"

"You might say that. I could probably teach you."

"To ski?"

"Yeah."

"That'd be nice."

We walked all the way to the Trailside Museum and had a look inside, before Michael checked his watch and said, "We better head back."

"Already?"

"It's after 2:00."

My teeth were chattering and I knew that my cheeks would be bright red from the wind. I didn't mind though. My father says I look good that way—very healthy.

When we were back in the car I rubbed my hands together, trying to get warm, while Michael started up the engine. It stalled a few times. When it finally caught he pumped the gas. "I better give it a minute to make sure," he said.

"Okay."

He turned to face me. "Can I kiss you, Katherine?"

"Do you always ask first?"

"No . . . but with you I don't know what to expect."

"Try me . . ." I said.

He took off his glasses and put them on the dashboard.

I wet my lips. Michael kept looking at me. "You're making me nervous," I told him. "Stop staring."

"I just want to see what you look like without my glasses."

"Well?"

"You're all blurred."

We both laughed.

Finally he kissed me. It was a nice kiss, warm but not sloppy.

Before he let me out at Sybil's house, Michael stopped the car and kissed me again. "You're delicious," he said.

No boy had ever told me that. As I opened the car door all I could think of to say was, "See you . . ." but that wasn't at all what I meant.

CHAPTER 3

"I MET A VERY nice boy," I told my mother that night, "even though he's still in high school." Mom was in her bathroom, trimming her toenails. "He has this reddish-blond hair and wears glasses. He likes to ski."

"What's his name?" Mom asked.

"Michael Wagner . . . isn't that a nice name?"

She looked up and smiled at me. "It must have been a good party."

"It was okay . . . I'm seeing him Friday night . . . and Saturday too."

"Where's he from?"

"Summit . . . he goes to school with Sybil. Can I borrow your nail scissors when you're done? I can't find mine."

"Here . . ." Mom handed them to me. "But don't forget to return them this time."

"I won't."

My mother's name is Diana—Diana Danziger. It sounds like she should be a movie star or something. Actually, she's a librarian, in charge of the children's room at the public library. Mom is naturally thin, so she can eat four cupcakes at one sitting or polish off as much beer as she wants. We are exactly the same size—five-feet-six and 109 pounds—but she is sort of flat chested and never wears a bra.

While I was cutting my toenails my sister, Jamie, came into my room, holding up a pair of jeans. "I embroidered them while you were at Sybil's. What do you think?"

"They're just great," I told her. "They're fantastic!"

"Want me to do a pair of yours?"

"Would you?"

"Sure."

"By next weekend?"

"Yeah . . . I guess I could."

"Jamie . . ." I said, hugging her, "you are an absolute angel!"

Jamie is in seventh grade and looks a lot like me but her eyes are fabulous—big and round—and if you look into them you get the feeling you can see deep inside her. Sometimes they seem very dark, with just a rim of green and other times they sparkle and are greenish-gray all over, like my grandfather's. The rest of us have ordinary brown eyes but my father's brows grow straight across the bridge of his nose. He told me that when he was in college he used to shave them up the center.

Jamie untangled herself from me. "What's next weekend?" she asked.

"I'm seeing someone I met last night," I told her, "and the truth is, I don't know how I'm going to live through this week."

"You mean you're in love again?"

"I have never been in love."

"What about Tommy Aronson?"

"That wasn't love . . . that was childish infatuation."

743

"You said it was love . . . I remember."

"Well, I didn't know anything then."

"Oh."

"Some day you'll understand."

"I doubt it," Jamie said.

I wish she hadn't brought up the subject of Tommy Aronson, because I did like him a lot last year, but only for a few months. Now he's at Ohio State and the news I get is he's so busy making it with every female on campus he may flunk out. I hope he does. Sex was all he was ever interested in, which is why we broke up—because he threatened that if I wouldn't sleep with him he'd find somebody who would. I told him if that was all he cared about he should go right ahead. So he did. Her name was Dorothy and she turned up in my English class this year.

Michael was different from Tommy Aronson right away. He called me every night.

"Hi . . . it's me, Michael," he said on Tuesday.

"Hi . . ."

"I'm sitting on the bed with this beautiful fifteen-year-old . . ."

"Oh?"

"Yeah . . . her name's Tasha . . . she's gray and furry and she's got a beard but I love her anyway."

I laughed. "A schnauzer?"

"How'd you guess?"

"The beard. Isn't fifteen kind of old for a dog?"

"In people years she'd be 105."

"Can she still get around?"

"Sure . . . she just doesn't bark much anymore. Wait a second and I'll put her on . . . say hello to Katherine, Tasha . . . don't be shy . . ."

"Hello, Tasha . . ." I said. "Arf . . . arf . . ."

The next night I asked Michael if he plays tennis.

"Not really . . . why, do you?"

"Uh huh . . . I'm on the school team," I said.

"Oh, a jock, huh?"

"Hardly . . . just that and modern dance . . ."

"A dancer too?"

"Um . . . sort of . . ."

"You jump around wearing one of those things?"

"What things?"

"You know . . ."

"A leotard, you mean?"

"That's it."

"I wear one."

"I'd like to see that."

"Some day, maybe . . . if you're lucky."

On Thursday night he said, "Did I tell you I'm trying to get my ski instructor's pin by next year?"

"No . . ."

"Yeah, I am. Do you by any chance like spinach?"

"Ugh, no . . . why, do you?"

"It's only my favorite food."

744

"Like Popeye?"

"Like Popeye."

"In that case, maybe I'll try to develop a taste for it . . . but I can't promise . . ."

"Hey . . . you know tomorrow's Friday?"

"I know."

"How's 7:30?"

"Fine."

"Well . . . see you then . . ."

"See you then. Oh, Michael . . ."

"Yeah?"

"I'll be ready."

I was nervous about seeing him again. On Friday, right after school, I washed my hair. I couldn't eat any dinner. My parents gave me a couple of funny looks but neither one said anything. Jamie had embroidered my jeans with tiny mushrooms and I'd bought a light blue sweater to go with them. I once read that boys like light blue on a girl better than any other color. I was ready half an hour early.

As soon as I opened the door we both started talking at the same time. Then we looked at each other, laughed, and I knew it was going to be all right between us.

Michael followed me into the living room.

My mother and father were stretched out on the floor, hooking a rug—Jamie's latest design. She paints the canvas and the three of us put in the colors. Hooking rugs is very easy and lots of fun but I wasn't sure what Michael would think and for a minute I was sorry I hadn't asked them to turn on the TV and just sit there.

"Michael," I said, "I'd like you to meet my parents." Then, "Mom . . . Dad . . . this is Michael Wagner."

My father stood up and he and Michael shook hands. Mom pushed her glasses up on her head so she could get a good look at him. She can see only close up when she's wearing them.

Michael cleared his throat and looked around. "This is really something," he said.

My mother was pleased. She said, "Thanks . . . we like it too."

I have to explain about our house. It's very ordinary on the outside but on the inside it's really something, like Michael said. All the walls are painted white and are hung with a million of Jamie's paintings and tapestries which are all done in bright, beautiful colors. Her artwork is not your everyday twelve-year-old's. She is what is called a gifted child. When you combine my mother's plants with Jamie's artwork you don't need anything else—our furniture is very plain and it's all kind of beige so that you don't notice it, which is the whole idea.

Jamie came tearing down the stairs then, yelling, "Is he here yet? Did I miss him?" When she saw Michael she blushed. "Oh . . . he's here."

Michael laughed.

"This is my sister, Jamie," I told him, ". . . in case you hadn't already guessed."

"Hi, Jamie," Michael said.

"Hi," she answered.

In many ways Jamie is still a little girl. She looks up to me—at least that's what my parents say. And I think they might be right. It took a long time for me to realize that, but when I did it helped me get over being jealous of all her talents. Not that I don't get a pang now and then, like when Michael admired everything she's made and I knew he wasn't just saying it to make her feel good but that he was really impressed.

As soon as I got into my jacket Michael and I left. We went to the Blue Star Cinema and held hands. All I could think about was later and being alone with him.

After the movie we stopped off at a diner on Route 22. When we'd finished eating Michael said, "Do you know any place to park around here?"

"No," I told him. "But we could go back to my house."

"Your parents won't mind?"

"They'd rather have me bring my friends home than sit in a car somewhere."

"Okay . . . it's back to your house, Katherine."

I really do know where people go to park. There's a dark, dead-end street not far from where I live and there is also the golf course and the hill. Erica lives on the hill. She's always finding used rubbers in the street. I can't understand how someone could just throw a thing like that out a car window and forget about it.

My mother and father talked to me about parking when I first started going with guys who drove. They explained how it isn't safe, not because of anything we might do, but because there are a lot of crazies in this world and they have been known to prey on couples who are out parking. So I've always invited my boyfriends home.

We have a den on one side of the living room that's very private. It's got a door and everything. It's small but there's a fireplace with two tilt-back chairs in front of it, a stereo built into the wall unit and a comfortable sofa under the windows, with the kind of cushions you sink into. There's a big, beautiful hooked rug on the floor with a lion's face in the middle.

My mother and father go to bed early—between 10:00 and 11:00, unless they go out or have company. They were already asleep when I got home with Michael. I have no curfew but I am supposed to let them know when I get in, and that I'm okay. I tiptoe upstairs and whisper, "Psst . . . I'm home." Usually my father hears me and mumbles something. Then he rolls over and goes back to sleep.

Michael had turned on the stereo and was poking the fire when I came back downstairs. I closed the den door and sat down on the sofa. He took off his glasses, put them on the side table, and joined me. We put our arms around each other and I lifted my face. But after a short kiss he said, "You brushed your teeth?"

"Yes."

"You taste like toothpaste."

"Is that bad?" I asked.

"I don't mind . . . but it makes your mouth cold."

"It does?"

"Yeah."

"I didn't know that."

"It's okay . . . it'll warm up in a minute."

"I hope so."

When we kissed again Michael used his tongue. I wanted him to.

We sat together on the sofa for an hour. Michael moved his hands around on the outside of my sweater but when he tried to get under it I said, "No . . . let's save something for tomorrow."

746

He didn't pressure me. He kissed my cheek, then my ear, and whispered, "Are you a virgin?"

No boy had ever come right out and asked me that—not even Tommy Aronson. I told Michael, "Yes, I am . . . does it matter?"

"No . . . but it's better if I know."

"Well, now you know."

"Don't get defensive, Katherine. It's nothing to be ashamed of."

"I'm not ashamed."

"Okay then . . . let's just forget it. I like you just the same. I like being with you."

"I like being with you too."

It occurred to me in the middle of the night that Michael asked if I was a virgin to find out what I expected of him. If I hadn't been one then he probably would have made love to me. What scares me is I'm not sure how I feel about that.

CHAPTER 4

M Y FATHER is a pharmacist. He owns Danziger's Drugs in town and Danziger's Two in Cranford. He is also very big on physical activity. He works out at a gym four times a week and plays tennis every morning from 7:30 to 8:30.

I suppose I get my physical coordination from him. I've been playing tennis since I was eight. I play a good game. One of Jamie's goals is to play tennis like me, even though when it comes to sports she is hopeless. I think she should stick to the things she does well. I mean, you can't excel at everything. I know better than to want to be great at music and art, like Jamie. I'm realistic about myself. I think a person has to be.

My father keeps warning my mother that if she doesn't start to work out at the gym soon, she'll wind up with flabby thighs. I can't imagine my mother with flab anywhere but just a few months ago I overheard her divorced friend tell her, "You really should take better care of yourself, Diana. Roger is so attractive and he's at that dangerous age."

"Bullshit," my mother answered. But when I was nine and Jamie was four we had this babysitter who had a *thing* for Dad. As soon as my parents left the house she would run up to his closet and touch all his things. She even smelled some of them. Finally, I told Mom and we never had that sitter again.

During Christmas vacation when both of our stores are fantastically busy I help out selling cosmetics and Jamie sometimes gift wraps. You wouldn't believe how many people buy last minute Christmas presents. They'll take absolutely anything they can get their hands on.

In January business slows down and toward the end of the month my parents go away for a week, usually to Mexico. Then my grandparents come to stay with us. They are my mother's parents. My father's are both dead. My grandmother, Hallie Gross, once ran for Congress, but she lost. She and my grandfather practice law together in New York. Since Grandpa had his stroke he hasn't handled any cases but he still goes to the office every day. My Uncle Howard, who is my mother's brother, really runs the show. Grandma is too busy with politics and Planned Parenthood[1] and NOW[2] to see many clients. I can't believe that she is almost seventy years old.

The night before my parents left for their vacation they said it would be all right for me to have some friends over. Michael brought Artie Lewin and I asked Erica. One thing about Erica—you never have to worry about her getting along with anyone. You can fix her up with the worst guy in the world and she'll act like he's someone special. That doesn't mean she'll make out with him but she will find something to talk about and he'll always call and ask to see her again. Grandma says Erica would make a great politician.

Artie turned out to be my height, with a good build, nice speckled eyes and terrific teeth. He was perfect for Erica. She goes for guys with good teeth.

For a while we all sat around and talked, then Artie said, "How about a game of backgammon?"

"We don't have it," I told him.

"Never mind that," Artie said, "I have mine in the car."

"You brought it with you?" Erica asked.

"I always bring it along . . . just in case."

"In case . . . what?" Erica said.

"In case we run out of things to do. But if you don't play backgammon I have Monopoly, Clue, Yahtzee, chess . . ."

"Scrabble," Michael added.

"Oh yeah . . . Scrabble . . ."

"A regular traveling game show," Erica said.

"So what do you say?" Artie asked.

"Backgammon," Erica told him.

"Great . . . don't go away . . . I'll be right back."

We laughed as Artie ran out to the car to get his set.

Erica's a whiz at backgammon. She plays a very offensive game. But by 10:00 she was down two games to Artie and the challenge was on.

Michael and I sat on the sofa. I reached for his hand and traced the lines of his palm with my finger. "Very interesting." I said.

"You read palms?" he asked.

"Sometimes."

"What do you see?"

"Oh . . . a long life line . . . that's good. And over here I see a girl with brown hair . . ."

"I see one too," he said, looking into my eyes.

My insides turned over. I moved as close to him as I could. I rested my head on his shoulder and held onto his hand. He put his arm around me.

At 10:30 we convinced Artie and Erica to take a break and go out for pizza and when we got back Mom and Dad had gone to sleep. Michael built us a fire in the den and we turned out all the lights. Erica and Artie sat together in a tilt-back chair but after a few minutes they got up and went into the other room, closing the door behind them.

---

1 *Planned Parenthood*   Planned Parenthood Federation of America, established in 1942 when Margaret Sanger's two organizations, the American Birth Control League and the Birth Control Clinical Research Bureau, merged. (See note on Margaret Sanger, Chp. 14.)

2 *NOW*   the National Organization for Women, founded in 1966. Headquartered in Washington, DC, it works to eliminate discrimination against women in industry, law, labor unions, religion, education, government, and medicine.

"I love your hair," Michael whispered, burying his face in it. "It always smells so good." He kissed my ears, my neck and my lips. Then he got up and walked across the room. "Lie down next to me, Kath . . . here, in front of the fire."

This was the fifth week in a row we'd seen each other. I'd asked him to go slow with me and he promised he would. I stretched out beside him. I felt his body against mine. He reached under my sweater and tried to unhook my bra but he had a lot of trouble and I wondered if I should help him out or just lie still and wait. He got it undone. His hands were cold at first but I didn't flinch. I pressed myself as tight against him as I could.

"I'm crazy about you." He touched me and we kissed until the same record had played three times. But when he fumbled with the snap on my jeans I sat up and said, "No . . . not now . . . not with them in the other room."

Michael rolled over onto his stomach and kind of groaned. I bent down and stroked his hair. "You're not mad, are you?"

"No."

"You're sure?"

"Yeah . . . but this is really rough . . ."

"I know it . . ."

"Give me a minute by myself, okay?" he asked.

"Sure." I needed a minute alone too. It wasn't easy to stop.

I opened the den door slowly, not sure what I would find on the other side, but Erica and Artie were sitting at the kitchen table, playing Monopoly. Erica never loses at that game. She steals from the bank.

"Well . . ." Erica said, looking me over, "we were beginning to give up on you two."

"We . . . uh . . ."

Erica held up her hand. "Please . . . spare us the gory details."

"Where's my buddy?" Artie asked.

"Oh . . . he'll be right out."

I went upstairs to the bathroom and splashed cold water on my face. If Artie and Erica hadn't been there I doubt that I'd have stopped Michael from unbuttoning my jeans. But I'm not sure. Now I wanted the boys to go home.

Michael had his jacket on when I came downstairs. "We have to take off now," he said. "It's late . . . see you next week." He gave me a quick kiss.

I was sorry I'd invited Erica to spend the night. While she was getting ready for bed I said, "I think I forgot to turn out the light in the den . . . I'll be right back . . ." I ran down-stairs. I'd already put out all the lights but Erica didn't know. I sat down on the rug where Michael and I had been together. Our rug, I thought. I ran my hands over it. It was still warm.

When I got back to my room Erica was in bed. "Must have been a lot of lights on," she said.

"Yeah." I looked at her. "Did you like Artie?"

"He's nice," she said, "but I think he's shy or something. He didn't try to kiss me."

"He didn't seem shy."

"I know . . . that's what's funny . . . I don't have bad breath or anything, do I?" She sat up, leaned over and breathed hard in my face.

"You smell fine."

"Maybe he wasn't attracted to me. Maybe he thinks I'm too little."

"It probably wasn't anything like that."

"He could be inexperienced, I suppose," Erica said. "If that's the case I could teach him. I really wouldn't mind . . . I love his teeth."

I pulled on my nightshirt. "I knew you would."

"Tell me about Michael, Kath."

"What about him?"

"Is he any good?"

"Uh huh . . . he knows what he's doing."

"Do you love him?"

"I like him a lot . . . that's all I know right now." I turned out the bedroom light. I wasn't going to say I loved Michael yet. I was too quick to think I'd loved Tommy Aronson and he and I never even got to be friends. I already knew Michael better than I'd ever known Tommy. And the way I'd felt about Tommy last year was nothing compared to what I felt for Michael.

"Are you still a virgin?" Erica asked.

"Yes."

"Is he?"

"I don't know . . . I haven't asked."

"I've been thinking," Erica said, "that it might not be a bad idea to get laid before college."

"Just like that?"

"Well . . . I'd have to be attracted to him, naturally."

"What about love?"

"You don't need love to have sex."

"But it means more that way."

"Oh, I don't know. They say the first time's never any good anyway."

"Which is why you should at least love him," I said.

"Maybe . . . but I'd really like to get it over with."

"What's the point?"

"I'm always thinking about it . . . wondering who's going to be the one . . . like tonight, I kept picturing myself with Artie . . . and in school I sit in class thinking how it would be with every guy . . ."

"Really?"

"Yes . . . even the teachers . . . I wonder about them too . . . especially Mr. Frazier, since he never zips his fly all the way. Tell the truth, Kath . . . don't you think about it?"

"Well, sure . . . but I want it to be special."

"You're a romantic," Erica said. "You always have been. I'm a realist."

"You're starting to sound like some kind of professor . . ."

"I mean it," Erica said, "we look at sex differently . . . I see it as a physical thing and you see it as a way of expressing love."

"That's not completely true . . ."

"Maybe not . . . but that's the picture I get."

"Well, you don't know Michael . . . that's all I can say."

CHAPTER 5

ANOTHER THING about Jamie is, she can cook. Not hotdogs and hamburgers like me, but real, honest-to-god gourmet stuff. When my grandparents came to stay with us the first week in February, Jamie did all the cooking. Every night, before they went to sleep, Grandma and Jamie pored over cookbooks deciding on the menu for the following day. While Jamie was at school Grandma did the grocery shopping. Once she drove all the way back to New York to get special spices for a recipe. After school they both went to work in the kitchen, preparing the feast. Jamie gave Grandma small jobs, like chopping shallots, but did all the important things herself. Since they went to so much trouble they usually invited guests for dinner. My grandmother knows everybody, from the mayor to the man behind the counter at the fish market, so you never could tell who might turn up.

While they cooked, Grandpa would wander into the kitchen, lifting lids off pots and sniffing inside. Since his stroke he walks with a cane and has trouble talking. He can't always get the right words out. It's sad to see him struggle over a simple sentence and hard to keep from trying to finish it for him. My mother was very close to Grandpa while she was growing up and now when they're together I can see how painful it is for her to watch him. But my grandmother treats him the same as always, like there's nothing wrong at all.

I've heard that people who come from happy homes, with parents who really care about each other, like my grandparents, tend to have good marriages themselves. And I believe it. My mother and father are certainly the happiest married couple I know. They really enjoy being together, which doesn't mean they agree on everything, because they definitely don't. But after an argument they laugh about it and I like that.

On Thursday night of the week my parents were away Michael picked me up at the hospital and drove me home. "What floor do you work on?" he asked.

"Third," I told him, "In geriatrics."

"Geriatrics . . . that's old people, isn't it?"

"Yes."

"Why'd they put you in there?"

"I requested it."

"How come?"

"Oh . . . it's a long story . . ."

"I'm listening"

"It's hard to explain . . ."

"Come on . . . I'm interested . . . really . . ."

"Well . . . when I was a little kid my father's mother lived in an old age home in Trenton and every Sunday we had to drive down to see her and I always wound up crying . . . you sure you want to hear this?"

"Uh huh . . ."

"Okay . . . so my parents would explain it by saying I was just overtired from the long ride . . . but the truth was, I hated the place. Just the smell of it made me feel sick . . . you know?"

"Go on . . ."

"Well . . . I never really knew my grandmother . . . as a person, that is . . . she was just some old lady with crooked fingers and wrinkled skin and I was kind of afraid of her . . . and of the other old people too . . . I was scared that one of them might grab me and hide me in a closet and my parents wouldn't be able to find me . . . ." I looked over at Michael before I went on. "Then, when I was about seven, my grandmother died, and I was glad . . . because we didn't have to go to Trenton anymore . . . God, I've never told anybody this story . . ." I took a deep breath. ". . . so anyway, when my grandfather—that's my mother's father . . . you'll meet him tonight—when he got sick last year and I went to the hospital to visit him I realized that he was old too . . . but I wasn't afraid of him . . .

because I loved him. I guess this doesn't make much sense to you . . . but that's why I asked to work in geriatrics . . ."

"It makes a lot of sense," Michael said.

"Look . . . don't get the wrong idea . . . I'm no Florence Nightingale . . . and I'm not big on blood and guts . . . I don't do much for the patients . . . just deliver the mail and flowers . . . and bring water and adjust beds . . . nothing special . . . but it makes me feel good . . ."

"It makes you look good too."

I pulled my coat around me and laughed. "I always feel funny in my uniform . . . like I'm dressed for a part in a play or something . . ."

"Say . . . that reminds me . . . our school play's in two weeks. Artie's got the lead."

"Artie . . . I can't picture him on stage."

"Why not?"

"I don't know . . . he doesn't seem like the type . . ."

"You'd be surprised."

"He's so self-conscious."

"Artie . . . self-conscious . . . never."

"Not with you . . ." I said.

"You mean with Erica!"

"Uh huh."

"I don't know about that . . ."

"Well, anyway, I'd like to see him in the play."

"Good . . . and there's a party after it . . . at Elizabeth Hailey's house."

"Didn't you used to go with her?"

"Not exactly."

"But New Year's Eve . . ."

"We were together but it wasn't anything special."

"Still . . . won't you feel funny bringing me to her house?"

"Why should I?" Michael took one hand off the wheel and reached for mine. "We go together, don't we? It's no big secret or anything." I tightened my fingers around his.

When we got to my house Grandma, Grandpa and Jamie were entertaining the DiNizios, from next door—I used to babysit for their kids—and Mr. and Mrs. Salamandre, our butcher and his wife. I introduced Michael to everyone, then Grandma insisted we join them for dessert, which was a chocolate mousse with almondine sauce. Michael said it was the greatest thing he'd ever tasted and Jamie positively beamed.

After that Michael had to leave and I had to study for a Spanish test. I walked him to his car and got in for a minute. We kissed goodbye.

Later, Grandma said, "He's a nice boy, Kath."

"I know."

"Intelligent."

"Uh huh."

"Attractive, too."

"I agree."

"Just be careful . . . that's my only advice."

"Of what?"

"Pregnancy."

"Grandma!"

"And venereal disease."

"Really . . ."

"Does it embarrass you to talk about it?"

"No, but . . ."

"It shouldn't."

"But listen, Grandma . . . we aren't sleeping together."

"Yet," Grandma said.

In the old days girls were divided into two groups—those who did and those who didn't. My mother told me that. Nice girls didn't, naturally. They were the ones boys wanted to marry. I'm glad those days are over but I still get angry when older people assume that everyone in my generation screws around. They're probably the same ones who think all kids use dope. It's true that we are more open than our parents but that just means we accept sex and talk about it. It doesn't mean we are all jumping into bed together. I was really surprised that Grandma thought Michael and I are lovers, in the true sense.

On the final night my grandparents stayed with us they had tickets to a concert at Lincoln Center. I said they should go and that I would stay home with Jamie and ask Michael over to keep us company. Jamie liked the idea of cooking something special for him. Finally, Grandma said, "I've checked with the DiNizios and they'll be home and you know the number in case of fire, don't you . . ."

"Yes," I said.

"Then I guess it's all right for us to go."

"I've been babysitting since ninth grade," I said.

"I know . . . I know . . . but with your mother and father away I feel responsible."

"Everything will be fine. You and Grandpa don't have to worry . . . just enjoy yourselves."

Jamie cooked all day. She made veal marsala, spinach salad and lemon chiffon pie. Michael devoured everything. When we were done I told her we'd do the dishes and she went downstairs to practice the piano. She has a kind of studio down there, where she can work on her music and her artwork undisturbed.

Michael and I loaded the dishwasher but there wasn't any room left for the pots and pans so I filled the sink with hot sudsy water and said, "I'll wash and you dry." I handed him a dish towel.

"Aren't you afraid of dishpan hands?" he asked.

"Nope . . . are you?"

"Oh, sure . . ." He held out his hands, pretending to admire them. "I only use Ivory . . . that's why everyone thinks I'm eighteen instead of thirty-eight. My hands don't give me away."

"You idiot!" I flicked some soap bubbles at him.

"Hey . . ." He reached into the sink, picked up a handful of suds and threw them at me.

So I tossed some more at him and he tossed them back and we had a terrific water fight until both of us were dripping and laughing hysterically. I cried, "No more, Michael . . . please . . ."

He wiped off his face with the dish towel, then started snapping it at me. "Work, slave, work . . . clean up this mess."

"Stop it . . ." I told him, jumping away, but he kept snapping the towel at my legs. I ran around the kitchen, shrieking, with Michael chasing me, only now he was aiming the towel at my behind.

753

"I'm going to get you," I said, reaching into the broom closet. I came out with the feather duster and tickled his face.

"You'll have to pay for that," Michael said, grabbing my wrists. I dropped the feather duster as he pushed me against the counter. He took off his glasses before he kissed me.

"Why do you always do that?" I asked him after.

"Did you every try to kiss with glasses on?"

"No."

"Well . . . they get in your way," he said. "Your hair's all wet."

"So's yours." I reached up and rumpled it. "We better dry off."

We went upstairs to the bathroom. When I looked in the mirror I was surprised. "Hey . . . I really do have soapy hair."

"Just remember who started it," Michael said.

"Hmph!"

"I'll shampoo it for you, if you want."

"You will?"

"Yeah."

"In the sink?"

"Unless you prefer the shower."

"Very funny."

"Well?"

"Okay." I handed him the shampoo and bent over the sink.

He did a good job on my hair and when he was done I wrapped a towel around my head, then shampooed him. We rubbed each other's heads until they were barely damp.

"I have to change my shirt," I said. "It's drenched."

"Go ahead."

I walked down the hall to my bedroom. Michael was right behind me. "I'll just be a minute," I told him as I started to close my door.

But he pushed it back open. "I'll stay."

"Oh, Michael . . . come on."

"I promise, I won't touch." He closed the door behind him.

I took a sweater and bra out of my dresser drawer while Michael bounced up and down on my bed. "Very nice," he said, "firm but not too hard."

"I'm glad you approve."

"Did you know that soft mattresses are no good for making love?"

"Michael . . ."

"Really . . . I mean it."

"That's very interesting . . . now would you please leave so I can change."

"Are you ashamed of your body, Katherine?"

"No . . . of course not."

"Then what's the difference if I stay?"

"Oh . . ." I shook my head at him, turned away and unbuttoned my shirt. I pulled it off and unhooked my bra, which was also wet. Then I hesitated for a minute and slipped that off too. I reached for my dry bra and put it on. All that time neither of us said anything.

Then Michael was behind me.

"You promised . . ." I reminded him.

"I'll hook it for you . . . that's all."

"Don't bother."

"It's no trouble." But instead of hooking it he slid his hands around to my breasts and kissed the back of my neck.

"Please, Michael . . . don't."

"Why not, Kath?"

"Because . . ."

There was a knock at my door then and Jamie called, "What are you two doing in there? The kitchen's a mess and it's almost time for the 9:00 movie."

"Coming . . ." I answered, hooking my bra and pulling on my sweater. Then I turned to Michael and whispered, "That's why . . ."

"Excuses, excuses," he said.

"Ha ha."

We finished up in the kitchen and sat in the den with Jamie, watching the Saturday night movie on TV. When it was over Michael kissed us both goodnight, me on the lips and Jamie on the cheek. She was still touching her face when I went in to tell her goodnight.

"I think Michael is the nicest boy in the whole world," she said.

"That makes two of us."

"I wish he had a younger brother."

"That would be fun . . . but he doesn't."

"Kath . . ."

"Hmmm?"

"What were you two doing in your bedroom?"

"Nothing . . . Michael just wanted to see it."

"Come on, Kath . . . I won't tell anybody."

"There's nothing to tell."

"I know all about sex."

"Congratulations!"

"Were you fucking?"

"Jamie!"

"That's not a bad word . . . hate and war are bad words but fuck isn't."

"I never said it was."

"So were you?"

"No . . . I wasn't . . . but even if I was I wouldn't tell you."

"Why not?"

"Because it's none of your damn business . . . that's why."

"Oh wow . . ." she said, clucking her tongue, "your generation is so hung up about sex."

CHAPTER 6

"HOW'D IT GO with Artie?" I asked Erica on Monday. We were in zoology, classifying mollusks.

"I'll tell you how it went," Erica said, ". . . it didn't!"

"He never showed up?"

"Oh, he showed up all right."

"So?"

"Still nothing . . . not even a kiss."

"Weird."

"And I'm sure he likes me. He asked me to his school play . . . he's got the lead."

"I heard. I'm going with Michael."

"I know . . . Artie said he'll arrange for you two to bring me."

"Fine."

"If he doesn't try anything after the play I'm going to do something about it. I can't sit around waiting forever."

Mr. Kolodny looked up from his desk. "Will you girls in the back please stop talking and get to work."

I pulled out a sheet of notebook paper, wrote *Like what?* and shoved it at Erica.

She wrote back, *Something drastic!*

On the night of the play Michael, Erica and I sat together in the fourth row of the auditorium at Summit High. The play was *Butterflies Are Free*[1] and Artie played the blind boy trying to make it on his own. Michael was right—Artie really surprised me. He was as good as a professional. Somehow, he seemed different on stage—more sure of himself. He made me forget he was Artie Lewin, game freak.

Sybil played his mother and Elizabeth played his girlfriend but they couldn't compare to Artie. It didn't help that Sybil looked fatter than ever and kept fidgeting with her gray wig. Elizabeth's costume consisted of the world's skimpiest bikini and when she first came on stage Erica nudged me with an elbow. For some stupid reason I felt I had to say something to Michael—something to show I'm not the jealous type. So I leaned over and whispered, "She's very pretty." How did I ever think up such a clever remark?

"Uh huh," Michael said.

When the play ended Artie got a standing ovation.

"I had no idea . . ." Erica said over and over. "I just can't believe it."

"Me neither."

"I told you," Michael said. "It's the most important thing in his life."

As I watched Artie take another bow I could see that Michael was right again.

We tried to go backstage but there were two teachers in charge of keeping everyone out since the custodians were anxious to lock up the school for the night. Erica said she'd wait for Artie and that we should go on to the party.

I wasn't looking forward to going to Elizabeth's house and facing her close up. But there was nothing I could do about it without being obvious. Besides, how would Artie feel if his best friend didn't show?

Elizabeth's house was on a street a lot like mine. Her mother answered the door.

"Michael . . ." Mrs. Hailey said, "it's so nice to see you again."

"Mrs. Hailey . . . this is Katherine Danziger," Michael told her.

"Hello," I said.

"Come in . . . come in . . ." Mrs. Hailey said, looking me over. "Everyone's downstairs . . . Michael, you know the way."

Could she have said that for my benefit, just to let me know that Michael had been there before?

It was a big party—maybe thirty or forty kids—and as soon as the cast arrived everyone surrounded them, offering congratulations. Michael gave Artie a cou-

---

1 Butterflies Are Free   Broadway play by Leonard Gershe, popular in the early 1970s.

ple of friendly slugs, then bent down and whispered something to him, and Artie smiled, nodded and said, "Thanks, buddy."

Elizabeth's father took movies of us for the next half hour. Artie really hammed it up. Michael kissed Elizabeth on the side of her face and said, "The part was made for you . . . you were great." And Elizabeth answered, "I'm glad you thought so."

I walked away with a sinking feeling in my stomach. Sybil was standing in the corner talking to some boy. I went over to her and said, "I enjoyed the play a lot . . . you were good."

Sybil laughed. "Thanks, but I know better . . . She introduced me to the boy who turned out to be Elizabeth's younger brother. I wondered if he would make her list.

Erica took me aside, looked in Artie's direction, and said, "He's flying very high . . . I wouldn't be surprised if tonight's the night . . ."

"Good luck," I said, without enthusiasm.

"Oh, here you are." Michael stood next to me and reached for my hand.

"Have we met?" I asked, pulling away.

"What's that supposed to mean?"

"Nothing," I said. "Just forget it." I made my way over to Artie, who was sitting on the couch surrounded by fans. When I got a chance I said, "I know you've heard this all night but you were really sensational."

"Thanks, Kath." He moved over, making room for me beside him.

"How'd you do it? You actually convinced me you were blind."

"I don't know . . . it just comes naturally."

"Seriously, Artie . . ."

"I'm serious. I don't know how I do it. I've always wanted to act . . . ever since I can remember."

"You mean for real . . . professionally?"

"Yeah . . . it's tough to get started but I'm going to give it a try."

"I think you're going to make it."

"I hope you're right . . . where's my buddy?"

"Over there . . . talking to Erica . . ."

"Hey . . ." Artie called, motioning for Michael and Erica to join us.

This time Michael didn't reach for my hand.

I watched and waited all night for some secret look to pass between Elizabeth and Michael but as far as I could tell nothing happened and when we finally got around to talking she was just plain friendly and even said that she remembered me from New Year's Eve, which only made me feel worse.

The party was still going strong when Michael said, "Let's get out of here."

"Why . . . aren't you having a good time?" I asked.

"Not especially . . . are you?"

I didn't answer. I went upstairs to get my coat and sulked all the way home. Michael didn't say a word. He didn't even look my way.

When we got to my house I unlocked the front door. "Are you coming in?" I asked him.

"Do you want me to?"

"If you want," I said, like it really didn't matter.

"It's up to you," he answered.

"Don't do me any favors." As if I hadn't been waiting all night to be alone with him. I stepped into the foyer.

757

Michael followed me. We took off our coats. "Did I do something . . . is that it?" he finally asked.

"No."

"Then what?"

"Oh, I don't know . . . just everything . . . thinking about you and Elizabeth . . ."

"You're jealous?" he asked.

"Maybe that's it . . . I'm not sure."

"That's why you've been such a bitch all night?"

"I guess."

He started to laugh. "I didn't know you were the jealous type."

"I'm not!" But as soon as I said it I realized how dumb it sounded and I laughed too.

"Hey . . . I dreamed about you last night," Michael said.

"What was I like?"

"Very sexy . . ."

I took his hand and we went into the den. "I'm sorry I was such an ass tonight."

"Forget it," he said. "It's nice to know you care. Just promise me one thing . . ."

"What?"

"From now on we're honest with each other. If something's bothering you, say it, and I'll do the same . . . agreed?"

"Agreed."

"Good."

We lay down on our rug and after a while, when Michael reached under my skirt I didn't stop him, not then and not when his hand was inside my underpants.

"I want you so much," he said.

"I want you too," I told him, "but I can't . . . I'm not ready, Michael . . ."

"Yes, you are . . . you are . . . I can feel how ready you are."

"No . . ." I pushed his hand away and sat up. "I'm talking about mentally ready."

"Mentally ready," Michael repeated.

"Yes."

"How does a person get mentally ready?" he asked.

"A person has to think . . . a person has to be sure . . ."

"But your body says you want to . . ."

"I have to control my body with my mind."

"Oh, shit . . ." Michael said.

"It's not easy for me either."

"I know . . . I know . . ." He put his arm around me. "Look . . . we can satisfy each other without the whole thing . . ."

"We will . . . soon . . ."

"If I didn't know better I'd think you were a tease."

"I'd never tease you."

"Yeah . . . I know that too."

"You want me to be honest, right?"

"Uh huh."

"Well . . . the thing is . . . I don't know exactly how to do it . . . satisfy you, I mean."

"It's the easiest thing in the world," Michael said, loosening his belt.

"Not now . . ." I told him.

“When?”
“Soon, but not tonight.”
“Promises . . . promises . . .”

After Michael went home and I was in bed, trying to fall asleep, I thought about making love with him—the whole thing, like he said. Would I make noises like my mother? I can always tell when my parents are making love because they shut their bedroom door after they think Jamie and I are asleep. It's hard not to listen. My room is right next to theirs. Sometimes I'll hear them laughing softly and other times my mother will let out these little moans or call *Roger . . . Roger . . .* Even though I know it's natural and I'm glad my parents love each other I can't help feeling embarrassed. What would it be like to be in bed with Michael? Sometimes I want to so much—but other times I'm afraid.

CHAPTER 7

“GUESS WHERE we're going over Washington's Birthday?” Michael asked. I shifted the phone to my other ear. “I give up.”
“Skiing.”
“But I don't know how.”
“I'm going to teach you.”
“Really?”
“Yeah . . . we're going to my sister's place in Vermont . . . she'll be calling in a little while to fill your mother in on the details.”
“You're serious?”
“You better believe it. Listen, you'll like Sharon, and her husband, Ike, is okay too.”
“It sounds great.”
“It will be . . . and Kath, wait till you see the snow.”
When I hung up I ran into the living room. “Guess where Michael's invited me?”
“To his prom?” Dad asked.
“No . . . nothing like that.”
“Well, tell us,” Mom said.
“To Vermont . . . to go skiing . . . his sister's got a place there. She's going to call you.”
My mother looked at my father.
“I can go, can't I?” I said.
“Well . . .” Dad began.
“Please!”
“You can't expect us to say *yes* just like that, Kath,” Mom said.
“We'll have to think about it,” Dad told me. “After we hear the details.”
Later, when the phone rang, I said, “That must be Michael's sister . . . her name's Sharon.”
“I'll take it upstairs,” Mom said, but by then Jamie had already answered and was calling, “Hey, Mom . . . telephone . . . somebody named Sharon something.”
“What'd she say?” I asked when my mother came back downstairs. “Did you tell her I can go?”

"She sounded very nice," Mom said.

"Go on . . ."

"She said she and her husband would drive you up to Vermont on Friday. It's about a seven hour trip. Their place is near Stowe."

"When would they come home?" Dad asked.

"Monday afternoon."

"That's three nights."

"What's the difference?" I said.

"They have plenty of room, Roger," Mom told him, and I knew then that she was on my side—that she would let me go. "They share the house with two other couples but they'll have it all to themselves over the weekend. She said there are three bedrooms."

"I don't know," my father said.

"Her husband's a resident in internal medicine," Mom said.

"So you won't have to worry about me getting sick," I told my father.

"Just breaking a leg or two," Dad said.

"I'll be very careful . . . I promise."

"I don't know . . . skiing is a dangerous sport."

"No more dangerous than riding in a car," I argued.

"Give us a chance to talk about it tonight," my father said. "And we'll let you know tomorrow."

"I don't see what there is to discuss . . . it's all very simple."

"I don't like making hasty decisions."

"Mom . . ."

"Dad's right. Let us sleep on it, Kath."

"I want to go very much."

"We know," they both said together.

I don't know how I got through the next day. Talking to Erica helped some.

"My mother will let me go but my father seemed kind of scared to say yes."

"That's logical," Erica said. "Fathers have complexes about their little girls. They can't stand the thought of their precious darlings having sex."

"You think that's what's bothering him?"

"Absolutely. It has nothing to do with breaking your leg, like he said . . . it has to do with breaking your cherry."

"Oh, Erica!"

She laughed. "But I'm willing to bet your mother talks him into letting you go."

"God . . . I hope so."

"I'd love to go away with Artie."

"I take it things have improved between the two of you."

"That depends on what you mean by *improved*."

"You know what I mean."

"They haven't improved that way . . . but at least we're getting honest with each other . . . and you can't have a decent relationship without honesty."

"That's just what we were talking about the other night . . . Michael said practically the same thing."

"It's true."

"Yes . . . but you said you were going to do something drastic if nothing happened after the play."

"I did . . . when he took me home from the party and kissed me goodnight on the cheek I came right out and asked him, *Artie, are you queer?*"

"You didn't!"

"Want to bet . . ."

"What'd he say?"

"He said, *I don't know, Erica, but I'm trying to find out.*"

"Jesus . . ."

"So I asked him, *Artie . . . how can you find out when all we ever do is play games . . . Monopoly, bingo, chess, backgammon . . . they're coming out of my ears.*"

"And?"

"He said, *I'm scared to try, Erica.* Now that's being honest, wouldn't you say?"

"Definitely."

"So I told him not to worry . . . that I'll help him find out and he said he'd really appreciate that. So next weekend, while you're in Vermont . . ."

"If I get to go," I said.

"If you get to go . . . Artie and I will be trying to get at the truth."

After school I walked over to the library. "It's okay," my mother said, before I could ask. "The stores are open late tonight and when I passed the *Sports Center* at lunchtime I noticed this terrific looking ski jacket in your size . . . reduced ten dollars."

"I really can go?"

"Why else would you need a ski jacket?" Mom asked.

"Oh Mom!" I hugged her as hard as I could. "You're the greatest . . . you're the best mother that ever was!"

"Remember that the next time we disagree."

Later that night, when Mom and I came home from shopping, I modeled my new ski clothes for Jamie and Dad. My jacket is yellow, red and blue and I bought navy ski pants and a hat to match out of my savings.

"At least it's bright enough for them to find you if you're buried in an avalanche," my father said.

"How can I get buried in an avalanche with Michael watching out for me?"

"They don't have avalanches in Vermont, anyway," Jamie said. "I wish I could go too."

"Not this time," I told her.

"I'd do all the cooking."

"Sorry, Jamie."

"Michael loves my cooking."

"No way."

"Drats!"

When Michael called I told him it was all set. "I even got ski clothes."

"You didn't have to go out and buy anything. Sharon was going to lend you a parka and warm-ups."

"Well . . . now she won't have to . . ."

"Yeah . . . but you'll still have to rent your boots and skis."

"I know . . . don't worry about it . . ."

"Your lift ticket's on me, though."

"Okay, if you insist . . . and Michael . . ."

"Yeah?"

"I can't wait until Friday."

"That makes two of us."

Before I went to sleep my father came into my room and sat down on the edge of my bed, like he used to do when I was little. He took my hand.

"I'm glad you decided I could go to Vermont, Dad."

"Well . . . you'll be off to college in the fall . . . I have to let you go sooner or later . . . I guess you're not a little girl anymore."

"I guess not."

"You have a lot of common sense, Kath. You've always made intelligent decisions . . . still, you and Michael are very young."

"We're not planning to elope, if that's what you're worried about."

"I'm not worried. I just don't want to see you get hurt."

"I told you, I'll be careful."

"Not that kind of hurt, Kath."

"Oh Dad . . ."

"I like Michael . . . and it's not that I don't trust him . . ."

"Daddy . . . he's not a sex fiend . . . so please stop worrying about us."

"I can't help it."

I sat up and hugged him. "Everything's going to be fine . . . really."

CHAPTER 8

AS SOON AS we got to the ski house Michael jumped out of the car and bombarded me with snowballs. There was beautiful fresh snow everywhere and miles and miles of woods, with icicles hanging from every tree. I ran from him, half-laughing and half-screaming, but he didn't listen until Ike grabbed him by the arm and said, "Work now . . . play later." He led Michael back to the car, opened the trunk and pointed to all the stuff that had to be lugged inside.

I helped Sharon unpack the groceries. She was tall and thin, like Michael, with the same color hair, but the shape of her eyes made her look like she was squinting, even when she wasn't. Ike was shorter than Sharon but very broad, with practically no neck. He had a bald spot on the top of his head. I wondered if it will grow until he's totally bald and if it does, will Sharon care? How would I feel if Michael was bald? I'm not sure. I love his hair—the color, the way it feels, the smell of it. I'd be disappointed if it all fell out.

After everything was put away in the kitchen I explored the house. There was one big room with a gray stone fireplace, a beat-up shaggy rug, and a bunch of pillows scattered on the floor. The kitchen opened right into it. Then there was Ike and Sharon's bedroom. They had a private bath. Upstairs there were two more bedrooms, connected by another bathroom, which meant that Michael and I would be sharing. I was glad I'd been honest with him when he picked me up that afternoon. I'd led him into the kitchen while my mother was talking with Sharon and Ike in the living room.

"I have something to tell you," I said.

"Go ahead."

"I got my period this morning."

"Oh."

"A week early."

"Oh."

"My mother says it probably happened because I was so excited . . . about going away and all . . . I just thought you should know."

"You're right."

"In case I have to make some stops on the drive up . . ."

"You don't feel sick or anything, do you?"

"No, I'm fine . . . just disappointed . . . I hope you're not."

"Hell, no . . . why should I be disappointed as long as you can still come with us," he'd said, taking my hand.

When Michael and Ike had finished unloading the car and we were all unpacked, the four of us sat around the fire, sipping mugs of steaming coffee laced with brandy. Sharon told me all about her job. She's an anthropologist, working for the Museum of Natural History, but she hopes to go on a field trip soon, maybe this summer. When I heard that I asked her if she'd be a speaker at our Career Day program in April, because most kids don't get to meet anthropologists every day. Sharon said she'd like that a lot. My guidance counselor, Mrs. Handelsman, will be pleased since she's having trouble finding enough interesting speakers, especially young women.

We were all tired from the trip and when Sharon started yawning the rest of us joined her. "Let's hit the sack," Ike said, and he and Sharon said goodnight and went to their room.

Michael and I looked at each other.

"You can use the bathroom first," he told me.

"Okay."

We went upstairs. "I'll wake you at 7:30 so we can get an early start."

"Okay . . . fine."

He kissed me on the cheek. "Just yell when you're done in the bathroom."

"I will."

"Well . . . goodnight."

"Goodnight . . ." I put my forehead against his chest. "You're sure you're not mad?"

"No . . . come on, Kath . . . it's okay. Get a good night's sleep and I'll see you in the morning."

I nodded, then went to my room while Michael went to his. I felt like crying. Our goodnight hadn't been at all the way I'd wanted it. I put on my long white nightgown. It's the prettiest one I own, made out of soft brushed nylon, with angel sleeves and tiny buttons shaped like hearts. I was hoping Michael would see me in it.

I used the bathroom, called, "Finished . . ." and got into bed. I listened as Michael ran the water and flushed the toilet. When it was quiet I called out again. "Goodnight, Michael . . ."

"Kath . . ."

"Yes?"

"Can I come in for a second?"

"Sure." I sat up in bed and hugged the covers to me.

Michael was wearing baggy blue pajamas. He sat down on the bed and I put my arms around him and a funny sound came out of his throat and we kissed.

"Your sister . . ." I muttered, when we came up for a breath.

"Don't worry."

We kissed again. Then Michael held me away and said, "I wasn't going to touch you tonight . . . just to prove I didn't get you up here for sex."

"I'd have been disappointed," I told him. "I even wore my best nightgown. Do you like it?"

"It covers too much of you but it's nice and soft." Michael reached over and turned out the lamp on the night table. "How do you work these crazy buttons?" he asked, trying to undo my nightgown.

I unbuttoned them myself.

"I want to feel you against me," Michael said and he took off the top of his pajamas. Then he lay down and put his arms around me.

"Oh . . . it feels nice this way," I whispered, as my hands wandered across his naked shoulders and down his back.

Michael kissed me and reached down between my legs but I caught his hand and moved it away. "No . . . not tonight . . ."

"I don't care."

"But I do." It wasn't so much that I didn't want him to touch me, because I did—it was just that I didn't think it was a good idea for either one of us to get carried away. "Michael . . . don't get too worked up . . . okay . . ."

"I'm already worked up."

He didn't have to tell me.

We kissed one more time and then he touched my face gently and said, "I love you, Katherine. I really mean it . . . I love you."

I could have said it back to him right away. I was thinking it all along. I was thinking, *I love you, Michael.* But can you really love someone you've seen just nineteen times in your life?

"I've never said that before," he told me.

"I'm glad."

"I want to hold you all night."

"I want you to."

We slept with our arms around each other till Ike's voice woke us in the morning.

CHAPTER 9

IT WAS A SUNNY cold day, but not windy. Michael said it was perfect for skiing. I got dressed in my long underwear, turtleneck shirt, ski pants, sweater, two pairs of socks and snow boots. I could hardly move.

Sharon was still asleep but Ike had breakfast on the table—cereal, eggs and buns. "No raisins," Michael said, passing the plate to me.

"How'd you know I don't like raisins?"

"New Year's Day . . . remember?"

"Oh, that . . ." I said, picturing myself at Sybil's table, picking raisins out of a bun. "You have a good memory."

"For some things," Michael said and he smiled.

After breakfast Ike gave Michael the car keys and told him to drive me into town to rent my equipment. "Their prices are better than at the lodge. With a little luck Sharon should be ready to go when you get back."

We went to the Alpine Ski Shop. When Michael was finally satisfied that I had the right size boots he showed me how to work the buckles and also how to walk in them without killing myself, which wasn't easy.

Sharon was dressed and ready to go when we got back to the house. From there it was just a short ride to the slopes. They had season tickets and Michael bought mine. When I saw the prices I said, "I never knew skiing was such an expensive sport."

"That's its only drawback," Michael told me.

"Let's go to the Ladies' Room before we get our skis on," Sharon said. "It's such a pain to have to come in before lunch."

I followed her into the lodge and downstairs. We both used the toilets. While we were washing our hands Sharon said that the reason so many beginners get hurt is because they try to learn to ski themselves. "I just want you to know that Michael is a qualified instructor . . . otherwise Ike and I would insist that you take class lessons."

"He's really that good?"

"Just wait till you see him in action."

I smiled. Sharon caught on and laughed. "I meant skiing action," she said.

"I know it."

"My brother's a very nice boy, isn't he?"

"I think so."

"But he seems so . . . well . . . vulnerable."

"How do you mean?"

"Oh . . . he's so open . . . I wouldn't want to see him get hurt."

She didn't look at me when she said that. She looked into the mirror and rubbed some kind of ointment on her lips. I didn't know what to say to her after that. Did she think Michael would get hurt because of me? Did she think I was just using him or what?

"Well . . . let's get going." Sharon put the tube of ointment into her pocket. "And Katherine . . ."

"Yes?"

"I'm sorry if I sounded like a mother hen just now . . . I've really got to stop worrying about Michael. After all, he's all grown up, isn't he?"

"Yes," I said, "he is." It's funny that Sharon worries about Michael in the same way that my father worries about me.

We went upstairs, found Michael and Ike waiting outside, and arranged to meet at the lodge at noon. Sharon and Ike went off to ski the more difficult slopes.

Michael got me onto my skis. They were very short and hardly stuck out at all behind me. He said it's much easier to learn with the short kind and as I improve I'll get longer ones. I didn't think that would be likely.

"First one foot and then the other," Michael said, as I tried to walk. But I got tangled up and tripped over myself. Both of us were laughing by then. "Let the ski slide across the snow . . . don't try to raise it."

"Oh . . . like this?" I asked.

"Very good," he said, taking my arm.

Somehow we made it to the chairlift. "Just grab the side and sit down when the lift comes," Michael told me. "Ready . . . now!" I sat down and was surprised that I landed in the chair and that Michael was right beside me. Before I had a chance to think about it we were going up.

Michael pulled the safety bar down, looked at me and said, "You're going to love it."

I nodded and tried to smile back.

"We're getting off at the beginners' slope so you don't have to worry."

"I'm not worried."

"You look scared to death."

"Don't be silly . . . I can't wait to learn to ski." But I was thinking, we're going up so high . . . how will I ever get down? My father was right . . . I am going to break a leg . . . I'm going to fall off this chairlift and break a leg . . . maybe even two . . . probably two legs and an arm . . . possibly more than that even.

"Getting off is tricky," Michael said and he flipped the safety bar up, leaving me free to fall off in mid-air. "Just do what I do . . . point your skis up."

I did what he said.

"That's it . . . now get ready . . . we're going to stand up in a minute and then just let the lift push you away . . . got it?" Michael grabbed me but I forgot everything he'd said and he had to push me out of the way or the lift would have whacked me in the head and naturally when he pushed me like that I fell over.

"Damn!"

Michael laughed.

"It's not funny."

"You better get used to it. You're going to be on the ground a lot today, but cheer up . . . tomorrow you'll be an expert."

"Ha!"

He helped me to my feet. My nose was running. "Here . . ." he said, pulling a tissue out of his pocket.

I blew my nose.

"I forgot to tell you . . . everybody's nose runs when they ski."

"Swell."

"Ready?"

"Are you sure I'm going to be able to do this?"

"Didn't you tell me how coordinated you are . . . a tennis whiz . . . a modern dance freak . . ."

"I never said *whiz* and I certainly never said *freak!*"

"Relax . . . anybody can learn to ski."

"I hope so. Just one simple question before we start, okay?"

"Sure . . . go ahead."

"How am I going to get down the mountain?"

"You're going to ski down, Kath."

"I was afraid you'd say that."

Michael was right. I spent more time on the ground than on my feet on my first try. But by noon I'd been up and down the beginners' slope three times. On my third try I didn't even fall when I got off the chairlift and if I wasn't skiing exactly, well, at least I was doing something.

Sharon and Ike were already at the lodge, saving a table for lunch. "Hey . . . how'd it go?" Ike asked.

"You wouldn't believe how good she's doing," Michael told them. "I'm really proud of her!"

"Did you enjoy it?" Sharon asked.

"Yes, it's fun . . . it's a very good feeling."

"Invigorating," Ike said.

"That's it . . . invigorating."

"And it builds up a good appetite," Sharon said. "I'm starving . . ."

"Let's get on line," Michael said. "I don't want to waste a lot of time in here . . . I want to get Kath back on the slopes."

After lunch we tried a different trail. "Skis together," Michael said, "let them run across the slope . . . glide . . . glide . . . good . . . okay . . . now, kick your heels down the mountain . . . that's it . . . great . . ."

"I did it," I called. "I actually stopped!"

"Yeah . . . now you won't have to sit down every time you lose your balance."

I scooped up some snow and threw it at him, but he ducked and laughed.

We skied until 4:00, when the lifts closed. "I've had the best time," I told Michael as he helped me out of my bindings. "I really loved it."

"I'm glad," he said. "You're not a bad student either . . . considering."

"Considering what?"

"Oh, just considering." He kissed me on the nose.

I had no idea how sore my muscles were until we got back to the house. Michael had to pull me out of the car. "I hurt all over," I said. "My legs don't want to hold me up."

"A bath will help," Sharon told me. "Soak a long time and keep adding hot water . . . there's plenty of time for a nap too. We don't eat until seven."

I bathed, then fell asleep and didn't wake up until Michael whispered in my ear. "Kath . . . time for dinner . . ."

"Mmmmm . . ." I rolled over.

He sat on the edge of the bed. "You need some help getting up?"

"Mmmmm . . ." I opened my eyes. His face was next to mine.

"Hi," he said.

"Hi . . ." I pulled him down and held him close.

"Later . . . it's time to get up now."

"No . . . not yet."

"I'll have to help you if you can't do it yourself . . ."

"Mmmmm . . . soon . . ."

Michael got off the bed and I closed my eyes again. I heard the water running in the bathroom. Then he was back, standing over me, calling, "Kath . . ." and when I opened my eyes he was holding a glass of water over my head, threatening.

"You wouldn't . . ." I cried, jumping out of bed.

"Now that you're up I won't have to," he told me, "but next time you don't get a second chance."

After dinner we sat around the fire and talked for a while, then Michael got up and went to the window. "The stars are out," he said. "You want to take a walk?" My insides still turn over when he looks at me that certain way.

I got my boots and jacket.

"Don't get frostbitten," Sharon called after us.

As soon as we were outside and away from the house we kissed. "I had to get out of there," Michael told me. "All I could think about was being alone with you."

"I know," I said, " . . . same here."

We held hands as we walked. "I've never seen so many stars," I said.

"That's because it's so dark and clear . . . no city lights, no traffic, no pollution . . ."

"I love to look at stars."

"I love to look at you."

"Oh, Michael . . . come on . . ." I gave him a friendly punch.

When we got back to the house Sharon and Ike were stretched out in front of the fire smoking grass. "Hi," Sharon said. "Did you freeze your tails off?"

"Almost," I told her. I was really surprised to see Sharon smoking. I thought she was so straight, especially after that business about Michael being vulnerable and getting hurt.

"Your cheeks are bright red," Ike told me.

"They always get that way."

"I like them," Michael said, putting his hand against my face.

Ike held the joint to his lips and took a long drag. Then he offered it to Michael.

"You want to?" Michael asked me.

"I don't think so," I said.

"We'll skip it," Michael told Ike, taking my hand. "Katherine's very tired."

"Goodnight," I said, as Michael and I headed upstairs.

"Get a good night's sleep," Sharon called.

"We will."

Michael lay down on the bed in my room.

"I thought you don't smoke," I said.

"I don't, anymore . . . except with them, sometimes . . ."

"Oh." I walked over to the window and opened it a little. I like plenty of fresh air in my bedroom. "I've only tried once . . . and nothing good happened . . . I felt sick to my stomach."

"It can be like that the first time."

"Besides," I said, going to the dresser and picking up my hairbrush, "I don't like to lose control of myself." I was thinking about later, wondering if he would get into bed with me again. Last night was so nice.

"I know it," Michael said.

"Would I . . . if I smoked again?"

"I don't know . . . probably not."

I started brushing my hair. Michael was watching me. I wanted to ask him *what next?* Did he have plans? Did he already know? I wished I had a script to follow so I wouldn't make any mistakes. *Don't forget about my period, Michael,* I felt like saying. "There are kids at school who are high all the time."

"That's different," he said.

"I suppose . . ." I put my brush down. "I'm surprised that Sharon and Ike smoke at all . . . I mean, Ike being a doctor and all." I opened the dresser drawer and pulled out my nightgown. I should wear it, shouldn't I? Yes, but leave it unbuttoned this time.

"They're not exactly addicts," Michael said.

"I know that . . . should I use the bathroom first?"

"Sure."

I put on my nightgown and bikini underpants and after I'd washed and brushed my teeth I said, "You can use the bathroom now."

I got into bed and waited. In a few minutes Michael opened my door. He was wearing his same blue pajamas. He kind of waved at me and said, "Hi."

"Hi," I answered.

He put his glasses on the night table, turned out the light and climbed into bed beside me. After we'd kissed for awhile he took off his pajama top, then said, "Let's take yours off too . . . it's in the way."

I slipped my nightgown over my head and dropped it to the floor. Then there were just my bikini pants and Michael's pajama bottoms between us. We

768

kissed again. Feeling him against me that way made me so excited I couldn't lie still. He rolled over on top of me and we moved together again and again and it felt so good I didn't ever want to stop—until I came.

After a minute I reached for Michael's hand. "Show me what to do," I said.

"Do whatever you want."

"Help me, Michael . . . I feel so stupid."

"Don't," he said, wiggling out of his pajama bottoms. He led my hand to his penis. "Katherine . . . I'd like you to meet Ralph . . . Ralph, this is Katherine. She's a very good friend of mine."

"Does every penis have a name?"

"I can only speak for my own."

In books penises are always described as hot and throbbing but Ralph felt like ordinary skin. Just his shape was different—that and the fact that he wasn't smooth, exactly—as if there was a lot going on under the skin. I don't know why I'd been so nervous about touching Michael. Once I got over being scared I let my hands go everywhere. I wanted to feel every part of him.

While I was experimenting, I asked, "Is this right?"

And Michael whispered, "Everything's right."

When I kissed his face it was all sweaty and his eyes were half-closed. He took my hand and led it back to Ralph, showing me how to hold him, moving my hand up and down according to his rhythm. Soon Michael moaned and I felt him come—a pulsating feeling, a throbbing, like the books said—then wetness. Some of it got on my hand but I didn't let go of Ralph.

We were both quiet for a while, then Michael reached for the tissue box by the side of the bed. He passed it to me. "Here . . . I didn't mean to get you."

"That's all right . . . I don't mind . . ." I pulled out some tissues.

He took the box back. "I'm glad," he said, wiping up his stomach.

I kissed the mole on the side of his face. "Did I do okay . . . considering my lack of experience?"

He laughed, then put his arms around me. "You did just fine . . . Ralph liked it a lot."

I settled next to Michael with my head on his chest.

"Kath . . ."

"Hmmmm?"

"Remember last night when I said I loved you?"

"Yes."

"Well . . . I really meant it . . . it's not just the sex thing . . . that's part of it . . . but it's more than that . . . you know?"

"I know . . . because I love you too," I whispered into his chest. Saying it the first time was the hardest. There's something so final about it. The second time I sat up and said it right to him. "I love you, Michael Wagner."

"Forever?" he asked.

"Forever," I said.

CHAPTER 10

"DO YOU STILL like each other?" Jamie said, as soon as I got back from Vermont. She and Mom and Dad were waiting up for me in the den. I collapsed on the sofa. Seven hours in a Volkswagen is a long time.

"Well, of course we do . . . why shouldn't we?"

"Daddy said sometimes spending a lot of time together can end a romance faster than anything else."

My father actually blushed when I looked at him. "Were you hoping this would end it?" I asked.

"Don't be silly, Kath," Dad said.

"Then why would you have said such a thing?"

"It was a general discussion . . . not one about you and Michael."

"We also discussed how being together can make a romance even stronger," my mother said, to rescue my father, I think.

"Well, that's more like it!" I said, looking at Dad. "Being together made ours stronger."

"I'm glad," Jamie said.

When I got into bed, half an hour later, my father came to my room. "You think I don't approve of you and Michael . . ." he began.

"Do you?"

"Of course I do. I'm just afraid you'll get too involved . . . that's all."

"What's wrong with being involved?"

"Maybe that's the wrong word. What I mean is, I don't want to see you tied down."

"Who's tied down?"

My father sighed. "Will you stop throwing questions back at me . . . what I'm trying to say is, you're too young to make lifetime decisions."

"I'm not making lifetime decisions."

"You have to consider the future, Kath."

"What about it?"

"There you go again."

"I'm sorry," I said, " . . . but the future will take care of itself."

The next morning I waited until my father had gone off to his tennis game and Jamie left for school. Then I caught my mother on her way into the shower and asked, "Does Daddy want me to stop seeing Michael?"

"Of course not."

"Because I won't . . . not even if he asks me to . . ."

"He's not going to ask you . . . he'd just like to see you get around more with other people . . . the way you used to . . ."

"But I don't want to . . . I don't want to be with any other boy."

"I understand, Kath . . . and deep down inside, so does Dad . . . he's just having trouble accepting it . . ."

"I can tell."

"Say, aren't you going to be late for school?"

"So I'll miss first period study hall . . . big deal!"

"If you want I'll drive you over as soon as I'm dressed."

"Okay."

I got my books together and found my clean gymsuit in the laundry room. Then I went out to the garage and started the car. I've had my license since September but I hardly ever get any driving practice.

Mom came out of the house pulling on her hat and gloves. She wears the same kind of white knitted hat that I do only she doesn't pull it over her forehead the right way. She shoves it back on her head because she says it makes her face itch.

"Brrr . . . it's cold out!" Mom opened the car door.

"Want me to drive?" I asked.

"No . . . the side streets are still icy."

I slid over and my mother got in behind the wheel.

On the way to school I said, "Mom . . . *were* you a virgin when you got married?"

My mother kept looking straight ahead but she tightened her grip on the wheel.

I quickly added, "I mean, I know you said you were, but . . ."

We stopped at a red light. Mom turned to me. "I was a virgin until we were engaged . . . not married."

"How about Dad . . ."

"There were double standards then . . . boys were supposed to get plenty of experience before marriage."

The car behind us tooted. "The light's green," I said.

"Oh . . ." We drove up East Broad Street and under the railroad tracks.

"Are you glad you waited?" I asked.

"I don't think of it in terms of waiting . . . I was just twenty."

"If you had it to do over again, would you still wait until you were engaged?"

"Everything's different now. I wouldn't have married so young in the first place."

"But would you have waited?"

"I can't answer that . . . I just don't know."

I didn't say anything more but when we got to school instead of just dropping me off my mother pulled into the lot and turned off the ignition. "Look, Kath . . ." she said, "I've always been honest with you about sex . . ."

"I know."

"But you have to be sure you can handle the situation before you jump into it . . . sex is a commitment . . . once you're there you can't go back to holding hands."

"I know it."

"And when you give yourself both mentally and physically . . . well, you're completely vulnerable."

"I've heard that before."

"It's true," my mother said. "It's up to you to decide what's right and what's wrong . . . I'm not going to tell you to go ahead but I'm not going to forbid it either. It's too late for any of that. I expect you to handle it with a sense of responsibility though . . . either way."

"I wasn't asking for personal reasons, Mom . . . I was just curious, really . . ."

"Of course . . ." She reached out and touched my face. "Well . . . have a good day."

We looked at each other for a minute and then I did something I haven't done in a while. I leaned over and kissed my mother.

"I absolutely can't believe it," Erica said, after I'd told her about my weekend. "You're still a virgin!"

"I'm not saying one way or the other."

"But I can tell."

"How?"

"I just can . . . I'd know in a second if you weren't."

We were in the cafeteria, at our usual table and Erica was eating a hotdog, the lunch special of the day. I am probably the only living American who doesn't like hotdogs so I had a cheese sandwich on my tray—that and a package of Oreos. "Look," I said, "what I do with Michael is private . . . it's not something I want to talk about . . ."

Erica gave me a hurt look, "Sure . . . okay . . ."

"Try to understand, Erica . . ."

"I do . . . I do . . ."

"When you're in love you want to keep it to yourself . . . that's all I'm saying."

"So you really do love him?"

"Yes."

"And he loves you?"

"Yes."

"He actually came right out and told you?"

"Uh huh."

"God . . . that's romantic!"

"I thought you don't believe in romance."

"I don't," Erica said, slurping up the end of her milk.

We carried our trays to the side table. "Don't you want to know about me and Artie?" Erica asked.

"Well, sure . . . but I don't want to pry."

"We played strip poker on Saturday night."

"You didn't!"

Erica laughed. "Right down to our birthday suits."

"Suppose your parents had walked in?"

"They respect my privacy."

"So do mine . . . but still . . ."

"Anyway, we didn't do a thing but touch. I'm beginning to feel like a therapist."

"You could be doing him more harm than good."

"I've thought about that . . . but he's very open about his problem. He's not gay . . . we've determined that. He's just impotent. I've been reading up on it and I'm almost sure I can help him."

"But Erica . . . if you want to get laid so badly why don't you find somebody else?"

"I could get laid tomorrow," she said, "but that's not the point anymore. I want to make it with Artie."

"Why?"

"Because I think I can help him, for one thing, and because . . . well, just because."

"I don't know . . . it still sounds to me like you'd both be better off if you'd just forget it."

"No chance . . . we really like each other . . . even though it's nothing like you and Michael . . . not everybody can be so lucky . . ."

CHAPTER 11

USUALLY MARCH is a slow month. There aren't any school holidays, the weather is still cold and dreary, the teachers get after you to work harder, and I can't believe that it will ever be spring.

This March was different. I felt on top of the world. Michael and I saw each other whenever we could. We went skiing at Great Gorge, twice, and one

Sunday we went to Madison Square Garden to a Rangers' game with Erica and Artie. The Rangers lost and Artie took it very hard, as if he'd been personally responsible or something. I tried to cheer him up on our way out of the Garden. "Win some . . . lose some . . ." I said.

Artie shook his head.

"Look . . . it was just a game."

"Nothing is *just* a game."

"So they'll win next time."

"Next time isn't good enough."

We walked to a Beef & Brew and were seated in a booth. While we were waiting to give our orders Erica said, "Did you know Artie's been accepted at the American Academy of Dramatic Arts?"

"Hey . . . that's great," I said. "You're really on your way now . . ."

"On my way nowhere . . ." Artie said. "My old man won't let me go."

Erica turned to him. "You didn't tell me that . . ."

"Yeah . . . well . . . he just made up his mind. It's a four year college or nothing."

"He can't do that," Erica said.

"No . . . who do you think's paying the tuition?"

"Listen . . ." I said, "you can major in drama anyway."

"The eternal optimist speaks again," Artie said.

"I'm sorry . . . I was just trying to look on the bright side of things." I glanced over at Michael, hoping he would come to my rescue but he didn't say anything. I guess he knew about Artie's father already.

"You've got to stand up for your rights!" Erica said. "Refuse to go anywhere but the American Academy . . ."

"Lay off!" Michael said, suddenly, and something in his voice made Erica stop.

All four of us studied our menus then, or pretended to, and the silence in our booth was uncomfortable. Finally the waitress came along and said, "Okay . . . what'll it be?"

Later, when Michael and I were at my house, alone, I said, "I've never seen Artie that way . . . he was so depressed."

"I know."

"Usually he's all fun and games."

"That's his public image."

"Is the private Artie different?"

"Just sometimes . . ."

"Did you hear him jump on everything I said?"

"I heard . . . but I've seen him that way before. He'll be okay in a couple of days. You've got to understand how he feels about school . . . he really hates it. I don't think he'll make it through one year of college, let alone four . . ."

"I didn't know . . ."

"It wasn't your fault."

"Do you think he and Erica are good for each other?"

"That's not my business . . . besides, every girl at school has the hots for him since the play and he's not interested . . . that must prove something."

"Would you be . . . interested . . ."

"Oh, sure. I only go with you because I can't get anything better." He pulled me down next to him. "We can't do anything to help Artie, right now."

"I suppose not . . ."

"We can help Ralph, though," he said, moving my hand to his belt buckle.

On Thursday Michael called to say that Sharon and Ike were taking some time off to go skiing and they'd asked him to join them and his parents said, yes, he could miss a week of school, because this was a special occasion, and the three of them were leaving the next morning and wouldn't be back until the following Sunday.

"Ten days?" I said. "Two entire weekends?"

"It's very important, Kath . . . I'm working toward my instructor's pin . . . you know that."

"I know . . . I know . . ."

That first weekend my parents didn't leave me alone for a minute. You'd have thought I was a widow. They took me out to dinner on Friday night, and on Saturday Jamie and I went shopping. Then Grandma called and asked me to stay overnight at her apartment so I packed a bag and Mom and Dad drove me into New York.

On Sunday morning Grandpa and I went for a walk in Central Park and that afternoon, Grandma took me to see a revival of *Gone With the Wind*, her all-time favorite picture, which she has seen sixteen times, so far. After it, when she asked me what I thought of Clark Gable, and I told her that his ears stuck out, she shook her head and said, "I'm disappointed in you, Kath." But I knew she was just teasing.

The school week dragged on. Jamie said I looked like a sick dog—well, that's how I felt. At dinner one night my father asked me if I'm going steady with Michael.

"We don't call it *going steady*," I told him. "But we are *going together*."

"Does that mean you can't see anyone else?" he asked.

"That means I don't want to see anyone else."

"I went steady once," Mom said, stirring a teaspoon of honey into her tea. "And I wore his school ring on a chain around my neck. His name was Seymour Mandelbaum."

"Seymour Mandelbaum?" Jamie said and cracked up.

"I was a junior and he was a senior," Mom told us. "I wonder what ever happened to him."

I got the feeling that Mom was talking about her old boyfriend so my father would see that it didn't matter about Michael and me going together.

Then Dad surprised me by saying, "I went steady twice."

"You?" I asked.

"Once when I was in tenth grade . . . I gave her my I.D. bracelet . . . and once when I was a freshman in college."

He and Mom started reminiscing about their college days. I didn't tell them that with Michael and me it's different. That it's not just some fifties fad, like going steady. That with us it is love—real, true honest-to-god love.

The next morning, at breakfast, Dad said, "I still think you'd be happier if you weren't tied down to one boy."

"You don't understand," I explained. "I'm not unhappy. I just miss him."

"What about next year?" Mom asked. "You're going to be apart then."

My mother's question sent me rushing to my guidance counselor first thing. When she saw me she said, "Oh, Katherine . . . I was just working on the final arrangements for Career Day . . . April 25 is just around the corner."

"This isn't about Career Day," I said.

"Then what?"

"I've got to apply to another school . . . right away."

"It's late to apply," she said.

"I know . . . but this is an emergency."

She took my folder out of her files. "Let's see . . ." she said, thumbing through it, "you've applied to Michigan, Penn State and Denver . . . all good schools."

"But I really want to go to University of Vermont . . . either there or Middlebury."

"Why this sudden change?"

"I've got a friend . . . and we want to be together."

"Have you discussed this with your parents?"

"Not yet . . ."

"I'll need their permission and even so . . . I can't promise you anything . . . Middlebury's tough and Vermont takes their own first."

"I'm sure I can get my parents' permission by tomorrow."

But later, when I told Mom, she said, "No!" Just like that. "I don't think that's wise . . . you've already applied to three schools."

"But Mom . . . you know what it's like for me this week . . . being away from him."

"You can see each other on vacations . . . and even weekends now and then . . . and if it's that serious between you it'll grow while you're apart."

"You really believe that?" I asked.

"Yes, Kath . . . I do. And you can always transfer after two years . . . or he can."

"I thought you'd be on my side," I said.

"I am," she told me.

Just when I was feeling really down, knowing that we can't be together next year, and that now I faced another weekend without him, the phone rang. It was Michael.

"I'm home," he said.

"But today's only Friday."

"I know . . . I took the train . . . I got back this morning."

"Wasn't the skiing any good?"

"It was super."

"Then why'd you come back early?"

"Do you really have to ask?"

When I answered the door, two hours later, he took my hand and kind of brushed my cheek with his face.

"Hi," I managed to say.

We went to the 8:00 movie and after it, on the way back to the car, Michael said, "Guess what I have?"

"VD?" I asked, laughing. I expected Michael to crack up over my joke, but he didn't.

"Why'd you say a stupid thing like that?" he said, seriously.

"I don't know . . . it just popped out."

"That means it's in your subconscious."

"It is not! It was just the way you said it . . . you sounded like that commercial where the boy calls the girl and then she calls another boy and he . . ."

"Yeah . . . I've seen it."

"I didn't mean for you to take it personally."

"Well, I did."

"I'm sorry . . ."

"I had it once."

We stopped walking and dropped hands. "You had VD?"

"I got it from this girl in Maine . . . the only time I ever got laid."

"You've only been laid once?"

"Well, twice . . . but with the same girl."

"That's all?"

"What do you mean, *that's all?* What'd you expect?"

"I don't know . . . I thought you had lots of experience."

"Yeah, well . . . the clap turned me off for a while."

"I can imagine," I said. We started walking again, this time without holding hands. "Did you tell the girl in Maine?"

"I couldn't . . . I didn't even know her last name. She was just somebody I met on the beach."

"Oh."

"Look, Kath . . . that was last summer . . . so don't go worrying about it . . . I'm fine now."

"Who said anything about worrying?" I asked, but I must have looked like something was wrong because Michael said, "Then what?"

"You should never take chances."

"That's easy for you to say . . . you always think of everything, don't you?"

"I try to . . ."

We got to the car and Michael unlocked the door. "You probably never took a chance in your life."

"What's that supposed to mean?" I said, sliding into my seat.

"Nothing . . . forget it." He got in, banged his fists against the steering wheel and said, "Oh, shit!"

"What's wrong?" I asked.

He looked straight ahead.

"Can't you at least tell me what's wrong?"

"I don't know . . ." he finally answered. "I've been waiting to be with you all week and now nothing's going right. I'm all tangled up inside."

"Same here." I said.

"Damn . . ." he reached for me. We held each other and then, for some stupid reason I started to cry, which I never do, especially in front of other people.

"Don't, Kath . . . please . . ."

"Same here," I said.

"Look," he said, "let's start over . . . okay?"

I nodded, then took out a tissue and blew my nose.

"Guess what I have?" Michael asked again.

This time I said, "I give up . . . what?"

"The key to my sister's apartment."

"That's what you were trying to tell me before?"

"Uh huh."

I started to laugh. I couldn't help it. The more I thought about it, the funnier it seemed, and the harder I laughed. In a minute Michael was laughing with me. He took my hand. "So . . . you want to go there?" he said.

"I'm not sure."

"We don't have to do anything . . . we can just talk."

S HARON AND IKE live in a garden apartment in Springfield. All the outside doors are painted green. "I hope nobody thinks we're trying to break in," I said, as Michael put the key in the lock, "because there's an old lady watching us." I pointed to a window.

"Don't worry about her." Michael pushed the door open. "That's Mrs. Cornick . . . she lives downstairs . . . she's always in the window." He waved at her and she dropped her shade. "Come on . . . their place is upstairs."

The stairs led into the living room. "It's nice," I said, looking around. There wasn't much furniture but they had a fantastic Persian rug and three posters of chimpanzees riding bicycles. I walked over to a plant and held up a leaf. "Too much water . . . that's why the edges are turning brown."

"I'll tell Sharon you said so."

"No, don't . . . then she'll know I've been here."

"So?"

"So, I just don't want her to know . . . okay?"

"I don't see why . . . but okay. You want something to eat?"

"Maybe . . ." We went to the kitchen which was small and narrow with no outside window.

Michael opened the refrigerator. "How about an apple . . . or a grapefruit? That's about all I see."

"I'll have an apple."

He polished it off on his shirt, then tossed it to me. "I'll show you around the place," he said.

Since I'd already seen the living room and the kitchen we started with the bathroom. "Notice the indoor plumbing." Michael demonstrated how to flush the toilet.

"Very interesting." I told him.

"And hot and cold running water." He turned on both faucets.

"Luxurious."

"Also, a genuine bathtub." He stepped into it and I pulled the curtain around him. While he was in there I wrapped the apple core in some toilet paper and hid it in my pocketbook. Michael jumped out of the tub, grabbed my hand and said, "Onward . . ."

We both knew there was just one room left to see. "Presenting . . ." Michael said, and he bowed, "the bedroom."

There was a brass bed, covered with a patchwork quilt and a LOVE poster hanging on the wall, above it. There were also two small chests, piled high with books.

Michael jumped up and down on the bed while I watched from the doorway. "Good mattress . . ." he said, "nice and firm . . . in case you're interested."

"For jumping, you mean?"

"For whatever . . ." He lay down and looked at the ceiling. "Kath . . ."

"Hmmm . . ."

"Come here . . ."

"I thought we were just going to talk."

"We are . . . but you're so far away . . . I don't want to shout."

"I can hear you fine."

"Cut it out . . . will you?"

I went to the bed and sat on the edge. "There's one thing I'd really like to know . . ."

"What's that?"

"Have you brought any other girls up here?"

"Your jealous streak is showing."

"I admit it . . . but I still want to know."

"Never," he said. "I've never brought a girl up here."

"Good."

"Because I just got my own key."

"You rat!" I yelled, grabbing a pillow and swatting him with it.

"Hey . . ." He knocked the pillow out of my hands and pinned me down on the bed. Then he kissed me.

"Let me go, Michael . . . please."

"I can't . . . you're too dangerous."

"I'll be good . . . I promise."

He let go of my arms and I wrapped them around him and we kissed again.

"You're beautiful," he said, looking down at me.

"Don't say things like that . . ."

"Why, do they embarrass you?"

"Yes."

"Okay . . . you're ugly! You're so ugly you make me want to puke." He turned away and leaned over the side of the bed making this terrible retching noise.

"Michael . . . you're crazy . . . stop it . . . I can't stand that!"

"Okay."

We lay next to each other kissing, and soon Michael unbuttoned my sweater and I sat up and unhooked my bra for him. While I slipped out of both, Michael pulled his sweater over his head. Then he held me. "You feel so good," he said, kissing me everywhere. "I love to feel you next to me. You're as soft as Tasha."

I started to laugh.

"What?" Michael asked.

"Nothing . . ."

"I love you, Kath."

"And I love you," I said, "even though you're an *outsy*."

"What's an *outsy?*"

"Your belly button sticks out," I said, tracing it with my fingers.

"That's not the only thing that sticks out."

"Michael . . . we're talking about belly buttons."

"You are . . ."

"I was explaining that you're an *outsy* and I'm an *insy* . . . you see how mine goes in?"

"Umm . . ." he said, kissing it.

"Do belly buttons have a taste?" I asked.

"Yours does . . . it's delicious . . . like the rest of you." He unbuckled my jeans, then his own.

"Michael . . . I'm not sure . . . please . . ."

"Shush . . . don't say anything."

"But Michael . . ."

"Like always, Kath . . . that's all . . ."

We both left on our underpants but after a minute Michael was easing mine down and then his fingers began exploring me. I let my hands wander across his stomach and down his legs and finally I began to stroke Ralph.

"Oh, yes . . . yes . . ." I said, as Michael made me come. And he came too.

We covered up with the patchwork quilt and rested. Michael fell asleep for a while and I watched him, thinking the better you know a person the more you can love him. Do two people ever reach the point where they know absolutely everything there is to know about each other? I leaned over and touched his hair. He didn't move.

The next night Michael picked me up at 7:30 and we headed straight for the apartment. I knew we would. Neither one of us could wait to be alone together. And when we were naked, in each other's arms, I wanted to do everything—I wanted to feel him inside me. I don't know if he sensed that or not but when he whispered, "Please, Kath . . . please let's keep going . . ." I told him, "Yes, Michael . . . yes . . . but not here . . . not on the bed."

"Yes . . . here . . ." he said, moving over me.

"No, we can't . . . I might bleed."

He rolled away from me. "You're right . . . I forgot about that . . . I'll get something."

He came back with a beach towel. "Down here," I called, because he couldn't find me in the dark.

"On the floor?" he asked.

"Yes."

"The floor's too hard."

"I don't mind . . . and we won't have to worry about stains."

"This is crazy."

"Please, Michael . . . just give me the towel . . . I hope it's not a good one."

He lay down next to me. "It's freezing down here," he said.

"I know . . ."

He jumped up and grabbed the quilt off the bed. We snuggled under it. "That's better." He put his arms around me.

"Look," I said, "you might as well know . . . I'm scared out of my mind."

"Me too."

"But you've at least had some experience."

"Not with anyone I love."

"Thank you," I said, kissing the side of his face.

He ran his hands up and down my body but nothing happened. I guess I was too nervous. "Michael . . . do you have something?" I asked.

"What for?" he said, nibbling my neck.

"You know . . ."

"Didn't you finish your period?"

"Last week . . . but I'm not taking any chances."

"If you're thinking about VD I promise I'm fine."

"I'm thinking about getting pregnant. Every woman has a different cycle."

"Okay . . . okay . . ." He stood up. "I've got a rubber in my wallet . . . if I can just find it." He looked around for his pants, found them on the floor next to the bed, then had to put on the light to find the rubber. When he did he held it up. "Satisfied?" he asked, turning the light off again.

"I will be when you put it on."

He kneeled beside me and rolled on the rubber. "Anything else?"

"Don't be funny now . . . please . . ."

"I won't . . . I won't . . ." he said and we kissed. Then he was on top of me and I felt Ralph, hard, against my thigh. Just when I thought, Oh God . . . we're really and truly going to do it, Michael groaned and said, "Oh no . . . no . . . I'm sorry . . . I'm sorry . . ."

"What's wrong?"

"I came . . . I don't know what to say. I came before I even got in. I ruined it . . . I ruined everything."

"It's all right," I told him. "It's okay . . . really."

"No, it's not."

"It doesn't matter."

"Maybe not to you . . ."

"It could have been all that talking. We shouldn't have talked so much."

"Next time it'll be better," Michael said. "I promise . . . Ralph won't fail me twice."

"Okay." I took his hand and kissed it.

"Let's just sleep for a while, then we can try again."

"I'm not tired," I said, "but I'm very hungry."

"There's nothing to eat here."

"We could go out."

"Get dressed and go out?"

"Why not?"

"Yeah . . . I suppose we could," he said.

We went to Stanley's for hamburgers and on the way back to the apartment we stopped at a drugstore so Michael could buy some more rubbers. I stayed in the car.

"Let's try the living room," Michael said when we got back.

"I couldn't . . . not on that beautiful rug."

"Oh, hell . . . it's got so many colors nothing would show on it anyway . . . and it's softer than the wood floor."

"I don't know . . ." I said, looking at the rug.

"I'll double up the towel." He spread it out. "There . . . that should take care of it."

This time I tried to relax and think of nothing—nothing but how my body felt—and then Ralph was pushing against me and I whispered, "Are you in . . . are we doing it?"

"Not yet," Michael said, pushing harder. "I don't want to hurt you."

"Don't worry . . . just do it!"

"I'm trying, Kath . . . but it's very tight in there."

"What should I do?"

"Can you spread your legs some more . . . and maybe raise them a little?"

"Like this?"

"That's better . . . much better."

I could feel him halfway inside me and then Michael whispered, "Kath . . ."

"What?"

"I think I'm going to come again."

I felt a big thrust, followed by a quick sharp pain that made me suck in my breath. "Oh . . . oh," Michael cried, but I didn't come. I wasn't even close. "I'm sorry," he said, "I couldn't hold off." He stopped moving. "It wasn't any good for you, was it?"

"Everybody says the first time is no good for a virgin. I'm not disappointed." But I was. I'd wanted it to be perfect.

"Maybe it was the rubber," Michael said. "I should have bought the more expensive kind." He kissed my cheek and took my hand. "I love you, Kath. I wanted it to be good for you too."

"I know."

"Next time it'll be better . . . we've got to work on it. Did you bleed?"

"I don't feel anything." I wrapped the beach towel around my middle and went to the bathroom. When I wiped myself with tissues I saw a few spots of blood, but nothing like what I'd expected.

On the way home I thought, I am no longer a virgin. I'll never have to go through the first-time business again and I'm glad—I'm so glad it's over! Still, I can't help feeling let down. Everybody makes such a big thing out of actually doing it. But Michael is probably right—this takes practice. I can't imagine what the first time would be like with someone you didn't love.

CHAPTER 13

W E WERE SITTING around the kitchen table the next day, having Sunday brunch. I thought for sure that as soon as my parents saw me they'd be able to tell. But after a while I realized that they were acting the same as always, so I guess my experience doesn't show, after all.

I smoothed some cream cheese on my bagel and decorated the top with a few dots of lox. My father and Jamie pile their bagels high but I can't eat mine that way. Mom is the same as me. She sort of mashes hers in, making a spread out of it.

When the phone rang, Dad said, "I'll get it . . ." He can reach the wall phone from his seat at the table. "Hello . . . who's calling, please . . . just a minute . . ." He covered the phone with one hand and said, "It's for you, Kath."

"Who is it?"

"Tommy Aronson."

Tommy Aronson? I mouthed his name and my father nodded. "I'll take it upstairs," I said.

I picked up the extension in my parents' bedroom and cleared my throat before I said, "Hello . . ."

"Katherine?"

"Yes?"

"This is Tom Aronson . . . remember me?"

"I remember."

"I'm home for the weekend."

"The weekend's just about over."

"I'm not going back until tomorrow morning."

"Have a nice trip."

"I see you haven't changed."

"Have you?"

"Why don't you come out with me tonight and decide for yourself?"

"Sorry . . . I can't make it."

"Oh, come on . . . I'll behave."

"It's not that . . ."

"Then what?"

"I'm going with someone."

"Oh . . . anyone I know?"

"No."

"Well . . . in that case . . . what's your girlfriend's number?"

"I have a lot of girlfriends."

"The little one . . . you know . . ."

"Erica?"

"That's the one."

"Her last name's Small and she's listed in the book." I hung up before he could say anything else. The nerve of him, coming back into my life today, of all days! And asking for Erica's number just to make me jealous—as if I care one way or the other!

I went back to the kitchen and sat down at the table. My cheeks were burning. "That was Tommy Aronson," I said.

"We know," Mom told me.

"What did he want?" Jamie asked.

"To go out tonight."

"Are you going?"

"Of course not . . . I wouldn't be caught dead with him!"

"You used to like him," Jamie said.

"A long time ago . . . things have changed."

"Is Michael going to be your only boyfriend?"

"For now," Mom answered, before I could. She smiled and offered me another half bagel.

I shook my head. The phone rang again. "That Tommy can't take no for an answer," I said, picking it up. "Hello . . ." I sounded irritated.

"Kath?" It was Michael.

"Oh, hi . . ."

"What's wrong?"

"Nothing . . . I thought you were someone else . . . hang on a second and I'll take it upstairs."

"How're you doing?" he asked me when I picked up the extension.

"I'm fine . . . and you?"

"Okay . . . I just wanted to tell you I thought about you all night."

"Same here . . . about you, that is."

"And that it was very special for me."

"For me, too . . ."

My mother came to my room that night. "I cut this article out of today's *Times*," she said, handing it to me. "I think it has a lot to say . . . you might find it interesting."

I got comfortable in bed, adjusted my lamp, and looked at the article. Maybe Mom could tell about me after all. The title was *What about the right to say 'no'?* and the subtitle was *Sexual liberation*. It was written by the director of medical clinics at Yale. He said that he always asks adolescents (am I still considered an adolescent?) four questions when he talks to them about sex.

1—Is sexual intercourse necessary for the relationship?

2—What should you expect from sexual intercourse?

3—If you should need help, where will you seek it?

4—Have you thought about how this relationship will end?

He went on to explain each question. In his discussion of question two he said that *enjoyable love-making, culminating in orgasm, isn't easy. It usually requires mutual education. It takes time, effort, and patience to learn to make love.*

That made me feel better about last night. It's funny, because I used to think if you read enough books you'd automatically know how to do everything the right way. But reading and doing are not the same at all.

Question three didn't interest me that much so I jumped ahead to question four, which made me very angry. Why should I have to think about *the end* with Michael when we are just at *the beginning?* And I didn't like the way he said, *Rejection is rejection whether we call it divorce, puppy love or adolescent turmoil.* Anyway, who says a relationship has to end?

"What did you think?" Mom asked over breakfast.

"About what?"

"That article?"

"Oh . . . well, it was pretty good."

"Did you agree?"

"With some of it . . . like a person shouldn't ever feel pushed into sex . . . or that she has to do it to please someone else . . ."

"I'm glad you feel that way," Mom said.

"I'm answering you hypothetically," I told her, "not personally."

"Yes, of course."

"You'll never believe who called me yesterday," Erica said. We were sitting in English, which we both have second period. Mr. Frazier wasn't there yet.

"Tommy Aronson?" I asked.

"He called you first?"

I could see that Erica was surprised, and hurt too. "Just to get your number," I said.

"Oh, wow . . . for a minute I really wondered."

"Did you go out with him?"

"No . . . but he came over." Erica must have seen some expression on my face that made her add, "We didn't make out, if that's what you're thinking."

"I'm not thinking anything . . . what you do is your own business."

"Not that he didn't try," Erica said, "and not that I wasn't curious . . . he has a very sexy body."

"So how come you didn't?"

"Because he's so dull . . . he doesn't have an idea in his head. Compared to Artie he's a real nothing . . . even if he does have a perpetual hard-on."

We both laughed as Mr. Frazier walked into the room, smoothing down his hair. His zipper was at half-mast, as usual.

I was surprised that Erica didn't say anything about the fact that I am no longer a virgin. She said she'd be able to tell in a minute. I was sure she'd ask me all about it. So in a way I will always be grateful to Tommy Aronson because if she hadn't had him on her mind she'd have put me through the third degree. And I'm not sure that I'd have told her the truth.

About school, I have two things to say. One, senior year is a bore, except for activities and history, and two, everyone is just marking time until graduation and all the teachers know it.

About my other friends, which I also haven't mentioned, I already know that after graduation we won't be seeing much of each other. It's funny how you can grow away from your friends, when just a few years ago they were the most important people in your life. We used to travel in a pack—there were eight of us and we did everything together. We still share a table at lunch but I don't talk to them on the phone every night, the way I used to, and I certainly don't share my innermost thoughts with them either. Erica is the only one of them I really care about now.

I used to be best friends with Janis Foster. Since ninth grade Janis has been going with Mark Flore. He's finishing his first year at Rutgers now. Naturally Janis is going to Douglass. She and Mark have their entire lives mapped out. They know exactly when they're going to get married and exactly when Baby One and Baby Two will be born. They've even picked out names. Sometimes, on Sundays, they go looking at houses, and at lunch on Monday Janis will tell us they know just where they want to live seven years from now. They make life seem so dull.

Lately, avoiding Janis and Mark has been tricky. She knows I'm going with Michael and wants to meet him. We're in modern dance together and Janis is always after me to make plans for us to go out together. I'm running out of excuses. Maybe it's selfish, but I don't want to waste a night with Michael by spending it with them. She must be really dense not to get the picture.

That night Michael called right after dinner. "Can I come over . . . just for a little while?"

"I have to finish a paper on Somerset Maugham," I told him.

"I'll only stay an hour. I miss you, Kath."

"I miss you too," I whispered.

"See you in a little while."

"Okay."

I raced upstairs and took a shower and shampoo. If I don't wash my hair at least every other day it gets oily and looks terrible. I put on a fresh pair of jeans and a sweatshirt.

"I brought my books," Michael said, after we'd kissed hello.

"Good . . . because if I don't get this paper in by Friday I'm going to fail. We can work at the kitchen table."

As soon as we got our books arranged Jamie wandered in. "I want a pretzel," she said.

"Take the box and please leave," I told her.

"Okay . . . okay . . ."

A few minutes later she was back. "They made me thirsty . . . I need some juice."

"Jamie . . ."

"Okay . . . I can take a hint."

"It's not that we don't want you in here," Michael told her. "It's just that we have a lot of studying to do."

"Sure."

At 10:00 Michael gathered his books and I walked him out to his car. "Get in for a minute," he said.

We put our arms around each other and kissed. "I don't know how I'll last until Friday," Michael said. "I can't think of anything else."

"Me neither."

We kissed again.

Like my mother said, you can't go back to holding hands and anyway, I don't want to.

784

"THERE'S NO school on Friday," Erica said. We were in the locker room, changing into our gymsuits.

"I know . . . some kind of special teacher's meeting."

"So you want to see a preview of a new Robert Redford picture?"

"Are you kidding? I'd love to!"

"We're taking the 8:45 train."

"I'll meet you at the station."

"No . . . we can pick you up . . . say around 8:30."

"Great . . . and tell your mother thanks for asking me."

When I got home from school I found a small package in the mail, from my grandmother. As I ripped it open I wondered if it could be a birthday present two weeks early. As soon as I saw what was inside I knew it wasn't. First I read the note.

Dear Kath,
I hear that you and Michael are officially going together. Thought these might come in handy. And remember, if you ever need to talk, I'm available. I don't judge, I just advise.

Love,
Grandma

I pulled out a whole bunch of pamphlets from Planned Parenthood on birth control, abortion and venereal disease.

At first I was angry. Grandma is jumping to conclusions again, I thought. But then I sat down and started to read. It turned out she had sent me a lot of valuable information. Could my mother have put her up to it?

I went to the phone and dialed her office.

"Gross, Gross and Gross . . . Good afternoon . . ."

"Haillie Gross, please," I said.

"Who's calling?"

"Katherine Danziger."

"One moment . . ."

"Kath?" It was Grandma.

"Hi," I said. "I got the stuff you sent."

"That was fast. I just mailed it yesterday."

"It was here when I got home from school."

"You're not angry, are you?" Grandma asked.

"Me? Why should I be angry?"

"You shouldn't be . . . but sometimes you jump to conclusions."

"Me . . . jump to conclusions?"

"You."

"Look . . . I'm glad you sent that stuff . . . it's very interesting . . . not personally or anything . . . but in general."

"I'm glad you think so. Do me a favor though . . . don't tell your mother and father . . ."

"Why not?"

"Sometimes it's hard for parents to accept the facts . . . so let's keep it between the two of us, okay?"

"Sure . . . okay. I'm coming into New York on Friday . . . maybe I could meet you and Grandpa for lunch."

"We'd love it," she said. "I'll make a reservation at Basil's . . . 12:30?"

"Fine."

"See you then."

"Right . . . bye."

That night I got into bed early and read all the pamphlets. When I'd finished I thought, well, I can start a service in school I know so much, which might not be a bad idea, considering there is a girl in my gym class who, until this year, never knew that intercourse was how you got pregnant, and she's already done it!

The next morning, during study hall, I went to the phone booth near the office and called Planned Parenthood of New York City. The phone rang three times before anyone answered. Either it was very hot in the booth or I was nervous because all of a sudden I was sweating like crazy.

"Hello . . . can I help you?"

"Yes," I said, coughing twice. "I'd like some information about birth control . . . that is, about getting it."

"One moment please . . ."

She connected me with someone else. "You wish to make an appointment?"

"I guess so."

"May I ask your age?"

"Does it matter?"

"No . . . we don't require parental permission . . . but if you're a teenager we have special sessions."

"Oh . . . I'll be eighteen in two weeks."

"Then you could come in this Thursday at 4:00."

"I was hoping I could get an appointment for Friday. You see, I live in New Jersey and I'll be in the city then."

"Hold on a minute, please." I heard a click. After a few seconds she came back on the line. "Friday afternoon will be fine."

"Oh, that's great."

"Your name, please?"

"Katherine Danziger."

"Would you spell the last name?"

"D-a-n-z-i-g-e-r."

"Very good . . . come to the Margaret Sanger[1] Clinic at 22nd Street and 2nd Avenue at 3:00."

"Thank you . . . I'll be there."

On Friday morning my father asked me if I needed any money for my day in New York.

"I've got some saved up," I told him.

"Then use this for train fare," he said, handing me a five.

"Thanks, Dad."

"And have a nice day."

---

1 *Margaret Sanger* (1883–1966) leader of the birth control movement in America. A nurse by profession, she established the first birth control clinic in America, in Brooklyn, NY, in 1916.

Going to a private screening with Juliette Small is a lot different than just going to the movies. This was the third time she'd invited me to join her. I like Mrs. Small. She acts like a regular person. You would never know she's famous. There were about twenty-five other people at the screening, besides us, and Erica said most of them were reviewers, like her mother.

After the picture Mrs. Small asked me, personally, what I thought of it.

"Well . . ." I told her, "I just love Robert Redford."

"Don't we all . . ." Mrs. Small said, "but I mean about the story."

"Oh, the story . . . I liked it . . ."

"But . . ."

"I don't think it could happen that way in real life . . ."

"Exactly!" she said. "But you wanted it to, didn't you . . . you were hoping it would turn out just that way."

"Yes," I told her.

"You see . . . that's the whole point."

"It's going to be a smash," Erica said.

"In spite of my review, you mean?"

"In spite of anybody's review."

"I agree with you, completely," Mrs. Small said. She got into her coat. "Well, that wraps it up . . . I'm yours for the rest of the day. Where shall we begin . . . the Guggenheim, the Whitney . . ."

"How about lunch?" Erica said.

"You're hungry already?"

"Famished . . ."

"Then lunch it is. Kath, want to join us?"

"Oh, thanks . . . but I'm meeting my grandparents."

"Of course . . . Erica did tell me that . . . how are they?"

"Just fine."

"Good . . . send them my love, will you?"

"I will. And thanks a lot for the show. I really enjoyed it."

Outside, I grabbed a cab and gave the driver the address of Basil's. It's my grandparents' favorite restaurant—a very small East Side place where Basil, the owner, will fix special dishes for his regular customers, like Grandpa, who's on a low sodium diet.

They were waiting for me in a booth, in the back, where they like to sit. Grandpa looked pale. I kissed him on the cheek, then hugged Grandma. She was wearing a big yellow felt hat. "Hey . . . I like that," I told her.

"It hides my hair." she said. "Whenever I need a shampoo I wear it."

Basil took our order himself and when I asked him about the special of the day, Chicken Kiev, be whipped out his pencil and drew a picture of it for me, right on the tablecloth, all the time explaining exactly how it's prepared. After that I felt I had to order it.

"So . . ." Grandma said, when Basil had finished with us, "let me get a good look at you." She narrowed her eyes and inspected me. I tried to keep a straight face. Finally she said, "Wonderful . . . glowing . . ."

"Oh, Grandma . . . people don't really glow . . . that's such a silly expression."

"What do you mean people don't really glow? Of course they do. Don't be embarrassed . . . It's very becoming." She looked across the table at Grandpa. "Doesn't she glow, Ivan?"

"To me, Katherine always glows," Grandpa said slowly.

"It must be love," Grandma said.

I could tell I was blushing, even though I didn't want to.

Grandpa raised his water glass. "To love . . ." he said.

Grandma clinked her glass against his. "To love . . ."

After dessert, Grandma and I went to the Ladies' Room. I thought about telling her that I have a 3:00 appointment at the Margaret Sanger Clinic. I knew she'd be pleased. But I decided against it because I want it to be my own experience, one I don't have to share with anyone, except Michael.

We said goodbye to Basil and went outside. It had turned very warm, like a beautiful spring day.

"Whew . . ." Grandma said, unbuttoning her coat. "I'm going back to the office for an hour. I have some work to finish . . ."

I checked my watch. "Well . . . I guess I'll be taking off now. I have a lot of shopping to do." I kissed them both goodbye. "Thanks for lunch." Grandpa hugged me extra hard.

I watched as Grandma helped him into a cab, then I started walking. There's something about walking in New York that really appeals to me, especially on a bright sunny day. I took off my jacket and hung it over my arm. I felt like smiling at everyone on the street even though I know you shouldn't do that in New York. It could lead to big trouble.

CHAPTER 15

I GOT TO THE CLINIC at 2:45. I went inside and gave my name to the receptionist. There were seven other people in my group session, including two young couples. First we had a general discussion with a physician and a social worker. They explained all the methods of birth control. You could ask questions if you wanted. I didn't.

Next came a private session called Personal Counseling—just me and a social worker. She was young and very pretty with long hair, tied back, and tinted glasses. Her name was Linda Kolker. I wondered if she was sexually experienced and decided she must be or else she wouldn't have the job.

We talked about the weather and my family for a minute and then she asked me my reason for coming to the clinic.

I told her, "I think it's my responsibility to make sure I don't get pregnant."

She nodded and said, "Do you have one special boyfriend?"

"Yes."

"Have you discussed this with him?"

"Not really."

"How do you think he'll feel about it?"

"I'm sure he'll be very happy. He approves of birth control."

"But coming here was all your idea?"

"Yes . . . absolutely."

"Good. Some of the questions I have to ask you are rather personal, Katherine . . . so that we can determine what method of birth control will be best for you."

"I understand."

"Have you already had sexual intercourse?"

"Yes."

"Have you been using a birth control device?"

"Yes."

"Which one?"

"A rubber . . . that is, a condom."

"Combined with foam or by itself?"

"By itself."

"And you find that method unacceptable?"

"Well . . . it's hard for me to say because we just did it one time."

"Oh . . . I see . . ."

Now I nodded.

"But you plan to have intercourse regularly?"

"Yes."

"About how often?"

"How often?" I repeated.

"Yes . . . how often do you plan to have intercourse?"

"Well . . . I don't know exactly."

"Would you say weekends and holidays or every day or once a month or a few times a year?"

"I guess on weekends mainly."

"Do you think you'll know in advance or will it be a spontaneous decision?"

"I guess I'll know in advance."

"Okay . . . so much for that. I'll need a little medical history now. How old were you when you began to menstruate?"

"Almost fourteen."

"And are your periods regular?"

"Sort of . . . I get it every four to five weeks."

"And how long does each period last?"

"About five days."

"Any bleeding in between periods?"

"No."

"Vaginal discharge?"

"Sometimes."

"Color?"

"Just clear."

"That's normal . . . any severe cramping?"

"No . . . just some low back pain the first day . . . nothing bad."

"How about your mother . . . is she in good health?"

"Yes, she's fine."

"Does she take birth control pills?"

"No . . . she uses a diaphragm."

"Quite a good method if it's used properly."

"I'd rather take the Pill."

"Yes . . . it has esthetic advantages but it's not the answer for everyone." I guess I must have looked unhappy when she said that because she added, "We'll see what the doctor has to say . . . okay? The whole idea of coming here is to find the birth control device that best suits the individual."

I nodded again.

"Now then . . . I need your written consent for the gonorrhea culture . . ." She hesitated for a moment, then added, "It's simple and painless."

"But I can't possibly have gonorrhea," I told her.

"There's always a possibility . . . and it's often difficult for the woman to tell . . ."

"But Michael . . . besides . . ."

"Look . . . it only takes a few seconds and it's so much safer to be sure . . ."

"All right," I said, deciding it was easier to agree. I signed my name. I tried not to think of Michael and that girl on the beach in Maine.

"Good," she said, standing up. She held out her hand and I shook it. "I'll see you after your physical, Katherine."

"Okay," I said. "And thank you."

My physical consisted of weight and blood pressure, a routine breast exam, with the doctor explaining how I should check my breasts each month, then my first pelvic examination. I tried to act as if I was used to it, but I didn't fool the doctor, who said, "Try to relax, Katherine. This isn't going to hurt." And it didn't either, but it was uncomfortable for a minute, like when he pushed with one hand from inside and with the other from outside.

Then he slipped this cold thing into my vagina and explained, "This is a vaginal speculum. It holds the walls of the vagina open so that the inside is easily seen. Would you like to see your cervix?"

"I don't know . . ."

"I think it's a good idea to become familiar with your body."

He held a mirror between my legs and I looked down while he explained what I was seeing. It reminded me of the time that Erica taught me to use tampons. I had to hold a mirror between my legs then too, to find the right hole.

"That's interesting." I told the doctor.

"Yes . . . the human body never ceases to amaze me." He took the mirror away and I lay back on the table.

"I'm almost done now, Katherine . . . just a Pap smear . . . there," he said, passing a long Q-tip kind of thing to his assistant. "And the gonorrhea culture . . . okay . . . that does it." He took off his rubber glove. "Now . . . do you have any preference concerning birth control devices?"

"Yes," I told him. "I'd like to try the Pill."

"I don't see any reason why you shouldn't . . . you're in excellent health . . . get dressed now and Ms. Kolker will see you back in her office."

"How did it go?" she asked.

"Oh, it was nothing," I told her.

"Here's your prescription." She passed it across her desk, then gave me a two-month supply of pills with instructions, making sure I understood every detail. We also discussed possible side-effects, in which case I am to call the clinic immediately.

I took a taxi to Penn Station and caught the 5:17 train. I couldn't wait to tell Michael my news.

But when I got home my mother said, "Michael called . . . he's got the flu."

CHAPTER 16

TWO DAYS LATER I came down with the same bug. My temperature went up to 104°. I could barely swallow, my head hurt something awful and I was so weak and dizzy I couldn't make it to the bathroom by myself. The doctor prescribed aspirin, bed rest and plenty to drink.

I felt like I was dying.

Mom and Dad took turns staying home from work to take care of me. My father is a super nurse. He concocts delicious fruit drinks in the blender, knows just when you need a cold compress on your head, and loves to play gin rummy.

I stayed in bed for four days. Jamie wasn't allowed anywhere near me but every night she stood in my doorway and told me about her day. On Thursday I got up for an hour and walked around. I'd lost five pounds and had no strength. That night I called Michael.

"Hi . . . how are you?" he asked.

"I'm a lot better . . . I walked around for a while today and tomorrow I'm getting out of bed for good."

"Don't be surprised if you feel like jumping back in . . ." He coughed.

"You don't sound so good . . . can't you take something for that?"

"Yeah . . . I've got a whole mess of stuff."

"I miss you," I said.

"You wouldn't if you could see me . . . I look like the creature from the green lagoon."

"I don't look so good myself. Are you going back to school tomorrow?"

"No . . . not till Monday."

"Can you come over this weekend?"

"I hope so . . . I'll call you tomorrow and let you know."

"Okay . . . and take it easy."

"You too." He coughed again.

On Sunday afternoon he was well enough to drive over for a short visit. I begged Mom to let me wash my hair but she wouldn't. So I tucked it up inside a beach hat, remembering that's what Grandma does. I knew I looked awful but so did he. He had dark circles under his eyes.

"What's with the hat?" he asked.

"It's hiding my hair . . . I don't want you to see it this way."

"You think it'd make a difference?"

"It might."

"You look tired."

"And you look green," I said, starting to laugh.

"I told you, didn't I?" He laughed with me until he started to cough. "Want a coughdrop?" he asked, popping one into his mouth.

"Thanks."

We sat in the den, holding hands, listening to music and talking.

I waited until my birthday, the following Friday, to tell Michael about the Pill. He had planned a special celebration. First we went to see *Candide* at the Paper Mill Playhouse and then we stopped at Mario's for a spaghetti supper. When we were just about through Michael reached into his pocket and pulled out a small black jewelry box. "Happy birthday," he said, pushing it across the table.

"For me?" I never know how to act when I get a present. I'm always embarrassed. "What is it?"

"Open the box."

"Okay . . ." I opened it slowly. Inside was a small silver disk, with *Katherine* engraved across it, on a slender silver chain. "Oh, Michael . . . it's just beautiful."

"Turn it over," he told me.

I did, and on the other side it said, *Forever . . . Michael.* Right away I knew I was going to cry. I bit my lip and tried to hold back the tears but nothing worked.

791

Michael called for the check while I hid my face behind a napkin. "I guess I should have waited till we were alone," he said.

I couldn't answer.

"Hey, Kath . . . come on . . . cut it out, will you . . ."

I nodded to show I was trying.

"It was supposed to make you happy . . . not sad."

"I'm not sad," I said in a squeaky voice.

"Let's get out of here." Michael paid the check, steered me through the restaurant, and led me to the car.

When we were inside he fastened the chain around my neck and kissed me. I looked down at the silver disk, touched it and said, "In my whole life nothing will ever mean more to me."

"I'm glad you like it."

We kissed again and then I whispered in his ear, "I've got a surprise for you, too."

"My birthday's still a month away."

"I know . . . this is a different kind of surprise."

"Oh, yeah . . . tell me . . ."

"You have to guess."

"At least give me a hint."

"Okay . . . it's something I've got."

"VD?" he asked.

I swatted him over the head with my pocketbook. "Not unless you gave it to me!"

"No chance."

"Then guess again."

"I'm no good at guessing games."

"Oh . . . all right," I said, opening my pocketbook. I took out a package of pills and held them up for him to see.

At first he didn't seem to understand but then this slow smile spread across his face and he said, "The Pill?"

"Yup."

"You're taking the Pill?"

"Uh huh."

"Since when?"

"I got them the day you got sick."

"But where . . . how . . ."

"I went to Planned Parenthood in New York."

"You're full of surprises, aren't you?"

"Well, it makes sense, doesn't it?"

"Oh, yeah . . . a lot."

I'd promised my parents we'd come home early, since according to them, I was still recuperating from the flu. They'd had friends in for dinner and everyone was still there when we got back, so Michael and I had no chance to be alone. We kissed goodnight on the front porch.

"Are Sharon and Ike away for the weekend?" I asked.

"No . . ."

"Oh . . . that's too bad." I put my arms around his waist and looked up at him.

"Don't worry," Michael said, "I'll think of something."

"Not your house," I told him the next night when he called for me, "I couldn't . . ."

"Why not? My mother and father won't be home before 12:00."

I checked my watch. It was 7:30. "I don't know . . ." I said. "I feel funny about going to your house."

"Look," he said, "we don't have to do anything . . . we can just go there and talk."

"I think I've heard that before!"

Michael's house is red brick with white shutters. It's near the company where his father works. As soon as he unlocked the front door Tasha jumped on me. "Hi, Tasha . . ." I patted her head.

"Down girl," Michael said, and Tasha obeyed. "Come on . . ." He took my hand and showed me around. Everything was very neat. Their furniture was big, heavy and dark and the drapes were drawn in the living and dining rooms.

The kitchen was brighter, with yellow wallpaper, and hanging plants. A note was attached to the refrigerator with a magnetic flower. It said, *M—soup in refrig. Heat, don't boil.*

"Want to see my room?" Michael asked.

"As long as I'm here I might as well," I laughed.

He led me upstairs, down a long hallway, to a room with cluttered bookcases and an unmade bed.

"Sorry about that," he said. "I'm supposed to make it every day but sometimes I forget."

"How can anybody forget to make a bed?"

"It's easy." He turned on some music while I walked around inspecting all the things on his shelves. He had lots of paperbacks, some team pennants, a picture of a chimpanzee dressed in jeans—his family must be very big on monkeys, I thought—and a cartoon showing a little boy, spelling out f-u-c-k with his alphabet soup. I held up a camp trophy. "Congratulations," I said, ". . . Most Improved Swimmer . . . wow!"

"Yeah . . . that was the year I got brave enough to jump into the deep water." We both laughed while Tasha curled up in the corner, under a chair.

"Can I look in your closet?" I asked.

"Sure . . . help yourself," Michael said and he began to straighten his bed.

I opened the closet. The floor was piled high with shoes, sports equipment and, I think, dirty laundry.

"Find what you're looking for?" he said.

"I'm not looking for anything special. I want to see everything . . . I want to know you inside out. So far I've discovered you're a slob."

"Only about some things," he said.

I opened what I thought was a second closet but it turned out to be a bathroom. There were towels strewn all around which Michael picked up in a hurry and dumped into the hamper.

"God . . ." I said, going through his bathroom cabinet, "you use more junk than I do." There were three kinds of deodorant, two shampoos, a tube of athlete's foot cream, acne soaps, medicated skin lotions, several prescriptions, and at least six different kinds of after shaves. "No wonder you always smell different," I said.

"Pick out your favorite and I'll throw the rest away."

"I don't know one from the other," I said, lining them up on the counter. I took off all the tops and started sniffing. "I like this one." I held up a bottle of green lotion called *Moustache*.

"You would . . . that's the most expensive of the lot."

"Mmmm . . ." I said, sniffing it again. "I have good taste."

He took the bottle from me and splashed some on his face.

"Do you ever put it on your balls?" I asked.

"I don't shave them," he said.

"I read that in a book . . . this guy put after shave on his balls before he went out with his girlfriends."

"Well . . . maybe I would too . . . if I thought anybody was going to smell them."

"Who did you have in mind?"

"Oh, I don't know . . . just anybody." He put the bottle on top of the toilet and unbuckled his jeans.

"What are you doing?"

"I'm going to try it now . . . so I'm ready . . . just in case." He stepped out of his jeans, then took off his underpants. "On second thought," he said, "why don't you do it for me?"

"Me . . . ?"

"It was your idea in the first place."

I felt funny about seeing Michael exposed from the waist down, because it's always been dark when we make love. I've touched him a lot but I've never looked carefully.

He sensed my feelings because he said, "You want to know me inside out, don't you?"

So I looked. His hair down there is almost the same color as on his head, but curlier. Mine is very dark, much darker than on my head. "Hello, Ralph . . ." I said, kneeling in front of Michael. Ralph was small and soft and just hung there. I shook some *Moustache* into the palm of my hand but when I reached out toward Michael, he caught my hand and said, "Don't . . . it stings . . ."

"How do you know?"

"I just do . . ."

"But you said . . ." He didn't let me finish. Instead, he kneeled with me and as we kissed Ralph grew bigger and hard. I undressed myself, while Michael watched. Ralph stuck straight out, as if he was watching too. We made love on the bathroom rug, but just when I was getting really excited, Michael came. I wondered if it would ever work out right between us.

"I'm sorry," he said. "I just couldn't wait . . . it's been a few weeks."

"That's okay."

We got into his bed and fell asleep for an hour and when we woke up Ralph was hard again. This time Michael made it last much, much longer and I got so carried away I grabbed his backside with both hands, trying to push him deeper and deeper into me—and I spread my legs as far apart as I could—and I raised my hips off the bed—and I moved with him, again and again and again—and at last, I came. I came right before Michael and as I did I made noises, just like my mother. Michael did too.

While he was still on top of me, catching his breath, I started laughing. "I came . . ." I told him. "I actually came."

"I know," he said, "I felt it . . . is that what's so funny?"

"I don't know why I'm laughing."

"Did you like it, Kath?"

"What a question . . . I felt so close to you . . . I've never felt so close to you before."

"Same here."

"Can we do it again?" I asked.

"Not right now . . . I've got to rest for a while."

"Oh. Michael . . ."

"Yeah?"

"How'd Ralph get his name?"

He looked at me and smiled. "I named him just for you."

Tasha jumped up on the bed and snuggled next to Michael. I'd forgotten she was in the room. Michael petted her for a few minutes, then put his arm around me and fell asleep again. I watched him. I love to watch him while he sleeps. Besides everything else he is really my best friend now. It's a different kind of friendship from the one I have with Erica. It makes me wish I could share every day with him—forever.

After half an hour I shook him gently. "It's 10:30," I said.

"Mmm . . . we better get going."

"I'm starving," I told him.

"Me too."

"I need a shower."

"Want company?"

"That'll be fun . . . are you sure we have enough time?"

"If we hurry."

We went into the bathroom and Michael got clean towels out for both of us and adjusted the water over the tub. "Do you always wear your necklace in the shower?" he asked.

"Of course," I said. "I never take it off."

He soaped my back. Then I did his.

We dried each other off and I used one of his deodorants. He put *Moustache* on his face, then we got dressed and went out for something to eat.

Over hamburgers I asked him, "Well . . . how does it feel to have made it with an older woman?" He gave me a blank look so I added, "I'm eighteen now, remember? But you won't be for another month."

He polished off his Coke. "There's a lot to be said for older women!"

On the way back to my house I said, "I'd like to meet your parents."

"You will . . . one of these days."

"What are they like?"

"They're okay . . . a little stuffier than yours, but basically they're good guys."

"What would they say if they knew about us?"

"My mother would think you'd seduced me . . . and my father would say I've got good taste."

"Oh, you!"

When we got to my house we sat in the den for an hour—otherwise my parents might have been suspicious. I thought how nice it would be if we could just go upstairs, to bed, together. I was hoping we'd make love again but Michael said he was kind of exhausted. Probably from just getting over the flu.

CHAPTER 17

JAMIE IS in love. His name is David and he's in her math class. She says he looks a lot like Michael. They've decided to act as if they hate each other in public so no one will be able to guess the truth and tease them.

When I hear that I'm glad I'm not thirteen anymore. He's been calling Jamie every night, tying up the phone for ages, which makes it hard for Michael to get through to me. So my parents have limited both our calls to fifteen minutes each.

This summer Jamie is going back to camp in New Hampshire. She says she can't wait. It doesn't seem to matter to her that she won't see David for seven weeks, which proves that love at thirteen is nothing like love at eighteen.

I don't know what I'm going to do about the summer. I've been job hunting, but so far, no luck. Mrs. Handelsman says I shouldn't worry, that something will turn up by June. But it's already the middle of April and I'm worried. So is Michael. He hasn't found anything either and he's counting on a good summer salary to help with next year's expenses at school.

On Monday morning Erica was waiting outside my homeroom. "I got the job on *The Leader*," she said.

The Leader is Westfield's weekly newspaper. There were at least a hundred kids after that job. "You're really lucky," I told her. "I wish I could find something exciting like that."

On Tuesday morning she was waiting for me again. "Sybil's pregnant," she said, shifting her books from one arm to the other. "I found out last night."

"Oh no . . ."

"And she doesn't know who the father is."

"Oh God . . ."

"And she's too far gone to have an abortion . . . the baby's due in early July."

I counted on my fingers. "That means she got pregnant in October . . ."

"Uh huh . . . and never even missed a day of school."

"Jesus . . . why didn't she say anything?"

"She wanted to have the baby and she knew if her parents found out they'd make her have an abortion."

"You mean they didn't notice?"

"She's so fat . . . you know . . . she just kept wearing those tents of hers and nothing showed . . ."

"Didn't she go to a doctor?"

"Yeah . . . but she told him she was married and gave him a phony name and address . . ."

"What's she going to do with a baby?"

"Oh, she knows she can't keep it. She'll put it up for adoption as soon as it's born."

"Then why have it in the first place?"

"For the experience, she told me."

"Will she be able to graduate?"

"I guess so . . . nobody knows but my aunt and uncle, my parents and us. And the only reason she told in the first place was they wanted to send her to Duke University for the summer . . . to this fat people's clinic."

I shook my head. "I can't believe it."

"I know . . . neither can I."

"I'd have an abortion . . . wouldn't you?"

"In a minute . . . my mother's so worked up about Sybil she made an appointment for me to see her gynecologist . . . she wants me to take the Pill. I told her, *Relax, Mom—I'm still a virgin*, but she said she'd feel better if she knew that I was prepared for college, in every way."

"Are you going to take it?"

"Sure . . . I like the idea of being ready for anything . . . and maybe it'll even help Artie . . . make him feel more secure."

The last Thursday in April is Career Day at our school. This year I was hostess to Sharon and my grandmother so I got to eat lunch in the teachers' cafeteria. The food wasn't any better there. Grandma and Sharon hit it off very well, trading anecdotes about their work.

After lunch there was a special assembly and all the guests gave short talks about their careers. Then the audience split up into groups and visited with the three speakers of their choice. Both Grandma and Sharon were among the most popular and had full classrooms at all three sessions.

At the end of the day Mrs. Handelsman couldn't thank me enough. We walked back to her office together. "I've been waiting to hear from you about those extra schools," she said. "What ever happened?"

"My parents wouldn't give me permission," I answered.

She touched my shoulder. "I'm sure everything will work out for the best."

"I hope so."

I didn't tell her that Michael and I have another plan. Since both the University of Vermont and Middlebury are on the trimester system, he will take off the winter semester and teach skiing in Colorado. He'll make up the lost credits at summer school and that way he can still graduate in four years and we can be together every weekend, all winter long. He's already written to Vail, Aspen and Steamboat Springs, stating his qualifications.

"But suppose I'm not accepted at Denver?" I said to him.

"You'll be accepted . . . don't worry."

So on Career Day my mind wasn't really on Sharon or Grandma or any other speakers. There was just one thing I could think about—college acceptances—which were due in the mail any day.

Two days later they arrived and I was rejected at Michigan, but accepted at Penn State and Denver. Michael got into University of Vermont but not Middlebury. A week after we heard from our schools, Erica was accepted at Radcliffe.

"I'm really not surprised," she said, when I called to congratulate her. "Did you hear about Sybil?"

"No . . . what now?"

"She got into Smith, Wellesley, Holyoke and Stanford . . . everywhere she applied. She didn't tell them she was pregnant."

"She's too much . . . What about Artie?" I asked, "anything new?"

"So far he's on the waiting list at Temple but that's it."

"Maybe if he's not accepted anywhere else his father will change his mind and let him go to the American Academy."

"That's what I said but Artie doesn't believe it."

I wrote to Denver right way, accepting, even though my parents felt I should wait a few weeks and think it over since Denver is so far away. Then I explained to them about Michael's plan. They weren't overjoyed.

CHAPTER 18

W HEN THE WEATHER turns warm we have a salad for supper once a week—tunafish, hard-boiled eggs, cheese and raw vegetables—usually on Wednesdays, because that's my mother's late day at the library.

I was peeling foil off a wedge of cheese when my father said, "How would you like to play tennis all summer *and* get paid for it?"

"Are you kidding . . . I'd love it," I told him, popping the cheese into my mouth.

He smiled. "I was hoping you'd say that."

"You're serious?" I asked. "Is the tennis club looking for someone?"

"No . . . but Foxy is."

"Foxy?"

"Sam Fox . . . the director of Jamie's camp," Dad said. "I spoke to him this morning . . . he's built three new courts . . . all weather composition . . . and he needs an assistant tennis counselor . . . the boy he originally hired has hepatitis."

"I can't go to Jamie's camp," I said, spearing an egg yolk.

"He'll pay you $350," Dad said.

"I don't care if it's $3000 . . . I'm not going to New Hampshire."

Mom and Dad exchanged looks.

"It's out of the question," I told them, suddenly having trouble getting the egg down.

"I told Foxy I was sure you'd be interested in the job . . ."

"Well, you can tell him you were wrong!"

"May I be excused?" Jamie asked.

"Go ahead," my mother said. When she was gone Mom turned to me. "Daddy went to a lot of trouble to find you a good job."

"Who asked him to?"

My mother put down her knife and fork. "I can't say I like your attitude."

I fought back tears. "Do you think I'm stupid . . . do you think I can't see what you're trying to do . . ."

"This had nothing to do with Michael," my father said.

"Don't lie . . . please!"

"All right," Mom said. "We both think you could use a change of scenery . . ."

"A change of scenery! Did you forget I'm going to Denver . . . you know Michael and I only have until September."

"Camp is just seven weeks," my father said.

"Just seven weeks!"

"Will you stop repeating everything I say," Dad shouted.

"Seven weeks may not be a lot to you but to me it's forever!"

"Let's try to discuss this rationally," Mom said.

My father lowered his voice. "Look, Kath . . . I already told Foxy it was a deal . . . that you'd take the job."

"You told him! What right have you to answer for me? I'm not a child anymore . . . I'm eighteen . . ." I didn't care that I was crying now. I wiped my nose and eyes with my dinner napkin.

"Last summer you said you'd love to be a counselor at Jamie's camp," Mom reminded me.

"That was last summer . . . things have changed!"

"I'd like you to give it some thought," Dad said.

"I already have . . . and my mind's made up . . . so you can call Foxy and tell him to find somebody else." I threw down my napkin and stood up.

"No," my father said. It hit me then that his mind was made up too. I understood the whole thing, just like that. "Let me get this straight," I said, very slowly. "You're telling me that I have no choice . . . is that right?"

798

"That's right," Dad said.

"Mom . . ." I began.

"I think you should give it a try," she said.

"What does that mean . . . an hour, a day, a week . . ."

"I think you should go for the summer."

"I can't believe this," I said. "I always thought you were really fair . . . both of you . . . but I can see I was wrong . . . way wrong . . ."

"I know how it seems now, Kath . . ." Mom said.

I held up a hand. "Don't feed me any of that crap about how grateful I'll be when I'm older . . ."

"I wasn't going to . . ." she answered, but I didn't stick around to listen. I ran out of the kitchen and upstairs, to my bedroom.

I was all cried out when Jamie knocked on my door, later. "I don't think they should make you go," she said.

"Did you tell them that?"

"Yes."

"And?"

"They said I should stay out of it."

"I could just walk out of here . . . I wonder if they ever thought of that . . . I could just pack my things and take off . . ."

"You won't though . . . will you?" Jamie asked. She looked really worried.

I rolled over on my bed and sighed. "No . . . I guess not . . ." It's strange, but when it comes right down to it I never do fall part—even when I'm sure I will.

"I'm glad," Jamie said.

We didn't discuss the situation at home the next day or the day after that but it was understood that I would take the job at camp.

And now I had to tell Michael.

I thought about waiting until his birthday. It's just a week away. I opened my bottom dresser drawer and pulled out the present I'd bought for him—a bluish-green Shetland sweater, the exact color of his eyes. I'd returned two others before I'd found this one. The first looked too big when I got it home and the second itched when I tried it on. This one was just right. I took the top off the box and held the sweater to my face. It smelled new. But would it be fair to wait until his birthday—would it be honest? No . . . I had to tell him right away.

When Erica heard about my parents and the summer job in New Hampshire she canceled her plans to spend the weekend at the beach with her family and asked me over instead. I thanked her for understanding and she said, "That's what friends are for . . . remember?"

"Why don't you invite her to stay with us instead?" Mom asked when I said I was going to keep Erica company while her parents were away.

"No . . . I'd rather go there."

On Saturday night Michael and Artie came over to Erica's for supper. We fixed hotdogs and beans, a whole package of spinach for Michael and a grilled cheese sandwich for me. Erica's dog, Rex, sat under the table and she fed him scraps from her plate. Both of us were careful not to bring up the subject of summer. Artie was in one of his high moods, entertaining us with family stories until I brought out the cupcake with the candle on it and set it down in front of Michael. I sang "Happy Birthday," even though his birthday isn't until next Thursday. He was surprised and pleased and made me help him blow out the candle, at which point Artie grew very somber. "Eighteen years . . ." he said.

"A quarter of our lives gone by . . . over . . . kaput . . . just like that . . ." He snapped his fingers. "From now on it's all downhill . . ."

"No, it's not," I said, "it's just the beginning . . . the best part is still coming . . ."

Artie said, "Sure . . . you spend your whole life trying to make it and for what . . . so you can wind up in some cancer ward full of needles and tubes with nobody giving a shit . . . that's what you've got to look forward to . . . that's what we've all got coming . . ."

Erica touched his arm. "You've got to enjoy whatever you can and forget about the rest."

"The odds are stacked against us . . ."

"Please, Artie . . ." I said, "don't spoil tonight."

"Hell, I'm not about to spoil it."

"Good." Erica jumped up to clear away the plates. "How about a game of dirty word Scrabble?"

"Sounds good to me," Michael said.

"Why not?" Artie asked. "Let's enjoy it while we can."

He snapped out of his glum mood and we had a fun game, then Michael and I went to the guest room and Erica and Artie headed upstairs, with Rex following them.

Michael took a long time getting me ready, or else it just seemed that way, and it worked out very well. We don't turn out all the lights anymore. It's much nicer being able to see as you make love. After, while we rested, I tried to think of how to tell him about the summer. Finally I decided there was no easy way and I said, "Michael . . . there's something I've got to tell you."

"Umm . . ." he said, playing with my hair.

"Are you listening?"

"Umm . . ." His eyes were still closed.

"It's about the summer . . ." I waited for some reaction from him. "You see . . . my parents . . . they arranged . . ." I sat up. "Oh God . . . I don't know how to tell you this . . ."

He opened his eyes and sat up too. "Just say it, Kath. Whatever it is . . . just say it."

"I've got to go to New Hampshire for seven weeks . . . my father got me this job at Jamie's camp . . . they needed an assistant tennis counselor . . . I said no . . . I told them to forget it . . . but they said I have no choice . . . they're making me go, Michael . . . but I figure you could drive up at least once, maybe twice, because I'm sure I'll get some time off . . . and . . ." I looked over at him. "I know what you're thinking," I said, "that I'm eighteen . . . that I should be more independent . . . I should have asserted myself . . . but, I don't know . . ." I stopped for a minute. "Say something, will you . . ."

"I've got a job too . . . in North Carolina."

"Oh, come on . . ."

"It's true. My uncle's got a lumber yard there and he's offered me a job for the summer . . . good pay and no expenses. I'll be staying with them."

He was serious. He was actually going to North Carolina. "How long have you known?"

"About three weeks."

I took a deep breath. "When were you going to tell me?"

"Tonight."

"Oh, sure . . ."

"I was . . ."

"You expect me to believe that?"

"It's the truth."

"I'll bet . . ."

"Look . . . I didn't want to tell you before because I kept hoping something else would turn up . . . some great job around here . . . and besides, I didn't want to think about facing the summer without you . . . if you don't believe me you can ask Artie . . . he knew I was going to tell you tonight . . ."

"You shouldn't have waited . . . that wasn't honest."

"Okay . . . so maybe I was wrong . . . I'm sorry if I was . . ."

"Whose idea was it . . . going to North Carolina?"

"Whose do you think?"

"Your parents?"

"You guessed it."

"Same here."

"So they'll find out that separating us won't change anything . . . and then maybe they'll leave us alone."

I nodded.

"Come here, Kath . . ."

I leaned over and kissed him. "We still have all of June," I said.

"I know . . . and we're going to make the most of it."

"Starting now?" I asked, kissing him again.

"Starting now . . ."

But Ralph wouldn't get hard. Even when I held him nothing happened.

"What's wrong?" I asked.

"I don't know!" Michael turned away from me. "Shit . . . this is just what I need . . ."

"Don't worry," I said, ". . . it's probably nothing." I ran my hands up and down his back. "Relax . . . it doesn't matter."

He rolled over, but Ralph stayed small and soft. Michael pushed my hand away. "Cut it out, will you . . . can't you see it's not going to work again tonight."

"Okay . . ." I said, "let's forget it."

We dressed side by side, not talking or laughing the way we usually do. I stripped the bed and put the sheets inside the pillow case.

Erica and Artie were sitting in the living room, waiting for us.

"You ready?" Michael asked Artie.

"Yeah."

"Let's get going then."

Erica just sat in the chair looking straight ahead. She and Artie didn't say goodnight to each other.

"I'll call you," Michael told me, without our usual goodnight kiss.

"Okay," I said. I walked him to the front door and when he and Artie were outside I saw Michael toss him the car keys. "I hope you don't mind driving because I've got a headache that's not to be believed."

"Take two aspirin," I called, but he didn't hear. I shut the door and went upstairs. Erica was on her bed, crying. "What is it?" I asked. I'd never seen her cry. Rex tried to lick her face.

"Everything . . . I just can't take it anymore."

"But Erica . . ."

"I've given him almost five months of my life! And I can't help him, Kath . . . it's no use . . . tonight was the end . . . I'm not going to see him again."

"Come on . . ." I said. "You're just upset. Everything will seem better in the morning."

That only made Erica cry harder. I found a tissue box and sat by her side.

"He locked himself in my bathroom and threatened to kill himself and I was scared he meant it . . . I was so scared . . . so I ran downstairs to get you and Michael but just as I was about to knock I heard you . . ." she was sobbing harder and harder.

"Please try to calm down, Erica . . . this isn't doing you any good."

"And then," she said, "when I got back to my room . . . there he was . . . sitting on the bed, all dressed, like nothing had happened and neither one of us said anything for the longest time and then I finally told him I don't want to see him anymore. And he looked right at me and he said, *I understand, Erica—you've been very kind and patient and I certainly don't blame you* . . . like he was acting a part in a play."

"You'll both change your minds," I said. "You'll see."

"No . . . it's over . . . don't you understand . . . it's over for good . . . and in a way I'm even glad."

CHAPTER 19

O N THURSDAY morning, Michael's birthday, Artie hung himself from the shower curtain rod in his bathroom. Luckily, the rod broke and he fell into the tub, winding up with a concussion and an assortment of cuts and bruises. He was stitched up at Overlook, then transferred to Carrier Clinic, a private psychiatric hospital near Princeton.

Both Michael and Erica blamed themselves. Neither one of them believed me when I said that maybe this was the best thing that could have happened because now, at least, Artie will get the kind of professional help he's needed all along.

Michael said he should have listened on Saturday night, when Artie was driving home. "He wanted to talk . . . I knew it but I didn't care . . . I was so wrapped up in my own problems I pretended to sleep all the way to my house. I wish I had it to do over again . . . I'd listen this time."

Erica was convinced it was all her fault. Wednesday afternoon, when she got home from school, Artie was parked out front, waiting for her. She told him that she'd meant what she'd said on Saturday night, and even though she still liked him as a person and always would, they were through and she didn't want him coming around anymore. "I shouldn't have ended it that way," she said. "I should have waited . . ."

We weren't in the mood to celebrate but I gave Michael his birthday present anyway. On the card I wrote, *To keep you warm next winter . . . until we can be together.* And I signed it, *Forever, Kath.*

"It's perfect," he said. "I'll wear it every day."

The next night Michael and Erica got drunk. The three of us went to The Playground, this singles bar on Route 22. We flashed our new I.D. cards at the bartender and ordered a round of screwdrivers. But even with her I.D. the bartender refused to serve Erica until she'd shown him her driver's license and her birth certificate, which she carries in her bag at all times.

Michael and Erica belted their drinks down and ordered a second round while I sipped my first slowly, the way my father said I should. After that I stuck to ginger ale. In less than two hours Michael and Erica each polished off another three drinks and were acting really dumb, singing school songs and laughing hysterically. Finally, I threatened to walk out and drive home myself if they wouldn't leave then and there.

Getting them to the car was another story. Neither one of them could walk and if it hadn't been for this very nice guy who offered to help we might still be there.

Erica got sick first, in the parking lot. When she was done we got her into the back seat of the car, where Michael was slumped in the corner. I thanked my friend and said goodbye. "Good luck," he told me. I waved. A few miles down the highway Michael heaved all over Erica, but she was so out of it she didn't even notice.

I brought them back to my house since I didn't know what else to do. My mother and father were very generous about helping them, because the truth is, they looked and smelled disgusting. Mom put Erica under the shower while Dad hosed off both Michael and his car. I made a pot of coffee.

I'd been very cool to my parents since the camp scene, but watching them help my friends, knowing that they cared, made me glad I hadn't done anything stupid.

Dad called the Wagners and the Smalls and explained the situation to them. We got Michael to bed in the den and Erica to bed in my room. Then I went to the bathroom, sat down on the toilet, and cried.

CHAPTER 20

JUNE—the month most seniors live for—the end of one life and the beginning of another. I read that once, on the cover of a paperback. And in a way it's true. I'd be lying if I said I wasn't caught up in the mood myself.

Yesterday I did something I've never done before. I cut all my afternoon classes. Michael picked me up right after lunch. His mother and father had gone up to the Shakespeare Festival at Stratford. We spent the rest of the day in his bed. We had no trouble with Ralph this time and I could tell that Michael was relieved. So was I. Somehow I thought I might have been to blame . . .

We didn't go to Michael's prom or mine. We'd talked about making one or the other, with Artie and Erica, but now it didn't seem right. Artie's parents told Michael there was no chance he'd be home for graduation. They asked him to write Artie short, cheerful notes, but not to expect any answers.

Jamie baked a special cake for Mom's fortieth birthday. We hid the layers in the downstairs freezer last week and defrosted them this morning, so they'd be ready to decorate when we got home from school. Jamie's icing flowers are better than any bakery's. We'd also chipped in for a big, beautiful plant that looks something like a palm tree. I drove down to the greenhouse to pick it up while Jamie put the finishing touches on the cake. I guess from now on I'll feel uneasy about birthday celebrations but as I helped Jamie get ready for Mom's party I tried to think of only happy things.

Grandma and Grandpa sent forty yellow tea roses, enough to fill up every vase in the house, plus a check. We had a really nice dinner and Mom got tears in her eyes when Jamie and I carried in her cake, singing "Happy Birthday." Then we gave her the plant. She loved it.

Dad's official present to her was a chunky silver bracelet she'd picked out in Mexico but he handed her a surprise package too—inside was a pink and orange bikini. She laughed when she saw it, kissed him, and told us it was great to be forty—that it sounded much worse than it felt. I wished Artie could have been there to see her.

Later, Mom tried on her new bikini and modeled it for us. When she came to my room she said, "Tell the truth, Kath . . . are my thighs getting flabby?"

I said, "No . . . of course not."

"Then what's this?" she asked, squeezing some extra flesh.

I didn't come right out and say it was flab. I told her, "I can teach you some exercises to get rid of it."

"I may take you up on that," she said. "And Kath . . . thank you for a lovely birthday."

"Any time," I answered.

The phone rang that night at 11:30. We never get calls that late because everyone knows my parents sack out early. I heard my father answer and say, ". . . just a minute . . . I'll see . . ."

He came to my door. "Are you awake?" he asked.

"Half . . . who is it?"

"Erica."

"At this hour?"

"She says it's important."

"Okay . . . I'll take it downstairs."

I picked up the phone in the kitchen and yawned. "Hello . . ."

"Sybil had a baby girl!"

I came awake very fast. "She did . . . when?"

"Tonight . . . her mother just called . . . six pounds, one ounce."

"But it's only the middle of June."

"I know . . . she was two weeks early."

"Is she okay?"

"Fine . . . so's the baby."

"I'm glad."

"Me too . . . see you tomorrow."

Erica and I went to visit Sybil in the hospital. Instead of going directly to her room we stopped off at the nursery first. Babies are on view twice a day, during afternoon and evening visiting hours. You can watch them through the glass wall. Sybil's baby had a headful of black hair and was fast asleep.

"What do you think?" Erica asked.

"She's very small."

"They all are."

"Yeah . . . I guess so."

"Do you think she looks like Sybil?" Erica said.

"I can't tell . . . they're not at their best until they're a few months old."

"I know . . . new ones look all shriveled up and distorted."

"I suppose if it's yours, you feel different," I said.

"Do you think just having a baby automatically makes you love it?"

"I'm not sure . . . you might have to learn to love it, like any other person."

We brought Sybil a bouquet of daisies. I arranged them in a disposable vase, the way I do when I'm working at the hospital. She was expecting us since Erica had phoned earlier to make sure she wanted company.

"Hi . . ." she said, and before either one of us had a chance to say anything she began to talk, "I want you to know it was no big deal . . . those movies showing women screaming in labor are plain bullshit . . . there's nothing to it . . . you just push and push and finally the baby pops out . . . to tell you the truth I don't even remember that much about it except there was this very nice guy standing over me and every time a strong contraction started he gave me a whiff of gas . . . did you see her yet? Isn't she adorable? Oh, thanks for the daisies . . . I love daisies . . . you know tonight's my graduation . . . I really planned to be there . . . but you can't fight Mother Nature . . . they're going to mail me my diploma . . . did I tell you I've decided to take off fifty pounds and go to Smith?"

She stopped to take a breath and Erica and I looked at each other.

"I'm getting an IUD so I won't get pregnant again because I've no intention of giving up sex . . . but the next time I have a baby I want to make sure I can keep it . . . did you see how much hair she has? My mother says it will probably all fall out and her regular hair will be completely different." She sighed, then smiled at us. "Thanks for coming. I'm glad you did. Are you going to Michael's graduation?" She directed this question to me.

"Yes."

"Then you'll hear them call my name."

"I'll clap for you . . . okay?"

"Sure . . . for me and Artie," Sybil said. Then she looked up at Erica and shook her head. "I'm sorry."

"It's okay."

"I'd rather be here than where he is," Sybil said.

"When are you coming home?" Erica asked.

"Day after tomorrow . . . but I'm supposed to take it easy for a week or two after that."

"Maybe you'll come to the the beach with us . . ."

"Maybe . . . the baby leaves on Friday with her adoptive parents . . . I hope she has a good life . . ." Sybil reached for a tissue and blew her nose. I hoped she wouldn't cry. I already had a lump in my throat.

"I figure two people who really want a kid will take good care of her . . . don't you think?"

"Sure," Erica said, "it's the best way."

"It's not like I could keep her . . . that wouldn't be fair . . ."

"You're doing the right thing," I told her, wondering why she hadn't thought about all that before.

"Are you sleeping with Michael?" she suddenly asked me.

"That's a very personal question," I answered.

She nodded. "I could have had an abortion but I wanted the experience of giving birth."

"Could have . . . should have . . ." Erica said, "it doesn't matter now . . . what's done is done."

"I've asked to see the baby one more time," Sybil told us, brightening. "The doctor said I can give her a bottle tonight . . . I hope they name her Jennifer . . ."

I T WAS A BEAUTIFUL, clear night and Michael's graduation was held outside. I sat with Sharon and Ike and finally met Michael's parents. His mother took my hand and said, "Well, at last . . . we've heard so much about you." She had red hair and freckles and wore eye make-up.

His father said, "So you're Katherine . . ."

And I told him, "Yes, I am."

He had a beer belly and a lot of grayish hair and a nice voice, deep, like a disc jockey's.

I choked up when Sybil's name was called, when Artie's wasn't, but should have been, and again when it was Michael's turn to accept his diploma. I kept dabbing my eyes, pretending I had something in one of them, in case Sharon or Ike were wondering.

After graduation there was a party at Michael's, a kind of Open House in the back yard, for his relatives. His mother introduced me to everyone as "Michael's little friend." I didn't much care for that but I wasn't about to say anything.

Sharon handed me a glass of champagne. "I hear you're going to be a tennis counselor this summer."

"Just an assistant."

"Sounds like fun. I'd love to get away for a while."

"What about your trip?"

"That fell through. I can't leave my job right now."

"Oh, that's too bad."

"There'll be other opportunities . . ."

I sipped my drink. Some of the bubbles went up my nose.

Ike said, "I like your hair that way."

"It's the same as always," I told him.

"Oh . . . I guess I never noticed." We each took a little hotdog in a blanket as Michael's mother passed with a tray. "You're graduating too, aren't you?" Ike asked.

"Thursday night." I had to answer with my mouth half open because the hotdog was burning my tongue.

"Well . . . congratulations in advance."

"Thank you."

Sharon wandered off and an uncle of Michael's joined us. "I hear you're going to Denver," he said.

I nodded and finished my champagne.

"Wonderful city . . . plenty of sunshine . . . fresh air . . ."

"Excuse me," Ike said, and left me alone with him.

"You have a lot to look forward to."

"Yes, I know," I said. "You're not from North Carolina, by any chance, are you?"

"No . . . that's my brother, Stephen."

"Oh." I looked around for Michael.

The uncle picked something out of his teeth, examined it, then flicked it off his finger. "So tell me," he said, "what do you want to do with your life?"

"Do?" I repeated.

"Yes . . . you've thought about it, haven't you?"

"Sure."

"So?"

"I want to be happy," I told him. "And make other people happy too."

"Very nice . . . but not enough."

"That's all I know right now." I turned and walked away from him.

My parents were asleep when Michael and I got to my house. We locked ourselves into the den, took off our clothes and held each other.

"Let's lie down on the rug," I said.

Michael looked at it. We were used to the sofa.

"For old time's sake . . ."

"Sure," he said, "why not . . ."

We stretched out on it, kissing. "Remember the first night we were together on the rug . . . with the fire . . ."

"And Erica and Artie in the other room . . ." Michael said.

"Yes . . . and after you left and Erica had gone upstairs I sat on the rug for a while thinking that it was very special . . . that it was ours . . ." I kissed his ears, running my tongue around the edges. I used my hands on his body while I worked my way down, kissing his neck, his chest, his belly.

"You're aggressive tonight . . ."

I hadn't thought about that until he said it. I was surprised myself. "Do you mind?"

"I like it."

I lay on top of him, feeling Ralph against my stomach. "Can we try it this way?" I whispered.

"Any way you want," he said.

I straddled him, helping Ralph find the right angle, and when he was inside me I moved slowly—up, down and around—up, down and around—until I couldn't control myself anymore. "Oh, God . . . oh, Michael . . . now . . . now . . ." And then I came. I came before he did. But I kept moving until he groaned and as he finished I came again, not caring about anything—anything but how good it felt.

"Happy graduation . . ." I laughed. After, we lay in each other's arms and I thought, there are so many ways to love a person. This is how it should be—forever.

*   *   *

My graduation was held indoors at the last minute because of a tremendous thunderstorm that began at 4:30 and lasted for hours, on and off. Each senior was allowed only two tickets for an indoor graduation so Michael had to wait for me at home, with Jamie and my grandparents. He didn't get to see me in my cap and gown.

We had a party at our house too, with a table full of sandwiches, fresh fruits and a big chocolate graduation cake.

The next morning Michael and I left for Long Beach Island. We'd been invited to Erica's house at Loveladies Harbor. It's a two hour trip from Westfield, straight down the parkway. We took turns driving.

Erica's house stands on stilts, right on the beach. From the outside it looks like three boxes—a big one in the middle and two smaller ones on either side. The side of the house facing the ocean is all glass. There's a large living room with a white tile floor and white wicker furniture with green cushions. Then there are two smaller wings, each with two bedrooms and a bathroom. Mr. and Mrs. Small use one wing for themselves. Erica's room is in the other. I was

807

sharing with her and Michael's room was opposite ours. None of us mentioned Artie or the fact that we'd planned this weekend long ago, for the four of us.

After lunch we walked up and down the beach, tossing a football around. Erica introduced us to all the summer kids—she's known them for ages. There's a surfing beach a few miles down, in Harvey Cedars, and we sat there for a while, watching a couple of guys trying to catch a wave. We used up a roll of film posing on their surfboards.

That night, after dark, most of the kids we'd met earlier dropped by. One girl brought her guitar and sang for us. Some kids smoked grass but I didn't want to, so Michael drank beer instead, but not enough to get sick. And later, when everyone had gone home and Erica went to bed, Michael and I took a sleeping bag out to the beach and we made love. We woke up at dawn and watched the sun come up together.

Four days later Jamie and I left for camp.

CHAPTER 22

Wednesday
June 26

Dear Michael,

Here I am at camp! The bus ride up was bad news. The air conditioning broke after an hour and we sweltered the rest of the way. One kid heaved in the aisle so we had to stop and let everyone out while the staff cleaned up the mess. I am considered staff!

There are 75 campers, all between the ages of 12 and 15 and every one of them is talented in music or art or both, like Jamie. Tennis is the only organized sport here, besides waterfront. The head tennis counselor is called Theo. He told me right off that I will be teaching the kids with less ability.

The girls live in a big old house and the boys have a sleeping dorm (a converted barn) and the 15 staff members are scattered around. My room is in the house and my roommate is from Seattle. She's a weaving expert. Her name is Angela and she doesn't believe in shaving any body hair and thinks natural body smells beat deodorant. Don't ask!!!

As soon as we got here, Foxy, the director, called a staff meeting and gave us a big lecture about drugs, which are prohibited. As far as I can tell that's the only rule.

To tell you the truth, I don't know what I'm doing here. I wish I was with you. Only 49 days until we can be together. I hope I live that long.

Love forever,
Kath

Friday night
June 28

Dear Kath,

I just got your letter. I read it eight times. I wish I could be your roommate instead of Angela. As you know I have plenty of deodorant. You wouldn't believe how hot it is here. It's impossible to breathe. I picked up my plane ticket today. I leave Wednesday night. Yesterday I ran into Erica. We were both ordering sandwiches to go at the Robert Treat

Deli. There are a lot of things I would like to tell you but I'm not very good at writing them down. If you were here I'd show you what I mean. I guess you get the picture.

I miss you so much!

Love forever,
Michael

P.S. Ralph also misses you.

Monday
July 1

Dear Michael,

I hope you get this before you leave. It rained all day today. This morning I was assigned a co-ed modern dance group. They weren't bad—I was really surprised. I slept all afternoon and I feel better now. I've been so tired since I got here. Do you know it's been eight days since we've been together!!! I'm trying hard not to think about that because every time I do I miss you more and more. I have all your pictures taped on the wall above my bed. Angela says you're very natural looking. I think that's supposed to be a compliment. I didn't tell her that you usually wear eyeshadow and color your hair. Ha ha.

Yesterday I waterskied and fell down in the middle of the lake. I almost lost my bathing suit. Luckily, only Kerrie was in the boat. She's Australian and is in charge of water sports with her husband, Poe.

Jamie says hello.

Have a safe trip to North Carolina but Do Not talk to any strangers on the plane, especially female ones. And don't forget that I love you! And that I miss you more than I can say.

Forever,
Kath

July 2
Tuesday night

Dear Kath,

I'm so excited! I wrote an editorial for The Leader and it's going to be printed in next week's issue. It deals with senior year. I'll send you a copy. I'm leaving for the beach tomorrow night for Fourth of July weekend. Sybil's coming too.

I ran into Michael at the Robert Treat a few days ago and tonight I saw him at Friendly's. We had an ice cream together and talked about you. He's all packed and ready to go. I kissed him goodbye for you—very platonically—on the cheek. I'm going to miss both of you this summer.

I'm enclosing Artie's address at the clinic. Michael said you asked for it. I wish I had it to do all over again with him. I'd handle things a lot differently. Oh well—as my mother says, we grow from our experiences. I hope that's true.

Have fun.

Love,
Erica

July 2

Dear Mom and Dad,

I guess you could say I'm adjusting to camp. Most of the staff is very nice. I like Nan, the photography counselor, best. Theo, the head of the tennis program, calls me

Kat, even though I have explained at least a million times that nobody calls me that. I got a letter from Grandma. I didn't know they were going to Martha's Vineyard next week. Did Jamie write that she has a new boyfriend? His name is Stuart. If she hasn't told you don't let on that you know. She'd kill me! He plays the oboe and has braces on his teeth. I never knew you could play that kind of instrument wearing braces. He's very good.

Last night Foxy called a special staff meeting telling us that the emphasis here is supposed to be on friendship, not sex! Don't worry about Jamie, though. I'm keeping an eye on her. Besides, Stuart is more interested in his oboe than in her.

See you on visiting day.

Love,
Kath

July 3
Wednesday

Dear Kath,

I'm at the airport waiting to board my plane. Don't worry about strange girls. I'm scared of them! Oh-oh ... they just announced my flight. Have to run. I love you. I'm counting the days too. Only 42 more.

Forever,
Michael

P.S. Keep that bathing suit on (until I get back).

Thurs. July 4

Dear Artie,

I'm an assistant tennis counselor at the camp in New Hampshire where my sister, Jamie, goes. It's not a bad job. The lake is really beautiful, but cold. I hope you're feeling okay. Just wanted to let you know I'm thinking of you.

Your friend,
Kath

Friday, July 5

Dear Erica,

When you get this you'll be back from the beach. I hope you had a good weekend. I wish you'd find a nice guy and get Artie off your mind. You can't go on blaming yourself forever. Remember your vow to get laid before college? Well, I've been thinking about that and I've decided it might be just what you need. And you know I wouldn't say that if I really didn't mean it.

You should see me. I'm a mess. My nose and forehead are peeling like mad. It's been very hot since Tuesday and I broil on the courts four hours a day. But that's better than at night—because at least my mind is occupied. Nights are the worst. You just don't know what it's like for me, trying not to think of Michael . . . knowing that we're going to be apart for so long. It's pure torture.

But here's some good news! My roommate, Angela, the smelly one, has moved in with Zack, the potter. He has a shack on the grounds. So now I have a room all to myself.

Most of the kids here are okay. There's just one 15 year old brat I can't stand. Her name is Marsha. Everyone says she's a fantastic ballerina but I haven't seen her dance yet. She's too busy hanging around the tennis courts because of Theo. When I compare us at 15 to Marsha, I can see that times are really changing . . . and not for the better, in my opinion. I wouldn't want to see Jamie carrying on like that in two years.

I'll say this for Theo—he's not impressed by silly kids. He doesn't say much about himself but my friend, Nan, knows that he is 21 and a senior at Northwestern. Nan is impossibly shy around guys but I'm going to try to fix things up between the two of them. He's not as bad as I first thought.

Time for supper now. Write soon.

Love,
Kath

July 9
Tuesday

Dear Kath,

We had a great weekend at the beach. The weather was perfect. I think I told you that Sybil was coming with us. She's on another one of her diets but this time with the doctor's approval. She didn't want to talk about the baby. I think the whole experience was more than she bargained for.

Thanks for your suggestions. But I've been doing a lot of thinking and have decided I don't want to fuck just for the hell of it. I want it to be special, like you and Michael. So I'm going to wait.

Theo and Nan sound nice. I'm glad you've found some friends. They should help make the time go faster.

Love,
Erica

Thursday, July 11

Dear Kath,

Dad and I enjoy hearing from you very much. We're glad you're adjusting to camp. It's been very hot here. Yesterday the air conditioning in the library broke down and we had to close early.

Let me know if there's anything you need on visiting day. We're looking forward to spending the day with you and Jamie. Grandma and Grandpa are off to Martha's Vineyard for ten days. Erica stopped in the library to say hello. That's about it.

Love,
Mom

CHAPTER 23

THE CAMPERS have to report to their rooms at 10:00 every night. Then the staff gets together in the retreat, which is a small cottage with some comfortable furniture. Usually I write my letters there.

Sometimes, while I'm trying to think of what to say I'll look up for a minute and catch Theo watching me. He doesn't get embarrassed and turn away but I do. His eyes are light green and Nan says every time she looks into them she melts. His hair is brown and hangs into his face. On the courts he has to wear a headband to keep it away so he can see the ball. He's got a moustache that turns down around the corners of his mouth and he's very tan, including his back and chest, because he hardly ever wears a shirt.

The other day, Theo, Nan and I were on the dock. I laughed when he took off his socks and sneakers because his feet were so white. So he picked me up and tossed me into the lake. I was wearing jeans and a shirt and I wanted to kill him.

The truth is, he's not the wise-ass I thought he was going to be when we first met. He's very patient with the kids and is even helping me improve my game. Sometimes, after dinner, we play a set or two. He says I'm the only one here who can give him a decent workout.

One night, during the first week of camp, Theo came over and pointed to my necklace. "What's it say?" he asked.

"This . . ." I said, holding up the disk.

"Yes."

"It says *Katherine* on one side and *Michael* on the other."

"The guy you're always writing to?"

"Uh huh."

"Can I see?"

"Sure."

He stood very close to me and took it in his hand. He looked at the side that said *Katherine* first, then turned it over. "What's *forever* supposed to mean?"

"What do you think?" I asked.

"I think forever's one hell of a long time for a kid like you."

"I'm not a kid. I happen to be eighteen."

"Congratulations," he said.

Right after that I asked him to please stop calling me Kat.

He said, "I can't stop now . . . I'm used to it . . . besides, it suits you."

Now everyone at camp calls me Kat. I don't mind as much as I did then.

I got a letter from Michael.

Dear Kath,

I'm getting settled here. I've got my own room since my cousin, Danny, is away for the summer. His twin sisters are thirteen and remind me of Jamie. Tell her I said hello. I'm getting to be a first rate lumber stacker. Next week I get to work the saw. That's a big step up! I think about you every night—all night.

Love forever,
Michael

Dear Michael,

Be careful with the saw! I don't want anything to happen to your hands. I love them (and the rest of you isn't bad either). Ha ha.

Love forever,
Kath

Each staff member gets two short and one long night off each week. A long night means you don't have to hang around for evening activity. You can leave right after supper and you don't have to report in until the next morning.

This week Theo asked if Nan and I would like to go into Laconia with him to see a movie. He has a car and we don't. Naturally we accepted.

I tried to arrange it so that I would sit next to Nan and she would sit between me and Theo but he decided it was only fair that he sit in the middle, since he was the only guy. He put one arm around each of us but I knew it was just a joke. It's funny, the way you get to know summer friends so well in a short period of time, especially at camp, when you are thrown together morning, noon and night.

Sometimes I dream that Michael and I are making love. I can understand that. But in the middle of the night after the movie, I woke up drenched with perspiration and ashamed—more ashamed than I've ever been in my life. I dreamed I was with Theo. It was so real—I could smell him, taste him, feel him—and I wanted him so much. I did things to him that I have only read about.

I wrote Michael a four-page letter the next day, to keep my mind where it belongs. I stayed as far away from Theo as I could. Even so, I knew there was something growing between us. Something I was afraid to even think about.

Every night, from 8:00 to 10:00, the canteen is open and the campers can hang out in there, listening to music, dancing and getting snacks. Theo dances with the younger kids, like Jamie, but avoids the older ones, like Marsha. You can tell he's not looking for trouble. Nan doesn't dance at all. She says she has two left feet. That presents a real problem because dancing can be a very good way to get two people together. And Theo likes to dance. If only he would look at Nan the way he looks at me. If only my insides didn't turn over every time our eyes meet.

Tonight, Marsha put on this slow song and all the kids booed her because they prefer hard rock. They don't even know how to touch-dance. But Marsha wouldn't change the record and she came slithering over to Theo and tried to drag him to his feet. He told her, "Sorry, Marsha . . . but I promised this one to Kat." And he took my hand and pulled me up. I shook my head but he didn't care. He said to the kids, "Watch carefully . . . and I'll show you a new way to dance." Then he put his arms around me and the kids whistled and cheered and Theo laughed and held me tighter. Soon, some of the kids got up to try touch-dancing and Theo started the record from the beginning again.

He's not much taller than I am—just three or four inches—and I was wearing clogs, so that as we danced our bodies came together. We didn't talk or look at each other but there was a lot going on between us. When the record ended I broke away from him and ran out of the canteen. I went down to the lake where it's cool and dark and I sat on a rock and I cried. How can you love one person and still be attracted to another?

The next day I got a long letter from Michael. I kissed it and showed it to Nan to prove that I am not the least bit interested in anyone but him.

On visiting day I spent the morning on the courts rallying with the campers so their parents could see how much their games had improved. Foxy gave me the afternoon off to be with Mom and Dad. I was the only counselor who had visitors. After lunch Jamie showed them her oils and watercolors and the fabric she's weaving with Angela's help. Then my father changed into tennis shorts and he and I played two sets. I beat him 6-3, 7-5. He was very impressed.

Later, I took Mom up to see my room. "It's nice and cozy." She sat on my bed and looked at the pictures of Michael taped to the wall. "You seem to be getting along very well . . . I'm glad."

"I'm managing . . ." I told her. I went to my closet and took out a shoe box full of letters. "Look at this," I said, ". . . all from Michael. We write every day."

813

Mom nodded.

"I'll bet you thought we wouldn't."

"No . . . I never thought that."

CHAPTER 24

O N THE FOLLOWING Sunday night I was in the retreat answering Erica's letter, when Foxy poked his head in and said there was a phone call for me. I looked at my watch. It was 10:30. Who would call me at 10:30?

Nan walked me over to the office.

My mother was on the line.

I said, "Mom . . . what's wrong?"

She said, "Bad news, Kath . . ."

"What is it?" I felt tears in my eyes before I even knew.

"It's Grandpa, honey . . ."

"What . . .?"

"Another stroke . . . he didn't make it this time, Kath. He died two hours ago."

"No . . ." I said and I started to cry for real. "No!"

"Yes, Kath . . . I'm sorry I have to tell you this way . . ." Her voice trailed off and my father got on. "Kath?"

I couldn't talk.

"Kath . . . are you still there?"

I made a small noise.

"Listen, Kath . . . he didn't suffer . . . he just passed out and when they got him to the hospital he was gone."

"Dead?"

"Yes . . . dead."

"Oh, Daddy . . . I didn't want him to die . . ."

"None of us did . . . but we didn't want him to suffer either."

"But he was so nice . . . so good . . ."

"I know . . ."

"What about Grandma?"

"She's okay."

"I want to talk to Mom again."

"Kath . . ." Mom said.

"I want to come home," I told her, "right away . . . I want to be with you and Grandma . . . I'll pack tonight and leave first thing in the morning."

"No, honey . . . we've talked it over and we don't want you to come home."

"But I have to . . ."

"Please listen . . . Grandpa didn't want a funeral . . . you know that . . . If you stay at camp with Jamie for another ten days Grandma will have a chance to get herself together. She wants you to do this for her."

"Is she all right . . . you're telling me the truth, aren't you?"

"She's right upstairs . . . resting . . . Uncle Howard's with her."

"I want to talk to her."

"Tomorrow."

"What about Jamie?" I asked. "Who's going to tell her?"

"Do you think you could do it?"

"I don't know."

"Please try . . . in the morning . . . and then call us."

"Okay . . . I'll try."

"Get some sleep now . . . and we'll talk tomorrow."

"Tell Grandma I'm sorry . . . will you?"

"I will."

"I loved him."

"We all did."

I told Nan what had happened and that I needed to be alone for a while. I went down to the lake and sat on my rock and I thought about Grandpa. I remembered how he'd played horsey with me when I was just a little kid and how he'd read aloud, using a different voice for each character. I thought of him sniffing around in the kitchen when Jamie and Grandma were preparing their feasts. I thought of how he'd looked after his first stroke—small and white and how he'd held out his hand to me when I visited him in the hospital. I tried to remember all the good things—the way he'd toasted Grandma in the restaurant—*To love*, he'd said, raising his glass.

And then I got the feeling I wasn't alone anymore. I turned away from the lake and saw Theo.

"Nan told me," he said. "I'm really sorry."

"He was very special . . . you just don't know . . ." I buried my face in my hands and I cried.

Theo sat on the grass, beside me. "It's hard to accept death," he said.

"He's the first person I've loved who's died."

"It's hard the first time."

"I don't know what to do," I told him.

He didn't talk until I was all cried out. Then he said, "I think you should get some rest now."

"I don't want to," I said. "I don't want to be alone."

"Maybe you could stay with Nan."

I shook my head.

"You can't sit here all night, Kat."

"I have to tell Jamie in the morning . . . how do you tell that to someone?"

"The simplest way possible."

"I'm not sure I'll be able to."

"I'll come with you if you want . . . but right now you've got to get to bed." He stood up and took my hand. "I'll walk you back to the house."

When we got there he smoothed my hair away from my face. "Goodnight, Kat . . ." he said, kissing my forehead.

I put my arms around him and pulled him close and I kissed him, the way I had in my dream, and at first he kissed me back—then he untangled himself from me and said, "Not like this . . . not with death for an excuse."

I ran to my room and started crying all over again.

It was a mistake to tell Jamie about Grandpa after breakfast. She threw up as soon as she heard. But all in all she took it better than I did and she didn't want to go home. We called Mom and Dad and I asked to talk to Grandma.

"We had forty-seven wonderful years together," she told me. "How many people can match that?"

"Not many," I said. Hearing her voice made me feel better.

Dear Michael,
    My grandfather died yesterday. He had another stroke. There's not going to be any funeral. He wanted to be cremated. I spoke to my grandmother this morning and she's okay. She's asked me to stay at camp with Jamie even though I want to go home and be with her. I won't believe this really happened until I get back and see that Grandpa's not there anymore. I'm going to miss him so much.

Love,
Kath

A few nights later Nan went into town with Kerrie and Poe but Theo stayed at camp with me, even though he had the night off too. We sat together on the steps of his cabin.

"About the other night . . ." he began.

But I told him, "I'd rather not talk about it."

"You have to, Kat."

I shook my head.

"You needed to be close to someone," he said, "and I happened to be handy." He kicked at the ground with his foot. "Sex is an antidote to death . . . did you know that?"

"No."

"Psychology Two . . . it's a very common reaction . . . somebody dies . . . you need to prove you're alive . . . and what better way is there?"

"I'm not sure that's how it was," I said.

He stood up, then went down to the lake and tossed in a few stones. I thought of that first day I'd spent with Michael.

"Look," he said, as if he could read my mind, "what about this *forever* business?"

I turned away but he walked up to me, put his hands on my shoulders and made me face him. "I want to see you again . . . after camp . . . but I won't until you get your head together."

"I need to think," I said.

July 31

Dear Kath,
    I'm really sorry about your grandfather. I liked him a lot. I wish I could be with you because it's hard for me to let you know I understand this way. Soon we'll be together. I love you and miss you.

Forever,
Michael

I couldn't answer that letter.

August 4

Dear Kath,
    I haven't heard from you. Is everything okay? Did you get my last letter? I meant what I said.

Love forever,
Michael

Dear Michael,

No, everything is not okay—but it's not your fault. I don't know how to say this but I'm going to try. I think I still love you but something's changed. I've met someone who's got me very mixed up. No, that's not exactly true. I mean it's true that I'm mixed up, but I can't blame him for that. I know this is hard for you to understand. It's hard for me, too. I made promises to you that I'm not sure I can keep. None of it has anything to do with you. It's just that I don't know what to do now. You must be thinking what a rotten person I am. Well, believe me, I'm thinking the same thing. I don't know how this happened or why. Maybe I can get over it. Do you think you can wait—because I don't want you to stop loving me. I keep remembering us and how it was. I don't want to hurt you . . . not ever . . .

I couldn't finish. Tears were stinging my eyes. Maybe there's something wrong with me. I don't know. Maybe if Michael and I had been together for the summer this never would have happened . . .

Later, when I read the letter over, I knew I could never send it. I ripped it into tiny pieces and threw them away.

CHAPTER 25

ON SATURDAY afternoon, right before activities ended, I was called to the office. Theo told the kids on the courts to rally by themselves and he walked me over, holding my hand, sensing how scared I was. Please don't let it be Grandma, I prayed . . . please don't let it be anything bad this time.

When we got there Foxy looked up from his desk and said, "Hi, Kat . . . you've got a visitor." He pointed to the bathroom but before I could ask any questions the door opened. And there was Michael.

Theo and I were standing side by side, both of us dressed in cut-off shorts, him with no shirt and me in a halter, covered with sweat, smudged with dirt and still holding hands, which we dropped immediately.

"Michael . . ." I said, going to him. "How can you be here?"

"I was worried," he said. "You didn't answer my letters so I flew in a few days early and decided to surprise you."

"Well . . . you did. You really did. Look at me . . . I'm a mess!"

"Not to me, you're not."

He hugged me hard, then I introduced him to Theo and they shook hands. "I've heard a lot about you," Theo said.

"I've heard a lot about you too," Michael told him, which wasn't exactly true because I only wrote about Theo now and then and it always had something to do with Nan.

Theo said, "I'll see you later . . . I've got to get cleaned up for supper." I wasn't sure if he'd meant that for me or for Michael. He walked out of the office.

Foxy said, "You can take a long night off, Kat."

I went back to the house, stood under a hot shower and shampooed my hair, thinking, what can I say to him—how can I explain—how can I make him understand without hating me? And now that he's here—now that I've seen him again—I don't know what I want. I let the water run off my hair into my face but it wasn't just the shampoo that made my eyes burn.

I put on the only dress I'd brought to camp. Michael was waiting for me downstairs. He took my hand and we walked to his car. He drove to a restaurant on the wharf and ordered lobsters and a bottle of white wine. We talked about Grandpa and Michael pulled two obituaries out of his pocket—one from *The New York Times* and one from *The Leader.* Erica had written it herself. Then we talked about North Carolina and lumber yards and tennis and Jamie and the weather and the food. We didn't get around to the most important thing at dinner, but I knew before long we would. And what then?

After dinner we went to Michael's room at the motel. He took off his shirt— a yellow polo with an alligator above the pocket—and tossed it onto a chair. We sat on the bed and as we kissed he unbuttoned my dress. All I had on under it was a pair of bikinis. He got out of his jeans, then his underpants. We lay side by side. Michael pushed my dress up, kissing me all the time. I couldn't really kiss him back. "I've missed you so much . . ." he said, "so much . . ." I didn't let my tongue wander into his mouth the way I used to. I just lay there, waiting. I couldn't let myself feel anything.

He put his hand inside my dress and held my breasts, squeezing one, then the other. I thought of pretending. Some people do that. They think of other things while they're making love. They pretend they are with other partners. He ran his hand up the inside of my thigh, resting it between my legs. I didn't wiggle out of my bikinis. I'm no good at pretending. And anyway, pretending isn't fair.

"Come on, Kath . . ." he whispered.

"No, wait," I said. "Wait, Michael . . ."

"I can't . . ."

I rolled away from him. "You have to." I got off the bed and crossed the room. "We've got to talk."

"I thought that's what we've been doing for the last couple of hours."

"This is different."

"You're thinking about your grandfather, aren't you?" he asked. "But he'd want us to be together . . . you don't have to feel guilty."

"That's not it."

"Then what?"

"I'm trying to explain . . . if you'll give me a chance."

"Go ahead . . . I'm listening . . ."

"Look," I told him, "it's not you. You haven't done anything . . . it's me . . . it's that . . . well . . ."

He gave me a long look, then jumped off the bed so fast he startled me. "There's another guy, isn't there?" He pulled on his underpants.

"In a way, I guess," I started to say, "but . . ."

"Did you sleep with him?"

"No . . . nothing like that."

He got into his jeans. "Then why did you have to tell me?"

"I didn't tell you . . . you guessed it . . ."

He put his shirt on inside out. "And you wanted me to, didn't you? I mean, Jesus . . . you lay there like a vegetable and I'm dumb enough to think it has to do with your grandfather . . . you must have thought I'd never catch on . . . that I'm really stupid."

"Come on, Michael . . . I don't think that and you know it. I'd have told you myself in another minute. We're supposed to be honest with each other, remember?"

"Yeah . . . I remember a lot of things . . ." He looked around for his sneakers. ". . . which is more than I can say for you."

"I haven't forgotten anything."

"No? What about forever . . . or is your memory failing at an early age?" He found his shoes and sat on the chair, putting them on but not tying the laces.

"I didn't forget . . . not about you and not about forever."

"Then what the hell's going on?"

"Please, Michael . . . don't . . ."

"Don't . . ." he shouted. "Hell, I'm not the one who's all fucked up!"

"I just don't want any lies between us."

"And you think it can be the same for us . . . now?"

"I don't know."

"Well, I'll tell you . . . it can't!" His voice broke. He went into the bathroom, slammed the door and flushed the toilet so I couldn't hear anything.

I didn't know what to do. I waited a while before I called, "Michael . . . are you okay?"

"Oh, sure . . ." he answered. "Just fine . . . just great . . ."

"Look . . . it could be that you rushed me so tonight . . . and I was too tense . . . oh, you know . . ."

"Don't give me any of that crap."

"It's not crap . . ."

He flushed the toilet again.

I buttoned my dress.

Finally he opened the bathroom door. His shirt was still inside out but he'd tied his sneakers. He walked over to the nightstand and put on his glasses. "I'm not about to share you," he said, sounding very calm. "I want it the way it was before . . . so make up your mind . . ."

I swallowed hard. "I can't make any promises . . . not now."

"That's what I thought."

"Are you saying it's over, then?"

"You said it . . . just now."

"Couldn't we sit on it a little while and see what happens?"

"You can't have it both ways."

"Then it's really over, isn't it?" Suddenly question number four popped into my mind. *Have you thought about how this relationship will end?*

"I guess so," he said.

I took off my necklace and held it out to him. My throat was too tight to talk.

"Keep it," he told me.

"I don't think I should." Our fingers touched as I handed it to him.

"What am I supposed to do with a necklace that says *Katherine?*"

"I don't know."

He picked up my pocketbook and dropped the necklace into it.

Neither one of us said anything on the drive back to camp. When we got there I opened the car door and stepped out, and as I did he leaned over and said, "You might as well know . . . I screwed my way around North Carolina . . ."

I shook my head to show I didn't believe him.

So he shouted, "I humped everything in sight!"

"Liar!" I shouted back. "You're just saying that to hurt me."

"You'll never know though . . . will you?" He took off so fast the tires shrieked and left marks on the road.

W E SAW each other one more time before we left for school. Erica and I were shopping in Hahne's and there he was, at the stationery counter.

I said, "Hi."

And he said, "Oh . . . hi."

I said, "How are you?"

And he said, "Okay . . . and you?"

"Okay . . . how's Artie?"

"He's home. I saw him yesterday."

"I'm glad."

Erica disappeared down another aisle and Michael and I stood there, looking at each other.

"Well . . ." I said, "good luck at school."

"You too."

"Thanks."

"Oh, by the way, I got that job in Vail . . ."

"Are you going to take it?"

He shrugged. "It all depends . . ."

"Michael . . ."

"Yeah?"

I wanted to tell him that I will never be sorry for loving him. That in a way I still do—that maybe I always will. I'll never regret one single thing we did together because what we had was very special. Maybe if we were ten years older it would have worked out differently. Maybe. I think it's just that I'm not ready for forever.

I hope that Michael knew what I was thinking. I hope that my eyes got the message through to him, because all I could manage to say was, "See you around . . ."

"Yeah," he answered, "see you around."

When I got home Jamie was out back with David and my mother was pruning her birthday tree.

"It looks nice," I said. "It's getting fatter."

"It needs a lot of water," she told me. "Did you get everything at Hahne's?"

"Almost everything."

"Are you all right . . . you don't look well . . ."

"I've had better days . . . but I'm okay. I think I'll take a shower before dinner."

"Go ahead . . . and Kath . . ."

"Yes?"

"Theo called."

Cynthia Voigt

1942–

O VER A MILLION people, many of them adults, have read *Homecoming*. Why? A few readers have said the book bored them. Many have called it one of the best books they ever read. Again, why? It is very long for a young adult novel: 372 pages in a popular paperback edition. Filled with details—of landscapes, water, clouds, light, houses, people's faces and actions, and the perceptions and feelings of Dicey Tillerman, the protagonist—the book's length may be both its weakness and its strength. *Homecoming* neither compromises with nor condescends to its reader. It asks for sustained attention, for earnest interest in every facet of life on the road for four children, and, above all, for a heart in the reader open to caring greatly about the full experience of two sisters and two brothers, abandoned by their parents, who wanted at any cost to stay together, to be a family, to find a home. For those readers who have entered deeply into the world of the Tillermans, who have appreciated their depth of character and their author's moving regard for them, the rewards have been, as reported over and over, great.

Born in Boston, on February 25, 1942, to Frederick and Elise (Keeney) Irving, Cynthia Voigt was the second of three daughters born not far apart (her brothers, twins, arrived thirteen years later). Raised in southern Connecticut, the setting for much of *Homecoming*, Voigt read such authors as Burnett, Tolstoy, and Shakespeare by the age of nine (as well as such popular children's series as the Cherry Ames, Black Stallion, and Nancy Drew books). She began writing poetry and short fiction while at the Dana Hall School, a boarding school for girls in Wellesley, Massachusetts.

After graduating in 1963 from Smith College for women (where she took courses in creative writing, among other courses), she did secretarial work in New York City with an ad agency. Next, she moved with her first husband to Santa Fe where she obtained her teacher certification. From 1965 to 1972 she lived in Maryland, gave birth to a daughter, Jessica, and taught English to various school grades. This experience opened her eyes to the riches of novels for youth, and Voigt started to plan and then write her own books. Divorced in 1972, she married in 1974 Walter Voigt, a teacher of Latin, Greek, and classical history at the Key School in Annapolis. Their son Peter was born in 1978, and Voigt, made chair of the English Department in 1981, continued her teaching at the Key school until 1988. Voigt's first published book, *Homecoming* (Atheneum 1981) was followed by other books in the Tillerman series: *Dicey's Song* (1982), *A Solitary Blue* (1983), *The Runner* (1985), *Come a Stranger* (1986), *Sons from Afar* (1987), and *Seventeen Against the Dealer* (1989). Voigt has written more than a dozen other young adult novels as well as fiction for children and for adults.

Homecoming planted its seed idea when Voigt observed children in a car, parked by a supermarket, who were apparently waiting for their caregiver to return. Voigt wondered what would happen if they were abandoned. The story is written from thirteen-year-old Dicey's point of view, not as "first-person" narrative but by a narrator (of "limited omniscience") who views Dicey as the only person whose thoughts and feelings are known from the inside. This view is handled with great delicacy as the narrator respects the likely range of Dicey's responses but also employs a vocabulary and deftness of observation somewhat beyond Dicey's probable grasp. The narrator, for example, uses terms such as "exuded," "macadam," "mottled," "tumultuous," and "burgeoned." Especially in some of the many fine views of natural beauty, the narrator ascends to a slightly elevated, "literary" tone: "the air was clear, clean, lucid, lying lightly upon the world that morning"; "twilight crept over the water towards them, dainty as a mouse." The effect is to nudge Dicey's sensibility, along with our own, toward a heightened sensitivity and maturity. At the same time, we as readers are encouraged to reflect upon Dicey's experience, not simply to identify with it.

What is at the heart of Dicey's experience? The two-word phrase that echoes throughout the book rings with plain yet talismanic authority: "her family." Dicey, whose outstanding trait may be her determined responsiveness to every threat ("I like to be ready"; "Dicey was the determined sort") will keep her family "together" (another signal term in the book) no matter what the price. The whole reason for their secretive mode of travel is to avoid official inspection and likely separation in foster homes. Still, the bond of their togetherness remains a believable mystery. Each child is distinct in character: Sammy muscular and kinesthetically attuned to life; Maybeth mild and musical (like Beth in *Little Women*); James all intellect and eagerness to figure things out; and Dicey (whose name suggests her capacity to take risks on their ever-chancy path) able to figure forth upon the world the fact and power of their togetherness. Though Dicey is never called their substitute mother, and though these four highly individuated children never talk of how much they love one another, their journeying struggle to stay together and to *be*, if they cannot *find*, a family home attests to their unalterable bond. The living emblem of this harmony is, moreover, their collective singing, the multi-part singing (usually old ballads marking loss and yearning for union) that echoes through the book, generally at moments of peace when the four can turn toward each other.

The songs of crossing wide water toward home, like the Stevenson poem "Home Is the Sailor," fit probable gestures of the narrative toward folk-tale journeys of seeking a home (such as "Hansel and Gretel" alluded to on the first page) and epic journeys to an old or new home (such as the *Odyssey, Aeneid, Pilgrim's Progress*, and *Adventures of Huckleberry Finn*). Of course the images of life as a journey and of all persons as lost children or lost souls seeking home are resonant in many cultures. Here, however, the "homecoming" is complicated by the point that the children, at the outset, have just *left* the only home they ever knew. If we think, however, of homecoming as return to an ancestral place or roots, we may see the children coming to the home of their mother and grandmother, to the Tillerman family home. "If it was Momma's home, it has to be ours too," says Maybeth, but their grandmother had other ideas: "My home, not yours," she declares at one point during the final, absorbing struggle Dicey wages for "her family."

Dicey's last name seems to connect both with tilling fields (as at the Crisfield family farm) and manning the tiller of a boat. Only twice in the story does Dicey touch a boat's tiller, but each time carries weight. The first is when Dicey helps to steer a sailboat across Chesapeake Bay:

Boat, waves, water and wind: through the wood she felt them working for her. She was not directing, but accompanying them, turning them to her use. She didn't work against them, but with them; and she made the boat do that too. It wasn't power she felt, guiding the tiller, but purpose. She could not stop smiling.

The second time is when Dicey enters Gram's barn:

A large shape loomed in the center. . . . She approached it with her hands behind her back. Dicey almost didn't dare name it. . . . A sailboat. . . . She touched the long arm of the tiller. . . .

Dicey is destined, of course, to sail that boat in the sequel, *Dicey's Song*. Part of her "purpose" is to guide the tiller both of sailboat and family.

The Tillerman children were raised near the ocean in Provincetown, Rhode Island. Their long walk takes them along the Connecticut shore and across wide and narrow waters. They sing of water, and water sings to them. Out on the water, Dicey finds her element: "Out here, the sun heated and the wind cooled, and the waves sang their constant song." From her deeply realized sense of elemental harmony, of water's transforming medium and nature's sustaining rhythms, Dicey shapes her vision that reconciles freedom and home. As she finds a way to "roll with the underwater currents" of her life, she accepts that she and her family will somehow always prevail, even if only to "be always a part of the changing."

The depth of Dicey's purpose and the cohesion in spirit of her family lie in poetic strata below and above the more mundane narrative line of their travels. The story works along familiar vectors of deft characterization and driving suspense. As the Tillermans first meet mainly unfriendly persons (the guard at the mall, the woman who shouts at them) and even seem unsure of their own solidarity ("nobody cares about me except Momma"), their plight seems perilous ("we're the kind that people go off from"). Much of *Homecoming*'s first part presents the now-familiar world of young adult alienation ("you can't tell who to trust"; "we're running away from everybody"; "the whole world was arranged against kids"). Gradually, the Tillermans learn the growing power of Dicey's leadership and of their determination to stay together, though an equal strengthening of forces arrayed against it sorely tests that power.

Homecoming does more than sketch in a believable world. *Homecoming* knows and shows its world in every grain and fiber—from the precise look of rain and feel of hunger in New Haven, Connecticut, to the difference between an animal dog and a human dog in Hurlock, Maryland, from the high heels and sausage curls of Eunice Logan in Bridgeport to the clean bare feet and iron gray curls of Abigail Tillerman in Crisfield, from exact habits of response in Sammy and Maybeth to particular traits of mind and heart in James and Dicey. To absorb the wealth of detail, to give in to the unhurried pace of the journey, and to care for the Tillermans' courageous path is, for a willing reader, to enter a world of memorable feeling and of sustaining beauty. The path of troubled youth, this earnest and enduring novel shows, may lead through shining portals of integrity.

HOMECOMING
Part One

CHAPTER 1

Tʜᴇ ᴡᴏᴍᴀɴ put her sad moon-face in at the window of the car. "You be good," she said. "You hear me? You little ones, mind what Dicey tells you. You hear?"

"Yes, Momma," they said.

"That's all right then." She slung her purse over her shoulder and walked away, her stride made uneven by broken sandal thongs, thin elbows showing through holes in the oversized sweater, her jeans faded and baggy. When she had disappeared into the crowd of Saturday morning shoppers entering the side doors of the mall, the three younger children leaned forward onto the front seat. Dicey sat in front. She was thirteen and she read the maps.

"Why'd we stop?" asked James. "We're not there yet. We've got food. There's no reason to stop." James was ten and wanted everything to have a reason. "Dicey?"

"I dunno. You heard everything she said, same as I did. You tell me."

"All she said was, *We gotta stop here*. She didn't say why. She never says why, you know that. Are we out of gas?"

"I didn't look." Dicey wanted some quiet for thinking. There was something odd about this whole trip. She couldn't put her finger on it, not yet. "Why don't you tell them a story?"

"What story?"

"Cripes, James, you're the one with the famous brain."

"Yeah, well I can't think of any stories right now."

"Tell them anything. Tell them Hansel and Gretel."

"I want HanselnGretel. And the witch. And the candy house with peppermint sticks," Sammy said, from the back seat. James gave in without a quarrel. It was easier to give in to Sammy than to fight him. Dicey turned around to look at them. Maybeth sat hunched in a corner, big-eyed. Dicey smiled at her and Maybeth smiled back. "Once upon a time," James began. Maybeth turned to him.

Dicey closed her eyes and leaned her head back. She put her feet on the dashboard. She was tired. She'd had to stay awake and read maps, to find roads without tolls. She'd been up since three in the morning. But Dicey couldn't go to sleep. She gnawed away at what was bothering her.

For one thing, they never took trips. Momma always said the car couldn't run more than ten miles at a stretch. And here they were in Connecticut, heading down to Bridgeport. For one thing.

But that might make sense. All her life, Dicey had been hearing about Momma's Aunt Cilla and her big house in Bridgeport that Momma had never seen, and her rich husband who died. Aunt Cilla sent Christmas cards year after year, with pictures of Baby Jesus on them and long notes inside, on paper so thin it could have been tissue paper. Only Momma could decipher the lacy handwriting with its long, tall letters all bunched together and the lines running into one another because of the long-tailed, fancy z's and f's and g's. Aunt Cilla kept in touch. So it made sense for Momma to go to her for help.

But driving off like that in the middle of the night didn't make sense. That was the second thing. Momma woke them all up and told them to pack paper bags of clothing while she made sandwiches. She got them all into the old car and headed for Bridgeport.

For a third—things had been happening, all at once. Things were always bad with them, but lately worse than ever. Momma lost her checker's job. Maybeth's teacher had wanted a meeting with Momma that Momma wouldn't go to. Maybeth would be held back another year. Momma said she didn't want to hear about it, and she had ripped up every note, without reading any of them. Maybeth didn't worry her family, but she worried her teachers. She was nine and still in the second grade. She never said much, that was the trouble, so everybody thought she was stupid. Dicey knew she wasn't. Sometimes she'd come out and say something that showed she'd been watching and listening and taking things in. Dicey knew her sister could read and do sums, but Maybeth always sat quiet around strangers. For Maybeth, everyone in the world was a stranger, except Momma and Dicey and James and Sammy.

Momma herself was the fourth thing. Lately she'd go to the store for bread and come back with a can of tuna and just put her hands over her face, sitting at the table. Sometimes she'd be gone for a couple of hours and then she wouldn't say where she had been, with her face blank as if she couldn't say. As if she didn't know. Momma didn't talk to them any more, not even to scold, or sing, or make up games the way she used to. Except Sammy. She talked to Sammy, but even then they sounded like two six-year-olds talking, not one six-year-old and his mother.

Dicey kept her feet on the dash, and her body slouched down. She looked out through the windshield, over the rows of parked cars, to where the sky hung like a bleached-out sheet over the top of the mall buildings. Bugs were spattered all over the windshield and the sky promised a heavy, hot day. Dicey slid still further down on the seat. Her skin stuck to the blue plastic seat covers.

James was describing the witch's house, listing the kinds of candy used for various parts of the building. This was the part James liked best in Hansel and Gretel, and he always did it a little differently from the time before. Picturing the almond Hershey bar roof and the shutters made of cinnamon licorice sticks, Dicey did fall asleep.

She woke covered with sweat from the hot sun pouring in through the windshield. She woke hungry. Maybeth was singing softly, one of Momma's songs, about making her love a baby with no crying.[1] "I fell asleep," Dicey said. "What time's it?"

"I dunno," James said. "You've been asleep a long time. I'm hungry."

"Where's Momma?"

"I dunno. I'm hungry."

---

1 *one of Momma's songs . . . no crying*   Most of the many versions of the very old "Riddle Song" have the speaker "give" the lover a baby who doesn't cry because it is sleeping. He also gives a cherry "with no stone," a cherry blossom.

"You're always hungry. Go ask someone what time it is, OK?"

James climbed out of the car. He crossed to the walkway and stopped a man in a business suit. "Twelve-thirty," James reported.

"But that means I slept for more than two hours," Dicey protested.

"I'm going to eat," Sammy announced from the back seat. He opened the bag of food and pulled out a sandwich before Dicey could say anything.

"What do you want me to do?" James asked, looking into Dicey's face. His narrow little face wore a worried expression. "Want me to go look for her?"

"No," Dicey said (*Now* what had Momma gone and done?) "Sammy, give Maybeth a sandwich too. Let her choose for herself. Then pass the bag up here."

When everyone had a sandwich, and James had two, Dicey reached a decision. "We have to wait here for a while more," she said. "Then we'll do something. I'm going to take a walk and see if I can find her."

"Don't you go away too," Maybeth said softly.

"I'll be right where you can see me," Dicey said. "I'll stay on the sidewalk—see?—just like a path in front of the stores. Then maybe later we can all go into the mall and look in the stores. You'd like that, wouldn't you?" Maybeth smiled and nodded her golden head.

Dicey did her best thinking when she walked. On this warm June afternoon, she walked so fast and thought so hard, she didn't even see the people going past her. If Momma went past she'd say something, so Dicey wasn't worried about that.

She was worried that Momma had wandered off. And would not come back.

("You always look for the worst," Momma had often told her. "I like to be ready," Dicey answered.)

If Momma was gone . . . But that wasn't possible. Was it? But if she was, what could they do? Ask for help, probably from a policeman. (Would he put them in homes or orphanages? Wouldn't that be just what the police or some social worker would do?) Go back to Provincetown, they could go back home. (Momma hadn't paid the rent, not for weeks, and it was almost summertime, when even their old cabin, set off alone in the dunes, could bring in a lot of money. Mr. Martinez wasn't sympathetic, not when it came to money, not when it came to giving something away for free. He'd never let them stay there to wait for Momma.) They could go on to Bridgeport. Dicey had never seen Aunt Cilla—Great-aunt Cilla. She knew the name and address, because Momma had made her write it down four times, on each paper bag, in case something happened: Mrs. Cilla Logan, 1724 Ocean Drive, Bridgeport, Connecticut. Aunt Cilla was family, the only family Dicey knew about.

The sun beat down on the parking lot and heated up the air so even in the shaded walkway Dicey was hot. The kids must be hot too, she thought, and turned to get them.

Momma must have gone away on purpose. (But she loved them, loved them all.) Why else the addresses on the bags? Why else tell them to mind Dicey? (Mothers didn't do things like going off. It was crazy. Was Momma crazy?) How did she expect Dicey to take care of them? What did she expect Dicey to do? Take them to Bridgeport, of course. (Dump it all on Dicey, that was what Momma did, she always did, because Dicey was the determined sort. "It's in your blood," Momma said, and then wouldn't explain.)

Anger welled up in Dicey, flooded her eyes with tears, and now she was swept away with the determination to get the kids to Bridgeport. Well, she'd do it somehow, if she had to.

Momma wasn't at the car when Dicey returned, so Dicey said they'd wait for her until the next morning.

"Where'll we sleep?" Sammy asked.

"Right here—and no complaints," Dicey said.

"Then Momma will come back and we'll go on tomorrow?" Sammy asked. Dicey nodded.

"Where is Momma? Why's she taking so long?" James asked.

"I dunno, James," Dicey answered. Maybeth was silent, staring.

After a few minutes, Dicey hustled them all out of the car and trailed after them as they entered the mall.

The mall was built like a fortress around a huge, two-story enclosed street, where store succeeded store, as far as you could see. At one end of the central section was a cage of live birds in a little park of plastic trees and shrubs. The floor of their cage was littered with pieces of popcorn and gum wrappers. At the other end, the builders had made a waterfall through which shone different colored lights. Outside, beyond the covered sidewalk that ran like a moat around the huge building, lay the huge, gray parking lot, a no-man's-land of empty cars.

But here inside was a fairyland of colors and sounds, crowded with people on this Saturday afternoon, artificially lit and planted. Inside was a miniature city where endless diversions from the work-day world offered everything delightful. If you had money, of course. And even without money, you could still stare and be amazed.

They spent a long time wandering through stores, looking at toys and records and pianos and birthday cards. They were drawn to restaurants that exuded the smell of spaghetti and pizza or fried chicken, bakeries with trays of golden doughnuts lined up behind glass windows, candy stores, where the countertop was crowded with large jars of jelly beans and sourballs and little foil-covered chocolates and peppermints dipped in crunchy white frosting; cheese shops (they each had two free samples), where the rich smell of aged cheeses mingled with fresh-ground coffee, and hot dog stands, where they stood back in a silent row. After this, they sat on a backless bench before the waterfall, tired and hungry. Altogether, they had eleven dollars and fifty cents, more than any one of them had ever had at one time before, even Dicey, who contributed all of her baby-sitting money, seven dollars.

They spent almost four dollars on supper at the mall, and none of them had dessert. They had hamburgers and french fries and, after Dicey thought it over, milkshakes. At that rate, they could have one more meal before they ran out of money, or maybe two more. It was still light when they returned to the car. The little ones horsed around in the back, teasing, wrestling, tickling, quarreling and laughing, while Dicey studied the map. People walked by their car, vehicles came and went, and nobody paid any attention to them. In parking lots, it's not unusual to see a car full of kids waiting.

At half-past eight, Dicey herded everybody back into the mall, to use the bathrooms they had found earlier. Later, Sammy and Maybeth fell asleep easily, curled up along the back seat. James moved up to the front with Dicey. Dicey couldn't see how they were both to sleep in the front seat, but she supposed they would manage it. James sat stiffly, gripping the wheel. James had a narrow head and sharp features, a nose that pointed out, pencil-thin eyebrows, a narrow chin. Dicey studied him in the darkening car. They were parked so far from the nearest lamppost that they were in deep shadows.

With her brothers and sister near, with the two youngest asleep in the back seat, sitting as they were in a cocoon of darkness, she should feel safe. But she didn't. Though it was standing still, the car seemed to be flying down a highway, going too fast. Even the dark inside of it was not deep enough to hide them. Faces might appear in the windows at any time, asking angry questions.

"Where's Momma gone?" James asked, looking out at the night.

"I just don't know," Dicey said. "Here's what I think, I think if she isn't back by morning we ought to go on to Bridgeport."

"On our own?"

"Yes."

"How'll we get there? You can't drive. Momma took the keys."

"We could take a bus, if we have enough money. If we don't, we'll walk."

James stared at her. Finally he spoke. "Dicey? I'm scared. I feel all jiggly in my stomach. Why doesn't Momma come back?"

"If I knew, James, I'd know what to do."

"Do you know the way?"

"To Bridgeport? I can read a map. Once we get there, we can ask directions to Aunt Cilla's house."

James nodded. "Do you think she's been killed? Or kidnapped?"

"Rich people get kidnapped; not Momma. I'm not going to think about what might have happened to her, and I don't think you should, either."

"I can't help thinking about it," James said in a small voice.

"Don't tell Sammy or Maybeth," Dicey warned.

"I wouldn't. I know better. You should know I'd know better than that."

Dicey reached out and patted him on the shoulder. "I do know," she said.

James grabbed her hand. "Dicey? Do you think Momma meant to leave us here?"

"I think Momma meant to take us to Bridgeport, but—"

"Is Momma crazy?"

Dicey turned her head to look at him.

"The kids said so, at school. And the way the teachers looked at me and loaned me their own books and talked to me. And Maybeth. Craziness can run in families."

Dicey felt a great weight settle on her shoulders. She tried to shrug it off, but it wouldn't move.

"Dicey?"

"She loves us," Dicey muttered.

"But that's the only reason I can think of that might be true."

"There's nothing wrong with Maybeth. You know that."

"It runs in families. Hereditary craziness."

"Well, you don't have to worry about it, do you? You're the smart one, with A's in school and the science projects that get entered in the state contest."

"Yeah," James said. He settled his head back on the seat.

"Listen, I'm going to go to a phone and see where the bus station is and call them up to find out how much tickets cost. You lay low."

"Why?"

Dicey decided to tell him the truth. "Just in case. I mean, three kids in a car in a parking lot at night . . . See, James, I think we've got to get to Bridgeport and I just don't know what would happen if a policeman saw us. Foster homes or something, I dunno. I don't want to risk it. But one kid . . . and I'm pretty old so it doesn't look funny."

828

"OK. That sounds OK."

"We've got to get to Bridgeport."

James thought about that, then nodded his head. "I never listened much to Momma's talk about her. What will she be like, Aunt Cilla?"

"Rich," Dicey said.

"It would be a long walk," James said.

"Long enough," Dicey agreed. She got out of the car fast.

It was full dark, an overcast night. The parking lot was nearly empty; only two cars besides theirs remained. Dicey wondered how many cars were left in the other three parking lots that spread out from the other sides of the building. It felt as empty as all of space must be. She hoped there were cars in each lot. The more cars there were, the safer their car was for them.

Dicey headed confidently for the walkway, as if she had every right to be where she was, as if she had an important errand to run, as if she knew just where she was going. She remembered a telephone at the far end of the building. It wasn't a real phone booth, but a kind of cubicle hung up on the wall, with an open shelf underneath to hold the directory. James could probably see her from the car, if he looked for her. From that distance, she would look small.

The walkway was lit up, and the store windows were lit, so she moved through patches of sharp light. At the phone, she took out the directory to look up bus companies in the yellow pages. She ran her finger down the names, selected one that sounded local and reached into her pocket for change.

She heard footsteps. A man approached her, in a uniform like a policeman's, but tan not blue, and without the badge. He took his time getting to her, as if he was sure she'd wait, sure of his own strength to hold her, even at that distance. He moved like he thought she was afraid of him, too afraid to run.

"Hey," the man said. His shirt had the word "Security" sewn onto it. Where his belly sagged, the shirt hung out over his pants. He carried a long-handled flashlight. He wore a pistol at his belt.

Dicey didn't answer, but she didn't look away.

"Hey kid," he said, as if she had shown signs of running and he needed to halt her. He was heavy, out of shape. He had a pig-person face, a coarse skin that sagged at the jowls, little blue eyes and pale eyebrows, and a fat, pushed-back nose. When he came up next to her, Dicey stepped back a pace, but kept her finger on the number in the book.

"You lost?"

"Naw. I'm making a phone call."

"Where do you live?"

"Just over there," Dicey said, pointing vaguely with her free hand.

"Go home and call from there. Run along now. If you were a girl, I'd walk you over, but—"

"Our phone's broken," Dicey said. "That's why my mom sent me here."

The guard shifted his flashlight, holding it like a club. "Phones don't break. How's a phone break?"

"We've got this dog that chews things up. Slippers, papers, you know. He chewed the phone. The cord, actually, but it's all the same—the phone's broken."

"Are you bulling me?"

"I wish I was."

"What's your name kid?"

"Danny."

She felt funny, strange, making up lies as quickly and smoothly as if she'd been doing it all her life.

The man took a piece of gum out of his pocket, unwrapped it, folded it in half and stuck it into his mouth, chewing on it a couple of times.

"Danny what?"

"Tillerman." Dicey couldn't make up a new last name, except Smith and nobody would believe that even if it was true.

"You don't look more than ten. Isn't it late to be out?"

Dicey shrugged.

The guard grew suspicious. "Who're you calling?"

"The bus company. My sisters and me are going down to Bridgeport some time soon, to stay with my aunt."

He chewed and thought. "Sometime soon wouldn't send you out after ten at night to phone. What's the rush?"

"My mom just got back from the clinic and she's gonna have her baby, any day now the doctor said, and my aunt needs to know what time the buses arrive so she can meet us on Monday. So's we can take a bus it's good for her to meet. My mom asked me to come find out so's she can call first thing in the morning, before my aunt goes to church. It's hard for my mom to get around now—you know."

"Where's your father?"

"Gone."

"Gone where?"

"Dunno. He just up and went, way back, last winter."

The guard nodded. He reached in his pocket and pulled out the pack of gum. He offered a piece to Dicey, but she shook her head.

"Can I call now, mister?"

"Sure thing," he said. "I wouldn't have bothered you except that there've been some windows broken around here. We think it's kids. I'm the security guard. I've got to be careful."

Dicey nodded. She inserted the coins and slowly dialed the numbers, hoping he'd go away. But he stood there and listened. Behind him lay the parking lot, a vast open space where occasional clumps of planted bushes spread long shadows over the ground.

An impersonal voice answered. Dicey asked about tickets to Bridgeport, how much they cost.

"From where to Bridgeport."

Dicey grabbed at a name. "Peewauket." That was what the map said. She pronounced it Pee-Walk-It. The guard, listening, narrowed his eyes.

"From Peewauket?" the voice asked, saying it Pwuk-it.

"Yeah."

"Two dollars and forty-five cents a person."

"What's the rate for children?"

"The same. The charge is for the seat. Unless you've got a child under two."

"What time do buses run?"

"Every other hour, from eight to eight."

Dicey thanked the voice and hung up the phone. She stood with her arms hanging down at her sides, waiting for the guard to leave.

He was studying her with his little piggly eyes. He held his flashlight now in one hand and slapped it into the palm of the other. "You better get back now," he said and then added, "You didn't write anything down."

"I've got a good memory."

"Yeah? I'll give you a test." His body blocked the way to the safe darkness of the parking lot. "You don't remember anything about broken windows in the mall, do you? For instance, just one for instance, at Record City."

"I don't know what you're talking about."

"I wonder about that. I really wonder, Danny. You said Danny, didn't you? Tillerman, wasn't it? You see, we figure it was probably kids did it, account of nothing's been stolen. Or maybe just one kid did it, that's what I'm thinking."

Dicey glared at him. "I said I don't know anything about that."

He put one arm out to bar her in, resting his hand against the side of the phone. "I can't think of why I should believe you. Nope, now I come to think of it, I don't think I do believe you. The only question in my mind is, what do I do with you?"

Dicey thought fast, then acted just as fast. She lifted her right knee as if to hit him in the groin where she knew it would hurt bad. He lowered his arm and stepped back, to protect himself. In that one second while he was off balance, Dicey took off. She sprinted into the darkness of the parking lot. As soon as she was in the cover of the shadows, she turned left around the corner of the building, away from their car. He thundered after her.

Dicey ran smoothly. She was used to running on beaches, where the sand gave way under your feet and each thrust of your legs was hindered. Running over asphalt was easier. Dicey pulled away from her pursuer. His steps were heavy and his breathing was heavy. He was out of shape and too fat to catch up with her. She had time to crouch behind one of the little islands of green that decorated the parking lot. She had on a dark shirt and jeans, her face was tanned and her hair brown; she was confident nothing would give her away.

He stopped by the front entrance shining his flashlight out over the parking lot, like one bright eye. Dicey watched him. He listened, but his chest was heaving so much that she was sure he couldn't hear anything but the blood pounding in his ears. She smiled to herself.

"You haven't got a chance," he called. "You better come out now, kid. You're only making it worse."

Dicey covered her mouth with her hand.

"I know you now. We'll find you out," he said. He turned quickly away from the parking lot and looked further along the front of the mall. He hunched behind the flashlight. He used the beam like a giant eye, to peer into the shadows. "There you are! I can see you!" he cried.

But he was looking the wrong way. Dicey giggled, and the sound escaped her even though she bit on her hand to stop it.

He turned back to the parking lot, listening. Then he swore. His light swooped over the dark lot, trying to search out her hiding place. "Danny? I'm gonna find you."

Dicey moved softly away on soundless sneakers through the covering shadows. He continued to call: "I'll remember your face, you hear? You hear me? Hear me?"

From halfway across the parking lot, safe in her own speed and in shadows, Dicey stopped. Her heart swelled in victory. "I hear you," she called softly back, as she ran towards the empty road and the patch of woods beyond.

Much later, when she returned to the car, James awoke briefly. "Everything's OK," Dicey whispered, curling down onto the cold seat to sleep.

ICEY awoke at the first light. A chilly dew beaded the windshield. James' body leaning against her side was the only warmth in the car. He still slept, so she didn't move, even though her stiff muscles ached to be stretched. She watched the sun rise into a cold gray sky that turned warmer and brighter as the first peach-colored beams of light grew golden, then yellow, then white. Surrounded by sleepers, Dicey sat content. The car was a cave within which they were safe. It held them together; and it protected them from outside forces, the cold, the damp, people.

At last James stirred, and his eyes opened. All four of them had the same hazel eyes, although Dicey and James had their father's dark hair, not the yellow hair their mother had passed on to Maybeth and Sammy.

James' hazel eyes looked at Dicey for a minute before he spoke. "It's still true." His voice was hollow and sad. Their momma was really gone.

Dicey nodded. Sammy surged over from the back seat. "I gotta go to the bathroom. Bad."

Dicey turned her head and a muscle protested all the way down her back. "Maybeth? You awake?"

Maybeth was awake.

"OK, then. Let's take our clothes bags and change. And the food bag too, if you'd like to eat breakfast outside." Dicey took the map of Connecticut and jammed it into her clothes bag.

It was Sunday and nothing moved in the parking lot, the same few cars stood empty. The air was clear, clean, lucid, lying lightly upon the world that morning. The children scrambled out of the car and Dicey led them across the highway to the woodsy patch where she had hidden the night before. She led them into the thickest clustering of trees, then they separated to go to the bathroom.

They ate the last peanut butter sandwiches sitting on a low stone wall, listening to a few birds and watching the sunlight fall in bright, moving patterns onto the leafy floor of the woods. The air grew warmer.

Dicey finished her sandwich and crumpled the wax paper up. She tossed it into the food bag. Then she stripped down to her underpants and put on a pair of cutoff jeans and a T-shirt. She also put on a pair of socks. The others changed too. Dicey insisted that they wear socks.

"Why?" James asked. "It's hotter with socks on."

"If we're going to walk they'll keep us from getting blisters."

"Is that true?" James demanded. "I never had a blister."

"Of course, it's true," Dicey answered. "Now let me look at the map and think, all of you."

The little ones explored the little patch of woods while Dicey studied the map. Route 1 was the road they'd been driving on. They could follow it for a while, then they'd have to go on the Turnpike to get over the Thames River, to New London. After that, they'd have to switch to a road that followed the coastline, because Route 1 turned into the Turnpike for a long while. There was the Connecticut River to cross, then Route 1 again, or maybe they could take a coastal road, to New Haven. After New Haven, the map showed a yellow patch connecting the cities, all the way down to Bridgeport. That meant heavily populated areas. But Route 1 ran the whole distance.

Dicey looked at the map. Maybe two or three days, she judged. They had about seven dollars, so they could spend about two dollars a day on food. Half what they'd spent on one meal yesterday. But that was OK, because you didn't starve in two or three days. You could get awfully hungry, but you wouldn't starve.

"James?" she called. "Maybeth. Sammy. Come here now."

They ran up and sat in a circle around the map. Dicey showed them where Bridgeport was and about where they were. Then she made her announcement: "We're going to walk down to Bridgeport." The idea was so factual in her mind that she was unprepared for questions.

"What about Momma?" Sammy asked.

"I don't know where she's got to," Dicey said.

"We can wait for her here," Sammy said. His mouth puckered up.

"No we can't," Dicey said, and she told them about the guard. "Momma will know we went on to Aunt Cilla's," Dicey said. Sammy's mouth set in a firm line. "We can't go back," Dicey said, "and we've got to go somewhere."

"That's all right," James spoke, "but why don't we take the bus?"

"Because we don't have enough money. Each ticket is two forty five. That makes nine dollars and eighty cents all together and we've only got seven dollars."

"If we hadn't had supper last night," James said.

Dicey had already been over that in her own mind. "But we did," she cut him off. "So it's no good thinking, if we didn't. We're going to have to walk. Maybeth?"

Maybeth looked up from a pile of stones she was making into a long circle around herself. "That's fine Dicey," she said. No questions, no worries in her round hazel eyes, just *that's fine.* Dicey felt like hugging her.

"How far is it?" James asked.

"I don't know for sure," Dicey said.

"How far can we walk in a day?" James asked.

"There's only one way to find out, isn't there?" Dicey asked. Only Sammy didn't smile in return.

"It'll be hard," she added. "We have to carry as little as possible. Just one bag for all of us."

They sorted through their bags. Sammy refused to speak or help, just sat cross-legged with his jaw set, picking at the dirt with his finger. Dicey took out two changes of underwear and two clean shirts for each, then she added a pair of extra socks and one comb. Toothbrushes they could get at Aunt Cilla's. There was about half a bag full when she was through. It felt light enough in the cool morning, but she knew that it would get heavier as the day went on. She inhaled the sun-sweetened air and looked around her.

"I'm not going," Sammy said. He glared up at Dicey.

"What'll you do?" James asked him, perfectly reasonably.

"Wait here for Momma. Not here exactly, in the car."

"Sammy, you've got to come with us," Dicey said. "First we're going to stash these other three bags in the car, then we start walking. So get up."

Sammy shook his head.

"Don't you understand?" Dicey asked. "Momma's not coming back, not here."

Sammy didn't answer her. Sammy's stubbornness was beyond measure. When he made his mind up, there was nothing you could do to move him. Threats didn't work. He didn't mind being spanked or slapped. Explaining was no good; it was as if he didn't even hear what you were saying to him. Even

Momma couldn't bully him into doing something. Even James couldn't trick him into it.

But you couldn't go off and leave a six-year-old alone, in the woods, in a strange place.

Dicey crouched down beside him. The other two stood silent behind her. "Sammy? Momma's not coming back here. That's what I think. I think she's forgotten."

"Momma wouldn't forget me."

"No, she wouldn't. But she's forgotten where we are I think. So if we go to Aunt Cilla's that's where she'll probably be. We have to go find her."

"I don't want to," Sammy said. But he was thinking about what she'd said.

"I don't want to, either," Dicey said. "But we have to."

"No, we don't," Sammy said.

Dicey stood up in frustration and stamped her foot on the ground. "Then I'll carry you," she announced.

"I'll kick you." He stood up.

Maybeth stepped forward. "No, you won't," she said to Sammy. "Momma said to do as Dicey tells us. You heard her."

The two stared at one another. They were both sturdy little blond figures, with round bellies. Sammy shorter than Maybeth, but almost as heavy.

"Please, Sammy," Maybeth said.

"OK," Sammy said.

At the edge of the woods, where the grassy roadside banked above the macadam, they stopped to wait for an opening in the traffic. It was Sunday morning. People were driving to church, or to the beach. The children could look back and see their own car, green and lonely, in the middle of the parking lot.

It was kind of like a home, the car, Dicey thought. She understood why Sammy wanted to stay there.

They crossed the road, but stopped at the edge of the parking lot. A blue police car was driving around the lot. It stopped by their car. A policeman got out and opened the door. He stuck his head in. He opened the glove compartment and went through the maps, as if he was looking for something. He walked all around the car. He wrote something down in a little notebook. Then he looked towards the mall.

"Walk." Dicey gave the order. She took Sammy's hand. "Don't anybody look at our car."

They walked on, away from the mall and the parking lot and the car. Dicey led them back to Route 1. There they turned south. They dumped the three grocery bags in the first trash can they saw. Nobody said a word.

Route 1 was mostly garages and small shopping centers and discount stores and quick food places. There were no green patches and few sidewalks. They walked along concrete or asphalt, or on roadside gravel. Soon their feet hurt. Dicey walked at half her normal speed, because of Sammy's short legs. Trucks roared by and the sun grew hotter. The air smelled of oil and gas and nothing else. After an hour and a half, Sammy began to complain. It was the first time any of them had spoken.

At the next McDonald's that had outside tables, Dicey let them sit down. One at a time, they went inside to the bathroom. They had to go through a room that smelled of hamburgers and french fries, and they all became aware of

834

how hungry they were. Dicey ordered two large Cokes which they all four shared.

That refreshed them. Sitting still also refreshed them.

"How much longer is it?" Sammy asked.

"A long way," Dicey said. "We'll have to sleep outside tonight."

"Good-o," Sammy said. "Can we have a fire?"

"I don't know. It depends on where we get to. This road is awful."

"That's for sure," James agreed. "Dicey? When do we get lunch?"

"I've been thinking," she answered. "If we walk for a while, then rest a little, that's the best way. So we'll walk another hour or so and I'll go into a supermarket. We should have fruit every day, and maybe some doughnuts and milk. I'll see what they have. We've got to make our money last."

It was hard to start off again. Sammy lagged back on Dicey's hand and she snapped at him time and again to keep up. He didn't like being snapped at, so he pulled back a little more, while pretending to be hurrying as fast as he could. Dicey turned her head and saw Maybeth and James trudging along. Traffic passed them, roaring and honking. They passed building after building, and an occasional vacant stretch where wispy trees looked like weeds grown up. Dicey's fingers cramped from holding onto the bag, so she moved it under her armpit, holding it by a hand across the base.

The minutes stretched out. Dicey checked the time at every garage they passed. At noon, she began looking for a place to buy lunch, and at the next shopping center they turned off the highway and walked to the front of a supermarket that was open for business on Sundays. Dicey left the little ones with James, sitting on a curb off around to one side, and entered the market alone.

The electric eye door swung open before her. Dicey headed for the produce aisle, not even bothering to take a cart. If she could spend just fifty cents for lunch, they'd have a dollar fifty for dinner. She picked out four apples, then searched for the kind of rack they have in every supermarket, a place where they offered items that were damaged or old. She found it back by the meat department. She stood before it a minute, selecting a box of doughnuts at half price. That would be three doughnuts and an apple apiece.

It cost eighty-eight cents.

They ate sitting on the curb, with the sun hot overhead. Sammy couldn't eat his third doughnut but he didn't want to give it away, so Dicey put it into their bag. They trooped by pairs into the market, first James and Sammy, then Dicey and Maybeth, to drink water from the fountain and use the toilets. The pair waiting outside watched the bag while the other pair was inside.

"Now we rest," Dicey said.

"How much longer is it?" asked Sammy.

"I told you. More than today."

"Where are we going to camp?" he asked.

"I'll tell you when we get there," she said.

"I haven't seen any place that looks good for sleeping," James said.

"I figure we'll have to get off this road to find something, otherwise the cars would keep us awake. I figure we'll turn off the road and see what we find. There was that woods this morning. That would have been all right. So there are bound to be others. Don't you think?"

"Walking is no fun," Sammy said.

"Think about the soldiers who had to march everywhere," Dicey said.

"We could pretend to be soldiers," James said. His eyes lit up. "You could be the general and I could be the major, and Sammy and Maybeth could be the army. And we could sing songs while we walk, so it would be like marching, and maybe give drill orders. We could be Revolutionary soldiers, going to Concord."

Dicey didn't see that wouldn't make any difference, they'd still be walking. She agreed to go along with it.

"Everybody who talks to you has to say sir." James elaborated the plan. "And you two have to say sir to me. We should have a drum."

When they set off again, they sang a song about marching to Pretoria and pretty Peggy-o[1] running down the stairs, letting down her golden hair. It was a song Momma sang. It even had a line in it, "What will your Momma think," because in the song pretty Peggy-o ran away with the captain.

The afternoon wore on, wore away. Each rest period got longer, each walking period got shorter. At midafternoon they lay back in an overgrown lot next to two tiny houses, the only houses they'd seen that afternoon.

"I wouldn't want to live on this road, would you?" Dicey said, to nobody in particular.

"I bet it wasn't always like this," James answered. "It might have been a nice road once. A country road. And these people might be old people, or poor people, who can't afford to move. Like us."

"Yeah, but our house was out in the dunes. We had the ocean. Our house was nicer than the ones other people wanted."

"The bathtub was in the kitchen," James reminded her. "It was small, even smaller than these houses."

"So what?"

"Nobody else would have lived in it. Only us. Some of the kids said their parents thought it should be torn down."

"What do I care what people say?" Dicey asked.

"They called it a shack," James went on.

"I liked it," Dicey said. "The ocean's better than fancy bathrooms, any day."

In the little one-story house next door, a door slammed. They turned their heads to watch as an energetic old woman came out, waving a broom over her head and shouting something.

She was shouting at them. Dicey couldn't hear the words, but she understood the expression of fierce anger on the woman's face. As she came closer, they could hear her voice. "Get out of here, get out. Go on, get! I'm counting to ten and then I'm calling the police. I've had it with you kids hanging around and taking down clean laundry and dumping it in the dirt and tossing your trash and bottles into my lawn and throwing rocks at my door and your cars and your noise. One—" She shrieked, her chin wagging up and down.

The four children sprang to their feet. "Here we go," Dicey said.

"I can't," Sammy said. "I'm tired."

"You've got to," James said.

"No, I can't."

---

1 *song . . . Peggy-o* "Marching to Pretoria" (in South Africa) is a marching song from the Boer War (1899–1902) repopularized in the 1970s by singing groups such as The Weavers; it opens with "I'm with you and you're with me and so we are all together." The old ballad of "Pretty Peggy-o" (there is a Bob Dylan version) opens with the regiment marching and the captain seeing and falling for Peggy-o.

Dicey tried to persuade him. "We're soldiers, remember?"

"No, we're not. That's just pretend. You have to carry me. Piggyback."

Dicey also was tired. "I'll just leave you here," she said.

"OK." Sammy sat down.

The old woman shrieked anew.

"I've got to carry the bag," Dicey pleaded.

His eyes regarded her calmly.

"OK, OK." She gave in. James took the paper bag. Sammy jumped up onto Dicey's back. They set off, to the accompaniment of the old woman's voice: "And don't come back. Ever!"

"We won't," Dicey muttered. "Don't worry."

The afternoon was bleached hot white, hotter and whiter for Dicey with Sammy on her back. The air tasted bad in her mouth, as she gasped for breath. The raucous cars roared past, unheeding. Dicey forced her feet to move, and her legs, and her hands to hold tight onto Sammy's feet, and her back to stay straight because in the long run that would hurt less.

It was only four when they stopped at a light, waiting for it to turn green, so they could cross the road. "Off," Dicey said to Sammy. He slid down.

There were at least three more hours of daylight. But Dicey could go no farther. She turned around and saw Maybeth's eyes big with unshed tears.

The light changed and they crossed. Dicey stopped on the other side. "OK," she said. "The next grocery store I'll get food. Then, we'll have to get off this road to find a place to sleep. It'll be hard, because it's got to be private enough."

Three faces nodded at her, eyes blank with exhaustion.

It was a small market where Dicey stopped next. Again she went in alone. She bought bananas (they were cheapest by pound) and a package of hot dogs and a loaf of bread (you could wrap a slice of bread around a hotdog, like a roll) and a half-gallon of milk (it was a little cheaper that way). It cost almost three dollars, but she couldn't think of what to do about the expense. They were running out of money.

When a narrow road ran off of Route 1, marked by a sign that said: PHILLIP'S BEACH 6 MILES, Dicey led them across the four-lane highway and onto it. She chose the road because of the Dead End sign, which, she reasoned, meant that there wouldn't be many cars on the road. It turned out to have been good thinking. The blacktop twisted through a wooded area like a river and soon the sound of the highway had faded away behind them.

The road made two sweeping curves before Dicey saw a ramshackle house with a "For Sale" sign in front of it. The house had such a small front lawn it sat almost on the road. It looked abandoned, its clapboard siding faded to splintery gray. "Stay here," Dicey said.

She walked across the front of the house, where tall grass on the short driveway told her no car had driven, not for a long time. She walked around to the back, alert to run should a face appear in the empty windows.

The yard, overgrown and long neglected, stretched out behind the house to a large tree, and beyond that to woods. The quiet stretched out, over the long grass and distant trees. An unscreened porch opened along the back of the worn house. That meant they could have some shelter.

Dicey trotted back and called her family to join her.

The yard was like a private park, without swings of course, but green, and scattered with trees. Dicey sat down in the middle of it between two brown bags, one holding clothes, one food. The others sat facing her.

"Feels good, doesn't it?" James asked, but didn't wait for an answer. "Maybe we should just stay here and live here. It wouldn't be too bad. I bet we can find a way into the house."

"That's trespassing," Dicey said severely.

"It's empty," Sammy pointed out.

"I'm just daydreaming," James said. He lay back on the long grass and spread out his arms and legs. He closed his eyes. A lazy smile floated over his narrow face. "It's a bed. Better than a bed. A cloud."

They all fell asleep. When they woke, long bars of sunlight lay across the lawn. Sammy woke up first and roused the rest of them by calling back from the far end of the yard, "Hey! It's a brook back here! James! Wake up and come see." Dicey, her back too stiff to jump up as the others had, stayed put and rolled over on her stomach to watch them run to join Sammy. They'd be OK for a while. She didn't have to worry about water. They could all swim, and they had good sense about water. Living next to the ocean, they had to.

She wondered what time it was, and how much daylight was left. The sun was still above the horizon. Maybe seven? That seemed about right. But she wanted to look at her map to see where they were before the light got bad, and they would need to gather some wood. She listened to the splashing and calls while she traced her finger down the map.

One day should put them about halfway there. She started at a dot named Madison and began moving her finger backwards. She saw no marking for Phillip's Beach.

She called to James. He had noticed a sign saying they were near Stonington. "What?" she called back. He spelled it for her.

But Stonington was almost next to Peewauket and they hadn't gone any distance at all. She called to James again. He was quite sure. Stonington. Then they had traveled maybe—Dicey measured with her finger from the legend at the bottom corner of the map—eight miles? Maybe ten. At that rate—she walked off sections of road with her fingers—it would be days. More than a week. Two weeks.

They'd have to conserve money, and food. Quickly she calculated a way to eat only half of the food tonight and the rest for their next dinner. No more Cokes, either; they'd cost sixty cents. No more small markets; they were more expensive. They could fish in Long Island Sound or the rivers (string and a hook, they'd have to buy those), and why didn't she have a knife? None of them did, not even a jackknife.

They hadn't planned this properly. They hadn't planned it at all. Dicey couldn't see how they'd make it to Bridgeport, and a cold panic settled in her stomach. There was nothing for it though, was there? Just going ahead. People might give them food. She might be able to earn food or money, somehow. She couldn't think how they'd manage it. But they would have to manage it, somehow. Then she didn't think any more about it. She couldn't.

They gathered wood, some twigs, and handfuls of dried leaves. Accustomed to building fires on the beach, they found it easy to light the small starting pile of leaves and twigs with the matches Dicey had taken from the counter in the store. They skewered hot dogs on green branches, and when they were cooked wrapped them in slices of bread. They passed the milk container around and around. Each had a half a banana for dessert, and a quarter of Sammy's doughnut. The fire, fed with the bigger branches, burned brightly in the darkening

air. Dicey wanted them to sleep on the porch. "It's more hidden away," she explained.

"I'm going to sleep by the fire where it's warm," Sammy said.

"We're not going to put any more wood on the fire," Dicey told him.

"Why not?"

"Dangerous. It could spread. It could burn you."

"I'd wake up first," Sammy said. "It couldn't burn me."

"Well I'm not going to take a chance," Dicey said.

"Well I'm going to sleep here anyway," Sammy said. He lay on his stomach
facing the fire, with the light drifting over his stubborn face.

"We've gotta sleep together," Dicey said.

"I don't see why," he answered and yawned.

"We've gotta stick together," she repeated.

"Momma didn't," he said.

"Well, we have to," Dicey said.

"Well, I don't care," he said. He refused to speak again and was soon asleep.

Maybeth curled up next to Dicey, resting her head against her sister's thigh.
"It's all right Dicey," she said. "I'm going to sing. Doesn't the fire make you feel
like singing?"

Dicey would have said no, but after Maybeth had sung through one verse of
Momma's song about the cherry that has no stone,[2] she joined in, and James did
too. The song put Maybeth to sleep.

"You tired?" Dicey asked James.

"Yeah, but not tired enough to sleep yet," he said.

"We'll let the fire go out, then carry them to the porch."

"If you say so, but I don't see why," James said.

"It'll be safer out of sight."

The fire crackled and spat. Its light made a hemisphere of warmth across
which Dicey looked to see her small sleeping brother. "James? Do you remember Sammy at the beach?"

James grinned. "I do. That was some fun, wasn't it?"

They gathered up the two sleepers and carried them back to the porch.
Sammy half-awoke, to protest, but slept again. He was too tired even to quarrel.
Poor kid, Dicey thought. James lay down with them, but Dicey returned to the
dying fire, to be sure it burned out entirely.

. . . Sammy at the beach, when he was only a year and a half old, and running.
Summer days, eight-year-old Dicey was responsible for taking them all down to
the beach. Sammy wore an old bathing suit of James' over his diapers. The first
thing he'd do, every time, was take off his clothes. Then he'd turn to see their
expressions and laugh and clap his hands together with a smile spread all over
his face. He had a little noise he made, to go with the clapping: "Aaayy." He'd
learned that from them, because they would applaud his mistakes and his learn-
ings and cry, "Yeaayy," as they clapped.

Dicey could still remember his short, plump little body, sturdy legs and
round blond head, and his tiny penis that bobbled up and down as he ran. He
had a game he played with the waves, of going down to them, then turning to
run back. Usually he tripped and fell, and the tip of the wave would wet him as

---

2 *song about the cherry that has no stone*   see Chapter 1, note 1.

it washed up the beach. He would raise a dripping face and laugh, then elevate his fanny, put his feet under him, and totter erect again. He would clap and cry, "Aaayy," and they all giggled and clapped back at him.

Sammy had been such a cheerful baby. He had been able to bring laughter even to Momma's face. They would watch him move around and explore, the way other people watched television. When had Sammy changed?

His first words were "hot" (he would grab out for anything) and "no" ("Doe," he would cry, waving his arms, his face dreadfully earnest). He emptied cupboards and drawers, he unmade his bed, he grabbed homework papers and ran away, laughing. He was naughty, but not mean. Not selfish. And he was stubborn, even then when he was a baby. Dicey had watched him learn to turn around in a circle, patiently practicing, tumbling over his own feet, falling in a heap, sitting down in surprise. It took him days to do it, but he learned.

He was no less stubborn now, no less determined to have his own way—but what had happened to that happiness? Could anyone change that much? It must have been gradual, or they would have noticed. Dicey tried to remember the last time she heard Sammy laugh, and that had been laughing at Maybeth because a doll she made out of sea grass had been washed away by a wave. But Dicey also remembered Sammy's merry eyes, and his mouth with only ten teeth, opened wide in the kind of laughter that took over his whole body and made him stumble and fall down laughing.

The fire was out. She stamped on it, just to be safe, and retired to the porch.

CHAPTER 3

DICEY woke from a dream about a big white house that faced the ocean. Aunt Cilla's house.

The sun was rising over the trees behind the brook, rising in waves of molten pink. James lay sprawled on his back. Sammy was curled up into a ball, and Maybeth had thrown one of her arms over him. Dicey tiptoed off the porch and down to the brook for a quiet wash.

Maybeth and James woke up immediately when she spoke their names. "It's still true then," James said.

Sammy moaned and turned away, burying his head under his arms. "It's time to get up, Sammy," Dicey said.

" 'Tisn't," he answered, squinching his eyes closed.

"You all go down and wash now. I'm going to check the map. We'll eat when you're ready."

Dicey tried to look at the map realistically. She considered the lines that were roads, the green patches that were parks, and the flat blue of the sound, so different from the tumultuous, gray-faced ocean, where she had grown up.

They ate half a banana apiece and finished the milk. Afterwards, prepared to set out but reluctant to leave their sanctuary, they sat in a row on the porch.

"There's a park, maybe two or three days down the road. We'll stay there for a couple of nights," Dicey offered. She showed them where it was marked on the map. Rockland State Park, with a tent to show there was camping. "It'll have a beach. We've got three dollars and eighty cents left. We're gonna have to think up some ways of getting money."

"Maybe we can find some on the ground," James suggested. "If we look."

"Anyway, we've already got dinner for tonight."

James studied the map. "Where were we yesterday?" he asked. Dicey showed him. "Only there? We'll never get to Bridgeport."

"Yes, we will. We've just got to keep moving, that's all."

"Why?" James asked.

"Because that's where Aunt Cilla is," Dicey said. "And Momma might be there too."

"What if she's not there?" James asked.

"She will be," Sammy said. "Don't say that. She knows we're going there."

"That's how much you know," James said.

Sammy attacked James. He hurtled his little body at his brother, using his feet to kick as fast as his hands pummeled. Dicey pulled him off.

"Cut that out Sammy. You hear me? Do that again and I'll whip you for sure."

Sammy stood, sullen and silent.

Maybeth had watched this. "Momma said to do what Dicey tells us," she reminded Sammy.

"Anyway, it's time to go," Dicey said. She took Sammy's hand and pulled him, none too gently, after her. In her other hand she carried the grocery bag that held their clothes and food.

It was another hot day. The white pavement of Route 1 shimmered in the heat and in the fumes from gas and oil. The noise of traffic pounded in Dicey's ears. Her feet marched beneath her, step, step, step, plodding. As repetitive, as relentless, her mind marched over the same problems: money, food, distance, where to sleep, Momma: step, step, step.

They marched, rested, marched, lunched on water and a box of stale doughnuts, walked, rested, and once again on the final lap, Dicey carried Sammy on her back.

They were more tired at the end of the second day than they had been the day before. They had spoken little all day. Once again, Dicey led them off Route 1 toward the water to find a place to sleep. This second night they sheltered in a small stand of pines, a few yards from the road, and within sight of a big brick house. They couldn't risk a fire, so they ate the hot dogs uncooked.

The one bright spot in the day had occurred in the afternoon, when Sammy spied a dime on the sidewalk outside of the supermarket where Dicey bought the doughnuts. Added to the two pennies Maybeth and James had picked up earlier, Dicey figured that they were only twenty-one cents out of pocket for food. That left her with three dollars and fifty-nine cents. Still enough.

On the morning of the third day, the sky was overcast. James awoke with his usual observation, "It's still true." He was the only one with the energy to speak. The others were too hungry and thirsty. They assembled themselves quickly to return to Route 1.

A breakfast of milk and bananas (fifty cents) gave them energy. As they came closer to New London and the busy Thames River, Route 1 became increasingly cluttered with restaurants, bars, quick food chains and shopping plazas. Sammy found a quarter on the roadside.

"I'm tired of doughnuts," Sammy said, as they approached a supermarket.

"What do you want then?" Dicey asked. "Doughnuts are cheap, that's why I get them."

"I want a hamburger and french fries. I want a Coke."

"Not possible," Dicey said. "How about peanut butter sandwiches? We could spread the peanut butter with our fingers. And if I get a whole loaf of bread, we would have them again for dinner, so that would be OK."

The younger children agreed without enthusiasm. She found a loaf of bread on sale for fifteen cents and a jar of peanut butter for seventy-one cents. That totaled eighty-six cents, for lunch and dinner. That would leave them with two dollars and forty-eight cents. Still enough?

Dicey didn't say to herself, *enough for what.* She couldn't have. Neither could she have said what amount of money would not be enough.

Before going to the checkout line, Dicey drifted by the meat counter. Hamburger was expensive. Chicken, on the other hand, wasn't too expensive, not by the pound. But would they be able to cook it? She lingered by a package of chicken wings, which, at twenty-nine cents a pound, held some interest for her. Then she wandered over to the fruit and vegetable counter and discovered potatoes. Potatoes were cheap. You could eat all of a potato. If they could just build a fire.

That night it was in an unfinished house in a new development that they slept. Dicey picked out the house, but would not let them go into it until dark. Until then, they wandered around the maze of roads in the development, watching the children at evening play. At last it was dark and Dicey let them return to the half-built house. Only the joists had been put in for walls, but the rough floors were down. They lay on plywood. Dicey gave Sammy and Maybeth the extra clothes from the bag to make pillows. Dicey lay on her back and looked up, past the roof frame to the sky. Low clouds reflected light from the ground, which blurred softly as she fell asleep.

Fear of being caught woke Dicey before dawn. She knew that construction work began early in the day. It was one thing to be seen camping in the woods; that might be kids having a night out with their parents' permission. But four kids sleeping in an unfinished house—that would be police business.

She woke them all at the first gray light. "It's still true," James said. But he seemed to expect no response.

After a skimpy breakfast of milk, they started out and soon were crossing the Thames River on a bridge that arched like a rainbow, high enough to allow huge cargo ships to travel under it. The river, seen from the height of the bridge, seemed blue and sparkling clean. They knew better, because they had seen it close up. But the look of it refreshed Dicey. It reminded her of the sea, and it reminded her that they were heading for the water.

Sammy, cranky since the time he'd gotten up, had to be dragged away from the railing of the bridge. He had to be scolded every few steps to keep up. He never answered, just kept his eyes fixed to the ground. His jaw muscles worked. Dicey ground her teeth and stamped her feet in anger, still walking.

Step, step, step, on hard concrete sidewalks that made their feet hurt. Stop at the lights, then start again. Horns blared. Engines roared.

They ate lunch sitting on a bench at a bus stop on Route 1, finishing the bread and peanut butter, scooping it out with their fingers and licking it off. It was not really enough for lunch, none of them was satisfied, but Dicey pushed them on, to get out of the city.

When the smaller, quieter Beach Road turned off of Route 1, she told them to go on it. Immediately, even though the sky hung low and heavy with moisture, even though James protested and Maybeth's eyes glistened, even though

Sammy lagged behind and her voice was hoarse with nagging at him, Dicey felt better. They were heading toward the water.

At a small supermarket, she purchased two pounds of chicken wings and four potatoes. Instead of starting right off, she pulled out her map and showed the younger children where they were. "It'll be less populated," she pointed out. "We'll be able to have a fire and—"

Rain began to fall, in fat drops that slapped the ground.

Dicey's heart sank. You couldn't build a fire outside in the rain. She hoped maybe the rain would stop, but she didn't think it would. She had never eaten a raw potato. She couldn't imagine eating uncooked chicken. She didn't know what to do.

So she urged them up and on.

"It's raining," Sammy said.

"I know that," Dicey said.

"It's like a bath," James said. "It'll clean us off."

"It's cold," Sammy said.

"Not that bad," Dicey answered.

"I'm not going anywhere," Sammy said. "And you can't make me any more. You can't."

Dicey's patience was at an end. She spoke bitterly. "No I can't. And maybe I don't even want to. You've been a pill all day. I'll tell you what, you don't think I'll leave you, but I will. I'll be glad to leave you behind."

"I know." Sammy's voice was low. "So go ahead. Go on, because nobody cares about me except Momma, and Momma will come find me but she won't find you, so go ahead."

"All right, I will. Come on you two." Dicey stood up and strode off. James followed hesitantly. Maybeth waited.

"He's been holding us up all day long," Dicey called back. "And now he's doing it again. It's not fair to the rest of us."

She saw Sammy bend over and pick up something. She saw Maybeth go back to Sammy and hold out her hand to the little boy. Sammy put his hand in hers and came trudging after.

Dicey walked ahead of the others through a rain that resolved itself into drifting mist. It was gray, cool, chilling. She clutched a grocery bag in each hand and then, as the brown paper grew sodden, under each arm. She didn't allow an afternoon rest, just kept moving ahead.

They came to marshlands, tall grasses and cattails, shadowy in the gray afternoon. They passed bigger houses that had larger lawns. Then Dicey saw water on the right, a large inland pond. You couldn't sleep near it though; it was surrounded by sharp-edged marsh grass that grew only on muddy ground. However, opposite it a sign pointed to a dirt road running off into sparse, piney woods. PUBLIC BEACH, the sign said.

Dicey turned and waited for the others to catch up with her. Rain had plastered their hair down over their foreheads. Beads of moisture hung from their eyelashes, and their faces glimmered with water.

"Let's go there," she said.

"How far is it?" James asked.

"I don't know," Dicey answered. "But it's sure to be deserted, isn't it?"

The growth of pines was not thick enough to do more than interfere with the rain, and the needle-carpeted ground underfoot was damp. Their feet squished in their sneakers.

The beach at the end of this road was backed by low, rolling dunes, which flattened out to a narrow belt of sand before giving way to the placid gray water. The four children stood atop the dunes and looked down over the empty sand. Three picnic shelters had been erected for the pleasure of the people of Noank, three open-sided structures with shingled roofs, tables, and in each shelter a stone fireplace for cooking.

"It's going to be all right here," Dicey said softly.

"Look," Sammy said, coming up beside her. "Look what I found, all together. Somebody must have had a hole in their pocket." He held out a little square hand to show Dicey a cluster of pennies and nickels.

"Good for you, Sammy," she said. Her relief at finding shelter and a way to build a fire had washed away the anger of the day. She smiled down at him. "And look what I have for us."

She pulled gently at the top of the smaller grocery bag. The bag split, but she caught it from the bottom. "Chicken. And potatoes."

All together they ran down toward the nearest shelter, through the gentle rain. Halfway down the incline, Sammy tripped. He rolled the rest of the way, not trying to stop himself. When he came to join them under the roof of the picnic shelter, he was a sight. Dicey giggled. Then she laughed helplessly. Sand coated his wet hair and face and clothing. He looked like a cookie rolled in sugar.

At first, she thought Sammy was going to get angry. Even so, she couldn't stop laughing; and James and Maybeth joined in with her. But instead, Sammy smiled, threw up his arms and executed a stiff little jig, joining in their laughter. For just that moment he was again the little boy Dicey remembered, who loved to wrestle and tickle and never asked you to stop, who made games out of everything and anything.

The younger children scoured the beach for pieces of wood. Dicey went back to the woods to get needles and dry branches of quick-burning pine.

When the fire had burned down to coals, Dicey spread the potatoes out on the grate. Then they all went back down the beach to find more driftwood. They returned with arms laden, and Dicey turned the potatoes, rinsed in rain drops, over and then arranged the chicken wings near to the edge of the fire so they wouldn't scorch. Rain padded softly on the beach and water. The fire spat when chicken fat dripped into it. The smell of cooking chicken rose faintly on the air. The four children stood watching by the stone hearth. Their skin dried, then their hair and finally their clothing.

They tried to pull one of the tables over nearer to the fire, but it was bolted to the cement floor, as was every bench, so they ate in the chilly air beyond the fire's heat. The food was hot enough to warm them from within.

They ate without speaking, first wolfing it down, then savoring each bite, chewing on the narrow bones, eating every scrap of potato. There was more than enough chicken. Everyone was stuffed full by the time the food was gone, even James.

"I wish we had some butter," Sammy said.

"Or salt," Dicey added.

"Barbecue sauce is what I want," James said, "and some corn on the cob and some watermelon for dessert or a sundae, a chocolate sundae. I wish we had that."

"I wish we had Momma," Maybeth said.

Silence fell again.

844

Dicey got up and put two fat pieces of wood on the fire. She sat down in front of it. James gathered up the bones, put them into the trash can and came to sit with her. Sammy and Maybeth followed him. The fire glowed feverishly on their faces. While the early evening light was still adequate, Dicey spread her map out.

"We'll go there tomorrow," she decided quickly, pointing her finger at a green square labeled "State Park." "It's the one I told you about. We'll rest a day there. How does that sound to you? We've been walking for four days now."

"It sounds great," James said. His finger traced the red Thruway markings down to Bridgeport. "It's a long way," he said. "Why is it all yellow there?"

"Densely populated area," Dicey said.

"Like yesterday?"

"Yeah."

"Where'll we sleep?"

"How should I know, James. We'll just have to worry about that when we come to it."

Dicey put her hand in her pocket and took out her money. She asked Sammy to give her the money he'd shown her. He didn't want to but she insisted, and he retreated to a sulky silence. They had one dollar and fifty-six cents left now. Still enough.

Dicey folded up the map and put it on top of a table. She went down to the water's edge and came back with a heavy rock, which she dried on her shirt and then placed on top of the map. Over the water, the air turned purple with twilight. She rejoined the others before the fire, sitting between Maybeth and Sammy. Maybeth moved closer to her and began to hum.

"I know an old lady who swallowed a fly," Dicey sang.

"I don't know why she swallowed a fly," James answered her.

Dicey leaned over towards Sammy. She pointed her finger at him.

"Perhaps she'll die," he sang out, his eyes lighting up.

They sang the whole song through until Dicey spoke the last line. She waited, just long enough, before saying, in a solemn voice, "She died, of course."[1]

Contentment blanketed them. Full bellies, the warm crackling fire, the rain pattering on the roof and falling gently on the sand pulled them together and held them close.

"Sometimes," Dicey remarked, "I feel as if we could do just about anything. Because we're the Tillermans."

"And I am too," Sammy said.

"You are," Dicey answered.

James spoke quietly. "Dicey? Do you know where Momma is? For sure?"

"No."

"Why did she go?"

Maybeth spoke when Dicey didn't. "Momma's gotten lost. That's what I think."

"How could she get lost?" Sammy asked. "She knew where we were."

"Not lost from us," Maybeth said.

---

1 "*She died, of course*" from swallowing a horse, in the many versions of this popular children's song.

"Lost from who?" Sammy asked.

"Not lost from anyone," Maybeth said. "Just lost. But we have Dicey to take care of us."

"Dicey's not our Momma," Sammy said.

"Lucky for us she isn't," James remarked.

Sammy turned on him. "Don't you say that. That's not nice."

"But it's true," James insisted. "Dicey wouldn't ever go off and leave us. You wouldn't, would you, Dicey?"

"No," Dicey said.

"See?" James asked Sammy.

"Momma loves me," Sammy said.

"You know what?" James asked. "We're the kind that people go off from. First our father and now Momma. I never thought of that before. Whadda you think, Dicey? Is there something wrong about us?"

"I don't know and I don't care."

"No, but think about it. We were always alone out there in our house; nobody came to see us. And Momma talked different from other people, sort of more slow. I can't think of anybody else like us in Provincetown. Did Momma ever talk to you about our father? Did she say where he went?"

"No," Dicey said.

"Do you remember him?" James insisted.

"A little."

"Tell," Maybeth said.

Dicey gathered together her few memories, like scattered marbles. "He was tall and dark-haired with hazel eyes like Momma's. We all have eyes like theirs. James reminds me of him, and I guess I do too. You little ones look more like Momma. He had a skinny head, like James and me. He had a big, loud laugh. He built our beds for us."

"I know that," James said.

"I remember him picking me up and sitting me on his shoulders. He'd call me his little only. I don't know why." This was vivid to her, the masculine voice crooning, *"the little only, only in the world, only only."* "He could pick Momma up too, when he was excited, and swing her around in a circle. They'd sing, sometimes, when just the two of them were home. But most of the time he had friends who'd come to see him, and Momma would take us to the beach—me and James and Maybeth. Once he bought Momma a bright red sweater and I saw her kiss him."

Dicey stared into the fire, trying to piece together something whole from her few vague memories.

"He knew about cars. During the summer, he'd work as a bartender. They had fights sometimes. Real fights."

"Is that why he left us?" James asked. "I don't blame him if it was, because Momma sometimes was—you know."

"Sometimes what?"

"Sometimes so drifty and moony she could drive you crazy."

"I don't think that's why. I don't know why he left. I remember when he did and Momma trying to explain something and crying." But she remembered more than that, she remembered that Momma was pregnant with Sammy and that made her father angry. Then, sometime, after he'd gone but before Sammy was born, two policemen had come into their house and didn't sit down but

846

asked Momma questions, and Momma just said, *"I don't know, I didn't know,"* over and over, when they asked her. One of them had knelt down to ask Dicey something, but Dicey wouldn't talk to him, just looked up at Momma and held her hand tight. So, the older Dicey reasoned, her father had probably broken the law. What law? How could she know? And then he'd run away.

"I never had a father," Sammy declared.

"You did so," James answered. "Everybody has a mother and father."

"Not me," Sammy said. "I never want to have one."

"Well, you can't do anything about it," James answered.

"We all have the same father," Maybeth said.

"And I don't even know his name," James said. "Dicey, do you remember his name?"

"No."

"But it wasn't Tillerman," James said. "That's Momma's own name, not his. You know what that means, don't you?"

"What?"

"We're bastards."

"I am not!" Sammy cried, leaping to his feet. "I'll fight you if you say that. I'll make your nose bleed."

"Don't you remember?" Dicey asked James, who held Sammy at arm's length.

"Remember what?"

"When Maybeth was little, still a baby. There was a big party at our house. Momma wore her yellow dress with the flounces, and she had flowers in her hair. They got married, right outside. There was a man in a blue suit, and they stood together in front of him and said the words. Don't you remember?"

James struggled to find the memory in his mind. "No, no I don't."

How could he, Dicey thought, since she was making it up.

"Somebody had a guitar and Momma danced with you and everybody watched and applauded."

"Maybe," James said. His eyebrows were squeezed together with the effort. "But why *do* we still have Momma's name and not his?"

"Because it's the best name," Dicey said. "It's a good, strong name. Momma said."

"Is that real?" Sammy asked. Dicey nodded. "And we can let the fire burn all night?"

"Sure. It'll be safe here."

Sammy lay down and put his head on his forearms. "I'm going to sleep now," he announced.

Soon Maybeth too was asleep, her head in Dicey's lap.

James emerged from a reverie. "I didn't know they got married," he said.

"You never asked."

"I won't say it again in front of Sammy, but I don't blame him for going. Now I won't mind as much."

"What does it matter?" Dicey asked.

"It wouldn't matter to you. You always knew how to fight. You'd fight anyone who said anything to you—like Sammy does. But I can't fight. And the kids—said things about Momma, bad things, about not being married."

"Nobody ever did to me."

"They wouldn't dare."

That was true, and the thought made Dicey proud.

"Would they say things to Sammy?" she asked.

"Yeah. Especially after Maybeth. I think Sammy really got it at school."

Dicey fell asleep before the fire that evening, thinking of Sammy and how he must have hated to go to school every morning and then come home, and if Momma was there she would talk to him—but less and less like a mother, and if she wasn't there he would wonder. That could change a person.

CHAPTER 4

Sometime during the night the rain stopped. They awoke to a sun already risen in the sky. They awoke to the last traces of mist floating above the water. They awoke to thirst. "It's still true," James said.

One by one, the little ones first, they went off behind the dunes to go to the bathroom. Waiting her turn, Dicey stared at the water. It seemed to stretch off endlessly, in shallow blue wavelets. The waves here didn't crash on the shore with a steady sound like muted thunder the way they did in Provincetown. Here, the little waves murmured and gurgled, like contented children. A light breeze came off the water, smelling of salt and marshlands.

They set off eagerly, to find something to drink, and in the knowledge that they would have to walk only a few miles to the park. They could wait to eat, after last night's dinner.

"What's the name of this park?" James asked.

"Rockland," Dicey said. They were walking abreast on the untraveled road.

"Why?" asked James. "What do you think? Named after somebody called Rockland? Or because the land is rocky there?"

"How should I know?" Dicey said.

"Most of the land so far has been flat down by the water," James continued. Dicey stopped listening.

They drank from a water hose at a gas station. The attendant, busy and incurious, barely looked at them, so they walked off, Dicey turning to look over her shoulder.

"He's not watching us," Maybeth said to Dicey.

"I don't want anyone to know who we are, or that we're alone."

"We're not alone," Maybeth answered.

"She means without adults," James said.

"But he let us drink the water. He didn't seem to notice us much."

"You can't tell," Dicey said. "You can't tell who to trust."

"Yes I can," Maybeth said, but not to quarrel. She said it simply, as if it was her name.

Dicey smiled at her and took her hand. "Well I can't," she said.

The road wound between occasional houses. It was hedged in low stone fences and went up hills and down hills and around hills. They saw few cars and no stores. Trees were in full leaf, the bright green of early summer. The sun warmed them, the shadows of trees cooled them. The houses they passed had smooth green lawns and long white stone driveways. Just before the road into the park, there was a small general store, its one plate glass window cluttered with signs for circuses, garage sales, and church suppers. Dicey went in alone.

Inside was a young man with red hair that sprang up all over his head in spurts. He had freckles and wore overalls over a plaid shirt. Dicey wandered over to the fresh produce counter. He came to watch her.

She picked out four potatoes and a bag of apples. She put these down on the counter by the cash register. Then, she got a half-gallon of milk. She went to the hardware shelves and looked at the knives, pans, fishing rods and nets.

"Can I get you something?" the young man asked.

"How much are hooks?" Dicey asked.

"You going fishing?"

Dicey nodded.

"There's not much to catch around here. The clamming's better. You ever been clamming?"

Dicey shook her head.

"You take one of these"—he pulled down a long-handled, claw-fingered rake—"and drag in the sandbars for clams. The clams dig in, just below the sand, and you can see their air holes. Or you can dig for them with your fingers. The rake is more efficient."

"But how much are hooks?"

"Ten cents each."

"I'll take one please. Do you have any fishing line?"

He offered her a spool, for $1.50. Dicey shook her head. They'd unravel some clothes, or something.

"What're you doing, anyway?" he asked as he rang up her purchases.

"We're going to the park, my brothers and sister and me. We're going to cook out. And fish. And maybe dig some clams."

"Your folks with you?"

"Naw. We're going on our own."

He looked at her. "Sounds like fun. Look"—he unrolled a long piece of fishing line from the spool, cut it off, wound it around three fingers to make a tight coil—"you'll need this if you want to try fishing. You got a map of the park?"

"Is there one? We just found the park on a state map and decided to come over and see what it's like."

He reached under the counter and pulled out a small folded brown map. "You'll have it pretty much to yourselves. People only come on weekends, this time of year. Take care now," he said, ringing up her money.

"We will. Thanks an awful lot."

"If you like the service, you come back." He smiled. Dicey hefted the bag and left quickly. They had twenty-six cents left. Not enough for anything.

Just inside the entrance to the park, the road turned to dirt. Woods grew up on both sides, pines and hardwoods, with none of the stone fences the children had come to expect. They walked down the entrance road a way, then Dicey led them off into the trees, out of sight of the road. They sat down and she gave each an apple to munch while she studied the map of the park.

Rockland State Park was the same general shape as the state of Connecticut, except in miniature. The two long sides of the rectangle were a little over three miles. The short sides measured a mile and a half. The eastern length ran along the Sound in an uneven line. One large cove made what the map called LONG BEACH. There was also a small cove farther north, called just BEACH. The rest of the shorefront seemed to be headlands and rocky promontories. The high land began at the southwest corner of the park and ran down to the water, which it met up with about halfway along the length of waterfront. In the southeast section the map showed marshlands, labeled BIRD SANCTUARY.

"It's four and a half square miles," James said. "Can I have another apple? Is this all there is for lunch?"

"I thought we'd fish," Dicey said.

The road they were on led through the center of the park until it branched apart about halfway through and went as two roads to the two different beaches. The map showed picnic areas and a playground off to the left, near the inland border. Opposite that, a small campground lay in the highlands on a path that branched off to the right. A larger campground, with six camping sites marked on it, was on a road that turned off the left fork. This campground lay on the headlands that overlooked the water, near the small beach. The picnic area had "Facilities" marked on it. "What do you think that means?" Dicey asked, pointing.

"Toilets I guess," James answered. "Do you think they have showers too?"

Dicey had been hoping for a kitchen house of some sort, with pans and a stove. Where you could make a soup. James didn't think that was likely.

"OK," Dicey announced. "I say we walk down to here"—she pointed to the large campground—"and put our stuff at this site." The site nearest to the water. That would feel more like their own home. "Then we better get down to the shore and see if we can find some clams. When we've solved the food problem for the day, we can take it easy."

Once again they set off, walking four abreast. Perhaps it was the deep silence around them, perhaps the salty wind off the water, perhaps the sense of forest and solitude; for whatever reason, this walk was a pleasure. Dicey's legs swung out and she began to sing the song about pretty Peggy-o. The others joined in. They sang softly, though, so that their music would contribute to the quiet, not destroy it.

They passed the playground area to their left. It had tennis courts, parking lots and a children's section with swings and slide and sandbox and seesaws.

They continued past to the campsites, which had fireplaces, water faucets and flat dirt spaces, where a tent could be pitched or a car pulled in. They put the two bags down and looked about them. It was high land, and trees soared above them. Hulking gray rocks broke through the earth at irregular intervals, some so large you could climb to the top and sit looking down. A faint path led off to the east. One behind the other, they followed the path. Soon they were standing on top of a rocky bluff, looking down to shallow water. The path ran on for several more yards along the front of the bluff, then descended to a small beach. The children ran down that section of path, slipping, tumbling, jumping from rock to rock.

The beach was nestled into the rocks, as if after hundreds of years of work the waves had succeeded in making themselves a little room to rest in. It was high tide. Dicey knew that by the closeness of the waves to the line of seaweed that etched the sand. There would be no clams for lunch—you clammed at low tide, on the sandbars. There would be no lunch then, and they'd just have to stand it. They could drink some milk.

She explained this to the others and they did not complain. Sammy took off his sneakers and waded in the water, which he reported as cold. "Not as cold as ours, but too cold for swimming." Maybeth gathered the fragments of shells that nestled among the grassy seaweed. James went off to climb the rocks at the water's edge. Dicey stood, looking out over the water.

You could see no land across the Sound, just unending, restless dark water. A couple of white sails skimmed along in the distance, bellied out in the wind. The sun toasted her face. She breathed deeply.

Somehow, they had to get some more money. Maybe she could go back to that store and offer to work. She could sweep and straighten out shelves. She could fetch things. But then she'd have to think up stories to tell the young red-headed man, and she was tired of making up stories, tired.

James called out, then came running back. "Dicey? There're mussels on the rocks." He held out two of the black, bearded mollusks. "You can eat mussels, can't you?"

"We sure can," Dicey said. "We can eat them right here."

Dicey and James pulled mussels from the rocks and washed them off in the water, while Maybeth and Sammy climbed back up the hill for twigs and larger pieces of wood. Soon they had a large mound of mussels waiting beside a crackling fire. Dicey gathered an arm-load of damp seaweed from the water's edge. When the fire was ready, she placed a layer of wet seaweed right on top of it. Steam hissed its way up through to the air. Quickly, Sammy dropped the mussels onto this bed, and Dicey covered them with another layer of seaweed.

"It's like a pie," she said.

"Or a sandwich," James said.

"It looks awful," Sammy said, poking at the fire with a stick.

"But they'll taste good," James answered. "Anything would taste good. It's funny, you know? When I thought there wasn't anything for lunch I wasn't that hungry. But now—"

"Now I'm staaaarr-ving!" Sammy shrieked. He jumped up, did two cart-wheels, which took him to the water's edge, and landed on his feet with his arms out. "And we're gonna eat!"

They ate the rich, meaty mussels for lunch. That evening, when the tide was low and the muddy sandbars appeared among puddles of water, as far as a hundred yards out, they gathered clams. These they steamed as they had the mussels. With supper, they drank part of the milk and had an apple apiece. They buried the fire in sand and tossed the shells into the water. Then they climbed back up the steep hill, to hurl apple cores into the woods and go to bed.

They slept behind the campsite rather than in it, in the woods nearer the water. Dicey couldn't relax. When she saw that the others were all soundly sleeping, she quietly got up and went back down the little beach. For a while she just sat in the sand, hearing and seeing the dark waters. Then she walked back and forth along the water's edge. The stars burned high overhead. Silence and solitude: she might have been alone in the world.

If she had been sitting when the voices approached, she would have kept still and tried to remain unnoticed. But she was standing by the water, clearly silhouetted there, and she could hear a woman's voice saying, "There's someone here."

Two figures approached, descending the hill cautiously, hand in hand.

"Hey, man," the man called.

Warily, Dicey nodded to him.

"Don't be afraid of us, we're harmless," the woman said. Only she was a girl, really. They were both young, in their teens.

"So am I," Dicey answered.

"Are your folks camping here?" the boy asked.

"No," Dicey said.

"We are," the girl said. She looked up at the boy's face. "We've been here for two weeks already, haven't we? Was that your fire we saw earlier?"

"Probably," Dicey said. "I had some clams."

"You live near here?" the boy asked.

"Yeah," Dicey said. Well, right now they were living about fifty yards from where she stood.

"We always come to this beach," the girl said. "It feels like our own private beach by now. Doesn't it Lou? It does to me. Except for weekends, it's empty. You're the first person we've met on it during the week."

Dicey made a grunting noise in answer.

"What's your name kid?" the boy asked.

"Danny."

"Danny what?"

"Don't pry, Lou. Leave him be," the girl interrupted. "I'm Edie. This is Lou, short for Louis. You'll scare him," she said to the boy.

"Naw I won't. Will I?"

"I dunno," Dicey said.

"I know about him and it's OK," Lou said. Dicey looked up in alarm. She couldn't see his face clearly. "You ran away, didn't you? It all got to be too much for you, and you cut out. Isn't that about it?"

"So what?" Dicey asked.

"So we're in the same boat, on the same trip. So you haven't got any reason to worry about us squealing on you, or laying a heavy go-home message on you. So, relax."

Dicey grinned. "OK," she said.

"Are you alone?"

"Not exactly."

"That's relaxed? I've seen people who thought they were about to be mugged more relaxed. OK, I won't bug you. We'll all enjoy the scenery together here and talk about cabbages and kings."

"I gotta go now."

"If you stick around here," the girl said, "we'll see you again. I'd like that, Danny. We're easy to find, at the small campground. We'll be there, or at the playground, or down here."

"OK," Dicey said. "Well—see you."

They had forgotten her by the time she reached the top of the bluff. They stood where she had left them, their arms around each other, facing out over the water. She returned quickly to her family and fell asleep easily.

First thing the next morning, while they munched apples and passed the milk carton around, Dicey told the others about her encounter of the night before. "I told them I was a boy," she said. "Named Danny. Can you remember that?" They nodded. "Maybeth? You too."

"But why?" James asked. "What does it matter?"

"It's safer to be a boy than a girl," Dicey said. "People leave boys alone more. Anyway, if we meet them again don't tell our last name. I told them I was a runaway. We'll all be runaways."

"Are we runaways?" Sammy asked.

"Sort of," Dicey said.

"We were running away with Momma." James worked it out. "But then Momma ran away from us. And now we're running away from everybody. But we're running to Aunt Cilla's house, and that makes it different. And Momma may be there. That's another difference. We're runaways *to*, not just runaways."

Dicey gave her orders for the morning. James and Sammy were to fish, while she and Maybeth washed out the clothes they had been wearing. They wouldn't wash the shorts, just the underwear and socks and shirts. She had seen a movie at school once, where the village women washed out the clothes and dried them in the sun.

Dicey carried the clothes down to the beach. James and Sammy came down later with some worms they had dug. The boys sat out on a rock surrounded by water, while the girls stood knee-deep in the waves, dipping and rubbing the clothing.

Half an hour later, James waded out to stand beside Dicey. "There are no fish here," he said.

"The map said there was fishing. That means there must be fish."

"Well nothing's happening."

"Go back and wait."

"Why? Sammy's there."

"Sammy is only six years old. How do you know he'll know what to do if he gets a bite?"

"He won't get a bite."

"James, do as I say," Dicey ordered sternly. He shuffled off, picking up stones and throwing them out into the water, loitering by the base of the bluff, and finally Dicey saw him climb back up by Sammy.

In another few minutes he was back where Dicey and Maybeth were spreading clothes out on the sand.

"It's no use," James said. "Why are you putting them out here? They'll get sandy."

"That'll blow away once they're dry."

"I don't want sand in my underpants," James said.

"Our job is laundry, yours is fishing," Dicey said, and she sent him back.

He was beside her again in another few minutes. "It's boring," he said.

"We've got to eat," Dicey muttered.

"We can eat mussels and clams."

"I need to know if there are fish."

"I know that already—there aren't."

"All right," she cried, exasperated. "Never mind. Just stop pestering me. I don't care what you do, but let me get on with my work."

James wandered to the far end of the beach. He scratched at the rocks with his nails. Dicey looked to be sure Sammy was all right. The little boy sat patiently, the line hanging down from his finger into the water.

When all the clothes had been soaked and scrubbed, then wrung out and laid on the sand, Dicey waded out to the rock where Sammy sat. She scrambled up to sit with him. "Hey Sammy," she said, "catch anything?"

Sammy shook his head. His mouth was set in a stubborn line. He glared down at the water.

"Tide's almost high," Dicey observed.

Sammy nodded.

"Maybe you should give up."

"Hush up, Dicey." Sammy spoke in a whisper. "Fish don't like noise."

"But James says there aren't any fish here," Dicey whispered.

"James is wrong. Look." He pulled up the string and showed Dicey a half-eaten worm still impaled on the hook. "I've lost two other worms. Something is down there eating them. I'll catch it."

Dicey left him there and went back to the beach. She started a small fire, more to let Sammy know she had faith in him than because she thought he would actually catch anything. Then she skipped stones across the water.

Maybeth stood swaying in a half-dance by the water's edge, singing to herself. James was climbing up among the big rocks that had tumbled down to the water. Dicey watched him scramble to the top of a rounded boulder and stand up. He saw her watching and waved his arm at her. Then, in a continuation of that motion, he began to fall over.

Dicey didn't see James fall, because when he lost his balance she had taken off down the beach. She didn't know what she would do when she got there, but she would be as close as possible in case there was something she could do. She climbed over the small boulders at the bottom of the pile before she looked for James. He had disappeared—except for one foot, which stuck up over a rock above her head.

Dicey found James cradled in among rocks. His eyes were closed. His face looked pale. "James?"

He didn't answer.

Was he dead? That couldn't happen, could it? And why not, considering the other things that had happened?

James' eyes fluttered and opened. He stared around, as if he couldn't see her. "Dicey? What happened?" he asked. He hunkered his body up.

So, she thought, no bones were broken.

"You fell," she said. "Are you OK?"

"I fell?"

"You were waving and you fell off the rock."

"Oh. Let me think. I don't—" he said. "My foot slipped, I remember. I shouldn't have been climbing with wet sneakers."

"But are you OK?" Maybeth was standing at the bottom of the rocks, looking up. "It's OK," Dicey yelled down. Sammy still concentrated on the water below the rock. He hadn't seen James fall. "Are you?" Dicey asked James.

"I think so." James moved his arms first, then his legs. "I guess my back's not broken," he remarked.

"How do you know?"

"If you move someone with a broken back, the spine separates and the person dies, right away," James stated. "Boy was that scary." He sat up beside Dicey. "Oooh . . ." He bent his head and covered the back of it with his hands. "Dizzy. I must have banged my head."

Dicey helped James make his slow, sliding way back down over the rocks. He leaned against her as they walked back to the fire. She sat him down beside the little blaze and examined the back of his head. "There's no blood, but it's swelling." She pushed the place. "Here."

"Don't Dicey!" James cried. "That hurts!"

Maybeth brought James a T-shirt soaked in the cool water. Dicey wrapped that around his head and told him to lie down. James said it felt better when he was sitting up and he thought he might have a concussion. Dicey asked him what that was and he told her the symptoms. "And I do have a headache," he said hopefully.

"Bad?"

"Pretty bad, not terrible," he said. "But if I fall asleep within about half an hour, you better call an ambulance. The danger is lapsing into a coma."

Sammy pushed through the shallow water to them, his hands behind his back. "Look!" he called, holding out three small fish. "I told you. Is something the matter with James?"

"I dunno," Dicey answered. "He fell off those rocks."

Sammy wasn't interested. While James sat aside, silent, they roasted the fish as they had the hotdogs and peeled off the hot meat with their fingers. James refused any. "It makes me sick to look at them," he said.

Dicey studied him while she chewed. He looked sort of bad. He was the one who knew what the symptoms of concussion were, so he could fake it. But she couldn't imagine James faking nausea and missing a meal. Should she take him to a doctor? How could she explain their situation to a doctor? How could she pay a doctor?

"Just as well you're not hungry," she commented. "There wouldn't be enough to go around."

James didn't respond.

They cleaned up the bones and innards and tossed them into the water. Dicey praised Sammy absentmindedly for catching the fish. Then they gathered up the sunbaked clothes and shook the sand from them. "Let's get back to the campsite," Dicey said. "James should be out of the sun. Don't you think, James?" James nodded, but cut the movement short, as if it hurt his head to move it.

Back at their camp they all sat around and stared at James. Dicey was pretty sure more than a half hour had passed. Sammy wandered around, tossing stones, hitting bushes with sticks. "What can we do?" he finally demanded.

"Nothing," Dicey said.

Sammy kicked at some stones. "Why not?"

"You could take them to the playground," James told Dicey. "My headache's not that bad, if I don't move. I'm sleepy. If I could just sit quiet. You know?"

"Are you sure I can leave you alone?" Dicey asked. "What about concussions, how long do they last?"

"You're supposed to keep the patient quiet for a few days, until the headaches stop," James told her.

"So we can't travel tomorrow," Dicey said.

James started to shake his head, but winced.

"Or until you get better," Dicey continued.

"That's probably right," James said. "I'm sorry."

Dicey swallowed back her crossness and impatience. "It's OK, I guess. I mean, it'll have to be, won't it."

She scratched with her finger in the dirt. How long would they have to stay? Days and days?

"I'm sorry," James repeated. "I'll tell you when it stops, Dicey."

"OK," she said. "Then we *will* go over to the playground. You won't go wandering off, will you?"

"What do you think?" James asked. He was leaning back against a rock, his face still pale.

"Then we're off. First stop the bathrooms. James, don't you have to go to the bathroom?"

"No," he said. "All I want is some quiet."

They cut through the woods rather than going down the road. Dicey picked up a long stick and swung it at tree trunks, trying to work things out. They would have to stay another day, at least. She would have to keep an eye on James too, to be sure he was all right. But she wanted to get going tomorrow morning. She broke her stick against a trunk and picked up another one. But she couldn't get going because it wouldn't be safe for James.

The longer they stayed in a place, the greater their danger of being noticed.

As they emerged from the woods, Dicey saw the boy and the girl who had talked to her on the beach. Louis and Edie. They looked at her. "Remember," she whispered to Sammy and Maybeth, "I'm Danny. Remember."

"Yes, Dicey," they said.

The boy and girl were even younger than they had seemed at night, maybe even sixteen. Edie had long heavy brown hair and protruding brown eyes. Louis had wildly curling brown hair and wore heavy-rimmed glasses, which he continually pushed up on his nose. His teeth were crooked, which made him look friendly.

"Hi Danny," Edie called.

"Hi," Dicey answered, approaching them. "Meet Maybeth and Sammy."

"I want to swing," Sammy said.

"First the bathrooms, then you can play."

"You coming with me?" Sammy asked.

"Of course," Dicey said, then remembered who she was, or, rather, who she wasn't. Sammy just grinned.

The men's bathroom was like a girls' except there were three urinals in a row, and only one toilet. The toilet had no door on it. It wasn't so bad. All the same, she hurried and her heart was beating fast when she pulled the clumsy wooden door closed behind her. Sammy was inside washing his hands and face, giggling, but Dicey didn't want to risk hanging around any longer than she had to.

Louis and Edie were standing around Maybeth when Dicey came out. She sent Maybeth and Sammy over to the swings.

"Not exactly alone," Louis said, facing Dicey.

"Not exactly."

"And there's another one," Louis said. "Maybeth shook her head when I asked was this all of you."

Dicey nodded.

"He's not with you now," Louis observed.

Dicey sighed. "He had a fall so he's resting."

"Is he all right?" Edie sounded worried. "What happened?"

"He fell," Dicey said. "He says he's OK."

"So—where you heading?" Louis asked.

"Up to Provincetown, on the Cape," Dicey told him. "We used to have some family there. It's a neat place in summer."

"Edie, want to go with them?" Louis asked. "It would be a good cover, in case your old man has the cops out."

Edie shook her head. She looked at Dicey with frightened eyes.

"Provincetown's a good place, from all I've heard," Louis went on. "Some jobs. Lots of people. Cops don't look too close."

"You said we'd stay here until our money ran out," Edie said.

"You scared?" Louis challenged her.

"You know I'm not. I proved it, didn't I?"

"Sure. You got ahold of the money just fine. You can relax, Edie—Danny here isn't about to tell anybody anything. Are you, kid?"

Dicey just stared at him.

"It's not as if she really robbed him," Louis went on explaining. He was talking to Dicey, but he was watching the effect of his words on Edie. "I mean, *I* wrote the checks. She just took the checkbook. Besides, the way I figure, I'm saving him a lot of money—on her college education. So he should be grateful to me. Right, Edie?"

"Sure."

"So—whaddayou say? Want to travel with these kids?"

Edie shook her head. "I like it here," she said.

"And if I decide I don't?" Louis asked.

Edie looked up at him. Her eyes had tears in them. "Hey," Louis said. He threw his arm around her. "Hey, I'm just kidding. Can't you take a joke?"

Dicey sidled away from them and went to the swings. Let it go on being a joke, she thought. She didn't know what to do if Louis and Edie tried to go with them.

She couldn't wait there long for worry about James, and for worry about when they'd be able to get moving again. Sammy complained, but she hurried the two little ones back to their campsite. James greeted them in his normal voice. His head, he said, was better now. His appetite, he said, was huge—he'd missed lunch, after all. They all went down to the little cove. James moved his body slowly and cautiously, as if he was afraid it might break.

They gathered clams for dinner while James watched the fire. Dicey wrapped the potatoes in seaweed, too, and baked them in the fire. They had brought the milk carton down with them. They picnicked in tired solitude, eating as much as they wanted. Behind them, the sun went quietly down. Twilight crept over the water towards them, dainty as a mouse.

CHAPTER 5

DICEY awoke to the beginning of a bright day. She lay still for a long time, looking at the cloudless sky through the branches and leaves of green maples and sycamores. The leaves made designs on the background of the sky, intricate patterns that shifted with any slightest breeze. She heard James stir and rolled over on her side to watch him.

James' eyes opened. He yawned and stretched. Dicey waited for him to say what he always said first thing, about it still being true. Then everything would be back to normal.

He caught her eye. "I wish I'd seen you going into the boys' bathroom," he said. "I thought I'd split when Sammy told me."

"I noticed," Dicey said. "How's your head?"

James rolled it back and forth. "Almost OK," he said.

"What do you mean, almost? Does it hurt?"

James thought. "It feels tender. As if it could hurt. It doesn't exactly *hurt*, but it feels like it will."

Dicey sat up. "We can't go until James is better," she said sternly to herself, "that's the most important thing." So, they'd have to wait another day.

They had only apples left in their food supply, and Dicey wanted to save them, in case. So they went down to the little beach, leaving James behind.

Three or four families already crowded the beach, and the Tillermans had to eat the apples for breakfast after all.

"It's a weekend," James explained. "That means a lot of people around, especially on the beaches, I bet."

"But what'll we do?" Dicey asked him. She answered herself. "We'll try fishing in the marsh. You'll have to stay here alone," she cautioned James.

"Danny?" a voice called from the road. "Is that you?" It was Edie, and Dicey stood up to show the girl where they were. Louis was with her. They had come, they said, to see how the third brother was and to warn the children that it was a weekend, so lots of people would be in the park.

Edie was carrying something bulky, an instrument. She sat down beside James and played on it a little, leaning it back against her shoulder. The sound was part banjo, part harp. "You like that?" she asked James.

"What is it?"

"An autoharp. Here," she said, and sang a song for them about a girl who wanted to follow her boyfriend to war.

"I like that," Maybeth said, when Edie finished.

"I do too, honey," Edie said. "Do you know any songs you'd like me to sing?" Maybeth shook her head.

Dicey looked at Edie over James' head and asked, "Do you know Pretty Peggy-o?"

"Sure," Edie said. She bent her head over the autoharp and her long hair fell down like a curtain. She strummed a couple of chords, then raised her face. But this wasn't their song. This song was about William the false lover and how he tricked pretty Peggy-o into running away with him but then murdered her. Edie sang the song quick and cruel, with sharp metallic sounds from her instrument.

"You're a good singer," James said.

"I thought we were going," Sammy said.

"Going where?" Edie asked.

"Fishing," Dicey told her.

"Do you have the hook and line?" James asked. Dicey nodded. "And worms?" She hadn't thought of bait. Count on James to think things through, Dicey thought, and forgave him for his lack of persistence the day before and for being careless and falling.

"Shall we stay with James?" Edie asked. Dicey didn't object.

When they had gotten out of earshot of the campsite, Sammy said he wasn't going fishing with them, he was going to the playground. He didn't want to walk any more ever. He didn't want to explore. He wouldn't get into any trouble. He didn't mind being left alone. And he would not go with them, no matter what Dicey said or did.

Dicey decided she could probably leave him safely at the playground. She instructed him to go back to the campsite if he got bored, not to go wandering about. "And don't talk to anyone."

"Why not?" Sammy demanded.

"Well, you know, don't talk about us."

"I wouldn't do that. I'm not stupid."

Maybeth and Dicey crossed the dirt road from the playground and found the path to the small campground. Another path led to a bluff overlooking the marshes. They walked without speaking through the warm morning. The only sounds were the rustling of the leaves above them and the rustling of their feet on the leafy ground. They emerged from the woods on top of a low bluff that marked the border of the marshlands. Below, the heavy grasses swayed. Narrow canals of water moved gently. The scene could have been painted in watercolors, so pale was the green of the grass, so subdued was the blue of the water.

They climbed down a short path and stood on the muddy ground of the lowlands. A heron looked up at them, curious but not afraid, before he flew to a more secluded spot. Clusters of gnats hovered in the air.

"It's so quiet," Dicey said. Maybeth nodded. "Think there are any fish?" Dicey asked, feeling her hunger. Maybeth didn't answer. Dicey walked out along the mudflat until she found a spot she liked. There she baited the hook with a worm from her pocket, put it into the water, and waited.

Maybeth sat beside her, braiding sea grass into long and useless lines. Dicey caught a fish almost right away, six or seven inches long. She rebaited the hook and caught another, even larger. She couldn't believe her luck. Every few minutes she could feel the tentative, jerking nibble on the end of her line.

When she had enough, Dicey took off her shirt and piled her catch into it. As long as they could fish, they wouldn't go hungry. She smiled at Maybeth. "Let's go back and eat," she said. It would be OK. They could wait for James to get well.

They stopped by the playground to pick up Sammy, but he wasn't there. Dicey hurried back to their camp. James sat alone, scratching at the ground with a stick. Fear clutched at Dicey's stomach. "Sammy?" she called. She shouldn't have left him alone for so long. "James, have you seen Sammy?"

Sammy stepped out from behind a boulder. Dicey let out a little snort of relief.

"Look." Dicey held up the fish she had caught. "Anybody hungry?"

"Why were you hiding?" Maybeth asked Sammy.

"We heard somebody coming. I didn't know who it was." His hazel eyes searched out Dicey's face: "I found something."

"What? Bring it over. We need some wood, too, to cook the fish."

Sammy went behind the boulder and came out holding a big grocery bag, which he set down before the fireplace. "Look at this," he said.

Egg salad sandwiches, a bag of potato chips, ham sandwiches, pieces of celery stuffed with peanut butter, a bag of cookies, paper plates, paper cups, paper napkins.

James sat silent, watching. "Where'd you find it?" Dicey asked.

"Left in the woods behind the bathrooms," Sammy said. "And some people gave me a hot dog too, but I ate it with them. They had catsup. I was so hungry," he said.

"Sammy," Dicey spoke slowly. "This looks like somebody's picnic."

"They might have forgotten it," Sammy said.

"That's not the truth," Dicey said.

"Is too," Sammy said.

"What's it matter?" James asked. "I mean, we're the hungry ones. They could probably go back to the store and buy food, whoever this belonged to. Or just go home and eat. We need it."

Dicey couldn't entirely disagree with him. "But it's stealing," she said.

"Just food," James argued. "Louis said it should be a natural right for everybody to have enough food."

"Does Louis know?"

"No. Sammy wasn't back."

"Sammy? Tell the truth," Dicey said.

"They left it on one of those tables. I don't know who they were. They left two bags on the table and I could see there was nobody watching, so I took one. I wanted you all to have something to eat. Dicey?" He made himself look straight at her. "I wanted to help out."

Dicey understood. "Well, you surely did that. But stealing—we don't steal." Not unless they had to, not unless they were starving, and then it should be Dicey herself to do it. Not a little boy six years old.

"I think it was pretty smart of him," James said. "And brave."

"I ran," Sammy boasted, "I ran so fast—it's hard to run with a big bag. Nobody caught me."

"I'm glad of that," Dicey said, reaching to pat his tangled hair. "I don't know how we would have gotten you back if you'd been caught."

"Would you get me back?" Sammy asked.

"Of course. What do you think?"

"I don't know," Sammy said.

"We're all together, aren't we?" Dicey asked him. "We'd just have to get you back. But it would be hard, really hard—so I'm glad."

They ate the celery and the egg salad sandwiches right away, because mayonnaise could spoil. The rest of Sammy's food they put away for some other time. Meanwhile, they built a fire and roasted Dicey's fish over it. Even James was full when they finished. They stayed put for the rest of that long, early summer afternoon, but when the evening cool came into the air and the families on the beach left, the Tillermans went down by the water. James sat quietly by the water's edge, while the rest played tag until dark. James wanted quiet; the heat had given him a headache. But he told Dicey she didn't have to worry about him.

When they returned to the campsite, Louis and Edie were waiting for them. "James? We got you something," Edie said. "It's convalescent food." She handed him a small grocery bag. It held two oranges.

"Thanks," James said. "They look terrific." He peeled an orange and ate it.

Dicey grabbed the other one from him, peeled it and split it in half. She gave half to Maybeth and half to Sammy. James looked like he wanted to say something to her, but he didn't.

"Guess what?" Edie said. Her voice came out of the dark.

"What?"

"When we went to get the oranges, there was some man in there buying food, who said his lunch had been stolen."

Louis took over the story. "He was a big, fat guy. Asking what the country was coming to when a family's picnic lunch was stolen in a public park. He said it was probably dope addicts. He was all for calling in the police. But the guy who runs the store said it was probably somebody's idea of a joke. The big guy said that if he could get his hands on the joker, he'd show him what he thought of it. He reminded me of your father, didn't he, Edie? Isn't that just what your father would do? Then, he pulls out a wallet a foot thick, crammed with bills. He peels off a couple and goes out, still complaining about his bad luck. I say good luck to whoever walked off with his lunch."

"Why?" James asked.

"Big guys like that, with thick bankrolls—they've got so much that they don't know what to do with it. And they're always the first ones to call in the police on little guys. Like us. Like you."

Dicey went over to the trash barrel to throw out the orange peels. Edie went with her. "Danny? I wondered if you kids had taken it."

"No," Dicey said. "No, how could we? We were fishing at the marsh."

"I thought—you know—if you were hungry enough," Edie said.

"We're not hungry," Dicey said. "We've got plenty."

"If you say so," Edie said.

Louis called over: "Hey Danny, James says you caught a mess of fish."

Glad at the change of subject, Dicey told him about the marsh and how easy it was to catch fish there. Louis said it was illegal to fish in the marsh, because that area was a game sanctuary. "So you better be careful. You don't want to get caught at it."

How were they supposed to eat then, Dicey asked herself. By buying food, she answered. The whole world was arranged for people who had money—for *adults* who had money. The whole world was arranged against kids. Well, she could handle it. Somehow.

"If you were caught," Louis said. "Kids have no legal rights at all. That's one reason I took off. What about you kids, Danny? How come you're on the road?"

"Huh?" Dicey asked, pretending she hadn't been listening.

"You're about the most secretive bunch I've ever met," Louis said. "I don't even know where you're from. Where are you from?"

"Nowhere special," Dicey said.

"You don't trust me." Louis' voice hovered in the darkness. He waited for an answer.

"Don't tease him, Lou."

"I don't trust anyone," Dicey said. "It's what you said, kids have no rights. So we have to be extra careful."

"Why don't kids have any rights?" James asked.

"Because parents own them," Louis answered quickly. "Your parents can beat you, steal your money, decide not to take you to a doctor—anything they want."

"There's a law I have to go to school," James said. "That's a right isn't it?"

"If you look at it that way."

"They couldn't kill me," James continued. "That would be murder."

"If it could be proved."

James thought about this. "Then the only person who will look out for me is myself."

"You got it. And you better learn how to do that, learn quick and learn good. Look out for yourself and let the rest go hang—because they're out to hang you, you can be sure of it."

"What about love?" Edie asked.

"You tell us all about it, tell us all about your old man; and then talk about love," Louis said. "Danny here knows what's what—he doesn't trust anyone."

"What do you two do when you're not camping here?" Dicey asked them.

She saw the two heads turn towards one another, and the look they exchanged.

"I can't remember," Edie said, in a soft voice. "Nothing before now seems real to me any more. Nothing before is worth remembering."

"So I guess you'd say we didn't do anything. And now we do something—we pluck the lotus.[1] Right, honey?"

Then they got up to leave. Edie said she'd come by tomorrow and bring James some soup. "That sounds good," James said. The two young people stole silently away. Dicey was listening, but she couldn't hear their footsteps. For a little while she wondered if they were hanging around, to overhear something.

The next morning, Sunday morning, dawned warm. Morning spread a haze of golden heat over the trees and boulders. James said it wasn't a good day for him to travel, it was too hot, it was too far, he just wasn't feeling right. So Dicey took her family across the top of the highland to the long beach. She guessed, correctly as it turned out, that that beach would be a favorite spot, that it would be crowded on this hot Sunday. She planned for the Tillermans to lose themselves among the mob of people there. James protested, saying he wanted to wait for Edie, but Dicey told him he had to come with them. The sun would give him a headache, he said. She said she thought he could stand that. "How much longer are we going to have to wait, anyway?" she demanded.

"I don't know. I told you, I'll say when I feel OK again," James said. "It's not my fault I'm sick."

Dicey didn't answer.

The long beach was a flat crescent that marked the edge of a shallow cove. Children straddled the water's edge and a few bolder ones were actually swimming. Towels crowded the sand, like bright pieces of confetti. On the towels lay people in bathing suits, surrounded by picnic baskets, paper bags, canvas totes, blaring radios and coolers full of ice and drinks.

The Tillermans walked about, unnoticed, and later returned to their camp for a quick lunch of ham sandwiches and potato chips, which finished off the food in Sammy's bag. Then they went back to the long beach. Dicey was glad not to meet Louis and Edie.

Later in the afternoon, when the beach began to empty, Dicey looked around, to gather James and Maybeth and Sammy together. They could leave tomorrow: she had watched James and she was pretty sure he was fine. Sammy was nowhere to be seen. Neither James nor Maybeth had spoken with him, not for a long time.

Dicey looked out over the low sandbars, not yet covered by the incoming tide. She knew she didn't have to worry about Sammy having drowned. She decided to wait a few minutes. He might, after all, just have slipped away to the woods to pee.

Sure enough, within ten minutes, she saw his sturdy body trudging down the path from the highlands. They went to meet him. As they walked along the cliff that fronted the Sound, Dicey asked him where he'd been. Sammy turned his head to look behind them, and then announced with swelling pride, "I got us another one."

"Another what?"

"Another food bag. It was all the leftovers a family couldn't finish. I watched them eat, then pack up the bag. Then they all went down to rinse off sand in the water, and I grabbed the bag, and I ran. It's at the camp."

"Good job, Sammy," James said.

---

1 *"pluck the lotus"*   take drugs. In Homer's *Odyssey* (Bk. 9), those venturing to the land of Lotus-eaters lose all desire to return home.

"No it isn't," Dicey said. She knelt down in front of him. "And Sammy knows that," she said, looking straight in his eyes. His mouth grew stubborn and he would not look at her. "Stealing isn't right," Dicey said.

"Not even if you're hungry?" Sammy argued.

"You're not hungry, not really hungry," Dicey said. "We never stole things. Tillermans don't have to steal."

"Well, maybe we should," James interrupted. "It's like a war, isn't it? Us against everyone so we can get to Bridgeport. Otherwise, you'd have asked a policeman for help right away, when there was one hanging around our car. Remember?" Dicey remembered. "So if it's like that, what's wrong with Sammy taking somebody's leftovers?"

"And more too." Sammy grinned up at James. "There's money. A wallet."

"Oh no." Dicey groaned. "Sammy, you can't take a wallet the way you can food. You just can't get away with that. We have to take it back."

"No!" Sammy cried.

"Yes," Dicey said firmly. "And on the double. I'm right, aren't I, James?"

Even James agreed.

Dicey sent James and Maybeth on to gather mussels and clams and firewood. She hurried Sammy back to the camp, and he showed her where he'd hidden the stolen bag. "But they're gone home," he protested. "Their towel was gone when I came back."

Worse and worse. Dicey thought hard and fast. She took the wallet out of the bag—it was a man's wallet, brown leather—and grabbing Sammy by the hand, ran back to the long beach. She wanted to make him give it back himself and apologize. But she couldn't, not at the risk.

The long beach was empty under shadows that fell from the cliff out toward the water. But Dicey heard voices coming from somewhere. She stood halfway down the steep hill and made Sammy point to where he had found the bag. She lifted her arm and hurled the wallet at that spot. She didn't wait to see where it landed, but turned and ran back laboriously, uphill. She didn't wait for Sammy.

Safe again under cover of the trees, Sammy spoke sullenly, "It had almost twenty dollars in it."

Dicey didn't answer. She couldn't think of what to say. Finally she said, "You have got to do what I tell you. What *I* tell you, not anybody else."

Sammy nodded as if he understood.

They had a fire on the beach that evening and steamed mussels so hot and chewy they burned their tongues on the tawny meat. The smell of damp seaweed, richer than the smell of wet wood, rose with the smoke from the fire and lingered over their faces. They were salty after the day at the water. They were together. The light dimmed, melting into early twilight. Stars became visible, pinpricks of light on the silken sky. If they hadn't known better, they would have thought that when the fire died out and the moon shone bright in the sky, they could turn and trudge slowly up over familiar dunes to their own home. Where Momma would look up absentmindedly to greet them and ask if they had a good day.

Sammy dug wells for the water to run into. Maybeth arranged shells and water-polished stones into an intricate design. James skimmed rocks out over the water.

"We'll get going again tomorrow," Dicey said.

"I'm not sure, Dicey," James protested. "I don't think I should, yet." Dicey looked at him. He looked like he meant what he said.

"We could stay here," Sammy added. "It's OK here."

Dicey sat down beside the fire, her knees drawn up under her chin, poking at the blaze with a long stick and thinking. They had to go. But what if James wasn't better and it hurt him? Should she wait another day?

Louis and Edie came up silently behind her and surprised her with some chords on the autoharp. Dicey welcomed the music, but she had wanted to avoid any further contact with them.

Edie played and sang. Louis took Maybeth by the hand and led her in a galloping dance up and down the beach. Sammy trailed them in a jig of his own, while James clapped time energetically. Dicey watched him—some brother! He was no more sick than she was. They were leaving tomorrow, if she had to drag them out of the park herself.

The dance over, they all relaxed around the fire while Edie continued to sing. Louis held Maybeth at his side. Sammy curled up against Dicey. The sky turned black velvet. Deep satin water curled against the sand.

"We gotta go to sleep," Dicey said, after a while.

"Don't go yet, Danny," Edie said, putting down the autoharp. "I don't know when I've had a better time."

Dicey stood up and dusted sand from her fanny. Barely awake, Sammy waited beside her. James stayed seated, his eyes reproachful.

"Maybeth?" Dicey spoke gently.

Maybeth came over.

"Goodnight, honey," Louis said.

Maybeth didn't answer.

"Doesn't she ever say anything?" Louis asked.

"Sure. Sometimes."

"Wait," Edie said, "we'll come with you."

They climbed up the steep path. At the top of the hill, Dicey turned to say good night, so they would go away, but Louis was holding onto Edie's arm and pointing.

Between the trees they saw a bright light that rhythmically flashed red.

"What is it?" Dicey asked.

"Shut up," Louis said. "Move it, Edie." They slipped away into the darkness.

He was right, Dicey realized. It was a police car going along the road that ran past the campsites. She pulled her family into the bushes and told them to lie down.

"It's a police car," James said quietly. "Heading towards our camp."

"I dumped the bag in the trash," Dicey said.

"That's where they'll look," James said.

"I can't see what's going on," Dicey said. "Lie quiet, everyone."

Darkness rustled through the trees. Faintly, the water lapped at the shore. Dicey thought. "We're going up to the woods past the playground, long way around," she said. "We'll sleep there and get out of here at first morning."

"But . . ." James said.

Dicey felt Maybeth's small hand on her arm. "But nothing. You've been fine all day today, and you know it. Don't lie to me, not any more. I won't believe you."

They waited a long time, then began a silent journey across the dark park. They made a wide circle around their campsite. They saw nothing, they heard nothing, only the insects and the noise of the wind. Dicey was sure of her direction, but she wasn't sure just where they were until she saw the pale emptiness of the playground before her. They were so tired by then that they just stumbled into the woods beyond and slept there, slept uneasily.

THEY awoke in pale, predawn light. Mist lay in patches along the ground. The wet, black trunks of trees loomed out of the foggy half-light.

"It's still true," James said.

It was damp, and their clothes were sodden. Dicey wanted to get moving, right away. "Ready? Let's use the bathrooms and then get out of here."

Dawn gilded the sky when they arrived at the park entrance. The fear, which had stayed beside them since the night before, retreated at the promise of a bright morning. The sound of a car motor gave Dicey warning. She drew her family back into the cover of the woods.

"Why?" James asked.

"Shut *up*," Dicey whispered fiercely. "Lie down. Lie still. I don't know, but I don't want anyone to see us."

A police car, followed by another police car, roared along the main road. Both slowed down and turned onto the dirt road. They stopped, just inside the gates, one behind the other. Leaving his motor running, a policeman got out of the first car and walked to the car behind him. His leather boots shone. He wore dark glasses and had a gun at his belt. He leaned into the window by the driver's side and unfolded a map that Dicey recognized as a map of the park. He pointed to parts of it.

Dicey strained to hear what they were saying, but the motors drowned out their voices.

The policeman nodded his head sharply, twice, and strode back to his own car. The flashing lights on top of the police cars were turned on. The two cars roared down the road.

"Let's go," Dicey said. "On the double."

They hurried down the road.

"What was it?" James said.

"I don't know," Dicey said.

"Were they after us?" James asked.

"I don't know," Dicey said.

"Or Louis and Edie," James said. "Nobody knew we were there. People knew Louis and Edie were there—they bought food every day."

"We bought food, too."

"Only that first day. How long ago was that?"

"I can't remember. But we did take those lunches."

"Sammy did that. That wasn't us."

Dicey thought aloud: "Louis and Edie are runaways; and maybe more. Anyway, we got away in time."

The children walked the long morning through. Conditioned by the earlier hard days, refreshed by the days at the park, both their muscles and spirits were in good tone. The road wound south, following the coastline.

At noon, they rested by the roadside, leaning back against one of the low stone fences that ran all over this countryside.

"I'm hungry," James said. "Aren't you?"

"We haven't passed a store of any kind since that one town," Dicey answered. "And no garages." Then, like a black fist punching at her head, she realized: "My map! I don't even know where we are. How could I forget the map?"

"Should we turn around?" James asked. "That town had a grocery store."

865

"That was miles back. Besides, you might as well know. We don't have much left, just twenty-six cents. I was going to try to get work at the store by the park, but I was afraid we'd get too conspicuous when we had to stay. So now, we have to keep going," Dicey said. "We've seen railroad tracks, right? That means there must be more towns ahead."

"But what'll we eat?" James asked.

"For now, nothing. We can't. We'll just have to keep going and see what happens. If I had my map I could see where the water is and we could fish or clam or find mussels. I need a map."

They were tired when they stood up, more tired than when they had sat down. The folds of the hills and the symmetry of the trees no longer had the power to please them. They walked more slowly than before. The feeling that she did not know what to expect, or when to expect it, made Dicey jumpy.

In an hour they passed a sign marking the limits of a town called Sound View. Dicey felt better. Soon the houses sat closer together and the welcome sight of a small shopping center placed on two sides of a crossroads greeted them. Shopping centers on this road were quite different from those on Route 1. These were small, fancier. They had no huge parking lots, just a row of parking places right up against the sidewalk. Instead of large glass windows plastered with sale signs, these stores had small panes, like house windows. Everything looked clean.

Dicey instructed the other three to stay where they were, while she crossed the street and went into a Texaco station. The office was occupied by one man with a fringe of hair around his shiny head who was dozing with his feet up on a wooden desk. He snored gently.

His head snapped up as Dicey closed the door loudly. His blue eyes studied her. "What can I do for you?"

"I'd like a map, please, of Connecticut."

He pulled out a drawer and selected one map from several file folders there. "That'll be fifty cents," he said.

"But I don't have any money," Dicey said.

"OK," he said. He replaced the map in its folder, closed the drawer, and once again raised his feet to the top of the desk.

"I have to have a map," Dicey said.

"Paper's expensive, kid. We don't give maps away anymore."

"Who does?"

"Nobody." He closed his eyes.

Dicey stood, chewing on her lip. Money, money, money, always money. And she couldn't get into the drawer, find the right map, and get out the door—not fast enough to make it. "Mister?" He opened his eyes. "I really want one."

"That's tough on you, kid. I'm sorry."

"Could I work for one?"

"Doing what?"

"I dunno. There must be some chore—something. Sweeping? Washing? Are the bathrooms clean?"

"My bathrooms are always sparkling clean," he said. He closed his eyes. Dicey stood thinking. She wondered if she could pump gas. It didn't look hard.

"That window," the man said. The office had a large plate glass window that faced the pumps and the street. "That window needs washing. You know how to use a squeegee?"

866

Dicey didn't even know what a squeegee was. "Sure," she said.

"I didn't get to it yesterday," the man said, lumbering into a closet and pulling out a bucket, a rag and a longarmed utensil that had to be the squeegee.

"Inside and out," he said.

Dicey nodded.

"All over and no streaks."

Dicey nodded. If he would just let her get to work on it.

"I'll give you the map and a quarter too. Fair enough?"

"Fair enough."

Dicey began on the outside of the window. She signaled her family to wait, and James nodded to show he understood. The three sat down on the curb, facing Dicey. Dicey filled the bucket, added some cleanser from a bottle she found in it, sloshed the mixture together and began spreading the water over the window. She did it in four sections, wetting the glass, pulling the squeegee down over it firmly, squeezing the squeegee out and repeating the last step twice. The glass gleamed. Then she went inside and did the same thing. A few cars pulled in, were filled with gas and pulled out again. Every time a car pulled away, Dicey looked to be sure her three were still there.

She finished, emptied the bucket and put it away. The man came in from filling a car. He handed her a map and a quarter. "You got an audience," he said.

"They're friends."

"Well, that's a good job. If you're around later in the week . . ."

"Thanks, mister," Dicey said.

"You earned it, kid."

Dicey returned to her family, the map in her hand.

"You were hours," James said. "I'm so hungry my stomach hurts."

"The map cost fifty cents. So I washed the window. And got a quarter more, too."

"Let's eat," Sammy said.

They walked along the front of the first section of the shopping center, but saw only a restaurant and some clothing stores. They crossed the street and entered a small market filled with specialty goods, delicatessen items and huge, fancy pieces of fruit. Everything on the shelves cost much more than fifty-one cents. The people who worked in the store stared at the Tillermans suspiciously, and Dicey hurried them out.

"But I want to eat," Sammy protested. "I'll die if I don't eat."

Dicey pulled him firmly out the door. "Hush up—you don't know what people will think," she whispered fiercely in his ear. He snuffled. "Look, you won't die, not in one day. Starvation takes days and days."

A small bakery, its windows filled with decorated cakes and layered pastries, also did business in the second part of the shopping center. Dicey would not let them linger before its windows, but she sat them down around her on the curb just beyond it. Their knees were up against the fenders of a blue Cadillac car.

"OK," Dicey said. "We've got to do this smart."

"What do you mean?" asked James.

"We've only got fifty-one cents, and around here that won't buy enough to feed even one of us. This is a ritzy area. So—we want some bakery goods, because they're cheapest, but not at full price. So, we've got to make that lady in there feel like giving us a lot for our money. So, we've got to make her feel sorry for us."

James nodded.

867

"I'll go tell her how hungry I am," Sammy volunteered.

"No, you won't and have her start asking questions," Dicey snapped. Her own stomach was taut within her, and she was having trouble thinking well. "It's got to be done right. By the right person."

"That's you, isn't it?" James asked.

"Not this time, it isn't. Nor you, either. People don't take to us the right way, not at first. Maybeth would be the best one."

Maybeth shook her head mutely. Her eyes grew large and stared at Dicey.

"I know." Dicey sighed. "So Sammy, it's you, after all."

"Good-o," Sammy said. "Give me the money."

"Not so fast. If she asks you, we're staying in a summer house—where?" Dicey searched her memory. "In Old Lyme and we went for a walk and got lost, and there's nobody home this afternoon to come and get us in the car. Do you have that? And we're hungry. That's if she asks you."

"What if she doesn't?"

"We need enough food for lunch, and maybe dinner too. For just fifty-one cents. So, unless she'll give you two loaves of bread for it, sort of hem and haw. Say that's too much. Tell her you've only got fifty-one cents. Ask her if this road will get us home. Be sort of brave and pitiful—do you know what I mean, Sammy? But whatever happens, don't tell her the truth."

He stood up, his legs sturdy and brown. He held out a dirty hand and Dicey put the money into it.

"Can you do it, Sammy?"

"I think so."

"If there isn't anything right to buy, don't buy anything."

"Dicey—I wouldn't do that."

No, he wouldn't. He couldn't be bullied. They watched him walk back and enter the bakery. They heard a jingle of bells as he closed the door. Then they waited, silently, for what seemed a very long time, studying the front of the big car. It stared back at them with empty glass eyes.

Dicey turned her head when she heard the shop door open with a jingling of bells. Sammy had a big white bakery bag in one hand. In the other, he had a round cookie, half-eaten. His eyes met Dicey's, and he quickly shoved the rest of the cookie into his mouth.

"It's fine," he said. "She had a couple of old doughnuts, and some rolls and a pie she said she couldn't sell after two days. She said she'd call our parents, but I said I didn't remember the phone number yet. She said maybe my sister would. So I said I'd come out and you'd tell her the number after you ate because I thought you were pretty hungry."

Dicey jumped to her feet. "Good job, Sammy," she said. "OK, let's go. I don't want to answer any more questions. We'll eat as soon as we're out of sight. We'll eat the pie—that's worth waiting a little for, isn't it?"

They trotted down the road and around a corner. Once out of sight, they sat on the grass to eat, breaking pieces of apple pie off with their fingers and licking all the sticky sauce before seizing another portion. They were too hungry to save much for later; only two rolls were left in the white bag when Dicey put her map into it, rolled down the top and led them off again. She wanted to get to a creek she had seen on the map. It was a little creek that fed into the mouth of the Connecticut River. There might be fish in it. If they could fish, then they could have breakfast before they set off. And then it wouldn't matter so much that they didn't have any money left.

They didn't have one penny left. Not one.

Four miles up the road they found the creek. Dicey led them up it, away from the road. The creek was bordered with marshes, but if you went a few yards back the land got higher, drier. It was posted: NO HUNTING. NO FISHING. NO TRESPASSING. But Dicey figured they had to risk it. A small fire, during daylight hours, that wouldn't be so noticeable.

She set James and Sammy fishing down by the creek and took Maybeth back into the trees. Together they cleared a place for a fire, surrounded it with stones, then gathered twigs, leaves and branches to burn, plus four slim branches on which they could thread the fish.

For all their patient waiting, James and Sammy caught only two fish. Those Dicey cooked and shared out among them, dividing the fish and the two rolls evenly. It was not enough, not after a long day's walk. They went silent to sleep hungry, thirsty, huddled together to keep warm.

Dicey woke early and dug up some worms. She took the line and hook down to the creek and tried to catch breakfast. Fish bit in the early morning. The fishing boats that went out from Provincetown went out when night was still dark, so that as the first light brought out the fish they could be there, nets down and ready.

Birds awoke. The sun came up, although you couldn't see it through overhanging clouds. The water gurgled quietly at Dicey's feet. She heard an occasional motorboat, far off, but no cars, However, off in the distance there was a humming that suggested heavy traffic. This noise was carried to her on a steady wind that blew from off the land toward the water.

No fish were biting. Not that morning.

She heard James calling her with panic in his voice. Slowly, she trudged back to her family.

"I told you," Sammy said to James, "because the fishing line was gone."

"I didn't know where you were," James said. "Why didn't you say where you were going?"

"You were asleep," Dicey answered. "Let's get going."

She did not say a word about eating. They did not ask her.

It was a subdued four children who returned to the road, walked over the little bridge and through a tiny town that didn't even have its own post office building, just one section of the laundromat set aside, and a small flag flying outside to show where the post office was. They walked through town and on, north along the Connecticut River. It was a low, gray morning, and Dicey thought someday soon it would rain again. She didn't have the energy to care about that. Besides, you could drink rain water.

By noon they were at the town of Old Lyme and Dicey had identified the distant rumble, grown louder now, as the Thruway. Here Route 1 joined the Thruway to cross over the broad river.

They passed the Thruway entry ramp and a shopping center backed up against the fast-moving highway. They cut through to the river's bank and stood looking up at the soaring metal that arched overhead to cross the river.

When Dicey realized that the bridge had no walkway, she stared out over the river. It wasn't terribly broad, but it was much too broad to swim.

If there was no walkway, they would have to walk on the shoulder of the road. Someone would be sure to stop them. If they didn't get run over first. Cars and trucks and buses—all hurtled over that bridge as if the devil himself was chasing them. He'd be chasing them from both directions then, Dicey thought; he'd catch you either way.

Dicey crouched down where she was and buried her face in her knees. How could they go forward from here? The railroad bridge downriver had a draw section in the middle that was raised up. They couldn't cross there. It was miles and miles upriver to the next bridge. Tears welled up behind her eyes and the corners of her mouth pulled sharply down.

You don't cry, she said to herself. Not you.

No money, no food, no way to go forward. The silence behind her told her that her brothers and sister were watching her. Maybe they could just all stay right here, without moving, and turn to stone. Then her troubles would be over. Dicey opened her eyes and studied the darkness of her knees. There was nothing more she could do. Nothing. She had done her best and that wasn't good enough and now she could do no more. That was it. The end.

She sighed and felt a small hand on her shoulder. Maybeth. She raised her head to look out again over the impassable river.

At least it was beautiful, with curves and marshy islands and yachts moored along the edges. At least the trees that crowded up to the top of the bluff spread above them, proud and growing. A solitary, two-masted sailboat glided down the river. She watched it.

"Dicey?" Maybeth said.

"Yes, Maybeth," Dicey answered, without turning her head. Food, money, a way forward. They had none.

"What's wrong?"

Dicey almost laughed. "What's right?" is what she wanted to answer, but she didn't speak. Never mind even the way forward, you couldn't get food without money and they had none.

Kids just couldn't earn money.

She had, yesterday. She had earned seventy-five cents in all. They could eat something today, if they had seventy-five cents now.

James asked, "What're we going to do now?"

"I dunno," Dicey said. So, she had to earn some money. But how? There was that shopping center. It had a big parking lot, and a supermarket. She pictured it carefully, and then pictured herself coming out of the market with two big bags filled with groceries after she had earned money somehow, bags filled with fruit and meat and breads and cans of vegetables and a pan to cook things in. And a can opener; it would be just her luck to forget the can opener.

In her daydream, the Dicey she saw walking out of the store with enough food for her family to eat for days, with her eyes smiling and a big grin stretching her mouth, that Dicey tripped and fell. The food scattered over the ground. The wheels of cars squashed the scattered oranges and bananas. A dog took the package of hamburger meat and ran away with it. The people around went off on their own ways, carrying their own heavy bags of groceries.

Was this how Momma felt? Was this why Momma ran away? Because she couldn't think of anything more to do and couldn't stand any more to try to take care of her children.

Dicey said to herself, I'm getting as bad as Momma. Imagination doesn't do any good. Then her mind flicked back to the people with their heavy bags.

That might be a way. If they all did it. They might earn something.

She turned her head and ran fingers through her hair. They had to look neat or people wouldn't trust them.

"Listen, we could carry groceries to cars out at that shopping center. People might tip us."

"I wanna eat first," Sammy said.

"We can't." Dicey looked directly into his eyes. "We don't have any money left, you know that. All we've got is this," and she held up the white bag in which she was carrying the map.

"Dicey? Is everything going to be all right?" Sammy looked scared.

Momma always reassured him, whenever he was afraid or when she'd been angry because she was worried. She always smiled at him and said everything would be all right. And somehow, it always was.

"I hope so," Dicey said. "I don't know. I'll tell you, if this idea works and we can earn some money, the first thing we'll do is buy a quart of milk. The first forty cents we have. That's a promise."

The fear stayed in Sammy's eyes, but he nodded his head. Dicey tidied them up as much as possible. She had not noticed how dirty they'd become. Maybeth's hair was a tangled mess. James' hands were brown with dirt and his nails were black. And Sammy looked—well, Sammy looked like most six-year-olds, so that might be OK. Her own shorts were grubby, her knees stained. But her dark hair was always kept short, so that must look all right. They'd just have to try it.

They stationed themselves outside of the entrance doors, where the paper bags were brought out on a rolling belt. Maybeth looked at the people going in and coming out and shook her head. Her eyes grew big and pleading. Dicey understood. She told Maybeth to sit quiet at the far end of the belt. Maybeth nodded and ran off. She sat and didn't move a muscle, just sat quiet as if she was waiting for her mother to come and take her home.

Most of the people the children approached said, "No, thank you," with a kind of puzzled look, as if it didn't often happen that someone offered to carry their grocery bags. Some, especially ladies with babies, said yes, with a grateful look, and Dicey or James or Sammy would carry huge bags out to large station wagons. The people would give them a dime, or some nickels.

True to her word, at the end of the first half hour, when they had forty cents, Dicey went inside to buy milk. They ducked around the corner of the building to drink it, careful not to spill any as they poured it into their mouths. The cool, rich liquid flowed down Dicey's throat and settled gently into her stomach. The carton was soon empty. "Better?" Dicey asked. "Better," they said. They returned to work.

All afternoon, they went up to strangers and asked if they would like their bags carried. Dicey learned to read the no or yes in people's eyes before they spoke it. Then, unexpectedly, the way good luck always surprises you, they had a piece of very good luck.

An older man and a little girl came out of the busy store. They stood waiting for their bags to emerge from the metal doors the rolling belt used.

Soon, the man moved to a group of three grocery bags. The little girl followed beside him. Dicey stepped up to him. "Would you like me to carry those bags?"

He looked at her. "We've got three," he said, hesitantly.

"My brother could help too," Dicey said.

"The car is across the lot, by the restaurant," he said.

"That's OK," Dicey said.

The man waited, hesitating, maybe, for her to say more, to ask again. When she didn't speak, that seemed to decide him and his eyes twinkled at her. "Why not?" he said to the little girl. "Sure," he said to Dicey, "you and your brother carry these two and I'll take the third. Be careful—there are some eggs in there somewhere. We did remember the eggs, didn't we?"

"Grandpa," the girl spoke. "You keep asking that. Stop teasing. But Grandpa"—her mouth puffed out sulky—"you said I could carry a bag. You said."

He shook his head at her.

"You said I could because I'm your helper on the boat."

He ignored her. Dicey ignored her too, not liking the tone of her voice.

"But I'm bigger than him," the little girl said, pointing at Sammy. "It's not fair."

They walked along to the car. Sammy carried the lightest bag. The man and Dicey carried the heavier ones. The little girl trailed behind. To make conversation, the man asked Dicey how much money they'd earned, and she answered that they hadn't counted yet. He asked her how long they'd been at it, and when she answered all afternoon he said she must like working. Dicey shrugged. He said he himself liked working, but he wasn't sure if he didn't like it because it made vacations so much more pleasant.

Dicey smiled at this.

"So you're all in it together," the man said. He didn't say it nosy, but as if he was really interested in her, Dicey.

Dicey wanted to answer, even though she couldn't tell him the truth. "We want to get our mother a birthday present," she said.

"What are you thinking of getting her?" he asked.

"She needs a new ironing board," Dicey answered.

"Your father can help you out a little, can't he?" the man said. Dicey knew that was the way this man would do it.

"He's not around," she said shortly.

The man just nodded. They had come to the car. It had Pennsylvania license plates. He held the rear door open while she and Sammy put the bags inside, and then he put his own bag in. He put his hand in his pocket. "How many of you are there?" he asked.

"Four," Dicey said.

He took out his wallet and gave her two dollars. "That's fifty cents apiece," he said.

"It's too much," Dicey protested. She would not take the money.

He folded the bills and stuffed them into the pocket of her shorts. "That, young lady, is for me to say. Now scoot and good luck to you."

Dicey thanked him and turned to go. By then the little girl had scuffed her way to the car. She stood up on tiptoe to speak to her grandfather, and he lifted her firmly into the car, talking to her. He was angry with her, but not rough. He plunked her down on the seat by the steering wheel.

Dicey and Sammy walked away. "How much did he give you?" Sammy asked, as soon as they were out of earshot.

Before Dicey could answer, she heard running feet and the little girl caught at her arm. "Wait," she said. She held another dollar in her hand. "This is from me. Grandpa said I could. Mommy gave it to me to buy her a present while I was spending the night with Grandpa on his boat, but everything was plastic and she doesn't like plastic. She says it's tack-y. She'd rather I wrote her a story anyway, and I can do that tonight. Grandpa got me some paper and crayons. To keep me quiet, that's what he said. I talk a lot. Maybe I'll write her a poem because it would be shorter. So this is for your mother. I'm sorry I got mad."

872

Dicey hesitated again. "Take it, Dicey," Sammy urged.

"Please take it." The little girl smiled. "I want you to, I do. Mommy likes my poems better than anything. She says they're stu-pendous. I'm going to write one about fish, because we're on a boat. Do you think fish would eat flowers, because I write good poems about flowers."

Dicey could barely keep up with the stream of chatter. She grinned and took the dollar. "OK," she said.

"OK," the little girl said, happily. She ran back to the car where her grandfather waited. Dicey did not watch them drive away.

"Good-o," was all Sammy said, but he strutted back to his post by the supermarket doors.

Shortly thereafter, Dicey called James and Sammy together, and they counted the money they had earned. Five dollars and fifteen cents. Dicey nodded in satisfaction.

"That sure is an improvement," she said. She went inside to buy peanut butter, bread and milk. She still had $3.85 when she came out. "And we got a good heavy bag, too."

They returned to their wooded post looking over the winding river. They could see only two houses, one on each side of where they sat, both built low to the bluff and designed to face out over the river, both with those walls of windows that modern houses have. After they had eaten, Dicey explained the next difficulty, that they couldn't walk over the river on the bridge. She no longer felt so hopeless, so she could say it without sounding defeated. They had earned money, more than enough money. And that grandfather and the little girl— Dicey didn't know why they had made her feel better, but they had, even though it wasn't going to get any easier.

The Tillermans sat in a row and looked down at the river flowing below. They looked at boats moored close together in marinas, or alone at the ends of long docks. Overhead, cars roared across the bridge.

"We could go upriver to the next bridge," James suggested.

"That'll take days," Dicey said. "But we may have to." She was reluctant to journey away from the water; she didn't want to go far from the Sound that was part of the sea.

"Does the river get narrow enough to swim across?"

"I don't know," Dicey said. "It would be too risky to light a fire, wouldn't it? I feel like sitting by a fire, don't you?"

Maybeth snuggled up to Dicey and hummed tunelessly. Dicey sat looking down, not thinking or worrying, just feeling her full belly and her sister's warm body, watching the river water shimmer in the sun, remembering with pride how James and Sammy had worked that afternoon, wondering which boat the little girl was sleeping on and thinking those two would remember her. A melody came into her head and she sang one of Momma's old, sad songs: " 'The water is wide,[1] I cannot get o'er. Neither have I wings to fly.' "

The melody floated out over the water, where she could not go.

" 'Give me a boat that will carry two, and two shall row—my love and I' "

The setting sun floated gold along the surface of the water.

" 'Oh, love is bonny, when it is young,' " Dicey sang. " 'Fair as a flower when first it is new.' " Then she stopped. "We'll take a boat," she said.

"Good-o," Sammy said.

---

1 *"The water is wide"* popular ballad published in 1724.

"Where will we get a boat?" asked James. "Where could we get a boat?"

"All these yachts have little dinghys that go with them, so the people on the yachts can get to and from their moorings. We'll take a dinghy and row across and tie it up on the other side. I can row and so can you, James, if you have to."

She led them down the steep bluff, clutching the bag with leftover food and the map in it. She wouldn't leave food or map behind again, no matter what. They slid most of the way down, bouncing on their fannies, giggling. At the foot of the bluff, Dicey turned upriver.

They found a rowboat easily. It was upended on the ground beside a long private dock. Waiting for dark, they watched nervously up the cliff to the house whose lighted windows looked out over the silver river. When full dark came, somebody inside pulled curtains over the long windows. Then the children stealthily approached the boat.

James and Dicey carried it down to the end of the dock and lowered it noiselessly into the water. James held the painter while Dicey went back for the bag, the oars and Maybeth and Sammy. They were accustomed to boats, so they had no trouble getting into it quietly. Maybeth sat at the bow, Sammy and James at the stern. Dicey shipped the oars and James pushed off. The boat slid away from the dock.

Dicey lifted the oars in their oarlocks. She brought them down cautiously, unused to their weight. The oars bit into the black water, and the boat shot ahead.

The current carried them slightly downstream, Dicey's strokes carried them across, the smooth water eased their passage. The bridge loomed overhead. Its thick pilings caused races in the current that could trap a small boat and maybe even overturn it. Dicey knew enough to simply follow these races until the boat had floated out of their currents. Then she dipped the oars once again into the dark water.

The sky was dark. The air was dark, so dark that they could barely make out one another's faces. The water flowed beneath them, black and bottomless.

Dicey headed for the lights on the opposite shore. It felt good to stretch the muscles in her back and arms, to lean back and then pull forward against the oars.

In the middle of the river the current eased and the boat shot straight ahead. Then, as they drew near the far bank, Dicey felt the twists and eddies begin again. James directed her to a huge marina, where lights burned in many buildings and in many of the small windows of the boats tied in rows along the docks. It looked sort of like a parking lot. They pulled up beside a boat that was dark and empty and tied their dinghy to its stern. Dicey thought that if she left the dinghy there it had a good chance of being claimed or returned.

They had come down close to the mouth of the river, where its water flowed out into the Sound. A small town lay on the low flatlands. They walked through the town, to the south. It was late at night and the houses became fewer, but there was no safe place to sleep. After an hour, they were all tired, and Sammy stumbled with every third step. Dicey put him on her back, giving James the grocery bag. She discovered then how much the long rowing had strained her muscles.

They came to a church, shining white in the dark air. Behind it stretched a graveyard, with groves of trees planted among the tombstones. Dicey turned toward the graveyard.

Behind her, James drew in his breath.

At the first grove of trees, Dicey put Sammy down. He was already half-asleep and just curled up on the ground. Maybeth settled beside him without a word. Dicey stood, looking at James.

"It's a graveyard, Dicey," James said.

"I know," she said. "But we're tired."

"Do you believe in ghosts?" he asked.

"I never saw one," Dicey said. She sat down. James sat down right beside her. They could see tombstones placed in neat rows. Some of them had statues on top.

"I don't believe in ghosts," James said. "All the same, I don't like this place. It's—too quiet."

Indeed, the silence was thick as fog around them. The silence vibrated, as if with things beneath it struggling to break through.

Dicey yawned. She was too tired, the day had been too long, for this kind of worrying. "I like quiet."

James flicked his eyes over the cemetery. "We're all gonna die, you know."

Dicey nodded. "Not for a long time."

"Do you think Momma's dead?"

"I don't know. How could I know that?"

"No matter what, we're all gonna die," James remarked. "So it doesn't matter what we do, does it?"

Dicey was thinking about other things, about maps and food. She didn't answer.

"Unless there's a Hell, to punish us. But I don't think there is. I really don't. Or Heaven. Or anything. Dicey?"

"Yeah?"

"You know the only thing you can count on, the only thing that's always true? It's the speed of light. Louis told me Einstein figured it out, 186,000 miles per second. That's the only sure thing. Everything else—changes. I was proud of Sammy for stealing that food, you know that?"

"So was I."

"You were? You sure didn't act it. You acted angry."

"Well, I was."

"Dicey, that doesn't make sense."

"I'm too tired to make sense, James. I'm trying to figure out where we might be. We came way downriver. We'll have sandwiches for breakfast and finish the food up so we don't have to carry it." Dicey let her mind wander. "Did you ever hear Momma talk about her father, James? We had to have a grandfather, you know."

"Probably dead," James said. "Everyone's either dead or dying."

"Go to *sleep*, James," Dicey said. "That's just morbid. You'll make yourself crazy."

"I make myself crazy when I try to figure out a good reason why I *shouldn't* be morbid," James answered.

"Go to sleep."

"I don't want to."

"Go to sleep, please. You're not crazy. You'll never be crazy. You're just too smart for your own good. Anyone who stays awake so he can have ideas like that . . . well, he ought to be going to sleep."

Dicey lay back and closed her eyes resolutely. James sighed.

MORNING broke low and cloudy. Streaks of smudged gray clouds covered the sky. "It's still true," James said. He looked out over the cemetery, where bright green grass contrasted with the faded marble of tombstones, and the tombstones reflected the cold gray of the sky.

"Some of them are bent over," James said. "I bet they're old, really old. Hundreds of years."

After breakfast, while Dicey gathered together their litter and packed it into the paper bag to be discarded at the first trash can they saw, the little ones explored the graveyard. Sammy stayed with James, because James could read everything to him. Maybeth wandered among the rows, studying the statues of angels and lambs.

Dicey had a sudden fear that she had forgotten where they were going, so she recited Aunt Cilla's address to herself. Mrs. Cilla Logan, 1724 Ocean Drive, Bridgeport. She ought to make the others memorize it. She made a mental note to do that as they walked that day.

Then she studied the map and admitted that they would have to go back to Route 1. She didn't want to. She wanted to stay among big houses and tall trees, on the shore road that would keep her close to the water. But Route 1 was the shorter way, even though it looped up north of the Thruway before entering New Haven.

Those decisions made, Dicey went to call the others. They had to start. They had money and a map, their stomachs were full—it wasn't a bad way to begin.

While she waited for Maybeth to return and for James and Sammy to finish working out what was written on a cracked stone that slanted back towards the earth, Dicey looked at the gravestones about her. She read an inscription: *Home is the hunter, home from the hill, and the sailor home from the sea.*[1]

What a thing to put on a grave.

As if to say that being dead was home. Home, for Dicey, was their house in Provincetown, where the wind made the boards creak in a way that was almost music. Or Aunt Cilla's big white house that faced over the water, the one she had dreamed about. Being dead wasn't going home, was it? Unless—and she remembered what James had been saying last night—home was the place where you finally stayed, forever and ever. Then this person *was* home, and nobody would be truly home until he, or she, died. It was an awful thought.

Only living people had homes. That was the difference.

(If Momma was dead, where was her grave? What was written on it? Nobody would even know her name or who she was or when she was born.)

If you took home to mean where you rested content and never wanted to go anywhere else, then Dicey had never had a home. The ocean always made her restless; so even Provincetown, even their own remembered kitchen, wasn't home. That was why Dicey always ran along the sand beside the ocean, as if she had to race the waves. The ocean wasn't home, then, and neither was anyplace else. Nobody could be home, really, until he was in his grave. Nobody could rest, really, until then.

It was a cold, hard thought written on that cold, hard stone. But maybe true.

---

1 Home . . . sea   from "Requiem" by Robert Louis Stevenson (1850–94).

If Dicey died, she guessed she wouldn't mind having this poem on her tombstone, now that she thought about it. She was the hunter and the sailor, and she guessed dead people did lie quietly in their graves.

"James," she said when he came back. "You know what you were saying last night?"

"Yeah?"

"You're pretty smart," Dicey said.

"I know," he said.

A pale sun showed behind the clouds. It looked like there were two layers of clouds now, one layer lower, like a gray veil spread before the other. Where the veil broke, you could see silvery islands of clouds on which tall angels might stand. Not cute little Christmas angels, but high, stern angels in white robes, whose faces were sad and serious from being near God all day and hearing His decisions about the world. Dicey was hypnotized by the molten silver of the cloudy islands and not until the veil of fuzzy gray blew across it again did she begin their march of the day.

Route 1 had not changed in their absence. Stores, shopping centers, garages, furniture outlets, restaurants, quick-food stands: the cement procession marched on, broken only by traffic lights dangling from heavy wires over the roadway. Traffic was heavier, and the exhaust and the diesel fumes could not rise into the sky on that first gray day, but hung over everything. Their faces and hands felt grimy all the time. Day by day, their money dwindled away.

When she thought back on this part of their journey, Dicey found that she could remember very little of it, that it all blurred together in her memory, all the long days, all the strange nights. They spent a night on a shaly beach, with no shelter and no fire. They spent a night in a grove of pines that stood at the entrance to an estate, where Dicey woke frequently with the fear that they would be discovered by the owners of the big stone house that lay at the end of the driveway. They spent a night by the entrance to another state park. As Route 1 looped north, they crossed under the Thruway and spent a miserable night huddled at the back of a shopping center. They slept sitting together on the concrete walkway, against the concrete wall. As they approached the large city of New Haven, the buildings were closer together and there were no more open spaces.

In all these days, the sun had come out only twice, once for an hour early in the morning, and once late in the evening to give them a fine sunset. Slowly, rain had been building. The rain finally began to fall during the night they spent in a tiny playground beside the Branford River. The next day they spent the last of their money, standing in the rain to eat cold doughnuts. The rain continued, steady and gentle, all that day. Dicey led them under the shelter of an empty car wash for that night and roused them early so they would be gone before anybody arrived to open the business or to wash a car. She roused them early even though nobody in his right mind would wash his car on a rainy day. You couldn't expect people to act as if they were in their right minds. Dicey was taking no chances.

They approached New Haven and Dicey took out the map, which she carried under her shirt, where the cloth and her arm would protect it. She planned their way through the city. She wanted to get across it before dark. She didn't like cities and didn't want to have to spend the night in one.

That they had nothing to eat and no money to buy food with, these facts she refused to think of. They would cross the city first, and then get some money. They would cross the city hungry because they had to.

James, Maybeth and Sammy greeted this announcement without a change in expression. They did not speak or sing any more, just followed Dicey meekly. If she had food to give them, they ate it. If there was no food, then they said nothing. Dicey thought she might prefer to have them complain, but that was another worry she could not deal with until they had crossed the city. That was a worry that went along with the limp James had developed from a hole worn into the sole of his left sneaker; with the gray under Maybeth's eyes and not having heard her voice for days; with Sammy's new habit of clinging to her hand and doing whatever she told him, right away, not even the start of a quarrel.

James, Maybeth and Sammy listened quietly while she recited the streets they would take to cross the city. "We have to get off Route 1 to cross the rivers," she said. "So we'll follow the train tracks for a while, then take a couple of blocks on a street named Quinnipiac, up to Ferry Street. That will take us over one branch of the river. When Ferry meets with Chapel Street, we'll turn left and start walking across the city. We'll go over a river, then by a big college. There, we'll be about halfway. OK?"

They nodded, three pale faces.

"Then, we're going to have to get back to Route 1, so we'll turn left onto a cross-street to meet up with it. It doesn't matter which street we take. We can follow Route 1 the rest of the way out of the city."

They nodded, six blank eyes.

"So let's go. Or we won't get across before dark."

Dicey walked with Maybeth and James took Sammy's hand. At first, most of the buildings were low, four or five stories of soiled brick. They walked beside the railroad tracks and saw only the backs of buildings, houses with no grass in the yards, ripped curtains in dirty windows, fences that looked like some giant rat had been gnawing at them. The empty windows of factories stared down. Rain fell steadily. Sometimes they would glimpse a face through an open window. Most often, except for the people looking out of train windows, they saw no one.

They crossed a small river, walking on a narrow, fenced-over walkway that was built to run beside the road. Rain showered down and made miniature puddles on the turgid river water. Green and oily slime floated on the river and gathered in stringy islands by its banks.

Chapel Street was wide, lined with stores. Groceries, five-and-dimes, an occasional movie theater, Army-Navy surplus stores, liquor stores with metal gates across the windows. The street passed a small park before it crossed another river. On the other side of the river, tall modern buildings, with whole walls of windows, lifted up out above the squat brick constructions.

The Tillermans walked on, over the Thruway. They passed hotels, clothing stores, jewelers and bookstores; then old brick churches, with signs out front saying what sermon would be given the next Sunday, and a few large old city homes. As evening thickened and lights were turned on, you could see inside where large mirrors hung on ivory-white walls and long curtains framed polished wood tables.

Dicey did not look in the store windows as the others did, or in the windows of the houses. She looked in the unsmiling faces of the people walking past her.

Night, hurrying down upon them, was not in their favor, nor was the rain, falling steadily. But they were all past hunger, she thought—she knew she wasn't hungry any more. Just tired.

It was after ten when they came to the college and the square park that lay at the center of the city, bordered by the college on one side, a chapel on the opposite and the city on the others.

Dicey finally admitted that they would have to sleep the night in the city. This park would have to do, even though it was too open. She chose a cluster of bushes far from any street lamp. "Look, you all go in there," she pointed to a kind of nest made by the low branches of the piney bushes. "You curl up there, as covered as you can. I'll stay out here and keep watch."

Without a word, they obeyed.

The rain pattered down. People hurried across the park, their heads bent. Dicey sat on a bench near her family's hiding place and looked across the park to a long wall of college dormitories. Some of the windows had lights in them. One had someone sitting in it.

Dicey sat and stared into the night without seeing, without thinking. Lights shone all around her. The street-light cast puddles of light on the wet sidewalks. The rain-drops caught the light from the lamps and glowed, falling, like yellow pebbles. Bright red neon light shone hazily on top of a building in the distance. The arch topped windows of the dormitories showed like yellow cutouts. The water on the roads and sidewalks reflected light with a silvery sheen.

Dicey sat and kept the watch. Three little children, alone in a city: she couldn't sleep.

How many more days until Bridgeport? And Aunt Cilla's big white house.

How would they get money? Why had she thrown away the twenty dollars Sammy found? How would they eat all those days until Bridgeport?

How was she going to see to it that they got there, when she didn't even know where it was?

Dicey thought the rain had grown warm, until a stuffiness in her nose and an ache in her throat (like she was trying to swallow an apple whole) told her she was crying. But she never cried! And now she couldn't stop.

She heard footsteps approaching, the first in a long time. Just one person. She bowed her chin down and folded her arms across her chest, trying to look as if she was asleep. She held her breath against a sob that was swelling in her throat. But she kept an eye out. If she needed to, she could break and run, away from the bushes where her family slept. They all knew Aunt Cilla's address.

Somebody—a man she guessed from his pants legs and loafers—sat down at the other end of her bench. His pants legs were wet, as if he had been walking for a long time. They clung against his calves. Dicey didn't move.

But the sob moved. It swelled up and broke through her clenched teeth. Dicey's panicked eyes moved to the face of the person beside her.

He had turned to look at her. He was young. He wore a yellow raincoat and his hands were jammed into the pockets. In the dim light, his eyes were dark and serious. His hair was plastered down over his forehead.

When he spoke, his voice was flat. "You looked like a girl crying. I thought you were a girl crying. Can I help?"

Dicey bit her lip and shook her head.

"You lost?"

Dicey shook her head again.

"OK." He seemed to believe her. "Can you walk home from here?"

This made Dicey feel like smiling, but not from laughter. She shook her head.

"Cat got your tongue?"

"Nope."

"OK. I'll tell you what I think. I think you don't have a place to sleep, you're probably hungry, you're frightened and worried, and you don't want to tell me anything. So far, am I right?"

"Yeah."

He shifted on the bench and turned to face Dicey. "OK. Now. You don't have to believe this, but you can trust me. I've been in your kind of jam myself, more than once. If it helps, I'm studying at the college, if that tells you anything about me."

"Schools are closed in summer."

"Not colleges. They have summer session. I'm taking a geology course because I flunked it this year and I have to pass it to graduate. I want to graduate next June."

"You don't sound stupid," Dicey said.

"Oh, I'm not. I just didn't work at it, so it's my own fault. Look, I have an idea for you."

"Yeah?"

"Yeah. Don't say no right away. OK? OK. Why don't you come with me and get some food and camp out in my room tonight. It's better than the Green—it's dry at least. I've got a roommate so you won't have to worry about being alone with me."

"I've got roommates too," Dicey said.

He smiled.

"No, three—over there."

He looked at her carefully. "OK then, we'll all go. All your age?"

"No. Younger. They're my brothers and my sister."

His jaw fell a little, and then he pulled it up sharply. His eyebrows twitched, as if he were keeping them from shooting up in surprise. "Will wonders never cease?" he asked. He stood up briskly. "Let's see the worst. I've made up my mind anyway and I guess four kids can sleep on our floor. You've made up your mind to trust me, haven't you?"

"I'm afraid so," Dicey said. That made him laugh, but she didn't know why. "Wait here," she said.

He stood absolutely still, as if to show that he would do exactly what she told him, and a smile played around his lips. He wasn't serious. He was teasing her. Dicey looked up at him through the rainy light, still trying to decide. He made his mouth still, and then she nodded at him. "OK," she said. "But we don't have any money."

"I do," he said.

Dicey roused her family. They woke easily, even Sammy, who usually slept deeply.

They rose up out of the bushes, Maybeth first, then James, then Sammy. Their eyes were surprised, but they didn't question her. She felt suddenly sorry for them. She wondered if she had done the right thing, when she began this whole journey. Was she doing the right thing now?

With one arm around Maybeth's shoulders, holding Sammy's hand tight, Dicey led her family back to where the young man stood waiting. James tagged behind, limping slightly.

The smile went out of the young man's eyes when he saw them. Dicey was briefly worried, but he crouched down on his heels, ignoring the puddles, and looked up at them all.

"You don't have to feel sorry for us," Dicey said. "You can back out."

"Not on your life. That's not it. I'm curious—intensely curious—about you. What are your names? Mine's Windy . . . well, Windy's what they call me here because they say I talk too much. How did you get here? Where are your parents? Are you hungry?"

"Yes," Sammy said fiercely.

"When's the last time you ate?"

"Yesterday, I think," Dicey said.

"Then what are we hanging around here for?" the young man asked. He stood up and took James' hand. James was too tired to protest this extraordinary gesture. "I know just the place," Windy said. He led them to one of the city sides of the Green and into a small diner that had a long counter and four booths. The clock read 1.30. Windy herded them into a booth, then brought over menus. He called the waitress before they had even opened the menus and ordered each of them a large glass of milk. He asked for a cup of coffee for himself.

Dicey could barely see the words and prices. Food smells filled the diner, and she was out of the rain. It was warm and bright. The words on the menu swam before her eyes. She looked at their rescuer.

He sat with James beside him. He had dark curly hair and a black mustache and black eyebrows that moved up and down or wrinkled as if they had a life all their own.

"Who'd believe this?" he asked, meeting Dicey's eyes. "I ask you."

The waitress put his coffee down before him and gave each child a tall glass of milk. "Y'want straws?"

Dicey shook her head and grabbed for the glass. They drank, in large gulps at first, and then, when their stomachs had welcomed the first eager swallows, more slowly. All four glasses were empty when the children put them down.

"What can I getcha?" the waitress asked.

Windy looked at them. They had forgotten the menus. He grinned. "Four hamburgers. No, make that eight. Four large orders of fries. That's all for now, but we'll probably have dessert. Do you have any apple pie?"

"Yeah."

"Give me a piece of pie now, please," he said. "And save four pieces for the kids."

She shuffled away, writing on her order pad. "Is that OK?" Windy asked Dicey. "We can change it if it's not OK. It wouldn't be any trouble. But I thought maybe it would be hard for you to decide, and the little one doesn't look old enough to read yet."

"I can too," Sammy said.

"Apologies for insulting you," Windy said, and his eyebrows waggled, as if they were laughing.

"I wanted hamburgers," Sammy said. "Anyway. And french fries. That's what I wanted."

"Ah," Windy said. "And what is your name?"

Sammy looked at Dicey. She nodded.

"Sammy," he said.

"How old are you?"

"Six. How old are you?"

"Twenty-one. Really very old."

Dicey remembered her manners. It was easier to remember manners with milk in her stomach and food on the way. "I'm Dicey and this is Maybeth and that's James." She answered the question in his eyes before he asked it: "I'm thirteen, Maybeth is nine, James is ten."

His dark eyes studied her. "I once ran away, when I was James' age," he said. He told them a long story about running away one morning when he was afraid to go to school because he was short and skinny and somebody was waiting there to beat him up. In the middle of the story their food was set before them. Dicey stopped listening. Windy could eat and talk at the same time. But the Tillermans ate in absolute silence, in huge bites, barely tasting what they chewed before they swallowed it. They all had apple pie for dessert. Throughout the meal, Windy's voice blew over them, smooth and steady. It didn't matter what he was saying.

Windy paid the bill and left a dollar on the table for the waitress. Dicey, warmed from within, tried to thank him, but he shrugged it off. He took them back to the Green, saying he wished he could stop the rain because he, for one, had had enough of it and he suspected they had too. He led them across the Green to the long dormitory building. There, the hallways were narrow and brown, like tunnels. They climbed up four flights of stairs, twisting past closed doors. Finally, Windy threw open a door and ushered them into a room.

It was a mess. Ashtrays overflowed with cigarette ashes and butts. A newspaper had been left scattered on the floor around one armchair. Books were piled on the three desks and on the low table before the sofa and along the mantelpiece. Beer cans lay around a wastebasket that was so full it looked as if it wanted to erupt like a volcano and spew trash all over the room. It was warm and messy and comfortable, and filled with yellow light. Outside, dark rain fell. But they were inside.

Windy went through a door and turned on a light in the next room. Dicey caught a glimpse of bunk beds and dressers. He returned with an armload of clothing, mostly T-shirts and sweat-shirts. "The bathroom's through that door." He pointed to the door beside the one they'd entered through. "Go get off your wet clothes and put some of these on. I guess you might want to go to the bathroom too."

"I do," Sammy said, so definitely that Dicey smiled.

"Meanwhile, I'll see if anyone's around."

When they had gone to the bathroom, they covered themselves with Windy's dry shirts which, if none too fresh, were dry and warm. They hung their own clothes on the towel racks to dry. Dicey washed out all of their underwear, using the cake of soap on the sink. They returned to the living room. Windy waited there and another young man was with him.

"Stewart," Windy said, "let me introduce my findings." He remembered all of their names and ages. "This is Stewart, my roommate," he said.

Stewart smoked on his pipe and looked at them. He was tall, taller than Windy, and skinny like Windy. He had blond hair, so pale it was almost white, hanging fine and straight down to his ears. He had a strong, square jaw and a moustache as blond as the hair on his head. His eyes, as he looked at the Tillermans, might have been gray or blue, Dicey couldn't decide which. It was as if his eyes changed back and forth between gray and blue, but she wasn't sure if that was possible.

"What's going on?" he asked Windy.

"I found them, as I said. Dicey first, and then the others. They need a place to sleep and it's raining cats and dogs, and mice and pterodactyls and God knows what else out there—so I thought to myself, why not here with us?"

Stewart smiled quietly. "Why not indeed? I'll come in with you and they can have my bunks."

James grinned at Dicey. Real beds.

Stewart took them into his room. He cleared books and papers off the top bunk, and James climbed up onto it. Sammy and Maybeth lay down on opposite ends of the bottom bunk. Dicey thought they looked like two little dolls in a dollhouse, lying there. James was half-asleep before she turned out the light and closed the door behind her.

She thought she would go back and sleep on the floor in that room, but Windy said she should take the sofa in the living room for her bed. He brought a pillow and blanket from his own room. "What do I need those for?" Dicey asked. "You keep them. I'll be fine."

Windy passed her the armload of linen. "Go ahead. Live it up. I can do without for one night."

"*You* can do without," Stewart said. "Listen, he took them off the bed where I'm going to sleep. And if you really don't want them, I'd be glad to have them." Dicey passed them over.

"Can we talk a little before you go to sleep, Dicey?" Windy asked. "Are you too tired?"

Dicey was so comfortable that she would have been glad to talk all night. She didn't want to go to sleep, because then she wouldn't be able to enjoy being comfortable. But she wasn't sure she wanted to answer any questions. She was too brain-tired to be as careful as she ought.

They all sat down. Dicey sat alone in the middle of the sofa, and the young men took two arm chairs.

Stewart started. "Windy says you're not lost."

"No. I know where we are."

"A fundamentalist," Windy said to Stewart. His eyebrows moved. He asked Dicey, "What about your family? Do they know where you are?"

Dicey shook her head. "But that doesn't matter."

"Why not?" Windy asked. Dicey didn't answer that.

"Are you in trouble?" Windy asked.

"I don't think so," Dicey said. "I hope not."

"OK," Windy said. He leaned forward and rested his chin on his hands. His eyebrows were temporarily still. "What *will* you tell us? We'd like to help if we can. Do you believe that?"

"Yeah," Dicey said. "Yeah, I do." She thought. "I mean, you already did, didn't you?"

"How about your parents?" Stewart asked. He was resting his head against the back of the chair, looking at her.

It wasn't that she couldn't lie to him. She could lie to anyone and make it good, if she had to—she'd certainly discovered that. But she didn't want to, not to him or to Windy. She wasn't going to lie to them, she decided.

"We don't have parents. We're on our own," she said. Stewart's eyes did not change, but waited, quiet as water.

"Wait a minute," Dicey said. "Let me think a minute, OK?" He nodded. "We come from Provincetown, in Massachusetts. On the Cape." He nodded his head, just a little. She heard Windy swallow a question. "My father walked out on us when I was about seven. Just before Sammy was born. We were OK until lately, when things happened wrong. My mother lost her job. And things. So she told us we were going to Bridgeport, where she has an aunt, and we all packed into our car."

Stewart held her eyes with his.

"We were in Peewauket and she left us to wait in the car while she went into a big mall. But she didn't come out, and we couldn't find her. So I decided that we should go ahead to Bridgeport and hope she'll meet us there."

Stewart asked, "How long did you wait for her?"

"All day and all night," Dicey said. "We waited in the car. She didn't come back. I'm hoping . . . I don't know. The only place I know she might be is Bridgeport."

"What if she isn't there?" Windy asked.

"There's this Aunt Cilla," Dicey explained.

"Do you know her?" Stewart asked.

"No. But she sends us cards every Christmas."

"You didn't ask anyone for help?" Stewart asked. "The police?"

Dicey shook her head firmly. "I don't know for sure what they would do. They might send us to a foster home. Or split us up. I don't know what Momma—she didn't say anything, she just disappeared . . . I have no idea what happened. No idea. I couldn't risk telling the police. And that's all true," Dicey said.

"How long ago was this?" Windy asked.

"In June. Maybe two weeks, maybe three."

"And you've been walking from Peewauket all this time?"

"We stayed at a park once. The little kids can't go very fast."

"Is that all you want to tell?" Windy asked.

"Please," Dicey answered.

He nodded his head and his eyebrows arched as he smiled at her. "Then I say we get some sleep. What do you say, Stew?"

"Just thinking about all that walking makes me tired," Stewart said.

"You OK here, Dicey?" Windy asked.

Dicey nodded. She hoped she hadn't made a mistake in telling them.

Windy turned off the lights and Dicey stretched out on the sofa. She didn't even hear the door close behind them.

CHAPTER 8

Dicey opened her eyes to the gray ceiling of the living room. She opened her ears to city noises floating in on warm air that came through the open windows. She sat up, alarmed at finding herself alone. Then the events of the night before came back to her, and she relaxed, stretched, bounced on the sofa and smiled to herself. She went to the window and looked out.

The rain had been swept away with the darkness. Everything on the Green below sparkled in the early morning air. It even smelled fresh outside.

Dicey remembered that in the bathroom she had seen a stall shower. She went in quietly. She folded up their clothes hanging on the rack, except for her own, and put them in a pile on the sofa. Then she went back and turned on the hot water, so it would be hot when she had gone to the bathroom. When she was ready, she stripped off Windy's T-shirt and stepped into the warm water, pulling the curtain closed behind her. The warm water beat down on her back and her chest and her hips and her arms. She revolved slowly, her eyes closed, like a wind-up toy that was running down. She had forgotten just how it felt to take a bath or a shower. It felt gentle and warm, like somebody's arms around you.

Dicey took a cake of soap and washed herself, head to foot, hair and ears, toes and fingers, face, torso. The soap slid onto the floor. She bent over to pick it up and the water tattooed on her fanny.

She took one last slow turn under the water that turned into five last slow turns. Then she turned both handles off and stepped out.

As she rubbed herself dry and dressed, she thought: I can do anything. Anything. We're going to be all right. It's all going to be all right.

She squeezed some toothpaste onto her finger and brushed her teeth. Her teeth squeaked and her mouth tasted minty. She grinned at herself in the mirror and ran her fingers through her damp hair.

She opened wide the door of the bathroom and saw, not only her brothers and sister, sleep still in their dazed eyes, but also wild-haired Windy, and Stewart. Maybeth came to take Dicey's hand.

Dicey asked Windy if they could all have showers. She turned on the water for Maybeth and returned to the living room.

"So. What's next?" Windy was asking. Stewart had sat down in the same chair he occupied the last night. He looked around, but didn't speak. His face looked fuzzy and confused, not quite awake. Windy answered himself:

"Breakfast is next. And then we have to see about getting these kids to Bridgeport."

"Really?" Dicey asked.

"Really," Windy said. "Stew has a car and it's only—an hour from here? You'll do it, won't you, Stew?"

The gray-blue eyes rested on Dicey. "I've got an eleven o'clock class."

"Then after the class," Windy said.

"OK. Sure. Do you mind waiting?" Stewart asked Dicey.

Dicey shook her head at his foolishness. "Do you know how long it would take us to walk it? Three days. Maybe four. I'd be a jerk to mind waiting a couple of hours," she said.

"And you're not a jerk," Windy said. He was leaning against the mantelpiece, looking down at her.

"Nope," Dicey said. Maybe she should have been more polite, but she felt too happy for that. "Other things. Bossy. And I lie and I fight, but I'm not a jerk."

Windy looked amused. He exchanged a glance with Stewart.

The little children paraded in and out of the bathroom, putting their clothes on in the bedroom. At last, everybody was dressed.

"Can you lend me some cash?" Windy asked. "Stewart?"

"I've got a twenty," Stewart said. He went into his bedroom.

The living room was filled with warm air and sunlight from the windows. The Tillermans were all fresh and clean and not starving. They would have breakfast. They would get a ride to Bridgeport.

It was almost over.

Stewart stood in the doorway of his room. Dicey looked at him and smiled, but he did not smile back at her. He waited there, silent, and looked over the small group of people standing between the sofa and the fireplace. His eyes were gray now, a distant wintry gray. "I can't find it," he said. He looked at Windy over the heads of the children.

"You sure?" Windy asked. "It's not like you to keep good track of your money." His eyebrows made dark arches over his eyes.

"I'm sure this time," Stewart said, still not looking at the children. "I just cashed the check yesterday and put the money in my wallet. I didn't spend any. My wallet was in the top drawer."

Despite the warmth of the day and the brightness of the room, Dicey felt a chill spread out from her stomach and everything grew shades darker, as if a big black cloud had just covered the sun. She looked at Sammy.

Sammy shook his head, decisively.

James' eyes were on the floor and his hands were clenched in his pockets. "James," Dicey said.

"Whyn'cha ask Sammy," James said. His eyes were hot and angry.

"Sammy said he didn't," Dicey answered. She held on to her temper.

"Then neither did I," James said.

Dicey looked at Stewart, who still stood in the doorway to his room where the little kids had slept last night. He looked back at her and she was ashamed.

"Give it to me, James," she said quietly.

James pulled one hand out of his pocket and opened it wide. A crumpled bill fell to the floor. "Get it yourself."

Dicey exploded. "I told you we don't steal and you just go ahead and do it. And then you try to lie to me about it. I could kill you, James. You hear me? You're so smart, but you can't even figure out—" She was so angry the words got jammed up in her throat. "Look what you've done!"

James stood with his head bowed. Silence filled the room, a cold silence.

The crumpled bill lay there on the floor. Dicey couldn't look at the faces of the young men.

"You've ruined everything," she said. She strode to the window and looked out, pounding with her fist on the windowsill. She tried to find something to say to James that would make him fall down onto the floor, that would knock him over and hurt him.

Finally James spoke. "You didn't yell at Sammy, you didn't say you wished he was dead."

"Sammy's six!" Dicey turned around. "And Sammy didn't take money, he took food. And Sammy didn't take it from someone who'd helped us. Even you can see the difference."

"He"—James kept his eyes on the floor but he jerked his head towards Stewart—"doesn't need the money like we do. He's got sweaters and guitars."

"So what!" Dicey hissed. "And who are you to say, anyhow? All I asked you was to do what I say, only that—and now—"

Maybeth went to James and looked up at him for a minute. Then she took hold of the hand he had out of his pocket.

"You're a thief," Dicey spat the words at James. His hazel eyes flicked up to hers. "You steal."

"Big deal," James answered, from deep within his own anger. "It doesn't matter."

886

"OK," Dicey matched anger to anger. "OK, if that's the way you want it. But until we get to Aunt Cilla's you will do exactly what I say to do—or I'll leave you behind. Do you understand?" James nodded. "Then we better get out of here."

James nodded.

"Apologize, James," Dicey ordered.

He had to obey her, so he apologized, looking into the empty fireplace. "I'm sorry."

"OK. Let's go," Dicey said to her family. She felt sick inside.

"Why?" Windy unexpectedly spoke. He bent down and picked up the bill, smoothed it with his fingers and held it out to Stewart, who came forward to take it. "As far as I'm concerned, we found Stew's money. Right, Stew?"

"No," Stewart said. "But you did want to borrow it, didn't you?" He handed it back to Windy.

Dicey wished they were out of the room and on their way again, on their own.

"Dicey?" Stewart said her name. She looked at him. "What did Sammy steal?"

"Some lunchbags at a park," Dicey said. "Two. It was different. We needed food, sort of. He thought we did anyway. He doesn't understand. He did it to help. There was a wallet in one bag, but we took that back. Sort of. Not just because it was stealing money though. Really because we didn't want to have police coming in. I guess James doesn't understand either. He's not bad."

Stewart looked at her and she looked right back at him. James was her brother and she would have to stick by him; and she wanted to stick by him. How could Stewart know James? He couldn't, but Dicey could.

"It does matter, James," said Stewart.

"Why? We all dic anyway," James said.

"Sure, but you can see to it that you like yourself when you die," Stewart answered. "You can be sure you don't hurt anybody while you're alive. Especially, you can be sure you don't hurt yourself. Are you a thief?"

James shook his head.

"But you stole," Stewart said. "Who did you hurt? You're right about me, I'm not rich but I can go to the bank and take out another twenty. So you didn't hurt me very much. You hurt yourself. More than anyone you hurt yourself."

"That doesn't make sense. Nothing matters. There's nothing you can count on—except the speed of light. And dying," James said.

"So that's what it is," Stewart said. He studied James' face. "Well that may be true but it's not a big enough truth to contain me. I plan to be a man when I get through. Not only a man, I plan to a be a good man."

"Why?" James asked.

"Because I owe it to myself," Stewart said.

"Is that all?"

"No," Stewart said, but he didn't add anything to it.

"I don't understand," James said.

Stewart didn't answer him.

"Can I learn to understand?"

"Maybe," Stewart said.

"I'm smart," James said. "Will that help?"

"Maybe," Stewart said. "Maybe not."

James nodded.

Dicey waited for the conversation to continue, but it didn't, and James just stood there looking at Stewart as if Stewart were a mountain or something terribly large. So she began to move towards the door, pulling Sammy with her.

"Hold it," Windy said. "Where are you going? Dicey? We've got breakfast to get and then Stew's going to drive you to Bridgeport. That's right, isn't it, Stew?" His eyebrows moved as he spoke, emphasizing his words.

"Of course," Stewart answered. "Get me some doughnuts and coffee will you?"

Windy took the Tillermans to the diner they had eaten at the night before. Dicey followed along, as quiet as Maybeth. She felt as if she was no longer in charge. In a way, she was relieved to let somebody else give directions and make decisions. In another way she was angry at these young men for taking over their lives, for telling them when and where to eat, for leaving her out of the conversation with James.

In the diner, which looked dingy by daylight, Dicey had fried eggs, while the others had pancakes. She had time now to enjoy the taste of her food. When she had eaten both eggs, she took one piece of toast and mopped up some yolk onto it.

Never had she enjoyed a meal more. She said so to Windy and he told her she looked like she'd like to climb onto the plate and roll around in the eggs. Dicey giggled and said she guessed she might. Windy finished his own breakfast and Maybeth's. Dicey took part of Sammy's pancakes and gave the rest to James, who was never full. They all drank milk.

When they returned to the room and Windy had given Stewart his coffee and doughnuts, he said goodbye to the Tillermans. "I've got a lab this morning and you'll probably be gone when I return," he said, shaking hands solemnly with each of them.

They thanked him, but he waved the words aside. "Any time," he said. "It was fun." He grinned at them and his eyebrows arched.

Stewart quickly wolfed down the four doughnuts and while he was sipping coffee he pulled out a guitar and played. The Tillermans sat quietly and listened.

His was not an ordinary guitar, although it looked like one; it had a belly and neck and six strings like ordinary guitars, but instead of cradling it against his arm, Stewart laid it on his lap. He held a metal bar to the strings of the neck and plucked the strings over the belly. The sound this odd guitar made was metallic and round and slidy. When he reached over his coffee cup, Dicey asked him what it was.

"A Dobro," he answered. He explained how it was made and how he played it. Then he played a slow, mournful melody on it, concentrating hard, biting his lip, leaning over the instrument and moving his shoulders with the rhythm.

Maybeth stood beside him and watched. "That's 'Greensleeves,'" she said.

Stewart nodded. "Do you know it? You want to sing it?"

Maybeth sang the old song in her clear voice. "'Alas, my love, you do me wrong, to cast me off discourteously.'"

At the conclusion, Stewart smiled at her. "You do know it."

"Momma sang to us," Maybeth said. "We know a lot of songs."

"What else do you sing?" Stewart asked. He looked around at all of them.

"Play something you like," Dicey answered him.

"I play blue grass," Stewart said. "You know what that is?"

888

They didn't, so he played a song about a miner's child who dreamed her daddy would die if he went to the mines that day, but he went anyway.

"That's silly," Maybeth said, when he had finished.

"OK, then, what about this?" Stewart asked. "'Oft I sing[1] for my friends,'" he sang. His voice was soft as clouds and clear as the sky could be. "'When death's dark form I see. When I reach my journey's end, who will sing for me?'"

It was a short song, and Maybeth asked him to sing it again, and she joined in with him.

When that was finished, he looked at them. "Do you all sing? Like that?"

Dicey nodded.

Then Stewart put down the Dobro and said he had to go to class, but as soon as he got back he'd take them to Bridgeport. He went into his room and came back with a guitar case, out of which he took a regular guitar. "You can mess around on these if you like," he said. Even after he left, the room was filled with the harmony they had made, and the singing.

James picked up the Dobro and plucked at it with his fingers. "Dicey? I'm sorry. Really. I won't ever do anything like that again."

"I know," Dicey said. Her anger was entirely forgotten. "I didn't mean most of what I said."

"You think Stewart is smarter than Louis?" James asked. "I do," he said.

"How should I know that?" Dicey asked. "I like him a lot better. I like Windy too. Maybeth?"

Maybeth nodded. She was looking at a book of pictures.

"Sammy?"

Sammy stared out the window. "How long do you think it'll be? Until we get there?"

"Not long. They said an hour."

"What's it like there?"

"I dunno, Sammy. Why?"

"Will Momma be there?"

Dicey looked at the back of his round little head, where the yellow hair stood out at crazy angles. *No*, her heart said inside her. "I dunno, Sammy," she said aloud. He didn't answer, just stood looking out.

Stewart's car was a battered old black VW bug. The three little ones sat in the back seat, crowded together. James sat in the middle because he could see out easiest. Dicey was in the front seat. "It's a good thing you don't have luggage," Stewart said. "We'd never fit it in."

The day had grown hot and muggy. City smells hung heavy on the air. The little car clattered, like a giant sewing machine.

They made their way onto the Thruway and joined the cars hurtling along there. Stewart stayed in the middle lane. Cars passed them on both sides.

"I left my map," Dicey said.

"We'll get another," Stewart answered her, without moving his eyes from the road. "I don't know Bridgeport at all. Do you?"

"How could we?"

They drove with the windows open. The air roared in their ears. Things went by so fast when you were in a car, you could barely look at anything before

---

1 *Oft I sing . . .*"   traditional ballad, "Who Will Sing for Me?" Voigt acknowledges the Carter Stanley version (1963).

it was gone. But this area, all concrete and sad little houses, was the kind you liked to pass by quickly.

Dicey leaned over and said loudly: "I don't know where we would have slept along this road."

"Where'd you sleep when you came to New Haven?" Stewart glanced quickly in the rearview mirror.

"Behind some stores. In a little park. Once in a carwash," Dicey told him.

"Then you'd have found someplace along here," Stewart said.

They went through a toll booth where Stewart paid a quarter, and then after a while saw signs saying: BRIDGEPORT. Stewart kept to the middle lane.

"Aren't we going to get off?" Dicey asked.

"Not yet. I'm hungry, aren't you?"

"Yes," Dicey said, "but—"

"I thought we'd go down to Fairfield—it's only ten or twenty miles on—and eat at McDonald's there. I know where that is, and I like going someplace that I know where it is. We can pick up a map of Bridgeport too, so we can see how to get there, to your aunt's house."

Ten or twenty miles, two days' walk. Four days there and back. Dicey just nodded. "If you want to," she said.

"What I don't want to do is drive into a strange city without a map," Stewart said. He studied the traffic behind him in the rearview mirror and turned on his signal blinker. "Besides, Fairfield's pretty."

"Do you live there?" Dicey asked.

He shook his head. They pulled off the Thruway and onto a four-lane road lined with low buildings, hung over with stoplights, bleached white by the heat.

"This is Route 1," Dicey said.

"You know it?"

"We've been on it most of the time."

"That's too bad."

Stewart stopped at a gas station and came back with a map. He pulled into the nearby McDonald's and they all ordered lunch. He carried their tray to a big table back in a corner. Dicey handed out the wrapped hamburgers and the parcels of french fries. She jammed straws into the Cokes.

Stewart had ordered two Big Macs. He ate them as if he were starving. When Dicey told him this, he said he felt like he *was* starving, most of the time. "But I'll outgrow it," he said. "It used to be worse. I used to eat much more—a whole large pizza—and still not be full. Now I'm sometimes full. When I was in high school, I felt like I could eat all day long and never fill up."

James nodded at him, chewing.

After they had cleared the table and thrown out the wrapping papers, Stewart unfolded his map. Dicey told him the address and he found the street easily. It was one of many little streets running across the map of the city.

"But it's not near the water," Dicey said.

"Why should it be?"

"It's called Ocean Drive. I thought it would be near the water. A big white house."

"Ocean Drive runs through the heart of town, a few blocks from the downtown section. But the street goes down to a main street that ends up at the harbor," Stewart pointed out. Dicey was unreasonably disappointed. "Maybe it was a joke," he suggested.

"Some joke."

"You like being near the water."

"In Provincetown, we were right next to it. Behind the dunes, but next to it. I'm used to it. Yeah, I like it. I don't feel right unless I'm near the ocean."

"You feel that way and you're going to Bridgeport? You're in trouble," Stewart said. "Listen, are you in a big hurry? Do you want to go to a beach for a while before you go to your aunt's?"

"Yes," James and Dicey said.

"No," Sammy said. "I want to see Momma. Right away."

"We don't even know whether she's there, Sammy," James argued. "You can wait an hour, can't you?"

"I don't want to wait any more," Sammy said. "Dicey?"

"Just for an hour, Sammy. Please?" she said. His face grew stubborn. "I've decided," Dicey said. "For an hour. No more."

Once they got off Route 1 in Fairfield, everything was clean and neat. The houses all looked freshly painted. The lawns all looked freshly mown. The cars all looked just washed. It was the kind of place where all the door handles shone with polishing.

They drove through a little village and then down by some big houses around some curves—and then Dicey could see the water. At first she only glimpsed it in the spaces between the large trees that grew around the houses; then she could see a long narrow beach ahead, with marshlands on the other side of the road.

Sammy wanted to stay in the car, but Dicey insisted that he come out with them at least to begin with. "Then you can go back and wait in the car if you want," she said. "That's fair, isn't it?"

They spent an hour at the beach, no more. Sammy kept track of the time on Stewart's watch. They waded and dug. The children wandered up and down while Stewart and Dicey sat watching the little waves that meandered up onto the smooth sand. Dicey stared out over the quiet blue water, knowing that although the surface was calm, the great tides were moving underneath. She listened to the rippling waves mingled with the voices of the other people at the beach. They didn't talk much. Stewart didn't seem to be a talkative person, and Dicey didn't mind. He only asked her one question:

"What'll you do if things don't work out at your aunt's?"

He could have been reading Dicey's mind. She turned quickly to look at his face, but he was looking out over the water, his gray-blue eyes glinting in its reflections.

"I don't expect Momma to be there, you know," she said. He nodded. "Aunt Cilla must be pretty old now. She's really Momma's aunt, not ours. So she might not want a mess of kids. Is that what you mean?" He nodded. "I don't know what I'll do. Or if she's not even there. I guess I'll have to go to the police then, won't I? Or somebody. For help." He nodded. "What do you think I should do if—"

His eyes turned to her. "I honestly don't know. Except stick together, all of you. That's the most important thing."

Dicey agreed.

"If you can," he said. "If you are able to. You might not be able to."

"You and Windy—you were a big help to us," Dicey said.

"That's OK," Stewart said.

"Especially Windy."

"Windy had a good time. You brightened up his life."

"Especially you, too."

"I didn't do anything. Sang you a couple of songs. Got you some bad ham-burgers."

"And took us to the beach, don't forget that."

They found 1724 Ocean Drive without any trouble. It was one of a long row of houses that stretched down treeless streets. It was a small house, shingled with gray asphalt. Three concrete steps led up to the plain front door. On one side of the door, two windows faced the street. There were thin curtains on the windows and you couldn't see in. The house looked flat-faced and empty. Dicey sat in the car and studied it before she got out. Was this going to be their home?

They clambered out of the car and said goodbye to Stewart. He left the motor running while he climbed out himself to shake hands with each one of them, James last, and wish them good luck.

Then he drove off, down the street, away, the little black car clattering busily. Dicey waved to him, but he must not have seen her because he didn't wave back. She turned to the closed door. She was nervous, but not in any way she had been nervous before. She looked at James and Maybeth and Sammy standing in a silent row and tried to smile at them. Then she went up the steps, hoping she looked more confident than she felt. At least they were all freshly washed. Dicey knocked on the door.

CHAPTER 9

NOBODY answered Dicey's knock. She could hear the echoes of her knock-ings inside, so she knew that she would have heard footsteps if someone had been hurrying to answer the door.

She knocked again, louder. While she waited, to be sure no one was at home, she studied the brown paint on the door. It was a thick reddish-brown color and in the inset panels you could see brush strokes.

Nobody was there. Dicey swallowed, as much in relief as in disappointment, and turned to face her family. "I guess we wait," she said. She sat on the bottom step. They sat behind her and beside her.

They had nothing other than what they wore. Even Dicey's map, rain-soaked and ripped, had been lost. Stewart had taken his with him.

"I thought Aunt Cilla was rich," James said. "This isn't a rich person's house."

"I must have been wrong about that," Dicey said.

"Momma said she was," James insisted.

"Then Momma was wrong."

"Do you think Momma's here?" Sammy asked. "If she's here why isn't she here?"

"I dunno," Dicey said. "It's Thursday, a working day, isn't it? So if she's got a job she'd be there, wouldn't she?"

"What about Aunt Cilla? Is she too old to work?" James asked.

"I don't know anything about her except what she wrote in her letters—and that wasn't true."

"Why would she lie?" James asked.

"I dunno," Dicey said.

"Dicey?"

"Yeah, Maybeth."

"Why did Momma go?"

Dicey looked at Maybeth's round and worried face. She looked down the quiet street, where no cars were parked, where all the houses were the same and had the same closed and empty faces.

"I don't know, Maybeth, but I can tell you what I think."

Maybeth waited.

"I think she got so worried about so many things, about money and us, about what she could do to take care of us, about not being able to do anything to make things better—I think it all piled up inside her so that she just quit. She felt so sad and sorry then, and lost—remember how she'd go out and not come back for hours? I think she got lost outside those times, the way she was lost inside."

"Amnesia," James suggested.

"Maybe. So she decided that she'd ask Aunt Cilla to help us, because she couldn't help us any more. And maybe, when she went off into the Mall, maybe she'd run out of money and she couldn't take us any farther and all the things that had piled up inside her head sort of exploded there. And she just forgot us. Like amnesia, where you forget everything, even who you are. She couldn't stand to think and worry any more. Everything she thought of, every place she went to, it all looked so sad and hopeless and she couldn't do anything about it—so it all exploded and left her brain empty." Empty. That was the way Momma had looked those last months. As if she were far away from them.

"Will she be better now?" Sammy asked. "Do you think?"

"Maybe she's not even here," James said.

"She has to be," Sammy said.

"Why?" James asked. Dicey thought of stopping the conversation, but decided not to.

"Because," Sammy said.

"Because is no reason," James said.

"Because, if she isn't here, then I don't know where she is. And she doesn't know where I am. And how can she find me?"

"Maybe she doesn't want to find you, or any of us," James said. "That's what Dicey said, that she had to get away from us."

"Momma loves me," Sammy said. His chin stuck out in the stubborn way.

"Yes, she does," Dicey said. "And so do I."

Because she did, she loved all of them. That had kind of sneaked up on her over their journey.

"See?" Sammy said to James. "I told you."

"But that doesn't prove anything," James protested.

Sammy didn't pay any attention to him.

The sun moved slowly across a white sky. At the end of the long summer afternoon, or at the beginning of the long summer evening, the street gradually filled up with traffic, and the sidewalk became crowded with people. One after another, buses stopped at the corner and a short parade of men and women climbed off. Some carried briefcases, some grocery bags. They walked on, down the street or up the street. Some went up the stoops of the gray houses, pulled out keys, unlocked doors and went in. Others walked on, around corners, out of sight. No children lived on these streets.

The Tillermans silently watched the people move to and fro past them. Nobody looked at them. Most of the men and women walked with their eyes toward the ground, or fixed blankly ahead. Sammy moved closer to Dicey and held onto her forearm with his small, tense hand. He did not say a word, but his eyes flicked back and forth. He was looking for Momma.

Dicey just watched the people, with no particular thought in her mind. She could not do any more. From now on, things would happen to them.

She saw men in workshirts with tired shoulders, carrying plain black lunchboxes. She saw women in brightly flowered summer dresses, the dresses wilted by the heat as if they were real flowers, the women's faces sagging after the work day.

A short round woman wearing high-heeled shoes walked towards the steps where they sat. She actually looked at them and seemed surprised, but she walked on past them. A man in a green khaki suit, carrying a scuffed briefcase, stared at them for a minute before he let himself into the house next door.

A few minutes later, a woman of the same age as the man, about fifty Dicey guessed, struggled up the steps to the next-door house, carrying two huge bags of groceries. She noticed the Tillermans just as she pulled the door closed behind her and her eyes widened.

The little round woman in high heels walked past again, from the opposite direction and on the opposite side of the street. She stared at them. She was wearing a plain black cotton dress and had short gray hair that was permanented into sausage-like curls that bounced and jiggled on her round head. She walked as if her feet hurt her, as if she had been standing and walking in the high-heeled shoes all day long. Dicey wondered where she was going.

The people coming home from work had filled the street for a while; now they thinned out, melted away into houses, out of sight. All the sounds were faint ones from distant traffic or from the humming of air conditioners up and down the block. A solitary man wearing shorts and sneakers walked his dog on the opposite side of the street.

The round woman came towards them again. This time, as at first, she was on their side of the street and looking at the ground. She held her purse in both hands, protectively close against her side. Dicey thought she must be old.

She stopped about three feet away and looked at them. At first only Dicey was looking back at her, into pale blue eyes that blinked behind plastic-framed glasses sitting high up on her nose. She wasn't that old after all, close up.

"What do you want?" the woman asked. "What are you doing here? What do you want here?" Her voice was high and a little scared. Her lips pursed.

Dicey stood up. "We're the Tillermans," she said. She named them all. The woman's expression did not change.

Dicey knew then that Momma was not here.

Dicey kept on talking. "I'm hoping you're our aunt, our great-aunt, Mrs. Cilla Logan."

Then the woman's expression did change. A little half-smile, a silly helpless smile, fluttered her mouth "That is Mother," she said. "Not me. I'm her daughter. That is, I was her daughter." She fumbled around in her purse and took out keys. "Mother passed on this last March," she said. Dicey had a sinking feeling in her stomach. "But do come in. There's no need to stand talking on the front stoop."

The woman unlocked the door and stepped inside. The Tillermans followed. It was dark and stuffy after the summer evening sunlight. They entered a narrow hallway that led to the rear of the house, passed a room with thin curtains, passed a narrow dark staircase going up and went into a kitchen.

894

The kitchen was large enough for all five of them, but not big. Sunlight made it brighter than the rest of the house. It was shiny clean. The gray linoleum floor gleamed, the refrigerator shone, the windows, looking over a tiny yard, were polished. There was a formica-topped table in the center of the room, and the woman told the Tillermans to sit at the four chairs that surrounded it. She opened the windows and the back door, then fetched herself a chair from the front room, putting it beside Maybeth. Before she sat down, she put some water into a kettle, put the kettle on the stove and took a mug out of a cupboard. As she did all this, she spoke to them in starts and stops. "Yes, Mother passed away. You couldn't have known. It was her heart. Her heart was always weak, but we never knew. She wouldn't complain, you see. She was only in her seventies. Seventy-two. A wonderful person—everybody said how wonderful she was. It was a shock to me. I found her, when I came back from work. Sitting in her chair by the window. A Wednesday it was. We had a high mass for her." She sighed, the kettle whistled, and she poured water into her mug. She dunked a teabag, in and out, in and out. "I have been—not quite the same since Mother went away. People have said that to me. It has been hard for me."

She turned to face them, and Dicey saw little tears gathering in her little eyes. She took off her glasses and polished them on a paper towel.

The Tillermans sat silent, their mouths clamped shut, not knowing what to say. The woman sat down at the table with them. She sipped at her tea. James looked at Dicey and raised and lowered his eyebrows, as Windy had. Dicey smothered a giggle.

"And then, of course, to see four children on my doorstep. Well, I had no idea. You don't mind, do you? You aren't offended? I was afraid. You hear of such strange things happening these days. Especially to women who live alone. I live alone now. I hoped you would go away. If Mother were here, of course. . . . " Her voice drifted off, her eyes drifted away from them and out to the windows.

Nobody spoke.

Finally, the woman gathered herself together with a kind of shake over her whole body. "But what am I thinking of? Are you thirsty? I don't know what I have for children to drink. Living alone, I don't keep much food in the house."

"Please," Maybeth said, "I would like a glass of water."

The woman looked at her. She smiled at Maybeth and said, "Of course, you all would like a drink of water, wouldn't you. What a pretty child you are. Really, like an angel. I was a pretty child too. Everyone said so—and we have photographs."

She got them each a little jelly glass full of water. They drank quickly and then Dicey refilled them once, twice, three times. The woman smiled absently.

"What are you doing here?" the woman asked, as if the question had just occurred to her. "Where are your parents? Who did you say you were?"

"We are the Tillermans," Dicey said again. She announced all of their names again, "James, Maybeth, Sammy, and I'm Dicey."

The woman repeated their names softly to herself. "My mother's maiden name was Hackett," she said.

"Our mother," Dicey began. She looked sharply at Sammy in case he might be about to interrupt, "is your mother's niece. We used to get a card and letter from your mother every Christmas, and Momma would read it to us. That's how we knew about Aunt Cilla, and her address. But I don't even know your name."

"Eunice Logan," the woman said, "Miss Eunice Logan. That makes us cousins, you know."

"Does it?"

"Yes, because your grandmother was my mother's sister. That means your mother and I are first cousins. Does that make us second cousins?"

"I don't know," Dicey said.

"Your grandmother would be Abigail Tillerman. Abigail Hackett she was before she married. Priscilla Hackett was my mother, you see. Before she married."

"Do we have a grandmother?" Dicey asked.

"Of course. Everyone does. But where are your parents? Are they visiting in Bridgeport?"

Dicey found herself ready to lie again. She could say they were visiting and the children had come to meet Aunt Cilla, and then later the Tillermans could go off and—and do what? If she lied, then she would get herself into a box. They had come such a long way. They had to have some kind of help from this cousin she'd never even heard of before. (That was strange too, that Aunt Cilla had never mentioned a daughter.) If Cousin Eunice didn't help them, they would have to go to the police. Dicey had to tell the truth.

But first she had to say it to Sammy. Say it out loud. "Momma's not here, Sammy," Dicey said.

He nodded, and tears welled up in his eyes. Dicey reached over and put her hand on top of his. He laid his forehead on her hand and closed his eyes.

"You don't know where your mother is?"

"No," Dicey said. "She ran away, I think. Anyway, she disappeared. We were on our way here to find Aunt Cilla, so we just came along. We hoped she'd be here."

"Where's your father?"

"He's been gone for years," James said, his voice sharp.

"You're alone?" Cousin Eunice asked. They nodded. "Oh dear. Oh dear, oh dear. You poor, sweet little things. I don't know what to think. I have to ask advice. Will you excuse me to make a phone call? You're absolutely alone? I don't know what should be done."

She hurried out of the room, swinging the door closed behind her. Sammy raised his head and Dicey retrieved her hand, now a little wet. "I don't understand," Sammy said.

"Neither do I," Dicey answered. "She'd never heard of us, you know that? And we'd never heard of her. But Momma answered those letters, every year."

"What should we do?" James asked.

"Tell the truth and see what happens," Dicey said. "We can't do anything else. Can we? James?"

"We could take off again, and look out for ourselves until—"

"Until what?" Dicey asked.

"Until we grow up?"

"We could," Dicey agreed. "We always might do that and we'd figure a way out, I guess. But for now I think we shouldn't, unless we have to. We don't have any idea where Momma is, and I want to find out. Maybe this Cousin Eunice will take care of us—I could work later and pay her back. That's what I'm hoping will happen. Just so we're together."

"Is Momma gone for always?" Maybeth asked.

"I don't know," Dicey said. "She might as well be."

896

"Don't say that!" Sammy cried. "Don't you ever!"

Cousin Eunice returned. "My friend—he's an advisor really, he's my spiritual counselor—he'll be by after supper. We have to get some more food—I have only two dinners in the freezer. Dicey? Can you go to a store and get three TV dinners? I don't know what kind you children prefer. Is that all right?"

"Of course," Dicey said. She flushed and said, "We don't have any money."

"None?"

"None. I'm sorry."

"Don't be sorry—I feel so sorry for you—I don't understand what has happened—"

"Neither do we," Dicey answered.

"How could you? You're only children." She reached for her purse and took out ten dollars. "This will be enough. You must want milk, children should drink milk. And fruit? Can you decide what you need? Will this be enough?"

Dicey nodded.

"The grocer is two blocks away, just around a corner. You go up the street, turn right, and you'll see it. But don't talk to strangers."

Dicey nodded, lowering her head to hide her smile.

"And you should call me 'Eunice.' Cousin Eunice. Because we're cousins. And could you pick out a cake from the frozen foods? Something light, perhaps lemon; something that will sit well with tea."

Dicey walked to the store, not thinking about anything in particular, just taking it slow. There was a kind of pool of sadness in her heart she thought, and she wondered why it should be so. Not only for Momma, because she had not expected to find Momma here. She didn't ever expect to see Momma again, she realized. The sadness was for themselves, even though they were much better off now than they had been, say, just last night at this time. Dicey picked out three chicken TV dinners and went to the fruit counter.

Once again, everything had changed on them. Perhaps it was all this changing that made her sad. Or perhaps the disappointment, after finally arriving at Aunt Cilla's house, and finding only Eunice there, whom they had never heard of. A stranger. Who pitied them.

Probably, they could never go back to New Haven. She wished they could have stayed there longer. She wished she knew something more about those two young men. She didn't even know their last names. Or phone numbers. Or address. Stewart hadn't even stayed to find out if the Tillermans would be all right. The Tillermans had just drifted through his life touch in, touch out, and gone without a thought.

Dicey paid for her purchases and walked slowly back to the little gray house. Maybe it was just that she was away from the ocean, the salt water with its tides and turbulence, that made her sad.

Father Joseph, Cousin Eunice's friend, was a priest, a slender, restless man with thick gray hair and deep lines in his forehead. He had cool, thoughtful light-brown eyes, deep set, and a thin mouth. He wore shiny black trousers and jacket, a black shirt-front, and the band of white, crisp and stiff, around his neck. Cousin Eunice introduced him and fluttered nervously around him on her high-heeled shoes, bringing him a cup of tea and offering him a tray with a little china pitcher of milk and a little china bowl of sugar cubes.

Father Joseph did not show pity for the Tillermans as Eunice had. They sat together in the living room, on the chairs and the floor. He asked them about their home in Provincetown and their school, about Momma, about living in a summer resort area, about the fishing fleet and about books. After a while, he suggested that the younger children go to bed, while he and Cousin Eunice and Dicey made some plans.

"But they have no nightclothes," Cousin Eunice said.

"We can sleep in our underwear," Dicey said. "We washed everything out last night."

The priest remarked, "You did? You do seem to have managed well."

Dicey took the younger ones upstairs. James protested, but she told him: "We're guests. We're strangers here. She didn't even know we existed, and she's trying to help us. Let's just do as we're told, OK?"

James and Sammy were to sleep in the small back bedroom that looked out over the yard, in a double bed. Maybeth would sleep in the other twin bed in Cousin Eunice's room. Maybeth looked small lying there, her curls spread behind her on the pillow, her hands folded over the clean sheets. "You OK, Maybeth?" Dicey asked.

The little girl nodded.

"I think I liked it better when we all slept in the same place," Dicey said, smiling at her. "Like that first night."

Maybeth nodded.

"I expect I'll be sleeping in with James and Sammy, on the floor, or downstairs on the sofa," Dicey said. "If you want me."

"It's OK, Dicey," Maybeth said. "I won't be lonely."

"Lonely? All cramped together here in this little house? Why I'll hear you if you roll over. I'll hear you if you sneeze—and come running."

Maybeth smiled at Dicey and closed her hazel eyes.

Dicey went back downstairs, where the adults awaited her in the living room, which was cluttered with the kinds of things collected over a lifetime, pictures and little china figurines and pillows stuffed with pine needles.

Father Joseph greeted her. "Sit down Dicey, we have to get to business now. That's an odd name, Dicey. What is your real name?"

Dicey sat cross-legged on the floor, between the two in their chairs, looking up at them. "Dicey's my name," she said. "I don't have another name."

"You just don't know it," the priest assured her. Dicey didn't argue. After all, maybe he was right.

He studied her, as if he wanted to see her thoughts. He made her uncomfortable.

"Your cousin has agreed to make you welcome here, until we can make inquiries about your mother, and your father."

Dicey looked at Cousin Eunice, who smiled foolishly at her and said, "It must be temporary, I'm afraid, but—"

"Your cousin has—certain plans, of which she may tell you later," Father Joseph said. He smiled at Cousin Eunice across the top of Dicey's head, and she blushed like a little girl. "However, the Church has summer activities in which your younger siblings can participate. A day camp for the little boy and the young girl. James will attend a school-camp. Will he object to that?"

"He likes school," Dicey said. "He's awfully smart."

"I thought so," Father Joseph said. "I'm one of the teachers there, so I can see that he gets into the proper classes. And of course there will be more active things to do in the afternoon."

"That sounds fine," Dicey said. "Thank you. Thank you both. I know we've just sort of fallen on you," she said to Cousin Eunice. "I'm sorry."

"Oh, don't be sorry," Cousin Eunice said, leaning forward, pushing her glasses back up her nose. "We are family, aren't we? And when I think of you, all alone—abandoned—like myself really, in a way. Why I couldn't do anything else, could I? Only, I work, you see, so I have to be gone all day, and there will be so much to do with four children in the house. Cleaning and shopping, laundry."

"But I can do that, can't I?" Dicey asked her.

"That is what we hoped," Father Joseph said. "And the Church, Eunice, can give you clothing, as well as all the support we can offer, and counsel. Have the children no other relatives?"

"None that I know of," Dicey said. She knew she had interrupted, but she didn't like him talking about them as if she weren't there.

"Mother had just one sister," Cousin Eunice said. "Abigail. She would be their grandmother. But I don't know much about her. She was much younger than Mother, twelve years, and then they never were close. I've never met her. They might have had a falling out. I did write to her when Mother passed away, but I received no answer."

"Was the letter returned to you?"

"No."

"So it must have been received. By someone."

Dicey was listening hard.

Cousin Eunice waved her little hands. "Let me see. Abigail married a man named John Tillerman."

"Where does she live?" Father Joseph asked.

"In Maryland, down south, on the Eastern Shore. A town called Crisfield. I don't know anything about it. It is where Mother lived as a girl."

Father Joseph nodded.

"This John Tillerman farmed, I think I remember." Cousin Eunice wrinkled her brows with the effort. "They had children." Dicey nodded her head. "I don't know how many but one daughter would be Dicey's mother. I don't know where they are now."

Crisfield, Eastern Shore, Maryland, Dicey said to herself, to fix it in her memory.

"By that time, Mother had been in the north for years and married to Father, and they lived here. Mother didn't like her sister. She didn't like to be reminded of her family. I don't know—she wouldn't speak of them. She became a part of Father's family. These are the first Hackett relations I've met. I'll try to remember more, Father Joseph. We have photograph albums."

"That would be most helpful. I myself will see what I can find out about the Tillerman family. Sometimes the Church can make the more sensitive personal inquiries, that the police authorities can't." He turned to Dicey. "What is your religion?"

"I don't know," Dicey said. "We never went to church." He frowned slightly.

"There is another question which I'm afraid I have to ask. The matter of your name. Tillerman, that would be your mother's name. Your parents were not married?"

Dicey shook her head. "I don't think so," she said. Cousin Eunice sucked in a noisy breath. Dicey did not look at her. She pulled at the laces of her sneakers, as if she had just noticed they were coming loose.

"Had you the same father, all of you? Would you know that?"

"Yes," Dicey said. Her head snapped up and her eyes met his. He did not seem surprised at her anger. "Sammy and Maybeth look like Momma, but James and me, we look like our father. I remember him, a little. Because I'm the oldest."

899

"Yes, yes," the priest said, smiling a little. "I'm sure you're right." He didn't sound sure.

"No, you're not," Dicey said, "but I am. And I know. Aren't there birth certificates? There have to be, don't there? We were all born in Provincetown—why don't you call the hospital there? They'll tell you. Momma wasn't—" She couldn't find the polite word. "She didn't have boyfriends, she didn't even go out on dates. She's nice. She's good. She loves us—and you probably don't believe that either, but she does. We'd know and you wouldn't."

He held up his hands. A smile lifted the corners of his mouth. Cousin Eunice fluttered in the background making little protests to tell Dicey she shouldn't talk like that to a priest.

"No, no, Eunice. The child is probably right. She *would* know better than we."

"Then why did she abandon them?" Eunice asked. "Oh, I'm sorry, I didn't mean to say that," she apologized to Dicey. Dicey didn't respond.

"That is what we'll try to find out," Father Joseph said. "I think, Dicey, if you can, I'd like you to speak to the Missing Persons Department."

"The police?" Dicey asked.

"The police."

Dicey thought. She didn't want to talk to the police. But how else could they find where Momma went? And what if something bad had happened to Momma and the police could help her? And if by not talking to them Dicey could hurt her? She had a sudden memory of Momma's sad moon-face and her sad moon-smile in the car window; and then of Momma running to comfort Sammy when he had fallen off a chair and was frightened, pulling the little boy onto her knees and wrapping her arms around him, saying crooning comforting things. The two round yellow heads bent towards each other, and Momma's strong hands cradled the back of Sammy's little head.

"OK," Dicey said. "They can't put us into foster homes when we're here with Cousin Eunice, can they? We're not runaways, are we? I don't want us to be separated," she explained to the priest.

"Neither do we, if it can be helped," he answered. "I'll contact the police and someone will come here to see you. Shall I come with him?"

"OK," Dicey said again. She was thinking furiously, trying to see if there was a trap in this, or danger.

"You really have no choice," the priest said.

Dicey nodded, with her eyes on his, but she was reciting to herself: *Crisfield. Eastern Shore. Maryland.*

Father Joseph left, then, and Cousin Eunice brought Dicey a cot that she kept in the cellar. Dicey put it into the last of the floor space in the boys' bedroom. Cousin Eunice wanted to object to having Dicey in with the boys, but she didn't want her own room to be crowded, so she didn't say much.

Dicey looked in on the sleeping Maybeth before she made her final stop in the bathroom and lay down on her cot. She could hear James breathing softly. Sammy turned and rustled in the sheets.

Dicey lay on her back with her arms under her head, staring at the blank, black ceiling. They had come here, had come here safely. If this was to be their home, then she could learn to get along here. She would have to. Stewart was right, they had to stay together. That was the only important thing.

She was lulled to sleep by the words repeating in her head: *Crisfield, Eastern Shore, Maryland.*

A SHARP KNOCK on the door woke Dicey. She opened her eyes wide. The window was dark. Dicey had slept and awakened in so many unknown places that she never had that first, morning feeling of being lost, or not knowing where she was. She knew where she was, or rather, where she wasn't.

The knock came again. Dicey jumped off the cot and squeezed around the corner of the bed where her brothers slept to open the door.

Cousin Eunice stood there, wearing the same black cotton dress, or its twin sister, and the same high-heeled shoes. "I am about to leave," she whispered. "Can you come downstairs for a word before I go?"

Dicey nodded. She closed the door and searched through the darkness for her shorts and her shirt.

A rustling noise in the bed made her turn her head as she was about to leave. James sat up. "It's still true," he said.

"Go back to sleep, James," Dicey said. He lay down obediently, and his eyes closed.

Dicey found Cousin Eunice in the kitchen, drinking a cup of tea. Beside her on the table lay a black purse, black gloves, and a little round black hat with a brim that tilted up.

"Good morning," Dicey said.

"I'm sorry to wake you so early," Cousin Eunice said. Her face was pale above all the black around her. "But I am going to six-thirty mass. I always do that," she said. "I get breakfast on my way to work. There's a diner on the way, quite clean. Mother didn't like making breakfast. And I've always gone to early mass."

Dicey nodded. She sat down facing her cousin.

"I pray for Mother, and for myself, and for the world," Cousin Eunice said. "This morning, I shall pray for you, and for your poor mother."

Dicey felt uncomfortable. "Thank you," she said. Was that what you were supposed to say to somebody who was praying for you?

"I thought of staying home today," Cousin Eunice went on. She talked without looking at Dicey. "But I've never missed a day of work, not for any reason. Not in twenty-one years. Somehow, I didn't want to miss today."

Dicey nodded.

"Father Joseph said he would come by this morning and bring some clothing for you. He will register the younger children at camp, so that they can begin right away. So you must be sure to be here when he arrives."

"We will."

"But there is shopping that needs to be done, and usually on Thursday evenings I clean the living room, dust and vacuum, wash the windows, damp mop the floors. I couldn't get that done last night."

"I can do that," Dicey said.

"Do be careful not to break anything," Cousin Eunice urged.

"I will," Dicey said.

"Here is some money. Try not to spend it all." Cousin Eunice handed her twenty dollars. "We'll need something for supper, I suppose. Can you cook?"

Dicey nodded.

"It has to be fish," Cousin Eunice said. "Today is Friday."

"I've cooked fish," Dicey said. Well, that was true. She had just never cooked fish on a stove, in a pan. What did Friday have to do with fish?

"I get home at five-forty. Will you be all right?"

"We'll be all right," Dicey said. "You don't need to worry about us."

"I don't know how you've managed it," Cousin Eunice said. "You must be a very resourceful child."

Dicey didn't know what to say.

"But you're here now, and I'll take care of you," Cousin Eunice said.

"That's awfully nice of you," Dicey answered. It sounded so flat. But she felt flat, flat and—she admitted it to herself—disappointed.

"How could a Christian do less?" Cousin Eunice asked. Then she got up and put her hat on her head. She drew her gloves on over her plump hands and picked up her purse. "Until this evening then. You're sure you'll be all right?" Dicey nodded. "Don't forget Father Joseph."

"I won't."

"And the living room."

"I won't. I mean, I'll do it."

"And the shopping."

Dicey nodded.

"Fish, remember. Why don't we have a tuna casserole?"

Dicey nodded. She hoped she could find a cookbook in this neat and tidy kitchen, maybe behind a cupboard door.

Cousin Eunice left, drawing the door quietly closed behind her. Dicey breathed a sigh of relief, but the door opened immediately. "Don't leave the house empty," Cousin Eunice said. "There must be someone home, at all times. Thieves come, even in broad daylight these days."

"All right," Dicey said.

"It's not as if I have anything valuable," Cousin Eunice said. "But they steal anything. And murder—and other things—I don't know—the world has gone crazy. I'll have a key made for you, just one. Until then, don't leave the house unlocked."

"I won't," Dicey said. "Don't worry about us. We'll be fine."

"How can I help worrying?" Cousin Eunice asked. She did not give Dicey time to answer.

Dicey looked at the clock hanging on the kitchen wall. It was shaped like a cat, with a long, curled tail that twitched the seconds. Six-fifteen. Dicey familiarized herself with the kitchen, cupboards (no cookbook), drawers, refrigerator and freezer. She took a dustcloth and the vacuum and went into the living room.

The room was cluttered, but not messy. Dicey didn't think it needed cleaning, but if Cousin Eunice wanted it cleaned then she would clean it. She dusted the wooden-backed chairs, the table tops, the windowsills, the one bookcase which held a Bible and two rows of photograph albums. Dicey thought she should ask permission before she looked through the albums. She dusted the pictures on the walls, of Jesus and Mary, like the ones that she used to see on Aunt Cilla's Christmas cards, of Jesus being crucified, and photographs, of a round-faced man standing beside a round-fendered car, of a sharp-eyed woman with a fur around her neck, of a little girl with curly hair and a flouncy white dress and a bouquet of flowers held in her white-gloved hands. Dicey dusted the row of china cats on top of the bookcase. She dusted the lamps and the doorhandles. Then she ran the vacuum over the pale blue rug, careful to clean under tables and chairs.

When she finished, it was seven-thirty. She set out bowls and spoons and glasses of milk. Cousin Eunice had two kinds of cold cereal, cornflakes with sugar frosting, and a fruit cereal which said it had fifteen flavors in its different-colored little balls. Dicey put both boxes in the middle of the table. She wished she could find some flowers to put in a glass in the middle, but there were none in the back yard. Nothing grew there except a straggly, neglected cover of grass.

Dicey enjoyed getting ready for this meal. The morning sun brightened the living room beyond. Light made things cheerful.

They ate a quick breakfast and then Dicey washed and dried the bowls and glasses and spoons. Maybeth helped her put them away. Sammy and Maybeth went out to the back yard. Dicey took James upstairs and made him help her make their beds. Cousin Eunice had made her own.

She left James in charge while she went to the store. There she purchased bread and milk and fruit, tuna fish and noodles and (after reading the instructions on the back of the bag of noodles) a can of mushroom soup, peanut butter, jelly. She also bought a dozen eggs, a box of pancake mix, a jar of syrup and a cheap red rubber ball (because if Sammy was going to spend most of the day waiting around, he'd need something to play with).

Returning, unpacking the groceries, piling the dollars and change beside the toaster, washing the apples before putting them in the refrigerator, Dicey heard herself humming the song about Peggy-o. It was like playing house.

James wandered in and took an apple. "There aren't any books in the house. Are we going to stay here?"

"I don't think we can do anything else," Dicey said. "So we've got to please Cousin Eunice, you know? And that Father Joseph too, I guess. We've got to be on best behavior all the time. Can you do that, James?"

"Sure," he said. "But it's an awful small house for four kids."

"Bigger than ours was."

"Yeah, but there we had the dunes and the beach."

Dicey went out into the tiny yard and called Sammy and Maybeth to her. To them she repeated what she had just said to James. They nodded solemnly at her, then she pulled out her hand from behind her back and tossed the red ball to Sammy.

He grabbed for it, missed, ran after it and caught it in two hands. He bounced it high. He turned and grinned at Dicey. Then he ran up to her and nearly knocked her over, hugging her. He called Maybeth to play catch.

Dicey watched them playing, proud that she had thought to get the ball. Glad in her heart that she had been able to give it to them.

They had finished lunch and washed and dried the plates and glasses by the time Father Joseph arrived. He carried two large shopping bags, which he passed to Dicey. "Clothes," he told her.

He gathered up the younger children and walked off down the street with them. James walked beside him. Sammy ran ahead. Maybeth trotted behind.

Dicey was alone in the house. It felt strange to be alone. Being alone inside was very different from being alone outside. Inside, there was nothing to do. And she felt full of energy.

She wanted to take a walk but she couldn't leave the house empty. So she sorted through the bags of clothes.

The clothes were worn, but clean and pressed. Their own clothes were worn out, but that was somehow different. Other people's old clothes—Dicey quelled the thought. She must remember to be grateful. For Dicey and Maybeth there were dresses, for the boys shirts and trousers. Dicey didn't like dresses. There was no underwear. No blue jeans. Two pairs of shoes, heavy leather shoes that tied with laces. She would have to tell Father Joseph what they needed. Or maybe Cousin Eunice could give them the money for shoes and underwear.

In an hour, Father Joseph returned. The children were not with him, but another man was. He wore a business suit of olive green and had a round face and yellow-brown eyes that protruded. Goggle eyes. He had round fat fingers, and he jingled the money in his pocket. He peered at Dicey.

They all went to sit at the kitchen table. "The children are staying at camp for the afternoon," Father Joseph said to Dicey. "You and I will go pick them up, so that you can learn the way. Is that all right?"

Dicey nodded. She wondered if she should have changed into one of the dresses.

"This is Sergeant Gordo. He works with the Missing Persons Bureau of the Police Department, and he is also a personal friend of mine."

"How do you do," Dicey said.

"How do. Hot enough for you?" Sergeant Gordo asked. He laughed at his own joke. "Well. I understand you've got a missing mother."

Dicey nodded.

He took a pad out of his rear pants pocket and prepared to write with a ballpoint pen. "Give me her particulars," he said.

Dicey didn't understand.

"Name, age, weight, description, any distinguishing marks, last seen."

"Liza Tillerman, thirty-six," Dicey said. "I don't know how much she weighs."

"How's she built? Fat? Thin?"

"She's regular," Dicey said. "Sort of thin, I guess, but she has a regular shape."

"Height?"

"Two or three inches taller than I am."

"How tall are you?"

"I don't know."

"Stand up, will you?" His eyes measured her. "She'd be about five-six or seven. Any scars or moles?"

"She's got a big mole on her chin, and one at the back of her neck, under her hair. There are more, but those are the big ones. She's got blond hair, long blond hair. Hazel eyes, like mine. A round face, with high cheek-bones."

"What was she wearing when she took off?"

"Blue jeans. A sweater—a big, red, man's sweater, with holes in the elbows. Sandals. A purse over her shoulder."

"Rings? Watch?"

Dicey shook her head. Momma didn't have jewelry.

"Wedding ring?"

Dicey shook her head. The two men exchanged a glance.

"When did you last see her?"

"I'm not exactly sure. It was early in June."

"Where was it?"

Dicey told him about the mall in Peewauket. She told him about the car and how they had left it there.

He snapped his notebook shut. "I'll see what I can do for you," he said.

Dicey swallowed. "Do you think she's dead?"

He pursed his lips. "I can't say that, not now. If she is, we'll find out soon enough. Dead bodies stink, so we find them."

Dicey nodded. She didn't trust herself to speak.

Father Joseph seemed to understand that and he changed the subject. "I've put in a call to the church in Maryland."

"Crisfield," Dicey said. His eyes studied her briefly.

"Yes. The priest there will see what he can find out. Your people aren't Catholic."

"No," Dicey said. "We aren't anything. At least, I don't think we are."

His eyebrows went up. "Your Cousin Eunice is a devout Catholic," he said. "She was raised in the Church. But of course it was her father who was a Catholic—her mother converted when they married. She herself is very traditional in her devotion—she still chooses to keep meatless Fridays, for example."

But none of this interested Dicey. Her attention remained with the officer.

"How long will it take you?" she asked Sergeant Gordo.

"I can't say now, can I? Maybe a day. Maybe a year."

"No, I mean if she's dead."

"That'll take less time. If there's any possibilities I'll show you some pictures—oh, within a week."

"So if you don't tell me anything in a week—"

"Then we can be reasonably sure she's alive. Father Joseph tells me you don't have any idea what made her leave you."

"She didn't say," Dicey said. She looked at him. She didn't like him, but he could help her. "Do you want to know what I think?"

He took out his pad again. "Anything might be useful."

"I think she ran out of money and didn't know what to do, so she just—forgot about us. Her mind just erased us. Because she was so worried about us. Does that make sense?"

"The kind of people we deal with? Anything makes sense. Was she worried about anything in particular?"

"Everything. Always. She lost her job. That was why we were coming to Aunt Cilla's house—here."

"What about welfare? Or unemployment compensation?"

Dicey shook her head. "Momma said she couldn't do that. She wouldn't even go talk to anyone. She said charity was not for the Tillermans."

"I wish more people felt that way," Sergeant Gordo said. He folded his notebook and put it away again. "Well, I've got work to do."

Father Joseph stood up too. "And we have some children to pick up."

"But I can't leave the house. Cousin Eunice said not to leave the house empty and unlocked, and I don't have a key. Can't you get James first and then the other two? James can show me the way on Monday morning."

Father Joseph looked doubtful.

"James will remember all right. He's smart."

"Oh yes, that's very clear. I guess we can do it that way."

Dicey saw them out, and when they had gone she sat waiting on the hall staircase for her family to return to her. It seemed like a long time, waiting there in the dim, silent hallway.

At last they were at the door, James thin and thoughtful, Maybeth who hurried up to take Dicey's hand, and Sammy who stood grinning by the doorway. Dicey thanked Father Joseph and said good-bye to him. She took her family out to the kitchen. She gave them fruit and then they all went out to the back yard. Sammy wanted to play catch with Dicey, but she wanted to talk.

"What did you do? What was it like?"

"I talked with the teachers," James said. "It's a school building and they have arts and crafts and games in the afternoons. All the teachers are priests," he said, taking a huge bite of banana and chewing it. "They've got a library just for the school and labs with Bunsen burners and chemicals in cupboards. I knew almost all the answers to their questions," he reported proudly. "I think I'll like it."

Dicey was glad to hear that.

"They talked to me as if I was a high school student," James added.

"What about you Sammy? What did you do?"

"Played."

"Played what?"

"Blocks, sandbox. We had running races and I came in second. Some of the boys I beat were in third grade."

"What about the girls?"

"No girls in my camp. All the girls are in one, all the boys in another."

"So yours was all girls?" Dicey asked Maybeth. She nodded. "What did you play?" Maybeth didn't answer. "Did you stand with the teacher all the time?" Dicey guessed.

"Yes," Maybeth said in a small voice, with a small smile.

Dicey rumpled her hair. She wanted to know more about what they had been doing. Each of them had had an entirely separate afternoon. "Did anybody look friendly?" she asked.

"I didn't see any of the guys," James said. "They were figuring out what classes to put me in. They asked me what prayers I knew, and what about the Gospels and the saints. I don't know anything about any of those. Catechism," he pronounced the new word. "They'll teach me."

"You sound glad about going to school."

"Boy, am I." James smiled at her, his hazel eyes smiling too. "These fathers, they're all so smart. Really smart. I never had a teacher like that, not even one. These guys know so much. And they really want to teach me what they know. You can tell that. Yeah, I guess I am glad. So would you be."

"I doubt it," Dicey said. "It takes different things to make me glad."

"Like what?"

"Like knowing we've got food."

"Be serious, Dicey."

"The ocean," Dicey said. "And lots of room outdoors. But mostly the ocean. And the food too, that *was* serious."

"Father Joseph said to tell you we're all enrolled. He said you should take us on Monday."

"What was it like where Sammy and Maybeth were?"

James shrugged. "Playgrounds mostly, next to schools. Blacktop. Lots of jungle gyms and swings. The teachers for the girls, where Maybeth is, are nuns."

"Did you like the nuns?" Dicey asked Maybeth.

Maybeth didn't answer.

"All the other girls were wearing dresses," James reported.

"We have some dresses," Dicey said to Maybeth. "Father Joseph brought them today. Do you want to go try them on? And see how they look?"

Maybeth nodded. Dicey took her upstairs and she tried on the dresses. Cousin Eunice had come home before they got back downstairs.

Dicey found Cousin Eunice sitting again in the kitchen, waiting for the kettle to come to a boil. The little woman looked tired. She had taken off her glasses and was resting her forehead on her hands, rubbing her eyes. Dicey sent the children outside to play in the back yard and cautioned James to keep them out there. She sat down facing Cousin Eunice. "Are you tired? Can I get you something?"

At that moment the kettle whistled. "I'll make the tea," Dicey said, hopping up. She poured the water and dipped the tea bag in.

"Thanks," Cousin Eunice said. "Yes, I am tired. And I have an instruction class tonight—"

"An instruction class?"

"Religious instruction. I am studying to . . . I am studying. But my feet hurt so, I don't know if I can go tonight. Well of course I can, but—"

"What kind of work do you do?" Dicey asked. The woman was almost curled over onto the tabletop. Her face was pale and her eyes lacked expression. Dicey couldn't imagine what kind of work would make a person look like that.

"I'm a junior foreman. We attach the lace insets to lingerie, my girls and I. You know, on slips and nighties there are lace panels, or the cups of brassieres." Dicey didn't know, but she nodded anyway. "I've been quite successful in my work. There are only half a dozen junior foremen who are women, and only one senior foreman. But it's tiring—the supervising and the sewing and the quality control. It's a responsibility. You wouldn't believe some of the pieces of lace they expect us to set. We have to mend some of the pieces before we can even baste them in. And I'm on my feet most of the day, what with one thing and another. When Mother was here, she knew how tired I was." Her small, high voice droned on. "She'd always have a cup of hot tea waiting for me when I came in the door. And dinner on the table at six. I do get so hungry."

"Do you always get home at the same time?"

"Oh yes, at twenty to six, precisely." Dicey made a mental note. "But I have to begin dinner if we're to eat before my class." Cousin Eunice replaced her glasses and pushed herself up from the table, tottering a little in her high heels. She put a pot of water on to boil. She opened the can of tuna and the can of soup. Dicey tried to help, but she felt clumsy—as if she was interfering, not helping. So she set the table and found the noodles for Cousin Eunice.

"And did you get the living room done?"

"Yes I did."

"Good. You washed the windows?"

"Oh no. I forgot that. I'll do it in the morning."

"Oh dear, In the morning we'll do the upstairs. And take the sheets and towels to the laundromat. And do our personal laundry. I think we'll have to let the windows go until next week. Although they get so dirty."

"I'll do them," Dicey assured her.

"And the floor. Did you damp mop?"

"No, no I'm sorry, I didn't. I didn't know what you meant by that."

"We'll just have to do the living room as well, tomorrow. Somehow."

"I'll do it, don't you worry about it."

Cousin Eunice poured the noodles into the boiling water.

"But Cousin Eunice?"

"Yes, Dicey."

"You know that Father Joseph brought us some clothes."

"That's nice."

"Yes, it was nice. We are grateful. You'll tell him, won't you?"

"Yes I will."

"But—we need underwear, and there wasn't any. And blue jeans or shorts, just one more each, so that when we play we won't ruin good clothes. And sneakers. At least, the others need sneakers. I can still wear mine for a long time. I guess I don't have to have a second pair of shorts."

"Oh dear."

Dicey pushed the forks around on the table, as if she was still setting it.

"So we'll have to go shopping tomorrow too," Cousin Eunice said.

"Thank you," Dicey said.

"I don't know how much things for children cost."

"Neither do I. I'm sorry," Dicey said. "Maybe I could get work?"

"I don't think so," Cousin Eunice said. She was stirring the noodles with a long-handled fork. "I was talking with my girls and they said someone your age could only get baby-sitting jobs. I don't know anybody who has small children. We might advertise in the paper I suppose, but who would take care of the housework then? The girls said—you know how silly some people are—that I was a saint to take you in, that anybody else would turn you over to social services. But I said, I can't do that, they're my own flesh and blood. Which in a way you are, you know."

"Yes," Dicey said. Then she added, because she knew it was true even though she didn't feel that it was true, "You are being awfully kind to us."

Cousin Eunice nodded and smiled her foolish smile.

"James is excited about school," Dicey told her. "Maybeth and Sammy are enrolled in day camp."

"That's nice. And you dusted?"

"Yes. Everything." Dicey was glad to be able to answer yes to one of the cleaning chores. "Are those your photograph albums in the bookcase?"

Cousin Eunice nodded as she put a colander in the sink.

"May I look through them?" Dicey asked.

"I guess so," Cousin Eunice said. "I didn't keep the albums. They're Mother's work. Some of the pictures are very, very old. You'll be careful won't you?"

"Yes," Dicey said. "Will you be late coming home tonight?"

"After ten. There's no need for you to wait up. Mother never did. I expect you'll all be in bed by the time I return. There's a television in my bedroom you can watch. As long as you don't play in there. Children like watching television, don't they?"

Dicey answered with more enthusiasm than she felt.

"And tomorrow we'll have to remember to have a key made for you." Cousin Eunice sighed and drained the noodles.

CHAPTER 11

SOMETHING about Aunt Cilla's house (even though she knew it belonged to Cousin Eunice, Dicey still thought of it as Aunt Cilla's house, and still regretted her lost dream of it) made Dicey's brain slow down. Maybe it was trying so hard to please Cousin Eunice that had that effect on her. Maybe it was the routine of every day, with meals, cleaning, times to drop off the little children and pick them up, shopping, mending and ironing, having the cup of tea ready for Cousin Eunice at precisely twenty of six. Maybe it was just fatigue after her long journey there. Or maybe it was that nothing seemed to happen, except the same thing happening over and over again.

Even that was not precisely true. Sergeant Gordo called up one morning when Dicey was alone in the house. He asked her to come down to the police station, and gave her careful instructions for getting there on the bus. She took just enough change for her fare from shopping money and rode the bus down to the old stone building, with bars on the windows of the second and third stories. There she sat in the midst of a large, busy room to look at some pictures of women who might be Momma. None of them were. All of them, Sergeant Gordo told her, were dead and unidentified. They had found the Tillermans' car, he told her, and the Peewauket police could sell it and send the money to Dicey. He didn't expect she would get very much for it, he said.

"Does that mean Momma's not dead?" Dicey asked.

"I think we can assume that," Sergeant Gordo said.

"Now, I'll start checking hospitals. Part of the problem is that we don't know where to look. If you'd reported her missing right away, we'd have a better chance."

"I'm sorry," Dicey said.

"Fat lot of good that does now," he answered. His phone rang then, and he waved her away. "I'll be in touch if anything turns up."

Dicey didn't have much time for thinking about her family. James, she knew, was perfectly happy. He studied at night and went through the heavy wooden doors into the school at a run, every morning. Now and then he would report some amazing fact to Dicey. One time he told her about Alaric's treasure, that disappeared long ago when Rome ruled the world and America wasn't even discovered. Nobody had ever found the treasure because Alaric hid it so well. He diverted a river, then buried the treasure in the riverbed, then rerouted the river back to its old path. The treasure was somewhere there, in Italy. Only Alaric had known where. He even killed all the men who had worked to hide it, so they couldn't tell. James pored over the maps in his history book, trying to think out where the treasure might be. James was always willing to tell Dicey what he was learning, even though he seemed to have no interest in discussing other things with her.

Sammy, on the other hand, demanded more and more of her attention. He ran up to her every afternoon, grabbed her hand and pulled her away from the gate where she waited with Maybeth silent beside her. "Let's go," he said. "Let's play ball. Will you play catch with me? Can we race on the sidewalk?" He wanted to wrestle with her after dinner and needed her to tuck him in every night.

Maybeth was Maybeth. Silent and peaceful, she went off to church with Cousin Eunice on Sundays dressed in a frilly pink dress Cousin Eunice had bought her, wearing a little straw hat with flowers on the brim and white gloves. She even had a little white purse. Cousin Eunice had taken a great liking to Maybeth.

Dicey wondered if she was losing touch with her family.

Dicey had looked through Aunt Cilla's photograph albums. She didn't know what it was she was looking for, just something. There were only two pictures of Aunt Cilla's childhood, before she met and married Mr. Logan and lived in Bridgeport.

The first picture was a posed photographer's picture, badly yellowed, of a man with a long beard and a woman with long hair piled on top of her head. The woman held a baby on her lap. Beside her stood a girl with curling blond hair and a silly smile. Underneath this picture Aunt Cilla had written in her lacy handwriting: *Mother, Father, Abigail and myself.* Dicey thought Abigail must be the baby, since Cousin Eunice said Aunt Cilla was twelve years older than her sister.

The other picture must have been taken at a birthday party, because there was a cake with candles at the center of the picture. A pretty young woman in a white summer dress held a knife to cut the cake. Beside her, on one side, stood her parents, the man's beard turning white and the woman grown fat. On the other side stood a girl with wildly curly dark hair and a sour expression. The three adults were looking at the photographer and smiling. The little girl scowled down at the cake. Her hands were behind her back. Dicey would have bet that her fists were clenched.

Dicey recognized the oldest daughter as Aunt Cilla. The younger girl was Abigail. The sour one. Her grandmother.

One afternoon Dicey went early to meet James. She went early on purpose and entered the school building rather than going around to the playground to where James usually waited for her. She found Father Joseph in a small office, sitting behind a wooden desk correcting papers.

"We're very pleased with James," he said to her. "Sit down." He pulled out a chair. "How is everything going for you? You've been with your cousin for about two weeks now, haven't you?"

"Yes," Dicey said.

"Is something wrong?" he asked her. Then he seemed to recall something that had slipped his mind. "I've been wanting to talk with you anyway and haven't gotten around to it. I'm glad you came in. Shall we deal with your business first, and then get on to mine?"

"But you said you were pleased with James," Dicey said. She was alarmed. "He's happy here. Awfully happy."

"James is fine, fine," Father Joseph said. He closed up his grade book, folded his hands and looked at her. "What brought you to see me?"

"I wondered if you had heard from your church in Crisfield," Dicey said. Her mind was working furiously. Was something wrong about Maybeth? Or Sammy? Or both of them? She knew something was wrong with Sammy at camp, she'd known that all along.

"What do you know about your mother's family?" Father Joseph asked.

"Nothing. Momma never talked about them, never at all. Except Aunt Cilla. And that wasn't the truth—but Momma didn't know that. I found a picture of my grandmother in Aunt Cilla's albums, but she was only a girl, Maybeth's age. Cousin Eunice doesn't know anything. Did you find out something?"

"A little. The family is not Catholic, you know."

Dicey nodded. He kept bringing that up.

"So they aren't parishioners. If they were parishioners, then we would know a great deal about them. But—your grandmother. Her name is Abigail Tillerman."

"I knew that. There were names under one of the pictures."

"She lives alone on a small farm, outside of Crisfield. She lives absolutely alone there. Her husband died some years ago."

So Dicey didn't have a grandfather.

"They weren't Catholics, but Crisfield is a small town, where everybody knows everybody else. So—the priest asked some questions of his older parishioners. They had known the Tillermans. None of them had been friends—the Tillermans didn't seem to have friends—but they knew about them. He told me there were three children in the family. A boy, John, named after his father. People say he is in California. Nobody has heard from him for years, not his mother, nobody—twenty years or more. A second son died in Vietnam. Do you know about the war in Vietnam?"

Dicey nodded. Well, she had heard of it, and James would be able to tell her about it.

"Then the daughter, your mother. She ran off when she was twenty-one, they say, to join a merchant mariner she had somehow met, a man named Francis Verricker."

"My father?" The man who had swung her to his shoulder and named her his little only.

Father Joseph rubbed his hand over his eyes. "Yes. At least, that is the name on the birth certificates from Provincetown. I have no reason to think he was not everyone's father. The police are trying to trace him for me. They had searched for him some years ago. He seems to have disappeared."

"I don't mind," Dicey said.

"I do." Father Joseph's voice was sharp and angry. That surprised Dicey, and, sensing his concern, she was grateful to him, for the first time in all the time in Bridgeport, truly grateful.

"Do you mind hearing unpleasant truths, Dicey?"

"Yes. But I'd rather know the truth than not, if that's what you mean."

"I thought so. The Tillerman home—it must have been unhappy. Do you know what that can mean?"

"I think so," Dicey said. "I mean, we were happy. We were—whether you believe it or not . . ."

"Oddly enough, I do believe it."

Dicey smiled at him. "You see, there were kids at school—they hated their parents or they hated other people so much that you knew—it wasn't just being angry, it was hating. I can't explain what I mean, but I could feel the unhappiness."

"I see that James doesn't have all the brains in the family," Father Joseph said.

Dicey was flattered. "He's the smart one. I'm just—practical."

"Well, the Tillermans seem to have had that kind of unhappiness. The priest—or his informants—seem to blame her parents, especially the father. Remember, this is conjecture, not fact. It may just be gossip, you know. This is just what someone told him and he told me. Your grandfather seems to have been a stern man. An unbending man. Overrighteous perhaps. Perhaps cruel. Nobody knows anything certain. Your grandmother always let him have his way. Nobody can say what she thought. She never spoke of it. He had his boys do a man's work, from the time they were eight. He used a whip for disobedience, a real whip. He did not tolerate disobedience of any sort. He quarreled with his neighbors. He was angry—probably hate-filled too. She—your grandmother— was apparently the kind of woman who sticks faithfully to her husband's rule. She may have thought he was right. Or something else."

"It doesn't really matter which, does it?"

"In effect, no. You *are* practical."

"I haven't had much choice."

"Speaking practically then, your other uncle is dead, your mother has disappeared, and I don't think your Uncle John wants to be found. Which leaves your Cousin Eunice."

What was wrong with her grandmother? Dicey didn't ask aloud. She sat silent for a while. "What a family," she finally said.

"You shouldn't judge unless you've been there and known what actually went on," Father Joseph said.

"Come on," Dicey protested. "And Momma's—but she gave us a good home in Provincetown. She took good care of us, as good as she could."

"Yes, I think so, in some ways. One wonders," he said carefully, his light brown eyes resting on Dicey's face, "if there isn't a strain of—mental weakness."

Was he reading her mind?

"Your grandmother's isolation—she has no phone, so the priest drove out from Crisfield to talk with her. She wouldn't let him into the house. She apparently screamed aloud so that she wouldn't hear what he was saying."

Dicey remembered Momma's strangeness and James' idea that craziness was inherited.

"I mention this to you because I want to tell you that, if it can be inherited, you have probably *not* inherited it. In my opinion," Father Joseph said.

"Are you sure?"

"No, of course not. But remember, you've already been through more trials than most people endure in a lifetime. You and James, you two at least, seem to have the strength and resilience to go on. Isn't that what sanity is?"

"I don't know," Dicey said. She rose to go, her mind filled with what he had said.

"But we *are* concerned about your sister. She is—so far behind her age group. She doesn't speak. She can't read or work with numbers."

This again.

"She can," Dicey sat down again. "She can do all that. She isn't—she doesn't in front of strangers. Her teachers always said she couldn't do things, but at home, with me or James, she could. You don't believe me."

"No, I don't."

"You didn't believe me about our father being the same," Dicey reminded him.

"That's true."

"You just have to give Maybeth time."

"How much time? There's Sammy, too. The brothers report that he is not mixing in well. He is hostile to his peers and hard to direct and control. He plays alone, because the other boys avoid him."

Dicey sighed. "It was hardest on Sammy when Momma left us. And before it was hardest because she paid so much attention to him. James told me on our way here that in Provincetown Sammy had it hardest of anyone. Because of coming after Maybeth. And the things people said about Momma."

"How did you and James manage?" Father Joseph asked.

"James is smart. He'd think his own thoughts and ignore people. I guess I just fought back too hard for people to want to tease me. But Sammy wouldn't. I mean, he'd fight, but he's not as fierce as I am." Father Joseph smiled. "When he was a baby, he was always happy and friendly. That's the way he really is. He can still be that way. Sometimes, on the way here, you could see it, you could see him getting to be more like himself."

"Sammy is a difficult child," Father Joseph said. "But I suppose his hostility isn't surprising when you think of causes. He needs a warm, loving home."

So do we all, Dicey thought. She looked quickly at Father Joseph. "I love Sammy," she said.

"Of course you do. You must consider, however, the effect of these burdens on your own life. I think you must. I think you must give some thought to adoption and foster homes. Sammy, despite his behavior, may prove the easiest to find a home for. It will be hard to place Maybeth. A retarded child—"

"She's not!"

"She has the symptoms," Father Joseph answered gently. "And you, an older child. You also would be hard to place. Your cousin—I don't know what her plans are now."

Dicey had no idea what he was talking about. She shrugged her shoulders.

"James also is old for adoption, but he would easily find a permanent home here at the school, or he might stay with one of our families. His academic promise makes him most desirable."

Dicey could think of nothing to say.

"You should think of these things," Father said, still gently. "I know you don't want to, but you must think them through and be ready. Think of yourself also. You are still a child yourself."

A child? Dicey felt a hundred years old. Or more.

"I'm not asking you to decide. Just to open your mind to other possibilities."

Dicey nodded. She knew she should thank him, but she couldn't. So she just walked out of the room, without a word.

That afternoon, in the mail, Dicey received a check from the Police Department of Peewauket, for fifty-seven dollars. The receipt with it said "Profits from the sale of one 1963 Chevrolet sedan, less costs." Dicey looked at the check and smiled, for the first time in days, it felt. She could give it to Cousin Eunice and that would make her cousin feel better about taking the Tillermans in. Or she could buy some blue jeans for herself and Maybeth, which would make them feel better. Or she could hide the money away, for what purpose she didn't know.

Dicey knew what she should do. She should give the money to Cousin Eunice. Instead, she cashed the check at the grocery store, where the man knew her, and put the money into the box Maybeth's church shoes had come in.

Having money made a difference. It woke Dicey up. She began to think of how she could earn more during the day when everybody was gone. She could easily spend less time on housework if she pushed herself to be faster and more efficient. If she did that she could have some time for earning. Dicey felt like her old self again.

Because she was young, Dicey couldn't get a regular job. Over the next few days, she thought hard about what she could do to earn money. She could wash windows, she knew how, she'd done it. She decided to try that. If that didn't work, she would try something else.

The first place Dicey asked for work was the grocery store. The manager-owner, Mr. Platernis, liked her, so she figured she'd try him first.

Dicey suggested to Mr. Platernis that she wash his windows three times a week, for two dollars each time. He studied her.

"I've only got two windows," he said.

"They're plate glass, and big. I'd do them inside and out, and then I'd restack the canned goods and dog food," Dicey countered.

"You'd need some special equipment," he said. "A long-handled washer, a bucket, cleanser."

"If I knew I'd be using them I'd buy them," Dicey said.

He considered this. Dicey enjoyed the bargaining. He enjoyed it too. "I'd buy them here," Dicey added. "I'd buy all my supplies here too."

"You going into the business?"

"I might be."

He thought some more. "Two dollars is a lot of money."

"A store with clean windows is more attractive to customers. Especially a grocery store. More people would come to shop here."

"I can do the windows myself."

"Three times a week? They get pretty dirty."

"I know, oh I know. How about a trial period of a week?"

"Two weeks," Dicey said. "It'll cost me that much to get the equipment."

He laughed at her. "All right, two weeks. And I'll call some other people who might be interested, some other store owners in this area. We'll see if they would like to employ your services."

"Would you, Mr. Platernis? You won't be sorry." Dicey grinned at him.

By bargaining this way, before she knew it, Dicey had six regular jobs, washing the city grime off the windows of neighborhood stores. She had two grocery stores, one hardware store, one shoe store, one pawn shop and one dress store. The dress store was her best job—they had four big windows they wanted washed three times a week, so she earned twelve dollars a week from there. That, added to the six dollars weekly from Mr. Platernis and four apiece from the other three stores, made a total income of thirty dollars a week. Her supplies, once she had made the original purchase of bucket and long-handled squeegee, cost her five dollars a week. Mr. Platernis let her store her equipment in the closet with his own cleaning equipment and supplies, just to keep an eye on her, he said. He didn't need to worry—Dicey liked her work, she liked making money. The money in the shoebox began to mount up. Dicey's spirits mounted with it.

She was working hard, but she seemed to have more energy than before. The July heat thickened and deepened, but Dicey wasn't slowed down by that. Mr. Platernis couldn't get over her high spirits. "You must have been raised in the tropics," he said, mopping at his face with a cloth handkerchief. He often stood outside and talked with Dicey while she worked. He would help her replace the soup cans and bags of dogfood she had to move before she could wash the inside windows.

"I like having something to do," Dicey said.

"I'd think you have enough to do keeping house for Miss Logan and your family. Since you arrived I haven't seen her, except passing by. You're doing all her shopping, and the rest of it too, I'm guessing."

"That's not the same," Dicey said.

"You don't like housework," Mr. Platernis concluded.

Dicey didn't contradict him, though she knew that wasn't it. She didn't mind housework. She'd always kept house in Provincetown, although Momma wasn't nearly as fussy as Cousin Eunice. But it wasn't the same when you always had to remember to feel grateful.

Dicey bought herself three maps: one of Connecticut, one of New York and New Jersey, one of Maryland and Delaware. She found Crisfield easily enough, way down at the end of Maryland, facing the Chesapeake Bay.

One night at dinner Dicey tried to find out something about her grandmother. "Did you ever visit your mother's family?" she asked.

Cousin Eunice looked up in surprise. "Of course not. Mother said she didn't want to go back, and she wouldn't have me going near the place. Sammy! What are you doing? Sit up! Don't lie on the table! Bring the fork to your face, not your face to the fork." Her eyes, sulking behind the glasses, went back to Dicey. "I don't know why you children can't work on your manners yourselves, instead of worrying me with them. Don't you think I have enough to do?"

Dicey cast a quick eye around the table. Maybeth put her left hand into her lap and straightened her back. Then she met Dicey's glance with a silly smile, half worried, half apologetic.

"I have enough to do," Cousin Eunice went on, "And added to—" she hesitated and seemed to remember something. "Sammy? Is that a cut on your hand?"

Sammy chewed and nodded.

"How did that happen?" Cousin Eunice asked.

Sammy stuck his jaw out. He did not answer.

"Answer me," Cousin Eunice said.

"I don't remember," Sammy muttered.

"That is a lie."

"How do you know?"

"I know because I heard about how you got cut, that's how I know."

"Then why did you ask me?" Sammy demanded.

Maybeth bowed her head lower over her plate. Dicey looked at Sammy, trying to will him to be cooperative. Or at least quiet.

Cousin Eunice spoke through stiff lips. "Don't be fresh. Don't you ever be fresh with me. You hear? The reason I asked you is because—because—because I wanted to hear what you would say," she finished lamely.

"I didn't say nothing," Sammy said.

"What was the fight about?" Cousin Eunice asked.

"Nothing," Sammy said.

"Sammy?" Dicey interrupted. "Cousin Eunice wants to hear your side."

"I can't remember what it was about," Sammy said stubbornly. Dicey could have picked him up and shaken him.

"Who won?" James asked.

"James!" cried Cousin Eunice.

Sammy lifted his head. "Me, I did."

"That has nothing to do with it," Cousin Eunice said.

Yes it does, Dicey said to herself. It does to Sammy.

"I don't want you to fight any more," Cousin Eunice announced. "I want you to promise me that you won't."

Sammy chewed silently. He kept his eyes on his plate. At least, Dicey thought, his mouth was closed.

"Sammy—" Cousin Eunice warned him.

He shook his head.

"Then you will go to your room. Right now." Cousin Eunice's voice sounded angry, and tired. "And you will stay there for the rest of the night. You tell lies. You won't promise not to fight. I won't have you at my table."

Sammy got down from his chair and trudged out of the room. They heard his slow footsteps going up the uncarpeted stairs. They heard the door slam behind him.

"I don't know. I just don't know," Cousin Eunice said. She shook her head and the sausage curls on it bounced. "At least I hear some fine things about James. James seems to be making quite a good impression." She smiled at him.

James wavered between saying something rude and being flattered. Dicey watched him nervously. "James is smart," she said, trying to tip the scales.

"It's not only that," Cousin Eunice said. "James conducts himself well, too. He is a credit."

"It's a good school," James finally said. Dicey let out her breath. James looked across at her, waggled his eyebrows the way Windy had, and kept on talking. "When you think of all there is to learn, in order to understand things. Like history and science—there's so much to learn. The fathers say that part of man's purpose is to increase his knowledge, so that he can understand better how great is God's work. A lot of people think knowledge is dangerous. But they're wrong. Did you ever think of that, Cousin Eunice?"

"Yes, of course," Cousin Eunice said. "God wants children to study hard and behave well in school."

James answered slowly. "I guess you could say that. But that's not the way the fathers talk about it, about learning. They don't treat it like a duty. They treat it like a gift. Like grace."

"I don't think you can be right about that," Cousin Eunice said. "Not grace. That's not what the Gospels say, is it? Nobody's ever told me the Gospels say that. I've always understood that duty is the most important, even the best."

James shrugged. "Maybe learning's just that way for me. Lucky for me, isn't it?"

Cousin Eunice smiled at him. The tension was gone from the table. But Sammy hadn't had much dinner and he was up in his room. Dicey tried not to think about that. It was his own fault anyway, for being so stubborn. But Dicey had never talked about her fights when she got home—you just didn't do that. That was squealing. Momma never asked about them. Why did Cousin Eunice have to ask?

After the dishes were done and Sammy was asleep and Maybeth was tucked into her bed and James was settled down to homework in the living room, Cousin Eunice called to Dicey to join her in the kitchen. Dicey saw that a cup of tea had been made for her, and for some reason that made her nervous.

"Sit down, Dicey," Cousin Eunice greeted her. She was wearing another one of her black dresses. Dicey had never seen her wearing colors. Her eyes looked out at Dicey from behind polished glass. "I was talking with Father Joseph today."

"I didn't know that," Dicey said. She wondered what was wrong now.

"He took me to lunch," Cousin Eunice said. "Well, I was surprised when he asked me. I wasn't sure it was right—but he insisted that it was. We didn't go to a real restaurant, but it was a very nice cafeteria, everything as clean as you could want. I had a fruit salad. There's something I haven't ever told you, you see, and Father Joseph thinks I should."

"What is that?" Dicey asked.

"Before you came, you and your family, I had certain—ambitions," Cousin Eunice said. Her voice was very soft and she stirred her tea thoughtfully. "Father Joseph knows of these, of course. He approved of them, with certain reservations. And since he had approved, I was sure it was the right thing."

"What was?"

"To enter a sisterhood. To become a nun. I was going to be a nun before . . . and Father Joseph had made the preliminary arrangements for me. It's a useful life. I have a substantial savings account, which would make up my dowry, that and the house. So you see, I could have managed well."

"It sounds—" Dicey tried to think of what she should say. "Nice. You'd make a good nun."

"Do you think so? I had hoped so. However, that is out of the question now." Cousin Eunice's eyes filmed with tears, and she shook her head. "Because of you children. You need me more, Father Joseph says. It is God's work, just as much, caring for the abandoned children." As she spoke, she looked over Dicey's shoulder at something Dicey couldn't see, something Dicey suspected wasn't there at all, and her eyes shone. "That is my duty. You will be my family now." Her soft voice vibrated with the pleasure of resolution and sacrifice.

"Are you sure?" Dicey asked.

"It is God's will," Cousin Eunice said, bowing her head.

Dicey sipped tea, which she had never liked, and thought about this. "That's awfully kind of you."

Cousin Eunice smiled at Dicey.

"You're giving up something you want," Dicey said.

"You are not to speak of that," Cousin Eunice said. "I wasn't going to tell you at all, but Father Joseph said that you and I especially must understand one another. So that if sometimes I grow sad . . . you will know why and sympathize with me rather than feeling you've done something wrong. Perhaps Maybeth is meant to be a nun, perhaps she has a vocation, and it will be my place to guide her to it. Perhaps she will be my purpose in life."

Dicey wanted to get up and run, but she made herself sit still.

"Father Joseph suggested that I adopt you, so that I will be the legal guardian."

"What if Momma comes back?"

"Surely she has shown herself unfit to raise children," Cousin Eunice answered. Her lips pursed.

Dicey couldn't answer that.

"However, Dicey, you and I must deal with Sammy. He's causing some trouble at camp. Not just today—constantly. Father Joseph said he had spoken to you about this. Sammy has to be brought into line. I couldn't adopt a child who will bring nothing but trouble. Could I? You saw how he behaved at supper. Sammy has to understand that his behavior is unacceptable."

"But—" Dicey said, and then changed her mind. "How would you do that?"

"I'll talk with Father Joseph. He's not sure that my house is the best place for Sammy, but he feels we should try it for a while, to see if we can keep your family together. He's concerned about Maybeth, too, he told me, but I could assure him that we would do well, Maybeth and I. But Sammy—I don't know. I'll see. Father Joseph knows about disciplining boys. James, fortunately, is biddable. Sammy has to be brought into line, so he doesn't shame me."

Dicey stayed absolutely still. She didn't even blink. She didn't trust herself to speak.

"I *do* feel better, now that we've talked. Don't you?" Cousin Eunice looked happy. Her curls bounced on her head. "You will be like a family of my own. If I'd had a daughter, she might be just your age. You'll grow up and have children of your own. So that when I'm older, I won't be alone. Just as Mother wasn't alone. In a way, I'm glad about this. Aren't you? And you children will have a good mother."

We already have a good mother, Dicey said angrily to herself. Hold on, she said to herself. This was what Father Joseph had decided. It might be for the best. The Tillermans would be able to stay together—maybe. They would have a home. Dicey knew she should feel grateful to Cousin Eunice. But she didn't. She felt like crying.

AUGUST choked the city. The morning sun had to burn its red path through low-hanging hazes and clouds of industrial smoke. The streets steamed, as concrete reflected heavy sunlight. The temperature climbed until one in the afternoon, and then continued climbing. When it rained, fat gray drops plopped down upon the roads, then bounced up, as if in a halfhearted effort to escape. At evening, darkness gradually smothered the sun, until night fell upon the city.

Dicey rose early every morning, cooked the breakfasts, cleaned the kitchen, walked her family to their daily activities and hurried back to pick up her equipment and wash whatever store windows were on her schedule for the day. Then she completed whatever housekeeping chores Cousin Eunice had assigned before she went to fetch her family, played briefly with them, prepared dinner and made Cousin Eunice's cup of tea.

Weekends were a little different. For those two afternoons, the Tillermans could go off to a park or a public beach after they had completed the morning chores, or after Maybeth had returned from church with Cousin Eunice.

Sometimes it was more convenient for Dicey to meet Maybeth at the church, if they were going to picnic at the park, or if Cousin Eunice had friends she wanted to visit with. Dicey would wait outside the big brick building, waiting for the heavy doors to be opened from within. The steeple stretched tall up into the sky. There was a gold cross on top of the steeple, and from below it looked like the tip of the cross scratched the bottom of the sky.

When the doors opened, Dicey watched carefully for her sister. Lots of children went to church with their parents, all of them dressed up. The girls wore organdy dresses and party shoes and ribbons in their hair, or hats. The boys wore real suits and ties. Cousin Eunice always walked out slowly, surrounded by a group of women who could have been her sisters. They dressed alike. They all wore those high-heeled shoes. They all had curled their hair into sausages.

These women made a pet out of Maybeth. She would stand in the middle and they would tell her how pretty she was, how lucky she was to have naturally curly hair, and what a sweet, quiet girl she was. "You're going to break some hearts for sure," they said, giggling.

Maybeth listened to this and smiled foolishly.

"An angel like you—nobody will be good enough for you. She's a treasure, Eunice," they said.

"Don't I know it?" Cousin Eunice answered, smugly.

"A doll, a perfect doll."

Dicey put her hands behind her back and clenched her fists, waiting for Cousin Eunice to see her.

When Cousin Eunice called her, the women stepped back and smiled primly at her. Maybeth put out her hand for Dicey to take. Her eyes were wide as she looked at Dicey, wide and pleased with the attention. The silly smile stayed.

Sunday afternoons the Tillermans chose to go to a small park nearby because on summer weekends it was less crowded than the beach. There were trees there, and grass. Several times Dicey saw Mr. Platernis in the park, who greeted her warmly with: "How's my go-getter today?" Nobody commented on this, except James, but Dicey abruptly changed the subject.

She found a time, soon after her talk with Cousin Eunice, to try to explain the situation to Sammy.

"You've got to be cooperative at camp," Dicey said.

"I don't like them," Sammy said.

"Don't like who? The boys? or the teachers?"

"Don't like any of them."

"Why not?"

"They're all bossy."

That was all he would say. His little jaw stuck out, and he pulled at blades of grass as they sat by the sandbox.

"We've got a problem, Sammy," Dicey said. "We have to please Cousin Eunice. The way for you to help is to cooperate at camp. Act more friendly."

"Why?" Sammy asked.

"So we can all stay together with Cousin Eunice," Dicey said.

"When Momma comes we won't have to. And I don't want to anyway."

Dicey sighed. She didn't much want to herself. She daydreamed about Crisfield and a farm; but she had learned her lesson about believing in daydreams, learned it from Cousin Eunice and her house that wasn't a big white house by the ocean.

"Would you do it for James and Maybeth and me?" Dicey asked him. "Would you try, for us? I know it's hard. I know you get angry. But we need you to try. When we were on our own, you stopped quarreling and helped. Remember?"

Sammy nodded.

"You liked that, didn't you?"

Sammy nodded.

"All I want you to do is be more that way at camp. Can you try?"

Sammy nodded. "You sound like Momma," he said.

"What do you mean?"

"Well you do. When she'd ask me to be gooder, that was the way she'd talk."

He ran off to join Maybeth on the swings. Dicey watched him catch a flying swing and leap onto it, then pump furiously with his sturdy little legs. When he caught up with Maybeth, he cheered for himself.

Day succeeded day in slow procession. Cousin Eunice treated Dicey differently since their talk. She wanted to sit with Dicey in the kitchen every night, with cups of tea which Dicey could never completely drink, and talk about religion and serving God and how when she was a girl she had wanted to be a nun. But her mother said she wasn't strong enough in spirit, didn't have a real calling, should wait to see if she got married.

Dicey listened. She began to feel sorry for Cousin Eunice, who had lived all of her life in this city, who had gone off to work every morning along the same gray city streets. Dicey didn't like the sound of Aunt Cilla. She had lied to Momma in her letters. It seemed to Dicey that Aunt Cilla had tried to keep Cousin Eunice all for herself. And then, Dicey thought to herself as the soft voice droned on about service and prayer, just when Cousin Eunice was about to do what she'd always wanted, the Tillermans turned up to tie her down again. Poor Cousin Eunice.

If that had happened to Dicey, she'd be angry. Cousin Eunice wasn't angry at all, just sad sometimes. As if this was the way her whole life had to be, not getting what she wanted, always giving it up for the sake of someone else.

Maybe she enjoyed giving things up for the sake of someone else. Some people liked that feeling. But even if that was the case, Dicey knew her cousin would rather have been a nun. That was what she really wanted.

It wasn't very much to want, and she didn't have even that.

The money in Dicey's shoebox increased slowly, day by day. Sixty-five, seventy, which, with the fifty dollars she had left from the car, made one hundred and twenty, then one hundred and forty dollars, one hundred and fifty.

Maybeth came home from camp with a note addressed to Miss Tillerman. The note requested Dicey to come to camp the next afternoon at two, an hour before the children went home. Somebody named Sister Berenice wanted to talk to her.

Dicey didn't want to go. She knew what the sister would say. She read the note and reread it. She considered throwing it away and pretending she had never gotten it, as Momma had done. She ripped it up into little pieces and dropped them into the wastepaper basket. She didn't want to hear whatever the sister had to say about Maybeth being retarded and needing a special school.

James was no help. He seemed convinced that the fathers, and the nuns too, couldn't make a mistake. "Go and talk to her. Maybe she knows something we don't. Maybe she knows something that can help Maybeth. Just plan to learn from her, about whatever she has to say. You've got to keep an open mind, Dicey. You've got to leave a door open so understanding can get in. That's one thing I've learned."

"It's not just minds," Dicey said. "You all think it's just smartness that counts. But Stewart didn't think that. And I don't think I do, either. I don't want to go."

"Suit yourself," James said. "I'd go."

"I'm not you," Dicey said.

But she kept the appointment, wearing one of the secondhand dresses that made her feel stiff and awkward because they never fit properly. She wore sneakers, because they were the only shoes she had. She held her chin high and a little angry—she knew Maybeth and this woman didn't.

Sister Berenice waited for Dicey in one of the classrooms next to the camp playground. It was a room for very small children. All the chairs were small. The tables didn't even come up to Dicey's knees.

Sister Berenice rose from her desk when Dicey came into the long room. The sister was very tall and very thin. She wore a black suit with a longish skirt, and her face was framed by the cowl she wore. She had pale blue eyes and her mouth looked stern. When she pulled up one of the little chairs for Dicey to sit on, Dicey saw with surprise that she wore a silver wedding ring on her right hand.

"You're a child," she said. Dicey nodded. "I asked Maybeth," Sister Berenice said, sounding cross, "I asked her who her guardian was and she said Dicey, her sister. I asked if you were married and Maybeth said no. Well, actually, she just shook her head. It is the longest conversation we have had. I didn't think to ask Father Joseph how old you were. Who is the person legally responsible for Maybeth?"

"Our Cousin Eunice, I guess," Dicey said. "Until they find our mother."

"Miss Logan," Sister Berenice murmured, in apparent disbelief.

"She took us in. She didn't have to do that," Dicey said. "She'd never even heard of us." She wanted Sister Berenice to appreciate what Cousin Eunice had done. She wanted to appreciate it herself.

"How old are you?" she asked Dicey.

Dicey's temper flared. "I'm thirteen. How old are you?"

A smile bent the corners of Sister Berenice's pale mouth. "Fifty-three, old enough to recognize spirit when I meet it. Tell me about your sister, Dicey."

Dicey stared at her in surprise. For a minute she couldn't think of anything to say. Usually, people told her about Maybeth, and she tried to explain that they were wrong. Nobody had ever asked her, first.

"She's shy," Dicey said. "She almost never speaks to strangers. And people always want to speak to her, because she's pretty. Usually, she stays stiff and quiet and stares, with big eyes. She doesn't even talk to us much. But when she does, it's always the right thing to say. Not right-polite, right-true."

Sister Berenice sat listening, with folded hands. So Dicey went on.

"I don't know why Maybeth is the way she is. But she's always been that way. From the time she started school, her teachers thought she was stupid. I guess I can understand that. She would be so quiet that you'd think she didn't know anything. She stayed back one year, in first grade. Then the teacher wanted to keep her back this year, or at least that's what I think. Momma never opened those notes."

"You said she almost never speaks to strangers. That means she sometimes does. Who did she speak to?"

Dicey told her how Maybeth had talked to Stewart and sung with him. "She sings—it's lovely when she sings. She learns songs fast, music and words. She couldn't be retarded and do that, could she?"

Sister Berenice just smiled.

"And she *can* read," Dicey said. "Not like James, but as well as Sammy. She used to read to me at home when I asked her to. And she *can* add and subtract." Dicey thought. "She's not quick, but she can work the problems out. It just takes her a longer time to learn school things, and she's too shy to say what she knows. When she plays, she builds gardens and castles and makes up stories about them." Dicey had never before defined so exactly just what Maybeth could and could not do. "I guess she's slow at school, but I don't think she's retarded. Or anything like that."

"Would you go look out the window at the children?" Sister Berenice asked Dicey. Puzzled, Dicey obeyed.

The playground was surrounded by a tall fence. Little groups of children were gathered about, playing or reading or listening to one of several nuns who were out there with them. Dicey's eyes searched for Maybeth among the many little girls.

She found her, sitting in a circle around a nun with a guitar. Maybeth sat behind the group. Her dress, like Dicey's, was long and dark. Her face was round and sad. All the other little girls were singing and clapping their hands, but Maybeth was staring at the nun's hands as they played on the instrument. She was not singing. She was not clapping.

The nun stopped playing and said something, at which all the little girls jumped up and ran to different parts of the playground. Maybeth didn't move. The nun bent to speak to her and she looked up.

"But she looks frightened," Dicey said. "Why does she look frightened?" She heard the rude, demanding tone of her own voice.

Sister Berenice didn't answer.

"I see what you mean," Dicey said. Maybeth did look different from all the other little girls. Dicey watched her sister walk slowly over to the swings. She stood there. Several girls were swinging energetically. There were some unoccupied swings, but Maybeth didn't get onto one. The other girls paid no attention to her.

It was as if Maybeth wasn't even there, not even to herself. What was wrong with her? She looked—empty.

"But she isn't that way," Dicey started to say.

"I wonder," Sister Berenice said in a voice that suggested doubt. Sister Berenice didn't believe Dicey. Why should she?

"Father Joseph said that you were unusual," Sister Berenice said to Dicey.

"He did?"

"Yes." The rich voice assured Dicey that this was the truth. "To keep your family together, and fed. But I wonder if you have faced the truth about Maybeth. I think you may be fooling yourself." This, too, Dicey recognized, was the truth.

Maybe she was, maybe . . .

"Do you know the kind of special schooling available to a child like Maybeth? Not through us, of course, but the state maintains excellent facilities for disabled children. There is much they can learn and do, such children, if they are properly taught. Is it fair to Maybeth to deny her the opportunity, just because you don't want to face the facts?"

"No," Dicey said. The word burst from her.

"I didn't think you wanted to do that to Maybeth."

"No," Dicey said again. "Those aren't the facts."

"Oh, now," the nun said. She sounded disappointed in Dicey.

Dicey sighed. "I'm sorry," she said. "I don't mean to be rude."

"Are you thinking of Maybeth or of yourself?" Sister Berenice asked quietly.

Dicey didn't know, and she didn't care; she was too tired and discouraged to think of an answer. This nun had already made up her mind anyway. Dicey didn't want to think about Maybeth any more. She was arguing more from habit than conviction. "You just don't know," she repeated.

"I think I probably know better than you do."

Dicey was finished arguing. She just wanted to get out of there and take Maybeth with her. "Can Maybeth come with me now? It's almost time."

The nun stared at her for a long time. Finally she answered, "Yes, of course." But her voice said more, it told Dicey that the sister was sorry she had asked Dicey to come in. Well, Dicey was sorry too. She nodded, and left the room.

Dicey entered the playground through the tall iron gates. She started to walk over to where Maybeth was, but a young nun came and asked her what she was doing there. She sounded important, as though she was accustomed to being obeyed without question. Dicey explained who she was. She said that she had been meeting with Sister Berenice and had permission to take Maybeth home. The young nun looked back at the windows behind them and stood aside.

Maybeth had seen Dicey. She smiled at her, but did not come running as Sammy would have. Dicey smiled back and hoped the way she was feeling didn't show in her face. "Let's go get Sammy," she said, holding out her hand.

*   *   *

Sammy had a cut on his forehead that someone had covered with a big Band-Aid. His lip was swollen. "Oh Sammy." Dicey could not keep the worry out of her voice. "You said you'd try."

"I did."

"You were in a fight," Dicey said. "And a pretty bad one."

"He said—"

"Who? Who said?"

"Johnny. I don't know his last name. And I don't care. He's a big kid. He's in fourth grade. I made him cry and I didn't cry."

"What did he say?"

"He said I was going to a foster home because nobody here likes me. He said he heard the fathers saying it. It's not true, is it Dicey? So I fought him."

"What did the fathers say?"

"Johnny's the one that heard them. He said they didn't know he could hear."

"No, no. I mean when they stopped the fight. They did stop it, didn't they?"

Sammy nodded. They were walking to James' school. Dicey held one hand of each of the little ones. There was too much bad news in this day.

"They didn't say nothing. We didn't tell 'em nothing."

"So they think it's all your fault, don't they?"

Sammy nodded. "I have to stay inside alone tomorrow. All day."

"Oh, Sammy. Why didn't you tell them what Johnny said?"

"Because they try to find out everything. What's a foster home?"

"You didn't know? And you fought about it?"

"It's not good is it? I could tell that. From how he said it."

Dicey sighed. "A foster home is where somebody not your own family takes you into their home to live. And somebody gives them an allowance, to pay for you."

"You wouldn't let them do that, would you Dicey? I told Johnny and he said you couldn't stop them."

Dicey felt helpless, absolutely helpless, with the two little ones holding her hands. She knew how Sammy felt. She wanted to fight somebody herself. Or to run, fast, not waiting for lights to change. But she had the two little ones holding onto her.

"There's James now," she said to Sammy. Sammy ran to meet his brother. James was walking quickly, a huge smile on his face. At least one of us is happy, Dicey thought.

Dicey called the bus station and found out that it cost twenty-six dollars to get to Crisfield. Fifty-two dollars there and back. She would still have some money, so she wouldn't be dependent. She would stay in a hotel or something, for a couple of days. It was only for a couple of days, until she took a look at this grandmother, to see for herself.

She purchased a small overnight case at the Goodwill store. She located the bus station in Bridgeport. There, she picked up a bus schedule and found out that if she left Bridgeport at ten o'clock in the morning, she would have to change at New York for Wilmington. At Wilmington, she decided by looking at a map, she could get a bus to take her down to Easton, then Salisbury, then Crisfield. Easton and Salisbury were yellow on the map so they were big towns. There would be sure to be buses.

This was on a Thursday. She thought she would go the next Monday, so that the little ones would be in camp during the day while she was away. James could take charge, for four days. That was all she'd be gone for. They would just have to get along without her for four days. There was no way she could take them with her. Just as there was no way she could tell Cousin Eunice she was going.

That evening, Cousin Eunice came home late from work carrying a bakery bag. "Father Joseph called me at work. He is bringing a friend by after supper, after the children are in bed," she said. "I got a cake on my way home. Did you get the living room done today? It's Thursday."

Dicey nodded.

"Father Joseph said you have already met this man, a policeman. I have not. Did you wash the windows?"

Dicey had forgotten that. She lied. Well, it wasn't an entire lie, since she had washed windows that day. She just hadn't washed the windows Cousin Eunice meant.

"And a good vacuuming? I don't know—the house gets so dirty with all you children. I don't know how you manage to collect so much dirt and bring it inside." She fluttered about the kitchen, fussing over one thing and another, looking in the icebox for lemons, in the cupboard to be sure her good teapot was clean and there was sugar in the sugar bowl.

It could not be good news they brought. Dicey knew that ahead of time. If it had been good news, the sergeant would have called her up right away, or Momma would have called her up, or Momma would have appeared at the house.

Father Joseph and Sergeant Gordo arrived late. The two men and Cousin Eunice sat in all the chairs there were in the living room. After she had passed around the teacups, milk, sugar, lemon and cake, Dicey sat on the floor. She was wearing one of the stiff dresses Father Joseph had brought. Cousin Eunice twittered as she poured tea, then fell silent.

"We have located your mother," Sergeant Gordo said. He held a teacup in one hand and a plate with cake in the other. He could neither eat nor drink, because he had no free hand. He looked around for a table to set the plate on. Cousin Eunice made a little *Oh* sound at this news.

"I thought so," Dicey said.

"I don't have anything good to tell you," Sergeant Gordo said.

"I didn't think so," Dicey said. She made her face expressionless.

"You're a smart kid," the sergeant said. "Your mother is in a state hospital in Massachusetts. She was found in Boston. She—do you know the term catatonic?"

Dicey shook her head.

"It means the patient won't respond to anything. Your mother—well she doesn't do anything, doesn't speak, doesn't seem to hear what's said to her, won't feed herself, won't move at all, not even to go to the bathroom. When they found out about her family, the doctors tried talking to her about you. No response. No response at all. Nothing. They think she's incurable."

Dicey nodded. "Are you sure it's Momma?"

"Her fingerprints match the ones the hospital took when you children were born."

"Why did they do that?" Dicey asked. She didn't know why she asked. She didn't care what he answered.

"So the mothers and babies can be sure they go together. They do the baby's feet. So nobody gets mixed up."

"Oh."

"And I've got a picture."

Dicey took the photograph. She looked at the vacant-faced woman lying in a bed, her hair cut off short and her hazel eyes staring at the camera without any expression, as if the camera and photographer were not there. Her face looked so flat and empty, so far away, as if it hung miles above the earth and could not be bothered by anything happening on the little planet below. "They cut her hair," Dicey said. "Are they sure she's incurable?"

"These head-shrinkers are never sure of anything. But they're as near to sure as they can be."

"I could go see her," Dicey suggested.

"I wouldn't do that, little girl. They'll get in touch with us if there's any change, and then maybe it might do some good."

"It would be best to forget her," Father Joseph said.

"What if I don't want to?" Dicey demanded, angry.

"I didn't mean that, child. I meant, it is better not to have false hopes."

Dicey clamped her mouth shut.

"Poor Liza," Cousin Eunice said. "She's only five years younger than I am. Do you know that?"

Cousin Eunice poured out more cups of tea, which Dicey passed around. The adults talked around her and above her, about adoption procedures and welfare applications. "Sammy is on trial here," Cousin Eunice said to Father Joseph.

He nodded. "As is Maybeth," he answered. Cousin Eunice shook her head but didn't say anything. Dicey walked out of the room. She heard Cousin Eunice start to call her back and Father Joseph say to let her go.

Maybeth was asleep and so was Sammy. James wasn't. Dicey undressed and lay down on her cot. Her mind was blank.

"What about Momma?" James whispered.

"How'd you know?"

"That policeman . . . they came in a police car."

"Momma's gone crazy," Dicey reported in a flat voice, "and they don't think she'll ever get better. She's in a mental hospital. She was in Boston. How do you think she got to Boston?"

James sat up. "What kind of crazy?"

"A kind where you just lie in bed and don't do anything. James, do you think Maybeth's like Momma?"

"Yes."

"Do you think Maybeth could go crazy like that?"

"Yes. If—if she had to. You know? Momma had four kids and no job. Our father walked out on her."

"But we were happy, weren't we? When we were in Provincetown. We were, I know it. Momma wasn't crazy then."

"Maybe. I don't know, Dicey. Does that mean this is our home?"

"Yeah. I guess so. I don't know, James. Would you like that?"

"It's a good school," James said. "I've never been in a school like this, where the teachers all know so much and they like it when you ask questions and they keep giving you more work. Nothing bothers the fathers, you know? Oh, swearing and things, those. But they're so sure they have the answers, they don't mind you asking questions. In this school, I'm really glad I'm me. I can learn anything—do you know how that feels, Dicey? The fathers show me how and I learn. You better believe I'm happy."

"Should we tell Sammy and Maybeth?"

"About Momma? I guess so, sometime. Not right now. Or is right away better?"

So they woke the two younger children and told them the bad news. Maybeth just nodded and sat closer to Dicey on the cot.

Sammy stuck his chin out. "She'll still get better maybe," he declared. "How do they know so much anyway. I don't care what they say. I won't believe them."

Dicey grinned at him, unable to stretch her mouth wide enough to let out all the feelings his silly stubbornness let her feel. Then she began to cry. "I'm sorry, Dicey," Maybeth said.

"Me too," Dicey said, burying her face in her sister's hair. "I'm sorry too."

Now she had to go on Monday and find out fast what Crisfield was like. What their grandmother was like. Cousin Eunice would flutter and flitter, and before they knew it the Tillermans would be adopted. Or something worse.

It was not that Dicey was ungrateful. They might end up here. Cousin Eunice's house might be the best place for them. Even for Sammy and Maybeth. It might be the best they could do, even if Sammy and Maybeth had to go somewhere else. But Dicey had to know that for sure.

That weekend she took the family to the beach. She was especially careful to pay attention to them. She laughed at Sammy's jokes and turned cartwheels on the sand with him and tossed him up over her shoulders into the water until he was exhausted. She built castles with Maybeth, decorating them with bits of shell and colored stones, telling stories about princesses and giants. She talked with James about history and science, listening with all her brain, so her questions would show that she was really interested.

Monday morning, she walked them all to camp and school. Sammy hesitated at the gate and said, "I wish it was always the weekend."

Dicey ruffled his hair.

Maybeth let go of Dicey's hand and walked slowly over to where the little girls were gathering. Her dress was too long for her. She looked clumsy.

Dicey asked James to pick up the little children. "I'll leave the door unlocked. I've got something to do," she explained. "Can you get them at the end of the day? And don't be late—Maybeth worries."

James smiled happily over his pile of books. "Sure thing," he said. He ran up the steps to the doorway and turned to wave before he went inside.

Dicey hurried back to the little gray house. She had already told her customers she was taking the week off. She pulled the overnight case out from under her bed, put underwear, toothbrush, clean shirts and shorts into it. She put in the shoebox with her money, the bus schedule and her map of Maryland. She would wear a dress for traveling.

Downstairs, Dicey wrote a hasty note to James, asking him to take charge until she got back, telling him where she was going, saying she was sorry but he would have to tell Cousin Eunice. She put her house key into the envelope and sealed it. She wrote James' name on the front and left it on the kitchen table. Suitcase in hand, Dicey opened the front door.

James sat on the stoop.

"I thought so!" he crowed, laughing at her as she stood, open-mouthed, the suitcase in one hand, the door knob in the other. "You can't fool me!"

"I left you a note," Dicey said. "I've got to hurry or I'll miss the bus."

"The next bus doesn't leave Bridgeport until ten," James answered. "You've got a whole hour." He smirked at her.

"James!" Dicey cried. "You've been snooping in my things."

"And here comes Sammy, right on schedule," James said. "I told him, when I found that money box. Besides, there was that man at the park, the grocer. I'd make a good detective. We're going with you."

"I don't have enough money," Dicey said. "What about Maybeth?"

"You'll think up a way," James said. "Where are we going anyway?"

"But what about your school?" Dicey asked. "I mean, you're the one who's really happy here. I will come back, you know that."

"How do I know it?" James told her. "I know you mean to—but what if you can't, or don't?"

"I wouldn't do that!" Dicey protested.

"How do you know? How does anybody know? I don't want you to leave me behind. Besides, school—well, Dicey? Listen. It's me that makes the school so good, my brain. Other kids don't like it as much as I do. So, there are books all over the world, in libraries. The fathers help me, an awful lot—but there must be other schools with good teachers. Even if there aren't, I'll always be me."

"Are you sure, James?"

"I'm sure I want to go with you. And so does Sammy."

Dicey couldn't think clearly. She couldn't think at all. Sammy marched up to them. "I crossed four streets with lights," he announced. "Hi, Dicey. I didn't believe James, but he was right."

Dicey didn't even try to argue further. They all went back inside. She sent the boys upstairs to get changes of underwear for everyone, and shorts and shirts. She changed into shorts herself. She wrote another note, to Cousin Eunice this time, a note much harder to write. Dicey knew that Cousin Eunice wouldn't understand, no matter what she said.

"We are going to Crisfield," she wrote. "I don't want you to worry about us, because I will take care of everyone. I don't know what will happen there. When we find out, I'll write to you." Dicey chewed on the end of the pencil and tried to think of some way to let Cousin Eunice know that they *were* grateful to her. "No matter what happens to us, I think you should go ahead and become a nun because it is what you really want to do," she wrote. "Your cousin, Dicey Tillerman." Once again, she put the house key in the envelope and sealed it.

Dicey went alone to fetch Maybeth. The boys waited at the corner, with the suitcase.

Dicey walked right into the playground. Groups of little girls ran around. The young nun approached her. Dicey took a deep breath. "I've come for Maybeth Tillerman," she said. "I'm her sister. Sister Berenice said I should pick her up now," she lied.

The nun hesitated. She squinted her eyes at Dicey.

"You can go and ask Sister Berenice if you like," Dicey said. "But then we'll be late for Maybeth's appointment and she'll be angry."

The nun called Maybeth from the sandbox where she was playing alone. Dicey took the little girl's hand and walked slowly out through the gates. She had to hold herself back from running.

"Where are we going?" Maybeth asked.

"We're going to see the place Momma lived in when she was a little girl," Dicey answered.

"All of us together?"

"All of us together," Dicey said. "That's the only way the Tillermans travel."

PART TWO

CHAPTER 1

T HE motor rumbled like hunger in the belly of the bus. The fumes that
floated in through the open windows were swollen with heat. They were
on their way. Again.

Dicey leaned back in her seat and tried to make herself relax. They had until
evening, when Cousin Eunice got home. Unless the camps wondered why all
the Tillermans were absent and called Cousin Eunice at work. She didn't think
that was likely.

James leaned towards Dicey. They were the only people sitting in the back of
the bus. Nobody would hear them over the sound of the motor.

"It's like a prison break, isn't it?"

Dicey knew what he meant. Even so, "That's not fair," she said. "Cousin Eunice wasn't a jailer."

James shrugged. "Whadda you think?" he asked out of the corner of his
mouth. "I think, if we can get to New York without being caught—we'll be
home free."

Home, Dicey thought. She remembered the inscription on the tombstone:
Home is the sailor, home is the hunter. Until she died, Dicey wouldn't expect any
place to be home. Home was with Momma—and Momma was in a hospital
where the doctors said she'd always stay. There could be no home for the
Tillermans. Home free—Dicey would settle for a place to stay. Stay free.

Cousin Eunice's house wasn't free; it was expensive. The price was always remembering to be grateful. And there was danger to Sammy and Maybeth, of
being sent to foster homes or special schools; danger to Dicey and James of forgetting and saying what they thought before wondering if it would sound ungrateful. At Cousin Eunice's house, they were kept busy so they wouldn't be a
bother, couldn't get in trouble.

Dicey had lowered her sights. She no longer hoped for a home. Now she
wanted only a place where the Tillermans could be themselves and do what was
good for them. Home was out of the question. Stay might be possible, if this
grandmother could be persuaded. . . .

Dicey stopped thinking. She wanted to keep it simple. Get to Crisfield and
see, that was her plan. That was all of it.

"Anyway, they know where we're going," Dicey told James.

"How could they know that?"

"I said so in the note I left."

"Dicey! Why'd you do that?"

"I don't think it would be fair to leave her to worry."

"She'll worry anyway. She likes worrying."

"I can't help that, James. I can't help what she's like. I can only help what
I'm like."

"You've ruined it," James went on. "We can't be running away if they know where we're going."

"We're not running away—we never were running away," Dicey said. "We're just going to see."

James shook his head. "I'm running away. Before—we were always the ones who were run away from. This time I want us to do it. What's your plan?"

Dicey didn't answer.

The road flowed under the wheels. They were back on Route 1. Maybe it was her doom, always to get back on Route 1. She squeezed Maybeth's fingers. "Maybeth? What's the matter? You scared?"

Maybeth looked at Dicey and nodded.

"So am I, a little," Dicey said. "We'll just wait and see. That's all we can do."

"I don't want to go back." Maybeth spoke in a small voice.

"I thought you liked it," Dicey said. "The church, the pretty dress you wore there, all the attention."

"I did," Maybeth said.

Dicey decided to tell the truth, now. "We might have to go back. Do you know that?"

Maybeth nodded.

Well, Dicey thought. She had underestimated Maybeth. She'd been fooled, like the nuns were fooled and Maybeth's teachers. She'd been fooled into thinking Maybeth wasn't who she knew Maybeth was.

"Look, Maybeth," Dicey said, "if we do have to go back I'll go with you to church, and we'll both talk to the nuns. To Sister Berenice. I won't leave you alone so much."

Maybeth smiled, a tenuous little smile, and turned back to the window.

Smog made the air seem thick, like light, yellowed fog. In the heavy traffic the bus stopped and started, stopped and started. Buildings soared up higher than Dicey could see out the window. She twisted her head down to see their tops.

The bus turned onto a new street and headed east. Dicey felt as if they were in a maze and would never make their way out. Cars honked. Lights changed. They traveled down a narrow channel over which other roads crossed on high bridges. All the traffic, all the people, the tall buildings—Dicey felt scared, and exhilarated. There was so much life, all here in one place, teeming, whirling about her. More than at the crowded summer beaches in Provincetown. It was like a pot of vegetable soup boiling on a stove, everything moving. A restlessness and excitement came into Dicey with the air she breathed. Anything can happen, she thought.

At last the bus turned off into a huge warehouse. It followed a ramp, up and around, then fitted itself into a slot before a wall of glass doors. It became one of a row of buses.

The Tillermans stood up. Dicey led them to the front of the bus and down the steps, one after another, onto the sidewalk before the doors. Everyone was hurrying. Everyone acted as if he or she or they knew exactly where to go.

"What now, Dicey?" asked James.

"An information booth," she answered briskly. "Then bathrooms, and maybe something to eat."

They entered a huge, hollow hall lined with benches and ticket windows. Emptiness hung high over their heads although the room was crowded with people. The information booth was in the center of this hall. Dicey stationed her family by a water fountain and went up to stand in line.

When her turn finally came, she couldn't think straight. The girl behind the glass window spoke without looking at Dicey: "Next? Little boy?"

Dicey gulped. "When's the next bus to Wilmington, Delaware?"

Without speaking, the girl handed her a schedule.

"Where are the bathrooms?" Dicey asked.

"Lower level, on the street side."

"Where can I buy a ticket?"

"Upper level, any window with a yellow or green light."

Dicey fled, dragging her suitcase.

"She thought I was a boy," she said to James.

"So did Louis and Edie," he answered.

Dicey put the suitcase down and opened the schedule. They had forty minutes to wait. She would play it safe. "OK, listen James. Take this money"—she gave him a ten dollar bill—"and go get two tickets for Wilmington. That ticket window over there with a green light."

"Why not four?"

"Just in case," Dicey answered. "Two and two is not the same as four."

James looked at her.

"Not in this case," Dicey said. "In this case, it is but it isn't."

"You can say so," James said. "And I'll do it. And I see what you mean. But you're wrong. Two and two is always four."

When they had all four tickets, Dicey started walking along the concourse. She found the escalators leading down. "Now we go to the bathroom."

The women's room could have held Cousin Eunice's house in it and had room to spare. Lines of women waited before each closed door, old, young, medium, some alone, some with friends, some with children, one with a tiny baby that rode in a pouch on her chest. The air smelled of perfume and cleanser. Maybeth and Dicey entered the cubicle together, because Maybeth didn't want to go in alone. Dicey protested, "But you're nine." Maybeth just shook her head.

They took turns, Maybeth first. Dicey set the suitcase on the floor and opened it. She took out shorts and a shirt for Maybeth and her shoebox of money. She put twenty more dollars in her pocket. As they left the room, they tossed Maybeth's rolled-up dress into the trash.

When they emerged from the women's room, Dicey could not see James and Sammy. People hurried past, some carrying suitcases, some shopping bags, some just purses or newspapers. You could get lost here in this crowded station. You could get swept away. Or grabbed by somebody.

"Maybeth? If we get separated—" Maybeth caught Dicey's free hand. "Just in case," Dicey said. "We'll meet back by that information booth I went to first. Remember it?"

James and Sammy joined them. They had a hot dog apiece, standing up at a counter, and a glass of orange drink. Dicey looked at a clock—only ten minutes until the bus left. The air hummed with voices, distant motors, and the muffled droning of the loudspeaker announcing what buses were leaving for what cities. If they could get on the bus all right, and out of the city, then they were on their way. And they might make it.

James and Sammy went onto the bus first. Dicey dawdled by the gate, with Maybeth beside her. Maybeth went first up into the bus. Dicey followed, pulling their two tickets out of her pocket and handing them to the driver.

He looked at her with a grimace. "What is this, kids' day out?"

Dicey tried to look as if she didn't know what he was talking about.

"Never mind. But I'll tell you what I told them. We've got a long drive and I don't stand any horsing around."

"We won't," she said.

"I know, I know. You're angels from heaven. Go on back."

After a few minutes, the driver closed the door and turned on the engine. He backed out of the parking lot. With every turn of the wheel, Dicey felt her stomach loosen and her muscles relax. By the time the bus entered a tunnel, a smile was beginning to turn up the corners of her mouth. She felt her back relaxing into the back of the seat. Beside her, Maybeth hummed softly. The bus zoomed out of the tunnel and into the light. Dicey stretched, smiled, yawned— and fell asleep.

When Dicey opened her eyes, she saw the sleek, straight lines of the rectangular interior of the bus. Out the windows, on both sides, lay farmlands. Fields of corn ripened under a bright sun. The corn swayed in the wind, like dancers with scarves.

Dicey wasn't tired any more. She was relaxed inside and out. She felt lazy and unworried. The bus rolled along.

It was as if, during that nap, Dicey had traveled days away from Cousin Eunice's house in Bridgeport. That time now felt like a distant memory, something so far behind them that they didn't have to concern themselves with it, not any more.

She looked past Maybeth's head, out the window. Fields, farmhouses, trees, sky with clouds; her eyes roamed lazily over them all. Her thoughts roamed lazily too, over memories and ideas. She rode outside of time and place.

She thought about Momma, and it seemed to her that she almost understood why all of this had happened to them, to the Tillermans, all this sadness and running away. She thought about the long walk from Peewauket to New Haven, and the grandfather who had tipped them two dollars and Stewart with his blue-gray eyes; then her mind switched to the journey ahead of them, as if the future were a road stretching ahead, twisting and turning. What did it matter where they were going, as long as they were going?

Sammy was asleep on James' shoulder. Dicey leaned over to ask softly where they were. James told her the last stop had been Trenton.

Dicey took a map out of her suitcase. She unfolded it halfway, to show Wilmington and the Chesapeake Bay. Beneath her, the wheels rumbled on the road.

Sammy woke up. He punched James. James hit him back. Dicey quelled them with a glance and instructed them to play odds-and-evens while she thought. "But I'm hungry," Sammy argued.

"I can't do anything about that," Dicey answered.

"Why not?"

"Because I'm not a hot dog tree," Dicey said.

"Why not?"

"Because if I were, then you'd be one too because you're my brother. Only you'd be a pickle tree," Dicey said, turning back to her map. "Pickle tree," Sammy repeated, trying to repress his giggles, not wanting to laugh at Dicey's joke.

Dicey studied the map. Just below Wilmington, the Chesapeake Bay drove up like a wedge between two sections of land. The eastern shore of Maryland, where Crisfield was, was on the land between the bay and the ocean. It looked about two hundred miles from Wilmington to Crisfield. So it might be a lot farther. Maybe as much as thirty days of walking. Too far. But there were some cities that must have buses running to them: Salisbury, Cambridge, Easton.

They'd already spent too much on bus tickets. Money was always the problem. Dicey wanted to have money left over, so they could get back to Bridgeport, if they had to. She figured they'd have to walk part of the way anyway, and she wanted to have some tools for camping. A jackknife, one with a can opener on it. A pan of some kind. Ponchos, for when it rained. She let her mind wander on briefly to other things, to a backpack and bedrolls, to a portable stove. No, those would be silly; but fishing line and hooks would be useful. There was a lot of water around, so there must be fishing.

They had another choice: they could go down the western shore, to Baltimore or Annapolis—it would have to be Annapolis because that was near the only bridge over the bay. That would leave them about half of the distance to Crisfield still to cover. Maybe two weeks of walking.

They would have to get over the bridge if they did that. The map said Toll Bridge, so they probably couldn't walk over it. They might hitchhike, but Dicey didn't like that idea. She didn't like being in somebody's car and not able to run away. Besides, who would pick up four kids? They might have to take another bus.

Definitely, then, the eastern shore was better. At Wilmington they would get on a bus going south. How far they went would depend on how much it cost. That was easy enough. She folded up the map and returned it to her suitcase.

The bus made its way through Philadelphia and then south through more farmland, more small cities. After another hour, after a bridge like a section of roller coaster, they came into Wilmington.

The Wilmington Bus Depot was a one-story building, a single room with wooden benches, a lunch counter, lockers where you could store your suitcases, six windows where tickets could be purchased and at its center an information booth with a clock on top of it. Three forty-five. Dicey told James to stay with Maybeth and Sammy by the door. Only one bus stood waiting, now that the one they had ridden on had gone on to Baltimore. That bus, she saw by the sign above its front window, was going to Annapolis.

Inside, Dicey picked out a schedule from the assortment at the information booth. The first thing she did was to see if Crisfield was there, at the bottom of the list of towns. It was. After Salisbury, Eden and Princess Anne, came Crisfield.

Her eye went back up to the top of the list, found Wilmington and traced the buses leaving for the eastern shore. There were several, but most went no farther than Cambridge. Only one went down to Crisfield, a morning bus.

Then Dicey saw that the last afternoon bus heading south to Cambridge left Wilmington at two-thirty. The only bus after that didn't leave until nine at night.

Nine. By nine, Cousin Eunice would have been home for almost three hours. By nine, she could call Father Joseph. By nine, they might be able to trace the Tillermans, and maybe find them, and stop them. She didn't know Dicey had money, did she? She might think the Tillermans were walking. But Dicey couldn't count on that. She couldn't count on anything. She rushed up to the information booth and asked when the bus for Annapolis was leaving. The man put his hand over the microphone and told her, "Five minutes."

Five minutes, how could she think it through in five minutes? Dicey hurried over to a ticket window and bought four tickets to Annapolis. They couldn't just sit around the bus station for five hours, waiting to be recognized. Cousin Eunice would have to do something to find them; she would think it was her responsibility.

Dicey joined her family. "We missed the last bus until nine."

"Tonight? We better stay here," James said.

"No," Dicey said. "We can't. We'll go to Annapolis. It's the only bus."

"But Dicey—"

"Do as I say James."

She wasn't thinking, she knew that. She wasn't thinking clearly. She hurried her family onto the bus just as the driver was closing the door. They sat at the back. Dicey chewed on her lip.

"Nobody will expect us to go to Annapolis," James said. "It was good luck that we missed the bus."

"I don't know about that," Dicey said.

The bus left Wilmington and headed south. This bus was air-conditioned, and you couldn't open the windows. The windows were smeared with grime, so you couldn't see out. The hour and a half to Baltimore seemed endless. At Baltimore, a lot of dressed-up people got on, commuters, Dicey guessed, going home from work. The bus grew crowded.

The circuitous route from Baltimore to Annapolis, where they kept getting on and off the same road to stop at little huts by the road and let off passengers, took another hour and a half. Dicey tried to control her impatience by reminding herself that if they had been walking it would have taken days and days. This was slow, but it was faster than walking. They'd be walking soon enough.

At last, the bus turned into a parking lot before a low brick building. The bus driver turned around and called, "Annapolis. End of the line."

The Tillermans hopped up and joined the few people waiting to get off the bus. Dicey just followed in the direction the majority took, turning left down a sidewalk, away from the bus station. Behind her, the sun lowered, so they were walking on their own shadows, heading east.

"Where we going?"

"We'll find a place to sit down and think," Dicey said. "I'm looking for a park."

They passed a drugstore and a finance company and three banks. They saw bookshops and card stores, clothing stores and a wine-and-cheese store. The road they walked along came up to a traffic circle. Cars and trucks whirled around it, circling a church that stood at its center.

Dicey led them around the circle. Streets led off, but none promised to go to a park, although one said it went to the hospital. At the top of one street, Dicey looked down and saw blue water with sails on it. She stood, staring.

It looked like the painted backdrop to a movie, not like anything real. The long main street went downhill and then fetched up at the water. On the blue water, boats sailed or motored as if they were in an entirely different world, and it wasn't clear, in the bright August light, where water ended and sky began.

They headed down the hill to the water, passing stores and shops and more banks. The street was crowded: parked cars lined both sides, while moving vehicles crawled bumper to bumper uphill and the sidewalks were crowded with people. At the foot of the street was another circle, around which cars traveled slowly, with a steady chorus of horns and many near collisions. Across this circle, a quiet finger of water, hemmed in by concrete, marked the corner of a narrow area where people thronged, eating, talking, sitting and watching one another. Dicey moved through the milling crowd and along beside the water. They passed boats crowded as closely together as the cars in a parking lot, motor boats, sailboats and old, worn fishing boats.

At the waterfront, beyond a huge parking lot jammed with cars, they found a public park. It had no grass, just trees in wooden boxes. The ground was covered by wooden flooring. Benches, however, there were plenty. The benches right at the water were all full, but one beneath a sparsely leaved young tree was empty. The Tillermans sat on that.

"It's hot," James said. His face was red. Sweat plastered his hair to his neck. The air hung moist and heavy over the park. A slight ripple of a breeze came off the water, but that did little to relieve them. Everybody seemed slowed down by heat. Nobody walked briskly, everybody sauntered. A lot of people were licking ice cream cones. Dicey's mouth watered.

"What time's it?" James asked. Without waiting for an answer, he hopped up and asked the same question of a man moving by, who held his suit jacket over his shoulder. "It's seven-thirty," James reported. "Time for supper."

"How about ice cream cones for supper?" Dicey asked. She didn't know just how much money she had in her pocket, not enough for a real dinner.

"We passed a hamburger joint," James countered.

"Ice cream," Sammy said.

"Hamburgers," James said.

Sammy stuck his jaw out.

"Ice cream's cheaper," Dicey said. "Double dip?"

"Can I have seconds?" James asked.

"We'll see how hungry you are," Dicey said.

James agreed.

"But first I've got to figure out a couple of things, OK?"

"Like what?" James asked.

"Like where to sleep, and how to find an Army-Navy surplus store. And how to get across the bay."

"Get across the bay? Why?"

Dicey pulled out the map again and showed him where they were. Then she pointed out Crisfield.

"Oh, Dicey. What are we doing on this side?"

"I told you, we missed the last bus."

"Yeah but—" James caught a glimpse of Dicey's face and stopped speaking.

"I know. I know. But if we can just get across, we'll be much nearer."

"How can we do that? OK, we're here. We need a place to sleep tonight, right?"

"I guess. The Army-Navy store will be closed, wherever it is."

"If there is one."

"I'm sorry, James," Dicey said. "I panicked. When I found out we'd missed the last bus—"

"It's OK, Dicey. I just thought you had it all planned."

"I did. For me to go."

"Are you angry at us?" Sammy asked this. It sounded like the beginning of a quarrel.

"No. Well, yes, a little, but that doesn't matter. I'd rather be all together. Really, I would. I'm just confused still because I didn't have any plan for all of us. Can you understand that?"

Sammy didn't answer.

"I was going to come back," Dicey said to him.

He looked at her, with the question in his hazel eyes. "Really?"

"Really. Really and truly. Don't you trust me, Sammy?"

"You said you didn't trust anyone."

"I didn't mean any of us. I didn't mean you. Would you leave me behind? Or James or Maybeth?"

"No!"

"Well I wouldn't leave you, either. I feel the same way."

"But you were going to leave us behind," Sammy said stubbornly. Dicey sighed.

They rose to find the ice cream store. James got a double-dip chocolate nut cone, explaining that nuts and chocolate were both rich and filling. Dicey got a scoop of chocolate and a scoop of butter almond. She noticed a pile of maps of Annapolis on the counter top and took one. Maybeth wanted pink sherbet and green, but Dicey told her to get real ice cream because of the milk. She chose two scoops of strawberry. Sammy asked for strawberry ripple ice cream topped with peanut butter ice cream. "Ugh," Dicey said, listening to his order. He grinned at her.

They sat at a small table to eat. The ice cream tasted rich and smooth and cold. You could tell that it was made from real cream, it was that rich. Dicey studied her map while her tongue made valleys in the ice cream and then smoothed them out. The cone was crunchy and sweet.

"There's a college," Dicey said. "Let's try that, OK?"

James had a single-dip cone for seconds, another scoop of chocolate nut. They walked out and onto the crowded sidewalk. What were all these people doing? It was like a carnival.

The college lay in summer twilight, set back from the road by a long, sloping lawn. It was brick and very old. Everything looked old about it, old and tended, the smooth brick sidewalks, the many-paned windows, the little dome on top of the main building. It had trees—huge, tall trees, with branches too high for climbing—all about on its lawn. There were plenty of people. Students lay scattered about, reading. Watchmen wandered around on the brick paths. Families were eating picnic suppers. Children ran everywhere.

The Tillermans stood on the sidewalk, separated by a briar hedge from this scene. "No good," Dicey said. "Too many people."

She did not move on, however. It looked—so quiet and solid; the air over it was lavender in the evening light, and mysterious. She wished . . . she didn't know what she wished.

Resolutely, she turned away.

Her map showed only something called the Historic District. They had walked through some of it. All the houses crowded up onto the sidewalk, close to one another.

Dicey moved on. The suitcase weighed heavy on her shoulder muscle and banged against her legs. The map showed the Naval Academy in one direction, closed in by a wall that ran all around it. She turned the other way and led them back toward the first circle they had seen. She chose the road leading to the hospital, and they walked on, past that large building.

The houses were bigger here and had front lawns. A residential area. A rich residential area.

She walked on.

They saw one vacant lot that had no cover to conceal them from the surrounding houses.

She walked on.

The air grew darker, gray-violet now. The heat did not abate. Sweat ran down her back.

She walked on.

On her left, she saw a long, narrow stretch of grass in the middle of a kind of courtyard of houses. On both sides of the stretch ran roads, and houses stood facing one another across the grass. At the end of this stretch, with all its many windows dark, stood a house larger than any other on the street. Dicey headed down towards it.

They walked down the middle of the grass. There was one broad clump of bushes the little kids could hide in, if it came to that.

When they stood before the large house, Dicey noticed oddly shaped piles. Old radiators had been dropped here and pipes and slate shingles from the roof and even a bathroom sink. They were pulled up right by the front porch.

"Let's go around back," she said quietly. "I think it's empty. It looks like somebody's fixing it up. If anybody calls out, don't run. Tell them we're looking for Prince George Street. Tell them we're lost. Don't look guilty."

Their feet silent on the unmown grass, they stepped around the side of the house.

A silver pool of water glimmered at the end of the long lawn. The back of the house was as dark as the front, and Dicey breathed easy. She put her suitcase beside one of the overgrown bushes that grew by the screened porch, and they all walked down to the water.

A long-fingered willow swept the top of the grass at the water's edge. Two towering pines stood silent guard. On the silver pool, which was part of a river, some sailboats floated.

There was a bulkhead at the end of the lawn made out of railroad ties. They sat on that and dangled their feet over the water.

Dicey's stomach had butterflies of excitement in it. "Remember that first house?" she asked James.

"Yeah. Think it's empty?"

"I think so. Let's risk it."

No other houses were visible, although patches of light from windows showed through high hedges or trees. It was a private lawn.

"No fires," Dicey said.

A sailboat, its sails down, motored up the river. It made little waves that streaked the silver with black and lapped gently against the bulkheading.

Dicey turned to look at the house behind her. Its windows were comfortingly blank.

"We'll have to be quiet and get out early," she said.

Her family watched out over the water with dream-dazed eyes. They nodded. The river was narrow enough to swim easily. Across it, houses looked back at them.

Dicey smiled. Sammy drummed at the wood with his heels, quietly. James lay back and looked at the sky. Maybeth hummed, a tune Dicey half-recognized. "What song is that?" she asked.

"Stewart's song," Maybeth said. "'Oft I sing for my friends,'" she sang softly. "Remember?"

Dicey shook her head. "We can't sing—but I sure feel like it," she said. "I don't really know why."

"Yes, you do," James said, but said no more. He was watching the first stars emerge in the gray sky.

And Dicey did. They had money and a good place to sleep. She had a map. They were together alone again, themselves again. The night air was warm, and the willow whispered behind her, and the water whispered before her.

"OK," she said, rousing them, rousing herself, "Let's go up and get to sleep."

CHAPTER 2

SAFE as she felt, Dicey woke early. She rolled over on her back. The lightening sky arched over her. Behind her, the empty house stood like a protecting wall. From the water came the cries of gulls. Their quarrels cut through the quiet slapping sound ropes and rigging made against masts. Dicey stretched lazily and sat up.

James lay sprawled on his stomach, one arm flung out. Sammy had curled into a tight ball. Maybeth lay on her back, her arms folded over her stomach.

To the east, the sky showed a lake of clear blue into which the sun would rise. It was a particular blue, made of light and darkness mingling, clear as glass, smooth as glass, as much like water as sky. Dicey stood up and went around the far corner of the house to pee behind a large evergreen bush. She decided to let her family sleep awhile longer. Even men eager to get started while the day was cool wouldn't come to work this early. Dicey returned to the bulkheading and sat.

The boats rocked at their moorings. The houses beside her and across the river from her slept. Quiet as kittens, the water lapped at the boats and the bulkheads. In the east, that first blue lake increased to an ocean. The sun rose.

The air shimmered in golden light. Water reflected and brightened the air. The masts and spars of the boats stood stiff and dark. The colors of the hulls became clear: whites, reds, yellows, greens, and one burnished mahogany.

Dicey walked back through the long grass. She called each of the sleepers by name.

"James?"

He stirred, rolled over, sat up, grinned. "Hey. Good morning. Is it late? I'm starving."

"Maybeth?"

Maybeth's eyes flew open. She lay still for a minute, staring blankly, remembering herself.

Dicey crouched next to Sammy. She put her hand on his shoulder and jostled him gently while calling his name. "Sammy. Sammy. Time to get up."

He mumbled something and curled up more tightly.

"You've got to. Sammy?"

One eyelid struggled to open, then fell closed.

"Wake up, Sammy. We can't stay here."

He opened both eyes. "OK," he said. He closed both eyes.

"That's right," Dicey encouraged him. James grinned at her. "C'mon Sammy—time to get up. Gotta go to the bathroom and get out of here."

He stumbled to his feet. He and James walked together to the bush, James holding Sammy's arm to keep the little boy from falling.

Dicey pulled her suitcase out from under the bush, opened it again and took out twenty more dollars. She wondered how much money she had left. She could worry about that later in the day. For now, she wanted breakfast and a phone book.

They returned to the circle with the church at its center and to the steep main street. Once again Dicey was surprised to see the backdrop of water that lay at its foot. Something was peculiar about the perspective here, she thought. It looked as if two photographs of two different places had been jammed together. The town looked as though it fell into the water.

Her eyes searched eastward, across the water. "I can see something," she said. She could see a distant looming of land, low and flat. "Do you think that's the eastern shore?"

"How should I know?" James asked. "Can we eat in a restaurant?"

"If one's open. It's pretty early."

Early as it was, no more than half-past seven, the water was already dotted with white sails. Everybody here must sail, Dicey thought. Everybody must have his own boat. "Did you ever see so many boats?" she asked James, as they descended the main street.

He paid no attention to her. He was looking for a place to eat. They passed three closed restaurants before they found one open. Its single narrow room wasn't air-conditioned, but the cool morning air came in through the open door and was moved around by big ceiling fans. They sat down in a tiny booth.

Dicey read the prices before she read the menu. "Pancakes," she said. "Maybeth, Sammy and I can split an order. James, you can have one to yourself, if you'll give me half of a pancake. Is that OK? And milk." James was too hungry to argue. Dicey realized that they hadn't had enough dinner the night before. She would have to be careful about that.

The counter was filled with people drinking coffee and reading papers. The little room hummed with activity as waitresses whisked about taking orders, bringing food. When Dicey paid the bill, she asked the man at the cash register where an Army-Navy surplus store was. He told her it was out beyond the bus station, and he took the time to be sure she understood his directions, even though there was a line of people behind her waiting to pay.

Fast and relaxed, that was what it was like in that restaurant.

It was that way out on the street, too. The temperature was climbing up, and the sky was bleaching yellow with heat. People were entering the little stores that lined the streets or standing in groups before the doors of the several banks. The working day was about to begin. But almost all of these people turned, before they entered, to look down the hill to the water and boats, and then up the hill to the church within its ring of trees, as if they could take their own sweet time going in to work. Some of them smiled at the Tillermans. Some wished them a good morning.

At the Army-Navy store, Dicey studied the shelves of goods before she made her purchases. It was like a library in there, tall stacks of rods, shirts, hats, pants, shoes and jackets, and tennis rackets and inflatable rafts lining the narrow aisles. Dicey picked out a one-quart aluminum saucepan, four ponchos in children's sizes, a packet of hooks and the smallest, lightest reel of fishing line she could find. After some thought, she chose a red canvas bookbag and went to the front of the store.

938

The jackknife she picked out of a glass-fronted case was the most expensive thing she bought. It had two blades, one large and one small, a gadget to open cans with, a little screwdriver and a file. The bill came to seventeen dollars altogether, seventeen dollars and twenty-four cents to be exact. Dicey sighed, but paid. She asked the salesman to put everything into the canvas bag, except the jackknife. She slipped the jackknife into her pocket. It felt heavy and good there.

Outside again, Dicey waited until they were out of sight of the store, then she transferred everything from the suitcase to the canvas bag. She gave James the empty suitcase to carry and slung the bag over her shoulder, holding it by the rope that pulled its neck closed. It was much easier to carry than the suitcase, so much easier that she wondered why she had brought a suitcase in the first place.

Dicey went into the small bus station and set her empty suitcase down by the door. She went out to rejoin her family. She was entirely pleased with herself.

"Now what?" she asked them.

"What do you mean?" James asked.

"What do you want to do now?" Dicey asked.

"Get going," Sammy said.

"I don't know how yet," Dicey answered. "I haven't figured that out. Are you tired?"

None of them was tired.

"Let's just wander around then, OK? I think better while I'm moving."

They walked the morning away. They stayed away from the hospital and their sleeping place and stuck to the historic section on the map. They wandered down narrow streets lined with narrow houses and up broader streets where the houses were grander, where the street-level windows rose from floor to ceiling of the rooms within. People in Annapolis, Dicey decided, must like bricks. The sidewalks were brick as were many of the houses and public buildings.

Dicey also decided that she liked brick. It was so sturdy looking and symmetrical, in the first place. And then, when it was very, very old, it achieved a gentle, mellowed look, like old photographs or long-burning fires or a pair of blue jeans you've had for so long that even when you take them off they still have the shape of your body in them. When brick aged long enough it could look soft.

They spent some time on the college lawn, watching other people wander about. They spent some time on the main street, walking down to the foot, where the crowds were just as thick as they had been the night before. At a stall in an open market, Dicey bought little sandwiches made of flat sausages in biscuits.

Nobody stared at them. There were lots of kids messing around, and almost everybody, adults and children alike, wore jeans and shirts. Not full, but no longer hungry, the Tillermans sat by the water and stared. Lots of bare feet and long hair, like Provincetown. But also lots of gold watches and big diamonds in rings. Boys and girls together, men and women, with arms around each other's waists.

"Too much lovey dovey stuff," Sammy announced.

Dicey noticed something else. Most of the young women wore no bras. Their breasts went jiggle-jiggle as they walked. Finally, she could hold her tongue no longer.

"James—the girls aren't wearing bras."

He turned red. "I noticed."

"Do you see how they all go jiggle-jiggle? No, look—see the one with the long red hair? The pretty one, with eye makeup? Jiggle, jiggle, jiggle—see what I mean?"

James giggled helplessly. Dicey joined in. Then she noticed a bridge, down the river, leading over to another part of the city. From where they sat it seemed that this other part was given over entirely to boatyards and docks.

"Let's go over there," she pointed. "Let's go look at some boats."

"Do you think the jiggling hurts?" James asked her. "I'd think it would."

"How would I know, James? I don't have bosoms."

"Yeah, but you will."

"I'll tell you about it if I do," Dicey said. "Do you want to go look at the boatyards?"

"Could we row it?" James asked her.

His brain, Dicey thought, must work twice as fast as hers. It had taken her all that time sitting there to think of the possibilities of a boatyard.

"I don't know," she said. "First, let's see what's there. It might be twenty miles across—I'll check the map later."

"We couldn't possibly row twenty miles, could we?"

"Let's worry about all that later, OK?"

They followed the water around to get to the drawbridge. Everywhere in Annapolis fingers of water would appear at the ends of streets or around corners, unexpectedly. Back in Provincetown, there was a belt of sandy beaches all around the town, except for the harbor side, where houses were built out over the water. Here, the town crowded down onto the water, trying to get as close to it as possible, all the time, at every opportunity.

They threaded their way through crowds of tourists. They passed countless cars, with license plates from many states, locked and empty.

The drawbridge humped over the water. The air around it was a little cooler, so they stood for a while, leaning against the railing, looking down at the busy harbor. There were no working boats, just pleasure craft.

The boatyards hummed with laboring. Some boats were up on racks, and men and women worked over the hulls, sanding, scraping, painting. One hull hung from a huge crane, ready to be returned to the water. Most of the boats were moored at docks that stretched out into the water. Many had people sitting on them, eating, reading. Others were empty, their sails furled, their hatch covers locked. The only rowboats the children saw were locked onto storage racks or tied on top of the cabins of the boats they belonged with.

Nobody stopped the children or asked them any questions. Many people seemed to be wandering like them, just looking at the activity. More were at work on their boats, polishing brass, sitting on deck splicing ropes, hosing down the sails.

Dicey led her family out to the end of one dock. The bag over her shoulder had grown heavy, so she put it down. They all sat, staring out across the water. The afternoon sun reflected off the water onto their faces and arms and legs. Next to them, two boys were scrubbing down the deck of a sailboat. They wore only bathing suits. Their bodies were tanned and their hair was bleached by the sunlight. They looked as if they spent all summer outdoors in bathing suits, on boats. One of them, the heavier one, whose stomach had ripples of fat on it, jumped lightly onto the dock to pick up a hose that was coiled there. Dicey watched him lazily.

He turned on the water, then leaped back onto the deck and rinsed off the suds their brushes had left.

Dicey knew what he would do before he did it. It was inevitable. It was what anybody would do with a hose in his hand and a friend who wasn't looking. He picked up the head of the hose, put his thumb over it and sprayed his friend.

The friend charged him, his hands up before his face. The heavy boy stood and sprayed him, holding him off at arm's length. The friend looked younger, because he was so much lighter and smaller. He spluttered and turned under the shaft of water, but he didn't stop trying to get it. Then, he stamped on the heavy boy's foot and grabbed the nozzle during that moment of distraction.

They wrestled for the hose, spraying one another, shooting the water over onto the dock, laughing and cursing each other. Neither of them could take the hose away from the other. Great, heavy arcs of water shot out from the boat, spraying everywhere.

"Hey!" Dicey yelled. "Look out!"

The two wet faces turned to her. The heavier boy spoke immediately. "I didn't see you," he said. "You really wet?"

"You could say so," Dicey said, wiping her hair off her face. "But it's a hot day and the water's cool."

"That's true," he said. "But still, come on up and dry off. Jerry? Doesn't your dad keep towels on board?"

The slimmer boy swung down out of sight. He reappeared with two large towels. "It's OK if you want to come on board. It's my dad's boat."

James looked at Dicey. Sammy was already standing by the bow. "Why not?" Dicey said.

The boys pulled on the bow mooring line until the boat was only two feet off the dock. "Can you jump?"

Dicey could, and did. She reached out a hand and helped Maybeth over. James swung over on the hand of the heavy boy. Sammy refused help. He stumbled as his feet hit the deck and fell on his face. Jerry leaned a worried face over him, but Sammy came up smiling. "I said I could do it," he said proudly.

"My name's Jerry," the slim boy said, "and this is Tom."

Dicey introduced her family.

They were given a tour of the boat, above and below decks. It was small, only thirty-two feet, but it had everything possible on board, and everything tucked away into its own place. There was even a shower in the head, and the walls and floor of the tiny space sloped down, following the curve of the hull, to a central drain.

"You could live on a boat," Dicey said.

"Lots of people do just that, especially in summer," Tom said.

"I've tried to talk Dad into letting me live on her," Jerry said. "He just says I should be grateful he lets me have a key to her. Grateful . . ." He grinned at Tom. "I do enough work for him."

"Let's take some Cokes up with us," Tom suggested. They were in the cabin at the end of their tour.

The icebox was a two-level locker holding a huge chunk of ice. Tom pulled out six cans of Coke and shut the heavy wooden door. Dicey took a last look around the cabin. A table was hinged so it could be pulled up flat against the wall and clamped there. This enabled the berth, which served as a sofa during the day, to pull out into a double bed. There was storage space behind and below the berths. The efficiency of it took Dicey's breath away.

After they had seated themselves around the cockpit, back in the blazing sunlight, Dicey asked, "Do you work on this boat?"

"Yeah. We're free labor right now. Next year, when we're sixteen, he'll have to pay us. Or we can get work at one of the yards. I know a lot of people," Jerry said.

"Can you take the boat out sailing whenever you want?" she asked.

"Well, I've gotta ask permission." The two boys exchanged a glance that Dicey could read—it meant they often didn't ask permission.

"You must be a pretty good sailor," James said.

"I guess you'd say so," Jerry answered. He stretched out his legs and admired his tanned feet.

"Do you sail too?" James asked Tom.

"Not like Jerry does. I just hack around."

"Are you brothers?"

"Naw," Tom said. "We're old friends. Since first grade."

They drank their Cokes silently for a bit, basking in the sunlight.

"Does your dad sail the boat?" James asked.

"On weekends," Jerry said. "During the week, she's pretty much my own."

"Gee," James said, admiration in his voice. He looked at Dicey, hard.

Dicey got the feeling there was something James wanted her to understand, but she didn't understand it yet. She tried to help by talking about the same topic. "What does your dad do?"

"Works in Washington," Jerry's voice had pride in it as he said that.

"Gee, is he a senator?" James asked.

"Not so important," Jerry said. "Just a representative—you know what they are?"

"House of Representatives," James said quickly.

"Yep. He's the representative from Ohio, third district. It's his first term."

"Gee," James said again. He looked significantly at Dicey again. She didn't pay any attention because she had sensed it was a lie. She was busy wondering why this boy would lie about his father's job, and why his friend would go along with it without saying anything.

"We live over here because my mom doesn't want to get all caught up in political circles. She says it's no good for kids. She's a regular hawkeye, my mom."

"She only wants to keep her baby boy as long as she can," Tom remarked.

Jerry flushed and bit his lip. "At least she cares about her kids."

Tom laughed. "You can't get me that way, old friend. My parents care about me—but I've made my declaration of independence, and they were smart enough to accept that. I've got my freedom."

"And I don't?"

"Not yet, old buddy. When you're ready, when you want it bad enough, you'll have the nerve to fight for it. But what the hell—it's summer—nothing's worth worrying about in the summer, is it?"

Sammy had lost interest in the conversation and was lying on his stomach on the deck, trying to dabble his hand in the water.

"Do you ever go to the eastern shore?" James asked Jerry.

At last, Dicey understood what James was driving at. She nodded her head at him, briskly. He raised an eyebrow at her, as if to say, "Well, it's about time."

"Go there?" Jerry asked. "I've spent almost as much time there as over here. When you sail the Chesapeake, you learn all about the eastern shore. Why?"

"We gotta go over tomorrow," James said.

942

"Yeah? Where?"

"Easton," Dicey said quickly. "We're visiting an aunt for a couple of weeks. Our parents sent us down from Wilmington. To get fresh air," she said, trying to sound disgusted.

"What are you doing in Annapolis?" Tom asked.

"There's this old lady my dad knows, from when he was a kid and his father was in the Navy," Dicey said. "She always says she's dying to see us—I guess because she never had any children of her own. We're spending the night with her first. But she sleeps all the time. She told us to go run around while she slept. She's awfully old. I dunno," Dicey said, "I think she'd rather just invite us and not have us come. But Mom says she really enjoys our visits, as long as we don't hang around the house too much."

"Where is this?"

"Over on Prince George Street—you know where that is? Everything in her house can't be touched. It's hard on Sammy."

The boys seemed to believe this.

"So, you're making the great trip to the eastern shore tomorrow," Tom said.

"On a bus," Dicey said. "It's crazy. My aunt and her kids aren't even going to be there until dinner, because she works and they go to some camp. I told our parents we should wait until tomorrow and take a late bus to Easton, but they said—you know how parents are."

"Man, do I know," Jerry said.

"It's too bad you can't sail over," Tom said to Dicey.

"It sure beats the bus," Jerry agreed.

They didn't sound like they were offering, so Dicey played it low. "Yeah. But it's a short trip. We'll survive."

"Yeah, it's too bad," Tom said to her. "We'd offer to sail you over, see, but Jerry would have to ask permission, and . . ."

Dicey nodded, as if she understood. Well, she did. She understood what he was up to.

Jerry studied his feet.

Dicey stood up. "We gotta get back now. Thanks for the Cokes."

"Wait a minute," Jerry said. "Would you really like to sail over?" he asked. He was looking at Tom, not at them, as he spoke.

"Gee, yes," James said.

"We could get back by dark, you know," Jerry said to Tom. Tom just smiled. "I'll tell my mom I'm having dinner at your house. Do you think we could? Get over and back?"

Tom looked doubtful.

"I'd like to try it, wouldn't you?" Jerry insisted.

"Oh, I'd like it, you know that. I'm always game for something out of the ordinary. But *I* don't have to be home by dark. *I* don't have the mother who has to know where I am every minute of the day."

"Cut it out, OK? Lay off that stuff. I mean what can they do to me after all? Lock me in the attic? Beat me with wet noodles? Send me away to school?"

Tom shrugged.

"Gee, I don't want to get you in trouble," James said.

"Trouble," Jerry said, as if there was no trouble he couldn't handle. "Let me worry about that. I'm game for a day's hard sailing. Think you can do it?" he challenged Tom.

"Anything you can do I can do," Tom answered.

"We'll see," Jerry said. "You kids get back here early tomorrow—eight o'clock. Can you be here that early?"

"I think so," Dicey said. "I think there's a seven o'clock bus we could say we were taking. It sure would be fun to sail over."

"It's not easy," Jerry warned her. "You have to keep out of the way."

"We can do that," Dicey said.

"And the little kids—can they swim?"

"I can swim good," Sammy said.

"OK, then. OK?"

"OK," Dicey agreed. They left the boat quickly. She picked up her bag from the dock and hustled everyone ahead of her down the dock. When they were well out of sight, she slowed down and turned to James.

"Gee, James," she said—and burst out laughing.

James joined in.

"I want hamburgers for supper tonight," he said.

"You deserve them," Dicey answered.

"I thought you'd never catch on," he said. "I thought that Jerry'd never catch on. You know, Dicey? We made them do what we wanted them to do."

"Tom really did it," Dicey said.

"Yeah. Why did he? Does he want to get his friend in trouble?"

"I dunno," Dicey said. "Is that what friends do?"

"Don't you know?"

"No. I never had a friend like that, a best friend from first grade. We never had many friends, did we?"

"I guess not." James thought about that. "None of us did. Maybe Tillermans don't."

They ate dinner at Burger King, hamburgers, french fries, milkshakes. It tasted good to them, after weeks of Cousin Eunice's frozen dinners and pot pies. They wandered around again until evening had settled in, milling with crowds of people who seemed to have nothing else to do but saunter down the streets and look in store windows, or peer at the little houses.

When they had drifted back to their own empty house, the little children fell asleep almost at once. Dicey and James sat for a long time down by the river. Occasional boats motored up and down. Voices floated across the water. The air was humid and hot. Altogether Dicey felt satisfied.

"What do you know about our grandmother?" James asked her.

"I think she's poor," Dicey said. "And maybe strange."

"Strange? Like Momma? Crazy?"

"Strange like all the Tillermans," Dicey said. "She lives all alone on a farm."

"Why do Tillermans always live alone?"

"We don't. We live together."

"Together, but all alone together," James said.

"Maybe every family feels that way," Dicey said. "Maybe that's what families are."

"I don't know," James said. "I don't think so."

Before she went to sleep that night, Dicey counted her money, peering at the bills in the dim light. She had forty-seven dollars left, and some change.

It had cost them a lot to get to Annapolis. Dicey decided that forty would be the amount to keep in her pocket. Once they got across the bay, they'd have to stop spending. They'd have to fish for food, and get clams; or something. And she'd have to earn money if she could. Seven dollars could go a long way, if it had to, if you made it. She'd make it go as far as she could, all the way to Crisfield. If she could.

CHAPTER 3

WHEN Dicey awoke, she was cool and damp, and even a little chilly. The morning air lay moist over her. She turned her eyes from the gray sky to her family.

Sammy wasn't there.

She sat up, peering towards the bush they used for a bathroom. She waited, long enough, she judged, but he did not appear. She jumped to her feet and looked around.

His little figure sat huddled on the bulkheading at the end of the lawn. In the mists rising from the water, he could have been a woeful little bush planted between the willow and the pine.

Dicey went to the bathroom, then walked down to join him. He knew who she was without turning his head. "What got you up?" she asked.

"I had to pee," he said. His fingers picked long splinters from the wood. "I was thinking," he said.

"You worried?"

He shook his head. "I'm not scared of sailing."

"I never said you were," Dicey answered. "You're not scared of anything, are you?"

Sammy looked at her then, his eyes questioning. "I had a dream that you were all on a bus and the door closed and I couldn't get on. I ran and ran after it, but it kept getting away."

Dicey nodded her head and watched the mists rising almost in straight lines, like rain going backwards. In the east, the sky lightened.

"Dicey? Can I ask you something?"

"Sure."

"Tell the truth?"

"I always do."

"No, you don't," Sammy said.

Dicey understood him. "I'll tell the truth Sammy, I promise."

Sammy asked his question: "Why were you going to go alone, before James caught you?"

The hulls of the boats were shadowy silhouettes on the water. Mist caught in the branches of the trees across the river. The mists would burn off, Dicey thought. There wasn't much wind.

"I don't know what we're going to find when we get there," Dicey said. "So I figured if I went down alone and saw what it's like, then I could come back and get you all. If it was OK. If it wasn't OK, I could just forget about it. Also, I had enough money to get there and back on a bus and stay on my own in a hotel. See, Sammy, I don't know what this grandmother will be like. I was trying to make things easiest for you all. Do you understand?"

"I guess so. I think so—like I fight when people say things, so they won't say them any more. Are you sorry that we're with you?"

945

"A little, yes. It's harder with four of us. And more expensive. And"—since Dicey had determined to tell the whole truth, she did—"I kind of liked the idea of traveling alone—you know? With no one to look after. But I was wrong, Sammy, or at least I think now I was. I made a mistake not telling you."

"Why?"

"Because we do things together. The trouble was, we didn't do things together at Cousin Eunice's and that got me thinking the wrong way."

"How can something get you thinking the wrong way, if you know how to think the right way?" Sammy asked. But he was sitting up straighter and kicking his heels.

"They just do. I don't know how."

"I always thought . . . well, you didn't make mistakes."

"Everybody makes mistakes!"

"Not you—you didn't!"

"Oh, Sammy. I made dozens of mistakes."

"Name one."

"Staying too long at Rockland. Not planning how to cross the Connecticut River. Not having any money in New Haven. Not telling Cousin Eunice what I thought, about you and Maybeth."

"Don't tell me," Sammy begged. "Don't tell me any more."

"But you asked me to!" Dicey protested.

The sun was rising, turning the sky and air a rosy gold color. Gulls wheeled through the air. A boat motored quietly down the river, the people on it dark figures.

"You did," Dicey insisted. "You did ask me." She reached over and tickled Sammy under his arm. He squirmed. She reached her other arm over and wrestled him down to the grass, tickling, crying, "You did, you did, you did. Say so."

Sammy screamed with laughter and wriggled under her hands. "All right, I did!"

Dicey stood up. She brushed her hands briskly together. "Let's get going," she said. They raced back up the lawn.

They were early down to the boat, early and hungry. James grumbled that he wanted breakfast but Dicey ignored him. She didn't want to spend any money until they got across the bay. She wanted everything to stay just as it was until they were actually on the other side.

The Tillermans sat on the end of the dock waiting. All around them, the boatyards came awake. Water traffic made many little waves. A slight breeze blew now, and little boats sailed down to the mouth of the river and the bay.

Time passed slowly. Dicey sensed that it was after eight o'clock. Cars streamed over the bridge, going toward town. People going to work, she thought. Her hunger mounted. She had been sure, at first, that she could wait to eat until they were across.

"Tonight," Dicey announced, "we've got to wash our underwear. And put on clean. Maybe shirts too. OK?"

"Do you think they forgot?" James asked. His head moved restlessly. "Or changed their minds?"

"Maybe," Dicey said. "Or they could have been lying to us."

At this, James smiled: "That would serve us right, wouldn't it?"

They had to eat. If Dicey was hungry, James must be starving. She went back to a gas station and bought crackers with peanut butter from a machine. Then she put in two more quarters and got chocolate bars.

When she returned, the two boys were there, busy working with sails on the deck. They were dressed just as they had been the day before. Dicey wondered if they slept in their swimming suits. She looked at James and raised her eyebrows. She handed out packets of crackers and offered some of hers to Jerry and Tom. "No thanks," they both said. "We just ate. You kids stay in the cockpit, OK?"

It was like sitting in a booth without a table, with the four Tillermans, two to a side, knees hitting knees, stiff and watchful. The boys spent a long time putting on the jib. Jerry came back and stood by the base of the mast. He pulled down on a rope. The jib rose slowly and hung flapping at its stay. Jerry told Tom to fend off from the bow while he backed out of the dock.

When Jerry returned to the cockpit, he looked at the Tillermans. "Ready to go?"

"You bet," Dicey answered.

"Drop your bag on one of the bunks below," Jerry told her. "Then I think you and your brother James had better go sit on the cabin. I need room for play on the tiller, and Tom'll be back here, handling the sails. You ever sail before?"

Dicey thought of lying and then thought better of it. "No," she said.

Jerry considered this. His face was thin and his hair was bleached to a metallic tone that matched the gold in his eyes. His mouth looked soft and sulky, but his body was lean. "OK," he said, "listen carefully. We're going to have to tack out a ways, then we can reach over to St. Mike's. Tacking means we zigzag, going as close to the wind as possible." His hand sketched a zigzag motion in the air. "At the end of each tack, I'll call 'ready about.' The boat will rotate, about sixty degrees, and the main-sail and boom will swing from one side to the other. The keel will reverse too."

"What?" James said. "I don't understand."

Jerry held his hand out stiffly, slanted one way, then reversed the slant. "That's what the keel does when we tack and come about," he said. "On a reach we'll ride pretty flat. All you have to do is hang on when we come about. There's no danger. I want you to sit where you're put, and sit quiet. But if I tell you to move, or give any order, you've got to obey right away. Got that?"

"We can do that," Dicey said. "All of us."

She leaned down and tossed her bag onto a bunk below. Then she and James went up forward to sit on the roof of the cabin. They could lean back against the mast, or slip down to the deck and lean against the cabin wall.

Jerry started the motor. Tom uncleated a heavy line with a floater tied on its end and dropped it into the water. James looked at Dicey: "I hope they know what they're doing," he said.

The sun was toasting warm. The water danced beneath the keel. The motor hummed. The boat slipped out into the river and turned east. The jib flapped.

Waterfront buildings glided slowly by, boatyards, condominiums with great glass windows looking out over the water, an occasional small house in the middle of a green lawn. Theirs was one of many boats headed out to the bay.

The motor stopped. Dicey turned her head. She smiled to Sammy and Maybeth, sitting straight up and still, one on each side of the cockpit. Tom stood up, holding the tiller. Jerry jumped up behind them to raise the mainsail. When he had it cleated, he jumped down into the cockpit and hauled in on a line.

The mainsail stiffened, then puffed out. The boat responded, surging forward underneath them.

Tom returned the tiller to Jerry and pulled in the jib. It was not the kind of jib Dicey knew. At Provincetown she had seen little, narrow triangular sails.

This jib was long. It curved back around, halfway down the length of the cockpit. Dicey turned her head back and yelled, "What kind of a jib is that?"

"It's a genoa," Tom answered. He seemed to be enjoying himself. His eyes squinted into the sunlight, and his smile showed big, square teeth.

The wind blew firmly against the sails. The water jostled the boat, wave after wave. When Dicey looked at the water, they seemed to be traveling quite fast. But when she looked at the shore, now falling away beside them, they seemed to be going very slowly.

Under the protection of the shore, the boat heeled only slightly. Jerry brought the boat about, and Dicey and James had to do no more than protect themselves from the genoa as it flapped across the bow in front of them. Dicey saw a shadow of shoreline, across the bay.

She also saw three huge tankers, moored one behind the other, lying across their path, like tall buildings. Jerry approached them, then passed between two, where there was much more room than there had first seemed to be. The metal walls soared up above the little boat. Some crewmen waved down at them, and Dicey waved back. The tanker came from Athens, from Athens across the Atlantic and down the length of the Mediterranean Sea.

Dicey looked up the bay to where Baltimore was. Two bridges, twin spans, crossed the bay in long arcs. They looked like something from the future, slender silver ropes flung over the broad water, beautiful and strong.

Dicey's eyes moved out, across again. Jerry brought the boat about, and—after shifting her weight to compensate for the heel—she found she could no longer see the far shore, for which they were headed. They had left most of the other boats behind, and now passed only an occasional fishing boat, rocking at the end of its anchor line.

The wind hummed in her ears, the sun poured over her face and arms and legs, the waves knocked against the keel, and the boat pulled forward. Like everything else in Annapolis, the movement was both lazy and fast, at once. She turned back and saw Sammy staring at Tom. Jerry sat with the long wooden tiller in his hand, his eyes on the sails.

Dicey slid down onto the deck and leaned her back against the cabin. The sky was clear, the sails shone white against it. She closed her eyes.

In the darkness behind her eyelids, Dicey felt part of the boat itself, riding the wind over the water. It was easy work, this. It was silent and serene. Her thoughts loosed themselves from their everyday moorings and wandered. Nothing mattered out here. Nobody talked and nobody listened. The waves went past them, maybe each different, maybe the same wave over and over again. Who knew which? Who cared?

Dicey opened her eyes. They had never sailed in Provincetown. They had never been asked. She had rowed in dinghies and been out once or twice on large fishing boats. But they were nothing like this quiet harnessing of wind and the sharp keel cutting through silken water.

Out here, there was salt on the wind itself that fell on your skin like rain. You could taste it. Out here the sun heated and the wind cooled, and the waves sang their constant song.

Dicey wished she could stop breathing and give herself entirely over to the movement and the being still. Maybe she could learn to sail. Maybe she could go to sea, somehow. A boat could be a home. The perfect home that could move around, a home that didn't close you in or tie you down: and a sailor would always be at home if he was on the sea.

Maybe life was like a sea, and all the people were like boats. There were big, important yachts and little rafts and motorboats and sailboats and working boats and pleasure boats. And some really big boats like ocean liners or tankers—those would be rich or powerful people, whose lives engulfed many other lives and carried them along. Or maybe each boat was a kind of family. Then what kind of boat would the Tillermans be? A little one, bobbling about, with the mast fallen off? A grubby, worn-down workboat, with Dicey hanging onto the rudder for dear life?

Everybody who was born was cast onto the sea. Winds would blow them in all directions. Tides would rise and turn, in their own rhythm. And the boats— they just went along as best they could, trying to find a harbor.

Dicey didn't feel like finding a harbor. She knew she needed one, and they needed one, but she would rather just sail along, dreaming, not caring where they were going or when they would get there or what they would do there.

Couldn't you live your whole life without going into harbor? The land would catch you at the end. *Home is the sailor.* But until then, you could keep free. And even then, even when you died, you could die at sea and your body would roll with the underwater currents until your flesh peeled off and you were white bones rocking in the waves on the sandy bottom of the ocean. Always part of the changing.

Dicey smiled to herself. The ocean at Provincetown had always sung at her too. As long as I'm near the water, she thought, that'll be enough, even if I'm on land. Because life wasn't really an ocean, and she wasn't really a little boat bobbling about on it. There were James and Maybeth and Sammy, for one thing. But for now, she was content to sit still and silent.

The sun beat down hotter, and her skin started to run with sweat. She was getting sticky, uncomfortable. The sails fell lifeless and quiet, flapping morosely. The boat no longer thrust ahead, slicing the waves; now it rolled from side to side. She crawled back over the cabin.

"What's the matter?" she asked.

The two boys were leaning back, drinking beer from cans. "Wind's died down," Tom said.

"That happens," Jerry added. "Especially in the middle of the bay. No worry. The only deadline we have is I've got to be back in Annapolis by dark."

"Yeah, or the ghosties and boogies will get him."

Jerry frowned, but ignored his friend. "We can always let you off and head right back."

"I've got some friends in St. Mike's," Tom said.

"We know about your friends in St. Mike's," Jerry answered.

"It beats sitting around watching TV," Tom answered. "Doesn't it? Your mom's not here, Jer, you can tell the truth."

Dicey interrupted. "Could I steer? I mean, we're not going anywhere—"

"We are, but not far," Jerry corrected.

"Go ahead, let her," Tom urged. Jerry agreed.

Jerry slid down towards Sammy and put Dicey's hand on the long tiller. The wood was smooth and warm. It responded to every vibration in the hull and every flapping of the sails. Dicey's hand seesawed gently back and forth. The tiller let her feel the boat under her hand. She grinned at Jerry. "I like it," she said.

He grinned back at her and taught her how to head up, into the wind, and point down, away from it. He showed her what changes in the mainsail to watch for. He pointed to the glassy water just ahead of them and then to a patch far ahead where little ripples danced in the sunlight. "There's wind up there," he said. He leaned back and drank from his can of beer.

"I'm going below for a snooze," Tom announced. He climbed down the ladder and disappeared.

Sammy went up to sit with James.

Jerry moved over to Tom's seat. "He doesn't like sailing," he said.

"Who, Sammy? I didn't notice."

"No, Tom."

"But—"

"He's got nothing better to do." Jerry shrugged, then smiled a little. "And he likes getting me in trouble."

"What about you?" Dicey asked.

"I need some help getting in trouble. I'd never dare do it on my own. You know? Rebellion is necessary for the development of character."

Dicey wondered about that.

"Most men lead lives of quiet desperation," Jerry said. "Somebody said that. He was right. So—I get in trouble, now and then—so I won't be like most men."

"You're going to lead a life of noisy desperation?" Dicey asked.

He laughed at that. He gave himself over to laughter and enjoyed it. Dicey decided she liked him after all.

"At least that much," he said. "More if I can, but at least that."

They sailed on, if this odd, rolling progress could be called sailing. Then, under her hand, Dicey felt the boat stir. She looked at the water and the sails. They had reached the ripply patch of water. The sails bellied out.

Jerry was watching her. She offered him the tiller, but he shook his head. His smile teased her. He pulled in on the genoa line and held it. The long sail lay nearly flat. The mainsail line he had already cleated down. "Watch the genoa," he instructed.

Dicey did. She watched the sail and the water ahead. She rested her hand lightly on the tiller, letting the boat tell her where it wanted to go. She sat alert, her body tuned to that gentle pull on the tiller.

Boat, waves, water and wind: through the wood she felt them working for her. She was not directing, but accompanying them, turning them to her use. She didn't work against them, but with them; and she made the boat do that too. It wasn't power she felt, guiding the tiller, but purpose. She could not stop smiling.

The wind built up, and Jerry took back the tiller, giving Dicey the genoa line. She played it, without being told, letting it out a fraction, pulling it in two fractions, responding to the pull of the wind in the sail

They didn't talk, sailing the boat. They didn't talk at all until Jerry pointed out the land approaching. Dicey saw short, narrow beaches, a few trees, some big houses.

"Another hour," Jerry said.

Dicey nodded.

"How old are you?" he asked.

"Thirteen," Dicey answered. "I turned thirteen in June."

"That's too bad," Jerry said. "If you were fifteen, or even fourteen . . . you really take to it, don't you? I've never seen anybody take to it like that. I never thought a girl could. You've got good hands, Dicey. And you're not scared."

"Thirteen isn't too young to sail," Dicey pointed out.

"No, it isn't," he agreed. He leaned his head down and called Tom awake. "We've got to come about and make the approach to St. Mike's."

Dicey nodded to show she understood, and she thought she did understand what he had said. She was too young to be a girlfriend. Her cheeks grew warm with the thought. Of course she was, much too young, and besides, she had more important things to do. She was surprised at herself, though, for the nice feeling it gave her. Maybe because she'd been so often taken for a boy.

She joined James and Sammy. Maybeth said she didn't want to move from her seat nestled up against the cabin wall, where she had sat silent for the whole trip. So Dicey returned to the foredeck. The boat heeled a little now, in the afternoon wind. She and James kept Sammy sitting between them. "I sailed it," Dicey said.

"I saw," James answered. "What was it like?"

Dicey couldn't explain. "Great," she said.

They watched the shoreline close them in as Jerry negotiated the channel into St. Mike's. This was low land, with large houses standing on bright green lawns. Buoys slipped by.

Jerry let down the mainsail and gathered it in, wrapping it around the boom and looping a line around it to hold it. Tom turned on the motor. Jerry loosed the genoa halyard and showed Dicey how to pull it down and hold it in at the same time. Great armloads of material surrounded her. She couldn't see anything. Jerry's voice, muffled by the sail he was packing into a sail bag, assured her that she was doing just fine.

They pulled into the front of a long dock, and Tom took a line from the bow and wrapped it around one of the posts. Jerry tied the stern. He held the boat close to the dock while the Tillermans climbed out.

The steadiness of the land under her feet felt strange to Dicey. She felt as if everything was reversed. On the boat, the deck had been unsteady and her leg muscles had worked to keep her balanced. On land, the ground was so steady that her leg muscles took up the motion of the boat. It was crazy.

Her family stood back while she thanked Jerry. Tom was talking to him about calling some people. "We got beer on the boat," he was saying.

Jerry hesitated.

"Just an hour. You can call your old lady and tell her where you are, if you're worried. Or better yet, call her and tell her you're here and can't get back before dark. She'll be mad at you for sailing over, but glad you called, so it'll be all right. Jerry? You wanna? Man, we're over here with the boat and beer—we can really have a party."

Jerry laughed, a light, high sound. He turned the idea over in his mind. "I don't know," he said.

Dicey knew. She knew also what he would decide. "We gotta find a bus," she said. "Thanks an awful lot."

"That's OK, kid," Tom answered.

Dicey waited for Jerry to say something. Finally he noticed. "It was fun," he said.

"Yeah it was. It really was."

"See you around, yeah?" he said.

"Probably not," Dicey said. She held out her hand and he shook it. "Yeah," he said, but he wasn't paying attention to her. He was looking at Tom, and a smile was creeping over his mouth. Dicey picked up her bag, slung it over her shoulder, took a last look at the boat and walked off fast.

St. Michael's was a small town huddled around its waterfront. It was like Annapolis, but without the hurrying quality of the city across the bay. It was pretty, but Dicey was not cheered by that as they walked out of town on the one main street. She felt vaguely sad. To make herself feel better, she vowed that she would sail again, and often, if she could. Crisfield was on the water. People there must sail.

The midafternoon sun pounded down on them. They walked two abreast on the side of the road, Dicey with Maybeth, James with Sammy. Dicey carried her bag over her shoulder.

Little town houses, with handkerchief lawns, gave way to fields where corn and soybeans grew. Driveways led off the highway. Sometimes you could see the roofs of houses back among the trees that began at the far ends of the fields. Some of the mailboxes had the names of houses on them, Windward, Petersons Landing, Oakwood, Second Chance.

They came to a wooded section, mostly pines, and walked at its edge, as far from the traffic as they could get. In the midst of this section, a driveway went off. Like the other driveways they'd passed, this was a dirt road. But this road had a name, Overview Circle, and a bunch of mailboxes clustered at its beginning.

Dicey peered down the highway and saw a small store ahead, with a gas pump out front.

"You all wait here," she said, putting down her bag. "I'm going up to the store to get some food, and we'll see if there's a place to camp down this driveway. I figure, these are big estates, and probably on the riverfront. OK?"

"It's not dark yet," James objected.

"It's getting late and we've got to find a place. This looks like there might be lots of privacy," Dicey explained.

"OK, if you say so," James said.

"And if I'm wrong there'll still be time to find another place," Dicey said.

They sat down within the first row of trees. Dicey walked on, scuffing her feet, to the store.

Dicey entered the store through the screen door. She saw mostly cans and dried foods. There was one small icebox that held milk, butter, eggs and cold cuts in plastic packaging. She picked out a can of chicken noodle soup, a quart of milk, a loaf of bread, a bar of soap, a box of safety matches and four tomatoes from a bushel basket. It cost two dollars and ten cents.

The storekeeper stood beside her while she made all these selections, watching her carefully. He didn't say a word. He was a bony man, with short grizzled hair and long, nervous fingers. When Dicey had piled everything on the counter, he said "That be it?" and rang up her purchases on an ancient cash register.

Something about his voice was familiar, but Dicey couldn't put her finger on it.

Outside Dicey recognized what had been familiar in the man's voice. He had Momma's way with the sounds of letters. They sounded, just a little, like Momma. Dicey smiled and rejoined her family.

The dirt driveway led off the road straight for a quarter of a mile before it began winding among the trees. At the turns, driveways entered. Dicey walked down one and saw a large house, white shingled, and water beyond it. Dogs barked at her, so she turned back.

The third house was silent, although a car waited in the long garage. The Tillermans skirted the trees at the edge of the property and cut down to the water when they saw it. They found a marshy beach, nestled back against the piney woods. It was not ideal, but it was private and, except for birds and frogs, quiet.

Dicey built a small fire and opened the soup can with her jackknife can opener. It was hard work, but it did the job. She mixed a can of milk into the condensed soup in the pan. Then she told everybody to strip and put on clean underwear. James stood in the muddy water and washed out their underwear, using the cake of soap. He brought it back for Dicey to inspect. "I dunno," she said.

"The water's muddy, not like a laundromat."

Maybeth spread the wet clothing over some bushes. They sat around the small fire and took turns drinking soup from the pan, soaking it up with flabby slices of bread. They passed the milk container around, and Dicey halved the tomatoes. They ate these eagerly, even Sammy, who didn't ordinarily like tomatoes. They were red, firm, juicy. They tasted fresher than anything Dicey had ever eaten before.

After supper, Dicey put out the fire ("We don't want to attract attention") and set Sammy fishing in the quiet river. After a while, James joined Sammy, holding his own line and hook.

The sun set quietly, flaming in the water. The boys caught five small fish, which they killed and then left lying in the water, so they'd be fresh for breakfast.

When the sun was only a band of burning red seen through the trees, Dicey took out the ponchos and spread them on the ground, rolling on them to crush the undergrowth beneath. Nobody wanted to go to sleep, however. They sat with their knees pulled up under their chins. Maybeth began to sing, and they joined in without thinking. They kept their voices down, just in case, but they sang eagerly. When darkness had fallen over everything, and the stars burned bright in a moonless sky, they went to sleep.

CHAPTER 4

T HEY slept late the next morning and were awakened by the roar of a racing motorboat as it headed down the river to the bay. They were all, even Sammy, shoved out of sleep into the hot morning, like falling out of bed.

Dicey raised her face from the poncho. Her cheek was damp with sweat. Her thighs stuck to the rubber. She rubbed at her eyes.

The woods rested behind them. The water and the opposite shore lay before them. Between these wandered the narrow river. The sun was high in the sky, high and hot.

They all peed in the woods and then gathered fuel for a small fire. Dicey pulled the five fish out of the water. With the jackknife, she gutted them and scraped off some of their scales. Then she and James threaded them onto supple branches. Nobody spoke.

They ate the fish and finished the milk and bread. James experimented with toasting the bread on a stick. He got a patchwork piece of toast, splotches of white, splotches of black and various shades of brown. Dicey gathered the underwear, almost dry, from the bushes where it had been hanging all night. James taught Sammy how to put out a fire properly; how to cover it with dirt and then stamp on it and wait, to be sure no telltale smoke rose from the ashes.

953

Maybeth helped Dicey fold up the ponchos and pack them into her bag. They gathered all their garbage into the brown grocery bag.

Dicey knew it was time to go, but she didn't want to start, not yet. She pulled out her map and studied it. They would go through Easton and then loop west. Dicey would have preferred to stick to the water's edge, to follow the shoreline down, but this countryside had too many fists and fingers of land that reached out into the water. If they followed the shoreline, they would travel many miles more than they had to, winding in and out along the points of land.

At the sound of another motor, they all froze. A small boat, really just a rowboat with an outboard, chugged downriver. Three boys were in it, all about James' age. They were tanned by the sun; all wore cutoffs, T-shirts and sneakers. Their hair looked shaggy, as if it hadn't been cut all summer. They trailed lazy hands in the water as they moved slowly, aimlessly, down the river and out of sight.

"You know," Dicey said, "they look like us. Don't they? James?"

He nodded. His eyes followed the wake the little boat left behind.

"Do you think we're like most of the kids over here, in the way we look?" Dicey asked.

"Natural camouflage," James said.

Dicey looked at them. They were all tan, and her day in the sun yesterday had caught her up in brownness for what she'd lost during hours inside at Bridgeport. Their hair was scruffy, and Maybeth's curls looked tangled. But they didn't look out of place, or unusual. They looked like kids running a little wild during the summer.

They returned to the road, hurrying down the dirt driveway. James carried the bag of trash and dumped it into a garbage can near the little store Dicey had shopped in the afternoon before. The clock within the store read ten. Late.

The children walked on beside the highway. This was Route 33, heading east. In Easton, they would change roads to go south. Traffic was light on this hot summer morning. They walked two by two on the shoulder of the road. Fields of corn hedged them in. Insects buzzed among the rows. Dicey wondered if they could take a few ears for supper. Her pan wasn't big enough to hold a whole ear of corn, but you could scrape off the kernels. Her curiosity was aroused by these fields, so unprotected from the road. Anybody could go in and steal the corn. There were no fences to stop them. Maybe that was why she didn't want to do it.

As they neared the town of Easton, they began to pass shopping centers and development houses, little, low one-story ranchers with sprigs of new grass and one or two puny trees. At one of the large markets, Dicey bought a pie on sale and four bananas. They cost ninety-two cents. She told her family that they would stop to eat after they has passed through Easton.

Sammy wanted to stop before the town. "It takes all day to get through a place."

"Not a little one like this," Dicey said.

"Are you sure?"

"Pretty sure," Dicey said. "Wanna bet?"

They wagered an hour's fishing time. If it took too long to get through Easton, Dicey would have to fish for an hour, while Sammy had free time. If it didn't, then Sammy would have to fish an extra hour. Sammy liked this. Either way, he won. He walked eagerly on.

Dicey won the wager, of course. As she said to herself, if she couldn't read a map by now, she'd be a pretty sore fool. The streets of Easton, even the main arteries that they walked on, were sleepy, treelined roads. The tallest buildings reached only four stories. Stop signs outnumbered traffic lights.

Their roads took them around the town rather than through its center. They passed by a long pond that ran behind the YMCA and then down across abandoned railroad tracks to where a big highway joined up with 322.

Here, Dicey took out her map again: Route 50—a four lane highway with a grass divider. Trucks, cars, campers, buses, vans, pickups, motorcycles, all thundered down the highway, hard on one another's heels, traveling fast. Dicey wanted to get off this road for two reasons. First, it was too heavily traveled, and the air was thick with fumes and noise. Second, Route 50 went due south, to Cambridge, before bearing east to Salisbury. It would be quicker to take a road that followed the third side of the triangle formed by Easton, Cambridge and Salisbury. A river lay across that route, the Choptank. It was broad down by Cambridge, but narrower up above, and would be easy to cross, she guessed, remembering the little river they'd camped by. She decided to turn off the main highway and cut cross-country.

A quarter of a mile south of Easton, she took a turn onto River Road. That had the right sound to it. They crossed the highway at a run. They raced across the southbound lanes, then had to wait several minutes before they could dash safely across the northbound traffic. Dicey saw fields ahead, and a few houses. Twenty yards from the highway, they were back in open countryside.

It was James who sighted the circus ahead, set up on a fallow field. He saw the ferris wheel. "Let's go there and eat," he said.

"We can't spend any money," Dicey said.

"That's OK, I like to look," James answered.

They ate the bananas as they approached the circus. They came to it from the rear, from behind a big tent. A short midway with a Ferris wheel and carousel and a dozen booths for games and food stands led away from the tent entrance. People were hurrying around, setting up games, carrying boxes marked with the names of soft drinks; a man tinkered with the engine that drove the ferris wheel. Dicey stopped by a trash can. She broke the pie into four pieces and handed them out. They dropped their garbage into the metal barrel. They stared for a while at the activity on the midway and then drifted back to the tent from which music and voices issued.

"Do you think they have elephants?" Sammy asked Dicey.

"It doesn't look big enough," she said. "I don't see any place where they'd keep animals, do you, James? It doesn't look like much of a circus."

James peered into the tent, standing in the doorway. "There's a tightrope," he reported.

"Out," ordered a sharp voice from the dimness within the tent. The Tillermans backed away. "You heard me." A woman stepped out into the hot sunlight.

She had bright red hair and wore a man's shirt over tight blue jeans. She wore sandals with very high heels. She carried a whip. Three terriers, like little white mobilized mops, swirled around her feet in eager circles. Somehow, she managed not to step on them or trip over them.

"What're you kids doing here?" she demanded. She sounded angry, angry at them.

"Nothing," Dicey said.

"Tell that to the Marines," the woman said. "You know we don't open until six."

"No, we didn't," Dicey said.

"You do now," she answered. She put her hands on her hips and glared at them. The whip dangled down, and one of the little dogs, the one with a pink ribbon on its head, jumped up to grab it out of her hand. The woman rocked on her heels and the dogs ran off in a row, the other two chasing the one carrying the whip.

Dicey started to smile.

"You heard me," the woman said. "Or should I call the police?"

"I don't think so." A slow, thick man's voice spoke from behind the Tillermans. Dicey turned to face this new person. He was a tall black man, with eyes so dark brown they looked almost black beneath thick eyebrows. He was clothed entirely in black, a black shirt and black pants and high black leather boots. His tightly curling hair was cut short, and he had a narrow, short beard along his jawbone. His face looked relaxed, as if nothing could upset him.

Maybeth moved closer to Dicey. James stood where he was, his mouth open. Sammy was poised to run.

The man spoke again. "Relax, kids, she won't hurt you. Claire? What is this?"

"They were snooping around," the woman told him. "This one," she indicated Dicey, "he said they didn't know we're closed until six."

"You go back to work," the man told her. "I'll take care of this." They waited while she whistled for the dogs and then stalked off, back into the tent.

"We are off-limits until the show opens," the man told the Tillermans.

"We really didn't know," Dicey said.

"Then you're strangers around here." His eyes studied her.

Dicey nodded. Looking at his calm face, with its studying eyes, she said what she was thinking: "Strangers about everywhere."

He looked quizzically at her.

"She had no cause to be angry," Dicey said.

He nodded. "I apologize for that. Claire's got a bad temper—but that's no excuse. Believe it or not, she's a good friend. A good person to have on your side."

"We owe you an apology, too," Dicey answered. "Even if we didn't mean to, we did trespass."

"I'll see you out," he said. "You came through the back? Where are you going, if you don't live in Easton?"

"South," Dicey said.

"Where you from?"

"North."

The man stopped two strides ahead of them and turned to look at them all. His leather boots creaked a little. The Tillermans stood in a row, facing him.

"Are you OK?" he asked.

"Yeah," Dicey said.

"You're not a boy," the man said, walking beside them now. He had a little smile hovering around his mouth.

"No, I'm not," Dicey agreed.

"Do you own this circus?" James asked.

"Yep," he said.

"Why?" James asked.

"It's my living. Name's Will, by the way. I like moving around, following the good weather."

956

"I wouldn't think you'd make any money," James observed.

"Why not?" Will asked.

"It's so small."

"That's right enough," Will agreed. "Still . . ." his warm voice drifted off without finishing the sentence.

At the road he said good-bye. "Good traveling," he said to Dicey.

"Thanks for rescuing us," Dicey said.

"You didn't need help," he answered. "Take care."

"You too," Dicey said.

"Oh I do, you can believe I do," he said. He turned back with a wave. The Tillermans walked away.

They were silent for a long time, each thinking his own thoughts in the steamy afternoon. The road wound through farm country. Here the farms were large. Several fields separated one farmhouse from another. The fields were flat. The farmhouses had only a few trees near them. Big barns and many sheds lay behind the houses. They were prosperous farms, you could tell, because the barns gleamed with fresh red paint and the houses often had swimming pools out front.

Finally, James broke the silence. "She probably figured she could be angry and mean to us and get away with it," he said. "Because we're kids."

"She didn't get away with it," Dicey reminded him. "Sammy? You were ready to run, weren't you?"

"I didn't know what she'd do," Sammy explained. "She said she'd call the police."

"That was smart," Dicey said.

"But—" James started to say, and then he stopped.

They walked on and sang as they walked.

They passed fields and more fields. Some of them had been picked bare. Some of the farms had a cardboard sign posted at their mailboxes: PICKERS WANTED.

At a crossroads, Dicey went into a general store and bought potatoes and tomatoes, a quart of milk and another loaf of bread. She also bought two Cokes in cans, because she was thirsty. All these cost two dollars and thirty-five cents. Except for the forty dollars she didn't want to spend, she was almost out of money.

They shared the Cokes. "We could pick for a day or two," Dicey said to her family, "and get some money."

"Do we need money?" James asked.

"Of course," Dicey said. "I've got some set aside, in case we have to go back to Bridgeport. I don't want to spend that. So we're not out of money, but we need more."

"Would they hire kids?" James asked.

"We could try," Dicey said. "Are you game to try? Could you pick for a day, Sammy?"

"Sure," Sammy said.

Dicey grinned at him. "I believe you could," she said.

"I'll try," Maybeth volunteered.

"I guess so," James said.

"Not today though," Dicey said. "Today—there's a creek up a ways, or down a ways. I thought we'd camp by that and fish. Somebody has a couple of fishing hours owed us. I will not say who."

"It's me!" Sammy cried. "Because I lost the bet. It's me!"

As they approached the creek Dicey had seen on the map—only the map called it a river—the land developed a few gentle rises. These were not hills like they'd found in Connecticut, not high, sharp hills. They were gentle roundings, mere ripples in the land. In contrast to the flat land all around, however, they stood up. Here, there were hardwood trees, sycamores and maples and oaks, as well as the pines that grew everywhere.

The road went over the little creek, and the Tillermans turned off the road, following the creek's dry banks until they judged they were far enough from road and farmhouse. Sammy dug a few worms and set himself to fishing. James and Dicey gathered wood for a fire. Maybeth spread out the ponchos under the green trees, as best she could. There wasn't room for more than two of them, because of the roots and bushes and the creek bank.

When everything was ready and they had only to wait for Sammy to catch something, Dicey and James and Maybeth went downstream to wade and wash. Sammy watched them go without a word. He stood very quiet in the center of the narrow creek, letting the water splash at his hips, holding the fishing line out from his hands.

The late afternoon wore away into early evening. Dicey came back and started the fire. Sammy had caught nothing and reported no nibbles. He was not quite ready to quit trying, he said.

Dicey shoved the potatoes into the fire. The skins would burn, maybe, but she didn't think she could get a pot of water boiling on the small fire she felt safe building.

They ate potatoes, tomatoes, and bread for supper and passed around the carton of milk. There was enough food to fill them, and they kept back some bread and milk for breakfast. James put out the fire, using dirt not water, because water would make more smoke.

The sun was going down, then. It grasped at the land with long yellow fingers and made the mottled trunks of sycamores look like people's skin. Flocks of birds made their evening journeys home, twittering to one another. Far off, an occasional motor sounded.

The Tillermans lay sprawled around with the creek at their feet and the slight hillside behind them. Clouds strayed across the darkening sky.

"You know," Dicey said, "we don't have to go anywhere. We could always travel like this, following the warm weather, like Will said he did. We can take care of ourselves."

"Yeah, but what's the point?" James asked.

"There doesn't have to be a point," Dicey said. "Just doing it. Like sailing."

"We have to go home," Maybeth said.

"Home? We don't have a home," Dicey said.

"I thought we were going to Momma's home," Maybeth said.

"Is that our home too?" Sammy asked.

"I don't know," Dicey said. "That's what we're trying to find out, I guess. Oh, well," she said, "I guess you're right, James. I mean, you have to go to school."

"So do you." He grinned at her. "So do we all. We're going to grow up. We have to."

"I know. I know," she said.

"If it was Momma's home, it has to be ours too," Maybeth said.

"We have this grandmother there," Dicey answered. "But we can't tell—what she'll think of us. What she'll want. Momma never talked about her," Dicey pointed out.

"Yes, she did," Sammy said, "but it made her sad. She'd cry."

"Is that right? What did she say?"

"I can't remember, only the sadness. I'm sorry, Dicey."

"That's OK. I didn't know Momma ever said anything about her. I just don't know what to expect there."

"Whatever," James said, "we can take care of ourselves. Wherever."

"'I know an old lady, who swallowed a fly,'" Dicey chanted. They sang all the silly songs they knew until darkness had gathered around them. Then they lay down close together and went gently to sleep.

CHAPTER 5

Early the next morning, after they had buried their garbage in the soft soil and washed briefly in the creek, they set off. By the time the sun had fully risen, the four children were back on the road.

The morning air tasted cool and clean. At a fork in the road Dicey headed south, because the Choptank River lay to the southeast. This road narrowed and ran straight between fields of tall, ripening corn. They passed farmhouses, barns and an occasional weathered gray shack raised off the ground on piles of bricks. Most of these shacks were guarded by thin dogs, that yapped at the children from the shade under the houses.

Many of the fields were being harvested. People moved up and down the rows gathering corn, squashes, tomatoes or cucumbers into bushel baskets. Their heads were wrapped with bright red and blue bandanas. They stooped, squatted or stretched. Even from the road their fatigue was evident.

"Hard work," James remarked.

"We need the money," Dicey said. "But I'm not sure the little kids can do it."

"We don't really need the money, do we? You have extra."

It was hot. The sun burned high. Dicey was thirsty and impatient. "I don't want to be stuck in Crisfield, James. I don't know how things will go there. We've got to have some extra money. We may need it."

James considered this. "What's our grandmother's name?"

"Abigail. It was in the album."

"Do you think we could go back to Bridgeport? Do you think Cousin Eunice would take us back?"

"I dunno, James."

They passed no stores, no gas stations, just farms surrounded by outbuildings and old pickup trucks.

"The map shows towns across the Choptank," Dicey said to her family. "So even if we don't get lunch we can eat after we cross it."

"Does this road go over it?" James asked.

Dicey shook her head.

"Then what are we doing? How're we going to cross it?"

"Swim. Or wade if it's shallow."

"Do you know how wide it is?"

"How could I know that?" Dicey demanded. "Stop asking questions."

"Why?"

"You're driving me crazy with them, that's why."

James quieted, but his eyes held doubts.

At midday, they saw another sign that said: PICKERS WANTED. Dicey looked down a long dirt driveway that ran between fields of corn turned to the color of August sunlight. Trees lined the driveway. No house could be seen, although a circle of trees was visible beyond the tops of the corn. "I say we try it," Dicey said. Without waiting for an answer, she turned onto the driveway. They followed her.

The driveway ran straight for about half a mile, then curved to the east. The air was thick and hot. It hummed with the activities of insects. Dicey shifted her bag onto her other shoulder and trudged on. With her free hand she slapped at bugs.

The farmhouse sat within the circle of trees they had seen from the driveway. It was a two-storied building covered with pale green asphalt shingles. It had a discouraged look to it.

The Tillermans approached the house slowly. A large, windowless barn, sided in silvery corrugated metal, made one side of the farmyard. The house made a second. Some small sheds made a third. Tall wire cyclone fences lay on both sides of the house itself. The yard was a three-sided cage.

A dog growled and barked, snarled and leaped angrily up against the fencing on the right side of the house. This must be a kennel. This dog needed a kennel. It was a large gray-and-brown creature, bigger than a setter, with a huge slavering mouth. Its teeth hung long and sharp. It charged against the fence, setting up a clamor that would rouse anyone in the house, Dicey thought. She couldn't make herself step any farther toward the screen door of the house, not with that dog there, not even to make money.

The screen door opened and a man holding a napkin in his hand stepped out. As soon as he appeared, the dog stopped barking and crouched, fawning and whimpering. The man started toward the children.

He was short and slender. He wore overalls and heavy working boots that laced up the front. The shirt under his overalls was dark blue with fancy red and yellow flowers printed all over it. His face was square and blunt; he had gray hair that he brushed back off his forehead and thin, straight eyebrows over cold eyes. He moved toward the Tillermans without hesitating, without hurrying, and stood silent before them. His skin was tanned and leathery. Deep lines ran across his forehead. He reached his napkin up and wiped his mouth.

"Yeah," he said.

Dicey spoke. "You have a sign out front, pickers wanted." She hesitated, but he didn't say anything. "We—my brother and me—we'd like to apply." She motioned James to come stand beside her.

The man didn't speak. He studied them, through hard gray eyes.

"We can work hard," Dicey said.

She waited. He didn't speak.

"What do you pay?" she asked.

"Fifty cents a bushel."

You could pick lots of bushels in a day. That would be OK. "Will you hire us?"

"Yes," he said. "What about the smaller ones?" he asked Dicey.

"They'll come with us and help," Dicey said. "They won't cause any trouble."

"Name's Rudyard," he said. "What's yours?"

"Verricker," Dicey said quickly. That seemed to be all he wanted to know. Except, "What's hers?" he demanded, pointing at Maybeth with his head. "Maybeth," Dicey said.

960

Something was wrong here, something she couldn't put her finger on. Well, it wasn't her problem; they would work an afternoon and take their money.

He told them to get up into the back of a dusty old pickup truck the color of canned peas. He drove them on a flat dirt road that led around the barn and behind it before heading straight up a slight incline, through an overgrown field, to another field. This was a long field of tomatoes. The plants were crowded with weeds, grasses and low vines. You could barely see the rows they had been planted in. But the tomatoes had grown red and plump. They shone out from the weeds like bulbs on a Christmas tree. At one corner of the field, a mound of bushel baskets waited. The Tillermans scrambled down.

Mr. Rudyard didn't even get out of the truck. "I'll be by at dark," he said. He backed the truck around and drove off. Dicey watched it go into the distance, back to the barn, then around it and out of sight.

"Creepy," James said.

"You can say that again," Dicey agreed. "Maybeth, you OK?"

Maybeth nodded, wide-eyed.

"How long do we have to stay?" Sammy asked.

They all felt uneasy. Dicey tried to reassure them. "Just this afternoon. Then we'll take our pay and get out of here. OK?"

They got to it. Because they were hungry, Dicey decided they could each eat two tomatoes. That was fair enough, she figured. Then they all worked together, pushing or pulling weeds away from the tomato plants. One would hold back the overgrowth, and the rest would reach in for tomatoes, wresting the fruit from the stems. Their legs and hands and faces were scratched. They had bug bites on every part of their bodies. Dirt was smeared across their faces and arms and legs. They left the filled baskets where they were when they finished with them.

After an hour they had completed one row. Two to a basket, they carried the bushels down to where the pile of empty baskets waited. They had six baskets. "Three dollars," Dicey said.

Dicey's back ached from bending over. Her hands stung where small scratches had accumulated. She had never felt such heat before, an air that closed down over her and made it hard to breathe.

"Hot," James said. "It's too hot, Dicey."

"You two take a break," Dicey said to Sammy and Maybeth. "Go off and explore a little. Stick together though. When you're rested, come back and help. Remember our name?"

"Verricker," Sammy said. "What's that?"

"Our father's name," Dicey said.

"That right?" James asked. "How do you know that?"

"So what," Sammy said. "I like Tillerman better."

Sammy and Maybeth wandered off down the edge of the field, going away from the house and the dog. Dicey and James got back to work.

This row took longer. James grew sloppy and Dicey had to nag at him to keep at it and find all the ripe tomatoes that grew on the plants and on the long vines that crawled along next to the dry earth. "My back hurts," he protested. "I'm hot." His face was streaked with dirt and sweat. His eyes wavered between anger and self-pity. He crouched unwilling by her side.

"It's only for an afternoon," Dicey snapped at him.

Sammy and Maybeth returned before they had finished the row. "There's another field," Sammy reported. "And a river. I wanted to go swimming but Maybeth wouldn't."

"The Choptank," Dicey said.

"Could we swim across it?" James asked Sammy.

Sammy nodded. Dicey shot a triumphant glance at James. "It's not wide," Sammy said. "I could swim it easy."

"Can we go now, Dicey?" Maybeth asked.

Dicey almost said yes. They all looked at her, waiting. She shook her head. "Not before we get paid," she said grimly. "Don't worry, we'll be all right. As long as we're together."

At late afternoon, when the sun was beginning to lower and the mosquitos were beginning to rise, the green pickup truck returned. The children went eagerly to meet it.

Mr. Rudyard had the dog in the front seat with him. He climbed down and pulled on a long rope to get the dog to follow him. The Tillermans crowded together. The dog snarled at them.

"There's a bag in the cab," Mr. Rudyard said to Dicey. "The missus said I had to feed you something." He walked off, down to the far end of the field.

"What's he going to do?" Maybeth whispered.

"I dunno," Dicey said. Fear climbed up from her stomach to her throat. A sour, metallic taste was in her saliva and she swallowed it down. She made herself climb up and get the paper bag from the seat of the cab. Mr. Rudyard had left the keys in the ignition.

Mr. Rudyard tied the dog to a tree, using the end of the long rope. When he came back, Dicey had decided what to do.

"We can't pick any more," she said. "We have to go now," she said.

He looked at her out of cold eyes. Then he said, "If he runs against that sapling it'll snap." He got back into the truck and leaned out the window. "I keep him hungry," he remarked. He backed the truck around and drove off.

In the silence, Dicey could hear insects humming. "What does he *want?*" she demanded.

Nobody could answer her.

"We might as well eat," Dicey said. They all sat down. Mrs. Rudyard had packed a tall thermos of milk and a package of tall biscuits slathered with butter and bright strawberry jam. They passed the thermos around. The biscuits looked delicious. Dicey took a bite of one, and her stomach closed against it. She put it down on the wax paper.

Even James couldn't eat. They looked at one another. "I'm sorry," Dicey said.

"Well, I don't care, I'm not picking any more," Sammy announced. He threw his unfinished biscuit into the pile and they scattered around, like fallen blocks. "And you can't make me," he said to Dicey.

Dicey couldn't help smiling at him and that made her feel better. "I won't try," she said. "James? What can we do?"

"I'd like to kill him and hit him," Sammy said. "He scares Maybeth." Maybeth had big tears in her eyes.

"There's the dog," James said, "and the man." Absent-mindedly, he picked up a biscuit. He took a bite, then tossed it down again. "He's crazy, Dicey."

"Bad crazy," she agreed. "Don't get on that truck again, no matter what."

"He wants us to be scared," Maybeth said. "He wants to hurt us."

Dicey nodded. Her mind was working and working, and she couldn't think of anything. James just stared at her. She picked up her maroon bag from where she had put it beside the bushels. She took out all of the money and jammed it into her pocket, with the jackknife. (With a jackknife, if she had to, she could try to fight the man or the dog.) She stuffed the map into the waistband of her shorts.

"We're going to have to run," she said. "When he comes back for the dog. James, you take Maybeth. Maybeth, no matter what, you stick with James." Sammy could take care of himself. "Go for the river."

"What about you?" James asked.

"I'm not sure," Dicey tried to keep her voice normal. She had gotten them into this mess, and if anyone got caught it should be her. "I'll do something. You just keep ready to run."

It was deep twilight, shadowy and still, when the truck returned. The Tillermans sat where Mr. Rudyard had left them. The headlights shone on them briefly. He backed the truck so that its back section was where the filled bushel baskets waited and its nose pointed almost straight down the road to the farmhouse. He got out and looked at them.

"You're not much use," he observed. Maybeth grabbed Dicey's hand as his eyes rested on her. "I'll just have to teach you. Now, load up," he ordered. He walked down to the dog, which barked a greeting.

"How does he know we're alone?" James wondered.

"Quiet," Dicey said. She looked into the cab to see if the keys had been left there. They had. "OK, now listen. When he's to the dog, tell me. And when I say run, you run, all of you, as fast as you can. You hear?"

They nodded. Dicey got up into the truck. She tried to forget about the man at the far corner of the field. She looked for the key and found it. She turned on the engine. Nothing happened. She looked at the transmission box. A needle pointed to *D*. Quickly, she shifted it to *N*. "Now, Dicey," James whispered.

She turned the key again, and the engine caught.

Dicey looked back over her shoulder. Mr. Rudyard ran toward them, his mouth open in a yell. The dog ran ahead of him, at full cry, but held back by the rope that his master had looped around his shoulder.

"James," Dicey yelled. "Now. Run."

She shifted into *D*, and turned the wheel so it would head straight down the road to the barn. If she got it started, she figured, the incline would keep it going. She pushed on the accelerator and threw herself out of the cab.

The ground surged up to meet her and the cab door slammed against her shoulder. It hurt, but she didn't have time to worry about that. She rolled onto her feet and looked to see her family, waiting, watching her. "Go!" she shrieked.

Dicey led them into the middle of the tomato field, away from the man and the dog. It was harder running, especially for Sammy with his short legs, but it would be harder for Mr. Rudyard too. She let James and Maybeth pass her and slowed until she was behind Sammy too.

They weren't going to go without her. She didn't have time to know how she felt about that. She glanced over her shoulder.

Mr. Rudyard was already letting the dog's rope fall from his shoulder as he ran after the truck. He would catch it easily, but how soon? The dog looked after his master for a second and then bent his head to the ground, snuffling something. Probably their scent, Dicey thought, turning her head back and making a burst of speed to catch up.

Across the tomato field, and then across the next field, where young corn made a narrow path for them to follow, they ran. Dicey tried to listen for the sound of the dog behind them, or the sound of the motor coming out of the darkness. But she could hear only their labored breathing and the stamping of their feet. She charged through the row of brush and small trees that separated the second field from the river, grabbing Sammy's hand, pulling him with her. The earth fell away from beneath her feet and she tumbled into water.

Water closed warm over Dicey's head. She shut her eyes. She held tight onto Sammy's hand. How deep was it?

Her toes touched muddy river bottom and she pushed up. She shot out of the water. It was only up to her chest.

"James? Maybeth?"

"Here," James spoke just beyond her.

"It's warm," Sammy said.

In the distance, a truck motor roared.

"Straight across, then right, downstream. OK? Stay close."

They set out into darkness, paddling quietly across. Through the gentle sounds of water, Dicey could hear their breathing. Dark water was all around them, and the dark land behind, and the dark land ahead. Every now and then she lowered a tentative foot to touch bottom.

The river was no more than fifty or sixty yards across, and it wasn't long before Dicey saw the opposite bank rise over her head, capped by a tangle of undergrowth and trees. She put her foot down again. It sank into mud.

Dicey and James were tall enough to touch bottom, but the water was over the heads of the smaller children. So Dicey and James each carried the weight of a younger one floating beside. They made their way cautiously, silently, quickly, downstream. They didn't speak, not even when they heard the man breaking through the bushes behind them upstream.

Sounds of someone walking hastily through underbrush across the river.

James moved doggedly on. Dicey followed him. They were near enough to get out and run, if Mr. Rudyard dove into the water to pursue them. They could hide in the bushes on this side. He didn't have the dog with him.

The sounds ceased, as if someone were standing still to listen. James stopped too, but she pushed him on with an impatient hand.

The water gurgled around them.

The crackling sounds began again, hurrying away.

The darkness around Dicey lifted, as if a blanket had been taken off her head. There was no actual change, of course. Only, the night seemed cool and empty, and the clear dark silhouettes of bushes and trees above them seemed to move back to give her more room, and the broad river seemed to float peacefully beside them.

They kept silence for another half hour, working their way downriver. At last, Dicey spoke. "Let's get out—James? Can you lift Sammy? Sammy? Do you mind being first?"

" 'Course not," Sammy said.

James hoisted the little boy up onto the bank. Sammy reached down to help Maybeth scramble up. Dicey pushed James from behind, and he turned around to pull her up, while her feet slipped against the muddy bank, searching for firm holds. They sat, huddling together, shivering but not from a chill.

Dicey turned to look behind them, where flat farmlands stretched off. No windows shone, but she could see a pair of headlights, far off, moving on a straight line. There must be a road.

964

"Not him," Dicey said. She kept her voice low. Danger lurked all around them, always, she knew that now. "It couldn't be him. There aren't but two bridges over the river and they're miles away."

"What about the dog?" Sammy asked.

"Dogs can't track through water," James said.

Dicey remembered the dog, snuffling at the ground for their scents. Then she began to giggle. "It was eating the biscuits!" she cried. "He couldn't get it to chase us because it was hungry. Doesn't that serve him right."

This set them all giggling, even Maybeth. They kept their laughter low, and after a while they lay back on the grassy bank and slept, close together.

CHAPTER 6

A T THE FIRST signs of dawn, the first pink glimmers, the first watery bird songs, Dicey opened her eyes. She lay on her back with James on one side and Maybeth curled against the other and Sammy on his belly beside James. Her eyes looked up through the delicate leaves of trees into a depthless sky. She smiled, and her eyes closed.

Later, when they opened again, the sun was fully risen. Faint voices floated to her across the fields that lay behind them. James had rolled away from her. The sky had blued above her. Dicey sat up.

The Choptank danced at her feet, deep and clear. It looked cleaner than any water she had seen. Grasses grew up its banks, and a musical silence stirred in its depths. She followed its path with her eyes to where it wound out of sight, going west.

When they were all awake, even Sammy, and when Dicey had pulled out her jackknife and dried it thoroughly on her shirt and counted her money (handling it delicately so that the damp paper wouldn't rip apart), she gently spread the map before them.

"We're about here," she said. She pointed to a place on the southern bank of the Choptank. "Let's head for that town." Her finger traced a path to a place named Hurlock.

James protested: "Secretary's closer."

"Hurlock's bigger. It's in the right direction," Dicey said. "If he comes after us—"

"You think he will?" Sammy asked.

"I don't know, but I don't want to take any chances."

"It'll be easier to hide in a bigger town," James said.

That was what Dicey was thinking. She was also thinking what a long, unknown way lay between here and Crisfield; and that Crisfield too was unknown.

They cut across fields. The ground underfoot was dry and crumbly, and although they tried to hurry, it was difficult because the furrows rose up to trip them. Walking across fields was like having one leg shorter than the other.

One of the fields they had to cross was being picked. Pickers were scattered among tomato plants that rose up from the tops of furrows. Weeds had been kept down in this field, and the plants had been trained up stakes. It looked like a painting, the ridges of brown earth, the tepees of dark green tomato plants with their bright red fruits, the bent figures of the pickers and the blue sky overhead.

Dicey led her family single file along the edge of this field. She set a brisk pace, so that anyone who saw them would think they had someplace to be and the right to be where they were. Nobody paid them the slightest attention.

After the field they came to a road. Dicey turned right on it. She wasn't sure of her direction, except that she wanted to go south, away from the river.

So began another morning's march. This part of the journey was often interrupted because at the faintest sound of a motor, the Tillermans ducked into the bushes at the side of the road and hid. Dicey didn't have to tell anybody this.

No green pickup passed them. He would have to search both sides of the river, Dicey thought. If he searched at all.

Their road made a fork with another road, and now they walked on a gravel shoulder. After an hour, they came to a crossroads that had signs. Hurlock was one and a half miles straight ahead. Dicey found herself looking at the houses they passed (whether the buildings were run-down or cared for, whether they were small or large, close to the road or set far back) with questions in her mind. Every house was a secret place, a fortress, within which anything might be going on. Every house was perhaps a trap.

They bought a cantaloupe from a boy at a roadside stand. Dicey cut it up with her jackknife. They pulled the seeds out with their fingers. The juices ran down their chins as they took huge bites of the warm fruit. It was mild, sweet and chewy. When they had finished it, they heaved the rinds into an empty field and continued on.

An hour later, they reached the outskirts of Hurlock, a dusty, sprawling little town, with one stoplight at its center. The windows of the stores were crammed with notices of church suppers and house tours. One poster advertised a circus and showed a lion jumping through a hoop. Hawkins Circus, it announced. Admission, $1.50 for adults, $.75 for children. Taped to the bottom was a hand-lettered notice that said that the circus would be in town for two nights only, on the grounds of the elementary school.

Dicey went into the second market, just after the stoplight at the center of town, and bought milk, peanut butter and bread. When she emerged, she saw James studying the circus poster.

"That's nothing to do with us," she said. He followed her down off the porch. Sammy and Maybeth stood up from the curb.

A dusty green pickup drove by them, driven by a square-faced man. The head and shoulders of a large dog were visible sitting beside him. The man and the dog looked straight ahead. The truck headed out of Hurlock, past the stoplight, back towards the Choptank.

Dicey's heart jumped. She clutched the bag of food to her chest.

James watched the back of the green truck. "He didn't see us. I don't think he saw us," he said. "What can he do, anyway?"

Dicey couldn't imagine what Mr. Rudyard could do, but she was afraid he would do something. "Let's run," she said. The elementary school might be on the far side of town. They hadn't passed it coming in. "Come on."

"He didn't even turn around," James protested.

"A circus is here now. There'll be people and if he does turn around and try to do something, we can get help. Call the police, or something."

"They wouldn't believe us."

"Stop arguing, James!"

Dicey grabbed Maybeth's hand and began to run. James and Sammy followed.

966

They ran along uneven sidewalks in front of stores, then houses. Nobody paid any attention to them. They cut past two women who were meandering along, talking. At corners, Dicey looked quickly up and down, for a building that might be an elementary school. It had to be in the town. When she didn't see it, she dashed across. She couldn't go as fast as she wanted because Maybeth's legs were shorter than hers.

At last she saw a modern building that nestled against the ground, down a low sloping hill. Behind the building rose the hoop of a Ferris wheel.

The sidewalk they were on went beside a playground, then up to the front door of the school. As the Tillermans, breathing in gasps, were passing the playground, a dusty green pickup swung into the road that circled before the school entrance.

Dicey swerved onto the grass. "James! Go around behind!" She grabbed Sammy's arm and pulled him. He struggled to keep his balance at Dicey's pace. Ahead of her, James and Maybeth ran side by side. Maybeth's legs pumped frantically.

Around the corner of the building, Dicey caught sight of the big tent. She pulled Sammy up even with James and Maybeth. "Into the tent," she gasped. They dodged around the base of the Ferris wheel. Dicey heard footsteps behind her now and the familiar snarling of a dog.

She turned her head. Mr. Rudyard was jogging along easily, pulled by the dog, which he held on a short chain. The rest of the chain he carried looped over his shoulder.

At the open space before the tent, Sammy tripped. He stumbled and fell, rolled over and sat up. Dicey stopped. She turned to face their pursuer. That would give Sammy time.

James and Maybeth had run into the tent. Dicey heard noises from within, voices and the yapping of dogs. She backed toward the entrance. Mr. Rudyard slowed his pace to a walk. He took the loops of chain down from his shoulder and began to play them out. The dog strained towards Dicey. She could see the yellow eyes and the saliva dripping from its tongue.

He was going to loose the dog on her.

Dicey put the paper bag up over her chest and throat, ready to jam it down the dog's throat if he should leap. Dogs went for the jugular. "There are people around here," Dicey panted. Her voice was hoarse. "You can't get away with it."

He didn't seem to hear her. He was intent upon her face and her slow backing away.

Suddenly, Dicey's legs were shoved from behind. Her knees buckled and she fell on the ground, flat on her back. She dropped the bag. Up she sprang to her feet, still facing Mr. Rudyard. He was not the kind of man you could turn your back to.

Three white terriers had charged out from behind her, bowling her over in their excitement. They yapped and yipped, happily. They ran up to the big dog, holding their tails up like little flags. The big dog snarled, growled and dove into their midst. A cacophony of noise burst out of the mass of tumbling dogs.

Claire rushed out from behind Dicey. She laid into the dogs, cracking her whip. The terriers danced away. Claire played her whip around the ears and eyes of the big dog, forcing him backwards until he stood at Mr. Rudyard's side.

Dicey turned around then. She saw a ring of people, with Will at the center and James beside him. Two men were dressed as clowns; three more large, muscular men in jeans and workshirts inched forward with clenched fists; a girl in

967

ballet tights stood tensely beside an older man who wore glasses and chewed on a fat cigar.

Claire looked Mr. Rudyard in the eye. In her high heels, she was six inches taller than he was. "Hold your dog," she said.

His hand took the leather collar. Dicey edged toward James.

"Where you going?" Mr. Rudyard's voice demanded. He surveyed the group. "They're my kids, foster kids," he said.

"No, we're not," Dicey said. She turned to Will. "We're not, you know that."

"You in charge?" Mr. Rudyard asked Will. He sounded surprised.

"I am," Will said. He stepped up beside Dicey.

"They gotta come back," Mr. Rudyard said. "I got papers."

"What kind?"

"Legal papers."

"Show me," Will said.

"I've got them back home," Mr. Rudyard said.

Dicey looked at James. She saw Maybeth and Sammy standing in the gloom just within the tent entrance. They could still run, maybe. How did Will know what was true? How could he possibly know they were telling the truth? He seemed to be thinking about what Mr. Rudyard was saying. Nobody knew the Tillermans, except back in Bridgeport, nobody even knew they were alive. Why should anyone care what happened to them?

And how was Dicey going to keep them safe?

"I want them kids back now," Mr. Rudyard said.

"I'd need to see those papers first," Will answered slowly. He took a couple of steps forward. His boots creaked.

Dicey's legs felt watery.

"I said, I'll take them now." Mr. Rudyard's voice was steely and he didn't bother to disguise the threat.

"I don't think so," Will said, still slowly. "Not until I see the papers."

Mr. Rudyard loosened his hand on the dog's collar.

"I wouldn't," Will said, still slowly. "Claire here—she's got one nasty temper—and a good hand with a whip. That so, Claire?" Claire smiled. "And I've been chased by dogs myself often enough not to be overly scared of them. Animal dogs or human dogs."

"Nigger!" Mr. Rudyard hissed the word.

Will didn't move a muscle of his face or body, but the three big men behind him did. Claire, however, was the one who attacked. She moved smoothly, like a snake. She cracked her whip before her, at the dog's feet and chest, at his head. The dog whined and growled and backed away. Mr. Rudyard was forced to move with him.

Claire moved steadily forward. She cracked the whip again, at Mr. Rudyard's feet, then at his knees, then at his hand where he held the dog, then at his shoulders. He was wearing another fancy shirt, red with long white fringe hanging from the shoulders. Claire snapped the whip at one shoulder, then the other, back and forth.

He backed steadily away from her. His eyes burned cold at her.

"Get out," she said. She didn't shriek it, she hissed it. "You make me sick."

Mr. Rudyard looked as if he wanted to say something. Instead, he spat into the dust at his feet. Then he turned his back to them and walked slowly away, the dog at his side. Claire lifted the whip and snapped it sharply against his fanny. He leaped forward.

Dicey held herself stiff until she heard the motor of the truck start, and then longer, until she saw the truck pull up the long slope before the school building and turn back to town. Then she let her legs collapse underneath her.

The people drifted away, leaving Claire, Will, the Tillermans and the three terriers, who ran happily in circles.

"Well, Claire," Will said.

"Well, Will," she answered, looking him straight in the eye. Her cheeks were red.

"I always said you've got quite some temper."

"You could use a little of it," she said shortly. "I'm going back to work."

Will turned to the Tillermans. "Why don't we talk this thing over?" He sat down beside Dicey. James, Maybeth and Sammy joined them. Dicey kept trying to speak, but her voice caught in her throat and she couldn't make words come out. The others waited for her to say something first.

"What's in the bag?" Will asked. "Food? Lunch?" Dicey nodded. "Go ahead and eat. If you've got enough, I'd like something too. I seem to have a bad taste in my mouth."

Making the sandwiches relaxed Dicey. It was such an ordinary thing to do. She spread the peanut butter with her jackknife, then wiped the blade clean on her shorts. She made everybody one sandwich and two for James. She opened the milk and set it on the ground.

"We're not foster kids," James finally said. "That's the truth. He—it's so crazy I wouldn't blame you if you didn't believe it—we took jobs as pickers and—"

"He never paid us!" Dicey realized.

Will chewed contentedly on his sandwich. "Happens I do believe you. That was one mean man."

"Boy, was he," Dicey said. Her voice had returned. "We—thanks, you know?" He waved that away with a hand.

"My idea is you ought to stay with us awhile," Will said. "We're going south to Salisbury for our next shows, then Berlin. After that down to Virginia. Where *are* you headed for? You ought to tell me. Don't you think?"

"We can work," Dicey said. "We can help out. We could pay you, too."

"Let's start somewhere solid," Will said, smiling. "Like names. I'm Will Hawkins."

Dicey introduced them. She picked up her sandwich and began to eat. Between bites, she told their destination, as briefly as she could, not about Momma and the journey to Bridgeport, nor about leaving Cousin Eunice's house, but about Crisfield and the grandmother there they'd never met and about needing some kind of home. He listened, nodded, asked no questions and made himself another peanut butter sandwich.

"We've got two nights here and then we break. We'll be a week in Salisbury," he said. "What say you stay with us and we run you down to Crisfield one of the days in Salisbury. That OK?"

"That's fine," Dicey said. "That's great. But do you have room for us?"

"It's a bit primitive. We live in trailers—you could go in with Claire."

"Wouldn't she mind?"

"I don't think so. I'll have to ask her, of course. But she has all those dogs in there, I don't see four kids would make such a big difference."

"We can sleep anywhere," Dicey said. "As long as we're together."

"We'll have to think some what to do about him," Will said. "But not now. I've got work to do now. Stick around—hear me? He might come back."

"I know," Dicey said. "We'll stay close."

They stayed near the tent all afternoon. Sammy hung around Claire until she finally let him help her by holding hoops and moving the little stools the dogs perched on. James went to watch the man with the cigar who operated the Ferris wheel. Soon, he too was working busily, passing tools and squirting oil. Dicey and Maybeth cleared away litter from the midway. They ate supper back where the trailers were parked, at a campsite that had only three trailers on it. Each of these had a picture painted on its side of a lion jumping through a flaming hoop and the words Hawkins Circus spelled out in bright letters. "But there aren't any lions," Dicey said to James. He shrugged.

At dinner, Maybeth helped with the serving and clearing. Dicey wanted to help too, but the cook, a tiny black woman with her hair grown out into an afro, said the two of them were just fine and she didn't think she'd ever had a better assistant. When Will asked them, James told how they met up with Mr. Rudyard. "We were walking down the road," James began, "feeling pretty good." Everybody listened. Dicey sometimes forgot to eat because she was so interested, as if this was a story that had happened to somebody else.

That night they went to the circus with Mattie, the cook, who was married to one of the big men Dicey noticed earlier, a man named Samson whose head was entirely bald even though he wasn't at all old. Dicey insisted on paying for all their rides and games, as if they were real customers. She was through worrying about money. While she had it she didn't need to worry. When she ran out, she would earn some more. They sat in the front row for the show. They clapped for Claire, who looked like the Snow Queen in the fairy tale, white and glittering. They smiled at Will in his black cape with red lining and a tall hat he swept off his head. They gasped when the tightrope walker fell off into a net and cheered when she climbed right back up to try again.

The Tillermans slept in Claire's trailer, James and Maybeth on the second bunk, Sammy among the nestled pile of terriers, Dicey on the floor. When Dicey awoke the next morning, she saw filmy shadows, as if the inside of the trailer was swathed in veils. She awoke to the quiet sounds of seven creatures deep in sleep. For a while, she lay and listened.

James turned restlessly, uneasily, and the sheets rustled around him. Maybeth was still. One of the dogs yipped gently: Dicey raised her head and saw his little legs moving as he lay on his side with his eyes closed. What did dogs dream? Sammy had an arm around another of the dogs. All that Dicey could see of Claire was her hair spread out on the pillow. She snored gently, like the waves on Long Island Sound, soft and regular.

Making no noise, Dicey slipped out to sit on the metal trailer steps. Animals stirred, birds and squirrels, two timid rabbits. Distant motors stirred beyond Dicey's sight. The branches of the tall pines stirred in a rain-bearing wind. These pines were not like the thick, cone-shaped trees of New England. On these pines, the needles hung like pompoms in sparse clusters along lank branches. As the trees grew taller, the lower branches fell off, so they grew into giant lollipops. Loblollies, Will called them, and it was a good name for them.

Mr. Rudyard could have caught the Tillermans so easily. Were they just more stupid and helpless than most people? And what about this farm they were going to, their grandmother's farm. When you walked down a road, you could be walking to anything. Anything. What if this grandmother, too . . .

Well then, Dicey thought, they would beg to return to Cousin Eunice, and Dicey would know enough to be grateful, really grateful, for someone who took them in and meant to take care of them. Cousin Eunice wasn't perfect, and she wasn't Momma, but they could work things out with Cousin Eunice.

If she would. Maybe she wouldn't take them back. Maybe, maybe, maybe.

A squirrel up in a tall oak tree set up a terrific chittering. He was furious, frantic. His tail thrashed up and down.

What good did it do, worrying and making plans, and more plans, if the first plans failed. It was like money. If you had it, good. If you didn't, then you had to find a way to earn it. There was nothing to be gained by fretting over maybes.

Dicey took a deep breath, which tasted of dampened sunlight and moist earth. They were living with a circus for a day or so. For a day or so they were safe. Something would happen after, but that was after. You had to keep alert and watchful, she'd learned that. You had to be ready to run. But if you wasted every day worrying about the next . . . And you never knew what was coming, anyway.

After breakfast, Will took Dicey into town. "To get some stuff," he said, "and see someone." The stuff, as it turned out, was clothing for the Tillermans, underpants (three new pairs each, because they came in packets of three), T-shirts and shorts. Will also got toothbrushes, toothpaste and a comb. They dropped the packages in the windows of Claire's big white station wagon. Then Will insisted on buying popsicles, which they ate as they walked to visit the somebody, a friend of his who was a Reverend. Will explained to the Reverend about Mr. Rudyard, and Dicey listened. The Reverend said he thought he could speak a word to the sheriff about it. He asked Dicey if she was sure she didn't want to speak to the sheriff herself. "She can't," Will said, and the Reverend didn't ask any more questions.

As they walked back to the car, Dicey said, "I used to think that everyone was the same, pretty much like us. They're not though, are they?"

"Not a bit of it," Will answered. A minute later he added, "Everybody's different, and everybody thinks everybody else is the same and they're the only one different." He smiled at Dicey then. "We've done the most we can, just about," he told her.

Back at the circus, Sammy dashed up to tell Dicey that he was going to be in the show with Claire, helping, as long as they stayed with the circus, that Claire thought he would be funny and he thought so too, that Maybeth and Mattie were making him a costume with spangles on it, like Claire's. James was busy with the machinery that ran the carousel. Dicey spent the day drifting around. She had passing, lazy conversations with people. After a conversation, she would walk away slowly and sit somewhere private to think over what she'd heard. She would sit and watch the people moving about, like characters on a TV screen with the sound off.

She was alone all afternoon. The sky got heavier with rain, but no rain fell. It was a gray afternoon, the kind of gray that darkens and deepens the greens of leaves and grasses. She had nothing to do, and she didn't want anything to do. Her thoughts whirled among bits of information and ideas that crowded into her brain, and blew about there, like dry leaves in a storm.

Sammy came to find her late in the afternoon. She was sitting in the grass by the playground, pulling out the blades and looking at them. But she wasn't seeing them, she was seeing the windy dunes at Provincetown and all the days they had lived there.

"Time for supper, Dicey," Sammy said. "What're you doing?"

"Thinking." He hadn't entirely awakened Dicey from her reverie. He stood in front of her, and she saw him and did not see him.

"Thinking what?"

"About Momma."

"We gotta go now." He tugged at her hand. He had already forgotten about Momma, Dicey thought, and probably that was better for him.

"I dream about her," Sammy said, hurrying Dicey back to Claire's station wagon. "A lot."

So he hadn't forgotten: and Dicey knew that, whatever anyone wiser or smarter might say, she didn't want him to forget. "What do you dream?" she asked.

"Nothing special. She's just there, in the dreams." He ran ahead.

That night, the tightrope lady fell off the wire in the same way, and the audience gasped in the same way and applauded with the same enthusiasm when she climbed back up the tall ladder. Dicey realized then that the fall was part of the act. The fall was as flawless as all the rest of the steps. It was a fake. Like the lion on the poster and the glittering costumes that made everybody look beautiful. Like the way everyone laughed at Sammy because they thought he was making mistakes with the dogs, when it was really part of the act. Like the way Maybeth looked like a princess when she circled under the cascading lights of the carousel. Fake.

Dicey looked at James. He shrugged his shoulders at her. He didn't care. But Dicey did, she discovered. It wasn't that she minded, exactly. Not exactly—because she had done too much lying of her own to mind about this. But—they didn't need to lie, did they?

The circus days floated by. They drove through the rain to Salisbury and set up the tent and booths in the rain. Dicey didn't do anything much, she didn't even go to the shows after the second night. James and Maybeth and Sammy were busy and contented.

Contentment was too small a word for what Dicey was feeling. They had food and a warm place to sleep, and Dicey had money in her pocket. They were traveling and had purpose and destination, but no conclusion. Dicey had nothing to worry about. Nothing except what lay ahead, in Crisfield, and she didn't want to think about that any more. She had thought all she could about that. You couldn't know what lay ahead. How could you know that? How could Dicey expect herself to know what this grandmother would be like? She couldn't; she realized that at last. She would have to wait and see. That part was easy, the waiting and the seeing.

These circus days drifted slowly. It would be something to live in a circus, Dicey thought, always moving around, always heading for somewhere new. If it was Dicey's circus, she would go everywhere. She planned it out herself, alone in Claire's trailer at night, with the noise from the fairgrounds behind her. First, all around the United States, then up to Canada and down to Mexico. She would make her circus get famous and get jobs in Europe, and maybe even China or Japan. They'd have trailers for land travel and a ship of their own for sea travel. She would have real lions.

Day after lazy day, night after long dreaming night passed Dicey by.

L ATE one morning, as Dicey stood in a blazing sunlight where the tent had been the night before coiling up the long ropes so that Samson could stack them evenly on the truck and find them when he needed to stake down the sides of the tent that evening in Berlin, James and Maybeth and Sammy approached her.

"Hey," James said.

"I don't need any help," Dicey told him. "Go on and do what you like."

"Are we going to go to Crisfield?" James asked. "We're all ready. We packed our things into a paper bag and your map too. Will says he can take us now, in Claire's car."

"Is it time?" Dicey asked.

"Will says so," James said.

"Let me just finish this, OK?"

More good-byes, Dicey thought to herself, coiling up the last rope into a dark brown hoop, piling loop upon loop. "I am unfond of good-byes," she said to herself. All of their good-byes lay like the coiled ropes on the ground, connected and unconnected, curling silently, finished things.

But the kids were right, and Will was right. It was time.

Dicey took a deep breath. Time to get moving.

She sat beside Will in the front seat. James and the little kids sat behind them. Dicey took out her map. Time to put the circus behind them.

The circus people stood around and waved and made jokes. Dicey looked around at them, gathered together there in the fairground, their hands held high, their friendly wishes for good luck floating around the car still, like cherry blossoms blowing down to the ground. The car pulled out of the fairgrounds. "Good-bye," everybody called. "Good-bye, good-bye."

After a while, Dicey turned to the map. There was nothing to look at on the road. It was just like Route 1. "What route are we on?" she asked Will.

"Thirteen. We follow that to just south of a place called Princess Anne, then get onto Three-thirteen," Will said. "How do you figure to find her?"

"Look up the address in a phone book," Dicey answered. "Then we'll ask directions."

"We've got lots of time," Will assured her. "All I have to do is go back, pick up Claire and the beasts and the trailer and make it to Berlin in time for supper."

"Are you going to take us right there?" Dicey asked.

He didn't turn his head. His profile was smooth lines, slightly curved except where his nose jutted out and his beard jutted out at the end of his chin. His skin was smooth and brown, like silk. He didn't answer, he just nodded.

"But why?" Dicey asked.

"To make sure you're OK," he said.

Dicey looked out the window. City clutter had fallen behind and now there was country clutter, junkyards, a trailer park, billboards advertising dog food and faraway hotels. Beyond these the land stretched away to low, flat country. The fields and woods all had shallow ditches dug around them to drain away water. Most of the land was being used for farms, interspersed with patches of loblollies and other trees.

"Crisfield's a small town," Dicey said to Will. "We'll be OK."

"You don't want me to take you right there, do you?"

Dicey leaned towards him. "It's not that. It's—she doesn't know about us. Not only that we're coming, but she doesn't even know we exist. We didn't know about her until our cousin in Bridgeport told us we had a grandmother. And—I don't know how she'll be. There was this priest in Bridgeport. He had somebody here come to see her and tell her. She wouldn't let him in, or listen. He said she screamed so she couldn't hear what he was saying. So I don't know how she'll act. Momma . . ." her voice faded away.

"There's a lot you haven't told me, isn't there?" Will asked.

"Yes." Dicey thought. "It gets so complicated."

"I'll tell you what," Will said. "How do you want to do it? I'll go along with you if you'll make me one promise. You keep your promises?"

"Yes."

"If you'll promise me that you'll come to me if you need help. We'll be in Berlin for a week, four shows and then three days off on the beaches. The police can always find me if you call. Will you promise?"

Dicey thought about that. "But what could you do?"

"Who knows? What do friends do for each other? Something. Whatever. Will you promise?"

"OK," Dicey said. "I promise."

"We'll be coming by again in eight months—but anything can happen in eight months. I can't just dump you kids off. Not and forget about you. I can't do that. But I can let you do it your own way if I know you'll call me if you need to—if it's not working out."

"Why?" Dicey asked. "I mean, why should you bother? You have your own life."

"You're a little bit of my life now. You can't get away, and I can't get rid of you. That's a fact."

Dicey understood. A lot of people had little bits of her life now, and they were tied to her now, or she was tied to them. To some of them, she owed something that she hadn't paid yet, like Windy and Stewart, or Cousin Eunice. You didn't just let people go, that's what Will meant. You always did what you could.

Dicey leaned back into her own corner by the door. Well.

"What I thought was," she said, "we'd go downtown and find out where she lives. Then just go out there." That was almost the truth.

"And you want me to leave you off and drive away," Will said. Dicey had no idea what he was thinking. "Are you scared?" he asked her.

"Some."

"Why?"

"It's a last chance for us," Dicey said.

"I don't know about that," Will said slowly. "You could say all of life is a series of last chances."

"OK," Dicey said, "but inside of houses—no matter what they look like from outside—even that one"—the car sped past a tall brick house, surrounded by old elm trees and seeming serene and wise, as if it had stood there for so many years that nothing could surprise or hurt it—"you can't tell what's inside. You can't tell what might happen. How do you know who to trust when you meet people? How can I tell about this grandmother? I know *I* can always run, but when there are four of us . . ."

"Wouldn't it be easier if I stuck with you?" Will asked.

Dicey shook her head. "Well, yes, of course it would. But I have to know by myself, for us."

"OK," Will said. "OK. You can have it your way."

As they neared Crisfield, entered the town limits, followed the main street, they all fell silent. Dicey could almost hear the worries that nobody said aloud. The air inside the car grew thick with them.

The road ran straight and broad until it came to the water. They looked around. Docks, most of them vacant now on this summer morning, stretched out into the bay. Sheds lined the land's edge. Piles of small wire boxes were everywhere, and oyster shells had been scattered like a layer of earth. A few people, mostly old men, sat in the sunlight, looking at nothing.

"Well," Dicey said.

"We'll meet again." Will turned to her. "One way or another. OK?"

"OK!" Sammy said.

The Tillermans climbed out of the car. They stood at the road's end by the water's edge. Will backed the car, turned it around, looked out the window to give them the thumbs up signal, and drove away.

Until the station wagon was out of sight, the Tillermans didn't move. Dicey held the grocery bag in one hand, and the other hand she held up in farewell, until she could no longer see the square back of the car.

They were on their own again.

"OK," Dicey said. She passed the bag to James. "You wait here. I'm going to find a phone book." She didn't wait for anything, not even to study the flat expanse of blue water. She walked back along the docks to the side-walk and entered a grocery store. There was a poster in its window advertising Will's circus.

The store was filled with darkness, dust and the smell of the food on its shelves. Dicey stood inside the screen door for a minute, while her eyes adjusted to the dim light. The only person in the store was a woman in a stained apron behind a glass-framed counter. Dicey walked up to her. The woman had thick, strong arms and her hands were mottled red. Her face was pale and thick with flesh. Her eyebrows were straight and bushy over little colorless eyes.

"Yeah?" she asked, leaning her elbows on the top of the counter. "What can I get you?" Her words came thick and slow, like molasses—again, something like Momma.

"I'm looking for a phone book," Dicey said. "Do you have one I can look at?"

The woman nodded. She plodded out from behind the meat counter and walked heavily down to the cash register at the front of the store. She pulled out a thin phone book from underneath the counter there. She watched Dicey open it.

There was a Peter Tillerman on a place called Deal Island, and a G. Ridgely Tillerman in Princess Anne. There was no Abigail Tillerman. There was no A. Tillerman, either.

Maybe their grandmother didn't have a phone. Or maybe it was listed under their grandfather's name. Only, there was no Tillerman listed for Crisfield.

Dicey looked at the page and chewed on her lip.

None of the Tillermans listed lived in Crisfield. Was her grandmother still here?

Yes, because that priest had gone to see her. He would have told Father Joseph if she'd moved or died. He knew where she lived.

"Something wrong?" the woman asked.

"I got work to do," the woman continued, to prod Dicey. She leaned down on the counter as if she needed the rest.

"I was looking for the telephone number for Abigail Tillerman," Dicey said.

"Why would you do that?"

"I was going to call her up. To see if she needed some help around the place," Dicey said.

"I've never seen you before," the woman remarked.

"We're new," Dicey said. "We just moved in."

"Ab won't hire you," the woman said. "She's letting the farm go."

"Selling it?" Dicey asked.

"Naw, she'd never sell that place. But she can't work it by herself."

"That's why I thought she might hire me," Dicey said.

The woman shook her head, closed up the phone book and put it away. "Besides, she hasn't had a phone since Bullet died. If you'd asked me I'd of told you. She came down and threw her phone through the telephone company window. You don't want to work for her."

The woman trudged back down the aisle to the meat counter. Dicey stood where she was, listening to the hum of a large refrigerator.

"Where is her farm, anyway?" she called to the back of the store.

"Down to the water, south," the woman answered.

"What road?"

"Landing Neck. It goes off South Main, half a mile inland. Maybe a mile. There's a bend on Landing Neck, and a new little house sits right on it. Next mailbox is Ab's. But it's seven miles. I wouldn't go out there. She's queer."

"Queer?"

"Crazy as a coot, that's my opinion. We leave her alone. You should too."

"Maybe you're right," Dicey said.

"No maybes about it."

Dicey left the store. She returned to her family. Their eyes held the same question.

Dicey sat on the edge of the dock, hanging her feet over the water. James, Maybeth and Sammy sat in a line beside her. You couldn't see the bottom of the water. It was muddy, so you could only see a little way down into it. The waves gurgled underneath them.

More bad news, Dicey thought to herself. But why didn't she feel bad? She looked around at the docks and the dozing men and the water and the shacks. She picked up an oyster shell and dropped it into the water.

The air smelled of salt and fish and motor oil.

"You know what this is like?" Dicey asked James. "It's like Provincetown. Isn't it? It smells like it."

"Yeah. What about our grandmother?"

"She lives seven miles out of town, on Landing Neck Road. She doesn't have a telephone."

"How do we get there?"

"I don't know yet. But I thought . . . James, I want to go out there alone. Just in case. I want you to stay here with the kids. And I'll come back for you when I know."

"Know what?"

"If it's OK for us there."

"I don't like that, Dicey. What if you get in trouble?"

"Better just me than all of us, right? Will said we could call the Berlin police to get him if we need help. So if I don't come back then you can call him. Here's the money, for lunch and anything. Can you keep an eye on Maybeth and Sammy?"

"Yeah, but I don't like it."

"I'm in charge, James. Remember."

"OK. But . . ."

Dicey gave him the money she had left, nine dollars. She leaned over to talk to Maybeth and Sammy. "You do what James says. You hear?"

They both nodded.

"That's all right then," Dicey said. She stood up quickly and hurried away, without looking back.

The business section of Crisfield lay next to the water, low buildings with big plate glass windows. The business section crowded as close as it could to the bay and looked out over the docks, as if that was where its real interest lay. Beyond that, residential streets branched out, circling around the town itself.

There seemed to be three kinds of houses. There were lots of churches, even on the one street Dicey followed out of town. These were mostly small stucco or clapboard buildings with short steeples. Then, there were the usual narrow clapboard houses on little handkerchief lawns, two stories high, two rooms wide. The third kind were large wooden houses with broad porches that ran around the buildings; they had odd shapes, round towers, octagonal bays, balconies. These houses had paint that had faded and peeled. Often, their screens were ripped or doors hung askew. But they spoke clearly of what they had once been: once they had been homes for large, rich families; once the spiraled pillars that held up the veranda roofs had gleamed with white paint; once the tall windows of the ground floors had opened into rooms crammed with plush furniture and oriental rugs, and the large trees in the yards had swarmed with climbing children. These were the kind of houses that might have treasures in the attic, or ghosts in the cellar. These were the kind of houses that could burst with life. Now they rotted quietly, neglected, sad, but filled with mysterious memories.

Dicey walked on, walking fast. She turned at the second stop sign and found herself on Landing Neck Road, in farm country, where broad fields burgeoned with corn or barbed wire contained cows and horses, where chickens and ducks wandered around the yards. The farmhouses sat next to the road, quiet and clean, secretive.

How would she know if their grandmother's house was safe for them? What questions did you ask a person to find out if you could like one another? If she could be trusted?

Dicey's sneakers made no noise on the roadway. No cars overtook her. There was no sound at all, except the occasional distant barking of a dog or a lowing of a cow. The silence wrapped around her like a quilt, a silence made up of trees growing and corn ripening, of the bright sky glowing and the distant water following its tides. This was not an empty silence.

Six miles outside of town, Dicey came to the expected bend in the road. A low, one-story white house looked out from a stand of pines. Behind it were stables. Two pastures, where long-legged horses grazed, came next.

Half a mile down the road, Dicey saw the mailbox, dented, rusted, its post awry; *llerma* was all that remained of sloppily painted black letters. The little door hung open, like a dog's tongue. Two or three old leaves lay inside, and a plastic glass with a straw sticking out of its cover.

Across the road, where the farm itself lay, overgrown fields stretched back to meet a thick woods of pine trees, oaks and tall, topheavy loblollies. The fields had small trees scattered over them, pine and maple saplings, and the grass was thick and tangled, as tall as Dicey's waist.

The driveway ran straight between the fields. It too was overgrown. You could barely make out the ruts where car wheels would fit.

The sun had risen high into the sky. Dicey turned into the driveway, walking slowly now, even reluctantly. She did not look ahead, but at the ground before her feet. Abandoned, that was the word this farm said to her.

She couldn't even see the house until she had passed under the pines, walking now on a thick carpet of needles that seemed never to have been disturbed. The air under the pines was thick and shady.

The house sat behind a small orchard, and beyond it, a barn was slowly falling down. The house was faded white clapboard, two stories high, and had a screened porch all along the front that ran around the sides. The roof, gray slate, slanted down in four directions from a central peak. Two chimneys stuck up through the roof.

The house was silent, vacant, neglected. Long weedy grass grew up, as high as the porch floor. Honeysuckle spread over the screens of the porch, and its long fingers reached for the trees in the yard. Most of the trees were short, heavily leaved. Some had tiny apples growing on them. They had the rough bark of fruit trees.

One larger tree grew right up in front of the house, hiding the front door, shading the lawn. This tree looked like an umbrella, held overhead by four trunks that spread out from their common source. Its broad leaves made a green canopy against the sunlight. It wouldn't be a good climbing tree, Dicey thought, walking up to it and past it, but you could make a platform tree house to rest on the four trunks and build steps out of pieces of wood to go up one trunk. Then, you would have a house like a boat, almost floating on air, and the long, leafy branches stretching above like sails.

Dicey pushed her way through the long grasses to the steps leading to the porch. The grass tickled her knees. Grasshoppers leaped aside to let her pass.

The steps were rotting away. The screen door hung from broken hinges. The sun couldn't penetrate the honeysuckle leaves, so the motionless air on the porch was as dark as twilight.

Dicey knocked on the door. It was a wooden door, once painted white. A rusted nail stuck out from its center, over Dicey's head.

Nobody answered. She knocked again and listened. She heard faint noises, like some night creature scurrying. But the noises did not come toward the door.

Somebody was in there, of that Dicey was sure. She knocked again, three loud raps. No voice called out. Dicey turned the knob and pushed against the door. It was locked.

She went back across the porch and down the steps. She walked around to the side of the house.

The side looked just like the front, except that it had no steps or door. There were two windows on the second floor and four on the first, which were barely visible through honeysuckle. The honeysuckle here had not grown as fast as that on the front of the house. The porch, she noticed, continued around the back. The whole house was surrounded by a broad porch.

All the second story windows had their shades down. Nobody could be seen inside, nor any light. Dicey went on, around to the back.

She saw the woman the moment the woman saw her. The woman sat on the bottom of some steps facing out, over more fields (only these had crops growing in them) and the distant dull green of marsh grass. She wore a shapeless blouse over a long, shapeless skirt. Her feet were bare.

Her dark eyes looked at Dicey angrily. Her skin was tanned. Her hair had been hacked short, so its iron gray curls burst heltershelter all over her narrow head.

Dicey stood where she was. She swallowed, twice. Her throat was suddenly dry. "Mrs. Tillerman?" she finally asked. Her voice squeaked.

"You're trespassing," the woman said. She had a thin, stiff voice, not like Momma's at all.

"I thought I heard—when I knocked—I didn't know if—" Dicey stepped forward. "The fact is, I wonder if you would hire me to work for you." She stood right in front of the woman now. Her grandmother.

Her grandmother's eyes seemed big for her face as she stared at Dicey. But maybe that was just because her face was small, the skin stretched tight over its bones. Her eyes, now that Dicey was closer, were not brown but dark hazel, browns and greens without any yellow to give them sparkle. Fine lines sprayed out from around her eyes.

These were the eyes of the girl in Cousin Eunice's photograph album. The rest of her was all different, but the eyes were the same.

"The fact is you're trespassing," her grandmother said. "Who told you to come here?"

"Nobody. I heard you were alone—so I thought I'd try."

"I don't know you, do I?"

Dicey shook her head. "We're new here."

"Why aren't you in school?"

"It's summer."

"Not for long."

Her grandmother stood up. She walked up the steps and through the screen door, without looking back. The back door stood open, and she went straight into a kitchen.

Dicey followed her.

Her grandmother opened a glass-fronted cupboard and pulled down a can of spaghetti. She took a can opener out of a drawer and opened the can. A saucepan waited on the stove. She opened another drawer, took out a big spoon and scooped the stiff red and yellow contents of the can into the saucepan. With a match, she lit the fire under the burner. She dropped the match into an ashtray and turned to take a bowl out from the cupboard.

Dicey might just as well not have been there.

Her grandmother waited by the stove, stirring in the pan.

"I didn't say come in," she said.

"You never said if you want me to work," Dicey answered.

Hazel eyes studied Dicey. Dicey studied the barefooted woman. Her feet were caked with earthy dirt.

"How do I know you're not going to rob me?" her grandmother said.

How could she know? Dicey thought. The people in the houses were in just as much danger as the people outside the houses. "I'm not," Dicey said. "It doesn't look like you have much to steal anyway."

"You have family?"

979

"Yes," Dicey said.

"Where do you live?"

"In town. I can work hard. Your barn needs painting, and the screens and the steps, and the lawn. I could take off the honeysuckle."

"I'm not too old to do that."

"I can pick and weed."

"So can I. So can anybody. You better get down a bowl, since you've invited yourself for lunch."

Dicey did as she was told.

They sat down at a long table, big enough for ten people. It was made of wood and had been scrubbed to a pale, smooth finish. Dicey sat across from her grandmother. She spooned the canned spaghetti into her mouth. After the first bite, she ate quickly, trying to fill up her stomach without tasting anything.

"You like my spaghetti?" her grandmother asked.

"No," Dicey said. "But I'm hungry. Do you like it?"

"It's easy to fix. You know what I sometimes think?" Her grandmother looked straight at her, her mouth chewing. "I sometimes think people might be good to eat. Cows and chickens eat corn and grass and turn it into good meat. People eat cows and chickens. In people, it might turn into something even better. Do you ever think that?"

Dicey shook her head.

"Especially babies," her grandmother said. She swallowed thoughtfully. "Or children. Do you have brothers and sisters?"

"Yes."

"Who told you I was alone?"

"A lady in the grocery store."

"Millie. She's the butcher. Can you imagine that? A lady butcher."

"Why not?" Dicey asked.

"I guess you might say so. Millie is one, and that's a fact. Facts are facts. What did she say about me?"

"Nothing much."

"Did she tell you I was crazy?" Her grandmother wasn't looking at her.

Dicey didn't answer.

"Maybe I am. You know? When you die all the gases build up in your body for weeks, like yeast in dough. And you swell and swell. Then, things start exploding. That's where the stink comes from. After that, you're fresh as a daisy and the worms and maggots have you. What do you think?"

Dicey put her spoon down. She was through eating.

Her grandmother's mouth twisted. "What do you think about death? Don't be smart with me, girl."

Dicey was puzzled.

"Or don't you think?"

"I saw a tombstone. *Home is the hunter, home from the hill, and the sailor home from the sea:* that was what it said. As if"—Dicey tried to explain her thoughts—"that was the quiet place at the end of things."

"It's not quiet," her grandmother said. "Not for the worms."

"I wouldn't care about that if I was dead," Dicey said.

"Maybe I am crazy," her grandmother said. "You know?"

Dicey was beginning to think she might be.

"Maybe not. Do you feel sorry for me?"

"Why should I?" Dicey asked.

"Old, alone, crazy—the farm falling down around me. My husband died these four years and more."

"I'm sorry," Dicey said.

"I'm not. I'm happy since he died."

"Why?" Dicey asked.

"He kept wanting his shoes polished. He never did polish them himself. First thing I did, I bought myself a washing machine. Do you play the piano?"

"No."

"Too bad," the woman said. "I've got one. Haven't played it myself, I never had time. My children did. They all died too, and that was a relief."

Dicey stood up. She didn't even feel bad. She didn't feel anything, except maybe glad she had come out here by herself.

"You're going," her grandmother said.

Dicey nodded.

"You didn't offer to help with the dishes. No, don't bother. I know what children are like."

"OK," Dicey said. It didn't matter. She'd go back and get her family, and then they'd call Will.

"Don't you want to know if I want you to work for me?" her grandmother said. She was still sitting in her chair, but she had turned around to watch Dicey leave. "Well, I don't. I couldn't pay you anyway."

Dicey nodded and turned her back to the room.

The woman's voice spoke from behind her: "I know who you are. You hear me? I know who you are, and you can't stay here."

CHAPTER 8

S LOWLY, Dicey turned. She looked all around the room before she answered. She didn't know what she should say. Why should she say anything? She'd been told to go away.

Sunlight poured into the kitchen through the door and windows. (So, her grandmother had kept the honeysuckle down on this side of the house.) It was a long bright plain room, the kitchen. Everything in it looked old and scrubbed, like the top of the table. Wooden counters, wooden cupboards, wooden chairs, wooden floor; only the refrigerator, sink and stove were porcelain. A single light hung down over the table. It had a pale yellow glass hood over it.

Her grandmother sat without moving, staring at Dicey.

"Then who am I?" Dicey asked.

"I knew the minute you knocked on the door. That's why I came outside. A polite person would have gone away." Her grandmother waited to see what Dicey would say.

Dicey didn't say anything.

"Oh, I know who you are; you're the oldest one, I can't remember your name. There's a foolish letter here, somewhere. It has all your names in it."

This wasn't good enough. "You don't know who I am," Dicey said.

"You're Liza's daughter. Some ungodly name she gave you, her and that Francis. I liked him, I did."

"Who's the letter from?" Dicey asked.

"Connecticut," her grandmother answered. "Where are the rest of you? One's retarded, the letter said. Maudlin, simpering fool. Can't blame her the right, Dicey saw the lopsided barn. It had once been red, but the paint had weathered, faded and peeled, until it looked pink as a bad sunburn. The tin roof was rusted in large patches.

"Anyway," Dicey said, "this is where Momma lived."

"It's beautiful," Maybeth said.

"It's a wreck," Dicey answered. "The fields out front—and look at that barn. It's gone to ruin. She hasn't taken care of it."

"But it's big," James said. "Big enough for all of us. Is it near the water?"

"There's a marsh first," Dicey said, "a long, empty marsh. Then the bay. There's a path, but the water's at least a quarter of a mile away. Not like Provincetown. Anyway, who cares? We won't be staying."

"True enough," her grandmother said from the side of the house. "But you'll be here for supper so there's work to be done. I see you found them." She started at James. "James," she said.

He tried to smile but her face discouraged him.

Her eyes flickered over Maybeth. "And Maybeth." She looked away quickly, as if nothing about Maybeth could interest her. The little girl moved closer to Dicey.

"I've got crab pots set down by the dock," their grandmother said. "Who'll fetch the crabs?"

"I will," Dicey said.

"Me too," Sammy said.

"James and Sammy will," their grandmother announced. "It's after four. I eat early, and so will you. I put a basket by the back steps."

The two boys ran off.

"You two come with me. I'll show you where to sleep."

She strode around to the back of the house. Dicey picked up the grocery bag and followed her. Maybeth clung to Dicey's hand.

They saw James and Sammy heading off down the path to the water. James carried a bushel basket by its two metal handles.

Their grandmother led them through the kitchen and into a dim hallway. "That's my room," she said, pointing at a closed door, "and my bathroom," pointing to the closed door next to it. They turned left down the hall and ascended a narrow staircase.

Upstairs, they saw a long, U-shaped hallway with five closed doors around it. A window at one end looked out over the front yard, through the leaves of the big tree. Their grandmother stood on the top step and let them go past her. "That's the bathroom at the far end. Sheets are in one of the bureaus. I can't recollect which."

Dicey went to look out the window. "What kind of tree is that?"

"Paper mulberry," her grandmother answered.

Dicey noticed from above what could not be seen from below. There were strong twisted wires running around the tree. "Why is it wired?" she asked.

"Because paper mulberries are fragile," her grandmother answered. "It's the way they spread out at the top, it's the way they grow. If you didn't brace it, the weight of the leaves and the growing branches would pull the tree apart. Like families." She went abruptly downstairs.

Dicey and Maybeth stood in the dim hallway. "Cripes," Dicey whispered. "It's like a ghost house."

The air was warm and old, as if the same air had been up here for hundreds of years. The closed doors looked like so many secrets.

Maybeth's eyes were round and frightened.

"Look at it this way, Maybeth, it's only for one night. And besides, this was Momma's house, when she was little. Isn't that right?"

That didn't make Maybeth feel any better, but it made Dicey feel better. She forced up the old window to let in fresh air. She braced it with a piece of wood lying on the sill. Their grandmother wasn't going to take any trouble for them, but Dicey would show her.

Dicey opened the nearest door and stepped boldly into the room. This was a bedroom with a plain iron bedstead overlaid with a thin white quilt. The pillow had no cover on it. The room held a dresser, a desk and chair and a wardrobe, all of plain wood. Dicey went to a window and snapped up the shade. This room faced the big tree. She snapped up a shade on the other wall and found a window that looked out to the barn. Between them, she and Maybeth got the four windows up, and braced them with pieces of wood. Fresh air filtered around the room and light came in.

The smaller room across the hall was almost identical, except the quilt was faded blue instead of white. On the front of the wardrobe somebody had painted a picture of Indians coming out of the woods, carrying bows and arrows, wearing warpaint and bright headdresses. It was a kid's painting with blobs of green paint for leaves and the sun a yellow circle with lines coming out. Dicey liked it. They opened this room too and returned to the hall. With two doors open and the sunlight and the clean air, the upstairs seemed more friendly. Dicey walked down the wooden floor to the opposite end.

First she opened the door opposite the hall window. This was a bathroom. It had a toilet with a wooden seat and a wooden box above the seat from which hung a long, wooden-handled chain. The bathtub was raised off the floor by four stubby legs that ended at four feet with claws on them. The sink stood on a tall pedestal. Above it was a shelf where you could put soap and toothpaste.

Dicey and Maybeth both went to the bathroom. They pulled on the chain to flush. When you flushed, you could hear the water gurgling down the pipes from the overhead box.

Then Dicey opened the window and looked out.

From this window you looked over the roof of the porch, over the back yard, over the planted fields, over the long stretch of marshes—to the water. The band of water lay blue and sparkling, out and away. A boat, tiny at this distance, moved up the bay, maybe heading back to Crisfield with its day's catch.

Dicey hurried into the room on the right. Here there were some small differences. There was the same iron bedstead, and the quilt was multicolored, faded but still cheerful with reds and blues and greens and yellows. The bureau and wardrobe had been painted white. The desk and chair were plain wood. A picture hung on the wall, a childish picture of a boat sailing on blue water. Fish swam on the water, and crabs ran about the sandy bottom. Gulls wheeled in the air and rode, with folded wings, on the waves. Dicey snapped up the side shades and held the windows while Maybeth put the braces under them. These windows looked to the barn. But the other two windows, as she had hoped, gave out over the marsh and to the bay.

The last bedroom had a ruffled quilt and picture of ladies in old-fashioned dresses on the walls, pictures cut out of magazines and pasted on a white background. The childish painter had put a picture on the wardrobe here too, of a castle and town and a queen, wearing an impossibly tall crown, walking in the garden.

987

"I can hear what you're thinking," her grandmother said.

Dicey swiveled her head around to meet those dark hazel eyes, the sullen, angry eyes she had seen in the photograph Aunt Cilla kept. Could her grandmother know what she was thinking? And so what if she could?

"Maybe you can," Dicey said, not dropping her glance. She'd think of a way. She'd been thinking up ways to get them in and out of trouble all summer long. As if she had been practicing for this occasion, warming up for this last struggle. Her grandmother didn't know Dicey. Her grandmother didn't know the kind of thinking and planning Dicey could do.

A fleeting expression that might have been unaccustomed mirth, or might have been a twinge of pain, went across her grandmother's face. For a second, the face came alive around the eyes. Then it was all gone.

Dicey turned back to the sink. She didn't want to be distracted. She had thinking to do.

They had crabs for dinner. It had taken the boys a while to learn how to shake the crabs out of the pots into the basket. The first pot they'd just opened, and the crabs had fled sideways in a turbulence of muddy water. Sammy had tried to grab a couple and been nipped for his pains.

"You should have seen them," he cried, telling the story. His cheeks were pink and his eyes shone. He was too pleased to let his grandmother's stony silence quiet him down. "They looked at the door and looked at us and then"—he thrust his arms straight out and waggled his fingers—"gone! I didn't know things could go sideways so fast. Boy are they smart."

James spoke to their grandmother: "We closed the doors and set the traps back where they were. Is that right?"

"Right enough. What did you use for bait?"

"I didn't think," James said. "What should we use?"

"Fish. You have to catch the fish."

"Good-o," Sammy said. "Can I go down after dinner? Do you have any line?"

"No point to it," their grandmother said. She was checking the boiling water in a huge pot on the stove. The potatoes were in the oven, the beans in a covered pan, the table set with forks and a platter of sliced tomatoes and glasses of water.

"So what?" Dicey answered quickly. "I'll go with you Sammy. We like fishing," she said defiantly to her grandmother.

The woman didn't answer, but instead lifted up the basket and poured the teeming mass of crabs into the water. She slammed the lid down on top of them. You could hear them scrambling around inside the metal pot, scrabbling up to escape the steam. Their grandmother stood with one hand holding the lid down, staring at the children.

Maybeth ran out of the room. Dicey felt like following her—she could imagine how those crabs felt, and she had had that feeling herself at times—but she wasn't going to back down before those eyes. So she stood, and pretty soon there was silence in the pan. She knew they were all dead then.

They ate the crabs from a big plate in the middle of the table. They were served individual plates with potato and beans on them. There was no butter for the potatoes, but there was salt.

The Tillermans had never eaten crabs before. They learned how to rip off the legs first, then lift back the top shell. Then you broke the crab in half, like a turnover, and picked out the meat from between sections of cartilage. Each crab had two larger chunks of meat in it, and an awful lot of stringy little pieces.

It was hard work getting full on the scraps of crabmeat. It took a time to get even a mouthful ready, once you'd taken out the two chunks. But it was a good dinner for talking at, if you wanted to talk. Everybody's hands were busy, and almost nobody's mouth was full.

Their grandmother seemed to want to talk, or seemed to want them to talk. She asked questions.

"Where's your mother?" she asked. She sent the question out to the middle of the table, as if she was asking the platter of crabs.

The children looked to Dicey.

"Momma's in a mental hospital in Massachusetts," Dicey said. "She doesn't recognize anybody. She doesn't do anything. They don't think she's ever going to get well."

"Who don't think?" her grandmother asked.

"The doctors," Dicey said.

"They don't know," Sammy said. "She might. Isn't that right, Dicey?"

Dicey nodded.

"So you know better than the doctors," his grandmother said to Sammy.

Sammy's jaw went out and he didn't answer.

"And you ran away from this silly chit in Bridgeport. You ran away from someone who was willing to take you in and take care of you. Why'd you do that?"

They looked to Dicey again.

"It wasn't right for us. Especially not for Sammy and Maybeth."

"Because Maybeth's retarded?"

The cruel question lay before them.

Dicey looked at Maybeth. Maybe she hadn't understood. But she had. Well, that was good because if she hadn't understood that would mean maybe she really was retarded. Maybeth's eyes filled with tears.

"She's not," Dicey said.

"What is it? Can't she speak for herself? Can't you?" Her grandmother glared at Maybeth. Maybeth sat staring at her lap. "Can't you?"

"Yes," Maybeth said softly.

Dicey fumed. She felt like throwing her plate at her grandmother.

"You keep out of this, girl," her grandmother said. "You, Dicey."

Maybeth looked up. Tears rolled out of her eyes, but she stayed at the table. "I don't think I am," she said. "I don't know just what it means, but if it's such a bad thing to be—why do you want to know?"

Their grandmother nodded once, briskly. She asked another question. "You do a lot of running away. Where's your father?"

"He's been gone for years," James said. James' voice was tight. "Six years. Longer. Since before Sammy."

"I remember him," their grandmother said.

"The police in Bridgeport tried to find him and couldn't," Dicey said.

"He was the kind of man who always sailed close to the wind," their grandmother said.

"What does that mean?" James asked. "What do you mean? Do you know him?"

"He used to come around here, whenever he was in the area, when his ship was in Baltimore," their grandmother said.

"What was he like?" James asked. "Only Dicey remembers him—I don't. What did he look like?"

"Slim, dark-haired. He was a quick, nervous, darting kind of man. Not steady, but lively. The kind who might cheat at cards if luck wasn't running his way. And he'd bet too much too, that would be his way. She should have come back here when he ran out on her."

"She didn't want to," Sammy said.

"How do you know?" their grandmother said. Then, before he could answer, she said, "What does it matter anyway?"

"Momma matters to me," Sammy said, his chin stubborn.

"She went off and left you," their grandmother said.

"She wanted to come back," Sammy said.

"How do you know that," their grandmother said. She didn't ask it, she said it.

"Because she loved me. Didn't she, Dicey?"

"Yes, she did. She loved all of us," Dicey said.

"Humph," their grandmother said, reaching for another crab.

The Tillermans had won that battle. Dicey knew it. She knew it as close to her bones as she knew that Momma did always love them. Dicey tried not to grin. It didn't do to grin when there was still the whole war to win.

The children washed the dishes while their grandmother watched them and told them where to put things away. When everything was finished, and Maybeth had scrubbed the wooden tabletop with mild soap and a stiff brush, Dicey announced that they would like to go down to the dock, to fish for crab bait and to swim.

"Can Sammy swim?" their grandmother asked.

"We can all swim. We were raised near the ocean," Dicey said.

"Suit yourselves," their grandmother said.

At the dock, they took turns fishing and swimming. They stripped down to their underwear and dove into the quiet water. The bay had no waves and no undertows. It was as calm as a swimming pool. You could swim miles in this quiet water.

Dicey swam out, away from land, in a slow crawl. Her mind was working fast. There was a way, if only she could see it. Sammy and James took the few bony fish they had caught and baited the crab traps. Maybeth jumped off the dock into the water, then climbed back onto the dock to jump again. When she hit the water, waves surged up around her and the water she sprayed out turned golden in the setting sun.

Evening fell across the water, toward them. The sky turned twilight purple. A molten pink band flowed across the horizon, where the sun had been.

The children dashed back to the house, trying to outrun the mosquitoes that swarmed up from the marshlands. Their grandmother sat in the same chair in the kitchen. They wished her good night, and she nodded her head but said nothing to them.

Dicey showed James and Sammy the rooms they could have. She unpacked the toothbrushes and toothpaste and comb into the bathroom. She put each one's underwear and clean clothes into his own room.

They gathered in Sammy's room, the one with the picture of Indians on the wardrobe, and sat on his bed. "What're we going to do tomorrow?" James asked Dicey.

"I dunno yet, James," she said. "She doesn't want us to stay. She said so."

"Well, neither do I," Sammy announced. He was in bed but sitting up. His hair was damp. "Even if it is fun."

"What about you, James?" Dicey asked. "People say she's crazy."

"Crazy like a fox," James said. He dismissed that question, without hesitation. "It would be OK here. It's sure big enough."

"Maybeth?"

Maybeth didn't answer. She looked down at her hands and across at Sammy. "You want to," she said to Dicey. "Don't you?"

"*That* we'll have to talk about in the morning," Dicey said. "How about a song, how about Peggy-o."

They sang softly, in case it might bother their grandmother, sitting alone downstairs at the empty kitchen table.

CHAPTER 9

DICEY woke herself up early the next morning, before the first gray signals of dawn, when the air outside lay black over fields, marshes and the glistening water she could just see from her window. For a time, she sat by the window and thought out the plan she had gone to sleep considering.

It all depended on what their grandmother was really like, inside herself where she was who she really was. Not outside. Dicey knew about the difference between outside and inside.

You could assume that everybody wasn't just the way they seemed. The question was, in what way was their grandmother not what she seemed. Did she really want the Tillermans to go away?

Dicey was sure that she didn't want the Tillermans to stay. But Dicey wasn't sure she wanted them to go away. Their grandmother was a Tillerman too, which made everything contradictory. If she wanted the Tillermans to go, then she wanted herself to go—in a contradictory way this was true. Dicey's job was to see through the contradictions and find out where they made sense together.

Why had their grandmother gone outside to the back when Dicey knocked? She could have stayed inside and not been found. Why had she asked all those questions at dinner? Cousin Eunice's letter would have explained about Momma. And what did she mean when she said to Dicey that she knew what Dicey was thinking. Unless it was what she herself was thinking.

Besides, their grandmother had taken the boat to town to find James and Maybeth and Sammy. That was something she wouldn't have done if she'd really wanted them to go away.

Maybe their grandmother didn't know just what she wanted. Or maybe she didn't really want anything, except to be left alone. Four kids, they were an awful bother. Cousin Eunice said so, again and again. And an expense.

Dicey could manage the bother and they'd figure out a way to cover the expenses. She was sure they could do that. They could leave their grandmother pretty much alone. It was the place Dicey wanted, the big house, the acres of farmland, the barn, the water and the boat. It didn't have anything to do with the woman.

The sky lightened. Over in the east, behind the house, the last star would be fading as the sun surged up. Above the marshes, a pale quarter moon waited in a light blue sky, with mares' tails clouds brushing against it. Time to get moving.

Dicey woke James and Sammy and Maybeth. They all met in Dicey's room over the kitchen, so that any noise they made wouldn't waken their grandmother. Dicey explained her plan:

"We have to get started on something useful before she wakes up. That way, she'll keep us here today. Or if she tells us to go, we can say we will, as soon as we finish the job."

"But—" James said.

"But what?"

"What if she means it?"

"She does mean it," Dicey said. "That's the trouble, isn't it? I figure, if we get her to put it off she'll get used to us and forget that she wants us to go away. We pretend we're not even thinking about staying here. But every day we do something that needs to be done so it's worth her while to keep us."

"She could call the police," James said.

"She doesn't have a phone. But if she does then we will go, I promise. If she really means it. Can't you tell? She doesn't want us to stay, but she doesn't want us to go, either."

"I don't think she likes me," Sammy said.

"That doesn't matter Sammy. It's not her I'm thinking about. It's us."

"She's mean," Sammy said. "She's not like Momma at all."

"That doesn't matter," Dicey repeated. "Besides, she's not really mean, not like Mr. Rudyard. Is she?"

"How do you know?" Sammy demanded.

"Remember when James took that money?" Maybeth asked him. "Remember how Dicey's face got all red and hot and she told us we had to go, and she told James he had to obey. Remember? That was like our grandmother. Mr. Rudyard was cold."

Sammy subsided. Dicey took advantage of the moment to announce their project for the day: Honeysuckle.

They dressed quietly, used the bathroom quickly and tiptoed down the stairs into the dark hall. The kitchen lay in shadows.

They began with the honeysuckle growing up around the front porch. It had formed a massed wall that wove around itself and clung to itself with tiny tendrils. The tendrils looped and looped around anything that would hold them up.

The Tillermans had no plan. They just reached into the plants and pulled. The honeysuckle vines emerged in long stringers, unwoven from the mass.

By the time the sun had risen and only the shadow of the paper mulberry tree kept an early morning coolness over the yard, they had a large mound of honeysuckle branches at the foot of the lawn. Dicey didn't know how they were going to get rid of it. In some patches, she could see the screen on the porch, but they hadn't gotten a quarter of the growth yet. Maybe it would burn, but she doubted that; it was lush summer growth, tensile vines and green leaves.

"I'm hungry," James said. "This is going to take all day."

"I hope so," Dicey grunted, jerking back on a fat vine. "Anyway, let's see what there is to eat."

They trooped around the side of the house and across the porch. At the kitchen door, they stopped. Their grandmother was up. She was at the stove, making pancakes on a griddle so large it covered two burners on the stove. She turned around when she heard them coming in.

"Wash your hands. I see that you don't make your beds."

"I'll do that," Dicey offered.

"No, you'll each do your own," their grandmother said. She turned her back on them. She was wearing another shapeless blouse over another long, shapeless skirt. Her feet were bare and clean. She had set the table.

When the children sat down, two platters of pancakes waited for them. There was no syrup or butter, but quart jars of strawberry jam were set out. Their grandmother didn't say a word. She just served herself two pancakes and spread jam over them.

The pancakes looked normal, but they tasted curiously flat. The jam, however, was delicious and the children ate with good appetites.

Finally their grandmother spoke. "I like that honeysuckle." She looked at Dicey.

Dicey's heart sank.

"That honeysuckle's been there a long time. It's the kind of tenacious plant I have to respect," their grandmother said.

"Honeysuckle is parasitic," James announced. "It can be trained and kept back, but when allowed to proliferate without controls, it chokes out other growth. It's begun to climb over the small trees out front."

His grandmother studied him. James ignored her and slathered jam on his seventh pancake.

"Where'd you learn a word like proliferate?" she asked him. His mouth was full so he couldn't answer. "The honeysuckle will take you all day, at least," their grandmother said.

Nobody answered. Dicey tried to look unconcerned with what her grandmother would say next.

"You can't just leave those vines piled up. They have to go out on the marsh," was what she said.

Dicey chewed hard, to keep herself from smiling. This was just a skirmish, not even a real battle. She looked up to meet her grandmother's eyes and swallowed hastily.

After the dishes were washed and the beds made, the children went back outside. The temperature had gone up and they stripped down to just their shorts. This meant that as they pulled the vines or piled them up they got mightily scratched, all over their arms and chests and legs, but it was cooler.

They sang as they worked, sometimes in harmony, sometimes all singing melody.

Dicey showed Maybeth how to wrap a long vine around her arm and pull back on it, with all her weight, taking the strain in her shoulder. Sammy used both his hands. Half the time he jerked so hard that he fell over backwards.

The overgrowth gradually gave way to a thin layer of the oldest, thickest vines. These had to be worked out of the screen netting, because if you pulled hard on them, the screen ripped out.

As they stood, patiently unraveling coiled tendrils, Dicey began to sing the song about the wide river and the small boat. She liked the way the melody held its notes and lingered over its phrases. This was a song they all sang together, but each of them sang it his own way, holding the notes and words he liked best.

The voice came from behind them: "Where'd you hear that song?"

They turned, wiping back sweat-dampened hair. Their grandmother had a cantaloupe cut up into thick slices. She had arranged the slices on a metal cookie sheet.

"Momma sang it," James answered her. "Is that for us?"

"I don't have lemons for lemonade," she said. "Don't have milk, eggs, butter—it's melons or nothing."

"Melons are fine, thanks," Dicey said quickly.

"Did you sing to our momma?" Maybeth asked.

"I don't recall," their grandmother said. She walked away from them, back around the house.

The children ignored her and fell upon the melons. As they sat and ate, Dicey looked at what they had accomplished. "We can finish the front and clear away around the trees. Then we'll eat lunch, OK?"

They agreed.

"And after that we'll move that pile of vines down to the marsh. I guess it might be safe to burn them there. And after that—how does a long swim sound?"

A long swim sounded fine.

When they went into the kitchen for lunch, their grandmother was not there. They couldn't call out to her, because they didn't know what name they were supposed to use. It sounded funny to say "Mrs. Tillerman," and it sounded just as funny to say "Grandmother." Dicey knocked on the closed door of the downstairs bedroom, but there was no answer.

Because Dicey didn't feel right about going into the refrigerator or the pantry, they ate tomatoes and cucumbers from the garden. As soon as they were finished, they jumped up to carry huge armloads of tangled vines out to the marsh. Dicey decided that the pile should be a good way into the marsh, but next to the path so they didn't have to tramp through the wet grasses. It made quite a hill, big enough to slide down if it had been hay.

Dicey didn't want to light a fire without checking with their grandmother. She didn't feel sure of what would happen when the leaves caught. So they left the vines and ran down to the water, single-file along the narrow path.

They tossed their shorts and sneakers on the end of the dock and leaped into the water. It was cool and cleansing. It washed the sweat off their bodies. They stretched muscles that were taut and tired from pulling and carrying. Dicey swam underwater, looking at the muddy bottom. The water soaked through her hair and cooled her head. She rolled and floated under water, as if she were a piece of seaweed.

After a while, she climbed out and sat on the dock. It was then she realized that the boat was gone. What was their grandmother up to?

The children lay on the dock, letting the hot sun dry them.

"We ought to trim back that honeysuckle by the barn," James said. He was lying on his back in the puddle made by the water dripping off of him. His eyes were closed tight against the bright sunlight. "She said she likes honeysuckle, didn't she? If we trimmed it, it would make a kind of hedge, and it wouldn't harm anything."

"We don't have anything to cut it with," Dicey said.

"You could ask."

"No, I can't. Don't you see? We can't ask, we just have to do things. We can't give her a chance to say no, because if we do then that's what she'll say. And we've got to get back to work. There are still the side porches. I've got to look in the barn for tools because the next job is to fix the screens on the porches." Dicey sprang up and put on her shorts. She hurried her family along.

James and Maybeth and Sammy pulled at the honeysuckle on the side near the barn, while Dicey explored the cobwebby barn inside. She forced the doors wide apart, so she would have enough light to see. She found a small workshop opposite the empty stalls. The tools looked clean and well-oiled, saws, hammers, pliers, axes, mallets, planes, drills, screwdrivers, a level. No cobwebs had been spun around the workbench, so she figured her grandmother kept it in order. Nearby, garden tools hung on the wall and lay on a long shelf, clippers in four different sizes, shovels, hoes, stiff metal rakes and long-fingered leaf rakes. A tiny cupboard with three dozen small drawers held nails and screws of every size.

Dicey did not let herself linger by the boat. The boat was the prize. Unless they could stay, she wouldn't think about fixing it up or sailing it. She hoisted herself up onto the side and checked under the bow to be sure the sails in a canvas bag were there. Then she picked out the two largest pairs of clippers and ran outside.

James and Maybeth began the slow task of trimming back the honeysuckle hedge. Sammy didn't want to. He enjoyed tearing down the vines, grabbing at them with both hands and holding hard, as his hands slipped down, ripping off the leaves. Then, when his grip held, he would lean back on the vine and swing his weight against it. He grunted as he pulled. He braced his sturdy little legs against the ground. Sammy was hard to stop once he'd made up his mind to do a job.

Dicey saw their grandmother walking through the vegetable fields carrying two large grocery bags. She called to James to go take them, or at least one, and continued pulling. The next time she looked, her grandmother was walking along, still carrying two bags, and James was nowhere in sight. Dicey let go of the vine in exasperation and ran to help.

She met her grandmother at the end of the lawn. She didn't even ask, she just took a bag. "Front must be clear, by the size of that pile out in the marsh," the woman said.

Their grandmother came around the side to inspect the work. Sammy decided he should show off. He leaned back and grunted, to show how hard he was working. He jerked his arms. His whole body pulled back against the vine.

The vine snapped free of the roof.

Sammy tumbled backwards onto his fanny. His feet flew up in the air. The vine came after him and wrapped around him, as if it had a life of its own, as if it was a boa constrictor attacking its dinner.

Their grandmother laughed, a thin, rusty sound. Sammy struggled to free his head and arms from the snaky leaves.

"What's so funny?" he demanded.

"You are," his grandmother said.

And Sammy laughed too.

James came up from the marsh, carrying two more bags of groceries.

"Can she use clippers?" the woman asked Dicey when she saw Maybeth. "Is it safe for her?"

This irritated Dicey. "Ask her yourself. She's not deaf. If you can't see for yourself."

"Well, you'd better rub the tools down carefully with the tack cloth before you put them away. Or they'll rust. I have groceries to put away."

They swam again before dinner. They came to the table with wet heads and shining faces. Their grandmother had fried pieces of chicken in a thin cornbread batter. She served mashed potatoes with butter in pools on the top, and green beans. She even had dessert, a store cake with stiff, over-sweet chocolate frosting, and a bowl of apples and bananas. By each child's place stood a tall glass of milk.

"You did a good day's work," their grandmother said. "I suppose you'll be moving on tomorrow."

Dicey took a deep breath. "There's still honeysuckle to be pulled."

"Don't know why you carried it so far into the marsh," their grandmother said. "You could leave it up to the near end, and it'll rot away by spring. James, you look like you could use another piece of chicken."

It was not what she said, but what she didn't say, that Dicey heard. The Tillermans had won another day.

After supper, the children washed up the dishes and their grandmother went out to the fields. As Maybeth soaped and rinsed, and the boys dried, and Dicey put away the glasses, dishes, knives, forks, pots and pans, they sang. Maybeth scrubbed down the wooden table and Dicey polished it dry. Maybeth sang the song about the man who sang for his dead friends. The others had forgotten the words, so she taught them again. Their voices blended in the yellow kitchen light, and filled the empty house as the world outside darkened into twilight. "'When I come to the cross of that silent sea, who will si-ing for me?'"[1]

They let the echoes of melody fade away before they moved again.

"I'll give you this much," their grandmother said from the doorway. "Your momma taught you how to sing." She stood with darkness behind her. Dicey couldn't read her expression. "Where'd you hear that song?"

"A friend taught it to us. Someone we met when we were going to Aunt Cilla's house," Dicey said.

"Stewart," Maybeth said.

"Stewart who?" their grandmother asked.

"I don't know," Dicey said. "It was at a college."

"What were you doing at a college?" their grandmother asked.

James told her about their time in New Haven. He started with the rain and the hunger. He even told about stealing the money. He finished it at the beach in Fairfield.

Their grandmother had stood silent in the doorway while he told it. "You're not helpless infants," she remarked. Then she added quickly, "If you want to wash anything, tonight's the time. I'm canning tomorrow and the next week."

Dicey washed out their dirty underwear in the sink. She stumbled through the dark outside to the far side of the house, the side they hadn't yet pulled honeysuckle from, to find the clothesline. Mosquitoes bit at her but she lingered outside anyway, listening to the wind in the pines and the frogs croaking across the marsh. Overhead, between the branches of the trees, stars shone. Clouds drifted across the moon's partial face. When she returned to the kitchen, it was dark and empty. She ran up the stairs two at a time to join her family.

That was how the first day went.

On the second day they pulled down the rest of the honeysuckle on both sides of the house and gathered all the piles together near the edge of the marsh. In the afternoon, James and Dicey started patching up the holes in the porch screens, where the screens had pulled out of the wood or just ripped.

Their grandmother spent the whole day in the kitchen, canning batches of tomatoes and carrying them out to cool on the back porch. Sammy and Maybeth emptied the crab pots for supper, and they ate at the trestle table on the porch. Some crabs were left over. Even James couldn't fit anymore in. So Maybeth picked out the meat and put it in a bowl in the refrigerator, for lunch the next day.

---

1 *sing . . . for me* see Part 1, Chapter 8, n. 1.

"I guess you'll be moving on tomorrow," their grandmother said again.

"There's still screens to be patched," Dicey said.

"Did you bait the traps?" the woman asked Sammy and Maybeth. They had. That was how the second day went.

On the third day they finished the screens and James set to work mending the front steps, with Maybeth to give him an extra hand. Sammy and Dicey mopped and waxed the floors inside. They even went into the dark dining room (which had a big table and eight chairs, and a fireplace at one end) and the living room. Dicey snapped up the shades and looked around there.

This room too had a fireplace, and a sofa in front of it, and a huge wooden desk and walls full of books. Dicey called James in to see it. A few of the books he'd read. Some he'd heard of. The rest he stood and looked at. "You could read for years," he said.

"Who wants to?" Sammy asked him. "Hurry up, so I can go swimming."

At dinner, James asked their grandmother about the books.

"My husband was a reading man," she said. "For all the good it did him."

"What do you mean?" James asked.

"He got all of his answers out of books," their grandmother said. "Books don't change, and he liked that. They made him feel right."

"What's the matter with that?" James wanted to know. "You can study books and think about what's in them. People put down what happened before you were even born, and you can understand and not make the same mistakes. Like history."

"The past is gone," their grandmother said.

"But it shouldn't be forgotten," James said. "Should it?"

"Sometimes," their grandmother said. "Sometimes it's better. My husband used his books to build a wall to keep things out. Oh I know." She cut off James' answer. "I know it doesn't have to be that way. But that's the way it was."

"Books let things in," James said.

His grandmother studied him. "I guess they could. For some. They didn't, not for him. But he knew a lot about history and ideas and the way things should be." James was listening carefully, but she changed the subject. "Will you be moving on tomorrow?"

"When the front hinges are set in," Dicey said. "Your mailbox needs bracing, and there's some patching to be done on the barn. You have lumber in there, don't you?"

"It's going to rain," their grandmother said. "There's storms brewing."

Dicey's heart fell.

That night. Dicey was awakened by thunder roaring about the house. Lightning snaked down out of a black sky. She started counting at the end of the thunder, and barely got to two when the lightning flashed again.

Maybeth entered her room. "Dicey?"

"Climb in."

"It's right over our heads," Maybeth said.

It certainly seemed to be. Thunder growled just outside the window, trying to get in. Lightning flashed down and cracked like a whip. Dicey reached for Maybeth's hand and they tiptoed down the hallway and down the stairs.

In the kitchen, Dicey turned on the light. Maybeth stood by the door, pale. "Come on. Sit down," Dicey urged her. "I didn't know you were afraid of thunderstorms. Don't worry. Lightning goes for the highest thing, so it'll hit a tree or one of the chimneys. Not us." She reached out and pulled at Maybeth's right hand.

The little girl winced and turned paler. She pulled back and rubbed at her arm, up by the elbow. The arm hung down by her side, as if it were a broken wing.

"Maybeth?" Dicey asked. "What's wrong with your arm?"

"It hurts. It hurts when I close my hand into a fist or try to hold something. Sometimes it just hurts when I don't do anything. It woke me up. I don't know what's wrong, Dicey."

"Maybe it'll go away by itself," Dicey said. She poured Maybeth a glass of milk and got one for herself. They sat and drank quietly. Maybeth held the glass awkwardly in her left hand.

The sky outside exploded with rain. It pounded on the tin roof of the porch. After a while the two girls went quietly upstairs again.

There was a bar of light under their grandmother's bedroom door. Dicey wondered if she was afraid of storms. Momma wasn't.

The morning of the fourth day dawned low and dark. The thunderstorm had passed, but the rain poured steadily down. It drummed on the roof, it splattered on the ground, it rattled softly among the trees. Dicey stood by the window, looking west. A low gray mist covered the marshes and you couldn't see the bay.

They couldn't work outside in the rain. But surely their grandmother wouldn't ask them to leave on a day like this. But then why shouldn't she? What did she care? Dicey stood, watching rain fall in sheets. The barn. They could clean out the barn.

She woke her brothers and sister. They dressed quietly. Quietly, they went to the bathroom and washed the sleep from their eyes and brushed their teeth. Quietly, they went down the stairs and into the kitchen.

Their grandmother, already dressed in shirt and skirt, stood by the sink. She was running water into a canning pot. Glass jars stood on the draining board. A bushel basket of tomatoes was on the kitchen table. The woman's hair was damp and curled wildly. Her feet were caked with mud.

Caught, the children could only wait.

"You could help me," the woman said. Her eyes were bright, but her face sagged with fatigue. "I need the ripe tomatoes picked, and the squashes and cukes that are along the ground. Drainage is so bad they'll rot if we don't get them in."

The children took off their sneakers and shirts and left them by the porch door. Dicey and James carried a towering pile of bushel baskets. They stepped out into the rain.

The drops of water hammered down on them, like a shower on at full force. They bent their heads and ran for the field. The long grass was wet and cold against their legs. They were soaked before they reached the field. Dicey told James and Maybeth to tackle the tomatoes. She showed Sammy where the cucumbers were and went back to the squashes herself.

Mud oozed up through her toes as her feet sank into the earth. She worked as fast as she could, around the mounds where zucchini and yellow squashes spread out. The squashes were hidden under leaves larger than her hand. Dicey knelt down into the chilly mud and picked them out. She tossed them into the basket beside her. The rain beat down on her bare back. Her wet shorts chafed against her waist and thighs. They might as well have taken off all their clothes, she thought.

In spite of her discomfort, she worked fast. Once she looked over to see how James and Maybeth were doing. When she checked on Sammy she saw that he had taken off his shorts and underpants and was standing stark naked over the cucumber plants. Sometimes, she thought, he has more sense than any of us.

Dicey carried the two baskets she and Sammy filled back to the porch, without going inside. She ran to help finish the tomatoes. Sammy's fanny gleamed white on his tan body as he stooped over to pick beside Maybeth. Maybeth was using only her left hand. She held her right arm stiff by her side.

James and Dicey carried the full baskets back. Maybeth ran ahead inside. Sammy didn't want to go in. He ran about in the long grass of the lawn. He turned cartwheels and the rain droned down around him.

When Dicey came up with the last basket, she saw him rolling about in the long grass, like a dog. His face was bright, entirely happy. She looked past him and saw their grandmother standing to hold the porch door open for James, who struggled up the steps with a basket of tomatoes in his arms. The woman was watching Sammy with a smile in her eyes. Their grandmother seemed to have a smile as sudden and complete as laughter.

Dicey called Sammy in. Maybeth had dressed and sat quietly at the table nursing her arm. Dicey ran the boys upstairs to dry off and change clothes.

The table was set for breakfast when they came down. The huge pot steamed and rattled as the glass jars boiled, to be sterile for the day's canning. Their grandmother served them bowls of hot oatmeal with brown sugar and milk to put on it.

Dicey sat beside Maybeth. "It still hurts?" she asked. Maybeth just nodded. She held the spoon in her left hand and ate sloppily. Dicey realized that she shouldn't have let Maybeth come out picking with them. She didn't know what could be wrong. What was it like when your arm was broken? How could Maybeth have broken her arm?

Maybeth reached across the cereal bowl for the pitcher of milk. She tried to pour it over her cereal, but it splashed onto the table.

Their grandmother stormed up from the table and threw a dishcloth across at Maybeth. "Can't you even feed yourself? Mop it up."

Maybeth mopped at the milk and knocked at her bowl. Dicey caught it before it spilled.

"What's the matter with her?" their grandmother demanded. Maybeth's face was white, and she stared at her cereal. Dicey mopped up the spilled milk. She touched Maybeth softly on the left shoulder, to let her know she wasn't angry.

"Answer me," their grandmother said. "Or is this the way she usually is, and it's all been an act until now."

"Something's wrong with her arm," Dicey said.

"What something?" The woman sat down and began eating again.

"I dunno," Dicey said. "It hurts."

Their grandmother turned her attention to Maybeth. "How long has it hurt?"

"Since yesterday morning," Maybeth said.

"Why didn't you say?" Dicey asked, exasperated.

Maybeth shrugged. Dicey subsided, because she knew why Maybeth hadn't said anything.

"What does it feel like?" their grandmother asked.

"It hurts. It feels burny and achy. When I close my hand and try to hold something, it's like a fire going up around my elbow." Maybeth swallowed. "It's getting worse, not better."

Their grandmother stormed up from the table and out of the room. The Tillermans looked at one another, surprised. "Maybe she doesn't like people being sick," Dicey said.

But the woman returned with a jar of ointment and a broad roll of gauze bandaging. She rubbed the ointment into Maybeth's elbow and down her forearm. Then she made a tight bracelet around Maybeth's wrist, ripping off the gauze with her teeth and tying it into a knot. She made another such bandage above the little girl's elbow.

"Probably a tendon," she announced. "Does that help?" Maybeth nodded. "It sounds like you've pulled down a tendon in your arm. Pulling down that honeysuckle—it doesn't surprise me. You'll have to take it easy with that arm for weeks. The bandages will ease the strain on the muscle."

"Thank you," Maybeth said.

"You should have spoken up sooner," her grandmother answered. "No need to bear pain unless you have to."

Maybeth nodded. "I was afraid it wouldn't ever feel better," she said.

"Tendons can be pretty bad," their grandmother answered. "What are your plans for the day?" she asked Dicey. There was a challenge in her words.

"Clean out the barn," Dicey said.

"Not without sunlight. It's dark as the tomb in there," the woman answered. She waited, her eyes snapping.

"We'll wash windows," Dicey said.

"In the rain?"

"It's not raining inside."

Her grandmother nodded. "I could use some help in the kitchen."

Dicey washed off the tomatoes. James cut them up and Maybeth ladled them awkwardly into jars with her left hand. Sammy got down some old towels and ripped them into cloths. Their grandmother put the tops on the jars and set them into the canning pot.

"You know those old houses in town," James said. "Who owned them?"

"Rich people. There was a time when Crisfield was a boom town," their grandmother said. "People made fortunes in oysters and crabs and built big houses."

"What happened?" James said.

"The usual," his grandmother said. "There was a lot of money and a lot of crime—gambling and drinking and people killing one another one way or another. So the town tried to clean itself up. They passed a law against whiskey and that had the usual result."

"Bootlegging? Moonshining?" James asked. She nodded.

"And the oysters had a few bad seasons. So there were no more big fortunes to be made here, legally or illegally. So people left. The trains stopped running. When I was a girl, this was quite a town. Not like it is now."

"Did you know any bootleggers?" James asked. "On the water, with boats, there must have been a lot of it around here."

"I suppose I did," their grandmother said. "But, they'd been doing it for so long—"

"Prohibition didn't last that long," James said.

"Around here it did. It started in 1875—and that was before my time, long before, in case you think of asking. There were families that had been bootlegging for two or three generations."

"Why did it start so early?" James asked. His eyes began to gleam and Dicey knew that he would pick information from the woman's brain as long as she would answer his questions. Dicey filled a bucket with water and ammonia and took Sammy upstairs with her to wash windows. They soaped the glass down with sponges and dried it with the pieces of towels. By midmorning, Sammy's restlessness had grown too large for the house to contain him. Dicey had worked slowly, dragging out the chore, but Sammy didn't see any sense in this.

At two o'clock, by the clock that ticked on the mantel in the living room, he was ready to quit. Dicey told him he couldn't, he had to be useful.

Sammy thought for a minute, then ran down the hallway to the kitchen. Dicey had polished dry all the windows before she wondered where he was.

He'd been gone an hour. He wasn't in the kitchen. He wasn't upstairs. Dicey ran out to the barn, but he wasn't in the gloom there, either.

She came inside again. Only her grandmother was in the kitchen, sitting with a cup of tea at the table, while two canning pots rattled on the stove. A huge bowl of cut squashes stood ready to be canned next. "Did you see Sammy?" Dicey asked.

"He ran through a while back, more than an hour. The other two are in the living room." Dicey heard the faint notes of the piano.

"I'm going down to the dock to look for him," Dicey said. "He's been gone too long."

"Didn't he say where he was going?" her grandmother asked. Dicey shook her head. "That boy needs some controlling, doesn't he? Your cousin said that."

"She didn't approve of us," Dicey said. "She—she wanted Sammy to be like James, only James isn't like what she thought, either. She just liked him because people praised her about him. And Maybeth—she wanted her to be a doll, a dressed-up doll to take places. Sammy wasn't easy enough for her, that's why she said that."

"What about you?" her grandmother asked.

"I dunno," Dicey said. "I never thought about it. I was busy."

"Busy sneaking out to earn money and never saying a thing about it to her."

Dicey bit back her anger. "She thinks we're not grateful enough, doesn't she?"

"Something like that. She says it's her duty, though, to take care of you. I've never seen such a foolish letter. She wrote me another one when her mother died."

"You didn't answer it."

"I couldn't answer such silliness. I'll have to write her now."

Dicey stared at her grandmother. She wasn't going to ask any questions. Her grandmother looked tired. "You were awake during the storm," Dicey said.

"So were you and Maybeth. Were you scared?"

Dicey shook her head. "Maybeth's arm hurt and it woke her up. Were you scared?"

"There's nothing to be frightened of in a thunderstorm. I was thinking. With four children in the house, the only time you can feel alone is at night."

Sammy burst into the kitchen. His hair was plastered down over his forehead. His shirt and shorts were sodden. He dripped onto the floor.

"Where have you been!" Dicey demanded. Before he could answer, she ran to get towels.

When she returned, her grandmother was in the middle of a lecture. "—running off without telling anyone where you're going. Your sister was worried."

"You weren't were you?" Sammy said. His grandmother shook her head. "Then why are you yelling at me about it?"

His grandmother stared at him. Sammy's jaw stuck out and he stared right back at her.

Dicey handed him a towel. "Don't be rude, Sammy," she said.

"But it's the truth," he protested. She dried his hair for him, and his voice came out muffled from beneath the terrycloth. "I'm sorry, Dicey—I thought I'd break something if I stayed inside. I was down at the dock. I bailed out the boat, so the motor won't get covered with water. Then I checked the crab pots. The water doesn't have any waves."

"Because there's no wind," Dicey said. "Next time, tell me where you're going, OK?"

"OK," Sammy answered.

Dicey knew Sammy. He wouldn't do things for politeness or because he was told. He would obey if he loved you and knew you loved him. You could trust Sammy.

"Go get into dry clothes. And hang up the towels," she said.

Her grandmother was looking at her. "Doesn't he get punished?" she asked.

Dicey wanted to go along with her, so that she would like the Tillermans and let them stay on her farm. She wanted to agree so badly that she had trouble saying the words to argue. But she had given Sammy her word, and Maybeth. She had said she'd stand up for them. And she had learned that she had to do what she thought was right for her family, not what someone else thought.

"No," Dicey said. She made her voice as pleasant and unquarrelsome as she could. "Why should he? It was a mistake."

"You'll ruin him. He's willful and needs to learn."

"No," Dicey said again. "He doesn't need to learn to give in and give up. That's what you mean, isn't it? The way Sammy is—he's not perfect, but he's all right. Stubbornness isn't bad."

"He fights," she said.

"So do I," Dicey answered. "And I'm glad he knows how to."

That was the end of the conversation, but not of the battle, for this was a battle, not a skirmish. Dicey knew it. She wondered if she won that battle, would she lose the whole war?

CHAPTER 10

THE next day, the fifth day, it rained again. Their grandmother continued with her canning. Dicey thought that the children should be out of the house (although James protested that he wanted to read and he wouldn't get into any trouble), so she made them all go into the barn. It was dark and gloomy in there, but after a while their eyes grew accustomed, and they could knock down the big spider webs and polish the tools with the tack rags and put the pieces of lumber into neat piles.

The rain splattered on the tin roof of the barn, like a drummer who was just learning how to play, uneven and off-beat. Dicey examined the places in the barn wall where the wood had been torn away, or fallen awry. She and James worked on figuring out how to make patches. There was a tall extension ladder in the barn, so they could reach all the damaged places.

Late in the morning they heard the sudden, sharp call of a car horn.

At first, Dicey couldn't think of what it was, but when it sounded again she realized that there must be a car outside. You couldn't hear anything from the road this far back.

Dicey and her family went to the door of the barn. They couldn't see anything, so they went around the house to the front yard.

Claire's white station wagon, with two people in it, was stopped under the paper mulberry tree.

"We figured you were still here since we didn't hear from you," Will said, climbing out. "This sure is the boonies."

Claire had come with him. She wore her same high-heeled sandals and blue jeans, and a yellow rain jacket. She had tied a clear plastic scarf around her hair. "How is everything?" she asked. "Are you doing OK?"

Dicey nodded. "OK," she said to Will, "but not terrific."

"Are you going to introduce us?" Will asked.

"I guess so," Dicey said. How could she introduce them when she never called her grandmother anything but *Umm-ah?*

"Something wrong?" he asked.

"Nothing's decided," Dicey said. "For us, I mean. She says we can't stay. But she hasn't made us go."

"Invite us in, OK, Dicey?" Will said. He and Claire looked at each other.

"Your feet'll get wet," Dicey said to Claire.

"Worse things have happened to me," Claire answered.

"Do the dogs miss me?" Sammy asked her.

"Of course," Claire said.

They waited on the broad back porch while Dicey called her grandmother from the stove. "I heard company," the woman said.

"Come and meet them," Dicey answered. "This is Mrs. Tillerman," she said. "Will and Claire, friends of ours."

Her grandmother shook hands with Claire, then Will, and asked them to sit down on the porch because the kitchen was so hot. She asked them if they wanted some lemonade and they asked what was wrong with Maybeth's arm. Dicey brought out a pitcher of lemonade made from a can, and seven glasses. The children sat silent while the adults talked about who Will and Claire were. Will called their grandmother, "Mrs. Tillerman, Ma'am," until she finally snapped at him to call her Ab.

"We had the devil of a time finding you," he said. "You don't have a phone."

"I know that," she said. "I took it out years ago."

"Why would you do that?" Claire asked.

"You have any children?" their grandmother asked Claire. Claire shook her head. "You wouldn't understand then. I used to. My boy, Bullet, he was in the army . . ." Her dark hazel eyes clouded while she talked, and her face stiffened. "They called me up on the telephone to tell me he got killed. I had to do something. What I did was, I went downtown and took the thing and threw it through the phone company's window. They were surprised, I can tell you that. It didn't help, of course—but it was better than doing nothing."

Will threw back his head and laughed. Their grandmother smiled her sudden, surprised smile.

"Did you hit anyone?" Sammy asked.

"All their desks were at the back," their grandmother said, "and there was a display shelf right by the window. I didn't aim to hurt anyone."

"What kind of a name is Bullet?" Sammy asked. "A nickname? What was his real name?"

"Sam. Samuel."

"Like me? Dicey, he had my name."

Dicey wondered if Momma had named Sammy after her brother because he was dead. How would Momma have known that? Maybe she had liked her brother Bullet.

"Claire," Will said. "The rain's let up a little. Why don't you take the kids out and show them what we have in the car?"

In the back of the station wagon were three bicycles, piled one on top of the other. A fourth was folded in behind the front seat.

James and Dicey had full-sized bikes, with three gears. Sammy and Maybeth had smaller models, but theirs too had gears and thin wheels.

"Oh," the children said.

And, "Oh," again.

Claire grinned at them. "They're not new. We're near Ocean City, right? And it's the end of the season there so the places that rent bicycles to tourists are selling off their old ones. Well, we all thought of you when we saw that. So everybody chipped in."

Sammy hopped onto his and wobbled for a few feet before he toppled off. "Did you see me ride?" he yelled.

Dicey and James had ridden on other kids' bikes in Provincetown, so they knew how. Claire took Maybeth aside to begin teaching her. Sammy needed no help, or so he thought. Dicey watched him for a minute and decided that he would manage on his own and that would be better than trying to get him to sit still and learn properly. She and James raced down the muddy driveway and back again. As they rode back, the rain intensified.

"We'd better get these in the barn," Dicey called over to him.

"If we'd had bikes I bet we could have gone twenty miles a day," James answered.

They took the bikes into the barn and dried them off with the tack cloth there. "If the rain lets up later, can I ride again?" Sammy asked. "I'm beginning to know how."

"Maybe," Dicey said. Claire had gone back to the porch. "We didn't say thank you," Dicey realized.

They quieted down when they came to the back porch. Maybeth went up to Will. "Thank you," she said. "It's more wonderful than anything. Will you tell everyone thank you?"

"I certainly will," Will answered.

"For me too," James said, and Dicey and Sammy added their thanks.

Will and Claire stood up then, while the rain poured down beyond the wire screens, over the trees and garden and marsh.

"Do you have to go?" Dicey asked. She felt that when they did go she and her family would be farther away from the circus than before, than just that morning. "Can't you stay for lunch? Can they?" she asked her grandmother.

Her grandmother looked hesitant.

"Perhaps you would allow us to take all of you to a restaurant for lunch," Will said. He spoke to their grandmother.

That seemed to decide her. "And pay good money for what we can make better ourselves? Nonsense. If James and Sammy will empty the crab pots and

Dicey will get us some tomatoes, I think I can feed us pretty well here. If you don't mind eating out on the porch. If it's not too cold for you."

So they had lunch together on the back porch, while the rain faded away outside. They ate and talked. Will told their grandmother about how he first met the children, and how they turned up again with Mr. Rudyard on their heels. Then James had to tell about Mr. Rudyard again, because he told it best. Their grandmother picked crab meat and chewed and listened. She studied James' face as he spoke. She looked from one to the other of them, especially at Maybeth. At the end she raised her eyebrows a little and said to Dicey, "You ran a risk to hire yourselves out."

"I had to," Dicey said.

"I can see that."

Then lunch was over and it really was time for Will and Claire to leave. The rain had stopped by then and the thick masses of gray clouds were beginning to break apart. A golden bar of sunlight would occasionally slip past the guard the clouds had put up. But the mood as the children stood around Claire's car, saying good-bye, was still rainy.

"Well," Dicey said.

"Well," Will said. Then, like a bolt of sunlight he changed the subject from good-bye. "It's turning into biking weather, wouldn't you say, Claire?"

Dicey grinned at him then. "Don't lose touch with us," she said. He reached into his shirt pocket and pulled out a calling card, printed with the name of the circus and an address in New York City.

"My booking agent," Will said. "He always knows where we are."

Dicey reached up and kissed him on the cheek. His short beard scratched at her cheek as his arms hugged her, round and strong, for the briefest of times.

"You'll be OK," he assured her. "I don't know what that old lady will do—I don't think even she knows—but you kids, remember you can always call on us."

Dicey nodded, and tried to smile. What was the matter with her today? Wasn't she used to saying good-bye?

The white car drove off, splashing through puddles, its wheels throwing muddy water aside.

Sammy asked if he could ride his bike and Dicey gave him permission. Maybeth went into the house to help her grandmother clear up. James and Dicey worked out plans for mending the biggest holes in the side of the barn.

"Whadda you think, Dicey," James finally asked. "Are we going to stay?"

"I think so," Dicey answered. "I think we've shown her we can be useful. And not too much trouble. I think she likes Sammy—maybe because he's named after her son—"

"Our uncle. Did you think of that?"

"And I'm pretty sure we'll be OK here. All of us."

"What about schools?"

"We can ride our bikes downtown and find out. Tomorrow. You want to?"

"Tomorrow's Sunday."

"Then the next day."

"That's Labor Day."

"Then Tuesday or next week. Why are you quarrelling, James? Don't you want to stay?"

"I guess so. I like it, and all those books. Do you think our grandfather was smart? Do you think he went to college or just read? What do you think he was like?"

"I don't know anything about him except what she said. Would it be OK with you if we stayed?"

"Sure. It's a good place. But Dicey, why did all of her children leave her? She's not so bad."

"Do you think there's something we don't know? Do you think it's dangerous for us?" Dicey asked him.

"Do you like her?" James asked.

Dicey considered this. "You know? I could. I mean, she's so odd and prickly. She fights us, or anyway I feel like I'm fighting her and she's fighting back, as if we both know what's going on but neither of us is saying anything. It's fun."

"You're crazy," James said.

"Maybe. But she's a good enemy—you know? In that way. Cousin Eunice wasn't." Dicey thought some more. "So she might make a good friend," Dicey said finally.

"You are crazy," James said. He looked at her. "But you might be right. You're smart too, Dicey, do you ever think about that?" Dicey hadn't. It didn't seem very important to her, not the way it was to James.

Sammy had ridden out of sight, beyond the long driveway. He wasn't back in an hour and he wasn't back in two hours. The rain clouds blew away, leaving room for a bright red sunset, where fiery lights burned behind the clouds that gathered around the lowering sun.

They had cold ham for supper, and Sammy hadn't returned when they sat down. Dicey was worried. She didn't dare say anything though. They sat down in a troubled silence.

When she heard Sammy's feet on the steps of the porch, Dicey's appetite revived. He burst in the door to the kitchen, his cheeks red, his eyes sparkling.

"Wash your hands," Dicey said. She could see him and he was fine, he was safe and back again. Relief dissolved into anger then. She looked at her grandmother.

"When you've done that, go to your room," their grandmother said.

Sammy turned. "But I'm hungry."

"That'll help you remember. Did you tell your sister where you were going?" Sammy's jaw went out. He wasn't going to answer, not to tell a lie.

"Did he tell you?" Dicey shook her head. "Did he have your permission?"

"Sort of," Dicey said.

"Sort of?" their grandmother said in a sharp, sarcastic voice. "Sort of? How do you sort of give permission to disappear for hours at a time? What do you say? 'OK, Sammy, go sort of run wild and sort of let people worry?' Are you stupid, girl?"

Dicey chewed her lip. Why did every adult send kids away from the table? Maybe because nobody sent *them* to bed hungry. Maybe they'd forgotten what hungry was. But it wasn't right. Dicey knew what hungry was, and so did Sammy.

"It's not Dicey's fault," Sammy said. "It's my fault. Don't yell at Dicey."

"I will yell at whom I please," his grandmother answered him. "I have told you to go to your room."

"No," Dicey said quietly.

"Dicey!" James whispered.

"It's not right, James," Dicey said. "It's not right to send him to bed hungry. I can't let that happen, and I was wrong when I let Cousin Eunice do it. Sit down and eat, Sammy," Dicey said.

Then she turned to try to explain to her grandmother. Her grandmother's eyes flashed. Her face was still and pale. Her lips were hard together.

"You," Dicey said. She wanted to call her by name, but she had no name to call her. "You don't understand, not what it is to be hungry. It doesn't serve any purpose to punish Sammy that way."

Her grandmother's fury burned behind her immobile face. Her hand clenched the handle of the fork.

Dicey was frightened, with a fear that swelled up deep within her. This fear had two heads, and Dicey was caught between them: she was afraid to speak and lose what they had gained of a place for themselves in this house; she was afraid to keep silent and lose what she felt was right for Sammy, for her family. This was more difficult danger than any she had faced before. It wasn't the kind of danger you could run away from, or fight back at. Dicey wasn't even sure she wanted to fight. She just knew she had to stand by her brother and her family.

"Whose house is this?" their grandmother said. "Whose food? Whose table?"

"You're right," Dicey said. "It's not our house, that's what you said from the beginning. But we're not your family, you meant that too, didn't you."

Her grandmother stared at her.

"Sit down and eat," Dicey said to Sammy. James and Maybeth were staring at her. Everybody was staring at her. "But you're not to ride the bike again for two days."

"Aw, Dicey," Sammy said. He slipped into his chair and cut his meat.

"I mean it. No matter what. Will you obey?"

Sammy nodded.

"You have to say when you're going off," Dicey said. She ignored her grandmother, who was sitting at the head of the table in a silence of furious anger.

Sammy nodded again. "I know. I will. I'm sorry, Dicey," he said, with a weak smile. Then he turned to his grandmother. "I'm sorry to you, too. I didn't mean to make trouble. But it's my fault, not Dicey's."

"You're a child," his grandmother answered.

"So is Dicey," Sammy said.

"I will not have this talking back!" their grandmother snapped.

"But it's not talking back," James said. His voice was high and frightened. "It's explaining. We're trying to get at the truth." His grandmother stared at him before she answered, as if he had said something she didn't understand.

"You are in my home," their grandmother said. She looked around the table at the four pairs of hazel eyes, none as dark as hers. And none, except Dicey's, as angry as hers. "My home, not yours," their grandmother said.

We might as well have it out now as any other time, Dicey said to herself. She felt as if she had been running away from this for days, and she had only the last of her strength left. She had to turn and fight now. She took a deep, shivering breath.

"Are you expecting us to stay then?" she demanded. Her voice sounded thin and hard.

Her grandmother's mouth worked, and she looked surprised, as if she hadn't understood what it was they were fighting about this time. Her mouth formed words, but no sounds came out. Finally she spoke:

"No."

The word ballooned out and filled all the air of the kitchen. Dicey didn't even try to argue. She just nodded her head and ate her supper in silence and helped with the dishes, and when the little children went up to bed she went with them. The *No* filled the whole air of the house. Every time she breathed in she breathed in that *No*. Dicey wasn't even frightened any more. She was simply defeated. She fell asleep suddenly and without any thought.

CHAPTER 11

DICEY awoke to a thick, black silence. She slipped out of bed and went to the window. Night smothered the land. A dark wind blew clouds over the face of the moon and over the little stars. This kind of wind blew in clear weather. So tomorrow would be a good day to begin traveling again.

They had only seven dollars left, but they had bicycles now, and Dicey had her jackknife and her map. What they didn't have was any place to go.

Back to Bridgeport, Dicey supposed, the long way back.

Will couldn't help them. They couldn't live with the circus. James had to go to school. And so did Maybeth, but for different reasons.

Could they hide out? Could they find the circus again and travel south and then pitch a permanent camp somewhere? Dicey thought they could manage that. She could lie to any school officials. She'd be eighteen in five years. She could say they lived back in the hills with their momma and their momma couldn't come in because she was working the farm. Nobody'd care enough to question, not as long as they showed up in school. There was a big boy Dicey knew in Provincetown who ran away from home and he just kept on coming to school and nobody knew, not for months.

The plan was possible, Dicey thought. Only she couldn't get excited about it. Having someplace in mind that you were traveling to was different from not having any place.

But it was a plan. She'd ask James what he thought. He might think they should go back to Bridgeport, and he might be right. One way or the other, north or south, they'd be moving on.

"OK," Dicey said to herself, "OK, that's what we'll do." She thought she'd go back to bed and sleep some more, if she could get to sleep again. She took a last look—seeing in her mind's eye the things she couldn't really see, the pines and the fields, the marshes and the bay beyond, the barn that held the sailboat like a buried treasure in its dark belly. Dicey belonged here. She belonged here; yet she was being blown away. Well, it wasn't her house, that was true. It was their grandmother's house and they were not welcome. They would stay together, at least that. She could go along with Cousin Eunice on everything except about that; she wouldn't agree to sending Sammy or Maybeth away. She'd say that right away.

Dicey noticed a yellow light flowing onto the lawn below the porch. Had somebody left the kitchen light on? She went downstairs to turn it off.

Her grandmother sat at the kitchen table wearing an old striped cotton bathrobe. She had a cup of tea before her and a pad of paper on which she was writing. Her hair was all in tousled curls. She looked up at Dicey when Dicey came in.

"I couldn't sleep so I'm writing that silly woman, Eunice," she said.

Dicey stared. Her grandmother was pretty. Her face had delicate straight bones, and those wide dark eyes.

"What're you staring at, girl?"

"You. You're pretty. I never noticed," Dicey said. "Never mind. I saw the light from my window. I didn't know anyone was here. I'm sorry."

"Sit down," her grandmother said. "Get a glass of milk first. I wondered who'd taken that room when I heard you up there. Get your milk and sit—I've got something I should say to you."

Dicey poured herself a glass of milk and sat down. She had never really looked at her grandmother before, just at the enemy she had to trick, just at her bare feet.

"It's OK," Dicey said. "I'm not going to argue about staying."

"Wouldn't do you any good," her grandmother said. She put the cap on the pen and twisted it shut. "But I should apologize for yelling at you."

Her grandmother's mouth twisted in her sudden smile. "That Will seems a good man. Could you go to him? Would you rather do that than go back to this woman?"

"I was thinking about that," Dicey said. "I was going to ask James what he thought. He's the one, really, he should go to school. Well, Maybeth should too."

"Maybeth's not retarded," her grandmother said.

"I know that. She is slow though. Not as slow as she seems in school, but . . ." Why go over this again? "There was a lady, a nun, in Bridgeport. She might help Maybeth."

Her grandmother sipped at her cup of tea and Dicey drank at her milk.

"I want to explain," Dicey's grandmother said. "I've never explained before, to anyone, but I have to now. Because, in a way, I do want to keep you here. But I can't."

Dicey nodded. She could feel how true that was. Her grandmother went on speaking.

"I'm old. Not very old yet, but getting older. You can't tell what will happen. What if I fell sick, for instance. And I've very little money. When my husband died he left some insurance. Enough to live on if I live carefully. I don't mind that. But it's expensive with children." She smiled again. "I'm already going to have to die a month sooner than I planned, with the food this week."

"That's crazy," Dicey said.

"It's a joke, girl," her grandmother said. "I mean to explain that I don't have the money. Will said Social Security would give me money for you. But I never took charity."

"Momma wouldn't, either. That's why she was taking us to Aunt Cilla's house," Dicey said. "I understand about that," she said.

"There's more too," her grandmother said. "I don't know whether you can understand this now, but if not now there's always later. I was married for thirty-eight years and my husband just died these four years ago. Until then, until he died—when you marry someone you make promises. I kept those promises, love and honor and obey. Even when I didn't want to I kept them. I kept quiet when I had things to say. I always went his way."

"That's hard to believe," Dicey said.

"It is, isn't it. Since he died, I've been different. It took a while, but—it's my own life I'm living now. I had a hard time getting it. I don't want to give it up. No lies, no pretending, no standing back quiet when I want to fight."

Dicey thought of Cousin Eunice. She couldn't picture her grandmother like Cousin Eunice. It would be awful if her grandmother was like that.

"It's OK," said Dicey. "I understand."

"That's more than your momma could," her grandmother said. "She felt sorry for me—do you know that?"

"No. She never talked about you. Except to Sammy and he couldn't remember."

"Your momma stuck around here a long time just because she felt sorry for me. I was glad when she began seeing Francis. He was handsome and cheerful. I thought, maybe she'll be happy, maybe she'll steady him down. But do you know what I said to her, just before she left this house? She was twenty-one then and her father couldn't stop her. I said—'We don't want to hear anything from you until we hear that you've been married.' He was right beside me then and I knew it was what he would say. So I was the one to say it, because I didn't want her thinking I wouldn't stand by him. I had to stand by him—he was my husband. Do you know what she said? She said, 'I'll never get married.' She wasn't angry. She never fought, not your mother. She was gentle—like Maybeth. Your father wasn't a fighter, either. I don't know where you get it from because you are."

Dicey knew where she got it from, but she had a more urgent question. "Why didn't Momma want to get married?"

"She had seen what happens. She didn't want to give her word, like I did. We keep our promises, we Tillermans. We keep them hard."

"But I don't understand. Can't you love somebody and fight with them? I fight with Sammy, and with James. I make Maybeth do things she's scared to do. But that's because I love them. If I didn't love them I wouldn't bother. And they fight back—like James walking out here instead of waiting, that's fighting back. It was OK too, because it was his own decision. I want him to make his own decisions. Didn't you love Momma?"

"Oh yes, I loved my children. I had a lot of love to give in those days, to my husband too. But it got turned around. I got turned around. I let myself get turned around." Her grandmother waved her hand, vaguely, to brush away the memories like you brush away cobwebs. "And it's all gone now and they're all gone now. So it's the past."

Dicey finished her milk. "Will you tell them about Momma not marrying? I lied to them about it. It was better then, to lie. Now it isn't; at least, I don't think so. I'll tell them if you won't, but if you would they'd understand better."

"Maybe. Maybe I'll try."

"I saw a picture of you when you were little," Dicey said. "Cousin Eunice had one. You looked angry."

"I was angry—most of my life," her grandmother said. "Not any more—if you can believe that. Just crazy now, and that's an improvement. Not really crazy. Eccentric. But those years, morning to night. All that anger—you can choke swallowing back anger. And it still sneaks out, in little ways, and everybody knows although nobody says anything. So they left, every one. They couldn't stay here. All of my children, they ran as fast and as far as they could. My Sammy, he died of it, and that was hard. Hard. And your poor momma— They shamed me. And I shamed myself." She chewed on her lip. Then she looked Dicey full in the eyes and said:

"I failed them. I let them go. I told them to go. There were times I could have killed him. He'd sit chewing and the anger and shame were sitting at the table with us. Chew and swallow, so sure he was right. But I'd promised him— and he didn't know why they each left. I did. So, I'm responsible. I won't have that responsibility again. Not to fail again."

"Are you sure you'd fail?" Dicey asked in a low voice. "We can't stay here, I know. Don't worry about that. But I don't think you'd fail with us. We had Momma. And I wouldn't let those things happen." That was true, Dicey knew it. They were safe, safer than her grandmother, even though her grandmother had this big house and what remained of the farm to keep her fed.

Her grandmother nodded. "You've got determination," she said.

"Momma said it was in my blood," Dicey answered. "I never knew what she meant before."

"Your Momma was a kind child," her grandmother said. "But she never forgave her father."

"Did you?" Dicey asked.

"No. Yes."

Somehow, this made sense to Dicey. It let her know that she would be all right, and her family would be all right. They wouldn't be children forever. They didn't have to have a place, they just had to have themselves. She yawned, fighting it off and losing.

"You'd better get back to bed. I'll finish this letter to that Eunice now. I'll try to tell her about Maybeth—but she's such a silly woman I doubt she's got two ounces of common sense rattling around in her head. Your cousin doesn't care much for you."

This didn't surprise Dicey. "That's OK," she said.

"Well I do," her grandmother said. "I care for all of you. Now get to bed. I'll wash out your glass. Scat!"

Dicey ran upstairs. She ran into her bed and pulled the covers up over her head. Cousin Eunice didn't want them, but she would take them in. Her grandmother wanted them, but wouldn't let them stay. And they—she, James, Maybeth and Sammy—they were the losers. Dicey cried herself to sleep. She couldn't stop. She tried, but she couldn't. She didn't know if she was crying for her family, or for herself, or for her grandmother—or for all of them, all the Tillermans, Momma too, lost up in Massachusetts, and Bullet lost in Vietnam. They were all lost. Dicey promised herself this was the last time she'd cry, ever, and wept until her eyes were swollen shut and she slept.

Sunlight was pouring over the house and yard and through the windows when Dicey awoke the next morning. She pulled on shorts and a shirt and looked into three empty bedrooms before she came downstairs.

Her grandmother was alone in the kitchen. She was kneading dough. "What's that?" Dicey asked.

"Bread. I haven't made it for years. You slept late."

Dicey nodded, without apologizing. She looked at her grandmother. She had gray splotches under her eyes, and the fine wrinkles that came out from the edges of her eyes and her mouth seemed deeper this morning. This was not quite the same woman Dicey had talked with in the dead of night; but this was not a different woman, either.

Dicey poured herself a glass of milk and took an apple from the bowl of fruit. She stood by the sink, drinking and chewing, and watching her grandmother knead the pale dough. Push-pull, slap, push-pull. Her grandmother leaned into the dough with her shoulders, but handled it gently at the same time.

Her grandmother was contradictory. Except for the fatigue, her grandmother looked perfectly ordinary this morning. Only now Dicey knew better.

There was a warm feeling in her stomach, as if she had swallowed sunshine. At least now, everything was settled, she wasn't battling any more. She liked her grandmother, her momma's mother. She liked her all prickly and contrary. She liked the way her grandmother said one thing and then the opposite, because it made sense to Dicey, the same kind of sense Dicey made to herself. She liked the way the woman had watched Sammy roll naked in the grass. She liked her bare feet.

This was a good way to feel to say good-bye.

"We'll be moving on today," Dicey said. "I wanted to thank you for letting us stay so long."

"Not today, you won't," her grandmother said. "You can't just bolt off like that. You've done enough running away, don't you think?"

Dicey couldn't see her face, but her voice sounded pleasant enough.

"I've written to your cousin. We have to wait and see what she answers. You'll stay here until then. I'll mail the letter Tuesday. We're going to town Tuesday, for food and to talk to the people at the school. What grade are you in?"

"Going into eighth," Dicey said. "But why?"

"Do you know how long it'll take that dithering woman to get advice from all the people she talks to and arrange to come and get you? You may, but I don't. Children should be in school. School starts Tuesday, or so James tells me and I have no reason to disbelieve him. Those bikes will give some trouble—I have no idea how to ship bicycles and I won't have them here, rusting in the barn."

"What if we don't want to go back to Bridgeport?" Dicey asked.

"First we find out if you can. For today, while the bread is rising, we might go take a look at Janes Island. It's all marsh and you can't land there. Don't know why they call it an island."

"Where are the little kids?" Dicey asked.

"Down by the dock, bailing out the boat. *They* have all agreed. *They* want to see the island." Her hands slapped at the bread. She poked at it with a finger, then began kneading it again. "I told them, what you wanted me to. Sammy"—she shook her head and slapped the dough down on the table—"he said I was lying and he said he didn't care. Then he said he was sorry he knew I wasn't lying, but he still didn't care. Maybeth didn't say a word. But James—he told Sammy he did care, and if it was what your momma wanted then that was OK with him because she might have been crazy in some ways but she was never crazy when it came to loving her kids. I asked him where he got ideas like that and he looked me straight in the eye and said, 'from books.'" She laughed briefly. "Yes, I told them, I also told them they ought to think twice before they held that lie against you."

Dicey ran down to the dock. The bay was lively, with crisp-topped blue waves under a steady breeze. Her family had bailed out the boat and now they were swimming.

"What's going on, James?" Dicey called. He swam over to her.

"I dunno, Dicey. We'll be here a little longer, that's all I know."

"We're going to an island!" Sammy called. "It's OK about Momma. She didn't want to get married. Did you know?" Dicey nodded.

They motored over to the stretch of marshland just off the town shore. There, they dropped an anchor on the bay side. Birds lived on Janes Island, but nothing else could. One snowy heron soared down, folding its wings in at the last minute, returning to its nest deep in the marsh grass. A few ducks wandered along the muddy shore, in and out of the tall grasses. They saw flocks of gulls, gossiping, bickering, bobbling on the waves, flying in noisy swarms.

Their grandmother had packed a bag of fruit and some cold crab, left over from yesterday's lunch. As they ate, she asked them about their travelings, so James and Dicey took turns telling her. "Well," she kept saying. And, "That was a piece of luck." She didn't ask them about Bridgeport.

Back at the farm, Dicey took Sammy to the barn to begin patching, while James and Maybeth rode their bikes up and down the driveway. "You don't have to do that," their grandmother said to Dicey.

"I know," she said.

The patched places showed up bleak against the wasted pink paint of the barn. They would hold, Dicey knew; they had been nailed into place firmly and the edges were sealed against the weather. If she'd had time, she would have liked to paint the whole barn. Just so there would be something here to say, "Dicey Tillerman stayed here awhile and she made a difference." Dicey figured they had a week, maybe two, before they had to go back to Bridgeport, to the little house and the fussing and fretting. She planned to enjoy the time and not worry about the future. Her grandmother seemed to feel the same way. It was as if now everything was decided, they could both relax.

So they passed two quiet days, hammering, bike riding (except Sammy), swimming, weeding, picking, fixing the mailbox—just living together. In the evenings, they went onto the back porch or into the living room. Their grandmother found an old checkers set, somewhere deep in a closet. Maybeth picked out tunes on the piano. Some of the songs they sang, the songs Momma had sung, their grandmother knew. Some of them she had to learn, and she wasn't very good at it.

Yet, the feelings in the air were not all placid. Dicey disagreed with her grandmother whenever she thought her grandmother was being unfair. "Ah-ummm," she would say, because they still had no name to call their grandmother, "Cousin Eunice tried to do her best. Sure she's silly, but that's not her fault is it?"

"Well, whose fault is it then?" their grandmother would answer sharply. "If it's not her own fault for what she's like, I'd like to know whose fault it is."

"OK," Dicey would say, giving ground because privately she thought her grandmother was right, "but she's not bad."

"Who mentioned bad?" their grandmother would say. "James? Did I? Maybeth, did I say bad? I said silly and I meant silly." Their grandmother would rush on before they could answer. "And there's an end on it."

"Dicey's the one who said silly," James would say.

"Aha!" their grandmother would say. "I told you Dicey, it's all your fault."

Then Dicey would swallow her disappointment and enjoy this temporary haven. For these two days, she stopped thinking ahead. She learned how to put the bandage on Maybeth's arm, which Maybeth said was better, but their grandmother said should be supported for two full weeks, especially since Maybeth was riding her bike so much.

They took one long ride, James and Dicey and Maybeth. They saw several farmhouses. Some of them had cows and horses. All of them had chickens. Most of them had fields of corn and tomatoes.

Dicey made herself stop thinking about the sailboat in her grandmother's barn. That was to have been the prize, her prize, if they had stayed. She wouldn't go near it now. She knew that if she did she'd begin planning again, and she'd get it down to the water, somehow. Once the boat was in the water, they could take it away and sail south, and hide. But they didn't have any place left to go to.

She had been beaten this time, down to her bones beaten. She had fought her hardest and her smartest, and she had lost. She could take that, and she could understand the whys of it. But not if the boat was in the water, and the sails fitted to the mast, and the wind blowing little clouds along the sky. So she shut the sailboat out of her mind, just as she shut out hoping and caring and the disappointment that waited for her to relax her guard so it could leap out and get its teeth into her. She just lived through the hours, taking them as they came, knowing they would never come again.

CHAPTER 12

O N TUESDAY MORNING, their grandmother started another batch of bread, then told them to take baths and put on fresh shorts and shirts. When the children came downstairs, their grandmother was waiting in the kitchen. She had combed her curly hair with water, but it wouldn't lie flat. She was wearing a dark blue suit, with her blouse tucked in, and lipstick, stockings and Loafers.

"You're all dressed up," Dicey said.

"It's old," her grandmother said. "But I'm old. Or do you mean the shoes? I hope you children appreciate what I'm going through for you." But she said that as if it was a joke.

"I don't care if you have bare feet," Sammy said, very serious.

"Neither do I," his grandmother said, "but there are them that do."

Maybeth stood shyly beside Dicey. "You look different," she said to the woman. "Pretty."

Their grandmother blushed. The dark red came up under her tanned cheeks. "I'll be getting vain the next thing you know. And that's a vice I never had. Let's go." She picked up a worn black purse from the table. "I'm bound to leave this behind somewhere. Keep an eye on it, somebody. James, you're reliable, will you?"

"I'll try," James said.

The wind blew their carefully combed hair all out of order, and the salt spray covered their bodies, so they arrived at the dock looking as they ordinarily did, except their grandmother. She led them down the main street, and down a side street, to a long, low building that had windows over most of its walls.

Inside, the air was noisy with children's voices. The halls were made of white-painted concrete blocks. A long, dim, windowless hallway went down the center of the building, with classrooms on both sides. It smelled like a school, of chalk and children's sweat, and warm food from the lunchroom. A teacher told their grandmother where the registration office was. The sign over the door said *Guidance*. In the tiny office, they found a fat young woman seated behind a big wooden desk.

"My name is Abigail Tillerman," their grandmother announced. "These children will be in Crisfield temporarily and they ought to be in school until they go back. What's your name?"

Their grandmother sounded nervous.

"Mrs. Jenkins," the woman said. "I'm the guidance counselor." She told them to come in and sit down. The room was so crowded with filing cabinets and plants and her big desk, there was room only for two straight chairs for visitors. Dicey and her grandmother sat in those. James and Maybeth and Sammy crowded into the corners of the room.

"What do you mean by temporarily?" Mrs. Jenkins asked.

"For a short time. I'm not sure how long exactly," their grandmother said. "If I could tell you I would."

Mrs. Jenkins asked their names and ages, and Dicey told her. She asked for their address, and Dicey looked at her grandmother, who told Mrs. Jenkins. Mrs. Jenkins asked what the last school they had been in was; her grandmother looked at Dicey, and Dicey told her.

"Parents?" Mrs. Jenkins asked.

"Not noticeably," their grandmother said. James gave a short snort of laughter.

"What then is your relationship to them, Mrs. Tillerman? I assume you will be responsible for them while they are attending school here."

"I am their mother's mother," their grandmother said.

Mrs. Jenkins looked at her for a long moment. Dicey watched her write down, *grandmother*.

"All right then. I will call the Provincetown school to have your records sent to us. I think it would be well to do that now, before we assign the children to classes. Would you like to walk around the school for a bit? Come back, in half an hour, I think."

They trooped out of the office. All the classroom doors were closed, so they went outside. The playground was a huge field of short grass. Scattered over it were jungle gyms and tall swings, sandboxes, slides and a baseball diamond. It was empty now, with the children inside. The equipment gleamed, as if it had never been played on.

"It looks brand new," Dicey said. "The whole school does."

"I should think it is," her grandmother said. Sammy and Maybeth ran off to the swings.

"Who pays for it?" Dicey asked.

"Me," her grandmother said.

Dicey stared at her.

"Taxes, girl."

"Do you pay taxes?"

"Indeed I do. Taxes on land, taxes on my house, death taxes, life taxes. I even pay taxes on the money I keep in the bank."

Dicey hadn't known that. "No wonder you're worried about money," she said.

"But with a farm, there must be ways to get money," James said. "Did you ever think of growing trees?"

His grandmother looked at him.

"No, Christmas trees, on those front fields. There are pine seedlings already there."

Dicey chimed in. "It shouldn't be hard to grow them and people always buy Christmas trees. Even we did, in Provincetown."

"Why should anyone buy what they can walk outside and cut down for free?"

"In many places," James said, as if he were talking to somebody a little stupid, "like Annapolis—there they can't just walk outside and cut down a tree."

"How would I get trees to Annapolis?"

"There must be ways." He dismissed that problem. "You could earn money that way. Or you could sell land—"

"No," their grandmother said.

"Or chickens—why don't you have chickens? A lot of other farms do."

"I don't care for the company of chickens."

"Maybe," James said. He leaned towards her, earnestly trying to explain his ideas. "But you can sell eggs. You could sell some of your vegetables, too, if you had a stand out front by the driveway. Or you could rent out your fields to some other farmer who wants more land. Or butter," his ideas dashed on. "People will pay for good butter, won't they? You'd need cows, but you've already got stalls in the barn. What about pigs?"

Their grandmother was looking at him, with a contradictory expression, half amusement and half interest.

"You've got to be careful with money and earn it whenever you can," Dicey said.

Her grandmother shook her head, as if Dicey didn't know what she was talking about. Maybe she didn't, Dicey thought. But maybe she did.

"I know what you're thinking, girl," her grandmother said.

"Then you know I might be right," Dicey answered.

Her grandmother humphed.

"She is," James said. "With inflation, and if you're on fixed income—you could lose the farm if you can't pay taxes."

"Could you?" Dicey asked. "Could that happen?"

"What's that to you?" her grandmother demanded.

"I guess nothing. But if we can't be there I want you to be. So it matters something. And you can't change that."

Her grandmother humphed again.

When they returned to Mrs. Jenkins' office, the counselor was waiting for them. She had papers on her desk, and a pad with notes all over it. She waited until they were all in, all five of them, before she said anything.

The first thing she said was, "You're in the wrong school, Dicey. You should be in the junior high. I've called and they'll expect you tomorrow morning. Mr. MacGuire will be your guidance counselor. Can you find the junior high?"

"She can," their grandmother said.

Dicey hadn't thought that she'd be in a different school.

"James will go into the accelerated section of fifth grade. We have some special programs for the gifted student. They should suit you, James. Your teacher will be Mr. Thomas."

James looked at Dicey and grinned. She knew what he was thinking: a man teacher. There weren't any men teachers in the elementary school in Provincetown, not one.

"Sammy will be in Miss Tieds' second grade."

"OK," said Sammy. "I don't care."

"James and Sammy," Mrs. Jenkins said, "I want you to meet your teachers today. If you go to the principal's office, they will come there when the recess bell rings. That will be in ten minutes. It's the third door on your right, as you go down the hall. You may go now."

The boys left together. James walked eagerly, but Sammy dragged his heels. James turned at the door. "Don't forget your purse," he said to their grandmother. She waved him away.

Mrs. Jenkins gathered her papers into a pile.

"What about Maybeth?" Dicey asked. She got herself ready to fight for Maybeth.

"I'm coming to that," Mrs. Jenkins said. Maybeth sidled over between the two chairs Dicey and their grandmother sat in. She didn't say anything.

"Your records—Maybeth, are you listening to me?" Mrs. Jenkins asked. She spoke without emphasis. Maybeth nodded. "Your records show that they wanted to hold you back in second grade. That would be the second time you have been kept back. Did you know that?" She turned to their grandmother. "Their recommendation is—most strong."

"But—" Dicey began.

Mrs. Jenkins cut her off, to say: "Our school, however, has a policy not to put brothers and sisters in the same grade. Do you want to be in Sammy's grade, Maybeth?"

Maybeth shook her head, no. She looked at Dicey.

"Why not?" Mrs. Jenkins asked.

Maybeth waited. No one else said anything. "Because I'm bigger than he is," she whispered.

"I thought so." Mrs. Jenkins smiled. When she smiled, with her short dark hair and bright cheeks, she looked like a kid herself, Dicey thought. She was as fresh as apples.

"I thought that would be the case. If you want to go into third grade—and mind you, I'm not promising anything—but if you want to try, you'll have to take some tests for me."

"What kind of tests?" their grandmother asked.

"A quick IQ then reading and math, achievement and aptitude. They're short and not precise, but they'll give a fairly good idea of where Maybeth can be put in school." Mrs. Jenkins waited for an answer.

"How long will it take?" their grandmother asked.

"An hour at the most. Will you do that, Maybeth?" Mrs. Jenkins kept talking to Maybeth. Maybeth looked at Dicey with wide eyes.

Their grandmother stood up. "We have errands to do, so if you'll tell James and Sammy to bring Maybeth and wait for us by the boat, I have no objections."

Maybeth's hand held onto Dicey's arm.

"But—can I stay?" Dicey asked Mrs. Jenkins. "It'll be better. You don't understand—"

"No," her grandmother said. "Maybeth will take the tests by herself."

"I would prefer that," Mrs. Jenkins said.

"Don't argue, girl," her grandmother said to Dicey, just as Dicey was opening her mouth to say she wasn't going to leave Maybeth there alone. Her grandmother spoke to Maybeth. "Maybeth? You've got two hard times coming. This, now, is the first. Tomorrow morning is the next. Nothing will make them easier. That's the way it is. Do you understand that?"

Maybeth nodded, but her hand stayed on Dicey's arm.

"Will you try?" their grandmother asked. "It'll take some courage, but I think you've got that. Do you have it?"

"I don't know," Maybeth said. "I'll try." She released Dicey's arm. "It'll be OK, Dicey."

Dicey wasn't sure.

"Come along," her grandmother ordered. "I'll see you tomorrow morning, Mrs. Jenkins. Mind you, she's ripped a tendon in her right arm so her writing won't be much."

"Yes, thank you," Mrs. Jenkins said. She stood up, and Dicey followed her grandmother out of the little office, leaving Maybeth behind.

When they stepped out of the building into the hot morning sunlight, her grandmother turned on Dicey. "You've got to let her make her own way."

"I know," Dicey said. "But—"

"But nothing. But hogwash. If she can't do that—"

"But she *is*," Dicey argued. "She's doing it right now."

Her grandmother nodded her head briskly. "Yes, so she is."

They strolled back to the main street and entered the grocery store Dicey had gone into days earlier. The storekeeper and butcher, Millie, looked like she wanted to say something when she saw them, she looked like she had several somethings to say, but she didn't dare. Dicey didn't know how her grandmother stopped the questions, but she did, by the glitter in her eye and the lift to her chin. Dicey took part of their list and went around the store finding cans of tuna, jars of peanut butter, bags of apples, and all the odds and ends that go to keeping house for a family. The store was warm and dim. Her grandmother spent a long time at the meat counter.

When they were ready to check out, Dicey stood awkwardly aside. The bill came to forty-seven dollars. Dicey chewed on her lip. Maybe she could find work. Maybe she could find work here, dusting the shelves and washing the windows and making the place look brighter, cleaner, more like someplace where you wanted to buy groceries.

Her grandmother paid the bill. Millie took the money and gave her back her change without a word. She packed the groceries into four large bags.

Then the shopkeeper could hold her tongue no longer. "I see you found work," she said to Dicey.

"Yes," Dicey said. She said no more. She turned her chin up the way her grandmother's chin was held. It worked in just the same way.

"Tell me, Millie," her grandmother said, with a side glance at Dicey. "Do you get Social Security money?"

"Of course, since Herbie died. It's my due. I paid into it every month, all my working life. It's a widow's due, I tell you. I couldn't get through the month without it, not with what the store brings in. Widow's due, that's what I call it, and there's no shame. You take it too, don't you?"

"I didn't work to pay in," Dicey's grandmother said.

"No more you didn't, Ab Tillerman, raising three children and working on that farm. Your John did, too, every year in his taxes. It's for widows and their children, as much as for people older than we are, and helpless. So don't raise your nose at me."

"Ever buy a Christmas tree?" Dicey's grandmother demanded.

The abrupt change of topic flustered Millie. "What?" she asked. "What do you mean? for Christmas? Why should I do that, when I can get one cut for me just by asking? I know a lady in Cambridge that bought one, but I never did. What kind of a question is that?"

"How much did she pay?"

"How should I know? Ten, fifteen dollars, I think she said. And it was a scrawny thing, too, some poor relation of a loblolly. She had more bulbs than branches on the thing, trying to make it look right. You feeling all right, Ab?"

Dicey looked at her grandmother, glad because it meant her grandmother was thinking of putting in a cash crop, to repay herself the money she'd spent on the Tillermans.

"See if your family's around, girl," her grandmother said. "We're going to need some extra hands with these bags."

Dicey went out through the door.

Sunlight burned on the street. She saw James across by the docks, leading Maybeth and Sammy down to the boat.

"Hey!" she called. "Hey! James! Over here."

They turned and strolled towards her. They looked tanned, healthy and perfectly ordinary. Dicey tried to read in Maybeth's face what had happened.

"I thought you were at the boat," James said.

"There are bags to carry. Maybeth?" Dicey asked.

Maybeth nodded and her eyes gleamed. "I can go into third grade. I read for her, the most I could. Out loud. I tried to sound out the words I didn't know, just like they said at school. It was easier, because it was the story about the little goats that get left at home and the wolf comes and tries to trick them into opening the door. So I knew the story. I told Mrs. Jenkins I already knew it and asked her if she wanted to find another story to test me with, but she said it was OK. She said even if I knew the story, I'd still have to read the words. I answered all her questions about it, but they were easy ones. I got two wrong on the adding and three on subtracting, and they don't start multiplication until third grade. But they know fractions already."

"I can show you fractions," Dicey said. "Was it hard?"

"Not as hard as I thought," Maybeth said. "Not as hard as tomorrow will be. But I think maybe I can do that too."

Their grandmother pushed the screen door aside. "What are you waiting for?"

Maybeth ran over to her and pulled on her arm. Their grandmother bent her gray curly head down to the bright yellow head. She listened to Maybeth and smiled at what she heard.

The children went inside. Sammy said he wasn't too small to carry a bag, but he was, so Millie divided one bag into two smaller bags, one for Sammy and one for Maybeth. Her eyes bugged out with curiosity.

"By the way, Millie," their grandmother finally said, "I don't believe you've met my grandchildren." One by one she introduced them. "Liza's brood," their grandmother said. "They'll be staying with me for a couple of weeks."

Their grandmother herded them outside before Millie could ask any questions. They walked together down the hot street and along the dock. Dicey got into the boat first. James handed the bags down to her.

Sammy had been thinking. "If you're our grandmother—I mean, if you say you are—I mean, you know you are but you never said so—now that you say so what do I call you?"

The boat was rocking under Dicey's feet. She wished they weren't going to be in different schools, even for this little time. In Bridgeport, there would be boys' schools and girls' schools, and they'd all be split up. She wished that here, just for this little while, they could still be in the same school. But it didn't matter. It was just another way things weren't working out.

"You'll call me Gram," their grandmother said to Sammy.

"Gram," Sammy repeated, trying it. He ran to the edge of the dock and wheeled around. "Hey, Gram!" he yelled. He ran back. "Gram?"

"Yes, Sammy." She sounded tired.

"You like us, don't you? You do, no matter what you say. I know."

"Never said I didn't," Gram said. "And I'm pretty proud of Maybeth at this moment."

"So am I," Dicey said.

"So am I," Maybeth said, with a smile at herself, a smile that had no silliness in it.

They all stood for a minute there. Little bright-topped waves rocked the boat gently on the way to pattering up against the seawalls. A salty wind blew from the land out over the water. The town of Crisfield lay in the sunlight before them, bleached white as the oyster shells scattered around the ground.

Dicey thought about the bread dough rising in the big earthenware bowl back on the scrubbed wooden table in her grandmother's kitchen. She was getting hungry. She looked at James. He was studying his grandmother, as if he was hungry too, but for something not food, hungry in a way that food could never fill.

It wasn't fair, not just for Dicey but for all of them. Well, Dicey said to herself, life isn't fair. Everybody said that to you. They had all tried, and they had lost, and they were going to have to make the best of it with Cousin Eunice.

She remembered the letter then. Gram hadn't mailed the letter. Dicey thought about not telling her grandmother; but not for long. What was the use of postponing it? When something bad was going to happen it got worse the longer you waited. If she didn't tell Gram, that would be like asking again. And Gram had said no. Dicey wasn't the kind to argue and beg when somebody said no.

"You forgot to mail your letter," she said.

Gram's face was surprised. She really had forgotten it. She was also surprised (Dicey knew this too) that Dicey had remembered and said something. She opened her purse and took it out. Dicey looked down at the floorboards of the little boat. She looked at her sneakers, worn with all the traveling they'd done. Her big toes stuck out through the canvas. Those sneakers had come a long way.

Wasn't it worth it, having come such a way, to fight a little harder? a little longer? Being told no twice couldn't be worse than being told no once.

"Gram?" Dicey said. She looked up. She was almost as tall as her grandmother, but now the woman loomed above her, standing on the dock. The dark hazel eyes stared down at her, forbidding her to speak.

"Well, you should," Dicey said fiercely. "You should let us live with you."

That was no way to ask.

"Would that suit you?" Gram asked Dicey.

Dicey was shocked into silence.

"I thought you were the one it didn't suit," James said.

"Well, it doesn't," Gram said. "But it will. I give up. I do, I give up. You've worn me out. You can stay, you can live with me. You hear that, girl?" she called down to Dicey.

"Do you mean it?" Dicey asked.

"I don't say what I don't mean. You should know that. You'll live with me and we'll see lawyers about adoption and take government money—and we'll plant Christmas trees and raise chickens, whatever we have to do, whatever ideas James cooks up that we can't talk him out of. But can we go now, please? My feet are itching me half to death."

But instead of getting into the boat, Gram held up the letter to Cousin Eunice and ripped it into little pieces. She tossed the scraps into the air. The breeze took them out and dropped them onto the dancing waves.

"I'll have to write to her again," Gram said, as if the idea gave her no pleasure.

"Gram," Dicey said. Her grandmother looked down at her again. "The boat, the sailboat in the barn. Can I fix it up and sail it? Can I have it?"

"Do you know how to sail?"

"No. But I could learn. Could you teach me?"

"Yes," Gram said.

"Yes, what?" Dicey asked.

"Yes to both—and no more questions; not until I get my shoes off."

Gram climbed down into the boat and held it steady against the dock while the little children jumped in. James threw the painter down to Dicey and leaped down himself.

"Ready to go home?" Gram asked Dicey. She was smiling.

Dicey just grinned back. "Ready," she said.

Gary Paulsen

1939–

O NE INCIDENT sums up Gary Paulsen's approach to life and work. It is a story he tells often. Sometime in 1979, while running his dogsled along the Minnesota trapline that provided a meager living for Paulsen and his family, he began to cross a frozen lake. It was midnight, thirty degrees below zero; the full moon shone over the tall pines. He had never seen anything so beautiful. He knew that at the top of the next hill, he could turn left and go home, or, "If I hung a right, I could stay in the beauty." It was the kind of pivotal moment few have. He turned right, and stayed in the beauty for eight days, alone with his dogs and the icy, mystical landscape.

Paulsen's physical courage, his now-legendary eagerness for risk, his love of animals and the outdoors, his total honesty—these qualities are matched only by his passion for writing. He is the most prolific of contemporary YA writers. Between 1991 and 1996, for example, he published fourteen young adult novels in addition to twenty-five other works in various genres. He once accepted—and won—a bet that he could write eleven articles and short stories in four days; he sold them all. His biographer Gary Salvner (*Presenting Gary Paulsen*, Twayne 1996) says he "writes as if possessed." Paulsen himself says he is not particularly driven; he writes because, for him, "it's all there is."

Born in 1939 in Minneapolis, Minnesota, Paulsen experienced a difficult childhood. His father, an Army officer, was in Europe for most of his young life. When his mother brought a man home to live with her, she sent Gary alone on a train to his grandmother in northern Minnesota. At the end of the war, Gary and his mother went to the Philippines to be with his father—a terrible journey he has described in *Eastern Sun, Winter Moon* (1993). There, his parents drank heavily and argued. By 1949 they were back in the states, where his father tried various occupations without much success. To escape from his parents' drinking and turmoil, he made periodic visits to relatives who lived in the country, where life seemed more pleasant for a while. During one summer of his high school years, he worked in North Dakota hoeing sugar beets and then ran with a carnival—anything to stay away from home.

Paulsen's schooling was irregular. Because his father was constantly on the move, he attended one school after another, showing up as little as he could get away with. Things got worse as he reached high school; he "pretty much" failed the ninth grade, had to repeat English and algebra, got in a lot of fights, and had no social life. He finally graduated in 1957 from Thief River Falls High School in Minnesota with "probably a D minus average."

But at fourteen, he had two positive experiences which would shape his life. Wanting some respect from his schoolmates, he decided to track a deer and touch it. He tracked a doe for two days, and when it was too exhausted to move, he approached and touched it. Although he realizes now it wasn't "that hard to do," and although it did not magically make him popular at school, his choice of this particular feat and his determination in carrying it out heralded his almost uncanny empathy with the natural world. His writing life may have begun on a cold night when he went into the Thief River Falls public library to get warm. The librarian, whose name he no longer recalls, asked him if he'd like a library card. The availability of the card and her lack of prejudice about his looks and schooling were revelations to him. She gave him a book—a Western, he remembers—and when he returned that one, kept supplying him with books as he became a voracious reader. Reading provided an escape from his turbulent home life, and an education in fine literature when she would "schlep in a Melville" along with the Westerns. This too is a story he loves to tell, especially when encouraging young people to read: "When she handed me the card, she handed me the world. I can't even describe how liberating it was."

He flunked out of college within a year and joined the Army; after his military service he found jobs in the aerospace industry in California. At age 26, he experienced another of those crucial moments. Reading a magazine article on flight testing, he suddenly realized that writing about something interesting would be a great way to make a living. He quit his job the next day and headed for Hollywood to learn the craft of writing by getting a job—with a slightly falsified resume—as an editor. He got hired, and spent a fruitful year editing during the day and writing at night, getting the advice he needed from three editors he had met. But he also realized that the artificiality of Hollywood was unhealthy for him. He went back to Minnesota and not long afterward, in 1967, sold his first book. His next one, *Mr. Tucket*, was his first work for young readers, a historical novel about a boy kidnapped by Indians.

Life seemed to be going Paulsen's way at last. But when he moved to the artist's colony in Taos, New Mexico, he began to drink. For the next six years, he was, as he puts it, a "bottom-level, hard-core drunk," unable to write, getting into fights, working only odd jobs. By this time he had two failed marriages. But when during this period he met artist Ruth Ellen Wright, he tried again, marrying her in 1971. Despite his alcoholism, she stayed with him. They had a son, Jim; when the boy was two years old, Paulsen realized he had to change. With Ruth's encouragement, Paulsen joined Alcoholics Anonymous, and stopped drinking in 1973.

There were two more years of hard work before he could again sell a book. He published a how-to manual about building a house, and several more books of nonfiction before he could write fiction. He and Ruth suffered serious financial hardship during this period and in 1979 moved back to a cabin in the Minnesota woods, barely scraping by. To add to his troubles, he was sued for libel because a Minnesota man believed an unattractive adult character in his 1976 YA novel *Winterkill* was based on him. His publisher offered little support; although the suit was unsuccessful, the experience left Paulsen bitter about the publishing business. On his return to Minnesota, he decided to make a living trapping. A neighbor gave him a used sled and four dogs, and Paulsen felt for the first time the exhilaration of running with the dogs. After that one remarkable night when he turned right and "stayed in the beauty" for eight days, he vowed never to kill another animal.

When someone suggested he try running the famous dogsled race across Alaska, the Iditarod, he went into training hardly knowing what would be required. In 1983, he made the run of his life—seventeen days and fourteen hours across the snow, without sleep, sometimes hallucinating, totally dependent on his dogs for survival. He came in forty-second out of seventy-two entries, a triumph of determination. He has said of this experience, "The Iditarod may sound like a macho thrill, but it's the opposite. You go where death goes . . . macho is a lie. It's testicular garbage. Core toughness and compassion are the opposite of macho."

He ran the Iditarod again in 1985. In 1988 he almost froze to death after falling asleep in the snow. In 1990, when he was training for a third Iditarod and going on one book-signing tour after another, he collapsed with angina and was ordered to stop running dogs. He and Ruth eventually moved to New Mexico, and there Paulsen continues to pour out his books, some of them now illustrated by Ruth.

Hatchet, published in 1987, represents Paulsen at the height of his literary powers and remains one of the most popular Young Adult novels, touching young readers so deeply and consistently that in 1996 Paulsen told biographer Gary Salvner that he still got 150 to 200 letters a day about it. "It's incredible," he said. "I honest to God don't know what I did." Great literature is always, ultimately, a mystery, but one thing he did was to bring the classic adventure story into the modern YA canon. Professor Martin Green, who has studied the literary phenomenon of the Robinson Crusoe tale, notes that among scholars such literature is usually regarded as not quite "literary" enough, because it blurs the distinction between reality and fiction and hence muddies the very idea of the *novel* (*The Robinson Crusoe Story*, Pennsylvania State University Press 1990). However, it has for centuries been a popular form of entertainment and a meditation on the fragility and meaning of life. In its focus on a specific task and on physical and moral triumph, it clearly embraces a male ethic, either eliminating women or making their concerns secondary. In this mode, Paulsen joins the ranks of those who write for boys: Henty, Marrayat, Ballantyne, and Scott in nineteenth century England, for example, and Alger, Tunis, Lipsyte, Brooks, and Crutcher in nineteenth and twentieth century America. But as Green points out, girls as well as boys have always enjoyed such literature, for in these tales, physical isolation and survival represent the challenges of young adulthood in all societies.

Part of Paulsen's accomplishment in *Hatchet* is its tone. There is no doubt that we are reading the thoughts of a terrified contemporary teenaged boy, yet the third person, past tense narrative voice is spare, dignified, slightly abstract even when describing highly emotional situations: "He stood away from the eggs for a moment, literally stood and turned away so that he could not see them. If he looked at them he would have to eat more." Paulsen repeats words and phrases to create Brian's mental panic and his efforts to control it, in a style reminiscent of Hemingway's in *The Old Man and the Sea*: "And there was still hunger there, but not like it was—not tearing at him. This was hunger that he knew would be there always, even when he had food—a hunger that made him look at things. A hunger to make him hunt."

Paulsen has added two elements to his basic survival tale that link it to the Crusoe tradition yet make it completely modern. One is what Brian calls "The Secret." He has discovered his mother's infidelity, plunging him into a morass of guilt, anger, longing, and bewilderment, a psychological undercurrent to his physical suffering. While the question "Why me?" torments other castaways in the Robinson tradition, Brian's ancestry here is more recent, recalling the protagonists of the problem novels which dominated Young Adult literature in the 1970s, most of whom suffered through divorce and other forms of parental inadequacy. The second element is a spiritual conversion. In Defoe's novel,

Robinson conveys his own Christianity to Friday, a motif that infuses many of the succeeding versions of the tale. Paulsen eliminates conventional religion and substitutes a spiritual connection with nature, as Brian gradually learns to listen, to observe, to respect, and ultimately to become one with his natural surroundings—so much so that when he recovers the rifle, he sets it carefully aside: "It somehow removed him from everything around him . . . he wasn't sure he liked the change very much." After his rescue, he recalls "the lake, the forest, the fire at night, the night birds singing and the fish jumping—[he would] sit in the dark alone and think of them and it was not bad and would never be bad for him."

Readers' fascination with *Hatchet* has prompted Paulsen to produce five more books directly related to it. The first came as a result of a request from the National Geographic Society, who wanted to interview Brian; they were convinced he was real. He had become real to so many readers, said Paulsen, that in 1991 he wrote *The River*, in which Brian returns to his crash site with a psychologist who wants to study him, a development Paulsen anticipates in the epilogue of *Hatchet*. In 1994, to address readers' questions about his own experiences of survival in the woods, he wrote *Father Water, Mother Woods: Essays on Fishing and Hunting in the North Woods*. To satisfy readers who asked what would have happened had Brian had to stay into the winter, Paulsen produced *Brian's Winter* in 1996. Still the questions came, and in 1999 he wrote *Brian's Return* to explore what happened to Brian after his return to civilization. His most recent return to Brian is *Guts: The True Stories Behind* Hatchet *and the Brian Books* (Delacorte 2001), in which Paulsen responds to readers' desires to know specific details about his own experiences with plane crashes, moose attacks, mosquitoes, and turtle eggs. Here he describes the change in himself as he came to understand nature, to feel "what the woods were about." Such learning, he says, "has been the one guiding part of living that has helped me more than anything else" (118). No other Young Adult novel conveys this learning as well as *Hatchet*, a classic survival tale honed to the basics, one of the most intense and dignified of all books for young adult readers.

HATCHET

CHAPTER 1

B RIAN ROBESON stared out the window of the small plane at the endless green northern wilderness below. It was a small plane, a Cessna 406—a bushplane—and the engine was so loud, so roaring and consuming and loud, that it ruined any chance for conversation.

Not that he had much to say. He was thirteen and the only passenger on the plane with a pilot named—what was it? Jim or Jake or something—who was in his mid-forties and who had been silent as he worked to prepare for take-off. In fact since Brian had come to the small airport in Hampton, New York to meet the plane—driven by his mother—the pilot had spoken only five words to him.

"Get in the copilot's seat."

Which Brian had done. They had taken off and that was the last of the conversation. There had been the initial excitement, of course. He had never flown in a single-engine plane before and to be sitting in the copilot's seat with all the controls right there in front of him, all the instruments in his face as the plane clawed for altitude, jerking and sliding on the wind currents as the pilot took off, had been interesting and exciting. But in five minutes they had leveled off at six thousand feet and headed northwest and from then on the pilot had been silent, staring out the front, and the drone of the engine had been all that was left. The drone and the sea of green trees that lay before the plane's nose and flowed to the horizon, spread with lakes, swamps, and wandering streams and rivers.

Now Brian sat, looking out the window with the roar thundering through his ears, and tried to catalog what had led up to his taking this flight.

The thinking started.

Always it started with a single word.

Divorce.

It was an ugly word, he thought. A tearing, ugly word that meant fights and yelling, lawyers—God, he thought, how he hated lawyers who sat with their comfortable smiles and tried to explain to him in legal terms how all that he lived in was coming apart—and the breaking and shattering of all the solid things. His home, his life—all the solid things. Divorce. A breaking word, an ugly breaking word.

Divorce.

Secrets.

No, not secrets so much as just the Secret. What he knew and had not told anybody, what he knew about his mother that had caused the divorce, what he knew, what he knew—the Secret.

Divorce.

The Secret.

Brian felt his eyes beginning to burn and knew there would be tears. He had cried for a time, but that was gone now. He didn't cry now. Instead his eyes burned and tears came, the seeping tears that burned, but he didn't cry. He wiped his eyes with a finger and looked at the pilot out of the corner of his eye to make sure he hadn't noticed the burning and tears.

The pilot sat large, his hands lightly on the wheel, feet on the rudder pedals. He seemed more a machine than a man, an extension of the plane. On the dashboard in front of him Brian saw the dials, switches, meters, knobs, levers, cranks, lights, handles that were wiggling and flickering, all indicating nothing that he understood and the pilot seemed the same way. Part of the plane, not human.

When he saw Brian look at him, the pilot seemed to open up a bit and he smiled. "Ever fly in the copilot's seat before?" He leaned over and lifted the headset off his right ear and put it on his temple, yelling to overcome the sound of the engine.

Brian shook his head. He had never been in any kind of plane, never seen the cockpit of a plane except in films or television. It was loud and confusing. "First time."

"It's not as complicated as it looks. Good plane like this almost flies itself." The pilot shrugged. "Makes my job easy." He took Brian's left arm. "Here, put your hands on the controls, your feet on the rudder pedals, and I'll show you what I mean."

Brian shook his head. "I'd better not."

"Sure. Try it . . ."

Brian reached out and took the wheel in a grip so tight his knuckles were white. He pushed his feet down on the pedals. The plane slewed suddenly to the right.

"Not so hard. Take her light, take her light."

Brian eased off, relaxed his grip. The burning in his eyes was forgotten momentarily as the vibration of the plane came through the wheel and the pedals. It seemed almost alive.

"See?" The pilot let go of his wheel, raised his hands in the air and took his feet off the pedals to show Brian he was actually flying the plane alone. "Simple. Now turn the wheel a little to the right and push on the right rudder pedal a small amount."

Brian turned the wheel slightly and the plane immediately banked to the right, and when he pressed on the right rudder pedal the nose slid across the horizon to the right. He left off on the pressure and straightened the wheel and the plane righted itself.

"Now you can turn. Bring her back to the left a little."

Brian turned the wheel left, pushed on the left pedal, and the plane came back around. "It's easy." He smiled. "At least this part."

The pilot nodded. "All of flying is easy. Just takes learning. Like everything else. Like everything else." He took the controls back, then reached up and rubbed his left shoulder. "Aches and pains—must be getting old."

Brian let go of the controls and moved his feet away from the pedals as the pilot put his hands on the wheel. "Thank you . . ."

But the pilot had put his headset back on and the gratitude was lost in the engine noise and things went back to Brian looking out the window at the ocean of trees and lakes. The burning eyes did not come back, but memories did, came flooding in. The words. Always the words.

Divorce.

The Secret.

Fights.

Split.

The big split. Brian's father did not understand as Brian did, knew only that Brian's mother wanted to break the marriage apart. The split had come and then the divorce, all so fast, and the court had left him with his mother except for the summers and what the judge called "visitation rights." So formal. Brian hated judges as he hated lawyers. Judges that leaned over the bench and asked Brian if he understood where he was to live and why. Judges with the caring look that meant nothing as lawyers said legal phrases that meant nothing.

In the summer Brian would live with his father. In the school year with his mother. That's what the judge said after looking at papers on his desk and listening to the lawyers talk. Talk. Words.

Now the plane lurched slightly to the right and Brian looked at the pilot. He was rubbing his shoulder again and there was the sudden smell of body gas in the plane. Brian turned back to avoid embarrassing the pilot, who was obviously in some discomfort. Must have stomach troubles.

So this summer, this first summer when he was allowed to have "visitation rights" with his father, with the divorce only one month old, Brian was heading north. His father was a mechanical engineer who had designed or invented a new drill bit for oil drilling, a self-cleaning, self-sharpening bit. He was working in the oil fields of Canada, up on the tree line where the tundra started and the forests ended. Brian was riding up from New York with some drilling equipment—it was lashed down in the rear of the plane next to a fabric bag the pilot had called a survival pack, which had emergency supplies in case they had to make an emergency landing—that had to be specially made in the city, riding in a bushplane with the pilot named Jim or Jake or something who had turned out to be an all right guy, letting him fly and all.

Except for the smell. Now there was a constant odor, and Brian took another look at the pilot, found him rubbing the shoulder and down the arm now, the left arm, letting go more gas and wincing. Probably something he ate, Brian thought.

His mother had driven him from the city to meet the plane at Hampton where it came to pick up the drilling equipment. A drive in silence, a long drive in silence. Two and a half hours of sitting in the car, staring out the window of the plane. Once, after an hour, when they were out of the city she turned to him.

"Look, can't we talk this over? Can't we talk this out? Can't you tell me what's bothering you?"

And there were the words again. Divorce. Split. The Secret. How could he tell her what he knew? So he had remained silent, shook his head and continued to stare unseeing at the countryside, and his mother had gone back to driving only to speak to him one more time when they were close to Hampton.

She reached over the back of the seat and brought up a paper sack. "I got something for you, for the trip."

Brian took the sack and opened the top. Inside there was a hatchet, the kind with a steel handle and a rubber handgrip. The head was in a stout leather case that had a brass-riveted belt loop.

"It goes on your belt." His mother spoke now without looking at him. There were some farm trucks on the roads now and she had to weave through them and watch traffic. "The man at the store said you could use it. You know. In the woods with your father."

Dad, he thought. Not "my father." My dad. "Thanks. It's really nice." But the words sounded hollow, even to Brian.

"Try it on. See how it looks on your belt."

And he would normally have said no, would normally have said no that it looked too hokey to have a hatchet on your belt. Those were the normal things he would say. But her voice was thin, had a sound like something thin that would break if you touched it, and he felt bad for not speaking to her. Knowing what he knew, even with the anger, the hot white hate of his anger at her, he still felt bad for not speaking to her, and so to humor her he loosened his belt and pulled the right side out and put the hatchet on and rethreaded the belt.

"Scootch around so I can see."

He moved around in the seat, feeling only slightly ridiculous.

She nodded. "Just like a scout. My little scout." And there was the tenderness in her voice that she had when he was small, the tenderness that she had when he was small and sick, with a cold, and she put her hand on his forehead, and the burning came into his eyes again and he had turned away from her and looked out the window, forgotten the hatchet on his belt and so arrived at the plane with the hatchet still on his belt.

Because it was a bush flight from a small airport there had been no security and the plane had been waiting, with the engine running when he arrived and he had grabbed his suitcase and pack bag and run for the plane without stopping to remove the hatchet.

So it was still on his belt. At first he had been embarrassed but the pilot had said nothing about it and Brian forgot it as they took off and began flying.

More smell now. Bad. Brian turned again to glance at the pilot who had both hands on his stomach and was grimacing in pain, reaching for the left shoulder again as Brian watched.

"Don't know, kid . . ." The pilot's words were a hiss, barely audible. "Bad aches here. Bad aches. Thought it was something I ate but . . ."

He stopped as a fresh spasm of pain hit him. Even Brian could see how bad it was—the pain drove the pilot back into the seat, back and down.

"I've never had anything like this . . ."

The pilot reached for the switch on his mike cord, his hand coming up in a small arc from his stomach, and he flipped the switch and said, "This is flight four six . . ."

And now a jolt took him like a hammerblow, so forcefully that he seemed to crush back into the seat, and Brian reached for him, could not understand at first what it was, could not know.

And then he knew.

Brian knew. The pilot's mouth went rigid, he swore and jerked a short series of slams into the seat, holding his shoulder now. Swore and hissed, "Chest! Oh God, my chest is coming apart!"

Brian knew now.

The pilot was having a heart attack. Brian had been in the shopping mall with his mother when a man in front of Paisley's store had suffered a heart attack. He had gone down and screamed about his chest. An old man. Much older than the pilot.

Brian knew.

The pilot was having a heart attack and even as the knowledge came to Brian he saw the pilot slam into the seat one more time, one more awful time he slammed back into the seat and his right leg jerked, pulling the plane to the side in a sudden twist and his head fell forward and spit came. Spit came from the corners of his mouth and his legs contracted up, up into the seat, and his eyes rolled back in his head until there was only white.

Only white for his eyes and the smell became worse, filled the cockpit, and all of it so fast, so incredibly fast that Brian's mind could not take it in at first. Could only see it in stages.

The pilot had been talking, just a moment ago complaining of the pain. He had been talking.

Then the jolts had come.

The jolts that took the pilot back had come, and now Brian sat and there was a strange feeling of silence in the thrumming roar of the engine—a strange feeling of silence and being alone. Brian was stopped.

He was stopped. Inside he was stopped. He could not think past what he saw, what he felt. All was stopped. The very core of him, the very center of Brian Robeson was stopped and stricken with a white-flash of horror, a terror so intense that his breathing, his thinking, and nearly his heart had stopped.

Stopped.

Seconds passed, seconds that became all of his life, and he began to know what he was seeing, began to understand what he saw and that was worse, so much worse that he wanted to make his mind freeze again.

He was sitting in a bushplane roaring seven thousand feet above the northern wilderness with a pilot who had suffered a massive heart attack and who was either dead or in something close to a coma.

He was alone.

In the roaring plane with no pilot he was alone.

Alone.

CHAPTER 2

F OR A TIME that he could not understand Brian could do nothing. Even after his mind began working and he could see what had happened he could do nothing. It was as if his hands and arms were lead.

Then he looked for ways for it not to have happened. Be asleep, his mind screamed at the pilot. Just be asleep and your eyes will open now and your hands will take the controls and your feet will move to the pedals—but it did not happen.

The pilot did not move except that his head rolled on a neck impossibly loose as the plane hit a small bit of turbulence.

The plane.

Somehow the plane was still flying. Seconds had passed, nearly a minute, and the plane flew on as if nothing had happened and he had to do something, had to do something but did not know what.

Help.

He had to help.

He stretched one hand toward the pilot, saw that his fingers were trembling, and touched the pilot on the chest. He did not know what to do. He knew there were procedures, that you could do mouth-to-mouth on victims of heart attacks and push their chests—C.P.R.—but he did not know how to do it and in any case could not do it with the pilot, who was sitting up in the seat and still strapped in with his seatbelt. So he touched the pilot with the tips of his fingers, touched him on the chest and could feel nothing, no heartbeat, no rise and fall of breathing. Which meant that the pilot was almost certainly dead.

"Please," Brian said. But did not know what or who to ask. "Please . . ."

The plane lurched again, hit more turbulence, and Brian felt the nose drop. It did not dive, but the nose went down slightly and the down-angle increased the speed, and he knew that at this angle, this slight angle down, he would ultimately fly into the trees. He could see them ahead on the horizon where before he could see only sky.

He had to fly it somehow. Had to fly the plane. He had to help himself. The pilot was gone, beyond anything he could do. He had to try and fly the plane.

He turned back in the seat, facing the front, and put his hands—still trembling—on the control wheel, his feet gently on the rudder pedals. You pulled back on the stick to raise the plane, he knew that from reading. You always pulled back on the wheel. He gave it a tug and it slid back toward him easily. Too easily. The plane, with the increased speed from the tilt down, swooped eagerly up and drove Brian's stomach down. He pushed the wheel back in, went too far this time, and the plane's nose went below the horizon and the engine speed increased with the shallow dive.

Too much.

He pulled back again, more gently this time, and the nose floated up again, too far but not as violently as before, then down a bit too much, and up again as before, then down a bit too much, and up again, very easily, and the front of the engine cowling settled. When he had it aimed at the horizon and it seemed to be steady, he held the wheel where it was, let out his breath—which he had been holding all this time—and tried to think what to do next.

It was a clear, blue-sky day with fluffy bits of clouds here and there and he looked out the window for a moment, hoping to see something, a town or village, but there was nothing. Just the green of the trees, endless green, and lakes scattered more and more thickly as the plane flew—where?

He was flying but did not know where, had no idea where he was going. He looked at the dashboard of the plane, studied the dials and hoped to get some help, hoped to find a compass, but it was all so confusing, a jumble of numbers and lights. One lighted display in the top center of the dashboard said the number 342, another next to it said 22. Down beneath that were dials with lines that seemed to indicate what the winds were doing, tipping or moving, and one dial with a needle pointing to the number 70, which he thought—only thought—might be the altimeter. The device that told him his height above the ground. Or above sea level. Somewhere he had read something about altimeters but he couldn't remember what, or where, or anything about them.

Slightly to the left and below the altimeter he saw a small rectangular panel with a lighted dial and two knobs. His eyes had passed it over two or three times before he saw what was written in tiny letters on top of the panel. TRANSMITTER 221, was stamped in the metal and it hit him, finally, that this was the radio.

The radio. Of course. He had to use the radio. When the pilot had—had been hit that way (he couldn't bring himself to say that the pilot was dead, couldn't think it), he had been trying to use the radio.

Brian looked to the pilot. The headset was still on his head, turned sideways a bit from his jamming back into the seat, and the microphone switch was clipped into his belt.

Brian had to get the headset from the pilot. Had to reach over and get the headset from the pilot or he would not be able to use the radio to call for help. He had to reach over . . .

His hands began trembling again. He did not want to touch the pilot, did not want to reach for him. But he had to. Had to get the radio. He lifted his hands from the wheel, just slightly, and held them waiting to see what would happen. The plane flew on normally, smoothly.

All right, he thought. Now. Now to do this thing. He turned and reached for the headset, slid it from the pilot's head, one eye on the plane, waiting for it to dive. The headset came easily, but the microphone switch at the pilot's belt was jammed in and he had to pull to get it loose. When he pulled, his elbow bumped the wheel and pushed it in and the plane started down in a shallow dive. Brian grabbed the wheel and pulled it back, too hard again, and the plane went through another series of stomach-wrenching swoops up and down before he could get it under control.

When things had settled again he pulled at the mike cord once more and at last jerked the cord free. It took him another second or two to place the headset on his own head and position the small microphone tube in front of his mouth. He had seen the pilot use it, had seen him depress the switch at his belt, so Brian pushed the switch in and blew into the mike.

He heard the sound of his breath in the headset. "Hello? Is there anybody listening on this? Hello . . ."

He repeated it two or three times and then waited but heard nothing except his own breathing.

Panic came then. He had been afraid, had been stopped with the terror of what was happening, but now panic came and he began to scream into the microphone, scream over and over.

"Help! Somebody help me! I'm in this plane and don't know . . . don't know . . . don't know . . ."

And he started crying with the screams, crying and slamming his hands against the wheel of the plane, causing it to jerk down, then back up. But again, he heard nothing but the sound of his own sobs in the microphone, his own screams mocking him, coming back into his ears.

The microphone. Awareness cut into him. He had used a CB radio in his uncle's pickup once. You had to turn the mike switch off to hear anybody else. He reached to his belt and released the switch.

For a second all he heard was the *whusssh* of the empty air waves. Then, through the noise and static he heard a voice.

"Whoever is calling on this radio net, I repeat, release your mike switch— you are covering me. You are covering me. Over."

It stopped and Brian hit his mike switch. "I hear you! I hear you. This is me . . . !" He released the switch.

"Roger. I have you now." The voice was very faint and breaking up. "Please state your difficulty and location. And say *over* to signal end of transmission. Over."

Please state my difficulty, Brian thought. God. My difficulty. "I am in a plane with a pilot who is—he can't fly. And I don't know how to fly. Help me. Help . . ." He turned his mike off without ending transmission properly.

There was a moment's hesitation before the answer. "Your signal is breaking up and I lost most of it. Understand . . . pilot . . . you can't fly. Correct? Over."

Brian could barely hear him now, heard mostly noise and static. "That's right. I can't fly. The plane is flying now but I don't know how much longer. Over."

" . . . lost signal. Your location please. Flight number . . . location . . . ver."

"I don't know my flight number or location. I don't know anything. I told you that, over."

He waited now, waited but there was nothing. Once, for a second, he thought he heard a break in the noise, some part of a word, but it could have been static. Two, three minutes, ten minutes, the plane roared and Brian listened but heard no one. Then he hit the switch again.

"I do not know the flight number. My name is Brian Robeson and we left Hampton, New York headed for the Canadian oil fields to visit my father and I do not know how to fly an airplane and the pilot . . ."

He let go of the mike. His voice was starting to rattle and he felt as if he might start screaming at any second. He took a deep breath. "If there is anybody listening who can help me fly a plane, please answer."

Again he released the mike but heard nothing but the hissing of noise in the headset. After half an hour of listening and repeating the cry for help he tore the headset off in frustration and threw it to the floor. It all seemed so hopeless. Even if he did get somebody, what could anybody do? Tell him to be careful?

All so hopeless.

He tried to figure out the dials again. He thought he might know which was speed—it was a lighted number that read 160—but he didn't know if that was actual miles an hour, or kilometers, or if it just meant how fast the plane was moving through the air and not over the ground. He knew airspeed was different from groundspeed but not by how much.

Parts of books he'd read about flying came to him. How wings worked, how the propellor pulled the plane through the sky. Simple things that wouldn't help him now.

Nothing could help him now.

An hour passed. He picked up the headset and tried again—it was, he knew, in the end all he had—but there was no answer. He felt like a prisoner, kept in a small cell that was hurtling through the sky at what he thought to be 160 miles an hour, headed—he didn't know where—just headed somewhere until . . .

There it was. Until what? Until he ran out of fuel. When the plane ran out of fuel it would go down.

Period.

Or he could pull the throttle out and make it go down now. He had seen the pilot push the throttle in to increase speed. If he pulled the throttle back out, the engine would slow down and the plane would go down.

Those were his choices. He could wait for the plane to run out of gas and fall or he could push the throttle in and make it happen sooner. If he waited for the plane to run out of fuel he would go farther—but he did not know which way he was moving. When the pilot had jerked he had moved the plane, but Brian could not remember how much or if it had come back to its original course. Since he did not know the original course anyway and could only guess at which display might be the compass—the one reading 342—he did not know where he had been or where he was going, so it didn't make much difference if he went down now or waited.

Everything in him rebelled against stopping the engine and falling now. He had a vague feeling that he was wrong to keep heading as the plane was heading, a feeling that he might be going off in the wrong direction, but he could not bring himself to stop the engine and fall. Now he was safe, or safer than if he went down—the plane was flying, he was still breathing. When the engine stopped he would go down.

So he left the plane running, holding altitude, and kept trying the radio. He worked out a system. Every ten minutes by the small clock built into the dashboard he tried to radio with a simple message: "I need help. Is there anybody listening to me?"

In the times between transmissions he tried to prepare himself for what he knew was coming. When he ran out of fuel the plane would start down. He guessed that without the propellor pulling he would have to push the nose down to keep the plane flying—he thought he may have read that somewhere or it just came to him. Either way it made sense. He would have to push the nose down to keep flying speed and then, just before he hit, he would have to pull the nose back up to slow the plane as much as possible.

It all made sense. Glide down, then slow the plane and hit.

Hit.

He would have to find a clearing as he went down. The problem with that was that he hadn't seen one clearing since they'd started flying over the forest. Some swamps, but they had trees scattered through them. No roads, no trails, no clearings.

Just the lakes, and it came to him that he would have to use a lake for landing. If he went down in the trees he was certain to die. The trees would tear the plane to pieces as it went into them.

He would have to come down in a lake. No. On the edge of a lake. He would have to come down near the edge of a lake and try to slow the plane as much as possible just before he hit the water.

Easy to say, he thought, hard to do.

Easy say, hard do. Easy say, hard do. It became a chant that beat with the engine. Easy say, hard do.

Impossible to do.

He repeated the radio call seventeen times at the ten-minute intervals, working on what he would do between transmissions. Once more he reached over to the pilot and touched him on the face, but the skin was cold, hard cold, death cold, and Brian turned back to the dashboard. He did what he could, tightened his seatbelt, positioned himself, rehearsed mentally again and again what his procedure should be.

When the plane ran out of gas he should hold the nose down and head for the nearest lake and try to fly the plane kind of onto the water. That's how he thought of it. Kind of fly the plane onto the water. And just before it hit he should pull back on the wheel and slow the plane to reduce the impact.

Over and over his mind ran the picture of how it would go. The plane running out of gas, flying the plane onto the water, the crash—from pictures he'd seen on television. He tried to visualize it. He tried to be ready.

But between the seventeenth and eighteenth radio transmissions, without a warning, the engine coughed, roared violently for a second and died. There was sudden silence, cut only by the sound of the wind-milling propellor and the wind past the cockpit.

Brian pushed the nose of the plane down and threw up.

CHAPTER 3

GOING TO DIE, Brian thought. Going to die, gonna die, gonna die—his whole brain screamed it in the sudden silence.

Gonna die.

He wiped his mouth with the back of his arm and held the nose down. The plane went into a glide, a very fast glide that ate altitude, and suddenly there weren't any lakes. All he'd seen since they started flying over the forest was lakes and now they were gone. Gone. Out in front, far away at the horizon, he could see lots of them, glittering blue in the late afternoon sun.

But he needed one right in front. He desperately needed a lake right in front of the plane and all he saw through the windshield were trees, green death trees. If he had to turn—if he had to turn he didn't think he could keep the plane flying. His stomach tightened into a series of rolling knots and his breath came in short bursts . . .

There!

Not quite in front but slightly to the right he saw a lake. L-shaped, with rounded corners, and the plane was nearly aimed at the long part of the L, coming from the bottom and heading to the top. Just a tiny bit to the right. He pushed the right rudder pedal gently and the nose moved over.

But the turn cost him speed and now the lake was above the nose. He pulled back on the wheel slightly and the nose came up. This caused the plane to slow dramatically and almost seem to stop and wallow in the air. The controls became very loose-feeling and frightened Brian, making him push the wheel back in. This increased the speed a bit but filled the windshield once more with nothing but trees, and put the lake well above the nose and out of reach.

For a space of three or four seconds things seemed to hang, almost to stop. The plane was flying, but so slowly, so slowly . . . it would never reach the lake. Brian looked out to the side and saw a small pond and at the edge of the pond some large animal—he thought a moose—standing out in the water. All so still looking, so stopped, the pond and the moose and the trees, as he slid over them now only three or four hundred feet off the ground—all like a picture.

Then everything happened at once. Trees suddenly took on detail, filled his whole field of vision with green, and he knew he would hit and die, would die, but his luck held and just as he was to hit he came into an open lane, a channel of fallen trees, a wide place leading to the lake.

The plane, committed now to landing, to crashing, fell into the wide place like a stone, and Brian eased back on the wheel and braced himself for the crash. But there was a tiny bit of speed left and when he pulled on the wheel the nose came up and he saw in front the blue of the lake and at that instant the plane hit the trees.

There was a great wrenching as the wings caught the pines at the side of the clearing and broke back, ripping back just outside the main braces. Dust and dirt blew off the floor into his face so hard he thought there must have been some kind of explosion. He was momentarily blinded and slammed forward in the seat, smashing his head on the wheel.

Then a wild crashing sound, ripping of metal, and the plane rolled to the right and blew through the trees, out over the water and down, down to slam into the lake, skip once on water as hard as concrete, water that tore the windshield out and shattered the side windows, water that drove him back into the seat. Somebody was screaming, screaming as the plane drove down into the water. Someone screamed tight animal screams of fear and pain and he did not know that it was his sound, that he roared against the water that took him and the plane still deeper, down in the water. He saw nothing but sensed blue, cold blue-green, and he raked at the seatbelt latch, tore his nails loose on one hand. He ripped at it until it released and somehow—the water trying to kill him, to end him—somehow he pulled himself out of the shattered front window and clawed up into the blue, felt something hold him back, felt his windbreaker tear and he was free. Tearing free. Ripping free.

But so far! So far to the surface and his lungs could not do this thing, could not hold and were through, and he sucked water, took a great pull of water that would—finally—win, finally take him, and his head broke into light and he vomited and swam, pulling without knowing what he was, what he was doing. Without knowing anything. Pulling until his hands caught at weeds and muck, pulling and screaming until his hands caught at last in grass and brush and he felt his chest on land, felt his face in the coarse blades of grass and he stopped, everything stopped. A color came that he had never seen before, a color that exploded in his mind with the pain and he was gone, gone from it all, spiraling out into the world, spiraling out into nothing.

Nothing.

CHAPTER 4

T HE MEMORY was like a knife cutting into him. Slicing deep into him with hate.

The Secret.

He had been riding his ten-speed with a friend named Terry. They had been taking a run on a bike trail and decided to come back a different way, a way that took them past the Amber Mall. Brian remembered everything in incredible detail. Remembered the time on the bank clock in the mall, flashing 3:31, then the temperature, 82, and the date. All the numbers were part of the memory, all of his life was part of the memory.

Terry had just turned to smile at him about something and Brian looked over Terry's head and saw her.

His mother.

She was sitting in a station wagon, a strange wagon. He saw her and she did not see him. Brian was going to wave or call out, but something stopped him. There was a man in the car.

Short blond hair, the man had. Wearing some kind of white pullover tennis shirt.

Brian saw this and more, saw the Secret and saw more later, but the memory came in pieces, came in scenes like this—Terry smiling, Brian looking over his head to see the station wagon and his mother sitting with the man, the time and temperature clock, the front wheel of his bike, the short blond hair of the man, the white shirt of the man, the hot-hate slices of the memory were exact.

The Secret.

Brian opened his eyes and screamed.

For seconds he did not know where he was, only that the crash was still happening and he was going to die, and he screamed until his breath was gone.

Then silence, filled with sobs as he pulled in air, half crying. How could it be so quiet? Moments ago there was nothing but noise, crashing and tearing, screaming, now quiet.

Some birds were singing.

How could birds be singing?

His legs felt wet and he raised up on his hands and looked back down at them. They were in the lake. Strange. They went down into the water. He tried to move, but pain hammered into him and made his breath shorten into gasps and he stopped, his legs still in the water.

Pain.

Memory.

He turned again and sun came across the water, late sun, cut into his eyes and made him turn away.

It was over then. The crash.

He was alive.

The crash is over and I am alive, he thought. Then his eyes closed and he lowered his head for minutes that seemed longer. When he opened them again it was evening and some of the sharp pain had abated—there were many dull aches—and the crash came back to him fully.

Into the trees and out onto the lake. The plane had crashed and sunk in the lake and he had somehow pulled free.

He raised himself and crawled out of the water, grunting with the pain of movement. His legs were on fire, and his forehead felt as if somebody had been pounding on it with a hammer, but he could move. He pulled his legs out of the lake and crawled on his hands and knees until he was away from the wet-soft shore and near a small stand of brush of some kind.

Then he went down, only this time to rest, to save something of himself. He lay on his side and put his head on his arm and closed his eyes because that was all he could do now, all he could think of being able to do. He closed his eyes and slept, dreamless, deep and down.

There was almost no light when he opened his eyes again. The darkness of night was thick and for a moment he began to panic again. To see, he thought. To see is everything. And he could not see. But he turned his head without moving his body and saw that across the lake the sky was a light gray, that the sun was starting to come up, and he remembered that it had been evening when he went to sleep.

"Must be morning now . . ." He mumbled it, almost in a hoarse whisper. As the thickness of sleep left him the world came back.

He was still in pain, all-over pain. His legs were cramped and drawn up, tight and aching, and his back hurt when he tried to move. Worst was a keening throb in his head that pulsed with every beat of his heart. It seemed that the whole crash had happened to his head.

He rolled on his back and felt his sides and his legs, moving things slowly. He rubbed his arms; nothing seemed to be shattered or even sprained all that badly. When he was nine he had plowed his small dirt bike into a parked car and broken his ankle, had to wear a cast for eight weeks, and there was nothing now like that. Nothing broken. Just battered around a bit.

His forehead felt massively swollen to the touch, almost like a mound out over his eyes, and it was so tender that when his fingers grazed it he nearly cried. But there was nothing he could do about it and, like the rest of him, it seemed to be bruised more than broken.

I'm alive, he thought. I'm alive. It could have been different. There could have been death. I could have been done.

Like the pilot, he thought suddenly. The pilot in the plane, down into the water, down into the blue water strapped in the seat . . .

He sat up—or tried to. The first time he fell back. But on the second attempt, grunting with the effort, he managed to come to a sitting position and scrunched sideways until his back was against a small tree where he sat facing the lake, watching the sky get lighter and lighter with the coming dawn.

His clothes were wet and clammy and there was a faint chill. He pulled the torn remnants of his windbreaker, pieces really, around his shoulders and tried to hold what heat his body could find. He could not think, could not make thought patterns work right. Things seemed to go back and forth between reality and imagination—except that it was all reality. One second he seemed only to have imagined that there was a plane crash, that he had fought out of the sinking plane and swum to shore; that it had all happened to some other person or in a movie playing in his mind. Then he would feel his clothes, wet and cold, and his forehead would slash a pain through his thoughts and he would know it was real, that it had really happened. But all in a haze, all in a haze-world. So he sat and stared at the lake, felt the pain come and go in waves, and watched the sun come over the end of the lake.

It took an hour, perhaps two—he could not measure time yet and didn't care—for the sun to get halfway up. With it came some warmth, small bits of it at first, and with the heat came clouds of insects—thick, swarming hordes of mosquitos that flocked to his body, made a living coat on his exposed skin, clogged his nostrils when he inhaled, poured into his mouth when he opened it to take a breath.

It was not possibly believable. Not this. He had come through the crash, but the insects were not possible. He coughed them up, spat them out, sneezed them out, closed his eyes and kept brushing his face, slapping and crushing them by the dozens, by the hundreds. But as soon as he cleared a place, as soon as he killed them, more came, thick, whining, buzzing masses of them. Mosquitos and some small black flies he had never seen before. All biting, chewing, taking from him.

In moments his eyes were swollen shut and his face puffy and round to match his battered forehead. He pulled the torn pieces of his windbreaker over his head and tried to shelter in it but the jacket was full of rips and it didn't work. In desperation he pulled his T-shirt up to cover his face, but that exposed the skin of his lower back and the mosquitos and flies attacked the new soft flesh of his back so viciously that he pulled the shirt down.

In the end he sat with the windbreaker pulled up, brushed with his hands and took it, almost crying in frustration and agony. There was nothing left to do.

And when the sun was fully up and heating him directly, bringing steam off of his wet clothes and bathing him with warmth, the mosquitos and flies disappeared. Almost that suddenly. One minute he was sitting in the middle of a swarm; the next, they were gone and the sun was on him.

Vampires, he thought. Apparently they didn't like the deep of night, perhaps because it was too cool, and they couldn't take the direct sunlight. But in that gray time in the morning, when it began to get warm and before the sun was full up and hot—he couldn't believe them. Never, in all the reading, in the movies he had watched on television about the outdoors, never once had they ever mentioned the mosquitos or flies. All they ever showed on the naturalist shows was beautiful scenery or animals jumping around having a good time. Nobody ever mentioned mosquitos and flies.

"Unnnhhh." He pulled himself up to stand against the tree and stretched, bringing new aches and pains. His back muscles must have been hurt as well—they almost seemed to tear when he stretched—and while the pain in his forehead seemed to be abating somewhat, just trying to stand made him weak enough to nearly collapse.

The backs of his hands were puffy and his eyes were almost swollen shut from the mosquitos, and he saw everything through a narrow squint.

Not that there was much to see, he thought, scratching the bites. In front of him lay the lake, blue and deep. He had a sudden picture of the plane, sunk in the lake, down and down in the blue with the pilot's body still strapped in the seat, his hair waving . . .

He shook his head. More pain. That wasn't something to think about.

He looked at his surroundings again. The lake stretched out slightly below him. He was at the base of the L, looking up the long part with the short part out to his right. In the morning light and calm the water was absolutely, perfectly still. He could see the reflections of the trees at the other end of the lake. Upside down in the water they seemed almost like another forest, an upside-down forest to match the real one. As he watched, a large bird—he thought it looked like a crow but it seemed larger—flew from the top, real forest, and the reflection-bird matched it, both flying out over the water.

Everything was green, so green it went into him. The forest was largely made up of pines and spruce, with stands of some low brush smeared here and there and thick grass and some other kind of very small brush all over. He couldn't identify most of it—except the evergreens—and some leafy trees he thought might be aspen. He'd seen pictures of aspens in the mountains on television. The country around the lake was moderately hilly, but the hills were small—almost hummocks—and there were very few rocks except to his left. There lay a rocky ridge that stuck out overlooking the lake, about twenty feet high.

If the plane had come down a little to the left it would have hit the rocks and never made the lake. He would have been smashed.

Destroyed.

The word came. I would have been destroyed and torn and smashed. Driven into the rocks and destroyed.

Luck, he thought. I have luck, I had good luck there. But he knew that was wrong. If he had had good luck his parents wouldn't have divorced because of the Secret and he wouldn't have been flying with a pilot who had a heart attack and he wouldn't be here where he had to have good luck to keep from being destroyed.

If you keep walking back from good luck, he thought, you'll come to bad luck.

He shook his head again—wincing. Another thing not to think about.

The rocky ridge was rounded and seemed to be of some kind of sandstone with bits of darker stone layered and stuck into it. Directly across the lake from it, at the inside corner of the L, was a mound of sticks and mud rising up out of the water a good eight or ten feet. At first Brian couldn't place it but knew that he somehow knew what it was—had seen it in films. Then a small brown head popped to the surface of the water near the mound and began swimming off down the short leg of the L leaving a V of ripples behind and he remembered where he'd seen it. It was a beaver house, called a beaver lodge in a special he'd seen on the public channel.

A fish jumped. Not a large fish, but it made a big splash near the beaver, and as if by a signal there were suddenly little splops all over the sides of the lake— along the shore—as fish began jumping. Hundreds of them, jumping and slapping the water. Brian watched them for a time, still in the half-daze, still not thinking well. The scenery was very pretty, he thought, and there were new things to look at, but it was all a green and blue blur and he was used to the gray and black of the city, the sounds of the city. Traffic, people talking, sounds all the time—the hum and whine of the city.

Here, at first, it was silent, or he thought it was silent, but when he started to listen, really listen, he heard thousands of things. Hisses and blurks, small sounds, birds singing, hum of insects, splashes from the fish jumping—there was great noise here, but a noise he did not know, and the colors were new to him, and the colors and noise mixed in his mind to make a green-blue blur he could hear, hear as a hissing pulse-sound and he was still tired.

So tired.

So awfully tired, and standing had taken a lot of energy somehow, had drained him. He supposed he was still in some kind of shock from the crash and there was still the pain, the dizziness, the strange feeling.

He found another tree, a tall pine with no branches until the top, and sat with his back against it looking down on the lake with the sun warming him, and in a few moments he scrunched down and was asleep again.

CHAPTER 5

H IS EYES snapped open, hammered open, and there were these things about himself that he knew, instantly.

He was unbelievably, viciously thirsty. His mouth was dry and tasted foul and sticky. His lips were cracked and felt as if they were bleeding and if he did not drink some water soon he felt that he would wither up and die. Lots of water. All the water he could find.

He knew the thirst and felt the burn on his face. It was midafternoon and the sun had come over him and cooked him while he slept and his face was on fire, would blister, would peel. Which did not help the thirst, made it much worse. He stood, using the tree to pull himself up because there was still some pain and much stiffness, and looked down at the lake.

It was water. But he did not know if he could drink it. Nobody had ever told him if you could or could not drink lakes. There was also the thought of the pilot.

Down in the blue with the plane, strapped in, the body . . .

Awful, he thought. But the lake was blue, and wet-looking, and his mouth and throat raged with the thirst and he did not know where there might be another form of water he could drink. Besides, he had probably swallowed a ton of it while he was swimming out of the plane and getting to shore. In the movies they always showed the hero finding a clear spring with pure sweet water to drink but in the movies they didn't have plane wrecks and swollen foreheads and aching bodies and thirst that tore at the hero until he couldn't think.

Brian took small steps down the bank to the lake. Along the edge there were thick grasses and the water looked a little murky and there were small things swimming in the water, small bugs. But there was a log extending about twenty feet out into the water of the lake—a beaver drop from some time before—with old limbs sticking up, almost like handles. He balanced on the log, holding himself up with the limbs, and teetered out past the weeds and murky water.

When he was out where the water was clear and he could see no bugs swimming he kneeled on the log to drink. A sip, he thought, still worrying about the lake water—I'll just take a sip.

But when he brought a cupped hand to his mouth and felt the cold lake water trickle past his cracked lips and over his tongue he could not stop. He had never, not even on long bike trips in the hot summer, been this thirsty. It was as if the water were more than water, as if the water had become all of life, and he could not stop. He stooped and put his mouth to the lake and drank and drank, pulling it deep and swallowing great gulps of it. He drank until his stomach was swollen, until he nearly fell off the log with it, then he rose and stagger-tripped his way back to the bank.

Where he was immediately sick and threw up most of the water. But his thirst was gone and the water seemed to reduce the pain in his head as well—although the sunburn still cooked his face.

"So." He almost jumped with the word, spoken aloud. It seemed so out of place, the sound. He tried it again. "So. So. So here I am."

And there it is, he thought. For the first time since the crash his mind started to work, his brain triggered and he began thinking.

Here I am—and where is that?

Where am I?

He pulled himself once more up the bank to the tall tree without branches and sat again with his back against the rough bark. It was hot now, but the sun was high and to his rear and he sat in the shade of the tree in relative comfort. There were things to sort out.

Here I am and that is nowhere. With his mind opened and thoughts happening it all tried to come in with a rush, all of what had occurred and he could not take it. The whole thing turned into a confused jumble that made no sense. So he fought it down and tried to take one thing at a time.

He had been flying north to visit his father for a couple of months, in the summer, and the pilot had had a heart attack and had died, and the plane had crashed somewhere in the Canadian north woods but he did not know how far they had flown or in what direction or where he was . . .

Slow down, he thought. Slow down more.

My name is Brian Robeson and I am thirteen years old and I am alone in the north woods of Canada.

All right, he thought, that's simple enough.

I was flying to visit my father and the plane crashed and sank in a lake.

There, keep it that way. Short thoughts.

I do not know where I am.

Which doesn't mean much. More to the point, *they* do not know where I am—*they* meaning anybody who might be wanting to look for me. The searchers.

They would look for him, look for the plane. His father and mother would be frantic. They would tear the world apart to find him. Brian had seen searches on the news, seen movies about lost planes. When a plane went down they mounted extensive searches and almost always they found the plane within a day or two. Pilots all filed flight plans—a detailed plan for where and when they were going to fly, with all the courses explained. They would come, they would look for him. The searchers would get government planes and cover both sides of the flight plan filed by the pilot and search until they found him.

Maybe even today. They might come today. This was the second day after the crash. No. Brian frowned. Was it the first day or the second day? They had gone down in the afternoon and he had spent the whole night out cold. So this was the first real day. But they could still come today. They would have started the search immediately when Brian's plane did not arrive.

Yeah, they would probably come today.

Probably come in here with amphibious planes, small bushplanes with floats that could land right here on the lake and pick him up and take him home.

Which home? The father home or the mother home. He stopped the thinking. It didn't matter. Either on to his dad or back to his mother. Either way he would probably be home by late night or early morning, home where he could sit down and eat a large, cheesy, juicy burger with tomatoes and double fries with ketchup and a thick chocolate shake.

And there came hunger.

Brian rubbed his stomach. The hunger had been there but something else—fear, pain—had held it down. Now, with the thought of the burger, the emptiness roared at him. He could not believe the hunger, had never felt it this way. The lake water had filled his stomach but left it hungry, and now it demanded food, screamed for food.

And there was, he thought, absolutely nothing to eat.

Nothing.

What did they do in the movies when they got stranded like this? Oh, yes, the hero usually found some kind of plant that he knew was good to eat and that took care of it. Just ate the plant until he was full or used some kind of cute trap to catch an animal and cook it over a slick little fire and pretty soon he had a full eight-course meal.

The trouble, Brian thought, looking around, was that all he could see was grass and brush. There was nothing obvious to eat and aside from about a million birds and the beaver he hadn't seen animals to trap and cook, and even if he got one somehow he didn't have any matches so he couldn't have a fire . . .

Nothing.

It kept coming back to that. He had nothing.

Well, almost nothing. As a matter of fact, he thought, I don't know what I've got or haven't got. Maybe I should try and figure out just how I stand. It will give me something to do—keep me from thinking of food. Until they come to find me.

Brian had once had an English teacher, a guy named Perpich, who was always talking about being positive, thinking positive, staying on top of things.

That's how Perpich had put it—stay positive and stay on top of things. Brian thought of him now—wondered how to stay positive and stay on top of this. All Perpich would say is that I have to get motivated. He was always telling kids to get motivated.

Brian changed position so he was sitting on his knees. He reached into his pockets and took out everything he had and laid it on the grass in front of him.

It was pitiful enough. A quarter, three dimes, a nickel, and two pennies. A fingernail clipper. A billfold with a twenty-dollar bill—"In case you get stranded at the airport in some small town and have to buy food," his mother had said—and some odd pieces of paper.

And on his belt, somehow still there, the hatchet his mother had given him. He had forgotten it and now reached around and took it out and put it in the grass. There was a touch of rust already forming on the cutting edge of the blade and he rubbed it off with his thumbs.

That was it.

He frowned. No, wait—if he was going to play the game, might as well play it right. Perpich would tell him to quit messing around. Get motivated. Look at *all* of it, Robeson.

He had on a pair of good tennis shoes, now almost dry. And socks. And jeans and underwear and a thin leather belt and a T-shirt with a windbreaker so torn it hung on him in tatters.

And a watch. He had a digital watch still on his wrist but it was broken from the crash—the little screen blank—and he took it off and almost threw it away but stopped the hand motion and lay the watch on the grass with the rest of it.

There. That was it.

No, wait. One other thing. Those were all the things he had, but he also had himself. Perpich used to drum that into them—"You are your most valuable asset. Don't forget that. You are the best thing you have."

Brian looked around again. I wish you were here, Perpich. I'm hungry and I'd trade everything I have for a hamburger.

"I'm hungry." He said it aloud. In normal tones at first, then louder and louder until he was yelling it. "I'm hungry, I'm hungry, I'm hungry."

When he stopped there was a sudden silence, not just from him but the clicks and blurps and bird sounds of the forest as well. The noise of his voice had startled everything and it was quiet. He looked around, listened with his mouth open, and realized that in all his life he had never heard silence before. Complete silence. There had always been some sound, some kind of sound.

It lasted only a few seconds, but it was so intense that it seemed to become part of him. Nothing. There was no sound. Then the bird started again, and some kind of buzzing insect, and then a chattering and a cawing, and soon there was the same background of sound.

Which left him still hungry.

Of course, he thought, putting the coins and the rest back in his pocket and the hatchet in his belt—of course if they come tonight or even if they take as long as tomorrow the hunger is no big thing. People have gone for many days without food as long as they've got water. Even if they don't come until late tomorrow I'll be all right. Lose a little weight maybe, but the first hamburger and a malt and fries will bring it right back.

A mental picture of hamburger, the way they showed it in the television commercials, thundered into his thoughts. Rich colors, the meat juicy and hot . . .

He pushed the picture away. So even if they didn't find him until tomorrow, he thought, he would be all right. He had plenty of water, although he wasn't sure if it was good and clean or not.

He sat again by the tree, his back against it. There was a thing bothering him. He wasn't quite sure what it was but it kept chewing at the edge of his thoughts. Something about the plane and the pilot that would change things . . .

Ahh, there it was—the moment when the pilot had his heart attack his right foot had jerked down on the rudder pedal and the plane had slewed sideways. What did that mean? Why did that keep coming into his thinking that way, nudging and pushing?

It means, a voice in his thoughts said, that they might not be coming for you tonight or even tomorrow. When the pilot pushed the rudder pedal the plane had jerked to the side and assumed a new course. Brian could not remember how much it had pulled around, but it wouldn't have had to be much because after that, with the pilot dead, Brian had flown for hour after hour on the new course.

Well away from the flight plan the pilot had filed. Many hours, at maybe 160 miles an hour. Even if it was only a little off course, with that speed and time Brian might now be sitting several hundred miles off to the side of the recorded flight plan.

And they would probably search most heavily at first along the flight plan course. They might go out to the side a little, but he could easily be three, four hundred miles to the side. He could not know, could not think of how far he might have flown wrong because he didn't know the original course and didn't know how much they had pulled sideways.

Quite a bit—that's how he remembered it. Quite a jerk to the side. It pulled his head over sharply when the plane had swung around.

They might not find him for two or three days. He felt his heartbeat increase as the fear started. The thought was there but he fought it down for a time, pushed it away, then it exploded out.

They might not find him for a long time.

And the next thought was there as well, that they might never find him, but that was panic and he fought it down and tried to stay positive. They searched hard when a plane went down, they used many men and planes and they would go to the side, they would know he was off from the flight path, he had talked to the man on the radio, they would somehow know . . .

It would be all right.

They would soon find him. Maybe not tomorrow, but soon. Soon. Soon.

They would find him soon.

Gradually, like sloshing oil his thoughts settled back and the panic was gone. Say they didn't come for two days—no, say they didn't come for three days, even push that to four days—he could live with that. He would have to live with that. He didn't want to think of them taking longer. But say four days. He had to do something. He couldn't just sit at the bottom of this tree and stare down at the lake for four days.

And nights. He was in deep woods and didn't have any matches, couldn't make a fire. There were large things in the woods. There were wolves, he thought, and bears—other things. In the dark he would be in the open here, just sitting at the bottom of a tree.

He looked around suddenly, felt the hair on the back of his neck go up. Things might be looking at him right now, waiting for him—waiting for dark so they could move in and take him.

He fingered the hatchet at his belt. It was the only weapon he had, but it was something.

He had to have some kind of shelter. No, make that more: He had to have some kind of shelter and he had to have something to eat.

He pulled himself to his feet and jerked the back of his shirt down before the mosquitos could get at it. He had to do something to help himself.

I have to get motivated, he thought, remembering Perpich. Right now I'm all I've got. I have to do something.

CHAPTER 6

TWO YEARS before he and Terry had been fooling around down near the park, where the city seemed to end for a time and the trees grew thick and came down to the small river that went through the park. It was thick there and seemed kind of wild, and they had been joking and making things up and they pretended that they were lost in the woods and talked in the afternoon about what they would do. Of course they figured they'd have all sorts of goodies like a gun and a knife and fishing gear and matches so they could hunt and fish and have a fire.

I wish you were here, Terry, he thought. With a gun and a knife and some matches . . .

In the park that time they had decided the best shelter was a lean-to and Brian set out now to make one up. Maybe cover it with grass or leaves or sticks, he thought, and he started to go down to the lake again, where there were some willows he could cut down for braces. But it struck him that he ought to find a good place for the lean-to and so he decided to look around first. He wanted to stay near the lake because he thought the plane, even deep in the water, might show up to somebody flying over and he didn't want to diminish any chance he might have of being found.

His eyes fell upon the stone ridge to his left and he thought at first he should build his shelter against the stone. But before that he decided to check out the far side of the ridge and that was where he got lucky.

Using the sun and the fact that it rose in the east and set in the west, he decided that the far side was the northern side of the ridge. At one time in the far past it had been scooped by something, probably a glacier, and this scooping had left a kind of sideways bowl, back in under a ledge. It wasn't very deep, not a cave, but it was smooth and made a perfect roof and he could almost stand in under the ledge. He had to hold his head slightly tipped forward at the front to keep it from hitting the top. Some of the rock that had been scooped out had also been pulverized by the glacial action, turned into sand, and now made a small sand beach that went down to the edge of the water in front and to the right of the overhang.

It was his first good luck.

No, he thought. He had good luck in the landing. But this was good luck as well, luck he needed.

All he had to do was wall off part of the bowl and leave an opening as a doorway and he would have a perfect shelter—much stronger than a lean-to and dry because the overhang made a watertight roof.

He crawled back in, under the ledge, and sat. The sand was cool here in the shade, and the coolness felt wonderful to his face, which was already starting to blister and get especially painful on his forehead, with the blisters on top of the swelling.

He was also still weak. Just the walk around the back of the ridge and the slight climb over the top had left his legs rubbery. It felt good to sit for a bit under the shade of the overhang in the cool sand.

And now, he thought, if I just had something to eat.

Anything.

When he had rested a bit he went back down to the lake and drank a couple of swallows of water. He wasn't all that thirsty but he thought the water might help to take the edge off his hunger. It didn't. Somehow the cold lake water actually made it worse, sharpened it.

He thought of dragging in wood to make a wall on part of the overhang, and picked up one piece to pull up, but his arms were too weak and he knew then that it wasn't just the crash and injury to his body and head, it was also that he was weak from hunger.

He would have to find something to eat. Before he did anything else he would have to have something to eat.

But what?

Brian leaned against the rock and stared out at the lake. What, in all of this, was there to eat? He was so used to having food just be there, just always being there. When he was hungry he went to the icebox, or to the store, or sat down at a meal his mother cooked.

Oh, he thought, remembering a meal now—oh. It was last Thanksgiving, last year, the last Thanksgiving they had as a family before his mother demanded the divorce and his father moved out in the following January. Brian already knew the Secret but did not know it would cause them to break up and thought it might work out, the Secret that his father still did not know but that he would try to tell him. When he saw him.

The meal had been turkey and they cooked it in the back yard in the barbecue over charcoal with the lid down tight. His father had put hickory chips on the charcoal and the smell of the cooking turkey and the hickory smoke had filled the yard. When his father took the lid off, smiling, the smell that had come out was unbelievable, and when they sat to eat the meat was wet with juice and rich and had the taste of the smoke in it . . .

He had to stop this. His mouth was full of saliva and his stomach was twisting and growling.

What was there to eat?

What had he read or seen that told him about food in the wilderness? Hadn't there been something? A show, yes, a show on television about air force pilots and some kind of course they took. A survival course. All right, he had the show coming into his thoughts now. The pilots had to live in the desert. They put them in the desert down in Arizona or someplace and they had to live for a week. They had to find food and water for a week.

For water they made a sheet of plastic into a dew-gathering device and for food they ate lizards.

That was it. Of course Brian had lots of water and there weren't too many lizards in the Canadian woods, that he knew. One of the pilots had used a watch crystal as a magnifying glass to focus the sun and start a fire so they didn't have to eat the lizards raw. But Brian had a digital watch, without a crystal, broken at that. So the show didn't help him much.

Wait, there was one thing. One of the pilots, a woman, had found some kind of beans on a bush and she had used them with her lizard meat to make a little stew in a tin can she had found. Bean lizard stew. There weren't any beans here, but there must be berries. There had to be berry bushes around. That's what everybody always said. Well, he'd actually never heard anybody *say* it. But he felt that it should be true.

There must be berry bushes.

He stood and moved out into the sand and looked up at the sun. It was still high. He didn't know what time it must be. At home it would be one or two if the sun were that high. At home at one or two his mother would be putting away the lunch dishes and getting ready for her exercise class. No, that would have been yesterday. Today she would be going to see *him*. Today was Thursday and she always went to see him on Thursdays. Wednesday was the exercise class and Thursdays she went to see him. Hot little jets of hate worked into his thoughts, pushed once, moved back. If his mother hadn't begun to see *him* and forced the divorce, Brian wouldn't be here now.

He shook his head. Had to stop that kind of thinking. The sun was still high and that meant that he had some time before darkness to find berries. He didn't want to be away from his—he almost thought of it as home—shelter when it came to be dark.

He didn't want to be anywhere in the woods when it came to be dark. And he didn't want to get lost—which was a real problem. All he knew in the world was the lake in front of him and the hill at his back and the ridge—if he lost sight of them there was a really good chance that he would get turned around and not find his way back.

So he had to look for berry bushes, but keep the lake or the rock ridge in sight at all times.

He looked up the lake shore, to the north. For a good distance, perhaps two hundred yards, it was fairly clear. There were tall pines, the kind with no limbs until very close to the top, with a gentle breeze sighing in them, but not too much low brush. Two hundred yards up there seemed to be a belt of thick, lower brush starting—about ten or twelve feet high—and that formed a wall he could not see through. It seemed to go on around the lake, thick and lushly green, but he could not be sure.

If there were berries they would be in that brush, he felt, and as long as he stayed close to the lake, so he could keep the water on his right and know it was there, he wouldn't get lost. When he was done or found berries, he thought, he would just turn around so the water was on his left and walk back until he came to the ridge and his shelter.

Simple. Keep it simple. I am Brian Robeson. I have been in a plane crash. I am going to find some food. I am going to find some berries.

He walked slowly—still a bit pained in his joints and weak from hunger—up along the side of the lake. The trees were full of birds singing ahead of him in the sun. Some he knew, some he didn't. He saw a robin, and some kind of sparrows, and a flock of reddish orange birds with thick beaks. Twenty or thirty of them were sitting in one of the pines. They made much noise and flew away ahead of him when he walked under the tree. He watched them fly, their color a bright slash in solid green, and in this way he found the berries. The birds landed in some taller willow type of undergrowth with wide leaves and started jumping and making noise. At first he was too far away to see what they were doing, but their color drew him and he moved toward them, keeping the lake in sight on his right, and when he got closer he saw they were eating the berries.

He could not believe it was that easy. It was as if the birds had taken him right to the berries. The slender branches went up about twenty feet and were heavy, drooping with clusters of bright red berries. They were half as big as grapes but hung in bunches much like grapes and when Brian saw them, glistening red in the sunlight, he almost yelled.

His pace quickened and he was in them in moments, scattering the birds, grabbing branches, stripping them to fill his mouth with berries.

He almost spit them out. It wasn't that they were bitter so much as that they lacked any sweetness, had a tart flavor that left his mouth dry feeling. And they were like cherries in that they had large pits, which made them hard to chew. But there was such a hunger on him, such an emptiness, that he could not stop and kept stripping branches and eating berries by the handful, grabbing and jamming them into his mouth and swallowing them pits and all.

He could not stop and when, at last, his stomach was full he was still hungry. Two days without food must have shrunken his stomach, but the drive of hunger was still there. Thinking of the birds, and how they would come back into the berries when he left, he made a carrying pouch of his torn windbreaker and kept picking. Finally, when he judged he had close to four pounds in the jacket he stopped and went back to his camp by the ridge.

Now, he thought. Now I have some food and I can do something about fixing this place up. He glanced at the sun and saw he had some time before dark.

If only I had matches, he thought, looking ruefully at the beach and lakeside. There was driftwood everywhere, not to mention dead and dry wood all over the hill and dead-dry branches hanging from every tree. All firewood. And no matches. How did they used to do it? he thought. Rub two sticks together?

He tucked the berries in the pouch back in under the overhang in the cool shade and found a couple of sticks. After ten minutes of rubbing he felt the sticks and they were almost cool to the touch. Not that, he thought. They didn't do fire that way. He threw the sticks down in disgust. So no fire. But he could still fix the shelter and make it—here the word "safer" came into his mind and he didn't know why—more livable.

Kind of close it in, he thought. I'll close it in a bit.

He started dragging sticks up from the lake and pulling long dead branches down from the hill, never getting out of sight of the water and the ridge. With these he interlaced and wove a wall across the opening of the front of the rock. It took over two hours, and he had to stop several times because he still felt a bit weak and once because he felt a strange new twinge in his stomach. A tightening, rolling. Too many berries, he thought. I ate too many of them.

But it was gone soon and he kept working until the entire front of the overhang was covered save for a small opening at the right end, nearest the lake. The doorway was about three feet, and when he went in he found himself in a room almost fifteen feet long and eight to ten feet deep, with the rock wall sloping down at the rear.

"Good," he said, nodding. "Good . . ."

Outside the sun was going down, finally, and in the initial coolness the mosquitos came out again and clouded in on him. They were thick, terrible, if not quite as bad as in the morning, and he kept brushing them off his arms until he couldn't stand it and then dumped the berries and put the torn wind-breaker on. At least the sleeves covered his arms.

Wrapped in the jacket, with darkness coming down fast now, he crawled back in under the rock and huddled and tried to sleep. He was deeply tired, and still aching some, but sleep was slow coming and did not finally settle in until the evening cool turned to night cool and the mosquitos slowed.

Then, at last, with his stomach turning on the berries, Brian went to sleep.

CHAPTER 7

"MOTHER!"

He screamed it and he could not be sure if the scream awakened him or the pain in his stomach. His whole abdomen was torn with great rolling jolts of pain, pain that doubled him in the darkness of the little shelter, put him over and face down in the sand to moan again and again: "Mother, mother, mother . . ."

Never anything like this. Never. It was as if all the berries, all the pits had exploded in the center of him, ripped and tore at him. He crawled out the doorway and was sick in the sand, then crawled still farther and was sick again, vomiting and with terrible diarrhea for over an hour, for over a year he thought, until he was at last empty and drained of all strength.

Then he crawled back into the shelter and fell again to the sand but could not sleep at first, could do nothing except lie there, and his mind decided then to bring the memory up again.

In the mall. Every detail. His mother sitting in the station wagon with the man. And she had leaned across and kissed him, kissed the man with the short blond hair, and it was not a friendly peck, but a kiss. A kiss where she turned her head over at an angle and put her mouth against the mouth of the blond man who was not his father and kissed, mouth to mouth, and then brought her hand up to touch his cheek, his forehead, while they were kissing. And Brian saw it.

Saw this thing that his mother did with the blond man. Saw the kiss that became the Secret that his father still did not know about, know all about.

The memory was so real that he could feel the heat in the mall that day, could remember the worry that Terry would turn and see his mother, could remember the worry of the shame of it and then the memory faded and he slept again . . .

Awake.

For a second, perhaps two, he did not know where he was, was still in his sleep somewhere. Then he saw the sun streaming in the open doorway of the shelter and heard the close, vicious whine of the mosquitos and knew. He brushed his face, completely welted now with two days of bites, completely covered with lumps and bites, and was surprised to find the swelling on his forehead had gone down a great deal, was almost gone.

The smell was awful and he couldn't place it. Then he saw the pile of berries at the back of the shelter and remembered the night and being sick.

"Too many of them," he said aloud. "Too many gut cherries . . ."

He crawled out of the shelter and found where he'd messed the sand. He used sticks and cleaned it as best he could, covered it with clean sand and went down to the lake to wash his hands and get a drink.

It was still very early, only just past true dawn, and the water was so calm he could see his reflection. It frightened him—the face was cut and bleeding, swollen and lumpy, the hair all matted, and on his forehead a cut had healed but left the hair stuck with blood and scab. His eyes were slits in the bites and he was—somehow—covered with dirt. He slapped the water with his hand to destroy the mirror.

Ugly, he thought. Very, very ugly.

And he was, at that moment, almost overcome with self-pity. He was dirty and starving and bitten and hurt and lonely and ugly and afraid and so completely miserable that it was like being in a pit, a dark, deep pit with no way out.

He sat back on the bank and fought crying. Then let it come and cried for perhaps three, four minutes. Long tears, self-pity tears, wasted tears.

He stood, went back to the water, and took small drinks. As soon as the cold water hit his stomach he felt the hunger sharpen, as it had before, and he stood and held his abdomen until the hunger cramps receded.

He had to eat. He was weak with it again, down with the hunger, and he had to eat.

Back at the shelter the berries lay in a pile where he had dumped them when he grabbed his windbreaker—gut cherries he called them in his mind now—and he thought of eating some of them. Not such a crazy amount, as he had, which he felt brought on the sickness in the night—but just enough to stave off the hunger a bit.

He crawled into the shelter. Some flies were on the berries and he brushed them off. He selected only the berries that were solidly ripe—not the light red ones, but the berries that were dark, maroon red to black and swollen in ripeness. When he had a small handful of them he went back down to the lake and washed them in the water—small fish scattered away when he splashed the water up and he wished he had a fishing line and hook—then he ate them carefully, spitting out the pits. They were still tart, but had a sweetness to them, although they seemed to make his lips a bit numb.

When he finished he was still hungry, but the edge was gone and his legs didn't feel as weak as they had.

He went back to the shelter. It took him half an hour to go through the rest of the berries and sort them, putting all the fully ripe ones in a pile on some leaves, the rest in another pile. When he was done he covered the two piles with grass he tore from the lake shore to keep the flies off and went back outside.

They were awful berries, those gut cherries, he thought. But there was food there, food of some kind, and he could eat a bit more later tonight if he had to.

For now he had a full day ahead of him. He looked at the sky through the trees and saw that while there were clouds they were scattered and did not seem to hold rain. There was a light breeze that seemed to keep the mosquitos down and, he thought, looking up along the lake shore, if there was one kind of berry there should be other kinds. Sweeter kinds.

If he kept the lake in sight as he had done yesterday he should be all right, should be able to find home again—and it stopped him. He had actually thought it that time.

Home. Three days, no, two—or was it three? Yes, this was the third day and he had thought of the shelter as home.

He turned and looked at it, studied the crude work. The brush made a fair wall, not weathertight but it cut most of the wind off. He hadn't done so badly at that. Maybe it wasn't much, but also maybe it was all he had for a home.

All right, he thought, so I'll call it home.

He turned back and set off up the side of the lake, heading for the gut cherry bushes, his windbreaker-bag in his hand. Things were bad, he thought, but maybe not that bad.

Maybe he could find some better berries.

When he came to the gut cherry bushes he paused. The branches were empty of birds but still had many berries, and some of those that had been merely red yesterday were now a dark maroon to black. Much riper. Maybe he should stay and pick them to save them.

But the explosion in the night was still much in his memory and he decided to go on. Gut cherries were food, but tricky to eat. He needed something better.

Another hundred yards up the shore there was a place where the wind had torn another path. These must have been fierce winds, he thought, to tear up places like this—as they had the path he had found with the plane when he crashed. Here the trees were not all the way down but twisted and snapped off halfway up from the ground, so their tops were all down and rotted and gone, leaving the snags poking into the sky like broken teeth. It made for tons of dead and dry wood and he wished once more he could get a fire going. It also made a kind of clearing—with the tops of the trees gone the sun could get down to the ground— and it was filled with small thorny bushes that were covered with berries.

Raspberries.

These he knew because there were some raspberry bushes in the park and he and Terry were always picking and eating them when they biked past.

The berries were full and ripe, and he tasted one to find it sweet, and with none of the problems of the gut cherries. Although they did not grow in clusters, there were many of them and they were easy to pick and Brian smiled and started eating.

Sweet juice, he thought. Oh, they were sweet with just a tiny tang and he picked and ate and picked and ate and thought that he had never tasted anything this good. Soon, as before, his stomach was full, but now he had some sense and he did not gorge or cram more down. Instead he picked more and put them in his windbreaker, feeling the morning sun on his back and thinking he was rich, rich with food now, just rich, and he heard a noise to his rear, a slight noise, and he turned and saw the bear.

He could do nothing, think nothing. His tongue, stained with berry juice, stuck to the roof of his mouth and he stared at the bear. It was black, with a cinnamon-colored nose, not twenty feet from him and big. No, huge. It was all black fur and huge. He had seen one in the zoo in the city once, a black bear, but it had been from India or somewhere. This one was wild, and much bigger than the one in the zoo and it was right there.

Right there.

The sun caught the ends of the hairs along his back. Shining black and silky the bear stood on its hind legs, half up, and studied Brian, just studied him, then lowered itself and moved slowly to the left, eating berries as it rolled along, wuffling and delicately using its mouth to lift each berry from the stem, and in seconds it was gone. Gone, and Brian still had not moved. His tongue was stuck to the top of his mouth, the tip half out, his eyes were wide and his hands were reaching for a berry.

Then he made a sound, a low: "Nnnnnnggg." It made no sense, was just a sound of fear, of disbelief that something that large could have come so close to him without his knowing. It just walked up to him and could have eaten him and he could have done nothing. Nothing. And when the sound was half done a thing happened with his legs, a thing he had nothing to do with, and they were running in the opposite direction from the bear, back toward the shelter.

He would have run all the way, in panic, but after he had gone perhaps fifty yards his brain took over and slowed and, finally, stopped him.

If the bear had wanted you, his brain said, he would have taken you. It is something to understand, he thought, not something to run away from. The bear was eating berries.

Not people.

The bear made no move to hurt you, to threaten you. It stood to see you better, study you, then went on its way eating berries. It was a big bear, but it did not want you, did not want to cause you harm, and that is the thing to understand here.

He turned and looked back at the stand of raspberries. The bear was gone, the birds were singing, he saw nothing that could hurt him. There was no danger here that he could sense, could feel. In the city, at night, there was sometimes danger. You could not be in the park at night, after dark, because of the danger. But here, the bear had looked at him and had moved on and—this filled his thoughts—the berries were so good.

So good. So sweet and rich and his body was so empty.

And the bear had almost indicated that it didn't mind sharing—had just walked from him.

And the berries were so good.

And, he thought, finally, if he did not go back and get the berries he would have to eat the gut cherries again tonight.

That convinced him and he walked slowly back to the raspberry patch and continued picking for the entire morning, although with great caution, and once when a squirrel rustled some pine needles at the base of a tree he nearly jumped out of his skin.

About noon—the sun was almost straight overhead—the clouds began to thicken and look dark. In moments it started to rain and he took what he had picked and trotted back to the shelter. He had eaten probably two pounds of raspberries and had maybe another three pounds in his jacket, rolled in a pouch.

He made it to the shelter just as the clouds completely opened and the rain roared down in sheets. Soon the sand outside was drenched and there were rivulets running down to the lake. But inside he was dry and snug. He started to put the picked berries back in the sorted pile with the gut cherries but noticed that the raspberries were seeping through the jacket. They were much softer than the gut cherries and apparently were being crushed a bit with their own weight.

When he held the jacket up and looked beneath it he saw a stream of red liquid. He put a finger in it and found it to be sweet and tangy, like pop without the fizz, and he grinned and lay back on the sand, holding the bag up over his face and letting the seepage drip into his mouth.

Outside the rain poured down, but Brian lay back, drinking syrup from the berries, dry and with the pain almost all gone, the stiffness also gone, his belly full and a good taste in his mouth.

For the first time since the crash he was not thinking of himself, or his own life. Brian was wondering if the bear was as surprised as he to find another being in the berries.

Later in the afternoon, as evening came down, he went to the lake and washed the sticky berry juice from his face and hands, then went back to prepare for the night.

While he had accepted and understood that the bear did not want to hurt him, it was still much in his thoughts and as darkness came into the shelter he took the hatchet out of his belt and put it by his head, his hand on the handle, as the day caught up with him and he slept.

CHAPTER 8

A T FIRST he thought it was a growl. In the still darkness of the shelter in the middle of the night his eyes came open and he was awake and he thought there was a growl. But it was the wind, a medium wind in the pines had made some sound that brought him up, brought him awake. He sat up and was hit with the smell.

It terrified him. The smell was one of rot, some musty rot that made him think only of graves with cobwebs and dust and old death. His nostrils widened and he opened his eyes wider but he could see nothing. It was too dark, too hard dark with clouds covering even the small light from the stars, and he could not see. But the smell was alive, alive and full and in the shelter. He thought of the bear, thought of Bigfoot and every monster he had ever seen in every fright movie he had ever watched, and his heart hammered in his throat.

Then he heard the slithering. A brushing sound, a slithering brushing sound near his feet—and he kicked out as hard as he could, kicked out and threw the hatchet at the sound, a noise coming from his throat. But the hatchet missed, sailed into the wall where it hit the rocks with a shower of sparks, and his leg was instantly torn with pain as if a hundred needles had been driven into it. "Unnnngh!"

Now he screamed, with the pain and fear, and skittered on his backside up into the corner of the shelter, breathing through his mouth, straining to see, to hear.

The slithering moved again, he thought toward him at first, and terror took him, stopping his breath. He felt he could see a low dark form, a bulk in the darkness, a shadow that lived, but now it moved away, slithering and scraping it moved away and he saw or thought he saw it go out of the door opening.

He lay on his side for a moment, then pulled a rasping breath in and held it, listening for the attacker to return. When it was apparent that the shadow wasn't coming back he felt the calf of his leg, where the pain was centered and spreading to fill the whole leg.

His fingers gingerly touched a group of needles that had been driven through his pants and into the fleshy part of his calf. They were stiff and very sharp on the ends that stuck out, and he knew then what the attacker had been.

A porcupine had stumbled into his shelter and when he had kicked it the thing had slapped him with its tail of quills.

He touched each quill carefully. The pain made it seem as if dozens of them had been slammed into his leg, but there were only eight, pinning the cloth against his skin. He leaned back against the wall for a minute. He couldn't leave them in, they had to come out, but just touching them made the pain more intense.

So fast, he thought. So fast things change. When he'd gone to sleep he had satisfaction and in just a moment it was all different. He grasped one of the quills, held his breath, and jerked. It sent pain signals to his brain in tight waves, but he grabbed another, pulled it, then another quill. When he had pulled four of them he stopped for a moment. The pain had gone from being a pointed injury pain to spreading in a hot smear up his leg and it made him catch his breath.

Some of the quills were driven in deeper than others and they tore when they came out. He breathed deeply twice, let half of the breath out, and went back to work. Jerk, pause, jerk—and three more times before he lay back in the darkness, done. The pain filled his leg now, and with it came new waves of self-pity. Sitting alone in the dark, his leg aching, some mosquitos finding him again, he started crying. It was all too much, just too much, and he couldn't take it. Not the way it was.

I can't take it this way, alone with no fire and in the dark, and next time it might be something worse, maybe a bear, and it wouldn't be just quills in the leg, it would be worse. I can't do this, he thought, again and again. I can't. Brian pulled himself up until he was sitting upright back in the corner of the cave. He put his head down on his arms across his knees, with stiffness taking his left leg, and cried until he was cried out.

He did not know how long it took, but later he looked back on this time of crying in the corner of the dark cave and thought of it as when he learned the most important rule of survival, which was that feeling sorry for yourself didn't work. It wasn't just that it was wrong to do, or that it was considered incorrect. It was more than that—it didn't work. When he sat alone in the darkness and cried and was done, all done with it, nothing had changed. His leg still hurt, it was still dark, he was still alone and the self-pity had accomplished nothing.

At last he slept again, but already his patterns were changing and the sleep was light, a resting doze more than a deep sleep, with small sounds awakening him twice in the rest of the night. In the last doze period before daylight, before he awakened finally with the morning light and the clouds of new mosquitos, he dreamed. This time it was not of his mother, not of the Secret, but of his father at first and then of his friend Terry.

In the initial segment of the dream his father was standing at the side of a living room looking at him and it was clear from his expression that he was trying to tell Brian something. His lips moved but there was no sound, not a whisper. He waved his hands at Brian, made gestures in front of his face as if he were scratching something, and he worked to make a word with his mouth but at first Brian could not see it. Then the lips made an *mmmmm* shape but no sound came. *Mmmmm—maaaa*. Brian could not hear it, could not understand it and he wanted to so badly; it was so important to understand his father, to know what he was saying. He was trying to help, trying so hard, and when Brian couldn't understand he looked cross, the way he did when Brian asked questions more than once, and he faded. Brian's father faded into a fog place Brian could not see and the dream was almost over, or seemed to be, when Terry came.

1057

He was not gesturing to Brian but was sitting in the park at a bench looking at a barbecue pit and for a time nothing happened. Then he got up and poured some charcoal from a bag into the cooker, then some starter fluid, and he took a flick type of lighter and lit the fluid. When it was burning and the charcoal was at last getting hot he turned, noticing Brian for the first time in the dream. He turned and smiled and pointed to the fire as if to say, see, a fire.

But it meant nothing to Brian, except that he wished he had a fire. He saw a grocery sack on the table next to Terry. Brian thought it must contain hot dogs and chips and mustard and he could think only of the food. But Terry shook his head and pointed again to the fire, and twice more he pointed to the fire, made Brian see the flames, and Brian felt his frustration and anger rise and he thought all right, all right, I see the fire but so what? I don't have a fire. I know about fire; I know I need a fire.

I know that.

His eyes opened and there was light in the cave, a gray dim light of morning. He wiped his mouth and tried to move his leg, which had stiffened like wood. There was thirst, and hunger, and he ate some raspberries from the jacket. They had spoiled a bit, seemed softer and mushier, but still had a rich sweetness. He crushed the berries against the roof of his mouth with his tongue and drank the sweet juice as it ran down his throat. A flash of metal caught his eye and he saw his hatchet in the sand where he had thrown it at the porcupine in the dark.

He scootched up, wincing a bit when he bent his stiff leg, and crawled to where the hatchet lay. He picked it up and examined it and saw a chip in the top of the head.

The nick wasn't large, but the hatchet was important to him, was his only tool, and he should not have thrown it. He should keep it in his hand, and make a tool of some kind to help push an animal away. Make a staff, he thought, or a lance, and save the hatchet. Something came then, a thought as he held the hatchet, something about the dream and his father and Terry, but he couldn't pin it down.

"Ahhh . . ." He scrambled out and stood in the morning sun and stretched his back muscles and his sore leg. The hatchet was still in his hand, and as he stretched and raised it over his head it caught the first rays of the morning sun. The first faint light hit the silver of the hatchet and it flashed a brilliant gold in the light. Like fire. That is it, he thought. What they were trying to tell me.

Fire. The hatchet was the key to it all. When he threw the hatchet at the porcupine in the cave and missed and hit the stone wall it had showered sparks, a golden shower of sparks in the dark, as golden with fire as the sun was now.

The hatchet was the answer. That's what his father and Terry had been trying to tell him. Somehow he could get fire from the hatchet. The sparks would make fire.

Brian went back into the shelter and studied the wall. It was some form of chalky granite, or a sandstone, but imbedded in it were large pieces of a darker stone, a harder and darker stone. It only took him a moment to find where the hatchet had struck. The steel had nicked into the edge of one of the darker stone pieces. Brian turned the head backward so he would strike with the flat rear of the hatchet and hit the black rock gently. Too gently, and nothing happened. He struck harder, a glancing blow, and two or three weak sparks skipped off the rock and died immediately.

He swung harder, held the hatchet so it would hit a longer, sliding blow, and the black rock exploded in fire. Sparks flew so heavily that several of them skittered and jumped on the sand beneath the rock and he smiled and struck again and again.

There could be fire here, he thought. I will have a fire here, he thought, and struck again—I will have fire from the hatchet.

CHAPTER 9

B RIAN FOUND it was a long way from sparks to fire. Clearly there had to be something for the sparks to ignite, some kind of tinder or kindling—but what? He brought some dried grass in, tapped sparks into it, and watched them die. He tried small twigs, breaking them into little pieces, but that was worse than the grass. Then he tried a combination of the two, grass and twigs.

Nothing. He had no trouble getting sparks, but the tiny bits of hot stone or metal—he couldn't tell which they were—just sputtered and died.

He settled back on his haunches in exasperation, looking at the pitiful clump of grass and twigs.

He needed something finer, something soft and fine and fluffy to catch the bits of fire.

Shredded paper would be nice, but he had no paper.

"So close," he said aloud, "so close . . ."

He put the hatchet back in his belt and went out of the shelter, limping on his sore leg. There had to be something, had to be. Man had made fire. There had been fire for thousands, millions of years. There had to be a way. He dug in his pockets and found the twenty-dollar bill in his wallet. Paper. Worthless paper out here. But if he could get a fire going . . .

He ripped the twenty into tiny pieces, made a pile of pieces, and hit sparks into them. Nothing happened. They just wouldn't take the sparks. But there had to be a way—some way to do it.

Not twenty feet to his right, leaning out over the water were birches and he stood looking at them for a full half-minute before they registered on his mind. They were a beautiful white with bark like clean, slightly speckled paper.

Paper.

He moved to the trees. Where the bark was peeling from the trunks it lifted in tiny tendrils, almost fluffs. Brian plucked some of them loose, rolled them in his fingers. They seemed flammable, dry and nearly powdery. He pulled and twisted bits off the trees, packing them in one hand while he picked them with the other, picking and gathering until he had a wad close to the size of a baseball.

Then he went back into the shelter and arranged the ball of birchbark peelings at the base of the black rock. As an after-thought he threw in the remains of the twenty-dollar bill. He struck and a stream of sparks fell into the bark and quickly died. But this time one spark fell on one small hair of dry bark—almost a thread of bark—and seemed to glow a bit brighter before it died.

The material had to be finer. There had to be a soft and incredibly fine nest for the sparks.

I must make a home for the sparks, he thought. A perfect home or they won't stay, they won't make fire.

He started ripping the bark, using his fingernails at first, and when that didn't work he used the sharp edge of the hatchet, cutting the bark in thin slivers, hairs so fine they were almost not there. It was painstaking work, slow work, and he stayed with it for over two hours. Twice he stopped for a handful of berries and once to go to the lake for a drink. Then back to work, the sun on his back, until at last he had a ball of fluff as big as a grapefruit—dry birchbark fluff.

He positioned his spark nest—as he thought of it—at the base of the rock, used his thumb to make a small depression in the middle, and slammed the back of the hatchet down across the black rock. A cloud of sparks rained down, most of them missing the nest, but some, perhaps thirty or so, hit in the depression and of those six or seven found fuel and grew, smoldered and caused the bark to take on the red glow.

Then they went out.

Close—he was close. He repositioned the nest, made a new and smaller dent with his thumb, and struck again.

More sparks, a slight glow, then nothing.

It's me, he thought. I'm doing something wrong. I do not know this—a cave dweller would have had a fire by now, a Cro-Magnon man would have a fire by now—but I don't know this. I don't know how to make a fire.

Maybe not enough sparks. He settled the nest in place once more and hit the rock with a series of blows, as fast as he could. The sparks poured like a golden waterfall. At first they seemed to take, there were several, many sparks that found life and took briefly, but they all died.

Starved.

He leaned back. They are like me. They are starving. It wasn't quantity, there were plenty of sparks, but they needed more.

I would kill, he thought suddenly, for a book of matches. Just one book. Just one match. I would kill.

What makes fire? He thought back to school. To all those science classes. Had he ever learned what made a fire? Did a teacher ever stand up there and say, "This is what makes a fire . . ."

He shook his head, tried to focus his thoughts. What did it take? You have to have fuel, he thought—and he had that. The bark was fuel. Oxygen—there had to be air.

He needed to add air. He had to fan on it, blow on it.

He made the nest ready again, held the hatchet backward, tensed, and struck four quick blows. Sparks came down and he leaned forward as fast as he could and blew.

Too hard. There was a bright, almost intense glow, then it was gone. He had blown it out.

Another set of strikes, more sparks. He leaned and blew, but gently this time, holding back and aiming the stream of air from his mouth to hit the brightest spot. Five or six sparks had fallen in a tight mass of bark hair and Brian centered his efforts there.

The sparks grew with his gentle breath. The red glow moved from the sparks themselves into the bark, moved and grew and became worms, glowing red worms that crawled up the bark hairs and caught other threads of bark and grew until there was a pocket of red as big as a quarter, a glowing red coal of heat.

And when he ran out of breath and paused to inhale, the red ball suddenly burst into flame.

"Fire!" He yelled. "I've got fire! I've got it, I've got, I've got it . . ."

But the flames were thick and oily and burning fast, consuming the ball of bark as fast as if it were gasoline. He had to feed the flames, keep them going.

Working as fast as he could he carefully placed the dried grass and wood pieces he had tried at first on top of the bark and was gratified to see them take.

But they would go fast. He needed more, and more. He could not let the flames go out.

He ran from the shelter to the pines and started breaking off the low, dead small limbs. These he threw in the shelter, went back for more, threw those in, and squatted to break and feed the hungry flames. When the small wood was going well he went out and found larger wood and did not relax until that was going. Then he leaned back against the wood brace of his door opening and smiled.

I have a friend, he thought—I have a friend now. A hungry friend, but a good one. I have a friend named fire.

"Hello, fire . . ."

The curve of the rock back made an almost perfect drawing flue that carried the smoke up through the cracks of the roof but held the heat. If he kept the fire small it would be perfect and would keep anything like the porcupine from coming through the door again.

A friend and a guard, he thought.

So much from a little spark. A friend and a guard from a tiny spark.

He looked around and wished he had somebody to tell this thing, to show this thing he had done. But there was nobody.

Nothing but the trees and the sun and the breeze and the lake.

Nobody.

And he thought, rolling thoughts, with the smoke curling up over his head and the smile still half on his face he thought: I wonder what they're doing now.

I wonder what my father is doing now.

I wonder what my mother is doing now.

I wonder if she is with him.

CHAPTER 10

H E COULD NOT at first leave the fire. It was so precious to him, so close and sweet a thing, the yellow and red flames brightening the dark interior of the shelter, the happy crackle of the dry wood as it burned, that he could not leave it. He went to the trees and brought in as many dead limbs as he could chop off and carry, and when he had a large pile of them he sat near the fire—though it was getting into the warm middle part of the day and he was hot—and broke them in small pieces and fed the fire.

I will not let you go out, he said to himself, to the flames—not ever. And so he sat through a long part of the day, keeping the flames even, eating from his stock of raspberries, leaving to drink from the lake when he was thirsty. In the afternoon, toward evening, with his face smoke smeared and his skin red from the heat, he finally began to think ahead to what he needed to do.

He would need a large woodpile to get through the night. It would be almost impossible to find wood in the dark so he had to have it all in and cut and stacked before the sun went down.

Brian made certain the fire was banked with new wood, then went out of the shelter and searched for a good fuel supply. Up the hill from the campsite the same windstorm that left him a place to land the plane—had that only been three, four days ago?—had dropped three large white pines across each other.

They were dead now, dry and filled with weathered dry dead limbs—enough for many days. He chopped and broke and carried wood back to the camp, stacking the pieces under the overhang until he had what he thought to be an enormous pile, as high as his head and six feet across the base. Between trips he added small pieces to the fire to keep it going and on one of the trips to get wood he noticed an added advantage of the fire. When he was in the shade of the trees breaking limbs the mosquitos swarmed on him, as usual, but when he came to the fire, or just near the shelter where the smoke eddied and swirled, the insects were gone.

It was a wonderful discovery. The mosquitos had nearly driven him mad and the thought of being rid of them lifted his spirits. On another trip he looked back and saw the smoke curling up through the trees and realized, for the first time, that he now had the means to make a signal. He could carry a burning stick and build a signal and perhaps attract attention.

Which meant more wood. And still more wood. There did not seem to be an end to the wood he would need and he spent all the rest of the afternoon into dusk making wood trips.

At dark he settled in again for the night, next to the fire with the stack of short pieces ready to put on, and he ate the rest of the raspberries. During all the work of the day his leg had loosened but it still ached a bit, and he rubbed it and watched the fire and thought for the first time since the crash that he might be getting a handle on things, might be starting to do something other than just sit.

He was out of food, but he could look tomorrow and he could build a signal fire tomorrow and get more wood tomorrow . . .

The fire cut the night coolness and settled him back into sleep, thinking of tomorrow.

He slept hard and wasn't sure what awakened him but his eyes came open and he stared into the darkness. The fire had burned down and looked out but he stirred with a piece of wood and found a bed of coals still glowing hot and red. With small pieces of wood and careful blowing he soon had a blaze going again.

It had been close. He had to be sure to try and sleep in short intervals so he could keep the fire going, and he tried to think of a way to regulate his sleep but it made him sleepy to think about it and he was just going under again when he heard the sound outside.

It was not unlike the sound of the porcupine, something slithering and being dragged across the sand, but when he looked out the door opening it was too dark to see anything.

Whatever it was it stopped making that sound in a few moments and he thought he heard something sloshing into the water at the shoreline, but he had the fire now and plenty of wood so he wasn't as worried as he had been the night before.

He dozed, slept for a time, awakened again just at dawn-gray light, and added wood to the still-smoking fire before standing outside and stretching. Standing with his arms stretched over his head and the tight knot of hunger in his stomach, he looked toward the lake and saw the tracks.

They were strange, a main center line up from the lake in the sand with claw marks to the side leading to a small pile of sand, then going back down to the water.

He walked over and squatted near them, studied them, tried to make sense of them.

Whatever had made the tracks had some kind of flat dragging bottom in the middle and was apparently pushed along by the legs that stuck out to the side.

Up from the water to a small pile of sand, then back down into the water. Some animal. Some kind of water animal that came up to the sand to . . . to do what?

To do something with the sand, to play and make a pile in the sand?

He smiled. City boy, he thought. Oh, you city boy with your city ways—he made a mirror in his mind, a mirror of himself, and saw how he must look. City boy with your city ways sitting in the sand trying to read the tracks and not knowing, not understanding. Why would anything wild come up from the water to play in the sand? Not that way, animals weren't that way. They didn't waste time that way.

It had come up from the water for a reason, a good reason, and he must try to understand the reason, he must change to fully understand the reason himself or he would not make it.

It had come up from the water for a reason, and the reason, he thought, squatting, the reason had to do with the pile of sand.

He brushed the top off gently with his hand but found only damp sand. Still, there must be a reason and he carefully kept scraping and digging until, about four inches down, he suddenly came into a small chamber in the cool-damp sand and there lay eggs, many eggs, almost perfectly round eggs the size of table tennis balls, and he laughed then because he knew.

It had been a turtle. He had seen a show on television about sea turtles that came up onto beaches and laid their eggs in the sand. There must be freshwater lake turtles that did the same. Maybe snapping turtles. He had heard of snapping turtles. They became fairly large, he thought. It must have been a snapper that came up in the night when he heard the noise that awakened him; she must have come then and laid the eggs.

Food.

More than eggs, more than knowledge, more than anything this was food. His stomach tightened and rolled and made noise as he looked at the eggs, as if his stomach belonged to somebody else or had seen the eggs with its own eyes and was demanding food. The hunger, always there, had been somewhat controlled and dormant when there was nothing to eat but with the eggs came the scream to eat. His whole body craved food with such an intensity that it quickened his breath.

He reached into the nest and pulled the eggs out one at a time. There were seventeen of them, each as round as a ball, and white. They had leathery shells that gave instead of breaking when he squeezed them.

When he had them heaped on the sand in a pyramid—he had never felt so rich somehow—he suddenly realized that he did not know how to eat them.

He had a fire but no way to cook them, no container, and he had never thought of eating a raw egg. He had an uncle named Carter, his father's brother, who always put an egg in a glass of milk and drank it in the morning. Brian had watched him do it once, just once, and when the runny part of the white left the glass and went into his uncle's mouth and down the throat in a single gulp Brian almost lost everything he had ever eaten.

Still, he thought. Still. As his stomach moved toward his backbone he became less and less fussy. Some natives in the world ate grasshoppers and ants and if they could do that he could get a raw egg down.

He picked one up and tried to break the shell and found it surprisingly tough. Finally, using the hatchet he sharpened a stick and poked a hole in the egg. He widened the hole with his finger and looked inside. Just an egg. It had a dark yellow yolk and not so much white as he thought there would be.

Just an egg.

Food.

Just an egg he had to eat.

Raw.

He looked out across the lake and brought the egg to his mouth and closed his eyes and sucked and squeezed the egg at the same time and swallowed as fast as he could.

"Ecch . . ."

It had a greasy, almost oily taste, but it was still an egg. His throat tried to throw it back up, his whole body seemed to convulse with it, but his stomach took it, held it, and demanded more.

The second egg was easier, and by the third one he had no trouble at all—it just slid down. He ate six of them, could have easily eaten all of them and not been full, but a part of him said to hold back, save the rest.

He could not now believe the hunger. The eggs had awakened it fully, roaringly, so that it tore at him. After the sixth egg he ripped the shell open and licked the inside clean, then went back and ripped the other five open and licked them out as well and wondered if he could eat the shells. There must be some food value in them. But when he tried they were too leathery to chew and he couldn't get them down.

He stood away from the eggs for a moment, literally stood and turned away so that he could not see them. If he looked at them he would have to eat more.

He would store them in the shelter and eat only one a day. He fought the hunger down again, controlled it. He would take them now and store them and save them and eat one a day, and he realized as he thought it that he had forgotten that *they* might come. The searchers. Surely, they would come before he could eat all the eggs at one a day.

He had forgotten to think about them and that wasn't good. He had to keep thinking of them because if he forgot them and did not think of them they might forget about him.

And he had to keep hoping.

He had to keep hoping.

CHAPTER 11

THERE WERE these things to do.

He transferred all the eggs from the small beach into the shelter, reburying them near his sleeping area. It took all his will to keep from eating another one as he moved them, but he got it done and when they were out of sight again it was easier. He added wood to the fire and cleaned up the camp area.

A good laugh, that—cleaning up the camp. All he did was shake out his windbreaker and hang it in the sun to dry the berry juice that had soaked in, and smooth the sand where he slept.

But it was a mental thing. He had gotten depressed thinking about how they hadn't found him yet, and when he was busy and had something to do the depression seemed to leave.

So there were things to do.

With the camp squared away he brought in more wood. He had decided to always have enough on hand for three days and after spending one night with the fire for a friend he knew what a staggering amount of wood it would take. He worked all through the morning at the wood, breaking down dead limbs and breaking or chopping them in smaller pieces, storing them neatly beneath the overhang. He stopped once to take a drink at the lake and in his reflection he saw that the swelling on his head was nearly gone. There was no pain there so he assumed that had taken care of itself. His leg was also back to normal, although he had a small pattern of holes—roughly star-shaped—where the quills had nailed him, and while he was standing at the lake shore taking stock he noticed that his body was changing.

He had never been fat, but he had been slightly heavy with a little extra weight just above his belt at the sides.

This was completely gone and his stomach had caved in to the hunger and the sun had cooked him past burning so he was tanning, and with the smoke from the fire his face was starting to look like leather. But perhaps more than his body was the change in his mind, or in the way he was—was becoming.

I am not the same, he thought. I see, I hear differently. He did not know when the change started, but it was there; when a sound came to him now he didn't just hear it but would know the sound. He would swing and look at it—a breaking twig, a movement of air—and know the sound as if he somehow could move his mind back down the wave of sound to the source.

He could know what the sound was before he quite realized he had heard it. And when he saw something—a bird moving a wing inside a bush or a ripple on the water—he would truly see that thing, not just notice it as he used to notice things in the city. He would see all parts of it; see the whole wing, the feathers, see the color of the feathers, see the bush, and the size and shape and color of its leaves. He would see the way the light moved with the ripples on the water and see that the wind made the ripples and which way that wind had to blow to make the ripples move in that certain way.

None of that used to be in Brian and now it was a part of him, a changed part of him, a grown part of him, and the two things, his mind and his body, had come together as well, had made a connection with each other that he didn't quite understand. When his ears heard a sound or his eyes saw a sight his mind took control of his body. Without his thinking, he moved to face the sound or sight, moved to make ready for it, to deal with it.

There were these things to do.

When the wood was done he decided to get a signal fire ready. He moved to the top of the rock ridge that comprised the bluff over his shelter and was pleased to find a large, flat stone area.

More wood, he thought, moaning inwardly. He went back to the fallen trees and found more dead limbs, carrying them up on the rock until he had enough for a bonfire. Initially he had thought of making a signal fire every day but he couldn't—he would never be able to keep the wood supply going. So while he was working he decided to have the fire ready and if he heard an engine, or even thought he heard a plane engine, he would run up with a burning limb and set off the signal fire.

Things to do.

At the last trip to the top of the stone bluff with wood he stopped, sat on the point overlooking the lake, and rested. The lake lay before him, twenty or so feet below, and he had not seen it this way since he had come in with the plane.

Remembering the crash he had a moment of fear, a breath-tightening little rip of terror, but it passed and he was quickly caught up in the beauty of the scenery.

It was so incredibly beautiful that it was almost unreal. From his height he could see not just the lake but across part of the forest, a green carpet, and it was full of life. Birds, insects—there was a constant hum and song. At the other end of the bottom of the L there was another large rock sticking out over the water and on top of the rock a snaggly pine had somehow found food and grown, bent and gnarled. Sitting on one limb was a blue bird with a crest and sharp beak, a kingfisher—he thought of a picture he had seen once—which left the branch while he watched and dove into the water. It emerged a split part of a second later. In its mouth was a small fish, wiggling silver in the sun. It took the fish to a limb, juggled it twice, and swallowed it whole.

Fish.

Of course, he thought. There were fish in the lake and they were food. And if a bird could do it . . .

He scrambled down the side of the bluff and trotted to the edge of the lake, looking down into the water. Somehow it had never occurred to him to look *inside* the water—only at the surface. The sun was flashing back up into his eyes and he moved off to the side and took his shoes off and waded out fifteen feet. Then he turned and stood still, with the sun at his back, and studied the water again.

It was, he saw after a moment, literally packed with life. Small fish swam everywhere, some narrow and long, some round, most of them three or four inches long, some a bit larger and many smaller. There was a patch of mud off to the side, leading into deeper water, and he could see old clam shells there, so there must be clams. As he watched, a crayfish, looking like a tiny lobster, left one of the empty clam shells and went to another looking for something to eat, digging with its claws.

While he stood some of the small, roundish fish came quite close to his legs and he tensed, got ready, and made a wild stab at grabbing one of them. They exploded away in a hundred flicks of quick light, so fast that he had no hope of catching them that way. But they soon came back, seemed to be curious about him, and as he walked from the water he tried to think of a way to use that curiosity to catch them.

He had no hooks or string but if he could somehow lure them into the shallows—and make a spear, a small fish spear—he might be able to strike fast enough to get one.

He would have to find the right kind of wood, slim and straight—he had seen some willows up along the lake that might work—and he could use the hatchet to sharpen it and shape it while he was sitting by the fire tonight. And that brought up the fire, which he had to feed again. He looked at the sun and saw it was getting late in the afternoon, and when he thought of how late it was he thought that he ought to reward all his work with another egg and that made him think that some kind of dessert would be nice—he smiled when he thought of dessert, so fancy—and he wondered if he should move up the lake and see if he could find some raspberries after he banked the fire and while he was looking for the right wood for a spear. Spearwood, he thought, and it all rolled together, just rolled together and rolled over him . . .

There were these things to do.

CHAPTER 12

T HE FISH SPEAR didn't work.

He stood in the shallows and waited, again and again. The small fish came closer and closer and he lunged time after time but was always too slow. He tried throwing it, jabbing it, everything but flailing with it, and it didn't work. The fish were just too fast.

He had been so sure, so absolutely certain that it would work the night before. Sitting by the fire he had taken the willow and carefully peeled the bark until he had a straight staff about six feet long and just under an inch thick at the base, the thickest end.

Then, propping the hatchet in a crack in the rock wall, he had pulled the head of his spear against it, carving a thin piece off each time, until the thick end tapered down to a needle point. Still not satisfied—he could not imagine hitting one of the fish with a single point—he carefully used the hatchet to split the point up the middle for eight or ten inches and jammed a piece of wood up into the split to make a two-prong spear with the points about two inches apart. It was crude, but it looked effective and seemed to have good balance when he stood outside the shelter and hefted the spear.

He had worked on the fish spear until it had become more than just a tool. He'd spent hours and hours on it, and now it didn't work. He moved into the shallows and stood and the fish came to him. Just as before they swarmed around his legs, some of them almost six inches long, but no matter how he tried they were too fast. At first he tried throwing it but that had no chance. As soon as he brought his arm back—well before he threw—the movement frightened them. Next he tried lunging at them, having the spear ready just above the water and thrusting with it. Finally he actually put the spear in the water and waited until the fish were right in front of it, but still somehow he telegraphed his motion before he thrust and they saw it and flashed away.

He needed something to spring the spear forward, some way to make it move faster than the fish—some motive force. A string that snapped—or a bow. A bow and arrow. A thin, long arrow with the point in the water and the bow pulled back so that all he had to do was release the arrow . . . yes. That was it.

He had to "invent" the bow and arrow—he almost laughed as he moved out of the water and put his shoes on. The morning sun was getting hot and he took his shirt off. Maybe that was how it really happened, way back when—some primitive man tried to spear fish and it didn't work and he "invented" the bow and arrow. Maybe it was always that way, discoveries happened because they needed to happen.

He had not eaten anything yet this morning so he took a moment to dig up the eggs and eat one, then he reburied them, banked the fire with a couple of thicker pieces of wood, settled the hatchet on his belt and took the spear in his right hand and set off up the lake to find wood to make a bow. He went without a shirt but something about the wood smoke smell on him kept the insects from bothering him as he walked to the berry patch. The raspberries were starting to become overripe, just in two days, and he would have to pick as many as possible after he found the wood but he did take a little time now to pick a few and eat them. They were full and sweet and when he picked one, two others would fall off the limbs into the grass and soon his hands and cheeks were covered with red berry juice and he was full. That surprised him—being full.

He hadn't thought he would ever be full again, knew only the hunger, and here he was full. One turtle egg and a few handfuls of berries and he felt full. He looked down at his stomach and saw that it was still caved in—did not bulge out as it would have with two hamburgers and a freezy slush. It must have shrunk. And there was still hunger there, but not like it was—not tearing at him. This was hunger that he knew would be there always, even when he had food—a hunger that made him look for things, see things. A hunger to make him hunt.

He swung his eyes across the berries to make sure the bear wasn't there, at his back, then he moved down to the lake. The spear went out before him automatically, moving the brush away from his face as he walked, and when he came to the water's edge he swung left. Not sure what he was looking for, not knowing what wood might be best for a bow—he had never made a bow, never shot a bow in his life—but it seemed that it would be along the lake, near the water.

He saw some young birch, and they were springy, but they lacked snap somehow, as did the willows. Not enough whip-back.

Halfway up the lake, just as he started to step over a log, he was absolutely terrified by an explosion under his feet. Something like a feathered bomb blew up and away in a flurry of leaves and thunder. It frightened him so badly that he fell back and down and then it was gone, leaving only an image in his mind.

A bird, it had been, about the size of a very small chicken only with a fantail and stubby wings that slammed against its body and made loud noise. Noise there and gone. He got up and brushed himself off. The bird had been speckled, brown and gray, and it must not be very smart because Brian's foot had been nearly on it before it flew. Half a second more and he would have stepped on it.

And caught it, he thought, and eaten it. He might be able to catch one, or spear one. Maybe, he thought, maybe it tasted like chicken. Maybe he could catch one or spear on and it probably did taste just like chicken. Just like chicken when his mother baked it in the oven with garlic and salt and it turned golden brown and crackled. . . .

He shook his head to drive the picture out and moved down to the shore. There was a tree there with long branches that seemed straight and when he pulled on one of them and let go it had an almost vicious snap to it. He picked one of the limbs that seemed right and began chopping where the limb joined the tree.

The wood was hard and he didn't want to cause it to split so he took his time, took small chips and concentrated so hard that at first he didn't hear it.

A persistent whine, like the insects only more steady with an edge of a roar to it, was in his ears and he chopped and cut and was thinking of a bow, how he would make a bow, how it would be when he shaped it with the hatchet and still the sound did not cut through until the limb was nearly off the tree and the whine was inside his head and he knew it then.

A plane! It was a motor, far off but seeming to get louder. They were coming for him!

He threw down the limb and his spear and, holding the hatchet, he started to run for camp. He had to get fire up on the bluff and signal to them, get fire and smoke up. He put all of his life into his legs, jumped logs and moved through brush like a light ghost, swiveling and running, his lungs filling and blowing and now the sound was louder, coming in his direction.

If not right at him, at least closer. He could see it all in his mind now, the picture, the way it would be. He would get the fire going and the plane would see the smoke and circle, circle once, then again, and waggle its wings. It would be a float plane and it would land on the water and come across the lake and the pilot would be amazed that he was alive after all these days.

All this he saw as he ran for the camp and the fire. They would take him from here and this night, this very night, he would sit with his father and eat and tell him all the things. He could see it now. Oh, yes, all as he ran in the sun, his legs liquid springs. He got to the camp still hearing the whine of the engine, and one stick of wood still had good flame.

He dove inside and grabbed the wood and ran around the edge of the ridge, scrambled up like a cat and blew and nearly had the flame feeding, growing, when the sound moved away.

It was abrupt, as if the plane had turned. He shielded the sun from his eyes and tried to see it, tried to make the plane become real in his eyes. But the trees were so high, so thick, and now the sound was still fainter. He kneeled again to the flames and blew and added grass and chips and the flames fed and grew and in moments he had a bonfire as high as his head but the sound was gone now.

Look back, he thought. Look back and see the smoke now and turn, please turn.

"Look back," he whispered, feeling all the pictures fade, seeing his father's face fade like the sound, like lost dreams, like an end to hope. Oh, turn now and come back, look back and see the smoke and turn for me. . . .

But it kept moving away until he could not hear it even in his imagination, in his soul. Gone. He stood on the bluff over the lake, his face cooking in the roaring bonfire, watching the clouds of ash and smoke going into the sky and thought—no, more than thought—he knew then that he would not get out of this place. Not now, not ever.

That had been a search plane. He was sure of it. That must have been them and they had come as far off to the side of the flight plan as they thought they would have to come and then turned back. They did not see his smoke, did not hear the cry from his mind.

They would not return. He would never leave now, never get out of here. He went down to his knees and felt the tears start, cutting through the smoke and ash on his face, silently falling onto the stone.

Gone, he thought finally, it was all gone. All silly and gone. No bows, no spears, or fish or berries, it was all silly anyway, all just a game. He could do a day, but not forever—he could not make it if they did not come for him someday.

He could not play the game without hope; could not play the game without a dream. They had taken it all away from him now, they had turned away from him and there was nothing for him now. The plane gone, his family gone, all of it gone. They would not come. He was alone and there was nothing for him.

CHAPTER 13

Brian stood at the end of the long part of the L of the lake and watched the water, smelled the water, listened to the water, was the water.

A fish moved and his eyes jerked sideways to see the ripples but he did not move any other part of his body and did not raise the bow or reach into his belt pouch for a fish arrow. It was not the right kind of fish, not a food fish.

The food fish stayed close in, in the shallows, and did not roll that way but made quicker movements, small movements, food movements. The large fish rolled and stayed deep and could not be taken. But it didn't matter. This day, this morning, he was not looking for fish. Fish was light meat and he was sick of them.

He was looking for one of the foolish birds—he called them foolbirds—and there was a flock that lived near the end of the long part of the lake. But something he did not understand had stopped him and he stood, breathing gently through his mouth to keep silent, letting his eyes and ears go out and do the work for him.

It had happened before this way, something had come into him from outside to warn him and he had stopped. Once it had been the bear again. He had been taking the last of the raspberries and something came inside and stopped him, and when he looked where his ears said to look there was a female bear with cubs.

Had he taken two more steps he would have come between the mother and her cubs and that was a bad place to be. As it was the mother had stood and faced him and made a sound, a low sound in her throat to threaten and warn him. He paid attention to the feeling now and he stood and waited, patiently, knowing he was right and that something would come.

Turn, smell, listen, feel and then a sound, a small sound, and he looked up and away from the lake and saw the wolf. It was halfway up the hill from the lake, standing with its head and shoulders sticking out into a small opening, looking down on him with wide yellow eyes. He had never seen a wolf and the size threw him—not as big as a bear but somehow seeming that large. The wolf claimed all that was below him as his own, took Brian as his own.

Brian looked back and for a moment felt afraid because the wolf was so . . . so right. He knew Brian, knew him and owned him and chose not to do anything to him. But the fear moved then, moved away, and Brian knew the wolf for what it was—another part of the woods, another part of all of it. Brian relaxed the tension on the spear in his hand, settled the bow in his other hand from where it had started to come up. He knew the wolf now, as the wolf knew him, and he nodded to it, nodded and smiled.

The wolf watched him for another time, another part of his life, then it turned and walked effortlessly up the hill and as it came out of the brush it was followed by three other wolves, all equally large and gray and beautiful, all looking down on him as they trotted past and away and Brian nodded to each of them.

He was not the same now—the Brian that stood and watched the wolves move away and nodded to them was completely changed. Time had come, time that he measured but didn't care about; time had come into his life and moved out and left him different.

In measured time forty-seven days had passed since the crash. Forty-two days, he thought, since he had died and been born as the new Brian.

When the plane had come and gone it had put him down, gutted him and dropped him and left him with nothing. The rest of that first day he had gone down and down until dark. He had let the fire go out, had forgotten to eat even an egg, had let his brain take him down to where he was done, where he wanted to be done and done.

To where he wanted to die. He had settled into the gray funk deeper and still deeper until finally, in the dark, he had gone up on the ridge and taken the hatchet and tried to end it by cutting himself.

Madness. A hissing madness that took his brain. There had been nothing for him then and he tried to become nothing but the cutting had been hard to do, impossible to do, and he had at last fallen to his side, wishing for death, wishing for an end, and slept only didn't sleep.

With his eyes closed and his mind open he lay on the rock through the night, lay and hated and wished for it to end and thought the word *Clouddown, Clouddown* through that awful night. Over and over the word, wanting all his clouds to come down, but in the morning he was still there.

Still there on his side and the sun came up and when he opened his eyes he saw the cuts on his arm, the dry blood turning black; he saw the blood and hated the blood, hated what he had done to himself when he was the old Brian and was weak, and two things came into his mind—two true things.

He was not the same. The plane passing changed him, the disappointment cut him down and made him new. He was not the same and would never be again like he had been. That was one of the true things, the new things. And the other one was that he would not die, he would not let death in again.

He was new.

Of course he had made a lot of mistakes. He smiled now, walking up the lake shore after the wolves were gone, thinking of the early mistakes; the mistakes that came before he realized that he had to find new ways to be what he had become.

He had made new fire, which he now kept going using partially rotten wood because the punky wood would smolder for many hours and still come back with fire. But that had been the extent of doing things right for a while. His first bow was a disaster that almost blinded him.

He had sat a whole night and shaped the limbs carefully until the bow looked beautiful. Then he had spent two days making arrows. The shafts were willow, straight and with the bark peeled, and he fire-hardened the points and split a couple of them to make forked points, as he had done with the spear. He had no feathers so he just left them bare, figuring for fish they only had to travel a few inches. He had no string and that threw him until he looked down at his tennis shoes. They had long laces, too long, and he found that one lace cut in half would take care of both shoes and that left the other lace for a bowstring.

All seemed to be going well until he tried a test shot. He put an arrow to the string, pulled it back to his cheek, pointed it at a dirt hummock, and at that precise instant the bow wood exploded in his hands sending splinters and chips of wood into his face. Two pieces actually stuck into his forehead, just above his eyes, and had they been only slightly lower they would have blinded him.

Too stiff.

Mistakes. In his mental journal he listed them to tell his father, listed all the mistakes. He had made a new bow, with slender limbs and a more fluid, gentle pull, but could not hit the fish though he sat in the water and was, in the end, surrounded by a virtual cloud of small fish. It was infuriating. He would pull the bow back, set the arrow just above the water, and when the fish was no more than an inch away release the arrow.

Only to miss. It seemed to him that the arrow had gone right through the fish, again and again, but the fish didn't get hurt. Finally, after hours, he stuck the arrow down in the water, pulled the bow, and waited for a fish to come close and while he was waiting he noticed that the water seemed to make the arrow bend or break in the middle.

Of course—he had forgotten that water refracts, bends light. He had learned that somewhere, in some class, maybe it was biology—he couldn't remember.

But it did bend light and that meant the fish were not where they appeared to be. They were lower, just below, which meant he had to aim just under them.

He would not forget his first hit. Not ever. A round-shaped fish, with golden sides, sides as gold as the sun, stopped in front of the arrow and he aimed just beneath it, at the bottom edge of the fish, and released the arrow and there was a bright flurry, a splash of gold in the water. He grabbed the arrow and raised it up and the fish was on the end, wiggling against the blue sky.

He held the fish against the sky until it stopped wiggling, held it and looked to the sky and felt his throat tighten, swell, and fill with pride at what he had done.

He had done food.

With his bow, with an arrow fashioned by his own hands he had done food, had found a way to live. The bow had given him this way and he exulted in it, in the bow, in the arrow, in the fish, in the hatchet, in the sky. He stood and walked from the water, still holding the fish and arrow and bow against the sky, seeing them as they fit his arms, as they were part of him.

He had food.

He cut a green willow fork and held the fish over the fire until the skin crackled and peeled away and the meat inside was flaky and moist and tender. This he picked off carefully with his fingers, tasting every piece, mashing them in his mouth with his tongue to get the juices out of them, hot steaming pieces of fish. . . .

He could not, he thought then, ever get enough. And all that first day, first new day, he spent going to the lake, shooting a fish, taking it back to the fire, cooking it and eating it, then back to the lake, shooting a fish, cooking it and eating it, and on that way until it was dark.

He had taken the scraps back to the water with the thought they might work for bait, and the other fish came by the hundreds to clean them up. He could take his pick of them. Like a store, he thought, just like a store, and he could not remember later how many he ate that day but he thought it must have been over twenty.

It had been a feast day, his first feast day, and a celebration of being alive and the new way he had of getting food. By the end of that day, when it became dark and he lay next to the fire with his stomach full of fish and grease from the meat smeared around his mouth, he could feel new hope building in him. Not hope that he would be rescued—that was gone.

But hope in his knowledge. Hope in the fact that he could learn and survive and take care of himself.

Tough hope, he thought that night. I am full of tough hope.

CHAPTER 14

MISTAKES.

Small mistakes could turn into disasters, funny little mistakes could snowball so that while you were still smiling at the humor you could find yourself looking at death. In the city if he made a mistake usually there was a way to rectify it, make it all right. If he fell on his bike and sprained a leg he could wait for it to heal; if he forgot something at the store he could find other food in the refrigerator.

Now it was different, and all so quick, all so incredibly quick. If he sprained a leg here he might starve before he could get around again; if he missed while he was hunting or if the fish moved away he might starve. If he got sick, really sick so he couldn't move he might starve.

Mistakes.

Early in the new time he had learned the most important thing, the truly vital knowledge that drives all creatures in the forest—food is all. Food was simply everything. All things in the woods, from insects to fish to bears, were always, always looking for food—it was the great, single driving influence in nature. To eat. All must eat.

But the way he learned it almost killed him. His second new night, stomach full of fish and the fire smoldering in the shelter, he had been sound asleep when something—he thought later it might be smell—had awakened him.

Near the fire, completely unafraid of the smoking coals, completely unfraid of Brian, a skunk was digging where he had buried the eggs. There was some sliver of a moon and in the faint-pearl light he could see the bushy tail, the white stripes down the back, and he had nearly smiled. He did not know how the skunk had found the eggs, some smell, perhaps some tiny fragment of shell had left a smell, but it looked almost cute, its little head down and its little tail up as it dug, kicking the sand back.

But those were his eggs, not the skunk's, and the half smile had been quickly replaced with fear that he would lose his food and he had grabbed a handful of sand and thrown it at the skunk.

"Get out of here . . ."

He was going to say more, some silly human words, but in less than half a second the skunk had snapped its rear end up, curved the tail over, and sprayed Brian with a direct shot aimed at his head from less than four feet away.

In the tiny confines of the shelter the effect was devastating. The thick sulfurous rotten odor filled the small room, heavy, ugly, and stinking. The corrosive spray that hit his face seared into his lungs and eyes, blinding him.

He screamed and threw himself sideways, taking the entire wall off the shelter; screamed and clawed out of the shelter and fell-ran to the shore of the lake. Stumbling and tripping, he scrambled into the water and slammed his head back and forth trying to wash his eyes, slashing at the water to clear his eyes.

A hundred funny cartoons he had seen about skunks. Cute cartoons about the smell of skunks, cartoons to laugh at and joke about, but when the spray hit there was nothing funny about it—he was completely blind for almost two hours. A lifetime. He thought that he might be permanently blind, or at least impaired— and that would have been the end. As it was the pain in his eyes lasted for days, bothered him after that for two weeks. The smell in the shelter, in his clothes, and in his hair was still there now, almost a month and a half later.

And he had nearly smiled.

Mistakes.

Food had to be protected. While he was in the lake trying to clear his eyes the skunk went ahead and dug up the rest of the turtle eggs and ate every one. Licked all the shells clean and couldn't have cared less that Brian was thrashing around in the water like a dying carp. The skunk had found food and was taking it and Brian was paying for a lesson.

Protect food and have a good shelter. Not just a shelter to keep the wind and rain out, but a shelter to protect, a shelter to make him safe. The day after the skunk he set about making a good place to live.

The basic idea had been good, the place for his shelter was right, but he just hadn't gone far enough. He'd been lazy—but now he knew the second most important thing about nature, what drives nature. Food was first, but the work for the food went on and on. Nothing in nature was lazy. He had tried to take a shortcut and paid for it with his turtle eggs—which he had come to like more than chicken eggs from the store. They had been fuller somehow, had more depth to them.

He set about improving his shelter by tearing it down. From dead pines up the hill he brought down heavier logs and fastened several of them across the opening, wedging them at the top and burying the bottoms in the sand. Then he wove long branches in through them to make a truly tight wall and, still not satisfied, he took even thinner branches and wove those into the first weave. When he was at last finished he could not find a place to put his fist through. It all held together like a very stiff woven basket.

He judged the door opening to be the weakest spot, and here he took special time to weave a door of willows in so tight a mesh that no matter how a skunk tried—or porcupine, he thought, looking at the marks in his leg—it could not possibly get through. He had no hinges but by arranging some cut-off limbs at the top in the right way he had a method to hook the door in place, and when he was in and the door was hung he felt relatively safe. A bear, something big, could still get in by tearing at it, but nothing small could bother him and the weave of the structure still allowed the smoke to filter up through the top and out.

All in all it took him three days to make the shelter, stopping to shoot fish and eat as he went, bathing four times a day to try and get the smell from the skunk to leave. When his house was done, finally done right, he turned to the constant problem—food.

It was all right to hunt and eat, or fish and eat, but what happened if he had to go a long time without food? What happened when the berries were gone and he got sick or hurt or—thinking of the skunk—laid up temporarily? He needed a way to store food, a place to store it, and he needed food to store.

Mistakes.

He tried to learn from the mistakes. He couldn't bury food again, couldn't leave it in the shelter, because something like a bear could get at it right away. It had to be high, somehow, high and safe.

Above the door to the shelter, up the rock face about ten feet, was a small ledge that could make a natural storage place, unreachable to animals—except that it was unreachable to him as well.

A ladder, of course. He needed a ladder. But he had no way to fashion one, nothing to hold the steps on, and that stopped him until he found a dead pine with many small branches still sticking out. Using his hatchet he chopped the branches off so they stuck out four or five inches, all up along the log, then he cut the log off about ten feet long and dragged it down to his shelter. It was a little heavy, but dry and he could manage it, and when he propped it up he found he could climb to the ledge with ease, though the tree did roll from side to side a bit as he climbed.

His food shelf—as he thought of it—had been covered with bird manure and he carefully scraped it clean with sticks. He had never seen birds there, but that was probably because the smoke from his fire went up right across the opening and they didn't like smoke. Still, he had learned and he took time to weave a snug door for the small opening with green willows, cutting it so it jammed in tightly, and when he finished he stood back and looked at the rock face—his shelter below, the food shelf above—and allowed a small bit of pride to come.

Not bad, he had thought, not bad for somebody who used to have trouble greasing the bearings on his bicycle. Not bad at all.

Mistakes.

He had made a good shelter and food shelf, but he had no food except for fish and the last of the berries. And the fish, as good as they still tasted then, were not something he could store. His mother had left some salmon out by mistake one time when they went on an overnight trip to Cape Hesper to visit relatives and when they got back the smell filled the whole house. There was no way to store fish.

At least, he thought, no way to store them dead. But as he looked at the weave of his structure a thought came to him and he moved down to the water.

He had been putting the waste from the fish back in the water and the food had attracted hundreds of new ones.

"I wonder . . ."

They seemed to come easily to the food, at least the small ones. He had no trouble now shooting them and had even speared one with his old fish spear now that he knew to aim low. He could dangle something in his fingers and they came right up to it. It might be possible, he thought, might just be possible to trap them. Make some kind of pond . . .

To his right, at the base of the rock bluff, there were piles of smaller rocks that had fallen from the main chunk, splinters and hunks, from double-fist size to some as large as his head. He spent an afternoon carrying rocks to the beach and making what amounted to a large pen for holding live fish—two rock "arms" that stuck out fifteen feet into the lake and curved together at the end. Where the arms came together he left an opening about two feet across, then he sat on the shore and waited.

When he had first started dropping the rocks all the fish had darted away. But his fish-trash pile of bones and skin and guts was in the pond area and the prospect of food brought them back. Soon, under an hour, there were thirty or forty small fish in the enclosure and Brian made a gate by weaving small willows together into a fine mesh and closed them in.

"Fresh fish," he had yelled. "I have fresh fish for sale . . ."

Storing live fish to eat later had been a major breakthrough, he thought. It wasn't just keeping from starving—it was trying to save ahead, think ahead.

Of course he didn't know then how sick he would get of fish.

CHAPTER 15

THE DAYS had folded one into another and mixed so that after two or three weeks he only knew time had passed in days because he made a mark for each day in stone near the door to his shelter. Real time he measured in events. A day was nothing, not a thing to remember—it was just sun coming up, sun going down, some light in the middle.

But events—events were burned into his memory and so he used them to remember time, to know and to remember what had happened, to keep a mental journal.

There had been the day of First Meat. That had been a day that had started like the rest, up after the sun, clean the camp and make sure there is enough wood for another night. But it was a long time, a long time of eating fish and looking for berries, and he craved more, craved more food, heavier food, deeper food.

He craved meat. He thought in the night now of meat, thought of his mother's cooking a roast or dreamed of turkey, and one night he awakened before he had to put wood on the fire with his mouth making saliva and the taste of pork chops in his mouth. So real, so real. And all a dream, but it left him intent on getting meat.

He had been working farther and farther out for wood, sometimes now going nearly a quarter of a mile away from camp for wood, and he saw many small animals. Squirrels were everywhere, small red ones that chattered at him and seemed to swear and jumped from limb to limb. There were also many rabbits—large, gray ones with a mix of reddish fur, smaller fast gray ones that he saw only at dawn. The larger ones sometimes sat until he was quite close, then bounded and jerked two or three steps before freezing again. He thought if he worked at it and practiced he might hit one of the larger rabbits with an arrow or a spear—never the small ones or the squirrels. They were too small and fast.

Then there were the foolbirds.

They exasperated him to the point where they were close to driving him insane. The birds were everywhere, five and six in a flock, and their camouflage was so perfect that it was possible for Brian to sit and rest, leaning against a tree, with one of them standing right in front of him in a willow clump, two feet away—hidden—only to explode into deafening flight just when Brian least expected it. He just couldn't see them, couldn't figure out how to locate them before they flew, because they stood so perfectly still and blended in so perfectly well.

And what made it worse was that they were so dumb, or seemed to be so dumb, that it was almost insulting the way they kept hidden from him. Nor could he get used to the way they exploded up when they flew. It seemed like every time he went for wood, which was every morning, he spent the whole time jumping and jerking in fright as he walked. On one memorable morning he had actually reached for a piece of wood, what he thought to be a pitchy stump at the base of a dead birch, his fingers close to touching it, only to have it blow up in his face.

But on the day of First Meat he had decided the best thing to try for would be a foolbird and that morning he had set out with his bow and spear to get one; to stay with it until he got one and ate some meat. Not to get wood, not to find berries, but to get a bird and eat some meat.

At first the hunt had not gone well. He saw plenty of birds, working up along the shore of the lake to the end, then down the other side, but he only saw them after they flew. He had to find a way to see them first, see them and get close enough to either shoot them with the bow or use the spear, and he could not find a way to see them.

When he had gone halfway around the lake, and had jumped up twenty or so birds, he finally gave up and sat at the base of a tree. He had to work this out, see what he was doing wrong. There were birds there, and he had eyes—he just had to bring the two things together.

Looking wrong, he thought. I am looking wrong. More, more than that I am being wrong somehow—I am doing it the wrong way. Fine—sarcasm came into his thoughts—I know that, thank you. I know I'm doing it wrong. But what is right? The morning sun had cooked him until it seemed his brain was frying, sitting by the tree, but nothing came until he got up and started to walk again and hadn't gone two steps when a bird got up. It had been there all the time, while he was thinking about how to see them, right next to him—right there.

He almost screamed.

But this time, when the bird flew, something caught his eye and it was the secret key. The bird cut down toward the lake, then, seeing it couldn't land in the water, turned and flew back up the hill into the trees. When it turned, curving through the trees, the sun had caught it, and Brian, for an instant, saw it as a shape; sharp-pointed in front, back from the head in a streamlined bullet shape to the fat body.

Kind of like a pear, he had thought, with a point on one end and a fat little body; a flying pear.

And that had been the secret. He had been looking for feathers, for the color of the bird, for a bird sitting there. He had to look for the outline instead, had to see the shape instead of the feathers or color, had to train his eyes to see the shape . . .

It was like turning on a television. Suddenly he could see things he never saw before. In just moments, it seemed, he saw three birds before they flew, saw them sitting and got close to one of them, moving slowly, got close enough to try a shot with his bow.

He had missed that time, and had missed many more, but he saw them; he saw the little fat shapes with the pointed heads sitting in the brush all over the place. Time and again he drew, held, and let arrows fly but he still had no feathers on the arrows and they were little more than sticks that flopped out of the bow, sometimes going sideways. Even when a bird was seven or eight feet away the arrow would turn without feathers to stabilize it and hit brush or a twig. After a time he gave up with the bow. It had worked all right for the fish, when they came right to the end of the arrow, but it wasn't good for any kind of distance—at least not the way it was now.

But he had carried his fish spear, the original one with the two prongs, and he moved the bow to his left hand and carried the spear in his right.

He tried throwing the spear but he was not good enough and not fast enough—the birds could fly amazingly fast, get up fast. But in the end he found that if he saw the bird sitting and moved sideways toward it—not directly toward it but at an angle, back and forth—he could get close enough to put the spear point out ahead almost to the bird and thrust-lunge with it. He came close twice, and then, down along the lake not far from the beaver house he got his first meat.

The bird had sat and he had lunged and the two points took the bird back down into the ground and killed it almost instantly—it had fluttered a bit—and Brian had grabbed it and held it in both hands until he was sure it was dead.

Then he picked up the spear and the bow and trotted back around the lake to his shelter, where the fire had burned down to glowing coals. He sat looking at the bird wondering what to do. With the fish, he had just cooked them whole, left everything in and picked the meat off. This was different; he would have to clean it.

It had always been so simple at home. He would go to the store and get a chicken and it was all cleaned and neat, no feathers or insides, and his mother would bake it in the oven and he would eat it. His mother from the old time, from the time before, would bake it.

Now he had the bird, but he had never cleaned one, never taken the insides out or gotten rid of the feathers, and he didn't know where to start. But he wanted the meat—had to have the meat—and that drove him.

In the end the feathers came off easily. He tried to pluck them out but the skin was so fragile that it pulled off as well, so he just pulled the skin off the bird. Like peeling an orange, he thought, sort of. Except that when the skin was gone the insides fell out the back end.

He was immediately caught in a cloud of raw odor, a kind of steamy dung odor that came up from the greasy coil of insides that fell from the bird, and he nearly threw up. But there was something else to the smell as well, some kind of richness that went with his hunger and that overcame the sick smell.

He quickly cut the neck with his hatchet, cut the feet off the same way, and in his hand he held something like a small chicken with a dark, fat, thick breast and small legs.

He set it up on some sticks on the shelter wall and took the feathers and insides down to the water, to his fish pond. The fish would eat them, or eat what they could, and the feeding action would bring more fish. On second thought he took out the wing and tail feathers, which were stiff and long and pretty—banded and speckled in browns and grays and light reds. There might be some use for them, he thought, maybe work them onto the arrows somehow.

The rest he threw in the water, saw the small round fish begin tearing at it, and washed his hands. Back at the shelter the flies were on the meat and he brushed them off. It was amazing how fast they came, but when he built up the fire and the smoke increased the flies almost magically disappeared. He pushed a pointed stick through the bird and held it over the fire.

The fire was too hot. The flames hit the fat and the bird almost ignited. He held it higher but the heat was worse and finally he moved it to the side a bit and there it seemed to cook properly. Except that it only cooked on one side and all the juice dripped off. He had to rotate it slowly and that was hard to do with his hands so he found a forked stick and stuck it in the sand to put his cooking stick in. He turned it, and in this way he found a proper method to cook the bird.

In minutes the outside was cooked and the odor that came up was almost the same as the odor when his mother baked chickens in the oven and he didn't think he could stand it but when he tried to pull a piece of the breast meat off the meat was still raw inside.

Patience, he thought. So much of this was patience—waiting and thinking and doing things right. So much of all this, so much of all living was patience and thinking.

He settled back, turning the bird slowly, letting the juices go back into the meat, letting it cook and smell and smell and cook and there came a time when it didn't matter if the meat was done or not; it was black on the outside and hard and hot, and he would eat it.

He tore a piece from the breast, a sliver of meat, and put it in his mouth and chewed carefully, chewed as slowly and carefully as he could to get all the taste and he thought:

Never. Never in all the food, all the hamburgers and malts, all the fries or meals at home, never in all the candy or pies or cakes, never in all the roasts or steaks or pizzas, never in all the submarine sandwiches, never never never had he tasted anything as fine as that first bite.

First Meat.

CHAPTER 16

A ND NOW he stood at the end of the long part of the lake and was not the same, would not be the same again.

There had been many First Days.

First Arrow Day—when he had used thread from his tattered old piece of windbreaker and some pitch from a stump to put slivers of feather on a dry willow shaft and make an arrow that would fly correctly. Not accurately—he never got really good with it—but fly correctly so that if a rabbit or a foolbird sat in one place long enough, close enough, and he had enough arrows, he could hit it.

That brought First Rabbit Day—when he killed one of the large rabbits with an arrow and skinned it as he had the first bird, cooked it the same to find the meat as good—not as rich as the bird, but still good—and there were strips of fat on the back of the rabbit that cooked into the meat to make it richer.

Now he went back and forth between rabbits and foolbirds when he could, filling in with fish in the middle.

Always hungry.

I am always hungry but I can do it now, I can get food and I know I can get food and it makes me more. I know what I can do.

He moved closer to the lake to a stand of nut brush. These were thick bushes with little stickler pods that held green nuts—nuts that he thought he might be able to eat but they weren't ripe yet. He was out for a foolbird and they liked to hide in the base of the thick part of the nut brush, back in where the stems were close together and provided cover.

In the second clump he saw a bird, moved close to it, paused when the head feathers came up and it made a sound like a cricket—a sign of alarm just before it flew—then moved closer when the feathers went down and the bird relaxed. He did this four times, never looking at the bird directly, moving toward it at an angle so that it seemed he was moving off to the side—he had perfected this method after many attempts and it worked so well that he had actually caught one with his bare hands   until he was standing less than three feet from the bird, which was frozen in a hiding attitude in the brush.

The bird held for him and he put an arrow to the bow, one of the feathered arrows, not a fish arrow, and drew and released. It was a clean miss and he took another arrow out of the cloth pouch, at his belt, which he'd made from a piece of his windbreaker sleeve, tied at one end to make a bottom. The foolbird sat still for him and he did not look directly at it until he drew the second arrow and aimed and released and missed again.

This time the bird jerked a bit and the arrow stuck next to it so close it almost brushed its breast. Brian only had two more arrows and he debated moving slowly to change the spear over to his right hand and use that to kill the bird. One more shot, he decided, he would try it again. He slowly brought another arrow out, put it on the string, and aimed and released and this time saw the flurry of feathers that meant he had made a hit.

The bird had been struck off-center and was flopping around wildly. Brian jumped on it and grabbed it and slammed it against the ground once, sharply, to kill it. Then he stood and retrieved his arrows and made sure they were all right and went down to the lake to wash the blood off his hands. He kneeled at the water's edge and put the dead bird and his weapons down and dipped his hands into the water.

It was very nearly the last act of his life. Later he would not know why he started to turn—some smell or sound. A tiny brushing sound. But something caught his ear or nose and he began to turn, and had his head half around, when he saw a brown wall of fur detach itself from the forest to his rear and come down on him like a runaway truck. He just had time to see that it was a moose—he knew them from pictures but did not know, could not guess how large they were—when it hit him. It was a cow and she had horns, but she took him in the left side of the back with her forehead, took him and threw him out into the water and then came after him to finish the job.

He had another half-second to fill his lungs with air and she was on him again, using her head to drive him down into the mud of the bottom. Insane, he thought. Just that, the word, insane. Mud filled his eyes, his ears, the horn boss on the moose drove him deeper and deeper into the bottom muck, and suddenly it was over and he felt alone.

He sputtered to the surface, sucking air and fighting panic, and when he wiped the mud and water out of his eyes and cleared them he saw the cow standing sideways to him, not ten feet away, calmly chewing on a lilypad root. She didn't appear to even see him, or didn't seem to care about him, and Brian turned carefully and began to swim-crawl out of the water.

As soon as he moved, the hair on her back went up and she charged him again, using her head and front hooves this time, slamming him back and down into the water, on his back this time, and he screamed the air out of his lungs and hammered on her head with his fists and filled his throat with water and she left again.

Once more he came to the surface. But he was hurt now, hurt inside, hurt in his ribs and he stayed hunched over, pretended to be dead. She was standing again, eating. Brian studied her out of one eye, looking to the bank with the other, wondering how seriously he was injured, wondering if she would let him go this time.

Insane.

He started to move, ever so slowly; her head turned and her back hair went up—like the hair on an angry dog—and he stopped, took a slow breath, the hair went down and she ate. Move, hair up, stop, hair down, move, hair up—a half-foot at a time until he was at the edge of the water. He stayed on his hands and knees—indeed, was hurt so he wasn't sure he could walk anyway, and she seemed to accept that and let him crawl, slowly, out of the water and up into the trees and brush.

When he was behind a tree he stood carefully and took stock. Legs seemed all right, but his ribs were hurt bad—he could only take short breaths and then he had a jabbing pain—and his right shoulder seemed to be wrenched somehow. Also his bow and spear and foolbird were in the water.

At least he could walk and he had just about decided to leave everything when the cow moved out of the deeper water and left him, as quickly as she'd come, walking down along the shoreline in the shallow water, with her long legs making sucking sounds when she pulled them free of the mud. Hanging on a pine limb, he watched her go, half expecting her to turn and come back to run over him again. But she kept going and when she was well gone from sight he went to the bank and found the bird, then waded out a bit to get his bow and spear. Neither of them was broken and the arrows, incredibly, were still on his belt in the pouch, although messed up with mud and water.

It took him most of an hour to work his way back around the lake. His legs worked well enough, but if he took two or three fast steps he would begin to breathe deeply and the pain from his ribs would stop him and he would have to lean against a tree until he could slow back down to shallow breathing. She had done more damage than he had originally thought, the insane cow—no sense at all to it. Just madness. When he got to the shelter he crawled inside and was grateful that the coals were still glowing and that he had thought to get wood first thing in the mornings to be ready for the day, grateful that he had thought to get enough wood for two or three days at a time, grateful that he had fish nearby if he needed to eat, grateful, finally, as he dozed off, that he was alive.

So insane, he thought, letting sleep cover the pain in his chest—such an insane attack for no reason and he fell asleep with his mind trying to make the moose have reason.

The noise awakened him.

It was a low sound, a low roaring sound that came from wind. His eyes snapped open not because it was loud but because it was new. He had felt wind in his shelter, felt the rain that came with wind and had heard thunder many times in the past forty-seven days but not this, not this noise. Low, almost alive, almost from a throat somehow, the sound, the noise was a roar, a far-off roar but coming at him and when he was fully awake he sat up in the darkness, grimacing with pain from his ribs.

The pain was different now, a tightened pain, and it seemed less—but the sound. So strange, he thought. A mystery sound. A spirit sound. A bad sound. He took some small wood and got the fire going again, felt some little comfort and cheer from the flames but also felt that he should get ready. He did not know how, but he should get ready. The sound was coming for him, just for him, and he had to get ready. The sound wanted him.

He found the spear and bow where they were hanging on the pegs of the shelter wall and brought his weapons to the bed he had made of pine boughs. More comfort, but like the comfort of the flames it didn't work with this new threat that he didn't understand yet.

Restless threat, he thought, and stood out of the shelter away from the flames to study the sky but it was too dark. The sound meant something to him, something from his memory, something he had read about. Something he had seen on television. Something . . . oh, he thought. Oh no.

It was wind, wind like the sound of a train, with the low belly roar of a train. It was a tornado. That was it! The roar of a train meant bad wind and it was coming for him. God, he thought, on top of the moose not this—not this.

But it was too late, too late to do anything. In the strange stillness he looked to the night sky, then turned back into his shelter and was leaning over to go through the door opening when it hit. Later he would think of it and find that it was the same as the moose. Just insanity. He was taken in the back by some mad force and driven into the shelter on his face, slammed down into the pine branches of his bed.

At the same time the wind tore at the fire and sprayed red coals and sparks in a cloud around him. Then it backed out, seemed to hesitate momentarily, and returned with a massive roar; a roar that took his ears and mind and body.

He was whipped against the front wall of the shelter like a rag, felt a ripping pain in his ribs again, then was hammered back down into the sand once more while the wind took the whole wall, his bed, the fire, his tools—all of it—and threw it out into the lake, gone out of sight, gone forever. He felt a burning on his neck and reached up to find red coals there. He brushed those off, found more in his pants, brushed those away, and the wind hit again, heavy gusts, tearing gusts. He heard trees snapping in the forest around the rock, felt his body slipping out and clawed at the rocks to hold himself down. He couldn't think, just held and knew that he was praying but didn't know what the prayer was—knew that he wanted to be, stay and be, and then the wind moved to the lake.

Brian heard the great, roaring sucking sounds of the water and opened his eyes to see the lake torn by the wind, the water slamming in great waves that went in all ways, fought each other and then rose in a spout of water going up into the night sky like a wet column of light. It was beautiful and terrible at the same time.

The tornado tore one more time at the shore on the opposite side of the lake—Brian could hear trees being ripped down—and then it was done, gone as rapidly as it had come. It left nothing, nothing but Brian in the pitch dark. He could find nothing of where his fire had been, not a spark, nothing of his shelter, tools, or bed, even the body of the foolbird was gone. I am back to nothing he thought, trying to find things in the dark—back to where I was when I crashed. Hurt, in the dark, just the same.

As if to emphasize his thoughts the mosquitos—with the fire gone and protective smoke no longer saving him—came back in thick, nostril-clogging swarms. All that was left was the hatchet at his belt. Still there. But now it began to rain and in the down-pour he would never find anything dry enough to get a fire going, and at last he pulled his battered body back in under the overhang, where his bed had been, and wrapped his arms around his ribs.

Sleep didn't come, couldn't come with the insects ripping at him, so he lay the rest of the night, slapping mosquitos and chewing with his mind on the day. This morning he had been fat—well, almost fat—and happy, sure of everything, with good weapons and food and the sun in his face and things looking good for the future, and inside of one day, just one day, he had been run over by a moose and a tornado, had lost everything and was back to square one. Just like that.

A flip of some giant coin and he was the loser.

But there is a difference now, he thought—there really is a difference. I might be hit but I'm not done. When the light comes I'll start to rebuild. I still have the hatchet and that's all I had in the first place.

Come on, he thought, baring his teeth in the darkness—come on. Is that the best you can do? Is that all you can hit me with—a moose and a tornado? Well, he thought, holding his ribs and smiling, then spitting mosquitos out of his mouth. Well, that won't get the job done. That was the difference now. He had changed, and he was tough. I'm tough where it counts—tough in the head.

In the end, right before dawn a kind of cold snap came down—something else new, this cold snap—and the mosquitos settled back into the damp grass and under the leaves and he could sleep. Or doze. And the last thought he had that morning as he closed his eyes was: I hope the tornado hit the moose.

When he awakened the sun was cooking the inside of his mouth and had dried his tongue to leather. He had fallen into a deeper sleep with his mouth open just at dawn and it tasted as if he had been sucking on his foot all night.

He rolled out and almost bellowed with pain from his ribs. They had tightened in the night and seemed to pull at his chest when he moved. He slowed his movements and stood slowly, without stretching unduly, and went to the lake for a drink. At the shore he kneeled, carefully and with great gentleness, and drank and rinsed his mouth. To his right he saw that the fish pond was still there, although the willow gate was gone and there were no fish. They'll come back, he thought, as soon as I can make a spear or bow and get one or two for bait they'll come back.

He turned to look at his shelter—saw that some of the wood for the wall was scattered around the beach but was still there, then saw his bow jammed into a driftwood log, broken but with the precious string still intact. Not so bad now—not so bad. He looked down the shoreline for other parts of his wall and that's when he saw it.

Out in the lake, in the short part of the L, something curved and yellow was sticking six or eight inches out of the water. It was a bright color, not an earth or natural color, and for a second he could not place it, then he knew it for what it was.

"It's the tail of the plane." He said it aloud, half expecting to hear somebody answer him. There it was, sticking up out of the water. The tornado must have flipped the plane around somehow when it hit the lake, changed the position of the plane and raised the tail. Well, he thought. Well, just look at that. And at the same moment a cutting thought hit him. He thought of the pilot, still in the plane, and that brought a shiver and massive sadness that seemed to settle on him like a weight and he thought that he should say or do something for the pilot; some words but he didn't know any of the right words, the religious words.

So he went down to the side of the water and looked at the plane and focused his mind, the way he did when he was hunting the foolbirds and wanted to concentrate, focused it on the pilot and thought: Have rest. Have rest forever.

CHAPTER 17

HE TURNED BACK to his campsite and looked to the wreckage. He had a lot to do, rebuild his shelter, get a new fire going, find some food or get ready to find some food, make weapons—and he had to work slowly because his ribs hurt.

First things first. He tried to find some dry grass and twigs, then peeled bark from a nearby birch to shred into a fire nest. He worked slowly but even so, with his new skill he had a fire going in less than an hour. The flames cut the cool damp morning, crackled and did much to bring his spirits up, not to mention chasing away the incessant mosquitos. With the fire going he searched for dry wood—the rain had driven water into virtually all the wood he could find—and at last located some in a thick evergreen where the top branches had covered the lower dead ones, keeping them dry.

He had great difficulty breaking them, not being able to pull much with his arm or chest muscles, but finally got enough to keep the fire going all day and into the night. With that he rested a bit, eased his chest, and then set about getting a shelter squared away.

Much of the wood from his original wall was still nearby and up in back of the ridge he actually found a major section of the weave still intact. The wind had torn it out, lifted it, and thrown it to the top of the ridge and Brian felt lucky once more that he had not been killed or more seriously injured—which would have been the same, he thought. If he couldn't hunt he would die and if he were injured badly he would not be able to hunt.

He jerked and dragged wood around until the wall was once more in place— crudely, but he could improve it later. He had no trouble finding enough pine boughs to make a new bed. The storm had torn the forest to pieces—up in back of the ridge it looked like a giant had become angry and used some kind of a massive meatgrinder on the trees. Huge pines were twisted and snapped off, blown sideways. The ground was so littered, with limbs and tree-tops sticking every which way, that it was hard to get through. He pulled enough thick limbs in for a bed, green and spicy with the new broken sap smell, and by evening he was exhausted, hungry, and hurting, but he had something close to a place to live again, a place to be.

Tomorrow, he thought, as he lay back in the darkness. Tomorrow maybe the fish would be back and he would make a spear and new bow and get some food. Tomorrow he would find food and refine the camp and bring things back to sanity from the one completely insane day.

He faced the fire. Curving his body, he rested his head on his arm, and began to sleep when a picture came into his head. The tail of the plane sticking out of the water. There it was, the tail sticking up. And inside the plane, near the tail somewhere, was the survival pack. It must have survived the crash because the plane's main body was still intact. That was the picture—the tail sticking up and the survival pack inside—right there in his mind as he dozed. His eyes snapped opened. If I could get at the pack, he thought. Oh, if I could get at the pack. It probably had food and knives and matches. It might have a sleeping bag. It might have fishing gear. Oh, it must have so many wonderful things—if I could get at the pack and just get some of those things. I would be rich. So rich if I could get at the pack.

Tomorrow. He watched the flames and smiled. Tomorrow I'll see. All things come tomorrow.

He slept, deep and down with only the picture of the plane tail sticking up in his mind. A healing sleep.

In the morning he rolled out before true light. In the gray dawn he built up the fire and found more wood for the day, feeling almost chipper because his ribs were much better now. With camp ready for the day he looked to the lake. Part of him half-expected the plane tail to be gone, sunk back into the depths, but he saw that it was still there, didn't seem to have moved at all.

He looked down at his feet and saw that there were some fish in his fish pen looking for the tiny bits of bait still left from before the wind came. He fought impatience to get on the plane project and remembered sense, remembered what he had learned. First food, because food made strength; first food, then thought, then action. There were fish at hand here, and he might not be able to get anything from the plane. That was all a dream.

The fish were real and his stomach, even his new shrunken stomach, was sending signals that it was savagely empty.

He made a fish spear with two points, not peeling the bark all the way back but just working on the pointed end. It took him an hour or so and all the time he worked he sat looking at the tail of the plane sticking up in the air, his hands working on the spear, his mind working on the problem of the plane.

When the spear was done, although still crude, he jammed a wedge between the points to spread them apart and went to the fish pond. There were not clouds of fish, but at least ten, and he picked one of the larger ones, a round fish almost six inches long, and put the spear point in the water, held it, then thrust with a flicking motion of his wrist when the fish was just above the point.

The fish was pinned neatly and he took two more with the same ease, then carried all three back up to the fire. He had a fish board now, a piece of wood he had flattened with the hatchet, that leaned up by the fire for cooking fish so he didn't have to hold a stick all the time. He put the three fish on the board, pushed sharpened pegs through their tails into cracks on the cooking board, and propped it next to the reddest part of the coals. In moments the fish were hissing and cooking with the heat and as soon as they were done, or when he could stand the smell no longer, he picked the steaming meat from under the loosened skin and ate it.

The fish did not fill him, did not even come close—fish meat was too light for that. But they gave him strength—he could feel it moving into his arms and legs—and he began to work on the plane project.

While making the spear he had decided that what he would have to do was make a raft and push-paddle the raft to the plane and tie it there for a working base. Somehow he would have to get into the tail, inside the plane—rip or cut his way in—and however he did it he would need an operating base of some kind. A raft.

Which, he found ruefully, was much easier said than done. There were plenty of logs around. The shore was littered with driftwood, new and old, tossed up and scattered by the tornado. And it was a simple matter to find four of them about the same length and pull them together.

Keeping them together was the problem. Without rope or crosspieces and nails the logs just rolled and separated. He tried wedging them together, crossing them over each other—nothing seemed to work. And he needed a stable platform to get the job done. It was becoming frustrating and he had a momentary loss of temper—as he would have done in the past, when he was the other person.

At that point he sat back on the beach and studied the problem again. Sense, he had to use his sense. That's all it took to solve problems—just sense.

It came then. The logs he had selected were smooth and round and had no limbs. What he needed were logs with limbs sticking out, then he could cross the limbs of one log over the limbs of another and "weave" them together as he had done his wall, the food shelf cover, and the fish gate. He scanned the area above the beach and found four dry treetops that had been broken off by the storm. These had limbs and he dragged them down to his work area at the water's edge and fitted them together.

It took most of the day. The limbs were cluttered and stuck any which way and he would have to cut one to make another fit, then cut one from another log to come back to the first one, then still another from a third log would have to be pulled in.

But at last, in the late afternoon he was done and the raft—which he called Brushpile One for its looks—hung together even as he pulled it into the water off the beach. It floated well, if low in the water, and in the excitement he started for the plane. He could not stand on it, but would have to swim alongside.

He was out to chest depth when he realized he had no way to keep the raft at the plane. He needed some way to tie it in place so he could work from it.

And for a moment he was stymied. He had no rope, only the bowstring and the other cut shoe-string in his tennis shoes—which were by now looking close to dead, his toes showing at the tops. Then he remembered his windbreaker and he found the tattered part he used for an arrow pouch. He tore it into narrow strips and tied them together to make a rope or tie-down about four feet long. It wasn't strong, he couldn't use it to pull a Tarzan and swing from a tree, but it should hold the raft to the plane.

Once more he slid the raft off the beach and out into the water until he was chest deep. He had left his tennis shoes in the shelter and when he felt the sand turn to mud between his toes he kicked off the bottom and began to swim.

Pushing the raft, he figured, was about like trying to push an aircraft carrier. All the branches that stuck down into the water dragged and pulled and the logs themselves fought any forward motion and he hadn't gone twenty feet when he realized that it was going to be much harder than he thought to get the raft to the plane. It barely moved and if he kept going this way he would just about reach the plane at dark. He decided to turn back again, spend the night and start early in the morning, and he pulled the raft once more onto the sand and wipe-scraped it dry with his hand.

Patience. He was better now but impatience still ground at him a bit so he sat at the edge of the fish pond with the new spear and took three more fish, cooked them up and ate them, which helped to pass the time until dark. He also dragged in more wood—endless wood—and then relaxed and watched the sun set over the trees in back of the ridge. West, he thought. I'm watching the sun set in the west. And that way was north where his father was, and that way east and that way south—and somewhere to the south and east his mother would be. The news would be on the television. He could visualize more easily his mother doing things than his father because he had never been to where his father lived now. He knew everything about how his mother lived. She would have the small television on the kitchen counter on and be watching the news and talking about how awful it was in South Africa or how cute the baby in the commercial looked. Talking and making sounds, cooking sounds.

He jerked his mind back to the lake. There was great beauty here—almost unbelievable beauty. The sun exploded the sky, just blew it up with the setting color, and that color came down into the water of the lake, lit the trees. Amazing beauty and he wished he could share it with somebody and say, "Look there, and over there, and see that . . ."

But even alone it was beautiful and he fed the fire to cut the night chill. There it is again, he thought, that late summer chill to the air, the smell of fall. He went to sleep thinking a kind of reverse question. He did not know if he would ever get out of this, could not see how it might be, but if he did somehow get home and go back to living the way he had lived, would it be just the opposite? Would he be sitting watching television and suddenly think about the sunset up in back of the ridge and wonder how the color looked in the lake?

Sleep.

In the morning the chill was more pronounced and he could see tiny wisps of vapor from his breath. He threw wood on the fire and blew until it flamed, then banked the flames to last and went down to the lake. Perhaps because the air was so cool the water felt warm as he waded in. He made sure the hatchet was still at his belt and the raft still held together, then set out pushing the raft and kick-swimming toward the tail of the plane.

As before, it was very hard going. Once an eddy of breeze came up against him and he seemed to be standing still and by the time he was close enough to the tail to see the rivets in the aluminum he had pushed and kicked for over two hours, was nearly exhausted and wished he had taken some time to get a fish or two and have breakfast. He was also wrinkled as a prune and ready for a break.

The tail looked much larger when he got next to it, with a major part of the vertical stabilizer[1] showing and perhaps half of the elevators.[2] Only a short piece of the top of the fuselage, the plane's body toward the tail, was out of the water, just a curve of aluminum, and at first he could see no place to tie the raft. But he pulled himself along the elevators to the end and there he found a gap that went in up by the hinges where he could feed his rope through.

With the raft secure he climbed on top of it and lay on his back for fifteen minutes, resting and letting the sun warm him. The job, he thought, looked impossible. To have any chance of success he would have to be strong when he started.

Somehow he had to get inside the plane. All openings, even the small rear cargo hatch, were underwater so he couldn't get at them without diving and coming up inside the plane.

Where he would be trapped.

He shuddered at that thought and then remembered what was in front of the plane, down in the bottom of the lake, still strapped in the seat, the body of the pilot. Sitting there in the water—Brian could see him, the big man with his hair waving up in the current, his eyes open . . .

Stop, he thought. Stop now. Stop that thinking. He was nearly at the point of swimming back to shore and forgetting the whole thing. But the image of the survival pack kept him. If he could get it out of the plane, or if he could just get into it and pull something out. A candy bar.

Even that—just a candy bar. It would be worth it.

But how to get at the inside of the plane?

He rolled off the raft and pulled himself around the plane. No openings. Three times he put his face in the water and opened his eyes and looked down. The water was murky, but he could see perhaps six feet and there was no obvious way to get into the plane. He was blocked.

CHAPTER 18

BRIAN WORKED around the tail of the plane two more times, pulling himself along on the stabilizer and the elevator, but there simply wasn't a way in.

Stupid, he thought. I was stupid to think I could just come out here and get inside the plane. Nothing is that easy. Not out here, not in this place. Nothing is easy.

He slammed his fist against the body of the plane and to his complete surprise the aluminum covering gave easily under his blow. He hit it again, and once more it bent and gave and he found that even when he didn't strike it but just pushed it, it still moved. It was really, he thought, very thin aluminum skin

---

1 *vertical stabilizer*   the typical airplane's upright tail, hinged at the back to form its rudder, which controls the plane's left and right movements.

2 *elevators*   the hinged rear sections of that part of the typical plane's tail known as the horizontal stabilizer, which controls the plane's up and down movements.

over a kind of skeleton and if it gave that easily he might be able to force his way through . . .

The hatchet. He might be able to cut or hack with the hatchet. He reached to his belt and pulled the hatchet out, picked a place where the aluminum gave to his push and took an experimental swing at it.

The hatchet cut through the aluminum as if it were soft cheese. He couldn't believe it. Three more hacks and he had a triangular hole the size of his hand and he could see four cables that he guessed were the control cables going back to the tail and he hit the skin of the plane with a frenzied series of hacks to make a still larger opening and he was bending a piece of aluminum away from two aluminum braces of some kind when he dropped the hatchet.

It went straight down past his legs. He felt it bump his foot and then go down, down into the water and for a second he couldn't understand that he had done it. For all this time, all the living and fighting, the hatchet had been every-thing—he had always worn it. Without the hatchet he had nothing—no fire, no tools, no weapons—he was nothing. The hatchet was, had been him.

And he had dropped it.

"Arrrgghhh!" He yelled it, choked on it, a snarl-cry of rage at his own care-lessness. The hole in the plane was still too small to use for anything and now he didn't have a tool.

"That was the kind of thing I would have done before," he said to the lake, to the sky, to the trees. "When I came here—I would have done that. Not now. Not now . . ."

Yet he had and he hung on the raft for a moment and felt sorry for himself. For his own stupidity. But as before, the self-pity didn't help and he knew that he had only one course of action.

He had to get the hatchet back. He had to dive and get it back.

But how deep was it? In the deep end of the gym pool at school he had no trouble getting to the bottom and that was, he was pretty sure, about eleven feet.

Here it was impossible to know the exact depth. The front end of the plane, anchored by the weight of the engine, was obviously on the bottom but it came back up at an angle so the water wasn't as deep as the plane was long.

He pulled himself out of the water so his chest could expand, took two deep breaths and swiveled and dove, pulling his arms and kicking off the raft bottom with his feet.

His first thrust took him down a good eight feet but the visibility was only five feet beyond that and he could not see bottom yet. He clawed down six or seven feet, the pressure pushing in his ears until he held his nose and popped them and just as he ran out of breath and headed back up he thought he saw the bottom—still four feet below his dive.

He exploded out of the surface, bumping his head on the side of the elevator when he came up and took air like a whale, pushing the stale air out until he wheezed, taking new in. He would have to get deeper yet and still have time to search while he was down there.

Stupid, he thought once more, cursing himself—just dumb. He pulled air again and again, pushing his chest out until he could not possibly get any more capacity, then took one more deep lungful, wheeled and dove again.

This time he made an arrow out of his arms and used his legs to push off the bottom of the raft, all he had in his legs, to spring-snap and propel him down.

As soon as he felt himself slowing a bit he started raking back with his arms at his sides, like paddles, and thrusting with his legs like a frog and this time he was so successful that he ran his face into the bottom mud.

He shook his head to clear his eyes and looked around. The plane disappeared out and down in front of him. He thought he could see the windows and that made him think again of the pilot sitting inside and he forced his thoughts from it—but he could see no hatchet. Bad air triggers were starting to go off in his brain and he knew he was limited to seconds now but he held for a moment and tried moving out a bit and just as he ran out of air, knew that he was going to have to blow soon, he saw the handle sticking out of the mud. He made one grab, missed, reached again and felt his fingers close on the rubber. He clutched it and in one motion slammed his feet down into the mud and powered himself up. But now his lungs were ready to explode and he had flashes of color in his brain, explosions of color, and he would have to take a pull of water, take it into his lungs and just as he opened his mouth to take it in, to pull in all the water in the lake his head blew out of the surface and into the light.

"*Tchaaak!*" It was as if a balloon had exploded. Old air blew out of his nose and mouth and he pulled new in again and again. He reached for the side of the raft and hung there, just breathing, until he could think once more—the hatchet clutched and shining in his right hand.

"All right . . . the plane. Still the plane . . ."

He went back to the hole in the fuselage and began to chop and cut again, peeling the aluminum skin off in pieces. It was slow going because he was careful, very careful with the hatchet, but he hacked and pulled until he had opened a hole large enough to pull his head and shoulders in and look down into the water. It was very dark inside the fuselage and he could see nothing—certainly no sign of the survival pack. There were some small pieces and bits of paper floating on the surface inside the plane—dirt from the floor of the plane that had floated up—but nothing substantial.

Well, he thought. Did you expect it to be easy? So easy that way? Just open her up and get the pack—right?

He would have to open it more, much more so he could poke down inside and see what he could find. The survival pack had been a zippered nylon bag, or perhaps canvas of some kind, and he thought it had been red, or was it gray? Well, that didn't matter. It must have been moved when the plane crashed and it might be jammed down under something else.

He started chopping again, cutting the aluminum away in small triangles, putting each one on the raft as he chopped—he could never throw anything away again, he thought—because they might be useful later. Bits of metal, fish arrowheads or lures, maybe. And when he finally finished again he had cleaned away the whole side and top of the fuselage that stuck out of the water, had cut down into the water as far as he could reach and had a hole almost as big as he was, except that it was crossed and criss-crossed with aluminum—or it might be steel, he couldn't tell—braces and formers and cables.[1] It was an awful tangled mess, but after chopping some braces away there was room for him to wiggle through and get inside.

---

1 *braces and formers and cables* an airplane's fuselage or body is shaped by upright wooden or metal formers, roughly oval in shape, held in place by horizontal braces; metal cables run from the cockpit controls to the plane's rudder, elevators, and other control surfaces.

He held back for a moment, uncomfortable with the thought of getting inside the plane. What if the tail settled back to the bottom and he got caught and couldn't get out? It was a horrible thought. But then he reconsidered. The thing had been up now for two days, plus a bit, and he had been hammering and climbing on it and it hadn't gone back down. It seemed pretty solid.

He eeled in through the cables and formers, wiggling and pulling until he was inside the tail with his head clear of the surface of the water and his legs down on the angled floor. When he was ready, he took a deep breath and pushed down along the floor with his legs, feeling for some kind of fabric or cloth—anything—with his bare feet. He touched nothing but the floor plates.

Up, a new breath, then he reached down to formers underwater and pulled himself beneath the water, his legs pushing down and down almost to the backs of the front seats and finally, on the left side of the plane, he thought he felt his foot hit cloth or canvas.

Up for more air, deep breathing, then one more grab at the formers and pushing as hard as he could he jammed his feet down and he hit it again, definitely canvas or heavy nylon, and this time when he pushed his foot he thought he felt something inside it; something hard.

It had to be the bag. Driven forward by the crash, it was jammed into the backs of the seats and caught on something. He tried to reach for it and pull but didn't have the air left and went up for more.

Lungs filled in great gulps, he shot down again, pulling on the formers until he was almost there, then wheeling down head first he grabbed at the cloth. It was the survival bag. He pulled and tore at it to loosen it and just as it broke free and his heart leaped to feel it rise he looked up, above the bag. In the light coming through the side window, the pale green light from the water, he saw the pilot's head only it wasn't the pilot's head any longer.

The fish. He'd never really thought of it, but the fish—the fish he had been eating all this time had to eat, too. They had been at the pilot all this time, almost two months, nibbling and chewing and all that remained was the not quite cleaned skull and when he looked up it wobbled loosely.

Too much. Too much. His mind screamed in horror and he slammed back and was sick in the water, sick so that he choked on it and tried to breathe water and could have ended there, ended with the pilot where it almost ended when they first arrived except that his legs jerked. It was instinctive, fear more than anything else, fear of what he had seen. But they jerked and pushed and he was headed up when they jerked and he shot to the surface, still inside the birdcage of formers and cables.

His head slammed into a bracket as he cleared and he reached up to grab it and was free, in the air, hanging up in the tail.

He hung that way for several minutes, choking and heaving and gasping for air, fighting to clear the picture of the pilot from his mind. It went slowly—he knew it would never completely leave—but he looked to the shore and there were trees and birds, the sun was getting low and golden over his shelter and when he stopped coughing he could hear the gentle sounds of evening, the peace sounds, the bird sounds and the breeze in the trees.

The peace finally came to him and he settled his breathing. He was still a long way from being finished—had a lot of work to do. The bag was floating next to him but he had to get it out of the plane and onto the raft, then back to shore.

He wiggled out through the formers—it seemed harder than when he came in—and pulled the raft around. The bag fought him. It was almost as if it didn't want to leave the plane. He pulled and jerked and still it wouldn't fit and at last he had to change the shape of it, rearranging what was inside by pushing and pulling at the sides until he had narrowed it and made it longer. Even when it finally came it was difficult and he had to pull first at one side, then another, an inch at a time, squeezing it through.

All of this took some time and when he finally got the bag out and tied on top of the raft it was nearly dark, he was bone tired from working in the water all day, chilled deep, and he still had to push the raft to shore.

Many times he thought he would not make it. With the added weight of the bag—which seemed to get heavier by the foot—coupled with the fact that he was getting weaker all the time, the raft seemed barely to move. He kicked and pulled and pushed, taking the shortest way straight back to shore, hanging to rest many times, then surging again and again.

It seemed to take forever and when at last his feet hit bottom and he could push against the mud and slide the raft into the shore weeds to bump against the bank he was so weak he couldn't stand, had to crawl; so tired he didn't even notice the mosquitos that tore into him like a gray, angry cloud.

He had done it.

That's all he could think now. He had done it.

He turned and sat on the bank with his legs in the water and pulled the bag ashore and began the long drag—he couldn't lift it—back down the shoreline to his shelter. Two hours, almost three he dragged and stumbled in the dark, brushing the mosquitos away, sometimes on his feet, more often on his knees, finally to drop across the bag and to sleep when he made the sand in front of the doorway.

He had done it.

CHAPTER 19

T REASURE.

Unbelievable riches. He could not believe the contents of the survival pack.

The night before he was so numb with exhaustion he couldn't do anything but sleep. All day in the water had tired him so much that, in the end, he had fallen asleep sitting against his shelter wall, oblivious even to the mosquitos, to the night, to anything. But with false gray dawn he had awakened, instantly, and began to dig in the pack—to find amazing, wonderful things.

There was a sleeping bag—which he hung to dry over his shelter roof on the outside—and foam sleeping pad. An aluminum cookset with four little pots and two frying pans; it actually even had a fork and knife and spoon. A waterproof container with matches and two small butane lighters. A sheath knife with a compass in the handle. As if a compass would help him, he thought, smiling. A first-aid kit with bandages and tubes of antiseptic paste and small scissors. A cap that said CESSNA[1] across the front in large letters. Why a cap? he wondered. It was adjustable and he put it on immediately. A fishing kit with four coils of line, a dozen small lures, and hooks and sinkers.

---

1 *CESSNA*   an airplane manufacturer.

Incredible wealth. It was like all the holidays in the world, all the birthdays there were. He sat in the sun by the doorway where he had dropped the night before and pulled the presents—as he thought of them—out one at a time to examine them, turn them in the light, touch them and feel them with his hands and eyes.

Something that at first puzzled him. He pulled out what seemed to be the broken-off, bulky stock of a rifle and he was going to put it aside, thinking it might be for something else in the pack, when he shook it and it rattled. After working at it a moment he found the butt of the stock came off and inside there was a barrel and magazine and action assembly, with a clip and a full box of fifty shells. It was a .22 survival rifle—he had seen one once in the sporting goods store where he went for bike parts—and the barrel screwed onto the stock. He had never owned a rifle, never fired one, but had seen them on television, of course, and after a few moments figured out how to put it together by screwing the action onto the stock, how to load it and put the clip full of bullets into the action.

It was a strange feeling, holding the rifle. It somehow removed him from everything around him. Without the rifle he had to fit in, to be part of it all, to understand it and use it—the woods, all of it. With the rifle, suddenly, he didn't have to know; did not have to be afraid or understand. He didn't have to get close to a foolbird to kill it—didn't have to know how it would stand if he didn't look at it and moved off to the side.

The rifle changed him, the minute he picked it up, and he wasn't sure he liked the change very much. He set it aside, leaning it carefully against the wall. He could deal with that feeling later. The fire was out and and he used a butane lighter and a piece of birchbark with small twigs to get another one started—marveling at how easy it was but feeling again that the lighter somehow removed him from where he was, what he had to know. With a ready flame he didn't have to know how to make a spark nest, or how to feed the new flames to make them grow. As with the rifle, he wasn't sure he liked the change.

Up and down, he thought. The pack was wonderful but it gave him up and down feelings.

With the fire going and sending up black smoke and a steady roar from a pitch-smelling chunk he put on, he turned once more to the pack. Rummaging through the food packets—he hadn't brought them out yet because he wanted to save them until last, glory in them—he came up with a small electronic device completely encased in a plastic bag. At first he thought it was a radio or cassette player and he had a surge of hope because he missed music, missed sounds, missed hearing another voice. But when he opened the plastic and took the thing out and turned it over he could see that it wasn't a receiver at all. There was a coil of wire held together on the side by tape and it sprung into a three-foot-long antenna when he took the tape off. No speaker, no lights, just a small switch at the top and on the bottom he finally found, in small print:

Emergency Transmitter.

That was it. He turned the switch back and forth a few times but nothing happened—he couldn't even hear static—so, as with the rifle, he set it against the wall and went back to the bag. It was probably ruined in the crash, he thought.

Two bars of soap.

He had bathed regularly in the lake, but not with soap and he thought how wonderful it would be to wash his hair. Thick with grime and smoke dirt, frizzed by wind and sun, matted with fish and foolbird grease, his hair had grown and stuck and tangled and grown until it was a clumped mess on his head. He could use the scissors from the first-aid kit to cut it off, then wash it with soap.

And then, finally—the food.

It was all freeze-dried and in such quantity that he thought, with this I could live forever. Package after package he took out, beef dinner with potatoes, cheese and noodle dinners, chicken dinners, egg and potato breakfasts, fruit mixes, drink mixes, dessert mixes, more dinners and breakfasts than he could count easily, dozens and dozens of them all packed in waterproof bags, all in perfect shape and when he had them all out and laid against the wall in stacks he couldn't stand it and he went through them again.

If I'm careful, he thought, they'll last as long as . . . as long as I need them to last. If I'm careful. . . . No. Not yet. I won't be careful just yet. First I am going to have a feast. Right here and now I am going to cook up a feast and eat until I drop and then I'll be careful.

He went into the food packs once more and selected what he wanted for his feast: a four-person beef and potato dinner, with orange drink for an appetizer and something called a peach whip for dessert. Just add water, it said on the packages, and cook for half an hour or so until everything was normal-size and done.

Brian went to the lake and got water in one of the aluminum pots and came back to the fire. Just that amazed him—to be able to carry water to the fire in a pot. Such a simple act and he hadn't been able to do it for almost two months. He guessed at the amounts and put the beef dinner and peach dessert on to boil, then went back to the lake and brought water to mix with the orange drink.

It was sweet and tangy—almost too sweet—but so good that he didn't drink it fast, held it in his mouth and let the taste go over his tongue. Tickling on the sides, sloshing it back and forth and then down, swallow, then another.

That, he thought, that is just fine. Just fine. He got more lake water and mixed another one and drank it fast, then a third one, and he sat with that near the fire but looking out across the lake, thinking how rich the smell was from the cooking beef dinner. There was garlic in it and some other spices and the smells came up to him and made him think of home, his mother cooking, the rich smells of the kitchen, and at that precise instant, with his mind full of home and the smell from the food filling him, the plane appeared.

He had only a moment of warning. There was a tiny drone but as before it didn't register, then suddenly, roaring over his head low and in back of the ridge a bushplane with floats fairly exploded into his life.

It passed directly over him, very low, tipped a wing sharply over the tail of the crashed plane in the lake, cut power, glided down the long part of the L of the lake, then turned and glided back, touching the water gently once, twice, and settling with a spray to taxi and stop with its floats gently bumping the beach in front of Brian's shelter.

He had not moved. It had all happened so fast that he hadn't moved. He sat with the pot of orange drink still in his hand, staring at the plane, not quite understanding it yet; not quite knowing yet that it was over.

The pilot cut the engine, opened the door, and got out, balanced, and stepped forward on the float to hop onto the sand without getting his feet wet. He was wearing sunglasses and he took them off to stare at Brian.

"I heard your emergency transmitter—then I saw the plane when I came over . . ." He trailed off, cocked his head, studying Brian. "Damn. You're him, aren't you? You're that kid? They quit looking, a month, no, almost two months ago. You're him, aren't you? You're that kid . . ."

Brian was standing now, but still silent, still holding the drink. His tongue seemed to be stuck to the roof of his mouth and his throat didn't work right. He looked at the pilot, and the plane, and down at himself—dirty and ragged, burned and lean and tough—and he coughed to clear his throat.

"My name is Brian Robeson," he said. Then he saw that his stew was done, the peach whip almost done, and he waved to it with his hand. "Would you like something to eat?"

EPILOGUE

THE PILOT who landed so suddenly in the lake was a fur buyer mapping Cree trapping camps for future buying runs—drawn by Brian when he unwittingly turned on the emergency transmitter and left it going. The Cree move into the camps for fall and winter to trap and the buyers fly from camp to camp on a regular route.

When the pilot rescued Brian he had been alone on the L-shaped lake for fifty-four days. During that time he had lost seventeen percent of his body weight. He later gained back six percent, but had virtually no body fat—his body had consumed all extra weight and he would remain lean and wiry for several years.

Many of the changes would prove to be permanent. Brian had gained immensely in his ability to observe what was happening and react to it; that would last him all his life. He had become more thoughtful as well, and from that time on he would think slowly about something before speaking.

Food, all food, even food he did not like, never lost its wonder for him. For years after his rescue he would find himself stopping in grocery stores to just stare at the aisles of food, marveling at the quantity and the variety.

There were many questions in his mind about what he had seen and known, and he worked at research when he got back, identifying the game and berries. Gut cherries were termed choke cherries, and made good jelly. The nut bushes where the foolbirds hid were hazelnut bushes. The two kinds of rabbits were snowshoes and cottontails; the foolbirds were ruffed grouse (also called fool hens by trappers, for their stupidity); the small food fish were bluegills, sunfish, and perch; the turtle eggs were laid by a snapping turtle, as he had thought; the wolves were timber wolves, which are not known to attack or bother people; the moose was a moose.

There were also the dreams—he had many dreams about the lake after he was rescued. The Canadian government sent a team in to recover the body of the pilot and they took reporters, who naturally took pictures and film of the whole campsite, the shelter—all of it. For a brief time the press made much of Brian and he was interviewed for several networks but the furor died within a few months. A writer showed up who wanted to do a book on the "complete adventure" (as he called it) but he turned out to be a dreamer and it all came to nothing but talk. Still Brian was given copies of the pictures and tape, and looking at them seemed to trigger the dreams. They were not nightmares, none of them was frightening, but he would awaken at times with them; just awaken and sit up and think of the lake, the forest, the fire at night, the night birds singing, the fish jumping—sit in the dark alone and think of them and it was not bad and would never be bad for him.

Predictions are, for the most part, ineffective; but it might be interesting to note that had Brian not been rescued when he was, had he been forced to go into hard fall, perhaps winter, it would have been very rough on him. When the lake froze he would have lost the fish, and when the snow got deep he would have had trouble moving at all. Game becomes seemingly plentiful in the fall (it's easier to see with the leaves off the brush) but in winter it gets scarce and sometimes simply nonexistent as predators (fox, lynx, wolf, owls, weasels, fisher, martin, northern coyote) sweep through areas and wipe things out. It is amazing what a single owl can do to a local population of ruffled grouse and rabbits in just a few months.

After the initial surprise and happiness from his parents at his being alive— for a week it looked as if they might actually get back together—things rapidly went back to normal. His father returned to the northern oil fields, where Brian eventually visited him, and his mother stayed in the city, worked at her career in real estate, and continued to see the man in the station wagon.

Brian tried several times to tell his father, came really close once to doing it, but in the end never said a word about the man or what he knew, the Secret.

Victor Martinez

1954–

VICTOR MARTINEZ was born in Fresno, California, the fourth child of parents who were migrant workers from Mexico. He eventually had eleven brothers and sisters. The family was not wealthy. Though his early and middle school years were marked by his academic progress, his teen years were troubled. Still he managed (with help from affirmative action) to enter California State at Fresno, where, he says, he tended to sit in the back of the classroom. A few of his teachers, however, recognized his creative writing talent, and he secured a graduate fellowship at Stanford where one teacher in particular, the well-known poet Philip Levine, encouraged him to pursue poetry while he worked at other jobs.

Martinez did write—poetry, short fiction, essays—while working variously as a crop-picker, welder, truck driver, firefighter, and office clerk. Some of his work was published, and Martinez for a time was poet-in-residence in the school system of San Francisco, where he had moved with his wife, Tina. Martinez has said he was hesitant to teach for fear he might not control his lively temper. He came to know and respect many of the students, however, and learned about the lives of some of the troubled ones. Out of this and his own experiences as a middle-teenager, together with the experiences of his siblings, Martinez fashioned his first novel, *Parrot in the Oven.*

He first sent the novel to Chicano publishers. Then, at his wife's urging, he dared to send it to mainstream publishers in New York. Joanna Cotler of HarperCollins read and liked it; she and other editors worked with Martinez to tighten the story line while keeping the poetic imagery.

When *Parrot in the Oven: mi vida*, appeared in 1996, the publishing world took notice. Reviewers praised this authentic Mexican American voice describing *barrio* life in prose at once poetic and vigorously honest. *Publisher's Weekly* named it among the best books of 1996; it appeared on the select "Fanfare Honor List" for 1996 sponsored by the *Boston Globe* and the *Horn Book Magazine*. Even more impressive was its 1996 National Book Award for Young People's Literature—recognition he found little short of miraculous. At a time when America's Hispanic population has reached new proportions, these prizes are an acknowledgement not only of the appearance of a new writing talent but of an element of American life that needs new attention.

YA Literature has had a Chicano voice, however, since the early 1990s, when Gary Soto began writing novels for YA readers. Soto, like Martinez, grew up in Fresno, California, of Mexican American heritage, and like Martinez, mines his early experiences there for his literary works. Two years older than Martinez, Soto was also encouraged by poet Philip Levine and published several collections of poetry for adults and one for young adults. Like Martinez, he blends a poetic awareness of language into his prose. His collection of stories *Baseball in April* was named by the American Library Association as one of the best books for young adults in 1990; since then he has written several other YA works. Until his 1997 novel *Buried Onions*, however, his work was lighter, more humorous, and aimed at a slightly younger audience than *Parrot*—probably the reasons it has not captured as much national attention as Martinez's novel.

Parrot in the Oven is more a collection of short stories than a carefully plotted novel, a quality that might be considered a literary weakness but that does, in fact, capture the random sense of life that typifies many adolescents' perceptions. Manny, the protagonist and narrator, is at the center of these vignettes of his home life with his father, mother, brother Nardo, and sisters Magda and Pedi, interspersed with glimpses of school, parties, part-time jobs, and gangs. We see the father's alcoholism, the family's poverty, the mother's desperation, the older sister Magda's need for acceptance, and Manny's frustrations about family responsibility, money, work, girls, and social status. *Parrot* shares these elements with a host of other Young Adult novels, for it is a modern coming-of-age tale. Manny stumbles through his days as *Catcher in the Rye*'s Holden Caulfield stumbles through his, somewhere between a boy and a man, accidentally doing good, and bumping into moments that change his perceptions of others and, ultimately, of himself.

What distinguishes this novel from lesser YA works, however, are its setting, its language, and two climactic moments that ground the novel in a kind of transcendent realism. The locale is apparently Fresno, California, in the 1970s, though this detail is less important than the setting of Manny's home, where his mother cleans obsessively as if to protect it from the grime of the outside world, where Magda hoards and plays her beloved phonograph records, and where his father's alcoholic rages threaten them all. Martinez creates place, action, and character simultaneously in such details: "He found some bullets, finally, inside Mom's dresser drawer, knotted up in one of her old bras. In his anxiousness to untie the straps, he scattered the bullets all over the floor. Rocking a little on his heels, he waited for Pedi to pick them up. She could get into corners and at one that spun like a pinwheel under the bed."

Manny's voice when he speaks to his family and friends is undistinguished, even ungrammatical. But his narrative voice reaches for perceptions that find beauty in unlikely places: "You could almost hear the strategies sizzling around in his head, like hot sand swirling inside a tin cup." At his grandmother's wake, he thinks, "She will flake away into dirt . . . Her shadow will be erased, and her soul will drift up to heaven like the fluff of a dandelion in the wind. And then it will blossom in another garden, so bright the colors will hurt your eyes." At times, these poetic flights seem a bit strained and intrusive ("My eyelashes were tiny wings beating in a fevery air, yet my face felt frozen, as if blasted by an arctic wind"), but they create a dimension to Manny that only the reader knows.

Parrot contains two moments of understated dramatic intensity that lift it beyond most YA novels. Manny remembers when his father had a job, when his homecoming made the house sparkle. Now his father is in constant pain from a bad back, but also drunk, murderous, manipulating, and insulting. When his sister Magda begins to abort her illegitimate baby, Manny and his mother try to hide her fever and hemorrhage from his sleeping father, terrified by the retribution he will take on Manny, Magda, and his mother. His father wakes suddenly, and, grasping everything "in a flash," lifts Magda from the bed into the bath—a loving act that saves her life and turns the novel toward its end. During the last part of the novel, after a humiliating encounter with white teens at a party, Manny flirts with the possibility of joining a gang. After his initiation and inadvertent participation in a purse-snatching, he escapes punishment because of a black man's generous act and goes home. There, he sees his sisters asleep on the couch; he sees the whole shabby room lit up with sunlight, and "it was wondrous, like a place I was meant to be." There is no preachiness, no overstatement of his feelings, just a joyful acceptance of his home with all its flaws.

One of the hallmarks of YA Literature is the rite of passage in which the protagonist moves from idealism to reality, which sometimes translates into cynicism, or at least sadness. Martinez's novel takes the rite of passage in the opposite direction. Manny's life has hardly been ideal; his dealings with the world—in school, jobs, the hospital—have already shown him that life isn't fair. But at the close of the novel Manny transcends his circumstances to embrace his family and his home, to see the beauty in this place that is his, as no other place on earth can be. Like Gary Paulsen, who as a young man discovered that "Macho is a lie," Manny has discovered that growing up is less about becoming strong than about becoming loving, accepting, and responsible.

Whether *Parrot in the Oven* will have the status of a classic twenty years from now, no one can say. We place it in this collection for its honest, intense depiction of a young man's maturation in a literary style that repays examination, and as a fine example—though not the only one—of recent YA novels which open a window onto the many cultures American young adults share with the world.

PARROT IN THE OVEN
MI VIDA

CHAPTER 1

The Baseball Glove

T HAT SUMMER my brother, Bernardo, or "Nardo," as we call him, flipped through more jobs than a thumb through a deck of cards. First he was a dishwasher, then a busboy, then a parking attendant and, finally, a patty turner for some guy who never seemed to be in his hamburger stand for more than ten minutes at a time. (Mom believed he sold marijuana, or did some other illegal shamelessness.) Nardo lost one job for not showing up regular enough, another for showing up too regular—the boss hated his guts. The last job lost him when the owner of the hamburger stand packed up unexpectedly and left for Canada.

The job Nardo misses most, though, was when he worked as a busboy for the Bonneville Lakes Golf and Catering Service. He says it was the only time he ever got to touch elbows with rich people. The parties they catered served free daiquiris, whisky drinks and cold beer, really cold, in big barrels choking with ice. At some parties, like the one he got fired from, they passed out tickets for juicy prizes like motorcycles, TV sets, stereos and snow skis. The last party had a six-piece band and a great huge dance floor so the "old fogies," as my brother called them, could get sloshed and make fools of themselves.

As it turns out, he and a white guy named Randy took off their busboy jackets and began daring each other to get a ticket and ask a girl to dance. Randy bet Nardo wouldn't do it, and Nardo bet he would, and after a two-dollar pledge he steered for the ticket lady.

"I could've hashed it around a bit, you know, Manny," he said. "I could've double- and triple-dared the guy a couple of times over, then come up with a good excuse. But that ain't my style."

Instead he tapped Randy's fingers smooth as fur and walked up to the ticket lady. She peered out from behind the large butcher-paper-covered table at the blotches of pasta sauce on his black uniform pants and white shirt—which were supposed to go clean with the catering service's light-orange busboy jacket, but didn't—and said, "Ah, what the hell," and tore him out a tag.

Before the little voice nagging inside him could talk louder, Nardo asked the nearest girl for a dance. She had about a million freckles and enough wire in her mouth to run a toy train over. They stumbled around the dance floor until the band mercifully ground to a halt. She looked down at his arm kind of shylike and said, "You dance real nice."

Now my brother had what you could call a sixth sense. *"Es muy vivo,"*[1] as my grandma used to say about a kid born that way, and with Nardo it was pretty

---

1 Es muy vivo.   He is very alive.

much a scary truth. He could duck trouble better than a champion boxer could duck a right cross. He made hairline escapes from baths, belt whippings and scoldings just by not being around when punishment came through the door. So I believed him when he said something ticklish crawled over his shoulder, and when he turned around, there, across the dance floor, in front of the band-leader about to make an announcement over the microphone, was his boss, Mr. Baxter—and boy was he steamed!

Mr. Baxter owned the catering service, and sometimes, my brother said, the way he'd yell at the busboys, it was like he owned them, too. Mr. Baxter didn't say anything, just pointed to the door, then at Nardo, and scratched a big X across his chest. Just like that, he was fired.

The way Nardo tells it, you'd think he did that man a favor working for him. "Don't you ever get braces, Manny," he said, as if that were the lesson he'd learned.

At first Nardo didn't want to go to the fields. Not because of pride, although he'd have used that excuse at the beginning if he could've gotten away with it. It was more because, like anyone else, he didn't like sobbing out tears of sweat in 110-degree sun. That summer was a scorcher, maybe the worst in all the years we'd lived in that valley desert, which our town would've been if the irrigation pumped in from the Sierra were turned off. I could tell how searing it was by the dragged-out way my mom's roses drooped every morning after I watered them. The water didn't catch hold. The roses only sighed a moment before the sun sucked even that little breather away.

Although it was hard for Nardo to duck my mom's accusing eyes, especially when Magda, my sister, came home slumped from the laundry after feeding bedsheets all day into a steam press, he was refusing to work anymore. Whether one tried threats, scoldings, or even shaming, which my mom tried almost every other day, nothing worked. We all gave it a shot, but none more vigorously than my dad. He'd yell and stomp around a little space of anger he'd cut in our living room, a branch of spit dangling from his lip. He'd declare to the walls what a good-for-nothing son he had, even dare Nardo to at least be man enough to join the Army. He vowed to sign the papers himself, since Nardo wasn't old enough.

The thing was, my dad wasn't working either. He'd just lost his job as a translator for the city because he'd drink beer during lunch and slur his words. Ever since losing his job, and even before, really, Dad had about as much pa-tience as you could prop on a toothpick. He was always zeroing in on things he wanted to be disappointed in, and when he found one, he'd loose a curse quicker than an eyeblink. Even when he wasn't cursing, you could still feel one simmering there under his lip, ready to boil over.

Even though he'd worked as a translator, my dad's English wasn't the great-est. Some syllables he just couldn't catch. Instead of saying "watch," he'd say "wash," and for "stupid," he'd slip in a bit of Spanish, "es-tupid." But when he said "ass" or "ounce," stretching the S with a long, lingering slowness, there was pure acid in the set of his teeth.

"If only Bernardo had jus whuan ounss, whuan ounss . . ." my dad would say, making the tiniest measure between his thumb and forefinger, but with a voice the size of our whole block.

For his part, Nardo stayed home lifting weights and doing sit-ups and push-ups, and nursing any piddling little pimple worth a few hours of panic. He was a nut about his handsome looks, and must have tenderly combed his hair at least twenty times a day in the mirror.

I wasn't like Nardo. I suppose years of not knowing what, besides work, was expected from a Mexican convinced me that I wouldn't pass from this earth without putting in a lot of days. I suppose Nardo figured the same, and wasn't about to waste his time. But I was of my grandpa Ignacio's line of useful blood. All his life, no matter what the job, my grandpa worked like a man trying to fill all his tomorrows with one solid day's work. Even in the end, when he got sick and couldn't move, he hated sitting on the couch doing nothing. He'd fumble around the house fixing sockets and floor trim, painting lower shelves and screwing legs back on to tables, although the finished chore was always more a sign of how much his mind had gotten older than anything else.

For a while, I hustled fruit with my cousins Rio and Pete. Their dad, my uncle Joe, owned a panel truck, and together we sold melons, apples, oranges—whatever grew in season—from door to door. But when my uncle hurt his leg tripping over some tree roots, and his ankle swelled up blue and tender as a ripened plum and he couldn't walk, except maybe to hobble on one leg to the refrigerator or lean over to change channels on the TV, he took the panel truck away.

Without work, I was empty as a Coke bottle. School was starting soon, and I needed money for clothes and paper stuff. I wanted a baseball mitt so bad a sweet hurt blossomed in my stomach whenever I thought about it. Baseball had a grip on my fantasies then, and I couldn't shake it loose. There was an outfielder's glove in the window of Duran's Department Store that kept me dreaming downright dangerous outfield catches. I decided to stir up Nardo to see if he'd go pick chili peppers with me.

"You can buy more weights!" I said a bit too enthusiastically, making him suspicious right off the bat.

He looked up at me from the middle of a push-up. "You think I'm lazy, don't you?"

"No," I lied.

"Yeah, you do. You think I'm lazy," he said, breathing tight as he pushed off the floor.

"I said no!"

"Yeah, you do." He forced air into his lungs, then got up miserably wiping his hands.

"But that's all right, little boy, if you think I'm lazy. Everybody else does." He started picking at a sliver in his palm. "I'm not really lazy, you know. I've been working off and on." He greedily bit the sliver, moving his elbow up and down like a bird's wing. "If Mom wants me to go," he said, finally, "I'll go. If that's what *she* wants. But I'm telling you right now, if it gets hot I'm quitting."

Miracles don't wait for doubters, so the next morning I asked my dad if we could borrow his car, a Plymouth, which Nardo could drive despite the tricky gearshift. Dad was pretty cheery about me getting Nardo out of hibernation. He gave us some paint cans for the chili peppers and practically put a Christmas ribbon on the large brimmed hats from Mexico he'd bought years ago. The headbands were already dark with sweat and the straw furry with dust, but they'd protect us from the sun.

When we arrived at the chili field, the wind through the window was warm on our shirt-sleeves. Already the sky was beginning to hollow out, the clouds rushing toward the rim of the horizon as if even they knew the sun would soon be the center of a boiling pot.

The foreman, wearing a pale-yellow shirt with a black-leather vest and cowboy boots with curled tips, refused at first to hire us, saying I was too young, that it was too late in the day—most field workers got up at the first wink of dawn. Besides, all the rows had been taken hours ago. He laughed at the huge lunch bag bulging under Nardo's arm, and said we looked like two kids strolling out on a picnic.

Although he could fake disappointment better than anybody, deep down I believed Nardo wanted to give picking chilies a try. But a good excuse was a good excuse, and any excuse was better than quitting. So he hurriedly threw his can into the car trunk and made a stagy flourish with his hand before opening the side door.

Seeing him so spunky, I thought it nothing less than torture when the foreman said that, fortunately for us, there was a scrawny row next to the road no one wanted. The foreman must have thought it a big joke, giving us that row. He chuckled and called us over with a sneaky offer of his arm, as if to share a secret.

"*Vamos, muchachos, aquí hay un surco muy bueno que pueden piscar,*"[2] he said, gesturing down at some limp branches leaning away from the road, as if trying to lift their roots and hustle away from the passing traffic. The leaves were sparse and shriveled, dying for air, and they had a coat of white pesticide dust and exhaust fumes so thick you could smear your hands on the leaves and rub fingerprints with them.

My brother shrugged. His luck gone, there was not much else he could do. The foreman hung around a bit to make sure we knew which peppers to pick and which to leave for the next growing, not that it mattered in that row.

We'd been picking about two hours when the sun began scalding the backs of our hands, leaving a pocket of heat crawling like a small animal inside our shirts. My fingers were as rubbery as old carrots, and it seemed forever before the peppers rose to the center of my can. Nardo topped his can before I did, patted the chilies down and lifted it over his shoulder, his rock of an arm solid against his cheek.

"I'm gonna get my money and buy me a soda," he said, and strode off toward the weighing area, carefully swishing his legs between the plants. I limped behind him, straining with my half-filled can of lungless chili peppers.

The weighing area wasn't anything special, just a tripod with a scale hook hanging from the center. People brought their cans and sagging burlap sacks and formed a line. After the scale pointer flipped and settled, heaving with the sack's weight, the peppers were dumped onto a wooden table-bed. Tiny slits between the boards let the mixed-in dirt and leaves sift through.

There was a line of older women and young girls with handkerchiefs across their faces. They stood along the sides, like train robbers in cowboy movies, cleaning the leaves and clods of dirt, pushing the peppers down through a chute. When the sack at the end bloated, one of the foremen unhooked it from the nails and sewed the opening. Then he stacked it on a pile near a waiting truck whose driver lay asleep in the cab with boots sticking out in the blurry currents of air.

Standing near the table-bed, my eyes flared and nose dribbled a mustache of watery snot. The dried leaves and the angry scent of freshly broken peppers was

---

2 Vamos, muchachos, aqui hay un surco muy bueno que pueden piscar.   Let's go, kids, there's a good row to pick.

like being swarmed by bees. No matter how hard I tried to keep my breath even, I kept coughing and choking like I had a crushed ball of sandpaper stuffed in my throat. I wondered how the women were able to stand it, even with the handkerchiefs.

The only good thing about the weighing area was that they paid right after announcing your load. This lured workers from Mexico needing quick cash for rent or emergency food, and people like me who had important baseball mitts to buy. It also brought business to a burrito truck behind the scales owned by the labor contractor. It sold everything from chicken tacos, chili beans and egg burritos, to snow cones and fudge bars.

The prices, though, made Nardo complain real loud: "You know how much I paid for this!" he exclaimed, when out of earshot of the foreman. "Eighty-five cents! Eighty-five cents for a damn soda! And to top it off, it's one of those cheap jobs with no fizzle or nothing."

We picked steadily on, but by noon both Nardo and I were burned out, with our tongues flagging in the heat, and a good sprint away from the nearest picker. Farther up, under clouds boiling like water on the horizon, a staggered string of men worked two and three rows apiece.

"They're wetbacks,"[3] my brother explained; "they pick like their goddamned lives depended on it."

I looked over at the Mexican man working on the rows next to ours and nodded agreement. He handled four rows all by himself, using two cans, and trading handfuls from one can to the other. He'd go up two rows, then down two rows, greeting us on his return with a smile and shy wave. To save time, he placed burlap sacks every twenty feet, and every half hour or so he'd pour a loaded can into the closest. Behind him, three sacks already lay fat and tightly sewn. We eyed him, amazed by his quickness.

"Maybe that's what we should do," I suggested.

Nardo shook his head. "Are you crazy?" he asked with conviction. "It'll take us the whole damn day just to fill one lousy sack."

He was right. We weren't the best pickers in the field; we weren't even close to being the worst. We stopped too much, my brother to eye the girls near the weigher, and me to watch the man and compare hands. His were wings in a blur of wonder, mine stirred a pot of warm honey. The way he moved, too, made me think he'd make a terrific shortstop, what with the way he shifted from plant to plant, his knees like a triangle, tilting first one way then another. He was a whirlwind when gathering up his cans and burlap sacks, and eyeing him this way, with admiration, almost made me forget my own tiredness, although he never seemed to tire, never seemed to rise much above the plant, but hid inside the quivering leaves until with one flickering toss, a rain of yellow peppers showered the air and dropped into his can.

I was marveling at him when Nardo tapped me on the shoulder. "Look what's coming," he said, pointing his chin at a van creeping up the road.

Cars had been insulting us with dust and exhaust fumes all morning, so when I saw how this van approached, like a dog sneaking up on a bush, I knew something was wrong.

The van was green, a dim, starved-for-light green, like the leaves on our row. Its windows were open and the man behind the wheel had his head out scan-

---

3 *wetbacks* Mexican laborers who illegally cross the U.S. border ("wet" because they often cross through the Rio Grande).

ning the rows. Suddenly people began to stand up, licking the air and stretching as if peering over a high wall. There was fast talking in Spanish and frenzied commotion as suddenly forty or so people all at once jumped up and started running. They didn't even bother going through the furrows in scissor steps like Nardo had done, but ran in waves, trampling over plants and tipping over cans. Those last to run brought up the rear, steadying their hats with one hand and thrashing their snapped-up coats in the other.

I still didn't know what was going on. My first thought was to run, but when I saw three more vans and a large labor bus pop out of a narrow road in the cornfield bordering ours, I knew that Immigration had come for the people.

No one had seen the other vans place themselves at points along the cornfield. The people just ran wildly in panic toward them as if their first thought was to hide in the stalks. The quicker ones got caught at once, their paths cut off by officers holding out their arms. They surrendered without a word. The slower ones veered off into the open spaces of the cordon and dove into the field. Most were caught in the first sweep, except for some who ducked under the arms of the officers and hustled down the road; but they, too, were quickly run down by another van and escorted inside.

The handful who hid in the cornstalks seemed to have gotten away. We all cheered and waved our arms as if our side had won. Some of us jeered at the officers, my brother Nardo the loudest.

Everyone quieted down, though, when some of the officers formed a line along the field and disappeared into the stalks. A while later they came out yanking on the shirt collars of those we thought had gotten away. Everybody sighed and said nothing.

The foreman who'd given us the scraggly row rushed over to see what was going on. He took off in a huff saying "son-ova-beeches," and worse. I thought he was going to cuss those Immigration guys off, but instead he stood by meekly watching the officers corral the people before loading them into the vans. I tried to find the Mexican on the row next to ours, but I didn't see him. I hoped he'd gotten away.

The officer in charge approached the foreman and said something we couldn't make out, but it sounded like a scolding. The foreman came back and knelt down by the water tank. "Damn son-ova-beeches," he said again, flicking his hat off and raising dust as he slapped it against his pant leg. He poured himself some water and glared over at the Immigration officers as they packed in the people and roared off in a boiling cloud of dust. A crowd of us stood around covering our eyes. No one bothered to go back to work.

When the air cleared, a man tottered back from the spot where the vans had assembled. He was an older man with salt-and-pepper stubble on his chin and a slightly longer and darker mustache. He was nursing his right knee.

At first I thought maybe he'd gotten away, but then someone recognized him and laughed, "Hey Joe, you're not a wetback. You're a *bracero*."[4]

Joe came slowly over and took off his hat and covered his stomach as if he'd been caught naked. He shrugged an apology and said he couldn't help it, when everyone else began to run, he got so excited he ran too. He looked down at his legs as if they'd betrayed him. He said Immigration let him go as soon as they saw he had too much meat on his bones to be a wetback. Everybody laughed. Then his family, whose confused uncle he was, came over and led him away.

---

4 *bracero*   temporary or seasonal farm laborer, especially a Mexican.

Nardo and I laughed too, but for some reason I thought he was the best man in the whole field.

Of the twenty or so people left, everyone claimed they encouraged the Mexicans not to run. They said Immigration guys usually don't go into the fields to check for citizenship unless they have a good reason. If you acted like you belonged, sometimes you could fool them. They said none of those ungratefuls took them at their word, though, and for that they had only themselves to blame.

One of the listeners, a tall pimple-faced guy with blotchy cheeks and the skin of a fig, only paler, shouted out, "*Pinches gavachos*[5] don't give a damn about harassing us! *Gavachos* do what they want." He didn't wait for anybody to answer back, nor did he pick up any cans or equipment, but walked quickly away, swung open the door of a rusty Buick and drove off.

"I guess he came alone," Nardo said musingly. He rubbed his eyes with the backs of his wrists, then became more alert. "Hey, we can pick on any row we want now."

"That man's crazy! Those people don't live here, anyway," said a short, moist-faced guy with tight bunched-in cheeks and pants that settled unevenly around his waist. When he walked, one of his legs looked shorter than the other. He went over to one of the rows a Mexican had been picking on and lifted up a pair of old shoes. The soles were crusted with mud and the leather scarred and furrowed like the faces of old men who've worked in the fields all their lives. He held them at the tips of his fingers and away from his precious nose. The man who wore them probably had taken them off in the heat to stick his toes in the moist, irrigated soil. A small chorus of laughter went up when he held them high, then fell when he dropped them back to earth. He rummaged some more down the row until he found a sack bulging with chili peppers.

"Hey, I'm gonna keep these," he declared, and began dragging the sack.

When everyone saw this they all began to scramble around for the other abandoned sacks, claiming their right by how close their rows had been to the Mexicans beside them. The sacks belonging to the man working on the rows next to ours were laying, tightly sewn, on their sides. Nardo walked over and placed his hand on one. Two other guys came over to argue about whom the others belonged to, but my brother was stronger, and after some half-serious pushing and shoving they walked away grumbling.

"Look, Manny," Nardo said, excitedly spearing up his shirtsleeves. He lifted one sack by its ears and pounded it on the ground, packing the peppers down its belly. "We got more here than it'd take us two days to pick. Hey, you can even buy your mitt."

I thought of the baseball glove, all clean and stiff and leather-smelling, and of myself in the cool green lawn of center field. I imagined already being on the baseball team at school, and people looking at me. Not these people picking chilies or those sent away in the vans, but people I had yet to know, watching me as I stood mightily in center field. I looked down at the sacks, then far out in the distance at the clouds of dust folding and unfolding where the vans were pulling away. I wondered how long I'd have had to work to fill those sacks. The weariness of it stretched as wide as the horizon.

---

5 pinches gavachos   rascally white people.

CHAPTER 2

Rico's Pool Hall

Rico's Pool Hall was Dad's favorite spot in the whole world. Among four pool tables made of solid wood, cobwebs of smoke drifting to the ceiling, the air smelling hearty of varnished wood, field sweat, beer and farts, he breathed easy. All day he talked to his buddies about Mexico, and about schemes for making money and escaping back to Mexico—although some of the men there were born in the United States.

Kids weren't allowed in the pool hall, but Rico let me stay sometimes while waiting for Dad. I'd sit on a stool at the far end of the bar, watching guys lean against pool cues, smoke and cuss one another out. I even saw a fight once where a guy threw a cue ball at a man in a Texas hat and smacked his teeth clean off the gums.

Because of his drinking, and because of the milk she said drained into the gutter whenever he drank, Mom hated to see Dad go to Rico's. She was always dragging me along with her to bring him home. On the day after the chili peppers, we were all piled in the car—my little sister Pedi whining about the heat, Magda clapping her hands to the rock-and-roll music inside her head, Dad complaining about a streak of clever pool shots he was working on before Mom yanked him rudely away. No telling how much money he could have won, he kept saying.

Steam puffed from my mouth and my nose ached from the heavy tar smell of melting asphalt. That's when I did a stupid thing. I put my arm on the car door and shouted, "Dammit!" as I jerked from the searing metal.

Sitting in the front seat, Mom heard me, and before I could plead excuses, she reached over her shoulder and smacked me one on the mouth. There were certain rules that needed no part of a brain's labor for Mom to smack me one. If she caught me cursing, or breaking a glass, she'd pound my arm. Twice if the curse had anything to do with girls, or the glass had milk. Also, whatever gossip could cling to our family for as long as people's memories lasted, I was to avoid.

With my Dad, it was more simple. If I grew a bit too raucous, he'd put a vise grip on my shoulder and whisper hot breath inside my ear. "Settle down quick, Manuel," he'd say, "or elsse."

Luckily, he was still too soaked from drinking at the pool hall to pay me any mind. He did get into it with the three Garcia brothers, though, who were lazying around their front yard.

"*¡Qué chingados!*"[1] he exclaimed, as we drove into the parking lot. "Those bastards, drinking beer and laughing out of their mouths. They'd suck their mother's last milk if she wasn't dead."

Dad was angry at the Garcias for destroying his dream. He had bought this croquet set, with which he planned to play with the neighbors while lounging away the hot afternoons. But on the first day we brought it home, the Garcias came over like wild chimpanzees. Bobby wrestled a mallet out of my hands and tossed it into a tree, and Stinky stole a wire wicket while Dad's back was turned. Dad vowed never again to favor our neighborhood with culture.

---

1 *que chingados!* What roughnecks!

I slunk my chin low while Dad slowed the car and gazed acidly at the Garcias. They pretended these big, idiot smiles, and seeing them act so disrespectful, Dad yelled out the window, "Where're your girlfriends. Did you send them off to work for you?"

This riled Bobby and Stinky, who were old enough to have girlfriends but didn't. They started pushing their chairs around searching for a rock, but Dad laughed and pumped the gas.

He was chuckling under his breath when he pulled up in front of our house, made of Sheetrock and a gravel-tile roof. Shaped like box hotels in a Monopoly set, the houses weren't pretty or stylish, but in spring the grass flowed to every porch like green water lapping against the hulls of houseboats, and that was beautiful. But now it was summer, and the heat had sucked the grass blond.

Dad seemed to like his clever joke, so I figured the next best thing for him was to start in about the Welfare, and sure enough, he fired his two cents into that one. Actually, Mom started him off, so I shouldn't blame Dad, totally. She mentioned how some men from the projects were earning money from jobs the Welfare gave them. She'd seen them coming home with metal lunch pails and shirts flagging out of their pants.

"But you know how the Welfare is," Dad said. "They want to know everything. A social worker comes over, acting like we're criminals. Then the whole neighborhood knows we're getting Welfare."

He looked dazed, Dad did, like if you tapped him on the shoulder he'd bolt off running down the street. Mom just pursed her lips. She knew he was just groping for something to complain about. Besides, half of the projects were already getting Welfare, and the other half were trying to get on. This didn't stop Dad, though.

"They'll make a copy of my driver's license, Rebecca," he insisted, "and it will stay in their files." After grinding his finger about fifty times in the air, he added, "Besides, I have never done anything in my whole life that would make me beg."

"Would you rather let the kids starve?" Mom asked, indignant and, as usual, making a ton of sense.

This reddened Dad's face more than the beer had already, but even he knew those canned meats and yellow bricks of butter the Welfare gave away wouldn't be half bad.

But it was no use. Dad believed weasely guys already owned the world, and anything you could do to get over on them was useless. He believed people were like money. If you were a million-dollar person, you had a grip on things, a big house maybe, and a crowd of suckers you could push around. You could be a thousand-dollar person or a hundred-dollar person—even a ten-, five-, or one-dollar person. Below that, everybody was just nickels and dimes. To my dad, we were pennies.

Finally, he slowed down the wheels in his brain. "I'll get a job," he said, sullenly, "don't worry about it, I'll get job." Then he got out of the car and rushed inside, slinking through the hydraulic screen door.

Mom just gazed at the empty space where he had disappeared, then smirked her lips away from her teeth. She'd heard it all before. Ever since he lost his job with the city, every day he'd zoom on about the Welfare, or about the Garcias, or how he was going to get another job, this time on a higher floor.

I always wondered why he got so tossed around by things, why he'd roughen his voice and tire himself out complaining. Mom was more quiet. Whenever she worried about something, she'd bite her nails and look up at the sky; not like she was staring at the clouds, but like the whole sky was the most marvelous sight she'd ever seen.

When they started shouting and throwing their arms around, which I knew they'd do as soon as Mom walked in through the door, it was best to disappear. Even the walls sweated. Mom's shrieks chased away the panicked air; Dad's voice was coarse paper shredding to pieces. Sometimes I'd climb the elm tree out back or race over to my friend Frankie's, where the TV talked all day with nobody listening.

As I left, I saw my sister Magda through the window listening to records. She was singing to herself, stabbing her hands in the air like a belly dancer. "Everything's awright. Everything's gonna be awright," she sang.

I speeded across the parking lot, my eyelids heavy under the sun, grumbling over my mom's criminal unfairness. My lip was pulsing from where she had slapped me, and a swatch of blood smeared when I dabbed it with my fingers. My steps were snapping crisply on the dry shoots of blond grass when I reached the Big Lawn, where almost all year round the guys in our projects either smacked a baseball around or ran football plays, while our mothers, on plastic chairs, visited with one another, drinking iced tea and sprinkling gossip on the backs of those who got up to do chores.

Suddenly a dog crashed out of some side bushes, grunting and hunkering low, froth blowing from his mouth. I was afraid he was coming to clamp his jaws on my leg, but then I saw the Garcia brothers, Bobby, Stinky and Little Tommy, chasing him with sticks. Stinky let fly a rock and it whizzed past my ear. Whether he was aiming at the dog or me, I wasn't sure, but they sure weren't going to catch the dog. Its paws were practically blistering on the asphalt.

The Garcias slowed down to a trot and veered toward me. Stinky, who was sweating enough to drip drops on the ground, was wearing a dingy gray T-shirt and jeans that looked as if they'd been scraped with rocks. Little Tommy had on a yellow-plaid shirt. Bobby wore a long green Pendleton shirt with red and gold patterns. His arms were straight at his sides, like he didn't want to wrinkle anything, and his mouth crooked funny when his head tilted back.

"Hey, it's the Hernandez boy," Bobby said over his shoulder to his brothers. Then, turning to me, he said, "Hey, Hernandez, I hear your fawder's got a job in the Welfare?"

I didn't bother denying it. Nothing anybody said could sink in with the Garcias.

"Hey, Manny." This time it was Stinky, twisting a stick in his hand, acting like he'd just thought up something terrific. He was in my grade at school, but about three years older than everybody else. He had ratty shoulders and two large can-opener teeth. His black hair was swatted smooth with pomade, and his voice sounded like two knife blades rubbing together.

I'd always been afraid of him. Every year at school he made it a habit of punching me around to show he was still boss. Once he broke a bone in my little finger, and I lied to Mom about it, saying that I got it sliding into second base. Another time he separated the soft rubber on the bridge of my nose, and I had to tell her I got hit by a pop fly.

Stinky was either hitching up his pants or trying to pull a knife out of his back pocket, I couldn't tell. "Where're *your* girlfriends, huh, Manny? You got any girls on you?"

Bobby, the oldest, came over and slung a lazy arm over my shoulder. I thought maybe he wanted to give my head a knuckle burn, but instead he looked into my ear as if peering into a microscope. He started fiddling with the collar of my shirt, twisting it like a necklace around his finger. His breath smelled gamy, of beer and sour pork. "You think your dad could get us some girls, Manny?" he said. "Your Dad knows a lot about that, huh?" He pulled on my collar. "What-aya say, Manny?"

Then he yanked hard again on my collar. I jerked back for balance but slipped and smashed my hip against the sidewalk. I stood up in an eye-blink, not wanting to be lying there with the Garcias around. Inside me something knotted, began to gel, then jiggle, as if shaking loose from under a trembling light. Even Little Tommy could tell I was scared. He was bouncing up and down, his scrawny legs working furiously, his fists clenched above his ears.

Stinky shoved his way back in and pressed his palm against my chest. "Hey, Manny," he said, "why don't you fix me a date with your sister, *ése*?"[2]

"She doesn't go on dates," I said, but right away knew that I'd made a mistake by talking.

"Oh yeah, why don't she go on dates, huh?" Stinky asked. "What? Does she think she's too good for me? Is that it, *ése*? Is she too good for me now?" Stinky's fist was wound tight and he was jabbing it close to my face. I could see little white lightning bolts between his knuckles.

"My dad says she's too young."

"Too young!" Stinky exploded, fanning open his fingers. He started flinching his arms. "Man, she must be nineteen or something!"

Then Little Tommy, looking ornery and offended, huffed over and planted his bony chest against mine. He had a big smudge of dirt on his cheek and a glob of gum stuck in his uncombed hair. He glared at me with his tiny anger, but Stinky wasn't finished, and again elbowed his way between us.

"Who in the hell does your sister think she is anyways . . . the Queen of Sheba? I oughta kick your frickin' ass right here, just ta show you no one's too good for me." He slowly cranked back his fist as if to clobber me, but then Bobby, who looked sleepy, like someone had poured Karo syrup over his face, shoved him away.

"Get back, Stinky! He's just a punk."

"Hey, it's Manny who *wants* to fight, not me," Stinky exclaimed, exaggerating his voice. "Look, Bobby, he's *making* a fist at me!" When Bobby turned, Stinky steered around him and flung a blow at my chin, his fingers whiffing the air near my nose. "Hey, you wanna fight?" he said, stepping back and shuffling his feet around like a boxer admiring his moves.

Stinky was wild about himself. He began clowning around, winding his arms and bluffing blows at my face. "I'll break your nose again, boy," he said, snapping his fingers. "I'll make that bump on your nose bigger. You'll lose ten pounds just taking in my punches."

Pushing Stinky away, Bobby turned to me with a creamy voice. "Whatsa matter with you, Manny, don't you *like* us?"

Just like that, they lost interest in me, and started walking across the Big Lawn toward the Yellow Projects. A cold ache of fear thawed in my chest, but I didn't move, thinking that if I did, they'd reel around and start bullying me again. When they were a little farther away, Stinky turned around, waving at me

---

2 ése   guy, dude.

like I was his best friend in the whole world—which, actually, even after all the times he beat me up, I really think he believed.

"Next time, Aw'm gonna kick your ass!" he said, smiling friendly.

I decided to head back home. I didn't want to risk running into them again. The sky was scarred with clouds shaped like giant hoof marks, but the sun was hot and sputtering on the rim of the horizon. It was like walking into an ocean of heat.

When I got home, everything was quiet. I saw Magda through the window of her room, cleaning bits of dust from her records. On the porch, Pedi was playing jacks with a golf ball Nardo had stolen from Bonneville Lakes Golf and Catering. I tousled her hair and stepped inside.

Dad was sitting on the living-room couch, his feet propped on the coffee table, drinking a can of beer and nipping little gulps of tequila from a pint bottle. In the kitchen, Mom was scrubbing the counter. She had her black hair braided into a solid coil in the back and was wearing a flower-print apron with the sleeves puffed like biscuits.

Mom was wild about daytime movies. When the music on the TV quickened, she'd angle her head through the doorway and watch the action. When there was a lot of talking, she'd scrub hard on the daisy-print linoleum. I thought she was going to grab me by the collar and plant me in front of the sink to wash dishes; instead, she said. "*Mijo,*[3] you're blocking the TV!"

"What are you watching?"

"A Tony Curtis movie."

Standing behind a liquor bar, Tony was rustling ice cubes in a glass and twirling a spoon in suave, romantic circles. He glinted his eyes enticingly at some jazzy-looking blond lady—Marilyn Monroe, or somebody—lounging on a billowy couch. The blond lady didn't suspect a thing. Or maybe she did. Mom sure in the hell did. She knew Tony.

While I was standing there watching the off-and-on squiggles on the TV, Mom grabbed me by the shoulder and shoved me aside. "Move, *mijo*!" she said, craning her neck.

Although sitting close to the TV, Dad was pretending like he wasn't watching. He'd get interested in the parts where Mom's eyes glued on Tony, though. He'd stretch his leg across the coffee table to block out part of the screen, knowing this annoyed her, although she was trying hard to ignore him.

After a while, Mom came into the living room like gravity was pulling at her. She sat on the arm of the couch and propped her chin on her palms. So close was Tony to the blond lady that you could practically zipper their eyelashes together.

That's when Dad got up, snatching angrily at the air, and huffed into the bathroom. He washed, slapped on aftershave and smoothed his hair back with Red Rose brilliantine. He came out wearing a white shirt and black pants, like he was dressing for a funeral. Fat chance he was going to stick around to watch Tony smooch with the blond lady, while Mom swooned. He was heading back to Rico's to see if he could connect again with his lucky shooting streak. He stood over Mom for about a minute to see if she'd lift her eyes, then grinned meanly, grabbed his keys and pint of tequila and stormed out.

Mom just kept watching the TV. I guess she figured she could scold him for starving us, scold him about the unpaid rent or the job somewhere in the world waiting for him to try harder, but she was tired of all that. She knew if she clut-

---

3 mijo   my son (affectionate term).

tered his ears with too much griping, it would only thicken his stubbornness. He'd smolder around the house for hours, grumbling and haranguing until he gnawed her patience down to shreds.

Outside, I heard the car starter winding, but it wouldn't kick over. "God dammit!" Dad shouted.

I pushed the curtains back and saw him wrestling with the arm of the gear shift, which sometimes stuck. He slammed his feet on the floor and shook the wheel; then, relaxing his hands, he stared hard at me, like I was weeds growing wild in a field that some day he'd have to chop.

Mom came up behind me and pressed down on my shoulders, her hands smelling of ammonia. We watched as Dad got out of the car and walked across the parking lot, grumbling. The hoof-mark clouds in the sky had burned away, and already I could see the wind beginning to smooth out the wrinkles of the afternoon heat. Pedi was still on porch, erasing some sparrows tracks on the dusty concrete.

Two of the Garcia brothers, Bobby and Stinky, snuck out from behind our neighbor Sophie's house and followed Dad, laughing and shoving each other with dares. They threw little pieces of gravel at him, trying to land them inside his neck collar, but he only swiped at the air behind his head and kept walking.

I turned around and saw the thick cords on Mom's neck, pulsing. She looked at me, and with a funny smile squeezed her fingers against my cheeks, sparking tiny needles of pain. When she let go, my face stung with a glowing warmth.

CHAPTER 3

Charity

T HE NEXT day, Mom began thinking about the future. She wanted me to go to a better school across town, where all the white kids got educated. So I grabbed the number 42 bus down Chandler Avenue, walked two blocks to the brown, ivy-rusted walls of my high school, and presented a note from my mom to Mrs. Kingsley, the secretary. Mom had heard rumors that they didn't like kids leaving my school and sometimes would mix things up for months, so she wanted me to get a record of my grades in person.

Mrs. Kingsley was an old white lady with cat-eye glasses dangling on a silver chain necklace. She had a pasty face, thick berry-painted lips and enough wrinkles on her neck to make a parachute. After giving her the note—she seemed to know what it was about, but asked me to read it anyway, I guess to test my English—she slid out a manila folder from a squeaky steel cabinet and, with an "I know more than you" smile, handed me the records. Her eyes casually dropped along the length of my arm, and just as I was about to grab the folder, she pushed it away like a worm had plopped down on it from the ceiling.

While waiting to catch the bus, I thought about calling Dad to see if he'd give me a ride home, but figured he was still numb from drinking the night before and would probably scold me for the hell of it. Besides, Mom wanted to keep it hush about me attending a school across town. She thought schooling could graduate me into places that would make her eyes gleam. Dad thought I should cut school altogether and get a dishwashing job. *Start on the bottom and work your way up*, that's what he'd say. Only most of the people he knew started on the bottom and worked their way sideways.

I got hooked watching cars swish by on the street. They'd skirt against the curb trying to crowd into a gas station at the corner. The pump man was this big, muscly guy with bleachy hair and angry clusters of pimples around his face and neck. He was tanking up the cars, banging the nozzle around like a cattleprod and pretty much doing a lousy job of wiping the windows. None of the customers seemed to work up a sweat about it, though, or maybe they just didn't want to tussle with a beefy guy spitting sunflower seeds.

I was watching this when my old history teacher, Mr. Hart, came up and stood beside me. I remembered him because his favorite subject was the Civil War. He was wild about General McClellan, who he swore was a military genius and only needed a chance to put his sophisticated designs of warfare to work. Of course, on the battlefield, McClellan got chopped up bad by Robert E. Lee, but that didn't matter to Mr. Hart a bit; it was the beauty of the plan that counted. Once, I remember during class, after he'd gotten all teary-eyed about the battle of Gettysburg, this smart-aleck guy named Malcolm Angustus leaked out this cheesy little snicker and the whole class bursted out laughing. Mr. Hart's face pumped red with embarrassment.

At first he pretended he didn't recognize me, then he raised his eyebrows. "What are you doing here!?"

"I came to get my grades."

"What on earth for?"

He sounded concerned, so I told him. "My mom wants me to go Hawthorne School across town."

"Mmm," he said, looking down at my shoes. "You *have* the grades. You're a pretty smart boy." He was thinking hard, but he kept staring at my shoes. They were my dad's old pair that had got chewed up by dogs when he left them outside. My feet slid around in two extra sizes of space. The tongue flopped out of the left, and a jagged crack split down the sole of the right from stomping on shovels. Neither shoe had enough lace to grip more than three rings.

"What have you been doing this summer?" Mr. Hart asked finally, snapping out of his thoughts.

"I have been working in a variety of jobs."

I spoke organized English to Mr. Hart, maybe a bit too organized. He was a twitchy kind of teacher who got all pushed out of shape if you talked to him natural. He was always wearing stay-pressed slacks and a white shirt with a black tie thin as an exclamation mark. I liked him because he wasn't one of those movie-star teachers who all the girls giggle over and guys respect, who act like they're your buddy and want to shoot the breeze when really they're just snoops and end up reporting you for smoking in the restroom.

"That's fine, real fine, Manuel," he said. "Most kids don't carry their own weight, you know."

I shifted the shoe with the floppy tongue behind the other, regretting I'd worn them.

"How much money did you make for school?" he asked, smiling but holding back his teeth.

"Well, sir," I said, "we made enough."

Searching for words—mostly to keep his eyes away from my shoes—I told him we went to San Jose, but that was to pick figs, and only for a week. We never got to see the city.

Mr. Hart smiled again, still holding back his teeth, and rubbed his chin. He kept flicking at his nose, sliding out little flakes that he'd leave dangling. It looked awful.

"Did you ever stop to think, Manuel, that maybe you have to go places, experience things?"

"Well, sir, I never thought about it, actually."

He studied my shoes some more.

"How about it if I give you a ride home?" he said, rubbing the back of his hand.

Before I could unclog the surprise from my throat, he poked into his pocket and brought out a small paper bag and a pencil and scribbled something down.

"I'll be heading your way in a little while. Why don't you come with me."

Just then the bus came and I edged to the curb, telling him thanks but no thanks. I talked with my hands to steer his eyes away from my shoes, but he kept staring. I was about to jump on the bus and bury myself in the crush of people when he smiled, this time agreeable and with a blare of teeth. He grabbed my arm, "Come on," he said. "You can keep me company."

My eyes followed the orange-lined bus as it pulled away from the curb. When I turned around, Mr. Hart was shaking his head and smiling at the ground where I'd been standing.

The school had been closed for summer, except for the administration building and some bungalows for half-day summer classes. Mr. Hart's room was on the second floor next to the typewriting class. Without all the ticking and tacking that goes on during regular school I could hear our footsteps whispering in the hallway.

Mr. Hart waved me into his office and asked where I lived. His room smelled salty; not ocean salty, or can of potted meat salty, but a musty, papery saltiness, like books sweating. He motioned me to sit down, but I stayed standing. Then he showed me what he had written on the paper bag. It said, *Give the Hernandez boy $20.* He pointed at the amount and asked if it was enough.

"Enough for what?"

"Enough for school supplies. You know, papers and pencils, binders, stuff like that. You'll need them at your new school." He was upping his voice to sound official.

Too embarrassed to tell him that attending another school was just a dream of my mom's—another one that probably wasn't going to hatch—I assured him that I had money by lightly patting my pocket. He nodded, then folded the paper. He reached back for his wallet anyway, and opened it to a spread of bills, tugging one out. Then, a shade embarrassed, and clearing his throat, he grabbed my hand and pretended to shake it, slipping me the money.

The sun was milky when we finally got going, and the air had a weight that made me swallow hard. Then a little wind came, but instead of being cool it snapped hot sparks in my face.

When we got to his car, Mr. Hart, antsy over the heat, revved the engine once and put it in gear. I cranked down the window as we pulled out of the parking lot, and the wind rolled in a small tidal wave of heat, splashing my face.

Mr. Hart decided against going down Chandler Avenue to the projects, where I lived. Instead, he took me in a roundabout journey across town, down Nestle Avenue, where he said I'd be going to school. From the window I could see the clean, green lawns of the houses closest to the road, the hoses neatly coiled, the driveways without a smear of oil. I'd only been there a few times to see the Christmas and Nativity scenes that during December were the main attractions. Antlered reindeers and cherry-cheeked Santas tramping on fake rooftop snow; Jesus as a swaddling baby; and camel caravans, complete with the Three Kings glowed among floodlights spread across the lawns. The whole avenue at that time of year was brilliant with lights and Christmas spangles.

I didn't really feel like talking. I mostly said "Yeah, yeah," whenever Mr. Hart shot his arms out to assemble some words above the steering wheel. There were houses behind forests of maple and pine trees that couldn't be seen from the road, except maybe a dip of a driveway or sun-splash of a window in the distance. I leaned my chin on the dashboard and asked, "Rich people live out here, huh?"

"It's just another place to live," Mr. Hart said blandly, "middle-class, some upper."

I could tell by the quickness of his voice that he was disappointed that I was excited, except that I wasn't excited, but scared; scared of all the new kids I'd be meeting; different kids, the kind that lived in houses like these. Mr. Hart smiled and patted me on the shoulder.

"You're sure right about that, Mr. Hart," I said, nervously.

When we finally neared our projects, I asked him to drive around back and drop me off by the irrigation ditch near Frankie's house. He didn't know our project was lousy with snoops. People hanging outside on their front porches saw something suspicious in a white guy driving somebody home in a cream-colored car.

If my mom happened to be in the front yard, for instance, watering her plants, she'd have a heart attack for sure. She'd think somebody from the public housing works was coming to complain; or worse, think it was one of those unmarked police cars bringing her son home to psychologically torture her before locking me up forever.

Mr. Hart ignored me about dropping me off by Frankie's, and instead drove straight into the parking lot. Luckily, Mom wasn't home. But my dad was. When we pulled up he was plucking mint leaves by the water faucet. He zeroed his eyes angrily on me, and an icy, powerful mist began peeling away the inside walls of my lungs.

My dad had it in for white guys like Mr. Hart, who had good jobs and dressed in white shirts and black ties. It didn't matter that he was my teacher and that he was nice enough to give me a ride home. It didn't matter that, for whatever else one could say about him, Mr. Hart was an okay guy. What mattered to my dad was the possible panic I might cause my mom, or worse, that he'd be beholden to some white man for giving his son a ride home. No matter how many sophisticated ways I could turn it over to convince him, nothing would make sense to my dad. Letting Mr. Hart take me home was the worst acid I could have poured into his stomach.

He didn't say anything, though. When we got out of the car, he was sifting through the spearmint stems and shaking off the loose dirt with his thumbs. He did nod hello to Mr. Hart.

"How are you doing, sir," Mr. Hart said, walking across the yard. He stretched out his hand.

Oh no, I thought, *Dad's gonna flip him.* Instead he said, "Oh, fine, I'm doing real fine."

He said this good-naturedly, begging off Mr. Hart's outstretched hand with a wave of the soily mint. With his mouth like clay that couldn't be massaged, he continued coolly prying apart the stems. When Mr. Hart turned to admire the yard, Dad lifted his eyes and gave me a look that could crack concrete.

You could tell Mr. Hart wanted to say something stupid, like how neat the yard was or what a fine impression our project house had on him. If he had, I think Dad would have mowed him down.

Luckily, he didn't say anything, and when he turned his back again, I put my head down quick. I could still feel Dad's eyes boring a hole through my skull. Toward Mr. Hart, though, he was a reservoir of calm water barely touched by the wind.

Finally, after a couple of minutes of nervously standing around, Mr. Hart waved a generous good-bye and tried again to shake Dad's hand. Dad just lifted the spearmint in one final excuse.

When Mr. Hart had gone, Dad came over and stared me square in the face. His eyes were dead and black, like a deep anger had eaten away the light. I wanted to run, but I couldn't signal my legs to move. My heart quickened as he threw down the spearmint and grabbed me roughly by the shoulders. He stuck his hand in my front shirt pocket. Being Nardo's hand-me-down shirt, it fit loose, and when Dad pulled, the pocket came down almost to my belly button. He yanked out a piece of smashed lint. Then he dug his fingers into my pants pockets and with grunting satisfaction pulled out the twenty-dollar bill.

"He give you this?" he asked, his voice croaking and the cords on his neck pulsing as he took in gulps of air. He didn't really expect an answer. He looked over at me with glazed eyes, then turned toward the house. As he reached the door, he swung back around and pointing right at the president's picture on the twenty-dollar bill, said, "Don't you think I know people like this?"

CHAPTER 4

The Bullet

THE TWENTY-DOLLAR BILL Dad took from me went into his drinking bankroll. Once he started a binge, he wouldn't stop until every cent drained from his pockets. For two days he didn't come home. On the second day, while we were sitting around the dinner table in front of some potatoes in red chili sauce and corn tortillas, our necks stiff, staring at the walls as if looking for scratches, Mom finally said we better go get him.

Having eaten only cornmeal that morning, my stomach gritting like hungry teeth, I sure wasn't in any mood to go to Rico's again. But I knew Mom. Until the problem of Dad was solved, she wouldn't let anybody eat. Already, the red chili sauce was thickening in the potatoes, and the corn tortillas were warping like records in the sun.

"Could you take care of the baby while we're gone?" Mom asked Magda, whose eyes stabbed angrily back at her. They'd been arguing all morning, and had established a polite buffer of silence between them.

At the pool hall, when Mom and I walked in through the doors, Dad's friends lifted their heads and rolled their eyes, pushing back their hair. Rico, who was always fidgeting with his collar, dropped his hands and cleared his throat. He had his hair combed in a pompadour and had the look of a finicky barber. Mom asked about Dad, and Rico, tapping his finger on the counter, said he'd gone home.

It was the way he said it, too nonchalant, too nervously offhand, too guilty, actually, that made Mom suspicious right away. She began roving her eyes around the bar in a slow wandering arc, then walked straight as a divining rod into the men's restroom. There she found Dad hiding in a toilet stall.

Although she really didn't want to embarrass him in front of his cronies, and even though Dad came out looking cool and unfluttered, you could tell he'd been cut down a notch. He went to the counter proud as possible and ordered a beer. Rico said he couldn't spare any more credit.

Hearing this, and turning around on his bar stool, Mr. Sanchez, our neighbor from the projects, said, "Mano, I'll buy you beer." He was sitting at the bar, and when he pulled out his money he almost flopped off his bar stool.

Rico twirled a quarter that spilled out of Sanchez's pocket. "Keep your money," he said, "Manuel has to go home."

"No, no, I want to buy him a drink," Mr. Sanchez said sincerely, as only someone who'd been drinking can.

"No, he is going home with his wife," Rico said, mildly insistent. In the light of the pool hall, the waves of his brilliantined hair shone like glints of tar. He strained a smile of apology at Mom, who touched her hair like it was a mess. Then Dad slapped his hand hard on the counter, startling them both, and shouted, "If I want a beer, I can have a beer!"

Rico just stared at him, unblinking.

Dad was sore, but not stoked enough to start shoving anybody around. At worst maybe he'd throw a few fake tomahawk chops at me. He turned to me like he was going to do just that, but stopped himself. "Ahhh, *el perico*. How are you doing today, *Perico*?"

Perico, or parrot, was what Dad called me sometimes. It was from a Mexican saying about a parrot that complains how hot it is in the shade, while all along he's sitting inside an oven. People usually say this when talking about ignorant people who don't know where they're at in the world. I didn't mind it so much, actually, because Dad didn't say it because he thought I was dumb, but because I trusted everything too much, because I'd go right into the oven trusting people all the way—brains or no brains.

That's when Mom began to sense that Dad was angrier than he was letting on. She grabbed me by the shoulder and steered me out the door. Some girls were coming out of the Azteca Theater down the street, giggling, pulling on each other's braids, and there was a station wagon parked on the curb loaded with about ten noisy kids. When I looked back I saw Dad through the window lean forward on the counter, rubbing his chin like it was sore.

Mom hurried me along, whisking her head back every once in a while to see if Dad was following. Her lips were twisting funny and churning on words I couldn't hear above the hum of car tires. Stretching my T-shirt, she hurried me along with shoves, a couple of times even punching me on the shoulder. Each car grinding its gears on the street I thought was Dad pulling up beside us and ordering us inside the car. Tiny splinters of light were flittering away from the grass when we got back to the projects.

Right away Mom told Magda, who was putting cold cream on her face, to go visit Linda, her girlfriend who lived down the block. She didn't have to tell her twice. It took about three seconds for Magda to rush out the door, wiping cold cream off her face with a towel.

Mom figured Dad would come home in a lousy mood, but that he wouldn't do anything to me, since really, deep down Dad liked me. She told me to stay home and watch over Pedi, who was asleep, then wrote something on a piece of paper, folded it, and laid it on the table.

When he came home, Dad threw his cigarette on the porch and stubbed it with his heel. The evening air must have built back the balance in his legs, because he was walking straighter. He was swishing and slapping a chinaberry branch against his pant leg. He pulled out another cigarette, but left it dead and bobbing on his lips.

Because Mom sometimes polished the floor in the late afternoon, he was careful to not step into any scary, heart-fluttering slides. Once inside the door, he strained to see in the half light, then leveled the stick under his eye, signaling that I should go to my room.

When he was working for the city, every payday Dad used to come home lugging in boxes of groceries. He'd walk into the living room, and all the pictures, tiny statues and glass animals Mom collected would sparkle from the light rushing in through the door. It was like his coming home made them sparkle. Now he came home late, usually, with nothing—no rent money, no car money, no food money, no sparkle. And mostly he came home drunk, his face drowsy with booze, rambling about how he lost his job, or how the pain in his back felt like a broken-tooth gear, cranking and cranking.

Dad tossed the stick onto the couch. He began talking to himself in this polite, official voice. He sometimes unlocked this voice from under his tongue when he wanted to pump his words up to impress himself. It also meant he wanted to distance himself from us, to make us all strangers, so that nothing we said could touch him.

"I'm home!" he announced, loudly. "I said, 'I'm home.' Did you hear me?" He looked at the floor, and although it was scrubbed clean, acted like there was a surf of dirt rising to his ankles. "What is this? What is this mess? How can a man come home to a mess like this?"

He roamed his eyes around the kitchen, opening his arms as if expecting the walls to agree with him. He took a step toward me, then changed his mind and sat down at the yellow Formica table. The paper on the table was still creased but folded open, because I'd read it.

"What the hell is this, goddamn it?" he said. He flicked down his unlit cigarette and picked up the paper. "She wants to leave me. That's what she wants to do," he said, glancing at the paper and tossing it back on the table.

"No, she doesn't, Dad," I said. "She says she went to get her hair done at Sophie's."

Burying his hands in his pockets and cradling in his shoulders, like he was cold, Dad said, "That *pinche*[1] Sophie, filling her head with ideas." His face, which he'd kept alert since walking through the door, softened, and his eyes floated around the kitchen. Then he got up and veered down the hallway, a skirt of hair oil, beer and cigarette smoke wafting in the ammonia air. He paused at the door of his room. "I'll fix her," he said.

Dad pulled out his rifle from the shelf of his closet, and after checking the loader began searching for bullets, waking up Pedi, who groaned and rubbed her eyes. He swung open the bathroom cabinet, his drunk hand shoveling and knocking over toothbrushes, shaving cream, half-empty bottles of cologne that

---

1 pinche   rascal.

he'd always buy and never finish. Remembering all the places where Mom hid his liquor bottles, he stumbled around opening cupboards, reaching far back into shelves and behind pipes under the kitchen sink. He scattered Mom's animal collection, slapping her little glass and ceramic cows, pigs, donkeys, even rhinos and an elephant off the shelves. With one swoosh of his arm, he thrashed to the floor my green plastic tyrannosaurus.

I was behind him all the way, picking up and putting things back the best I could, trying not to trample over Pedi, awake and helping Dad look for the bullets. I was begging him to please respect reason, but quickly found myself saying, "But Dad, if you shoot Mom, they'll only throw you in jail. Then what will happen to us?"

"I don't care what happens to you," Dad clipped, "only Pedi. Isn't that right, *mija?*"[2] he said to Pedi. "You're the only one your dad cares about?"

Pedi was really awake now, and excited, working her legs and stabbing her chubby hands in the air. In the pantry, she tipped over cans of tomatoes and string beans. She thought Daddy was playing a game, that he was going to show her how to shoot the gun. She wanted to hear it go *khurrr*, like in the movies. She wanted to see something collapse at the end of the barrel when the sound trailed off.

"Pedi, cut that out!" I said.

"You shut up! My *mija* is helping me, not you!" Dad said, kicking away clothes that he'd flung out of the closet.

"Dad," I said, trying to be calm. "You have to understand, you'll only get in trouble. . . ."

My words weren't worth a penny in his ears.

"I don't care about trouble," he said. "It's that *bruja*, that witch, I've had it up to here with her." He jerked the rifle up to show how high he'd had it up to with my mom and smacked the barrel against his forehead. He shifted the rifle to his other hand and touched the hurt, relieved when his fingers came away clean.

He found some bullets, finally, inside Mom's dresser drawer, knotted up in one of her old bras. In his anxiousness to untie the straps, he scattered the bullets all over the floor. Rocking a little on his heels, he waited for Pedi to pick them up. She could get into corners and at one that spun like a pinwheel under the bed. I also picked up a bullet, but stashed it in my pocket.

"Here you go, Daddy, here," Pedi gushed, handing him three copper-headed .22 bullets. She ducked her head down and was about to scurry for more when Dad stepped out the door. "Wait, Daddy, wait for me!" Pedi yelled, running down the hall after him. At the door, Dad strained the hydraulic screen wide, and when it sprung back, it slammed against Pedi's face. She fell back on her butt and began to cry.

"Oh, Pedi, you stupid!" I said, then rushed out searching for Dad.

The sky was a soft glow, pushing the houses, trees and electric posts forward in relief. I found Dad hammering on the kitchen door of Sophie's house, swearing at Sophie and Mom to quit being cowards and let him in. The lights of the kitchen blinked off, blacking the house, but then turned on again and another weaker light came on in the living room.

I rushed over to the front just in time to see Mom bolt across the porch, scared out of her mind. She had pink roller sponges cinched into her hair and an apron tied clumsily around her neck. Bobby pins dangled from her half-

---

2 mija   my daughter (affectionate term).

finished curls. She knew Dad was angry. She was just trying to blossom herself up, but Dad didn't understand that. He didn't know how awful she felt about embarrassing him at the pool hall. She ran toward the crowd of maple trees where the trunks were thick and black against the soft night.

I yelled, "Mom!" and realized my mistake right away. Dad heard me, and came swerving around the corner. He was trying to slide a bullet into the chamber of the rifle, but it slipped through his fingers onto the ground. He left it there in a dark cradle of dirt and tried another, but that one got stuck in the loader. He wrestled with the bolt arm. "Where? Where's your mother?" he said, stumbling.

"Over there!" I yelled, pointing to the other side of Sophie's house.

Dad didn't even turn to where I pointed. From the corner of his eye, he caught the dark clump of Mom running, and ran after her. When she disappeared behind a tree, he froze, shifting his knees, the barrel of the rifle alert and ready. For an instant I caught a glimpse of her tiptoeing away from a tree. Dad saw her too and banged on the bolt arm. She started with a jolt and began running again, ducking and dodging from tree to tree, as Dad, frustrated with the loader because it wouldn't eat the bullet, and not wanting her to escape, pretended to lock a bullet in the chamber and level aim. He even lifted the barrel and made a shooting noise with his lips. *Kapow. Kapow.* Mom flinched her shoulders every time he did it, too.

Then I heard the police. Not the siren of the police or the *blink blink* of quick lights, but the hush of deep-threaded tires pressing against asphalt, an engine that wound and gathered like a powerful animal. I felt a pressure in my throat, and my legs were full of cement. "Get back to the house," I yelled in a thick voice. "Get back to the house!"

Dad stopped and turned around. He saw the police car pulling up from the street bordering our projects, then the lights, *flash flash*, and rushed back toward the house.

"Come on, Mom," I shouted, waving her in like into home plate. "The police are coming!" She started bustling toward me. When she passed me, she was breathing fast and her hair smelled of perm solution.

When we got back to the house, Dad was standing in the middle of the living room like he was lost, the rifle dangling in his right hand. Mom snatched up Pedi, still whimpering, and smacked her on the butt to get her moving. She splashed the curtains shut, and turned off the lamp, then headed for the hallway. Before reaching it, we all heard police shoes grating on the sidewalk, and Mom turned quickly toward Dad, who was holding the rifle like it was too much weight for him. I thought she was going to slap him, but instead she wrestled the rifle out of his hands and ran with it down the hallway.

That's when the two cops arrived. Seeing Dad through the screen door, they stiffened, pressing their hands against their leather holsters. But then they loosened their shoulders when they saw that he was just standing there. They slowly stretched back the hydraulic door and came into the room, crouching at the knees, just to be safe, their eyes roving around.

Unfortunately, they also saw Mom's shadow against the hallway wall, shoved out by the light of Magda's room. She must have been frozen there, wondering what to do with the rifle. I thought the police were going to panic and start shooting, thinking maybe Mom was there to ambush them, but they seemed to guess right away what was going on.

When Mom moved away, the cop in front asked Dad about the rifle. He was a large man with burly arms, soft with a yellow fur of hair. The two stomach buttons on his shirt were open wide enough to stick a softball through.

"What rifle?" Dad said, trying to straighten himself to appear sober.

"Are you Mr. Hernandez?"

"Yes, officer, I am," Dad said, tossing his hand in the air.

"Well, sir," said the policeman. "We have a report here that a man from this house was pointing a weapon around the neighborhood." He switched on a flashlight, and flicked the beam around the room, lighting a moon on Mom's glass-top table and pausing on the large picture of the Last Supper, framed in gold plastic and with cherub angels mounted on each corner. Then he relaxed his wrist and crossed the beam from Dad to me with a careless flicker.

"I don't know what you're talking about," Dad said.

"The report we received, Mr. Hernandez, claims you were trying to shoot your wife."

"That's crazy! My wife's over there." He pointed to Mom, who came down the hallway with Pedi, her eyes big as wheels, clutching at her skirt.

"Mrs. Hernandez?" the officer asked, as if trying to make her out in the dark.

Mom nodded, shielding her hair. She pressed at a drooping curl near her ear and glanced over at Dad, who dropped his eyes.

"Mrs. Hernandez," the officer said again, lifting his fist to his mouth and letting out a loud, ratchety cough, "as I was explaining to your husband, we received a report that a man was trying to shoot his wife. The report mentions this address and both your names."

Mom didn't say anything. Instead, she raised her eyes to the ceiling, breathing deep, as if gathering enough air to blow up a balloon. She stood like that for a while, hands on her hips, holding in her lungs. Her face appeared calm and lifted, as if she were listening to soft guitar music from far away.

Both officers studied her curiously and exchanged glances, the one in back still alert, his hand stiff on his holster and thumb cocked like a talon over the gun hammer.

Mom's curious silence nudged Dad into a small panic. "We don't know what you're talking about, officer," he said, shuffling toward her. "No one is trying to do anything here. Besides, we don't have a gun. Rebecca, tell him we don't have a gun."

Her eyes, which had opened wide from holding in her breath, blinked and glazed over, then she released the air from her lungs and began breathing deeply, evenly, fingering a curl of hair near her ear. Dad egged her again with his palm to please say something, but she only stared at a blank spot on the wall.

"You can see nothing's wrong here, officer," Dad said, nervously.

"Well, Mr. Hernandez, the truth is, that when we came in through the door, we saw your wife here taking away what looked to us like a firearm."

"But we don't have a firearm," Dad said again, trying to staunch their worries.

The first officer grimaced suspiciously, then he raised his flashlight and nodded to the other who, with eyes shifting and hand still braced on his pistol, walked past Mom and disappeared down the hallway. We all stood there—Dad, Mom, Pedi, the first officer, and me—looking, not looking at each other. A moment later, the other officer came out holding the .22.

"I found it in the last room, under the bed," he said, waving it in the air in reluctant triumph.

The first officer slowly shook his head and sighed, rubbing his finger reflectively along a deep crease on his forehead. "Now, Mr. Hernandez. I don't want to hear any more about how we don't have a rifle, because there's obviously a rifle here. And I don't want to hear anything about this particular rifle *not* being yours, because I'm fairly sure that it is." He sighed again and with a slow shake of his head took the rifle from the other officer's hand. He shined the flashlight on it, inspecting it, turning it over in his hand and squinching his eyes at a mark under the barrel.

"Mr. Hernandez," he said, finally, straightening his shoulders. "I don't want to have to tell you this, but I'm sorry, we're going to have to confiscate this rifle."

I saw ice freeze around Dad's eyes. "You can't take my rifle," he said abruptly, in a voice I knew meant trouble.

"Mr. Hernandez," the officer said, unbinding his shoulders some more, "there doesn't seem to be any registration number on this rifle. It's against the law to have an unregistered firearm."

That's when Mom, dragging Pedi along with her, went over and stuck her finger inside Dad's belt loop.

Seeing this, the first officer waved a cautious hand at her and stepped over to his partner. He leaned into his ear, nodded and turned back to Dad. "Mr. Hernandez, we're taking the rifle. If you want it back, you'll have to come to the station. But I don't advise you do that, sir. I really don't. I'm sure the Chief will want to ask a lot more questions about this rifle."

"Don't take it," Dad said. His voice was thick, and he was beginning to breathe harder. I saw a redness flow up the vein of his neck and gather in a puddle of wine under his ear.

That's when Mom pulled on his belt loop, enough to bend him a bit at the waist, and to my relief Dad loosened a little. "Look," he said, more calmly, "you can't take it. I wasn't doing anything."

The officer narrowed his eyes and lowered the rifle along his leg. He tucked his chin into his shoulder and signaled with one eye to the other officer, who instantly became alert. "I'm sorry then, Mr. Hernandez," he said, "we're going to have to take you in for possession of an illegal firearm."

Before any more talk, and moving as if studying his own movements, the second officer walked over to Mom and slowly, as if trying to be polite, lifted her hand away from Dad's belt loop. Then with a smooth, relaxed quickness, he took hold of Dad's arms and just like that handcuffed him. Dad seemed to be stunned into feebleness by the speed in which the officer worked. All he could say was "You can't take my rifle . . . you can't take my rifle," his voice sinking into a plea.

The first officer turned to Mom and raised a hand of apology. "Mrs. Hernandez, I sure am sorry about this. I sure am, believe me."

But Mom wasn't listening. She seemed to still be hearing something in the air. Then her face became more alert, and she turned to the officer leading Dad out of the door. "Take him," she said, softly at first, then with decided anger. "Go ahead, take him!"

After the police had gone, Mom sat on the couch a long time staring at the floor. I noticed that she didn't appear tired, but more like the muscles needed to move her face were numb. The curtains were closed, and there were no lights, but my eyes adjusted to the dark. The walls of the room, like in all the houses in our neighborhood, were Sheetrock, painted white, but in the darkness everything looked gray. The frame of the Last Supper, with its gold-colored flange and cherub angels, looked as gray as a plastic-model battleship. Even the glass-top table mirrored a reflection of gray.

Seeing a dark spot on the floor, Mom bent over and picked up a little donkey, staring at it, and delicately turning it over in her fingers as if expecting a hoof to suddenly click off. "You know," she said, "I don't even have a vacuum cleaner. Sophie has a vacuum cleaner. So does Mrs. Lopez. When the police came, I heard Mrs. Lopez's vacuum cleaner. It sounded like it was really picking up dirt."

Ever since seeing a demonstration by a plaid-suited man who came to our door, Mom had always wanted a vacuum cleaner. The man threw dirt and cigarette ash on our bathroom drop rug and to our amazed eyes sucked it all away. "There's an attachment you can hold in your hand," he had said. "That way you can get into cabinets and corners. You don't need any cloth rags. You don't need a broom. It does all the work for you."

My legs weakened, like someone had pulled a plug from my ankles and drained all my energy, so I sat down on the couch. "Mom," I said, "Mom. . . ."

She wasn't listening. She lay back on the couch and lifted her arm, resting it on her forehead, as if the heat were unbearable.

"Mom," I said again. "When do you think they're going to let Dad out?"

"When I go pay the bail."

"How much is the bail?"

"I don't know. But it's too much, I know that." Her voice sounded muffled, as though she were talking through stuffed cotton. She carefully placed the donkey on the glass table. "They'll just have to let him out when they decide to let him out."

After sitting quietly there with Mom for a while, I got up and went into Pedi's room. Her face was moist and fevery, and she was whimpering. All the excitement had opened up something bad inside her, and with her two fists pressed tightly against her chest, she was trying to close it. I reached into my pocket and pulled out the bullet I'd picked up earlier and wedged it between her fingers. That seemed to quiet her a little.

CHAPTER 5

The Garden

D EEP DOWN I hoped Mom would wise up and leave Dad for good, or maybe go live with Grandma for a while, or run off on her own, if that's what she wanted. Either that, or that Dad would finally open his eyes to see how close it was to being his last chance. But none of what I wished was going to happen.

On the day Dad got out of jail, Mom ordered us to clean this and clean that, she was so excited. Singing church hymns she learned as a girl, she took a long bath with some of Magda's creamy soap, and dusted powder on her neck and shoulders. We went on the bus to pick him up, and after we returned home, I lingered in the living room reading my science magazine. I'd found it thrown away in the alley behind Giddens's Pharmacy, a big boot print tracking the front cover, and its slippery paper warped by rain, but still amazing with pictures of flashy-colored planets whirling around in a thick, black space, and grinning dinosaurs fighting.

All afternoon they talked over the kitchen table about how things were going to get better. Dad promised he'd never go anywhere unless he said what time he'd be back, and how he was going to find a job and not just look for a job, since looking for a job kept him at the pool hall with all the other guys just looking for jobs. Mom promised she would never again embarrass him in front of his friends. And some other things I couldn't make out. Finally, when they were done promising each other everything, night was beginning to push away the light, and they went to sleep, laying slowly down on their squeaky bed.

After staying up for the longest time, with everything inside me scary and about to collapse, I heard rustling outside by the elm tree, and then Nardo's round face appeared at the window. He was drunk, mushy around the mouth, his eyes watery and stained. After losing his grip and stumbling a couple of times, he finally hoisted his belly over the window ledge and flopped into the room. He rose clumsily to his feet, and sat on the bed, staring at the floor as if over a cliff. He tried to take off his shoes but only knotted the laces. Seeing me awake, he started to ask about Dad, but I shushed him with my finger.

"Well," he said, swaying, "did he get out?"

"He got out, now shut up!" I hissed.

He sat there staring at me for a while. "What??? Are they going to make it all right again?"

"That's what they say."

"Yeah, those two, they're crazy, you know that? They're crazy."

"They ain't as crazy as you," I said, rolling over and covering my shoulder, then turning back around. "If you keep talking, they're going to come in here and gang up on you."

"Like I care."

"You better care, because I think they'd rather be fighting with you than with each other. If I was you, I'd lay down and go to sleep."

Nardo curled his arm around the bedpost and smiled. "Yeah, that's funny. That sure is funny," he said, moving his head up and down. "They'll probably be picking fights with us tomorrow, huh?"

"Shut up and go to sleep," I said, tiredly.

He looked at the mirror over by the door and noticed a swirl of his hair out of place. He tried clumsily to press it down but it kept popping up. Then he walked over to the mirror and peered into it, as if noticing something he hadn't before, pointing a lazy finger at himself. For a long time he stared at the mirror, pointing, then walked slowly back to his bed and plopped down, asleep.

I woke to the bare bulb stinging my eyes. It was morning, and Dad was in the room, breathing heavy, like he'd just gotten out of a shower. He grunted at me and roughly shook Nardo awake, who got up digging his fists in his eyes, still starched from drinking the night before. Dad slid out his belt from around the loops of his pants and began slapping it against the mattress, threatening to burn our legs if we didn't listen. He stood around bullying us into our clothes and without breakfast drove us to Grandma's.

Dad must have sizzled on some smart plans while he was in jail, and now, after all the smooth talk with Mom was over, he was ready to get into action. I'd rather have gotten dragged across a cactus desert and dropped thirsty in a lake of salt than listen to him, but he had us there in the car, muscling his voice so our minds wouldn't wander.

Grandma lived in a clapboard house at the corner of two old gray roads that the city, after scrimping for years, finally paved over with asphalt. The asphalt came cheap, without curbs, and on the first dangerous sun it melted and became lumpy. From then on cars driving over it jostled in a chorus of springs, and people's heads bounced wildly.

Dad pushed the car door open, leaned back on the seat and said he wanted the yard raked and hoed before he came back. "And I mean spotless," he said, pointing a menacing finger at us. He leaned over and slammed the door shut.

Cleaning a yard to my dad meant even the grass edges had to be trimmed and plants polished. He reminded us that he'd check on our work, making sure we dug out to his satisfaction the tufts of grass near Grandma's roses and pinched out whatever mealy bugs and aphids were chewing on the stems. We could tell it was going to be one of those hot days when asphalt softens and ants foam up from the dirt with the scratch of a stick, and when dogs bark, the sound is dry, like hollow wood. But it was still morning, and the first hour was a smile and thoughts of lunch; nothing but a few shrubs to chop and leaves to rake.

Nardo had trouble coming back from his hangover. He moved like a ground sloth, and kept gulping water from the garden hose. He sobered up a little when we began to clip off the small yellow weeds choking the roses. The bigger shoots over by the *nopal* cactus had to be pulled. The roots sunk deep and we knew in a month they'd spring up again, so we pulled with every muscle until a big chunk of the main stalk plucked out.

We wore our arms out pulling those weeds, as well as stacking the bricks Dad had once stored in the corner of the yard to build a barbecue pit. We found a couple of centipedes numb underneath an old plank and crushed them under our heels. We sent chips soaring from the axe as we cut out the roots of a dead trunk and dropped its bulk thundering into a wheelbarrow.

When Horacio, my grandma's cat, came around, we were chopping the last weeds growing inside the flowerbeds. Nardo called to him, but he was stalking near the cherry tree. When the chirp of a bird skeetered in the air, he stiffened, his nose twitching and ears cupped like radar antennae, then he darted away, clawing up the tree trunk.

When we stopped, finally, the sun was prickling like a hot rash on the back of my neck, and a piece of lava was wedged in my spine. My brother's face was swollen and burnished as a new penny. A channel of sweat slipped down the bridge of his nose and plopped on the dirt near his feet. His eyes, drowsy with sun, watched it like someone who didn't deserve sweat.

"Hey, you know what?" he said, stretching. He pulled his shoulders back and the muscles tightened under his T-shirt. With one last punch of the hoe, he exploded a puff of dirt. "I'm gonna get some Kool-Aid. How about that? You want some Kool-Aid?"

"Why don't we finish first, we only got this to do," I said, knowing that once he went inside, work was over. I looked at the cherry tree standing brilliant at the end of the garden, its leaves twirling and echoing light. It wasn't just a cherry tree. Long ago Grandpa had chopped off limbs and grafted saplings of different fruit. One branch sprouted plums, another almonds, and still another, peaches. Most were cherries, though. When in season, they glowed ripe and flashed like Christmas balls.

"I'll wait for you right over there," I said, pointing to the tree.

"No, you just keep on working, I'll be right back. Don't worry, I'll be right back." Nardo made a move to leave, but seeing me straighten up, he put his hand assuringly on my shoulder. "Don't you believe me?" he asked. "I *said* I'll be right back."

"No, I *believe* you," I said. "I just want to make sure you're not going to take a nap."

"I'm not gonna take a nap! What's the matter with you, anyway?" he asked. "You been so suspicious lately. You act like I'm gonna quit or something."

When I didn't say anything, he slid the hoe along his knee, levered it in the air, then snatched it quickly by the neck. "I'll be right back, believe me!"

It was no use arguing with Nardo. He could go around the same point from twenty different angles. "You do what you want," I said, waving my hand like it weighed a ton, "but I'm going to sit down."

Now that I'd given up, he was pretty springy. He hurdled the back steps in one leap and stopped at the door. "Man," he said, smiling, "and they call *me* lazy."

I shuffled over to the faucet, swishing the dirt from my pants. My joints felt slack, and my lips were cracked enough to bleed if I mouthed a zero. I'd taken my shirt off hours ago, and when I pressed my finger against the skin of my shoulder, I felt the numb warning of sunburn. Splashing water on myself came to mind, but my neck and shoulders chilled at the thought. Instead I hosed water into the cup of my hands and washed my face, drying it with my shirt before putting it back on.

As the sun winked over the ledge of the roof, the shadows of the cherry tree stretched across the yard, smudging Grandma's row of cactus. Pinching the waterspout, I flecked some water on them and watched as curling wisps of hot dust exploded from the spiked, green skin.

When Nardo came back, he had two clinking glasses in one hand and an ice pitcher of Kool-Aid in another. He watched the clouds herding west and frowned at the puddle of water foaming like dirty milk near the faucet.

"Are you gonna work anymore or what?" he asked, accusingly.

"No," I said, inspecting my fingernails, half-mooned with dirt.

"Hell then, let's quit." He hunched back his shoulders and blew up his lungs; then, tilting his head back, he began drinking from the pitcher in huge, noisy gulps. Then he filled a glass and finished that, shaking the purple-stained ice cubes. He put the pitcher on a wood stool nearby.

"Besides," he said, breathing heavy, "Grandma's awake."

"Grandma's awake?"

"Yeah." He pressed his arms against his sides, feigning fear. "She said she just woke up from a dream where Grandpa was sitting on the bed beside her."

He lay down on the shaded grass, linking his fingers behind his neck. Like my dad's, his hair was swirly and glinted in the sun like splashes of water. I looked at the muscles along his ribs where the T-shirt had ridden up and thought of my own flabby waist. Nardo only had a mulberry birthmark on his shoulder, which he always rubbed when thinking. I had a face Dad said would look handsome on a horse.

Grandma came around from the front wearing a flowery Japanese kimono. Her eyes weren't too strong, so she groped around, homing in on our faces. Ropes pulled at her from the ground when she walked and her sighs sounded like roots releasing from moist earth.

Nardo put the pitcher on the ground and brought Grandma the stool, which she stared at a while before sitting down. It belonged to my grandpa, who had died some years back after his brain got fevery and he couldn't recognize anyone, even himself in the mirror when we held it up one day for him to comb his hair. A sickness broke down the muscles in his legs, then broke down the stories about Mexico that smoldered in his heart. In the end, his only memory was of the desert he crossed to plant his foot in this country.

Grandma used to keep her face pretty like a baby doll, dabbing cold cream on it every night. She used to tighten her hair in knots and dye it black like a young girl's. Now her face was webbed with wrinkles, and her hair sworly white and frazzled. She still sprinkled on perfume, and was still wild about painting her lips, except now the sprinkles became palmfuls and the lipstick wandered, smearing her face eerie.

She gazed dreamily over the yard. It was beautiful back then, she said. It was a garden, and every house had one so bright a person's eyesight blurred. She remembered browsing among the flowers, smelling odors that even people in heaven would envy. My brother and I scanned around, trying to imagine the same wonder, but what we saw wasn't as sweet as Grandma remembered. I even tried to imagine neighbors, which she no longer had, except far down the road. One by one, they had all moved away.

She must have sensed our confusion, because she said it was true, the yard wasn't as joyful as when she and Grandpa were young. She said it was mostly the drought that sucked all the gardens away, but we knew that wasn't altogether true. There were still reservoirs of water, even if the rings showed how much the drought had shrunk them. It was more that the city planned to build a freeway, and was slowly buying and wrecking the houses, plowing the gardens gray. Grandpa and his neighbor, Mr. Vuksanivich, refused to sell, and for a while the city held back its plans for a freeway. Grandpa kept the garden alive and Mr. Vuksanivich kept his pasture green. Then Mr. Vuksanivich died, and the city bought the land from his son, and then Grandpa also died, and with him, the garden. Since Mom was the oldest, my dad figured she'd get the house when Grandma died.

The sun was a spot of dried blood on the rim of the horizon when Grandma waved at the cherry tree with her finger. "*Allí*," she said. "There." A few puckered cherries lay on the ground; a mantis unfurled a blue sail and skittered across the grass. "There," she said, again. "There!"

Long ago, under the drooping branches, was once a small girl, our mother, with a handkerchief covering her dark, pony eyes. She was swinging a stick at a bull *piñata* slung on a rope. By a chance hit, she burst open the clay pot nestled inside the bull's belly. Fistfuls of chocolates and candy came cascading out of the wound. Everyone screamed with excitement. The children, from the once full neighborhood of children, scurried about, eyes watery and chubby hands stashing candies into their pockets. They laughed with a cute, greedy look Grandma said only a child can make. "*Qué curiositos se miraban*," she said. "How curious they looked."

Grandma Rosa died a few months later, and after the burial we gathered at her house. The sun was as bright as an egg yolk leaking an orange finger across a porcelain plate, and there was a smell of bruised plums and burning grapevines drifting through the trees.

My aunt Letty cried so loud my uncle Joe scolded her by twirling his finger. "Now, now Leticia," he said to her, "there's nothing you can do for her now." With a shredded throat, Letty told him to shut up.

Although moist around the cheeks, Mom didn't cry. She sat on the living room couch next to the shuffling cooler. She didn't wear black because she

had no black dress, and my dad could only scrounge up seven dollars and
twenty-eight cents. Mom claimed this was as good as could be expected,
considering the funeral costs, but not half enough for a respectable black
dress. She used the money instead to buy Mexican sweet bread, and make
buñuelos, fried tortillas sprinkled with cinnamon, and sweet potatoes that bled
a dark syrup.

Sitting there, Nardo, my cousin Rio and I stared at Grandma's old chair. I remembered once sleeping on the floor and a mouse scuttling across my stomach.
I awoke to see Grandma under the tulip lamp, asleep, her head circled by a
glowing moon of light. Then I heard scuffling, as a mouse scratched across on
the wooden floor. Suddenly, there was a cushiony thud, and the mouse let out a
tiny, piercing *yeek*, as though driven through with an icepick. It was Horacio,
my grandma's cat, who'd spotted the mouse from his perch on the mantel and
pounced on it, pinning it between his claws. As my eyes brightened in the dark,
I saw Horacio's fur glowing, as he sort of smiled down at the mouse. Then he
released it, and it scurried away to search for a hole; but Horacio leaped again,
clasping and pawing the mouse around the floor like a ball of yarn. I watched in
fascination as he let the mouse go three or four times, rolling it around with
crisp, playful, precision until he finally snatched it up and throddled it down his
throat, the tail churning around his mouth.

Grandma's chair had bark designs on its wooden legs and carved bear claws
for handrests. Already frayed on the cushion, wobbly in the struts, its wooden
legs scratched, no one except Grandma ever sat in it. I began wondering about
what would happen to it now that it was empty of her.

I leaned forward on the couch and in a half whisper told Nardo that the night
before I had dreamt about Grandma. She and I were walking together in the
mountains, when suddenly, under our feet, a huge earthquake erupted, with fire
tearing open the earth like a sharp knife through seams of old leather. I woke up
shivering and soaked in cold sweat. The walls of my room were like blue ice,
like the sky after a clean rain.

Dreams fascinated Nardo. He could analyse people's sleep. Grandma claimed
this was because he had a birthmark in the shape of an eagle's wing on his
shoulder. Nardo said that before leaving for heaven the dead sometimes sprinkle messages inside the ears of those they love. He didn't know why Grandma
would want to leave a message for me, but the dream sounded like a warning. I
would die alone, he predicted, in a very cold place.

I leaped from the couch and hammered him on the arm. We wrestled around
the living-room floor in front of Mom, too buried in her grief to pay us any
mind. Dad wasn't too buried in grief, though. Irked by our noisy tumbling, he
burst in from the kitchen and with one of his shoes, crowned us both on the
head. He pointed the shoe threateningly at everybody and said that we all better
get the message quick about how to behave, or else.

After Dad's scolding, we sat quietly on the couch across from Mom. She was
looking down at the floor as if searching for scuff marks. We all became bored
and antsy. My cousin Rio pretended to be mournful, and Nardo coolly studied
the dust on the windowpane, grinning because the blow Dad had given him
hadn't even hurt.

Only Pedi was having fun. She came into the room revving her lips like an
airplane and spanning her arms. She circled us at an angle, swooping past
Nardo and snagging her wing on his pants pocket. She flew on a crippled half
wing a little way before crashing.

When she started playing at making faces, we giggled, but stopped when Dad poked his head in from the kitchen. "I'm gonna *burn* somebody's legs," he warned.

Everybody really shut up after that and stared at the walls. I munched on a sweet potato and gazed at the ringed stains inside my coffee cup. Finally, ignoring everybody's eyes licking after my heels, I snuck out the door.

Outside, the air was a sleek powdery ash. It dusted Dad's car and uncle Joe's panel truck, parked grille to grille on the gravel driveway. Steam rose from the hoods in thin ghostly clouds, and blanched by the sun, the windshields shone like morning frost. I climbed over the hood of my uncle's truck and walked over to the cherry tree, clambering up on a branch.

Over the wood shingles of the house, I could see a blond strip of Mr. Vuksanivich's old pasture. The grapevines had been plowed over and the house lifted on struts, then trucked away, but I could almost see old Mr. Vuksanivich standing there in a gray sweater, raking and burning leaves, a great plume of smoke rising into a cloud.

In the kitchen, I heard Dad talking loud. Everybody else's voices made tiny booms of sound against the walls, but my dad's voice cut through the walls. He was talking to my uncle Joe about how impossible it was going to be to keep up the place, and how he'd have to sell it. You could almost hear the strategies sizzling around inside his head, like hot sand swirling inside a tin cup.

I sat there imagining the cherry tree's roots slithering down into the earth, and how it would have to be pulled out by a strong tractor; and also, I thought about how, in the end, Grandma couldn't read anymore under the tulip lamp, only sit on her armchair, looking up at the ceiling, swallowing and swallowing; and once, when she put her arm on my shoulder, I felt the dead weight of her strength abandoning her.

In my family, we're taught to touch the hand of the one who has died. So at the wake, when my mother called, I walked toward the casket, and in the full bloom of my family's eyes, I touched Grandma's hand. A lump of salt caught in my throat, closing like a fist, as I studied the bark skin of her face—each crack sealed with perfect makeup.

She will flake away into dirt, I thought, just as the sun does the bottom of a pond during a drought. Her shadow will be erased, and her soul will drift to heaven like the fluff of a dandelion in the wind. And then it will blossom in another garden, so bright the colors will hurt your eyes. That's how I imagined it. For Grandma, that's how I wanted it to be.

CHAPTER 6

The Rifle

M Y SISTER Magda lived and breathed to caress her records. She was wild-eyed about them, and danger threatened anyone who touched even the most needle worn and milky surfaced. She had a stack as thick as an elephant's spine in the corner of her room, and copies, sometimes three, of her most precious favorites. She'd either slip them inside the flanges of a metal rack, or save them in a wooden box with a lever switch that locked with a miniature key.

On her wall, she thumbtacked magazine photos of her two dream stars, Elvis Presley and Smokey Robinson, surrounding them with a rainbow of paper colors. Elvis had a tough-guy sneer and tossed-back flame of black hair. Smokey had slit, romantic eyes. More than once I caught her drooping her head over them, dreaming.

The money for her records came from working at the Valley Laundry, a place she hated more than anything in the world. Her friend Linda said she was moody spirited and argued too much with the supervisor. Linda worked beside her on the steam press. She was in love with Nardo, but he didn't pay her any mind, mostly because blocks of fat sagged on her hips like a belt of thick Bibles, and she dressed in those elastic skirts, the kind with stretchy waists and no belt. Only with Linda, belts were the last worry, what with skin spilling out in all the worst places and buttons missing where you didn't want buttons missing.

Linda always showed wrinkles of concern over Magda, but when alone she confided to me that Magda had to learn how things worked at the laundry. You had to flirt a little with the supervisor. Pay attention to his lousy conversation. Flatter him a bit about his muscles. Two other flirty girls who worked there were already pushed over to Loading, and in another month they were going to push her over to Processing, but Magda's mouth was too smart-alecky for her own good, and the supervisor vowed he'd never in a million years move her up.

"Manny," Magda said, "that supervisor tells me I ain't doing the sheets right, that they ain't coming out of the machine right. Too many wrinkles. And I'm just sweating there, trying to do it right the best way I can. But you know, there ain't no *right* way of doing bedsheets. He just gets a big bang out of showing how he's got me under his thumb."

She was talking fast in front of her dresser mirror. She pressed a blunt pencil of mascara against her eyebrow, then picked up a tool shaped like a torture rack and stretched her eyelashes. She worked hard for beauty, teasing her hair high as an ocean wave, blushing pink on her cheeks and sometimes smearing her lips dark as pomegranate syrup. To me she was pretty enough with a naked face, but she never listened to me. Instead she bribed me when she wanted something. Like that day she promised me a cherry pie and a root beer.

"Keep an eye on Baby for a while, will you, Manny?" she begged, and just as quickly, hissed, "but don't say anything to Mom."

"Where're you going?"

"Out."

"Out where?"

"Out, out. That's all you need to know."

Magda bit at her pink-lacquered nails that she ate sometimes down to slivers. Even painted, her fingertips were scalded red and puss-y.

She had a secret boyfriend, and since Mom was at Grandma's putting things away, and Dad was again at Rico's, she got me to stay home and baby sit Pedi while she smooched with him over by the maple trees. If Mom found out she'd have fainted dead away; Dad would have boiled over faster than salted water.

Adjusting the belt of her skirt, Magda straightened her collar. "I'll be right back," she said.

I watched her walk out the screen door and cross the yard separating our house from the grove of maple trees. Her hips had a confident swing and her shoulders were proud and sassy. When she reached the edge of the grass, a guy in a T-shirt and jeans came out from behind a tree and stood watching her. He had blond hair sleeked back with pomade, except for one wave which veered over his face like a broken hinge. It was obvious he'd spruced himself up. His chin glowed with a fresh shave, and his shoes were mirror polished. They walked into the trees.

When I turned around, Pedi was sitting on the couch, smearing chocolate from a half-eaten candy bar all over her face. I really had to keep an eye on her. Usually, she wouldn't unglue from the hem of Magda's skirt unless given a candy. Left alone, she'd tumble off the couch or reach for boiling water. The day before, I caught her rubbing a stick in her hands until she rasped a splinter. She also suffered from allergies, which Mom first thought were congestion and shoved steaming water under her nose to loosen her lungs. When that didn't help, a doctor stuck tiny needle pricks along her back. Each prick swelled red, which meant practically everything alive in the wind—pollen, grass, smoke, even certain siftings of dust—could bring tears and wheezing fits.

I took a chair from the kitchen and propped it on the door of Dad's closet, reaching far back into the shelf. I scraped my knuckle on the aimer of his rifle. He'd gotten it back from the police by spending a hundred and fifty dollars on a lawyer for a rifle that had cost fifty bucks. Mom said that was the stupidest thing she ever heard, but she didn't say anything to him about it.

With my finger, I traced a zero around the barrel hole, feeling the cold dead steel and imagining a bullet, tiny as a sliver, racing up my arm and zinging into my brain. I searched around some more and found what I was looking for, the box of dominoes.

"Come on, Pedi," I said, wiping chocolate from her face. "Let's build a house."

Most kids act like your fingers are made of hot glass when you touch them, but not Pedi. She liked people to wipe her face or squish the soft pillows of her arms. If you rubbed her head, she'd get drowsy and knock out in a minute.

I stood the dominoes up one by one. After settling Pedi's hands on her lap, I announced a *tah dah* and tapped the first domino. They collapsed in a riffling click of doom, but Pedi didn't notice the spectacle. At the last second she turned her head to the door, her eyes anxious for Magda's return.

"Come on now, Pedi," I pleaded, gathering the dominoes into a pile. "Look, let's build a house."

Pedi rose and climbed onto the couch. She stretched her neck in the direction Magda had gone, pressing her temple against the window-pane, her breath blurring a small balloon on the glass.

"Did she go to the store?"

"Yeah, she went to the store."

"Why'd she go to the store for?"

"She went to get some root beer." I noticed her dirt-black tennis shoes crushing smudges on the couch. "You know, Pedi, you shouldn't be stepping on the cushions. You know how Mom gets."

"There's root beer in the 'figerator."

"Not the kind that tastes like vanilla."

"Uh huh! There's that kind, too."

"Did I say vanilla? No, I meant chocolate."

"Chocolate?"

"Yeah, chocolate."

Pedi's eyes narrowed keen with suspicion. "You're lying, ain't you?" she said.

"Hey, I'm no liar."

"Yeah, you're a liar. A big fat *gordo*[1] liar!"

"No I'm not," I said, although I could tell by her face that she knew I was lying.

Pedi slapped a hand on her pant leg and turned back to the window. When smaller, she was always arguing jibberish. Her speech was hard to understand, but you could tell when she was mad at you. She'd scrunch her face, and her fists would open and close with fury.

Usually, though, I had fun teasing her into tantrums, but only when Mom or Magda were around to quiet down her hysterics. Besides, at that moment, seeing her face empty of any trust in me didn't make me feel good about bothering her.

"Come on, Pedi," I said, "look, look at the house I built."

Actually, I was surprised myself, because without thinking, I had put together a three-story domino house. One piece remained to be put on top, and I was about to do it when Pedi climbed down off the couch.

"Hey, now, check this out," I coaxed. "It ain't even just any old house. It's a regular palace."

Avoiding my eyes, Pedi knelt on the floor, shuffling her knees closer. As she did, she placed her fist on the floor and pushed it forward. Before I could stop her, she bulldozed the domino house to rubble.

"Now, what did you do that for?!" I said, my voice lengthening into a whine.

She didn't say anything, only inched back a little on her knees. Instead of getting up, though, she suddenly splashed all the domino ruins across the floor. "Because you're a liar!"

There wasn't much to do after that. Afraid she'd start screeching, I quietly collected the dominoes and slipped them back into the cardboard box.

Sulking, her eyes squeezed shut, she sat back on the couch. I thought how Magda, if she were there, would probably toss around pouty faces with her for hours. She liked to argue and backbite with her, and laugh when Pedi pressed her hands to her sides in anger.

When I noticed her sneaking glances at me, measuring my patience, which by then I had to admit was pretty much punched out of air, I didn't even blink— blank was how I played it, blank. I just kept picking up the scattered dominoes like all I did my whole life was pick up dominoes. When I finished packing them in the box, I sat down opposite her on the couch.

After a while, she stood up, roughly tucking her T-shirt into her pants. Peering once at me with tight eyebrows, she looked down at the floppy laces of her tennis shoes and after another lightning glance at me, knelt down to tie them. Then she went into the kitchen, sliding her chin haughtily over her shoulder.

I heard the refrigerator swoosh open and the crack of an ice tray. After what sounded like trouble reaching the faucet, she came to the doorway, a long plastic Tupperware cup in her hand. She sipped from the rim, watching me, shaking her head in little yeses and nos.

I answered her with a sizzling stare, then turned quickly around, like the sight of her had offended my eyes.

After a while I felt a little tap on my head. When I turned around, Pedi nudged her forehead into my shoulder. She didn't say anything at first, only looped her wrist around my neck. "You're not a liar," she said, finally, in a forgiving voice.

---

1 gordo   fat guy.

"It's okay," I said, wiping my shirt. A small slink of snot had dripped from her nose onto my shirt.

After a while, Pedi fell asleep with her head cradled on my lap, but I eased out from under her and went back to the closet. I was curious about Dad's rifle. I wondered why he loved it so much, why he was willing to argue with the police over keeping it, and why he'd spend every cent we had in the bank plus what he could borrow to get it back. Then it was in my hands, and I began working the bolt arm as if inside were all the secrets.

Even then, it remained jammed. I began to work it, and suddenly it slid smooth and easy and I saw the round heel of a bullet rise and flutter a moment in the air, as if to pop out and fall on the floor, but instead it sank back into the chamber. Startled, I lifted my head, my eyes falling straight along the barrel, then on the aimer, and above it, Pedi, walking through the door, her tiny fists unscrewing sleep from her eyes.

The sound of the gun going off was like a huge mouth swallowing a noise, and Pedi was eaten by that mouth. Thoughts ran together inside my head and blurred, like currents of fast water flowing together. Loud shrieks inside my lungs were bursting to get out, but couldn't. Pedi was dead, I knew it. The way she fell back on the floor, she could only be dead. I was afraid to go up to her, thinking I'd see a gory gash where the bullet entered her head and I'd lose my mind.

My muscles felt weak and droopy. I thought I was going to pass out, but then I heard her crying, and when I speeded over to her, her mouth was fluttering. Tears sprouted from her eyes and leaked down past her ears, but this only made me laugh; my heart felt like it was being squeezed between two hands; joy and grief pressing and unpressing.

As she lay there on the floor, sucking air, I said, "Pedi, Pedi. Shhh, shhh!!!" My hands were jittering, as if tied to puppet strings, and my voice leaked through a wet sponge. I stopped to massage my cheeks, thawing them little by little.

If Mom had seen what happened, all the wrinkles on her face would have snapped shut. But she hadn't. No one had, not even Pedi, really. She hardly knew what happened.

I hid the rifle back in the closet right away, and after calming my mind down and staunching Pedi's crying, I put her back to sleep on the living room couch. That's when Magda came home. I turned on the TV fast and pretended to watch an old John Wayne movie.

Magda was glowing with perspiration and breathing in little gulps of air when she walked through the door. She took off her earrings and looked at me. Her hair was mashed down in the back and she was trying to fluff it with her fingers. "Did anybody come?"

"No."

"What about Pedi, did she cry?"

"No."

The TV was buzzing a loud, comforting current of electricity. Magda tilted her head around in a swivel, dabbing at stray hair. She went over to the TV and turned it off just as John Wayne, in the midst of squiggles, was dying on a bulldozer. The humming stopped, but the sound buzzed in the air before the current finally died away. "What was that noise a little while ago?" she asked.

"Why's your hair all messed up?"

"Well, not that it's any of your business, but there's a lot of wind out there you know."

"Oh yeah?"

"Yeah!" She pursed her lips and tugged menacingly at a tuft of my hair. "If you're thinking of telling any lies to Mom about me, you better think again." She gave my hair a yank and held on with a twisting pinch. "Do you *hear* me!?"

"Hear what?" Mom said, coming in through the door. She had a bag of groceries under her arm. "Did he hear what?"

Magda quickly let go my hair. Seeing her dressed like she was, and me with my face rubbery, Mom was suspicious.

"Nothing's going on, Mom. Manny's just being a pest, that's all," she said, sidling up against me. She wanted me to know that she'd give me pain if I spilled my guts.

Mom put the bag of groceries down on the glass-top table. "What's really going on here?"

Just then Pedi woke up, her eyes drowsy and focusing. I felt a heavy pressing on my chest. When she saw Mom, she crawled across the couch and clamped her arms around her waist. "Mama . . . you know what? Manny . . ."

"Wait a minute, *mija*." Mom said, hoisting her up by the armpits and sitting her back on the couch. Not altogether awake, Pedi flopped back asleep. Mom looked about the room like small flames were beginning to sprout on the floor. "What the hell is going *on* here, Magda? Why are you dressed up like that? Did anybody come?"

"Nobody came, Momma," Magda said, dryly.

"Then why are you dressed up like that?"

"I'm just trying on new clothes for tomorrow, that's all. We're supposed to go to work dressed up sometimes."

"You never dressed up for work before."

"Yeah, I have. I've gone to work dressed up!"

"No, never." Mom sounded sure, but also a touch disappointed that she'd caught Magda in a lie. She never scolded her, since she was too grown up and the only one in the family working steady.

"I've dressed up before," Magda said, glancing at me. She expected a nod of agreement, but I didn't give her one. She pursed her lips and twirled back with an innocent smile. "How's Grandma's house? Is Dad still going to sell it?"

About to open her mouth to answer, Mom instead curled her finger slowly, as if trying to pluck something delicate out of the air. "Don't make the same mistake I did, Magdalena," she said. "Don't ruin your life, *mija*."

"I'm not ruining my life, Mom! You keep saying I'm going to ruin my life."

Mom shook her head like she wasn't listening. She'd gathered up her own thoughts, and would use *them* to do the figuring. "Your father and I ran off together when I was sixteen. You were already big in my belly." For a moment she looked to put her hand on Magda's shoulder, but held back, rubbing her arms. "Don't make the same mistake I did, that's all I have to say."

At first Magda said nothing. If she'd kept quiet everything might have blown over. But then an angry heat began seeping into her face. She could understand Mom being angry at her. She could accept any punishment, but she couldn't accept the fact that she'd already been judged—especially in the voice Mom used, a voice like an accusing needle—and there was nothing left for her to do but be guilty.

Magda, breathing heavily, pinched her eyelids tight. "You don't tell me what to do," she said, in an even voice, but squeezing her fists. Then she widened her mouth. "You shouldn't *ever* tell me what to do!"

"I'm not telling you what to do!" Mom said, surprised by her sudden anger.

"Yes, you are . . . you are," Magda said, unclamping one finger from her starchy knuckles. "If you ever tell me about my business again I'm going to leave. You hear me!? Me and Linda, we'll get our own place. What will you do then, huh, Mom, with no money? What will you do then?"

Mom looked like she'd been poked in the chest with an icepick. She stammered. There was a squeak in her voice. "*Mija*, I only . . ."

Her voice sparked a watery trickle in my throat, but there was nothing I could do. When Mom and Magda warred against each other, it was their war, and anyone who got in between them became an enemy. Magda's face was fierce, and loaded with hurt. She braced her legs and wiped a splash of spit from the side of her twisted mouth. Whatever scolding or advice Mom had once been able to give her, she wasn't going to take anymore.

That's when Mom's eyes began to weaken, and she bent down slowly to pick up the groceries from the glass-top table. She walked into the kitchen and set the bag rustling on the linoleum counter. It tipped over, and a can of pork and beans rolled out, stopping on the metal flange of the counter and bobbing back. Mom watched it, then turned to open the closet door next to the pantry. She grabbed a broom, shrugged, and began sweeping, the straw bristles scraping the floor. First one corner then another, she herded the dirt to the center of the room.

I pulled out a bedsheet from the hamper, and for the rest of the afternoon lay down in the hallway underneath the water cooler, relieved that Mom hadn't found out about me almost shooting Pedi. I crunched lightning out of ice cubes and watched the sun slowly whittle away the shadows from the walls. The sun, pressing down on everything, was too crippling to let anyone do anything other than drag oneself around. In that heat even the birds squirmed, and if you stood in the sun, it was like your shadow was groaning to escape.

My mother kept coming in and telling me to get out of her way. Once to bring in chairs from the kitchen, while she mopped the floor, another time to string a clothesline from one end of the hallway to the other. Water swished in the kitchen sink as she squeezed clothes against the scrub-board, churning, then wracking and splatting them as she ruffled the wetness out.

"Mom, how're those gonna dry under the cooler?" I asked, raising up on my elbow.

"Oh, they'll dry. Don't you worry about that. In this heat even ice will dry. Besides, you don't have to worry, the cooler's going off."

"Off!"

"Yes, off!" she said, shoving me with her foot. "Do you think electricity is free?"

She didn't turn off the cooler, though. Her hand paused over the switch, and she sort of half turned her head toward me. Then she bustled back into the kitchen.

I don't know how long I lay there not thinking anything, watching the clothes flutter under the cooler breeze. I saw one of Magda's dresses hanging above me on the clothesline, a flower print with fluffy shoulders and gardenia patterns stitched on the bottom hem. I saw Nardo's white shirt that he used when he was a busboy, with ghosts of smudges on it. Whenever he sprouted beyond his sleeve size, Mom trimmed his clothes and passed them down to me.

Then I began thinking about a lot of things. I thought about this girl in school, Maria, how she sat behind me in class and I could feel her breath on my neck, smelling of caramel candy. The way her hair was soft around her ears made my stomach landslide with a strange, delirious emotion. For a long time, I remember, I couldn't touch anything without feeling a little current of mystery traveling inside it.

All my thoughts were coming forward, one by one, then flying away. I thought about the time in spring, after the rains came and everything sighed, how I climbed the largest maple in the Big Lawn and looked around. I could see people walking under me, hear their voices, as I lazily veered on the branches, the wind twittering the leaves. I thought about Nardo, who was hardly ever home anymore. Always on the move, drinking with his wino friends, snatching up his coat while feeding a long line of excuses to Mom's disbelieving ears. I thought about how Mom kept cleaning the house, shifting dirt from one place to another. Maybe she thought she could get the house so spanking shiny that someday it'd disappear in one great sparkle, and she'd be free. I thought about Dad, how on his breezier days, he'd unhook the buttons on his sleeve and fix something around the house. When was he going to quit butting his head against a wall? When was he either going to break it, or break his head? I thought about happy times, too. I thought about Grandma; how when she got new eyeglasses, she discovered Mexican movies. She liked to see the singer Flor Silvestre cradled in her costumes of spun radiance, and watch westerns from Mexico, with brick-red sunsets and a ribbon of blue mountains in the distance.

For a long time I lay there, thinking, my head pillowed on my arm. Thoughts came like damp, echoing coughs, and the air felt empty. I sort of began to feel like no gravity was holding me, and I was spiraling down a long, black tunnel. Looking up, I remembered the bullet, which I figured got buried inside the cooler shaft. I prayed no one would ever see it. The thought of how close I'd come to killing Pedi gave my lungs a peculiar sponginess, as if apart from my body they'd been sobbing for hours.

CHAPTER 7

The Boxing Match

WHEN SUMMER ENDED, I was again at the same school. Mom's plans to get me transferred didn't work out. The administration said it was too late. There were already too many kids in that school. There was an imbalance in the student body—whatever that meant. They said lots of things, but it all ended with me not transferring.

So I was sitting with my friend Albert Sosa, eating lunch on the picnic table over by the maple trees, when all of a sudden Lencho Dominguez came and parked his big beefy shadow above us. We liked eating lunch there, because every day around twelve o'clock one of the English teachers, Miss Van der Meer, would step out of her classroom and swoon our minds with the gorgeous way she'd fluff her hair and fix the collar of her ruffly blouse. Her legs dangled from the hem of her skirt like two shapely white bowling pins, and her shoulders were straight as a geography book.

We acted like that wasn't why we ate lunch there, but it was. Anybody could see how cold it got. The wind already had glass edges to it, stiffening muscles and practically cutting through the stitches of our clothes. When it blew, the chill stabbed our teeth like icicles, and our voices jiggled every time we talked. Yet our eyes melted when Miss Van der Meer appeared at the door.

Anyway, Lencho came over and eyed us like we were hopeless. He was dressed in Big Ben pants, starched stiff as ironing-boards, and a plaid Pendleton shirt with the lap and tail out. Hardly a smile of a wrinkle showed anywhere. He cleared his throat with an exaggerated gutter.

"You *vatos*[1] are real screwy, you know that?" he said, in his strep-throaty voice.

Rumor had it that Lencho stripped his voice by smoking cartons of Lucky Strike cigarettes and drinking Jack Daniel's whisky straight from a thermos bottle stashed in his locker. He leaned over and fingered about a dozen of Albert's fried potatoes. "That white bitch teaches a class of *gavachos*, and you guys hang around waiting to see her ass."

"Whataya mean?" Albert said, acting sore about Lencho thieving his potatoes. He knew better than to complain, though. No one complained to Lencho. I once saw him grab Mark Calavasos by the tits and squeeze until he grit his teeth and begged Lencho to please, please let him go.

"You guys ever been in that room?" Lencho mumbled, snatching and pushing another load of Albert's potatoes into his mouth.

"No," I said, pretending to not be interested. Actually, I must have wondered a thousand times about what was behind that door.

Daintily flicking salt from his fingers, Lencho did a curious thing. He wet his two fingers on his tongue, and pinching the crease of his pants, ran them down to his knee. He did the same with the other pant leg. We watched him with open-mouthed fascination.

"Well, let me tell you *vatos*," he said, finishing his grooming with a swipe of his pocket. "There's couches and sofas in there. You guys ever seen couches and sofas in a *class*room?" He laughed, a sort of half chuckle, half sneering laugh. We looked dumbly at him, and he laughed again, only louder. "You *vatos* are screwy—you know that? You're a couple of real sissies."

He didn't say it like an insult, but more a statement of fact. If he'd have asked us, we'd have agreed with him in a second. Compared to Lencho, *everybody* was a sissy. He had lumpy sacks of potatoes for shoulders, and even the weight of his breathing made you feel puny.

He put his knuckle to his mouth and cleared a big wad of phlegm and spat it out. "I want to talk to you about something, Manny," he said, seriously. "Do you think that maybe Bernardo might wanna join my boxing team?"

"I don't know," I said.

"He's a pretty tough *vato*, ain't he?"

"I guess so."

"What do you mean you *guess* so? Don't you know anything about your own brother?"

"He doesn't tell me everything!" I said, trying to toughen my voice. I must have sounded whiny, though, because Albert ducked his eyes.

It was the truth about Nardo. He mostly told me what he had done and how he felt about what he had done, but never anything about what he was planning to do or anything about what he wanted to do. If he thought about something, he'd ask me in a question, like, 'Hey, Manny, do you think I should join Lencho's boxing team?' He hadn't asked me a thing like that lately, so I didn't know.

---

1 vatos guys, dudes.

"Well, anyway, ask your brother if he wants to join," Lencho said. He stamped his Stacy Adams shoes on the bench and walked away, eyeing his snazzy polish.

That's when Miss Van der Meer came out of her classroom. She had a load of books crooked under her arm and was mangling a cluster of keys against her hip. As usual, there were some white students pattering like puppies behind her. She fished a key out and locked the door. Lencho walked toward her, tiptoeing—with dignity—trying not to get any grass on his shoes. He hopped on the concrete walkway.

"Hey, Lench!" I yelled. "Albert says he wants to join. He says he could whip anybody in the whole school—even Boise. He says he'll even take on Boise." I got up and gave Albert's shoulders a champion's massage.

Annoyed, but not wanting to make a big commotion around a teacher, Lencho turned and shot a hidden Screw You finger at me from his hip; then, coolly deadening his face, he zipped past Miss Van der Meer, almost bumping her shoulder.

As he passed, the white students cold-stared Lencho like he'd just peed on the Queen of England. They weren't about to say anything, though. They knew his reputation. Besides, Miss Van der Meer pretended like she hadn't noticed a thing. That's the kind of teacher she was, too precious to notice anything.

That's when I yelled out, "Hi, Miss Van der Meer!" It was one of those phony-baloney hi's that always comes out sounding smoochy. She turned around and automatically started to wave back, but then recognized that she didn't know who I was. She tossed a polite hand at me anyway, and her students hurried her away.

"You jerk! What the hell you do that for?" Albert moaned after Miss Van der Meer and her pack of puppies rounded the corner. He was steamed. He snatched angrily at his hair. He stood up, grabbed his books like he was about to huff off, then changed his mind and plunked them back down on the table. "Man," he said, in a mopey voice, "now she's gonna think we're a coupla idiots."

"We *are* a coupla idiots, you idiot," I said, defiantly, but I could see regret tightening on Albert's face. He was convinced that we'd never get another chance to moon over Miss Van der Meer on the sly. But to me, Lencho was right. It was stupid sitting out there stuffed in a mountain of double sweaters, waiting for some teacher to make a grand appearance. She paid us less mind than she would a wad of chewing gum stuck on the sidewalk. That much I could tell by the way she waved at me.

I wanted to tell Albert this, but he was looking like he just got plugged on the shoulder with an arrow. "Man, Lencho's gonna have it *in* for you!" he said finally, perking up in almost a gleeful way, like he wouldn't be *too* sorry if Lencho knocked in my teeth.

"He won't do anything," I said.

"Oh, no!?" Albert stressed, anxious to prove me wrong.

"No," I said. "He doesn't want to mess with Nardo."

"Oh, yeah."

He was glum again. He didn't have a brother, only a sister, and she'd as soon slap him in the face as smile. When you're like Albert, and you don't have protection, any day of the week, on any street corner, a guy like Lencho can kick in your rib cage and nobody would give a damn.

All in all, I thought it amazing that Lencho even *tried* to spark up the Chicano guys to join his boxing team. Not that the Chicano guys couldn't fight or anything. There were a lot of ornery *vatos* around, but they just hung around and smoked and ditched class and acted like the school was some kind of contaminated nuclear zone. They'd never join any team that wasn't a gang.

Lencho did recruit two suckers, though. One was a guy named Chico. A nice guy, but as my brother Nardo once said about him, the only shining he ever did came from his teeth. He could draw a neat picture of a naked girl and follow the numbers in a bingo game, but putting his finger on an algebra problem would probably burn him to ashes. Chico once tried out for the basketball team, but he was too short and couldn't dribble to save his life. When scratched from the roster, he blamed Coach Rogers, the basketball and boxing coach. The coach wore tortoise-shell glasses and talked in a Marine voice. He had a head that reflected the sun and a blue-black carpet of hair over his muscular arms. Where Chico got the story, I don't know, but he said the coach once caught a Mexican guy frisking around with his daughter and ever since then he didn't like Mexican guys.

The other fish Lencho hooked—and no one could believe it at first, especially me—was "Skinny Boy" Albert Sosa, my friend. I thought this was a pretty sorry thing for Lencho to do, considering Albert couldn't punch the air out of a soap bubble. Of course, it was a robustly stupid thing for Albert to do, too, since teachers lifted their eyebrows with appreciation when handing back his test papers.

But Albert wanted to show something about himself. He wanted to impress his dad maybe, who sat around watching TV all day, making fun of the white actors, or maybe he wanted to impress Miss Van der Meer, who you could tell sent fingers of ice down his neck.

I tried warning him. I tried explaining how ribs crack easy as dry twigs, and how a punch sometimes welcomes paralysis. But he wouldn't listen. He practically begged to sign up, and you could tell Lencho was disappointed at such a scrawny catch. He wanted guys like Nardo and Sammy Fuentes—dangers known to everyone.

But I think it was enough for Lencho to know that Chico and Albert would yank in whatever direction he pulled. They hung on his every word, and he could sure pump guys up with confidence. He belonged to this group called the Berets; older guys, mostly, already out of school. Actually, Lencho was only a Junior Beret, him still being in school and all. But to him, being a Junior Beret was still halfway better than a plain nobody.

The Berets believed that white people were our worst enemy, and if they had one purpose in mind, it was to keep brown people down. We, on the other hand, were descendants of Indians blessed with a color that was as necessary as dirt to the earth, as important as the sun to all the trees. We had treasures buried deep inside our blood, hidden treasures we hardly knew existed.

This is the kind of stuff I listened to from Lencho, who figured if he made me his equipment manager and handler, then maybe Nardo might change his mind and put on the leather.

For three weeks, I hung out with the boxers. Training was held after school in the weight room, where the guys bounced around swiveling their necks, skipping rope and running in place until wet as fish. Then, with faces swelling, they'd groan out a few dozen sit-ups. (Lencho didn't let them lift iron because he said weights make muscles bulky, and they needed to be quick and springy in the exchanges.)

1139

For equipment, we had an old, hobo-looking punching bag and one of those rubber tetherballs suspended on a bungee cord. On the first day, Albert hit the ball with a left, then came over—or *tried* to come over—with a right. The ball snapped back in a wobble and the cord gashed his fist. Between his two big knuckles, a flap of skin the size of a postage stamp opened a jagged eye.

Unwinding a jump rope in his hand, Lencho told him to skip the day's training, but to stick around for the pep talk. He didn't mean that, of course. What he really meant to say was that Albert should show his fireball commitment by toughing it out. He didn't say this, exactly; Lencho never said anything, exactly. Instead, he coolly started jumping rope and talking about how *real* fighters never let little chicken stuff like cuts put the coward's bite on them. After a long stare at the blood creeping under the Band-Aid he'd put on, Albert wrapped his hand in a T-shirt and began shuffling his feet around, jabbing at the air.

One of the fighters in Coach Rogers's stable was a black guy named Boise Johnson. During training Lencho took particular attention to stink up his name. Clapping his hands, he'd roughen his voice and say we were going to pluck him like a chicken, crush him like a pasta shell. These putdowns were meant to lift the guys' confidence, but both Chico and Albert blessed their skinny bones they weren't going to fight Boise.

There was also a feud going on between Lencho and Coach Rogers. The coach didn't appreciate him mavericking fighters on his own. He was a former Golden Gloves boxing champion, and he considered that a big deal. I think every student at J. Edgar Hoover High knew the coach was a Golden Gloves boxing champion. Even in junior high I remember knowing, and I think even my dad knew, and my dad didn't give a rat's ass about anything that happened in my school.

Coach Rogers selected his fighters from those who scored highest on the school's physical exams, which included climbing the high rope and squat-jumping and running windsprints until our lungs collapsed; but he depended, mostly, on who could lift the heaviest weights, or repeat the lighter weights the longest. This torture of selection dragged on for about two weeks, after which the guys who scored Excellent were given free gold trunks to wear and were invited later to join the football, basketball and boxing teams. The guys who scored Average could buy purple trunks with silver trim to announce their standing. Those who scored Poor, like me, had to wear those gray gym trunks like a flag of shame.

What mostly fired us up, though, was Lencho's inspirational talks. He spoke with braids of lightning in his voice, saying stuff he'd learned in the Berets about Mexicans and Chicanos being a special people, how power slept in our fists and we could awaken it with a simple nod of our heroic will. He piled it on about being proud, about how marvelous it was going to be after we pulverized those other guys. Lencho could really swell the chest muscles.

After a couple of weeks of watching punches pop deeper into the bag, and guys skip blurs on the jump rope—Albert actually hit the tetherball four swipes in a row!—I began to get a little swell-headed about our chances. Sure, at first I was a bit leery, since those other guys were bigger and could cross their arms when jumping rope, but they weren't any better than us, not really.

One day, while walking over by B Hall, I was surprised to hear my name called from behind. "Oh, Manuel! Manuel!"

It was Miss Van der Meer, bustling over, a pile of books shoved up against her breasts. She was walking in that cute, pigeon-toed way that used to make Albert and me do crazy rolls with our eyes.

"Do you think Leonard will win the contest?" she asked, stopping in front of me. She began to busily shuffle the order of her books on her chest.

"Yeah, I guess so," I said. "He's pretty confident."

"Yes, I noticed that about him," she said, waving her finger in the air. "He's a regular Hotspur."[2]

"A hot what?" I asked. I thought maybe she was talking about some kind of bullsticker or thorn.

"Hotspur, in Shakespeare, you know."

I must have looked blank, because she got this disappointed frown on her face.

"Well, it's not important," she said, matter-of-factly. Her face was sprayed with sun freckles, and with her finger she delicately crooked back her bangs. She was beautiful, with swirls of glowing sunlight floating on her hair.

I was going to grab her free hand and shake it, but she started fiddling with the bindings of her books.

"Anyway," she said, "you tell Leonard for me that I wish him all the luck in the world. Will you do that, Manuel?" She made her hand straight as a Ping-Pong peddle and patted me a couple of times on the shoulder.

My heart lumped in my throat, and when I said, "Yeah, sure, Miss Van der Meer," my voice was thick as oatmeal.

Of course I didn't tell Lencho anything. He'd probably have spit at my shoes and said, *What a bitch!* He'd probably say something nasty, too, like why was a dog like me still sniffing after her tail. He talked like that sometimes when he wasn't getting all glorious about the Mexican race.

Not until Miss Van der Meer walked away did I wonder how she knew my name. I figured she must have asked someone, or looked it up in the administration files. Whichever way, I could tell by her eyes that she knew something about me. But then, I'd found out some things about her, too. For one, she wasn't one of the regular teachers, but a sort of extra teacher for the white students bussed in from Alemany High. I also found out about the couches and sofas in her classroom, because I asked the janitor, an El Salvadoran man who once worked with my dad in the onion fields. He scratched the back of his neck, and said, "*O sí, allí tienen sofás, lámparas y todo.*"[3] He thought it was a teachers' lounge.

What all this has to do with the fight, I don't know. Usually I didn't like thoughts about teachers browsing around inside my head, but Miss Van der Meer was special. I hoped, in fact, that by some wildcard of luck they'd transfer me over from Mr. Shattler's class, where all we did was read magazines and play bingo games, to hers, where students read detective books and stuff by that Shakespeare guy. Except for Albert, the guys I hung with thought that if they even flicked through the pages of a book, ink would rub off on their hands and mark them sissies for life. I could imagine them in a classroom like Miss Van der Meer's, getting all cushy on the couches; throwing spit-wads at her butt.

The boxing tournament was announced in every home room in the school, and on flyers stapled in the hallways. Hardly a word passed across anyone's lips that didn't include the thrill they *hoped* they'd get when somebody got knocked out cold.

---

2 *Hotspur*   character in Shakespeare's *Henry IV, Part 1*, known for his quick temper.
3 O sí, allí tienen sofas, lamparas y todo.   Oh, yes, here they have sofas, lamps, everything.

Being an official trainer, I got a reputation among a couple of girls, Rachel and Mary, who hung over by the baseball diamond. Their attitudes toward me couldn't have changed more completely. They said hi to me now, whereas before I would've died if just one of them had thrown me her eyes.

The day of the tournament, the basketball gym was packed from hoop to hoop. Waves of nervous anticipation washed like an ocean surf across the bleachers, and there was barely standing room by the push-open doors, where it was so pressed no one dared breathe.

The boxing ring was four brass stands taken from the school auditorium, linked by a long, furry velvet rope. They were just for show. A fighter would have to be crazy to lean against those ropes. The actual ring was a square of thick brown masking tape in the center of a huge wrestling mat.

Lencho invited his cronies from the Berets to come witness his spectacle. Decked out in khaki shirts and brown beret hats, their shoes polished to a smooth military sheen, they stood over by the exit doors intimidating anyone who happened to walk into their space. I was surprised to see Miss Van der Meer there, trying not to look excited. Old Mr. Hart, my history teacher, was there too, pacing on the sidelines and bogusly snuffling his nose with a crumpled handkerchief. Being the timekeeper and bell ringer, he was sweating diamonds.

I waited at ringside. I saw Nardo pump a fist at me as he and his friends Felix Contreras and Johnny Martinez crowded their way to a middle bleacher. He called to me, but I couldn't hear. The noise in the gym sounded warped, like a blackboard bending, about to splinter and crack. Blood hissed along my temples and my earlobes pulsed like tiny engines. *This is the biggest moment of my life*, I thought.

I was supposed to get the ring corner organized, so I gave everything an anxious onceover; Lencho didn't want to be bothered by details. I had gym towels, water bottles, an already melting ice pack stuffed in a plastic bucket, and three mouthpieces wrapped in a clean white handkerchief. I had tape and Vaseline and those stretch wraps used for sprained ankles, although what I'd actually use them for was a mystery. The Berets paid for all the equipment, so I'd grabbed everything on the shelf.

The first fight was Albert's. He was to take on Boise's brother, Rochel Johnson, and from the look of Roach's arms, I knew somebody didn't keep an eye on the weight scales. Albert, if he breathed deep, probably weighed no more than an ounce above a hundred and nine pounds. Rochel looked, not a little, but a lot heavier.

I saw worry leaking out of Lencho's face. Unfortunately, Albert saw this too, because he stared at Rochel like he was Godzilla about to trample over Tokyo.

The fight was lopsided from the beginning, and lasted only about two minutes, although for me it was a hundred and twenty long, painfully slow seconds. Albert kept backing away and backing away until the crowd started whistling. The whistling soon turned to jeering and the jeering into sneering disgust. But that was okay, since the sneers shrunk the noise down enough for Lencho to holler, "Throw a combination! Throw a combination!" He punched his fists in the air to demonstrate, but Albert just looked at him like he'd been slapped on the face with a wet towel. "Charge, then; goddam it. Charge!" Lencho urged.

Unfortunately, Albert charged. But Rochel saw him coming from a mile away, and with his gloves up and head leaning to one side he moved smartly out of the way. Albert stumbled past him, tripped and smacked his nose on one of the auditorium stands. Everybody oohhed and awwhed and mangled their collars like it was them that got their noses smashed. Coach Mazzini mercifully waved the fight over.

Albert's face was awful with defeat; Lencho's was a torment of disappointment. He stuffed some ice in a towel and roughly pinched Albert's nose shut. The nosebleed bloomed a rose of blood in the towel, and Albert started to cry in wet, little puppy whimpers. Lencho, with a sigh, told me to grab the towel and take him into the locker room.

That sure was a mistake. I knew it as soon as I walked into the locker room because there, dressing for his fight, was Chico—late as usual. Before I could tell him it was just a plain bloody nose, Chico took one look at the blood sopping the towel, and his face glazed over with shock.

"Hey, it's okay," I said, reassuringly. I left Albert by his locker. "It's only a bloody nose."

"Only a bloody nose!" Chico cried, clutching at his hair. He was stiff with panic. If somebody at that moment had pushed him over, he'd have landed flat on the back of his head.

I tried to grab his arm and lead him into the gym, but he shrugged me off and walked like a zombie down the locker aisle. I was afraid he'd suddenly bolt for the exit doors. *Oh no*, I said to myself. *What am I going to do?* I ran down the aisle and grabbed him by the shoulder.

"Hey, you're not *scared*, are you?" I said, trying to be peppy.

Chico stared blank at me for a while, then a little spark of embarrassment flashed in his eyes. "Hell, no, I was just, I was just going to get my towel."

"No, no," I insisted, "I got towels, I got plenty of towels! Hey man," I said with exaggerated pride, "I came *prepared*!"

This seemed to boost Chico's spirit a little, and he let me steer him through the swinging rubber doors and into the gym.

As soon as Chico and I walked in, a stampede began in the bleachers. The Mexicans, both guys and girls, began hammering the floorboards and hooting like wild Yaquis.[4] It was a big cheer, considering the school was mostly black, with a few whites bussed in from across town.

When Chico and I reached the corner, Lencho was clapping these hard, buffeting claps, like he was a thousand times relieved to see us. He practically popped the knuckles out of my hand when he grabbed it.

I looked over and saw Nardo jamming his arm in the air, and could hear Rachel and Mary screeching Chico's and my names. The girlish pitch of their voices sliced through the noise like a paper cut. It touched down softly on my heart and opened a tiny slit that spilled sweet and aching all around inside me.

Lencho hurriedly sat Chico on the stool. "You hear that?" he said, stoking his courage. "That's for you! That's so you can show this guy who the real man is. Now, don't let your *Raza*[5] down."

I left off listening and glanced about hoping to spot Rachel or Mary. I saw them, hair teased high and stiff, excitedly smacking their lips and rolling gum over their teeth. I saw Nardo again, too, standing on the bleachers. He was winding his shoulders as if readying to fight himself. Feeling proud and nervous at the same time, I flipped the towel over my shoulder, but it landed on the floor.

---

4 *Yaquis*   a California Native American tribe.
5 *Raza*   Latino people.

Lencho had revved Chico up. When the bell rang, he shot off his stool like a man in a desperate search for dropped money. He started punching at the guy, aiming for his stomach, but mostly hitting arms and shoulders.

The guy Chico fought was Malcolm Augustus, who was now in my biology class. He was the only one in the whole class who knew the answer to the teacher's question about how much blood spills when a girl's on her period. Guys were saying a gallon and girls were acting like they knew it already, but nobody really knew—except Malcolm, who said it was about six tablespoons. Imagine, six tablespoons!

Surprised at first by Chico's aggressiveness, Malcolm soon calmed down and stabbed him with some head jabs. When Chico ducked low to avoid getting his head snapped back, Malcolm unhinged an uppercut right under his chin. Chico stumbled back, looking like he'd stuck a fork into a light socket. I thought, *Oh no, we're doomed!* But Chico sparked up again and in a flutter of blows drove Malcolm outside the ring tape.

"You see that, did you see that uppercut!" Lencho shouted when Chico stumbled back to the corner. "That was the stupidest move the *vato* could've done. When he does that, just ignore it and come over the top with a left hook. You'll knock him out, I'm not kidding, you'll knock him out!" Lencho grabbed one of the bottles from my hand and splashed water on Chico's face. He fumbled when handing the bottle back and clunked me on the forehead. "Now, I want you to body punch that bastard until he squirms," he said, turning to Chico again, "and remember, remember the left hook!"

Chico didn't remember the left hook. He couldn't have remembered his name if you asked him. Halfway through the round his legs were making wobbly journeys around the ring. He did toss some slaps and chicken-wing flutters, but at the end of the second round he looked so winded you couldn't have put a baby to sleep in his arms.

In the third round Chico tried to duck a jab and come inside, but instead ran smack into Malcolm's elbow, and was knocked out cold. They had to carry him out flat on a blanket. People's eyes widened as they took him out the exit doors. His own eyes were ditched back inside his head, and he was slobbering all over one of the blanket carrier's hands. A smart aleck from the rafters yelled out, "Emergency! Emergency!" That got a big laugh from everybody, except Coach Rogers, who shoved his way up the bleachers and gave the guy the heave-ho out of the gym.

Right away talk turned to Boise and Lencho. All the excitement became sharp as a cone.

What happened first, though, was that the leader from the Berets, a guy named Miguel, wearing a cadet's starched khaki uniform, took over my job at the corner just as I was putting Lencho's gloves on. "Take a seat, Ace," he said, and without so much as an Excuse Me, he swished the towel off my shoulder and draped it over his own.

I tried to say something in Lencho's ear about uppercuts and strategy, but Miguel pushed me away. Lencho was too nervous to listen, anyway. And no wonder. Miguel right away started nudging him on the ribs, nodding up, and reminding him how many people were in the audience. Lencho's face wrung stiff as a twisted rope.

In the other corner, Coach Rogers and Boise seemed like two cozy sweet potatoes in the dirt. Boise's face was smooth from his warm-up, dark and shiny, like an icy glass of Coca-Cola. He wasn't wearing a shirt, and a tiny sapphire necklace of sweat strung across his lean belly. Just another fight to old Boise, I thought. Cool, that's what he was, cool, with nothing jumping around in his face and nobody in his corner giving him the jitters.

Lencho and Boise being about the same size, and the two guys in the school whose muscles were the most crowded together, it was natural that people would get excited about pitting them against each other. Seeing Lencho, proud and ready for action, you couldn't help but back him. And then there was Boise. He didn't strain against the threads of his clothes like Lencho, but he was what everybody in the Boys' Gym called "ribbed." He even looked like a boxer, his nose square and puffy around the eyes, like he'd just awakened from a dream of beating up people.

The referee was Coach Mazzini. He had this big watersack gut that got in the way of everything, but otherwise he knew what to do, which was mostly to keep fighters from chickening out of the ring. When Mr. Hart clanged the bell announcing the start of the fight, everyone screwed their butts tight to their seat.

After a moment of staring at each other hard enough to shove a crowbar across a table, Lencho right away began wrenching left hooks and long winding right crosses; Boise ducked and upper-cutted to the body. It was a mean fight, a blur that even if you slowed it down by half, it would still be a blur. Even Coach Mazzini, fat belly and all, sprinted out of the ring and didn't go back in until Mr. Hart smacked the bell ending the first round.

The whole gym busted open with screams and foot stomping that almost brought the bleachers crashing down. Lencho came back to the corner, breathing huge and proud in his sweaty T-shirt, a fat grin on his face.

In the bleachers, it was a circus. Guys were dancing and girls collapsing over each other. The girls pawed over the guys and the guys pretended to hug them as they fainted on their laps. But then needling stuff, like arguing and weasely bragging, sparked between some black and brown guys. A few even began to shove each other and spit into arguments. Then the bell to the second round clanged and everybody right away sat down.

Boise was still calm, a gob of Vaseline dangling on his chin. At first he'd dip his shoulder and ease over to the side when Lencho charged. Then he began grinding punches into Lencho's belly, and suddenly, like a tidal wave, rise up to hammer him on the side of the head. A queery smile smeared across Lencho's face a couple of times.

That's when he began to shy away, stirring his gloves in the air like he was waving away flies. To show he wasn't stunned when he came back to the corner, he sunk his lips into a confident smirk. You could tell, though, that this was a sloppy excuse. In the bleachers, it was so quiet you could practically hear people breathing.

Whatever Lencho's plans were for the third round, they weren't very good. Boise began laying up for him, butting him on the jaw with jabs and swinging catapult blows against his ribs, making him grunt deep. To protect himself, Lencho crossed his arms and began stepping back, stubbornly jerking his chin from side to side to avoid blows. When Boise sledgehammered him on the side of the ear, his shoulders stiffened and his jaw squinched like a little electricity had run through it.

My heart was jerking around inside my chest, I was so nervous. My eyelashes were tiny wings beating in a fevery air, yet my face felt frozen, as if blasted by an arctic wind. I couldn't tell if my mouth was smiling or grinning.

Lencho didn't even bother coming in anymore, but just stood there gritting tighter on his mouthpiece, following Boise around the ring with beaten eyes. You could tell then that he was finished.

I pressed the sides of my cheeks to settle the nerves down, but my face kept on jumbling. Miguel, beside me, was yelling for Lencho to go forward. "Come on, Lencho! Come on! Attack! Attack!"

I felt like screaming for him to shut up. The truth was, I was afraid that Lencho would go down. If he did, I didn't know what I'd do. I had expected and wanted so much from him, that for him to disappoint me then would hurt, really hurt. I suddenly realized that the whole fight shouldn't have been given so much meaning. When pumped up with pride, something so ugly as a boxing match could only grow too cruel to maintain; it could only burst, right in everybody's faces.

When old Mr. Hart finally clanged the bell, ending the fight, I was relieved. It was obvious who had won. Coach Rogers gave Boise a big bear hug of victory. Then he rushed over and—real corny!—like he really meant it, cupped Lencho behind the neck like a proud father, staring into his eyes.

Miguel left the ringside in a hurry to talk with the Beret guys standing over by the exit doors. You could see their faces had hardened against showing what they really felt. Later, when it was all over, after they had *analysed* it and all, they decided to kick Lencho out of the Berets. They said that he brought embarrassment to them, and worse, caused a loss of unity between them and their black brothers.

But that was later. Right then no one was around, except me, and Lencho kept searching for somebody to take off his gloves. Even when Boise came over—his own gloves off and, with his two naked hands, shook Lencho's arms— Lencho looked down at his gloves sort of funny, the way you look at a dog that has just dug up your garden, halfway angry at the dog and halfway sad about the garden. A hunk of concrete weighed on my chest and gopher teeth were gnawing at my heart, but I went over and began peeling the tape and undoing the laces—because Lencho wanted somebody to take off his gloves.

CHAPTER 8

Family Affair

THE DAY we took Magda to the hospital, the wind against my ears sounded like sizzling, it was so cold. I remember tears of ice dripping from the trees and frozen pools clasping the blackened soil near the roots. My fingers felt like snapping off the bone when I opened and closed them. Across from the hospital was the bus stop made of mortared cinderblocks. When we got off the bus, a scrap of paper tumbled up the sidewalk and stuck on the wrought-iron gate of the hospital entrance.

We went to the hospital because Magda had come home crying with pain. She splashed vomit on the front step, and when she tried to rise, swooned and crashed against the screen door. Mom and I were in the kitchen. She was sewing a button on a shirt, and I was scraping the dirty moons under my fingernails. Mom jumped up right away and rushed out the door screaming in panic.

Not knowing what the screaming was about, I thought something crazy had happened, like maybe some rabid dog had snuck into the kitchen or a giant rat poked its head out of a hole, two things of which I knew my mom was terrified. I dashed out behind her.

At first I thought Magda had gotten hit by a car. The crosswalk over by Walnut Street had no stop sign, and the street winds around a curve so sharp that cars boom down on you before you know it. But the way she was cramping and bundling her stomach, I thought it was food poisoning, like my aunt Letty, who came back from Mexico with amoebas. But Magda didn't look stiff and glassy-eyed like I'd seen dogs that had been hit by a car look, and she wasn't moaning in a way that showed amoebas had knotted her up. When I got close, I noticed a red carnation of blood blooming on the lap of her dress.

Mom had her suspicions. She pulled me over and told me to help drag Magda inside. Gossip had a way of spreading around the housing projects quicker than dry burning grass.

Mom's suspicions proved right. Magda was losing a baby. Mom figured it out by the stiff way Magda clutched her belly which you could see was swollen even under the loose dress. Mom had lost two babies herself; one was born dead; the other birthed too early to start life complete, and died in the hospital incubator after only a couple of hours of sucking air. Mom said you could have put her little baby girl inside a shoebox, she was so tiny.

We dragged Magda, muscle stiff and clumsy, across the cement floor to the bathroom. She was hooking her fingers into tiny crevices in the air and whenever she whined, a menthol chill the size of a maple leaf touched on my neck.

It took some pulling to drag her to the bathroom, but as soon as we stopped, Mom said to me, "Get out!," and grabbed my arm to shove me back through the door. I didn't know why we were in the bathroom, or what the hell exactly was the matter with Magda, so I sort of wrestled with Mom there at the door. I didn't really try too hard, and she was strong as a bear. She slammed the door against my hands.

I stood outside not knowing how long and not really thinking about anything. Then I opened the door. Magda had her coat off, and her head was leaning against the toilet. Right beside her, as if it had just spit out between her legs, was this tiny baby laying there like a slimy puppy with a big head and no hair and smeared in a dirty blue-purple jam. Its mouth was puckered shut, its teeny arms were raised and tight like a wrestler flexing victory, and its bitsy fingers spread out as if to grab a marble. Mom fumbled a little with the braid it was tied to and threw the baby in the toilet.

On the bus ride to the hospital, Mom cried and moaned about not following her instincts and asking questions. She should have pulled the *bruta*,[1] my sister, weeks ago by the hair and demanded explanations. She was only thankful to the Lord that Dad wasn't home. She forced her voice through gritted teeth and warned me not to tell him.

Hearing Dad's name, Magda started whining and blubbering, and people on the bus turned around. The way the nosy bus driver eyed us in the rearview, I could tell he thought we were some crazies. I gave him a criminal stare, and showed all the people in the bus that we weren't a family to be messed with.

It was after we reached our stop in front of the hospital and began steering Magda toward the Emergency entrance that I noticed the cold. It was warmer

---

1 *bruta* stupid girl.

in the Emergency Room, though. While Mom filled out the admission forms, I sat with Magda on the scratchy orange seats made of plastic and black tubing. Her hair was sweaty and plastered on her forehead, and she kept drawing up her legs, cradling herself small. She shuddered and moaned, and every time she did, a shovel blade churned earth inside my stomach. Once I made the mistake of touching her head, and she whimpered, loud.

The receptionist, a Mexican lady like us, kept sighing and shaking her head. Mom kept opening and closing her old lint-bally coat, then finally took it off. She had tried for months to get Dad to buy her a long beige coat with buttons big as fifty-cent pieces that she'd seen at Penney's. Dad mostly refused, raising his hand as if to visor his eyes against the sun. Sometimes he'd promise to buy her one at the end of the month, knowing that the bills would always manage to wedge in between her and the coat. One day she came home saying that she'd gone to the store and the coat wasn't there. The saleslady said they'd run out of stock. It didn't matter, Mom said. She'd gotten used to wearing her old linty coat and double sweaters. You could tell by the watery way her voice sounded, though, that she hated that coat. She just didn't want to give my dad the satisfaction of denying her something he knew she wanted.

She came out from behind the cubicle and creeped over to whisper in my ear. "That lady could make Santa Claus grumble," she said, pointing to where the receptionist was watching.

That was just like my mom, I thought, always making jokes about things people did to us. She'd tell it later to our neighbor Sophie, for sure, like it was the funniest story in the world. When she said this about the receptionist, I knew then that the lady's sighs were not out of sympathy, or embarrassment, or even curiosity; they were sighs of disapproval.

In the waiting room, there were two people with sick, droopy faces, and another with a broken finger or wrist. Sitting next to us was a man with a gash on his head. He was pressing a ball of baby diapers against his forehead. His wife told us that they'd been standing on a curb when one of those plumbing trucks cut around the corner, and a pipe sticking out of the back hit her husband smack on the forehead, knocking him out. She said she was terrified and couldn't find help. She thought at first that the guys in the truck didn't notice, but now that she remembers it, she did hear the engine winding down as if to stop, then pick up speed again. She said it was funny how she didn't remember this before, and how her memory came back to her at that very moment. Her husband, with his one eye peeking, gave her a look like, *Oh, please.*

She made me nervous, that lady, the way she kneaded her hands and fussed over her husband who got all steamed when he heard how those guys gassed the pedal after knocking him out. What made it worse was that he couldn't talk. Every time he widened his throat to say something, a tiny trickle of blood streamed down the lobe of his ear. He couldn't tilt back on the seats either, because of the angle of his wound. So he just sat there, shoulders straight and forehead pointing to the ceiling.

After a while, Mom grabbed my arm and said Magda needed to go pee. I helped walk her down the hall. We were so busy keeping her head from flopping over that we walked into the men's restroom. I knew right away by the stink, and no doors on the toilet stalls, and all the crappers sprinkled with gold drops.

Before we could pull Magda out though, she fainted, and Mom panicked and ordered me to get the receptionist. As I ran out, sliding on the tile floor, I noticed Magda's head lying near some black heel scuffs.

I ran over to the receptionist, who was sitting stiffly behind her desk. She must have heard Mom shout, but looked at me without a smidgen of sympathy.

"We gotta get a doctor," I said when I reached her desk. "My sister's fainted. She's right there on the floor, fainted."

"Is that the men's restroom you went into?" the receptionist asked.

"Yeah, but . . ."

The receptionist surveyed me up and down, her face a windless puddle of water. She picked up some papers on her desk and shuffled them carefully in order, then removed an ink pen and flat marble penholder and placed them inside her desk drawer. She jiggled out a key from her pocket and locked it. Looking at me, her lips pressed and eyebrows like black lightning bolts, I couldn't tell whether she was embarrassed or angry.

When I got back to the restroom, Magda was on the floor, her muscles slack as water inside a balloon. I thought she was dead. The receptionist, who didn't seem panicky at all, stood straight over her with her arms and legs set in triangles. "She'll be all right," she said. "She's just weak, that's all. Once we get her inside the doctor will fix her right up." She tried to say this cheerfully, but when she saw my mother's face, she put her frown back on.

Mom stuck her hands under Magda's shoulders and lifted. "Let's go, honey, let's go see the doctor." Her hands kept sliding out from under Magda's armpits, and she kept drooping back to the floor. "Manny, get over here and help me," she said. "We got to get her inside the clinic." She turned to the receptionist and said in the politest voice she knew if she could please get a wheelchair.

"Okay, I will, but I'm sorry you won't be able to see the doctor right now."

My mother started to stand up but didn't. If she had, Magda's head would have whacked on the floor.

"It's only that the doctor can't see her right away," the receptionist explained. She had her eyes fixed on the scuff marks on the floor, blinking, her lips firm. "If you just go back to the waiting room, as soon as he's free, I'll call him, okay?"

Before Mom could answer, the receptionist snapped her eyes from the floor and rushed out, saying something I couldn't hear.

I was trying to get a hold under Magda's shoulders when the receptionist came back, slamming a wheelchair against the hydraulic door, making me jump from the sudden bang and hiss.

I guess the receptionist hadn't finished with her lecture about the doctor, because as soon as she came in she started in on how all the doctors work nonstop ten hours a day, sometimes nights, how the whole staff are so dedicated. She knew, because she herself had typed up the duty rosters. She blew some more smoke about how people like us expect everything to be fed to them on silver spoons. How we never take responsibility. She said that's why we're so confused and screwed up. Only she didn't say "confused" and "screwed up," but said "neurotic" and another medical word I couldn't make out.

Mom's shoulders began twitching, and any minute I thought she was going to jump up and tear the lady's hair out. But she was too busy grabbing Magda under the arms and trying to prop the wheelchair, which kept slipping, against the door handle.

I was going to get up and tell the lady myself to leave, but just then Magda turned to me, and said my name, "Manny," real low and weak.

Finally, we got her into the wheelchair. The receptionist held the hydraulic door and watched, her eyes a mushy boredom. She wasn't preaching anymore.

She didn't even look embarrassed about her slobbery speech. If anything, it was my mom who looked embarrassed. She was rattled, too, by what the lady had said. She wasn't surprised, though. Nothing surprised my mom. She *expected* people to treat her mean. Then a little anger sparked inside her. When she turned the chair to wheel Magda out, she said in a gruff voice for me, *not* the lady, to hold open the door.

In the waiting room we sat down near the guy clenching his bloody diapers. I couldn't see much under the compress, but he was a bald guy with bulby, alcoholic ears and a sunburned neck. His wife had come over when she heard the commotion. Her fat rolled in different directions when she walked with us down the hallway.

The lady stopped at the coffee machine and plopped in some coins. The spout squirted out a dark, rusty water. She planned to give it to her husband, but from under his mountain of diapers, he peered at her like she was an idiot for even thinking he could drink from a cup.

She asked Mom if she wanted the coffee. Mom took the coffee, gulped a mouthful, and braced it on her lap.

"These people," the lady said, sitting down beside my mom. "I can't stand them, either. It's like they care more about the *gavachos* than they do about us." She shook her head and stared at the floor.

I was sitting behind my mom and the lady. I saw Mom's shoulders begin to jiggle. She was crying. The lady reached out and put her hand on Mom's lap. As she did, a tear from Mom's eye dropped on her arm, and quickly, the lady rubbed it off, as if it burned. Then she looked up at her husband peeking at her from behind his barricade of diapers. He flinched his head, signaling with gritted teeth. He wanted her to keep to her own business and get back to taking care of him.

When we got back from the hospital it was early, but already dark. Dad was asleep and Nardo nowhere to be found. Pedi was at Sophie's. I went to my room and nestled under the covers, feeling wound-up and anxious, cringing down in bed. I must have fallen asleep, because when I heard moaning, I sat up in an eyeblink, and there was a gray shaft of morning light under the door, and Nardo was beside me, asleep.

I heard Mom through the walls, talking to herself. I wasn't sure if she was saying something about Magda or reminding herself of the chores needing to be done. Flopping off my side of the blankets, I called to her, then knocked lightly on the wall to see if I could get her attention. Dad heard me, and began mumbling curses about the pesty annoyance of kids, but he didn't get up.

Beside me, Nardo was a dark clump on the bed. I whispered to him, but there was no answer. His face could barely be seen in the murky darkness. I wondered whether I should wake him, but just as I was about to touch his shoulder, he snatched at the blanket and tucked himself into a cocoon. I saw a shadow flicker under the door and slipped out of bed.

Magda had been tumbling in fever, strangling phlegm in her throat and making gruff, coughy barks. When I got to her room, the bedsheet was moist and the blanket mussed from all her twisting. Sweat had glued her eyelids shut, and spit leaked out of her mouth and pushed a wet dent on the pillow. Mom, her eyes worried to slits, was sitting on the bed beside her, wondering aloud whether to take her back to the hospital. Her fever was worse than the doctor had said it'd get.

When she heard me, she ordered me to stay by the door. She didn't want me tugging her brain with questions. So I stayed where I was, staring over Mom's back as she loaded up a towel from a bowl of water, squeezed it, and washed away a smear of milky wetness from Magda's nose.

"Are we going to take her to the hospital?" I asked, worrying my finger on my T-shirt.

Mom turned, and after settling her eyes on me for about a second she looked above my shoulder. I followed her eyes and there, through a slit in the hallway, I could see my dad lying, the blankets kicked to his feet and his arm dangling over the side of the bed. He'd fallen back asleep as soon as he shouted for Mom to shut up the noise. He looked like a huge baby, but with a mustache and graying hair.

"Go back to sleep," Mom said, her face soft, "quit worrying about your sister." She went back to dampening her with a towel.

I stayed where I was, my eyes locked on the ruffles of her blue nightgown. "Mom, I think you better get Dad's keys so we can take her to the hospital again," I said, twisting my finger more on my shirt.

Mom shrunk her eyes narrow. "You listen to me, Manuel," she said, "if you don't get back to bed . . ." She stopped there. This was the voice she often used on me, but I was getting too big now to bow to her threats. If I remained stubborn, she'd usually call on Dad to come threaten me. But Dad didn't know what had happened, and she didn't want him finding out.

"I think we ought to take her to the hospital," I said as a low whine flowed from Magda.

Mom laid Magda's head gently back on the pillow. When she turned to me, a wildness showed in her eyes, and her right cheek fluttered like a nerve had blown out on that side of her face. She took the moistened rag and threw it with a splat near my feet. "I told *you* to go back to sleep," she said icily.

Then, suddenly, before I could say anything, or even lift my eyes from the wet rag, she rose, and with her hand cupped like a spoon, smacked me hard on the ear. I just stood there, bracing, but the blow was like a spike inside my ear, and I stumbled, my head butting against the side of the door. I collapsed on one knee and stayed there, gazing at the floor. When Mom spoke again, I lifted my face. I wasn't angry or afraid but could only plead at her with my eyes.

"Now, go back to sleep!" she said, her voice breaking.

I refused to budge. I kept holding my ear like it was an abscessed tooth. "You just don't want him to be mad at you," I said, with crevices in my voice.

Looking around like there was no place for her to hide her eyes, Mom shrieked, "We don't have any money!" Then, her face reddening with panic, she covered her mouth, afraid that any more yelling might wake up Dad.

Then, maybe to keep me from saying anything more, she struck me again, this time with mean, chopping strokes. Zigzags of lightning connected the seconds as she cut down smack after smack on my neck and on my shoulder. The air had a sharp, splintery edge. I arched my back, cowering, but I didn't want to raise my arm to cover myself, thinking she'd stop hitting me sooner if I didn't do anything.

When I finally looked up, Mom backed away, her eyes circles of panic and her long liquid hair drooping across her face. She pushed back some strands of hair and stood there, her nose flaring and her cheeks watery with tears. "*Mijo*, please, do what I say," she pleaded, sucking back a ribbon of saliva. Then her voice became tender, and she began to cajole me, saying, "Please, I *can't* wake him. He'll blame it on you for not watching over her. He'll say it's your fault. Come on, honey, go back to bed, I'll fix Magda up. Don't worry." Her last words wound to a slur, and a glassy trickle weeped over her chin.

I leaned against the wall, my arm dead to the coldness. "How's he gonna blame me?" I asked, in a voice that sounded like a girl's. "Who's he got to blame other than hisself?"

An aching, heavy gravity pulled down on my stomach when Mom looked at me, her face twisted with hurt over what I'd said. She hurt, I knew, because she didn't want to admit it to herself, afraid that she too was to blame. But just then, Dad sat up in bed with a jerking snort, his body creaking the bed springs. He was moaning from pain. From years of cranking tools and lifting sacks, the heels of his palms were anvils of yellow callus, and his back had slipped a disc. He couldn't move in the easy way he once did. Every time he rose from a couch or bed, he'd groan.

Mom turned to me with a stiff stare. I thought she'd stay frozen that way forever, when suddenly her eyes lifted over my shoulder. There, suddenly, in the doorway, was Dad. He put his hand on my shoulder, peering into the room. Even with his half-painful, half-sleepy eyes he figured out everything in a flash.

"Put her in water," he said to my mom in Spanish.

"But . . ."

"Put her in water," he said again, brusquely this time, then walked away wobbly and absentminded.

I thought he was going back to bed, but then I saw a light blink on at the end of the hallway and heard water drumming into the bathtub. He came back pushing his way past me, and without a word grabbed Magda from the bed and with a mighty groan lifted her up.

Like an ant carrying a giant statue of bread, Dad carried Magda out of the room. I slid up beside him, bracing his arms. I knew his back was hurting. In the bathroom, Dad put Magda, nightgown and all, inside the tub and bobbed her steady. She floated a little, her gown blossoming in the water like a boat sail, and after a long while her eyes blinked open. She looked up at us staring down at her, and then, with a surprise that showed the fever had died, she looked at Dad, amazed. I don't know if it was because of the pain in his back, or the pain of seeing Magda sick, or both, but his face was trembling and red, as if blown by a hot, blurry wind.

CHAPTER 9

Dying of Love

To Mom's surprise, Dad actually found a job doing office work for the Awoni Building Company. To everyone's surprise, Nardo got a job delivering medicine for Giddens's Pharmacy. I helped him with his route on Saturdays, when the weather was either snips of cold snagging fishhooks through your clothes, or just plain icy, with steam flowing from every breath. Nardo would keep the engine running while I bolted for the cash, or Medi-Cal card, whichever arrangement those old retired geezers had with the pharmacy.

Afterward, we'd go to lunch in Chinatown and order hot plates of chow mein noodles and sweet-and-sour pork.

That Saturday I roused myself from bed, put on my red hunter's jacket and right away walked out into the thin ghosts of fog. I heard the kitchen faucet hissing, and saw Mom through the kitchen window squeezing a mop in the sink, humming as she shook out dirt from the strands. She was wearing her flower print dress, the one with the flowers faded, and rumpled like she'd crushed it in her hands before putting it on.

She always did chores before the sun blinked on the horizon, when she could think clear without a lot of kids yelling, or Sanchez, our neighbor with the blue Virgin tattooed across his back, gunning his car engine.

She began slapping the mop wildly on the floor, shuffling around in my dad's old hightop boots, the ones with the buckles torn out and tongues wagging. Most of the time she mopped the floor barefoot, since her feet had enough calluses to step on my dad's cigarette butts without making her wince, but that day it was too cold.

I heard more water moaning through the pipes, then a drumming in the bathtub. Dad was taking a bath and singing. For as long as I remember, especially when in a good mood, he sang this Mexican ballad that I never could figure out the words to. He'd repeat this one line over and over, *"Quiero morir de amor,"* or *"Quiero vivir con amor." I want to die of love;* or, *I want to live with love.* One or the other, I wasn't sure. Both phrases in Spanish sounded so alike.

When I neared the pharmacy, the sun was knifing a big blue hand through the ghosts of fog, sweeping them away like cobwebs. The maple trees on that street were dreary and weeping moisture, their stripped bark dusted with a glassy talcum of mist. But that, too, was melting. And when the wind came, little sneezes of drizzle sprayed on my face.

Nardo, who'd taken off earlier, should have been waiting outside, since he didn't want Mr. Giddens to find out I was working with him. I doubted if he'd get fired, though, since Nardo with my help was the fastest deliverer that old boss man had.

I waited outside, trying to keep my teeth from chattering. Finally, against the nagging in my head, I stepped inside.

Mr. Giddens was behind the counter, pouring pills with a plastic shovel into a jar. He had parched hands and a face hacked as if by baseball cleats. I acted casual over by the Get Well cards, pretending to read them and then jamming them back into the slots.

From the corner of my eye, I saw Mr. Giddens sizing me up. He put down what he was doing and came over. He had a mustache of sweat and tiny diamond necklaces under his eyes. Figuring he'd lose more money from thievery than gas bills, he kept the store steaming hot, so that everybody who came in would have to take off their coats and hang them on a tree rack by the door. I didn't take off my coat, and that's why Mr. Giddens noticed me.

Steering his finger toward the storage room in the back, he said, "You and Bernard better get your butts cracking, all the other boys are gone."

"Yes sir, Mr. Giddens," I said, hurrying down the aisle. "We'll get going right away. . . . I mean, I'll tell my brother to get going."

"Don't think I don't know about you two working together," he shouted after me, wiping his face with a handkerchief. "I wasn't born yesterday."

Nardo was busy sorting out prescriptions in a cardboard box. Other guys hoarded routes that gave tips, or had addresses near their homes, so they could knock off for lunch. Nardo didn't need to, since most of the guys lived across town, and our side of town didn't give any tips.

Acting annoyed when I came in, Nardo nodded and kept counting the bags of prescriptions. In the storage room there were packing crates full of empty soda bottles. I put my finger into the hole of a Dr Pepper. "You ready?"

"Yeah, let's get going."

"We still going to Chinatown?"

"Yeah, we're still going to Chinatown!" he said, still annoyed. "I think we should finish all the deliveries before we eat, though, don't you?"

"If you say so."

"Yeah, I say so," he said. "Hey, and what's the deal coming in through the store?" He put the box down on a chair and shook his coat before putting it on. "What did the old fart say, anyway?"

"I think he knows we're working together."

"For crying out loud—I knew he'd find out," he said, pushing his fingers through his hair. "Well, if we don't admit it, I think it'll be all right."

To keep up the pretending, I went back in through the store with the idea of going around to the alley, where Nardo would pick me up.

That's when I saw Dorothy, Mr. Giddens's daughter, although I didn't know her name or who she was at the time. She was standing over by the Get Well cards where I'd stood, raising her arms in the air and talking excitedly to Mr. Giddens. She kept turning heatedly away from him, as if to puzzle over some hot question, then she'd whirl around and say stuff like, "You're kidding!" or "That's hard to believe!"

When she saw me, she smiled, like she recognized me, then turned back around to Mr. Giddens who looked at me like suddenly an idea had popped into his head.

"Oh, Manuel! Could you come over here a minute," he said, bending his arm around in a little corral. "I want to introduce you to my daughter."

He kept circling his hand for me to come over, but I couldn't get my shoes to budge. Something was screwed on wrong. Mr. Giddens inviting me over to introduce me to his daughter wasn't natural. He hardly ever talked to Nardo, and the only time he'd ever even talked to me was on that day, and then only to yell at me.

"Dorothy, this is one of my delivery boys, Manuel, uh, Hernandez—or is it Herrera?"

"Hernandez."

"Oh yeah," he said, tossing his hand flightily in the air. "I get Bernard confused as well." He smiled and looped his arm around me.

Dorothy wore a beige skirt and a thinly woven sweater with cord designs. Her hair was clipped in high bangs on her forehead. Close up, her shoulders and hair smelled like a peach orchard with the wind coming through it, and there was a sort of mushy softness to her face, like she'd carefully massaged oils and special creams into it. Her nose was small, with the most delicious angles, and she had a moony way of looking at me that got me all buttery inside.

"Hi, Dorothy!" I said, anxious to meet her, yet stiffening a little against Mr. Giddens's push.

"Hi," she said, smiling.

She wanted to talk more with her father, but he didn't want to. He clamped both his hands on my shoulders.

"You know, Dorothy," he said, "one day Manuel is going to be my best deliverer. Right now I have him training with his brother Bernard. He's too young to have a license, but as soon as he gets one, he's going to have a job right here."

"But Dad! What about the cards?" she said, taking a big step forward.

"Oh, the cards! Is that all you want? Well, go ahead, take as many as you like." He waved his hand carelessly along the aisle. "If you want more, there's boxes of them in the back. Here, I'll get Manuel to help you."

"I already have the ones I want," Dorothy said, tapping the stack of cards she had in her hand against her other wrist.

"Oh, well, I'll tell you what. How many do you have there?"

Dorothy tilted her head slightly, and one of her eyes shrunk with suspicion. "Fifteen?" she said.

"Fifteen, huh. I'll tell you what. Get one more. Make it an even sixteen. I'm sure Manuel here would like to go. What do you say? Would you like to come to Dorothy's party? Lots of food and punch?"

He said this enthusiastically, wiping his face with a handkerchief, but while he did, Dorothy was tightening her shoulders and her smile collapsed a little. "Dad!!" she said, stressing her voice.

"No—no—I'm serious about this, now. I think Manuel would like to come. Wouldn't you, Manuel? Sure—sure, you'd like to come."

"Daad!!!" Dorothy said again, and this time her smile vanished. She struggled to hold her hands to her sides. I could see the bones on her chest stretching from the muscle, like little wing-blades about to take flight.

"Do you know what, dear?" Mr. Giddens said, his eyes sparkling. "Now that I think of it. Maybe some of the *other* delivery boys would like to come to your party. Maybe I'll ask *them*."

"They're too old!" Dorothy exclaimed. "You're going to spoil it, Dad. You're going to mess it all up like you always do!" Her face was glowing with defiance.

"Well, maybe you're right, honey," Mr. Giddens said, putting his hand on his waist and eyeing Dorothy as if figuring out a complicated math problem. "Maybe just Manuel, then—huh, sweetheart?"

An idea snapped inside Dorothy's head. She turned hopefully to me. "Maybe he doesn't *want* to come, Dad?"

"Sure he wants to come! Don't you Manuel?" Mr. Giddens said, egging me on.

"Well," I said. I didn't know what to say, really; didn't know what was going on. Whatever was going on, though, I knew words wouldn't help.

"But he won't *know* anybody," Dorothy pleaded.

"That's what you'll be there for, honey," Mr. Giddens said with assurance, "to introduce him around, make him feel welcome. I'm positive he'll have a good time."

"Okay . . . okay. I give up!" Dorothy said, gritting her teeth and dropping her arms, exasperated. She handed me an invitation card. "Here, you're invited," she said halfheartedly.

Despite being angry, Dorothy had a smooth, floating look about her as she walked quickly away, like she was being lifted by the applause in a theater full of people. I remembered then a vase I once saw at the Kern Museum.[1] It belonged to some rich people who first settled our town, and it was beautiful. Not the vase, actually, but everything inside and around the vase. The tinted petals of the roses, the white flowers, tiny as gnats, and the deep, glowing nut-color of

---

1 *the Kern Museum* the Kern County Museum, in Bakersfield, California.

the mahogany table. Everything seemed so perfect. And the vase held it all together. I remembered thinking if somebody were to come in at that exact moment and lift that vase off the table, the whole room and everything in it would collapse.

Before walking out of the door, Dorothy turned and smiled. It was a smile that would tumble around inside my brain for days. I wanted to believe that it meant that somehow she'd changed her mind about me, and that I'd be welcome at her party, but deep down I knew it didn't. In any case I didn't care, and only later, when I realized that I *should* have cared, did it really hurt.

Just then I felt someone's eyes on the back of my neck. It was Nardo near the storage door staring at me. He was smiling, too, but a mocking smile, like he sure didn't envy my predicament.

We went straight home after work, not stopping in Chinatown. Nardo was anxious to tell everybody in the world about Dorothy. He took off his coat and flung it into the living room, missing by a breath the shelf where Mom displayed her miniature animals. He rushed over to Magda, who was eating cornmeal mush at the yellow Formica table, and said, "Hey, do you know what? Manny's got the hots for Mr. Giddens's daughter!"

"Mr. Giddens has a daughter?"

"Yeah, and pretty, too. At least I think she's pretty, underneath all that snobby makeup. But you shoulda seen Manny." He pointed at me. "He got all mushy and red over her. Boy, was it a sad sight. I thought his jaw was going to drop off."

"My jaw wasn't doing nothing," I said sullenly.

"Hey, what can I say?" He arched his eyebrows and sprouted ten, innocent fingers. "If Mr. Giddens notices, anybody can."

"Nobody notices nothing," I said, sinking into a chair.

"*Nobody notices nothing*," Nardo mimicked. He shook me teasingly on the shoulder. "You should of heard what he said when you went out through the front door. Aw, you don't want to know about that?" He slapped me on the shoulder.

I was dying to know, but I wasn't about to admit it to him. If I even hinted that I was interested, he wouldn't tell me for as long as he could torture me by not telling. I could feel his and Magda's superior eyes on me, grins stretching back to their ears. When I looked up, they shut down their smiles and exchanged nods.

"Is there any more cornmeal?" Nardo asked, his voice a deep echo inside the open refrigerator.

"No, I just made this for me," Magda said, innocently pinching cornmeal from her lip. "Mom said to wait till she got back. She's gonna buy Fig Newtons to eat until she fixes dinner."

"Fig Newtons, huh?" Nardo said, casual as could be. He acted like nothing was going on, but I could tell he knew he had me hooked. He closed the door and stared at the ceiling, his eyes icing over.

"Don't you know what's going on, stupid!?" he burst out suddenly. "Mr. Giddens and his wife are going to be out of town. He just wants you to spy on his daughter's party while he's away."

Shaking her head, Magda lurched forward. She had food in her mouth and had to swallow before talking. "You mean she didn't invite him?" she asked, choking.

"No."

"Yeah, she did!"

"Boy, are you going to be out of place there!" Magda said, shaking her head.

"He don't listen. He thinks he's really been invited."

"She gave me an invitation," I said, hotly.

"Yeah, an invitation with nothing written on it."

"They'll probably make him wash dishes," Magda put in.

"No, they'll tell him to feed the dog."

Magda pushed her cornmeal away, afraid she'd tip it over while she laughed, but spilled some anyway.

"Aw, you guys could kiss lemons for all I care," I said, pushing back my chair.

"Yeah, I know what *you* wanna kiss," Nardo howled.

"Is that true?" Magda asked, glassy-eyed with laughter, but fighting to be serious. "Do you really *like* that white bitch?"

"She's not a bitch!" I said, even hotter.

"So, you do! You do like her!" she exclaimed. She leaned back on her chair, beaming, as if remembering something savory. "Boy, I thought you had better sense than to fall for some white girl."

"You guys ain't funny—you know that? You ain't funny!"

"Oh, I wasn't trying to be funny. It was Nardo who was trying to be funny," Magda said, jerking her thumb at him. "I was trying to figure out why Chicano guys are always falling for white girls—that's all."

That's when, my skin blazing, I stomped out the door, knowing that their teasing wasn't going to let up. I began rushing across the yard when suddenly I stopped, remembering that it was best not to go more than a sprinter's distance from the house, since the Garcia brothers roamed the projects like a pack of ferocious dogs. I lingered over my mom's pruned rosebushes, fingering the ashy thorns on the stems. I pricked my finger and out popped a small globe of blood. It tasted like copper.

Inside the kitchen, I could hear them laughing in lightning spurts, gorging on their own stupid wisecracks. Magda kept calming herself, then bursting out again in wild giggles. Finally, she said something about what a poor baby I was and scolded Nardo for being so mean. Then Nardo said something nasty that started her laughing all over again.

Maybe they were right, though. Maybe this was all a big joke to Mr. Giddens. All I knew was that for days after I couldn't pluck Dorothy's smile out of my mind. I was locked in long mental tortures of remembering her every move, her defiant eyes when arguing with Mr. Giddens, the fast fall of her blond hair when she crooked her neck, her bored fingers fluttering along the shelves when she pretended not to be listening. I even found myself thinking for hours over the designs of wind that wove behind her when she walked out of the store.

A flash of shame bloomed in my face, because when I focused my eyes, there, suddenly, in front of me, was Magda. "Boy, you really *are* hurting," she said, shaking her head. "You're going to get in trouble, you know that? If I was you I wouldn't go to that party," she warned.

"Well, you're not me. Besides, look who's talking about white people."

Magda just stared at me like she didn't believe what I'd said. She went back inside, listlessly waving her hand in the air. "Just don't get burned, that's all I gotta say. Don't get burned."

Once she had closed the door behind her, Nardo right away began laughing again, but she didn't join in.

For days I suffered the joy and terror of wanting to go to Dorothy's party, and knowing that it would be a big mistake. It was like a loose tooth you keep wiggling with your tongue, slow and deliberate, teasing the pain. The pain, however, wasn't in my mouth, but inside my chest. I fought against it. I'd stare hard into the mirror and order myself over and over to be strong . . . be a man! But then a cold fluttering would begin in the pit of my chest and before I could stop it, it'd spurt up a misty burning in my throat and eyes. My mind was speeding anxiously, gobbling up whole chunks of anticipation. At first, time seemed slow and heavy, but then faster and lighter—lighter until the day of the party, when the waiting became like no weight at all. Even so, I began to panic when Nardo pulled our Plymouth up in front of Mr. Giddens's house.

It was a cold night, but I was soaked in dread and could barely breathe. I was trying to be casual, so that Nardo wouldn't catch on and tease me, but he knew something was up and snatched me by the arm. "Hey, don't stick your foot in shit in there. You know what I mean?"

"No."

"It might stink."

"Oh."

When I opened the car door, the cold gushed in. The car had no heater, so when I spoke, clouds puffed from my mouth.

"Hey, Nardo," I said, turning back, "what do you think I should do?"

Nardo revved the engine lightly. It turned off if you didn't gas the pedal. "I don't know," he said, thinking. "Maybe you should try to have fun." He let the engine rumble. "What's wrong with that?"

"Nothing."

"Well, hey, don't worry. They're just a bunch of stuck-up *gavachos*." He smiled, pinched his lips shut and crunched the car into reverse. The car wound backward down the street and veered before going forward.

I walked toward the house, my breath fogging the air, my shoes cracking lines of geometry on the frozen lawn. The grasping night air, the far-off streetlights flashing, and the windows of the other houses on the block closing like eyelids too tired to stay awake, left me stiff with dread. Then a chill wind prowled under my jacket-wing and climbed to my ribs, making my lips burr. I zippered the jacket up and went up the porch steps.

A friend of Dorothy's answered the door. He was a husky, autumn-leaf-haired guy with a face spattered with freckles. He stood by the door, I suppose to welcome people as they came. I figured he was Dorothy's boyfriend, because he stood beside her, his brilliant white kernels of teeth blaring.

Dorothy had on a pleated gray skirt and white blouse ironed even under her arms and on the tips of her collar. Her hair, flared back in curls, was clasped by a black barrette with tiny diamonds on it, and she was wearing earrings. She had a drowsiness to her eyes, but when she smiled, her whole face gladdened like she was admiring a cute baby.

"How are you *doing*, Manuel?" she said, like these were the first words she'd used all day.

"I'm doing real good, thank you," I said, surprised that words even came from my mouth.

"Well, come inside, it's cold out there," she said, fussily.

I put on this big, smeary smile and urged my legs forward. My lungs felt big as balloons. There was a song by the Rolling Stones on the record player. I was nervous, but once I put my hand on the back of my neck, trying to look casual, I felt better.

Even in the darkness, I sensed the eyes of Dorothy's friends wondering who I was. Silent messages passed down the line of girls sitting on the long leather couch. The guys, standing by the large frosted windows, were staring hard at me. They were about my age or a little older, dressed in ironed slacks, wool sweaters and blazers.

One guy left a window and offered a hand to a girl sitting on one of the couches. She refused with a bored shrug, signaling the side of her face toward me. The guy nodded, and walked into the brightly-lit kitchen.

Then a girl with hair fluffed airy and wispy like cotton candy came over. She was tiny waisted, her face spotted with brown freckles. "Hi," she said, eyeing me up and down. "I'm Gloria."

"I'm Manuel. I work at Dorothy's father's store." I sort of stumbled with the words "Dorothy's father's store," but she nodded her head like she understood.

"Oh, I know," said the girl. "I know—she told me all about it."

Dorothy was not far away. She was talking in whispers to the red-haired guy, who was nodding his head up and down. Then she drifted around the room, speaking into people's ears and looking up at me. I snuck glances at her as she moved around the room, knowing that something about me was being exchanged, yet at the same time not caring. I remembered her smile at the store, and for some strange reason its effect on me was like a powerful light splashing around inside me, chasing away the shadows.

The turntable spun a slow song and the lights dimmed. Everybody began to dance, melting into a warm darkness of bodies. I was relieved, for a moment, because I felt that maybe they'd forgotten about me. I was almost sure of it when Gloria clasped my arm and led me to the middle of the dance floor. She linked her hands in mine, and a guy I didn't know cheerfully saluted us from across the room with a Dixie cup. We breathed on each other, Gloria breathing normal and me almost not at all, although I could smell the powder of her shoulders and perfume behind her ears.

As we danced, I saw Dorothy with the red-haired guy not far from us, her hand pressed against his chest. He had a drink of rum in one hand, and in the other, a cigarette, which he casually puffed on, but removed when he leaned over to whisper into Dorothy's ear. He said something, and dropped his eyes down the neck of her blouse.

Dorothy looked cool and fresh, as if carved from night air. The way her shoulders lifted, the way her heels didn't sway when she danced, the way the hem of her skirt fluttered, as if the air itself was swishing out of her way, touched my skin with a strange warmth, like I was being deliciously licked all over by tiny tongues of flame. I envied Red-Hair.

But this dreamy stumbling over Dorothy caused me to hug Gloria a bit too close, and not fit into her dancing rhythm. My leg accidentally slid between her legs. She got angry right away. "Hey, what's going on here? What do you think you're doing?"

I stepped back, startled, the brittle feeling of my dream collapsing, but I didn't say anything. Later, when I thought about it, after I ran it over and over in my mind, I realized that that was a mistake. I should have said I was sorry right away. I should have kept my voice close. By stepping back, everybody's eyes focused on us. When I told Nardo later what had happened, he said that it wouldn't have mattered what I did.

The lights blinked on, and the guy playing the records abruptly took the needle off the grooves. People groaned.

Although he looked like he didn't totally know what was going on, Red-Hair grabbed my arm and pulled me away—not hard or jerking, but firm, as if ushering me out of a place I wasn't supposed to be.

"I told you what he's up to," I heard Dorothy say with coughy dryness.

Before I could half free my arm to say something, I noticed her from the corner of my eye twirl around and walk swiftly into the kitchen, her skirt flapping.

Still a bit puzzled but determined that it was his show now, Red-Hair let my arm go. There was a group of about four older guys in front of me, blocking my way to the door. They weren't big guys, nor did they look particularly mean, but there were four, and I didn't know them. For a short, dissolving second, I thought of shouldering my way through them and hurrying for the door, but they had these tense, questioning looks, and I was beginning to feel needles on my skin.

Instead of bumping into them, I took a step toward a sliding glass door on my right, and slid it open enough to squeeze out.

It led to a backyard, which like the house, was enormous. There were trees and bushes everywhere, and the grass went on for about a half a block and glowed with an icy sheen. I looked up, and the sky had a sort of bright raspiness to it, like dark water becoming slack after boiling. The air was chilly, but my chest hurt not from the cold, but from a feeling of everything being empty, as if inside my lungs there were only echoes.

I began to walk anxiously back and forth along the side of the house, searching for an opening. The yard was surrounded by a high cedar fence, brown and slivering where some of the wood had curled with age. If I climbed it, I'd get splinters. I passed the glass door, and from the light of the outside lamp I saw the reflection of a ridiculous boy, a clumsy boy. It was me, looking at myself, except that it wasn't me, but someone ghostly and strange.

Then a shadow came across my reflection. Thinking for a second that it was Dorothy, my heart gulped.

"What are you doing out here, pal?" Red-Hair said, his voice like an electrical current traveling underwater. He was standing near me, his head glowing in the bright light that just then darkened with the heads of more guys. "I hear crazy things about you, buddy. Crazy things."

Red-Hair was rolling a piece of gum between his teeth and looking back at his friends as they began to fan out around the side of the house as though inspecting the grass and flowerbeds for snails. He leaned up close to me, almost touching my shoulder, then looked off to the far end of the yard. The outside lamp shone hard on half his face, and I could see the muscles of his jaw pulsing.

"You know, guys like you are weird ducks," he said, in a loud, but lazy voice. "You just hang around, quacking and flapping your little paddle feet. Do you know what I mean?"

I felt like a piece of cold steel was caught in my throat.

Noticing that I wasn't saying anything, Red-Hair went on, moving his chin in little jerks. "Well, let me just say this, pal. I don't care if you are supposed to be a guest. This is not your party, and I don't like you coming around here bothering Dorothy." The last part he said with a hard pop of his gum as he ground his teeth into it.

I wanted to tell him that it was all a mistake, that Mr. Giddens made me come, and that I wasn't dying of love anymore, but I knew my brain was just searching for excuses.

Whether Red-Hair sensed what I was thinking, or whether he just thought he'd said enough, he smiled and shook his head at his friends. He put his thick palm on my shoulder, and in an almost friendly way, conked me a couple of times on the head with the large knuckle of his hand. Then, still chewing his gum hard, he turned toward the sliding glass door.

There, standing by the open curtain, was Dorothy. She was delicately biting a cuticle and looking worriedly at us, a crowd of curious girlfriends behind her.

Cocking his head back, Red-Hair walked toward her. He didn't say anything, but nodded and raised both his hands, first at me, then at her, as if to say, *Was this enough?*

CHAPTER 10

A Test of Courage

THE WHOLE disaster with Dorothy Giddens made me realize that I wasn't anywhere close to being smooth with girls. Not so much because I was ugly, although I was *kind* of ugly, or that I was a pest, although my sister Magda would argue different. It was because I was too chicken to ever say anything to a girl—chicken with the sourest yellow. Just thinking about telling a girl I liked her clamped the muscles on my chest and made my lungs pull hard to catch a breath.

Not that girls spit on my shadow or anything, but I would never be sweet enough to threaten cavities even to a girl like Imelda Rodriguez, who wore bottle glasses and had teeth going every which way. Imelda wore clodhopper shoes and dragged a heavy shadow. I imagined her love would be a terrible howl of loneliness. But I would have adored her forever if, just once, she'd have tapped me with a shy finger of love.

I told my friend Frankie about this. He lived near the irrigation canal at the far end of our projects, banked with scraggly oak trees and tall, speary grasses. Polliwogs wiggled away from approaching shadows and striped-green garter snakes twined inside the leafy beds of dead stumps. It was a fun place to play, sometimes.

Frankie said he knew what I meant, but that girls nowadays were impossible to talk to, although he knew where I could get to know this girl real good, if I wanted, and easy. I gulped like I'd just swallowed a delicious worm and said, "Really?"

"Yeah, really. Tomorrow—I'll show you."

A red blush of sky was giving in to silver patches of moonlight when Frankie and I set out for Mondo's house in the Callaway Projects. There, we found some guys hanging around a backyard. One was Mondo, another was his half-brother, Eddie. A guy called Gody whose real name was Guillermo was also there. And there were two girls named Rita and Patty inside the house.

Somebody had been using the yard to fix cars; it didn't have a lick of grass on it, only packed-in dirt stained with oil. Bald tires lay scattered around, and a chinaberry tree near the fence had a pulley chain hanging from a branch. The greasy chinaberries crudded my tennis shoes.

Frankie said if I wanted to sit down I could stand up a tire and crunch it down with my butt. I looked at the streaks of black grime on the rump of one of the tires and decided to stay standing.

Along the backyard was an alley with a gapped-out wooden fence. Broken boards dangled from rusted nails. Frankie told me that Eddie, Mondo's half-brother, cracked the planks with his foot when he drank too much and got angry about his mom dying of cancer. He warned me not to mention anything about mothers to Eddie. "When he starts going on about how you don't know shit, just shut your mouth, okay?"

Rita and Patty were inside Mondo's room, which you could get into from the back porch. I wanted to join the gang because Frankie promised that I could kiss and make out with one of the girls when I passed the initiation. I was anxious about it, and curious about how the girls looked.

That's when Patty came out. She had beer-color eyes and black hair plowed down the middle, flowing down almost to her hips. I remembered seeing her at school, her hair in the sun glowing like a fiery blue jelly. She wore cowboy boots and high black socks that led up to a miniskirt so tight against her hips that she had to turn her legs a little sideways to walk.

Patty smiled daisies at Frankie and play-tugged on Gody's sleeve, but her best eyes she saved for Mondo, making flirty winks and talking with a throaty voice. He craned his neck back, rubbed his wrist and smiled with slit eyes. Me, she ignored, and went back into the house.

She was supposed to be Mondo's girlfriend, but Frankie didn't know for sure. He searched the clouds whenever I asked about her. That didn't stop him from making up stories when I got cold about joining the gang. He also said Rita wasn't as pretty as Patty, but said she'd let anybody kiss her, and that thought clawed at my throat, as did the way he referred to the girls as *pollitas*, which in Spanish meant "little chicks." The word sent a current of excitement rushing through my chest.

With the brim of his *pachuco* hat[1] turned down, Mondo went around collecting dues. The plan was to buy a car. They figured he could drive, him being seventeen and having a beginner's license. His aunt signed the papers at the DMV because he promised he'd take her to buy groceries when he bought the car. She wasn't so smart.

In any case, Mondo didn't want a bunch of guys hogging up the seats, so they figured a few *vatos firmes*, firm guys, would do the trick.

"Hey, *ése*, are you a *vato firme*?" he said holding out the hat. His eyes stared at me from far away.

"Yeah, *ése*." I dug into my pocket and took out all my change, about eighteen cents, and dropped it in the hat.

"Did you give him the lowdown?" he asked Frankie.

"Yeah, I told him."

The lowdown was that I had to pass the Test of Courage to become a member of the Callaway Projects gang. I'd also get to make out with Rita, which, as I found out later, was a rule made up while trying to decide if girls were even going to be in the gang. Rita suggested it, although she added that she wouldn't let anybody actually lie down with her. She didn't mind making it seem close, though.

It was one of those evenings when the moon comes out early and looks scarred with a dark rash. Mondo passed around some Lucky Strike cigarettes, shoving them out like tubes and watching to see if we were thankful or greedy. "So," he said, "Frankie says you been to Juvy."

---

1 pachuco *hat*   a wide-brimmed hat associated with rebellious fashion among Mexican American young men beginning in the 1940s.

"No—I never been to Juvy," I said. I was embarrassed about having to admit it. Frankie must have told him I'd been in Juvenile Hall to impress him.

"Well, I been to Juvy," Mondo said, "once." He nodded slowly, getting everybody's attention and lit his cigarette. He handed me the match, and when he did, I caught a glimpse of a tattoo in the shape of a C on the fleshy bridge between his thumb and forefinger. "Me and some guys from Holloway Projects got caught stealing this car. We didn't mean nothing by it. We was jus' going to cruise around and drink beer, go check out the *rucas*[2] on Belmont Avenue. We used to do it all the time, you know. We'd take the car and dump it over by Chinatown. The owner'd get it back the next day, sometimes with more gas in the tank than when we got it."

He winked over at Frankie, his cigarette pinched between his fingers, then took a giant drag, letting the smoke pour out between his lips in a tight blue vapor. "You ever stole a car?" he asked, choking a little.

"No, sorry," I said, regretting again my mousy admission.

"Never!" Mondo asked, in mock surprise. He turned sideways and raised an eyebrow at the guys. I thought he was going to make fun of me, but then he said, "Ahh, don't worry about it. It ain't no big deal, really, it ain't no big deal." He spit out a speck of tobacco, then walked over to the fence and flipped his cigarette into the alley. It hit a puddle somewhere and made a sizzle. "Besides, we ain't stealing any more cars. Ain't that right, Frankie?"

Frankie was searching for matches. He found a book and began lighting everybody's cigarettes, all except Eddie's, who had hooked his behind his ear. I hadn't smoked my own cigarette either and couldn't remember what I did with the match Mondo handed me.

"*Chale*,[3] those days are gone," Frankie said, arching his shoulders.

"*Simón ése*, those days are gone," Mondo agreed. He puffed his cigarette again, then crooked his fingers in the shape of a claw and circled them around. "We're going to buy a car, *ése*—all of us, except, maybe . . . you." He shook his fingers out, sweeping them over everybody, then curled them in again, leaving only his thumb out, the one with the tattoo. He pointed it at me. "It depends on whether you pass the test. Right, Frankie?"

"I tell you," Frankie said, with exaggerated toughness, "he's Bernardo's brother. He'll prob'ly kick all our asses."

"Not mine. He won't kick my ass!" Eddie said, stepping out of the dark of the alley. He'd been listening near the fence. There was threat in his voice, and his face was gluey from drinking Night Train.[4] He had long hair, almost as straight as mine, moss thin and blond, and a pale, bedsheet-color face. His eyes were nickel blue, like light flitting off the shank of a sharpened knife.

"Calm down, Eddie," Frankie said. "I was *only* kidding."

Eddie smiled, like he got one over on Frankie, then lit his cigarette.

When Frankie had first told me about the initiation, I pumped my fists in the air with showy bravery. The initiation was to test a guy's courage. You could either sissy out, or have Mondo think you brave enough to stand the punishment.

Actually, it wasn't the pain of getting socked and kicked that bothered me, but more the pain of feeling afraid. When chicken feathers choke in your

---

2 rucas   literally "old women" or "wives"; slang for "girls."
3 chale   No way!
4 *Night Train*   a cheap wine.

veins, being afraid could be a real knife in the ribs. Then any disgrace is possible. I worried that I'd start begging, maybe even drop to the ground, paralyzed with fear, like in the war movies when the bombs drop, shocking the dirt.

When Mondo announced the beginning of the initiation, a rash of alarm broke over my skin. Patty and Rita came out from the back porch, Patty still wearing her tight skirt, and Rita a rusty leather jacket about three sizes too big. She was giggling one of those long streamer giggles, and looking at her, I felt mushy around my shoulders. She had on those wrinkly short pants that flared like trombones. There was a crease between her legs, like somebody had lightly tapped a finger there.

As they walked slowly down the concrete steps, past the blistered paint on the screen door, the late moonlight shadows stretched lazily across the greasy yard.

Mondo invited the girls to watch. But only if they weren't squeamish, he said, winking at me. Then, without a word of warning or even a nod signaling a beginning, Mondo and Eddie began circling around me. Frankie and Gody snuck glances at each other, their faces rubbery, like they'd been slapped. I knew they weren't the serious ones.

Suddenly Eddie dropped to the ground, and before I could lift my leg, he hooked his left ankle behind my heel and shoved at my knee with his right foot. My knee hinge locked and I fell backward on my butt. I whirled around quickly, almost flailing to stand up, but before I did, Mondo clamped his hands on my head and forced me down.

Next came a thud against my ribs as he sunk his knee into me, and a glancing heel burn on my neck from Eddie. The circle shrank in around me. From the corner of my eye, moist and dripping, I saw Gody, Rita and Patty inch closer. Frankie stayed back. Suddenly, I felt a foot press down on my hand. It sprung alive with needles, and jerking my chin sideways, I saw Rita, her mouth scrunched tight, grinding her heel into my hand.

From then on, I only remember a storm of cuffs and chops and kicks hitting me as I thrashed under Mondo's grip. He crunched his knee against my head, scraping my eyebrow against the oil-crudded dirt. I tried twisting my body around to get up, yet for every strain, Mondo pressed harder, shifting the weight of his knees to counter my thrusts.

I could smell the acidy stink of the dirt, but strangely enough, there was no fear. Nor could I feel the blows, which felt like instead of me, they were hitting a slab of meat on a table. In my mind I kept saying, *Okay, you bastards, go ahead. Go ahead! See where it gets you!*

I knew that this had to be about the stupidest thing I could think about at the time, but somewhere in the back of my mind I had a thought that, once whatever it was I was being tested for came out, I'd get to go to the back room, where a couch lay against the wall and there I'd kiss Rita, or Patty, just like Frankie had promised—finally, I would hug a girl full in my arms, smell the mustiness of her breath brooding deep inside my nose, feel her lips smashing, like a kick against my mouth.

When they finally let me up, I sat there for the longest time dabbing my lips, swelling fast, flaring alive with throbs. There was also a bruise on my hand, trimmed black around the edges. My muscles felt weak, like mush, and all over my body, my bones echoed little pinpoints of pain.

I was squinching my eyes, trying to squeeze every last shudder of hurt and trembling away, when I heard Patty laughing behind me. She had a snappy laugh, like she expected everybody to crack a rib alongside her.

"Ahh, quit worrying about your lip!" Eddie scolded.

"Shut up, Eddie!" Frankie said, flicking dirt off my hair. "You'll be okay," he said, soothingly. He put his arm around my shoulders. "You'll be okay."

CHAPTER 11

Going Home

T HE NEXT DAY I woke up still bruised, but got dressed quick, feeling in my muscles a satisfying ache, like I'd done something really dangerous and survived it. We were going to hang around uptown, under the maple trees near Long's Drugstore. The guys figured we could steal some flashlight batteries, bottles of lotion or aspirin and then sell them to people looking for a bargain. While I was thinking about it, I remembered that I promised my mother I'd clean my room and rake the yard. Usually, my shoulders got slippery when my mother's hand came asking to do chores. Mops, brooms, sometimes dishes popped mysteriously out of my hands. But I was trying to help more around the house, and I was anxious to go out with the gang and didn't want Mom's eyes to narrow suspiciously.

I swept the floor of my room. I stuffed my dirty clothes in the closet, and fighting against whirlwinds from a coming storm, raked the leaves in the yard. After I was done, I rushed into the bathroom to wash up.

A feather was tickling the back of my throat. I stared into the mirror, imagining myself a brown Cary Grant and thinking about Rita, about how the night before she fluttered her eyelashes against my cheek, and stabbed the inside of my ear with the moist tip of her tongue. When she dropped hints that there'd be more surprises to come, my lungs became heavy as soaked towels.

The lightbulb in the bathroom was blazing a white star in the mirror, and looking at it, I was surprised by how much pleasure and agony could burst from one's heart at the same time. For once, I understood what my grandma used to say about happiness. She'd say that it came from breathing air that escaped from a tiny hole in heaven. But if you breathed too much of it, you became sick with the desire to go there, and you couldn't live your life properly.

At the door, I remembered my mom and yelled to her that I was going to play baseball. She was in the kitchen shifting cans around in the storage pantry. She shouted back that I should stay home since she was making chicken soup for lunch, and later planned to go with Dad to negotiate something about Grandma's house.

I picked up my old baseball mitt. I'd sort of lost the magic for baseball, and it showed in my old glove. The seams along the heel were bursting and the bootstring webbings were loose. The few times I did play, fastballs kept squirting out and popping me in the face. I knew it'd serve as a good excuse for going out, though.

I went down the hall, past Magda's room. She was in front of her old beaten-up dresser, combing her hair. She hadn't teased it yet, and her hair was a smooth current of dark, moonless water. When she saw me in the reflection of the mirror, she frowned and clacked the brush down. "What are you looking at?"

"Nothing."

She picked her brush back up and held it poised in front of the mirror. "What do you think if I peroxide my hair?" she asked, gently plucking at her eyebrow.

"You'll look like Conchita Rodriguez."*

"She's a monster!"

"Well, that's how you'd look."

"Who asked you anyway," Magda said, straightening her face in the mirror.

As I went back into the kitchen I heard the electricity in the refrigerator click on. Chicken soup was bubbling on the stove, its aroma roaming like a spirit throughout the room. I found Mom inside the pantry and waved the baseball mitt in her face. "Mom, this is an important game."

"They're all important games, *mijo*," she said, putting her cleaning rag down. I followed her around the kitchen as she busied over finding a can opener. She fussed with her hair, unknotting the tangles. "What I need is a hairbrush, not a can opener."

"But, Mom, this is different. Really."

"You're going to play baseball in this weather?" She peered outside the window. The wind was splashing hard on the maple trees. "You quit playing baseball months ago, Manuel. I know that. Don't try to fool me. Besides, you came home pretty late last night."

She stopped plucking at her hair and sized me up and down. I guess my face was bruised in spots. I had put on a cotton sweatshirt and a baseball cap with the word BASEBALL knitted in big red letters on the top. I lowered the brim so that she couldn't see all that much, turned and unpinched the glove from under my arm and began smacking my fist inside it. It made a dry, hollow sound.

"Well, I *suppose* it's okay," she said, finally. "But don't come back late."

I knew she believed me about as far as she could throw the refrigerator, but I guess she was sort of surprised I even tried to *make* an excuse. Nardo wouldn't have even bothered. She'd made up her mind to leave him alone and hope for the best. I thought at first she was wishing the same for me, but the way she looked at me was different, like she knew I'd do the right thing.

After tossing my glove and baseball cap in some bushes, I ran to Long's Drugstore. It was far away, and I had to walk sometimes, and when I did I noticed how furious the wind was getting. A storm was darkening the clouds. Telephone wires whirred and papers scorched across the sidewalk. When caught in the bushes, they scrabbled noisily around like castanets before shooting out again stiff as shotgun blasts.

The guys were sitting on the stone bench when I finally got there, except Mondo, who had his hands shoved in his pockets and was leaning against the wind. Even though it was cold, he had his shirttail out, but over it he wore a dark-blue industrial jacket, unzipped. He watched a woman scramble to her car, her knees bent low and arms crossed to pin down her skirt, and cackled so loud the woman turned and scowled at him.

There was this black guy selling newspapers in front of the store. He had on a gray knit cap curled around his ears and a letterman jacket with the collar turned up. He never said anything when customers snatched a paper and rudely dished a coin at him. Then he caught Eddie eyeing him and moved over by the department store further down the mall.

---

*Apparently a well-known media figure in California in the 1960s and 1970s.

Gody, wearing only a sweatshirt, kept rubbing his hands and burring his lips. His voice came with a clatter of teeth. "Maybe we shhould snatch some old lady's purse," he said, hunching over. "We'rre bound to make twenty, maaaybe thirty dollars."

Mondo smoothed back his wind-mussed hair and thought about Gody's plan. "It's true," he said. "Old white ladies sure have a *chorro*[1] of money. Besides, their arms are so weak they almost break off when you grab their purse." He imitated an old lady trying to get her joints moving, and we laughed. Finally, he said, "Naah, ladies with money don't shop around here. They hang more around the white side of town."

"What about the newspaper guy?" Eddie suggested. "I can catch 'em."

"Naah," Mondo stressed again, this time a little less nasty. He didn't want to spoil anybody's ideas.

By then the wind was like icy fish nibbling around our pant legs. Frankie and Gody sparked a match feud, but they got more interested in watching the match suddenly puff out and flit sideways. Frankie suggested we sneak in to see the new horror movie at the Azteca Theater. Mondo squelched that with another prolonged Naaah. I didn't suggest anything.

The parking lot was almost empty. People weren't staying long to shop, but rushed around anxious to get back home. Eddie suggested again that we nab the newspaper guy before he got too far. Last time we looked, he had distanced himself from us a good half block. "Come on, you cowards," Eddie coaxed.

"Where is he then?" Mondo asked, pretending interest. We all turned around, but the guy was gone. "Well," he said, looking around, "I'm going home. Besides, there's not enough people in the store for us to steal anything without getting noticed."

As he was shaking the cold out of his legs, a huge gust of wind came splashing against the tree above us, heaving over a branch and knocking it against one of the electric wires. "That's not good," Mondo said, nodding ominously at the tree. Then, without saying good-bye, he stretched his arms, made a military salute and walked across the parking lot.

Frankie, Gody and I offered to tag along with him, but he waved us off, saying he and Patty planned to watch television, alone.

As Mondo walked across the parking lot, some old geezer came out of the store fiddling with his car keys. When he reached for the door Mondo came up behind him and twirled a fist over his bald head. Eddie moved forward, but Mondo walked quickly away, massaging and winding his arm as if he was only kidding.

"Gee, I thought he wanted to jump that guy," Eddie said glumly, walking back to us. He looked over at Mondo, edging into the wind before disappearing behind a corner building. "I guess he's too chicken, like some people I know." He upped his chin toward us.

"Yeah, but he's got a girl," Gody said, clacking his teeth.

"I got a girl, too," Eddie said, but before he could say anything more, another huge wind set off what sounded like a catapult in the tree above us. We all jerked up thinking we'd be crushed by a collapsing branch, or struck dead by a sparking power line. Instead, the whole tree jolted, as if pulled suddenly from above by the fist of a cloud. The tree snapped back cracking and groaning against the power lines.

---

1 chorro   flood.

"Heeyyy, we better get outta here," Frankie said. "Sometimes these frickin' trees kill people!"

That's when Eddie, his hand like a shovel, stopped me and said that I should stay with him.

"What're you going to do?" Frankie asked.

"Go down the mall."

"Go down the mall where?"

"Hey, who the hell do you think you are asking me questions, the FBI?" Eddie flipped the book of matches he had in his hand at Frankie's shoes.

"No," Frankie said, looking at the matches.

"Well, it's none of your damn *business*, okay. Me and Manny are just going to check out the *rucas*."

"There ain't no *rucas*," Frankie said. "We've just been talking for an hour about what we're gonna do, and now you want to go down the mall?"

"Well, so what?"

"Hey, look," Frankie said, opening his palm in appeal. "I jus' don't want you guys to try anything, that's all. We got to be together, you know, and plan it out."

"Gaaah," Eddie said, exaggerating Frankie's accusation. "Who the hell do you think we are? Are we gonna steal something? Do you think we're thieves or what?"

"Whatta you talking about?" Frankie asked, confused. He *knew* Eddie was a thief.

"I'm talking about you, *pendejo!*[2] You stand there accusing us of stealing and then say what am *I* talking about."

"Well, I'm not accusing you of anything."

"Yeah you are. And if you don't watch it, you're going to find some teeth in your hand."

Frankie scraped his lower lip with his upper teeth, thinking. "You want to go with him?" he asked, shifting his eyes to me.

"Yeah, I'll go with him. What's the big deal?"

"Really?"

"Yeah, what's the big deal?" Eddie piped in.

You could tell by Frankie's face it was obviously a big deal. Frankie said Eddie liked to walk down the street and just for the kick of it punch some white guy in the mouth. He said Eddie liked to hit white guys square on the jaw, because their faces reddened with surprise. He hated white guys, especially those dressed in button sweaters, cotton pants and loafers, which was curious, since Eddie was a white guy himself. In fact, Mondo and Eddie weren't full brothers. Mondo's dad was named Montez, and he was in prison for assaulting a police officer, and Eddie's dad was named Owens, and he died a long time ago, knifed by a man who said he cheated at cards. But even without the splitting of names, anybody could tell they weren't all of the same blood. Mondo had curly black hair, thick enough to bend combs, and sprinkles of pimples on his cheeks and forehead. Eddie was so white, when he got agitated, little rosebuds bloomed on his face, then closed again like tiny fists.

I wished I had remembered all this when I agreed to go with Eddie, but I followed him anyway, snatching glances at Frankie and hoping maybe he'd wave me back. Instead, Frankie walked across the parking lot as if to go home, shading his eyes from blusters of dusty wind.

---

2 pendejo   fool.

"What are you looking at?" Eddie asked.

"Frankie."

"Screw him! He don't make the rules." Eddie was walking fast, still angry. An empty soda can came hammering down the mall, and Eddie, with a sneer kicked it back into the shifting wind.

The day sure was wild and blustery. Trees were creaking and whining like rusty wheels, a few shreds of sunlight twisted in the branches. Shadows grew and slipped around under the trees like dolphins frolicking about, and more than once when I glanced to the side I had the feeling that a tree was walking alongside me.

Eddie didn't seem to feel the trees at all. He walked with a heavy purpose to his heels, swiveling his head, his eyes making popping noises when he blinked. Not much other than the weather was happening in the mall. A knot of cars tried to untangle at an intersection. A flying pigeon was swept crazily away by a sudden burst of wind.

Then I heard a little buffeting sound on the trees like a whole audience of people were tapping their fingers lightly on paper. I checked with my open palm and a cold needle of rain pricked my skin. I was about to tell Eddie that maybe we ought to head for home when I saw the soft blue cords in his throat tighten. He began to move faster.

Across the street, a lady with a black dress and clear plastic raincoat came rushing out of the Guarantee Savings Bank. She had a flat black purse covering her head and was hunched against the wind. Eddie paused at the curb, eyeing the woman. He glanced both ways down the street, which I thought strange, since he usually walked across streets, practically daring cars to run over him.

The lady stopped by her car and began to root for something inside her purse. The rain was beginning to tap harder on everything. While she leaned against the door, the wind flailed her plastic raincoat, and she beat it down with her hand. Finally, she plucked out some keys and opened the door.

By then the rain was splatting hard on the asphalt and glazing the windshield, and Eddie had crossed the street, moving fast, blotches of red flaming in his cheeks and his mouth set in a mean clench. Suddenly, with his legs hinging like a jackknife, he lunged and blasted his foot against the car door. The door didn't close, but instead sprung back, stopped by the lady's hand.

She was stunned. She skitted her heel on the sleek asphalt and plopped down on her butt with a splashy thud. As she did, her purse dropped, and Eddie knelt down quickly to grab it, pushing her leg away. The lady sat there, surprised, her left ankle crooked and the white slip of her dress showing through, wet and ruffled. She didn't look so pretty as when she had first walked out of the bank, and I was surprised to feel a small trickle of excitement seep down my throat.

The lady's hand must have awoken to the pain, because she looked at it like it'd been struck by lightning. The corners of her mouth twitched, and her eyes opened, amazed. Then she burst into a sudden blubbering, but stopped right away, starring numb at Eddie as he shoveled back what spilled out of her purse. For a moment I thought she wanted to touch him. Not to grab back her purse, but to touch him to see if he was really there.

Eddie was there, all right. He rose, and seeing her outstretched hand, slapped it down like a naughty child's. Then he ran back across the street, not even bothering to scan for cars.

He rushed past me, not saying anything. His lungs were pumping for air. I called for him to wait, but he didn't even turn around. I ran after him down the mall, the wind pressing my back and legs pounding hard on the sidewalk. I was afraid I'd bust a knee joint, I was running so hard. I was too hurt and bruised from the beating the day before to catch him, though. Already, he was shrinking in the distance.

Before rounding the corner of Long's Drugstore, Eddie finally turned, and that's when I recognized him as Magda's boyfriend. The distance was the same as when I first saw him near the maple trees. That's how I knew it was him. Magda wasn't seeing him anymore, because she said she never really liked him, but only wanted somebody to be with her. I tried calling again, louder, but all that came out of my throat was a tremble of vocal cords.

In that instant of trying to call out to Eddie, everything changed. It was like I'd finally seen my own face and recognized myself; recognized who I really should be. Then I didn't feel like catching up to Eddie anymore. Instead, I wanted to grab him, and scold him about how to treat people, how to be somebody who knows how to treat people: like my sister; like that lady. But I didn't really feel like running anymore. Forget Eddie, I thought. Even if I caught him, he wouldn't understand anything I'd say. I slowed down to a walk just as the wind and rain were dying.

I stopped at the parking lot and halfheartedly searched around. It was empty of cars. Puddles of rain mirrored a hundred cloudy skies. Eddie was nowhere to be seen. The newspaper guy had migrated back to his spot in front of the drugstore, although he was packing his things. Some newspapers, soggy in his hand, were bleeding ink between his knuckles. He tossed them into a trash can, wrung the ink from his fingers and gazed at me with pitying eyes.

A thought rushed through my mind that maybe he had seen what had happened, but I figured it happened too far away.

"Where did he go?" I asked.

The guy shifted his eyes across the street, the same corner where Mondo, Frankie and Gody had gone. He flicked more ink off his fingers and hunched over his bag as if crouching over a fire. I shrugged and rubbed my forehead with the back of my hand.

Suddenly, the guy's head lifted and eyes focused over my shoulder. Down the mall, over by the department store, a black-and-white cop car came cruising in and out of the line of trees. Two cops were inside, and the passenger one pointed his finger at me and shouted to the driver. The driver pressed down the pedal and the car jerked forward, wobbling as it climbed over a curb.

I was about to bolt down the street, but the newspaper guy stopped me, saying, "Hey man. Just cool it."

The cops were on us instantly, swerving to a stop. My neck was hot as radiation and my brain racing for excuses. A sponge was in my throat and I was afraid that if I tried to talk, instead of words, a sob would squeeze out. What surprised me, though, was that the cops were not getting out of the car. I thought for sure they'd wrestle the handcuffs on me in a second.

The passenger cop, a blueberry-faced guy with a swollen, boozer's nose, and a glassy look on his face, started banging on the side door with his palm. "Hey you! Kid! Were you the one chasing that guy who stole the lady's purse?"

Before I could answer, the black guy shouted across my ear. "Yeah officer, he's the one. He came chasing that guy through the mall."

"Which way did he go?"

"He don't know, officer. He come over here to ask me, and I says I just seen him run around that corner over there not two minutes ago." He raised a finger in the direction Eddie had gone, and the car, as if pushed by the magic of his pointed finger, lurched backward, cranked into gear and gunned across the parking lot, spraying through the puddles.

As the cop car swung and squealed around the corner, the guy with the newspapers hurried to finish packing. In the trees, a silky rain was again falling with long, gathering sighs.

After packing his stuff, the guy turned to me and this time without a smile, said, "I know. I know you was with him. But they don't have to know everything. Let them deal with their own kind as they see fit." He left among coughs so ratchety you'd think he was dying of double pneumonia.

I began to walk home. The rain had died, but trash started crawling across the sidewalk again. As I neared our projects, I watched the branches of the elm trees creaking sluggishly back and forth. I stopped once to listen to some leaves falling. They'd *tap tap tap* on the branches before hitting the sidewalk, then a toss of wind would fling them in the air.

When I neared the Garcias' house, I saw them on their front porch, bundled up in coats, eating apples. I was surprised that a prickle of fear didn't rise behind my neck. Instead I felt numb, except that it was a glowing sort of numbness pushing out from me in slow, easy pulses.

Stinky, a saltshaker pinched under his forearm, was trying to pry open a green apple with his thumbs. When he couldn't, he licked it, sprinkled some salt on the moisture and crunched a bite, squeezing his face away from the tartness. Noticing me, he stared at me a while, as if he'd noticed something he'd never, in all the years he'd known me, seen. Then he winked and gestured to me if I wanted some of his apple. I waved my hand no, and he began unclogging the holes of the saltshaker.

When I opened the door to our house, the sun, out again, came rushing into the living room. Shadows lifted from the floor like a flock of birds rising into the horizon, and light guttered through the room, slapping away the dark for good. A huge splash of light even bounced off the glass-top coffee table and raked my eyes; a snake of it slithered on the painting of the Last Supper. So much brightness made me realize how tired my eyes were, and I wobbled into the room on soft legs.

Magda and Pedi were lying asleep, on opposite sides of the couch, each crunching their end of the blanket against their chest. Magda's hair was fanned out on a pillow, unteased. I watched her as she lay there, her mouth half open, a thin line of black mascara leaking from the corner of one eye. I went over and wiped it, and she snuffled and turned her face away.

Then I sat down on Dad's cushioned chair and watched them. I won't say why, because there's no way of explaining why, even if I could or wanted to, but I knew, as my eyes got drowsy and the bright walls of the room glowed around me, that I'd never again see anything so wondrous as my two sisters lying on the couch. And it wasn't just them, but the whole room: the squiggly TV, the lumpy cherub angels on the frame of the painting, the glass-top coffee table, my mother's animals, gleaming in the sunlight. This room was what my mother spent so much energy cleaning and keeping together, and what my father spent so much energy tearing apart. And it was wondrous, like a place I was meant to be. A place, I felt, that I had come back to after a long journey of being away. My home. The light in the room was closing in around me, I was so sleepy. It was dissolving and sifting in through my eyelashes in thin, filtered streams, and then there was only the dull blood under my eyelids, then dark, then sleep.

AWARDS FOR YOUNG
ADULT LITERATURE

B ECAUSE the definition of Young Adult Literature remains fluid among publishers, readers, and librarians, compiling a full list of award winners in this
category is extremely difficult. We list here the most prestigious awards, those
with the longest history, and those that seem most clearly to distinguish Young
Adult Literature for a reading audience of those aged twelve to twenty. As with
our selections for the anthology, we have chosen not to include Newbery Award
winners, even though their designated age range is up to and including age 14.
We thank nationally known Young Adult (YA) expert Pat Scales, Librarian at
the Governor's School for the Arts in Greenville, South Carolina, for her advice
in compiling this list.

THE MICHAEL PRINTZ AWARD

This annual award is given by the Young Adult Library Services Association of
the American Library Association. Organized in 1999, it honors Michael
Printz, librarian at Topeka West (Kansas) High School. It may be for fiction,
nonfiction, poetry, or drama, and is not limited to works first published in the
United States of America. This award designates ages twelve to eighteen as
the age range for YA. The award committee may name up to four Honor
Books in addition to the winner. Michael Cart, who chaired the feasibility
committee which designed the award, has said that it "serves notice on the
reading, publishing, and bookselling communities that young adult literature
has come of age."

2002 Winner: An Na, *A Step from Heaven*
2002 Honor Books: Jan Greenberg, ed., *Heart to Heart: New Poems Inspired by
    20th Century American Art*
Chris Lynch, *Free Will*
Peter Dickinson, *The Ropemaker*
Virginia Euwer Wolff, *True Believer*

2001 Winner: David Almond, *Kit's Wilderness*
2001 Honor Books: Carolyn Coman, *Many Stones*
Carol Plum-Ucci, *The Body of Christopher Creed*
Louise Rennison, *Angus, Thongs, and Full Frontal Snogging: Confessions
    of Georgia Nicolson*
Terry Trueman, *Stuck in Neutral*

2000 Winner: Walter Dean Myers, *Monster*
2000 Honor Books: David Almond, *Skellig*
Laurie Halse, *Speak*
Ellen Wittlinger, *Hard Love*

THE MARGARET A. EDWARDS AWARD

The Margaret A. Edwards Award honors an author's lifetime achievement in writing books that have been popular with teenagers. Edwards was a librarian who designed a training program for librarians just beginning their work with adolescents. Established in 1988, it recognizes, according to its website, an author's work "in helping adolescents become aware of themselves and addressing questions about their role and importance in relationships, society, and the world."

2002: Paul Zindel
2001: Robert Lipsyte
2000: Chris Crutcher
1999: Anne McCaffrey
1998: Madeleine L'Engle
1997: Gary Paulsen
1996: Judy Blume
1995: Cynthia Voigt
1994: Walter Dean Myers
1993: M. E. Kerr
1992: Lois Duncan
1991: Robert Cormier
1990: Richard Peck
1989: no award given
1988: S. E. Hinton

THE NATIONAL BOOK AWARD FOR YOUNG PEOPLE'S LITERATURE

The National Book Awards are the preeminent book awards in the United States. Established in 1950 by a consortium of book publishers, the National Book Awards first added an award for Children's Literature in 1969, expanding in 1980 to awards both in hardcover and paperback, and by 1982, awards in picture books and nonfiction as well. Several of the award-winning children's books might be considered YA today. In 1984, the awards were trimmed to only three, none for children's. In 1996 however, the National Book Award reaffirmed its interest in young readers by creating its "Young People's Literature" category. The awards are now administered by a nonprofit organization, the National Book Foundation.

2001: Virginia Euwer Wolff, *True Believer*
2000: Gloria Whelan, *Homeless Bird*

1999: Kimberly Willis Holt, *When Zachary Beaver Came to Town*
1998: Louis Sachar, *Holes*
1997: Han Nolan, *Dancing on the Edge*
1996: Victor Martinez, *Parrot in the Oven*

AWARDS FOR
YOUNG
ADULT
LITERATURE

THE YOUNG READER'S CHOICE AWARD

This award is among the oldest for young readers. Established in 1940 by the Pacific Northwest Library Association, it solicits nominations from children, teachers, parents, and librarians from the Pacific Northwest: Washington, Oregon, Alaska, Idaho, Montana, British Columbia, and Alberta. The nominees have been published three years previously and are "already readers' favorites." Voting students must be in grades 4 through 12. The Senior Division especially for grades 9–12 was created in 1991. In 2002, the organization designated an Intermediate Division for grades 7–9 and limited the Senior Division to grades 10–12.

2002 Senior Division Nominees: Martha Grimes, *Biting the Moon*
Sherryl Jackson, *Raging Quiet*
William Sleator, *Rewind*
Lensey Namoika, *Ties That Bind, Ties That Break*
Randy Powell, *Tribute to Another Dead Rock Star*
2001 Winner: William Sleator, *The Boxes*

THE ALAN AWARD

Each year, the Assembly on Literature for Adolescents of the National Council of Teachers of English (NCTE) honors someone who has made an outstanding contribution to the field of adolescent (YA) literature. The recipient may be an author, publisher, scholar, librarian, editor, or someone who has served the organization. The honoree is chosen by the Executive Board of ALAN.

2002: Paul Zindel, author
2001: Patty Campbell, librarian and scholar
2000: M. E. Kerr, author
1999: Robert Lipsyte, author
1998: S. E. Hinton, author
1997: Mildred Taylor, author
1996: Bill Morris, publisher
1995: Robert C. Small, Jr., scholar
1994: Walter Dean Myers, author
1993: Chris Crutcher, author
1992: Don Gallo, scholar
1991: Gary Paulsen, author
1990: Richard Peck, author
1989: Cynthia Voigt, author
1988: Ted Hipple, scholar

CREDITS

INDEX